social
psychology

8th edition

social psychology

David G. Myers

Hope College
Holland, Michigan

Boston   Burr Ridge, IL   Dubuque, IA   Madison, WI   New York   San Francisco   St. Louis
Bangkok   Bogotá   Caracas   Kuala Lumpur   Lisbon   London   Madrid   Mexico City
Milan   Montreal   New Delhi   Santiago   Seoul   Singapore   Sydney   Taipei   Toronto

Higher Education

SOCIAL PSYCHOLOGY
Published by McGraw-Hill, a business unit of The McGraw-Hill Companies, Inc., 1221 Avenue of the Americas, New York, NY, 10020. Copyright © 2005, 2002, 1999, 1996, 1993, 1990, 1987, 1983, by The McGraw-Hill Companies, Inc. All rights reserved. No part of this publication may be reproduced or distributed in any form or by any means, or stored in a database or retrieval system, without the prior written consent of The McGraw-Hill Companies, Inc., including, but not limited to, in any network or other electronic storage or transmission, or broadcast for distance learning.
Some ancillaries, including electronic and print components, may not be available to customers outside the United States.

This book is printed on acid-free paper.

2 3 4 5 6 7 8 9 0 DOW/DOW 0 9 8 7 6 5

ISBN 0-07-291694-X

Publisher: *Stephen Rutter*
Executive editor: *Michael J. Sugarman*
Director of development and new media: *Judith Kromm*
Editorial coordinator: *Katherine C. Russillo*
Marketing manager: *Melissa S. Caughlin*
Media technology producer: *Ginger Bunn*
Senior project manager: *Rebecca Nordbrock*
Production supervisor: *Janean A. Utley*
Design manager: *Laurie Entringer*
Cover designer: *Srdjan Savanovic*
Lead media project manager: *Marc Mattson*
Photo research coordinator: *Alexandra Ambrose*
Art manager: *Robin Mouat*
Photo researcher: *Toni Michaels*
Art director: *Jeanne Schreiber*
Permissions editor: *Marty Granahan*
Cover image: © *Superstock*
Typeface: *10/12 Palatino*
Compositor: *Cenveo*
Printer: *R.R. Donnelley and Sons Inc.*

Library of Congress Cataloging-in-Publication Data

Myers, David G.
    Social psychology / David G. Myers.— 8th ed.
      p. cm.
    Includes bibliographical references and index.
    ISBN 0-07-291694-X (alk. paper)
    1. Social psychology. I. Title
    HM1033.M897 2005
    302—dc22

                                        2004050453

www.mhhe.com

The McGraw-Hill Social Psychology Series

This popular series of paperback titles is written about the author's particular field of expertise and is meant to complement any social psychology course. The series includes:

Brief contents

Table of contents

Part Three   Social Relations

Preface

When first invited to write this book, I envisioned a text that would be at once solidly scientific and warmly human, factually rigorous and intellectually provocative. It would reveal social psychology as an investigative reporter might, by providing an up-to-date summary of important social phenomena, as well as how scientists uncover and explain such phenomena. It would be reasonably comprehensive, yet would also stimulate students' *thinking*—their readiness to inquire, to analyze, to relate principles to everyday happenings.

How does one select material for inclusion in a "reasonably comprehensive" introduction to one's discipline—one long enough to allow rich narrative (to weave a story) but crisp enough not to overwhelm? I have sought to present theories and findings that are neither too esoteric for the typical undergraduate nor better suited to other courses in sociology or psychology. I have chosen instead to emphasize material that casts social psychology in the intellectual tradition of the liberal arts. By the teaching of great literature, philosophy, and science, liberal education seeks to expand our thinking and awareness and to liberate us from the confines of the present. Social psychology can contribute to these goals. Many undergraduate social psychology students are not psychology majors; virtually all will enter other professions. By focusing on humanly significant issues, one can present the fundamental content that preprofessional psychology students need in ways that are stimulating and useful to all students.

And what a feast of ideas social psychology offers! In all of recorded history, human social behavior has been studied scientifically for barely more than one century—the one just past. Considering that we have barely begun, the results are gratifying. We have amassed significant insights into belief and illusion, love and hate, conformity and independence.

Much about human behavior remains a mystery, yet social psychology can now offer partial answers to many intriguing questions:

- Will people act differently if they first adopt new attitudes? If so, how can we best persuade them?
- What leads people sometimes to hurt and sometimes to help one another?
- What kindles social conflict, and how can we transform closed fists into helping hands?

Answering such questions—my mission in the pages that lie ahead—expands our self-understanding and sensitizes us to the social forces that work upon us.

Organization

The book opens with a single chapter that introduces social psychological methods of inquiry. The chapter then warns students how findings can seem obvious—once you know them—and how social psychologists' own values permeate the discipline. In addition, a new section, "Some Big Ideas in Social Psychology," introduces the book's overarching themes of how we construct our social reality, social intuition, social influences, personal attitudes and dispositions, biological behavior, and applications to everyday life. The intent is to give students just enough to prepare them for what follows.

The book then unfolds around its definition of social psychology: the scientific study of how people *think about* (Part One), *influence* (Part Two), and *relate to* (Part Three) one another, and the application of the principles of social psychology in everyday life (Part Four).

Part One examines *social thinking*—how we view ourselves and others. It assesses the accuracy of our impressions, intuitions, and explanations.

Part Two explores *social influence*. By appreciating the cultural sources of our attitudes and by learning the nature of conformity, persuasion, and group influence, we can better recognize subtle social forces at work upon us.

Part Three considers the attitudinal and behavioral manifestations of both negative and positive *social relations*. It flows from prejudice to aggression, and from attraction to helping, and concludes by exploring the dynamics of conflict and peacemaking.

Part Four examines how the concepts learned in earlier chapters are applied in society. Applications of social psychology are woven throughout every chapter in the book, but they are the focus of Chapter 14 (Social Psychology in the Clinic), Chapter 15 (Social Psychology in Court), and Chapter 16 (Social Psychology and the Sustainable Future).

This edition, like its predecessors, has a multicultural emphasis that can be seen in the treatment of cultural influences in Chapter 6 and integrated throughout the text in the inclusion of research from various cultural settings. All authors are creatures of their cultures, and I am no exception. Yet by reading the world's social psychology literature, by corresponding with researchers worldwide, and by traveling abroad, I have sought to present the *world* of social psychology to a worldwide student audience. The book's focus remains *the fundamental principles of social thinking, social influence, and social relations as revealed by careful empirical research*. But hoping to broaden our awareness of the whole human family, I aim to illustrate these principles transnationally.

To assist readers, I have organized chapters into three or four sections. Each begins with a preview and ends with a summary highlighting the organization and key concepts.

Believing with Thoreau that "anything living is easily and naturally expressed in popular language," I have sought, paragraph by paragraph, to craft the most engaging and effective book possible. A bright, four-color design complements the text revisions and enhances the impact of the photos and figures. As before, definitions of key terms appear both in the margins and in the Glossary.

Eighth edition features

This eighth edition offers

- **Current Research:** A thorough updating, with more than 500 new citations and examples and many new figures and tables, keeps the text on the cutting edge of social psychology.

- **The Story Behind the Research:** This feature offers interviews with researchers to illuminate the thinking behind contemporary, cutting-edge studies, as well as classic research.
- **Focus on:** This feature examines current events related to social psychology and the role of social psychology in everyday life.
- **Making the Social Connection:** Located at the end of each chapter, this section links content across chapters and encourages the reader to view a related video clip on the *SocialSense* CD-ROM that comes with the book.
- **Personal Postscripts:** Each chapter concludes with a reflection on the significance of a topic from the chapter, followed by a "What do you think?" question encouraging readers to apply ideas in social psychology to their experience.
- **Media icons:** Each chapter offers two types of margin icons to alert students to related content and activities that can be found on the *SocialSense* CD-ROM or the Online Learning Center. The *SocialSense* CD-ROM icon appears both within and at the end of each chapter, prompting students to view brief video clips of researchers and important concepts. The Online Learning Center icon directs students to visit the text's website at www.mhhe.com/myers8, where they will find scenarios, interactivities, quizzes, and additional study aids related to concepts in the text.

Eighth edition chapter-by-chapter revisions

1 **Introducing Social Psychology**
- New section "Some Big Ideas in Social Psychology" covers overarching themes of how we construct our social reality, social intuition, social influences, personal attitudes and dispositions, biological behavior, and applications to everyday life
- New figure "Some Big Ideas in Social Psychology"

PART 1 SOCIAL THINKING

2 **The Self in a Social World**
- New coverage of the spotlight effect
- New research on predicting our behavior, self, and self-esteem, and secure self-esteem
- New *Focus on: Self-serving bias*

3 **Social Beliefs and Judgments**
- Updated coverage on the limits of intuition and on self-fulfilling beliefs

4 **Behavior and Attitudes**
- Current events examples of cognitive dissonance, foot-in-the-door phenomenon
- New figure and updated coverage of cognitive dissonance
- New research study on amnesia and self-justification

PART 2 SOCIAL INFLUENCE

5 Genes, Culture, and Gender
- Updated coverage of genetics, plus culture, cross-cultural norms
- New research on universal behavior and language patterns, male and female sexuality, biology and culture, plus universal dimensions of social beliefs
- New figure on gender differences

6 Conformity
- New research on reactance

7 Persuasion
- New coverage of persuasion and group identification
- New table on persuasion principles
- Current research on the persuasive message, counterarguments, and attitude inoculation
- Updated and expanded coverage on inoculating children against advertising, plus the Motherhood Project, and attitude inoculation

8 Group Influence
- New figure on the effects of social arousal
- Current events examples of deindividuation, and defections from the majority
- Updated coverage of physical anonymity, polarization, group brainstorming, and recent research on the symptoms of groupthink

PART 3 SOCIAL RELATIONS

9 Prejudice: Disliking Others
- Significantly revised and updated with chapter co-author, Steven Spencer
- Updated coverage of weight discrimination, gender discrimination, distinctiveness, and perceiving people who stand out
- New research on racial discrimination with new figure
- New sections on social dominance orientation, the motivation to avoid prejudice, and the consequences of prejudice

10 Aggression: Hurting Others
- Updated material on genetic influences of aggression, frustration response, observational learning
- New figure on revised frustration-aggression theory
- Updated coverage of media influences on pornography and sexual violence, plus updates on television's effect on behavior and television's effect on thinking
- New section and research on media influence/video games

11 Attraction and Intimacy: Liking and Loving Others
- New research and new table on relationship distress
- Updated coverage of ostracism, similarity and complementarity, perceived equity, and satisfaction

- New *Focus on: Implicit egotism*
- Significantly updated section on who is considered attractive

12 Helping
- New *Focus on* features on the benefits and costs of empathy-based altruism
- New research on helping strangers around the world, and on modeling altruism

13 Conflict and Peacemaking
- Updated material on competition breeding conflict, external threats breeding internal unity, and updates on desegregation
- New research on simplistic thinking and on misperceptions
- New *Focus on: Why do we care who wins?*

PART 4 APPLYING SOCIAL PSYCHOLOGY

14 Social Psychology in the Clinic
- Updated coverage of making clinical judgments, explanatory style and illness, and close relationships and health
- New Personal Postscript on enhancing happiness

15 Social Psychology in Court
- Updated coverage of eyewitness testimony, influences on eyewitness testimony, police interviewing, and double-blind testing
- Updated information on jurors and number of jurors

16 Social Psychology and the Sustainable Future
- New figures on world population growth and overshooting our capacity
- New section on global warming
- New research on materialism and happiness, adaptation level phenomenon, and social comparison
- New Personal Postscript: "How does one live responsibly in the modern world?"

In appreciation

Although only one person's name appears on this book's cover, the truth is that a whole community of scholars has invested itself in it. Although none of these people should be held responsible for what I have written—nor do any of them fully agree with everything said—their suggestions made this a better book than it could otherwise have been.

A special "thank you" goes to Steven Spencer, University of Waterloo, for his contribution to Chapter 9 (Prejudice). Drawing on his extensive knowledge of stereotyping and prejudice, Spencer updated and revised this chapter.

This new edition still retains many of the improvements contributed by consultants and reviewers on the first seven editions. To the following esteemed colleagues I therefore remain indebted:

Mike Aamodt, Radord University

Robert Arkin, Ohio State
   University

Susan Beers, Sweet Briar College

George Bishop, National University
   of Singapore

Galen V. Bodenhausen, Northwestern University

Martin Bolt, Calvin College

Amy Bradfield, Iowa State University

Dorothea Braginsky, Fairfield University

Fred B. Bryant, Loyola University Chicago

Shawn Meghan Burn, California Polytechnic State University

David Buss, University of Texas

Thomas Cafferty, University of South Carolina

Jerome M. Chertkoff, Indiana University

Russell Clark, University of North Texas

Diana I. Cordova, Yale University

Karen A. Couture, New Hampshire College

Cynthia Crown, Xavier University

Jack Croxton, State University of New York at Fredonia

Anthony Doob, University of Toronto

Philip Finney, Southeast Missouri State University

Carie Forden, Clarion University

Kenneth Foster, City University of New York

Dennis Fox, University of Illinois at Springfield

Carrie B. Fried, Winona State University

William Froming, Pacific Graduate School of Psychology

Stephen Fugita, Santa Clara University

David A. Gershaw, Arizona Western College

Mary Alice Gordon, Southern Methodist University

Ranald Hansen, Oakland University

Allen Hart, Amherst College

Elaine Hatfield, University of Hawaii

James L. Hilton, University of Michigan

Bert Hodges, Gordon College

William Ickes, University of Texas at Arlington

Marita Inglehart, University of Michigan

Chester Insko, University of North Carolina

Jonathan Iuzzini, Texas A&M University

Meighan Johnson, Shorter College

Edward Jones, Princeton University [deceased]

Judi Jones, Georgia Southern College

Martin Kaplan, Northern Illinois University

Timothy J. Kasser, Knox College

Janice Kelly, Purdue University

Douglas Kenrick, Arizona State University

Norbert Kerr, Michigan State University

Charles Kiesler, University of Missouri

Marjorie Krebs, Gannon University

Travis Langley, Henderson State University

Helen E. Linkey, Marshall University

Diane Martichuski, University of Colorado

John W. McHoskey, Eastern Michigan University

Daniel N. McIntosh, University of Denver

Annie McManus, Parkland College

David McMillen, Mississippi State University

Robert Millard, Vassar College

Arthur Miller, Miami University

Teru Morton, Vanderbilt University

Todd D. Nelson, California State University

K. Paul Nesselroade, Jr., Simpson College

Darren Newtson, University of Virginia

Stuart Oskamp, Claremont Graduate University

Chris O'Sullivan, Bucknell University

Ellen E. Pastorino, Valencia Community College

Sandra Sims Patterson, Spelman College

Paul Paulus, University of Texas at Arlington

Scott Plous, Wesleyan University

Nicholas Reuterman, Southern Illinois University of Edwardsville

Robert D. Ridge, Brigham Young University

Nicole Schnopp-Wyatt, Pikeville College

Wesley Schultz, California State University, San Marcos

Vann Scott, Armstrong Atlantic State University

Linda Silka, University of Massachusetts–Lowell

Royce Singleton, Jr., College of the Holy Cross

Stephen Slane, Cleveland State University

Christine M. Smith, Grand Valley State University

Richard A. Smith, University of Kentucky

Mark Snyder, University of Minnesota

Sheldon Solomon, Skidmore College

Matthew Spackman, Brigham Young University

Garold Stasser, Miami University

Charles Stangor, University of Maryland at College Park

Homer Stavely, Keene State College

JoNell Strough, West Virginia University

Eric Sykes, Indiana University Kokomo

Elizabeth Tanke, University of Santa Clara

William Titus, Arkansas Tech University

Tom Tyler, New York University

Rhoda Unger, Montclair State University

Billy Van Jones, Abilene Christian College

Mary Stewart Van Leeuwen, Eastern College

Ann L. Weber, University of North Carolina at Asheville

Daniel M. Wegner, Harvard University

Gary Wells, Iowa State University

Bernard Whitley, Ball State University

Kipling Williams, Purdue University

Midge Wilson, DePaul University

I have additionally benefited from feedback on the seventh edition provided by many instructors who responded to a survey they received by e-mail prior to the creation of the eighth edition. My sincere thanks also to the following seventh edition reviewers, who provided detailed comments that helped to shape this edition:

Charles Daniel Batson, University of Kansas

Jonathon D. Brown, University of Washington

David Dunning, Cornell University

Alice H. Eagly, Northwestern University

Leandre Fabrigar, Queen's University

Tom Gilovich, Cornell University

Tim Kasser, Knox College

Norbert L. Kerr, Michigan State University

C.R. Snyder, University of Kansas

Mike Wessells, Randolph-Macon College

Finally, a number of teacher-scholars reviewed these new chapters, rescuing me from occasional mistakes and offering constructive suggestions (and encouragement):

Steve Baumgardner, University of Wisconsin–Eau Claire

Timothy C. Brock, Ohio State University

Deana Julka, University of Portland

Joachim Krueger, Brown University

Maurice J. Levesque, Elon University

Terry F. Pettijohn, Mercyhurst College

Carolyn Whitney, Saint Michael's University

I am indebted to each of these colleagues.

Hope College, Michigan, has been wonderfully supportive of these successive editions. Both the people and the environment have helped make the gestation of *Social Psychology* a pleasure. At Hope College, poet Jack Ridl helped shape the voice you will hear in these pages. Kathy Adamski has again contributed her good cheer and secretarial support. Brandi Siler and Stacey Zokoe faithfully sent for and photocopied the hundreds of articles from which this new edition is updated. And Kathryn Brownson did library research, edited and prepared the manuscript, managed the paper flow, proofed the pages and art, and prepared the page-referenced bibliography and name index. All in all, she midwifed this book.

Were it not for the inspiration of Nelson Black of McGraw-Hill, writing a textbook never would have occurred to me. Alison Meersschaert guided and encouraged the formative first edition. Senior Sponsoring Editors Rebecca Hope and Mike Sugarman and Director of Development and New Media Judith Kromm helped envision the execution of this eighth edition and its teaching supplements. With warmth and creativity, developmental editor Ann Greenberger collaborated with me every step of the way, envisioned new ways to summarize research and concepts in visual diagrams, and organized the *SocialSense* CD-ROM. Editorial coordinator Kate Russillo engaged the reviewers, managed the supplements, and organized the end-of-book glossary. Senior Project Manager Rebecca Nordbrock patiently guided the process of converting the manuscript into finished book, assisted by copyeditor Laurie McGee's perceptive fine-tuning.

After hearing countless dozens of people say that this book's supplements have taken their teaching to a new level, I also pay tribute to Martin Bolt (Calvin College), both for his authoring the study guide and for his pioneering the extensive instructor's resources, with their countless ready-to-use demonstration activities.

How fortunate we are now to have added to our team Jon Mueller (North Central College) as author of the new instructor's resources. Jon is able to draw on the accumulated resources in his acclaimed online resources for the teaching of social psychology and his monthly listserv offering resources to social psychology instructors (see jonathan.mueller.faculty.noctrl.edu/crow).

Also new to our author team is Kristine Anthis, Southern Connecticut State University. Hats off to her for professionally refining, extending, and updating our extensive testing resources, and also to Martha Hubertz of Florida Atlantic University for contributing questions for student use in the Online Learning Center and the *SocialSense* CD-ROM and to Terry Pettijohn, Ohio State University at Marion, for the interactive "scenarios" he created for the Online Learning Center.

To all in this supporting cast, I am indebted. Working with all these people has made the creation of this book a stimulating, gratifying experience.

David G. Myers
davidmyers.org

Supplements

Social Psychology, eighth edition, is accompanied by a comprehensive and fully integrated array of supplemental materials, both print and electronic, written specifically for instructors and students of social psychology.

The supplements listed here may accompany Myers, *Social Psychology*, eighth edition. Please contact your McGraw-Hill representative for details concerning policies, prices, and availability as some restrictions may apply.

For the instructor:

Instructor's Manual
Revised by Jon Mueller, North Central College

This manual has been highly praised as an excellent and useful tool for social psychology instructors, whether they are new to teaching or veterans of the course. For each chapter, the manual contains a chapter outline, lecture and discussion ideas, demonstrations and project ideas for the classroom, as well as student assignments. In addition, media resources are provided, along with contact information for each producer and distributor. To facilitate classroom activities and student review, the Instructor's Manual provides chapter outlines, demonstration, and project materials on separate pages for easy duplication and distribution to students.

Test Bank and Computerized Test Bank
Kristine Anthis, Southern Connecticut State University

The Test Bank contains more than 1,500 multiple-choice questions. Each item is classified as definition, factual, or conceptual for easier selection and use by the instructor. A page reference ties each item back to the text. The Test Bank is available on the Instructor's Resource CD-ROM in Microsoft Word™ files and in a computerized format that works with both Macintosh and Windows platforms.

Instructor's Resource CD-ROM

This tool allows instructors to customize their lecture presentations using McGraw-Hill materials. Resources for instructors include the Instructor's Manual, PowerPoint presentation slides by Curtis Brant of Baldwin-Wallace College, the Test Bank, and a link to the text's Online Learning Center.

The Test Bank and Computerized Test Bank form an integral part of the Instructor's Resource CD-ROM. The Test Bank has been revised by Kristine Anthis of Southern Connecticut State University. The Computerized Test Bank works with both Macintosh and Windows platforms and includes a fully functioning editing feature that enables instructors to integrate their own questions, scramble items, and modify questions.

Classroom Performance System Guide and CD-ROM
by Donelson Forsyth, Virginia Commonwealth University

The Classroom Performance System (CPS) from **eInstruction** allows instructors to gauge immediately what students are learning during lectures. With CPS, instructors can ask questions, take polls, host classroom demonstrations, and get instant feedback. In addition, CPS makes it easy to take attendance, give and grade pop quizzes, or give formal paper-based class tests with multiple versions of the test using CPS for immediate grading.

For instructors who want to use CPS in their classroom, we are pleased to offer a guide containing strategies for implementing the system, specific multiple-choice questions designed for in-class use (tied to key concepts in the book), and classroom demonstrations that make use of the system. The Instructor's Resource CD-ROM includes an electronic version of the multiple-choice questions and classroom demonstrations that can be easily ported into teaching notes. For a quick, easy demonstration of CPS, go to http://www.mhhe.com/wmg/cps/psychology.

Online Learning Center (www.mhhe.com/myers8)

This extensive website, designed specifically for *Social Psychology*, eighth edition, offers an array of resources for instructors and students. On the password-protected instructor's website is a full set of PowerPoint presentation slides, the complete Instructor's Manual, the *Social Psychology* image gallery, the McGraw-Hill Image Gallery, professional resource links, a link to PowerWeb (McGraw-Hill's online database of current articles related to social psychology), and topical Web links to related Web pages.

The *Social Connection* Video Modules

McGraw-Hill teamed up with Frank Vattano and Colorado State University's Office of Instructional Services, along with Martin Bolt of Calvin College, to produce this series of video modules. The *Social Connection* video modules feature leading researchers discussing and illustrating their research and its applications to everyday life. The modules also incorporate footage from classic research studies and new reenactments of social psychology studies. A Faculty Guide prepared by Martin Bolt accompanies the *Social Connection* video modules.

PageOut!—Build your own course website in less than an hour

You don't have to be a computer whiz to create a website. Especially with an exclusive McGraw-Hill product called PageOut. It requires no prior knowledge of HTML; no long hours of coding; and no design skills on your part. Visit us at http://www.pageout.net for more information.

For the student:
Student Study Guide,
Martin Bolt, Calvin College

For many students, the most helpful supplement to this text will be Martin Bolt's *Student Study Guide*. This highly rated study tool provides abundant materials enabling students to test their comprehension of each chapter in *Social Psychology,* eighth edition. Included for each chapter are chapter objectives, an interactive chapter review, matching terms, true/false questions, multiple-choice questions, and short essay questions. In addition, answers are provided at the end of the study guide so students can check their progress.

Online Learning Center (www.mhhe.com/myers8)

This extensive website, designed specifically for *Social Psychology,* eighth edition, offers the following resources for students: The website offers quizzes, scenarios, interactivities, the glossary from the book , topical Web links to relevant social psychology Web pages, psychology in the news, an Internet primer, and a careers in psychology feature. For each chapter in the text, there are chapter objectives, a chapter outline, a quiz, and an image gallery.

SocialSense CD-ROM

A *SocialSense* Student CD-ROM is packaged at no additional cost with each new copy of *Social Psychology,* eighth edition. This CD-ROM includes short clips of interviews with social psychology researchers as well as video clips of real-life situations. Each clip is accompanied by pedagogy created to increase understanding of research and concepts in social psychology. An icon within the chapter reminds students to watch a video clip on the CD. The CD also contains multiple-choice practice test questions prepared by Martha Hubertz of Florida Atlantic University, and each question includes immediate feedback. The CD also contains an assortment of interactive study resources.

A Visual Walkthrough

chapter outline
provides an overview of the chapter's organization and topic coverage.

The following is the sample chapter page content shown:

chapter 8

Group Influence

"Never doubt that a small group of thoughtful, committed citizens can change the world."
Anthropologist Margaret Mead

Tawna is nearing the end of her daily jog. Her mind prods her to keep going; her body begs her to walk the remaining six blocks. She compromises and does a slow jog home. The next day conditions are identical, except that two friends run with her. Tawna runs her route two minutes faster. She wonders, "Did I run better merely because Gail and José went along? Would I always run better if in a group?"

At almost every turn, we are involved in groups. Our world contains not only 6.4 billion individuals, but 200 nation-states, 4 million local communities, 20 million economic organizations, and hundreds of millions of other formal and informal groups—couples on dates, families, churches, housemates in bull sessions. How do these groups influence individuals?

Group interactions often have dramatic effects. Intellectual college students hang out with other intellectuals, and they strengthen one another's intellectual interests. Deviant youth hang out with other deviant youth, amplifying one another's antisocial tendencies. But how do these groups affect the attitudes of the

chapter opening vignettes
highlights a story or situation of great relevance to students of social psychology that helps the reader make important connections with the chapter concepts.

"the story behind the research"
interviews with famous social psychology researchers both classic and contemporary discussing how they became interested in their areas of research.

the *SocialSense* CD icon
appears in the margins throughout the text as a reminder to view a short video clip that illustrates the topic or research discussed in that section. Use the *SocialSense* CD-ROM, packaged for free with new copies of this text, to access the video clip.

Prejudice: Disliking others   chapter 9   **373**

the story behind the research:
Claude Steele on stereotype threat

During a committee meeting on campus diversity at the University of Michigan in the late 1980's, I noticed an interesting fact: at every level of entering SAT score, minority students were getting lower college grades than their non-minority counterparts. Soon, Steven Spencer, Joshua Aronson, and I found that this was a national phenomenon; it happened at most colleges and it happened to other groups whose abilities were negatively stereotyped, such as women in advanced math classes. This underperformance wasn't caused by group differences in preparation. It happened at all levels of preparation (as measured by SATs).

Eventually, we produced this underperformance in the laboratory by simply having motivated people perform a difficult task in a domain where their group was negatively stereotyped. We also found that we could eliminate this underperformance by making the same task irrelevant to the stereotype, by removing the "stereotype threat," as we had come to call it. This latter finding spawned more research: figuring out how to reduce stereotype threat and its ill effects. Through this work, we have gained an appreciation for two big things: first, the importance of life context in shaping psychological functioning, and second, the importance of social identities like age, race, and gender in shaping that context.

Claude Steele

performance on hard tests (O'Brien & Crandall, 2003; Ben-Zeev, Fein & Inzlicht, 2004). (Recall from Chapter 8, Group Influence, that arousal from others; presence tends to strengthen performance on easy tasks and disrupt performance on hard tasks.)

Why do non-White students tend to underachieve? Go to the *SocialSense* CD-ROM to view a video clip on stereotype threat.

If stereotype threats can disrupt performance, could *positive* stereotypes enhance it? Margaret Shih, Todd Pittinsky, and Nalini Ambady (1999) confirmed this possibility. When Asian American females were asked biographical questions that reminded them of their gender identity before taking a math test, their performance plunged (compared with a control group). When similarly reminded of their Asian identity, their performance rose. Negative stereotypes disrupt performance, and positive stereotypes, it seems, facilitate performance.

DO STEREOTYPES BIAS JUDGMENTS OF INDIVIDUALS?

Yes, stereotypes bias judgments, but here is good news: *People often evaluate individuals more positively than the groups they compose* (Miller & Felicio, 1990). Anne Locksley, Eugene Borgida, and Nancy Brekke have found that once someone knows a person, "Stereotypes may have minimal, if any, impact on judgments about that person" (Borgida & others, 1981; Locksley & others, 1980, 1982). They discovered this by giving University of Minnesota students anecdotal information about recent incidents in the life of "Nancy." In a supposed transcript of a telephone conversation, Nancy told a friend how she responded to three different situations (for example, being harassed by a seedy character while shopping). Some of the students read transcripts portraying Nancy responding assertively (telling the seedy character to leave); others read a report of passive responses (simply ignoring the character until she finally drifts away). Still other

Attractive communicators, such as Serena and Venus Williams endorsing Reebok and Puma, often trigger peripheral route persuasion. We associate their message or product with our good feelings toward the communicator, and we approve and believe.

WHAT IS SAID? THE MESSAGE CONTENT

It matters not only who says something, but *what* that person says. If you were to help organize an appeal to get people to vote for school taxes or to stop smoking or to give money to world hunger relief, you might wonder how to concoct a recipe for central route persuasion. Common sense could lead you to either side of these questions:

www.mhhe.com/**myers8**
How can the person who delivers a message be persuasive? Visit the Online Learning Center for a scenario on persuasion.

- Is a purely logical message most persuasive—or one that arouses emotion?
- Will you get more opinion change by advocating a position only slightly discrepant from the listeners' existing opinions or by advocating an extreme point of view?
- Should the message express your side only, or should it acknowledge and refute the opposing views?
- If people are to present both sides—say, in successive talks at a community meeting—is there an advantage to going first or last?

Let's take these questions one at a time.

Reason versus emotion

Suppose you were campaigning in support of world hunger relief. Would you best itemize your arguments and cite an array of impressive statistics? Or would you be more effective presenting an emotional approach—perhaps the compelling story of one starving child? Of course, an argument can be both reasonable and emotional. You can marry passion and logic. Still, which is *more* influential—reason or emotion? Was Shakespeare's Lysander right: "The will of man is by his reason sway'd"? Or was Lord Chesterfield's advice wiser: "Address yourself generally to the senses, to the heart, and to the weaknesses of mankind, but rarely to their reason"?

"The truth is always the strongest argument."
—Sophocles, *Phaedra*, 496–406 B.C.

---

the Online Learning Center icon

appears in the margins throughout the text as a reminder to go to the text's website [www.mhhe.com/myers8] for interactivities, scenarios, and additional information on the topic discussed in that section.

quotations

appear throughout the text in the margins to help promote further thought and discussion about a particular topic.

focus on

features demonstrate how an important concept is used or applied in research or real life. These illustrate key ideas in social psychology.

I was a Seattle 11-year-old at the time. I recall searching our windshield, frightened by the explanation that a Pacific H-bomb test was raining fallout on Seattle. On April 16, however, the newspapers hinted that the real culprit might be mass suggestibility. After April 17 there were no more complaints. Later analysis of the pitted windshields concluded that the cause was ordinary road damage. Why did we notice this only after April 14? Given the suggestion, we had looked carefully at our windshields instead of *through* them.

In real life, suggestibility is not always so amusing. Hijackings, UFO sightings, and even suicides tend to come in waves (see "Focus on: Mass Delusions"). Sociologist David Phillips and his colleagues (1985, 1989) report that known suicides, as well as fatal auto accidents and private airplane crashes

focus on   mass delusions

Suggestibility on a mass scale appears as collective delusions—spontaneous spreading of false beliefs. Occasionally, this appears as "mass hysteria"—the spread of bodily complaints within a school or workplace with no organic basis for the symptoms. One 2,000-student high school was closed for two weeks as 170 students and staff sought emergency treatment for stomach ailments, dizziness, headaches, and drowsiness. After investigators looked high and low for viruses, germs, pesticides, herbicides—anything that would make people ill—they found . . . nothing (Jones & others, 2000).

After 9/11, groups of children at schools scattered across the United States started breaking out with itchy red rashes without any apparent cause (Talbot, 2002). Unlike a viral condition, the rash spread by "line of sight." People got the rash as they *saw* others getting it (even if they had no close contact). Also, everyday skin conditions—eczema, acne, dry skin in overheated classrooms—got noticed, and perhaps amplified by anxiety. As with so many mass hysterias, rumors of a problem had caused people to notice their ordinary, everyday symptoms and to attribute them to their school.

Sociologists Robert Bartholomew and Erich Goode (2000) report on other mass delusions from the last millennium. During the Middle Ages, European convents reportedly experienced outbreaks of imitative behaviors. In one large French convent, at a time when it was believed that humans could be possessed by animals, one nun began to meow like a cat. Eventually, "all the nuns meowed together every day at a certain time." In a German convent, a nun reportedly fell to biting her companions, and before long "all the nuns of this convent began biting each other." In time, the biting mania spread to other convents.

In British South Africa in 1914, newspapers erroneously reported that German planes were flying over the country in preparation for an imminent attack. The reported maneuvers and length of flight were beyond the capabilities of 1914 aircraft. Nevertheless, thousands of people misperceived ambiguous, nighttime stimuli, such as stars and planets, as examples of the enemy planes.

On June 24, 1947, Kenneth Arnold, while piloting his private plane near Mount Rainier, spotted nine glittering objects in the sky. Worried that he may have seen foreign guided missiles, he tried reporting what he saw to the FBI. Discovering its office closed, he went to his local newspaper and reported crescent-shaped objects that moved "like a saucer would if you skipped it across the water." When the Associated Press then reported the sighting of "saucers" in more than 150 newspapers, the term "flying saucers" was created by headline writers, triggering a worldwide wave of flying saucer sightings during the rest of the summer of 1949.

key terms

are bolded in the main text and appear in the margin directly across from the relevant discussion for easier review.

Summing up

appears at the end of each major section as a review of the major concepts before the next section of the chapter.

---

even at the level of labeling phenomena, is a human activity. It is therefore natural and inevitable that prior beliefs and values will influence what social psychologists think and write.

There is no bridge from "is" to "ought"

A seductive error for those who work in the social sciences is sliding from a description of *what is* into a prescription of *what ought to be*. Philosophers call this the **naturalistic fallacy**. The gulf between "is" and "ought," between scientific description and ethical prescription, remains as wide today as when philosopher David Hume pointed it out more than 200 years ago. No survey of human behavior—say, of sexual practices—logically dictates what is "right" behavior. If most people don't do something, that does not make it wrong. If most people do it, that does not make it right. We inject our values whenever we move from objective statements of fact to prescriptive statements of what ought to be.

In both obvious and subtle ways, social psychologists' personal values influence their work. And what is true of them is true of each of us. Our values and assumptions color our views of the world. To discover how much our assumed values and social representations shape what we take for granted, we need to encounter different cultures. If you assume without question that people should, above all, be true to themselves; that women are (or aren't) better suited than men to certain roles; or that romantic love should come before marriage, stay tuned.

Should we dismiss science because it has its subjective side? Quite the contrary: The realization that human thinking always involves interpretation is precisely why we need researchers with varying biases to undertake scientific analysis. By constantly checking our beliefs against the facts, as best we know them, we check and restrain our biases. Systematic observation and experimentation help us clean the lens through which we see reality.

naturalistic fallacy
The error of defining what is good in terms of what is observable. For example: What's typical is normal; what's normal is good.

Summing up   Social psychologists' values penetrate their work in obvious ways, such as their choice of research topics, and in subtler ways, such as their hidden assumptions when forming concepts, choosing labels, and giving advice. There is a growing awareness of the subjectivity of scientific interpretation, of values hidden in social psychology's concepts and labels, and of the gulf between scientific description of what is and ethical prescription of what ought to be. This penetration of values into science is not unique to social psychology. That human thinking is seldom dispassionate is precisely why we need systematic observation and experimentation if we are to check our cherished ideas against reality.

I knew it all along: Is social psychology simply common sense?

Do social psychology's theories provide new insight into the human condition? Or do they only describe the obvious?

Many of the conclusions presented in this book may have already occurred to you, for social psychology is all around you. We constantly observe people

---

Another implication is that, for the persuader, an ineffective appeal can be worse than none. Can you see why? Those who reject an appeal are inoculated against further appeals. Consider an experiment in which Susan Darley and Joel Cooper (1972) invited students to write essays advocating a strict dress code. Because this was against the students' own positions and the essays were to be published, all chose *not* to write the essay—even those offered money to do so. After turning down the money, they became even more extreme and confident in their anti-dress-code opinions. Having made an overt decision against the dress code, they became more resistant to it. Those who have rejected initial appeals to quit smoking may likewise become immune to further appeals. Ineffective persuasion, by stimulating the listener's defenses, may be counterproductive. It may "harden the heart" against later appeals.

Summing up   How do people resist persuasion? A *prior public commitment* to one's own position, stimulated perhaps by a mild attack on the position, breeds resistance to later persuasion. A mild attack can also serve as an *inoculation*, stimulating one to develop counterarguments that will then be available if and when a strong attack comes. This implies, paradoxically, that one way to strengthen existing attitudes is to challenge them, though the challenge must not be so strong as to overwhelm them.

Personal Postscript: Being open but not naïve

As recipients of persuasion, our human task is to live in the land between gullibility and cynicism. Some people say that being persuadable is a weakness. "Think for yourself," we are urged. But is being closed to informational influence a virtue, or is it the mark of a fanatic? How can we live with humility and openness to others and yet be critical consumers of persuasive appeals?

To be open, we can assume that every person we meet is, in some ways, our superior. Each person I encounter has some expertise that exceeds my own and thus has something to teach me. As we connect, I hope to learn from this person and perhaps to be able to reciprocate by sharing my knowledge.

To be critical thinkers, we might take a cue from inoculation research. Do you want to build your resistance to persuasion without becoming closed to valid messages? Be an active listener and a critical thinker. Force yourself to counterargue. After hearing a political speech, discuss it with others. In other words, don't just listen; react. If the message cannot withstand careful analysis, so much the worse for it. If it can, its effect on you will be that much more enduring.

What do you think?

When have you been persuaded? Are you glad you were? If not, what might you have done to inoculate yourself?

Making the Social Connection

This chapter highlights Richard Petty's ideas about persuasion through his theory and research. We also reported Petty's ideas about dissonance in Chapter 4: Behavior and Attitudes. Go to the *SocialSense* CD-ROM to view Richard Petty on the central and peripheral routes to persuasion.

Personal Postscripts

from the author conclude every chapter and reflect on social psychology's human significance with an opportunity to apply these ideas with a "What do you think?" question.

Making the Social Connection

This section, found at the end of each chapter, offers connections across chapters and is a prompt to view a related video clip on the *SocialSense* CD-ROM.

About the author

S ince receiving his PhD from the University of Iowa, David Myers has spent his career at Michigan's Hope College, where he is the John Dirk Werkman Professor of Psychology and has taught dozens of social psychology sections. Hope College students have invited him to be their commencement speaker and voted him "outstanding professor."

Myers' scientific articles have appeared in some three dozen scientific books and periodicals, including *Science,* the *American Scientist, Psychological Science,* and the *American Psychologist.* In addition to his scholarly writing and his textbooks, he also communicates psychological science to the general public. His writings have appeared in three dozen magazines, from *Today's Education* to *Scientific American.* He also has published general audience books, including *The Pursuit of Happiness* and *Intuition: Its Powers and Perils.*

David Myers has chaired his city's Human Relations Commission, helped found a thriving assistance center for families in poverty, and spoken to hundreds of college and community groups. Drawing on his own experience, he also has written articles and a book (*A Quiet World*) about hearing loss, and he is advocating a revolution in American hearing assistance technology (hearingloop.org).

He bikes to work year-round and plays daily pick-up basketball. David and Carol Myers are parents of two sons and a daughter.

social psychology

chapter 1

Introducing Social Psychology

"Our lives are connected by a thousand invisible threads."

Herman Melville

There once was a man whose second wife was a vain and selfish woman. This woman had two daughters who were similarly vain and selfish. The man's own daughter, however, was sweet and kind. This sweet, kind daughter, whom we all know as Cinderella, learned early on that she had best do as she was told, accept insults, and not upstage her vain stepsisters.

But then, thanks to her fairy godmother, Cinderella was able to escape her situation and go to a grand ball, where she attracted a handsome prince. When the love-struck prince later encountered a homelier Cinderella back in her degrading home, he at first failed to recognize her.

Implausible? The folktale demands that we accept the power of the situation. In one situation, playing one role in the presence of her oppressive stepmother, the meek and unattractive Cinderella was a different person from the charming and beautiful Cinderella whom the prince met. At home, she cowered. At the ball, Cinderella felt more beautiful and walked and talked and smiled as if she were.

What is social psychology?

The French philosopher-novelist Jean-Paul Sartre (1946) would have had no problem accepting the Cinderella premise. We humans are "first of all beings in a situation," he believed. "We cannot be distinguished from our situations, for they form us and decide our possibilities" (pp. 59–60, paraphrased). **Social psychology** is a science that studies the influences of our situations, with special attention to how we view and affect one another. More precisely said, it is *the scientific study of how people think about, influence, and relate to one another*. It does so by asking questions that have intrigued us all (Figure 1–1).

social psychology
The scientific study of how people think about, influence, and relate to one another.

BIG QUESTIONS IN SOCIAL PSYCHOLOGY

How Much of Our Social World Is Just in Our Heads? As we will see in later chapters, our social behavior varies not just with the objective situation, but with how we construe it. Happily married people will attribute their spouse's acid remark ("Can't you ever put that where it goes?") to something external ("He must have had a frustrating day"). Unhappily married people will attribute the same remark to a mean disposition ("Is he ever hostile!") and may therefore respond with a counterattack. Moreover, expecting hostility from their spouse, they may behave resentfully, thereby eliciting the hostility they expect.

As we will also see, people who expect a professor's child to be bright, an attractive person to be warm, or a rival to be uncooperative also often get what they expect. Smile broadly at each person as you cross campus and the return smiles will make your school seem very friendly. Social beliefs can be similarly self-fulfilling. Others may prejudge us in ways that influence our reactions. For example, someone might construe your shyness as unfriendliness, snub you—leading you to bad-mouth the person, thereby confirming her suspicion of your "antagonism."

figure 1–1

Social psychology is . . .

Social psychology is the scientific study of . . .

Social thinking	Social influence	Social relations
• How we perceive ourselves and others • What we believe • Judgments we make • Our attitudes	• Culture and biology • Pressures to conform • Persuasion • Groups of people	• Prejudice • Aggression • Attraction and intimacy • Helping

Would You Be Cruel If Ordered? How did Nazi Germany conceive and implement the inconceivable slaughter of 6 million Jews? These evil acts occurred partly because thousands of people followed orders. They put the prisoners on trains, herded them into crowded showers, and poisoned them with gas. How could people engage in such horrific actions? Were these folks normal human beings?

Stanley Milgram (1974) wondered. So he set up a situation where people were ordered to administer increasing levels of electric shock to someone who was having difficulty learning a series of words. As we will see in Chapter 6, the experimental results were quite disturbing: Nearly two-thirds of the participants fully complied.

To Help? Or to Help Oneself? As bags of cash tumbled from an armored truck one fall day, $2 million was scattered along a Columbus, Ohio, street. Some motorists who stopped to help returned $100,000. Judging from what disappeared, many more stopped to help themselves. When similar incidents occurred several months later in San Francisco and Toronto, the results were the same: Passersby grabbed most of the money (Bowen, 1988). People have also helped themselves to what wasn't theirs in other incidents—in Montreal during a 1969 police strike, in Los Angeles during a 1992 riot in an area abandoned by police, and in Baghdad during the 2003 unpoliced gap between the end of Saddam Hussein's reign and the imposition of new military and police control. In each case, thousands of looters ransacked buildings and gleefully ran off with goods and treasures.

What situations trigger people to be helpful or greedy? Do some cultural contexts—perhaps villages and small towns—breed greater helpfulness?

Throughout this book, sources for information are cited parenthetically. The complete source is provided in the reference section that begins on page R-1.

A common thread runs through these questions: They all deal with how people view and affect one another. And that is what social psychology is all about. Social psychologists study attitudes and beliefs, conformity and independence, love and hate.

Social psychology is still a young science. We keep reminding people of this, partly as an excuse for our incomplete answers to some of its questions. But it's true. The first social psychology experiments were reported barely more than a century ago (1898), and the first social psychology text was published just three-quarters of a century ago (1924). Not until the 1930s did social psychology assume its current form. And it was not until World War II, when psychologists contributed

Tired of looking at the stars, Professor Mueller takes up social psychology.

Reprinted with permission by Jason Love at www.jasonlove.com

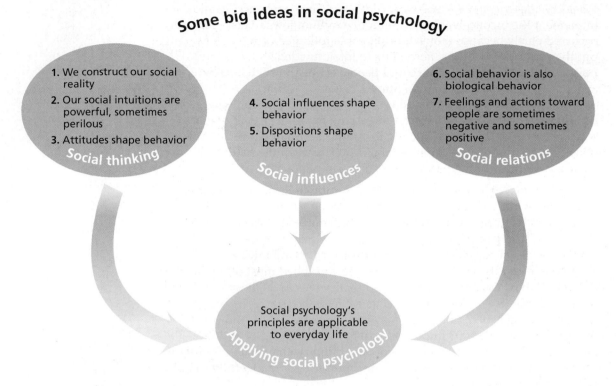

figure 1–2

Some big ideas in social psychology.

imaginative studies of persuasion and soldier morale, that it began to emerge as the vibrant field it is today.

SOME BIG IDEAS IN SOCIAL PSYCHOLOGY

What are social psychology's big lessons—its overarching themes? In many academic fields, the results of tens of thousands of studies, the conclusions of thousands of investigators, and the insights of hundreds of theorists can be boiled down to a few central ideas. Biology offers us principles such as natural selection and adaptation. Sociology builds on concepts such as social structure and organization. Music harnesses our ideas of rhythm, melody, and harmony.

What concepts are on social psychology's short list of big ideas? What themes, or fundamental principles, will be worth remembering long after you have forgotten most of the details? My short list of "great ideas we ought never forget" includes these, each of which we will unpack in chapters to come (Figure 1–2).

We construct our social reality

We humans have an irresistible urge to explain behavior, to attribute it to some cause, and therefore to make it seem orderly, predictable, and controllable. You and I may react differently to similar situations because we *think* differently. How we react to a friend's insult depends on whether we attribute it to hostility or to a bad day.

In a way, we are all intuitive scientists. We explain people's behavior, usually with enough speed and accuracy to suit our daily needs. When someone's behavior is consistent and distinctive, we attribute their behavior to their personality. For example, if you observe someone who makes repeated snide comments, you may infer that person has a nasty disposition, and then you might try to avoid the person.

Our beliefs about ourselves also matter. Do we have an optimistic outlook? Do we see ourselves as in control of things? Do we view ourselves as relatively superior or inferior? Our answers influence our emotions and actions. How we construe the world, and ourselves, matters.

Our social intuitions are often powerful but sometimes perilous

Our intuitions shape our fears (is flying dangerous?), impressions (can I trust him?), and relationships (does she like me?). Intuitions influence presidents in times of crisis, gamblers at the table, jurors in their assessments of guilt, and personnel directors when eyeing applicants. Such intuitions are commonplace.

Indeed, psychological science reveals a fascinating unconscious mind—an intuitive backstage mind—that Freud never told us about. More than we realized a decade or more ago, thinking occurs not onstage, but offstage, out of sight. As we will see, studies of "automatic processing," "implicit memory," "heuristics," "spontaneous trait inference," instant emotions, and nonverbal communication unveil our intuitive capacities. Thinking, memory, and attitudes all operate on two levels—one conscious and deliberate, the other unconscious and automatic. "Dual processing," today's researchers call it. We know more than we know we know.

So, intuition is huge. More than we realize, thinking occurs off-screen, with the results occasionally displayed on-screen. But intuition is also perilous. An example: While driving through life, mostly on automatic, we intuitively judge the likelihood of things by how readily instances come to mind. Especially since 9/11, we carry readily available images of plane crashes. Thus, most people fear flying more than driving, and many will drive great distances to avoid risking the skies. Actually, we're about three dozen times safer (per mile traveled) in a commercial plane than in a motor vehicle.

Even our intuitions about ourselves often err. We intuitively trust our memories more than we should. We misread our own minds; in experiments, we deny being affected by things that do influence us. We mispredict our own feelings—how bad we'll feel a year from now if we lose our job or our romance breaks up, and how good we'll feel a year from now if we win our state's lottery. And we often mispredict our own future—when buying clothes, people approaching middle age will still buy snug ("I anticipate shedding a few pounds"); rarely does anyone say, more realistically, "I'd better buy a relatively loose fit; people my age tend to put on pounds").

So, our social intuitions are noteworthy for both their ineffable powers and their troublesome perils. Our lives are empowered by subterranean intuitive thinking and occasionally imperiled by predictable errors. By reminding us of intuition's gifts and alerting us to its pitfalls, social psychologists aim to fortify our thinking. In most situations, "fast and frugal" snap judgments serve us well enough. But in others, where accuracy matters—as when needing to fear the right things and spend our resources accordingly—we had best restrain our impulsive intuitions with critical thinking.

Social influences shape our behavior

We are, as Aristotle long ago observed, social animals. We speak and think in words we learned from others. We long to connect, to belong, and to be well thought of. Matthias Mehl and James Pennebaker (2003) quantified their University of Texas students' social behavior by inviting them to wear microcassette recorders and microphones. Once every 12 minutes during their waking hours, the computer-operated recorder would imperceptibly record for 30 seconds. Although the observation period only covered weekdays (including class time), almost 30 percent of their time was spent talking. Relationships are a large part of being human.

As social creatures, we respond to our immediate contexts. Sometimes the power of a social situation leads us to act in ways that depart from our espoused attitudes. Indeed, powerful evil situations sometimes overwhelm good intentions, inducing people to agree with falsehoods or comply with cruelty. Under Nazi influence, many decent-seeming people became instruments of the Holocaust. Other situations may elicit great generosity and compassion. After the 9/11 catastrophe, New York City was overwhelmed with donations of food, clothing, and help from eager volunteers.

The power of the situation was also dramatically evident in varying attitudes toward the 2003 war against Iraq. Opinion polls revealed that Americans and Israelis overwhelmingly favored this waging of war. Their distant cousins elsewhere in the world overwhelmingly opposed it. Tell me where you live and I'll make a reasonable guess as to what your attitudes were as the war began. (Tell me your educational level and what media you watch and read and I'll make an even more confident guess of how you construed the war.) Regardless of how history judges the war, this much is evident: Our situations matter.

Our cultures help define our situations. Our standards regarding promptness, frankness, and clothing vary with our cultural situation. Whether you equate female beauty with slimness or shapeliness likewise depends on when and where in the world you live. Whether you define social justice as equality (all receive the same) or as equity (those who earn more receive more) depends on whether your ideology has been shaped more by socialism or capitalism. Whether you tend to be expressive or reserved, casual or formal, hinges partly on your culture and ethnicity. Whether you focus primarily on yourself—your personal needs, desires, and morality—or on your family, clan, and communal groups, depends on how much you are a product of modern Western individualism. Our attitudes and behavior are shaped by external social forces.

Personal attitudes and dispositions also shape behavior

Internal forces also matter. We are not passive tumbleweeds, merely blown this way and that by the social winds. Our inner attitudes affect our behavior. Our political attitudes influence our voting behavior. Our smoking attitudes influence our susceptibility to peer pressures to smoke. Our attitudes toward the poor influence our willingness to support them. (As we will see, attitudes also follow behavior, which leads us to believe strongly in those things for which we have committed ourselves or suffered.)

Personality dispositions also affect behavior. Facing the same situation, different people may react differently. Emerging from years of political imprisonment, one person exudes bitterness and seeks revenge. Another, such as

South Africa's Nelson Mandela, seeks reconciliation and unity with onetime enemies.

When we feel coerced by blatant social pressure, we may also react in ways that restore our sense of freedom. Moreover, those in a numerical minority will sometimes oppose and sway the majority. As individuals, we are not only the creatures of our social worlds, but also its creators. Treat others warmly and they will become more likable. The bottom line: Our worlds arise from the interactions between situations and persons.

Social behavior is also biological behavior

Early twenty-first-century social psychology is calling our attention to the biological foundations of social behavior. How we think about situations is important, but underneath our thinking lies biological wisdom. Everyone who has taken introductory psychology knows that nature and nurture together form who we are. As the area of a field is determined by both its length and width, so do biology and experience together create us. As *evolutionary psychologists* remind us (see Chapter 5), our inherited human nature predisposes us to behave in ways that helped our ancestors survive and reproduce. We carry the genes of those whose traits enabled them to survive and reproduce (and whose children did the same). Thus, evolutionary psychologists ask how natural selection might predispose our actions and reactions when dating and mating, hating and hurting, caring and sharing. Nature also endows us with an enormous capacity to learn and adapt. We are sensitive and responsive to our social context.

If every psychological event (every thought, every emotion) is simultaneously a biological event, then we can also examine the neurobiology that underlies social behavior. What brain areas enable our experiences of love and contempt, helping and aggression, perception and belief? How do brain, mind, and behavior function together as one coordinated system? What does the timing of brain events reveal about how we process information? Such questions are asked by those in "social cognitive neuroscience" (Ochsner & Lieberman, 2001).

Social neuroscientists do not aim to reproduce complex social behaviors, such as helping and hurting, to simple neural or molecular mechanisms. Yet to understand love and hate, we must consider both under-the-skin (biological) and between-skins (social) influences. Stress hormones affect how we feel and act; social ostracism elevates blood pressure; social support strengthens the disease-fighting immune system. Mind and body are one grand system. We are bio-psycho-social organisms.

Social psychology's principles are applicable in everyday life and in other disciplines

Social psychology is all about life, your life: your beliefs, your attitudes, your relationships. It therefore has the potential to illuminate your life, to make visible the subtle forces that guide your thinking and acting. And, as we will see, it offers many ideas about how to know ourselves better, how to win friends and influence people, how to transform closed fists into open arms.

Scholars are also applying social psychological insights to other disciplines. Principles of social thinking, social influence, and social relations have implications for human health and well-being, for judicial procedures and juror decisions in courtrooms, and for the encouragement of behaviors that will enable an environmentally sustainable human future.

But how does social psychology differ from sociology and from other areas of psychology? Are social psychologists influenced by their own values? What are social psychology's research tactics, and how might we apply these in everyday life? These are this chapter's questions.

Social psychology and related disciplines

Social psychologists are keenly interested in how people think about, influence, and relate to one another. But so are sociologists and personality psychologists. How does social psychology differ? What might social psychologists glean from evolutionary biology and neuroscience?

SOCIAL PSYCHOLOGY AND SOCIOLOGY

Sociologists and social psychologists share an interest in studying how people behave in groups. While most sociologists study groups, from small to very large (societies and their trends), most social psychologists study average *individuals*—how one person at a time thinks about others, is influenced by them, relates to them. These studies include how groups affect individual people and how an individual affects a group.

Some examples: In studying close relationships, a sociologist might study trends in marriage, divorce, and cohabitation rates; a social psychologist might examine how certain individuals become attracted to one another. Or a sociologist might investigate how the racial attitudes of middle-class people as a group differ from those of lower-income people. A social psychologist might study how racial attitudes develop within the individual.

Although sociologists and social psychologists use some of the same research methods, social psychologists rely much more heavily on experiments in which they *manipulate* a factor, such as the presence or absence of peer influence, to see its effect. The factors that sociologists study, such as socioeconomic class, are typically difficult or unethical to manipulate.

SOCIAL PSYCHOLOGY AND PERSONALITY PSYCHOLOGY

Social psychology and personality psychology are allies in their focus on the individual. Thus, the American Psychological Association includes the two subfields in the same journals (the *Journal of Personality and Social Psychology* and the *Personality and Social Psychology Bulletin*). Their difference lies in social psychology's social character. Personality psychologists focus on private internal functioning and on *differences* between individuals—for example, why some individuals are more aggressive than others. Social psychologists focus on our common humanity—on how people, in general, view and affect one another. They ask how social situations can lead *most* individuals to act kindly or cruelly, to conform or be independent, to feel liking or prejudice.

There are other differences: Social psychology has a shorter history. Many of personality psychology's heroes—people like Sigmund Freud, Carl Jung, Karen Horney, Abraham Maslow, and Carl Rogers—lived and worked during the first two-thirds of the last century. Most of the social psychologists whom you will meet in this book are still alive. Social psychology also has fewer

"You can never foretell what any man will do, but you can say with precision what an average number will be up to. Individuals may vary but percentages remain constant."
—Sherlock Holmes, in
Sir Arthur Conan Doyle's
A Study in Scarlet, 1887

famous theorists and more unsung ones—creative researchers who contribute smaller-scale concepts. We will meet a handful of these people in the autobiographical "The Story Behind a Classic Theory" boxes throughout this book.

LEVELS OF EXPLANATION

We study human beings from the differing perspectives of the academic disciplines. These perspectives range from basic sciences, such as physics and chemistry, to integrative disciplines, such as philosophy and theology. Which perspective is relevant depends on what you want to talk about. Take love, for example. A physiologist might describe the brain chemistry associated with passionate love. A social psychologist might examine how various characteristics and conditions—good looks, the partners' similarity, sheer repeated exposure—enhance the feeling we call love. A poet might extol the sublime experience love can sometimes be. We needn't assume that any one of these levels is the *real* explanation. The physiological and emotional perspectives on love, for example, are simply two ways of looking at the same event. Likewise, an evolutionary explanation of universal incest taboos (in terms of the genetic penalty offspring pay for inbreeding) does not replace a sociological explanation (which might see incest taboos as a way of preserving the family unit) or a theological one (which might focus on morality). The various explanations can complement one another (Figure 1–3).

If all truth is part of one fabric, then different levels of explanation should fit together to form a whole picture. Steven Pinker (2002) illustrates: "A geographer might explain why the coastline of Africa fits into the coastline of the Americas by saying that the landmasses were once adjacent but sat on different plates, which drifted apart. The question of why the plates move gets passed on to the geologists, who appeal to an upwelling of magma that pushes them apart. As for how the magma got so hot, they call in the physicists to explain the reactions in the Earth's core and mantle" (p. 70).

"Knowledge is one. Its division into subjects is a concession to human weakness."
—Sir Halford John MacKinder, 1887

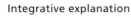

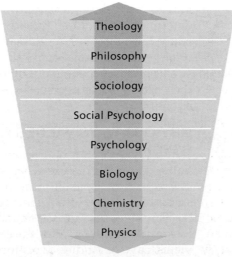

Integrative explanation

Theology

Philosophy

Sociology

Social Psychology

Psychology

Biology

Chemistry

Physics

Elemental explanation

figure 1–3

Partial hierarchy of disciplines.

The disciplines range from basic sciences that study nature's building blocks up to integrative disciplines that study complex systems. A successful explanation of human functioning at one level need not contradict explanations at other levels.

Recognizing the complementary relationship of various explanatory levels liberates us from useless argument over whether we should view human nature scientifically or subjectively: It's not an either/or matter. "Try as it might," explained sociologist Andrew Greeley (1976), "psychology cannot explain the purpose of human existence, the meaning of human life, the ultimate destiny of the human person." Social psychology is one important perspective from which we can view and understand ourselves, but it is not the only one.

Summing up

Social psychology is the scientific study of how people think about, influence, and relate to one another. Its central themes concern how we construe our social worlds, how our social intuitions guide and sometimes deceive us, and how our social behavior is shaped by other people, by our attitudes and personality, and by our biology. Sociology and psychology are social psychology's parent disciplines. Social psychology tends to be more individualistic in its content and more experimental in its method than sociology. Compared with personality psychology, social psychology focuses less on differences among individuals and more on how people, in general, view and affect one another.

Social psychology is an environmental science; it reveals how the social environment influences behavior. There are many additional perspectives on human nature, each of which asks its own set of questions and provides its own set of answers. These different perspectives are complementary, not contradictory.

Different sciences offer different perspectives. © 2004. Sidney Harris. Reprinted with permission.

Social psychology and human values

Social psychologists' values penetrate their work in ways both obvious and subtle. What are such ways?

Social psychology is less a collection of findings than a set of strategies for answering questions. In science, as in courts of law, personal opinions are inadmissible. When ideas are put on trial, evidence determines the verdict. But are social psychologists really this objective? As human beings, don't their *values*—their personal convictions about what is desirable and how people ought to behave—seep into their work? If so, can social psychology really be scientific?

OBVIOUS WAYS VALUES ENTER PSYCHOLOGY

Values enter the picture when social psychologists *choose research topics*. It was no accident that the study of prejudice flourished during the 1940s as fascism raged in Europe; that the 1950s, a time of look-alike fashions and intolerance of differing views, gave us studies of conformity; that the 1960s saw interest in aggression increase with riots and rising crime rates; that the feminist movement of the 1970s helped stimulate a wave of research on gender and sexism; that the 1980s offered a resurgence of attention to psychological aspects of the arms race; and that the 1990s were marked by heightened interest in how people respond to diversity in culture, race, and sexual orientation. Social psychology reflects social history.

Values also influence the *types of people* who are attracted to various disciplines (Campbell, 1975; Moynihan, 1979). At your school, too, do the students attracted to the humanities, the natural sciences, and the social sciences noticeably differ? Do social psychology and sociology attract people who are relatively eager to challenge tradition, people more inclined to shape the future than preserve the past?

Finally, values obviously enter the picture as the *object* of social-psychological analysis. Social psychologists investigate how values form, why they change, and how they influence attitudes and actions. None of this, however, tells us which values are "right."

NOT-SO-OBVIOUS WAYS VALUES ENTER PSYCHOLOGY

We less often recognize the subtler ways in which value commitments masquerade as objective truth. Consider three not-so-obvious ways in which values enter psychology.

The subjective aspects of science

Scientists and philosophers now agree: Science is not purely objective. Scientists do not simply read the book of nature. Rather, they interpret nature, using their own mental categories. In our daily lives, too, we view the world through the lens of our preconceptions. Pause a moment: What do you see in Figure 1–4?

"Science does not simply describe and explain nature; it is part of the interplay between nature and ourselves; it describes nature as exposed to our method of questioning."
—Werner Heisenberg, *Physics and Philosophy*, 1958

figure 1–4

What do you see?

Can you see a Dalmatian sniffing the ground at the picture's center? Without this preconception, most people are blind to the Dalmatian. Once your mind has the concept, it controls your interpretation of the picture—so much so that it becomes difficult *not* to see the dog.

This is the way our minds work. While reading these words you have been unaware that you are also looking at your nose. Your mind blocks from awareness something that is there, if only you were predisposed to perceive it. This tendency to prejudge reality based on our expectations is a basic fact about the human mind. A 1951 Princeton-Dartmouth football game provided a classic demonstration of how opinions control interpretations (Hastorf & Cantril, 1954; see also Loy & Andrews, 1981). The game lived up to its billing as a grudge match; it turned out to be one of the roughest and dirtiest games in the history of either school. A Princeton All-American was gang-tackled, piled on, and finally forced out of the game with a broken nose. Fistfights erupted, and there were further injuries on both sides. The whole performance hardly fit the Ivy League image of upper-class gentility.

Not long afterward, two psychologists, one from each school, showed films of the game to students on each campus. The students played the role of scientist-observer, noting each infraction as they watched and who was responsible for it. Could they set aside their loyalties? The Princeton students, for example, saw twice as many Dartmouth violations as the Dartmouth students saw. The moral: There *is* an objective reality out there; but we always view it through the lens of our beliefs and values.

Because scholars at work in any given area often share a common viewpoint or come from the same **culture,** their assumptions may go unchallenged. What we take for granted—the shared beliefs that European social psychologists call our **social representations** (Augoustinos & Innes, 1990; Moscovici, 1988)—are often our most important yet most unexamined convictions. Sometimes, however, someone from outside the camp will call attention to these assumptions. During the 1980s, feminists and Marxists exposed some of social psychology's unexamined assumptions. Feminist critics called attention to subtle biases—for example, the political conservatism of some scientists who favored a biological interpretation of gender differences in social behavior (Unger, 1985). Marxist critics called attention to competitive, individualist biases—for example, the assumption that conformity is bad and that individual rewards are good. Marxists and feminists, of course, make their own assumptions, as critics of academic "political correctness" are fond of noting. In Chapter 3 we will see more ways in which our preconceptions guide our interpretations. What guides our behavior is less the situation-as-it-is than the situation-as-we-construe-it.

Psychological concepts contain hidden values

Values also influence concepts. Consider attempts to specify the good life. Psychologists may refer to people as mature or immature, as well adjusted or poorly adjusted, as mentally healthy or mentally ill. They may talk as if they were stating facts, when really they are making *value judgments*. The personality psychologist Abraham Maslow, for example, was known for his sensitive descriptions of "self-actualized" people—people who, with their needs for survival, safety, "belongingness," and self-esteem satisfied, go on to fulfill their human potential. Few readers noticed that Maslow himself, guided by his own

culture
The enduring behaviors, ideas, attitudes, and traditions shared by a large group of people and transmitted from one generation to the next.

social representations
Socially shared beliefs—widely held ideas and values, including our assumptions and cultural ideologies. Our social representations help us make sense of our world.

values, selected the sample of self-actualized people he described. The resulting description of self-actualized personalities—as spontaneous, autonomous, mystical, and so forth—reflected Maslow's personal values. Had he begun with someone else's heroes—maybe Napoleon, Alexander the Great, and John D. Rockefeller—his resulting description of self-actualization would have differed (Smith, 1978).

Psychological advice also reflects the advice giver's personal values. When mental health professionals advise us how to live our lives, when child-rearing experts tell us how to handle our children, and when some psychologists encourage us to live free of concern for others' expectations, they are expressing their personal values. (In Western cultures, those values usually will be individualistic—encouraging what feels best for "me." Nonwestern cultures more often encourage what's best for "we.") Many people, unaware of the hidden values, defer to the "professional." But professional psychologists cannot answer questions of ultimate moral obligation, of purpose and direction, and of life's meaning.

Hidden values even seep into psychology's research-based *concepts*. Pretend you have taken a personality test and the psychologist, after scoring your answers, announces: "You scored high in self-esteem. You are low in anxiety. And you have exceptional ego-strength." "Ah," you think, "I suspected as much, but it feels good to know that." Now another psychologist gives you a similar test. For some peculiar reason, this test asks some of the same questions. Afterward the psychologist informs you that you seem defensive, for you scored high in "repressiveness." "How could this be?" you wonder. "The other psychologist said such nice things about me." It could be because all these labels describe the same set of responses (a tendency to say nice things about oneself and not to acknowledge problems). Shall we call it high self-esteem or defensiveness? The label reflects a value judgment.

That value judgments are often hidden within our social-psychological language is no reason to fault social psychology. This is true of everyday language. Whether we label someone engaged in guerrilla warfare a "terrorist" or a "freedom fighter" depends on our view of the cause. Whether we view wartime civilian deaths as "the loss of innocent lives" or as "collateral damage" affects our acceptance of such. Whether we call public assistance "welfare" or "aid to the needy" reflects our political views. When "they" exalt their country and people, it's nationalism; when "we" do it, it's patriotism. Whether someone involved in an extramarital affair is practicing "open marriage" or "adultery" depends on one's personal values. "Brainwashing" is social influence we do not approve of. "Perversions" are sex acts we do not practice. Remarks about "ambitious" men and "aggressive" women convey a hidden message.

To repeat, values lie hidden within our cultural definitions of mental health and self-esteem, our psychological advice for living, and our psychological labels. Throughout this book I will call your attention to additional examples of hidden values. The point is never that the implicit values are necessarily bad. The point is that scientific interpretation,

Hidden (and not-so-hidden) values seep into psychological advice. They permeate popular psychology books that offer guidance on living and loving.

even at the level of labeling phenomena, is a human activity. It is therefore natural and inevitable that prior beliefs and values will influence what social psychologists think and write.

There is no bridge from "is" to "ought"

naturalistic fallacy
The error of defining what is good in terms of what is observable. For example: What's typical is normal; what's normal is good.

A seductive error for those who work in the social sciences is sliding from a description of *what is* into a prescription of *what ought to be.* Philosophers call this the **naturalistic fallacy.** The gulf between "is" and "ought," between scientific description and ethical prescription, remains as wide today as when philosopher David Hume pointed it out more than 200 years ago. No survey of human behavior—say, of sexual practices—logically dictates what is "right" behavior. If most people don't do something, that does not make it wrong. If most people do it, that does not make it right. We inject our values whenever we move from objective statements of fact to prescriptive statements of what ought to be.

In both obvious and subtle ways, social psychologists' personal values influence their work. And what is true of them is true of each of us. Our values and assumptions color our views of the world. To discover how much our assumed values and social representations shape what we take for granted, we need to encounter different cultures. If you assume without question that people should, above all, be true to themselves; that women are (or aren't) better suited than men to certain roles; or that romantic love should come before marriage, stay tuned.

Should we dismiss science because it has its subjective side? Quite the contrary: The realization that human thinking always involves interpretation is precisely why we need researchers with varying biases to undertake scientific analysis. By constantly checking our beliefs against the facts, as best we know them, we check and restrain our biases. Systematic observation and experimentation help us clean the lens through which we see reality.

Summing up

Social psychologists' values penetrate their work in obvious ways, such as their choice of research topics, and in subtler ways, such as their hidden assumptions when forming concepts, choosing labels, and giving advice. There is a growing awareness of the subjectivity of scientific interpretation, of values hidden in social psychology's concepts and labels, and of the gulf between scientific description of what is and ethical prescription of what ought to be. This penetration of values into science is not unique to social psychology. That human thinking is seldom dispassionate is precisely why we need systematic observation and experimentation if we are to check our cherished ideas against reality.

I knew it all along: Is social psychology simply common sense?

Do social psychology's theories provide new insight into the human condition? Or do they only describe the obvious?

Many of the conclusions presented in this book may have already occurred to you, for social psychology is all around you. We constantly observe people thinking about, influencing, and relating to one another. It pays to discern what that facial expression predicts, how to get someone to do something, or whether to regard another as friend or foe. For centuries, philosophers, novelists, and poets have observed and commented on social behavior. Social psychology is everybody's business.

So is social psychology only common sense in different words? Social psychology faces two contradictory criticisms: One is that it is trivial because it documents the obvious; the second is that it is dangerous because its findings could be used to manipulate people. Is the first objection valid—does social psychology simply formalize what any amateur already knows intuitively?

Writer Cullen Murphy (1990) thought so: "Day after day social scientists go out into the world. Day after day they discover that people's behavior is pretty much what you'd expect." Nearly a half-century earlier, historian Arthur Schlesinger, Jr., (1949) reacted with similar scorn to social scientists' studies of American World War II soldiers.

What did these studies find? Another reviewer, sociologist Paul Lazarsfeld (1949), offered a sample with interpretive comments, a few of which I paraphrase:

1. Better-educated soldiers suffered more adjustment problems than did less-educated soldiers. (Intellectuals were less prepared for battle stresses than street-smart people.)
2. Southern soldiers coped better with the hot South Sea Island climate than did Northern soldiers. (Southerners are more accustomed to hot weather.)
3. White privates were more eager for promotion than were Black privates. (Years of oppression take a toll on achievement motivation.)
4. Southern Blacks preferred Southern to Northern White officers (because Southern officers were more experienced and skilled in interacting with Blacks).

One problem with common sense, however, is that we invoke it after we know the facts. Events are far more "obvious" and predictable in hindsight than beforehand. Experiments reveal that when people learn the outcome of an experiment, that outcome suddenly seems unsurprising—certainly less surprising than it is to people who are simply told about the experimental procedure and the possible outcomes (Slovic & Fischhoff, 1977). With new knowledge at hand, our efficient memory system purges its outdated presumption (Hoffrage & others, 2000).

"A first-rate theory predicts; a second-rate theory forbids; and a third-rate theory explains after the event."
—Aleksander Isaakovich Kitaigorodskii

You perhaps experienced this phenomenon when reading Lazarsfeld's summary of findings. For Lazarsfeld went on to say, *Every one of these statements is the direct opposite of what was actually found.* In reality, the book reported that less-educated soldiers adapted more poorly. Southerners were not more likely than Northerners to adjust to a tropical climate. Blacks were more eager than Whites for promotion, and so forth. "If we had mentioned the actual results of the investigation first [as Schlesinger experienced], the reader would have labeled these 'obvious' also."

Likewise, in everyday life we often do not expect something to happen until it does. *Then* we suddenly see clearly the forces that brought the event about and feel unsurprised. After elections or stock market shifts, most commentators find the turn of events unsurprising: "The market was due for a correction."

www.mhhe.com/myers8
Visit the Online Learning Center for an interactivity on the science of common sense.

hindsight bias
The tendency to exaggerate, after learning an outcome, one's ability to have foreseen how something turned out. Also known as the I-knew-it-all-along phenomenon.

After the 2003 war in Iraq, the result—for Coalition forces victory came swiftly, but not civility and democracy—seemed obvious. Some argued that with the United States' $330 billion to $1.6 billion annual military spending advantage over Iraq, anyone could have predicted the rout, but the American forces should have foreseen the need to protect Baghdad's museums, libraries, and schools from looters. As the Danish philosopher-theologian Søren Kierkegaard put it, "Life is lived forwards, but understood backwards."

If this **hindsight bias** (also called the I-knew-it-all-along phenomenon) is pervasive, you may now be feeling that you already knew about it. Indeed, almost any conceivable result of a psychological experiment can seem like common sense—*after* you know the result.

You can demonstrate the phenomenon. Give half a group one psychological finding and the other half the opposite result. For example, tell half as follows:

> Social psychologists have found that, whether choosing friends or falling in love, we are most attracted to people whose traits are different from our own. There seems to be wisdom in the old saying, "Opposites attract."

Tell the other half:

> Social psychologists have found that, whether choosing friends or falling in love, we are most attracted to people whose traits are similar to our own. There seems to be wisdom in the old saying, "Birds of a feather flock together."

Ask the people first to explain the result. Then ask them to say whether it is "surprising" or "not surprising." Virtually all will find whichever result they were given "not surprising."

Indeed, we can draw on our stockpile of proverbs to make almost any result seem to make sense. If a social psychologist reports that separation intensifies romantic attraction, Joe Public responds, "You get paid for this? Everybody knows that 'absence makes the heart grow fonder.'" Should it turn out that separation weakens attraction, Judy Public may say, "My grandmother could have told you, 'Out of sight, out of mind.'"

Karl Teigen (1986) must have had a few chuckles when he asked University of Leicester (England) students to evaluate actual proverbs and their opposites. When given the proverb, "Fear is stronger than love," most rated it as true. But so did students who were given its reversed form, "Love is stronger than fear." Likewise, the genuine proverb "He that is fallen cannot help him who is down" was rated highly; but so too was "He that is fallen can help him who is down."

My favorites, however, were two highly rated proverbs: "Wise men make proverbs and fools repeat them" (authentic) and its made-up counterpart, "Fools make proverbs and wise men repeat them." (For more dueling proverbs, see "Focus on: I Knew It All Along.")

The hindsight bias creates a problem for many psychology students. Sometimes results are genuinely surprising (for example, that Olympic *bronze* medalists take more joy in their achievement than do silver medalists). More often, when you read the results of experiments in your textbooks, the material seems easy, even obvious. When you later take a

In hindsight, events seem obvious and predictable.
© 2004 Sidney Harris. Reprinted with permission.

INSTITUTE for ADVANCED HINDSIGHT
RESEARCH INTO WHAT SHOULD HAVE BEEN

focus on   I knew it all along

Cullen Murphy (1990), managing editor of the *Atlantic*, faulted "sociology, psychology, and other social sciences for too often merely discerning the obvious or confirming the commonplace." His own casual survey of social science findings "turned up no ideas or conclusions that can't be found in *Bartlett's* or any other encyclopedia of quotations." Nevertheless, to sift through competing sayings, we need research. Consider some dueling proverbs:

Is it more true that . . .	*Or that . . .*
Too many cooks spoil the broth.	Two heads are better than one.
The pen is mightier than the sword.	Actions speak louder than words.
You can't teach an old dog new tricks.	You're never too old to learn.
Blood is thicker than water.	Many kinfolk, few friends.
He who hesitates is lost.	Look before you leap.
Forewarned is forearmed.	Don't cross the bridge until you come to it.

multiple-choice test on which you must choose among several plausible conclusions, the task may become surprisingly difficult. "I don't know what happened," the befuddled student later moans. "I thought I knew the material."

The I-knew-it-all-along phenomenon can have pernicious consequences. It is conducive to arrogance—an overestimation of our own intellectual powers. Moreover, because outcomes seem as if they should have been foreseeable, we are more likely to blame decision makers for what are in retrospect "obvious" bad choices than to praise them for good choices, which also seem "obvious." Starting *after* the morning of 9/11 and working backward, signals pointing to the impending disaster seemed obvious. A U.S. Senate investigative report listed the missed or misinterpreted clues (Gladwell, 2003). The CIA knew that al Qaeda operatives had entered the country. An FBI agent sent a memo to headquarters that began by warning "the Bureau and New York of the possibility of a coordinated effort by Osama bin Laden to send students to the United States to attend civilian aviation universities and colleges." The FBI ignored this accurate warning and failed to relate it to other reports that terrorists were planning to use planes as weapons. "The dumb fools!" it seemed to hindsight critics. "Why couldn't they connect the dots?"

But what seems clear in hindsight is seldom clear on the front side of history. The intelligence community is overwhelmed with "noise"—the piles of useless information surrounding the shreds of useful information. Analysts must therefore be selective in deciding which to pursue. In the six years prior to 9/11, the FBI's counterterrorism unit had 68,000 uninvestigated leads. In hindsight, the few useful ones are now obvious.

Likewise, we sometimes blame ourselves for "stupid mistakes"—perhaps for not having handled a person or a situation better. Looking back, we see how we should have handled it. "I should have known how busy I would be at the semester's end and started that paper earlier." But sometimes we are too hard on ourselves. We forget that what is obvious to us *now* was not nearly so obvious at the time.

Physicians who are told both a patient's symptoms and the cause of death (as determined by autopsy) sometimes wonder how an incorrect diagnosis could have been made. Other physicians, given only the symptoms, don't find the diagnosis nearly so obvious (Dawson & others, 1988). (Would juries be slower to assume malpractice if they were forced to take a foresight rather than a hindsight perspective?)

So what do we conclude—that common sense is usually wrong? Sometimes it is. Common sense and medical experience assured doctors that bleeding was an effective treatment for typhoid fever, until someone in the middle of the nineteenth century bothered to experiment—to divide patients into two groups, one bled, the other given mere bed rest.

Other times, conventional wisdom is right—or it falls on both sides of an issue: Does happiness come from knowing the truth or preserving illusions? From being with others or living in peaceful solitude? Opinions are a dime a dozen; no matter what we find, there will be someone who foresaw it. (Mark Twain jested that Adam was the only person who, when saying a good thing, knew that nobody had said it before.) But which of the many competing ideas best fit reality?

The point is not that common sense is predictably wrong. Rather, common sense usually is right *after the fact*. We therefore easily deceive ourselves into thinking that we know and knew more than we do and did. And this is precisely why we need science—to help us sift reality from illusion and genuine predictions from easy hindsight.

"It is easy to be wise after the event."
—Sherlock Holmes, in Arthur Conan Doyle's story "The Problem of Thor Bridge"

"Everything important has been said before."
—Philosopher Alfred North Whitehead (1861–1947)

Summing up

Like many of life's happenings, social psychology's findings sometimes seem obvious. Experiments, however, reveal that outcomes are more "obvious" *after* the facts are known. This hindsight bias often makes people overconfident about the validity of their judgments and predictions.

Research methods: How we do social psychology

Social psychologists propose theories that organize their observations and imply testable hypotheses and practical predictions. Social psychologists also do research that predicts behavior using correlational studies, often conducted in natural settings. And they seek to explain behavior by conducting experiments that manipulate one or more factors under controlled conditions.

Unlike other scientific disciplines, social psychology has nearly 6 billion amateur practitioners. People-watching is a universal hobby—in parks, on the street, at school. As we observe people, we form ideas about how human beings think about, influence, and relate to one another. Professional social psychologists do the same, only more systematically (by forming theories) and painstakingly (often with experiments that create miniature social dramas that pin down cause and effect). And they do it frequently, in 25,000 studies of 8 million people by one recent count (Richard & others, 2003).

"Nothing has such power to broaden the mind as the ability to investigate systematically and truly all that comes under thy observation in life."
—Marcus Aurelius, *Meditations*

FORMING AND TESTING HYPOTHESES

We social psychologists have a hard time thinking of anything more fascinating than human existence. If, as Socrates counseled, "The unexamined life is not worth living," then simply "knowing thyself" seems a worthy enough goal.

As we wrestle with human nature to pin down its secrets, we organize our ideas and findings into theories. A **theory** is *an integrated set of principles that explain and predict* observed events. Theories are a scientific shorthand.

In everyday conversation, "theory" often means "less than fact"—a middle rung on a confidence ladder from guess to theory to fact. But to a scientist, facts and theories are apples and oranges. Facts are agreed-upon statements about what we observe. Theories are *ideas* that summarize and explain facts. "Science is built up with facts, as a house is with stones," said Jules Henri Poincaré, "but a collection of facts is no more a science than a heap of stones is a house."

Theories not only summarize, they also imply testable predictions, called **hypotheses.** Hypotheses serve several purposes. First, they allow us to *test* a theory by suggesting how we might try to falsify it. In making predictions, a theory puts its money where its mouth is. Second, predictions give *direction* to research. Any scientific field will mature more rapidly if its researchers have a sense of direction. Theoretical predictions suggest new areas for research; they send investigators looking for things they might never have thought of. Third, the predictive feature of good theories can also make them *practical*. A complete theory of aggression, for example, would predict when to expect it and how to control it. As Kurt Lewin, one of modern social psychology's founders, declared, "There is nothing so practical as a good theory."

Consider how this works. Say we observe that people who loot, taunt, or attack often do so in groups or crowds. We might therefore theorize that the presence of other people makes individuals feel anonymous and lowers their inhibitions. Let's play with this idea for a moment. Perhaps we could test it by constructing a laboratory experiment simulating aspects of execution by electric chair. What if we asked individuals in groups to administer punishing shocks to a hapless victim without knowing which one of the group was actually shocking the victim? Would these individuals administer stronger shocks than individuals acting alone, as our theory predicts?

We might also manipulate anonymity: Would people deliver stronger shocks hiding behind masks? If the results confirm our hypothesis, they might suggest some practical applications. Perhaps police brutality could be reduced by having officers wear large name tags and drive cars identified with large numbers, or by videotaping their arrests— all of which have, in fact, recently become common practice in many cities.

But how do we conclude that one theory is better than another? A good theory (1) effectively summarizes a wide range of observations and (2) makes clear predictions that we can use to (a) confirm or modify the theory, (b) generate new exploration, and (c) suggest practical application. When we discard theories, usually it's not because they have been proved false. Rather, like old cars, they get replaced by newer, better models.

theory
An integrated set of principles that explain and predict observed events.

hypothesis
A testable proposition that describes a relationship that may exist between events.

www.mhhe.com/myers8
Visit the Online Learning Center for a scenario on research methods.

For humans, the most fascinating subject is people.

CORRELATIONAL RESEARCH: DETECTING NATURAL ASSOCIATIONS

Most of what you will learn about social-psychological research methods you will absorb as you read later chapters. But let us go backstage now and take a brief look at how social psychology is done. This glimpse behind the scenes will be just enough for you to appreciate findings discussed later and to think critically about everyday social events.

Social-psychological research varies by location. It can take place in the *laboratory* (a controlled situation) or in the **field** (everyday situations). And it varies by method—whether **correlational** (asking whether two or more factors are naturally associated) or **experimental** (manipulating some factor to see its effect on another). If you want to be a critical reader of psychological research reported in newspapers and magazines, it pays to understand the difference between correlational and experimental research.

Using some real examples, let's first consider the advantages of correlational research (often involving important variables in natural settings) and the disadvantage (ambiguous interpretation of cause and effect). As we will see in Chapter 14, today's psychologists relate personal and social factors to human health. Among the researchers have been Douglas Carroll at Glasgow Caledonian University and his colleagues, George Davey Smith and Paul Bennett (1994). In search of possible links between socioeconomic status and health, the researchers ventured into Glasgow's old graveyards. As a measure of health, they noted from grave markers the life spans of 843 individuals. As an indication of status, they measured the height of the pillars over the graves, reasoning that height reflected cost and therefore affluence. As Figure 1–5 shows, taller grave markers were related to longer lives, for both men and women.

Carroll and his colleagues explain how other researchers, using contemporary data, have confirmed the status-longevity correlation. Scottish postal-code

field research
Research done in natural, real-life settings outside the laboratory.

correlational research
The study of the naturally occurring relationships among variables.

experimental research
Studies that seek clues to cause-effect relationships by manipulating one or more factors (independent variables) while controlling others (holding them constant).

figure 1–5

Correlating status and longevity.
Tall grave pillars commemorated people who also tended to live longer.

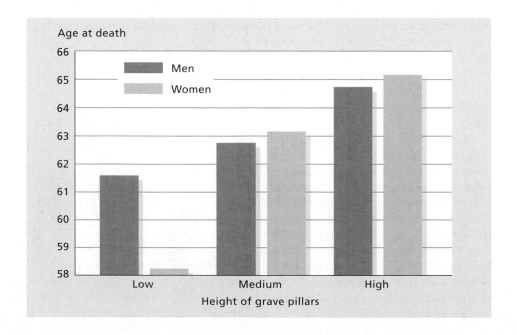

regions having the least overcrowding and unemployment also have the greatest longevity. In the United States, income correlates with longevity (poor and lower-status people are more at risk for premature death). In contemporary Britain, occupational status correlates with longevity. One study followed 17,350 British civil service workers over 10 years. Compared with top-grade administrators, those at the professional-executive grade were 1.6 times more likely to have died. Clerical workers were 2.2 times and laborers 2.7 times more likely to have died (Adler & others, 1993, 1994). Across times and places, the status-health correlation seems reliable.

Correlation versus causation

The status-longevity question illustrates the most irresistible thinking er-

Commemorative markers in Glasgow Cathedral graveyard.

ror made by both amateur and professional social psychologists: When two factors like status and health go together, it is terribly tempting to conclude that one is causing the other. Status, we might presume, somehow protects a person from health risks. Or might it be the other way around? Maybe health promotes vigor and success. Perhaps people who live longer accumulate more wealth (enabling them to have more expensive grave markers). Correlational research allows us to *predict*, but it cannot tell us whether changing one variable (such as social status) will *cause* changes in another (such as health).

The correlation-causation confusion is behind much muddled thinking in popular psychology. Consider another very real correlation—between self-esteem and academic achievement. Children with high self-esteem tend also to have high academic achievement. (As with any correlation, we can also state this the other way around: High achievers tend to have high self-esteem.) Why do you suppose this is (Figure 1–6)?

Researchers have found a modest but positive correlation between adolescents' preference for heavy metal music and their having attitudes favorable to premarital sex, pornography, satanism, and drug and alcohol use (Landers, 1988). What are some possible explanations for this correlation?

Some people believe a "healthy self-concept" contributes to achievement. Thus, boosting a child's self-image may also boost school achievement. Believing so, 30 U.S. states have enacted more than 170 self-esteem-promoting statutes.

But other people, including psychologists William Damon (1995), Robyn Dawes (1994), Mark Leary (1998), Martin Seligman (1994), and Roy Baumeister and colleagues (2003), doubt that self-esteem is really "the armor that protects kids" from underachievement (or drug abuse and delinquency). Perhaps it's the other way around: Perhaps problems and failures cause low self-esteem. Perhaps self-esteem often reflects the reality of how things are going for us. Perhaps self-esteem grows from hard-won achievements. Do well and you will feel good about yourself; goof off and fail and you will feel like a dolt. A study of 635 Norwegian schoolchildren suggests that a string of gold stars by one's name on the spelling chart and praise from the admiring teacher can boost a child's

figure 1–6
Correlation and causations.
When two variables correlate, any combination of three explanations is possible.

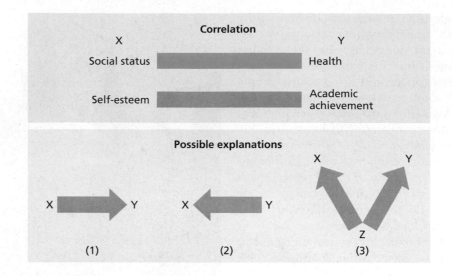

self-esteem (Skaalvik & Hagtvet, 1990). It's also possible that self-esteem and achievement correlate because both are linked to underlying intelligence and family social status.

That possibility was raised in two studies—one a nationwide sample of 1,600 young American men, another of 715 Minnesota youngsters (Bachman & O'Malley, 1977; Maruyama & others, 1981). When the researchers statistically removed the effect of intelligence and family status, the correlation between self-esteem and achievement evaporated.

Advanced correlational techniques can suggest cause-effect relations. *Time-lagged* correlations reveal the *sequence* of events (for example, by indicating whether changed achievement more often precedes or follows changed self-esteem). Researchers can also use statistical techniques that extract the influence of "confounded" variables as when the correlation between self-esteem *and* achievement evaporated after extracting intelligence and family status. (Among people of similar intelligence and family status, the self-esteem-achievement relationship was minimal.) The Scottish research team wondered whether the status-longevity relationship would survive their removing the effect of cigarette smoking, which is now much less common among those higher in status. It did, which suggested that some other factors, such as increased stress and decreased feelings of control, must also account for the greater mortality of the poor.

So the great strength of correlational research is that it tends to occur in real-world settings where we can examine factors like race, gender, and social status that we cannot manipulate in the laboratory. Its great disadvantage lies in the ambiguity of the results. The point is so important that, even if it fails to impress people the first 25 times they hear it, it is worth making a 26th time: Knowing that two variables change together enables us to predict one when we know the other; but correlation does not specify cause and effect.

Survey research

How do we measure variables such as status and health? One way is by surveying representative samples of people. Survey researchers obtain a representative

Even exit polls require a random (and therefore representative) sample of voters.

group by taking a **random sample**—*one in which every person in the population being studied has an equal chance of inclusion.* With this procedure any subgroup of people—blondes, joggers, liberals—will tend to be represented in the survey to the extent that they are represented in the total population.

It is an amazing fact that whether we survey people in a city or in a whole country, 1,200 randomly selected participants will enable us to be 95 percent confident of describing the entire population with an error margin of 3 percentage points or less. Imagine a huge jar filled with beans, 50 percent red and 50 percent white. Randomly sample 1,200 of these, and you will be 95 percent certain to draw out between 47 percent and 53 percent red beans—regardless of whether the jar contains 10,000 beans or 100 million beans. If we think of the red beans as supporters of one presidential candidate and the white beans as supporters of the other candidate, we can understand why, since 1950, the Gallup polls taken just before U.S. national elections have diverged from election results by an average of less than 2 percent. As a few drops of blood can speak for the whole body, so can a random sample speak for a population.

Bear in mind that polls do not literally *predict* voting; they only *describe* public opinion as of the moment they are taken. Public opinion can shift. To evaluate surveys, we must also bear in mind four potentially biasing influences: unrepresentative samples, order of questions, response options, and wording of the questions.

Unrepresentative samples.   Sample size is not all that matters in a survey; how closely the sample represents the population under study also matters. In 1984, columnist Ann Landers accepted a letter writer's challenge to poll her readers on the question of whether women find affection more important than sex. Her question: "Would you be content to be held close and treated tenderly and forget about 'the act'?" Of the more than 100,000 women who replied, 72 percent said yes. An avalanche of worldwide publicity followed. In response to critics, Landers (1985, p. 45) granted that "the sampling may not be representative of all American women. But it does provide honest—valuable—insights from a

random sample
Survey procedure in which every person in the population being studied has an equal chance of inclusion.

cross section of the public. This is because my column is read by people from every walk of life, approximately 70 million of them." Still, one wonders, are the 70 million readers representative of the entire population? And are the 1 in 700 readers who participated representative of the 699 in 700 who did not?

The importance of representativeness was effectively demonstrated in 1936, when a weekly newsmagazine, *Literary Digest,* mailed a postcard presidential election poll to 10 million Americans. Among the more than 2 million returns, Alf Landon won by a landslide over Franklin D. Roosevelt. When the actual votes were counted a few days later, Landon carried only two states. The magazine had sent the poll only to people whose names it had obtained from telephone books and automobile registrations—thus omitting all those who could afford neither (Cleghorn, 1980).

Order of questions.   Given a representative sample, we must also contend with other sources of bias, such as the order in which we ask questions. Asked whether "the Japanese government should be allowed to set limits on how much American industry can sell in Japan," most Americans answered no (Schuman & Ludwig, 1983). Simultaneously, two-thirds of an equivalent sample were answering yes to the same question because they were first asked whether "the American government should be allowed to set limits on how much Japanese industry can sell in the United States." Most of these people said the United States has the right to limit imports. To appear consistent, they then said that Japan should have the same right.

Response options.   Consider, too, the dramatic effects of the response options. When Joop van der Plight and his co-workers (1987) asked English voters what percentage of Britain's nuclear energy they wished came from nuclear power, the average preference was 41 percent. They asked others what percentage they wished came from (1) nuclear, (2) coal, and (3) other sources. Their average preference for nuclear power was 21 percent.

A similar effect occurred when Howard Schuman and Jacqueline Scott (1987) asked Americans, "What do you think is the most important problem facing this country today—the energy shortage, the quality of public schools, legalized abortion, or pollution—or if you prefer, you may name a different problem as most important." Given these choices, 32 percent felt that the quality of public schools was the biggest problem. Among others they simply asked, "What do you think is the most important problem facing this country today?" Only 1 percent named the schools. So remember: The form of the question may guide the answer.

Wording of questions.   The precise wording of questions may also influence answers. One poll found that only 23 percent of Americans thought their government was spending too much "on assistance to the poor." Yet 53 percent thought the government was spending too much "on welfare" (*Time*, 1994). Likewise, most people favor cutting "foreign aid" and *increasing* spending "to help hungry people in other nations" (Simon, 1996). Even subtle changes in the tone of a question can have large effects (Krosnick & Schuman, 1988; Schuman & Kalton, 1985).

"Forbidding" something may be the same as "not allowing" it. But in 1940, 54 percent of Americans said the United States should "forbid" speeches against democracy, and 75 percent said the United States should "not allow" them. And

SRC's Survey Services Laboratory at the University of Michigan's Institute for Social Research has interviewing carrels with monitoring stations. Staff and visitors must sign a pledge to honor the strict confidentiality of all interviews.

in late 2003, one national survey found 55 percent of Americans favoring a constitutional amendment that "would allow marriage only between a man and a woman," whereas in a simultaneous survey, only 40 percent favored "an amendment banning gay marriage" (Moore, 2004). Survey questioning is a very delicate matter. Even when people say they feel strongly about an issue, a question's form and wording may affect their answer.

Order, response, and wording effects enable political manipulators to use surveys to show public support for their views. Consultants, advertisers, and physicians can have similar disconcerting influences upon our decisions by how they "frame" our choices. No wonder the meat lobby in 1994 objected to a new U.S. food labeling law that requires declaring ground beef, for example, as "30 percent fat," rather than "70 percent lean, 30 percent fat."

The moral: The way choices are worded can make a big difference. The story is told of a sultan who dreamed he lost all his teeth. Summoned to interpret the dream, the first interpreter said, "Alas! The lost teeth mean you will see your family members die." Enraged, the sultan ordered 50 lashes for this bearer of bad news.

Survey researchers must be sensitive to subtle and not-so-subtle biases.
DOONESBURY © G. B. Trudeau. Reprinted with permission of Universal Press Syndicate. All rights reserved.

DOONESBURY   **by Garry Trudeau**

A young monk was once rebuffed when asking if he could smoke while he prayed. Ask a different question, advised a friend: Ask if you can pray while you smoke (Crossen, 1993).

When a second dream interpreter heard the dream, he explained the sultan's good fortune: "You will outlive your whole clan!" Reassured, the sultan ordered his treasurer to go and fetch 50 pieces of gold for this bearer of good news.

On the way, the bewildered treasurer observed to the second interpreter, "Your interpretation was no different from that of the first interpreter." "Ah yes," the wise interpreter replied, "but remember: What matters is not only what you say, but how you say it."

EXPERIMENTAL RESEARCH: SEARCHING FOR CAUSE AND EFFECT

The near impossibility of discerning cause and effect among naturally correlated events prompts most social psychologists to create laboratory simulations of everyday processes whenever this is feasible and ethical. These simulations are roughly similar to aeronautical wind tunnels. Aeronautical engineers don't begin by observing how flying objects perform in a wide variety of natural environments. The variations in both atmospheric conditions and flying objects are so complex that they would surely find it difficult to organize and use such data to design better aircraft. Instead, they construct a simulated reality that is under their control. Then they can manipulate wind conditions and observe the precise effect of particular wind conditions on particular wing structures.

Control: Manipulating variables

independent variable
The experimental factor that a researcher manipulates.

Like aeronautical engineers, social psychologists experiment by constructing social situations that simulate important features of our daily lives. By varying just one or two factors at a time—called **independent variables**—the experimenter pinpoints how changes in these one or two things affect us. As the wind tunnel helps the aeronautical engineer discover principles of aerodynamics, so the experiment enables the social psychologist to discover principles of social thinking, social influence, and social relations. The ultimate aim of wind tunnel simulations is to understand and predict the flying characteristics of complex aircraft. Social psychologists experiment to understand and predict complex human behaviors. They aim to understand why behavior varies among people, across situations, and over time.

Historically, social psychologists have used the experimental method in about three-fourths of their research studies (Higbee & others, 1982), and in two out of three studies the setting has been a research laboratory (Adair & others, 1985). To illustrate the laboratory experiment, consider two experiments that typify research from upcoming chapters on prejudice and aggression. Each suggests possible cause-effect explanations of correlational findings.

The first experiment concerns prejudice against people who are obese. People often perceive the obese as slow, lazy, and sloppy (Ryckman & others, 1989). Do such attitudes spawn discrimination? In hopes of finding out, Steven Gortmaker and his colleagues (1993) studied 370 obese 16- to 24-year-olds. When they restudied them seven years later, two-thirds of the women were still obese and were less likely to be married and earning high salaries than a comparison group of some 5,000 other women. Even after correcting for any differences in aptitude test scores, race, and parental income, the obese women's incomes were $7,000 a year below average.

Correcting for certain other factors makes it look like discrimination might explain the correlation between obesity and lower status. But we can't be sure.

(Can you think of other possibilities?) Enter social psychologists Mark Snyder and Julie Haugen (1994, 1995). They asked 76 University of Minnesota male students to have a getting acquainted phone conversation with 1 of 76 female students. Each man was shown a photo *said* to picture his conversational partner. Half were shown an obese woman (not the actual partner); the other half a normal weight woman. In one part of the experiment, the men were asked to form an impression of the women's traits. Later analysis of just the women's side of the conversation revealed that, when women were being evaluated, they spoke less warmly and happily if they were presumed obese. Clearly, the men's beliefs induced them to behave in a way that led their supposedly obese partners to confirm the idea that such women are undesirable. Prejudice and discrimination were having an effect. Recalling the effect of the stepmother's attitudes, perhaps we should call this "The Cinderella effect."

As a second example of how experiments clarify causation, consider the correlation between television viewing and children's behavior. Children who watch many violent television programs tend to be more aggressive than those who watch few. This suggests that children might be learning from what they see on the screen. As I hope you now recognize, this is a correlational finding. Figure 1–6 on p. 24 reminds us that there are two other cause-effect interpretations that do not implicate television as the cause of the children's aggression. (What are they?)

Social psychologists have therefore brought television viewing into the laboratory, where they control the amount of violence the children see. By exposing children to violent and nonviolent programs, researchers can observe how the amount of violence affects behavior. Chris Boyatzis and his colleagues (1995) showed some elementary school children, but not others, an episode of the 1990s most popular—and violent—children's television program, "Power Rangers." Immediately after viewing the episode, the viewers committed seven times as many aggressive acts per two-minute interval as the nonviewers. The

Does viewing violence on TV or in other media lead to imitation, especially among children? Experiments suggest that it does.

table 1–1   Recognizing correlations and experimental research

	Can Participants Be Randomly Assigned to Condition?	Independent Variable	Dependent Variable
Are early-maturing children more confident?	No → Correlational		
Do students learn more in online or classroom courses?	Yes → Experimental	Take class online or in classroom	Learning
Do school grades predict vocational success?	No → Correlational		
Does playing violent video games increase aggressiveness?	Yes → Experimental	Play violent or nonviolent game	Aggressiveness
Do people find comedy funnier when alone or with others?	(you answer)		
Do higher-income people have higher self-esteem?	(you answer)		

dependent variable
The variable being measured, so called because it may depend on manipulations of the independent variable.

observed aggressive acts we call the **dependent variable.** Such experiments indicate that television can be one cause of children's aggressive behavior.

So far we have seen that the logic of experimentation is simple: By creating and controlling a miniature reality, we can vary one factor and then another and discover how these factors, separately or in combination, affect people. Now let's go a little deeper and see how an experiment is done.

Every social-psychological experiment has two essential ingredients. We have just considered one—*control*. We manipulate one or two independent variables while trying to hold everything else constant. The other ingredient is *random assignment.*

Random assignment: The great equalizer

Recall that we were reluctant, on the basis of a correlation, to assume that obesity *caused* lower status (via discrimination) or that violence viewing *caused* aggressiveness (see Table 1–1 for more examples). A survey researcher might measure and statistically extract other possibly pertinent factors and see if the correlations survive. But one can never control for all the factors that might distinguish obese from nonobese, and viewers of violence from nonviewers. Maybe violence viewers differ in education, culture, intelligence—or in dozens of ways the researcher hasn't considered.

random assignment
The process of assigning participants to the conditions of an experiment such that all persons have the same chance of being in a given condition (Note the distinction between random assignment in experiments and random sampling in surveys. Random assignment helps us infer cause and effect. Random sampling helps us generalize to a population.)

In one fell swoop, **random assignment** eliminates all such extraneous factors. With random assignment, each person has an equal chance of viewing the violence or the nonviolence. Thus, the people in both groups would, in every conceivable way—family status, intelligence, education, initial aggressiveness—average about the same. Highly intelligent people, for example, are equally likely to appear in both groups. Because random assignment creates equivalent groups, any later aggression difference between the two groups must have something to do with the only way they differ—whether or not they viewed violence (Figure 1–7). And thanks to random assignment of the

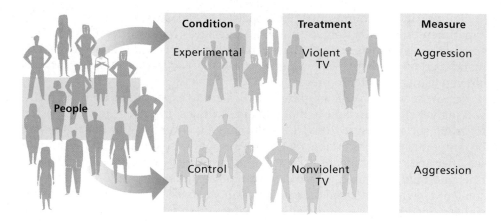

Experimental

Treatment
Violent TV

Measure
Aggression

People

Control

Nonviolent TV

Aggression

figure 1–7

Random assignment.

Experiments randomly assigning people either to a condition that receives the experimental treatment or to a control condition that does not. This gives the researcher confidence that any later difference is somehow caused by the treatment.

Minnesota students to the photo conditions, the women's behavior *must* have been influenced by the men's beliefs about their obesity.

The ethics of experimentation

Our television example illustrates why there are ethical issues with some conceivable experiments. Social psychologists would not, over long time periods, expose one group of children to brutal violence. Rather, they briefly alter people's social experience and note the effects. Sometimes the experimental treatment is a harmless, perhaps even enjoyable, experience to which people give their knowing consent. Sometimes, however, researchers find themselves operating in a gray area between the harmless and the risky.

Social psychologists often venture into that ethical gray area when they design experiments that engage intense thoughts and emotions. Experiments need not have what Elliot Aronson, Marilynn Brewer, and Merrill Carlsmith (1985) call **mundane realism.** That is, laboratory behavior (for example, delivering electric shocks as part of an experiment on aggression) need not be literally the same as everyday behavior. For many researchers, that sort of realism is indeed mundane—not important. But the experiment *should* have **experimental realism**—it should absorb and involve the participants. Experimenters do not want their people consciously play-acting or ho-humming it; they want to engage real psychological processes. Forcing people to choose whether to give intense or mild electric shock to someone else can, for example, be a realistic measure of aggression. It functionally simulates real aggression.

Achieving experimental realism sometimes requires deceiving people with a plausible cover story. If the person in the next room actually is not receiving the shocks, the experimenter does not want the participants to know this. That would destroy the experimental realism. Thus, about one-third of social-psychological studies (though a decreasing number) have used **deception** in their search for truth (Korn & Nicks, 1993; Vitelli, 1988).

Experimenters also seek to hide their predictions lest the participants, in their eagerness to be "good subjects," merely do what's expected or, in an ornery mood, do the opposite. Small wonder, says Ukrainian professor Anatoly Koladny, that 15 percent of Ukrainian survey respondents declared themselves "religious" while under Soviet communism in 1990 when religion was oppressed by the government—and that 70 percent declared themselves

mundane realism
Degree to which an experiment is superficially similar to everyday situations.

experimental realism
Degree to which an experiment absorbs and involves its participants.

deception
Occurs in research when participants are misinformed or misled about the study's methods and purposes.

**demand
characteristics**
*Cues in an experiment
that tell the participant
what behavior is expected.*

"religious" in postcommunist 1997 (Nielsen, 1998). In subtle ways, too, the experimenter's words, tone of voice, and gestures may call forth desired responses. To minimize such **demand characteristics**—cues that seem to "demand" certain behavior—experimenters typically standardize their instructions or even use a computer to present them.

Researchers often walk a tightrope in designing experiments that will be involving yet ethical. To believe that you are hurting someone, or to be subjected to strong social pressure to see if it will change your opinion or behavior, may be temporarily uncomfortable. Such experiments raise the age-old question of whether ends justify means. The social psychologists' deceptions are usually brief and mild compared with many misrepresentations in real life, or even on some of television's *Candid Camera* and reality shows. Nevertheless, do the insights gained justify deceiving and sometimes distressing people?

University ethics committees now review social-psychological research to ensure that it will treat people humanely. Ethical principles developed by the American Psychological Association (2002), the Canadian Psychological Association (2000), and the British Psychological Society (2000) urge investigators to do the following:

informed consent
*An ethical principle
requiring that research
participants be told
enough to enable them to
choose whether they wish
to participate.*

- Tell potential participants enough about the experiment to enable their **informed consent.**
- Be truthful. Use deception only if essential and justified by a significant purpose and not "about aspects that would affect their willingness to participate."
- Protect people from harm and significant discomfort.
- Treat information about the individual participants confidentially.
- **Debrief** participants. Fully explain the experiment afterward, including any deception. The only exception to this rule is when the feedback would be distressing, say by making people realize they have been stupid or cruel.

debriefing
*In social psychology, the
postexperimental
explanation of a study to
its participants.
Debriefing usually
discloses any deception
and often queries
participants regarding
their understandings and
feelings.*

The experimenter should be sufficiently informative *and* considerate that people leave feeling at least as good about themselves as when they came in. Better yet, the participants should be repaid by having learned something about the nature of psychological inquiry. When treated respectfully, few participants mind being deceived (Epley & Huff, 1998; Kimmel, 1998). Indeed, say social psychology's defenders, professors provoke far greater anxiety and distress by giving and returning course exams than researchers provoke in their experiments.

GENERALIZING FROM LABORATORY TO LIFE

As the research on children, television, and violence illustrates, social psychology mixes everyday experience and laboratory analysis. Throughout this book we will do the same by drawing our data mostly from the laboratory and our illustrations mostly from life. Social psychology displays a healthy interplay between laboratory research and everyday life. Hunches gained from everyday experience often inspire laboratory research, which deepens our understanding of our experience.

This interplay appears in the children's television experiment. What people saw in everyday life suggested experimental research. Network and government policymakers, those with the power to make changes, are now aware of the results. The consistency of findings on television's effects—in the lab and in the field—is true of research in many other areas, including studies of helping, leadership style, depression, and self-efficacy. The effects one finds in the lab have been mirrored by effects in the field. "The psychology laboratory has generally produced psychological truths rather than trivialities," note Craig Anderson and his colleagues (1999).

We need to be cautious, however, in generalizing from laboratory to life. Although the laboratory uncovers basic dynamics of human existence, it is still a simplified, controlled reality. It tells us what effect to expect of variable *X*, all other things being equal—which in real life they never are. Moreover, as you will see, the participants in many experiments are college students. Although this may help you identify with them, college students are hardly a random sample of all humanity. Would we get similar results with people of different ages, educational levels, and cultures? This is always an open question.

Nevertheless, we can distinguish between the *content* of people's thinking and acting (their attitudes, for example) and the *process* by which they think and act (for example, how attitudes affect actions and vice versa). The content varies more from culture to culture than does the process. People from various cultures may hold different opinions yet form them in similar ways. Consider:

- College students in Puerto Rico report greater loneliness than do collegians on the U.S. mainland. Yet in both cultures the ingredients of loneliness are much the same—shyness, uncertain purpose in life, low self-esteem (Jones & others, 1985).
- Ethnic groups differ in school achievement and delinquency, but the differences are "no more than skin deep," report David Rowe and his colleagues (1994). To the extent that family structure, peer influences, and parental education predict achievement or delinquency for one ethnic group, they do so for other groups.

Our behaviors may differ, yet be influenced by the same social forces.

Summing up

Social psychologists organize their ideas and findings into theories. A good theory will distill an array of facts into a much shorter list of predictive principles. We can use these predictions to confirm or modify the theory, to generate new research, and to suggest practical application.

Most social psychological research is either correlational or experimental. Correlational studies, sometimes conducted with systematic survey methods, discern the relationship between variables, such as between amount of education and amount of income. Knowing two things are naturally related is valuable information, but it seldom indicates what is causing what.

When possible, social psychologists prefer to conduct experiments that explore cause and effect. By constructing a miniature reality that is under their control, experimenters can vary one thing and then another and discover how these things, separately or in combination, affect behavior. We randomly assign participants to an experimental condition, which receives the experimental treatment, or to a control condition, which does not. We can then attribute any resulting difference between the two conditions to the independent variable (Figure 1–8).

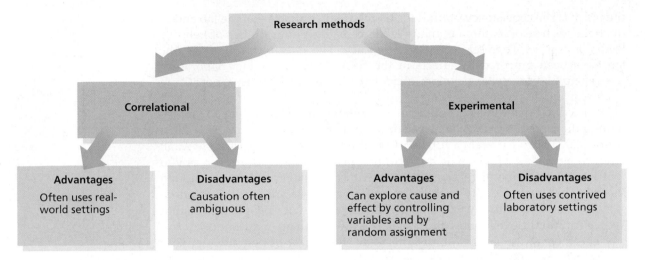

figure 1–8

Two methods of doing research: Correlational and experimental.

In creating experiments, social psychologists sometimes stage situations that engage people's emotions. In doing so, they are obliged to follow professional ethical guidelines, such as obtaining people's informed consent, protecting them from harm, and fully disclosing afterward any temporary deceptions. Laboratory experiments enable social psychologists to test ideas gleaned from life experience and then to apply the principles and findings to the real world.

PS Personal Postscript: Why I wrote this book

I write this text gladly giving you, and hoping that you will gladly receive, social psychology's powerful, hard-wrought principles. They have, I believe, the power to expand your mind and enrich your life. If you finish this book with sharpened critical thinking skills and with a deeper understanding of how we view and affect one another—and why we sometimes like, love, and help one another and sometimes dislike, hate, and harm one another—then I will be a satisfied author and you, I trust, will be a rewarded reader.

I conclude each chapter with a brief, personal reflection on social psychology's human significance. Then, I invite your own reflections.

I write with what I hope is disciplined passion, knowing that many readers are in the process of defining their life goals, identities, values, and attitudes. The novelist Chaim Potok recalls being urged by his mother to forgo writing: "Be a brain surgeon. You'll keep a lot of people from dying; you'll make a lot more money." Potok's response: "Mama, I don't want to keep people from dying; I want to show them how to live" (quoted by Peterson, 1992, p. 47).

Many of us who teach and write psychology are driven not only by a love for giving psychology away, but also by wanting to help students live better lives—wiser, more fulfilling, more compassionate lives. In this we are like teachers and writers in other fields. "Why do we write?" asks theologian Robert McAfee Brown. "I submit that beyond all rewards . . . *we write because we want to change things*. We write because we have this [conviction that we] can make a difference. The 'difference' may be a new perception of beauty, a new insight into self-understanding, a new experience of joy, or a decision to join the revolution" (quoted by Marty, 1988). Indeed, I write hoping to do my part to restrain intuition with critical thinking, refine judgmentalism with compassion, and replace illusion with understanding.

What do you think?

Take a minute to reflect on how social psychology might relate to your life. Are there situations where you'd like to sharpen your social intuitions? to win friends or influence people? redirect others' hostilities into empathic understanding?

Making the Social Connection

As you read this book, you'll find many interesting connections: connections between one researcher's work and other social psychology topics; connections between a concept discussed in one chapter and in other chapters.

Also, you will notice that many concepts introduced in early chapters connect to our everyday lives. Some of these social psychological concepts are also applicable in clinical psychology, the courtroom, and the care for our environment. These applications appear throughout the book and particularly in Part 4: Applying Social Psychology.

So, keep an eye out for each of these connections—to the work of researchers, to other topics in social psychology, and to applications to everyday life.

We make some of these connections for you, right here in Making the Social Connection. As a way to broaden your understanding of these connections, you are invited to view a video clip of either an important concept discussed in the chapter or of a famous social psychologist discussing what sparked his or her research interests. These short videos offer examples of how social psychology's topics relate to one another and to everyday experiences.

Go to the *SocialSense* CD-ROM to view the video clip "How Dave Myers became a social psychologist."

part one

Social Thinking

This book unfolds around its definition of social psychology: the scientific study of how we *think about* (Part One), *influence* (Part Two), and *relate to* (Part Three) one another. Part Four covers how the research and theories of social psychology are applied to real life.

Part One examines the scientific study of how we think about one another (also called social cognition). Each chapter confronts some overriding questions: How reasonable are our social attitudes, explanations, and beliefs? Are our impressions of ourselves and others generally accurate? How does our social thinking form? How is it prone to bias and error, and how might we bring it closer to reality?

Chapter 2 explores the interplay between our sense of self and our social worlds. How do our social surroundings shape our self-identities? How does self-interest color our social judgments and motivate our social behavior?

Chapter 3 looks at the amazing and sometimes rather amusing ways in which we form beliefs about our social worlds. It also alerts us to some pitfalls of social thinking and suggests how to avoid them and think smarter.

Chapter 4 explores the links between our thinking and our actions, between our attitudes and our behaviors: Do our attitudes determine our behaviors? Do our behaviors determine our attitudes? Or does it work both ways?

chapter 2

The Self in a Social World

"There are three things extremely hard, Steel, a Diamond, and to know one's self."

Benjamin Franklin

If you are a person with vision loss, you have dealt with it. You wear glasses or contact lenses. If you are a person with hearing loss, the odds are three in four that you have not dealt with it, that you don't wear hearing aids. As a hard-of-hearing person, I have often wondered about this discrepancy. Why don't we hard-of-hearing people, unless our need is profound, regard hearing aids as mere "glasses for the ears"?

For Americans, part of the answer is that hearing technology costs more. But even in Britain and Australia, where national health systems provide hearing aids, many people who would benefit from hearing technology don't. Worried about our self-image—we are the species that spends billions on hair dye, teeth whiteners, Botox, and face-lifts—we wouldn't want anyone to think that (horrors) our hearing is imperfect or that we may be aging.

But do others really care that I have little objects in my ears? Or are they so preoccupied with themselves that they hardly notice? In conversation, is my hearing loss (without hearing aids) actually more conspicuous than hearing aids would be?

spotlight effect
The belief that others are paying more attention to one's appearance and behavior than they really are.

This much is clear: At the center of our worlds, more pivotal for us than anything else, is ourselves. From our self-focused perspective, we overestimate our conspicuousness. This **spotlight effect** means that we tend to see ourselves at center stage, and so intuitively overestimate the extent to which others' attention is aimed at us.

Thomas Gilovich, Victoria Medvec, and Kenneth Savitsky (2000) explored the spotlight effect by having individual Cornell University students don embarrassing Barry Manilow T-shirts before entering a room with other students. The self-conscious T-shirt wearers guessed that nearly half their peers would notice the shirt. But only 23 percent actually did.

What's true of our dorky clothes, bad hair, and hearing aids is also true of our emotions: our anxiety, irritation, disgust, deceit, or attraction (Gilovich & others, 1998). Fewer people notice than we presume. Keenly aware of our own emotions, we often suffer an **illusion of transparency.** If we're happy and we know it, then our face will surely show it and others will notice, we presume. Actually, we can be more opaque than we realize.

illusion of transparency
The illusion that our concealed emotions leak out and can be easily read by others.

We also overestimate the visibility of our social blunders and public mental slips. When we trigger the library alarm, or are the only guest who shows up for the dinner without a gift for the host, we may be mortified ("everyone thinks I'm a jerk"). But research shows that what we agonize over, others may hardly notice and soon forget (Savitsky & others, 2001). Others just aren't as focused on us as we are.

The spotlight effect and the related illusion of transparency are but two of many examples of the interplay between our sense of self and our social worlds, between what's going on in our heads and in the world around us. Here are more examples:

- *Social surroundings affect our self-awareness.* As individuals in a group of a different culture, race, or gender, we notice how we differ and how others are reacting to our difference. On the day I wrote these words, a European American friend just back from Nepal explained how self-consciously White he felt while living in a rural village; an hour later an African American friend told me how self-consciously American she felt while in Africa.

- *Self-interest colors social judgment.* We are not objective, dispassionate judges of events. When problems arise in a close relationship such as marriage, we usually attribute more responsibility to our partners than to ourselves. Few divorced people blame themselves. When things go well at home or work or play, we see ourselves as more responsible. In competing for prizes, scientists seldom underrate their own contributions. After Frederick Banting and John Macleod received a 1923 Nobel Prize for discovering insulin, Banting claimed that Macleod, who headed the laboratory, had been more of a hindrance than a help. Macleod omitted Banting's name in speeches about the discovery (Ross, 1981).

- *Self-concern motivates our social behavior.* Our actions are often strategic. In hopes of making a positive impression, people agonize about their appearance. (Even if clothes and little imperfections get noticed less than we suppose, one's overall attractiveness does have effects, as we will see.) Like savvy politicians, we also monitor others' behavior and expectations and adjust our behavior accordingly. Concern for self-image drives much of our behavior.

- *Social relationships help define our self.* In our varied relationships, we have varying selves, note Susan Andersen and Serena Chen (2002). We may be one self with Mom, another with friends, another with teachers. How we think of ourselves is linked to who we are in relationship with at the moment.

As these examples suggest, the traffic between ourselves and others runs both ways. Our ideas and feelings about ourselves affect how we interpret events, how we recall them, and how we respond to others. Others, in turn, help shape our sense of self.

For these reasons, no topic in psychology today is more researched than the self. In 2002 the word "self" appeared in 10,343 book and article summaries in *Psychological Abstracts*—seven times the number that appeared in 1970. Our sense of self organizes our thoughts, feelings, and actions. Our sense of self enables us to remember our past, assess our present, and project our future—and thus to behave adaptively. No wonder, note Mark Leary and Nicole Buttermore (2003), that self-awareness is keener in humans than it is in chimps or was (judging from such things as art, body adornment, and language) in early Neanderthals. We therefore begin our tour of social psychology with a look at self-concept (how we come to know ourselves) and at the self in action (how our sense of self drives our attitudes and actions).

> "No topic is more interesting to people than people. For most people, moreover, the most interesting person is the self."
>
> —Roy F. Baumeister, *The Self in Social Psychology,* 1999

Self-concept: Who am I?

Whatever we do in our fourscore years on this global spaceship, whatever we observe and interpret, whatever we conceive and create, whomever we meet and greet will be filtered through our selves. How, and how accurately, do we know ourselves? What determines our self-concept?

As a unique and complex creature, you have many ways to complete the sentence "I am ____." (What five answers might you give?) Taken together, your answers define your **self-concept.**

AT THE CENTER OF OUR WORLDS: OUR SENSE OF SELF

The elements of your self-concept, the specific beliefs by which you define yourself, are your **self-schemas** (Markus & Wurf, 1987). *Schemas* are mental templates by which we organize our worlds. Our *self*-schemas—our perceiving ourselves as athletic, overweight, smart, or whatever—powerfully affect how we process social information. They influence how we perceive, remember, and evaluate both other people and ourselves. If athletics is a central part of your self-concept (if being an athlete is one of your self-schemas), then you will tend to notice others' bodies and skills. You will quickly recall sports-related experiences. And you will welcome information that is consistent with your self-schema (Kihlstrom & Cantor, 1984). The self-schemas that make up our self-concepts help us catalogue and retrieve our experiences.

self-concept
A person's answers to the question, "Who am I?"

self-schema
Beliefs about self that organize and guide the processing of self-relevant information.

Self-reference

Consider how the self influences memory, a phenomenon known as the **self-reference effect:** *When information is relevant to our self-concepts, we process it quickly and remember it well* (Higgins & Bargh, 1987; Kuiper & Rogers, 1979; Symons & Johnson, 1997). If asked whether a specific word, such as "outgoing," describes us, we later remember that word better than if asked whether it describes someone else. If asked to compare ourselves with a character in a short story, we remember that character better. Two days after a conversation with someone, our recall is best for what the person said about us (Kahan & Johnson, 1992). Thus, memories form around our primary interest: ourselves. When we think about something in relation to ourselves, we remember it better.

What determines a teenager's self-concept? Go to the *SocialSense* CD-ROM to view a video clip.

The self-reference effect illustrates a basic fact of life: Our sense of self is at the center of our worlds. Because we tend to see ourselves on center stage, we overestimate the extent to which others' behavior is aimed at us. We often see ourselves as responsible for events in which we played only a small part (Fenigstein, 1984). When judging someone else's performance or behavior, we often spontaneously compare it with our own (Dunning & Hayes, 1996). And if, while talking to one person, we overhear our name spoken by another in the room, our auditory radar instantly shifts our attention.

Possible selves

Our self-concepts include not only our self-schemas about who we currently are, they also include who we might become—our **possible selves.** Hazel Markus and her colleagues (Inglehart & others, 1989; Markus & Nurius, 1986) note that our possible selves include our visions of the self we dream of becoming—the rich self, the thin self, the passionately loved and loving self. They also include the self we fear becoming—the underemployed self, the unloved self, the academically failed self. Such possible selves motivate us with specific goals for a vision of the life we long for.

DEVELOPMENT OF THE SOCIAL SELF

The self-concept has become a major social psychological focus because it helps organize our thinking and guide our social behavior (Figure 2–1). But what determines our self-concepts? Studies of twins point to genetic influences on personality and self-concept, but social experience also plays a part. Among these influences are

- the roles we play,
- the social identifies we form,
- the comparisons we make with others,
- our successes and failures,
- how other people judge us, and
- the surrounding culture.

The roles we play

As we enact a new role—college student, parent, salesperson—we initially feel self-conscious. Gradually, however, what begins as play-acting in the theater of life gets absorbed into our sense of self. For example, while playing our roles we

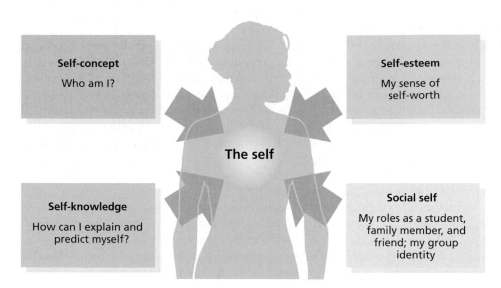

figure 2–1
The self.

may support something we haven't really thought much about. Having made a pitch on behalf of our organization, we then justify our words by believing more strongly in it. Moreover, observing ourselves can be self-revealing; we may now perceive ourselves as holding the views we expressed. Role playing becomes reality (see Chapter 4).

Social identity

Your self-concept—your sense of who you are—contains not just your personal identity (your sense of your personal attributes) but your social identity. The social definition of who you are—your race, religion, gender, academic major, and so forth—implies a definition of who you are not. The circle that includes "us" excludes "them."

When we're part of a small group surrounded by a larger group, we are often conscious of our social identity; when our social group is the majority, we think less about it. As a solo female in a group of men, or as a solo Canadian in a group of Europeans, we are conscious of our uniqueness. To be a Black student on a mostly White campus, or a White student on a mostly Black campus, is to feel one's ethnic identity more keenly and to react accordingly. In Canada, most people identify themselves as "Canadian"—except in Quebec, where the French-origin minority feels more "Provincial" (Québéçois) (Kalin & Berry, 1995).

In Britain, where the English outnumber the Scots 10 to 1, Scottish identity defines itself partly through differences with the English. "To be Scottish is, to some degree, to dislike or resent the English" (Meech & Kilborn, 1992). The English, as the majority, are less conscious of being not-Scottish. In the guest book of one Scottish hotel where I checked in recently, all the English guests reported "British" nationality, and all the Scots (who are equally British) reported their nationality as "Scottish." Moreover, the more students at English universities identify themselves as British, the less they identify themselves as European (Cinnirella, 1997).

For more on ethnic identity, see Chapters 9 and 13.

Social comparisons

How do we decide if we are rich, smart, or short? One way is through **social comparisons** (Festinger, 1954). Others around us help to define the standard by which we define ourselves as rich or poor, smart or dumb, tall or short: We compare ourselves with them and consider how we differ. Social comparison explains why students tend to have a higher academic self-concept if they attend a school with few exceptionally capable students (Marsh & others, 2000). After finishing secondary school near the top of the class, many academically confident students find their academic self-esteem threatened upon entering big, selective universities where many students graduated near the top of their classes. Given a little pond, a fish feels bigger.

Much of life revolves around social comparisons. We feel handsome when others seem homely, smart when others seem dull, caring when others seem callous. When we witness a peer's performance, we cannot resist comparing ourselves (Gilbert & others, 1995). We may, therefore, privately take some pleasure in a peer's failure, especially when it is the failure or misfortune of an envied person and when we don't feel vulnerable to such misfortune (Lockwood, 2002; Smith & others, 1996).

Social comparisons can also breed misery. When people experience an increase in affluence, status, or achievement, they raise the standards by which they evaluate their own attainments. When they are feeling good and climbing the ladder of success, people look up, not down (Gruder, 1977; Suls & Tesch, 1978; Wheeler & others, 1982). When facing competition, we often protect our shaky self-esteem by perceiving the competitor as advantaged (for example, in one study of collegiate swimmers—Shepperd & Taylor, 1999—as having better coaching and more practice time).

Success and failure

Self-concept is not only fed by our roles, our social identity, and our comparisons but also by our daily experiences. To undertake challenging yet realistic tasks and to succeed is to feel more competent. After mastering the physical skills needed to repel a sexual assault, women feel less vulnerable, less anxious, and more in control (Ozer & Bandura, 1990). After experiencing academic success, students develop higher appraisals of their academic ability, which often stimulate them to work harder and achieve more (Felson, 1984; Marsh & Young, 1997). To do one's best and achieve is to feel more confident and empowered.

As noted in Chapter 1, the success-feeds-self-esteem principle has led several research psychologists to question efforts to boost achievement by raising self-esteem with positive messages ("You are somebody! You're special!"). Low self-esteem does sometimes cause problems. Compared with those with low self-esteem, people with a sense of self-worth are happier, less neurotic, less troubled by ulcers and insomnia, less prone to drug and alcohol addictions, and more persistent after failure (Brockner & Hulton, 1978; Brown, 1991; Tafarodi & Vu, 1997). But it's at least as true the other way around, the critics argue: Problems and failures cause low self-esteem. Feelings follow reality. As we conquer challenges and learn skills, our successes breed a more hopeful, confident attitude. Self-esteem comes not only from telling children how wonderful they are but also from hard-earned achievements.

Other people's judgments

Recognized achievements boost self-concept because we see ourselves in others' positive appraisals. When people think well of us, it helps us think well of ourselves. Children whom others label as gifted, hard working, or helpful tend to incorporate such ideas into their self-concepts and behavior (see Chapter 3). If minority students feel threatened by negative stereotypes of their academic ability, or if women feel threatened by low expectations for their math and science performance, they may "disidentify" with these realms. Rather than fight such prejudgments, they may identify their interests elsewhere (Steele, 1997, and see Chapter 9).

The looking-glass self is how sociologist Charles H. Cooley (1902) described our habit of using how we imagine another perceives us as a mirror for perceiving ourselves. We perceive our reflections in how we think we appear to others, said Cooley. Fellow sociologist George Herbert Mead (1934) refined this concept, noting that what matters for our self-concepts is not what others actually think of us, but what we *perceive* them as thinking. We generally feel freer to praise than to criticize others. (We voice our compliments and restrain our gibes.) Others may, therefore, overestimate our appraisal, and their self-images will become a tad inflated (Shrauger & Schoeneman, 1979).

Self-inflation, as we will see, is found most strikingly in Western countries. Shinobu Kitayama (1996) reports that Japanese visitors to North America are routinely struck by the many words of praise that friends offer one another. When he and his colleagues asked people how many days ago they last complimented someone, the modal American response was one day. In Japan, where people are socialized less to feel pride in personal achievement than shame in failing others, the modal response was four days. Moreover, if told they're doing well on a task, North Americans persist more than if told they're not. With the Japanese, persistence is fueled more by failure (Heine & others, 2001).

Our ancestors' fate depended on what others thought of them. Their survival chances increased when protected by their group. When they perceived their group's disapproval, there was biological wisdom to their feeling shame and low self-esteem. As their heirs, having a similar deep-seated need to belong, we feel the pain of low self-esteem when we face social exclusion, notes Mark Leary (1998). Self-esteem, he argues, is a psychological gauge by which we monitor and react to how others appraise us.

SELF AND CULTURE

How did you complete the "I am ____" statement on page 41? Did you give information about your personal traits, such as "I am honest," "I am tall," or "I am outgoing"? Or did you also describe your social identity, such as "I am a Pisces," "I am a MacDonald," or "I am a Muslim"?

For some people, especially those in industrialized Western cultures, **individualism** prevails. Identity is pretty much self-contained. Adolescence is a time of separating from parents, becoming self-reliant, and defining one's personal, *independent self*. Uprooted and placed in a foreign land, one's identity—as a unique individual with particular abilities, traits, values, and dreams—would remain intact. The psychology of Western cultures assumes that your life will be

individualism
The concept of giving priority to one's own goals over group goals and defining one's identity in terms of personal attributes rather than group identifications.

table 2–1   **Voices of modern individualism**

• Do your own thing	• Cut my taxes
• Follow your bliss	• Avoid losing yourself in a codependent relationship
• If it feels good, do it	• To love others first love yourself
• Be true to yourself	• Prefer solo spirituality to faith communities
• Shun conformity	• Believe in yourself
• Don't force your values on others	• Think differently
• Don't constrain my rights to own guns, distribute pornography, do unregulated business	

enriched by defining your possible selves and believing in your power of personal control. By the last century's end, individualism had become the dominant voice in popular culture (see Table 2–1).

Western literature, from the *Iliad* to *The Adventures of Huckleberry Finn*, celebrates the self-reliant individual more than the person who fulfills others' expectations. Movie plots feature rugged heroes who buck the establishment. Songs proclaim "I Did It My Way" and "I Gotta Be Me" and revere "The Greatest Love of All"—loving oneself (Schoeneman, 1994). Individualism flourishes when people experience affluence, mobility, urbanism, and mass media (Freeman, 1997; Marshall, 1997; Triandis, 1994).

Cultures native to Asia, Africa, and Central and South America place a greater value on **collectivism.** They nurture what Shinobu Kitayama and Hazel Markus (1995) call the *interdependent self.* People are more self-critical and have less need for positive self-regard (Heine & others, 1999). Identity is defined more in relation to others. Malaysians, Indians, Japanese, and traditional Kenyans such as the Maasai, for example, are much more likely than Australians, Americans, and the British to complete the "I am" statement with their group identities (Kanagawa & others, 2001; Ma & Schoeneman, 1997). When speaking, people using the languages of collectivist countries say "I" less often (Kashima & Kashima, 1998, 2003). A person might say "Went to the movie" rather than "I went to the movie," with the subject made clear by the grammar or context.

Collectivism has a long history, with roots, for example, in Chinese agricultural villages, where harmony and cooperation enabled good crop production. The result is not only social relations that differ from the more individualist West, contends social psychologist Richard Nisbett in *The Geography of Thought* (2003), but also differing ways of thinking. Consider: Which two—of a panda, a monkey, and a banana—go together? Perhaps a monkey and panda, because they both fit the category "animal"? Asians more often than Americans see relationships: monkey eats banana.

When shown an animated underwater scene (Figure 2–2), Japanese spontaneously recalled 60 percent more background features than did Americans, and they spoke of more relationships (the frog beside the plant). Americans attend

collectivism

Giving priority to the goals of one's groups (often one's extended family or work group) and defining one's identity accordingly.

more to the focal object, such as a single big fish and attend less to the surroundings (Nisbett, 2003). Shinobu Kitayama and his colleagues (2003) also found Japanese to be more responsive to the perceptual context. Shown the stimulus in Figure 2–3 and asked to draw in a smaller empty box a similarly proportioned line, they did so more accurately than did Americans. Asked to draw a line of the same absolute length, Americans more accurately ignored the context and drew an identical line. Nisbett concludes from such studies that East Asians think more holistically—perceiving and thinking about objects and people in relationship to one another and to their environment.

figure 2–2

Asian and Western thinking.

When shown an underwater scene, Asians often describe the environment and the relationships among the fish. Americans attend more to a single big fish (Nisbett, 2003).

The original stimulus

Square = 90 mm tall
Line = 30 mm
(one-third of the height of the square)

figure 2–3

Perceiving in different cultures.

Shinobu Kitayama and his colleagues (2003) showed people a stimulus such as this, then asked them to reproduce, in a smaller or larger box, a line of the same length or of the same proportion relative to the box. American students were most accurate when drawing same-length lines; Japanese students when drawing same-proportion lines.

Pigeonholing cultures as individualist or collectivist oversimplifies, however, because within any culture individualism varies from person to person (Oyserman & others, 2002 a, b). It also varies across a country's regions and political views. In the United States, Hawaiians and those living in the deep South

Self-construal as independent or interdependent.

The independent self acknowledges relationships with others. But the interdependent self is more deeply embedded in others (Markus & Kitayama, 1991).

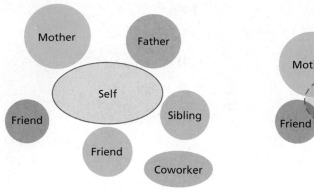
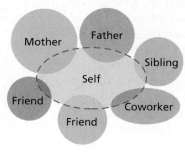

Independent view of self   Interdependent view of self

exhibit greater collectivism than do those in Mountain West states such as Oregon and Montana (Vandello & Cohen, 1999). Conservatives tend to be economic individualists ("don't tax or regulate me") and moral collectivists ("do legislate against immorality"). Liberals tend to be economic collectivists and moral individualists.

With an *inter*dependent self one has a greater sense of belonging. Uprooted and cut off from family, colleagues, and loyal friends, interdependent people would lose the social connections that define who they are. They have not one self but many selves: self-with-parents, self-at-work, self-with-friends (Cross & others, 1992). As Figure 2–4 and Table 2–2 suggest, the interdependent self is embedded in social memberships. Conversation is less direct and more polite (Holtgraves, 1997). The goal of social life is not so much to enhance one's individual self as to harmonize with and support one's communities. The individualized latte—"decaf, single shot, skinny, extra hot"—that seems just right at a North American espresso shop would seem a bit weird in Seoul, note Heejung Kim and Hazel Markus (1999). In Korea, people place less value on expressing their uniqueness and more on tradition and shared practices (Choi & Choi, 2002). Korean advertisements less often highlight personal choice and freedom and more often feature people together (Markus, 2001).

table 2–2   **Self-concept: Independent or interdependent**

	Independent	**Interdependent**
Identity is	Personal, defined by individual traits and goals	Social, defined by connections with others
What matters	Me—personal achievement and fulfillment; my rights and liberties	We—group goals and solidarity; our social responsibilities and relationships
Disapproves of	Conformity	Egotism
Illustrative motto	"To thine own self be true"	"No one is an island"
Cultures that support	Individualistic Western	Collectivistic Asian and Third World

figure 2–5

Which pen would you choose?

When Heejun Kim and Hazel Markus (1999) invited Americans to choose one of these pens, 77 percent chose the uncommon color (regardless of whether it was orange, as here, or green). Given the same choice, 31 percent of Asians picked the pen with the different color. This result illustrates differing cultural preferences for uniqueness and conformity, noted Kim and Markus.

Self-esteem in collectivist cultures correlates closely with "what others think of me and my group." Self-concept is malleable (context-specific) rather than stable (enduring across situations). In one study, four in five Canadian students but only one in three Chinese and Japanese students agreed that "the beliefs that you hold about who you are (your inner self) remain the same across different activity domains" (Tafarodi & others, 2004).

For those in individualistic cultures, and especially for minorities who have learned to discount others' prejudices, "outside" appraisals of oneself and one's group matter somewhat less (Crocker, 1994; Kwan & others, 1997). Self-esteem is more personal and less relational. Threaten our *personal* identity and we'll feel angrier and gloomier than when someone threatens our collective identity (Gaertner & others, 1999).

> "One needs to cultivate the spirits of sacrificing the *little me* to achieve the benefits of the *big me*."
> —Chinese saying

So when, do you suppose, are university students in collectivist Japan and individualist United States most likely to report positive emotions such as happiness and elation? For Japanese students, report Kitayama and Markus (2000), happiness comes with positive social engagement—with feeling close, friendly, and respectful. For American students, it more often comes with disengaged emotions—with feeling effective, superior, and proud. Conflict in collectivist cultures often is between groups; individualist cultures breed more crime and divorce between individuals (Triandis, 2000).

When Kitayama (1999), after ten years of teaching and researching in America, visited his Japanese alma mater, Kyoto University, graduate students were "astounded" when he explained the Western idea of the independent self. "I persisted in explaining this Western notion of self-concept—one that my American students understood intuitively—and finally began to persuade them that, indeed, many Americans do have such a disconnected notion of self. Still, one of them, sighing deeply, said at the end, 'Could this *really* be true?' "

How do various cultures view their sense of "self"? Go to the *SocialSense* CD-ROM to view Hazel Markus speaking on this topic.

When East meets West—as happens, for example, thanks to Western influences in urban Japan and to Japanese exchange students visiting Western countries—does the self-concept become more individualized? Are the Japanese, for example, influenced when exposed to a Western bombardment of promotions based on individual achievement rather than seniority, with admonitions to "believe in one's own possibilities," and with movies in which the heroic individual police officer catches the crook *despite* others' interference? They seem to be, report Steven Heine and his co-researchers (1999). Personal self-esteem increased among Japanese exchange students after spending seven months at the University of British Columbia. In Canada, individual self-esteem is also higher among long-term Asian immigrants to Canada than among more recent immigrants (and than among those living in Asia).

the story behind the research: Hazel Markus on cultural psychology

We began our collaboration by wondering out loud. Shinobu wondered why American life was so weird. Hazel countered with anecdotes about the strangeness of Japan. Cultural psychology is about making the strange familiar and the familiar strange. Our shared cultural encounters astonished us and convinced us that when it comes to psychological functioning, place matters.

After weeks of lecturing in Japan to students with a good command of English, Hazel wondered why the students did not say anything—no questions, no comments. She assured students she was interested in ideas that were different from hers, so why was there no response? Where were the arguments, debates, and signs of critical thinking? Even if she asked a straightforward question, "Where is the best noodle shop?" the answer was invariably an audible intake of air followed by, "It depends." Didn't Japanese students have preferences, ideas, opinions, and attitudes? What is inside a head if it isn't these things? How could you know someone if she didn't tell you what she was thinking?

Shinobu was curious about why students shouldn't just listen to a lecture and why American students felt the need to be constantly interrupting each other and talking over each other and the professor. Why did the comments and questions reveal strong emotions and have a competitive edge? What was the point of this arguing? Why did intelligence seem to be associated with getting the best of another person, even within a class where people knew each other well?

Shinobu expressed his amazement at American hosts who bombard their guests with choices. Do you want wine or beer, or soft drinks or juice, or coffee or tea? Why burden the guest with trivial decisions? Surely the host knew what would be good refreshment on this occasion and could just provide something appropriate and good.

Choice as a burden? Hazel wondered if this could be the key to one particularly humiliating experience in Japan. A group of eight was in a French restaurant, and everyone was following the universal restaurant script and was studying the menu. The waiter approached and stood nearby. Hazel announced her choice of appetizer and entrée. Next was a tense conversation among the Japanese host and the Japanese guests. When the meal was served, it was not what she had ordered. Everyone at the table was served the same meal. This was deeply disturbing. If you can't choose your own dinner, how could it be enjoyable? What was the point of the menu if everybody is served the same meal?

Could a sense of sameness be a good or a desirable feeling in Japan? When Hazel walked around the grounds of a Temple in Kyoto, there was a fork in the path and a sign that read: "ordinary path." Who would want to take the ordinary path? Where was the special, less traveled path? Choosing the non-ordinary path may be an obvious course for Americans, but in this case it led to the temple dump outside the temple grounds. The ordinary path did not denote the dull and unchallenging way, but meant the appropriate and the good way.

These exchanges inspired our experimental studies and remind us that there are ways of life beyond the ones that each of us knows best. So far, most of psychology has been produced by psychologists in middle-class European American settings studying middle-class European American respondents. In other sociocultural contexts, there can be different ideas and practices about how to be a person and how to live a meaningful life, and these differences have an influence on psychological functioning. It is this realization that fuels our continuing interest in collaboration and in cultural psychology.

Hazel Rose Markus, Stanford University

Shinobu Kitayama, University of Michigan

Collectivism in action: People resisted the temptation to loot and acted with civility following the 1995 earthquake in Kobe, a major Japanese city. Here they line up for water.

SELF-KNOWLEDGE

"Know thyself," admonished the Greek philosopher Socrates. We certainly try. We readily form beliefs about ourselves, and we don't hesitate to explain why we feel and act as we do. But how well do we actually know ourselves?

"There is one thing, and only one in the whole universe which we know more about than we could learn from external observation," noted C. S. Lewis (1952, pp. 18–19). "That one thing is [ourselves]. We have, so to speak, inside information; we are in the know." Indeed. Yet sometimes we *think* we know, but our inside information is wrong. This is the unavoidable conclusion of some fascinating research.

Explaining our behavior

Why did you choose your college? Why did you lash out at your roommate? Why did you fall in love with that special person? Sometimes we know. Sometimes we don't. Asked why we have felt or acted as we have, we produce plausible answers. Yet, when causes are subtle, our self-explanations are often wrong. We may dismiss factors that matter and inflate others that don't. In studies, people have misattributed their rainy-day gloom to life's emptiness and their excitement while crossing a suspension bridge to their attraction to a passerby (Schwarz & Clore, 1983; Dutton & Aron, 1974). And people routinely deny being influenced by the media, which, they acknowledge, affects *others*.

Richard Nisbett and Stanley Schachter (1966) demonstrated people's misreading of their own mind after asking Columbia University students to take a series of electric shocks of steadily increasing intensity. Beforehand, some took a fake pill that, they were told, would produce heart palpitations, breathing irregularities, and butterflies in the stomach—the very typical reactions to being shocked. Nisbett and Schachter anticipated that people would attribute the shock symptoms to the pill and thus should tolerate more shock than people

"In sooth, I know not why I am so sad."
—*The Merchant of Venice*, William Shakespeare, 1596

not given the pill. Indeed, the effect was enormous. People given the fake pill took four times as much shock. When asked why they withstood so much shock, they didn't mention the fake pill. When told the predicted pill effect, they granted that others might be influenced but denied its influence on them. "I didn't even think about the pill," was a typical reply.

Also thought provoking are studies in which people recorded their moods—every day for two or three months (Stone & others, 1985; Weiss & Brown, 1976; Wilson & others, 1982). They also recorded factors that might affect their moods: the day of the week, the weather, the amount they slept, and so forth. At the end of each study, the people judged how much each factor had affected their moods. Remarkably (given that their attention was being drawn to their daily moods), there was little relationship between their perceptions of how well a factor predicted their mood and how well it actually did so. These findings raise a disconcerting question: How much insight do we really have into what makes us happy or unhappy?

And how much insight do we have into our own freedom of will? As Daniel Wegner shows in *The Illusion of Conscious Will* (2002), people will *feel* that they have willed an action when their action-related thought precedes a behavior that seems otherwise unexplainable. In one of Wegner's experiments, two people jointly control a computer mouse that glides over an "I-spy" board covered with little pictures. As the mouse roams, the participants hear the names of objects over headphones, and then stop on any picture they wish. Even when one person is a confederate who, on some trials, forces the mouse to a particular picture, the actual participants will typically perceive that *they* willed the mouse to the chosen picture. In this and other situations, the brain generates an intuition of personal efficacy. Other times, such as when dowsing for water or when one's arms raise under hypnotic suggestion, people misperceive that some external will is operating upon them. So, whether perceiving that they have (or have not) caused their actions, people sometimes err.

Predicting our behavior

People also err when predicting their behavior. If asked whether they would obey demands to deliver severe electric shocks or would hesitate to help a victim if several other people were present, people overwhelmingly deny their vulnerability to such influences. But as we will see, experiments have shown that many of us are vulnerable. Moreover, consider what Sidney Shrauger (1983) discovered when he had college students predict the likelihood that they would experience dozens of different events during the ensuing two months (becoming romantically involved, being sick, and so forth): Their self-predictions were hardly more accurate than predictions based on the average person's experience.

People also err frequently when predicting the fate of their relationships. Dating couples predict the longevity of their relationships through rose-colored glasses. Focusing on the positives, lovers may feel sure they will always be lovers. Their friends and family often know better, report Tara MacDonald and Michael Ross (1997) from studies with University of Waterloo students. The less optimistic predictions of their parents and roommates tend to be more accurate. (Many a parent, having seen their child lunge confidently into an ill-fated relationship against all advice, nods yes.) When predicting negative behaviors such as crying or lying, self-predictions are more accurate than predictions by one's

"O wad some Power the giftie gie us
To see oursels as ithers see us!"
—Robert Burns, "To a Louse," 1786

mother and friends (Shrauger & others, 1996). Nevertheless, the surest thing we can say about your individual future is that it is sometimes hard for even you to predict. When predicting behavior, the best advice is to consider past behavior in similar situations (Osberg & Shrauger, 1986, 1990). Observing such, the people who know you can probably predict your behavior better than you can (for example, how nervous and chatty you will be when meeting someone new [Kenny, 1994]). So, to predict your future, consider your past.

Nicholas Epley and David Dunning (2000) discovered that we can sometimes better predict people's behavior by asking them to predict *others'* actions rather than their own. Five weeks ahead of Cornell University's annual "Daffodil Days" charity event, Epley and Dunning asked students to predict whether they would buy at least one daffodil for charity, and also to predict what proportion of their fellow students would do so. More than four in five predicted they would buy a daffodil. But only 43 percent actually did, which was close to their prediction that 56 percent of others would buy one. In a laboratory game played for money, 84 percent predicted they would cooperate with another for their mutual gain, though only 61 percent did (again, close to their prediction of 64 percent cooperation by others.) If Lao-tzu was right that "He who knows others is learned. He who knows himself is enlightened," then most people, it would seem, are more learned than enlightened.

Predicting our feelings

Many of life's big decisions involve predicting our future feelings. Would marrying this person lead to lifelong contentment? Would entering this profession make for satisfying work? Would going on this vacation produce a happy experience? Or would the likelier results be divorce, job burnout, and holiday disappointment?

Sometimes we know how we will feel—if we fail that exam, win that big game, or soothe our tensions with a half-hour jog. We know what exhilarates us, and what makes us anxious or bored. Other times we may mispredict our responses. Asked how they would feel if asked sexually harassing questions on a job interview, most women studied by Julie Woodzicka and Marianne LaFrance (2001) said they would feel angry. When actually asked such questions, however, women more often experienced fear. Studies of "affective forecasting" reveal that people nevertheless have greatest difficulty predicting the *intensity* and the *duration* of their future emotions (Wilson & Gilbert, 2003). People have mispredicted how they would feel some time after a romantic breakup, receiving a gift, losing an election, winning a game, and being insulted (Gilbert & Ebert, 2002; Loewenstein & Schkade 1999). Some examples:

- When male youths are shown sexually arousing photographs, then exposed to a passionate date scenario in which their date asks them to "stop," they admit that they might not stop. If not shown sexually arousing pictures first, they more often deny the possibility of being sexually aggressive. When not aroused, one easily mispredicts how one will feel and act when aroused—a phenomenon that leads to professions of love during lust, to unintended pregnancies, and to repeat offenses among sex abusers who have sincerely vowed "never again."

- Hungry shoppers do more impulse buying ("Those doughnuts would be delicious!") than when shopping after scarfing a quarter-pound

"When a feeling was there, they felt as if it would never go; when it was gone, they felt as if it had never been; when it returned, they felt as if it had never gone."
—George MacDonald, *What's Mine's Mine*, 1886

Predicting behavior, even one's own, is no easy matter, which may be why this visitor goes to an astrologer for help.

blueberry muffin (Gilbert & Wilson, 2000). When hungry, one mispredicts how gross those deep-fried doughnuts will seem when sated. When stuffed, one mispredicts how yummy a doughnut might be with a late-night glass of milk.

- Only one in seven occasional smokers (of less than a cigarette per day) predict they will be smoking in five years. But they underestimate the power of their drug cravings, for nearly half will still be smoking (Lynch & Bonnie, 1994).

- People overestimate how much their well-being would be affected by warmer winters, losing weight, more television channels, or more free time. Even extreme events, such as winning a state lottery or suffering a paralyzing accident, affect long-term happiness less than most people suppose.

Our intuitive theory seems to be: We want. We get. We are happy. If that were true, this chapter would have fewer words. In reality, note Daniel Gilbert and Timothy Wilson (2000), we often "mis-want." People who imagine an idyllic desert island holiday with sun, surf, and sand may be disappointed when they discover "how much they require daily structure, intellectual stimulation, or regular infusions of Pop Tarts." We think that if our candidate or team wins we will be delighted for a long while. But study after study reveals that the emotional traces of such good tidings evaporate more rapidly than we expect.

It's after *negative* events that we're especially prone to "impact bias"—to overestimating the enduring impact of emotion-causing events. When people being tested for HIV predict how they will feel five weeks after getting the results, they expect to be feeling misery over bad news and elation over good news. Yet five weeks later, the bad news recipients are less distraught and the good news recipients are less elated than they anticipated (Sieff & others, 1999). And when Gilbert and his colleagues (1998) asked assistant professors to predict their happiness a few years after achieving tenure or not, most believed a favorable outcome was important for their future happiness. "Losing my job would crush my life's ambitions. It would be terrible." Yet when surveyed several years after the event, those denied tenure were about as happy as those who received it.

Let's make this personal. Gilbert and Wilson invite us to imagine how we might feel a year after losing our nondominant hands. Compared with today, how happy would you be?

Thinking about this, you perhaps focused on what the calamity would mean: no clapping, no shoe tying, no competitive basketball, no speedy keyboarding. Although you likely would forever regret the loss, your general happiness some time after the event would be influenced by "two things: (a) the event, and (b) everything else." In focusing on the negative event, we discount the

"Weeping may tarry for the night, but joy comes with the morning."
—Psalm 30:5

importance of everything else that contributes to happiness and so overpredict our enduring misery. "Nothing that you focus on will make as much difference as you think," concur researchers David Schkade and Daniel Kahneman (1998).

Moreover, say Wilson and Gilbert (2003), people neglect the speed and power of their psychological immune system, which includes their strategies for rationalizing, discounting, forgiving, and limiting emotional trauma. Being largely ignorant of our "psychological immune system" (a phenomenon Gilbert and Wilson call *immune neglect*), we accommodate to disabilities, romantic breakups, exam failures, tenure denials, and personal and team defeats more readily than we would expect. Ironically, Gilbert and his colleagues report (2004), major negative events (which activate our psychological defenses) can be less enduringly distressing than minor irritations (which don't activate our defenses). In other words, we are resilient.

The wisdom and illusions of self-analysis

So, to a striking extent, our intuitions are often dead wrong about what has influenced us and what we will feel and do. But let's not overstate the case. When the causes of our behavior are conspicuous and the correct explanation fits our intuition, our self-perceptions will be accurate (Gavanski & Hoffman, 1987). Peter Wright and Peter Rip (1981) found that California high school juniors *could* discern how such features of a college as its size, tuition, and distance from home influenced their reactions to it. But when the causes of behavior are not obvious to an observer, they are not obvious to the person, either.

As Chapter 3 will explain, we are unaware of much that goes on in our minds. Studies of perception and memory show that we are more aware of the *results* than the process of our thinking. Gazing across our mental sea, we behold little below its conscious surface. We do, however, experience the results of our mind's unconscious workings when we set a mental clock to record the passage of time and to awaken us at an appointed hour, or when we somehow achieve a spontaneous creative insight after a problem has unconsciously "incubated." Creative scientists and artists, for example, often cannot report the thought processes that produced their insights.

Timothy Wilson (1985, 2002) offers a bold idea: The mental processes that *control* our social behavior are distinct from the mental processes through which we *explain* our behavior. Our rational explanations may therefore omit the gut-level attitudes that actually guide our behavior. In nine experiments, Wilson and his co-workers (1989) found that expressed attitudes toward things or people usually predicted later behavior reasonably well. If they first asked the participants to *analyze* their feelings, however, their attitude reports became useless. For example, dating couples' happiness with their relationship predicted whether they would still be dating several months later. But other participants first listed all the *reasons* they could think of why their relationship was good or bad before rating their happiness. After doing so, their attitude reports were useless in predicting the future of the relationship! Apparently the process of dissecting the relationship drew attention to easily verbalized factors that actually were less important than aspects of the relationship that were harder to verbalize. We are often "strangers to ourselves," says Wilson (2002).

In a later study, Wilson and his co-workers (1993) had people choose one of two art posters to take home. Those asked first to identify *reasons* for their choice preferred a humorous poster (whose positive features they could more

"Self-contemplation is a curse
That makes an old confusion worse."
—Theodore Roethke, *The Collected Poems of Theodore Roethke*, 1975

easily verbalize). But a few weeks later, they were less satisfied with their choice than were those who just went by their gut feelings and generally chose the other poster. Compared with reasoned judgments of people with various facial attributes, gut-level reactions also are more consistent, report Gary Levine and colleagues (1996). First impressions can be telling.

Such findings illustrate that we have a **dual attitude system,** say Wilson and his colleagues (2000). Our automatic *implicit* attitudes regarding someone or something often differ from our consciously controlled, *explicit* attitudes. From childhood, for example, we may retain a habitual, automatic fear or dislike of people for whom we now verbalize respect and appreciation. Although explicit attitudes may change with relative ease, notes Wilson, "implicit attitudes, like old habits, change more slowly." With repeated practice—acting on the new attitude—new habitual attitudes can, however, replace old ones.

Murray Millar and Abraham Tesser (1992) believe that Wilson overstates our ignorance of self. Their research suggests that, yes, drawing people's attention to *reasons* diminishes the usefulness of attitude reports in predicting behaviors that are driven by *feelings*. If, instead of having people analyze their romantic relationships, Wilson had first asked them to get more in touch with their feelings ("How do you feel when you are with and apart from your partner?"), the attitude reports might have been more insightful. Other behavior domains—say, choosing which school to attend based on considerations of cost, career advancement, and so forth—seem more cognitively driven. For these, an analysis of reasons rather than feelings may be most useful. Although the heart has its reasons, sometimes the mind's own reasons are decisive.

This research on the limits of our self-knowledge has two practical implications. The first is for psychological inquiry. *Self-reports are often untrustworthy.* Errors in self-understanding limit the scientific usefulness of subjective personal reports.

The second implication is for our everyday lives. The sincerity with which people report and interpret their experiences is no guarantee of the validity of these reports. Personal testimonies are powerfully persuasive (as we will see in Chapter 15, "Social Psychology in Court"). But they may also be wrong. Keeping this potential for error in mind can help us feel less intimidated by others and be less gullible.

dual attitudes
Differing implicit (automatic) and explicit (consciously controlled) attitudes toward the same object. Verbalized explicit attitudes may change with education and persuasion; implicit attitudes change slowly, with practice that forms new habits.

www.mhhe.com/myers8
Visit the Online Learning Center for an interactivity on self-reporting.

Summing up

Our sense of self helps organize our thoughts and actions. When we process information with reference to ourselves, we remember it well (a phenomenon called the self-reference effect). The elements of our self-concept are the specific self-schemas that guide our processing of self-relevant information and the possible selves that we dream of or dread. Our self-esteem is an overall sense of self-worth that influences how we appraise our traits and abilities.

What determines our self-concepts? There are multiple influences, including the roles we play, the comparisons we make, our social identities, how we perceive others appraising us, and our experiences of success and failure. Cultures shape the self, too. Some people, especially in individualistic Western cultures, assume an independent self. Others, often in Asian and Third World cultures, assume a more interdependent self. As Chapter 5 will further explain, these contrasting ideas contribute to cultural differences in social behavior.

Our self-knowledge is curiously flawed. We often do not know why we behave the way we do. When powerful influences upon our behavior are not so conspicuous that any observer could spot them, we, too, can miss them. The subtle, implicit processes that control our behavior may differ from our conscious, explicit explanations of it. We also tend to mispredict our emotions. We underestimate the power of our psychological immune systems and thus tend to overestimate the durability of our emotional reactions to significant events.

Perceived self-control

Several concepts and lines of research point to the significance of perceived control over one's life.

So far we have considered what a self-concept is, how it develops, and how well we know ourselves. Now let's see why our self-concepts matter, by viewing the self in action.

The self's action capacity has limits, note Roy Baumeister and his colleagues (1998, 2000; Muraven & others, 1998). People who exert self-control—by forcing themselves to eat radishes rather than chocolates, or by suppressing forbidden thoughts—subsequently quit faster when given unsolvable puzzles. People who tried to control their emotions to an upsetting movie exhibit decreased physical stamina. Effortful self-control depletes our limited willpower reserves. Self-control operates similarly to muscular strength, conclude Baumeister and Julia Exline (2000): Both are weaker after exertion, replenished with rest, and strengthened by exercise.

Nevertheless, our self-concepts do influence our behavior (Graziano & others, 1997). Given challenging tasks, people who imagine themselves as hardworking and successful outperform those who imagine themselves as failures (Ruvolo & Markus, 1992). Envision your positive possibilities and you become more likely to plan and enact a successful strategy. Perceived self-control matters.

SELF-EFFICACY

Stanford psychologist Albert Bandura (1997, 2000) captured the power of positive thinking in his research and theorizing about **self-efficacy.** An optimistic belief in our own competence and effectiveness pays dividends (Bandura & others, 1999; Maddux and Gosselin, 2003). Children and adults with strong feelings of self-efficacy are more persistent, less anxious, and less depressed. They also live healthier lives and are more academically successful.

In everyday life, self-efficacy leads us to set challenging goals and to persist in the face of difficulties. More than a hundred studies show that self-efficacy predicts worker productivity (Stajkovic & Luthans, 1998). When problems arise, a strong sense of self-efficacy leads workers to keep calm and seek solutions rather than ruminate on their inadequacy. Competence plus persistent striving equals accomplishment. And with accomplishment, self-confidence grows. Self-efficacy, like self-esteem, grows with hard-won achievements.

self-efficacy
A sense that one is competent and effective, distinguished from self-esteem, one's sense of self-worth. A bombardier might feel high self-efficacy and low self-esteem.

Even subtle manipulations of self-efficacy can affect behavior. Becca Levy (1996) discovered this when she subliminally exposed 90 older adults to words that activated (primed) either a negative or a positive stereotype of aging. Some subjects viewed .066-second presentations of words like "decline," "forgets," and "senile," or of words like "sage," "wise," and "learned." The participants consciously perceived only a flash or blur of light. Yet being given the positive words led to heightened "memory self-efficacy" (confidence in one's memory). Viewing the negative words had the opposite effect. Older adults in China, where positive images of aging prevail and memory self-efficacy may be greater, seem to suffer less memory decline than commonly observed in Western countries (Schacter & others, 1991).

Your self-efficacy is how competent you feel to do something. If you believe you can do something, will this belief necessarily make a difference? That depends on a second factor: Do you have *control* over your outcomes? You may, for example, feel like an effective driver (high self-efficacy), yet feel endangered by drunken drivers (low control). You may feel like a competent student or worker but, fearing discrimination based on your age, gender, or appearance, you may think your prospects are dim.

LOCUS OF CONTROL

"I have no social life," complained a 40-something single man to student therapist Jerry Phares. At Phares's urging, the patient went to a dance, where several women danced with him. "I was just lucky," he later reported, "it would never happen again." When Phares reported this to his mentor, Julian Rotter, it crystallized an idea he had been forming. In Rotter's experiments and in his clinical practice, some people seemed to persistently "feel that what happens to them is governed by external forces of one kind or another, while others feel that what happens to them is governed largely by their own efforts and skills" (quoted by Hunt, 1993, p. 334).

What do you think? Are people more often captains of their destinies or victims of their circumstances? Are they the playwrights, directors, and actors of their own lives or prisoners of their situations? Rotter called this dimension **locus of control.** With Phares, he developed 29 paired statements to measure a person's locus of control. Imagine yourself taking their test. Which do you more strongly believe?

locus of control
The extent to which people perceive outcomes as internally controllable by their own efforts and actions or as externally controlled by chance or outside forces.

In the long run, people get the respect they deserve in this world.	or	Unfortunately, people's worth passes unrecognized no matter how hard they try.
What happens to me is my own doing.	or	Sometimes I feel that I don't have enough control over the direction my life is taking.
The average person can have an influence in government decisions.	or	This world is run by the few people in power, and there is not much the little guy can do about it.

Do your answers to such questions from Rotter (1973) indicate that you believe you control your own destiny (*internal* locus of control)? Or that chance or

figure 2–6
Locus of control.

outside forces determine your fate (*external* locus of control, as in Figure 2–6)? Those who see themselves as internally controlled are more likely to do well in school, successfully stop smoking, wear seat belts, deal with marital problems directly, make lots of money, and delay instant gratification in order to achieve long-term goals (Findley & Cooper, 1983; Lefcourt, 1982; Miller & others, 1986). How much control we feel depends on how we explain setbacks. Perhaps you have known students who view themselves as victims—who blame poor grades on things beyond their control, such as their feelings of stupidity or their "poor" teachers, texts, or tests. If such students are coached to adopt a more hopeful attitude—to believe that effort, good study habits, and self-discipline can make a difference—their grades tend to go up (Noel & others, 1987; Peterson & Barrett, 1987). In general, students who feel in control—who, for example, agree that "I am good at resisting temptation" and disagree that "I spend too much money"—get better grades, enjoy better relationships, and exhibit better mental health (Tangney & others, 2004).

Successful people are more likely to see setbacks as a fluke or to think, "I need a new approach." New life insurance sales representatives who view failures as controllable ("It's difficult, but with persistence I'll get better") sell more policies. They are half as likely as their more pessimistic colleagues to quit during their first year (Seligman & Schulman, 1986). Among college swim team members, those with an optimistic "explanatory style" are more likely than pessimists to perform beyond expectations (Seligman & others, 1990). As the Roman poet Virgil said in the Aeneid, "They can because they think they can."

LEARNED HELPLESSNESS VERSUS SELF-DETERMINATION

The benefits of feelings of control also appear in animal research. Dogs taught that they cannot escape shocks while confined will learn a sense of helplessness. Later these dogs cower passively in other situations when they *could* escape

"If my mind can conceive it and my heart can believe it, I know I can achieve it. Down with dope! Up with hope! I am somebody!"
—Jesse Jackson, The March on Washington, 1983

"Argue for your limitations, and sure enough they're yours."
—Richard Bach, *Illusions: Adventures of a Reluctant Messiah*, 1977

figure 2–7

Learned helplessness.
When animals and people experience uncontrollable bad events, they learn to feel helpless and resigned.

learned helplessness
The hopelessness and resignation learned when a human or animal perceives no control over repeated bad events.

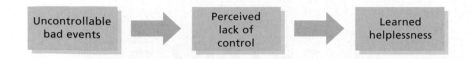

punishment. Dogs that learn personal control (by escaping their first shocks successfully) adapt easily to a new situation. Researcher Martin Seligman (1975, 1991) has noted similarities to this **learned helplessness** in human situations. Depressed or oppressed people, for example, become passive because they believe their efforts have no effect. Helpless dogs and depressed people both suffer paralysis of the will, passive resignation, even motionless apathy (Figure 2–7).

Here is a clue to how institutions—whether malevolent, like concentration camps, or benevolent, like hospitals—can dehumanize people. In hospitals, "good patients" don't ring bells, don't ask questions, don't try to control what's happening (Taylor, 1979). Such passivity may be good for hospital efficiency, but it is bad for people's health and survival. Losing control over what you do and what others do to you can make unpleasant events profoundly stressful (Pomerleau & Rodin, 1986). Several diseases are associated with feelings of helplessness and diminished choice. So is the rapidity of decline and death in concentration camps and nursing homes. Hospital patients who are trained to believe they can control stress require fewer pain relievers and sedatives and exhibit less anxiety (Langer & others, 1975).

Ellen Langer and Judith Rodin (1976) tested the importance of personal control by treating elderly patients in a highly rated Connecticut nursing home in one of two ways. With one group the benevolent caregivers stressed "our responsibility to make this a home you can be proud of and happy in." They gave the passive patients their normal well-intentioned, sympathetic care. Three weeks later, most were rated by themselves, by interviewers, and by nurses as further debilitated. Langer and Rodin's other treatment promoted personal control. It stressed opportunities for choice, the possibilities for influencing nursing-home policy, and the person's responsibility "to make of your life whatever you want." These patients were given small decisions to make and responsibilities to fulfill. Over the ensuing three weeks, 93 percent of this group showed improved alertness, activity, and happiness.

The experience of the first group must have been similar to that of James MacKay (1980), an 87-year-old psychologist:

> I became a nonperson last summer. My wife had an arthritic knee which put her in a walker, and I chose that moment to break my leg. We went to a nursing home. It was all nursing and no home. The doctor and the head nurse made all decisions; we were merely animate objects. Thank heavens it was only two weeks. . . . The top man of the nursing home was very well trained and very compassionate; I considered it the best home in town. But we were nonpersons from the time we entered until we left.

Studies confirm that systems of governing or managing people that promote personal control will indeed promote health and happiness (Deci & Ryan, 1987).

- Prisoners given some control over their environments—by being able to move chairs, control TV sets, and operate the lights—experience less stress, exhibit fewer health problems, and commit less vandalism (Ruback & others, 1986; Wener & others, 1987).

- Workers given leeway in carrying out tasks and making decisions experience improved morale (Miller & Monge, 1986).

- Institutionalized residents allowed choice in matters such as what to eat for breakfast, when to go to a movie, whether to sleep late or get up early, may live longer and certainly are happier (Timko & Moos, 1989).

- Homeless shelter residents who perceive little choice in when to eat and sleep, and little control over their privacy, are more likely to have a passive, helpless attitude regarding finding housing and work (Burn, 1992).

Personal control: Inmates of Spain's modern Valencia prison can, with appropriate behavior, gain access to classes, sports facilities, and cultural opportunities. Salary earned for work is credited to an account, which they can charge for extra snacks.

Can there ever be too much of a good thing like freedom and self-determination? Swarthmore College psychologist Barry Schwartz (2000, 2004) contends that individualistic modern cultures indeed have "an excess of freedom," causing decreased life satisfaction and increased clinical depression. Too many choices can lead to paralysis, or what Schwartz calls "the tyranny of freedom." After choosing between 30 kinds of jams or chocolates, people express less satisfaction with their choices than those choosing among six options (Iyengar & Lepper, 2000). With more choice comes information overload and more opportunities for regret.

In other experiments, people have expressed greater satisfaction with irrevocable choices (like those made in an "all purchases final" sale) than with reversible choices (as when allowing refunds or exchanges). Ironically, people like and will pay for the freedom to reverse their choices. Yet that freedom "can inhibit the psychological processes that manufacture satisfaction" (Gilbert & Ebert, 2002). Owning something irreversibly makes it feel better. This principle may help explain a curious social phenomenon (Myers, 2000a): National surveys show that people expressed more satisfaction with their marriages back when marriage was more irrevocable ("all purchases final"). Today, despite greater freedom to escape bad marriages and try new ones, people tend to express somewhat less satisfaction with the marriage that they have.

A concluding reflection: Although freedom can be taken to an extreme, personal control generally supports human thriving. Psychological research on perceived self-control is relatively new, but the emphasis on taking charge of one's life and realizing one's potential is not. The you-can-do-it theme of Horatio Alger's rags-to-riches books is an enduring idea. We find it in Norman Vincent Peale's 1950s best-seller, *The Power of Positive Thinking*—"If you think in positive terms you will get positive results. That is the simple fact." We find it in the many self-help books and videos that urge people to succeed through positive mental attitudes.

Research on self-control gives us greater confidence in traditional virtues such as perseverance and hope. Yet Bandura emphasizes that self-efficacy does not grow primarily by self-persuasion ("I think I can, I think I can") or by

"This gives my confidence a real boost."

puffing people up like hot-air balloons ("You're terrific!"). Its chief source is the experience of success. If your initial efforts to lose weight, stop smoking, or improve your grades succeed, your self-efficacy increases. A team of researchers led by Roy Baumeister (2003) concurs. "Praising all the children just for being themselves," they contend, "simply devalues praise." Better to praise and bolster self-esteem "in recognition of good performance. . . . As the person performs or behaves better, self-esteem is encouraged to rise, and the net effect will be to reinforce both good behavior and improvement. Those outcomes are conducive to both the happiness of the individual and the betterment of society."

Summing up

Several lines of research show the benefits of a sense of efficacy and feelings of control. People who believe in their own competence and effectiveness, and who have an internal locus of control, cope better and achieve more than do those who have learned a helpless, pessimistic outlook.

Self-esteem

self-esteem
A person's overall self-evaluation or sense of self-worth.

Is **self-esteem**—our overall self-evaluation—the sum of all our self-schemas and possible selves? If we see ourselves as attractive, athletic, smart, and destined to be rich and loved, will we have high self-esteem? That's what psychologists assume when they suggest that to help people feel better about themselves, we should first make them feel more attractive, athletic, smarter, and so forth. This is especially so, Jennifer Crocker and Connie Wolfe (2001) argue, for the particular domains important to their self-esteem. "One person may have self-esteem that is highly contingent on doing well in school and being physically attractive, whereas another may have self-esteem that is contingent on being loved by God and adhering to moral standards." Thus the first person will feel high self-esteem when made to feel smart and good looking, the second person when made to feel moral.

But Jonathon Brown and Keith Dutton (1994) argue that this "bottom-up" view of self-esteem is not the whole story. The causal arrow, they believe, also goes the other way. People who value themselves in a general way—those with high self-esteem—are more likely then to value their looks, abilities, and so forth. They are like new parents who, loving their infant, delight in its fingers, toes, and hair. (The parents do not first evaluate their infant's fingers or toes and then decide how much to value the whole baby.)

Oprah Winfrey's imagined possible selves, including the dreaded overweight self, the rich self, and the helpful self, motivated her to work to achieve the life she wanted.

To test their idea that global self-esteem affects specific self-perceptions ("top down"), Brown and Dutton introduced University of Washington students to a supposed trait called "integrative ability." They gave the students sets of three words—for example, "car," "swimming," "cue"—and challenged them to think of a word that linked the three words. (Hint: The word begins with *p*.) High-self-esteem people were more likely to report having this ability if told it was very important than if told it was useless. Feeling good about oneself in a general way, it seems, casts a rosy glow over one's specific self-schemas ("I have integrative ability") and possible selves.

SELF-ESTEEM MOTIVATION

A motivational engine powers our cognitive machinery (Dunning, 1999; Kunda, 1990). Facing failure, high-self-esteem people sustain their self-worth by perceiving other people as failing, too, and by exaggerating their superiority over others (Agostinelli & others, 1992; Brown & Gallagher, 1992). The more physiologically aroused people are after a failure, the more likely they are to excuse the failure with self-protective attributions (Brown & Rogers, 1991). We are not just cool, information-processing machines.

Abraham Tesser (1988) at the University of Georgia reports that a "self-esteem maintenance" motive predicts a variety of interesting findings, even friction among brothers and sisters. Do you have a sibling of the same gender who is close to you in age? If so, people probably compared the two of you as you grew up. Tesser presumes that people's perceiving one of you as more capable than the other will motivate the less able one to act in ways that maintain his or her self-esteem. (Tesser thinks the threat to self-esteem is greatest for an older child with a highly capable younger sibling.) Men with a brother with markedly different ability typically recall not getting along well with him; men with a similarly able brother are more likely to recall very little friction.

Self-esteem threats occur among friends, whose success can be more threatening than that of strangers (Zuckerman & Jost, 2001). And it can occur among

Among sibling relationships, the threat to self-esteem is greatest for an older child with a highly capable younger brother or sister.

married partners, too. Although shared interests are healthy, *identical* career goals may produce tension or jealousy (Clark & Bennett, 1992). Similarly, people feel greater jealousy toward a romantic rival whose achievements are in the domain of their own aspirations (DeSteno & Salovey, 1996).

What underlies the motive to maintain or enhance self-esteem? Mark Leary (1998, 1999) believes that our self-esteem feelings are like a fuel gauge. Relationships enable surviving and thriving. Thus, the self-esteem gauge alerts us to threatened social rejection, motivating us to act with greater sensitivity to others' expectations. Studies confirm that social rejection lowers our self-esteem, strengthening our eagerness for approval. Spurned or jilted, we feel unattractive or inadequate. Like a blinking dashboard light, this pain can motivate action—self-improvement and a search for acceptance and inclusion elsewhere.

THE DARK SIDE OF SELF-ESTEEM

Low self-esteem predicts increased risk of depression, drug abuse, and some forms of delinquency. High self-esteem fosters initiative, resilience, and pleasant feelings (Baumeister & others, 2003). Yet teen males who engage in sexual activity at an "inappropriately young age" tend to have *higher* than average self-esteem. So do teen gang leaders, extreme ethnocentrists, and terrorists, notes Robyn Dawes (1994, 1998).

Finding their favorable self-esteem threatened, people often react by putting others down, sometimes with violence. A youth who develops a big ego, which then gets threatened or deflated by social rejection, is potentially dangerous. In one experiment, Todd Heatherton and Kathleen Vohs (2000) threatened some undergraduate men, but not those in a control condition, with a failure experience on an aptitude test. In response to the failure, only high-self-esteem men became considerably more antagonistic (Figure 2–8).

In another experiment, Brad Bushman and Roy Baumeister (1998) had 540 undergraduate volunteers write a paragraph, in response to which another supposed student gave them either praise ("great essay!") or stinging criticism

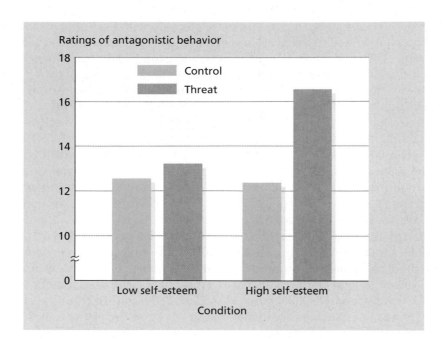

figure 2–8

When big egos get challenged.

When feeling threatened, only high-self-esteem people became significantly more antagonistic—arrogant, rude, and unfriendly (from Heatherton & Vohs, 2000).

("one of the worst essays I have read!"). Then each essay writer played a reaction time game against the other student. When the opponent lost, the writer could assault him or her with noise of any intensity and for any duration. After criticism, the people with the biggest egos—those who agreed with "narcissistic" statements such as "I am more capable than other people"— were "exceptionally aggressive." They delivered three times the auditory torture of those with normal self-esteem. Wounded pride motivates retaliation.

"The enthusiastic claims of the self-esteem movement mostly range from fantasy to hogwash," says Baumeister (1996), who suspects he has "probably published more studies on self-esteem than anybody else." "The effects of self-esteem are small, limited, and not all good." High-self-esteem folks, he reports, are more likely to be obnoxious, to interrupt, and to talk at people rather than with them (in contrast to the more shy, modest, self-effacing folks with low self-esteem). "My conclusion is that self-control is worth 10 times as much as self-esteem."

Do the big egos of people who sometimes do bad things conceal inner insecurity and low self-esteem? Do assertive, narcissistic people actually have weak egos that are hidden by a self-inflating veneer? Many researchers have tried to find low self-esteem beneath such an outer crust. But studies of bullies, gang members, genocidal dictators, and obnoxious narcissists have turned up no sign of it. "Hitler had very high self-esteem," note Baumeister and his co-authors (2003).

"Hidden lack of self-esteem is the New Age psychologist's ether," concludes Dawes (1994). "The ether was a substance that was supposed to fill all space as a vehicle for the travel of light waves. It proved undetectable, and the concept was discarded when Einstein introduced the special theory of relativity. A belief in undetected low self-esteem as a cause of undesirable behavior is even less plausible; all the available evidence directly contradicts it."

The dark side of high self-esteem exists in tension with the findings that people expressing low self-esteem are somewhat more vulnerable to assorted clinical problems, including anxiety, loneliness, and eating disorders. When feeling bad or threatened, they are more likely to view everything through dark glasses—to notice and remember others' worst behaviors and to think their partners don't love them (Murray & others, 1998, 2002; Ybarra, 1999).

Moreover, bullies exhibit a defensive, self-aggrandizing form of self-esteem, report Christina Salmivalli and her University of Turkey (Finland) colleagues (1999). Those with "genuine self-esteem"—who feel secure self-worth without seeking to be the center of attention or being angered by criticism—are more often found defending the victims of bullying. When feeling securely good about ourselves, we are less defensive (Epstein & Feist, 1988; Jordan & others, 2003). We are also less thin-skinned and judgmental—less likely to inflate those who like us and berate those who don't (Baumgardner & others, 1989).

Unlike a fragile self-esteem, a secure self-esteem—one rooted more in feeling good about who one is than on grades, looks, money, or others' approval—is conducive to long-term well-being (Kernis, 2003; Schimel & others, 2001). Jennifer Crocker and her colleagues (2002, 2003, 2004) confirmed this in studies with University of Michigan students. Those whose self-worth was most fragile—most contingent on external sources—experienced more stress, anger, relationship problems, drug and alcohol use, and eating disorders than did those whose worth was rooted more on internal sources, such as personal virtues. Ironically, note Crocker and Lora Park (2004), those who pursue self-esteem, perhaps by seeking to become beautiful, rich, or popular, may lose sight of what really makes for quality of life. Moreover, if feeling good about ourselves is our goal, then we may become less open to criticism, more likely to blame than empathize with others, and more pressured to succeed at rather than simply to enjoy activities. Over time, such pursuit of self-esteem can fail to satisfy our deep needs for competence, relationship, and autonomy, note Crocker and Park. To focus less on one's self-image, and more on developing one's talents and relationships, eventually leads to greater well-being.

Self-serving bias

As we process self-relevant information, a potent bias intrudes. We readily excuse our failures, accept credit for our successes, and in many ways see ourselves as better than average. Such self-enhancing perceptions enable most people to enjoy the bright side of high self-esteem, while occasionally suffering the dark side.

It is widely believed that most of us suffer low self-esteem. A generation ago, humanistic psychologist Carl Rogers (1958) concluded that most people he knew "despise themselves, regard themselves as worthless and unlovable." Many popularizers of humanistic psychology concurred. "All of us have inferiority complexes," contended John Powell (1989). "Those who seem not to have such a complex are only pretending." As Groucho Marx (1960) lampooned, "I don't want to belong to any club that would accept me as a member."

Actually, most of us have a good reputation with ourselves. In studies of self-esteem, even low-scoring people respond in the midrange of possible scores. (A low-self-esteem person responds to statements such as "I have good ideas" with a qualifying adjective, such as "somewhat" or "sometimes.") Moreover, one of social psychology's most provocative yet firmly established conclusions concerns the potency of **self-serving bias.**

self-serving bias
The tendency to perceive oneself favorably.

EXPLAINING POSITIVE AND NEGATIVE EVENTS

Dozens of experiments have found that people accept credit when told they have succeeded. They attribute the success to their ability and effort, but they attribute failure to external factors such as bad luck or the problem's inherent "impossibility" (Campbell & Sedikides, 1999). Similarly, in explaining their victories, athletes commonly credit themselves, but they attribute losses to something else: bad breaks, bad referee calls, or the other team's super effort or dirty play (Grove & others, 1991; Lalonde, 1992; Mullen & Riordan, 1988). And how much responsibility do you suppose car drivers tend to accept for their accidents? On insurance forms, drivers have described their accidents in words such as these: "An invisible car came out of nowhere, struck my car, and vanished"; "As I reached an intersection, a hedge sprang up, obscuring my vision, and I did not see the other car"; "A pedestrian hit me and went under my car" (*Toronto News*, 1977).

Situations that combine skill and chance (games, exams, job applications) are especially prone to the phenomenon: Winners can easily attribute their successes to their skill, while losers can attribute their losses to chance. When I win at Scrabble, it's because of my verbal dexterity; when I lose, it's because, "Who could get anywhere with a *Q* but no *U*?" Politicians similarly tend to attribute their wins to themselves (hard work, constituent service, reputation, and strategy) and their losses to factors beyond their control (their district's party makeup, their opponent's name, political trends) (Kingdon, 1967). When corporate profits are up, the CEOs welcome big bonuses for their managerial skill. When profits turn to losses, well, what could you expect in a down economy?

Michael Ross and Fiore Sicoly (1979) observed a marital version of self-serving bias. They found that young married Canadians usually believed they took more responsibility for such activities as cleaning the house and caring for the children than their spouses credited them for. In one national survey, 91 percent of wives but only 76 percent of husbands credited the wife with doing most of the food shopping (Burros, 1988). In other studies, wives estimated they did proportionally more of the housework than their husbands credited them with (Bird, 1999; Fiebert, 1990). Every night, my wife and I used to pitch our laundry at the foot of our bedroom clothes hamper. In the morning, one of us would put it in. When she suggested that I take more responsibility for this, I thought, "Huh? I already do it 75 percent of the time." So I asked her how often she

"Thanks a lot, pal! Maybe next time you'll be a little more considerate and look both ways!"

By permission of Leigh Rubin and Creators Syndicate, Inc.

© Jean Sorensen.

thought she picked up the clothes. "Oh," she replied, "about 75 percent of the time."

Such biases in allocating responsibility contribute to marital discord, dissatisfaction among workers, and impasses when bargaining (Kruger & Gilovich, 1999). Small wonder that divorced people usually blame their partner for the breakup (Gray & Silver, 1990), or that managers often blame poor performance on workers' lack of ability or effort (Imai, 1994; Rice, 1985). (Workers are more likely to blame something external—inadequate supplies, excessive workload, difficult co-workers, ambiguous assignments.) Small wonder, too, that people evaluate reward distributions such as pay raises as fairer when they receive more than most others (Diekmann & others, 1997).

We help maintain our positive self-images by associating ourselves with success and distancing ourselves from failure. For example, "I got an A on my econ test" versus "The prof gave me a C on my history exam." Blaming failure or rejection on something external, even another's prejudice, is less depressing than seeing oneself as undeserving (Major & others, 2003). We more readily acknowledge our distant past failings—those by our "former" self, note Anne Wilson and Michael Ross (2001). Describing their old precollege selves, the University of Waterloo students offered nearly as many negative as positive statements. When describing their present selves, they offered three times more positive statements. "I've learned and grown, and I'm a better person today," most people surmise. Chumps yesterday, champs today.

Students also exhibit self-serving bias. After receiving an exam grade, those who do well tend to accept personal credit. They judge the exam to be a valid measure of their competence (Arkin & Maruyama, 1979; Davis & Stephan, 1980; Gilmor & Reid, 1979; Griffin & others, 1983). Those who do poorly are much more likely to criticize the exam.

Dilbert   Scott Adams

Reading this research, I couldn't resist a satisfied "knew-it-all-along" feeling. But consider teachers' ways of explaining students' good and bad performances. When there is no need to feign modesty, those assigned the role of teacher tend to take credit for positive outcomes and blame failure on the student (Arkin & others, 1980; Davis, 1979). Teachers, it seems, are likely to think, "With my help, Maria graduated with honors. Despite all my help, Melinda flunked out."

CAN WE ALL BE BETTER THAN AVERAGE?

Self-serving bias also appears when people compare themselves with others. If the sixth-century B.C. Chinese philosopher Lao-tzu was right that "at no time in the world will a man who is sane over-reach himself, over-spend himself, over-rate himself," then most of us are a little insane. For on most *subjective* and *socially desirable* dimensions, most people see themselves as better than the average person. Compared with people in general, most people see themselves as more ethical, more competent at their job, friendlier, more intelligent, better looking, less prejudiced, healthier, and even more insightful and less biased in their self-assessments (see "Focus on: Self-Serving Bias—How Do I Love Me? Let Me Count the Ways").

Every community, it seems, is like Garrison Keillor's fictional Lake Wobegon, where "all the women are strong, all the men are good-looking, and all the children are above average." Perhaps one reason for this optimism is that although 12 percent of people feel old for their age, many more—66 percent—think they are young for their age (*Public Opinion*, 1984). All of which calls to mind Freud's joke about the husband who told his wife, "If one of us should die, I think I would go live in Paris."

www.mhhe.com/myers8
Visit the Online Learning Center for a scenario on self-serving bias.

Subjective behavior dimensions (such as "disciplined") trigger greater self-serving bias than objective behavioral dimensions (such as "punctual"). Students are more likely to rate themselves superior in "moral goodness" than in "intelligence" (Allison & others, 1989; Van Lange, 1991). And community residents overwhelmingly see themselves as *caring* more than most others about the environment, about hunger, and about other social issues, though they don't see themselves as *doing* more, such as contributing time or money to those issues (White & Plous, 1995). Education doesn't eliminate self-serving bias; even social psychologists exhibit it, by believing themselves more ethical than most social psychologists (Van Lange & others, 1997).

Subjective qualities give us leeway in constructing our own definitions of success (Dunning & others, 1989, 1991). Rating my "athletic ability," I ponder my basketball play, not the agonizing weeks I spent as a Little League baseball player hiding in right field. Assessing my "leadership ability," I conjure up an image of a great leader whose style is similar to mine. By defining ambiguous criteria in our own terms, each of us can see ourselves as relatively successful. In one College Entrance Examination Board survey of 829,000 high school seniors, 0 percent rated themselves below average in "ability to get along with others" (a subjective, desirable trait), 60 percent rated themselves in the top 10 percent, and 25 percent saw themselves among the top 1 percent!

We also support our self-images by assigning importance to the things we're good at. Over a semester, those who ace an introductory computer science course come to place a higher value on being a computer-literate person in today's world. Those who do poorly are more likely to scorn computer geeks

focus on | self-serving bias—How do I love me? Let me count the ways

"The one thing that unites all human beings, regardless of age, gender, religion, economic status or ethnic background," notes Dave Barry (1998), "is that deep down inside, we all believe that we are above average drivers." We also believe we are above average on most any other subjective and desirable trait. Among the many faces of self-serving bias are these:

- *Ethics.* Most business people see themselves as more ethical than the average business person (Baumhart, 1968; Brenner & Molander, 1977). One national survey asked, "How would you rate your own morals and values on a scale from 1 to 100 (100 being perfect)?" Fifty percent of people rated themselves 90 or above; only 11 percent said 74 or less (Lovett, 1997).

- *Professional competence.* Ninety percent of business managers rate their performance as superior to their average peer (French, 1968). In Australia, 86 percent of people rate their job performance as above average, 1 percent as below average (Headey & Wearing, 1987). Most surgeons believe their patients' mortality rate to be lower than average (Gawande, 2002).

- *Virtues.* In the Netherlands, most high school students rate themselves as more honest, persistent, original, friendly, and reliable than the average high school student (Hoorens, 1993, 1995).

- *Driving.* Most drivers—even most drivers who have been hospitalized for accidents—believe themselves to be safer and more skilled than the average driver (Guerin, 1994; McKenna & Myers, 1997; Svenson, 1981).

- *Intelligence.* Most people perceive themselves as more intelligent, better looking, and much less prejudiced than their average peer (*Public Opinion*, 1984; Wylie, 1979). When someone outperforms them, people tend to think of the other as a genius (Lassiter & Munhall, 2001).

- *Tolerance.* In a 1997 Gallup Poll, only 14 percent of white Americans rated their prejudice against Blacks as 5 or higher on a 0 to 10 scale. Yet Whites perceived high prejudice (5 or above) among 44 percent of *other* Whites.

- *Parental support.* Most adults believe they support their aging parents more than do their siblings (Lerner & others, 1991).

- *Health.* Los Angeles residents view themselves as healthier than most of their neighbors, and most college students believe they will outlive their actuarially predicted age of death by about 10 years (Larwood, 1978; C. R. Snyder, 1978).

- *Insight.* Others' words and deeds reveal their natures, we presume. Our *private* thoughts do the same. Thus, most of us believe we know and understand others better than they know and understand us. We also believe we know ourselves better than others know themselves (Pronin & others, 2001). Few college students see themselves as more naïve or more gullible than others; many more think they're less naïve and gullible (Levine, 2003).

- *Freedom from bias.* People see themselves as less vulnerable to various biases than most others (Pronin & others, 2002). They even think themselves less subject to self-serving bias than most others!

and to exclude computer skills as pertinent to their self-images (Hill & others, 1989).

UNREALISTIC OPTIMISM

Optimism predisposes a positive approach to life. "The optimist," notes H. Jackson Brown (1990, p. 79), "goes to the window every morning and says, 'Good morning, God.' The pessimist goes to the window and says, 'good god, morning.' " Many of us however, have what researcher Neil Weinstein (1980, 1982) terms "an unrealistic optimism about future life events." Due partly to their relative pessimism about others' fates (Shepperd, 2003), students perceive themselves as far more likely than their classmates to get a good job, draw a good salary, and own a home, and as far less likely to experience negative events, such as developing a drinking problem, having a heart at-

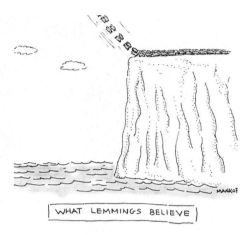

WHAT LEMMINGS BELIEVE

tack before age 40, or being fired. In Scotland and the United States, most older teens think they are much less likely than their peers to become infected by HIV (Abrams, 1991; Pryor & Reeder, 1993). After experiencing the 1989 earthquake, San Francisco Bay area students did lose their optimism. They felt as vulnerable as their school classmates to injury in a natural disaster, but within three months their illusory optimism had rebounded (Burger & Palmer, 1991).

Linda Perloff (1987) notes how illusory optimism increases our vulnerability. Believing ourselves immune to misfortune, we do not take sensible precautions. In one survey, 137 marriage license applicants accurately estimated that half of marriages end in divorce, yet most assessed their chance of divorce as 0 percent (Baker & Emery, 1993). Sexually active undergraduate women who don't consistently use contraceptives perceive themselves, compared with other women at their university, as much *less* vulnerable to unwanted pregnancy (Burger & Burns, 1988).

> "Views of the future are so rosy that they would make Pollyanna blush."
> —Shelley E. Taylor, *Positive Illusions*, 1989

Those who cheerfully shun seat belts, deny the effects of smoking, and stumble into ill-fated relationships remind us that blind optimism, like pride, may go before a fall. When gambling, optimists more than pessimists persist, even when piling up losses (Gibson & Sanbonmatsu, 2004). If those who deal in the stock market or in real estate perceive their business intuition to be superior to that of their competitors, they, too, may be in for severe disappointment. Even the seventeenth-century economist Adam Smith, a defender of human economic rationality, foresaw that people would overestimate their chances of gain. This "absurd presumption in their own good fortune," he said, arises from "the overweening conceit which the greater part of men have of their own abilities" (Spiegel, 1971, p. 243).

Optimism definitely beats pessimism in promoting self-efficacy, health, and well-being (Armor & Taylor, 1996; Segerstrom, 2001). Being natural optimists, most people believe they will be happier with their lives in the future—a belief that surely helps create happiness in the present (Robinson & Ryff, 1999).

Half of 18- to 19-year-old Americans cheer themselves with the thought that they are "somewhat" or "very" likely to "be rich" (a belief shared by progressively fewer people with age (Moore, 2003). Yet a dash of realism—or what Julie Norem (2000) calls "defensive pessimism"—can save us from the perils of unrealistic optimism. Students who enter university with inflated assessments of their academic ability often suffer deflating self-esteem and well-being (Robins & Beer, 2001). Defensive pessimism anticipates problems and motivates effective coping. As a Chinese proverb says, "Be prepared for danger while staying

> "O God, give us grace to accept with serenity the things that cannot be changed, courage to change the things which should be changed, and the wisdom to distinguish the one from the other."
> —Reinhold Niebuhr, *The Serenity Prayer*, 1943

Illusory optimism: Most couples marry feeling confident of long-term love. Actually, in individualistic cultures, half of marriages fail.

in peace." Students who exhibit excess optimism (as do many students destined for low grades) can benefit from having some self-doubt, which motivates study (Prohaska, 1994; Sparrell & Shrauger, 1984). (Such illusory optimism often disappears as the time approaches for receiving the exam back—Taylor & Shepperd, 1998.) Students who are overconfident tend to underprepare. Their equally able but more anxious peers, fearing that they are going to bomb on the upcoming exam, study furiously and get higher grades (Goodhart, 1986; Norem & Cantor, 1986; Showers & Ruben, 1987).

The moral: Success in school and beyond requires enough optimism to sustain hope and enough pessimism to motivate concern.

FALSE CONSENSUS AND UNIQUENESS

false consensus effect
The tendency to overestimate the commonality of one's opinions and one's undesirable or unsuccessful behaviors.

We have a curious tendency to further enhance our self-images by overestimating or underestimating the extent to which others think and act as we do. On matters of *opinion,* we find support for our positions by overestimating the extent to which others agree —a phenomenon called the **false consensus effect** (Krueger & Clement, 1994; Marks & Miller, 1987; Mullen & Goethals, 1990). If we favor a Canadian referendum or support New Zealand's National Party, we wishfully overestimate the extent to which others agree (Babad & others, 1992; Koestner, 1993). The sense we make of the world seems like common sense.

When we behave badly or fail in a task, we reassure ourselves by thinking that such lapses also are common. After one person lies to another, the liar begins to perceive the other as dishonest (Sagarin & others, 1998). They guess that others think and act as they do: "I lie, but doesn't everyone?" If we cheat on our income taxes or smoke, we are likely to overestimate the number of other people who do likewise. If we feel sexual desire toward another, we may overestimate the other's reciprocal desire. Four recent studies illustrate:

• People who sneak a shower during a shower ban believe (more than nonbathers) lots of others are doing the same (Monin & Norton, 2003).

- Those thirsty after hard exercise imagine that lost hikers would become more bothered by thirst than by hunger. That's what 88 percent of thirsty postexercisers guessed in a study by Leaf Van Boven and George Lowenstein (2003), compared with 57 percent of people who were about to exercise.

- As people's own lives change, they see the world changing. Protective new parents come to see the world as a more dangerous place. People who go on a diet judge food ads to be more prevalent (Eibach & others, 2003).

- People who harbor negative ideas about another racial group presume that many others also have negative stereotypes (Krueger, 1996). Thus our perceptions of others' stereotypes may reveal something of our own.

"We don't see things as they are," says the Talmud. "We see things as we are."

False consensus may occur because we generalize from a limited sample, which prominently includes ourselves (Dawes, 1990). Lacking other information, why not "project" ourselves; why not impute our own knowledge to others and use our responses as a clue to their likely responses? Also, we're more likely to associate with people who share our attitudes and behaviors and then to judge the world from the people we know.

On matters of *ability* or when we behave well or successfully, a **false uniqueness effect** more often occurs (Goethals & others, 1991). We serve our self-image by seeing our talents and moral behaviors as relatively unusual. Thus those who drink heavily but use seat belts will *over*estimate (false consensus) the number of other heavy drinkers and *under*estimate (false uniqueness) the commonality of seat belt use (Suls & others, 1988). This seems a natural result of our tendency to ascribe positive more than negative traits to ourselves (Gross & Miller, 1997; Krueger, 1997; Krueger & Clement, 1997). The less common a behavior, the more we overestimate its frequency. (If 20 percent of people are selfish, there is lots of room for people to overestimate the extent to which others [relative to themselves] are selfish.) Thus we may see our failings as relatively normal and our virtues as less commonplace than they are.

To sum up, these tendencies toward self-serving attributions, self-congratulatory comparisons, illusory optimism, and false consensus for our failings are major sources of self-serving bias (Figure 2–9, page 74).

EXPLAINING SELF-SERVING BIAS

Why do people perceive themselves in self-enhancing ways? One explanation sees the self-serving bias as a by-product of how we process and remember information about ourselves. Recall the study in which married people gave themselves credit for doing more housework than their spouses did. Might this not be due, as Michael Ross and Fiore Sicoly (1979) believe, to our greater recall for what we've actively done and our lesser recall for what we've not done or merely observed others doing? I can easily picture myself picking up the laundry, but I am less aware of the times when I absentmindedly overlooked it.

"I think few people have conventional family relationships."
—Madonna, 2000

"Everybody says I'm plastic from head to toe. Can't stand next to a radiator or I'll melt. I had (breast) implants, but so has every single person in L.A" (Talbert, 1997).
—Actress Pamela Lee

false uniqueness effect
The tendency to underestimate the commonality of one's abilities and one's desirable or successful behaviors.

Can we all be better than average? William W. Haefeli, *Saturday Review,* 1/20/79

"I admit it does look very impressive. But you see nowadays everyone graduates in the top ten percent of his class."

figure 2–9

How self-serving bias works.

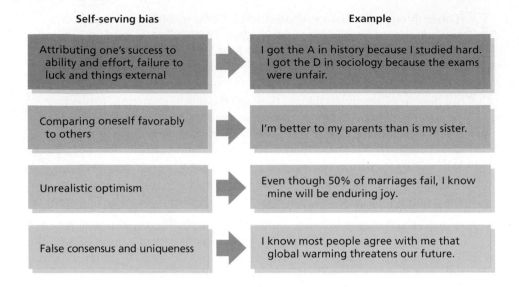

Self-serving bias		Example
Attributing one's success to ability and effort, failure to luck and things external	→	I got the A in history because I studied hard. I got the D in sociology because the exams were unfair.
Comparing oneself favorably to others	→	I'm better to my parents than is my sister.
Unrealistic optimism	→	Even though 50% of marriages fail, I know mine will be enduring joy.
False consensus and uniqueness	→	I know most people agree with me that global warming threatens our future.

Are the biased perceptions, then, simply a perceptual error, an unemotional bent in how we process information? Or are self-serving *motives* also involved? It's now clear from research that we have multiple motives. Questing for self-knowledge, we're eager to assess our competence (Dunning, 1995). Questing for self-confirmation, we're eager to *verify* our self-conceptions (Sanitioso & others, 1990; Swann, 1996, 1997). Questing for self-affirmation, we're especially motivated to *enhance* our self-image (Sedikides, 1993). Self-esteem motivation helps power self-serving bias.

REFLECTIONS ON SELF-EFFICACY AND SELF-SERVING BIAS

No doubt many readers are finding the self-serving bias either depressing or contrary to their own occasional feelings of inadequacy. To be sure, the people who exhibit the self-serving bias may feel inferior to specific individuals, especially those who are a step or two higher on the ladder of success, attractiveness, or skill. And not everyone operates with a self-serving bias. Some people *do* suffer from low self-esteem.

In experiments, people whose self-esteem is temporarily bruised—by being told they did miserably on an intelligence test, for example—are more likely to disparage others (Beauregard & Dunning, 1998). Those whose egos have recently been wounded also are more prone to self-serving explanations of success or failure than are those whose egos have recently received a boost (McCarrey & others, 1982). So threats to self-esteem may provoke self-protective defensiveness. When they feel unaffirmed, people may offer self-affirming boasts, excuses, and put-downs of others. More generally, people who are down on themselves tend also to be overly reactive to slights—they see rejection where none exists and tend to get down on others (Murray & others, 2002; Wills, 1981). Mockery says as much about the mocker as the one mocked.

Nevertheless, high self-esteem goes hand in hand with self-serving perceptions. Those who score highest on self-esteem tests (who say nice things about themselves) also say nice things about themselves when explaining their successes and failures, when evaluating their group, and when comparing themselves with others (Brown, 1986; Brown & others, 1988; Schlenker & others, 1990).

The self-serving bias as adaptive

Self-esteem has its dark side, but also its bright side. When good things happen, high more than low self-esteem people tend to savor and sustain the good feelings (Wood & others, 2003). Even illusory self-enhancement correlates with many mental health indicators. "Believing one has more talents and positive qualities than one's peers allows one to feel good about oneself and to enter the stressful circumstances of daily life with the resources conferred by a positive sense of self," note Shelley Taylor and her co-researchers (2003). Self-serving bias and its accompanying excuses also help protect people from depression and the biological costs of stress (Snyder & Higgins, 1988; Taylor & others, 2003). Nondepressed people excuse their failures on laboratory tasks or perceive themselves as being more in control than they are. Depressed people's self-appraisals and their appraisals of how others really view them are not inflated (more on this in Chapter 14).

In their "terror management theory," Jeff Greenberg, Sheldon Solomon, and Tom Pyszczynski (1997) propose another reason why positive self-esteem is adaptive—it buffers anxiety, including anxiety related to our certain death. In childhood we learn that when we meet the standards taught us by our parents, we are loved and protected; when we don't, love and protection may be withdrawn. We therefore come to associate viewing ourselves as good with feeling secure. Greenberg and colleagues argue that positive self-esteem—viewing oneself as good and secure—even protects us from feeling terror over our eventual death. Their research shows that reminding people of their mortality (say, by writing a short essay on dying) motivates them to affirm their self-worth. Moreover, when facing threats, increased self-esteem leads to decreased anxiety.

As this new research on depression and anxiety suggests, there may be some practical wisdom in self-serving perceptions. It may be strategic to believe we are smarter, stronger, and more socially successful than we are. Cheaters may give a more convincing display of honesty if they believe themselves honorable. Belief in our superiority can also motivate us to achieve—creating a self-fulfilling prophecy—and can sustain a sense of hope in difficult times.

The self-serving bias as maladaptive

Although self-serving pride may help protect us from depression, it can at times be maladaptive. People who blame others for their social difficulties are often unhappier than people who can acknowledge their mistakes (C. A. Anderson & others, 1983; Newman & Langer, 1981; Peterson & others, 1981).

Research by Barry Schlenker (1976; Schlenker & Miller, 1977a, 1977b) has also shown how self-serving perceptions can poison a group. As a rock band guitarist during his college days, Schlenker noted that "rock band members typically overestimated their contributions to a group's success and underestimated their contributions to failure. I saw many good bands disintegrate from the problems caused by these self-glorifying tendencies." In his later life as a

"Victory finds a hundred fathers but defeat is an orphan."
—Count Galeazzo Ciano, *The Ciano Diaries*, 1938

University of Florida social psychologist, Schlenker explored group members' self-serving perceptions. In nine experiments, he had people work together on some task. He then falsely informed them that their group had done either well or poorly. In every one of these studies, the members of successful groups claimed more responsibility for their group's performance than did members of groups that supposedly failed at the task. Most presented themselves as contributing more than the others in their group when the group did well; few said they contributed less.

If most group members believe they are underpaid and underappreciated relative to their better-than-average contributions, disharmony and envy are likely. College presidents and academic deans will readily recognize the phenomenon. Ninety percent or more of college faculty members rate themselves as superior to their average colleague (Blackburn & others, 1980; Cross, 1977). It is therefore inevitable that when merit salary raises are announced and half receive an average raise or less, many will feel themselves victims of injustice.

Self-serving biases also inflate people's judgments of their groups. When groups are comparable, most people consider their own group superior (Codol, 1976; Jourden & Heath, 1996; Taylor & Doria, 1981).

- Most university sorority members perceive those in their sorority as far less likely to be conceited and snobby than those in other sororities (Biernat & others, 1996).
- Fifty-three percent of Dutch adults rate their marriage or partnership as better than that of most others; only 1 percent rate it as worse than most (Buunk & van der Eijnden, 1997).
- Sixty-six percent of Americans give their oldest child's public schools a grade of A or B. But nearly as many—64 percent—give the nation's public schools a grade of C or D (Whitman, 1996).
- Most corporation presidents and production managers overpredict their own firms' productivity and growth (Kidd & Morgan, 1969; Larwood & Whittaker, 1977).

Self-serving pride in group settings can become especially dangerous.

"Then we're in agreement. There's nothing rotten here in Denmark. Something is rotten everywhere else."

That people see themselves and their groups with a favorable bias is hardly new. The tragic flaw portrayed in ancient Greek drama was *hubris*, or pride. Like the subjects of our experiments, the Greek tragic figures were not self-consciously evil; they merely thought too highly of themselves. In literature, the pitfalls of pride are portrayed again and again. In theology, pride has long been first among the "seven deadly sins."

If pride is akin to the self-serving bias, then what is humility? Is it self-contempt? Or can we be self-affirming and self-accepting without a self-serving bias? To paraphrase the English scholar-writer C. S. Lewis, humility is not handsome people trying to believe they are ugly and clever people trying to believe they are fools. False modesty can actually be a cover for pride in one's better-than-average humility. (James Friedrich [1996] reports that most students congratulate themselves on being better than average at not thinking themselves better than average!) True humility is more like self-forgetfulness than false modesty. It leaves people free to rejoice in their special talents and, with the same honesty, to recognize the talents of others.

Contrary to the presumption that most people suffer from low self-esteem or feelings of inferiority, researchers consistently find that most people exhibit a self-serving bias. In experiments and everyday life, we often blame failures on the situation while taking credit for successes. We typically rate ourselves as better than average on subjective, desirable traits and abilities. Believing in ourselves, we exhibit unrealistic optimism about our futures. And we overestimate the commonality of our opinions and foibles (false consensus) while underestimating the commonality of our abilities and virtues (false uniqueness). Such perceptions arise partly from a motive to maintain and enhance self-esteem, a motive that protects people from depression but contributes to misjudgment and group conflict.

Summing up

Self-presentation

Humans seem motivated not only to perceive themselves in self-enhancing ways but also to present themselves favorably to others. How might people's tactics of "impression management" lead to false modesty or to self-defeating behavior?

So far we have seen that the self is at the center of our social worlds, that self-esteem and self-efficacy pay some dividends, but that self-serving pride biases self-evaluations. Perhaps you have wondered: Are self-enhancing expressions always sincere? Do people have the same feelings privately as they express publicly? Or will they put on a positive face even while living with self-doubt?

FALSE MODESTY

There is indeed evidence that people sometimes present a different self than they feel. The clearest example, however, is not false pride but false modesty. Perhaps you have by now recalled times when someone was not self-praising but self-disparaging. Such put-downs can be subtly self-serving, for often they elicit reassuring "strokes." "I felt like a fool" may trigger a friend to reassure that "you did fine!" Even a remark such as "I wish I weren't so ugly" may elicit at least a "Come now. I know a couple of people who are uglier than you."

There is another reason people disparage themselves and praise others. Think of the coach who, before the big game, extols the opponent's strength. Is the coach utterly sincere? When coaches publicly exalt their opponents, they convey an image of modesty and good sportsmanship and set the stage for a favorable evaluation no matter what the outcome. A win becomes a praiseworthy achievement, a loss attributable to the opponent's "great defense." Modesty, said the seventeenth-century philosopher Francis Bacon, is but one of the "arts of ostentation."

Robert Gould, Paul Brounstein, and Harold Sigall (1977) found that, in a laboratory contest, their University of Maryland students similarly aggrandized their anticipated opponent, but only when the assessment was made publicly.

"Humility is often but a trick whereby pride abases itself only to exalt itself later."
—La Rochefoucauld, *Maxims*, 1665.

Anonymously, they credited their future opponent with much less ability. Understating one's own ability also serves to reduce performance pressure and lower the baseline for evaluating performance (Gibson & Sachau, 2000).

False modesty also appears in people's autobiographical accounts of their achievements. At awards ceremonies, honorees graciously thank others for their support. Upon receiving an Academy Award, Maureen Stapleton thanked "my family, my children, my friends, and everyone I have ever met in my entire life." Does such generous sharing of credit contradict the common finding that people readily attribute success to their own effort and competence?

To find out, Roy Baumeister and Stacey Ilko (1995) invited students to write a description of "an important success experience." Those whom they asked to sign their names and who anticipated reading their story to others often acknowledged the help or emotional support they had received. Those who wrote anonymously rarely made such mentions; rather, they portrayed themselves achieving their successes on their own. To Baumeister and Ilko, these results suggest "shallow gratitude"—superficial gratitude offered to *appear* humble, while "in the privacy of their own minds" the students credited themselves.

Shallow gratitude may surface when, like Maureen Stapleton, we outperform others around us and feel uneasy about other people's feelings toward us. If we think our success will make others feel envious or resentful—a phenomenon that Julia Exline and Marci Lobel (1999) call "the perils of outperformance"—we may downplay our achievements and display gratitude. For superachievers, modest self-presentations come naturally.

SELF-HANDICAPPING

Sometimes people sabotage their chances for success by creating impediments that make success less likely. Far from being deliberately self-destructive, such behaviors typically have a self-protective aim (Arkin & others, 1986; Baumeister & Scher, 1988; Rhodewalt, 1987): "I'm really not a failure—I would have done well except for this problem."

"With no attempt there can be no failure; with no failure no humiliation."
—William James, *Principles of Psychology*, 1890

Why would people handicap themselves with self-defeating behavior? Recall that we eagerly protect our self-images by attributing failures to external factors. Can you see why, *fearing failure,* people might handicap themselves by partying half the night before a job interview or playing video games instead of studying before a big exam? When self-image is tied up with performance, it can be more self-deflating to try hard and fail than to procrastinate and have a ready excuse. If we fail while handicapped in some way, we can cling to a sense of competence; if we succeed under such conditions, it can only boost our self-image. Handicaps protect both self-esteem and public image by allowing us to attribute failures to something temporary or external ("I was feeling sick"; "I was out too late the night before") rather than to lack of talent or ability.

self-handicapping
Protecting one's self-image with behaviors that create a handy excuse for later failure.

This analysis of **self-handicapping,** proposed by Steven Berglas and Edward Jones (1978), has been confirmed. One experiment was said to concern "drugs and intellectual performance." Imagine yourself in the position of their Duke University participants. You guess answers to some difficult aptitude questions and then are told, "Yours was one of the best scores seen to date!" Feeling incredibly lucky, you are then offered a choice between two drugs before answering more of these items. One drug will aid intellectual performance and the other will inhibit it. Which drug do you want? Most students wanted the drug that would supposedly disrupt their thinking and thus provide a handy excuse for anticipated poorer performance.

Researchers have documented other ways in which people self-handicap. Fearing failure, people will do the following:

- Reduce their preparation for important individual athletic events (Rhodewalt & others, 1984)
- Give their opponent an advantage (Shepperd & Arkin, 1991)
- Perform poorly at the beginning of a task in order not to create unreachable expectations (Baumgardner & Brownlee, 1987)
- Not try as hard as they could during a tough, ego-involving task (Hormuth, 1986; Pyszczynski & Greenberg, 1987; Riggs, 1992; Turner & Pratkanis, 1993)

IMPRESSION MANAGEMENT

Self-serving bias, false modesty, and self-handicapping reveal the depth of our concern for self-image. To varying degrees, we are continually managing the impressions we create. Whether we wish to impress, to intimidate, or to seem helpless, we are social animals, playing to an audience.

Self-presentation refers to our wanting to present a desired image both to an external audience (other people) and to an internal audience (ourselves). We work at managing the impressions we create. We excuse, justify, or apologize as necessary to shore up our self-esteem and verify our self-images (Schlenker & Weigold, 1992). In familiar situations, this happens without conscious effort. In unfamiliar situations, perhaps at a party with people we would like to impress or in conversation with someone we have romantic interest in, we are acutely self-conscious of the impressions we are creating and we are therefore less modest than when among friends who know us well (Leary & others, 1994; Tice & others, 1995). Preparing to have our photographs taken, we may even try out different faces in a mirror.

Given our concern for self-presentation, it's no wonder that people will self-handicap when failure might make them look bad (Arkin & Baumgardner, 1985). It's no wonder that people take health risks—tanning their skin with wrinkle- and cancer-causing radiation; becoming anorexic; yielding to peer pressures to smoke, get drunk, and do drugs (Leary & others, 1994). It's no wonder that people express more modesty when their self-flattery is vulnerable to being debunked, perhaps by experts who will be scrutinizing their self-evaluations (Arkin & others, 1980; Riess & others, 1981; Weary & others, 1982). Professor Smith will express less confidence in the significance of her work when presenting it to professional colleagues than when presenting to students.

For some people, conscious self-presentation is a way of life. They continually monitor their own behavior and note how others react, then adjust their social performance to gain a desired effect. Those who score high on a scale of **self-monitoring** tendency (who, for example, agree that "I tend to be what people expect me to be") act like social chameleons—they adjust their behavior in response to external situations (Snyder, 1987; Gangestad & Snyder, 2000). Having attuned their behavior to the situation, they are more likely to espouse attitudes they don't really hold (Zanna & Olson, 1982). Being conscious of others, they are less likely to act on their own attitudes. For high self-monitors, attitudes serve a social adjustment function; they help these people adapt to new jobs, roles, and relationships.

Those who score low in self-monitoring care less about what others think. They are more internally guided and thus more likely to talk and act as they feel

"If you try to fail, and succeed, what have you done?"
—Anonymous

After losing to some younger rivals, tennis great Martina Navratilova confessed that she was "afraid to play my best. . . . I was scared to find out if they could beat me when I'm playing my best because if they can, then I am finished" (Frankel & Snyder, 1987).

self-presentation
The act of expressing oneself and behaving in ways designed to create a favorable impression or an impression that corresponds to one's ideals.

self-monitoring
Being attuned to the way one presents oneself in social situations and adjusting one's performance to create the desired impression.

"Hmmm... what shall I wear today...?"

and believe (McCann & Hancock, 1983). If asked to list their thoughts about gay couples, they just express what they think, regardless of the attitudes of their anticipated audience (Klein & others, in press). Most of us fall somewhere between the high self-monitoring extreme of the con artist and the low self-monitoring extreme of stubborn insensitivity.

Presenting oneself in ways that create a desired impression is a very delicate matter. People want to be seen as able, but also as modest and honest (Carlston & Shovar, 1983). Modesty creates a good impression, and unsolicited boasting creates a bad impression. Thus, the false modesty phenomenon: We often display less self-esteem than we privately feel (Miller & Schlenker, 1985). But when we have obviously done extremely well, false disclaimers ("I did well, but it's no big deal") may come across as feigned humility. To make good impressions—as modest yet competent—requires social skill.

Self-presented modesty is greatest in cultures that value self-restraint, such as those of China and Japan (Brown & Kobayashi, 2003; Heine & others, 2000, 2002; Yik & others, 1998). In China and Japan, people exhibit less self-serving bias. Children learn to share credit for success and to accept responsibility for failures. "When I fail, it's my fault, not my group's" (Anderson, 1999). In Western countries, children learn to feel pride in success while attributing failure to the situation. The result, reports Philip Zimbardo (1993), is greater modesty and shyness among the self-effacing Japanese.

Despite such self-presentational concerns, people worldwide are privately self-enhancing (Brown, 2003). Self-serving bias has been noted among Dutch high school and university students, Belgian basketball players, Indian Hindus, Japanese students and drivers, Israeli and Singaporean schoolchildren, Australian students and workers, Chinese students, Hong Kong students and sports writers, and French people of all ages (Brown & Kobayashi, 2002, 2003; Codol, 1976; de Vries & van Knippenberg, 1987; Falbo & others, 1997; Feather, 1983; Hagiwara, 1983; Hallahan & others, 1997; Jain, 1990; Liebrand & others, 1986; Lefebvre, 1979; Murphy-Berman & Sharma, 1986; Ruzzene & Noller, 1986; Sedikides & others, 2003; Yik & others, 1998, respectively).

"Public opinion is always more tyrannical towards those who obviously fear it than towards those who feel indifferent to it."
—Bertrand Russell, *The Conquest of Happiness*, 1930

"If an American is hit on the head by a ball at the ballpark, he sues. If a Japanese person is hit on the head he says, "'It's my honor. It's my fault. I shouldn't have been standing there.'"
—Japanese bar-association official Koji Yanase, explaining why there are half as many lawyers in his country as in the greater Washington area alone, *Newsweek*, February 26, 1996

Group identity. In Asian countries, self-presentation is restrained. Children learn to identify themselves with their groups.

As social animals, we adjust our words and actions to suit our audiences. To varying degrees, we self-monitor; we note our performance and adjust it to create the impressions we desire. Such impression management tactics explain examples of false modesty, in which people put themselves down, extol future competitors, or publicly credit others when privately they credit themselves. Sometimes people will even self-handicap with self-defeating behaviors that protect self-esteem by providing excuses for failure.

Summing up

P̧s Personal Postscript: Twin truths—The perils of pride, the power of positive thinking

This chapter offered two memorable truths—the truth of self-efficacy and the truth of self-serving bias. The truth concerning *self-efficacy* encourages us not to resign ourselves to bad situations. We need to persist despite initial failures and to exert effort without being overly distracted by self-doubts. High self-esteem is likewise adaptive. When we believe in our positive possibilities, we are less vulnerable to depression and we increase our chances for success.

The truth concerning illusory optimism and other forms of *self-serving bias* reminds us that self-efficacy is not the whole story of the self in a social world. If positive thinking can accomplish anything, then we have only ourselves to blame if we are unhappily married, poor, or depressed. For shame! If only we had tried harder, been more disciplined, less stupid. Failing to appreciate that difficulties sometimes reflect the oppressive power of social situations can tempt us to blame people for their problems and failures, or even to blame ourselves too harshly for our own. Life's greatest achievements, but also its greatest disappointments, are born of the highest expectations.

These twin truths—self-efficacy and self-serving bias—remind me of what Pascal taught 300 years ago: No single truth is ever sufficient, because the world is complex. Any truth, separated from its complementary truth, is a half-truth.

What do you think?

Recall a specific situation where you exerted effort and were not distracted by self-doubt—where self-efficacy enabled you to succeed. Now, think of a time when, despite all your efforts and positive thinking, a situation did not turn out how you had hoped—a situation where you experienced the limits of self-efficacy. Did illusory optimism affect your judgment in the second instance?

Making the Social Connection

This chapter's discussion of self and culture explored research on individualism and collectivism by Hazel Markus and Shinobu Kitayama. We will consider their work again in chapters on conformity (Chapter 6) and conflict and peacemaking (Chapter 13). Go to the *SocialSense* CD-ROM to view Shinobu Kitayama speaking about how the interdependent and independent views of self differ.

chapter 3

Social Beliefs and Judgments

"You don't know your own mind."

Jonathan Swift,
Polite
Conversation,
1738

Soon after driving out the back entrance of the Ritz Hotel on an August night in 1997, Henri Paul was on a Paris highway alongside the River Seine. With his passengers, Princess Diana, her companion Dodi Fayed, and their bodyguard, he sped faster and faster as he dipped into a tunnel. With the car careening out of control, Paul suddenly smashed head-on into a pillar, leaving the Mercedes a crumpled wreck and killing all but the bodyguard.

In the weeks that followed people analyzed and debated endlessly. To what should the crash be attributed? To the driver and his alcohol intake earlier that evening? To the situation, especially the paparazzi photographers chasing the car and shooting their flash cameras? "I am disgusted and nauseated," said the anchor of a French evening news program, comparing the paparazzi to "rats." But the popular press responded with outrage at this explanation: "The driver was totally drunk and that is the essence of the story," said one newspaper editor.

On another fateful day, in April of 1999, Eric Harris and Dylan Klebold slaughtered 13 of their classmates at Colorado's Columbine High School. For the gunmen's devastated parents, classmates, and for much of their nation, why became the consuming question. Should we attribute their homicides to a psychiatric disorder? To "the negligence of the parents and possibly others," as alleged in a later lawsuit? To the hours the two reportedly had spent playing splatter games such as Doom and watching crazy kids commit carnage in *Natural Born Killers* and *Basketball Diaries*? To the taunting and ostracism they reportedly suffered at the hands of some classmates? To Harris's recent rejection by a prom date, by certain colleges, and by the Marines?

To what do we attribute the calculated evil of 9/11? What drove those 19 men to commit their suicidal violence? Were they uniquely evil? Crazy? Insane? (Had we been their neighbors, would we have found them noticeably demonic or mad?) Or were they unexceptional-seeming men whose cultural history bred hatred and a strategic plan to attack what they despised (and whose situation might be breeding more such persons)?

As these cases illustrate, our judgments of people depend on how we explain their behavior. Depending on our explanation, we may judge killing as murder, manslaughter, self-defense, or heroism. Depending on our explanation, we may view a homeless person as indolent or as victimized by job and welfare cutbacks. Depending on our explanation, we may attribute someone's friendly behavior as affection or ingratiation.

This chapter addresses these and other issues:

- To what do we attribute others' behavior?
- How do we perceive and recall our social worlds?
- What are the ways we judge each other?
- When do we tend to fulfill someone's expectations of us?

How do we explain others?

People make it their business to explain other people, and social psychologists make it their business to explain people's explanations. So, how—and how accurately—do people explain others' behavior? Attribution theory suggests some answers.

The human mind struggles to make sense of its world. If worker productivity declines, do we assume the workers are getting lazier? Or has their equipment become less efficient? Does a young boy who hits his classmates have a hostile personality? Or is he responding to relentless teasing? When a salesperson says, "That outfit really looks nice on you," does this reflect genuine feeling? Or is it a sales ploy?

ATTRIBUTING CAUSALITY: TO THE PERSON OR THE SITUATION

We endlessly analyze and discuss why things happen as they do, especially when we experience something negative or unexpected (Bohner & others, 1988; Weiner, 1985). Amy Holtzworth-Munroe and Neil Jacobson (1985, 1988) report that married people often analyze their partners' behaviors, especially their negative behaviors. Cold hostility is more likely than a warm hug to leave the partner wondering "why?"

The answers spouses choose correlate with their marriage satisfaction. Those in unhappy relationships typically offer distress-maintaining explanations for negative acts ("she was late because she doesn't care about me"). Happy couples more often externalize ("she was late because of heavy traffic"). With positive partner behavior, their explanations similarly work either to maintain distress ("he brought me flowers because he wants sex") or to enhance the relationship ("he brought me flowers to show he loves me") (Hewstone & Fincham, 1996; Weiner, 1995).

A question of attribution? In some sexual harassment or assault cases, men misattribute women's friendly behavior as sexual interest and therefore behave inappropriately. Some observers wondered if Kobe Bryant, accused of rape, perceived an invitation to sex that his accuser didn't intend.

Antonia Abbey (1987, 1991, 1998) and her colleagues have repeatedly found that men are more likely than women to attribute a woman's friendliness to mild sexual interest. This misreading of warmth as a sexual come-on (called *misattribution*) can contribute to behavior that women (American women, especially) regard as sexual harassment or rape (Johnson & others, 1991; Pryor & others, 1997; Saal & others, 1989). Many men believe women are flattered by repeated requests for dates, which women more often see as harassing (Rotundo & others, 2001).

Misattribution is especially likely when men are in positions of power. The boss may misinterpret a subordinate woman's submissive or friendly behavior and, full of himself, may see women only in sexual terms (Bargh & Raymond, 1995). Men more often than women think about sex (see Chapter 5). Men also tend to assume that others, including women, share their feelings (recall from Chapter 2 the "false consensus effect"). Thus, men can easily overestimate the sexual significance of a woman's courtesy smile (Nelson & LeBoeuf, 2002). What Jane intends as "just a smile" may give John the wrong idea.

Such misattributions help explain the greater sexual assertiveness exhibited by men across the world and the greater tendency of men in various cultures, from Boston to Bombay, to justify rape by blaming the victim's behavior (Kanekar & Nazareth, 1988; Muehlenhard, 1988; Shotland, 1989). Women more often judge the same behavior as meriting conviction and a stiff sentence. (Schutte & Hosch, 1997). Misattributions also help explain why the 23 percent of American women who say they have been forced into unwanted sexual behavior is eight times the 3 percent of American men who say they have ever forced a woman into a sexual act (Laumann & others, 1994). Sexually aggressive men are especially likely to misread women's communications (Malamuth & Brown, 1994). They "just don't get it."

Attribution theory analyzes how we explain people's behavior. The variations of attribution theory share some common assumptions. As Daniel Gilbert and Patrick Malone (1995) explain, each "construes the human skin as a special boundary that separates one set of 'causal forces' from another. On the sunny side of the epidermis are the external or situational forces that press inward

attribution theory
The theory of how people explain others' behavior; for example, by attributing it either to internal dispositions (enduring traits, motives, and attitudes) or to external situations.

"So! If it's good, it's Mister Coffee. If it's bad, it's me."

We tend to attribute someone's behavior or the outcome of an event either to internal (dispositional) or external (situational) causes.

dispositional attribution
Attributing behavior to the person's disposition and traits.

situational attribution
Attributing behavior to the environment.

upon the person, and on the meaty side are the internal or personal forces that exert pressure outward. Sometimes these forces press in conjunction, sometimes in opposition, and their dynamic interplay manifests itself as observable behavior."

Fritz Heider (1958), widely regarded as attribution theory's originator, analyzed the "commonsense psychology" by which people explain everyday events. Heider concluded that people tend to attribute someone's behavior to *internal* causes (for example, the person's disposition) or *external* causes (for example, something about the person's situation). A teacher may wonder whether a child's underachievement is due to lack of motivation and ability (a **dispositional attribution**) or to physical and social circumstances (a **situational attribution**).

This distinction between internal (dispositional) and external (situational) causes often blurs, because external situations produce internal changes (White, 1991). To say a schoolchild "is fearful" may be a short semantic leap from saying, "School frightens the child." Nevertheless, social psychologists have discovered that we often attribute the behavior of others *either* to their dispositions *or* to the situation. Thus when Constantine Sedikides and Craig Anderson (1992) asked American students why Americans have defected to the former Soviet Union, 8 in 10 attributed the behavior to a "confused," "ungrateful," or "traitorous" *personality*. But 9 in 10 attributed Russian defections to the oppressiveness of the Russian *situation*.

Inferring traits

Edward Jones and Keith Davis (1965) noted that we often infer that other people's intentions and dispositions correspond to their actions. If I observe Rick making a sarcastic comment to Linda, I infer that Rick is a hostile person. Jones and Davis's "theory of correspondent inferences" specified the conditions

To what should we attribute this student's sleepiness? To lack of sleep? To boredom? Whether we make internal or external attributions depends on whether we notice him consistently sleeping in this and other classes, and on whether other students react as he does to this particular class.

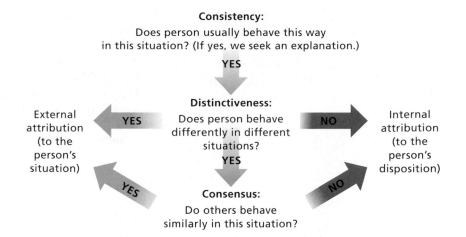

Consistency:
Does person usually behave this way
in this situation? (If yes, we seek an explanation.)

YES

Distinctiveness:
Does person behave
differently in different
situations?

YES   NO

External
attribution
(to the
person's
situation)

Internal
attribution
(to the
person's
disposition)

YES   NO

Consensus:
Do others behave
similarly in this situation?

figure 3–1

Harold Kelley's theory of attributions.

Three factors—consistency, distinctiveness, and consensus—influence whether we attribute someone's behavior to internal or external causes. Try creating your own examples such as: If Mary and many others criticize Steve (with consensus), and if Mary isn't critical of others (high distinctiveness), then we make an external attribution (it's something about Steve). If Mary alone (low consensus) criticizes Steve, and if she criticizes lots of other people, too (low distinctiveness), then we are drawn to an internal attribution (it's something about Mary).

under which such attributions are most likely. For example, normal or expected behavior tells us less about the person than does unusual behavior. If Samantha is sarcastic in a job interview, where a person would normally be pleasant, this tells us more about Samantha than if she is sarcastic with her friends.

The ease with which we infer traits is remarkable. In experiments at New York University, James Uleman (1989) gave students statements to remember, such as "The librarian carries the old woman's groceries across the street." The students would instantly, unintentionally, and unconsciously infer a trait. When later they were helped to recall the sentence, the most valuable clue word was not "books" (to cue librarian) or "bags" (to cue groceries) but "helpful"—the inferred trait that I suspect you, too, spontaneously attributed to the librarian.

Commonsense attributions

As these examples suggest, attributions often are rational. In testimony to the reasonable ways in which we explain behavior, attribution theorist Harold Kelley (1973) described how we use information about "consistency," "distinctiveness," and "consensus" (Figure 3–1). When explaining why Edgar is having trouble with his XYZ computer, most people use, appropriately, information concerning *consistency* (Is Edgar usually unable to get his computer to work?), *distinctiveness* (Does Edgar have trouble with other computers, or only the XYZ?), and *consensus* (Do other people have similar problems with the XYZ?). If we learn that Edgar alone consistently has trouble with this and other computers, we likely will attribute the troubles to Edgar, not to defects in the XYZ.

So our commonsense psychology often explains behavior logically. But Kelley also found that people often discount a contributing cause of behavior if other plausible causes are already known. If I can specify one or two sufficient reasons a student might have done poorly on an exam, we often ignore or discount alternate possibilities (McClure, 1998).

THE FUNDAMENTAL ATTRIBUTION ERROR

As later chapters will reveal, social psychology's most important lesson concerns the influence of our social environment. At any moment, our internal state, and therefore what we say and do, depends on the situation (as well as on what we bring to the situation). In experiments, a slight difference between two situations sometimes greatly affects how people respond. I have seen this when

figure 3–2

The fundamental attribution error.

When people read a debate speech supporting or attacking Fidel Castro, they attributed corresponding attitudes to the speech writer, even when the debate coach assigned the writer's position. **Source:** Data from Jones & Harris, 1967.

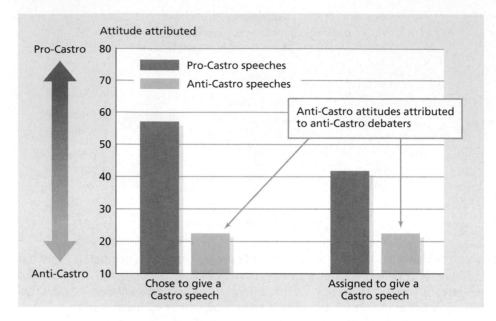

teaching classes at both 8:30 a.m. and 7:00 p.m. Silent stares would greet me at 8:30; at 7:00 I had to break up a party. In each situation some individuals were more talkative than others, but the difference between the two situations exceeded the individual differences.

Attribution researchers have found a common problem with our attributions. When explaining someone's behavior, we often underestimate the impact of the situation and overestimate the extent to which it reflects the individual's traits and attitudes. Thus, even knowing the effect of the time of day on classroom conversation, I found it terribly tempting to assume that the people in the 7:00 p.m. class were more extraverted than the "silent types" who come at 8:30 a.m.

fundamental attribution error

The tendency for observers to underestimate situational influences and overestimate dispositional influences upon others' behavior. (Also called correspondence bias, *because we so often see behavior as corresponding to a disposition.)*

This discounting of the situation, dubbed by Lee Ross (1977) the **fundamental attribution error,** appears in many experiments. In the first such study, Edward Jones and Victor Harris (1967) had Duke University students read debaters' speeches supporting or attacking Cuba's leader, Fidel Castro. When the position taken was said to have been chosen by the debater, the students logically enough assumed it reflected the person's own attitude. But what happened when the students were told that the debate coach had assigned the position? People who are merely feigning a position write more forceful statements than you'd expect (Allison & others, 1993; Miller & others, 1990). Thus, even knowing that the debater had been told to take a pro-Castro position did not prevent students from inferring that the debater in fact had some pro-Castro leanings (Figure 3–2). People seemed to think, "Yeah, I know he was assigned that position, but to some extent I think he really believes it."

Peter Ditto and his colleagues (1997) replicated the phenomenon when they asked men to meet a woman who was actually working for the experimenters. The woman wrote her supposed impressions of each man, who was then to guess how much she liked him. When she wrote only negative statements, the men discounted her criticisms when told she was under orders to be negative. But when the woman wrote only positive impressions, the typical man inferred

When viewing a movie actor playing a "good-guy" or "bad-guy" role, we find it difficult to escape the illusion that the scripted behavior reflects an inner disposition. Perhaps this is why Leonard Nimoy, who played Mr. Spock in the original Star Trek, *entitled one of his books* I Am Not Spock.

that she *really* liked him—and it didn't matter whether he believed she did so freely or was under orders to be positive. The fundamental attribution error looms large when it serves our self-interest.

The error is so irresistible that even when people *know* they are causing someone else's behavior, they still underestimate external influences. If individuals dictate an opinion that someone else must then express, they still tend to see the person as actually holding that opinion (Gilbert & Jones, 1986). If people are asked to be either self-enhancing or self-deprecating during an interview, they are very aware of why they are acting so. But they are *un*aware of their effect on another person. If Juan acts modestly, his naive partner Bob is likely to exhibit modesty as well. Juan will easily understand his own behavior, but he will think that poor Bob suffers low self-esteem (Baumeister & others, 1988). In short, we tend to presume that others *are* the way they act. Observing Cinderella cowering in her oppressive home, people (ignoring the situation) infer that she is meek; dancing with her at the ball, the prince sees a suave and glamorous person.

The discounting of social constraints was evident in a thought-provoking experiment by Lee Ross and his collaborators (Ross & others, 1977). The experiment re-created Ross's firsthand experience of moving from graduate student to professor. His doctoral oral exam had proved a humbling experience as his apparently brilliant professors quizzed him on topics they specialized in. Six months later, *Dr.* Ross was himself an examiner, now able to ask penetrating questions on *his* favorite topics. Ross's hapless student later confessed to feeling exactly as Ross had a half-year before—dissatisfied with his ignorance and impressed with the apparent brilliance of the examiners.

In the experiment, with Teresa Amabile and Julia Steinmetz, Ross set up a simulated quiz game. He randomly assigned some Stanford University students to play the role of questioner, some to play the role of contestant, and others to observe. The researchers invited the questioners to make up difficult questions that would demonstrate their wealth of knowledge. Any one of us

figure 3–3

Both contestants and observers of a simulated quiz game assumed that a person who had been randomly assigned the role of questioner was far more knowledgeable than the contestant. Actually the assigned roles of questioner and contestant simply made the questioner seem more knowledgeable. The failure to appreciate this illustrates the fundamental attribution error. **Source:** Data from Ross, Amabile, & Steinmetz, 1977.

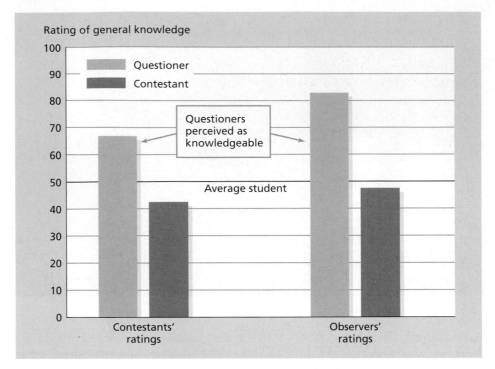

can imagine such questions using one's own domain of competence: "Where is Bainbridge Island?" "How did Mary, Queen of Scots, die?" "Which has the longer coastline, Europe or Africa?" If even these few questions have you feeling a little uninformed, then you will appreciate the results of this experiment.*

Everyone had to know that the questioner would have the advantage. Yet both contestants and observers (but not the questioners) came to the erroneous conclusion that the questioners *really were* more knowledgeable than the contestants (Figure 3–3). Follow-up research shows that these misimpressions are hardly a reflection of low social intelligence. If anything, intelligent and socially competent people are *more* likely to make the attribution error (Block & Funder, 1986).

The fundamental attribution error in everyday life

We commit the fundamental attribution error when we explain *other people's* behavior. Our own behavior we often explain in terms of the situation. So Ian might attribute his behavior to the situation ("I was angry because everything was going wrong"), while Rosa might think, "Ian was hostile because he is an angry person." When referring to ourselves, we typically use verbs that describe our actions and reactions ("I get annoyed when . . ."). Referring to someone else, we more often describe what that person is ("He is nasty") (Fiedler & others, 1991; McGuire & McGuire, 1986; White & Younger, 1988). Husbands who attribute their wives' criticisms to *her* being "mean and cold" are more

* Bainbridge Island is across Puget Sound from Seattle. Mary was ordered beheaded by her cousin, Queen Elizabeth I. Although the African continent is more than double the area of Europe, Europe's coastline is longer. (It is more convoluted, with lots of harbors and inlets, a geographical fact that contributed to its role in the history of maritime trade.)

likely to become violent (Schweinle & others, 2002). When she expresses distress about their relationship, he hears the worst and reacts angrily.

In real life, those with social power usually initiate and control conversations, which often leads underlings to overestimate their knowledge and intelligence. Medical doctors, for example, are often presumed to be experts on all sorts of questions unrelated to medicine. Similarly, students often overestimate the brilliance of their teachers. (As in the experiment, teachers are questioners on subjects of their special expertise.) When some of these students later become teachers, they are usually amazed to discover that teachers are not so brilliant after all.

People often attribute keen intelligence to those, such as teachers and quiz show hosts, who test others' knowledge.

To illustrate the fundamental attribution error, most of us need look no further than our own experiences. Determined to make some new friends, Bev plasters a smile on her face and anxiously plunges into a party. Everyone else seems quite relaxed and happy as they laugh and talk with one another. Bev wonders to herself, "Why is everyone always so at ease in groups like this while I'm feeling shy and tense?" Actually, everyone else is feeling nervous, too, and making the same attribution error in assuming that Bev and the others *are* as they *appear*—confidently convivial.

Attributions of responsibility are at the heart of many judicial decisions (Fincham & Jaspars, 1980). During the week following O. J. Simpson's 1994 arrest for the alleged murders of his ex-wife and her friend, a UCLA research team led by Sandra Graham (1997) questioned a sample of Los Angeles people who believed Simpson committed the crimes. Those who perceived his alleged act as an uncontrollable response to the situation advocated a relatively mild punishment. Those who believed he committed a self-initiated act advocated more severe punishment. The case exemplifies many judicial controversies: The prosecution argues, "You are to blame, for you could have done otherwise"; the defendant replies, "It wasn't my fault; I was a victim of the situation" or, "Under the circumstance I did no wrong."

WHY DO WE MAKE THE ATTRIBUTION ERROR?

So far we have seen a bias in the way we explain other people's behavior: We often ignore powerful situational determinants. Why do we tend to underestimate the situational determinants of others' behavior but not of our own?

Perspective and situational awareness

An actor-observer difference.   Attribution theorists point out that we observe others from a different perspective than we observe ourselves (Jones & Nisbett, 1971; Jones, 1976). When we act, the *environment* commands our attention. When we watch another person act, that *person* occupies the center of our attention and the environment becomes relatively invisible. Although professing inner anguish over his actions—"pity so great that I longed to vanish from the scene"—Auschwitz commandant Rudolph Höss (1959) was a "good SS officer"

The fundamental attribution error: observers under-estimating the situation. Driving into a gas station, we may think the person parked at the second pump (blocking access to the first) is inconsiderate. That person, having arrived when the first pump was in use, attributes her behavior to the situation.

who could "not show the slightest trace of emotion." Yet he inferred that his similarly stoic Jewish inmates were uncaring— a "racial characteristic," he presumed—as they led others to the gas chambers.

To use the perceptual analogy of figure and ground, the person is the figure that stands out from the surrounding environmental ground. So the person seems to cause whatever happens. If this theory is true, what might we expect if the perspectives were reversed? What if we could see ourselves as others see us and if we saw the world through their eyes? Shouldn't this eliminate or reverse the typical attribution error?

See if you can predict the result of a clever experiment conducted by Michael Storms (1973). Picture yourself as a participant in Storms's experiment. You are seated facing another student with whom you are to talk for a few minutes. Beside you is a TV camera that shares your view of the other student. Facing you from alongside the other student are an observer and another TV camera. Afterward, both you and the observer judge whether your behavior was caused more by your personal characteristics or by the situation.

Question: Which of you—participant or observer—will attribute the least importance to the situation? Storms found it was the observer (another demonstration of the fundamental attribution tendency). What if we reverse points of view by having you and the observer each watch the videotape recorded from the other's perspective? (You now view yourself, while the observer views what you saw.) This reverses the attributions: The observer now attributes your behavior mostly to the situation you faced, while you now attribute it to your person. *Remembering* an experience from an observer's perspective— by "seeing" oneself from the outside—has the same effect (Frank & Gilovich, 1989).

The camera perspective bias.   In some experiments, people have viewed a videotape of a suspect confessing during a police interview. If they viewed the confession through a camera focused on the suspect, they perceived the confession as genuine. If they viewed it through a camera focused on the detective, they perceived it as more coerced (Lassiter & others, 1986, in press). The camera perspective influenced people's guilt judgments even when the judge instructed them not to allow it to (Lassiter & others, 2002).

In courtrooms, most confession videotapes focus on the confessor. As we might expect, noted Daniel Lassiter and Kimberly Dudley (1991), such tapes yield a nearly 100 percent conviction rate when played by prosecutors. Aware of this research, reports Lassiter, New Zealand has made it a national policy that police interrogations be filmed with equal focus on the officer and suspect, such as by filming them with side profiles of both.

Perspectives change with time.   As the once-visible person recedes in their memory, observers often give more and more credit to the situation. Immediately after hearing someone argue an assigned position, people assume that's how the person really felt. A week later they are much more ready to credit the situational constraints (Burger, 1991). The day after a presidential election, Jerry Burger and Julie Pavelich (1994) asked voters why the election turned out as it did. Most attributed the outcome to the candidates' personal traits and positions (the winner from the incumbent party was likable). When they asked other voters the same question a year later, only a third attributed the verdict to the candidates. More people now credited circumstances, such as the country's good mood and the robust economy.

Perspective influences attributions. To television audiences, presidential candidate Howard Dean's screaming "Yeeeee-haaaa" to supporters after losing the Iowa primary election—taped with a microphone that cancelled out the noise of the crowd and with a camera focused solely on the candidate—made him seem like a maniac. Those present and aware of the excited crowd he was trying to speak over better understood how his behavior was partly in response to the situation.

Editorial reflections on the six U.S. presidential elections between 1964 and 1988 show the same growth in situational explanations with time (Burger & Pavelich, 1994). Just after the 1978 election, editorial pundits focused on the candidates' campaigns and personalities. Two years later the situation loomed larger: "The shadows of Watergate . . . cleared the way for [Carter's] climb to the Presidency," noted one editorial in the *New York Times*.

Future time perspective also matters. Predict someone's behavior a day from now—"Will Tamika come to my birthday party this weekend?"—and the current situation will loom large. Predict someone's behavior in the more distant future—"Will Tamika come to my birthday party next year?"—and her perceived traits seem to matter much more.

How did Howard Dean's speech sound to the crowd? Go to the *SocialSense* CD-ROM to view video clips from two perspectives.

Self-awareness.   Circumstances can also shift our perspective on ourselves. Seeing ourselves on television redirects our attention to ourselves. Seeing ourselves in a mirror, hearing our tape-recorded voices, having our pictures taken, or filling out biographical questionnaires similarly focus our attention inward, making us *self*-conscious instead of *situation*-conscious. Looking back on ill-fated relationships that once seemed like the unsinkable *Titanic*, people can see the icebergs (Berscheid, 1999).

Robert Wicklund, Shelley Duval, and their collaborators have explored the effects of **self-awareness** (Duval & Wicklund, 1972; Silvia & Duval, 2001). When our attention focuses upon ourselves, we often attribute more responsibility to ourselves. Allan Fenigstein and Charles Carver (1978) demonstrated this by having students imagine themselves in hypothetical situations. Some students were made self-aware by thinking they were hearing their own heartbeats while pondering the situation. Compared with those who thought they were just hearing extraneous noises, the self-aware students saw themselves as more responsible for the imagined outcome.

Some people are typically quite self-conscious. In experiments, people who report themselves as privately self-conscious (who agree with statements such

self-awareness
A self-conscious state in which attention focuses on oneself. It makes people more sensitive to their own attitudes and dispositions.

Focusing on the person. Would you infer that your professor for this course, or the professor shown here, is naturally outgoing?

as, "I'm generally attentive to my inner feelings") behave similarly to people whose attention has been self-focused with a mirror (Carver & Scheier, 1978). Thus, people whose attention focuses on themselves—either briefly during an experiment or because they are self-conscious persons—view themselves more as observers typically do; they attribute their behavior more to internal factors and less to the situation. (An exception would be after a failure, when self-consciousness might trigger defensiveness.)

All these experiments point to a reason for the attribution error: *We find causes where we look for them.* To see this in your own experience, consider: Would you say your social psychology instructor is a quiet or a talkative person?

My guess is you inferred that he or she is fairly outgoing. But consider the situation further: Your attention focuses on your instructor while he or she behaves in a public context that demands speaking. The instructor also observes his or her own behavior in many different situations—in the classroom, in meetings, at home. "Me talkative?" your instructor might say. "Well, it all depends on the situation. When I'm in class or with good friends, I'm rather outgoing. But at conventions and in unfamiliar situations I feel and act rather shy." Because we are acutely aware of how our behavior varies with the situation, we see ourselves as more variable than other people (Baxter & Goldberg, 1987; Kammer, 1982; Sande & others, 1988). "Nigel is uptight, Fiona is relaxed. With me it varies."

The less opportunity we have to observe people's behavior in contexts, the more we attribute to their personalities. Thomas Gilovich (1987) explored this by showing people a videotape of someone and then having them describe the person's actions to other people. The secondhand impressions were more extreme, partly because retellings focus attention on the person rather than on the situation (Baron & others, 1997). Similarly, people's impressions of someone they have heard about from a friend are typically more extreme than their friend's firsthand impressions (Prager & Cutler, 1990). Observing someone directly, or better yet, knowing them really well and seeing them in different situations, makes us more sensitive to their context (Idson & Mischel, 2001). Trait labels get applied most readily when describing strangers.

Cultural differences

Cultures also influence the attribution error (Ickes, 1980; Watson, 1982). A Western worldview predisposes people to assume that people, not situations, cause events. Internal explanations are more socially approved (Jellison & Green, 1981). "You can do it!" we are assured by the pop psychology of positive-thinking Western culture.

The assumption here is that, with the right disposition and attitude, anyone can surmount almost any problem: You get what you deserve and deserve what you get. Thus we often explain bad behavior by labeling a person "sick," "lazy," or "sadistic." As children grow up in Western culture, they learn to explain behavior in terms of the other's personal characteristics (Rholes & others, 1990; Ross, 1981). As a first-grader, one of my sons brought home an example. He unscrambled the words "gate the sleeve caught Tom on his" into "The gate caught Tom on his sleeve." His teacher, applying the Western cultural assumptions of the curriculum materials, marked this wrong. The "right" answer located the cause within Tom: "Tom caught his sleeve on the gate."

Culture influences attribution. Who is to blame for employees making unauthorized financial trades—the individual or the organization?

The fundamental attribution error occurs across all cultures studied (Krull & others, 1999). Yet people in Eastern Asian cultures are somewhat more sensitive to the importance of situations. Thus, when aware of the social context, they are less inclined to assume that others' behavior corresponds to their traits (Choi & others, 1999; Farwell & Weiner, 2000; Masuda & Kitayama, in press).

An example comes from the 1990s' "rogue trader" scandals that caused huge losses for several banks and investment firms when employees made unauthorized trades. Who was to blame? American newspapers attributed the mess-ups to the individuals ("Salomon's errant cowboy," was the *New York Times*' description of one trader). Japanese papers attributed the problems to lack of organizational controls (Menon & others, 1999).

Some languages promote external attributions. Instead of "I was late," Spanish idiom allows one to say, "The clock caused me to be late." In collectivist cultures, people less often perceive others in terms of personal dispositions (Lee & others, 1996; Zebrowitz-McArthur, 1988). They are less likely to spontaneously interpret a behavior as reflecting an inner trait (Newman, 1993). When told of someone's actions, Hindus in India are less likely than Americans to offer dispositional explanations ("She is kind") and more likely to offer situational explanations ("Her friends were with her") (Miller, 1984).

HOW FUNDAMENTAL IS THE FUNDAMENTAL ATTRIBUTION ERROR?

Like most provocative ideas, the presumption that we're all prone to a fundamental attribution error has its critics. Granted, say some, there is an attribution *bias*. But in any given instance, this may or may not produce an "error," just as parents who are biased to believe their child does not use drugs may or may not be correct (Harvey & others, 1981). We can be biased to believe what is true.

Moreover, some everyday circumstances, such as being in church or on a job interview, are like the experiments we have been considering: They involve clear constraints. Actors realize the constraints more than observers—hence the

The fundamental attribution error: People are biased to assume that people's behavior corresponds to their inner dispositions. Such assumptions are sometimes, but not always, correct. Some weekend bikers are weekday professionals.

attribution error. But in other settings—in one's room, at a park—people exhibit their individuality. In such settings, people may see their own behavior as *less* constrained than do observers (Monson & Snyder, 1977; Quattrone, 1982; Robins & others, 1996). So it's an overstatement to say that at all times and in all settings observers underestimate situational influences. For this reason, some social psychologists follow Edward Jones in referring to the fundamental attribution error—seeing behavior as corresponding to an inner disposition—as the *correspondence bias.*

Nevertheless, experiments reveal that the bias occurs even when we are aware of the situational forces—when we know that an assigned debate position is not a good basis for inferring someone's real attitudes (Croxton & others, 1984; Croxton & Miller, 1987; Reeder & others, 1987) or that the questioners' role in the quiz game gives the questioners an advantage (Johnson & others, 1984). It is sobering to think that you and I can know about a social process that distorts our thinking and still be susceptible to it. Perhaps that's because it takes more mental effort to assess social effects on people's behavior than it does merely to attribute it to their dispositions (Gilbert & others, 1988, 1992; Webster, 1993). It's as if the busy person thinks, "This isn't a very good basis for making a judgment, but it's easy and all I've got time to look at."

In many ways, this process is adaptive (psychologists generally assume that even our biases serve a purpose, because nature selected those who exhibit them). Attributing behavior to dispositions rather than to situations is efficient. Furthermore, our dispositions often lead us to choose our situations. If bankers dress conservatively, note Daniel Gilbert and Patrick Malone (1995), that may reflect not only their profession's demands but also the conservative person's choice of a profession. Assume that the banker really is more conservative than the artist and you are likely right.

The attribution error is, however, *fundamental* because it colors our explanations in basic and important ways. Researchers in Britain, India, Australia, and the United States have found that people's attributions predict their attitudes toward the poor and employed (Furnham, 1982; Pandey & others, 1982; Skitka, 1999; Wagstaff, 1983; Zucker & Weiner, 1993). Those who attribute poverty and unemployment to personal dispositions ("They're just lazy and undeserving") tend to adopt political positions unsympathetic to such people (Figure 3–4). This *dispositional attribution* attributes behavior to the person's disposition and traits. This differs from those who make external attributions ("If you or I were to live with the same overcrowding, poor education, and discrimination, would we be any better off?"). French investigators Jean-Leon Beauvois and Nicole Dubois (1988) report that "relatively privileged" middle-class people are more likely than less-advantaged people to assume that people's behaviors have internal explanations. (Those who have achieved success tend to assume that you get what you deserve.) This is also called *situational attribution*—when behavior is attributed to the environment.

Can we benefit from being aware of the attribution error? I once assisted with some interviews for a faculty position. One candidate was interviewed by six of

"Most poor people are not lazy. . . . They catch the early bus. . . . They raise other people's children. . . . They clean the streets. No, no, they're not lazy."
—The Reverend Jesse Jackson, address to the Democratic National Convention, July 1988

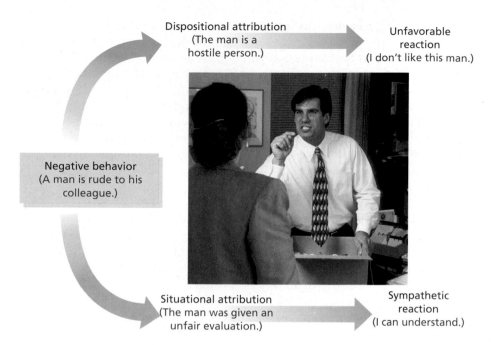

Dispositional attribution
(The man is a
hostile person.)

Unfavorable
reaction
(I don't like this man.)

Negative behavior
(A man is rude to his
colleague.)

Situational attribution
(The man was given an
unfair evaluation.)

Sympathetic
reaction
(I can understand.)

figure 3–4

Attributions and reactions.

How we explain someone's negative behavior determines how we feel about it.

us at once; each of us had the opportunity to ask two or three questions. I came away thinking, "What a stiff, awkward person he is." The second candidate I met privately over coffee, and we immediately discovered we had a close, mutual friend. As we talked, I became increasingly impressed by what a "warm, engaging, stimulating person she is." Only later did I remember the fundamental attribution error and reassess my analysis. I had attributed his stiffness and her warmth to their dispositions; in fact, I later realized, such behavior resulted partly from the difference in their interview situations.

WHY WE STUDY ATTRIBUTION ERRORS

This chapter, like the one before it, explains some foibles and fallacies in our social thinking. Reading about these may make it seem, as one of my students put it, that "social psychologists get their kicks out of playing tricks on people." Actually, the experiments are not designed to demonstrate "what fools these mortals be" (although some of the experiments are rather amusing); their purpose is to reveal how we think about ourselves and others.

If our capacity for illusion and self-deception is shocking, remember that our modes of thought are generally adaptive. Illusory thinking is often a by-product of our mind's strategies for simplifying complex information. It parallels our perceptual mechanisms, which generally give us useful images of the world but sometimes lead us astray.

A second reason for focusing on thinking biases such as the fundamental attribution error is humanitarian. One of social psychology's "great humanizing messages," note Thomas Gilovich and Richard Eibach (2001), is that people should not always be blamed for their problems. "Failure, disability, and misfortune are more often than people are willing to acknowledge the product of real environmental causes."

A third reason for focusing on biases is that we are mostly unaware of them. My hunch is that you will find more surprises, more challenges, and more benefit in an analysis of errors and biases than you would in a string of testimonies to the human capacity for logic and intellectual achievement. This is also why world literature so often portrays pride and other human failings. Liberal education exposes us to fallacies in our thinking in the hope that we will become more rational, more in touch with reality.

The hope is not in vain: Psychology students explain behavior less simplistically than similarly intelligent natural science students (Fletcher & others, 1986). So remembering this overriding aim—*developing our capacity for critical thinking*—let us continue looking at how the new research on social thinking can enhance our social reasoning.

Summing up

Attribution researchers study how we explain people's behavior. When will we attribute someone's behavior to a person's disposition and when to the situation? In most cases, we make reasonable attributions. When explaining other people's behavior, however, we often commit the *fundamental attribution error* (also called *correspondence bias*). We attribute their behavior so much to their inner traits and attitudes that we discount situational constraints, even when these are obvious. If a balloon moves because it is pushed by an invisible wind, we don't assume it is internally propelled. But people are not inanimate objects; thus, when a person acts, we more often discount the situational winds and assume internal propulsion.

We make this attribution error partly because when we watch someone act, that *person* is the focus of our attention and the situation is relatively invisible. When *we* act, our attention is usually on what we are reacting to—the situation is more visible. Thus we are more sensitive to the situational influences upon ourselves.

How do we perceive and recall our social worlds?

Striking research reveals the extent to which prejudgments can bias our perceptions and interpretations, and misinformation can bias our recall.

Chapter 1 noted a significant fact about the human mind—that our preconceptions guide how we perceive and interpret information. We construe the world through theory-tinted glasses. "Sure, preconceptions matter," people will agree, yet they fail to realize how great the effect is.

Let's consider some provocative experiments. The first group examines how *pre*judgments affect the way people perceive and interpret information. The second group plants a judgment in people's minds *after* they have been given information to see how after-the-fact ideas bias recall. The overarching point: *We respond not to reality as it is but to reality as we construe it.*

PERCEIVING AND INTERPRETING EVENTS

The effects of prejudgments and expectations are standard fare for psychology's introductory course. Recall the Dalmatian photo in Chapter 1. Or consider this phrase:

A
BIRD
IN THE
THE HAND

Did you notice anything wrong with it? There is more to perception than meets the eye. The same is true of social perception. Because social perceptions are very much in the eye of the beholder, even a simple stimulus may strike two people quite differently. Saying Canada's Paul Martin is "an okay prime minister" may sound like a put-down to one of his ardent admirers and like praise to someone who regards him with contempt. When social information is subject to multiple interpretations, preconceptions do matter (Hilton & von Hippel, 1990).

An experiment by Robert Vallone, Lee Ross, and Mark Lepper (1985) reveals just how powerful preconceptions can be. They showed pro-Israeli and pro-Arab students six network news segments describing the 1982 killing of civilian refugees at two camps in Lebanon. As Figure 3–5 illustrates, each group perceived the networks as hostile to its side. The phenomenon is commonplace:

- When Kimberly Matheson and Sanela Dursun (2001) showed Bosnian Serb and Muslim partisans independent media coverage of a Sarajevo market bombing, each side viewed the coverage as biased against their group.
- Presidential candidates and their supporters nearly always view the news media as unsympathetic to their cause.
- Sports fans perceive referees as partial to the other side.
- People in conflict (married couples, labor and management, opposing racial groups) see impartial mediators as biased against them.

People everywhere perceive media and mediators as biased against their position. "There is no subject about which people are less objective than

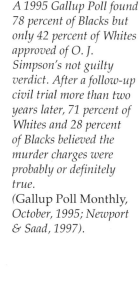

A 1995 Gallup Poll found 78 percent of Blacks but only 42 percent of Whites approved of O. J. Simpson's not guilty verdict. After a follow-up civil trial more than two years later, 71 percent of Whites and 28 percent of Blacks believed the murder charges were probably or definitely true.
(Gallup Poll Monthly, October, 1995; Newport & Saad, 1997).

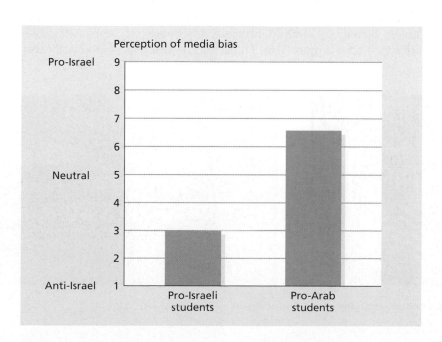

figure 3–5

Pro-Israeli and pro-Arab students who viewed network news descriptions of the "Beirut massacre" believed the coverage was biased against their point of view. **Source:**   Data from Vallone, Ross, & Lepper, 1985.

"Of course I care about how you imagined I thought
you perceived I wanted you to feel."

"Once you have a belief, it influences how you perceive all other relevant information. Once you see a country as hostile, you are likely to interpret ambiguous actions on their part as signifying their hostility."
—Political scientist Robert Jervis (1985)

objectivity," noted one media commentator (Poniewozik, 2003). Indeed, people's perceptions of bias can be used to assess their attitudes (Saucier & Miller, 2003). Tell me where you see bias, and you will clue me into your attitudes.

Our assumptions about the world can even make contradictory evidence seem supportive. For example, Ross and Lepper assisted Charles Lord (1979) in asking students to evaluate the results of two supposedly new research studies. Half the students favored capital punishment and half opposed it. One study confirmed and the other disconfirmed the students' beliefs about the deterrent effect of the death penalty. The results: Both proponents and opponents of capital punishment readily accepted evidence that confirmed their belief but were sharply critical of disconfirming evidence. Showing the two sides an *identical* body of mixed evidence had not lessened their disagreement but *increased* it. In follow-up studies, people exposed to mixed information have been provoked to think more about the issues and to refute the contrary evidence (Edwards & Smith, 1996; Kuhn & Lao, 1996; Munro & Ditto, 1997). Thus each side ends up perceiving the evidence as supporting its belief and now believes even more strongly.

Is this why, in politics, religion, and science, ambiguous information often fuels conflict? U.S. presidential debates have mostly reinforced predebate opinions. By nearly a 10-to-1 margin, those who already favored one candidate or the other perceived their candidate as having won (Kinder & Sears, 1985). Geoffrey Munro and his colleagues (1997) observed this belief-confirming phenomenon in the first 1996 presidential debate; thus people on both sides became even more supportive of their candidate after viewing the debate.

Other experiments have manipulated preconceptions, with astonishing effects upon how people interpret and recall what they observe. Myron Rothbart and Pamela Birrell (1977) had University of Oregon students assess the facial expression of a man (Figure 3–6). Those told he was a Gestapo leader responsi-

Supporters of a particular cause tend to see the media as favoring the other side.

ble for barbaric medical experiments on concentration camp inmates during World War II intuitively judged his expression as cruel. (Can you see that barely suppressed sneer?) Those told he was a leader in the anti-Nazi underground movement whose courage saved thousands of Jewish lives judged his facial expression as warm and kind. (On second thought, look at those caring eyes and that almost smiling mouth.)

figure 3–6

Judge for yourself: Is this person's expression cruel or kind? If told he was a Nazi, would your reading of his face differ?

Filmmakers can control people's perceptions of emotion by manipulating the setting in which they see a face. They call this the "Kulechov effect," after a Russian film director who would skillfully guide viewers' inferences by manipulating their assumptions. Kulechov demonstrated the phenomenon by creating three short films that presented the face of an actor with a neutral expression after viewers had first been shown a dead woman, a dish of soup, or a girl playing—making the actor seem sad, thoughtful, or happy. The moral: There is a reality out there, but our minds actively construe it. Other people may construe reality differently and may therefore behave differently.

"The error of our eye directs our mind: What error leads must err."
—Shakespeare, *Troilus and Cressida,* 1601–1602

Construal processes also color others' perceptions of us. When we say something good or bad about another, people will tend to associate that trait with us, report Lynda Mae, Donal Carlston, and John Skowronski (1999). If we go around talking about others being gossipy, people may then unconsciously associate "gossip" with us. Call someone a jerk and folks may later construe *you* as one. Describe someone as sensitive, loving, and compassionate, and you may seem more so. There is, it appears, intuitive wisdom in the old taunt, "I'm rubber, you're glue; what you say bounces off me and sticks to you."

"We hear and apprehend only what we already half know."
—Henry David Thoreau, 1817–1862

The bottom line: There is an objective reality out there, but we view it through the spectacles of our beliefs, attitudes, and values. This is one reason our beliefs are so important; they shape our interpretation of everything else.

BELIEF PERSEVERANCE

Imagine a baby-sitter who decides, during an evening with a crying infant, that bottle feeding produces colicky babies: "Come to think of it, cow's milk obviously suits calves better than babies." If the infant turns out to be suffering a high fever, will the sitter nevertheless persist in believing that bottle feeding causes colic (Ross & Anderson, 1982)? To find out, Lee Ross, Craig Anderson, and their colleagues planted a falsehood in people's minds and then tried to discredit it.

Their research reveals that it is surprisingly difficult to demolish a falsehood, once the person conjures up a rationale for it. Each experiment first *implanted a belief,* either by proclaiming it true or by showing people some anecdotal evidence. Then the people were asked to *explain why* it is true. Finally, the researchers totally *discredited* the initial information by telling the person the truth: The information was manufactured for the experiment, and half the people in the experiment had received opposite information. Nevertheless, the new belief survived about 75 percent intact, presumably because the people still retained their invented explanations for the belief. This phenomenon, named **belief perseverance,** shows that beliefs can grow their own legs and survive the discrediting of the evidence that gave them birth.

For instance, Anderson, Lepper, and Ross (1980) asked people, after giving them one of two concrete cases to inspect, to decide whether people who take risks make good or bad firefighters. One group considered a risk-prone person who was a successful firefighter and a cautious person who was an unsuccessful one. The other group considered cases suggesting the opposite conclusion. After forming their theory that risk-prone people make better or worse firefighters, the individuals wrote explanations for it—for example, that risk-prone people are brave or that cautious people are careful. Once each explanation was formed, it could exist independently of the information that initially created the belief. When that information was discredited, the people still held their self-generated explanations and therefore continued to believe that risk-prone people really do make better or worse firefighters.

These experiments also show that the more we examine our theories and explain how they *might* be true, the more closed we become to information that challenges our beliefs. Once we consider why an accused person might be guilty, why an offending stranger acts that way, or why a favored stock might rise in value, our explanations may survive challenging evidence to the contrary (Davies, 1997; Jelalian & Miller, 1984).

The evidence is compelling: Our beliefs and expectations powerfully affect how we mentally construct events. Usually we benefit from our preconceptions, just as scientists benefit from creating theories that guide them in noticing and interpreting events. But the benefits sometimes entail a cost: We become prisoners of our own thought patterns. Thus the supposed "canals" that were so often seen on Mars turned out to be the product of intelligent life—an intelligence on earth's side of the telescope.

Is there a remedy for belief perseverance? There is: *Explain the opposite.* Charles Lord, Mark Lepper, and Elizabeth Preston (1984) repeated the capital punishment study described earlier and added two variations. First, they asked some of their participants when evaluating the evidence to be "as *objective* and *unbiased* as possible." This instruction was to no avail; whether for or against capital punishment, those who received this plea made evaluations as biased as those who did not.

The researchers asked a third group of individuals to consider the opposite—to ask themselves "whether you would have made the same high or low evaluations had exactly the same study produced results on the *other* side of the issue." After imagining an opposite finding, these people were much less biased in their evaluations of the evidence for and against their views. In his experiments, Craig Anderson (1982; Anderson & Sechler, 1986) consistently found that explaining why an opposite theory might be true—why a cautious rather than a risk-taking person might be a better firefighter—reduces or eliminates belief perseverance. Indeed, explaining any alternative outcome, not just the opposite, drives people to ponder various possibilities (Hirt & Markman, 1995).

belief perseverance
Persistence of one's initial conceptions, as when the basis for one's belief is discredited but an explanation of why the belief might be true survives.

"Two-thirds of what we see is behind our eyes."
—Chinese proverb

"No one denies that new evidence can change people's beliefs. Children do eventually renounce their belief in Santa Claus. Our contention is simply that such changes generally occur slowly, and that more compelling evidence is often required to alter a belief than to create it."
—Lee Ross & Mark Lepper (1980)

CONSTRUCTING MEMORIES OF OURSELVES AND OUR WORLDS

Do you agree or disagree with this statement?

> Memory can be likened to a storage chest in the brain into which we deposit material and from which we can withdraw it later if needed. Occasionally, something is lost from the "chest," and then we say we have forgotten.

About 85 percent of college students have agreed (Lamal, 1979). As one magazine ad put it, "Science has proven the accumulated experience of a lifetime is preserved perfectly in your mind."

Actually, psychological research has proved the opposite. Many memories are not copies of experiences that remain on deposit in a memory bank. Rather, we construct memories at the time of withdrawal. Like a paleontologist inferring the appearance of a dinosaur from bone fragments, we reconstruct our distant past by using our current feelings and expectations to combine information fragments (Hirt, 1990; Ross & Buehler, 1994). Thus we can easily (though unconsciously) revise our memories to suit our current knowledge. When one of my sons complained, "The June issue of *Cricket* never came," and was then shown where it was, he delightedly responded, "Oh good, I knew I'd gotten it."

When an experimenter or a therapist manipulates people's presumptions about their past, a sizable fraction will construct false memories. Asked to imagine vividly a childhood time when they ran, tripped, fell, and stuck their hand through a window, or a time when they knocked over a punch bowl at a wedding, about one-fourth will later recall the fictitious event as something that actually happened (Garry & others, 1996; Hyman & others, 1995, 1996; Loftus & Pickrell, 1995). In its search for truth, the mind sometimes constructs a falsehood.

"Memory isn't like reading a book: it's more like writing a book from fragmentary notes."
—John F. Kihlstrom, 1994

Reconstructing our past attitudes

Five years ago, how did you feel about nuclear power? About President George W. Bush, or Prime Minister Paul Martin, or Tony Blair? About your parents? If your attitudes have changed, do you know the extent of the change?

Experimenters have explored such questions, and the results have been unnerving. People whose attitudes have changed often insist that they have always felt much as they now feel. Daryl Bem and Keith McConnell (1970) took a survey among Carnegie-Mellon University students. Buried in it was a question concerning student control over the university curriculum. A week later the students agreed to write an essay opposing student control. After doing so, their attitudes shifted toward greater opposition to student control. When asked to recall how they had answered the question before writing the essay, they "remembered" holding the opinion that they *now* held and denied that the experiment had affected them. After observing Clark University students similarly denying their former attitudes, researchers D. R. Wixon and James Laird (1976) commented, "The speed, magnitude, and certainty" with which the students revised their own histories "was striking." As George Vaillant (1977, p. 197) noted after following adults through time, "It is all too common for caterpillars to become butterflies and then to maintain that in their youth they had been little butterflies. Maturation makes liars of us all."

The construction of positive memories brightens our recollections. Terence Mitchell, Leigh Thompson, and their colleagues (1994, 1997) report that people often exhibit *rosy retrospection*—they recall mildly pleasant events more favorably than they experienced them. College students on a three-week bike trip,

"A man should never be ashamed to own that he has been in the wrong, which is but saying in other words, that he is wiser today than he was yesterday."
—Jonathan Swift, *Thoughts on Various Subjects*, 1711

older adults on a guided tour of Austria, and undergraduates on vacation all reported enjoying their experiences as they were having them. But they later *recalled* such experiences even more fondly, minimizing the unpleasant or boring aspects and remembering the high points. Thus, the pleasant times during which I have sojourned in Scotland I now (back in my office facing deadlines and interruptions) romanticize as pure bliss. The mist and midges are but dim memories. The beauty and fresh sea air are still with me. With any positive experience, some of the pleasure resides in the anticipation, some in the actual experience, and some in the rosy retrospection.

Cathy McFarland and Michael Ross (1985) found that we also revise our recollections of other people as our relationships with them change. They had university students rate their steady dating partners. Two months later, they rated them again. Students who were more in love than ever had a tendency to recall love at first sight. Those who had broken up were more likely to recall having recognized the partner as somewhat selfish and bad-tempered.

Diane Holmberg and John Holmes (1994) discovered the same phenomenon among 373 newlywed couples, most of whom reported being very happy. When resurveyed two years later, those whose marriages had soured recalled that things had always been bad. The results are "frightening," say Holmberg and Holmes: "Such biases can lead to a dangerous downward spiral. The worse your current view of your partner is, the worse your memories are, which only further confirms your negative attitudes."

It's not that we are totally unaware of how we used to feel, just that when memories are hazy, current feelings guide our recall. Parents of every generation bemoan the values of the next generation, partly because they misrecall their youthful values as being closer to their current values. Teens of every generation, depending on their current mood, describe their parents as wonderful or woeful.

Reconstructing our past behavior

Memory construction enables us to revise our own histories. Hartmuk Blank and his colleagues (2003) showed as much when inviting University of Leipzig students, after a surprising German election outcome, to recall their voting predictions from two months previous. The students demonstrated hindsight bias, by misrecalling their predictions as closer to the actual results.

Our memories reconstruct other sorts of past behaviors as well. Michael Ross, Cathy McFarland, and Garth Fletcher (1981) exposed some University of Waterloo students to a message convincing them of the desirability of toothbrushing. Later, in a supposedly different experiment, these students recalled brushing their teeth more often during the preceding two weeks than did students who had not heard the message. Likewise, projecting from surveys, people report smoking many fewer cigarettes than are actually sold (Hall, 1985). And they recall casting more votes than were actually recorded (Census Bureau, 1993).

Social psychologist Anthony Greenwald (1980) noted the similarity of such findings to happenings in George Orwell's novel *1984*—in which it was "necessary to remember that events happened in the desired manner." Indeed, argued Greenwald, we all have "totalitarian egos" that revise the past to suit our present views. Thus, we underreport bad behavior and overreport good behavior.

Sometimes our present view is that we've improved—in which case we may misrecall our past as more unlike the present than it actually was. This tendency resolves a puzzling pair of consistent findings: Those who participate in psychotherapy and self-improvement programs for weight control, anti-smoking, and exercise show only modest improvement on average. Yet they often claim considerable benefit (Myers, 2004). Michael Conway and Michael Ross (1985, 1986) explain why: Having expended so much time, effort, and money on self-improvement, people may think, "I may not be perfect now, but I was worse before; this did me a lot of good."

Reconstructing our experiences: Misinformation and priming

In experiments involving more than 20,000 people, Elizabeth Loftus has revealed our tendency to construct memories we recall with great confidence but sometimes little accuracy. In the typical experiment, people witness an event, receive misleading information about it (or not), and then take a memory test. The repeated finding is the **misinformation effect.** People incorporate the misinformation into their memories: They recall a yield sign as a stop sign, hammers as screwdrivers, *Vogue* magazine as *Mademoiselle,* Dr. Henderson as "Dr. David-son," breakfast cereal as eggs, and a clean-shaven man as a fellow with a mustache (Loftus & others, 1989). Suggested misinformation may even produce false memories of supposed child sexual abuse, argues Loftus (1993).

This process affects our recall of social as well as physical events. Jack Croxton and his colleagues (1984) had students spend 15 minutes talking with someone. Those who were later informed that this person liked them recalled the person's behavior as relaxed, comfortable, and happy. Those informed that the person disliked them recalled the person as nervous, uncomfortable, and not so happy.

To understand why, think of memories as stored in a web of associations. To retrieve a memory, we need to activate one of the strands that leads to it, a process called **priming** (Bower, 1986). Priming is what the philosopher-psychologist William James described as the "wakening of associations."

Events may awaken or prime our associations without our realizing it. Watching a scary movie while alone at home can prime our thinking—by activating frightening memories that cause us to interpret furnace noises as an intruder. For many psychology students, reading about psychological disorders primes how they interpret their own anxieties and gloomy moods. In experiments, ideas implanted in people's minds act like preconceptions: They automatically—unintentionally, effortlessly, and without awareness—prime how people interpret and recall events (Bargh & Chartrand, 1999). Having

How does misinformation effect influence memories? Go to the *SocialSense* CD-ROM to view a video clip.

misinformation effect
Incorporating "misinformation" into one's memory of the event, after witnessing an event and receiving misleading information about it.

priming
Activating particular associations in memory.

Pause to recall a scene from a favorite past experience, then read the rest of this note on the following page.

Our interpretation of the second sign is primed by our reading of the first. © 1999 Patrick Hardin.

Did you see yourself in the scene? If so, your memory must be a reconstruction, for in reality you did not see yourself.

recently seen words such as "adventurous" and "self-confident," people will later, in a different context, form positive impressions of an imagined mountain climber or Atlantic sailor. If their thinking instead is primed with such negative words as "reckless," their impressions are more negative (Higgins & others, 1977).

Summing up

Our preconceptions strongly influence how we interpret and remember events. In research, people's prejudgments have striking effects on how they perceive and interpret information. Other experiments have planted judgments or false ideas in people's minds *after* they have been given information. These experiments reveal that as *before-the-fact judgments* bias our perceptions and interpretations, so *after-the-fact judgments* bias our recall.

In Chapter 15 we will see that psychiatrists and clinical psychologists are not immune to these human tendencies. We all selectively notice, interpret, and recall events in ways that sustain our ideas. Our social judgments are a mix of observation and expectation, reason and passion.

How accurately do we make judgments?

As we have already noted, our cognitive mechanisms are efficient and adaptive, yet occasionally error-prone. Usually they serve us well. But sometimes clinicians misjudge patients, employers misjudge employees, people of one race misjudge another, and spouses misjudge their mates. The results are misdiagnoses, labor strife, prejudices, and divorces. So, how—and how well—do we make intuitive social judgments?

When historians describe social psychology's first century, they will surely record the last 30 years as the era of social cognition. By drawing on advances in cognitive psychology—in how people perceive, represent, and remember events—social psychologists have shed welcome light on how we form judgments. Let's look at what this research reveals of the marvels and mistakes of our social intuition.

INTUITIVE JUDGMENTS

What are our powers of intuition—of immediately knowing something without reasoning or analysis? Advocates of "intuitive management" believe we should tune into our hunches. When judging others, they say, we should plug into the nonlogical smarts of our "right brain." When hiring, firing, and investing, we should listen to our premonitions. In making judgments, we should follow the example of *Star Wars'* Luke Skywalker by switching off our computer guidance systems and trusting the force within.

Are the intuitionists correct that important information is immediately available apart from our conscious analysis? Or are the skeptics right in saying that intuition is "our knowing we are right, whether we are or not"?

Priming research suggests that the unconscious indeed controls much of our behavior. As John Bargh and Tanya Chartrand (1999) explain, "Most of a person's everyday life is determined not by their conscious intentions and deliberate choices but by mental processes that are put into motion by features of the environment and that operate outside of conscious awareness and guidance." For example, people quickly recognize that "beautiful" is a good word. But after viewing an imperceptible flashed puppy image (rather than a cockroach) they make that classification more instantly (Giner-Sorolla & others, 1999). Such priming is routine in daily life. When the light turns red, we react and hit the brake before consciously deciding to do so. Indeed, reflect Neil Macrae and Lucy Johnston (1998), "to be able to do just about anything at all (e.g., driving, dating, dancing), action initiation needs to be decoupled from the inefficient (i.e., slow, serial, resource consuming) workings of the conscious mind, otherwise inaction inevitably would prevail."

The powers of intuition

"The heart has its reasons which reason does not know," observed seventeenth-century philosopher-mathematician Blaise Pascal. Three centuries later, scientists have proved Pascal correct. We know more than we know we know. Studies of our unconscious information processing confirm our limited access to what's going on in our minds (Bargh, 1997; Greenwald & Banaji, 1995; Strack & Deutsch, 2004). Our thinking is partly **controlled** (reflective, deliberate, and conscious) and—more than most of us once supposed—partly **automatic** (impulsive, effortless, and without our awareness). Automatic thinking occurs not "on-screen" but off-screen, out of sight, where reason does not go. Consider these examples of automatic thinking, or what we often call intuition:

- *Schemas*—mental templates—automatically, intuitively, guide our perceptions and interpretations of our experience. Whether we hear someone speaking of religious *sects* or *sex* depends not only on the word spoken but on how we automatically interpret the sound.

- *Emotional reactions* are often nearly instantaneous, before there is time for deliberate thinking. One neural shortcut takes information from the eye or ear to the brain's sensory switchboard (the thalamus) and out to its emotional control center (the amygdala) before the thinking cortex has had any chance to intervene (LeDoux, 1994, 1996).

  Simple likes, dislikes, and fears typically involve little analysis. Although our intuitive reactions sometimes defy logic, they may still be adaptive. Our ancestors who intuitively feared a sound in the bushes were usually fearing nothing, but they were more likely to survive to pass their genes down to us than their more deliberative cousins.

- Given sufficient *expertise*, people may intuitively know the answer to a problem. The situation cues information stored in their memory. Without knowing quite how we do it, we recognize a friend's voice after the first spoken word of a phone conversation. Master chess players intuitively recognize meaningful patterns that novices miss and often make their next move with only a glance at the board.

- Some things—facts, names, and past experiences—we remember explicitly (consciously). But other things—skills and conditioned dispositions—we remember *implicitly*, without consciously knowing and declaring that we know. It's true of us all, but most strikingly evident in people with brain damage who cannot form new explicit memories. One

controlled processing
"Explicit" thinking that is deliberate, reflective, and conscious.

automatic processing
"Implicit" or intuitive thinking that is effortless, habitual, and without awareness.

such person never could learn to recognize her physician, who would need to reintroduce himself with a handshake each day. One day the physician affixed a tack to his hand, causing the patient to jump with pain. When the physician next returned, he was still unrecognized (explicitly). But the patient, retaining an implicit memory, would not shake his hand (LeDoux, 1996).

- Equally dramatic are the cases of *blindsight*. Having lost a portion of the visual cortex to surgery or stroke, people may be functionally blind in part of their field of vision. Shown a series of sticks in the blind field, they report seeing nothing. After correctly guessing whether the sticks are vertical or horizontal, the patients are astounded when told, "You got them all right." Again, these people know more than they know they know. There are, it seems, little minds—parallel processing units—operating unseen.

- Consider your own taken-for-granted capacity to recognize a face intuitively. As you look at a scene, your brain breaks the visual information into subdimensions such as color, depth, movement, and form and works on each aspect simultaneously before reassembling the components. Finally, somehow, your brain compares the perceived image with previously stored images. Voilà! Instantly and effortlessly, you recognize your grandmother. If intuition is immediately knowing something without reasoned analysis, then perceiving is intuition par excellence.

- *Subliminal* stimuli may nevertheless have intriguing effects. Shown certain geometric figures for less than 0.01 second each, people will deny having seen anything more than a flash of light. Yet they will later express a preference for the forms they saw. Sometimes we intuitively feel what we cannot explain. Likewise, invisible flashed words can prime our responses to later questions. If the word "bread" is flashed too briefly to recognize, we may then detect a flashed, related word such as "butter" more easily than an unrelated word such as "bottle."

So, many routine cognitive functions occur automatically, unintentionally, without awareness. Our minds function rather like big corporations. Our CEO—our controlled consciousness—attends to the most important or novel issues and assigns routine affairs to subordinates. This delegation of resources enables us to react to many situations quickly, efficiently, intuitively. Such is the "automaticity of everyday life."

The limits of intuition

Today's researchers affirm that unconscious information processing can produce flashes of intuition. The unconscious is less simple-minded and irrational than some researchers contend, argues John Bargh (1997). Automatic thinking can "make us smart" as well as create error, agree Gerd Gigerenzer and Peter Todd (1999). Thanks to a repository of experience, a tennis player automatically—and intelligently—knows just where to run to intercept the ball, with just the right racquet angle. As champion tennis player Venus Williams smacks the ball, conscious attention and unconscious perception and coordination integrate seamlessly. The result is her near-perfect intuitive physics.

Elizabeth Loftus and Mark Klinger (1992) speak for other cognitive scientists in having doubts about the brilliance of intuition. They report "a general consensus that the unconscious may not be as smart as previously believed." For example, although subliminal stimuli can trigger a weak, fleeting response—enough to evoke a feeling if not conscious awareness—there is no evidence that commercial subliminal tapes can "reprogram your unconscious mind" for success. (A significant body of evidence indicates that they can't [Greenwald, 1992].)

Social psychologists have explored our error-prone hindsight judgments (our intuitive sense, after the fact, that we knew-it-all-along). Other domains of psychology have explored our capacity for illusion—perceptual misinterpretations, fantasies, and constructed beliefs. Michael Gazzaniga (1992) reports that patients whose brain hemispheres have been surgically separated will instantly fabricate—and believe—explanations of their own puzzling behaviors. If the patient gets up and takes a few steps after the experimenter flashes the instruction "walk" to the patient's nonverbal right hemisphere, the verbal left hemisphere will instantly invent a plausible explanation ("I felt like getting a drink").

Illusory thinking also appears in the vast new literature on how we take in, store, and retrieve social information. As perception researchers study visual illusions for what they reveal about our normal perceptual mechanisms, social psychologists study illusory thinking for what it reveals about normal information processing. These researchers want to give us a map of everyday social thinking, with the hazards clearly marked.

As we examine some of these efficient thinking patterns, remember this: Demonstrations of how people create counterfeit beliefs do not prove that all beliefs are counterfeit. Still, to recognize counterfeiting, it helps to know how it's done. So let's explore how efficient information processing can go awry, beginning with our self-knowledge.

THE TENDENCY TO BE OVERCONFIDENT

So far we have seen that our cognitive systems process a vast amount of information efficiently and automatically. But our efficiency has a trade-off; as we interpret our experiences and construct memories, our automatic intuitions often err. Usually, we are unaware of our flaws. The "intellectual conceit" evident in judgments of past knowledge ("I knew it all along") extends to estimates of current knowledge and predictions of future behavior. Although we know we've muffed up in the past, we have more positive expectations for the future—how well we'll meet deadlines, manage relationships, follow an exercise routine (Ross & Newby-Clark, 1998). As we consider our past and our future we construe different selves.

To explore this **overconfidence phenomenon,** Daniel Kahneman and Amos Tversky (1979) gave people factual questions and asked them to fill in the blanks, as in the following: "I feel 98 percent certain that the air distance between New Delhi and Beijing is more than _____ miles but less than _____ miles." Most individuals were overconfident: About 30 percent of the time, the correct answers lay outside the range they felt 98 percent confident about.

To find out whether overconfidence extends to social judgments, David Dunning and his associates (1990) created a little game show. They asked Stanford University students to guess a stranger's answers to a series of questions, such as "Would you prepare for a difficult exam alone or with others?" and "Would you rate your lecture notes as neat or messy?" Knowing the type of question but not the actual questions, the participants first interviewed their target person about background, hobbies, academic interests, aspirations, astrological

"People are good enough to get through life, poor enough to make predictable and consequential mistakes."
—Baruch Fischhoff, 1981

overconfidence phenomenon
The tendency to be more confident than correct—to overestimate the accuracy of one's beliefs.

The air distance between New Delhi and Beijing is 2,500 miles.

DOONESBURY   by Garry Trudeau

DOONESBURY © G. B. Trudeau. Reprinted with permission of Universal Press Syndicate. All Rights Reserved.

sign—anything they thought might be helpful. Then, while the targets privately answered 20 of the two-choice questions, the interviewers predicted their target's answers and rated their own confidence in the predictions.

The interviewers guessed right 63 percent of the time, beating chance by 13 percent. But, on average, they *felt* 75 percent sure of their predictions. When guessing their own roommates' responses, they were 68 percent correct and 78 percent confident. Moreover, the most confident people were most likely to be overconfident. People also are markedly overconfident when judging whether someone is telling the truth or when estimating things such as the sexual history of their dating partner or the activity preferences of their roommates (DePaulo & others, 1997; Swann & Gill, 1997).

Ironically, incompetence feeds overconfidence. It takes competence to recognize what competence is, note Justin Kruger and David Dunning (1999). Students who score at the bottom on tests of grammar, humor, and logic are most prone to overestimating their gifts at such. Those who don't know what good logic or grammar is are often unaware that they lack it. If ignorance can beget confidence, then—yikes!—where, we may ask, are we unknowingly deficient?

In Chapter 2 we noted how poorly people overestimate their long-term emotional responses to good and bad happenings. Are people better at predicting their own behavior? To find out, Robert Vallone and his colleagues (1990) had college students predict in September whether they would drop a course, declare a major, elect to live off campus next year, and so forth. Although the students felt, on average, 84 percent sure of these self-predictions, they were wrong nearly twice as often as they expected to be. Even when feeling 100 percent sure of their predictions, they erred 15 percent of the time.

In estimating their chances for success on a task, such as a major exam, people's confidence runs highest when removed in time from the moment of truth. By exam day, the possibility of failure looms larger and confidence typically drops (Gilovich & others, 1993). Roger Buehler and his colleagues (1994, 2002, 2003) report that most students also confidently underestimate how long it will take them to complete papers and other major assignments. They are not alone:

- Planners routinely underestimate the time and expense of projects. In 1969, Montreal Mayor Jean Drapeau proudly announced that a $120 million stadium with a retractable roof would be built for the 1976 Olympics. The roof was completed in 1989 and cost $120 million by itself. In 1985, officials estimated that Boston's "Big Dig" highway project would cost $2.6 billion and take until 1998. By 2003, the cost had ballooned to $14.6 billion and the project was still unfinished.

- Investment experts market their services with the confident presumption that they can beat the stock market average, forgetting that for every stockbroker or buyer saying "Sell!" at a given price there is another saying "Buy!" A stock's price is the balance point between these mutually confident judgments. Thus, incredible as it may seem, economist Burton Malkiel (1999) reports that mutual fund portfolios selected by investment analysts have not outperformed randomly selected stocks.

- Editors' assessments of manuscripts also reveal surprising error. Writer Chuck Ross (1979), using a pseudonym, mailed a typewritten copy of Jerzy Kosinski's novel *Steps* to 28 major publishers and literary agencies. All rejected it, including Random House, which had published the book in 1968 and watched it win the National Book Award and sell more than 400,000 copies. The novel came closest to being accepted by Houghton Mifflin, publisher of three other Kosinski novels: "Several of us read your untitled novel here with admiration for writing and style. Jerzy Kosinski comes to mind as a point of comparison. . . . The drawback to the manuscript, as it stands, is that it doesn't add up to a satisfactory whole."

- Overconfident decision makers can wreak havoc. It was a confident Adolf Hitler who from 1939 to 1945 waged war against the rest of Europe. It was a confident Lyndon Johnson who in the 1960s invested U.S. weapons and soldiers in the effort to salvage democracy in South Vietnam. It was a confident Saddam Hussein who in 1990 marched his army into Kuwait and in 2003 promised to defeat invading armies. It was a confident George W. Bush who proclaimed that peaceful democracy would soon prevail in a liberated Iraq, with its alleged weapons of mass destruction newly destroyed.

> "The wise know too well their weakness to assume infallibility; and he who knows most, knows best how little he knows."
> —Thomas Jefferson, *Writings*

> Regarding the atomic bomb: "That is the biggest fool thing we have ever done. The bomb will never go off, and I speak as an expert in explosives."
> —Admiral William Leahy to President Truman, 1945

President Lyndon Johnson on a Vietnam visit, 1966. Overconfidence, such as he exhibited in committing troops to a failed war, underlies many blunders, both large and small.

What produces overconfidence? Why doesn't experience lead us to a more realistic self-appraisal? There are several reasons. For one thing, people tend to recall their mistaken judgments as times when they were almost right. Phillip Tetlock (1998, 1999) observed this after inviting various academic and government experts to project—from their viewpoint in the late 1980s—the future governance of the Soviet Union, South Africa, and Canada. Five years later communism collapsed, South Africa had become a multiracial democracy, and Canada continued undivided. Experts who had felt more than 80 percent confident were right in predicting these turns of events less than 40 percent of the time. Yet, reflecting on their judgments, those who erred believed they were still basically right. I was

"When you know a thing, to hold that you know it; and when you do not know a thing, to allow that you do not know it; this is knowledge."
—Confucius, *Analects*

"almost right," said many. "The hardliners almost succeeded in their coup attempt against Gorbachev." "The Quebeçois separatists almost won the secessionist referendum." "But for the coincidence of de Klerk and Mandela, there would have been a lot bloodier transition to black majority rule in South Africa." Among political experts—and stock market forecasters, mental health workers, and sports prognosticators—overconfidence is hard to dislodge.

Confirmation bias

People also tend not to seek information that might disprove what they believe. P. C. Wason (1960) demonstrated this, as you can, by giving people a sequence of three numbers—2, 4, 6—that conformed to a rule he had in mind (the rule was simply *any three ascending numbers*). To enable the people to discover the rule, Wason invited each person to generate sets of three numbers. Each time Wason told the person whether or not the set conformed to his rule. When they were sure they had discovered the rule, the people were to stop and announce it.

The result? Seldom right but never in doubt: 23 of the 29 people convinced themselves of a wrong rule. They typically formed some erroneous belief about the rule (for example, counting by twos) and then searched for *confirming* evidence (for example, by testing 8, 10, 12) rather than attempting to *disconfirm* their hunches. We are eager to verify our beliefs but less inclined to seek evidence that might disprove them, a phenomenon called the **confirmation bias.**

confirmation bias
A tendency to search for information that confirms one's preconceptions.

The confirmation bias helps explain why our self-images are so remarkably stable. In experiments at the University of Texas at Austin, William Swann and Stephen Read (1981; Swann & others, 1992a, b, 1994) discovered that students seek, elicit, and recall feedback that confirms their beliefs about themselves. People seek as friends and spouses those who bolster their own self views—even if they think poorly of themselves (Swann & others, 1991, 1992, 2000). Swann and Read liken this *self-verification* to how someone with a domineering self-image might behave at a party. Upon arriving, the person seeks those guests whom she knows acknowledge her dominance. In conversation she then presents her views in ways that elicit the respect she expects. After the party, she has trouble recalling conversations in which her influence was minimal and more easily *recalls* her persuasiveness in the conversations that she dominated. Thus her experience at the party confirms her self-image.

Remedies for overconfidence

What lessons can we draw from research on overconfidence? One lesson is to be wary of other people's dogmatic statements. Even when people seem sure they are right, they may be wrong. Confidence and competence need not coincide.

Two techniques have successfully reduced the overconfidence bias. One is prompt feedback (Lichtenstein & Fischhoff, 1980). In everyday life, weather forecasters and those who set the odds in horse racing both receive clear, daily feedback. Experts in both groups, therefore, do quite well at estimating their probable accuracy (Fischhoff, 1982).

When people think about why an idea *might* be true, it begins to seem true (Koehler, 1991). Thus, another way to reduce overconfidence is to get people to think of one good reason *why their judgments might be wrong;* that is, force them to consider disconfirming information (Koriat & others, 1980). Managers might foster more realistic judgments by insisting that all proposals and recommendations include reasons why they might not work.

Still, we should be careful not to undermine people's self-confidence to a point where they spend too much time in self-analysis or where self-doubts begin to cripple decisiveness. In times when their wisdom is needed, those lacking self-confidence may shrink from speaking up or making tough decisions. Overconfidence can cost us, but realistic self-confidence is adaptive.

HEURISTICS: MENTAL SHORTCUTS

With precious little time to process so much information, our cognitive system is fast and frugal. It specializes in mental shortcuts. With remarkable ease, we form impressions, make judgments, and invent explanations. We do so by using **heuristics**—simple, efficient thinking strategies. In many situations, our snap generalizations—"That's dangerous!"—are adaptive. The speed of these intuitive guides promotes our survival. The biological purpose of thinking is less to make us right than to keep us alive. In some situations, however, haste makes error.

heuristic
A thinking strategy that enables quick, efficient judgments.

Representativeness heuristic

A panel of psychologists interviewed a sample of 30 engineers and 70 lawyers and summarized their impressions in thumbnail descriptions. The following description has been drawn at random from the sample of 30 engineers and 70 lawyers:

> Twice divorced, Frank spends most of his free time hanging around the country club. His clubhouse bar conversations often center around his regrets at having tried to follow his esteemed father's footsteps. The long hours he had spent at academic drudgery would have been better invested in learning how to be less quarrelsome in his relations with other people.

> *Question:* What is the probability that Frank is a lawyer rather than an engineer?

Asked to guess Frank's occupation, more than 80 percent of University of Oregon students surmised he was one of the lawyers (Fischhoff & Bar-Hillel, 1984). Fair enough. But how do you suppose their estimates changed when the sample description was changed to say that 70 percent were engineers? Not in the slightest. The students took no account of the base rate of engineers and lawyers; in their minds Frank was more *representative* of lawyers, and that was all that seemed to matter.

To judge something by intuitively comparing it to our mental representation of a category is to use the **representativeness heuristic.** Like most heuristics, representativeness (typicalness) usually is a reasonable guide to reality. But not always. Consider Linda, who is 31, single, outspoken, and very bright. She majored in philosophy in college. As a student she was deeply concerned with discrimination and other social issues, and she participated in antinuclear demonstrations. Based on this description, would you say it is more likely that

representativeness heuristic
The tendency to presume, sometimes despite contrary odds, that someone or something belongs to a particular group if resembling (representing) a typical member.

a. Linda is a bank teller.
b. Linda is a bank teller and active in the feminist movement.

Most people think *b* is more likely, partly because Linda better *represents* their image of feminists (Mellers & others, 2001). Consider: Is there a better chance that Linda is *both* a bank teller *and* a feminist than that she's a bank teller (whether feminist or not)? As Amos Tversky and Daniel Kahneman (1983) reminded us, the conjunction of two events can't be more likely than either event alone.

table 3–1 **Fast and frugal heuristics**

Heuristic	Definition	Example	But May Lead to
Representativeness	Snap judgments of whether someone or something fits a category	Deciding that Carlos is a librarian rather than a trucker because he better represents one's image of librarians	Discounting other important information
Availability	Quick judgments of likelihood of events (how available in memory?)	Estimating teen violence after school shootings	Overweighting vivid instances and thus, for example, to fearing the wrong things

The availability heuristic

Consider the following: Question 1—Does the letter *k* appear in print more often as the first letter of a word or as the third letter? Question 2—Do more people live in Cambodia or in Tanzania? (See page 115.)

You probably answered in terms of how readily *k*'s, Cambodians, and Tanzanians come to mind. If examples are readily *available* in our memory—as letters beginning with *k* and as Cambodians tend to be—then we presume that such are commonplace. Usually it is, so we are often well served by this cognitive rule, called the **availability heuristic** (Table 3–1).

But sometimes the rule deludes us. If people hear a list of famous people of one sex (Mother Teresa, Madonna, Hilary Clinton) intermixed with an equal size list of unfamous people of the other sex (Donald Scarr, William Wood, Mel Jasper), the famous names will later be more cognitively available. Most people will therefore recall having heard more (in this instance) women's names (McKelvie, 1995, 1997; Tversky & Kahneman, 1973). Vivid, easy-to-imagine events, such as diseases with easy-to-picture symptoms, may likewise seem more likely than harder-to-picture events (MacLeod & Campbell, 1992; Sherman & others, 1985). Even fictional happenings in novels, television, and movies leave images that later penetrate our judgments (Gerrig & Prentice, 1991; Green & others, 2002). The more absorbed and "transported" the reader ("I could easily picture the events"), the more the story affects the reader's later beliefs (Diekman & others, 2000). Readers who are captivated by romance novels, for example, may gain readily available sexual scripts that influence their own sexual attitudes and behaviors.

Our use of the availability heuristic highlights a basic principle of social thinking: People are slow to deduce particular instances from a general truth, but they are remarkably quick to infer general truth from a vivid instance. No wonder that after hearing and reading stories of rapes, robberies, and beatings, 9 out of 10 Canadians overestimate—usually by a considerable margin—the percentage of crimes that involve violence (Doob & Roberts, 1988).

The availability heuristic explains why powerful anecdotes can nevertheless be more compelling than statistical information and why perceived risk is therefore often badly out of joint with real risks (Allison & others, 1992). Because news footage of airplane crashes is a readily available memory for most of us,

---

availability heuristic
A cognitive rule that judges the likelihood of things in terms of their availability in memory. If instances of something come readily to mind, we presume it to be commonplace.

"Most people reason dramatically, not quantitatively."
—Jurist Oliver Wendell Holmes, Jr., 1809–1894

TROUBLETOWN   BY LLOYD DANGLE

Answer to Question 1:
The letter k *appears in print two to three times more often as the third letter. Yet most people judge that* k *appears more often at the beginning of a word. Words beginning with* k *are more readily available to memory, surmise Amos Tversky and Daniel Kahneman (1974), and ease of recall—availability—is our heuristic for judging the frequency of events.*

Answer to Question 2:
Tanzania's 35 million people greatly outnumber Cambodia's 12 million. Most people, having more vivid images of Cambodians, guess wrong.

especially since 9/11, we often suppose we are more at risk traveling in commercial airplanes than in cars. Actually, U.S. travelers during the last half of the 1990s were more likely to die in a car crash than on a commercial flight covering the same distance (National Safety Council, 2001). For most air travelers, the most dangerous part of the journey is the drive to the airport.

Counterfactual thinking

Easily imagined (cognitively available) events also influence our experiences of guilt, regret, frustration, and relief. If our team loses (or wins) a big game by one point, we can easily imagine how the game might have gone the other way, and thus we feel greater regret (or relief). Imagining worse alternatives helps us feel better. Imagining better alternatives, and pondering what we might do differently next time, helps us prepare to do better in the future (Boninger & others, 1994; Roese, 1994, 1997).

In Olympic competition, bronze medalists (for whom an easily imagined alternative was finishing without a medal) exhibited more joy than silver medalists (who could more easily imagine having won the gold) (Medvec & others, 1995). Similarly, the higher a student's score within a grade category (such as B+), the *worse* they feel (Medvec & Savitsky, 1997). The B+ student who misses

"Testimonials may be more compelling than mountains of facts and figures (as mountains of facts and figures in social psychology so compellingly demonstrate)."
—Mark Snyder (1988)

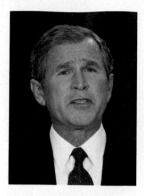

After the disputed 2000 U.S. presidential election, partisans for Al Gore, who got more votes but lost by a whisker in the deciding Florida recount, engaged in much counterfactual thinking. If only . . .

counterfactual thinking
Imagining alternative scenarios and outcomes that might have happened, but didn't.

People are, however, more often apologetic about actions than inactions (Zeelenberg & others, 1998).

illusory correlation
Perception of a relationship where none exists, or perception of a stronger relationship than actually exists.

an A− by a point feels worse than the B+ student who actually did worse and just made a B+ by a point.

Such **counterfactual thinking**—*mentally simulating what might have been*—occurs when we can easily picture an alternative outcome (Kahneman & Miller, 1986; Markman & McMullen, 2003). If we barely miss a plane or bus, we imagine making it *if only* we had left at our usual time, taken our usual route, not paused to talk. If we miss our connection by a half hour or after taking our usual route, it's harder to simulate a different outcome, so we feel less frustration. The team or the political candidate that barely loses will simulate over and over how they could have won (Sanna & others, 2003). If only . . .

Counterfactual thinking underlies our feelings of luck. When we have barely escaped a bad event—avoiding defeat with a last-minute goal or standing nearest a falling icicle—we easily imagine a negative counterfactual (losing, being hit) and therefore feel "good luck" (Teigen & others, 1999). "Bad luck," on the other hand, refers to bad events that did happen but easily might not have.

The more significant the event, the more intense the counterfactual thinking (Roese & Hur, 1997). Bereaved people who have lost a spouse or child in a vehicle accident, or a child to sudden infant death syndrome, commonly report replaying and undoing the event (Davis & others, 1995, 1996). One friend of mine survived a head-on collision with a drunk driver that killed his wife, daughter, and mother. He reported "For months I turned the events of that day over and over in my mind. I kept reliving the day, changing the order of events so that the accident wouldn't occur" (Sittser, 1994).

Across Asian and Western cultures most people, however, live with less regret over things done than over things they failed to do, such as, "I wish I had been more serious in college" or "I should have told my father I loved him before he died" (Gilovich & Medvec, 1994; Gilovich & others, 2003; Savitsky & others, 1997). (In one survey of adults, the most common regret was not taking their education more seriously [Kinnier & Metha, 1989].) Would we live with less regret if we dared more often to reach beyond our comfort zone—to venture out, risking failure, but at least having tried? The fruit is out on the limb.

ILLUSORY THINKING

Another influence on everyday thinking is our search for order in random events, a tendency that can lead us down all sorts of wrong paths.

Illusory correlation

It's easy to see a correlation where none exists. When we expect to find significant relationships, we easily associate random events, perceiving an **illusory correlation.** William Ward and Herbert Jenkins (1965) showed people the results of a hypothetical 50-day cloud-seeding experiment. They told their subjects which of the 50 days the clouds had been seeded and which days it rained. This information was nothing more than a random mix of results: Sometimes it rained after seeding; sometimes it didn't. People nevertheless became convinced—in conformity with their ideas about the effects of cloud seeding—that they really had observed a relationship between cloud seeding and rain.

Other experiments confirm that people easily misperceive random events as confirming their beliefs (Crocker, 1981; Jennings & others, 1982; Trolier & Hamilton, 1986). If we believe a correlation exists, we are more likely to notice and recall confirming instances. If we believe that premonitions correlate with events, we notice and remember the joint occurrence of the premonition and the event's later occurrence. We seldom notice or remember all the times unusual events do not coincide. If, after we think about a friend, the friend calls us, we notice and remember this coincidence. We don't notice all the times we think of a friend without any ensuing call or receive a call from a friend about whom we've not been thinking.

People see not only what they expect, but also correlations they *want* to see. In one experiment, Mariette Berndsen and her co-researchers (1996) showed University of Amsterdam students supposed student statements favoring or opposing a switch from Dutch to English lectures at Dutch universities and told them that the policy would be tried at a university where surveys found the most support. The students were then shown identical opinion distributions from Amsterdam and another university. For students with a vested interest, the result was an illusory correlation; students opposed to the language switch were especially likely to misperceive student statements from their own university as more opposed than those from the other university.

Illusion of control

Our tendency to perceive random events as related feeds an **illusion of control**—*the idea that chance events are subject to our influence.* This keeps gamblers going and makes the rest of us do all sorts of unlikely things.

Gambling.   Ellen Langer (1977) demonstrated the illusion of control with experiments on gambling. Compared with those given an assigned lottery number, people who chose their own number demanded four times as much money when asked if they would sell their ticket. When playing a game of chance against an awkward and nervous person, they bet significantly more than when playing against a dapper, confident opponent. Throwing the dice or spinning the wheel increases peoples' confidence (Wohl & Enzle, 2002). In these and other ways, more than 50 experiments have consistently found people acting as if they can predict or control chance events (Presson & Benassi, 1996; Thompson & others, 1998).

Observations of real-life gamblers confirm these experimental findings. Dice players may throw softly for low numbers and hard for high numbers (Henslin, 1967). The gambling industry thrives on gamblers' illusions. Gamblers attribute wins to their skill and foresight. Losses become "near misses" or "flukes," or for the sports gambler, a bad call by the referee or a freakish bounce of the ball (Gilovich & Douglas, 1986).

Stock traders also like the "feeling of empowerment" that comes from being able to choose and control their own stock trades, as if their being in control can enable them to outperform the "efficient market." One ad declared that online investing "is about control." Alas, the illusion of control breeds overconfidence, and frequent losses after trading costs are factored in (Barber & Odean, 2001).

Regression toward the average.   Tversky and Kahneman (1974) noted another way by which an illusion of control may arise: We fail to recognize the statistical phenomenon of **regression toward the average.** Because exam scores fluctuate

illusion of control
Perception of uncontrollable events as subject to one's control or as more controllable than they are.

regression toward the average
The statistical tendency for extreme scores or extreme behavior to return toward one's average.

Regression to the average. When we are at an extremely low point, anything we try will often seem effective. "Maybe kickboxing will improve my life." Events seldom continue at an abnormal low.

www.mhhe.com/myers8
Visit the Online Learning Center for an interactivity on the illusion of control.

partly by chance, most students who get extremely high scores on an exam will get lower scores on the next exam. Because their first score is at the ceiling, their second score is more likely to fall back ("regress") toward their own average than to push the ceiling even higher. (This is why a student who does consistently good work, even if never the best, will sometimes end a course at the top of the class.) Conversely, the lowest-scoring students on the first exam are likely to improve. If those who scored lowest go for tutoring after the first exam, the tutors are likely to feel effective when the student improves, even if the tutoring had no effect.

Indeed, when things reach a low point, we will try anything, and whatever we try—going to a psychotherapist, starting a new diet-exercise plan, reading a self-help book—is more likely to be followed by improvement than by further deterioration. Sometimes we recognize that events are not likely to continue at an unusually good or bad extreme. Experience has taught us that when everything is going great, something will go wrong, and that when life is dealing us terrible blows, we can usually look forward to things getting better. Often, though, we fail to recognize this regression effect. We puzzle at why baseball's rookie of the year often has a more ordinary second year—did he become overconfident? Self-conscious? We forget that exceptional performance tends to regress toward normality.

By simulating the consequences of using praise and punishment, Paul Schaffner (1985) showed how the illusion of control might infiltrate human relations. He invited Bowdoin College students to train an imaginary fourth-grade boy, "Harold," to come to school by 8:30 each morning. For each school day of a three-week period, a computer displayed Harold's arrival time, which was always between 8:20 and 8:40. The students would then select a response to Harold, ranging from strong praise to strong reprimand. As you might expect, they usually praised Harold when he arrived before 8:30 and reprimanded him when he arrived after 8:30. Because Schaffner had programmed the computer to display a random sequence of arrival times, Harold's arrival time tended to improve (to regress toward 8:30) after being reprimanded. For example, if Harold arrived at 8:39, he was almost sure to be reprimanded, and his randomly selected next-day arrival time was likely to be earlier than 8:39. Thus, *even though their reprimands were having no effect*, most students ended the experiment believing that their reprimands had been effective.

This experiment demonstrates Tversky and Kahneman's provocative conclusion: Nature operates in such a way that we often feel punished for rewarding others and rewarded for punishing them. In actuality, as every student of psychology knows, positive reinforcement for doing things right is usually more effective and has fewer negative side effects.

MOOD AND JUDGMENT

Social judgment involves efficient, though fallible, information processing. It also involves our feelings: Our moods infuse our judgments. We are not cool computing machines, we are emotional creatures. The extent to which feeling infuses cognition appears in new studies comparing happy and sad individuals (Myers, 1993, 2000). Unhappy people—especially those bereaved or depressed—tend to be more self-focused and brooding. Short of utter hopelessness, a depressed mood motivates intense thinking—a search for information that makes one's environment more understandable and controllable (Weary & Edwards, 1994).

Happy people, by contrast, are more trusting, more loving, more responsive. If people are made temporarily happy by receiving a small gift while mall-shopping, they will report, a few moments later on an unrelated survey, that their cars and TV sets are working beautifully—better, if you took their word for it, than those belonging to folks who didn't receive gifts.

Moods pervade our thinking. To West Germans enjoying their team's World Cup soccer victory (Schwarz & others, 1987) and to Australians emerging from a heartwarming movie (Forgas & Moylan, 1987), people seem good-hearted, life seems wonderful. After (but not before) a 1990 football game between rivals Alabama and Auburn, victorious Alabama fans deemed war less likely and potentially devastating than did the gloomier Auburn fans (Schweitzer & others, 1992). In a happy mood, the world seems friendlier, decisions are easier, good news more readily comes to mind (Johnson & Tversky, 1983; Isen & Means, 1983; Stone & Glass, 1986).

Let a mood turn gloomy, however, and thoughts switch onto a different track. Off come the rose-colored glasses; on come the dark glasses. Now the bad mood primes our recollections of negative events (Bower, 1987; Johnson & Magaro, 1987). Our relationships seem to sour. Our self-images take a dive. Our hopes for the future dim. Other people's behavior seems more sinister (Brown & Taylor, 1986; Mayer & Salovey, 1987).

University of New South Wales social psychologist Joseph Forgas (1999) had often been struck by how moody people's "memories and judgments change with the color of their mood." To understand this "mood infusion" he began to experiment. Imagine yourself in one such study. Using hypnosis, Forgas and his colleagues (1984) put you in a good or bad mood and then have you watch a videotape (made the day before) of yourself talking with someone. If made to feel happy, you feel pleased with what you see, and you are able to detect many instances of your poise, interest, and social skill. If you've been put in a bad mood, viewing the same tape seems to reveal a quite different you—one who is frequently stiff, nervous, and inarticulate (Figure 3–7). Given how your mood colors your judgments, you feel relieved at how things brighten when the experimenter switches you to a happy mood before leaving the experiment. Curiously, note Michael Ross and Garth Fletcher (1985), we don't attribute our changing perceptions to our mood shifts. Rather, the world really seems different.

Our moods color how we see our worlds partly by bringing to mind past experiences associated with the mood. In a bad mood we have more depressing thoughts. Mood-related thoughts may distract us from complex thinking about

A temporary good or bad mood strongly influenced people's ratings of their videotaped behavior. Those in a bad mood detected far fewer positive behaviors. **Source:** Forgas & others, 1984.

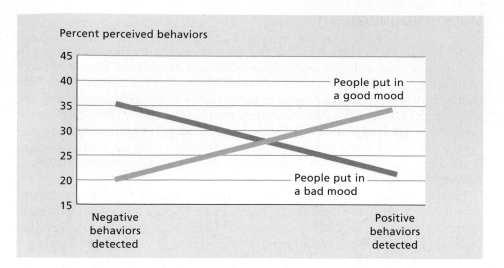

Percent perceived behaviors

People put in a good mood

People put in a bad mood

Negative behaviors detected

Positive behaviors detected

something else. Thus, when emotionally aroused—when angry or even in a very good mood—we become more likely to make snap judgments and evaluate others based on stereotypes (Bodenhausen & others, 1994; Paulhus & Lim, 1994). (Besides, why risk a postgame great mood by thinking deeply about some issue, such as the likelihood of a war?)

Our moods affect simple, "automatic" thinking less than complex, "effortful" thinking (Hartlage & others, 1993). Thus, notes Forgas (1994, 1995), moods are most likely to invade thinking when we evaluate unusual rather than typical people and explain complex rather than simple human conflicts. The more we think, the more our moods may infuse our thinking.

Summing up

Research psychologists have for a long time explored the mind's impressive capacity for processing information. We have an enormous capacity for automatic, efficient, intuitive thinking. Our cognitive efficiency, though generally adaptive, comes at the price of occasional error. Since we are generally unaware of these errors entering our thinking, it is useful to identify ways in which we form and sustain false beliefs—"reasons for unreason."

First, we often overestimate our judgments. This *overconfidence phenomenon* stems partly from the much greater ease with which we can imagine why we might be right than why we might be wrong. Moreover, people are much more likely to search for information that can confirm their beliefs than information that can disconfirm them.

Second, when given compelling anecdotes or even useless information, we often ignore useful base-rate information. This is partly due to the later ease of recall (*availability*) of vivid information.

Third, we are often swayed by illusions of correlation and personal control. It is tempting to perceive correlations where none exist (*illusory correlation*) and to think we can predict or control chance events (the *illusion of control*).

Finally, moods infuse judgments. Good and bad moods trigger memories of experiences associated with those moods. Moods color our interpretations of current experiences. And by distracting us, moods can also influence how deeply or superficially we think when making judgments.

Do our beliefs tend to be self-fulfilling?

Having considered how we explain and judge others—efficiently, adaptively, but sometimes erroneously—we conclude by pondering the effects of our social judgments. Do our social beliefs matter? Do they change reality?

Our social beliefs and judgments do matter because they have effects. They influence how we feel and act, and by so doing may generate their own reality. When our ideas lead us to act in ways that produce their apparent confirmation, they have become what sociologist Robert Merton (1948) termed **self-fulfilling prophecies**—false beliefs that lead to their own fulfillment. If, led to believe that their bank is about to crash, its customers race to withdraw their money, their false perceptions may create reality, noted Merton. If people are led to believe that stocks are about to soar, they will indeed (see "Focus on: The Self-Fulfilling Psychology of the Stock Market").

In his well-known studies of "experimenter bias," Robert Rosenthal (1985) found that research participants sometimes live up to what is expected of them. In one study, experimenters asked individuals to judge the success of people in various photographs. The experimenters read the same instructions to all their participants and showed them the same photos. Nevertheless, experimenters led to expect high ratings obtained higher ratings than did those who expected their participants to see the photographed people as failures. Even more startling—and controversial—are reports that teachers' beliefs about their students similarly serve as self-fulfilling prophecies. If a teacher believes a student is good at math, will the student do well in the class? Let's examine this.

self-fulfilling prophecy
A belief that leads to its own fulfillment.

www.mhhe.com/myers8
Visit the Online Learning Center for a scenario on self-fulfilling beliefs.

TEACHER EXPECTATIONS AND STUDENT PERFORMANCE

Teachers do have higher expectations for some students than for others. Perhaps you have detected this after having a brother or sister precede you in school, or after receiving a label such as "gifted" or "learning disabled," or after being tracked with "high-ability" or "average-ability" students. Perhaps conversation in the teachers' lounge sent your reputation ahead of you. Or perhaps your new teacher scrutinized your school file or discovered your family's social status. Do such teacher expectations affect student performance? It's clear that teachers' evaluations correlate with student achievement: Teachers think well of students who do well. That's mostly because teachers accurately perceive their students' abilities and achievements (Jussim & others, 1996; Smith & others, 1998, 1999; Trouilloud & others, 2002).

But are teachers' evaluations ever a *cause* as well as a consequence of student performance? One correlational study of 4,300 British schoolchildren by William Crano and Phyllis Mellon (1978) suggested yes. Not only is high performance followed by higher teacher evaluations, but the reverse is true as well.

Could we test this "teacher-expectations effect" experimentally? Pretend we gave a teacher the impression that Dana, Sally, Todd, and Manuel—four

focus on the self-fulfilling psychology of the stock market

On the evening of January 6, 1981, Joseph Granville, a popular Florida investment adviser, wired his clients: "Stock prices will nose-dive; sell tomorrow." Word of Granville's advice soon spread, and January 7 became the heaviest day of trading in the previous history of the New York Stock Exchange. All told, stock values lost $40 billion.

Nearly a half-century ago, John Maynard Keynes likened such stock market psychology to the popular beauty contests then conducted by London newspapers. To win, one had to pick the six faces out of a hundred that were, in turn, chosen most frequently by the other newspaper contestants. Thus, as Keynes wrote, "Each competitor has to pick not those faces which he himself finds prettiest, but those which he thinks likeliest to catch the fancy of the other competitors."

Investors likewise try to pick not the stocks that touch their fancy but the stocks that other investors will favor. The name of the game is predicting others' behavior. As one Wall Street fund manager explained, "You may or may not agree with Granville's view—but that's usually beside the point." If you think his advice will cause others to sell, then you want to sell quickly, before prices drop more. If you expect others to buy, you buy now to beat the rush.

The self-fulfilling psychology of the stock market worked to an extreme on Monday, October 19, 1987, when the Dow Jones Industrial average lost 20 percent. Part of what happens during such crashes is that the media and rumor mill focus on whatever bad news is available to explain them. Once reported, the explanatory news stories further diminish people's expectations, causing declining prices to fall still lower. The process also works in reverse by amplifying good news when stock prices are rising.

In April of 2000, the volatile technology market again demonstrated a self-fulfilling psychology, now called "momentum investing." After two years of eagerly buying stocks (because prices were rising), people started frantically selling them (because prices were falling). Such wild market swings—"irrational exuberance" followed by a crash—are mainly self-generated, noted economist Robert Shiller (2000).

randomly selected students—are unusually capable. Will the teacher give special treatment to these four and elicit superior performance from them? In a now famous experiment, Rosenthal and Lenore Jacobson (1968) reported precisely that. Randomly selected children in a San Francisco elementary school who were said (on the basis of a fictitious test) to be on the verge of a dramatic intellectual spurt did then spurt ahead in IQ score.

This dramatic result seemed to suggest that the school problems of "disadvantaged" children might reflect their teachers' low expectations. The findings were soon publicized in the national media as well as in many college textbooks in psychology and education. Further analysis revealed the teacher-expectations effect to be not as powerful and reliable as this initial study had led many people to believe (Spitz, 1999). By Rosenthal's own count, in only about 4 in 10 of the nearly 500 published experiments did expectations significantly affect performance (Rosenthal, 1991, 2002). Low expectations do not

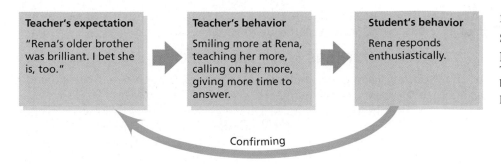

figure 3–8

Self-fulfilling prophecies.

Teacher expectations can become self-fulfilling prophecies.

doom a capable child, nor do high expectations magically transform a slow learner into a valedictorian. Human nature is not so pliable.

High expectations do seem to boost low achievers, for whom a teacher's positive attitude may be a hope-giving breath of fresh air (Madon & others, 1997). How are such expectations transmitted? Rosenthal and other investigators report that teachers look, smile, and nod more at "high-potential students." Teachers also may teach more to their "gifted" students, set higher goals for them, call on them more, and give them more time to answer (Cooper, 1983; Harris & Rosenthal, 1985, 1986; Jussim, 1986).

In one study, Elisha Babad, Frank Bernieri, and Rosenthal (1991) videotaped teachers talking to, or about, unseen students for whom they held high or low expectations. A random 10-second clip of either the teacher's voice or face was enough to tell viewers—both children and adults—whether this was a good or poor student and how much the teacher liked the student. (You read that right: 10 seconds.) Although teachers may think they can conceal their feelings, students are acutely sensitive to teachers' facial expressions and body movements (Figure 3–8).

Reading the experiments on teacher expectations makes me wonder about the effect of *students'* expectations upon their teachers. You no doubt begin many of your courses having heard "Professor Smith is interesting" and "Professor Jones is a bore." Robert Feldman and Thomas Prohaska (1979; Feldman & Theiss, 1982) found that such expectations can affect both student and teacher. Students in a learning experiment who expected to be taught by an excellent teacher perceived their teacher (who was unaware of their expectations) as more competent and interesting than did students with low expectations. Furthermore, the students actually learned more. In a follow-up experiment, Feldman and Prohaska videotaped teachers and had observers rate their performances. Teachers were judged most capable when assigned a student who nonverbally conveyed positive expectations.

To see whether such effects might also occur in actual classrooms, a research team led by David Jamieson (1987) experimented with four Ontario high school classes taught by a newly transferred teacher. During individual interviews, they told students in two of the classes that both other students and the research team rated the teacher very highly. Compared with the control classes, the students given positive expectations paid better attention during class. At the end of the teaching unit, they also got better grades and rated the teacher as clearer

To judge a teacher or professor's overall warmth and enthusiasm also takes but a thin slice of behavior—mere seconds (Ambady & Rosenthal, 1992, 1993).

in her teaching. The attitudes that a class has toward its teacher are as important, it seems, as the teacher's attitude toward the students.

GETTING FROM OTHERS WHAT WE EXPECT

So the expectations of experimenters and teachers, though usually reasonably accurate assessments, occasionally act as self-fulfilling prophecies. How widespread are self-fulfilling prophecies? Do we get from others what we expect of them? Studies show that self-fulfilling prophecies also operate in work settings (with managers who have high or low expectations), in courtrooms (as judges instruct juries), and in simulated police contexts (as interrogators with guilty or innocent expectations interrogate and pressure suspects) (Kassin & others, 2003; Rosenthal, 2003).

Do self-fulfilling prophecies color our personal relationships? There are times when negative expectations of someone lead us to be extra nice to that person, which induces them to be nice in return—thus *dis*confirming our expectations. But a more common finding in studies of social interaction is that, yes, we do to some extent get what we expect (Olson & others, 1996).

In laboratory games, hostility nearly always begets hostility: People who perceive their opponents as noncooperative will readily induce them to be noncooperative (Kelley & Stahelski, 1970). Each party's perception of the other as aggressive, resentful, and vindictive induces the other to display these behaviors in self-defense, thus creating a vicious self-perpetuating circle. Whether I expect my wife to be in a bad mood or in a warm, loving mood may affect how I relate to her, thereby inducing her to confirm my belief.

So do intimate relationships prosper when partners idealize one another? Are positive illusions of the other's virtues self-fulfilling? Or are they more often self-defeating, by creating expectations that can't be met and that ultimately spell doom? Among University of Waterloo dating couples followed by Sandra Murray and her associates (1996, 2000), positive ideals of one's partner were good omens. Idealization helped buffer conflict, bolster satisfaction, and turn self-perceived frogs into princes or princesses. When someone loves and admires us, it helps us become more the person he or she imagines us to be.

Among married couples, too, those who worry that their partner doesn't love and accept them interpret slight hurts as rejections, which motivates them to devalue the partner and distance themselves. Those who presume their partner's love and acceptance respond less defensively, and even may be closer to their partner (Murray & others, 2003). Love helps create its presumed reality.

behavioral confirmation
A type of self-fulfilling prophecy whereby people's social expectations lead them to behave in ways that cause others to confirm their expectations.

Several experiments conducted by Mark Snyder (1984) at the University of Minnesota show how, once formed, erroneous beliefs about the social world can induce others to confirm those beliefs, a phenomenon called **behavioral confirmation.** In a now-classic study, Snyder, Elizabeth Tanke, and Ellen Berscheid (1977) had men students talk on the telephone with women they thought (from having been shown a picture) were either attractive or unattractive. Analysis of just the women's comments during the conversations revealed that the supposedly attractive women spoke more warmly than the supposedly unattractive women. The men's erroneous beliefs had become a self-fulfilling prophecy by leading them to act in a way that influenced the women to fulfill the men's stereotype that beautiful people are desirable people.

Behavioral confirmation also occurs as people interact with partners holding mistaken beliefs. People who are believed lonely behave less sociably

(Rotenberg & others, 2002). Men who are believed sexist behave less favorably toward women (Pinel, 2002). Job interviewees who are believed to be warm behave more warmly.

Imagine yourself as one of the 60 young men or 60 young women in a recent experiment by Robert Ridge and Jeffrey Reber (2002). Each man is to interview one of the women to assess her suitability for a teaching assistant position. Before doing so, he is told either that she feels attracted to him (based on his answers to a biographical questionnaire) or not attracted. (Imagine being told that someone you were about to meet reported considerable interest in getting to know you and in dating you, or none whatsoever.) The result was behavioral confirmation: Applicants believed to feel an attraction exhibited more flirtatiousness (and without being aware of doing so). This process may be one of the roots of sexual harassment, Ridge and Reber believe. If a woman's behavior seems to confirm a man's beliefs, he may then escalate his overtures until they become sufficiently overt for the woman to recognize and interpret them as inappropriate or harassing.

Expectations influence children's behavior, too. After observing the amount of litter in three classrooms, Richard Miller and his colleagues (1975) had the teacher and others repeatedly tell one class that they should be neat and tidy. This persuasion increased the amount of litter placed in wastebaskets from 15 to 45 percent, but only temporarily. Another class, which also had been placing only 15 percent of its litter in wastebaskets, was repeatedly congratulated for being so neat and tidy. After eight days of hearing this, and still two weeks later, these children were fulfilling the expectation by putting more than 80 percent of their litter in wastebaskets. Tell children they are hardworking and kind (rather than lazy and mean), and they may live up to their labels.

> "The more he treated her as though she were really very nice, the more Lotty expanded and became really very nice, and the more he, affected in his turn, became really very nice himself; so that they went round and round, not in a vicious but in a highly virtuous circle."
> —Elizabeth von Arnim, *The Enchanted April,* 1922

These experiments help us understand how social beliefs, such as stereotypes about people with disabilities or about people of a particular race or sex, may be self-confirming. We help construct our own social realities. How others treat us reflects how we and others have treated them.

As with every social phenomenon, the tendency to confirm others' expectations has its limits. Expectations often predict behavior simply because they are accurate (Jussim, 1993). Also, people who are forewarned about another's

Behavioral confirmation. When English soccer fans came to France for the 1998 World Cup they were expected to live up to their reputation as aggressive "hooligans." Local French youth and police, expecting hooligan behavior, reportedly displayed hostility toward the English, who retaliated, thus confirming the expectation (Klein & Snyder, 2003).

expectation may work to overcome it (Hilton & Darley, 1985; Swann, 1987). If Chuck knows Jane thinks he's an airhead, he may strive to disprove her impression. If Jane knows that Chuck expects her to be aloof, she may actively refute his expectation.

William Swann and Robin Ely (1984) report another condition under which we are unlikely to confirm others' expectations: when their expectations clash with our clear self-concepts. For example, Swann and Ely found that when a strongly outgoing person was interviewed by someone who expected her to be introverted, the interviewer's perceptions changed, not the interviewee's behavior. In contrast, interviewees who were unsure of themselves more often lived up to the interviewer's expectations.

Our beliefs about ourselves can also be self-fulfilling. In several experiments, Steven Sherman (1980) found that people often fulfill predictions they make of their own behavior. When Bloomington, Indiana, residents were called and asked to volunteer three hours to an American Cancer Society drive, only 4 percent agreed to do so. When a comparable group of other residents were called and asked to *predict* how they would react if they were to receive such a request, almost half predicted they would agree to help—and most of these did indeed agree to do so when they were contacted by the Cancer Society. When we formulate plans for how we would want to act in a given situation, we become more likely to do it.

Summing up

Our beliefs sometimes take on lives of their own. Usually, our beliefs about others have a basis in reality. But studies of experimenter bias and teacher expectations show that an erroneous belief that certain people are unusually capable (or incapable) can lead teachers and researchers to give those people special treatment. This may elicit superior (or inferior) performance and, therefore, seem to confirm an assumption that is actually false. Similarly, in everyday life we often get *behavioral confirmation* of what we expect.

Conclusions

Social cognition studies reveal that our information-processing powers are impressive for their efficiency and adaptiveness ("in apprehension how like a god!" exclaimed Shakespeare's Hamlet), yet vulnerable to predictable errors and misjudgments ("headpiece filled with straw," said T. S. Eliot). What practical lessons, and what insights into human nature, can we take home from this research?

We have reviewed some reasons why people sometimes come to believe what may be untrue. We cannot easily dismiss these experiments: Most of their participants were intelligent people, often students at leading universities. Moreover, these predictable distortions and biases occurred even when payment for right answers motivated people to think optimally. As one researcher concluded, the illusions "have a persistent quality not unlike that of perceptual illusions" (Slovic, 1972).

Research in cognitive social psychology thus mirrors the mixed review given humanity in literature, philosophy, and religion. Many research psychologists have spent lifetimes exploring the awesome capacities of the human mind. We are smart enough to have cracked our own genetic code, to have invented talking computers, to have sent people to the moon. Three cheers for human reason.

Well, two cheers—because the mind's premium on efficient judgment makes our intuition more vulnerable to misjudgment than we suspect. With remarkable ease, we form and sustain false beliefs. Led by our preconceptions, overconfident, persuaded by vivid anecdotes, perceiving correlations and control even where none may exist, we construct our social beliefs and then influence others to confirm them. "The naked intellect," observed novelist Madeleine L'Engle, "is an extraordinarily inaccurate instrument."

But have these experiments just been intellectual tricks played on hapless participants, thus making them look worse than they are? Richard Nisbett and Lee Ross (1980) contend that, if anything, laboratory procedures overestimate our intuitive powers. The experiments usually present people with clear evidence and warn them that their reasoning ability is being tested. Seldom does life say to us: "Here is some evidence. Now put on your intellectual Sunday best and answer these questions."

"In creating these problems, we didn't set out to fool people. All our problems fooled us, too."
—Amos Tversky (1985)

Often our everyday failings are inconsequential, but not always so. False impressions, interpretations, and beliefs can produce serious consequences. Even small biases can have profound social effects when we are making important social judgments: Why are so many people homeless? Unhappy? Homicidal? Does my friend love me or my money? Cognitive biases even creep into sophisticated scientific thinking. Human nature has hardly changed in the 3,000 years since the Old Testament psalmist noted that "no one can see his own errors."

Lest we succumb to the cynical conclusion that all beliefs are absurd, I hasten to balance the picture. Social psychology has become unbalanced in its preoccupation with human foibles, note Joachim Krueger and David Funder (2003a, b), in their argument for "a more positive view of human nature." The elegant analyses of the imperfections of our thinking are themselves a tribute to human wisdom. (Were one to argue that all human thought is illusory, the assertion would be self-refuting, for it, too, would be but an illusion. It would be logically equivalent to contending, "All generalizations are false, including this one.")

"The purposes in the human mind are like deep water, but the intelligent will draw them out."
—Proverbs 20:5

As medical science assumes that any given body organ serves a function, so behavioral scientists find it useful to assume that our modes of thought and behavior are generally adaptive (Funder, 1987; Kruglanski & Ajzen, 1983; Swann, 1984). The rules of thought that produce false beliefs and striking deficiencies in our statistical intuition usually serve us well. Frequently, the errors are a by-product of our mental shortcuts that simplify the complex information we receive.

Nobel laureate psychologist Herbert Simon (1957) was among the modern researchers who first described the bounds of human reason. Simon contends that to cope with reality, we simplify it. Consider the complexity of a chess game: The number of possible games is greater than the number of particles in the universe. How do we cope? We adopt some simplifying rules—heuristics.

focus on | how journalists think: cognitive bias in newsmaking

"That's the way it is," concluded CBS anchor-person Walter Cronkite at the end of each newscast. And that's the journalistic ideal—to present reality the way it is. *The Wall Street Journal* reporters' manual states the ideal plainly: "A reporter must never hold inflexibly to his preconceptions, straining again and again to find proof of them where little exists, ignoring contrary evidence. . . . Events, not preconceptions, should shape all stories to the end" (Blundell, 1986, p. 25).

We might wish that it were so. But journalists are human, conclude Indiana University journalism professor Holly Stocking and New York psychologist-lawyer Paget Gross in their book *How Do Journalists Think?* Like laypeople and scientists, journalists "construct reality." The cognitive biases considered in this chapter therefore color newsmaking in at least six ways.

1. *Preconceptions may control interpretations.* Typically, reporters "go after an idea," which may then affect how they interpret information. Beginning with the idea that homelessness reflects a failure of mental health programs, a reporter may interpret ambiguous information accordingly while discounting other complicating factors.

2. *Confirmation bias may guide them toward sources and questions that will confirm their preconceptions.* Hoping to report the newsworthy story that a radiation leak is causing birth defects, a reporter might interview someone who accepts the idea and then someone else recommended by the first person.

3. *Belief perseverance may sustain preconceptions in the face of discrediting.* While "greedy" Ivan Boesky awaited sentencing on a 1987 Wall Street insider-trading scandal, he looked for volunteer work, something "a lot of white-collar crooks do to impress sentencing judges,"

noted a contemptuous reporter. On the other hand, a politician caught lying can, if respected, be reported as "confused" or "forgetful."

4. *Compelling anecdotes may seem more informative than base-rate information.* Like their readers, journalists may be more persuaded by vivid stories of ESP and other psychic happenings than by dispassionate research. They may be more taken by someone's apparent "cure" by a new therapy than by statistics on the therapy's success rate. After an air crash, they may describe "the frightening dangers of modern air travel," without noting its actual safety record.

5. *Events may seem correlated when they are not.* A striking co-occurrence—say three minority athletes' problems with drugs—may lead reporters to infer a relationship between race and drug use in the absence of representative evidence.

6. *Hindsight makes for easy after-the-fact analysis.* President Carter's ill-fated attempt to rescue American hostages in Iran was "doomed from the start"; so said journalists *after* they knew it had failed. Decisions that turn out poorly have a way of seeming *obviously* dumb, after the fact.

Indeed, surmise Stocking and Gross, given all the information that reporters and editors must process quickly, how could they avoid the illusory thinking tendencies that penetrate human thinking? But on the positive side, exposing these points of bias may alert journalists to ways of reducing them—by considering opposite conclusions, by seeking sources and asking questions that might counter their ideas, by seeking statistical information first and then seeking representative anecdotes, and by remembering that well-meaning people make decisions without advance knowledge of their consequences.

These heuristics sometimes lead us to defeat. But they do enable us to make efficient snap judgments.

Illusory thinking can likewise spring from useful heuristics that aid our survival. In many ways, heuristics "make us smart" (Gigerenzer & Todd, 1999). The belief in our power to control events helps maintain hope and effort. If things are sometimes subject to control and sometimes not, we maximize our outcomes by positive thinking. Optimism pays dividends. We might even say that our beliefs are like scientific theories—sometimes in error yet useful as generalizations. As social psychologist Susan Fiske (1992) says, "Thinking is for doing."

As we constantly seek to improve our theories, might we not also work to reduce errors in our social thinking? In school, math teachers teach, teach, teach until the mind is finally trained to process numerical information accurately and automatically. We assume that such ability does not come naturally; otherwise, why bother with the years of training? Research psychologist Robyn Dawes (1980)—who was dismayed that "study after study has shown [that] people have very limited abilities to process information on a conscious level, particularly social information"—suggested that we should also teach, teach, teach how to process social information.

Richard Nisbett and Lee Ross (1980) believe that education could indeed reduce our vulnerability to certain types of error. They propose that we do the following:

- We train people to recognize likely sources of error in their own social intuition.
- We set up statistics courses geared to everyday problems of logic and social judgment. Given such training, people do in fact reason better about everyday events (Lehman & others, 1988; Nisbett & others, 1987).
- We make such teaching more effective by illustrating it richly with concrete, vivid anecdotes and examples from everyday life.
- We teach memorable and useful slogans, such as: "It's an empirical question," "Which hat did you draw that sample out of?" or "You can lie with statistics, but a well-chosen example does the job better."

"Cognitive errors . . . exist in the present because they led to survival and reproductive advantages for humans in the past."
—Evolutionary psychologists Martie Haselton and David Buss (2000)

"The spirit of liberty is the spirit which is not too sure that it is right; the spirit of liberty is the spirit which seeks to understand the minds of other men and women; the spirit of liberty is the spirit which weighs their interests alongside its own without bias."
—Learned Hand, "The Spirit of Liberty," 1952

Research on social beliefs and judgments reveals how we form and sustain beliefs that usually serve us well, but sometimes lead us astray. Even our misjudgments are by-products of thinking strategies (*heuristics*) that usually serve us well, just as visual illusions are by-products of perceptual mechanisms that help us organize sensory information. But they are still errors, errors that can warp our perceptions of reality and prejudice our judgments of others. A balanced social psychology will therefore appreciate both the powers and the perils of social thinking.

Summing up

Personal Postscript: Reflecting on intuition's powers and limits

Is research on pride and error too humbling? Surely we can acknowledge the hard truth of our human limits and still sympathize with the deeper message that people are more than machines. Our subjective experiences are the stuff of our humanity—our art and our music, our enjoyment of friendship and love, our mystical and religious experiences.

The cognitive and social psychologists who explore illusory thinking are not out to remake us into unfeeling logical machines. They know that emotions enrich human experience and that intuitions are an important source of creative ideas. They add, however, the humbling reminder that our susceptibility to error also makes clear the need for disciplined training of the mind. Norman Cousins (1978) called this "the biggest truth of all about learning: that its purpose is to unlock the human mind and to develop it into an organ capable of thought—conceptual thought, analytical thought, sequential thought."

Research on error and illusion in social judgment reminds us to "judge not"—to remember, with a dash of humility, our potential for misjudgment. It also encourages us not to feel intimidated by the arrogance of those who cannot see their own potential for bias and error. We humans are wonderfully intelligent yet fallible creatures. We have dignity but not deity.

Such humility and distrust of human authority is at the heart of both religion and science. No wonder many of the founders of modern science were religious people whose convictions predisposed them to be humble before nature and skeptical of human authority (Hooykaas, 1972; Merton, 1938). Science always involves an interplay between intuition and rigorous test, between creative hunch and skepticism. To sift reality from illusion requires both open-minded curiosity and hard-headed rigor. This perspective could prove to be a good attitude for approaching all of life: to be critical but not cynical; curious but not gullible; open but not exploitable.

What do you think?

As you read this chapter, did you have any hunches or intuitions about human behavior? Maybe you were reminded of a situation you or someone you know were once in. What did that experience tell you about how others explain situations they are in? What did it tell you about how others judge people? Now, devise a way to test your hunch. In other words, develop a research study based on the hunch (theory) you have about people—using your personal experience.

Making the Social Connection

SS This chapter reported on Lee Ross's formation of the fundamental attribution error concept, which you will encounter later in this text. For example, how do we explain the actions of ethnic minorities (Chapter 9: Prejudice)? What misperceptions fuel conflict (Chapter 13: Conflict and Peacemaking)? Go to the *SocialSense* CD-ROM to view a short video explaining the fundamental attribution error. Keep the fundamental attribution error in mind as you read future chapters, and notice how people explain others' behavior.

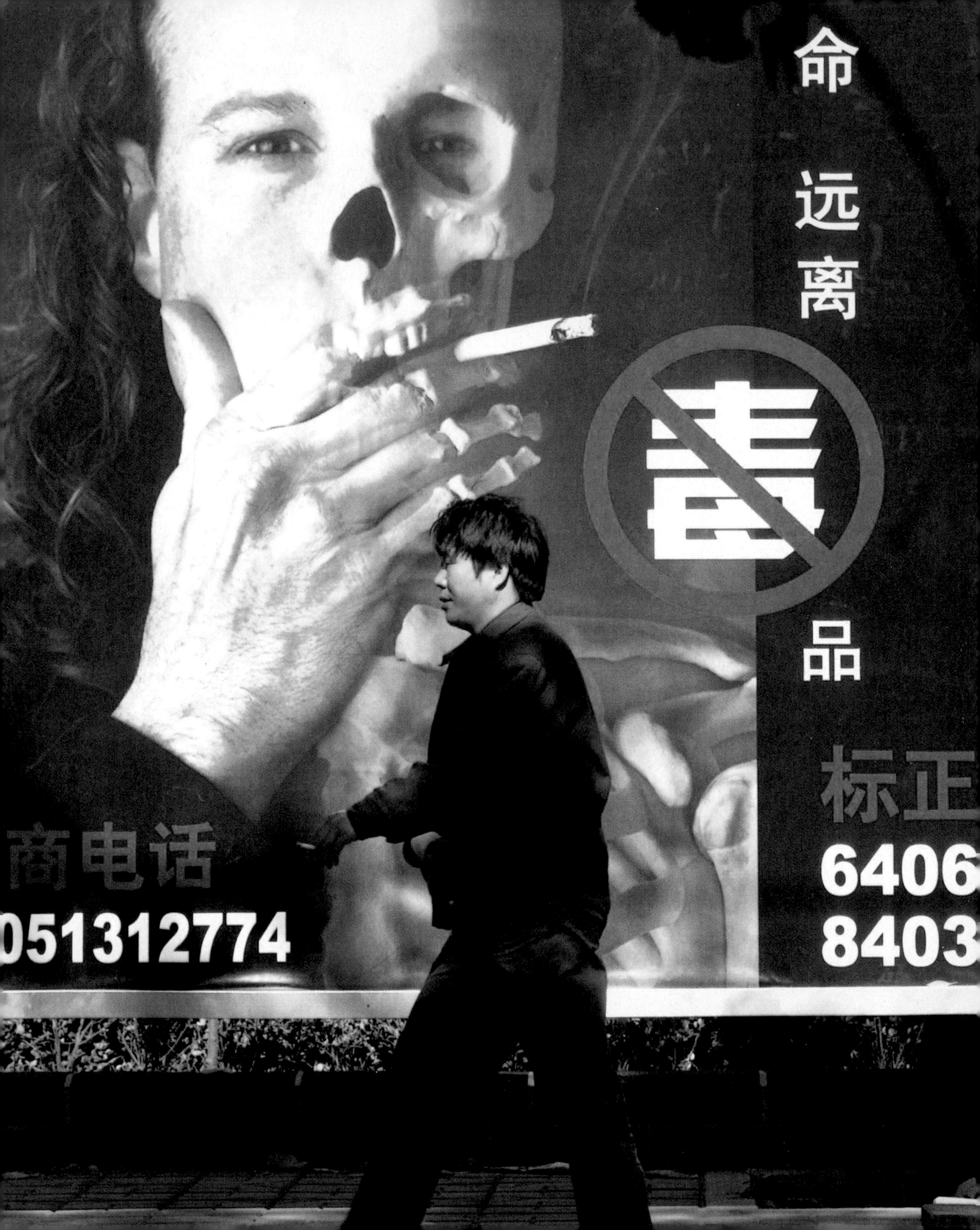
命
远离
毒
品
标正
6406
8403
商电话
051312774

chapter 4

Behavior and Attitudes

"One does what one is; one becomes what one does."

Robert Musil,
Kleine Prosa, *1930*

Worldwide concern recently focused on a fast-spreading and sometimes fatal virus causing Severe Acute Respiratory Syndrome (SARS), which claimed some 800 lives during 2002 and 2003. Meanwhile, the tobacco industry, aided by government subsidies, was killing nearly that many people every hour—4.9 million per year (WHO, 2002). The World Health Organization estimates that *half a billion* people alive today will be killed by tobacco. In the United States, for example, smoking kills 420,000 people a year—surpassing the combined fatalities from homicide, suicide, AIDS, car accidents, and alcohol and drug abuse. Although assisted suicide may be illegal, suicide assisted by the tobacco industry is not.

With the tobacco industry responsible for fatalities equal to 14 loaded and crashed jumbo jets a day (not including those in the expanding but harder to count Third World market), how do tobacco company executives live with themselves? At Philip Morris, one of the world's two largest tobacco advertisers, upper-level executives—mostly intelligent, family-oriented,

Attitudes and actions: Many sports events, which glorify health and physical prowess, are sponsored by manufacturers of products like cigarettes, which are dangers to health. And the ads themselves are incongruous.

community-minded people—resent being called "mass murderers." They were less than pleased when former U.S. Surgeon General C. Everett Koop (1997) called them "a sleazy bunch of people who misled us, deceived us and lied to us for three decades." Moreover, they defend smokers' right to choose. "Is it an addiction issue?" asks one vice-president. "I don't believe it. People do all sorts of things to express their individuality and to protest against society. And smoking is one of them, and not the worst" (Rosenblatt, 1994).

- Do these statements reflect privately held attitudes?
- If this executive really thinks smoking is a comparatively healthy expression of individuality, how are such attitudes internalized?
- Or do his statements reflect social pressure to say things he doesn't believe?

When people question someone's attitude, they refer to beliefs and feelings related to a person or event and the resulting behavior tendency. Taken together, favorable or unfavorable evaluative reactions toward something—whether exhibited in beliefs, feelings, or inclinations to act—define a person's **attitude** (Olson & Zanna, 1993). Attitudes provide an efficient way to size up the world. When we have to respond quickly to something, the way we feel about it can guide how we react. For example, a person who *believes* a particular ethnic group is lazy and aggressive may *feel* dislike for such people and therefore intend to act in a discriminatory manner. You can remember these three dimensions as the ABCs of attitudes: affect (feelings), behavior tendency, and cognition (thoughts) (Figure 4–1).

attitude

A favorable or unfavorable evaluative reaction toward something or someone, exhibited in one's beliefs, feelings, or intended behavior.

The study of attitudes is close to the heart of social psychology and was one of its first concerns. From the beginning, researchers wondered how much our attitudes affect our actions.

figure 4–1

The ABCs of attitudes.

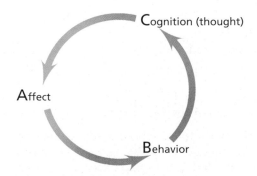

Do our attitudes determine our behavior?

To what extent, and under what conditions, do the attitudes of the heart drive our outward actions? Why were social psychologists at first surprised by a seemingly small connection between attitudes and actions?

What is the relationship between what we *are* (on the inside) and what we *do* (on the outside)? Philosophers, theologians, and educators have long speculated about the connection between thought and action, character and conduct, private word and public deed. The prevailing assumption, which underlies most teaching, counseling, and child rearing, has been that our private beliefs and feelings determine our public behavior, and that to alter behavior we need to change hearts and minds.

"The ancestor of every action is a thought."
—Ralph Waldo Emerson, *Essays, First Series,* 1841

ARE WE ALL HYPOCRITES?

In the beginning, social psychologists agreed: To know people's attitudes is to predict their actions. The 19 hijackers whose anti-American attitudes led to the 9/11 suicidal terrorism illustrate that extreme attitudes can produce extreme behavior. But in 1964, Leon Festinger concluded that the evidence did not show that changing attitudes changes behavior. Festinger believed the attitude-behavior relation works the other way around; our behavior is the horse, our attitudes the cart. As Robert Abelson (1972) put it, we are "very well trained and very good at finding reasons for what we do, but not very good at doing what we find reasons for."

A further blow to the supposed power of attitudes came when social psychologist Allan Wicker (1969) reviewed several dozen research studies covering a wide variety of people, attitudes, and behaviors. Wicker offered a shocking conclusion: People's expressed attitudes hardly predicted their varying behaviors.

- Student attitudes toward cheating bore little relation to the likelihood of their actually cheating.
- Attitudes toward the church were only modestly linked with church attendance on any given Sunday.
- Self-described racial attitudes provided little clue to behaviors in actual situations.

An example of the disjuncture between attitudes and actions is what Daniel Batson and his colleagues (1997, 2001, 2002) call "moral hypocrisy" (appearing moral while avoiding the costs of being so). Their studies presented their people with an appealing task (where the participant could earn raffle tickets toward a $30 prize) and a dull task with no positive consequences. The participants had to assign themselves to one task and a supposed second participant to the other. Only 1 in 20 believed that assigning the positive task to themselves was the most moral thing to do, yet 80 percent did so. In follow-up experiments on moral hypocrisy, participants were given coins they could flip privately if they wished. Even if they chose to flip, 90 percent assigned themselves to the positive task! Was this because they could specify the consequences of heads and tails after the coin toss? In yet another experiment, Batson put a sticker on each side of the coin, indicating what the flip outcome would signify. Still, 24 of 28 people who made the toss assigned themselves to the positive task. When morality and greed were put on a collision course, greed won.

If people don't play the same game that they talk, it's little wonder that attempts to change behavior by changing attitudes often fail. Warnings about the dangers of smoking affect only minimally those who already smoke. Increasing public awareness of the desensitizing and brutalizing effects of a prolonged diet of television violence has stimulated many people to voice a desire for less violent programming—yet they still watch media coverage of murder as much as ever. Appeals for safe driving have had far less effect on accident rates than have lower speed limits, divided highways, and drunk driving penalties (Etzioni, 1972).

While Wicker and others were describing the weakness of attitudes, some personality psychologists found personality traits equally ineffective in predicting behavior (Mischel, 1968). If we want to know how helpful people are going to be, we usually won't learn much by giving them tests of self-esteem, anxiety, or defensiveness. In a situation with clear-cut demands, we are better off knowing how most people react.

All in all, the developing picture of what controls behavior emphasizes external social influences and plays down internal factors, such as attitudes and personality. The original thesis that attitudes determine actions was countered during the 1960s by the antithesis that attitudes determine virtually nothing.

Thesis. Antithesis. Is there a synthesis? The surprising finding that what people *say* often differs from what they *do* sent social psychologists scurrying to find out why. Surely, we reasoned, convictions and feelings *must* sometimes make a difference.

Indeed. In fact, what I am about to explain now seems so obvious that I wonder why most social psychologists (myself included) were not thinking this way before the early 1970s. I must remind myself that truth never seems obvious until it is known.

> "It may be desirable to abandon the attitude concept."
> —Allan Wicker, 1971

WHEN ATTITUDES PREDICT BEHAVIOR

Our behavior and our expressed attitudes differ because both are subject to other influences. One social psychologist counted 40 separate factors that complicate their relationship (Triandis, 1982; see also Kraus, 1995). If we could just neutralize the other influences on behavior—make all other things equal—might attitudes accurately predict behaviors?

When social influences on what we say are minimal

Unlike a physician measuring heart rate, social psychologists never get a direct reading on attitudes. Rather, we measure *expressed* attitudes. Like other behaviors, expressions are subject to outside influences. This was vividly demonstrated when the U.S. House of Representatives once overwhelmingly passed a salary increase for itself in an off-the-record vote, then moments later overwhelmingly defeated the same bill on a roll-call vote. Fear of criticism had distorted the true sentiment on the roll-call vote. In late 2002, many U.S. legislators, sensing their country's post-9/11 fear, anger, and patriotic fervor, publicly voted support for President Bush's planned war against Iraq while privately having reservations (Nagourney, 2002). We sometimes say what we think others want to hear.

Today's social psychologists have some clever means at their disposal for subtly assessing attitudes. One is to measure facial muscle responses to statements (Cacioppo & Petty, 1981). Do the facial muscles reveal a microsmile or a microfrown? Another, the "implicit association test," uses reaction times to measure how quickly people associate concepts (Greenwald & others, 2002, 2003). One can, for example, measure implicit racial attitudes by assessing whether people take longer to associate positive words with Black rather than with White faces.

Knowing that people don't wear their hearts on their sleeves, social psychologists have longed for a "pipeline to the heart." Edward Jones and Harold Sigall (1971) therefore devised a **bogus pipeline** method that fools people into exposing their real attitudes. In one experiment, conducted with Richard Page, Sigall (1971) had University of Rochester students hold a locked wheel that, if unlocked, could turn a pointer to the left, indicating disagreement, or to the right, indicating agreement. When electrodes were attached to their arms, the fake machine supposedly measured tiny muscular responses said to gauge their tendency to turn the wheel left (disagree) or right (agree). To demonstrate this amazing new machine, the researcher asked the students some questions. After a few moments of impressive flashing lights and whirring sounds, a meter on the machine announced the student's attitude—which was nothing more than an attitude the student had earlier expressed as part of a now-forgotten survey. The procedure convinced everyone.

Once the students were convinced, the attitude meter was hidden and they were asked questions concerning their attitudes toward African Americans and requested to guess what the meter revealed. How do you suppose these White collegians responded? Compared with other students who responded through a typical questionnaire, those responding by the bogus pipeline admitted more negative belief. Unlike those responding to the paper-and-pencil scale—who rated African Americans as being more sensitive than other Americans—those responding through the bogus pipeline reversed these judgments. It was as if they were thinking, "I'd better tell the truth or the experimenter will think I'm out of touch with myself."

No wonder people who are first persuaded that lie detectors work may then admit the truth (in which case, the lie detector has worked!). And no wonder there is sometimes a weak attitude-behavior link: Under everyday conditions, such as those faced by tobacco executives and politicians, people sometimes express attitudes they don't privately hold.

bogus pipeline
A procedure that fools people into disclosing their attitudes. Participants are first convinced that a machine can use their psychological responses to measure their private attitudes. Then they are asked to predict the machine's reading, thus revealing their attitudes.

When other influences on behavior are minimal

On any occasion, it's not only our inner attitudes that guide us but also the situation we face. As Chapters 5 to 8 will illustrate again and again, social influences can be enormous—enormous enough to induce people to violate their deepest convictions. Presidential aides may go along with actions they know are wrong. Jesus' outspoken disciple Peter denied ever knowing him. Prisoners of war may lie to placate their captors.

So, would *averaging* many occasions enable us to detect more clearly the impact of our attitudes? Predicting people's behavior is like predicting a baseball or cricket player's hitting. The outcome of any particular time at bat is nearly impossible to predict, because it is affected not only by the batter but also by what the pitcher throws and by chance factors. When we aggregate many times at bat, we neutralize these complicating factors. Knowing the players, we can predict their approximate batting *averages*.

To use a research example, people's general attitude toward religion poorly predicts whether they will go to worship next weekend (because the weather, the preacher, how one is feeling, and so forth also influence attendance). But religious attitudes predict quite well the total quantity of religious behaviors over time (Fishbein & Ajzen, 1974; Kahle & Berman, 1979). The findings define

"Do I contradict myself? Very well then I contradict myself. (I am large, I contain multitudes.)"
—Walt Whitman, *Song of Myself*, 1855

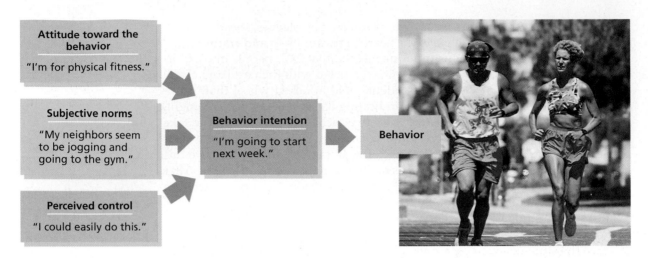

Compared to their general attitudes toward a healthy lifestyle, people's specific attitudes regarding jogging predict their jogging behavior much better.

figure 4–2

The theory of planned behavior.

Icek Ajzen, working with Martin Fishbein, has shown that one's (a) attitudes, (b) perceived social norms, and (c) feelings of control together determine one's intentions, which guide behavior.

a *principle of aggregation:* The effects of an attitude become more apparent when we look at a person's aggregate or average behavior rather than at isolated acts.

When attitudes specific to the behavior are examined

Other conditions further improve the predictive accuracy of attitudes. As Icek Ajzen and Martin Fishbein (1977; Ajzen, 1982, 2002) point out, when the measured attitude is general—say, an attitude toward Asians—and the behavior is very specific—say, a decision whether to help a particular Asian—we should not expect a close correspondence between words and actions. Indeed, report Fishbein and Ajzen, in 26 out of 27 such research studies, attitudes did not predict behavior. But attitudes did predict behavior in all 26 studies they could find in which the measured attitude was directly pertinent to the situation. Thus, attitudes toward the general concept of "health fitness" poorly predict specific exercise and dietary practices. Whether people jog is more likely to depend on their opinions about the costs and benefits of jogging. Better yet for predicting behavior, says Ajzen in his and Fishbein's "theory of planned behavior," is knowing someone's *intended* behaviors, and their perceived self-efficacy and control (Figure 4–2).

Further studies—more than 700 studies with 276,000 participants—confirmed that specific, relevant attitudes do predict intended and actual behavior (Armitage & Conner, 2001; Six & Eckes, 1996; Wallace & others, 2004). For example, attitudes toward condoms strongly predict condom use (Albarracin & others, 2001). And attitudes toward recycling (but not general attitudes toward environmental issues) predict participation in recycling (Oskamp, 1991). To change health habits through persuasion, we had best alter people's attitudes toward *specific* practices.

So far we have seen two conditions under which attitudes will predict behavior: (1) when we minimize other influences upon our attitude statements and on our behavior, and (2) when the attitude is specifically relevant to the observed behavior. There is a third condition: An attitude predicts behavior better when the attitude is potent.

When attitudes are potent

When we act automatically, our attitudes often lie dormant. We act out familiar scripts, without reflecting on what we're doing. We respond to people we meet in the hall with an automatic, "Hi." We answer the restaurant cashier's question, "How was your meal?" by saying, "Fine," even if we found it tasteless. Such mindless reaction is adaptive. It frees our minds to work on other things. As the philosopher Alfred North Whitehead argued, "Civilization advances by extending the number of operations which we can perform without thinking about them." But when we are on automatic pilot, our attitudes are dormant. For habitual behaviors—seat belt use, coffee consumption, class attendance—conscious intentions hardly get activated (Ouellette & Wood, 1998).

In novel situations our behavior is less automatic; lacking a script, we think before we act. If prompted to think about their attitudes before acting, will people be truer to themselves? Mark Snyder and William Swann (1976) wanted to find out. So two weeks after 120 of their University of Minnesota students indicated their attitudes toward affirmative-action employment policies, Snyder and Swann invited them to act as jurors in a sex-discrimination court case. Attitudes predicted verdicts only for those who were first induced to remember their attitudes—by giving them "a few minutes to organize your thoughts and views on the affirmative-action issue." Our attitudes guide our behavior if we think about them.

> "Thinking is easy, acting difficult, and to put one's thoughts into action, the most difficult thing in the world."
> —German poet Goethe, 1749–1832

Self-conscious people usually are in touch with their attitudes (Miller & Grush, 1986). This suggests another way to induce people to focus on their inner convictions: *Make* them self-conscious, perhaps by having them act in front of a mirror (Carver & Scheier, 1981). Maybe you can recall suddenly being acutely aware of yourself upon entering a room with a large mirror. Making people self-aware in this way promotes consistency between words and deeds (Gibbons, 1978; Froming & others, 1982).

Edward Diener and Mark Wallbom (1976) noted that nearly all college students say that cheating is morally wrong. But will they follow the advice of Shakespeare's Polonius, "To thine own self be true"? Diener and Wallbom set University of Washington students to work on an anagram-solving task (said to predict IQ) and told them to stop when a bell in the room sounded. Left alone, 71 percent cheated by working past the bell. Among students made self-aware—by working in front of a mirror while hearing their tape-recorded voices—only 7 percent cheated. It makes one wonder: Would eye-level mirrors in stores make people more self-conscious of their attitudes about stealing?

> "Without doubt it is a delightful harmony when doing and saying go together."
> —Montaigne, *Essays*, 1588

Remember Batson's studies of moral hypocrisy described on page 135? In a final experiment, Batson and his colleagues (1999) found that mirrors did bring behavior into line with espoused moral attitudes. When people flipped a coin while facing a mirror, the coin flip became scrupulously fair. Exactly half of the self-conscious participants assigned the other person to the positive task.

To summarize, it is now plain that, depending on the circumstances, the relationship between expressed attitudes and behavior can range from no relationship to a strong one (Kraus, 1995). Our attitudes predict our actions if

> "It is easier to preach virtue than to practice it."
> —La Rochefoucauld, *Maxims*, 1665

- other influences are minimal,
- the attitude is specific to the action, and
- the attitude is potent as when we are reminded of it.

Summing up

How do our inner attitudes relate to our external behavior? Social psychologists agree that attitudes and behavior feed each other. Popular wisdom stresses the impact of attitudes on behavior. Surprisingly, attitudes—usually assessed as feelings toward some object or person—are often poor predictors of behaviors. Moreover, changing people's attitudes typically fails to produce much change in their behavior. These findings sent social psychologists scurrying to find out why we so often fail to play the game we talk. The answer: Our expressions of attitudes and our behaviors are each subject to many influences.

Our attitudes will predict our behavior (1) if these "other influences" are minimized, (2) if the attitude corresponds very closely to the predicted behavior (as in voting studies), and (3) if the attitude is potent (because something reminds us of it, or because we acquired it by direct experience). Thus there is, under these conditions, a connection between what we think and feel and what we do.

When does behavior determine attitudes?

If social psychology has taught us anything during the last 25 years, it is that we are likely not only to think ourselves into a way of acting but also to act ourselves into a way of thinking. What evidence supports this assertion?

Now we turn to the more startling idea that behavior determines attitudes. It's true that we sometimes stand up for what we believe. But it's also true that we come to believe in what we stand up for. Social-psychological theories inspired much of the research that underlies this conclusion. Instead of beginning with these theories, however, let's first see what there is to explain. As we engage the evidence that behavior affects attitudes, speculate *why* actions affect attitudes and then compare your ideas with social psychologists' explanations.

Consider the following incidents:

"Thought is the child of Action."
—Benjamin Disraeli, *Vivian Grey*, 1826

- Sarah is hypnotized and told to take off her shoes when a book drops on the floor. Fifteen minutes later a book drops, and Sarah quietly slips out of her loafers. "Sarah," asks the hypnotist, "why did you take off your shoes?" "Well . . . my feet are hot and tired," Sarah replies. "It has been a long day." The act produces the idea.

- George has electrodes temporarily implanted in the brain region that controls his head movements. When neurosurgeon José Delgado (1973) stimulates the electrode by remote control, George always turns his head. Unaware of the remote stimulation, he offers a reasonable explanation for his head turning: "I'm looking for my slipper." "I heard a noise." "I'm restless." "I was looking under the bed."

- Carol's severe seizures were relieved by surgically separating her two brain hemispheres. Now, in an experiment, psychologist Michael Gazzaniga (1985) flashes a picture of a nude woman to the left half of Carol's field of vision and thus to her nonverbal right brain hemisphere. A sheepish smile spreads over her face, and she begins chuckling. Asked why, she invents—and apparently believes—a plausible explanation: "Oh—that funny machine." Frank, another split-brain patient, has the word "smile" flashed to his nonverbal right hemisphere. He obliges and forces a smile. Asked why, he explains, "This experiment is very funny."

The mental aftereffects of our behavior appear in many social psychological phenomena as well. The following examples illustrate self-persuasion—attitudes following behavior.

ROLE PLAYING

The word **role** is borrowed from the theater and, as in the theater, refers to actions expected of those who occupy a particular social position. When enacting new social roles, we may at first feel phony. But our unease seldom lasts.

Think of a time when you stepped into some new role—perhaps your first days on a job, or at college, or in a sorority or fraternity. That first week on campus, for example, you may have been supersensitive to your new social situation and tried valiantly to act appropriately and to root out your high school behavior. At such times you may have felt self-conscious. You observed your new speech and actions because they weren't natural to you. Then one day you noticed something amazing: Your enthusiasm for a sorority or your pseudo-intellectual talk no longer feels forced. The role has begun to fit as comfortably as your old jeans and T-shirt.

In one study, college men volunteered to spend time in a simulated prison constructed in Stanford's psychology department by Philip Zimbardo (1971; Haney & Zimbardo, 1998). Zimbardo was wondering: Is prison brutality a product of evil prisoners and malicious guards? Or do the institutional roles of guard and prisoner embitter and harden even compassionate people? Do the people make the place violent? Or does the place make the people violent?

So, by a flip of a coin, Zimbardo designated some students as guards. He gave them uniforms, billy clubs, and whistles and instructed them to enforce the rules. The other half, the prisoners, were locked in cells and made to wear humiliating outfits. After a jovial first day of "playing" their roles, the guards and prisoners, and even the experimenters, got caught up in the situation. The guards began to disparage the prisoners, and some devised cruel and degrading routines. The prisoners broke down, rebelled, or became apathetic. There developed, reported Zimbardo (1972), a "growing confusion between reality and illusion, between role-playing and self-identity. . . . This prison which we had created . . . was absorbing us as creatures of its own reality." Observing the emerging social pathology, Zimbardo was forced to call off the planned two-week simulation after only six days.

The effect of behavior on attitude appears even in the theater. Self-conscious acting may diminish as the actor becomes absorbed in the role and experiences genuine emotion. "My whole personality changed during the time I was doing the part," said Ian Charleson on his role as serene and devout Olympic

role
A set of norms that defines how people in a given social position ought to behave.

"No man, for any considerable period, can wear one face to himself and another to the multitude without finally getting bewildered as to which may be true."
—Nathaniel Hawthorne, 1850

Guards and prisoners in the Stanford prison simulation quickly absorbed the roles they played.

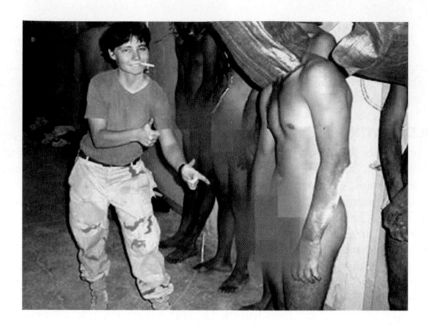

After the degradation of Iraqi prisoners by some U.S. military personnel, Philip Zimbardo (2004a, b) noted "direct and sad parallels between similar behavior of the 'guards' in the Stanford Prison Experiment." Such behavior, he contends, is attributable to a toxic situation that can make good people into perpetrators of evil. "It's not that we put bad apples in a good barrel. We put good apples in a bad barrel. The barrel corrupts anything that it touches."

hero Eric Liddell in *Chariots of Fire*. The point is not that we are powerless to resist imposed roles. In one modified reenactment of a prison simulation, albeit with BBC television cameras rolling, the guards did not become sadistic (Reicher & Haslam, 2002; Muldoon, 2003). The deeper lesson of role-playing studies concerns how what is unreal (an artificial role) can subtly evolve into what is real. In a new career, as teacher, soldier, or businessperson, we enact a role that shapes our attitudes. Imagine playing the role of slave—not just for six days but for decades. If a few days altered the behavior of those in Zimbardo's "prison," then imagine the corrosive effects of decades of subservient behavior. The master may be even more profoundly affected, because the master's role is chosen. Frederick Douglass, a former slave, recalls his slave mistress's transformation as she absorbed her role:

> My new mistress proved to be all she appeared when I first met her at the door— a woman of the kindest heart and finest feelings. . . . I was utterly astonished at her goodness. I scarcely knew how to behave towards her. She was entirely unlike any other white woman I had ever seen. . . . The meanest slave was put fully at ease in her presence, and none left without feeling better for having seen her. Her face was made of heavenly smiles, and her voice of tranquil music.
>
> But, alas! this kind heart had but a short time to remain such. The fatal poison of irresponsible power was already in her hands, and soon commenced its infernal work. That cheerful eye, under the influence of slavery, soon became red with rage; that voice, made all of sweet accord, changed to one of harsh and horrid discord; and that angelic face gave place to that of a demon. (Douglass, 1845, pp. 57–58)

WHEN SAYING BECOMES BELIEVING

"Fake it until you make it."
—Alcoholics Anonymous

People often adapt what they say to please their listeners. They are quicker to tell people good news than bad, and they adjust their message toward their listener's position (Manis & others, 1974; Tesser & others, 1972; Tetlock, 1983).

"Good God! He's giving the white-collar voters' speech to the blue collars."

Impression management: In expressing our thoughts to others, we sometimes tailor our words to what we think the others will want to hear.

When induced to give spoken or written witness to something they doubt, people will often feel bad about their deceit. Nevertheless, they begin to believe what they are saying—*provided* they weren't bribed or coerced into doing so. When there is no compelling external explanation for one's words, saying becomes believing (Klaas, 1978).

Tory Higgins and his colleagues (Higgins & Rholes, 1978; Higgins & McCann, 1984) illustrated how saying becomes believing. They had university students read a personality description of someone and then summarize it for someone else, who was believed either to like or dislike this person. The students wrote a more positive description when the recipient liked the person. Having said positive things, they also then liked the person more themselves. Asked to recall what they had read, they remembered the description as more positive than it was. In short, it seems that we are prone to adjust our messages to our listeners, and, having done so, to believe the altered message.

"I had thought I was humoring [my captors] by parroting their clichés and buzz words without personally believing in them. . . . In trying to convince them I convinced myself."
—Kidnap victim Patricia Campbell Hearst, *Every Secret Thing,* 1982

focus on | saying becomes believing

University of Oregon psychologist Ray Hyman (1981) described how acting the role of a palm reader convinced him that palmistry worked.

I started reading palms when I was in my teens as a way to supplement my income from doing magic and mental shows. When I started I did not believe in palmistry. But I knew that to "sell" it I had to act as if I did. After a few years I became a firm believer in palmistry. One day the late Stanley Jaks, who was a professional mentalist and a man I respected, tactfully suggested that it would make an interesting experiment if I deliberately gave readings opposite to what the lines indicated. I tried this out with a few clients. To my surprise and horror my readings were just as successful as ever. Ever since then I have been interested in the powerful forces that convince us, [palm] reader and client alike, that something is so when it really isn't. (p. 86)

THE FOOT-IN-THE-DOOR PHENOMENON

Most of us can recall times when, after agreeing to help out with a project or an organization, we ended up more involved than we ever intended, vowing that in the future we would say no to such requests. How does this happen? Experiments suggest that if you want people to do a big favor for you, an effective strategy is this: Get them to do a small favor first. In the best-known demonstration of this **foot-in-the-door phenomenon,** researchers posing as drive-safely volunteers asked Californians to permit the installation of huge, poorly lettered "Drive Carefully" signs in their front yards. Only 17 percent consented. Others were first approached with a small request: Would they display three-inch "Be a safe driver" window signs? Nearly all readily agreed. When approached two weeks later to allow the large, ugly signs in their front yards, 76 percent consented (Freedman & Fraser, 1966). One project helper who went from house to house later recalled that, not knowing who had been previously visited, "I was simply stunned at how easy it was to convince some people and how impossible to convince others" (Ornstein, 1991).

Other researchers have confirmed the foot-in-the-door phenomenon with altruistic behaviors.

- Patricia Pliner and her collaborators (1974) found 46 percent of Toronto suburbanites willing to give to the Cancer Society when approached directly. Others, asked a day ahead to wear a lapel pin publicizing the drive (which all agreed to do), were nearly twice as likely to donate.
- Anthony Greenwald and his co-researchers (1987) approached a sample of registered voters the day before the 1984 U.S. presidential election and asked them a small question: "Do you expect that you will vote or not?" All said yes. Compared with other voters not asked their intentions, they were 41 percent more likely to vote.
- Angela Lipsitz and others (1989) report that ending blood-drive reminder calls with, "We'll count on seeing you then, OK? [pause for response]," increased the show-up rate from 62 to 81 percent.
- In Internet chatrooms, Paul Markey and his colleagues (2002) requested help ("I can't get my e-mail to work. Is there any way I can get you to send me an e-mail?"). Help increased—from 2 to 16 percent—by including a smaller prior request ("I am new to this whole computer

foot-in-the-door phenomenon
The tendency for people who have first agreed to a small request to comply later with a larger request.

"You will easily find folk to do favors if you cultivate those who have done them."
—Publilius Syrus, 42 B.C.

The foot-in-the-door phenomenon. Reprinted with special permission of King Features Syndicate. Blondie by Dean Young and Stan Drake.

thing. Is there any way you can tell me how to look at someone's profile?"). Nicolas Guéguen and Céline Jacob (2001) tripled the rate of French Internet users contributing to child landmine victims organizations (from 1.6 to 4.9 percent) by first inviting them to sign a petition against landmines.

Note that in these, as in many of the 100+ foot-in-the-door experiments, the initial compliance—signing a petition, wearing a lapel pin, stating one's intention—was voluntary (Burger & Guadagno, 2003). We will see again and again that when people commit themselves to public behaviors *and* perceive these acts to be their own doing, they come to believe more strongly in what they have done.

Social psychologist Robert Cialdini [chal-DEE-nee] is a self-described "patsy." "For as long as I can recall, I've been an easy mark for the pitches of peddlers, fund-raisers, and operators of one sort or another." To better understand why one person says yes to another, he spent three years as a trainee in various sales, fund-raising, and advertising organizations, discovering how they exploit "the weapons of influence." He also put these weapons to the test in simple experiments. In one, Cialdini and his collaborators (1978) explored a variation of the foot-in-the-door phenomenon by experimenting with the **low-ball technique,** a tactic reportedly used by some car dealers. After the customer agrees to buy a new car because of its great price and begins completing the sales forms, the salesperson removes the price advantage by charging for options the customer thought were included or by checking with a boss who disallows the deal because, "We'd be losing money." Folklore has it that more customers now stick with the higher-priced purchase than would have agreed to it at the outset.

Real-life applications

Airlines and hotels have also used the tactic by attracting inquiries with great deals available on only a few seats or rooms, then hoping the customer will agree to a higher-priced option. Cialdini and his collaborators found that this technique indeed works. When they invited introductory psychology students to participate in an experiment at 7:00 a.m., only 24 percent showed up. But if the students first agreed to participate without knowing the time and only then were asked to participate at 7:00 a.m., 53 percent came.

low-ball technique
A tactic for getting people to agree to something. People who agree to an initial request will often still comply when the requester ups the ante. People who receive only the costly request are less likely to comply with it.

The low-ball technique. The Born Loser reprinted by permission of Newspaper Enterprise Association, Inc.

Marketing researchers and salespeople have found that the principle works even when we are aware of a profit motive (Cialdini, 1988). A harmless initial commitment—returning a card for more information and a gift, agreeing to listen to an investment possibility—often moves us toward a larger commitment. Salespeople sometimes exploit the power of small commitments by trying to bind people to purchase agreements. Many states now have laws that allow customers of door-to-door salespeople a few days to think over their purchases and cancel. To combat the effect of these laws, many companies use what the sales-training program of one encyclopedia company calls "a very important psychological aid in preventing customers from backing out of their contracts" (Cialdini, 1988, p. 78). They simply have the customer, rather than the salesperson, fill out the agreement. Having written it themselves, people usually live up to their commitment.

The foot-in-the-door phenomenon is well worth learning about. Someone trying to seduce us—financially, politically, or sexually—usually will try to create a momentum of compliance. The practical lesson: Before agreeing to a small request, think about what may follow.

EVIL ACTS AND ATTITUDES

The attitudes-follow-behavior principle works with immoral acts as well. Evil sometimes results from gradually escalating commitments. A trifling evil act can make a worse act easier. Evil acts gnaw at the actor's moral sensitivity. To paraphrase La Rochefoucauld's *Maxims* (1665), it is not as difficult to find a person who has never succumbed to a given temptation as to find a person who has succumbed only once.

For example, cruel acts corrode the consciences of those who perform them. Harming an innocent victim—by uttering hurtful comments or delivering electric shocks—typically leads aggressors to disparage their victims, thus helping them justify their behavior (Berscheid & others, 1968; Davis & Jones, 1960; Glass, 1964). We tend not only to hurt those we dislike but to dislike those we hurt. In studies establishing this, people would justify an action especially when coaxed into it, not coerced. When we agree to a deed voluntarily, we take more responsibility for it.

Cruel acts, such as the massacre of these Rwandan Tutsis, breed even crueler and more hate-filled attitudes.

The phenomenon appears in wartime. Concentration camp guards would sometimes display good manners to inmates in their first days on the job, but not for long. Soldiers ordered to kill may initially react with revulsion to the point of sickness over their act, but not for long (Waller, 2002). Often they will denigrate their enemies with dehumanizing nicknames.

Attitudes also follow behavior in peacetime. A group that holds another in slavery will likely come to perceive the slaves as having traits that justify their oppression. Actions and attitudes feed one another, sometimes to the point of moral numbness. The more one harms another and adjusts one's attitudes, the easier harm-doing becomes. Conscience mutates.

Evil acts shape the self, but so, thankfully, do moral acts. Character, it is said, is reflected in what we do when we think no one is looking. Researchers have tested character by giving children temptations when it seems no one is watching. Consider what happens when children resist the temptation. In a dramatic experiment, Jonathan Freedman (1965) introduced elementary school children to an enticing battery-controlled robot, instructing them not to play with it while he was out of the room. Freedman used a severe threat with half the children and a mild threat with the others. Both were sufficient to deter the children.

Several weeks later a different researcher, with no apparent relation to the earlier events, left each child to play in the same room with the same toys. Of the 18 children who had been given the severe threat, 14 now freely played with the robot; but two-thirds of those who had been given the mild deterrent still resisted playing with it. Having earlier chosen consciously *not* to play with the toy, the mildly deterred children apparently internalized their decisions. This new attitude controlled their subsequent actions. So they internalized the conscientious act if the deterrent was strong enough to elicit the desired behavior yet mild enough to leave them with a sense of choice. Moral action, especially when chosen rather than coerced, affects moral thinking.

"Our self-definitions are not constructed in our heads; they are forged by our deeds."
—Robert McAfee Brown, *Creative Dislocation: The Movement of Grace,* 1980

INTERRACIAL BEHAVIOR AND RACIAL ATTITUDES

If moral action feeds moral attitudes, will positive interracial behavior reduce racial prejudice—much as mandatory seat belt use has produced more favorable seat belt attitudes? This was part of social scientists' testimony before the U.S. Supreme Court's 1954 decision to desegregate schools. Their argument ran like this: If we wait for the heart to change—through preaching and teaching—we will wait a long time for racial justice. But if we legislate moral action, we can, under the right conditions, indirectly affect heartfelt attitudes.

This idea runs counter to the presumption that "you can't legislate morality." Yet attitude change has, in fact, followed desegregation. Consider some correlational findings from this mammoth social experiment:

- Following the Supreme Court decision, the percentage of White Americans favoring integrated schools more than doubled and now includes nearly everyone. (For other examples of old and current racial attitudes, see Chapter 9.)
- In the 10 years after the Civil Rights Act of 1964, the percentage of White Americans who described their neighborhoods, friends, co-workers, or other students as all-White declined by about 20 percent for each of these measures. Interracial behavior was increasing. During the same period,

"We become just by the practice of just actions, self-controlled by exercising self-control, and courageous by performing acts of courage."
—Aristotle

Our political rituals—the daily flag salute by schoolchildren, singing the national anthem—use public conformity to build private allegiance.

the percentage of White Americans who said that Blacks should be allowed to live in any neighborhood increased from 65 percent to 87 percent (ISR Newsletter, 1975). Attitudes were changing, too.

- More uniform national standards against discrimination were followed by decreasing differences in racial attitudes among people of differing religions, classes, and geographic regions. As Americans came to act more alike, they came to think more alike (Greeley & Sheatsley, 1971; Taylor & others, 1978).

"We do not love people so much for the good they have done us, as for the good we have done them."
—Leo Tolstoy, *War and Peace*, 1867–1869

Experiments confirm that positive behavior toward someone fosters liking for that person. Doing a favor for an experimenter or another subject, or tutoring a student, usually increases liking of the person helped (Blanchard & Cook, 1976). It is a lesson worth remembering: If you wish to love someone more, act as if you do.

In 1793, Benjamin Franklin tested the idea that doing a favor engenders liking. As clerk of the Pennsylvania General Assembly, he was disturbed by opposition from another important legislator. So Franklin set out to win him over:

> I did not . . . aim at gaining his favour by paying any servile respect to him but, after some time, took this other method. Having heard that he had in his library a certain very scarce and curious book I wrote a note to him expressing my desire of perusing that book and requesting he would do me the favour of lending it to me for a few days. He sent it immediately and I return'd it in about a week, expressing strongly my sense of the favour. When we next met in the House he spoke to me (which he had never done before), and with great civility; and he ever after manifested a readiness to serve me on all occasions, so that we became great friends and our friendship continued to his death. (Quoted by Rosenzweig, 1972, p. 769)

Celebrating Canada Day: Patriotic actions strengthen patriotic attitudes.

SOCIAL MOVEMENTS

The effect of a society's behavior on its racial attitudes suggests the possibility, and the danger, of employing the same idea for political socialization on a mass scale. For many Germans during the 1930s, participation in Nazi rallies, wearing uniforms, demonstrating, and especially the public greeting "Heil Hitler" established a profound inconsistency between behavior and belief. Historian Richard Grunberger (1971) reports that for those who had their doubts about Hitler, "The 'German greeting' was a powerful conditioning device. Having once decided to intone it as an outward token of conformity, many experienced . . . discomfort at the contradiction between their words and their feelings. Prevented from saying what they believed, they tried to establish their psychic equilibrium by consciously making themselves believe what they said" (p. 27).

The practice is not limited to totalitarian regimes. Political rituals—the daily flag salute by schoolchildren, singing the national anthem—use public conformity to build a private belief in patriotism. I recall participating in air-raid drills in an elementary school not far from the Boeing Company in Seattle. After we acted repeatedly as if we were the objects of Russian attack, many of us came to fear the Russians. Observers noted how the civil rights marches of the 1960s strengthened the demonstrators' commitments. Their actions expressed an idea whose time had come and drove that idea more deeply into their hearts. The move toward gender-inclusive language in the 1980s similarly strengthened inclusive attitudes, and the recycling programs of the 1990s helped boost environmental concern.

Many people assume that the most potent social indoctrination comes through *brainwashing,* a term coined to describe what happened to American prisoners of war (POWs) during the 1950s Korean war. Although the "thought-control" program was not nearly as irresistible as this term suggests, the results still were disconcerting. Hundreds of prisoners cooperated with their captors.

Twenty-one chose to remain after being granted permission to return to America. And many of those who did return came home believing "although communism won't work in America, I think it's a good thing for Asia" (Segal, 1954).

Edgar Schein (1956) interviewed many of the POWs during their journey home and reported that the captors' methods included a gradual escalation of demands. The captors always started with trivial requests and gradually worked up to more significant ones. "Thus after a prisoner had once been 'trained' to speak or write out trivia, statements on more important issues were demanded." Moreover, they always expected active participation, be it just copying something or participating in group discussions, writing self-criticism, or uttering public confessions. Once a prisoner had spoken or written a statement, he felt an inner need to make his beliefs consistent with his acts. This often drove prisoners to persuade themselves of what they had done. The "start-small-and-build" tactic was an effective application of the foot-in-the-door technique, as it continues to be today in the socialization of terrorists and torturers (Chapter 6).

Now let me ask you, before reading further, to play theorist. Ask yourself: Why in these studies and real-life examples did attitudes follow behavior? Why might playing a role or making a speech influence how you feel about something?

"You can use small commitments to manipulate a person's self-image; you can use them to turn citizens into 'public servants,' prospects into 'customers,' prisoners into 'collaborators.'"
—Robert Cialdini, *Influence*, 1988

Summing up

The attitude-action relation also works in the reverse direction: We are likely not only to think ourselves into action but also to act ourselves into a way of thinking. When we act, we amplify the idea underlying what we have done, especially when we feel responsible for it. Many streams of evidence converge on this principle. The actions prescribed by social roles mold the attitudes of the role players.

Research on the foot-in-the-door phenomenon reveals that committing a small act later makes people more willing to do a larger one. Actions also affect our moral attitudes: That which we have done we tend to justify as right. Similarly, our racial and political behaviors help shape our social consciousness: We not only stand up for what we believe, we also believe in what we have stood up for.

Why does our behavior affect our attitudes?

What theories help explain the attitudes-follow-behavior phenomenon? How does the contest between these competing theories illustrate the process of scientific explanation?

We have seen that several streams of evidence merge to form a river: the effect of actions on attitudes. Do these observations contain any clues to why action affects attitude? Social psychology's detectives suspect three possible sources. *Self-presentation theory* assumes that for strategic reasons we express attitudes that make us appear consistent. *Cognitive dissonance theory* assumes that to reduce discomfort, we justify our actions to ourselves. *Self-perception theory* assumes that our actions are self-revealing (when uncertain about our feelings or beliefs, we look to our behavior, much as anyone else would). Let's examine each.

SELF-PRESENTATION: IMPRESSION MANAGEMENT

The first explanation for why actions affect attitudes began as a simple idea that you may recall from Chapter 2. Who among us does not care what people think? We spend countless dollars on clothes, diets, cosmetics, and now plastic surgery—all because of our fretting over what others think. To make a good impression is often to gain social and material rewards, to feel better about ourselves, even to become more secure in our social identities (Leary, 1994, 2001).

No one wants to look foolishly inconsistent. To avoid seeming so, we express attitudes that match our actions. To appear consistent, we may pretend attitudes. Even if it means displaying a little insincerity or hypocrisy, it can pay to manage the impression one is making. Or so self-presentation theory suggests.

Does our eagerness to appear consistent explain why expressed attitudes shift toward consistency with behavior? To some extent, yes—people exhibit a much smaller attitude change when a bogus pipeline inhibits them from trying to make a good impression (Paulhus, 1982; Tedeschi & others, 1987).

But there is more to the attitude changes we have reviewed than self-presentation, for people express their changed attitudes even to someone who doesn't know how they have behaved. Two other theories explain why people sometimes internalize their self-presentations as genuine attitude changes.

"My not wearing a hairpiece indicates to others that I'm comfortable with myself."

Self-presentation theory assumes that our behavior aims to create desired impressions. Copyright © The New Yorker Collection, 1987, Robert Weber, from cartoonbank.com. All Rights Reserved.

SELF-JUSTIFICATION: COGNITIVE DISSONANCE

One theory is that our attitudes change because we are motivated to maintain consistency among our cognitions. This is the implication of Leon Festinger's (1957) famous **cognitive dissonance theory.** The theory is simple, but its range of application is enormous. It assumes we feel tension ("dissonance") when two simultaneously accessible thoughts or beliefs ("cognitions") are psychologically inconsistent—as when we decide to say or do something we have mixed feelings about. Festinger argued that to reduce this unpleasant arousal, we often adjust our thinking. This simple idea, and some surprising predictions derived from it, have spawned more than 2,000 studies (Cooper, 1999).

Dissonance theory pertains mostly to discrepancies between behavior and attitudes. We are aware of both. Thus, if we sense some inconsistency, perhaps some hypocrisy, we feel pressure for change. That helps explain why, in a British survey, half of cigarette smokers therefore disagreed with nonsmokers, who nearly all believed that smoking is "really as dangerous as people say" (Eiser & others, 1979). In the United States, too, 40 percent of smokers—and 13 percent of nonsmokers—judge smoking as not very harmful (Saad, 2002).

After the 2003 Iraq war, noted the director of the Program of International Policy Attitudes, some Americans struggled to reduce their "experience of

cognitive dissonance
Tension that arises when one is simultaneously aware of two inconsistent cognitions. For example, dissonance may occur when we realize that we have, with little justification, acted contrary to our attitudes or made a decision favoring one alternative despite reasons favoring another.

www.mhhe.com/**myers8**
Visit the Online Learning Center for a scenario on behavior and attitudes.

cognitive dissonance" (Kull, 2003). The war's main premise had been that Saddam Hussein, unlike most other brutal dictators whom the world was tolerating, had weapons of mass destruction that threatened U.S. and British security. As the war began, only 38 percent of Americans said the war was justified even if Iraq did not have weapons of mass destruction (Gallup, 2003). Nearly four in five Americans believed their invading troops would find such, and a similar percentage supported the just-launched war (Duffy, 2003; Newport & others, 2003).

When no such weapons were used during the war or found in sufficient quantity to pose a threat, the war-supporting majority experienced dissonance, which was heightened by their awareness of the war's financial and human costs, by scenes of Iraqi chaos in the war's aftermath, by surging anti-American attitudes in Europe and in Muslim countries, and by inflamed pro-terrorist attitudes. (In Indonesia, Jordan, and the Palestinian Authority, majorities now expressed confidence in Osama bin Laden to "do the right thing in world affairs" [Pew, 2003].) To reduce such dissonance, noted the Program of International Policy Attitudes, some American revised their memories of their government's primary rationale for going to war. The reasons now became construed as liberating an oppressed people from tyrannical and genocidal rule, and laying the groundwork for a more peaceful and democratic Middle East. A month after the war, the once-minority opinion was now the majority view: 58 percent of Americans now supported the war even if there were none of the proclaimed weapons of mass destruction (Gallup, 2003). "Whether or not they find weapons of mass destruction doesn't matter," suggested Republican pollster Frank Luntz (2003), "because the rationale for the war changed."

Cognitive dissonance theory offers an explanation for self-persuasion, and it offers several surprising predictions. See if you can anticipate them.

Insufficient justification

Imagine you are a participant in a famous experiment staged by the creative Festinger and his student, J. Merrill Carlsmith (1959). For an hour, you are required to perform dull tasks, such as turning wooden knobs again and again. After you finish, the experimenter (Carlsmith) explains that the study concerns how expectations affect performance. The next participant, waiting outside, must be led to expect an interesting experiment. The seemingly distraught experimenter, whom Festinger had spent hours coaching until he became extremely convincing, explains that the assistant who usually creates this expectation couldn't make this session. Wringing his hands, he pleads, "Could you fill in and do this?"

It's for science and you are being paid, so you agree to tell the next participant (who is actually the experimenter's real assistant) what a delightful experience you have just had. "Really?" responds the supposed participant. "A friend of mine was in this experiment a week ago, and she said it was boring." "Oh, no," you respond, "it's really very interesting. You get good exercise while turning some knobs. I'm sure you'll enjoy it." Finally, someone else who is studying how people react to experiments has you complete a questionnaire that asks how much you actually enjoyed your knob-turning experience.

Now for the prediction: Under which condition are you most likely to believe your little lie and say the experiment was indeed interesting? When paid $1 for doing so, as some of the participants were? Or when paid a then-lavish $20, as

the story behind the theory: Leon Festinger on dissonance reduction

Following a 1934 earthquake in India, there were rumors outside the disaster zone of worse disasters to follow. It occurred to me that these rumors might be "anxiety-justifying"—cognitions that would justify their lingering fears. From that germ of an idea, I developed my theory of dissonance reduction—making your view of the world fit with how you feel or what you've done.

Leon Festinger
1920–1989

others were? Contrary to the common notion that big rewards produce big effects, Festinger and Carlsmith made an outrageous prediction: Those paid just $1 (hardly sufficient justification for a lie) would be most likely to adjust their attitudes to their actions. Having **insufficient justification** for their actions, they would experience more discomfort (dissonance) and thus be more motivated to believe in what they had done. Those paid $20 had sufficient justification for what they had done and hence should have experienced less dissonance. As Figure 4–3 (page 154) shows, the results fit this intriguing prediction.*

In dozens of later experiments, the attitudes-follow-behavior effect was strongest when people felt some choice and when their actions had foreseeable consequences. One experiment had people read disparaging lawyer jokes into a recorder (for example, "How can you tell when a lawyer is lying? His lips are moving"). The reading produced more negative attitudes toward lawyers when it was a chosen rather than a coerced activity (Hobden & Olson, 1994). Other experiments have engaged people to write essays for a measly $1.50 or so. When the essay argues something they don't believe in—say, a tuition increase—the underpaid writers begin to feel somewhat greater sympathy with the policy. Advocating a policy favorable to another race may improve your attitudes not only toward the policy but toward the race. This is especially so if something makes you face the inconsistency or if you think important people will actually read an essay with your name on it (Leippe & Eisenstadt, 1994; Leippe & Elkin, 1987). Feeling responsible for statements they have made, people then believe them more strongly. Pretense becomes reality.

Earlier we noted how the insufficient justification principle works with punishments. Children were more likely to internalize a request not to play with an attractive toy if they were given a mild threat that insufficiently justified their compliance. When a parent says, "Clean up your room, Johnny, or I'll knock

insufficient justification effect
Reduction of dissonance by internally justifying one's behavior when external justification is "insufficient."

---

* There is a seldom-reported final aspect of this 1950s experiment. Imagine yourself finally back with the experimenter, who is truthfully explaining the whole study. Not only do you learn that you've been duped, but the experimenter asks for the $20 back. Do you comply? Festinger and Carlsmith note that all their Stanford student participants willingly reached into their pockets and gave back the money. This is a foretaste of some quite amazing observations on compliance and conformity discussed in Chapter 6. As we will see, when the social situation makes clear demands, people usually respond accordingly.

figure 4–3

Insufficient justification.

Dissonance theory predicts that when our actions are not fully explained by external rewards or coercion, we will experience dissonance, which we can reduce by believing in what we have done. **Source:** Data from Festinger & Carlsmith, 1959.

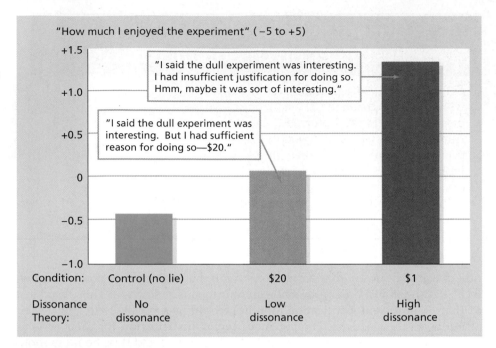

"How much I enjoyed the experiment" (−5 to +5)

"I said the dull experiment was interesting. I had insufficient justification for doing so. Hmm, maybe it was sort of interesting."

"I said the dull experiment was interesting. But I had sufficient reason for doing so—$20."

| Condition: | Control (no lie) | $20 | $1 |
| Dissonance Theory: | No dissonance | Low dissonance | High dissonance |

Dissonance theory suggests that parents should aim to elicit desired behavior noncoercively, thus motivating children to internalize the appropriate attitudes.

your block off," Johnny won't need to internally justify cleaning his room. The severe threat is justification enough.

Note that cognitive dissonance theory focuses not on the relative effectiveness of rewards and punishments administered after the act, but rather on what induces a desired action. It aims to have Johnny say, "I am cleaning up my room because I want a clean room," rather than, "I am cleaning up my room because my parents will kill me if I don't." Students who perceive their required community service as something they would have chosen to do are more likely to anticipate future volunteering than those who feel coerced (Stukas & others, 1999). The principle: *Attitudes follow behaviors for which we feel some responsibility.*

Authoritarian management will be effective, the theory predicts, only when the authority is present—because people are unlikely to internalize forced behavior. Bree, a formerly enslaved talking horse in C. S. Lewis's *The Horse and His Boy* (1974), observes, "One of the worst results of being a slave and being forced to do things is that when there is no one to force you any more you find you have almost lost the power of forcing yourself" (p. 193). Dissonance theory insists that encouragement and inducement should be enough to elicit the desired action. But it suggests that managers, teachers, and parents should use only enough incentive to elicit the desired behavior.

Dissonance after decisions

The emphasis on perceived choice and responsibility implies that decisions produce dissonance. When faced with an important decision—what college to

Big decisions can produce big dissonance when one later ponders the negative aspects of what is chosen and the positive aspects of what was not chosen.

attend, whom to date, which job to accept—we are sometimes torn between two equally attractive alternatives. Perhaps you can recall a time when, having committed yourself, you became painfully aware of dissonant cognitions—the desirable features of what you had rejected and the undesirable features of what you had chosen. If you decided to live on campus, you may have realized you were giving up the spaciousness and freedom of an apartment in favor of cramped, noisy dorm quarters. If you elected to live off campus, you may have realized that your decision meant physical separation from campus and friends and having to cook for yourself.

After making important decisions, we usually reduce dissonance by upgrading the chosen alternative and downgrading the unchosen option. In the first published dissonance experiment (1956), Jack Brehm had University of Minnesota women rate eight products, such as a toaster, a radio, and a hair dryer. Brehm then showed the women two objects they had rated closely and told them they could have whichever they chose. Later, when rerating the eight objects, the women increased their evaluations of the item they had chosen and decreased their evaluations of the rejected item. It seems that after we have made our choices, the grass does not then grow greener on the other side of the fence.

With simple decisions, this deciding-becomes-believing effect can breed overconfidence (Blanton & others, 2001). "What I've decided must be right." The effect can occur very quickly. Robert Knox and James Inkster (1968) found that racetrack bettors who had just put down their money felt more optimistic about their bets than did those who were about to bet. In the few moments that intervened between standing in line and walking away from the betting window, nothing had changed—except the decisive action and the person's feelings about it. There may sometimes be but a slight difference between two options, as I can recall in helping make faculty tenure decisions. The competence of one faculty member who barely makes it and that of another who barely loses seem not very different—until after you make and announce the decision.

www.mhhe.com/myers8
Visit the Online Learning Center for an interactivity on cognitive dissonance.

"Every time you make a choice you are turning the central part of you, the part of you that chooses, into something a little different from what it was before."
—C. S. Lewis, *Mere Christianity*, 1942

Once made, decisions grow their own self-justifying legs of support. Often, these new legs are strong enough that when one leg is pulled away—perhaps the original one—the decision does not collapse. Alison decides to take a trip home if it can be done for an airfare under $400. It can, so she makes her reservation and begins to think of additional reasons why she is glad she is going. When she goes to buy the tickets, however, she learns there has been a fare increase to $475. No matter, she is now determined to go. As when being lowballed by a car dealer, it never occurs to people, reports Robert Cialdini (1984, p. 103), "that those additional reasons might never have existed had the choice not been made in the first place."

SELF-PERCEPTION

Although dissonance theory has inspired much research, an even simpler theory explains its phenomena. Consider how we make inferences about other people's attitudes. We see how a person acts in a particular situation, and then we attribute the behavior either to the person's traits and attitudes or to environmental forces. If we see parents coercing their little Susie into saying, "I'm sorry," we attribute Susie's apology to the situation, not to her personal regret. If we see Susie apologizing with no apparent inducement, we attribute the apology to Susie herself (Figure 4–4).

self-perception theory
The theory that when we are unsure of our attitudes, we infer them much as would someone observing us, by looking at our behavior and the circumstances under which it occurs.

Self-perception theory (proposed by Daryl Bem, 1972) assumes that we make similar inferences when we observe our own behavior. When our attitudes are weak or ambiguous, we are in the position of someone observing us from the outside. We discern people's attitudes by looking closely at their actions when they are free to act as they please. We similarly discern our own attitudes. Hearing myself talk informs me of my attitudes; seeing my actions provides clues to how strong my beliefs are. This is especially so when I can't

figure 4–4
Attitudes follow behavior.

Why do actions affect attitudes?

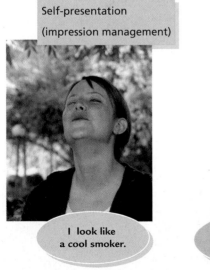

Self-presentation (impression management)

I look like a cool smoker.

Self-justification (cognitive dissonance)

I know smoking is bad for me.

Ah . . . I've been waiting all day for this.

Oh well . . . the statistics aren't as awful as they say. Anyway, I'm very healthy. I won't get sick.

Self-perception (self-observation)

Here I am smoking again. I must like smoking.

easily attribute my behavior to external constraints. The acts we freely commit are self-revealing.

William James proposed a similar explanation for emotion a century ago. We infer our emotions, he suggested, by observing our bodies and our behaviors. A stimulus such as a growling bear confronts a woman in the forest. She tenses, her heartbeat increases, adrenaline flows, and she runs away. Observing all this, she then experiences fear. At a college where I am to lecture, I awake before dawn and am unable to get back to sleep. Noting my wakefulness, I conclude that I must be anxious.

Do people who observe themselves agreeing to a small request indeed come to perceive themselves as the helpful sort of person who responds positively to requests for help? Is that why, in the foot-in-the-door experiments, people will then later agree to larger requests? Indeed, yes, report Jerry Burger and David Caldwell (2003). Behavior can modify self-concept.

Expressions and attitude

You may be skeptical of the self-perception effect, as I initially was. Experiments on the effects of facial expressions, however, suggest a way for you to experience it. When James Laird (1974, 1984) induced college students to frown while attaching electrodes to their faces—"contract these muscles," "pull your brows together"—they reported feeling angry. It's more fun to try out Laird's other finding: Those induced to make a smiling face felt happier and found cartoons more humorous. Those induced to repeatedly practice happy (versus sad or angry) expressions may recall more happy memories and find the happy mood lingering (Schnall & Laird, 2003). Viewing one's expressions in a mirror magnifies the self-perception effect (Kleinke & others, 1998).

We have all experienced this phenomenon. We're feeling crabby, but then the phone rings or someone comes to the door and elicits from us warm, polite behavior. "How's everything?" "Just fine, thanks. How are things with you?" "Oh, not bad. . . ." If our feelings are not intense, this warm behavior may change our whole attitude. It's tough to smile and feel grouchy. When Miss Universe parades her smile, she may, after all, be helping herself feel happy. As

What is the effect of facial expressions? Go to the *SocialSense* CD-ROM to view a video clip on motivation and the emotional language of the face.

According to German psychologist Fritz Strack and colleagues (1988), people find cartoons funnier while holding a pen with their teeth (using a smiling muscle) than while holding it with their lips (using muscles incompatible with smiling).

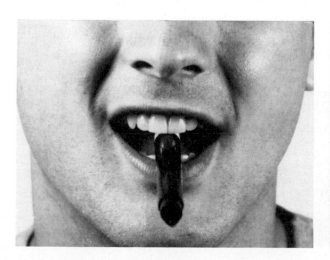
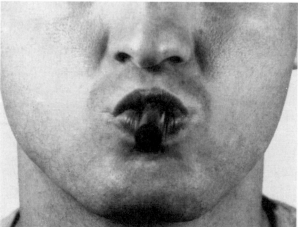

"I can watch myself and my actions, just like an outsider."
—Anne Frank, *The Diary of a Young Girl,* 1947

"The free expression by outward signs of emotion intensifies it. On the other hand, the repression, as far as possible, of all outward signs softens our emotions."
—Charles Darwin, *The Expression of the Emotions in Man and Animals,* 1897

More than self-perception may be at work here, Pablo Briñol and Richard Petty (2003) now believe. When listening to a persuasive message, head nodding appears to validate people's thoughts (favorable or unfavorable).

Natural mimicry and emotional contagion. People in sync, like these volunteers videotaped during a study by Frank Bernieri and colleagues (1994), feel more rapport with each other.

Rodgers and Hammerstein reminded us, when we are afraid, it may help to "whistle a happy tune." Going through the motions can trigger the emotions.

Even your gait can affect how you feel. When you get up from reading this chapter, walk for a minute taking short, shuffling steps, with eyes downcast. It's a great way to feel depressed. "Sit all day in a moping posture, sigh, and reply to everything with a dismal voice, and your melancholy lingers," noted William James (1890, p. 463). Want to feel better? Walk for a minute taking long strides with your arms swinging and your eyes straight ahead.

If our expressions influence our feelings, then would imitating others' expressions help us know what they are feeling? An experiment by Katherine Burns Vaughan and John Lanzetta (1981) suggests it would. They asked Dartmouth College students to observe someone receiving electric shock. They told some of the observers to make a pained expression whenever the shock came on. If, as Freud and others supposed, expressing an emotion allows us to discharge it, then the pained expression should be inwardly calming (Cacioppo & others, 1991). Actually, compared with other students who did not act out the expressions, these grimacing students perspired more and had faster heart rates whenever they saw the person shocked. Acting out the person's emotion apparently enabled the observers to feel more empathy. The implication: To sense how other people are feeling, let your own face mirror their expressions.

Actually, you hardly need try. Observing others' faces, postures, and voices, we naturally and unconsciously mimic their moment-to-moment reactions (Hatfield & others, 1992). We synchronize our movements, postures, and tones of voice with theirs. Doing so helps us tune in to what they're feeling. It also makes for "emotional contagion," which helps explain why it's fun to be around happy people and depressing to be around depressed people (Chapter 14).

Our facial expressions also influence our attitudes. In a clever experiment, Gary Wells and Richard Petty (1980) had University of Alberta students "test headphone sets" by making either vertical or horizontal head movements while listening to a radio editorial. Who most agreed with the editorial? Those who had been nodding their heads up and down. Why? Wells and Petty surmised that positive thoughts are compatible with vertical nodding and incompatible with horizontal motion. Try it yourself when listening to someone: Do you feel more agreeable when nodding rather than shaking your head?

In an even zanier experiment, John Cacioppo and his colleagues (1993) had people rate Chinese characters when pressing their arms upward (as when lifting food) or downward (as when pushing something or someone away). Which

flex condition do you suppose triggered the most positive ratings? It was the upward flex. Try it out: Do you get a more positive feeling while lifting a table edge with upturned hands rather than pressing down? Might this motion-affects-emotion phenomenon predispose people to feel better at parties while holding food or drink? In a follow-up experiment, Roland Neumann and Fritz Strack (2000) had University of Wurzburg students see how fast they could recognize words as positive or negative. Each student reacted to the words by pressing a left or right key (using two fingers of one hand). Meanwhile, the other hand was either pressing up (the approach muscles) or down and away. Can you guess the result? The students more speedily classified the positive words if their other hand was activating the positive, approach muscular response.

Overjustification and intrinsic motivations

Recall the insufficient justification effect—the smallest incentive that will get people to do something is usually the most effective in getting them to like the activity and keep on doing it. Cognitive dissonance theory offers one explanation for this: When external inducements are insufficient to justify our behavior, we reduce dissonance by justifying the behavior internally.

Self-perception theory offers another explanation: People explain their behavior by noting the conditions under which it occurs. Imagine hearing someone proclaim the wisdom of a tuition increase after being paid $20 to do so. Surely the statement would seem less sincere than if you thought the person was expressing those opinions for no pay. Perhaps we make similar inferences when observing ourselves.

"I don't sing because I am happy. I am happy because I sing."

Self-perception at work.

Self-perception theory goes even a step further. Contrary to the notion that rewards always increase motivation, it suggests that unnecessary rewards sometimes have a hidden cost. Rewarding people for doing what they already enjoy may lead them to attribute their action to the reward. If so, this would undermine their self-perception that they do it because they like it. Experiments by Edward Deci and Richard Ryan (1991, 1997) at the University of Rochester, by Mark Lepper and David Greene (1979) at Stanford, and by Ann Boggiano and her colleagues (1985, 1987) at the University of Colorado have confirmed this **overjustification effect.** Pay people for playing with puzzles, and they will later play with the puzzles less than those who play without being paid. Promise children a reward for doing what they intrinsically enjoy (for example, playing with magic markers), and you will turn their play into work (Figure 4–5).

A folktale illustrates the overjustification effect. An old man lived alone on a street where boys played noisily every afternoon. The din annoyed him, so one

overjustification effect
The result of bribing people to do what they already like doing; they may then see their actions as externally controlled rather than intrinsically appealing.

figure 4–5

Intrinsic and extrinsic motivation.

When people do something they enjoy, without reward or coercion, they attribute their behavior to their love of the activity. External rewards undermine intrinsic motivation by leading people to attribute their behavior to the incentive.

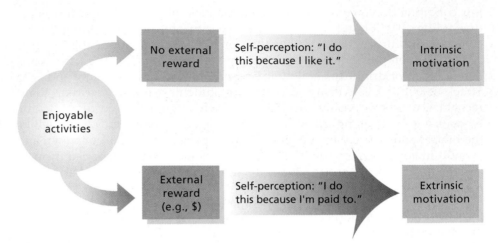

day he called the boys to his door. He told them he loved the cheerful sound of children's voices and promised them each 50 cents if they would return the next day. Next afternoon the youngsters raced back and played more lustily than ever. The old man paid them and promised another reward the next day. Again they returned, whooping it up, and the man again paid them; this time 25 cents. The following day they got only 15 cents, and the man explained that his meager resources were being exhausted. "Please, though, would you come to play for 10 cents tomorrow?" The disappointed boys told the man they would not be back. It wasn't worth the effort, they said, to play all afternoon at his house for only 10 cents.

As self-perception theory implies, an unanticipated reward does not diminish intrinsic interest, because people can still attribute their actions to their own motivation (Bradley & Mannell, 1984; Tang & Hall, 1994). (It's like the heroine who, having fallen in love with the woodcutter, now learns that he's really a prince.) And if compliments for a good job make us feel more competent and successful, this can actually increase our intrinsic motivation. When rightly administered, rewards may also boost creativity (Eisenberger & others, 1999, 2001).

The overjustification effect occurs when someone offers an unnecessary reward beforehand in an obvious effort to control behavior. What matters is what a reward implies: Rewards and praise that inform people of their achievements (that make them feel, "I'm very good at this") boost intrinsic motivation. Rewards that seek to control people and lead them to believe it was the reward that caused their effort ("I did it for the money") diminish the intrinsic appeal of an enjoyable task (Rosenfeld & others, 1980; Sansone, 1986).

How then can we cultivate people's enjoyment of tasks that are not intrinsically appealing? Young Maria may find her first piano lessons frustrating. Tommy may not have an intrinsic love of fifth-grade science. Sandra may not look forward to making those first sales calls. In such cases, the parent, teacher, or manager should probably use some incentives to coax the desired behavior (Boggiano & Ruble, 1985; Workman & Williams, 1980). After the person complies, suggest an intrinsic reason for doing so: "I'm not surprised that sales call went well, because you meet people so well."

Sally Forth

If we provide students with just enough justification to perform a learning task and use rewards and labels to help them feel competent, we may enhance their enjoyment and their eagerness to pursue the subject on their own. When there is too much justification—as happens in classrooms where teachers dictate behavior and use rewards to control the children—child-driven learning may diminish (Deci & Ryan, 1985, 1991). My younger son eagerly consumed 6 or 8 library books a week—until our library started a reading club that promised a party to those who read 10 books in three months. Three weeks later he began checking out only one or two books during our weekly visits. Why? "Because you only need to read 10 books, you know."

COMPARING THE THEORIES

We have seen one explanation of why our actions might only seem to affect our attitudes (self-presentation theory). And we have seen two explanations of why our actions genuinely affect our attitudes: (1) the dissonance-theory assumption that we justify our behavior to reduce our internal discomfort, and (2) the self-perception-theory assumption that we observe our behavior and make reasonable inferences about our attitudes, as we do when observing other people.

The last two explanations seem to contradict one another. Which is right? It's difficult to find a definitive test. In most instances they make the same predictions, and we can bend each theory to accommodate most of the findings we have considered (Greenwald, 1975). Daryl Bem (1972), the self-perception theorist, even suggested it boils down to a matter of loyalties and esthetics. This illustrates the human element in scientific theorizing (see Chapter 1). Neither dissonance theory nor self-perception theory has been handed to us by nature. Both are products of human imagination—creative attempts to simplify and explain what we've observed.

It is not unusual in science to find that a principle, such as "attitudes follow behavior," is predictable from more than one theory. Physicist Richard Feynman

(1967) marveled that "one of the amazing characteristics of nature" is the "wide range of beautiful ways" in which we can describe it: "I do not understand the reason why it is that the correct laws of physics seem to be expressible in such a tremendous variety of ways" (pp. 53–55). Like different roads leading to the same place, different sets of assumptions can lead to the same principle. If anything, this strengthens our confidence in the principle. It becomes credible not only because of the data supporting it but also because it rests on more than one theoretical pillar.

Dissonance as arousal

Can we say that one of our theories is better? On one key point, strong support has emerged for dissonance theory. Recall that dissonance is, by definition, an aroused state of uncomfortable tension. To reduce this tension, we supposedly change our attitudes. Self-perception theory says nothing about tension being aroused when our actions and attitudes are not in harmony. It assumes merely that when our attitudes are weak to begin with, we will use our behavior and its circumstances as a clue to those attitudes (like the person who said, "How do I know how I feel until I hear what I say?").

Are conditions that supposedly produce dissonance (for example, making decisions or acting contrary to one's attitudes) indeed uncomfortably arousing? Clearly yes, providing that the behavior has unwanted consequences for which the person feels responsible (Cooper, 1999). If, in the privacy of your closet, you say something you don't believe, dissonance will be minimal. It will be much greater if there are unpleasant results—if someone hears and believes you, if the negative effects are irrevocable, and if the person harmed is someone you like. If, moreover, you feel responsible for these consequences—if you can't easily excuse your act because you freely agreed to it and if you could foresee its consequences—then uncomfortable dissonance will be aroused. Moreover, the arousal will be detectable as increased perspiration and heart rate (Cacioppo & Petty, 1986; Croyle & Cooper, 1983; Losch & Cacioppo, 1990). So, *if you feel responsible for an aversive happening, you will experience the arousal of dissonance.*

Why is "volunteering" to say or do undesirable things so arousing? Because, suggests Claude Steele's (1988) **self-affirmation theory,** such acts are embarrassing. They make us feel foolish. They threaten our sense of personal competence and goodness. Justifying our actions and decisions is therefore *self-affirming;* it protects and supports our sense of integrity and self-worth.

What do you suppose happens, then, if we offer people who have committed self-contradictory acts a way to reaffirm their self-worth, such as doing good deeds? In several experiments Steele found that, with their self-concepts restored, people (especially those who came to the experiments with strong self-concepts) felt much less need to justify their acts (Steele & others, 1993). People with high and secure self-esteem also engage in less self-justification (Holland & others, 2002).

So dissonance conditions do indeed arouse tension, especially when they threaten positive feelings of self-worth. But is this arousal necessary for the attitudes-follow-behavior effect? Steele and his colleagues (1981) believe the answer is yes. When drinking alcohol reduces dissonance-produced arousal, the attitudes-follow-behavior effect disappears. In one of their experiments, they induced University of Washington students to write essays favoring a big tuition

self-affirmation theory
A theory that (a) people often experience a self-image threat, after engaging in an undesirable behavior; and that (b) they can compensate by affirming another aspect of the self. Threaten people's self-concept in one domain and they will compensate by either refocusing or by doing good deeds in some other domain.

increase. The students reduced their resulting dissonance by softening their antituition attitudes—*unless* after writing the unpleasant essays they drank alcohol, supposedly as part of a beer- or vodka-tasting experiment.

Nearly five decades after Festinger first proposed his theory, social psychologists continue to study and debate alternative views of what causes dissonance. Some say Festinger was right to think that merely behaving inconsistently with one's attitudes is enough to provoke some attitude change (Harmon-Jones & others, 1996, 2000; Johnson & others, 1995; McGregor & others, 1998). In fact, in studies with people suffering amnesia—and thus with an inability to explicitly remember their behavior—attitudes still changed following behavior (Lieberman & others, 2001). (This startling result suggests that there's more to the effect than conscious self-justification. Unconscious processing also seems to be at work.)

Others argue that the crucial inconsistency is between one's behavior and one's self-concept (Prislin & Pool, 1996; Stone & others, 1999). Japanese people are less concerned with affirming their personal sense of self. Thus, they don't exhibit the behavior rationalization that is so commonly found in dissonance experiments—unless primed to be aware of what others might think of them (Heine & Lehman, 1997; Kitayama & others, 2004). Although the dust has not settled on the issue, this much is clear, say Richard Petty, Duane Wegener, and Leandre Fabrigar (1997): "Dissonance theory has captivated the imagination of social psychologists as virtually no other, and it has continued to generate interesting new research."

"No, Hoskins, you're not going to do it just because I'm telling you to do it. You're going to do it because you believe in it."

People rarely internalize coerced behavior. Copyright © The New Yorker Collection, 1988, Charles Barsotti, from cartoonbank.com. All Rights Reserved.

Self-perceiving when not self-contradicting

Dissonance procedures are uncomfortably arousing, and that makes for self-persuasion after acting contrary to one's attitudes. But dissonance theory cannot explain all the findings. When people argue a position that is in line with their opinion, although a step or two beyond it, procedures that usually eliminate arousal do not eliminate attitude change (Fazio & others, 1977, 1979). Dissonance theory also does not explain the overjustification effect, since being paid to do what you like to do should not arouse great tension. And what about situations where the action does not contradict any attitude—when, for example, people are induced to smile or grimace. Here, too, there should be no dissonance. For these cases, self-perception theory has a ready explanation.

In short, it appears that dissonance theory successfully explains what happens when we act contrary to clearly defined attitudes: We feel tension, so we adjust our attitudes to reduce it. Dissonance theory, then, explains attitude *change*. In situations where our attitudes are not well formed, self-perception theory explains attitude *formation*. As we act and reflect, we develop more readily accessible attitudes to guide our future behavior (Fazio, 1987; Roese & Olson, 1994).

"Rather amazingly, 40 years after it publication, the theory of cognitive dissonance looks as strong and as interesting as ever."
—Social psychologist Jack W. Brehm (1999)

Summing up

Three competing theories explain why our actions affect our attitude reports. *Self-presentation theory* assumes that people, especially those who self-monitor their behavior hoping to create good impressions, will adapt their attitude reports to appear consistent with their actions. The available evidence confirms that people do adjust their attitude statements out of concern for what other people will think. But it also shows that some genuine attitude change occurs.

Two theories propose that our actions trigger genuine attitude change. Dissonance theory explains this attitude change by assuming that we feel tension after acting contrary to our attitudes or making difficult decisions. To reduce this arousal, we internally justify our behavior. *Dissonance theory* further proposes that the less external justification we have for our undesirable actions, the more we feel responsible for them, and thus the more dissonance arises and the more attitudes change.

Self-perception theory assumes that, when our attitudes are weak, we simply observe our behavior and its circumstances and infer our attitudes. One interesting implication of self-perception theory is the "overjustification effect": Rewarding people to do what they like doing anyway can turn their pleasure into drudgery (if the reward leads them to attribute their behavior to the reward). Evidence supports predictions from both theories, suggesting that each describes what happens under certain conditions.

℞ Personal Postscript: Changing ourselves through action

To make anything a habit, do it.
To not make it a habit, do not do it.
To unmake a habit, do something else in place of it.

—Greek stoic philosopher, Epictetus

"If we wish to conquer undesirable emotional tendencies in ourselves we must . . . cold-bloodedly go through the outward motions of those contrary dispositions we prefer to cultivate."
—William James, "What Is an Emotion?" 1884

This chapter's attitudes-follow-behavior principle offers a powerful lesson for life: If we want to change ourselves in some important way, it's best not to wait for insight or inspiration. Sometimes we need to act—to begin to write that paper, to make those phone calls, to see that person—even if we don't feel like acting. Jacques Barzun (1975) recognized the energizing power of action when he advised aspiring writers to engage in the act of writing even if contemplation had left them feeling uncertain about their ideas:

> If you are too modest about yourself or too plain indifferent about the possible reader and yet are required to write, then you have to pretend. Make believe that you want to bring somebody around to your opinion; in other words, adopt a thesis and start expounding it. . . . With a slight effort of the kind at the start—a challenge to utterance—you will find your pretense disappearing and a real concern creeping in. The subject will have taken hold of you as it does in the work of all habitual writers. (pp. 173–174)

This attitudes-follow-behavior phenomenon is not irrational or magical. That which prompts us to act may also prompt us to think. Writing an essay or role-playing an opposing view forces us to consider arguments we otherwise might have ignored. Also, we remember information best when we have explained it actively in our own terms. As one student wrote me, "It wasn't until I tried to verbalize my beliefs that I really understood them." As a teacher and a writer, I must therefore remind myself not always to lay out finished results. It is better to stimulate students to think through the implications of a theory, to make them active listeners and readers. Even taking notes deepens the impression. The philosopher-psychologist William James (1899) made the same point a century ago: "No reception without reaction, no impression without correlative expression—this is the great maxim which the teacher ought never to forget."

What do you think?

Do you recall a time when taking an action changed your attitude? Describe the experience. What action can you take now that will help you change an attitude? Is there someone or some class you would like to feel better about? If so, might it help to begin acting as if you did?

Making the Social Connection

As part of a discussion of attitudes and behavior, this chapter recounts Philip Zimbardo's classic Stanford Prison Experiment. In Chapter 8 we will meet Zimbardo again, through his work on lost self-consciousness in crowd situations. Go to the *SocialSense* CD-ROM to view Zimbardo explaining his famous prison experiment.

part two

Social Influence

So far we have considered mostly "within-the-skin" phenomena—how we think about one another. Now we consider "between-skins" happenings—how we influence and relate to one another. Therefore, in Chapters 5 through 8 we probe social psychology's central concern: the powers of social influence.

What are these unseen social forces that push and pull us? How powerful are they? Research on social influence helps illuminate the invisible strings by which our social worlds move us about. This part reveals these subtle powers, especially the cultural sources of attitudes and behavior (Chapter 5), the forces of social conformity (Chapter 6), the principles of persuasion (Chapter 7), the consequences of participation in groups (Chapter 8), and how all these influences operate together in everyday situations.

Seeing these influences, we may better understand why people feel and act as they do. And we may ourselves become less vulnerable to unwanted manipulation and more adept at pulling our own strings.

chapter 5

Genes, Culture, and Gender

"We recognize that we are the products of many cultures, traditions and memories; that mutual respect allows us to study and learn from other cultures; and that we gain strength by combining the foreign with the familiar."

U. N. Secretary-General Kofi Annan, Nobel Peace Prize lecture, 2001

approaching Earth from light-years away, alien scientists assigned to study the species *Homo sapiens* feel their excitement rising. Their plan: to observe two randomly sampled humans. Their first subject, Jan, is a verbally combative Los Angeles trial lawyer who grew up in Nashville but moved west seeking the "California lifestyle." After an affair and a divorce, Jan is enjoying a second marriage. Friends describe Jan as an independent thinker who is self-confident, competitive, and somewhat domineering.

Their second subject, Tomoko, lives with a spouse and their two children in a rural Japanese village, a walk from the homes of both their parents. Tomoko is proud of being a good child, loyal spouse, and protective parent. Friends describe Tomoko as kind, gentle, respectful, sensitive, and supportive of extended family.

From their small sample of two people of differing genders and cultures, what might our alien scientists conclude about human nature? Would they wonder whether the two are from different subspecies? Or would they be struck by deeper similarities beneath the surface differences?

The questions faced by our alien scientists are those faced by today's earth-bound scientists: How do we humans differ? How are we alike? These questions are central to a world where social diversity has become, as historian Arthur Schlesinger (1991) said, "the explosive problem of our times." In a world ripped apart by cultural differences, can we learn to accept our diversity, value our cultural identities, and recognize the extent of our human kinship? I believe we can. To see why, let's consider the evolutionary and cultural roots of our humanity. Then let's see how each might help us understand gender similarities and differences.

How are we influenced by human nature and cultural diversity?

In viewing human similarities and differences, two perspectives dominate current thinking: an evolutionary perspective, emphasizing human kinship, and a cultural perspective, emphasizing human diversity. Nearly everyone agrees that we need both: Our genes design an adaptive human brain—a hard drive that receives the culture's software.

In many important ways, Jan and Tomoko are more alike than different. As members of one great family with common ancestors, they share not only a common biology but also common behavior tendencies. Each perceives the world, feels thirst, and develops language through identical mechanisms. Jan and Tomoko both prefer sweet tastes to sour and divide the visual spectrum into similar colors. They and their kin across the globe all know how to read one another's frowns and smiles.

Jan and Tomoko—and humans everywhere—are intensely social creatures. They join groups, conform, and recognize distinctions of social status. They return favors, punish offenses, and grieve a child's death. As children, beginning at about 8 months of age, they displayed fear of strangers, and as adults they favor members of their own groups. Confronted by those with dissimilar attitudes or attributes, they react warily or negatively. Our alien scientists could drop in anywhere and find humans feasting and dancing, laughing and crying, singing and worshiping. Everywhere, humans prefer living with others—in families and communal groups—to living alone. Anthropologist Donald Brown (1991, 2000) has, in fact, identified several hundred such universal behavior and language patterns. To sample among just those beginning with "v," all human societies have verbs, violence, visiting, and vowels.

Such commonalities define our shared human nature. We're indeed all kin beneath the skin.

GENES, EVOLUTION, AND BEHAVIOR

The universal behaviors that define human nature arise from our biological similarity. Some 100,000 years ago, most anthropologists believe, we humans were all Africans. Feeling the urge to "be fruitful and multiply, and fill the earth," many of our ancestors moved out of Africa, displacing cousins such as Europe's Neanderthals. In adapting to their new environments, these early humans developed differences that, measured on anthropological scales, are relatively recent and superficial. Those who stayed in Africa had darker skin pigment—"sunscreen for the tropics" (Pinker, 2002). Those who went far north of the equator, for example, evolved lighter skins capable of synthesizing vitamin D in less direct sunlight. Still, historically, we all are Africans.

Indeed, we were Africans recently enough, when our ancestors had dwindled to a small number, that "there has not been much time to accumulate many new versions of the genes," notes Steven Pinker (2002, p. 143). Thus, if our alien scientist studied our genes, we humans—even Jan and Tomoko—would seem strikingly similar, like members of one tribe. We may be more numerous than chimpanzees, but chimps are more genetically varied.

To explain the traits of our species, and all species, the British naturalist Charles Darwin (1859) proposed an evolutionary process. Follow the genes, he advised. As organisms vary, nature selects those best equipped to survive and reproduce in particular environments. Genes that predisposed traits that increased the odds of leaving descendants became more abundant. In the snowy Arctic environment, for example, polar bear genes programming a thick coat of camouflaging white fur have won the genetic competition and now predominate. This process of **natural selection,** long an organizing principle of biology, recently has become an important principle for psychology as well.

Evolutionary psychology studies how natural selection predisposes not just physical traits suited to particular contexts—polar bear coats, bats' sonar, humans' color vision—but psychological traits and social behaviors that enhance the preservation and spread of one's genes. We humans are the way we are, say evolutionary psychologists, because among our ancestors' descendants, nature selected those who had our traits—those who, for example, preferred nutritious, energy-providing foods and who disliked bitter, sour, often toxic tastes. Those who lacked such preferences were less likely to survive to contribute their genes to posterity. As mobile gene machines, we carry the legacy of our ancestors' adaptive preferences. We long for whatever helped them survive, reproduce, and nurture their offspring to survive and reproduce. Biologically speaking, one major purpose of life is to leave grandchildren. "The purpose of the heart is to pump blood," notes evolutionary psychologist David Barash (2003). "The brain's purpose," he adds, is to direct our organs and our behavior "in a way that maximizes our evolutionary success. That's it."

The evolutionary perspective highlights our universal human nature. We not only maintain certain food preferences, we also share answers to social questions such as: Whom should I trust, and fear? Whom should I help? When, and with whom, should I mate? To whom should I defer, and whom may I control? Evolutionary psychologists contend that our emotional and behavioral answers to these questions are the same answers that worked for our ancestors.

Because these social tasks are common to people everywhere, humans everywhere tend to agree on the answers. For example, all humans rank others by authority and status. And all have ideas about economic justice (Fiske, 1992). Evolutionary psychologists highlight these universal characteristics that have evolved through natural selection. Cultures, however, provide the specific rules for working out these elements of social life.

CULTURE AND BEHAVIOR

Perhaps our most important similarity, the hallmark of our species, is our capacity to learn and adapt. Evolution has prepared us to live creatively in a changing world and to adapt to environments from equatorial jungles to arctic

---

natural selection
The evolutionary process by which nature selects traits that best enable organisms to survive and reproduce in particular environmental niches.

evolutionary psychology
The study of the evolution of behavior using principles of natural selection.

"Psychology will be based on a new foundation."
—Charles Darwin, *The Origin of Species*, 1859

Somehow the adherents of the 'nurture' side of the argument have scared themselves silly at the power and the inevitability of genes and missed the greatest lesson of all: the genes are on their side."
—Matt Ridley, *Nature via Nurture*, 2003

figure 5–1

Culture matters.

These responses to a 1997 World Gallup survey illustrate our cultural diversity. **Source:** Gallup & Lindsay, 1999.

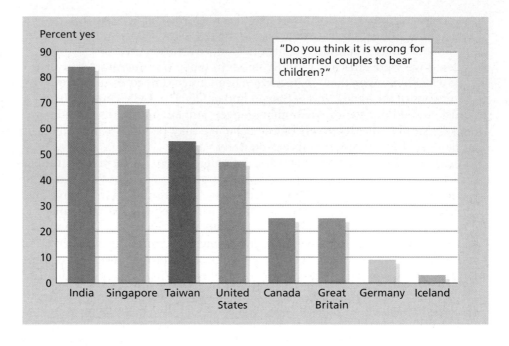

culture

The enduring behaviors, ideas, attitudes, and traditions shared by a large group of people and transmitted from one generation to the next.

"Stand tall, Bipedal Ape. The shark may outswim you, the cheetah outrun you, the swift outfly you, the capuchin outclimb you, the elephant outpower you, the redwood outlast you. But you have the biggest gifts of all."
—Richard Dawkins, *The Devil's Chaplain,* 2003

icefields. Compared with bees, birds, and bulldogs, nature has us on a looser genetic leash. Ironically, therefore, our shared human biology enables our cultural diversity. It enables those in one **culture** to value promptness, welcome frankness, or accept premarital sex, while those in another culture do not (Figure 5–1). Whether we equate beauty with slimness or shapeliness depends on when and where we live. Whether we define social justice as equality (all receive the same) or as equity (those who produce more receive more) depends on whether Marxism or capitalism shapes our ideology. Whether we tend to be expressive or reserved, casual or formal, hinges partly on whether we have spent our lives in an African, a European, or an Asian culture.

Evolutionary psychology incorporates environmental influences. We humans have been selected not only for big brains and biceps but also for social competence. We come prepared to learn language and to bond and cooperate with others in securing food, caring for young, and protecting ourselves. Nature therefore predisposes us to learn, whatever culture we are born into (Fiske & others, 1998). The cultural perspective, while acknowledging that all behavior requires our evolved genes, highlights human adaptability.

Cultural diversity

The diversity of our languages, customs, and expressive behaviors suggests that much of our behavior is socially programmed, not hardwired. Genes are not fixed blueprints: their expression depends on the environment (Lickliter & Honeycutt, 2003). Thus, the genetic leash is long. As sociologist Ian Robertson (1987) has noted:

> Americans eat oysters but not snails. The French eat snails but not locusts. The Zulus eat locusts but not fish. The Jews eat fish but not pork. The Hindus eat pork but not beef. The Russians eat beef but not snakes. The Chinese eat snakes but not people. The Jalé of New Guinea find people delicious. (p. 67)

If we all lived as homogeneous ethnic groups in separate regions of the world, as some people still do, cultural diversity would be less relevant to our daily living. In Japan, where there are 127 million people, of whom 126 million are Japanese, internal cultural differences are minimal compared with those found in Los Angeles, where the public schools have coped with 82 different languages (Iyer, 1993).

Increasingly, cultural diversity surrounds us. More and more we live in a global village, connected to our fellow villagers by e-mail, jumbo jets, and international trade. "American" jeans were invented by German immigrant Levi Strauss by combining Genes, the trouser style of Genoese sailors, with denim cloth from a French town (Legrain, 2003). The death of Princess Diana, an unknown pundit has said, typifies globalization. "An English princess with an Egyptian boyfriend crashes in a French tunnel, driving a German car with a Dutch engine, driven by a Belgian who was high on Scotch whiskey, followed closely by Italian paparazzi on Japanese motorcycles, and gets treated by an American doctor using medicines from Brazil." Cultural diversity exists within nations, too. The United Kingdom, Canada, the United States, and Australia each offer a national culture, with a prevalent language, national media, national holidays, and a democratic political system. But they also offer distinct regional cultures marked by clustered immigrant populations, various languages, and distinct climates, dialects, and values. In the United States, for example, New Englanders' valuing of broadmindedness and autonomy ("Live Free or Die" is the New Hampshire motto) differs from Southerners' greater valuing of warmth, cooperation, and honor (Plaut & others, 2002).

Migration and refugee evacuations are mixing cultures more than ever. "East is East and West is West, and never the twain shall meet," wrote the nineteenth-century British author Rudyard Kipling. But today, East and West, and North and South, meet all the time. Italy is home to many Albanians, Germany to Turks, England to Pakistanis, and the result is both friendship and hate crimes. For North Americans and Australians, too, one's country is more and more a mingling of cultures. One in six Canadians is an immigrant. As we work, play, and live with people from diverse cultural backgrounds, it helps to understand how our cultures influence us and to appreciate important ways in which cultures differ. In a world divided by conflicts, genuine peace requires respect for differences and appreciation for similarities.

To realize the impact of our own culture, we need only confront another one. American males may feel uncomfortable when Middle Eastern heads of state greet the U.S. president with a kiss on the cheek. A German student, accustomed to speaking

Cultures mixing. As these London schoolmates illustrate (one of Muslim heritage, the other Anglo Saxon), immigration and globalization are bringing once-distant cultures together.

"Women kiss women good night. Men kiss women good night. But men do not kiss men good night— especially in Armonk."

Although some norms are universal, every culture has its own norms—rules for accepted and expected social behavior. Copyright © The New Yorker Collection, 1979, J. B. Handelsman, from cartoonbank.com. All Rights Reserved.

norms
Rules for accepted and expected behavior. Norms prescribe "proper" behavior. (In a different sense of the word, norms also describe *what most others do—what is normal.)*

rarely to "Herr Professor," considers it strange that at my institution most faculty office doors are open and students stop by freely. An Iranian student on her first visit to an American McDonald's restaurant fumbles around in her paper bag looking for the eating utensils until she sees the other customers eating their french fries with, of all things, their hands. In many areas of the globe, your best manners and mine are serious breaches of etiquette. Foreigners visiting Japan often struggle to master the rules of the social game—when to take their shoes off, how to pour the tea, when to give and open gifts, how to act toward someone higher or lower in the social hierarchy.

Norms: Expected behavior

As etiquette rules illustrate, all cultures have their accepted ideas about appropriate behavior. We often view these social expectations, or **norms,** as a negative force that imprisons people in a blind effort to perpetuate tradition. Norms do restrain and control us—so successfully and so subtly that we hardly sense their existence. Like fish in the ocean, each of us is so immersed in our cultures that we must leap out of them to understand their influence. "When we see other Dutch people behaving in what foreigners would call a Dutch way," note Dutch psychologists Willem Koomen and Anton Dijker (1997), "we often do not realize that the behavior is typically Dutch."

There is no better way to learn the norms of our culture than to visit another culture and see that its members do things *that* way, whereas we do them *this* way. When living in Scotland, I acknowledged to my children that, yes, Europeans eat meat with the fork facing down in the left hand. "But we Americans consider it good manners to cut the meat and then transfer the fork to the right hand. I admit it's inefficient. But it's the way *we* do it."

To those who don't accept them, such norms may seem arbitrary and confining. To most in the Western world, the Muslim woman's veil seems arbitrary and confining, but not to most in Muslim cultures. But just as a play moves smoothly when the actors know their lines, so social behavior occurs smoothly when people know what to expect. Norms grease the social machinery. In unfamiliar situations, when the norms may be unclear, we monitor others' behavior and adjust our own accordingly. An individualist visiting a collectivist culture, or vice versa, may at first feel anxious and self-conscious (see Chapter 2). In familiar situations, our words and acts come effortlessly.

Cultures also vary in their norms for expressiveness and personal space. To someone from a relatively formal northern European culture, a person whose roots are in an expressive Mediterranean culture may seem "warm, charming, inefficient, and time-wasting." To the Mediterranean person, the northern European may seem "efficient, cold, and overconcerned with time" (Triandis, 1981). Latin American business executives who arrive late for a dinner engagement may be mystified by how obsessed their North American counterparts are with punctuality.

Personal space is a sort of portable bubble or buffer zone that we like to maintain between ourselves and others. As the situation changes, the bubble varies in size. With strangers we maintain a fairly large personal space, keeping a distance of 4 feet or more between us. On uncrowded buses, or in restrooms or libraries, we protect our space and respect others' space. We let friends come closer, often within 2 or 3 feet.

Individuals differ: Some people prefer more personal space than others (Smith, 1981; Sommer, 1969; Stockdale, 1978). Groups differ, too: Adults maintain more distance than children. Men keep more distance from one another than do women. For reasons unknown, cultures near the equator prefer less space and more touching and hugging. Thus the British and Scandinavians prefer more distance than the French and Arabs; North Americans prefer more space than Latin Americans.

To see the effect of encroaching on another's personal space, play space invader. Stand or sit a foot or so from a friend and strike up a conversation. Does the person fidget, look away, back off, show other signs of discomfort? These are the signs of arousal noted by space-invading researchers (Altman & Vinsel, 1978).

Cultural similarity

Thanks to human adaptability, cultures differ. Yet beneath the veneer of cultural differences, cross-cultural psychologists see "an essential universality" (Lonner, 1980). As members of one species, the processes that underlie our differing behaviors are much the same everywhere. Humans even have cross-cultural norms for conducting war. In the midst of killing one's enemy, there are agreed-upon rules. You are to wear identifiable uniforms, surrender with a gesture of submission, and humanely treat prisoners. (If you can't kill them before they surrender, you should feed them thereafter.) When Iraqi forces violated these norms by showing surrender flags and then attacking, and by dressing soldiers as liberated civilians to set up ambushes, a U.S. military spokesperson complained that "Both of these actions are among the most serious violations of the laws of war" (Clarke, 2003).

Although norms vary by culture, humans hold some norms in common. Best known is the taboo against incest: Parents are not to have sexual relations with their children, nor siblings with one another. Although the taboo apparently is violated more often than psychologists once believed, the norm is still universal. Every society disapproves of incest. Given the biological penalties for inbreeding, evolutionary psychologists can easily understand why people everywhere are predisposed against incest.

People everywhere also have some common norms for friendship. From studies conducted in Britain, Italy, Hong Kong, and Japan, Michael Argyle and Monika Henderson (1985) noted several cultural variations in the norms that define the role of friend (in Japan it's especially important not to embarrass a friend with public criticism). But there are also some apparently universal norms: Respect the friend's privacy; make eye contact while talking; don't divulge things said in confidence. These are among the rules of the friendship game. Break them and the game is over.

Around the world, people tend to describe others as more or less stable, outgoing, open, agreeable, and conscientious (John & Srivastava, 1999; McCrae & Costa, 1999). If a test specifies where you stand on these "Big Five" personality dimensions, it pretty well describes your personality, no matter where you live.

personal space
The buffer zone we like to maintain around our bodies. Its size depends on our familiarity with whoever is near us.

"Some 30 inches from my nose, the frontier of my person goes."
—W. H. Auden, 1907–1973

www.mhhe.com/myers8
What are the effects of personal space? Visit the Online Learning Center for an interactivity.

"I am confident that [if] modern psychology had developed in, let us say, India, the psychologists there would have discovered most of the principles discovered by the Westerners."
—Cross-cultural psychologist John E. Williams (1993)

figure 5–2
Leung and Bond's universal social belief dimensions.

The Big Five Social Beliefs	Sample Questionnaire Item
Cynicism	"Powerful people tend to exploit others."
Social complexity	"One has to deal with matters according to the specific circumstances."
Reward for application	"One will succeed if he/she really tries."
Spirituality	"Religious faith contributes to good mental health."
Fate control	"Fate determines one's success and failures."

In The Female Eunuch, *Germaine Greer notes how the language of affection reduces women to foods and baby animals—honey, lamb, sugar, sweetie-pie, kitten, chick.*

Likewise, say Hong Kong social psychologists Kwok Leung and Michael Harris Bond (2004), there are five universal dimensions of social beliefs. In each of the 38 countries they studied, people vary in the extent to which they endorse and apply these social understandings in their daily lives: cynicism, social complexity, reward for application, spirituality, and fate control (Figure 5–2). People's adherence to these social beliefs appears to guide their living. Those who espouse cynicism express lower life satisfaction and favor assertive influence tactics and right-wing politics. Those who espouse reward for application are inclined to invest themselves in study, planning, and competing.

Roger Brown (1965, 1987; Kroger & Wood, 1992) noticed another universal norm. Wherever people form status hierarchies, they also talk to higher-status people in the respectful way they often talk to strangers. And they talk to lower-status people in the more familiar, first-name way they speak to friends. Patients call their physician "Dr. So and So"; the physician often replies using the patients' first names. Students and professors typically address one another in a similarly nonmutual way.

Most languages have two forms of the English pronoun "you": a respectful form and a familiar form (for example, *Sie* and *du* in German, *vous* and *tu* in French, *usted* and *tu* in Spanish). People typically use the familiar form with intimates and subordinates (not only with close friends and family members but also in speaking to children and dogs). A German child receives a boost when strangers begin addressing the child as "Sie" instead of "du."

Norms—rules for accepted and expected behavior—vary by culture.

"Look, everyone here loves vanilla, right? So let's start there."

This first aspect of Brown's universal norm—that *forms of address communicate not only social distance but also social status*—correlates with a second aspect: *Advances in intimacy are usually suggested by the higher-status person.* In Europe, where most twosomes begin a relationship with the polite, formal "you" and may eventually progress to the more intimate "you," someone obviously has to initiate the increased intimacy. Whom do you suppose does so? On some congenial occasion, the elder or richer or more distinguished of the two may say, "Why don't we say *du* to one another?"

This norm extends beyond language to every type of advance in intimacy. It is more acceptable to borrow a pen from or put a hand on the shoulder of one's intimates and subordinates than to behave in such a casual way with strangers or superiors. Similarly, the president of my college invites faculty to his home before they invite him to theirs. In general, then, the higher-status person is the pacesetter in the progression toward intimacy.

So, some norms are culture-specific, others are universal. The force of culture appears in varying norms, and also in the roles that people play. Cultures everywhere influence people by engaging them in playing certain roles. Chapter 4 illustrated a powerful phenomenon: Playing a role often leads people to internalize their behavior. Acting becomes believing. So let's consider how roles vary within and across cultures.

SOCIAL ROLES

> All the world's a stage,
> And all the men and women merely players:
> They have their exits and their entrances;
> And one man in his time plays many parts.
> —William Shakespeare

Role theorists assume, as did William Shakespeare, that social life is like acting on a theatrical stage, with all its scenes, masks, and scripts. Like the role of Jaques, who speaks these lines in *As You Like It,* social roles outlast those who play them. The roles of parent, student, and friend will continue after we have discontinued. These roles allow some freedom of interpretation to those who act them out; great performances are defined by the way the role is played. Some aspects of any role *must* be performed, however. A student must at least show up for exams, turn in papers, and maintain some minimum grade point average.

When only a few norms are associated with a social category (for example, sidewalk pedestrians should keep to the right and not jaywalk), we do not regard the position as a social role. It takes a whole cluster of norms to define a role. I could readily generate a long list of norms prescribing my activities as a professor or as a father. Although I may acquire my particular image by violating the least important norms (valuing efficiency, I rarely arrive early for anything), violating my role's most important norms (failing to meet classes, abusing my children) could lead to my being fired or having my children removed from my care.

Roles have powerful effects. In Chapter 4, we noted that we tend to absorb our roles. On a first date or on a new job, you may act the role self-consciously. As you internalize the role, self-consciousness subsides. What felt awkward now feels genuine.

This is the experience of many refugees, immigrants, missionaries, Peace Corps workers, and international students and executives. After arriving in a new country, it takes time to learn how to talk and act appropriately in the new context. Once adapted, the almost universal experience of those who repatriate back to their home country is reentry distress (Sussman, 2000). Home sweet home is no longer quite so sweet. In ways one may not have been aware, one's behavior, values, and identity will have shifted to accommodate the role of citizen in a different place. One must reacculturate before being back in sync.

The case of kidnapped newspaper heiress Patricia Hearst illustrates the power of role playing. In 1974, while held by some young revolutionaries who called themselves the Symbionese Liberation Army (SLA), Hearst renounced her former life, her wealthy parents, and her fiancé. Announcing that she had joined her captors, she asked that people "try to understand the changes I've gone through." Twelve days later, a bank camera recorded her participation in an SLA armed holdup.

Heiress Patricia Hearst as "Tanya" the revolutionary and as a suburban socialite.

Nineteen months later, Hearst was apprehended and, after two years' incarceration and "deprogramming," she resumed her role as an heiress. Then she became a suburban Connecticut mother and author who devotes much of her time to charitable causes (Johnson, 1988; Schiffman, 1999). If Patricia Hearst had really been a dedicated revolutionary all along, or had she only pretended to cooperate with her captors, people could have understood her actions. What they could not understand (and what therefore helped make this one of the biggest news stories of the 1970s) was, as Philip Brickman wrote, "that she could really be an heiress, really a revolutionary, and then perhaps really an heiress again." It's mind-blowing. Surely, this could not happen to you or me—or could it?

Yes and no. As we'll see in the last section of this chapter, our actions depend not only on the social situation but also on our dispositions. Not everyone responds in the same way to pressure. In Patricia Hearst's predicament, you and I might respond differently. Nevertheless, some social situations can move most "normal" people to behave in "abnormal" ways. This is clear from experiments that put well-intentioned people in bad situations to see whether good or evil prevails. To a dismaying extent, evil wins. Nice guys often don't finish nice.

High- and low-status roles

In George Orwell's *Animal Farm*, the livestock overthrow their human masters and form an egalitarian society in which "all animals are equal." As the story unfolds, the pigs—who assume the managerial role—soon evade chores and accept comforts they consider appropriate to their status. "All animals are equal," they affirm, "but some animals are more equal than others."

Lawrence Messé, Norbert Kerr, and David Sattler (1992) note that the effects of status on self-perceptions aren't limited to Orwell's pigs. In many everyday and laboratory situations, people who are assigned a superior status come to see themselves as meriting favorable treatment or as capable of superior performance. Ronald Humphrey (1985) showed this when he set up a simulated business office. By lottery, some people became managers, others clerks. As in real offices, the managers gave orders to the clerks and did higher-level work. Afterward, both clerks and managers perceived the equally able (randomly assigned) managers as more intelligent, assertive, and supportive—as really being more like leaders.

Likewise, playing a *subservient* role can have demeaning effects. Ellen Langer and Ann Benevento (1978) discovered this when they had pairs of New York City women solve arithmetic problems. After solving the problems individually, the women solved some problems together, with one of the women designated "boss" and the other "assistant." When they then went back to working individually, the "bosses" now solved more problems than they had in the first round, and the "assistants" solved fewer. Similar effects of assigned status on performance have been found in experiments with elementary schoolchildren (Jemmott & Gonzalez, 1989; Musser & Graziano, 1991). Demeaning roles undermine self-efficacy.

> "It is the peculiar triumph of society—and its loss—that it is able to convince those people to whom it has given inferior status of the reality of this decree."
> —James Baldwin, *Notes of a Native Son*, 1955

Role reversal

Role playing can also be a positive force. By intentionally playing a new role, people sometimes change themselves or empathize with people whose roles differ from their own. In George Bernard Shaw's *Pygmalion*, Eliza Doolittle, the

Cockney flower vendor, discovers that if she plays the role of a lady and is viewed by others as a lady, then she in fact is a lady. What wasn't real now is.

Roles often come in pairs defined by relationships—parent and child, husband and wife, teacher and student, doctor and patient, employer and employee, police and citizen. Role reversals can help each understand the other. The problem with much human conversation and argument, observed La Rochefoucauld, is that people pay more attention to their own utterances than to giving exact answers to questions. "Even the most charming and clever do little more than appear attentive . . . so anxious are they to return to their own ideas" (1665, No. 139). A negotiator or group leader can therefore create better communication by having the two sides reverse roles, with each arguing the other's position. Or each side can be asked to restate the other party's point (to the other's satisfaction) before replying. The next time you get into a difficult argument with a friend or parent, try to stop it in the middle. If each of you will restate the other's perceptions and feelings before going on with your own, your mutual understanding will increase.

"Great Spirit, grant that I may not criticize my neighbor until I have walked for a moon in his moccasins."
—Native American prayer

So far in this chapter we have affirmed our biological kinship as members of one human family. We have acknowledged our cultural diversity. And we have noted how norms and roles vary within and across cultures. Remember that our primary quest in social psychology is not to catalog differences but to identify universal principles of behavior. Our aim is what cross-cultural psychologist Walter Lonner (1989) calls "a universalistic psychology—a psychology that is as valid and meaningful in Omaha and Osaka as it is in Rome and Botswana."

Attitudes and behaviors will always vary with culture, but the processes by which attitudes influence behavior vary much less. People in Nigeria and Japan define teen roles differently than do those in Europe and North America, but in all cultures role expectations guide social relations. G. K. Chesterton had the idea nearly a century ago: When someone "has discovered why men in Bond Street wear black hats he will at the same moment have discovered why men in Timbuctoo wear red feathers."

Summing up

How are we humans alike, how do we differ—and why? Evolutionary psychologists study how natural selection favors traits that promote the perpetuation of one's genes. Although part of evolution's legacy is our human capacity to learn and adapt (and therefore to differ from one another), the *evolutionary perspective* highlights the kinship that results from our shared human nature.

The *cultural perspective* highlights human diversity—the behaviors, ideas, and traditions that help define a group and that are transmitted across generations. The remarkable diversity of attitudes and behaviors from one culture to another indicates the extent to which we are the products of cultural norms and roles.

Yet cross-cultural psychologists also seek to identify the "essential universality" of all people. For example, despite their differences, cultures share some norms in common. One apparently universal norm concerns how people of unequal status relate to one another.

All cultures assign people to social roles. Playing cultural roles often leads people to internalize their behavior. Switching roles can therefore change our perspective.

How are gender similarities and differences explained?

Both evolutionary psychologists and psychologists working from a cultural perspective have sought to explain gender variations. Before considering their views, let's look at the basic issues: As males and females, how are we alike? How do we differ? And why?

There are many obvious dimensions of human diversity—height, weight, hair color, to name just a few. But for people's self-concepts and social relationships, the two dimensions that matter most, and that people first attune to, are race and, especially, sex (Stangor & others, 1992). Height and hair may influence our self-concepts and identities, our selecting of friends and mates, and how others regard and treat us. But ethnicity and sex matter much more. When you were born, the first thing people wanted to know about you was, "Is it a boy or a girl?" When a hermaphrodite child is born with a combination of male and female sex organs, physicians and family traditionally have felt compelled to assign the child a sex and to diminish the ambiguity surgically. The simple message: Everyone *must* be assigned a sex. Between day and night there is dusk. But between male and female there is, socially speaking, essentially nothing.

In Chapter 9, we will consider how race and sex affect the way others regard and treat us. For now, let's consider **gender**—the characteristics people associate with male and female. What behaviors *are* universally characteristic and expected of males? Of females?

"Of the 46 chromosomes in the human genome, 45 are unisex," notes Judith Rich Harris (1998). Females and males are therefore similar in many physical traits, such as age of sitting, teething, and walking. They also are alike in many psychological traits, such as overall vocabulary, creativity, intelligence, self-esteem, and happiness. Women and men feel the same emotions and longings, both dote on their children, and have similar-appearing brains (though men have more neurons and women have more neural connections). Your "opposite sex" is actually your nearly identical sex.

So shall we conclude that men and women are essentially the same, except for a few anatomical oddities that hardly matter apart from special occasions? Actually, there are some differences, and it is these differences, not the many similarities, that capture attention and make news. In both science and everyday life, differences excite interest. Compared with males, the average female

- has 70 percent more fat, 40 percent less muscle, and is five inches shorter;
- is more sensitive to smells and sounds; and
- is doubly vulnerable to anxiety disorders and depression.

Compared with females, the average male is

- slower to enter puberty (by two years) but quicker to die (by five years);
- three times more likely to commit suicide, four times more likely to be taking Ritalin for ADHD, five times more likely to become alcoholic, and six times more likely to be killed by lightning; and
- more likely to be capable of wiggling the ears.

gender
In psychology, the characteristics, whether biological or socially influenced, by which people define male and female.

Even in physical traits, individual differences among men and among women far exceed the average differences between the sexes. Don Schollander's world-record-setting 4 minutes, 12 seconds in the 400-meter freestyle swim at the 1964 Olympics would have placed him seventh against the women racing in the 2000 Olympics and 7 seconds behind winner Brooke Bennett.

"There should be no qualms about the forthright study of racial and gender differences; science is in desperate need of good studies that . . . inform us of what we need to do to help underrepresented people to succeed in this society. Unlike the ostrich, we cannot afford to hide our heads for fear of socially uncomfortable discoveries."
—Developmental psychologist Sandra Scarr (1988)

"In the different voice of women lies the truth of an ethic of care."
—Carol Gilligan, *In a Different Voice*, 1982

During the 1970s, many scholars worried that studies of such gender differences might reinforce stereotypes. Would gender differences be construed as women's deficits? Focusing attention on gender differences will provide "battle weapons against women" warned sociologist Jesse Bernard (1976, p. 13). Explanations for differences usually do focus on the group that's seen as different. In discussing the "gender gap" in national elections, for example, commentators more often wonder why women so often vote liberal than why men so often vote conservative. People ask why Asian heritage students so often excel in math and science, not why other groups less often excel. In each case, people define the standard by one group and wonder why the other is "different." People more often wonder what causes homosexuality than what causes heterosexuality (or what determines sexual orientation). From "different" it sometimes is but a short leap to "deviant" or "substandard."

Since the 1980s scholars have felt freer to explore gender diversity. Initially, gender difference research supported gender equality by reducing overblown stereotypes. Then, during the 1980s and 1990s, reports Alice Eagly (1995), many studies revealed gender differences—differences as large as "important" behavior differences in other areas of psychology. Although the findings confirm some stereotypes of women—as less physically aggressive, more nurturant, and more socially sensitive—those are traits that many feminists celebrate and most people prefer (Prentice & Carranza, 2002; Swim, 1994). Small wonder, then, that most people rate their beliefs and feelings regarding "women" as more *favorable* than their feelings regarding "men" (Eagly, 1994; Haddock & Zanna, 1994).

Let's compare men's and women's social connections, dominance, aggressiveness, and sexuality. Having described these differences, we can then consider how the evolutionary and cultural perspectives might explain them. Do gender differences reflect tendencies predisposed by natural selection? Are they culturally constructed—a reflection of the roles that men and women often play and the situations in which they act? Or do both genes and culture bend the genders?

INDEPENDENCE VERSUS CONNECTEDNESS

Individual men display outlooks and behavior that vary from fierce competitiveness to caring nurturance. So do individual women. Without denying that, psychologists Nancy Chodorow (1978, 1989), Jean Baker Miller (1986), and Carol Gilligan and her colleagues (1982, 1990) have contended that women more than men give priority to close, intimate relationships.

Compared with boys, girls talk more intimately and play less aggressively, notes Eleanor Maccoby (2002) from her decades of research on gender development. And as they each interact with their own gender, their differences grow.

As adults, women in individualist cultures describe themselves in more relational terms, welcome more help, experience more relationship-linked emotions, and are more attuned to others' relationships (Addis & Mahalik, 2003; Gabriel & Gardner, 1999; Tamres & others, 2002; Watkins & others, 1998, 2003). In conversation, men more often focus on tasks and on connections with large groups, women on personal relationships (Tannen, 1990). When on the phone, women's conversations with friends last longer (Smoreda & Licoppe, 2000). When on the computer, women spend more time sending e-mails, in which they express more emotion (Crabtree, 2002; Thomson & Murachver, 2001). When in groups, women share more of their lives, and offer more support

Girls' play is often in small groups and imitates relationships. Boys' play is more often competitive or aggressive.

(Dindia & Allen, 1992; Eagly, 1987). When facing stress, men tend to respond with "fight or flight"; often, their response to a threat is combat. In nearly all studies, notes Shelley Taylor (2002), stressed women more often "tend and befriend"; they turn to friends and family for support. Among first-year college students, 5 in 10 males and 7 in 10 females say it is *very* important to "help others who are in difficulty" (Sax & others, 2002).

In general, report Felicia Pratto and her colleagues (1997), men gravitate disproportionately to jobs that enhance inequalities (prosecuting attorney, corporate advertising); women gravitate to jobs that reduce inequalities (public defender, advertising work for a charity). Studies of 640,000 people's job preferences reveal some tendency for men more than women to value earnings, promotion, challenge, and power, and for women more than men to value good hours, personal relationships, and opportunities to help others (Konrad & others, 2000). Indeed, in most of the North American caregiving professions, such as social worker, teacher, and nurse, women outnumber men. Women also seem more charitable: Among individuals leaving estates worth more than $5 million, 48 percent of women and 35 percent of men make a charitable bequest, and women's colleges have unusually supportive alumni (National Council for Research on Women, 1994).

Women's connections as mothers, daughters, sisters, and grandmothers bind families (Rossi & Rossi, 1990). Women spend more time caring for both preschoolers and aging parents (Eagly & Crowley, 1986). Compared with men, they buy three times as many gifts and greeting cards, write two to four times as many personal letters, and make 10 to 20 percent more long distance calls to friends and family (Putnam, 2000). Asked to provide photos that portray who they are, women include more photos of parents and of themselves with others (Clancy & Dollinger, 1993). For women, especially, a sense of mutual support is crucial to marital satisfaction (Acitelli & Antonucci, 1994).

Smiling, of course, varies with situations. Yet across more than 400 studies, women's greater connectedness has been expressed in their generally higher rate of smiling (LaFrance & others, 2003). For example, when Marianne LaFrance (1985) analyzed 9,000 college yearbook photos and when Amy Halberstadt and Martha Saitta (1987) studied 1,100 magazine and newspaper

"Contrary to what many women believe, it's fairly easy to develop a long-term, stable, intimate, and mutually fulfilling relationship with a guy. Of course this guy has to be a Labrador retriever."
—Dave Barry, *Dave Barry's Complete Guide to Guys*, 1995

Empathy is feeling what another feels, as 7-year-old Lamar Pugh seemingly does.

empathy
The vicarious experience of another's feelings; putting oneself in another's shoes.

photos and 1,300 people in shopping malls, parks, and streets, they consistently found that females were more likely to smile.

When surveyed, women are far more likely to describe themselves as having **empathy,** or being able to feel what another feels—to rejoice with those who rejoice and weep with those who weep. Although to a lesser extent, the empathy difference extends to laboratory studies. Shown slides or told stories, girls react with more empathy (Hunt, 1990). Given upsetting experiences in the laboratory or in real life, women more than men express empathy for others enduring similar experiences (Batson & others, 1996). Women are more likely to cry or report feeling distressed at another's distress (Eisenberg & Lennon, 1983). Twelve percent of American men, and 43 percent of women, report having cried as a result of the war in Iraq (Gallup, 2003). Autism, which is a deficiency in empathy, is mostly a disorder of males.

All this helps explain why, compared to friendships with men, both men and women report friendships with women to be more intimate, enjoyable, and nurturing (Rubin, 1985; Sapadin, 1988). When they want empathy and understanding, someone to whom they can disclose their joys and hurts, both men and women usually turn to women.

One explanation for this male-female empathy difference is that women tend to outperform men at reading others' emotions. In her analysis of 125 studies of men's and women's sensitivity to nonverbal cues, Judith Hall (1984) discerned that women are generally superior at decoding others' emotional messages. For example, shown a 2-second silent film clip of the face of an upset woman, women guess more accurately whether she is criticizing someone or discussing her divorce. Women's sensitivity to nonverbal cues helps explain their greater emotional responsiveness in both depressing and joyful situations (Grossman & Wood, 1993; Sprecher & Sedikides, 1993; Stoppard & Gruchy, 1993). Women also

foresee more complex and nuanced emotions when given possible scenarios (if a friend in your line of work received a work-related prize, how would your friend feel and how would you feel [Barrett & others, 2000]?).

To study people's "empathic accuracy," William Ickes (2003) and his colleagues have videotaped many interactions between two people (sometimes strangers, sometimes friends or spouses or client and therapist). Then they ask each conversation partner to watch the tape, stopping at whatever points they had a specific thought or feeling (and recording what it was). Then the tape is replayed again, and an observer (sometimes the other conversation partner) is asked to guess what the first person was thinking or feeling at each of those moments.

Empathic accuracy is greatest when reading the minds of friends rather than strangers. But some people are generally easier to read. And some people are better readers. Women's empathic accuracy tends, on average, to surpass men's (Thomas & Fletcher, 2003). Women also have been found to more accurately remember facial features and other aspects of appearance (Horgan & others, 2004).

Women also are more skilled at *expressing* emotions nonverbally, reports Hall. This is especially so for positive emotion, report Erick Coats and Robert Feldman (1996). They had people talk about times they had been happy, sad, and angry. When shown 5-second silent video clips of these reports, observers could much more accurately discern women's than men's emotions when recalling happiness. Men, however, were slightly more successful in conveying anger.

Whether considered feminine or human, traits such as gentleness, sensitivity, and warmth are a boon to close relationships. In a study of married couples in Sydney, Australia, John Antill (1983) found that when either the husband or wife had these traditionally feminine qualities—or better, when *both* did—marital satisfaction was higher. People find marriage rewarding when their spouses are nurturant and emotionally supportive.

What do you think: Should Western women become more self-reliant and more attuned to their culture's individualism? Or might women's relational approach to life help transform power-oriented Western societies (marked by high levels of child neglect, loneliness, and depression) into more caring communities?

SOCIAL DOMINANCE

Imagine two people: One is "adventurous, autocratic, coarse, dominant, forceful, independent, and strong." The other is "affectionate, dependent, dreamy, emotional, submissive, and weak." If the first person sounds more to you like a man and the second like a woman, you are not alone, report John Williams and Deborah Best (1990a, p. 15). From Asia to Africa and Europe to Australia, people rate men as more dominant, driven, and aggressive.

These perceptions and expectations correlate with reality. In essentially every society, men *are* socially dominant. In no known societies do women dominate men (Pratto, 1996). As we will see, gender differences vary greatly by culture, and gender differences are shrinking over time as women assume more managerial and leadership positions. Yet consider:

- Women in 2002 were but 14 percent of the world's legislators and 5 percent of prime ministers and presidents (CIA, 2002; IPU, 2002). Women are 1 percent of the chief executives of the world's 500 largest corporations (Eagly & others, 2003).
- Men more than women are concerned with social dominance and are more likely to favor conservative political candidates and programs that

preserve group inequality (Eagly & others, 2003; Sidanius & Pratto, 1999).

- Men are half of all jurors but 90 percent of elected jury leaders and most of the leaders of ad hoc laboratory groups (Davis & Gilbert, 1989; Kerr & others, 1982).
- Women's wages in industrial countries average 77 percent of men's. About one-fifth of the wage gap is attributable to gender differences in education, work experience, or job characteristics (World Bank, 2003).

As is typical of those in higher-status positions, men still initiate most of the inviting for first dates, do most of the driving, and pick up most of the tabs (Laner & Ventrone, 1998, 2000).

Men's style of communicating undergirds their social power. In situations where roles aren't rigidly scripted, men tend to be directive, women to be democratic (Eagly & Johnson, 1990). In leadership roles, men tend to excel as directive, task-focused leaders; women excel more often in the "transformational" leadership that is favored by more and more organizations, with inspirational and social skills that build team spirit (Eagly & others, 2003). Men more than women place priority on winning, getting ahead, and dominating others (Sidanius & others, 1994). They also take more risks (Byrnes & others, 1999). When they lead democratically, women leaders are evaluated as favorably as men. When they lead autocratically, women are evaluated less favorably than men (Eagly & others, 1992). People will accept a man's "strong, assertive" leadership more readily than a woman's "pushy, aggressive" leadership.

In writing, women tend to use more communal prepositions ("with"), fewer quantitative words, and more present tense. One computer program, which taught itself to recognize gender differences in word usage and sentence structure, successfully identified the author's gender of 80 percent of 920 British fiction and nonfiction works (Koppel & others, 2002).

In conversation, men's style reflects their concern for independence, women's for connectedness. Men are more likely to act as powerful people often do—talking assertively, interrupting intrusively, touching with the hand, staring more, smiling less (Anderson & Leaper, 1998; Carli, 1991; Ellyson & others, 1991). Stating the results from a female perspective, women's influence style tends to be more indirect—less interruptive, more sensitive, more polite, less cocky.

So is it right to declare (in the title words of one 1990s best seller) *Men Are from Mars, Women Are from Venus*? Actually, note Kay Deaux and Marianne LaFrance (1998),

"After years of analyzing what makes leaders most effective and figuring out who's got the Right Stuff, management gurus now know how to boost the odds of getting a great executive: Hire a female."

—Rochelle Sharpe, in *Business Week*, 2000

"That was a fine report, Barbara. But since the sexes speak different languages, I probably didn't understand a word of it."

men's and women's conversational styles vary with the social context. Much of the style we attribute to men is typical of people (men and women) in positions of status and power. Moreover, individuals vary; some men are characteristically hesitant and deferential, some women direct and assertive. Clearly, it oversimplifies to suggest that women and men are from different emotional planets.

Aware of the varying yet oft-reported gender communication difference, Nancy Henley (1977) has argued that women should stop feigning smiles, averting their eyes, and tolerating interruptions and should instead look people in the eye and speak assertively. When Jean Twenge (2001) studied women's self-reported assertiveness over the years since 1931, she found that in eras when women's social status rose, they *did* become more assertive. Judith Hall (1984), nevertheless, values women's less autocratic communication style, noting, "Whenever it is assumed that women's nonverbal behavior is undesirable, yet another myth is perpetuated: that male behavior is normal and that it is women's behavior that is deviant and in need of explanation" (pp. 152–153).

AGGRESSION

By **aggression,** psychologists mean behavior intended to hurt. Throughout the world, hunting, fighting, and warring are primarily male activities. In surveys, men admit to more aggression than do women. In laboratory experiments, men indeed exhibit more physical aggression, for example, by administering what they believe are hurtful electric shocks (Knight & others, 1996). In Canada, the male-to-female arrest ratio is 8 to 1 for murder (Statistics Canada, 2001). In the

United States, where 92 percent of prisoners are male, it is 10 to 1 (FBI, 2001). But once again, the gender difference fluctuates with the context. When there is provocation, the gender gap shrinks (Bettencourt & Miller, 1996). And within less assaultive forms of aggression—say, slapping a family member, throwing something, or verbally attacking someone—women are no less aggressive than men (Björkqvist, 1994; White & Kowalski, 1994). Indeed, says John Archer (2000, 2002) from his statistical digests of dozens of studies, women may be slightly more likely

aggression
Physical or verbal behavior intended to hurt someone. In laboratory experiments, this might mean delivering electric shocks or saying something likely to hurt another's feelings.

"It's a guy thing."

to commit an aggressive act. But men are more likely to inflict an injury; 62 percent of those injured by a partner are women.

SEXUALITY

There is also a gender gap in sexual attitudes and assertiveness. It's true that, in their physiological and subjective responses to sexual stimuli, women and men are "more similar than different" (Griffitt, 1987). Yet consider:

- "I can imagine myself being comfortable and enjoying 'casual' sex with different partners," agreed 48 percent of men and 12 percent of women in an Australian survey (Bailey & others, 2000).
- The American Council on Education's recent survey of a quarter million first-year college students offers a similar finding. "If two people really like each other, it's all right for them to have sex even if they've known each other for only a very short time," agreed 53 percent of men but only 30 percent of women (Sax & others, 2002).
- In a survey of 3,400 randomly selected 18- to 59-year-old Americans, half as many men (25 percent) as women (48 percent) cited affection for the partner as a reason for first intercourse. How often do they think about sex? "Every day" or "several times a day," said 19 percent of women and 54 percent of men (Laumann & others, 1994).

The gender difference in sexual attitudes carries over to behavior. "With few exceptions anywhere in the world," report cross-cultural psychologist Marshall Segall and his colleagues (1990, p. 244), "males are more likely than females to initiate sexual activity." Compared with lesbians, gay men also report more interest in uncommitted sex, more responsiveness to visual stimuli, and more concern with partner attractiveness (Bailey & others, 1994). "It's not that gay men are oversexed," observes Steven Pinker (1997). "They are simply men whose male desires bounce off other male desires rather than off female desires."

Indeed, observe Roy Baumeister and Kathleen Vohs (in press; Baumeister & others, 2001), men not only fantasize more about sex, have more permissive attitudes, and seek more partners, they also are more quickly aroused, desire sex more often, masturbate more frequently, are less successful at celibacy, refuse sex less often, take more risks, expend more resources to gain sex, and prefer more sexual variety. One survey asked 16,288 people from 52 nations how many sexual partners they desired in the next month. Among those unattached, 29 percent of men and 6 percent of women wanted more than one partner (Schmitt, 2003). These results were nearly identical for both straight and gay people (29 percent of gay men and 6 percent of lesbians desired more than one partner).

"Everywhere sex is understood to be something females have that males want," offered anthropologist Donald Symons (1979, p. 253). Small wonder, say Baumeister and Vohs, that cultures everywhere attribute greater value to female than male sexuality, as indicated in gender asymmetries in prostitution and courtship, where men generally offer money, gifts, praise, or commitment in implicit exchange for a woman's sexual engagement. In human sexual economics, they note, women rarely if ever pay for sex. Like labor unions opposing "scab labor," which undermines the value of their own labor, most women oppose other women's offering "cheap sex," which reduces the value of their own sexuality. Across 185 countries, the more scarce are available men, the *higher* is the

MALE PROSTITUTE

GREGORY

"Oh yeah, baby, I'll listen to you—I'll listen to you all night long."

teen pregnancy rate—because when men are scarce "women compete against each other by offering sex at a lower price in terms of commitment" (Barber, 2000; Baumeister & Vohs, in press). When women are scarce, the market value of their sexuality rises and they demand greater commitment.

Sexual fantasies express the gender difference (Ellis & Symons, 1990). In male-oriented erotica, women are unattached and lust driven. In romance novels, whose primary market is women, a tender male is emotionally consumed by his devoted passion for the heroine. Social scientists aren't the only ones to have noticed. "Women can be fascinated by a four-hour movie with subtitles wherein the entire plot consists of a man and a woman yearning to have, but never actually having a relationship," observes humorist Dave Barry (1995). "Men HATE that. Men can take maybe 45 seconds of yearning, and they want everybody to get naked. Followed by a car chase. A movie called 'Naked People in Car Chases' would do really well among men."

Summing up

Boys and girls, and men and women, are in many ways alike. Yet their differences attract more attention. Although individual differences among women and among men exceed their gender differences, social psychologists have explored gender differences in *independence* versus *connectedness*. Women typically do more caring, express more empathy and emotion, and define themselves more in terms of relationships. Men and women also tend to exhibit differing social dominance, aggression, and sexuality.

As detectives are more intrigued by crime than virtue, so psychological detectives are more intrigued by differences than similarities. Let us therefore remind ourselves: *Individual* differences far exceed gender differences. Females and males are hardly opposite (altogether different) sexes. Rather, they differ like two folded hands—similar but not the same, fitting together yet differing as they grasp each other.

Evolution and gender: Doing what comes naturally?

In explaining gender differences, inquiry has focused on two culprits: evolution and culture.

www.mhhe.com/myers8
Visit the Online Learning Center for a scenario on gender and dating preferences.

"What do you think is the main reason men and women have different personalities, interests, and abilities?" asked the Gallup Organization (1990) in a national survey. "Is it mainly because of the way men and women are raised, or are the differences part of their biological makeup?" Among the 99 percent who answered the question (apparently without questioning its assumptions), nearly equal numbers answered "upbringing" and "biology."

There are, of course, those salient biological sex differences. Men have the muscle mass to hunt game; women can breast-feed. Are biological sex differences limited to such obvious distinctions in reproduction and physique? Or do men's and women's genes, hormones, and brains differ in ways that also contribute to behavioral differences?

GENDER AND MATING PREFERENCES

Noting the worldwide persistence of gender differences in aggressiveness, dominance, and sexuality, evolutionary psychologist Douglas Kenrick (1987) suggested, as have many others since, that "we cannot change the evolutionary history of our species, and some of the differences between us are undoubtedly a function of that history." Evolutionary psychology predicts no sex differences in all those domains in which the sexes faced similar adaptive challenges (Buss, 1995b). Both sexes regulate heat with sweat, have similar taste preferences to nourish their bodies, and grow calluses where the skin meets friction. But evolutionary psychology does predict sex differences in behaviors relevant to dating, mating, and reproduction.

Consider, for example, the male's greater sexual initiative. The average male produces many trillions of sperm in his lifetime, making sperm cheap compared with eggs. (If you happen to be an average man, you will make more than 1,000 sperm while reading this sentence.) Moreover, while a female brings one fetus to term and then nurses it, a male can spread his genes by fertilizing many females. Thus, say evolutionary psychologists, females invest their reproductive opportunities carefully, by looking for signs of health and resources. Males compete with other males for chances to win the genetic sweepstakes by sending their genes into the future. Women seek to reproduce wisely, men widely. Men seek fertile soil in which to plant their seed. Women seek men who will help them tend the garden—resourceful and monogamous dads rather than wandering cads. Or so the theory goes.

Moreover, evolutionary psychology suggests, physically dominant males

"I hunt and she gathers—otherwise, we couldn't make ends meet."

gained more access to females, which over generations enhanced male aggression and dominance. Whatever genetically influenced traits enabled Montezuma II to become Aztec king were also perpetuated through offspring from some of his 4,000 women (Wright, 1998). If our ancestral mothers benefited from being able to read their infants' and suitors' emotions, then natural selection may have similarly favored emotion-detecting ability in females. Underlying all these presumptions is a principle: *Nature selects traits that help send one's genes into the future.*

Little of this process is conscious. Few people in the throes of passion stop to think, "I want to give my genes to posterity" (much less, "Oh, how I want to have and raise a baby and have grandchildren!"). Men are not, having done the calculations, driven to line up outside sperm banks. Rather, say evolutionary psychologists, our natural yearnings are our genes' way of making more genes. Emotions execute evolution's dispositions, much as hunger executes the body's need for nutrients.

Lewis Thomas (1971) captured the idea of hidden evolutionary predispositions in his fanciful description of a male moth responding to a female's release of bombykol, a single molecule of which will tremble the hairs of any male within miles and send him driving upwind in a confusion of ardor. But it is doubtful if the moth has an awareness of being caught in an aerosol of chemical attractant. On the contrary, he probably finds suddenly that it has become an excellent day, the weather remarkably bracing, the time appropriate for a bit of exercise of the old wings, a brisk turn upwind.

"Humans are living fossils—collections of mechanisms produced by prior selections pressures," says David Buss (1995a). And that, evolutionary psychologists believe, helps explain not only male aggression but also the differing sexual attitudes and behaviors of females and males. Although a man's interpretation of a woman's smile as sexual interest usually proves wrong, occasionally being right can have reproductive payoff.

Evolutionary psychology also predicts that men will strive to offer what women will desire—external resources and physical protection. Male peacocks strut their feathers, and male humans, their abs, Audis, and assets. In one experiment, teen males rated "having lots of money" as more important if put alone in a room with a teen female (Roney, 2003). "Male achievement is ultimately a courtship display," says Glenn Wilson (1994). Women may balloon their breasts, Botox their wrinkles, and liposuction their fat to offer men the youthful, healthy appearance (connoting fertility) that men desire. Sure enough, note Buss (1994a) and Alan Feingold (1992), women's and men's mate preferences confirm these predictions. Consider:

- Studies in 37 cultures, from Australia to Zambia, reveal that men

Secretariat, one of the greatest racehorses of modern times, sired 400 foals.

"A hen is only an egg's way of making another egg."
—Samuel Butler, 1835–1901

"I thought that sperm-bank donors remained anonymous."

figure 5–3

Human mating preferences.

David Buss and 50 collaborators surveyed more than 10,000 people from all races, religions, and political systems on six continents and five islands. Everywhere, men preferred attractive physical features suggesting youth and health—and reproductive fitness. Everywhere, women preferred men with resources and status.

Source: From Buss, 1994b.

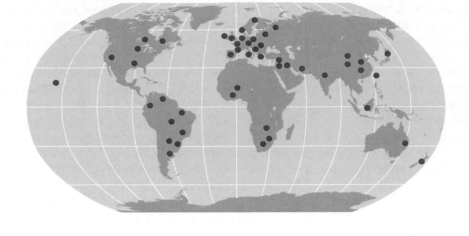

Larry King, 25 years older than seventh wife, Shawn Southwick King.

everywhere feel attracted to women whose physical features, such as youthful faces and forms, suggest fertility. Women everywhere feel attracted to men whose wealth, power, and ambition promise resources for protecting and nurturing offspring (Figure 5–3). Men's greater interest in physical form also makes them the consumers of most of the world's visual pornography. But there are gender similarities, too: Whether residing on an Indonesian island or in urban São Paulo, both women and men desire kindness, love, and mutual attraction.

- Men everywhere tend to marry younger women. Moreover, the older the man, the greater the age difference he prefers when selecting a mate. In their twenties, men prefer, and marry, women only slightly younger. In their sixties, men prefer, and marry, women averaging about ten years younger (Kenrick & Keefe, 1992). Women of all ages prefer men just slightly older than themselves. Once again, say the evolutionary psychologists, we see that natural selection predisposes men to feel attracted to female features associated with fertility.

Reflecting on these findings, Buss (1999) reports feeling somewhat astonished "that men and women across the world differ in their mate preferences in precisely the ways predicted by the evolutionists. Just as our fears of snakes, heights, and spiders provide a window for viewing the survival hazards of our evolutionary ancestors, our mating desires provide a window for viewing the resources our ancestors needed for reproduction. We all carry with us today the desires of our successful forebearers."

GENDER AND HORMONES

If genes predispose gender-related traits, they must do so by their effects on our bodies. In male embryos, the genes direct the formation of testes, which begin to secrete testosterone, the male sex hormone that influences masculine appearance (Berenbaum & Hines, 1992; Hines & Green, 1991). Do hormone differences also predispose psychological gender differences?

The gender gap in aggression does seem influenced by testosterone. In various animals, administering testosterone heightens aggressiveness. In humans, violent male criminals have higher than normal testosterone levels; so do National Football League players and boisterous fraternity members (Dabbs, 2000). Moreover, for both humans and monkeys, the gender difference in aggression appears early in life (before culture has much effect) and wanes as testosterone levels decline during adulthood. No one of these lines of evidence is conclusive. Taken together, they convince many scholars that sex hormones matter. But so, as we will see, does culture.

As people mature to middle age and beyond, a curious thing happens. Women become more assertive and self-confident, men more empathic and less domineering (Lowenthal & others, 1975; Pratt & others, 1990). Hormone changes are one possible explanation for the shrinking gender differences. Role demands are another. Some speculate that during courtship and early parenthood, social expectations lead both sexes to emphasize traits that enhance their roles. While courting, providing, and protecting, men play up their macho sides and forgo their needs for interdependence and nurturance (Gutmann, 1977). While courting and rearing young children, young women restrain their impulses to assert and be independent. As men and women graduate from these early adult roles, they supposedly express more of their restrained tendencies. Each becomes more *androgynous*—capable of both assertiveness and nurturance.

> "The finest people marry the two sexes in their own person."
> —Ralph Waldo Emerson, *Journals*, 1843

REFLECTIONS ON EVOLUTIONARY PSYCHOLOGY

Without disputing natural selection—nature's process of selecting physical and behavioral traits that enhance gene survival—critics see two problems with evolutionary explanations. First, evolutionary psychologists sometimes start with an effect (such as the male-female difference in sexual initiative) and then work backward to construct an explanation for it. This approach is reminiscent of functionalism, a dominant theory in psychology during the 1920s. "Why does that behavior occur? Because it serves such and such a function." The theorist can hardly lose at this hindsight explanation, note biologists Paul Ehrlich and Marcus Feldman (2003). It is, scorned paleontologist Stephen Jay Gould (1997), mere "speculation [and] guesswork in the cocktail-party mode."

The way to prevent the hindsight bias is to imagine things turning out otherwise. Let's try it. Imagine that women were stronger and more physically aggressive. "But of course!" someone might say, "all the better for protecting their young." And if human males were never known to have extramarital affairs, might we not see the evolutionary wisdom behind their fidelity? After all, argues Dorothy Einon (1994), women will mate throughout the menstrual cycle and while pregnant or lactating—which means that a faithful married man is hardly less likely to fertilize a woman than is a similarly sexually active unfaithful man. Moreover, because there is more to bringing offspring to maturity than merely depositing sperm, men and women both gain by investing jointly in their children. Males who are loyal to their mates and offspring are more apt to ensure that their young will survive to perpetuate their genes. Monogamy also increases men's certainty of paternity. (These are, in fact, evolutionary explanations for why humans, and certain other species whose young require a heavy parental investment, tend to pair off and be monogamous. Love between man and woman is universal because of its genetic payoffs: The offspring of devoted males were less vulnerable to predators.)

"Sex differences in behavior may have been relevant to our ancestors gathering roots and hunting squirrels on the plains of Northern Africa, but their manifestations in modern society are less clearly 'adaptive.' Modern society is information oriented—big biceps and gushing testosterone have less direct relevance to the president of a computer firm."

—Douglas Kenrick (1987)

Evolutionary psychologists reply that such criticisms are "flat out wrong." Hindsight, they say, plays no less a role in cultural explanations: Why do women and men differ? Because their culture *socializes* their behavior! When people's roles vary across time and place, "culture" *describes* those roles better than it explains them. And far from being mere hindsight conjecture, say evolutionary psychologists, their field is an empirical science that tests evolutionary predictions with data from animal behavior, cross-cultural observations, and hormonal and genetic studies. As in many scientific fields, observations inspire a theory that generates new, testable predictions (Figure 5–4). The predictions alert us to unnoticed phenomena and allow us to confirm, refute, or revise the theory.

Critics nevertheless worry that evolutionary speculation about sex and gender "reinforces male-female stereotypes" (Small, 1999). Might evolutionary explanations for gang violence, homicidal jealousy, and rape reinforce and justify male aggression as natural? And if evolutionary psychologists persuade more and more people that it is natural, should we all buy home security systems? But remember, reply the evolutionary psychologists, evolutionary wisdom is

figure 5–4

Sample predictions derived from evolutionary psychology by David Buss (1995a).

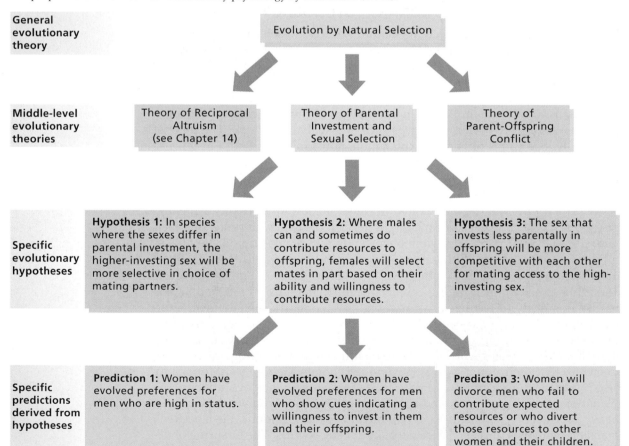

past wisdom. It tells us what behaviors worked in the past. Whether such tendencies are still adaptive is a different question. For example, although people tend to be attracted to potential mates whose appearance and behavior fit typical masculine or feminine images, people actually report more satisfying relationships with those who are androgynous (Ickes, 1993).

Evolutionary psychology's critics acknowledge that evolution helps explain both our commonalities and our differences (a certain amount of diversity aids survival). But they contend our common evolutionary heritage does not, by itself, predict the enormous cultural variation in human marriage patterns (from one spouse to a succession of spouses to multiple wives to multiple husbands to spouse swapping). Nor does it explain cultural changes in behavior patterns over mere decades of time. The most significant trait that nature has endowed us with, it seems, is the capacity to adapt—to learn and to change. Therein lies what all agree is culture's shaping power.

Summing up

Evolutionary psychologists theorize how evolution might have predisposed gender differences in behaviors such as aggression and sexual initiative. Nature's mating game, they suggest, favors males who take sexual initiative toward females—especially those with physical features suggesting fertility—and who seek aggressive dominance in competing with other males. Females, who have a greater stake in not squandering their fewer reproductive chances, place a greater priority on selecting mates with the ability to commit resources to protecting and nurturing their young. Critics say that evolutionary explanations are sometimes after-the-fact conjectures that fail to account for the reality of cultural diversity. What's agreed is that nature endows us with a remarkable capacity to adapt to differing contexts.

Culture and gender: Doing as the culture says?

Culture's influence is vividly illustrated by differing gender roles across place and time.

Culture, as we noted earlier, is what's shared by a large group and transmitted across generations—ideas, attitudes, behaviors, and traditions. We can see the shaping power of culture in ideas about how men and women should behave—and in the scorn that they endure when violating expectations (Kite, 2001). In countries everywhere, girls spend more time helping with housework and child care, while boys spend more time in unsupervised play (Edwards, 1991). Even in contemporary, dual-career, North American marriages, men do most of the household repairs and women arrange the child care (Bianchi & others, 2000; Biernat & Wortman, 1991).

Gender socialization, it has been said, gives girls "roots" and boys "wings." In twentieth-century Caldecott Award children's books, girls were four times more often than boys shown using household objects (such as broom, sewing needle, or pots and pans), and boys were five times more often than girls shown using production objects (such as pitchfork, plow, or gun) (Crabb & Bielawski, 1994). The adult result: "Everywhere," reported the United Nations (1991),

In Western countries, gender roles are becoming more flexible. No longer is preschool teaching necessarily women's work and piloting necessarily men's work.

gender role
A set of behavior expectations (norms) for males and females.

Do you ever present one self to members of your own gender and a different self to members of the other gender?

"women do most household work." And "everywhere, cooking and dishwashing are the least shared household chores." Such behavior expectations for males and females define **gender roles.**

In an experiment with Princeton University undergraduate women, Mark Zanna and Susan Pack (1975) showed the impact of gender-role expectations. The women answered questionnaires on which they described themselves to a tall, unattached, male senior student whom they expected to meet. Those led to believe the man's ideal woman was home oriented and deferential to her husband presented themselves as more traditionally feminine than did women expecting to meet a man who liked strong, ambitious women. Moreover, given a problem-solving test, those expecting to meet the nonsexist man behaved more intelligently: They solved 18 percent more problems than those expecting to meet the man with the traditional views. This adapting of themselves to fit the man's image was much less pronounced if the man was less desirable—a short, already attached freshman. In a companion experiment by Dean Morier and Cara Seroy (1994), men similarly adapted their self-presentations to meet desirable women's gender-role expectations.

Does culture construct gender roles? Or do gender roles merely reflect behavior naturally appropriate for men and women? The variety of gender roles across cultures and over time shows that culture indeed constructs our gender roles.

GENDER ROLES VARY WITH CULTURE

Is life more satisfying when both spouses work and share child care, or when women stay home and care for the children while the husband provides? When the Pew Global Attitudes (2003) survey posed that question to 38,000 people, majorities in 41 of 44 countries said the more satisfying way of life was when both spouses worked in both domains. But as Figure 5–5 shows, the country-to-country differences were considerable. Egyptians disagreed with the world majority opinion by 2 to 1, while Vietnamese concurred by 11 to 1. In industrialized societies, roles vary enormously. Women fill 1 in 10 managerial positions in Japan and Germany and nearly 1 in 2 in Australia and the United States (ILO, 1997; Wallace, 2000). In North America, most doctors and dentists are men; in Russia most doctors are women, as are most dentists in Denmark.

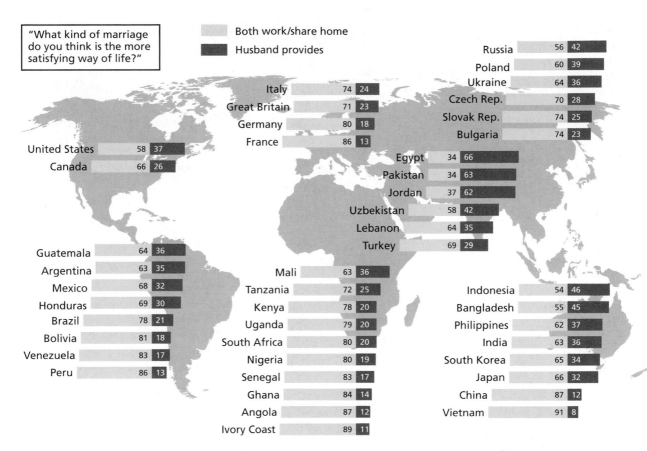

"What kind of marriage do you think is the more satisfying way of life?"

Both work/share home
Husband provides

Italy 74 | 24
Great Britain 71 | 23
Germany 80 | 18
France 86 | 13

United States 58 | 37
Canada 66 | 26

Russia 56 | 42
Poland 60 | 39
Ukraine 64 | 36
Czech Rep. 70 | 28
Slovak Rep. 74 | 25
Bulgaria 74 | 23

Egypt 34 | 66
Pakistan 34 | 63
Jordan 37 | 62
Uzbekistan 58 | 42
Lebanon 64 | 35
Turkey 69 | 29

Guatemala 64 | 36
Argentina 63 | 35
Mexico 68 | 32
Honduras 69 | 30
Brazil 78 | 21
Bolivia 81 | 18
Venezuela 83 | 17
Peru 86 | 13

Mali 63 | 36
Tanzania 72 | 25
Kenya 78 | 20
Uganda 79 | 20
South Africa 80 | 20
Nigeria 80 | 19
Senegal 83 | 17
Ghana 84 | 14
Angola 87 | 12
Ivory Coast 89 | 11

Indonesia 54 | 46
Bangladesh 55 | 45
Philippines 62 | 37
India 63 | 36
South Korea 65 | 34
Japan 66 | 32
China 87 | 12
Vietnam 91 | 8

figure 5–5

Approved gender roles vary with culture.

Source: Data from the 2003 Pew Global Attitudes survey.

GENDER ROLES VARY OVER TIME

In the last half-century—a thin slice of our long history—gender roles have changed dramatically. In 1938, one in five Americans approved "of a married woman earning money in business or industry if she has a husband capable of supporting her." By 1996, four in five approved (Niemi & others, 1989; NORC, 1996). In 1967, 57 percent of first-year American collegians agreed that "the activities of married women are best confined to the home and family." In 2002, only 22 percent agreed (Astin & others, 1987; Sax & others, 2002).

Behavioral changes have accompanied this attitude shift. Between 1960 and 1998, the proportion of 40-year-old married U.S. women in the workforce doubled—from 38 to 75 percent (Bureau of the Census, 1999). A similar influx of women in the workforce has occurred in Canada, Australia, and Britain.

In 1965, the Harvard Business School had never graduated a woman. At the turn of the century, 30 percent of its graduates were women. From 1960 to the end of the century, women as a proportion of graduates rose from 6 to 43 percent in American medical schools and from 3 to 45 percent in law schools (Hunt, 2000). In the mid-1960s, American married women devoted *seven times* as many hours to housework as did their husbands; by the mid-1990s this was down to twice as many hours (Figure 5–6, see page 198). This striking variation of roles across cultures and over time signals that evolution and biology do not fix gender roles: Culture also bends the genders.

Gallup polls: Is it all right for a girl to telephone a boy to ask for a date?

	Percent "Yes"
1950	29%
1999	70%

figure 5-6

Who is doing the housework?

From 1965 to 1995, women were devoting fewer hours to housework tasks, and men more. **Source:** From Bianchi & others, 2000.

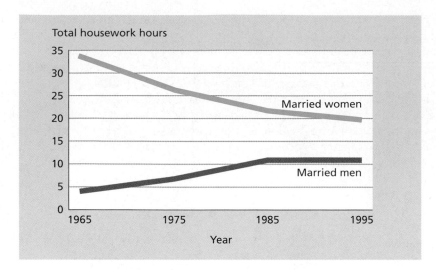

In Western cultures, gender roles are changing, but not this much. DOONESBURY © G. B. Trudeau. Reprinted with permission of Universal Press Syndicate. All Rights Reserved.

PEER-TRANSMITTED CULTURE

Cultures, like ice cream, come in many flavors. On Wall Street, men wear mostly suits and women wear mostly skirts and dresses; in Scotland many men wear pleated skirts (kilts) as formal dress; in some equatorial cultures (but not others) men and women wear virtually nothing at all. How are such traditions preserved across generations?

The prevailing assumption is what Judith Rich Harris (1998) calls *The Nurture Assumption:* Nurture, the way parents bring their children up, governs who their children become. On that much Freudians and behaviorists—and the person in front of you—agree. Comparing the extremes of loved and abused children suggests that parenting *does* matter. Moreover, children do absorb many of their values, including their political affiliation and religious faith, at home. But if children's personalities are molded by parental example and nurture, then children who grow up in the same families should be noticeably alike, yes?

That presumption is refuted by the most astonishing, agreed-upon, and dramatic recent finding of developmental psychology. In the words of behavior geneticists Robert Plomin and Denise Daniels (1987), "Two children in the same family [are on average] as different from one another as are pairs of children selected randomly from the population."

The evidence from studies of twins and biological and adoptive siblings indicates that genetic influences explain roughly 50 percent of individual variations in personality traits. Shared environmental influences—including the shared home influence—account for only 0 to 10 percent of their personality differences. So what accounts for the other 40 to 50 percent? It's *peer influence*, Harris argues. What children and teens care most about is less what their parents think than what peers think. Children and youth learn their games, their musical tastes, their accents, even their dirty words mostly from peers. In hindsight, this makes sense. It's their peers with whom they play and eventually will work and mate. Consider:

- Preschoolers will often refuse to try a certain food despite parents' urgings—until they are put at a table with a group of children who like it.

This Scottish wedding photo illustrates a cultural dress tradition maintained across many generations.

- Although children of smokers have an elevated smoking rate, the effect seems largely peer mediated. Such children more often have friends who model smoking, who suggest its pleasures, and who offer cigarettes.

- Nazi youth group members 60 years ago mostly came from emotionally supportive, middle-class homes, notes David Rowe (1994). What corrupted them was not bad parenting but the "heavier weight" of cultural change around them.

- Young immigrant children whose families are transplanted into foreign cultures usually grow up preferring the language and norms of their new peer culture. They may "code-switch" when they step back into their homes, but their hearts and minds are with their peer groups. Likewise, deaf children of hearing parents who attend schools for the deaf usually leave their parents' culture and assimilate into deaf culture.

Ergo, if we left a group of children with their same schools, neighborhoods, and peers but switched the parents around, says Harris (1996) in taking her argument to its limits, they "would develop into the same sort of adults." As it happens, the sort of adults they develop into often resemble their parents. But the cultural transmission is less from individual parent to child, she contends, than from the parental group to the children's group. The parents help define their children's schools, neighborhoods, and peers, which in turn influence their children's odds of becoming delinquent, using drugs, or getting pregnant. Moreover, children often take their cues from slightly older children, who get their cues from older youth, who take theirs from young adults in the parents' generation.

The links of influence from parental group to child group are loose enough that the cultural transmission is never perfect. And in both human and primate cultures, change comes from the young. When one monkey discovers a better way of washing food or when people develop a new idea about fashion or gender roles, the innovation usually comes from the young and is more readily embraced by younger adults. Thus, cultural traditions continue, yet cultures change.

Summing up

The most heavily researched of roles, gender roles, illustrate culture's impact. Gender roles vary sharply from culture to culture and from time to time. Much of culture's influence is transmitted not directly by parents but via peers.

Conclusions

Biology and culture do not exist in isolation, because culture works upon what is biologically given. How, then, do biology and culture interact? And how do our individual personalities interact with our situations?

BIOLOGY *AND* CULTURE

We needn't think of evolution and culture as competitors. Cultural norms subtly but powerfully affect our attitudes and behavior, but they don't do so independent of biology. Everything social and psychological is ultimately biological. If others' expectations influence us, that is part of our biological programming. Moreover, what our biological heritage initiates, culture may accentuate. If genes and hormones predispose males to be more physically aggressive than females, culture may amplify this difference through norms that expect males to be tough and females to be the kinder, gentler sex.

interaction
The effect of one factor (such as biology) depends on another factor (such as environment).

Biology and culture may also **interact.** Today's genetic science indicates how experience uses genes to change the brain (Quarts & Sejnowski, 2002). Environmental stimuli can turn on genes that produce new brain cell branching receptors. Visual experience turns on genes that develop the brain's visual area. Parental touch turns on genes that help offspring cope with future stressful events. Genes don't just constrain us, they respond adaptively to our experiences.

Biology and experience interact as biological traits influence how the environment reacts. People respond differently to a David Beckham than to a Woody Allen. Men, being 8 percent taller and averaging almost double the proportion of muscle mass, may likewise have different experiences than women. Or consider this: A very strong cultural norm dictates that males should be taller than their female mates. In one study, only 1 in 720 married couples violated this norm (Gillis & Avis, 1980). With hindsight, we can speculate a

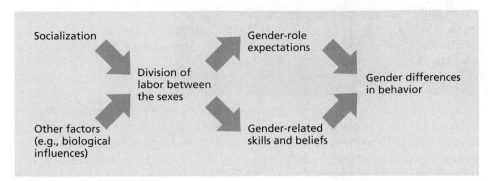

figure 5–7

A social-role theory of gender differences in social behavior.
Various influences, including childhood experiences and factors, bend males and females toward differing roles. It is the expectations and the skills and beliefs associated with these differing roles that affect men's and women's behavior. **Source:** Adapted from Eagly, 1987, and Eagly & Wood, 1991.

psychological explanation: Perhaps being taller (and older) helps men perpetuate their social power over women. But we can also speculate evolutionary wisdom that might underlie the cultural norm: If people preferred partners of the same height, tall men and short women would often be without partners. As it is, evolution dictates that men tend to be taller than women, and culture dictates the same for couples. So the height norm might well be a result of biology *and* culture.

Alice Eagly and Wendy Wood (1999; Eagly, 1987) theorize how biology and culture interact (Figure 5–7). They believe that a variety of factors, including biological influences and childhood socialization, predispose a sexual division of labor. In adult life the immediate causes of gender differences in social behavior are the *roles* that reflect this sexual division of labor. Men, because of their strength and speed, tend to be found in roles demanding physical power. Women's capacity for childbearing and nursing inclines them to more nurturant roles. Each sex then tends to exhibit the behaviors expected of those who fill such roles and to

Only very occasionally do couples violate the male-taller norm.

have their skills and beliefs shaped accordingly. Nature and nurture are a "tangled web."

Analyses of who does what in 185 societies reveals that men hunt big game and harvest lumber, women do about 90 percent of the cooking and laundry, and the sexes are equally likely to plant and harvest crops and to milk cows. As role assignments become more equal, Eagly predicts that gender differences "will gradually lessen."

the story behind the research:
Alice Eagly on gender similarities and differences

I began my work on gender with a project on social influence in the early 1970s. Like many feminist activists of the day, I initially assumed that, despite negative cultural stereotypes about women, the behavior of women and men is substantially equivalent. Over the years, my views have evolved considerably. I have found that some social behaviors of women and men are somewhat different, especially in situations that bring gender roles to mind.

People should not assume that these differences necessarily reflect unfavorably on women. Women's tendencies to be more attuned to other people's concerns and to treat others more democratically are favorably evaluated and can be assets in many situations. In fact, my research on gender stereotypes shows that, if we take both negative and positive qualities into account, the stereotype of women is currently more favorable than the stereotype of men. However, the qualities of niceness and nurturance that are important in expectations about women may decrease their power and effectiveness in situations that call for assertive and competitive behavior.

Alice Eagly,
Northwestern University

How are boys and girls socialized? Go to the *SocialSense* CD-ROM to view Alice Eagly on how biology and culture shape social roles.

Indeed, note Eagly and Wendy Wood (1999), in cultures with greater equality of gender roles the gender difference in mate preferences (men seeking youth and domestic skill, women seeking status and earning potential) is less. Likewise, as women's employment in formerly male occupations has increased, the gender difference in self-reported masculinity/femininity has decreased (Twenge, 1997). As men and women enact more similar roles, their psychological differences shrink. Although biology predisposes men to strength tasks and women to infant care, Wood and Eagly (2002) conclude that "the behavior of women and men is sufficiently malleable that individuals of both sexes are fully capable of effectively carrying out organizational roles at all levels." In addition to the diminishing importance of male size and aggressiveness for today's high-status roles, lowered birthrates mean that women are less constrained by pregnancy and nursing. The end result, when combined with laws against discrimination and with competitive pressures to hire the best talent (regardless of gender), is the inevitable rise in gender equality.

The effects of biology and socialization may be important insofar as they influence the social roles that people play, for the roles we play influence who we become. If men are more assertive and women more nurturing, this may be an *effect* of their playing powerful versus caregiving roles. When workers (men and women) shift from talking with their supervisors to talking with supervisees, they become more assertive (Moskowitz & others, 1994).

THE POWER OF THE SITUATION *AND* THE PERSON

"There are trivial truths and great truths," declared the physicist Niels Bohr. "The opposite of a trivial truth is plainly false. The opposite of a great truth is also true." Each chapter in this unit on social influence teaches a great truth: the power of the social situation. This great truth about the power of external pressures would sufficiently explain our behavior if we were passive, like tumbleweeds. But unlike tumbleweeds, we are not just blown here and there by the environment. We act; we react. We respond, and we get responses. We can resist the social situation and sometimes even change it. Thus each of these "social influence" chapters concludes by calling attention to the opposite of the great truth: the power of the person.

Perhaps stressing the power of culture leaves you somewhat uncomfortable. Most of us resent any suggestion that external forces determine our behavior; we see ourselves as free beings, as the originators of our actions (well, at least of our good actions). We sense that believing in social determinism can lead to what philosopher Jean-Paul Sartre called "bad faith"—evading responsibility by blaming something or someone for one's fate.

Actually, social control (the power of the situation) and personal control (the power of the person) no more compete with one another than do biological and cultural explanations. Social and personal explanations of our social behavior are both valid, for at any moment we are both the creatures and the creators of our social worlds. We may well be the products of the interplay of our genes and environment. But it is also true that the future is coming, and it is our job to decide where it is going. Our choices today determine our environment tomorrow.

Social situations do profoundly influence individuals. But individuals also influence social situations. The two *interact.* Asking whether external situations or inner dispositions (or culture or evolution) determine behavior is like asking whether length or width determines the area of a field.

The interaction occurs in at least three ways (Snyder & Ickes, 1985). First, a given social situation often *affects different people differently.* Because our minds do not see reality identically, each of us responds to a situation as we construe it. And some people are more sensitive and responsive to social situations than others (Snyder, 1983). The Japanese, for example, are more responsive to social expectations than the British (Argyle & others, 1978).

Second, interaction between persons and situations occurs because people often *choose their situations* (Ickes & others, 1997). Given a choice, sociable people elect situations that evoke social interaction. When you chose your college, you were also choosing to expose yourself to a specific set of social influences. Ardent political liberals are unlikely to settle in Orange County, California, and join the Chamber of Commerce. They are more likely to live in San Francisco or Toronto and join Greenpeace (or to read the *Manchester Guardian* rather than the *Times of London*)—in other words, to choose a social world that reinforces their inclinations.

Third, people often *create their situations.* Recall again that our preconceptions can be self-fulfilling: If we expect someone to be extraverted, hostile, feminine, or sexy, our actions toward the person may induce the very behavior we

Food for thought: If Bohr's statement is a great truth, what is its opposite?

"The words of truth are always paradoxical."
—Lao-tzu, *The Simple Way*

expect. What, after all, makes a social situation but the people in it? A liberal environment is created by liberals. What takes place in the sorority is created by the members. The social environment is not like the weather—something that just happens to us. It is more like our homes—something we make for ourselves.

Summing up

Biological and cultural explanations need not be contradictory. Indeed, they interact. Biological factors operate within a cultural context, and culture builds on a biological foundation.

The great truth about the power of social influence is but half the truth if separated from its complementary truth: the power of the person. Persons and situations interact in at least three ways. First, individuals vary in how they interpret and react to a given situation. Second, people choose many of the situations that influence them. Third, people help create their social situations. Thus power resides both in persons and in situations. We create and are created by our social worlds.

PS Personal Postscript: Should we view ourselves as products or architects of our social worlds?

The reciprocal causation between situations and persons allows us to see people as either *reacting to* or *acting upon* their environment. Each perspective is correct, for we are both the products and the architects of our social worlds. Is one perspective wiser, however? In one sense, it is wise to see ourselves as the creatures of our environments (lest we become too proud of our achievements and blame ourselves too much for our problems) and to see others as free actors (lest we become paternalistic and manipulative).

"If we explain poverty, or emotional disorders, or crime and delinquency or alcoholism, or even unemployment, as resulting from personal, internal, individual defect . . . then there simply is not much we can do about prevention."
—George Albee, 1979

Perhaps we would do well more often to assume the reverse, however—to view ourselves as free agents and to view others as influenced by their environments. We would then assume self-efficacy as we view ourselves, and we would seek understanding and social reform as we relate to others. (If we view others as influenced by their situations, we are more likely to empathize than smugly to judge unpleasant behavior as freely chosen by "immoral," "sadistic," or "lazy" persons.) Most religions encourage us to take responsibility for ourselves but to refrain from judging others. Is this because our natural inclination is to excuse our own failures while blaming others for theirs?

What do you think?

Read the margin quotation by George Albee. Do you know people who have one of the problems mentioned in the quotation? What would you say to be supportive to them if you believed their problem was due to their own incompetence, or avoidable negligence?

And what would you say if you believed their situation caused their problem?

Now, think about the three ways that people and situations interact and describe how one of these people interacted with his or her situation.

Making the Social Connection

Gender and culture pervade social psychology. For example, does culture predict how people will conform (Chapter 6: Conformity)? How do cultures vary in the way they see love? How do men and women see love differently (Chapter 11: Attraction and Intimacy)? Do you want to learn how gestures vary from one culture to another? Go to the *SocialSense* CD-ROM to find out more about cultural variations in nonverbal behavior.

chapter 6

Conformity

"Whatever crushes individuality is despotism, by whatever name it may be called."

John Stuart Mill,
On Liberty, *1859*

"The social pressures community brings to bear are a mainstay of our moral values."

Amitai Etzioni,
The Spirit of
Community, *1993*

You have surely experienced the phenomenon: As a controversial speaker or music concert finishes, the adoring fans near the front stand to applaud. The approving folks just behind them follow their example and join the standing ovation. Now the wave of people standing reaches people who, unprompted, would merely be giving polite applause from their comfortable seats. Seated among them, part of you wants to stay seated ("this speaker doesn't represent my views at all"). But as the wave of standing people sweeps by, will you alone stay seated? It's not easy, being a minority of one.

Such scenes of conformity raise this chapter's questions:

- Why, given the diversity of individuals in large groups, is their behavior so often uniform?
- Under what circumstances do people conform?
- Are certain people more likely to conform?
- Who resists the pressure to conform?
- Is conformity as bad as my image of a docile "herd" implies? Should I instead be describing their "group solidarity" and "social sensitivity"?

Let us take the last question first. Is conformity good or bad? This is a question that has no scientific answer, but, assuming the values most of us share, we can say that conformity is at times bad (when it leads someone to drink and drive or to join in racist behavior), at times good (when it inhibits people from cutting into a theater line), and at times inconsequential (when it disposes tennis players to wear white).

What is conformity?

The word "conformity" does, however, carry a negative value judgment. How would you feel if you overheard someone describing you as a "real conformist"? I suspect you would feel hurt, because you are probably from a Western culture that doesn't prize submitting to peer pressure. Hence North American and European social psychologists, reflecting their individualistic cultures, give it negative labels (conformity, submission, compliance) rather than positive ones (communal sensitivity, responsiveness, cooperative team play).

In Japan, going along with others is a sign not of weakness but of tolerance, self-control, and maturity (Markus & Kitayama, 1994). "Everywhere in Japan," observed Lance Morrow (1983), "one senses an intricate serenity that comes to a people who know exactly what to expect from each other."

The moral: We choose labels to suit our values and judgments. Some have viewed legislators who cast unpopular votes against the Iraq war as "independent" and "inner-directed" but those who cast unpopular votes against civil rights legislation as "reactionary" and "self-centered." Labels both describe and evaluate, and they are inescapable. We cannot discuss the topics of this chapter without labels. So let us be clear on the meanings of the following labels: conformity, compliance, acceptance.

Conformity is not just acting as other people act; it is being affected by how they act. It is acting differently from the way you would act alone. Thus **conformity** is a change in behavior or belief to accord with others. When, as part of a crowd, you rise to cheer a game-winning goal, are you conforming? When, along with millions of others, you drink milk or coffee, are you conforming? When you and everyone else agree that women look better with longer hair than with crewcuts, are you conforming? Maybe, maybe not. The key is whether your behavior and beliefs would be the same apart from the group. Would you rise to cheer the goal if you were the only fan in the stands?

conformity
A change in behavior or belief to accord with others.

"Sure, I follow the herd—not out of brainless obedience, mind you, but out of a deep and abiding respect for the concept of community."

There are several varieties of conformity (Nail & others, 2000). Consider two: compliance and acceptance. Sometimes we conform to an expectation or request without really believing in what we are doing. We put on the necktie or dress, though we dislike doing so. This outward conformity is **compliance.** We comply primarily to reap a reward or avoid a punishment. If our compliance is to an explicit command, we call it **obedience.**

Sometimes we genuinely believe in what the group has convinced us to do. We may join millions of others in drinking milk because we are convinced that milk is nutritious. This sincere, inward conformity is called **acceptance.** Acceptance sometimes follows compliance. As Chapter 4 emphasized, attitudes follow behavior. Unless we feel no responsibility for our behavior, we usually become sympathetic to what we have stood up for.

compliance
Conformity that involves publicly acting in accord with an implied or explicit request while privately disagreeing.

obedience
Acting in accord with a direct order.

acceptance
Conformity that involves both acting and believing in accord with social pressure.

Authorities may impose public compliance, but private acceptance is another matter. Copyright © The New Yorker Collection, 1997, George Booth, from cartoonbank.com. All Rights Reserved.

What are the classic conformity studies?

How have social psychologists studied conformity in the laboratory? What do their findings reveal about the potency of social forces and the nature of evil?

Researchers who study conformity construct miniature social worlds—laboratory microcultures that simplify and simulate important features of everyday social influence. Consider three noted sets of experiments. Each provides a method for studying conformity—and some startling findings.

SHERIF'S STUDIES OF NORM FORMATION

The first of the three classics bridges Chapter 5's focus on culture's power to create and perpetuate arbitrary norms and this chapter's focus on conformity. Muzafer Sherif (1935, 1937) wondered whether it was possible to observe the emergence of a social norm in the laboratory. Like biologists seeking to isolate a virus so they can then experiment with it, Sherif wanted to isolate and then experiment with norm formation.

As a participant in one of Sherif's experiments, you might have found yourself seated in a dark room. Fifteen feet in front of you a pinpoint of light appears. At first, nothing happens. Then for a few seconds it moves erratically and finally disappears. Now you must guess how far it moved. The dark room gives you no way to judge distance, so you offer an uncertain "six inches." The experimenter repeats the procedure. This time you say, "Ten inches." With further repetitions, your estimates continue to average about eight inches.

The next day you return, joined by two others who the day before had the same experience. When the light goes off for the first time, the other two people offer their best guesses from the day before. "One inch," says one. "Two inches," says the other. A bit taken aback, you nevertheless say, "Six inches." With successive repetitions of this group experience, both on this day and for the next two days, will your responses change? The Columbia University men whom Sherif tested changed their estimates markedly. As Figure 6–1 illustrates, a group norm typically emerged. (The norm was false. Why? The light never moved! Sherif had taken advantage of an optical illusion called the **autokinetic phenomenon.**)

autokinetic phenomenon
Self (auto) *motion* (kinetic). *The apparent movement of a stationary point of light in the dark.*

Sherif and others have used this technique to answer questions about people's suggestibility. When people were retested alone a year later, would their estimates again diverge or would they continue to follow the group norm? Remarkably, they continued to support the group norm (Rohrer & others, 1954). (Does this suggest compliance or acceptance?)

Struck by culture's seeming power to perpetuate false beliefs, Robert Jacobs and Donald Campbell (1961) studied the transmission of false beliefs in their Northwestern University laboratory. Using the autokinetic phenomenon, they had a **confederate** give an inflated estimate of how far the light moved. The confederate then left the experiment and was replaced by another real participant, who was in turn replaced by a still newer member. The inflated illusion persisted (although diminishing) for five generations of participants. These people had become "unwitting conspirators in perpetuating a cultural fraud." The lesson of these experiments: Our views of reality are not ours alone.

confederate
An accomplice of the experimenter.

In everyday life the results of suggestibility are sometimes amusing. One person coughs, laughs, or yawns, and others are soon doing the same. Comedy

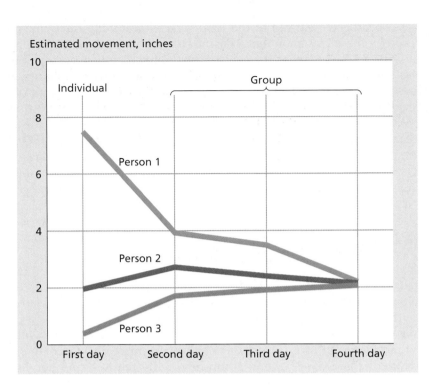

Estimated movement, inches

figure 6–1

A sample group from Sherif's study of norm formation.

Three individuals converge as they give repeated estimates of the apparent movement of a point of light. **Source:** Data from Sherif & Sherif, 1969, p. 209.

show laugh tracks capitalize on our suggestibility. Just being around happy people can help us feel happier, a phenomenon that Peter Totterdell and his colleagues (1998) call "mood linkage." In their studies of British nurses and accountants, people within the same work groups tended to share up and down moods.

Another form of social contagion is what Tanya Chartrand and John Bargh (1999) call "the chameleon effect." Picture yourself in one of their experiments, working alongside a confederate who occasionally either rubbed her face or shook her foot. Would you—like their participants—be more likely to rub your face when with a face-rubbing person and shake your foot when with a foot-shaking person? If so, it would quite likely be an automatic behavior, done without any conscious intention to conform, and it would incline you to feel what the other feels (Neumann & Strack, 2000).

Suggestibility can also occur on a large scale. In late March 1954, Seattle newspapers reported damage to car windshields in a city 80 miles to the north. On the morning of April 14, similar windshield damage was reported 65 miles away and later that day only 45 miles away. By nightfall, the windshield-pitting agent had reached Seattle. Before the end of April 15, the Seattle police department had received complaints of damage to more than 3,000 windshields (Medalia & Larsen, 1958). That evening the mayor of Seattle called on President Eisenhower for help.

"Why doth one man's yawning make another yawn?"
—Robert Burton, *Anatomy of Melancholy,* 1621

"I don't know why. I just suddenly felt like calling."

I was a Seattle 11-year-old at the time. I recall searching our windshield, frightened by the explanation that a Pacific H-bomb test was raining fallout on Seattle. On April 16, however, the newspapers hinted that the real culprit might be mass suggestibility. After April 17 there were no more complaints. Later analysis of the pitted windshields concluded that the cause was ordinary road damage. Why did we notice this only after April 14? Given the suggestion, we had looked carefully *at* our windshields instead of *through* them.

In real life, suggestibility is not always so amusing. Hijackings, UFO sightings, and even suicides tend to come in waves (see "Focus on: Mass Delusions"). Sociologist David Phillips and his colleagues (1985, 1989) report that known suicides, as well as fatal auto accidents and private airplane crashes

focus on | mass delusions

Suggestibility on a mass scale appears as collective delusions—spontaneous spreading of false beliefs. Occasionally, this appears as "mass hysteria"—the spread of bodily complaints within a school or workplace with no organic basis for the symptoms. One 2,000-student high school was closed for two weeks as 170 students and staff sought emergency treatment for stomach ailments, dizziness, headaches, and drowsiness. After investigators looked high and low for viruses, germs, pesticides, herbicides—anything that would make people ill—they found . . . nothing (Jones & others, 2000).

After 9/11, groups of children at schools scattered across the United States started breaking out with itchy red rashes without any apparent cause (Talbot, 2002). Unlike a viral condition, the rash spread by "line of sight." People got the rash as they *saw* others getting it (even if they had no close contact). Also, everyday skin conditions—eczema, acne, dry skin in overheated classrooms—got noticed, and perhaps amplified by anxiety. As with so many mass hysterias, rumors of a problem had caused people to notice their ordinary, everyday symptoms and to attribute them to their school.

Sociologists Robert Bartholomew and Erich Goode (2000) report on other mass delusions from the last millennium. During the Middle Ages, European convents reportedly experienced outbreaks of imitative behaviors. In one large French convent, at a time when it was believed that humans could be possessed by animals, one nun began to meow like a cat. Eventually, "all the nuns meowed together every day at a certain time." In a German convent, a nun reportedly fell to biting her companions, and before long "all the nuns of this convent began biting each other." In time, the biting mania spread to other convents.

In British South Africa in 1914, newspapers erroneously reported that German planes were flying over the country in preparation for an imminent attack. The reported maneuvers and length of flight were beyond the capabilities of 1914 aircraft. Nevertheless, thousands of people misperceived ambiguous, nighttime stimuli, such as stars and planets, as examples of the enemy planes.

On June 24, 1947, Kenneth Arnold, while piloting his private plane near Mount Rainier, spotted nine glittering objects in the sky. Worried that he may have seen foreign guided missiles, he tried reporting what he saw to the FBI. Discovering its office closed, he went to his local newspaper and reported crescent-shaped objects that moved "like a saucer would if you skipped it across the water." When the Associated Press then reported the sighting of "saucers" in more than 150 newspapers, the term "flying saucers" was created by headline writers, triggering a worldwide wave of flying saucer sightings during the rest of the summer of 1949.

(which sometimes disguise suicides), increase after well-publicized suicides. For example, following Marilyn Monroe's August 6, 1962, suicide, there were 200 more August suicides in the United States than normal. Moreover, the increase happens only in areas where the suicide story is publicized. The more publicity, the greater the increase in later fatalities.

Although not all studies have found the copycat suicide phenomenon, it has surfaced in Germany, in a London psychiatric unit that experienced 14 patient suicides in one year, and in one high school that, within 18 days, suffered two suicides, seven suicide attempts, and 23 students reporting suicidal thoughts (Joiner, 1999; Jonas, 1992). In both Germany and the United States, suicide rates rise slightly following fictional suicides on soap operas, and, ironically, even after serious dramas that focus on the suicide problem (Gould & Shaffer, 1986; Hafner & Schmidtke, 1989; Phillips, 1982). Phillips reports that teenagers are most susceptible, a finding that would help explain the occasional clusters of teen copycat suicides.

ASCH'S STUDIES OF GROUP PRESSURE

Participants in Sherif's autokinetic experiments faced an ambiguous reality. Consider a less ambiguous perceptual problem faced by a young boy named Solomon Asch (1907–1996). While attending the traditional Jewish Seder at Passover, Asch recalled,

> I asked my uncle, who was sitting next to me, why the door was being opened. He replied, "The prophet Elijah visits this evening every Jewish home and takes a sip of wine from the cup reserved for him."
>
> I was amazed at this news and repeated, "Does he really come? Does he really take a sip?"
>
> My uncle said, "If you watch very closely, when the door is opened you will see—you watch the cup—you will see that the wine will go down a little."
>
> And that's what happened. My eyes were riveted upon the cup of wine. I was determined to see whether there would be a change. And to me it seemed it was tantalizing, and of course, it was hard to be absolutely sure—that indeed something was happening at the rim of the cup, and the wine did go down a little (Aron & Aron, 1989, p. 27).

Years later, social psychologist Asch re-created his boyhood experience in his laboratory. Imagine yourself as one of Asch's volunteer subjects. You are seated sixth in a row of seven people. After explaining that you will be taking part in a study of perceptual judgments, the experimenter asks you to say which of the three lines in Figure 6–2 matches the standard line. You can easily see that it's line 2. So it's no surprise when the five people responding before you all say, "Line 2."

The next comparison proves as easy, and you settle in for what seems a simple test. But the third trial startles you. Although the correct answer seems just as clear-cut, the first person gives a wrong answer. When the second person gives the same wrong

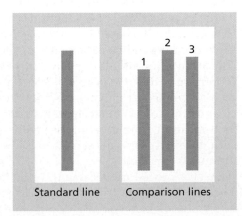

figure 6–2

Sample comparison from Solomon Asch's conformity procedure.

The participants judged which of three comparison lines matched the standard.

In one of Asch's conformity experiments (top), subject number 6 experienced uneasiness and conflict after hearing five people before him give a wrong answer.

answer, you sit up in your chair and stare at the cards. The third person agrees with the first two. Your jaw drops; you start to perspire. "What is this?" you ask yourself. "Are they blind? Or am I?" The fourth and fifth people agree with the others. Then the experimenter looks at you. Now you are experiencing an epistemological dilemma: "How am I to know what is true? Is it what my peers tell me or what my eyes tell me?"

Dozens of college students experienced this conflict during Asch's experiments. Those in a control condition who answered alone were correct more than 99 percent of the time. Asch wondered: If several others (confederates coached by the experimenter) gave identical wrong answers, would people declare what they would otherwise have denied? Although some people never conformed, three-quarters did so at least once. All told, 37 percent of the responses were conforming (or should we say "*trusting* of others"?). Of course, that means 63 percent of the time people did not conform. Despite the independence shown by many of his participants, Asch's (1955) feelings about the conformity were as clear as the correct answers to his questions: "That reasonably intelligent and well-meaning young people are willing to call white black is a matter of concern. It raises questions about our ways of education and about the values that guide our conduct."

Asch's procedure became the standard for hundreds of later experiments. These experiments lacked what Chapter 1 called the "mundane realism" of everyday conformity, but they did have "experimental realism." People became

"He who sees the truth, let him proclaim it, without asking who is for it or who is against it."
—Henry George, *The Irish Land Question*, 1881

emotionally involved in the experience. The Sherif and Asch results are startling because they involved no obvious pressure to conform—there were no rewards for "team play," no punishments for individuality. If people are this conforming in response to such minimal pressure, how compliant will they be if they are directly coerced? Could someone force the average American or British Commonwealth citizen to perform cruel acts? I would have guessed not: Their humane, democratic, individualistic values would make them resist such pressure. Besides, the easy verbal pronouncements of these experiments are a giant step away from actually harming someone; you and I would never yield to coercion to hurt another. Or would we? Social psychologist Stanley Milgram wondered.

MILGRAM'S OBEDIENCE EXPERIMENTS

Milgram's (1965, 1974) experiments tested what happens when the demands of authority clash with the demands of conscience. These have become social psychology's most famous and controversial experiments. "Perhaps more than any other empirical contributions in the history of social science," notes Lee Ross (1988), "they have become part of our society's shared intellectual legacy—that small body of historical incidents, biblical parables, and classic literature that serious thinkers feel free to draw on when they debate about human nature or contemplate human history."

Here is the scene staged by Milgram, a creative artist who wrote stories and stage plays: Two men come to Yale University's psychology laboratory to participate in a study of learning and memory. A stern experimenter in a gray technician's coat explains that this is a pioneering study of the effect of punishment on learning. The experiment requires one of them to teach a list of word pairs to the other and to punish errors by delivering shocks of increasing intensity. To assign the roles, they draw slips out of a hat. One of the men, a mild-mannered, 47-year-old accountant who is the experimenter's confederate, pretends that his slip says "learner" and is ushered into an adjacent room. The "teacher" (who has come in response to a newspaper ad) takes a mild sample shock and then looks on as the experimenter straps the learner into a chair and attaches an electrode to his wrist.

Teacher and experimenter then return to the main room (see Figure 6–3), where the teacher takes his place before a "shock generator" with switches ranging from 15 to 450 volts in 15-volt increments. The switches are labeled "Slight Shock," "Very Strong Shock," "Danger: Severe Shock," and so forth. Under the 435- and 450-volt switches appears "XXX." The experimenter

Ethical note: Professional ethics usually dictate explaining the experiment afterward (see Chapter 1). Imagine you were an experimenter who had just finished a session with a conforming participant. Could you explain the deception without making the person feel gullible and dumb?

figure 6–3
Milgram's obedience experiment.

Source: Milgram, 1974.

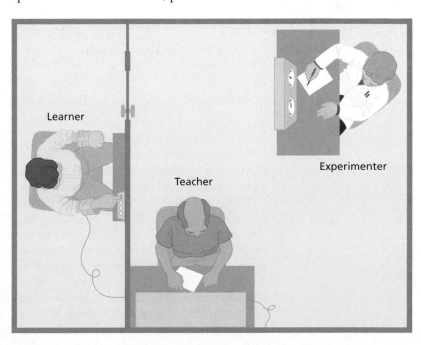

Learner

Teacher

Experimenter

table 6–1   **The learner's schedule of protests in Milgram's "heart disturbance" experiments**

75 volts	Ugh!
90 volts	Ugh!
105 volts	Ugh! (*Louder*)
120 volts	Ugh! Hey, this really hurts.
135 volts	Ugh!!
150 volts	Ugh!!! Experimenter! That's all. Get me out of here. I told you I had heart trouble. My heart's starting to bother me now. Get me out of here, please. My heart's starting to bother me. I refuse to go on. Let me out.
165 volts	Ugh! Let me out! (*Shouting*)
180 volts	Ugh! I can't stand the pain. Let me out of here! (*Shouting*)
195 volts	Ugh! Let me out of here. Let me out of here. My heart's bothering me. Let me out of here! You have no right to keep me here! Let me out! Let me out of here! Let me out! Let me out of here! My heart's bothering me. Let me out! Let me out!
210 volts	Ugh! Experimenter! Get me out of here. I've had enough. I won't be in the experiment any more.
225 volts	Ugh!
240 volts	Ugh!
255 volts	Ugh! Get me out of here.
270 volts	(*Agonized scream*) Let me out of here. Let me out of here. Let me out of here. Let me out. Do you hear? Let me out of here.
285 volts	(*Agonized scream*)
300 volts	(*Agonized scream*) I absolutely refuse to answer any more. Get me out of here. You can't hold me here. Get me out. Get me out of here.
315 volts	(*Intensely agonized scream*) I told you I refuse to answer. I'm no longer part of this experiment.
330 volts	(*Intense and prolonged agonized scream*) Let me out of here. Let me out of here. My heart's bothering me. Let me out. I tell you. (*Hysterically*) Let me out of here. Let me out of here. You have no right to hold me here. Let me out! Let me out! Let me out! Let me out of here! Let me out! Let me out!

Source: From *Obedience to Authority* by Stanley Milgram. New York: Harper & Row, 1974, pp. 56–57.

tells the teacher to "move one level higher on the shock generator" each time the learner gives a wrong answer. With each flick of a switch, lights flash, relay switches click, and an electric buzz sounds.

If the participant complies with the experimenter's requests, he hears the learner grunt at 75, 90, and 105 volts. At 120 volts the learner shouts that the shocks are painful. And at 150 volts he cries out, "Experimenter, get me out of here! I won't be in the experiment anymore! I refuse to go on!" By 270 volts his protests have become screams of agony, and he continues to insist to be let out. At 300 and 315 volts, he screams his refusal to answer. After 330 volts he falls silent (Table 6–1). In answer to the "teacher's" inquiries and pleas to end the experiment, the experimenter states that the nonresponses should be treated as wrong answers. To keep the participant going, he uses four verbal prods:

Prod 1: Please continue (or Please go on).

Prod 2: The experiment requires that you continue.

Prod 3: It is absolutely essential that you continue.

Prod 4: You have no other choice; you must go on.

How far would you go? Milgram described the experiment to 110 psychiatrists, college students, and middle-class adults. People in all three groups guessed that they would disobey by about 135 volts; none expected to go beyond 300 volts. Recognizing that self-estimates may reflect self-serving bias, Milgram asked them how far they thought *other* people would go. Virtually no one expected anyone to proceed to XXX on the shock panel. (The psychiatrists guessed about one in a thousand.)

But when Milgram conducted the experiment with 40 men—a vocational mix of 20- to 50-year-olds—26 of them (65 percent) progressed to 450 volts. In fact, all who reached 450 volts complied with a command to *continue* the procedure until, after two further trials, the experimenter called a halt.

Having expected a low rate of obedience, and with plans to replicate the experiment in Germany and assess the culture difference, Milgram was disturbed (A. Milgram, 2000). So instead of going to Germany, Milgram next made the learner's protests even more compelling. As the learner was strapped into the chair, the teacher heard him mention his "slight heart condition" and heard the experimenter's reassurance that "although the shocks may be painful, they cause no permanent tissue damage." The learner's anguished protests were to little avail; of 40 new men in this experiment, 25 (63 percent) fully complied with the experimenter's demands (Figure 6–4).

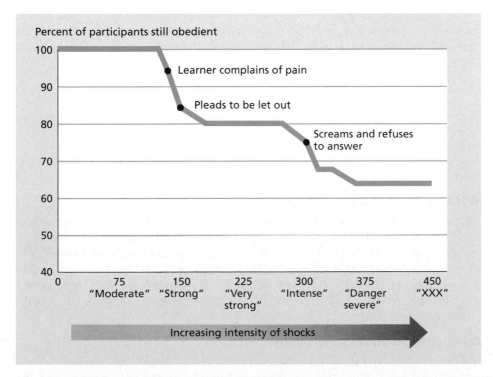

figure 6–4
The Milgram obedience experiment.
Percentage of participants complying despite the learner's cries of protest and failure to respond.
Source: From Milgram, 1965.

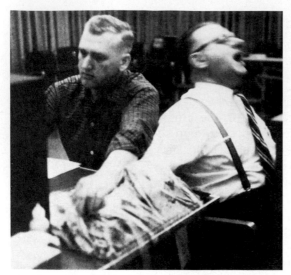

An obedient participant in Milgram's "touch" condition forces the victim's hand onto the shock plate. Usually, however, "teachers" were more merciful to victims who were this close to them.

The ethics of Milgram's experiments

The obedience of his subjects disturbed Milgram. The procedures he used disturbed many social psychologists (Miller, 1986). The "learner" in these experiments actually received no shock (he disengaged himself from the electric chair and turned on a tape recorder that delivered the protests). Nevertheless, some critics said that Milgram did to his participants what they did to their victims: He stressed them against their will. Indeed, many of the "teachers" did experience agony. They sweated, trembled, stuttered, bit their lips, groaned, or even broke into uncontrollable nervous laughter. A *New York Times* reviewer complained that the cruelty inflicted by the experiments "upon their unwitting subjects is surpassed only by the cruelty that they elicit from them" (Marcus, 1974).

Critics also argued that the participants' self-concepts may have been altered. One participant's wife told him, "You can call yourself Eichmann" (referring to Nazi death camp administrator Adolf Eichmann). CBS television depicted the results and the controversy in a two-hour dramatization starring William Shatner, of *Star Trek* fame, as Milgram. "A world of evil so terrifying no one dares penetrate its secret. Until Now!" declared a *TV Guide* ad for the program (Elms, 1995).

In his own defense, Milgram pointed to the lessons taught by his nearly two dozen experiments with a diverse sample of more than 1,000 participants. He also reminded critics of the support he received from the participants after the deception was revealed and the experiment explained. When surveyed afterward, 84 percent said they were glad to have participated; only 1 percent regretted volunteering. A year later, a psychiatrist interviewed 40 of those who had suffered most and concluded that, despite the temporary stress, none was harmed.

The ethical controversy was "terribly overblown," Milgram believed:

> There is less consequence to subjects in this experiment from the standpoint of effects on self-esteem, than to university students who take ordinary course examinations, and who do not get the grades they want. . . . It seems that [in giving exams] we are quite prepared to accept stress, tension, and consequences for self-esteem. But in regard to the process of generating new knowledge, how little tolerance we show. (quoted by Blass, 1996)

WHAT BREEDS OBEDIENCE?

Milgram did more than reveal the extent to which people will obey an authority; he also examined the conditions that breed obedience. In further experiments, he varied the social conditions and got compliance ranging from 0 to 93 percent fully obedient. Four factors that determined obedience were the victim's emotional distance, the authority's closeness and legitimacy, whether or not the authority was institutionalized, and the liberating effects of a disobedient fellow participant.

Emotional distance of the victim

Milgram's participants acted with least compassion when the "learners" could not be seen (and could not see them). When the victim was remote and the

focus on | personalizing the victims

Innocent victims trigger more compassion if personalized. In a week when a soon-forgotten earthquake in Iran kills 3,000 people, a lone boy dies, trapped in a well shaft in Italy, and the whole world grieves. The projected death statistics of a nuclear war are impersonal to the point of being incomprehensible. So international law professor Roger Fisher proposed a way to personalize the victims:

> It so happens that a young man, usually a navy officer, accompanies the president wherever he goes. This young man has a black attaché case which contains the codes that are needed to fire nuclear weapons.
>
> I can see the president at a staff meeting considering nuclear war as an abstract question. He might conclude, "On SIOP Plan One, the decision is affirmative. Communicate the Alpha line XYZ." Such jargon keeps what is involved at a distance.
>
> My suggestion, then, is quite simple. Put that needed code number in a little capsule and implant that capsule right next to the heart of a volunteer. The volunteer will carry with him a big, heavy butcher knife as he accompanies the president. If ever the president wants to fire nuclear weapons, the only way he can do so is by first, with his own hands, killing one human being.
>
> "George," the president would say, "I'm sorry, but tens of millions must die." The president then would have to look at someone and realize what death is—what an *innocent* death is. Blood on the White House carpet: it's reality brought home.
>
> When I suggested this to friends in the Pentagon, they said, "My God, that's terrible. Having to kill someone would distort the president's judgment. He might never push the button."

Source: Adapted from "Preventing Nuclear War" by Roger Fisher, *Bulletin of the Atomic Scientists*, March 1981, pp. 11–17.

"teachers" heard no complaints, nearly all obeyed calmly to the end. This situation minimized the learner's influence relative to the experimenter's. But what if we made the learner's pleas and the experimenter's pleas more equally visible? When the learner was in the same room, "only" 40 percent obeyed to 450 volts. Full compliance dropped to 30 percent when teachers were required to force the learner's hand into contact with a shock plate.

In everyday life, too, it is easiest to abuse someone who is distant or depersonalized. People will be unresponsive even to great tragedies. Executioners often depersonalize those being executed by placing hoods over their heads. The ethics of war allow one to bomb a helpless village from 40,000 feet but not to shoot an equally helpless villager. In combat with an enemy they can see, many soldiers either do not fire or do not aim. Such disobedience is rare among those given orders to kill with the more distant artillery or aircraft weapons (Padgett, 1989).

On the positive side, people act most compassionately toward those who are personalized. That is why appeals for the unborn, for the hungry, or for animal rights are nearly always personalized with a compelling photograph or description. Perhaps even more compelling is an ultrasound picture of one's own developing fetus. When queried by John Lydon and Christine Dunkel-Schetter (1994), expectant women expressed more commitment to their pregnancies if they had seen ultrasound pictures of their fetuses that clearly displayed body parts.

Imagine you had the power to prevent either a tidal wave that would kill 25,000 people on the planet's other side, a crash that would kill 250 people at your local airport, or a car accident that would kill a close friend. Which would you prevent?

Closeness and legitimacy of the authority

The physical presence of the experimenter also affected obedience. When Milgram gave the commands by telephone, full obedience dropped to 21 percent (although many lied and said they were obeying). Other studies confirm that when the one making the request is physically close, compliance increases. Given a light touch on the arm, people are more likely to lend a dime, sign a petition, or sample a new pizza (Kleinke, 1977; Smith & others, 1982; Willis & Hamm, 1980).

The authority, however, must be perceived as legitimate. In another twist on the basic experiment, the experimenter received a rigged telephone call that required him to leave the laboratory. He said that since the equipment recorded data automatically, the "teacher" should just go ahead. After the experimenter left, another person, who had been assigned a clerical role (actually a second confederate), assumed command. The clerk "decided" that the shock should be increased one level for each wrong answer and instructed the teacher accordingly. Now 80 percent of the teachers refused to comply fully. The confederate, feigning disgust at this defiance, sat down in front of the shock generator and tried to take over the teacher's role. At this point most of the defiant participants protested. Some tried to unplug the generator. One large man lifted the zealous confederate from his chair and threw him across the room. This rebellion against an illegitimate authority contrasted sharply with the deferential politeness usually shown the experimenter.

It also contrasts with the behavior of hospital nurses who in one study were called by an unknown physician and ordered to administer an obvious drug overdose (Hofling & others, 1966). The researchers told one group of nurses and nursing students about the experiment and asked how they would react. Nearly all said they would not have followed the order. One said she would have replied, "I'm sorry, sir, but I am not authorized to give any medication without a written order, especially one so large over the usual dose and one that I'm unfamiliar with. If it were possible, I would be glad to do it, but this is against hospital policy and my own ethical standards." Nevertheless, when 22 other nurses were actually given the phoned-in overdose order, all but one obeyed without

Given orders, most soldiers will torch people's homes or kill—behaviors that in other contexts they would consider immoral.

delay (until being intercepted on their way to the patient). Although not all nurses are so compliant (Krackow & Blass, 1995; Rank & Jacobson, 1977), these nurses were following a familiar script: Doctor (a legitimate authority) orders; nurse obeys.

Compliance with legitimate authority was also apparent in the strange case of the "rectal ear ache" (Cohen & Davis, 1981). A doctor ordered ear drops for a patient suffering infection in the right ear. On the prescription, the doctor abbreviated "place in right ear" as "place in R ear." Reading the order, the compliant nurse put the required drops in the compliant patient's rectum.

Institutional authority

If the prestige of the authority is this important, then perhaps the institutional prestige of Yale University legitimized the Milgram experiment commands. In postexperimental interviews, many participants said that had it not been for Yale's reputation, they would not have obeyed. To see whether this was true, Milgram moved the experiment to Bridgeport, Connecticut. He set himself up in a modest commercial building as the "Research Associates of Bridgeport." When the usual "heart disturbance" experiment was run with the same personnel, what percentage of the men do you suppose fully obeyed? Though reduced, the rate remained remarkably high—48 percent.

In everyday life, too, authorities backed by institutions wield social power. Robert Ornstein (1991) tells of a psychiatrist friend who was called to the edge of a cliff above San Mateo, California, where one of his patients, Alfred, was threatening to jump. When the psychiatrist's reasoned reassurance failed to dislodge Alfred, the psychiatrist could only hope that a police crisis expert would soon arrive.

Although no expert came, another police officer, unaware of the drama, happened onto the scene, took out his power bullhorn, and yelled at the assembled cliffside group: "Who's the ass who left that Pontiac station wagon double-parked out there in the middle of the road? I almost hit it. Move it *now*, whoever you are." Hearing the message, Alfred obediently got down at once, moved the car, and then without a word got into the policeman's car for a trip to the nearby hospital.

The liberating effects of group influence

These classic experiments give us a negative view of conformity. But conformity can also be constructive. Perhaps you can recall a time you felt justifiably angry at an unfair teacher but you hesitated to object. Then one or two other students spoke up about the unfair practices, and you followed their example which had a liberating effect. Milgram captured this liberating effect of conformity by placing the teacher with two confederates who were to help conduct the procedure. During the experiment, both confederates defied the experimenter, who then ordered the real participant to continue alone. Did he? No. Ninety percent liberated themselves by conforming to the defiant confederates.

REFLECTIONS ON THE CLASSIC STUDIES

The common response to Milgram's results is to note their counterparts in recent history: the "I was only following orders" defenses of Adolf Eichmann in Nazi Germany; of Lieutenant William Calley, who in 1968 directed the unprovoked slaughter of hundreds of Vietnamese in the village of My Lai; and of the

"If the commander-in-chief tells this lieutenant colonel to go stand in the corner and sit on his head, I will do so."
—Oliver North, 1987

the story behind the research:
Stanley Milgram on obedience
research

While working for Solomon E. Asch, I wondered whether his conformity experiments could be made more humanly significant. First, I imagined an experiment similar to Asch's, except that the group induced the person to deliver shocks to a protesting victim. But a control was needed to see how much shock a person would give in the absence of group pressure. Someone, presumably the experimenter, would have to instruct the subject to give the shocks. But now a new question arose: Just how far would a person go when ordered to administer such shocks? In my mind, the issue had shifted to the willingness of people to comply with destructive orders. It was an exciting moment for me. I realized that this simple question was both humanly important and capable of being precisely answered.

The laboratory procedure gave scientific expression to a more general concern about authority, a concern forced upon members of my generation, in particular upon Jews such as myself, by the atrocities of World War II. The impact of the Holocaust on my own psyche energized my interest in obedience and shaped the particular form in which it was examined.

Source: Abridged from the original for this book and from Milgram, 1977, with permission of Alexandra Milgram.

Stanley Milgram (1933–1984)

"ethnic cleansing" occurring more recently in Iraq, Rwanda, Bosnia, and Kosovo.

Soldiers are trained to obey superiors. Thus one participant in the My Lai massacre recalled:

> [Lieutenant Calley] told me to start shooting. So I started shooting, I poured about four clips into the group. . . . They were begging and saying, "No, no." And the mothers were hugging their children and. . . . Well, we kept right on firing. They was waving their arms and begging. (Wallace, 1969)

The United States military trains soldiers to disobey inappropriate, unlawful orders.

The "safe" scientific contexts of the obedience experiments differ from the wartime contexts. Moreover, much of the mockery and brutality of war and genocide goes beyond obedience (Miller, 2004). The obedience experiments also differ from the other conformity experiments in the strength of the social pressure: Compliance is explicitly commanded. Without the coercion, people did not act cruelly. Yet both the Asch and Milgram experiments share certain commonalities. They showed how compliance can take precedence over moral sense. They succeeded in pressuring people to go against their own consciences. They did more than teach an academic lesson; they sensitized us to moral conflicts in our own lives. And they illustrated and affirmed some familiar social psychological principles: the link between behavior and attitudes, the power of the situation, and the strength of the fundamental attribution error.

Behavior and attitudes

In Chapter 4 we noted that attitudes fail to determine behavior when external influences override inner convictions. These experiments vividly illustrate this

"Maybe I was too patriotic" So said ex-torturer Jeffrey Benzien, shown here demonstrating the "wet bag" technique to South Africa's Truth and Reconciliation Commission. He would place a cloth over victims' heads, bringing them to the terrifying brink of asphyxiation over and over again. Such terror by the former security police, who routinely denied such acts, were used to get an accused person to disclose, for example, where guns were hidden. "I did terrible things," Benzien admitted with apologies to his victims, though he claimed only to be following orders.

principle. When responding alone, Asch's participants nearly always gave the correct answer. It was another matter when they stood alone against a group.

In the obedience experiments, a powerful social pressure (the experimenter's commands) overcame a weaker one (the remote victim's pleas). Torn between the pleas of the victim and the orders of the experimenter, between the desire to avoid doing harm and the desire to be a good participant, a surprising number of people chose to obey.

Why were the participants unable to disengage themselves? How had they become trapped? Imagine yourself as the teacher in yet another version of Milgram's experiment, one he never conducted. Assume that when the learner gives the first wrong answer, the experimenter asks you to zap him with 330 volts. After flicking the switch, you hear the learner scream, complain of a heart disturbance, and plead for mercy. Do you continue?

I think not. Recall the step-by-step entrapment of the foot-in-the-door phenomenon (Chapter 4) as we compare this hypothetical experiment to what Milgram's participants experienced. Their first commitment was mild—15 volts—and it elicited no protest. You, too, would agree to do that much. By the time they delivered 75 volts and heard the learner's first groan, they already had complied five times. On the next trial, the experimenter asked them to commit an act only slightly more extreme than what they had already repeatedly committed. By the time they delivered 330 volts, after 22 acts of compliance, the participants had reduced some of their dissonance. They were therefore in a different psychological state from that of someone beginning the experiment at that point. As we saw in Chapter 4, external behavior and internal disposition can feed one another, sometimes in an escalating spiral. Thus, reported Milgram (1974, p. 10):

> Many subjects harshly devalue the victim as a consequence of acting against him. Such comments as, "He was so stupid and stubborn he deserved to get shocked," were common. Once having acted against the victim, these subjects found it necessary to view him as an unworthy individual, whose punishment was made inevitable by his own deficiencies of intellect and character.

During the early 1970s, the military junta then in power in Greece used this "blame-the-victim" process to train torturers (Haritos-Fatouros, 1988, 2002; Staub, 1989, 2003). There, as in the earlier training of SS officers in Nazi Germany, the military selected candidates based on their respect for and submission to authority. But such tendencies alone do not a torturer make. Thus they would first assign the trainee to guard prisoners, then to participate in arrest squads, then to hit prisoners, then to observe torture, and only then to practice it. Step by step, an obedient but otherwise decent person evolved into an agent of cruelty. Compliance bred acceptance.

As a Holocaust survivor, University of Massachusetts social psychologist Ervin Staub knows too well the forces that can transform citizens into agents of death. From his study of human genocide across the world, Staub (2003) shows where this process can lead. Too often, criticism produces contempt, which licenses cruelty, which, when justified, leads to brutality, then killing, then systematic killing. Evolving attitudes both follow and justify actions. Staub's disturbing conclusion: "Human beings have the capacity to come to experience killing other people as nothing extraordinary" (1989, p. 13).

Humans also have a capacity for heroism. During the Nazi Holocaust, 3,500 French Jews and 1,500 other refugees destined for deportation to Germany were sheltered by the villagers of Le Chambon. The villagers were mostly Protestants, descendants of a persecuted group, and people whose own authorities, their pastors, had taught them to "resist whenever our adversaries will demand of us obedience contrary to the orders of the Gospel" (Rochat, 1993; Rochat & Modigliani, 1995). Ordered to divulge the sheltered Jews, the head pastor modeled disobedience: "I don't know of Jews, I only know of human beings." Without knowing how terrible the war would be or how much they would suffer, the resisters made an initial commitment and then—supported by their beliefs, by their own authorities, and by one another—remained defiant to the war's end. Here and elsewhere, the ultimate response to Nazi occupation usually came early. The first acts of compliance or resistance bred attitudes that influenced behavior, which strengthened attitudes. Initial helping heightened commitment, leading to more helping.

The power of the situation

The most important lesson of Chapter 5—that culture is a powerful shaper of lives—and this chapter's most important lesson—that immediate situational forces are just as powerful—reveal the strength of the social context. To feel this for yourself, imagine violating some minor norms: standing up in the middle of a class; singing out loud in a restaurant; playing golf in a suit. In trying to break with social constraints, we suddenly realize how strong they are.

Even in an individualistic culture, few of us desire to challenge our culture's clearest norms, as did Stephen Gough in his 2003 effort to walk the length of Britain naked (apart from hat, socks, boots, and a rucksack). Between June and January he made it from Lands End, England's most southerly point, to John O'Groats, Scotland's most northerly mainland point. During his 847 mile trek he was arrested 16 times and spent about five months behind bars. "My naked activism is firstly and most importantly about me standing up for myself, a declaration of myself as a beautiful human being" Gough (2003) declared from his website.

Some of Milgram's own students learned this lesson when he and John Sabini (1983) asked their help in studying the effects of violating a simple social norm: asking riders on the New York City subway system for their seats. To their surprise, 56 percent gave up their seats, even when no justification was given. The students' own reactions to making the request were as interesting: Most found it extremely difficult. Often, the words got stuck in their throats, and they had to withdraw. Once having made their requests and gotten seats, they sometimes justified their norm violation by pretending to be sick. Such is the power of the unspoken rules governing our public behavior.

The students in a recent Pennsylvania State University experiment found it similarly difficult to get challenging words out of their mouths. Some students imagined themselves discussing with three others whom to select for survival on a desert island. They were asked to imagine one of the others, a man, injecting three sexist comments, such as, "I think we need more women on the island to keep the men satisfied." How would they react to such sexist remarks? Only 5 percent predicted they would ignore each of the comments or wait to see how others reacted. But when Janet Swim and Lauri Hyers (1999) engaged other students in discussions where such comments were actually made by a male confederate, 55 percent (not 5 percent) said nothing. This once again demonstrates the power of normative pressures and how hard it is to predict behavior, even our own behavior.

Milgram's experiments also offer a lesson about evil. Evil sometimes results from a few bad apples. That's the image of evil symbolized by depraved killers in suspense novels and horror movies. In real life we think of Hitler's extermination of Jews, of Saddam Hussein's extermination of Kurds, of Osama bin Laden's plotting terror. But evil also results from social forces—from the heat, humidity, and disease that help make a whole barrel of apples go bad. As these experiments show, situations can induce ordinary people to agree to falsehoods or to capitulate to cruelty.

> "History, despite its wrenching pain, cannot be unlived, and if faced with courage, need not be lived again."
> —Maya Angelou, *Presidential Inaugural Poem,* January 20, 1993

This is especially true when, as happens often in complex societies, the most terrible evil evolves from a sequence of small evils. "Indeed," notes John Darley (1996),

> it may be difficult to identify the individual who perpetrates the evil; the harm [as when Ford knowingly marketed a Pinto with its vulnerable gas tank] may seem to be an organizational product, with no clear stamp of any individual actor on it. . . . When one probes behind evil actions, one normally finds, not an evil individual viciously forwarding diabolical schemes, but instead ordinary individuals who have done acts of evil because they were caught up in complex social forces.

German civil servants surprised Nazi leaders with their willingness to handle the paperwork of the Holocaust. They were not killing Jews, of course; they were merely pushing paper (Silver & Geller, 1978). When fragmented, evil becomes easier. Milgram studied this compartmentalization of evil by involving yet another 40 men more indirectly. With someone else triggering the shock, they had only to administer the learning test. Now, 37 of the 40 fully complied.

So it is in our everyday lives: The drift toward evil usually comes in small increments, without any conscious intent to do evil. Procrastination involves a similar unintended drift, toward self-harm (Sabini & Silver, 1982). A student knows the deadline for a term paper weeks ahead. Each diversion from work on the paper—a video game here, a TV program there—seems harmless enough. Yet gradually the student veers toward not doing the paper without ever consciously deciding not to do it.

The fundamental attribution error

Why do the results of these classic experiments so often startle people? Is it because we expect people to act in accord with their dispositions? It doesn't surprise us when a surly person is nasty, but we expect those with pleasant dispositions to be kind. Bad people do bad things; good people do good things. The "senseless" 9/11 horror was perpetrated, we heard over and again, by "madmen," by "evil cowards," by "demonic" monsters.

When you read about Milgram's experiments, what impressions did you form of the obedient participants? Most people when told about one or two of the obedient persons, judge them to be aggressive, cold, and unappealing—even after learning that their behavior was typical (Miller & others, 1973). Cruelty, we presume, is inflicted by the cruel at heart.

Günter Bierbrauer (1979) tried to eliminate this underestimation of social forces (the fundamental attribution error). He had university students observe a vivid reenactment of the experiment or play the role of obedient teacher themselves. They still predicted that, in a repeat of Milgram's experiment, their friends would be only minimally compliant. Bierbrauer concluded that although social scientists accumulate evidence that our behavior is a product of our social histories and current environments, most people continue to believe that people's inner qualities reveal themselves—that good people do good and that evil people do evil.

It is tempting to assume that Eichmann and the Auschwitz death camp commanders were uncivilized monsters. But after a hard day's work, the commanders would relax by listening to Beethoven and Schubert. Of the 14 men who attended the January 1942 Wannsee Conference and formulated the Final Solution leading to the Nazi Holocaust, 8 had European university doctorates (Patterson, 1996). Like most other Nazis, Eichmann himself was outwardly indistinguishable from common people with ordinary jobs (Arendt, 1963; Zillmer & others, 1995). Mohamed Atta, the leader of the 9/11 attacks, reportedly had been a "good boy" and an excellent student from a healthy family. Zacarias Moussaoui, the alleged would-be 20th 9/11 attacker, had been very polite when applying for flight lessons and buying knives. He called women "ma'am." If these men had lived next door to us, they would hardly have fit our image of evil monsters.

Or consider the German police battalion responsible for shooting nearly 40,000 Jews in Poland, many of them women, children, and elderly people who were shot in the backs of their heads, gruesomely spraying their brains. Christopher Browning (1992) portrays the "normality" of these men. Like the many others who ravaged Europe's Jewish ghettos, operated the deportation trains, and administered the death camps, they were not Nazis, SS members, or racial fanatics. They were laborers, salesmen, clerks, and artisans—family men who were too old for military service, but who, when directly ordered to kill, did not refuse.

Milgram's conclusion also makes it hard to attribute the Nazi Holocaust to unique character traits in the German people: "The most fundamental lesson of our study," he noted, is that "ordinary people, simply doing their jobs, and without any particular hostility on their part, can become agents in a terrible

"The assaulting quality of the Milgram experiment is really a valuable attack on the denial and indifference of all of us. Whatever upset follows facing the truth, we must eventually face up to the fact that so many of us are, in fact, available to be genociders or their assistants."
—Israel W. Charny, Executive Director, International Conference on the Holocaust and Genocide, 1982

"Eichmann did not hate Jews, and that made it worse, to have no feelings. To make Eichmann appear a monster renders him less dangerous than he was. If you kill a monster you can go to bed and sleep, for there aren't many of them. But if Eichmann was normality, then this is a far more dangerous situation."
—Hannah Arendt, *Eichmann in Jerusalem*, 1963

table 6–2   **Summary of classic obedience studies**

Topic	Researcher	Method	Real-Life Example
Norm formation	Sherif	Assessing suggestibility regarding seeming movement of light	Interpreting events differently after hearing from others; appreciating a tasty food that others love
Conformity	Asch	Agreement with others' obviously wrong perceptual judgments	Doing as others do; fads such as tattoos
Obedience	Milgram	Complying with commands to shock another	Soldiers or employees following questionable orders

destructive process" (Milgram, 1974, p. 6). As Mister Rogers often reminded his preschool television audience, "Good people sometimes do bad things." Perhaps then, we should be more wary of political leaders whose charming dispositions lull us into supposing they would never do evil. Under the sway of evil forces, even nice people are sometimes corrupted as they construct moral rationalizations for immoral behavior (Tsang, 2002). So it is that ordinary soldiers may, in the end, follow orders to shoot defenseless civilians, ordinary employees may follow instructions to produce and distribute degrading products, and ordinary group members may heed commands to brutally haze initiates.

Finally, a comment on the experimental method used in conformity research (see synopsis, Table 6–2): Conformity situations in the laboratory differ from those in everyday life. How often are we asked to judge line lengths or administer shock? As combustion is similar for a burning match and a forest fire, so we assume that psychological processes in the laboratory and in everyday life are similar (Milgram, 1974). We must be careful in generalizing from the simplicity of a burning match to the complexity of a forest fire. Yet controlled experiments on burning matches can give us insights into combustion that we cannot gain by observing forest fires. So, too, the social-psychological experiment offers insights into behavior not readily revealed in everyday life. The experimental situation is unique, but so is every social situation. By testing with a variety of unique tasks, and by repeating experiments in different times and places, researchers probe for the common principles that lie beneath the surface diversity.

Summing up

Conformity—changing one's behavior or belief as a result of group pressure—comes in two forms. *Compliance* is outwardly going along with the group while inwardly disagreeing. *Acceptance* is believing as well as acting in accord with social pressure.

Three classic sets of experiments illustrate how researchers have studied conformity. Muzafer Sherif observed that others' judgments influenced people's estimates of the illusory movement of a point of light. Norms for "proper" answers emerged and survived both over long periods of time and through succeeding generations of research participants. This laboratory suggestibility parallels suggestibility in real life.

Solomon Asch used a task that was as clear-cut as Sherif's was ambiguous. Asch had people listen to others' judgments of which of three comparison lines was equal to a standard line and then make the same judgment themselves. When the others unanimously gave a wrong answer, the participants conformed 37 percent of the time.

Sherif's procedure elicited acceptance; Stanley Milgram's obedience experiments, on the other hand, elicited an extreme form of compliance. Under optimum conditions—a legitimate, close-at-hand commander, a remote victim, and no one else to exemplify disobedience—65 percent of his adult male participants fully obeyed instructions to deliver what were supposedly traumatizing electric shocks to a screaming innocent victim in an adjacent room.

These classic experiments expose the potency of social forces and the ease with which compliance breeds acceptance. Evil is not just the product of bad people in a nice world but also of powerful situations that induce people to conform to falsehoods or capitulate to cruelty.

The classic conformity experiments answered some questions but raised others: (1) Sometimes people conform; sometimes they do not. When do they conform? (2) Why do people conform? Why don't they ignore the group and "to their own selves be true?" (3) Is there a type of person who is likely to conform? Let's take these questions one at a time.

What predicts conformity?

Some situations trigger much conformity, others little conformity. If you want to produce maximum conformity, what conditions would you choose?

Social psychologists wondered: If even Asch's noncoercive, unambiguous situation could elicit a 37 percent conformity rate, would other settings produce even more? Researchers soon discovered that conformity did grow if the judgments were difficult or if the participants felt incompetent. The more insecure we are about our judgments, the more influenced we are by others.

Group attributes also matter. Conformity is highest when the group has three or more people and is cohesive, unanimous, and high in status. Conformity is also highest when the response is public and made without prior commitment. Let's look at each of these conditions.

GROUP SIZE

In laboratory experiments, a group need not be large to have a large effect. Asch and other researchers found that three to five people will elicit much more conformity than just one or two. Increasing the number of people beyond five yields diminishing returns (Gerard & others, 1968; Rosenberg, 1961). In a field experiment, Milgram and his colleagues (1969) had 1, 2, 3, 5, 10, or 15 people pause on a busy New York City sidewalk and look up. As Figure 6–5 shows, the percentage of passersby who also looked up increased as the number looking up increased from one to five persons.

The way the group is "packaged" also makes a difference. Rutgers University researcher David Wilder (1977) gave students a jury case. Before giving their own judgments, the students watched videotapes of four confederates giving their judgments. When the confederates were presented as two independent

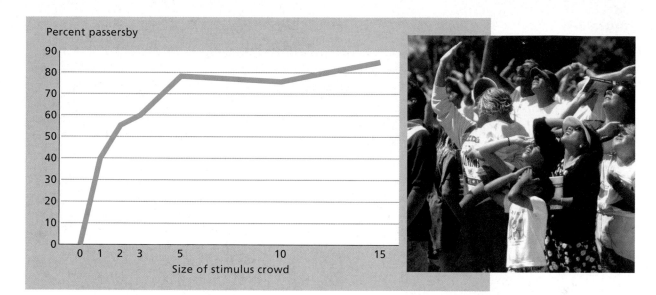

figure 6–5

Group size and conformity.

The percentage of passersby who imitated a group looking upward increased as group size increased to five persons.

Source: Data from Milgram, Bickman, & Berkowitz, 1969.

groups of two people, the participants conformed more than when the four confederates presented their judgments as a single group. Similarly, two groups of three people elicited more conformity than one group of six, and three groups of two people elicited even more. Evidently, the agreement of several small groups makes a position more credible.

UNANIMITY

Imagine yourself in a conformity experiment in which all but one of the people responding before you give the same wrong answer. Would the example of this one nonconforming confederate be as liberating as it was for the individuals in Milgram's obedience experiment? Several experiments reveal that someone who punctures a group's unanimity deflates its social power (Allen & Levine, 1969; Asch, 1955; Morris & Miller, 1975). As Figure 6–6 illustrates, people will nearly always voice their own convictions if just one other person has also done so. The participants in such experiments often later say they felt warm toward and close to their nonconforming ally. Yet they deny that the ally influenced them: "I would have answered just the same if he weren't there."

It's difficult to be a minority of one; few juries are hung because of one dissenting juror. These experiments teach the practical lesson that it is easier to stand up for something if you can find someone else to stand up with you. Many religious groups recognize this. Following the example of Jesus, who sent his disciples out in pairs, the Mormons send two missionaries into a neighborhood together. The support of the one comrade greatly increases a person's social courage.

Observing someone else's dissent—even when it is wrong—can increase our own independence. Charlan Nemeth and Cynthia Chiles (1988) discovered this after having people observe a lone individual in a group of four misjudge blue stimuli as green. Although the dissenter was wrong, observing him enabled the observers to exhibit their own form of independence—76 percent of the time they correctly labeled red slides "red" even when everyone else was calling

"My opinion, my conviction, gains infinitely in strength and success, the moment a second mind has adopted it."
—Novalis, Fragment

figure 6–6

The effect of unanimity on conformity.

When someone giving correct answers punctures the group's unanimity, individuals conform only one-fourth as often.

Source: From Asch, 1955.

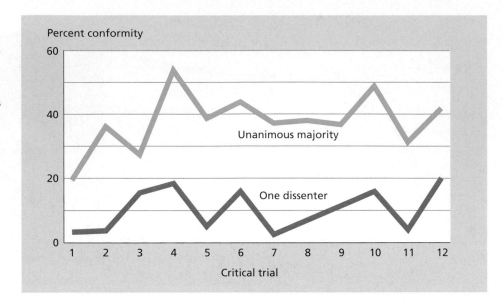

Go to the *SocialSense* CD-ROM to view a clip on girls and body image.

cohesiveness
A "we feeling"; the extent to which members of a group are bound together, such as by attraction for one another.

them "orange." Others, lacking this model of courage, conformed 70 percent of the time.

COHESION

A minority opinion from someone outside the groups we identify with—from someone at another college or of a different religion—sways us less than the same minority opinion from someone within our group (Clark & Maass, 1988). A heterosexual arguing for gay rights would more effectively sway heterosexuals than would a homosexual. People even comply more with requests from those said to share their birthday, their first name, or features of their fingerprint (Burger & others, 2004).

The more **cohesive** a group is, the more power it gains over its members. In college sororities, for example, friends tend to share binge-eating tendencies,

It is difficult to stand alone as a minority of one. But doing so sometimes makes a hero, as was the lone dissenting jury member played by Henry Fonda in the classic movie, 12 Angry Men.

especially as they grow closer (Crandall, 1988). People within an ethnic group may feel a similar "own-group conformity pressure"—to talk, act, and dress as "we" do. Blacks who "act White" or Whites who "act Black" may be mocked by their peers (Contrada & others, 2000).

In experiments, too, group members who feel attracted to the group are more responsive to its influence (Berkowitz, 1954; Lott & Lott, 1961; Sakurai, 1975). They do not like disagreeing with other group members. Fearing rejection by those they like, they allow them, especially those who most typify the group, a certain power (Hogg, 2001). In his *Essay Concerning Human Understanding*, the seventeenth-century philosopher John Locke recognized the cohesiveness factor: "Nor is there one in ten thousand who is stiff and insensible enough to bear up under the constant dislike and condemnation of his own club."

STATUS

As you might suspect, higher-status people tend to have more impact (Driskell & Mullen, 1990). Sometimes people actually avoid agreeing with low-status or stigmatized people. Janet Swim, Melissa Ferguson, and Lauri Hyers (1999) observed this when they placed heterosexual women students as the fifth and last persons to respond in an Asch-type conformity experiment. When all were asked, "Where would you go for a romantic evening with a member of the opposite sex?" the fourth person sometimes replied, "I wouldn't go out for a romantic evening with a man because I'm a lesbian." When so identified, the actual participants thereafter tended, when asked whether they thought discrimination against women was a problem, to avoid her answers.

Studies of jaywalking behavior, conducted with the unwitting aid of nearly 24,000 pedestrians, reveal that the baseline jaywalking rate of 25 percent decreases to 17 percent in the presence of a nonjaywalking confederate and increases to 44 percent in the presence of another jaywalker (Mullen & others, 1990). The nonjaywalker best discourages jaywalking when well dressed. Clothes seem to "make the person" in Australia, too. Michael Walker, Susan Harriman, and Stuart Costello (1980) found that Sydney pedestrians were more compliant when approached by a well-dressed survey taker than one who was poorly dressed.

Milgram (1974) reported that in his obedience experiments people of lower status accepted the experimenter's commands more readily than people of higher status. After delivering 450 volts, a 37-year-old welder turned to the experimenter and deferentially asked, "Where do we go from here, Professor?" (p. 46). Another participant, a divinity school professor who disobeyed at 150 volts, said "I don't understand why the experiment is placed above this person's life" and plied the experimenter with questions about "the ethics of this thing" (p. 48).

The entire parliament fell dead silent. For the first time since anyone could remember, one of the members voted "aye."

A cohesive group.

"Dress for success." A high-status appearance can increase a person's influence.

"If you worry about missing the boat—remember the Titanic."
—Anonymous

PUBLIC RESPONSE

One of the first questions researchers sought to answer was this: Would people conform more in their public responses than in their private opinions? Or would they wobble more in their private opinions but be unwilling to conform publicly, lest they appear wishy-washy? The answer is now clear: In experiments, people conform more when they must respond in front of others rather than writing their answers privately. Asch's participants, after hearing others respond, were less influenced by group pressure if they could write answers that only the experimenter would see. It is much easier to stand up for what we believe in the privacy of the voting booth than before a group.

NO PRIOR COMMITMENT

In 1980, Genuine Risk became the second filly to win the Kentucky Derby. In her next race, the Preakness, she came off the last turn gaining on the leader, Codex, a colt. As they came out of the turn neck and neck, Codex moved sideways toward Genuine Risk, causing her to hesitate and giving him a narrow victory. Had Codex brushed Genuine Risk? Had his jockey even whipped Genuine Risk in the face? The race referees huddled. After a brief deliberation they judged that no foul had occurred and confirmed Codex as the winner. The decision caused an uproar. Televised instant replays showed that Codex had indeed brushed Genuine Risk, the sentimental favorite. A protest was filed. The officials reconsidered their decision, but they did not change it.

Did their declared judgment immediately after the race affect officials' openness toward reaching a different decision later? We will never know for sure. We can, however, put people through a laboratory version of this event—with and without the immediate commitment—and observe whether the commitment makes a difference. Again, imagine yourself in an Asch-type experiment. The experimenter displays the lines and asks you to respond first. After you have given your judgment and then heard everyone else disagree, the experimenter offers you an opportunity to reconsider. In the face of group pressure, do you now back down?

Did Codex brush against Genuine Risk? Once race referees publicly announced their decision, no amount of evidence could budge them.

People almost never do (Deutsch & Gerard, 1955): Once having made a public commitment, they stick to it. At most, they will change their judgments in later situations (Saltzstein & Sandberg, 1979). We may therefore expect that judges of diving or gymnastic competitions, for example, will seldom change their ratings after seeing the other judges' ratings, although they might adjust their later performance ratings.

Prior commitments restrain persuasion, too. When simulated juries make decisions, hung verdicts are more likely in cases when jurors are polled by a show of hands rather than by secret ballot (Kerr & MacCoun, 1985). Making a public commitment makes people hesitant to back down.

Smart persuaders know this. Salespeople ask questions that prompt us to make statements for, rather than against, what they are marketing. Environmentalists ask people to commit themselves to recycling, energy conservation, or bus riding—and find that behavior then changes more than when environmental appeals are heard without inviting a commitment (Katzev & Wang, 1994). Teens 14 to 17 who make a public virginity-till-marriage pledge reportedly become somewhat more likely to remain sexually abstinent, or to delay intercourse, than similar teens who don't make the pledge (Bearman & Brueckner, 2001).

"All right! Have it your own way. It was a ball."

Prior commitment: Once they commit themselves to a position, people seldom yield to social pressure. Real umpires and referees rarely reverse their initial judgments. Copyright © The New Yorker Collection, 1980, Robert Mankoff, from cartoonbank.com. All Rights Reserved.

"Those who never retract their opinions love themselves more than they love truth." —Joubert, *Pensèes*

Summing up

Using conformity testing procedures, experimenters have explored the circumstances that produce conformity. Certain situations appear to be especially powerful. For example, conformity is affected by the characteristics of the group: People conform most when faced with the unanimous reports of three or more attractive, high-status people. People also conform most when their responses are public (in the presence of the group) and made without prior commitment.

Why conform?

"Do you see yonder cloud that's almost in the shape of a camel?" asks Shakespeare's Hamlet of Polonius. "Tis like a camel indeed," replies Polonius. "Methinks it is a weasel," says Hamlet a moment later. "It is backed like a weasel," acknowledges Polonius. "Or like a whale?" wonders Hamlet. "Very like a whale," agrees Polonius. Question: Why does Polonius so readily agree with the Prince of Denmark?

There I was, an American attending my first lecture during an extended visit at a German university. As the lecturer finished, I lifted my hands to join in the clapping. But rather than clap, the other people began rapping the tables with their knuckles. What did this mean? Did they disapprove of the speech? Surely, not everyone would be so openly rude to a visiting dignitary. Nor did their faces express displeasure. No, I decided, this must be a German ovation. Whereupon, I added my knuckles to the chorus.

What prompted this conformity? Why had I not clapped even while the others rapped? There are two possibilities: A person may bow to the group (a) to be

normative influence
Conformity based on a person's desire to fulfill others' expectations, often to gain acceptance.

informational influence
Conformity occurring when people accept evidence about reality provided by other people.

accepted and avoid rejection or (b) to obtain important information. Morton Deutsch and Harold Gerard (1955) named these two possibilities **normative influence** and **informational influence.**

Normative influence is "going along with the crowd" to avoid rejection, to stay in people's good graces, or to gain their approval. Perhaps Polonius sought the favor of Hamlet, the higher-status Prince of Denmark. In the laboratory and in everyday life, groups often reject those who consistently deviate (Miller & Anderson, 1979; Schachter, 1951). This is especially so when dissent is not just "within the family" but when one's group is engaged with another group (Matheson & others, 2003). It's socially permissible for members of Parliament or Congress to disagree with their country's war plans during the internal debate before a war. But once the conflict has begun, everyone is expected to "support our troops." As most of us know, social rejection is painful; when we deviate from group norms, we often pay an emotional price. Gerard (1999) recalls that in one of his conformity experiments an initially friendly participant became upset, asked to leave the room, and returned looking

> sick and visibly shaken. I became worried and suggested that we discontinue the session. He absolutely refused to stop and continued through all 36 trials, not yielding to the others on a single trial. After the experiment was over and I explained the subterfuge to him, his entire body relaxed and he sighed with relief. Color returned to his face. I asked him why he had left the room. 'To vomit,' he said. He did not yield, but at what a price! He wanted so much to be accepted and liked by the others and was afraid he would not be because he had stood his ground against them. There you have normative pressure operating with a vengeance.

"Do as most do and men will speak well of thee."
—Thomas Fuller, *Gnomologia*

Normative influence: Newly elected politicians often dream of changing the system. Then, seeking to climb within the system, normative influences compel them to comply with its social rules.

Sometimes the high price of deviation compels people to support what they do not believe in or at least to suppress their disagreement. "I was afraid that Leideritz and others would think I was a coward," reported one German officer, explaining his reluctance to dissent from mass executions (Waller, 2002). Fearing a court-martial for disobedience, some of the soldiers at My Lai participated in the massacre. Normative influence leads to compliance especially for people who have recently seen others ridiculed or who are seeking to climb a status ladder (Hollander, 1958; Janes & Olson, 2000). As John F. Kennedy (1956) recalled, " 'The way to get along,' I was told when I entered Congress, 'is to go along' " (p. 4).

Informational influence, on the other hand, leads people to acceptance. When reality is ambiguous, as it was for participants in the autokinetic situation, other people can be a valuable source of information. The individual may reason, "I can't tell how far the light is moving. But this guy seems to know." Even the Declaration of Independence says we owe "a decent respect to the opinion of mankind."

Others' responses may also affect how we interpret ambiguous stimuli. Viewing a changing cloud shape, Polonius may actually see what Hamlet helps him see. People who witness others agreeing that "free speech should be limited" may infer a different meaning in the statement than do those who witness others disagreeing (Allen & Wilder, 1980). *After* concurring with a group, people are especially likely to construe a meaning that justifies their decision (Buehler & Griffin, 1994).

So, concern for social image produces normative influence. The desire to be correct produces informational influence. In day-to-day life, normative and informational influence often occur together. I was not about to be the only person in that German lecture hall clapping (normative influence), yet the others' behavior also showed me how to express my appreciation (informational influence).

Experiments on "when people conform" have sometimes isolated either normative or informational influence. Conformity is greater when people respond before a group; this surely reflects normative influence (because people receive the same information whether they respond publicly or privately). On the other hand, conformity is greater when participants feel incompetent, when the task is difficult, and when the individuals care about being right—all signs of informational influence. Why do we conform? For two main reasons: Because we want to be liked and approved of, or because we want to be right.

Nine times out of ten, it's all about peer pressure.

Normative influence.
Reprinted with special permission of King Features Syndicate.

Summing up

Experiments reveal two reasons people conform. *Normative influence* results from a person's desire for acceptance. *Informational influence* results from others' providing evidence about reality. The tendency to conform more when responding publicly reflects normative influence. The tendency to conform more on difficult decision-making tasks reflects informational influence.

Who conforms?

Conformity varies not only with situations but also with persons. How much so? And in what social contexts do personality traits shine through best?

Are some people generally more susceptible (or, should I say, more open) to social influence? Among your friends, can you identify some who are "conformists" and others who are "independent"? In their search for the conformer, researchers have focused on two predictors: personality and culture.

PERSONALITY

During the late 1960s and 1970s, efforts to link personal characteristics with social behaviors, such as conformity, found only weak connections (Mischel, 1968). In contrast to the demonstrable power of situational factors, personality scores were poor predictors of individuals' behavior. If you wanted to know

www.mhhe.com/**myers8**
Visit the Online Learning Center for a scenario on conformity.

how conforming or aggressive or helpful someone was going to be, it seemed you were better off knowing the details of the situation than the person's scores on a battery of psychological tests. As Milgram (1974) concluded: "I am certain that there is a complex personality basis to obedience and disobedience. But I know we have not found it" (p. 205).

Reflecting on his prison simulation and other experiments, Philip Zimbardo argued that the ultimate message

> is to say what it is we have to do to break through your egocentricism, to say you're not different, anything any human being has ever done cannot be alien to you, you can't divorce it! We must break through this "we-they" idea that our dispositional orientation promotes and understand that the situational forces operating on a person at any given moment could be so powerful as to override everything—prior values, history, biology, family, church. (quoted by Bruck, 1976)

During the 1980s, the idea that personal dispositions make little difference prompted personality researchers to pinpoint the circumstances under which traits do predict behavior. Their research affirms a principle that we met in Chapter 4: While internal factors (attitudes, traits) seldom predict precisely a specific action, they do better at predicting a person's average behavior across many situations (Epstein, 1980; Rushton & others, 1983). An analogy may help: Just as your response to a single test item is hard to predict, so is your behavior in a single situation. And just as your total score across the many items of a test is more predictable, so is your total conformity (or outgoingness or aggressiveness) across many situations.

Personality also predicts behavior better when social influences are weak. Milgram's obedience experiments created "strong" situations; their clear-cut demands made it difficult for personality differences to operate. Even so, Milgram's participants differed widely in how obedient they were, and there is good reason to suspect that sometimes his participants' hostility, respect for authority, and concern for meeting expectations affected their obedience (Blass, 1990, 1991). In the Nazi extermination camps, too, some guards displayed kindness; others used live infants as shooting targets or hurled them into the fire. Personality matters. In "weaker" situations—as when two strangers sit in a waiting room with no cues to guide their behavior—individual personalities are even freer to shine (Ickes & others, 1982; Monson & others, 1982). If we compare two similar personalities in very different situations, the situational effect will overwhelm the personality difference. If we compare a group of Saddam Hussein types with a group of Mother Teresa types in a smattering of everyday situations, the personality effect will look much stronger.

It is interesting to note how the pendulum of professional opinion swings. Without discounting the undeniable power of social forces, the pendulum is now swinging back toward an appreciation of individual personality and its genetic predispositions. Like the attitude researchers we considered earlier, personality researchers are clarifying and reaffirming the connection between who we are and what we do. Thanks to their efforts, today's social psychologists agree with pioneering theorist Kurt Lewin's (1936) dictum: "Every psychological event depends upon the state of the person and at the same time on the environment, although their relative importance is different in different cases" (p. 12).

Personality effects loom larger when we note people's differing reactions to the same situation, as when one person reacts with terror and another with delight to a roller coaster ride.

CULTURE

Does cultural background help predict how conforming people will be? Indeed it does. James Whittaker and Robert Meade (1967) repeated Asch's conformity experiment in several countries and found similar conformity rates in most— 31 percent in Lebanon, 32 percent in Hong Kong, 34 percent in Brazil—but 51 percent among the Bantu of Zimbabwe, a tribe with strong sanctions for non-conformity. When Milgram (1961) used a different conformity procedure to compare Norwegian and French students, he consistently found the French students to be less conforming.

When researchers in Australia, Austria, Germany, Italy, Jordan, South Africa, Spain, and the United States repeated the obedience experiments, how do you think the results compared with those with American participants? The obedience rates were similar, or even higher—85 percent in Munich (Blass, 2000).

However, cultures may change. Replications of Asch's experiment with university students in Britain, Canada, and the United States sometimes trigger less conformity than Asch observed two or three decades earlier (Lalancette & Standing, 1990; Larsen, 1974, 1990; Nicholson & others, 1985; Perrin & Spencer, 1981).

"I don't want to get adjusted to this world."
—Woody Guthrie

So conformity and obedience are universal phenomena, yet they vary across cultures and eras (Bond, 1988; Triandis & others, 1988). An analysis by Rod Bond and Peter Smith (1996) of 133 studies in 17 countries confirms that cultural values have an impact on conformity. Compared with people in individualistic countries, those in collectivist countries (where harmony is prized and connections help define the self) are more responsive to others' influence.

The question "Who conforms?" has produced few definitive answers. Global personality scores are poor predictors of specific acts of conformity but better predictors of average tendencies to conformity (and other social behaviors). Trait effects are strongest in "weak" situations where

Summing up

social forces do not overwhelm individual differences. Although conformity and obedience are universal, culture socializes people to be more or less socially responsive.

How can we resist social pressure to conform?

Will people ever actively resist social pressure? When compelled to do A, will they instead do Z? What would motivate such anticonformity?

This chapter, like Chapter 5, emphasizes the power of social forces. It is therefore fitting that we conclude by again reminding ourselves of the power of the person. We are not just billiard balls moving where pushed; we act in response to the forces that push upon us. Knowing that someone is trying to coerce us may even prompt us to react in the *opposite* direction.

REACTANCE

Individuals value their sense of freedom and self-efficacy. So when social pressure becomes so blatant that it threatens their sense of freedom, they often rebel. Think of Romeo and Juliet, whose love was intensified by their families' opposition. Or think of children asserting their freedom and independence by doing the opposite of what their parents ask. Savvy parents therefore offer their children choices instead of commands: "It's time to clean up: Do you want a bath or a shower?"

The theory of psychological **reactance**—that people do indeed act to protect their sense of freedom—is supported by experiments showing that attempts to restrict a person's freedom often produce an anticonformity "boomerang effect" (Brehm & Brehm, 1981; Nail & others, 2000). After today's Western university women give thought to how traditional culture expects women to behave, they become less likely to exhibit traditional feminine modesty (Cialdini & others, 1998). Or suppose someone stops you on the street and asks you to sign a petition advocating something you mildly support. While considering the petition, you are told someone else believes "people absolutely should not be allowed to distribute or sign such petitions." Reactance theory predicts that such blatant attempts to limit freedom will actually increase the likelihood of your signing.

"To do just the opposite is also a form of imitation."
—Lichtenberg, *Aphorismen,* 1764–1799

reactance
A motive to protect or restore one's sense of freedom. Reactance arises when someone threatens our freedom of action.

Reactance. NON SEQUITUR © 1997 Wiley. Dist. by Universal Press Syndicate.

Reactance at work? Underage students have been found to be less often abstinent and more often drinking to excess than students over the legal drinking age.

When Madeline Heilman (1976) staged this experiment on the streets of New York City, that is precisely what she found.

Reactance may contribute to underage drinking. A survey of 18- to 24-year-olds by the Canadian Centre on Substance Abuse (1997) revealed that 69 percent of those over the legal drinking age (21) had been drunk in the last year, as had 77 percent of those *under* 21. In the United States, a survey of students on 56 campuses revealed a 25 percent rate of abstinence among students of legal drinking age (21) but only a 19 percent abstinence rate among students under 21 (Engs & Hanson, 1989). Reactance may also contribute to rape and sexual coercion, suggest Roy Baumeister, Kathleen Catanese, and Henry Wallace (2002). When a woman refuses to comply with a man's desire for sex, he may react with frustration over his restricted freedom and increased desire for the forbidden activity. Mix reactance with narcissism—a self-serving sense of entitlement and low empathy for others—and the unfortunate result can be forced sex.

ASSERTING UNIQUENESS

Imagine a world of complete conformity, where there were no differences among people. Would such a world be a happy place? If nonconformity can create discomfort, can sameness create comfort?

People feel uncomfortable when they appear too different from others. But, at least in Western cultures, they also feel uncomfortable when they appear exactly like everyone else. As experiments by C. R. Snyder and Howard Fromkin (1980) have shown, people feel better when they see themselves as moderately unique. Moreover, they act in ways that will assert their individuality. In one experiment, Snyder (1980) led Purdue University students to believe that their "10 most important attitudes" were either distinct from or nearly identical to the attitudes of 10,000 other students. Then, when they participated in a conformity experiment, those deprived of their feeling of uniqueness were most likely to assert their individuality by nonconformity. In another experiment, people who heard others express attitudes identical to their own altered their positions to maintain their sense of uniqueness.

Both social influence and the desire for uniqueness appear in popular baby names. People seeking less commonplace names often hit upon the same ones at the same time. Among the top 10 U.S. girls' names for 2002 were Madison (2), Alexis (5), and Olivia (10). Those who, in the 1960s, broke out of the pack by naming their baby Rebecca, thinking they were bucking convention, soon

www.mhhe.com/myers8
Visit the Online Learning Center for an interactivity on the "who's" and "why's" of conformity.

When shoulder tattoos come to be perceived as pack behavior—as displaying conformity rather than individuality—we may expect their popularity to similarly decline.

discovered their choice was part of a new pack, notes Peggy Orenstein (2003). Hillary, a popular late '80s, early '90s name, became less original-seeming and less frequent (even among her admirers) after Hillary Clinton became famous. Although the popularity of such names then fades, observes Orenstein, it may resurface with a future generation. Max, Rose, and Sophie sound like the roster of a retirement home—or a play group.

Seeing oneself as unique also appears in people's "spontaneous self-concepts." William McGuire and his Yale University colleagues (McGuire & Padawer-Singer, 1978; McGuire & others, 1979) report that when children are invited to "tell us about yourself," they are most likely to mention their distinctive attributes. Foreign-born children are more likely than others to mention their birthplace. Redheads are more likely than black- and brown-haired children to volunteer their hair color. Light and heavy children are the most likely to refer to their body weight. Minority children are the most likely to mention their race.

Likewise, we become more keenly aware of our gender when we are with people of the other gender (Cota & Dion, 1986). When I attended an American Psychological Association meeting with 10 others—all women as it happened— I immediately was aware of my gender. As we took a break at the end of the second day, I joked that the line would be short at my bathroom, triggering the woman sitting next to me to notice what hadn't crossed her mind—the group's gender makeup.

The principle, says McGuire, is that "one is conscious of oneself insofar as, and in the ways that, one is different." Thus, "If I am a Black woman in a group of White women, I tend to think of myself as a Black; if I move to a group of Black men, my blackness loses salience and I become more conscious of being a woman" (McGuire & others, 1978). This insight helps us understand why any minority group tends to be conscious of its distinctiveness and how the surrounding culture relates to it. The majority group, being less conscious of race, may see the minority group as hypersensitive. When occasionally living in Scotland, where my American accent marks me as a foreigner, I am conscious of my national identity and sensitive to how others react to it. For those of us in

"When I'm in America, I have no doubt I'm a Jew, but I have strong doubts about whether I'm really an American. And when I get to Israel, I know I'm an American, but I have strong doubts about whether I'm a Jew."
—Leslie Fiedler, *Fiedler on the Roof*, 1991

"Self-consciousness, the recognition of a creature by itself as a 'self,' [cannot] exist except in contrast with an 'other,' a something which is not the self."
—C. S. Lewis, *The Problem of Pain*, 1940

Asserting our uniqueness. While not wishing to be greatly deviant, most of us express our distinctiveness through our personal styles and dress.

Western cultures, our distinctiveness is central to our identity (Vignoles & others, 2000).

When the people of two cultures are nearly identical, they still will notice their differences, however small. Even trivial distinctions may provoke scorn and conflict. Jonathan Swift satirized the phenomenon in *Gulliver's Travels* with the story of the Little-Endians' war against the Big-Endians. Their difference: The Little-Endians preferred to break their eggs on the small end, the Big-Endians on the large end. On a world scale, the differences may not seem great between Scots and English, Serbs and Croatians, or Catholic and Protestant Northern Irelanders. But small differences can mean big conflicts (Rothbart & Taylor, 1992). Rivalry is often most intense when the other group most closely resembles you.

It seems that, while we do not like being greatly deviant, we are, ironically, all alike in wanting to feel distinctive and in noticing how we are distinctive. But as research on the self-serving bias (Chapter 2) makes clear, it is not just any kind of distinctiveness we seek but distinctiveness in the right direction. Our quest is not merely to be different from the average, but *better* than average.

Summing up

Social psychology's emphasis on the power of social pressure must be joined by a complementary emphasis on the power of the person. We are not puppets. When social coercion becomes blatant, people often experience *reactance*—a motivation to defy the coercion in order to maintain their sense of freedom. When group members experience reactance simultaneously, the result may be rebellion.

We are not comfortable being too different from a group, but neither do we want to appear the same as everyone else. Thus, we act in ways that preserve our sense of uniqueness and individuality. In a group, we are most conscious of how we differ from the others.

℔ Personal Postscript: On being an individual within community

Do your own thing. Question authority. If it feels good, do it. Follow your bliss. Don't conform. Think for yourself. Be true to yourself. You owe it to yourself.

We hear words like these over and again *if* we live in an individualistic Western nation, such as those of western Europe, Australia, New Zealand, Canada, or, especially, the United States. The unchallenged assumption that individualism is good and conformity is bad is what Chapter 1 called a "social representation," a collectively shared idea. Our mythical cultural heroes—from Huckleberry Finn to Sherlock Holmes to Luke Skywalker to Neo of the *Matrix* trilogy standing up against institutional rules—assume the preeminence of individual rights and celebrate the one who stands against the group.

In 1831, the French writer Alexis de Tocqueville, coined the term "individualism" after traveling America. Individualists, he noted, owe no one "anything and hardly expect anything from anybody. They form the habit of thinking of themselves in isolation and imagine that their whole destiny is in their hands." A century and a half later, therapist Fritz Perls (1972) epitomized this radical individualism in his "Gestalt prayer":

> I do my thing, and you do your thing.
> I am not in this world to live up to your expectations.
> And you are not in this world to live up to mine.

Psychologist Carl Rogers (1985) agreed: "The only question which matters is, 'Am I living in a way which is deeply satisfying to me, and which truly expresses me?'"

As we noted in Chapter 2, that is hardly the only question that matters to people in many other cultures, including those of Asia. Where *community* is prized, conformity is accepted. Schoolchildren often display their solidarity by wearing school uniforms. Attachments run deep. To maintain harmony, confrontation and dissent are muted. "The stake that stands out gets pounded down," say the Japanese.

Amitai Etzioni (1993), a recent president of the American Sociological Association, urges us toward a "communitarian" individualism that balances our nonconformist individualism with a spirit of community. Fellow sociologist Robert Bellah (1996) concurs. "Communitarianism is based on the value of the sacredness of the individual," he explains. But it also "affirms the central value of solidarity . . . that we become who we are through our relationships."

As Westerners in various nations, most readers of this book enjoy the benefits of nonconformist individualism. But communitarians believe there is a cost to our communal well-being. We humans like to feel unique and in control of our lives, but we also are social creatures having a basic need to belong. Conformity is neither all bad nor all good. As individuals, we therefore need to balance our needs for independence and attachment, privacy and community, individuality and social identity.

What do you think?

In what ways are you independent? In what ways are you attached? How do you feel about the balance? Do you think Westerners should be more individualist or more communitarian?

Making the Social Connection

This chapter introduced Ervin Staub's work on obedience and cruelty. We will meet Staub again in Chapter 10: Aggression when we discuss genocide and later, on the happier topic of how we can teach helping (Chapter 12). Is it obedience to authority that brings about genocide? Go to the *SocialSense* CD-ROM to view Staub discussing the roles that authority and respect for authority play in genocide.

"To swallow and follow, whether old doctrine or new propaganda, is a weakness still dominating the human mind."

Charlotte Perkins Gilman, Human Work, *1904*

"Remember that to change thy mind and to follow him that sets thee right, is to be none the less a free agent."

Marcus Aurelius Antoninus, Meditations, *viii. 16, 121–180*

persuasion
The process by which a message induces change in beliefs, attitudes, or behaviors.

chapter 7

Persuasion

Joseph Goebbels, Germany's minister of "popular enlightenment" and propaganda from 1933 to 1945, understood the power of **persuasion.** Given control of publications, radio programs, motion pictures, and the arts, he undertook to persuade Germans to accept Nazi ideology. Julius Streicher, another member of the Nazi group, published *Der Stürmer,* a weekly anti-Semitic (anti-Jewish) newspaper with a circulation of 500,000 and the only paper read cover to cover by his intimate friend, Adolf Hitler. Streicher also published anti-Semitic children's books and, with Goebbels, spoke at the mass rallies that became part of the Nazi propaganda machine.

How effective were Goebbels, Streicher, and other Nazi propagandists? Did they, as the Allies alleged at Streicher's Nuremberg trial, "inject poison into the minds of millions and millions" (Bytwerk, 1976)? Most Germans were not persuaded to feel raging hatred for the Jews. But many were. Others became sympathetic to anti-Semitic measures. And most of the rest became either sufficiently uncertain or sufficiently intimidated to staff the huge genocidal program, or at least to allow it to happen. Without the complicity of millions of people, there would have been no Holocaust (Goldhagen, 1996).

The powers of persuasion were more recently apparent in what a Pew survey (2003) called the "rift between Americans and Western Europeans" over the Iraq war. Surveys shortly before the war, for example, revealed that Europeans (and

Canadians) opposed military action against Iraq by about two to one, while Americans favored it by the same margin (Burkholder, 2003; Moore, 2003; Pew, 2003). Once the war began, Americans' support for the war rose to more than three to one (Newport & others, 2003). Except for Israel, people surveyed in all other countries were opposed to the attack.

Without taking sides regarding the wisdom of the war—that debate we can leave to history—the huge rift between Americans and their distant cousins in other countries points to persuasion at work. What persuaded Americans to favor the war? What persuaded most people elsewhere to oppose it? (Tell me where you live and I will guess whether you view the United States more as protector or predator.)

One possible reason is that people tend to identify with their groups and express their groups' attitudes (see Chapter 9, Prejudice). Attitudes regarding capital punishment, for example, tend to follow a nation's practice. The United States allows the death penalty for murder, and three in four of its citizens support this (Jones, 2003). Most other nations do not have a death penalty, and most of their citizens oppose it (readers in Canada, western Europe, Australia, New Zealand, and most of South America will nod their heads).

In addition to possible rationalization of "my country's" actions, attitudes were also being shaped by persuasive messages that led half of Americans to believe that Saddam was directly involved in the 9/11 attacks and four in five to believe that weapons of mass destruction would be found (Duffy, 2003; Gallup, 2003; Newport & others, 2003). Sociologist James Davison Hunter (2002) notes that culture-shaping usually occurs top-down, as cultural elites control the dissemination of information and ideas. Thus, Americans and people elsewhere learned about and watched a different war (della Cava, 2003; Friedman, 2003; Goldsmith, 2003; Krugman, 2003; Tomorrow, 2003). Depending on where you lived, you may have witnessed

- "America's liberation of Iraq" or "America's invasion of Iraq."
- "Operation Iraqi Freedom" or "The War in Iraq."
- the Iraqi "death squads" or the "Fedayeen" irregulars.
- headlines such as "Tense Standoff Between Troops and Iraqis Erupts in Bloodshed" (ambiguous passive voice headline of *Los Angeles Times*) or "U.S. Troops Fire on Iraqis; 13 Reported Dead" (active voice headline of the same incident by Canada's CBC).
- scenes of captured and dead Iraqis or scenes of captured and dead Americans.
- brief clips of "the usual protestors" (Fox News) or features on massive antiwar rallies.

To many Americans, the media of other nations appeared to combine a pervasive anti-American bias with a blindness to the threat posed by Saddam. To many people elsewhere, the "embedded" American war journalists seemed to feel it their patriotic duty to sell the war. Were they, as the German press wondered, going through *Gleichschaltung*—an ominous word used to describe how the Nazis brought the German media into line (Goldsmith, 2003)? Regardless of where bias lay or whose perspective was better informed, this much seems clear: Depending on where they lived, people were fed (and discussed and believed) somewhat differing information. Persuasion matters.

Persuasive forces also have been harnessed to promote healthier living. Thanks partly to health promotion campaigns, the Centers for Disease Control reports that the American cigarette smoking rate has plunged to 23 percent, barely more than half the rate of 40 years ago. *Statistics Canada* reports a similar smoking decline in Canada. And the rate of new U.S. collegians reporting abstinence from beer has increased—from 25 percent in 1981 to 53 percent in 2002 (Sax & others, 2002). More than at any time in recent decades, health- and safety-conscious educated adults are shunning cigarettes and beer.

Persuasion is everywhere. When we approve it, we may call it "education."

As these examples show, efforts to persuade are sometimes diabolical, sometimes beneficial. Persuasion is neither inherently good nor bad. It is a message's purpose and content that elicit judgments of good or bad. The bad we call "propaganda." The good we call "education." Education is more factually based and less coercive than propaganda. Yet generally we call it "education" when we believe it, "propaganda" when we don't (Lumsden & others, 1980).

"A fanatic is one who can't change his mind and won't change the subject."
—Winston Churchill, 1954

Our opinions have to come from somewhere. Persuasion—whether it be education or propaganda—is therefore inevitable. Indeed, persuasion is everywhere—at the heart of politics, marketing, courtship, parenting, negotiation, evangelism, and courtroom decision making. Social psychologists therefore seek to understand what leads to effective, long-lasting attitude change. What factors affect persuasion? And how, as persuaders, can we most effectively "educate" others?

Imagine that you are a marketing or advertising executive. Or imagine that you are a preacher, trying to increase love and charity among your parishioners. Or imagine that you want to promote energy conservation, to encourage breastfeeding, or to campaign for a political candidate. What could you do to make yourself and your message persuasive? If you are wary of being manipulated by such appeals, to what tactics should you be alert?

To answer such questions, social psychologists usually study persuasion the way some geologists study erosion—by observing the effects of various factors in brief, controlled experiments. The effects are small and are most potent on weak attitudes that don't touch our values (Johnson & Eagly, 1989; Petty & Krosnick, 1995). Yet they enable us to understand how, given enough time, such factors could produce big effects.

What paths lead to persuasion?

What two paths lead to influence? What type of cognitive processing does each involve—and with what effects?

While serving as chief psychologist for the U.S. War Department during World War II, Yale professor Carl Hovland and his colleagues (1949) helped the war effort by studying persuasion. Hoping to shore up soldier morale, Hovland and his colleagues systematically studied the effects of training films and historical documentaries on new recruits' attitudes and opinions toward the war. Back at Yale after the war, they continued studying what makes a message

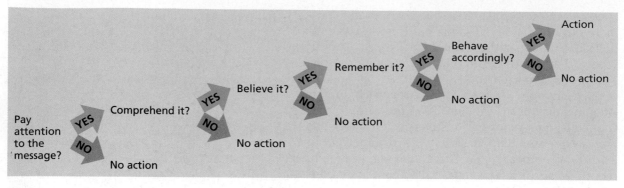

figure 7–1

To elicit action, a persuasive message must clear several hurdles. What is crucial, however, is not so much remembering the message itself, but remembering one's own thoughts in response. **Source:** Adapted from W. J. McGuire. "An Information-Processing Model of Advertising Effectiveness," *Behavioral and Management Sciences in Marketing*, edited by H. L. Davis and A. J. Silk, 1978. Copyright © 1978. Reprinted by permission of John Wiley & Sons, Inc.

persuasive. They varied factors related to the communicator, the content of the message, the channel of communication, and the audience.

As shown in Figure 7–1, persuasion entails clearing several hurdles. Any factors that help people clear the hurdles in the persuasion process increase the likelihood of persuasion. For example, if an attractive source increases your attention to a message, then the message should have a better chance of persuading you. The Yale group's approach to studying persuasion provides us with a good understanding of *when* persuasion is likely to occur.

Researchers at Ohio State University in the '60s, '70s, and '80s suggested that people's thoughts in response to persuasive messages also matter. If a message is clear and easy to comprehend but full of unconvincing arguments, then you will easily counterargue the message and won't be persuaded. If the message offers convincing arguments, then your thoughts will be more favorable, and you will most likely be persuaded. This "cognitive response" approach helps us understand *why* persuasion occurs more in some situations than in others.

THE CENTRAL ROUTE

central route to persuasion
Occurs when interested people focus on the arguments and respond with favorable thoughts.

Richard Petty and John Cacioppo (Cass-ee-OH-poh) (1986; Petty & Wegener, 1999) and Alice Eagly and Shelly Chaiken (1993, 1998) took this one step further. They theorized that persuasion is likely to occur via one of two routes. When people are motivated and able to think systematically about an issue, they are likely to take the **central route to persuasion**—focusing on the arguments. If those arguments are strong and compelling, persuasion is likely. If the message only contains weak arguments, thoughtful people will notice that the arguments aren't very compelling and will counterargue.

THE PERIPHERAL ROUTE

"All effective propaganda must be limited to a very few points and must harp on these in slogans until the last member of the public understands."
—Adolf Hitler, *Mein Kampf*

But sometimes the strength of the arguments doesn't matter. Sometimes we're not all that motivated or able to think carefully. If we're distracted, uninvolved, or just plain busy, we may not take the time to think carefully about the message content. Rather than noticing whether the arguments are particularly compelling, we might follow the **peripheral route to persuasion**—focusing on cues that trigger acceptance without much thinking. When people are distracted or not motivated to think, easily understood familiar statements are more persuasive than novel statements with the same meaning. Thus, for uninvolved or distracted people, "Don't put all your eggs in one basket" has more impact than "Don't risk everything on a single venture" (Howard, 1997).

Smart advertisers adapt ads to their consumers' thinking. Billboards and television commercials—media that consumers are only able to take in for brief amounts of time—typically use visual images as peripheral cues. Our opinions regarding products such as food and drink, cigarettes, and clothing are often based more on feelings than on logic. Ads for such products often use visual peripheral cues. Instead of providing arguments in favor of smoking, cigarette ads associate the product with images of beauty and pleasure. So do soft-drink ads that promote "the real thing" with images of youth, vitality, and happy polar bears. On the other hand, computer ads, which interested, logical consumers may pore over for some time, seldom feature Hollywood stars or great athletes; instead they offer customers information on competitive features and prices. Matching the type of message to the route that message recipients are likely to follow also increases their attention to it (Shavitt, 1990; Petty, Wheeler, & Bizer, 2000).

The ultimate goal of the advertiser, the preacher, and even the teacher is not just to have people pay attention to the message and move on. Typically, the goal involves some sort of behavior change. Are both routes to persuasion equally likely to fulfill this goal? Petty and his colleagues (1995) note how central route processing can lead to more enduring change. When people are thinking carefully and mentally elaborating on issues, they rely not just on the strength of persuasive appeals but on their own thoughts in response as well. It's not so much the arguments that are persuasive as what they get people thinking. And when people think deeply rather than superficially, any changed attitude will more likely persist, resist attack, and influence behavior (Petty & others, 1995; Verplanken, 1991). So the central route is more likely to lead to attitude and behavior changes that "stick," while the peripheral route may lead simply to superficial and temporary attitude change. If you really want someone to stop smoking as a result of the message you've just delivered, it's best both to provide strong, compelling arguments and to increase people's motivation and ability to think about those arguments.

Even thinking people sometimes form tentative opinions using the peripheral route to persuasion. Sometimes it's just easier for us to use simple rule-of-thumb heuristics, such as "trust the experts" or "long messages are credible" (Chaiken & Maheswaran, 1994). Residents of my community once voted on a complicated issue involving the legal ownership of our local hospital. I didn't have the time or interest to study this question myself (I had this book to write). But I noted that referendum supporters were all people I either liked or regarded as experts. So I used a simple heuristic—friends and experts can be trusted—and voted accordingly. We all make snap judgments using other heuristics: If a speaker is articulate and appealing, has apparently good motives, and has several arguments (or better, if the different arguments come from different sources), we usually take the easy peripheral route and accept the message without much thought (Figure 7–2, see page 250).

peripheral route to persuasion
Occurs when people are influenced by incidental cues, such as a speaker's attractiveness.

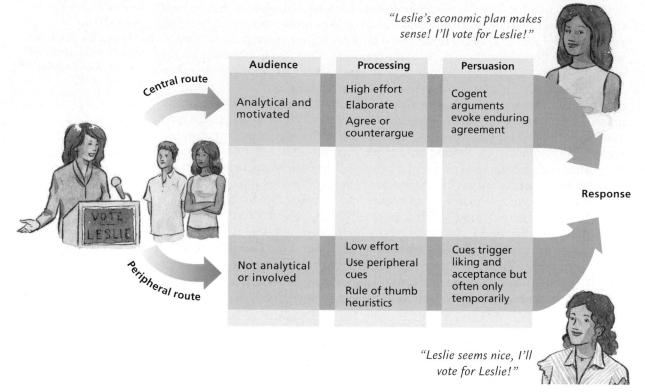

"Leslie's economic plan makes sense! I'll vote for Leslie!"

"Leslie seems nice, I'll vote for Leslie!"

figure 7–2

The central and peripheral routes to persuasion.

Computer ads typically take the central route, by assuming their audience wants to systematically compare features and prices. Soft-drink ads usually take the peripheral route, by merely associating their product with glamour, pleasure, and good moods. Central route processing more often produces enduring attitude change.

Summing up

Sometimes persuasion occurs as people focus on arguments and respond with favorable thoughts. Such systematic, or "central route," persuasion occurs when people are naturally analytical or involved in the issue. When issues don't engage systematic thinking, persuasion may occur through a faster "peripheral route," as people use heuristics or incidental cues to make snap judgments. Central route persuasion, being more thoughtful and less superficial, is more durable and more likely to influence behavior.

What are the elements of persuasion?

Among the primary ingredients of persuasion explored by social psychologists are these four: (1) the communicator, (2) the message, (3) how the message is communicated, and (4) the audience. In other words, who *says* what *by what means to whom? How do these factors affect the likelihood that we will take either the central or peripheral route to persuasion?*

"If I seem excited, Mr. Bolling, it's only because I know that I can make you a very rich man."

WHO SAYS? THE COMMUNICATOR

Imagine the following scene: I. M. Wright, a middle-aged American, is watching the evening news. In the first segment, a small group of radicals is shown burning an American flag. As they do, one shouts through a bullhorn that whenever any government becomes oppressive, "it is the Right of the People to alter or to abolish it. . . . It is their right, it is their duty, to throw off such government!" Angered, Mr. Wright mutters to his wife, "It's sickening to hear them spouting that Communist line." In the next segment, a presidential candidate speaking before an antitax rally declares, "Thrift should be the guiding principle in our government expenditure. It should be made clear to all government workers that corruption and waste are very great crimes." An obviously pleased Mr. Wright relaxes and smiles: "Now that's the kind of good sense we need. That's my kinda guy."

Now switch the scene. Imagine Mr. Wright hearing the same revolutionary line about "the Right of the People" at a July 4 oration of the Declaration of Independence (from which the line comes) and hearing a Communist speaker read the thrift sentence from *Quotations from Chairman Mao Zedong* (from which it comes). Would he now react differently?

Social psychologists have found that who is saying something affects how an audience receives it. In one experiment, when the Socialist and Liberal leaders in the Dutch parliament argued identical positions using the same words, each was most effective with members of his own party (Wiegman, 1985). It's not just the message that matters, but also who says it. What makes one communicator more persuasive than another?

Credibility

Any of us would find a statement about the benefits of exercise more believable if it came from the Royal Society or National Academy of Sciences rather than from a tabloid newspaper. But the effects of source **credibility** (perceived expertise and trustworthiness) diminish after a month or so. If a credible person's message is persuasive, its impact may fade as its source is forgotten or dissociated from the message. The impact of a noncredible person may correspondingly increase over time (if people remember the message better than the reason

credibility
Believability. A credible communicator is perceived as both expert and trustworthy.

for discounting it) (Cook & Flay, 1978; Gruder & others, 1978; Pratkanis & others, 1988). This delayed persuasion, after people forget the source or its connection with the message, is called the **sleeper effect.**

sleeper effect
A delayed impact of a message occurs when an initially discounted message becomes effective, as we remember the message but forget the reason for discounting it.

Perceived expertise.   How does one become an authoritative "expert"? One way is to begin by saying things the audience agrees with, which makes one seem smart. Another is to be introduced as someone who is *knowledgeable* on the topic. A message about toothbrushing from "Dr. James Rundle of the Canadian Dental Association" is much more convincing than the same message from "Jim Rundle, a local high school student who did a project with some of his classmates on dental hygiene" (Olson & Cal, 1984). After spending more than a decade studying high school marijuana use, University of Michigan researchers (Bachman & others, 1988) concluded that scare messages from unreliable sources did not affect marijuana use during the 1960s and 1970s. From a credible source, however, scientific reports of the biological and psychological results of long-term marijuana use "can play an important role in reducing . . . drug use."

"Believe an expert."
—Virgil, *Aeneid*, 19 B.C.

Another way to appear credible is to speak confidently. Bonnie Erickson and her collaborators (1978) had University of North Carolina students evaluate courtroom testimony given in a straightforward manner or in a more hesitant manner. For example:

QUESTION: Approximately how long did you stay there before the ambulance arrived?

ANSWER: [*Straightforward*] Twenty minutes. Long enough to help get Mrs. David straightened out.
[*Hesitating*] Oh, it seems like it was about uh, twenty minutes. Just long enough to help my friend Mrs. David, you know, get straightened out.

The students found the straightforward witnesses much more competent and credible.

Perceived trustworthiness.   Speech style also affects a speaker's apparent trustworthiness. Gordon Hemsley and Anthony Doob (1978) found that if, while testifying, videotaped witnesses looked their questioner *straight in the eye* instead of gazing downward, they impressed people as more believable.

Trustworthiness is also higher if the audience believes the communicator is *not trying to persuade* them. In an experimental version of what later became the "hidden-camera" method of television advertising, Elaine Hatfield and Leon Festinger (Walster & Festinger, 1962) had some Stanford University undergraduates eavesdrop on graduate students' conversations. (What they actually heard was a tape recording.) When the conversational topic was relevant to the eavesdroppers (having to do with campus regulations), supposedly unsuspecting speakers were more influential than speakers said to be aware that someone was listening. After all, if people don't know someone's listening, why would they be less than fully honest?

We also perceive as sincere those who *argue against their own self-interest*. Alice Eagly, Wendy Wood, and Shelly Chaiken (1978) presented University of Massachusetts students with a speech attacking a company's pollution of a river. When they said the speech was given by a political candidate with a business background or to an audience of company supporters, it seemed unbiased and was persuasive. When the same antibusiness speech was supposedly given to environmentalists by a proenvironment politician, listeners could attribute the politician's arguments to personal bias or to the audience. Being willing to suffer for one's beliefs—which Gandhi, Martin Luther King, Jr., and other great leaders have done—also helps convince people of one's sincerity (Knight & Weiss, 1980).

These experiments all point to the importance of attribution: To what do we attribute a speaker's position—to the speaker's bias and selfish motives or to the evidence? Wood and Eagly (1981) report that when a speaker argues an unexpected position, we are more likely to attribute the message to compelling evidence and to find it persuasive. Arguments for generous compensation in a personal-injury case are most persuasive when they come from a stingy person. Arguments for stingy compensation are most persuasive when they come from a normally generous person (Wachtler & Counselman, 1981).

Norman Miller and his colleagues (1976) at the University of Southern California found that trustworthiness and credibility increase when people *talk fast*. People who listened to tape-recorded messages rated fast speakers (about 190 words per minute) as more objective, intelligent, and knowledgeable than slow speakers (about 110 words per minute). They also found the more rapid speakers more persuasive. John F. Kennedy, an exceptionally effective public speaker, sometimes spoke in bursts approaching 300 words per minute.

To Americans (though not to Koreans) fast speech conveys power and competence (Peng & others, 1993). Although fast speech doesn't leave listeners time to elaborate with favorable thoughts, it also cuts short any unfavorable thoughts (Smith & Shaffer, 1991). If an advertiser is persuading you at 70 miles per hour, it's tough to counterargue at the same speed.

Some television ads are obviously constructed to make the communicator appear both expert and trustworthy. Drug companies peddle pain relievers using a speaker in a white lab coat, who declares confidently that most doctors recommend their key ingredient (the ingredient, of course, is aspirin). Given such peripheral cues, people who don't care enough to analyze the evidence may automatically infer the product's value. Other ads seem not to use the credibility principle. It's not primarily for his expertise about sports apparel that Nike pays Tiger Woods $100 million to appear in its ads.

Attractiveness and liking

Most people deny that endorsements by star athletes and entertainers affect them. Most people know that stars are seldom knowledgeable about the product they endorse. Besides, we know the intent is to persuade us; we don't just accidentally eavesdrop on Tiger Woods discussing clothes or cars. Such ads are based on another characteristic of an effective communicator: attractiveness. We may think we are not influenced by attractiveness or likability, but researchers have found otherwise. We're more likely to respond to those we like, a phenomenon well known to those organizing charitable solicitations, candy sales, and Tupperware parties. Even a mere fleeting conversation with someone is enough to increase our liking for someone, and our responsiveness to their influence (Burger & others, 2001). Our liking may open us up to the communicator's arguments (central route persuasion), or it may trigger positive associations when we see the product later (peripheral route persuasion). As with credibility, the liking begets persuasion principle suggests applications (see Table 7–1, see page 254).

table 7–1   Six persuasion principles

In his book *Influence: Science and Practice,* persuasion researcher Robert Cialdini (2000) illustrates six principles that underlie human relationships and human influence.

Principle	Application
Authority: People defer to credible experts.	Establish your expertise; identify problems you have solved and people you have served.
Liking: People respond more affirmatively to those they like.	Win friends and influence people. Create bonds based on similar interests, praise freely.
Social proof: People allow the example of others to validate how to think, feel, and act.	Use "peer power"—have respected others lead the way.
Reciprocity: People feel obliged to repay in kind what they've received.	Be generous with your time and resources. What goes around, comes around.
Consistency: People tend to honor their public commitments.	Have others write or voice their intentions. Don't say "Please do this by. . . ." Instead, elicit a "yes" by asking.
Scarcity: People prize what's scarce.	Highlight genuinely exclusive information or opportunities.

attractiveness

Having qualities that appeal to an audience. An appealing communicator (often someone similar to the audience) is most persuasive on matters of subjective preference.

Attractiveness varies in several ways. *Physical appeal* is one. Arguments, especially emotional ones, are often more influential when they come from beautiful people (Chaiken, 1979; Dion & Stein, 1978; Pallak & others, 1983). *Similarity* is another. As Chapter 11 will emphasize, we tend to like people who are like us. We also are influenced by them. For example, Theodore Dembroski, Thomas Lasater, and Albert Ramirez (1978) gave African American junior high students a taped appeal for proper dental care. When a dentist assessed the cleanliness of their teeth the next day, those who heard the appeal from an African American dentist had cleaner teeth. As a general rule, people respond better to a message that comes from someone in their group (Van Knippenberg & Wilke, 1992; Wilder, 1990).

Is similarity more important than credibility? Sometimes yes, sometimes no. Timothy Brock (1965) found paint store customers more influenced by the testimony of an ordinary person who had recently bought the same amount of paint they planned to buy than by an expert who had recently purchased 20 times as much. But recall that a leading dentist (a dissimilar but expert source) was more persuasive than a student (a similar but inexpert source) when discussing dental hygiene.

Such seemingly contradictory findings bring out the detective in the scientist. They suggest that an undiscovered factor is at work—that similarity is more important given the presence of factor X, and credibility is more important given the absence of factor X. Factor X, as George Goethals and Erick Nelson (1973) discovered, is whether the topic is more one of *subjective preference* or *objective reality.* When the choice concerns matters of personal value, taste, or way of life, *similar* communicators have the most influence. But on judgments of *fact*—Does Sydney have less rainfall than London?—confirmation of belief by a *dissimilar* person does more to boost confidence. A dissimilar person, better yet an expert, provides a more independent judgment.

Attractive communicators, such as Serena and Venus Williams endorsing Reebok and Puma, often trigger peripheral route persuasion. We associate their message or product with our good feelings toward the communicator, and we approve and believe.

WHAT IS SAID? THE MESSAGE CONTENT

It matters not only who says something, but *what* that person says. If you were to help organize an appeal to get people to vote for school taxes or to stop smoking or to give money to world hunger relief, you might wonder how to concoct a recipe for central route persuasion. Common sense could lead you to either side of these questions:

www.mhhe.com/**myers8**
How can the person who delivers a message be persuasive? Visit the Online Learning Center for a scenario on persuasion.

- Is a purely logical message most persuasive—or one that arouses emotion?
- Will you get more opinion change by advocating a position only slightly discrepant from the listeners' existing opinions or by advocating an extreme point of view?
- Should the message express your side only, or should it acknowledge and refute the opposing views?
- If people are to present both sides—say, in successive talks at a community meeting—is there an advantage to going first or last?

Let's take these questions one at a time.

Reason versus emotion

Suppose you were campaigning in support of world hunger relief. Would you best itemize your arguments and cite an array of impressive statistics? Or would you be more effective presenting an emotional approach—perhaps the compelling story of one starving child? Of course, an argument can be both reasonable and emotional. You can marry passion and logic. Still, which is *more* influential—reason or emotion? Was Shakespeare's Lysander right: "The will of man is by his reason sway'd"? Or was Lord Chesterfield's advice wiser: "Address yourself generally to the senses, to the heart, and to the weaknesses of mankind, but rarely to their reason"?

"The truth is always the strongest argument."
—Sophocles, *Phaedra,* 496–406 B.C.

The answer: It depends on the audience. Well-educated or analytical people are more responsive to rational appeals than are less educated or less analytical people (Cacioppo & others, 1983, 1996; Hovland & others, 1949). Thoughtful, involved audiences travel the central route; they are most responsive to reasoned arguments. Disinterested audiences travel the peripheral route; they are more affected by how much they like the communicator (Chaiken, 1980; Petty & others, 1981).

To judge from interviews before major elections, many voters are uninvolved. Americans' voting preferences have been more predictable from emotional reactions to the candidates than from their beliefs about the candidates' traits and likely behaviors (Abelson & others, 1982). It also matters how people's attitudes were formed. When people's initial attitudes are formed primarily through emotion, they are more persuaded by later emotional appeals; when their initial attitudes are formed primarily through reason, they are more persuaded by later intellectual arguments (Edwards, 1990; Fabrigar & Petty, 1999). New emotions may sway an emotion-based attitude. But to change an information-based attitude, more information may be needed.

Advertising research, as in one study of the persuasiveness of 168 television commercials (Agres, 1987), reveals that the most effective ads often invoke both reason ("You'll get whiter whites with Detergent X") and emotion ("Choosy mothers choose Jif").

The effect of good feelings. Messages also become more persuasive through association with good feelings. Irving Janis and his colleagues (1965; Dabbs & Janis, 1965) found that Yale students were more convinced by persuasive messages if they were allowed to enjoy peanuts and Pepsi while reading the messages (Figure 7–3). Similarly, Mark Galizio and Clyde Hendrick (1972) found that Kent State University students were more persuaded by folk-song lyrics accompanied by pleasant guitar music than they were by unaccompanied lyrics. Those who like conducting business over sumptuous lunches with soft background music can celebrate these results.

Good feelings often enhance persuasion—partly by enhancing positive thinking (if people are motivated to think) and partly by linking good feelings

figure 7–3

People who snacked as they read were more persuaded than those who read without snacking.

Source: Data from Janis, Kaye, & Kirschner, 1965.

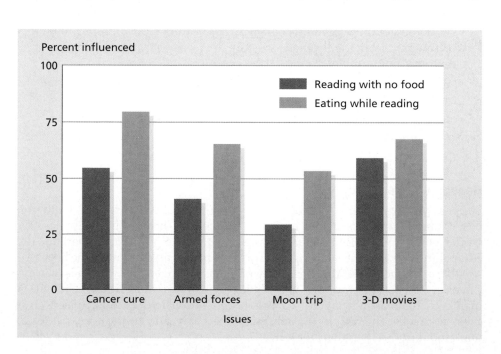

with the message (Petty & others, 1993). As noted in Chapter 3, in a good mood, people view the world through rose-colored glasses. But they also make faster, more impulsive decisions; they rely more on peripheral cues (Bodenhausen, 1993; Schwarz & others, 1991). Unhappy people ruminate more before reacting, so they are less easily swayed by weak arguments. Thus, if you can't make a strong case, you might want to put your audience in a good mood and hope they'll feel good about your message without thinking too much about it.

"If the jury had been sequestered in a nicer hotel, this would probably never have happened."

Good feelings help create positive attitudes. Copyright © The New Yorker Collection, 1997, Frank Cotham, from cartoonbank.com. All Rights Reserved.

The effect of arousing fear.   Messages can also be effective by evoking negative emotions. When trying to convince people to cut down on smoking, brush their teeth more often, get a tetanus shot, or drive carefully, a fear-arousing message can be potent (Muller & Johnson, 1990). The Canadian government is counting on the fact that showing cigarette smokers the horrible things that can happen

Canadian cigarette warnings, sampled here, use fear-arousal.

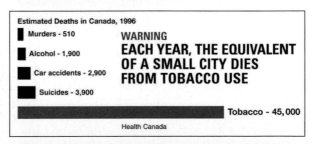

to people who smoke adds to persuasiveness by requiring cigarette makers to include graphic representations of the hazards of smoking on each new pack of cigarettes (Newman, 2001). But how much fear should you arouse? Should you evoke just a little fear, lest people become so frightened that they tune out your painful message? Or should you try to scare the daylights out of them? Experiments by Howard Leventhal (1970) and his collaborators at the University of Wisconsin and by Ronald Rogers and his collaborators at the University of Alabama (Robberson & Rogers, 1988) show that, often, the more frightened people are, the more they respond.

The effectiveness of fear-arousing communications is being applied in ads discouraging not only smoking, but also risky sexual behaviors and drinking and driving. When Claude Levy-Leboyer (1988) found that attitudes toward alcohol and drinking habits among French youth were changed effectively by fear-arousing pictures, the French government incorporated such pictures into its TV spots. To have one's fears aroused is to become more intensely interested in information about a disease, and in ways to prevent it (Das & others, 2003; Ruiter & others, 2001). Moreover, compared with positively framed messages ("abstinence indicates responsibility, self-respect, and planning for the future"), negatively framed messages ("engaging in sex indicates irresponsibility, lack of self-respect, and poor planning for the future") lead people to perceive a stronger norm for the advocated behavior (sexual abstinence). And that should strengthen the persuasive appeal (Stuart & Blanton, 2003).

Fear-arousing communications are increasing people's detection behaviors, such as getting mammograms, doing breast or testicular self-exams, and checking for signs of skin cancer. Sara Banks, Peter Salovey, and their colleagues (1995) had women aged 40–66 who had not obtained mammograms view an educational video on mammography. Of those who received a positively framed message (emphasizing that getting a mammogram can save your life through early detection), only half got a mammogram within 12 months. Of those who received a fear-framed message (emphasizing that not getting a mammogram can cost you your life), two-thirds got a mammogram within 12 months.

Playing on fear won't always make a message more potent. Many people who have been made afraid of AIDS are *not* abstaining from sex or using condoms. Many people who have been made to fear an early death from smoking continue to smoke. When the fear pertains to a pleasurable activity, notes Elliot Aronson (1997), the result often is not behavioral change but denial.

People may engage in denial because, when they aren't told how to avoid the danger, frightening messages can be overwhelming (Leventhal, 1970; Rogers & Mewborn, 1976). Fear-arousing messages are more effective if you lead people not only to fear the severity and likelihood of a threatened event but also to perceive a solution and to feel capable of implementing it (DeVos-Comby & Salovey, 2002; Maddux & Rogers, 1983; Ruiter & others, 2001). Anxiety-creating health messages about, say, the risks of high cholesterol can increase people's intentions to eat a low-fat, low-cholesterol diet (Millar & Millar, 1996).

Many ads aimed at reducing sexual risks aim both to arouse fear—"AIDS kills"—and to offer a protective strategy: Abstain or wear a condom or save sex for a committed relationship. During the 1980s, fear of AIDS did persuade many men to alter their behavior. One study of 5,000 gay men found that, as the AIDS crisis mushroomed between 1984 and 1986, the number saying they were celibate or monogamous rose from 14 to 39 percent (Fineberg, 1988).

Vivid propaganda often exploits fears. Streicher's Der Stürmer aroused fear with hundreds upon hundreds of unsubstantiated anecdotes about Jews who were said to have ground rats to make hash, seduced non-Jewish women, and cheated families out of their life savings. Streicher's appeals, like most Nazi propaganda, were emotional, not logical. The appeals also gave clear, specific instructions on how to combat "the danger": They listed Jewish businesses so readers would avoid them, encouraged readers to submit for publication the names of Germans who patronized Jewish shops and professionals, and directed readers to compile lists of Jews in their area (Bytwerk & Brooks, 1980).

Then, after the Holocaust, there emerged the vivid diary of one girl, one story—"and so much impact," note Steven Sherman, Denise Beike, and Kenneth Ryalls (1999). Hundreds of books have been written about the Nazi atrocities. Yet "one book by one girl has been translated into virtually every language and has sold more books than all the historical documentation of the Nazi occupation combined. More people, in fact, visit [the Anne Frank House] than any other site in Amsterdam, a city of countless museums and of much history."

"If those who have studied the art of writing are in accord on any one point, it is on this: the surest way to arouse and hold the attention of the reader is by being specific, definite, and concrete."
—William Strunk and E. B. White, *The Elements of Style,* 1979

Discrepancy

Picture the following scene: Wanda arrives home on spring vacation and hopes to convert her portly, middle-aged father to her new "health-fitness lifestyle." She runs 5 miles a day. Her father says his idea of exercise is "channel surfing." Wanda thinks, "Would I be more likely to get Dad off his duff by urging him to try a modest exercise program, say a daily walk, or by trying to get him involved in something strenuous, say a program of calisthenics and running? Maybe if I asked him to take up a rigorous exercise program, he would compromise and at least take up something worthwhile. But then again maybe he'd think I'm crazy and do nothing."

Like Wanda, social psychologists can reason either way. Disagreement produces discomfort, and discomfort prompts people to change their opinions (recall from Chapter 4 the effects of dissonance). So perhaps greater disagreement will produce more change. Then again, a communicator who proclaims an uncomfortable message may get discredited. People who disagree with conclusions drawn by a newscaster rate the newscaster as more biased, inaccurate, and untrustworthy. People are more open to conclusions within their range of acceptability (Liberman & Chaiken, 1992; Zanna, 1993). So perhaps greater disagreement will produce less change. With a sexually active population, health educators might best advocate safer sex. With a not-yet-active population, they might advocate abstinence (DeVos-Comby & Salovey, 2002).

Elliot Aronson, Judith Turner, and Merrill Carlsmith (1963) reasoned that when advocating a position *greatly discrepant* from the recipient's, a *credible source*—one hard to discount—would elicit the most opinion change. Sure enough, when credible T. S. Eliot was said to have highly praised a disliked poem, people changed their opinion more than when he gave it faint praise. But when "Agnes Stearns, a student at Mississippi State Teachers College," evaluated a disliked poem, high praise was no more persuasive than faint praise. Thus, as Figure 7–4 (see page 260) shows, discrepancy and credibility *interact:* The effect of a large versus small discrepancy depends on whether the communicator is credible.

So the answer to Wanda's question—"Should I argue an extreme position?"—is, "It depends." Is Wanda in her adoring father's eyes a highly

figure 7–4

Discrepancy interacts with communicator credibility.

Only a highly credible communicator maintains effectiveness when arguing an extreme position. **Source:**   Data from Aronson, Turner, & Carlsmith, 1963.

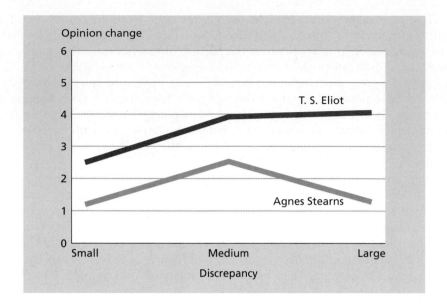

prestigious, authoritative source? If so, Wanda should push for a complete fitness program. If not, Wanda would be wise to make a more modest appeal.

The answer also depends on how involved her father is in the issue. Deeply involved people tend to accept only a narrow range of views. To them, a moderately discrepant message may seem foolishly radical, especially if the message argues an opposing view rather than being a more extreme version of a view with which they already agree (Pallak & others, 1972; Petty & Cacioppo, 1979; Rhine & Severance, 1970). If Wanda's father has not yet thought or cared much about exercise, she can probably take a more extreme position than if he is strongly committed to not exercising. *So, if you are a credible authority and your audience isn't much concerned with your issue, go for it:* Advocate a discrepant view.

One-sided versus two-sided appeals

Persuaders face another practical issue: how to deal with opposing arguments. Once again, common sense offers no clear answer. Acknowledging the opposing arguments might confuse the audience and weaken the case. On the other hand, a message might seem fairer and be more disarming if it recognizes the opposition's arguments.

Carol Werner and her colleagues (2002) showed the disarming power of a simple two-sided message in experimental messages that promoted aluminum can recycling. Signs added to wastebaskets in a University of Utah classroom building said, for example, "No Aluminum Cans Please!!!!! Use the Recycler Located on the First Floor, Near the Entrance." When a final persuasive message acknowledged and responded to the main counterargument—"It May Be Inconvenient. But It Is Important!!!!!!!!!!!"—recycling reached 80 percent (double the rate before any message, and more than in other message conditions).

After Germany's defeat in World War II, the U.S. Army did not want soldiers to relax and think that the still ongoing war with Japan would become easy. So social psychologist Carl Hovland and his colleagues (1949) in the Army's Information and Education Division designed two radio broadcasts arguing that the war in the Pacific would last at least two more years. One broadcast was

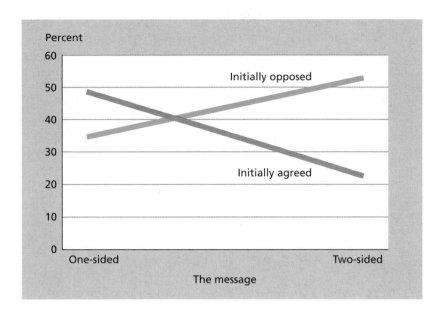

figure 7–5

The interaction of initial opinion with one- versus two-sidedness.
After Germany's defeat in World War II, American soldiers skeptical of a message suggesting Japan's strength were more persuaded by a two-sided communication. Soldiers initially agreeing with the message were strengthened more by a one-sided message. **Source:** Data from Howland, Lumsdaine, & Sheffield, 1949.

one-sided; it did not acknowledge the existence of contradictory arguments, such as the advantage of fighting only one enemy instead of two. The other broadcast was two-sided; it mentioned and responded to the opposing arguments. As Figure 7–5 illustrates, the effectiveness of the message depended on the listener. A one-sided appeal was most effective with those who already agreed. An appeal that acknowledged opposing arguments worked better with those who disagreed.

Experiments also reveal that if people are (or will be) aware of opposing arguments, a two-sided presentation is more persuasive and enduring (Jones & Brehm, 1970; Lumsdaine & Janis, 1953). In simulated trials, a defense case becomes more credible when the defense brings up damaging evidence before the prosecution does (Williams & others, 1993). Apparently, a one-sided message stimulates an informed audience to think of counterarguments and to view the communicator as biased. Thus, a political candidate speaking to a politically informed group would indeed be wise to respond to the opposition. So *if your audience will be exposed to opposing views, offer a two-sided appeal.*

This interaction effect typifies persuasion research. For optimists, positive persuasion works best ("The new plan reduces tuition in exchange for part-time university service."). For pessimists, negative persuasion is more effective ("All students will have to work part-time for the university, lest they pay out-of-state tuition.") (Geers & others, 2003). We might wish that persuasion variables had simple effects. (It would make this an easier chapter to study.) Alas, most variables, note Richard Petty and Duane Wegener (1998), "have complex effects—increasing persuasion in some situations and decreasing it in others."

As students and scientists we cherish "Occam's razor"—seeking the simplest possible principles. But if human reality is complex, well, our principles will need to have some complexity as well.

Primacy versus recency

Imagine that you are a consultant to a prominent politician who must soon debate another prominent politician regarding a proposed global warming treaty.

"Opponents fancy they refute us when they repeat their own opinion and pay no attention to ours."
—Goethe, *Maxims and Reflections*

Three weeks before the vote, each politician is to appear on the nightly news and present a prepared statement. By the flip of a coin, your side receives the choice of whether to speak first or last. Knowing that you are a former social psychology student, everyone looks to you for advice.

You mentally scan your old books and lecture notes. Would first be best? People's preconceptions control their interpretations. Moreover, a belief, once formed, is difficult to discredit, so going first could give people ideas that would favorably bias how they perceive and interpret the second speech. Besides, people may pay most attention to what comes first. Then again, people remember recent things best. Might it really be more effective to speak last?

Your first line of reasoning predicts what is most common, a **primacy effect:** Information presented early is most persuasive. First impressions *are* important. For example, can you sense a difference between these two descriptions?

- John is intelligent, industrious, impulsive, critical, stubborn, and envious.
- John is envious, stubborn, critical, impulsive, industrious, and intelligent.

When Solomon Asch (1946) gave these sentences to college students in New York City, those who read the adjectives in the intelligent-to-envious order rated the person more positively than did those given the envious-to-intelligent order. The earlier information seemed to color their interpretation of the later information, producing the primacy effect. A similar effect occurs in experiments where people succeed on a guessing task 50 percent of the time. Those whose successes come early seem more able than those whose successes come mostly after early failures (Jones & others, 1968; Langer & Roth, 1975; McAndrew, 1981).

Is primacy the rule in persuasion as well as judgment? Norman Miller and Donald Campbell (1959) gave Northwestern University students a condensed transcript from an actual civil trial. They placed the plaintiff's testimony and arguments in one block, those for the defense in another. The students read both blocks. When they returned a week later to declare their opinions, most sided with the information they had read first. What about the opposite possibility? We have all experienced what the book of Proverbs observed: "The one who first states a case seems right, until the other comes and cross-examines." So will our better memory for recent information ever create a **recency effect?** We know from our experience (as well as from memory experiments) that today's events can temporarily outweigh significant past events. To test this, Miller and Campbell gave another group of students one block of testimony to read. A week later the researchers had them read the second block and then immediately state their opinions. The results were the reverse of the other condition—a recency effect. Apparently the first block of arguments, being a week old, had largely faded from memory.

Forgetting creates the recency effect (1) when enough time separates the two messages *and* (2) when the audience commits itself soon after the second message. When the two messages are back to back, followed by a time gap, a primacy effect usually occurs (Figure 7–6). This is especially so when the first message stimulates thinking (Haugtvedt & Wegener, 1994). What advice would you now give to the political debater?

primacy effect
Other things being equal, information presented first usually has the most influence.

recency effect
Information presented last sometimes has the most influence. Recency effects are less common than primacy effects.

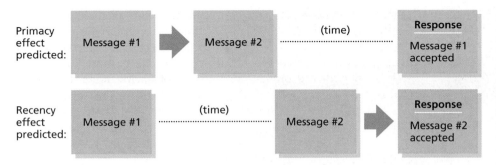

figure 7–6
Primacy effect versus recency effect.
When two persuasive messages are back to back and the audience then responds at some later time, the first message has the advantage (primacy effect). When the two messages are separated in time and the audience responds soon after the second message, the second message has the advantage (recency effect).

channel of communication
The way the message is delivered—whether face to face, in writing, on film, or in some other way.

HOW IS IT SAID? THE CHANNEL OF COMMUNICATION

In Chapter 4 we noted that our actions shape who we are. When we act, we amplify the idea behind what we've done, especially when we feel responsible. We also noted that attitudes rooted in our own experience are more likely to endure and to affect our behavior. Compared with attitudes formed passively, experience-based attitudes are more confident, more stable, and less vulnerable to attack.

Commonsense psychology nevertheless places faith in the power of written words. How do we try to get people out to a campus event? We post notices. How do we get drivers to slow down and keep their eyes on the road? We put "Drive Carefully" messages on billboards. How do we discourage students from dropping trash on campus? We post antilitter messages on campus bulletin boards and in mailboxes.

Are people so easily persuaded? Consider two well-intentioned efforts. At Scripps College in California, a week-long antilitter campaign urged students to "Keep Scripps' campus beautiful," "Let's clean up our trash," and so forth. Such slogans were placed in students' mailboxes each morning and displayed on prominent posters across the campus. The day before the campaign began, social psychologist Raymond Paloutzian (1979) placed litter near a trash can along a well-traveled sidewalk. Then he stepped back to record the behavior of 180 passersby. No one picked up anything. On the last day of the campaign, he repeated the test with 180 more passersby. Did the pedestrians now race one another in their zeal to comply with the appeals? Hardly. Only 2 of the 180 picked up the trash.

Active experience or passive reception?

Are spoken appeals more persuasive? Not necessarily. Those of us who speak publicly, as teachers or persuaders, become so enamored of our spoken words that we are tempted to overestimate their power. Ask college students what aspect of their college experience has been most valuable or what they remember from their first year, and few, I am sad to say, recall the brilliant lectures that we faculty remember giving.

Thomas Crawford (1974) and his associates tested the impact of the spoken word by going to the homes of people from 12 churches shortly before and after they heard sermons opposing racial bigotry and injustice. When asked during the second interview whether they had heard or read anything about racial prejudice or discrimination since the previous interview, only 10 percent recalled the sermons spontaneously. When the remaining 90 percent were asked

Advertising power. Cigarette advertising campaigns have correlated with teen smoking increases among the targeted gender (Pierce & others, 1994, 1995). This photo shows models practicing the "correct" pucker and blow technique for a 1950s TV ad.

In study after study, most people agree that mass media influence attitudes—other people's attitudes, but not their own (Duck & others, 1995).

directly whether their priest had "talked about prejudice or discrimination in the last couple of weeks," more than 30 percent denied hearing such a sermon. The end result: The sermons left racial attitudes unaffected.

When you stop to think about it, an effective preacher has many hurdles to surmount. As Figure 7–1 showed, a persuasive speaker must deliver a message that not only gets attention but also is understandable, convincing, memorable, and compelling. A carefully thought-out appeal must consider each of these steps in the persuasion process.

Passively received appeals, however, are not always futile. My drugstore sells two brands of aspirin, one heavily advertised and one unadvertised. Apart from slight differences in how fast each tablet crumbles in your mouth, any pharmacist will tell you the two brands are identical. Aspirin is aspirin. Our bodies cannot tell the difference. But our pocketbooks can. The advertised brand sells to millions of people for three times the price of the unadvertised brand.

With such power, can the media help a wealthy political candidate buy an election? In presidential primaries those who spend the most usually get the most votes (Grush, 1980). Advertising exposure helps make an unfamiliar candidate into a familiar one. As we will see in Chapter 11, mere exposure to unfamiliar stimuli breeds liking. Moreover, mere repetition can make things believable. People rate trivial statements such as "Mercury has a higher boiling point than copper" as more truthful if they read and rated them a week before. Researcher Hal Arkes (1990) calls such findings "scary." As political manipulators know, believable lies can displace hard truths. Repeated clichés can cover complex realities.

Mere repetition of a statement also serves to increase its fluency—the ease with which it spills off our tongue—which increases believability (McGlone & Tofighbakhsh, 2000). Other factors, such as rhyming, also increase fluency, and believability. "Variety presents satiety" may say essentially the same thing as "variation prevents satiety," but it seems more true. Whatever makes for fluency (familiarity, rhyming) also makes for credibility.

Would the media be as effective with important issues and familiar candidates? Europeans watched and read about a different Iraq war than presented to Americans and developed different attitudes. Yet researchers have time and again found that political advertising has little effect on voters' attitudes in general presidential elections (although, of course, even a small effect could swing a close election) (Kinder & Sears, 1985; McGuire, 1986).

Because passively received appeals are sometimes effective and sometimes not, can we specify in advance the topics on which a persuasive appeal will be successful? There is a simple rule: Persuasion *decreases* as the significance and familiarity of the issue *increase*. On minor issues, such as which brand of aspirin to buy, it's easy to demonstrate the media's power. On more familiar and important issues, such as racial attitudes in racially tense cities, persuading people is like trying to push a piano uphill. It is not impossible, but one shove won't do it.

Personal versus media influence

Persuasion studies demonstrate that the major influence on us is not the media but our contact with people. Two field experiments illustrate the strength of personal influence. Some years ago, Samuel Eldersveld and Richard Dodge (1954) studied political persuasion in Ann Arbor, Michigan. They divided citizens intending not to vote for a revision of the city charter into three groups. Among those exposed only to what they saw and heard in the mass media, 19 percent changed their minds and voted for the revision on election day. Of a second group, who received four mailings in support of the revision, 45 percent voted for it. Among people in a third group, who were visited personally and given the appeal face to face, 75 percent cast their votes for the revision.

In another field experiment, a research team led by John Farquhar and Nathan Maccoby (1977; Maccoby & Alexander, 1980; Maccoby, 1980) tried to reduce the frequency of heart disease among middle-aged adults in three small California cities. To check the relative effectiveness of personal and media influence, they interviewed and medically examined 1,200 people before the project began and at the end of each of the following three years. Residents of Tracy, California, received no persuasive appeals other than those occurring in their regular media. In Gilroy, California, a two-year multimedia campaign used TV, radio, newspapers, and direct mail to teach people about coronary risk and what they could do to reduce it. In Watsonville, California, this media campaign was supplemented by personal contacts with two-thirds of those whose blood pressure, weight, and age put them in a high-risk group. Using behavior-modification principles, the researchers helped people set specific goals and reinforced their successes.

As Figure 7–7 (see page 266) shows, after one, two, and three years, the high-risk people in Tracy (the control town) were about as much at risk as before. High-risk people in Gilroy, which was deluged with media appeals, improved their health habits and decreased their risk somewhat. Those in Watsonville, who received personal contacts as well as the media campaign, changed most.

Do you recognize the potency of personal influence in your own experience? In retrospect, most college students say they have learned more from their friends and other students than from contact with books or professors. Educational researchers have confirmed the students' intuition: Out-of-class personal relationships powerfully influence how students mature during college (Astin, 1972; Wilson & others, 1975).

Although face-to-face influence is usually greater than media influence, we should not underestimate the media's power. Those who personally influence our opinions must get their ideas somewhere, and often their sources are the media. Elihu Katz (1957) observed that many of the media's effects operate in a **two-step flow of communication**—from media to opinion leaders to the rank

two-step flow of communication
The process by which media influence often occurs through opinion leaders, who in turn influence others.

figure 7–7

Percentage change from baseline (0) in coronary risk after one, two, or three years of health education.
Source: Data from Maccoby, 1980.

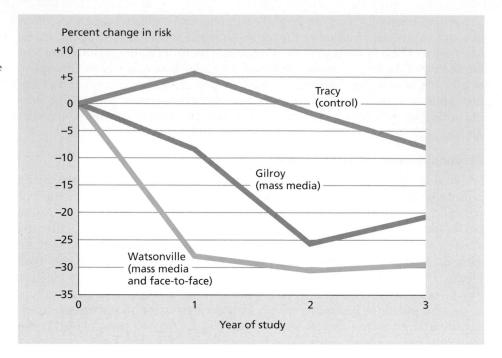

and file. If I want to evaluate computer equipment, I defer to the opinions of my son, who gets many of his ideas from the printed page.

The two-step flow model reminds us that media influences penetrate the culture in subtle ways. Even if the media had little direct effect on people's attitudes, they could still have a big indirect effect. Those rare children who grow up without watching television do not grow up beyond television's influence. Unless they live as hermits, they will join in TV-imitative play on the school ground. They will ask their parents for the TV-related toys their friends have. They will beg or demand to watch their friend's favorite programs. Parents can just say no, but they cannot switch off television's influence.

Lumping together all media, from mass mailings to television, oversimplifies. Studies comparing different media find that the more lifelike the medium, the more persuasive its message. Thus the order of persuasiveness seems to be: live, videotaped, audiotaped, and written. To add to the complexity, messages are best *comprehended* and *recalled* when written. Comprehension is one of the first steps in the persuasion process (recall Figure 7–1). So Shelly Chaiken and Alice Eagly (1976) reasoned that if a message is difficult to comprehend, persuasion should be greatest when the message is written, because readers will be able to work through the message at their own pace. The researchers gave University of Massachusetts students easy or difficult messages in writing, on audiotape, or on videotape. Figure 7–8 displays their results: Difficult messages were indeed most persuasive when written; easy messages, when videotaped. The TV medium takes control of the pacing of the message away from the recipients. It also encourages people to focus on peripheral cues, such as the communicator's attractiveness, by drawing attention to the communicator and away from the message itself (Chaiken & Eagly, 1983).

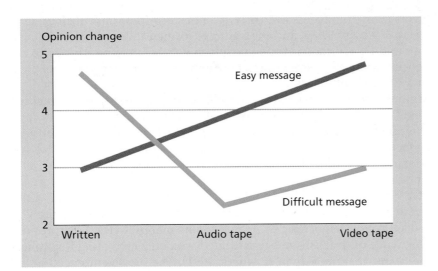

figure 7–8
Easy-to-understand
messages are most
persuasive when
videotaped. Difficult
messages are most
persuasive when written.
Thus the difficulty of the
message interacts with the
medium to determine
persuasiveness. **Source:**
Data from Chaiken & Eagly,
1978.

TO WHOM IS IT SAID? THE AUDIENCE

As we saw in Chapter 6, people's traits often don't predict their responses to social influence. A particular trait may enhance one step in the persuasion process
(Figure 7–1) but work against another. Take self-esteem. People with low self-
esteem are often slow to comprehend a message and therefore hard to persuade. Those with high self-esteem may comprehend yet remain confident of
their own opinions. The conclusion: People with moderate self-esteem are the
easiest to influence (Rhodes & Wood, 1992).

Let's also consider two other characteristics of those who receive a message:
age and thoughtfulness.

How old are they?

People tend to have different social and political attitudes depending on their
age. Social psychologists give two explanations for the difference. One is a *life
cycle explanation:* Attitudes change (for example, become more conservative) as
people grow older. The other is a *generational explanation:* The attitudes older
people adopted when they were young persist largely unchanged; because
these attitudes are different from those being adopted by young people today, a
generation gap develops.

The evidence mostly supports the generational explanation. In surveys and
resurveys of groups of younger and older people over several years, the attitudes of older people usually show less change than do those of young people.
As David Sears (1979, 1986) puts it, researchers have "almost invariably found
generational rather than life cycle effects."

Older adults are not inflexible; most people in their fifties and sixties have
more liberal sexual and racial attitudes than they had in their thirties and forties
(Glenn, 1980, 1981). Few of us are utterly uninfluenced by changing cultural
norms. Moreover, research by Penny Visser and Jon Krosnick (1998) suggests
that older adults, near the end of the life cycle, may again become more susceptible to attitude change, perhaps due to a decline in the strength of their
attitudes.

Nevertheless, the teens and early twenties are important formative years (Krosnick & Alwin, 1989), and the attitudes formed then tend to remain stable through middle adulthood. Young people might therefore be advised to choose their social influences—the groups they join, the media they imbibe, the roles they adopt—carefully.

Vermont's Bennington College provides a striking example. During the late 1930s and early 1940s, Bennington students—women from privileged, conservative families—encountered a free-spirited environment led by a left-leaning young faculty. One of those professors, social psychologist Theodore Newcomb, later denied that the faculty was trying to make "good little liberals" out of its students. But the faculty succeeded. The students became much more liberal than was typical of those from their social backgrounds. Moreover, attitudes formed at Bennington endured. A half-century later, the Bennington women, now 70ish, voted Democratic by a three-to-one margin in the 1984 presidential election, while other 70ish college-educated women were voting Republican by a three-to-one margin (Alwin & others, 1991). The views embraced at an impressionable time had survived a lifetime of wider experience.

Adolescent and early adult experiences are formative partly because they make deep and lasting impressions. When Howard Schuman and Jacqueline Scott (1989) asked people to name the one or two most important national or world events of the previous half century, most recalled events from their teens or early twenties. For those who experienced the Great Depression or World War II as 16- to 24-year-olds, those events overshadowed the civil rights movement and the Kennedy assassination of the early sixties, the Vietnam War and moon landing of the late sixties, and the women's movement of the seventies—all of which were imprinted on the minds of those who experienced them as 16- to 24-year-olds. We may therefore expect that today's young adults will include phenomena such as e-mail, the Web, and 9/11 as the memorable turning points in world history.

What are they thinking?

The crucial aspect of central route persuasion is not the message but the responses it evokes in a person's mind. Our minds are not sponges that soak up whatever pours over them. If the message summons favorable thoughts, it persuades us. If it provokes us to think of contrary arguments, we remain unpersuaded.

Forewarned is forearmed—If you care enough to counterargue.   What circumstances breed counterargument? One is a warning that someone is going to try to persuade you. If you had to tell your family that you wanted to drop out of school, you would likely anticipate their pleading with you to stay. So you might develop a list of arguments to counter every conceivable argument they might make.

Jonathan Freedman and David Sears (1965) demonstrated the difficulty of trying to persuade people under such circumstances. They warned one group of California high schoolers that they were going to hear a talk: "Why Teenagers Should Not Be Allowed to Drive." Those forewarned did not budge in their opinions. Others, not forewarned, did. In courtrooms, too, defense attorneys sometimes forewarn juries about prosecution evidence to come. With mock juries, such "stealing thunder" neutralizes its negative impact (Dolnik & others, 2003).

"To be forewarned and therefore forearmed . . . is eminently rational if our belief is true; but if our belief is a delusion, this same forewarning and forearming would obviously be the method whereby the delusion rendered itself incurable."
—C. S. Lewis, *Screwtape Proposes a Toast*, 1965

Sneak attacks on attitudes are especially useful with involved people. Given several minutes' forewarning, involved people will prepare defenses (Chen & others, 1992; Petty & Cacioppo, 1977, 1979). When forewarned people regard an issue as trivial, however, they may agree even before receiving the message, to avoid later seeming gullible (Wood & Quinn, 2003).

Distraction disarms counterarguing.   Verbal persuasion is also enhanced by distracting people with something that attracts their attention just enough to inhibit counterarguing (Festinger & Maccoby, 1964; Keating & Brock, 1974; Osterhouse & Brock, 1970). Political ads often use this technique. The words promote the candidate, and the visual images keep us occupied so we don't analyze the words. Distraction is especially effective when the message is simple (Harkins & Petty, 1981; Regan & Cheng, 1973).

Uninvolved audiences use peripheral cues.   Recall the two routes to persuasion—the central route of systematic thinking and the peripheral route of heuristic cues. Like the road through town, the central route has starts and stops as the mind analyzes arguments and formulates responses. Like the freeway around town, the peripheral route zips people to their destination. Analytical people—those with a high **need for cognition**—enjoy thinking carefully and prefer central routes (Cacioppo & others, 1996). People who like to conserve their mental resources—those with a low need for cognition—are quicker to respond to such peripheral cues as the communicator's attractiveness and the pleasantness of the surroundings.

need for cognition
The motivation to think and analyze. Assessed by agreement with items such as "The notion of thinking abstractly is appealing to me" and disagreement with items such as "I only think as hard as I have to."

But the issue matters, too. All of us actively struggle with issues that involve us while making snap judgments about things that matter little (Johnson & Eagly, 1990). As we mentally elaborate on an important issue, the strength of the arguments and of our own thoughts determine our attitudes (Figure 7–9, top panel). But if the issue seems unimportant, peripheral cues such as the expertise of the source have more of an effect on our attitudes than the strength of the message arguments (Figure 7–9, bottom panel).

This simple theory—that *what we think in response to a message is crucial*, especially if we are motivated and able to think about it—helps us understand several findings. For example, we more readily believe trustworthy, expert communicators if we're following the peripheral route. When we trust the source, we think favorable thoughts and are less likely to counterargue. Mistrusting the source makes us more likely to follow the central route. If we don't trust those who sell, we'll probably think critically about their sales pitch.

The theory has also generated many predictions, most of which have been confirmed by Petty, Cacioppo, and others (Axsom & others, 1987; Harkins & Petty, 1987; Leippe & Elkin, 1987). Many experiments have explored ways to stimulate people's thinking—by using *rhetorical questions,* by presenting *multiple speakers* (for example, having each of three speakers give one argument instead of one speaker giving three), by making people *feel responsible* for evaluating or passing along the message, by using *relaxed postures* rather than standing ones, by *repeating* the message, and by getting people's *undistracted attention.* Their consistent finding with each of these techniques: *Stimulating thinking makes strong messages more persuasive and* (because of counterarguing) *weak messages less persuasive.*

The theory also has practical implications. Effective communicators care not only about their images and their messages but also about how their audience is likely to react. The best instructors tend to get students to think actively. They

figure 7–9

Central versus peripheral routes to attitude change.

The central route: When involved college students received a persuasive message advocating a departmental exam before graduation, they found weak arguments unpersuasive but strong arguments convincing (top panel). **Source:** From R. E. Petty, T. J. Cacioppo and R. Goldman, "Personal Involvement as a Determinant of Argument-Based Persuasion," *Journal of Personality and Social Psychology*, 41, 1981, pp. 847–855. Copyright © 1981 by the American Psychological Association. Reprinted with permission.

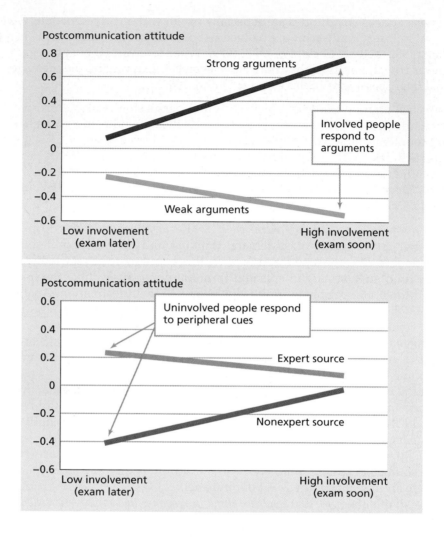

"Are you better off than you were four years ago?" Ronald Reagan soared to victory with a memorable rhetorical question that triggered voters' thinking.

ask rhetorical questions, provide intriguing examples, and challenge students with difficult problems. All these techniques are likely to foster a process that moves information through the central route to persuasion. In classes where the instruction is less engaging, you can provide your own central processing. If you think about the material and elaborate on the arguments, you are likely to do better in the course.

During the final days of a closely contested 1980 presidential campaign, Ronald Reagan effectively used rhetorical questions to stimulate desired thoughts in voters' minds. His summary statement in the presidential debate began with two potent rhetorical questions that he repeated often during the campaign's remaining week: "Are you better off than you were four years ago? Is it easier for you to go and buy things in the stores than it was four years ago?" Most people answered no, and Reagan, thanks partly to the way he prodded people to take the central route, won by a bigger-than-expected margin.

What makes persuasion effective? Researchers have explored four factors: the *communicator*, the *message*, the *channel*, and the *audience*.

Who says? Credible communicators are perceived as trustworthy experts. People who speak unhesitatingly, who talk fast, and who look listeners straight in the eye seem more credible. So are people who argue against their own self-interest. An *attractive communicator* also is effective on matters of taste and personal values.

What is said? Associating a message with good feelings makes it more convincing. People often make snappier, less reflective judgments while in good moods. Messages that arouse fear can also be effective, especially if the recipients can take protective action.

How discrepant a message should be from an audience's existing opinions depends on the communicator's credibility. And whether a one- or two-sided message is most persuasive depends: When the audience already agrees with the message, is unaware of opposing arguments, and is unlikely later to consider the opposition, a one-sided appeal is most effective. With more sophisticated audiences or with those not already in agreement, two-sided messages are most successful.

When two sides of an issue are included, do the arguments presented first or second have the advantage? The common finding is a *primacy effect*. If a time gap separates the presentations, the effect of the early information diminishes; if a decision is made right after hearing the second side, which is therefore still fresh in the mind, the result will likely be a *recency effect*.

How is it said? Another important consideration is how the message is communicated. Usually, face-to-face appeals work best. Print media can, however, be effective for complex messages. And the mass media can be effective when the issue is minor (such as which brand of aspirin to buy) or unfamiliar (such as deciding between two otherwise unknown political candidates).

To whom is it said? Finally, it matters who receives the message. What does the audience think while receiving a message? Do they think favorable thoughts? Do they counterargue? Were they forewarned? The age of the audience also makes a difference. Researchers who have resurveyed people over time find that young people's attitudes are less stable.

Real-life persuasion: How do cults indoctrinate?

What persuasion and group influence principles are harnessed by new religious movements ("cults")?

On March 22, 1997, Marshall Herff Applewhite and 37 of his disciples decided the time had come to shed their bodies—mere "containers"—and be whisked up to a UFO trailing the Hale-Bopp Comet, en route to heaven's gate. So they put themselves to sleep by mixing phenobarbital into pudding or applesauce, washing it down with vodka, and then fixing plastic bags over their heads so they would suffocate in their slumber. On that same day, a cottage in the French Canadian village of St. Casimir exploded in an inferno, consuming five people—the latest of 74 members of the Order of the Solar Temple to have committed suicide in Canada, Switzerland, and France. All were hoping to be transported to the star Sirius, nine light-years away.

The question on many minds: What persuades people to leave behind their former beliefs and join these mental chain gangs? Shall we attribute their strange behaviors to strange personalities? Or do their experiences illustrate the common dynamics of social influence and persuasion?

Bear two things in mind. First, this is hindsight analysis. It uses persuasion principles as categories for explaining, after the fact, a fascinating and some-times disturbing social phenomenon. Second, explaining *why* people believe something says nothing about the *truth* of their beliefs. That is a logically separate issue. A psychology of religion might tell us *why* a theist believes in God and an atheist disbelieves, but it cannot tell us who is right. Explaining either belief does not explain it away. So if someone tries to discount your beliefs by saying, "You just believe that because . . . ," you might recall Archbishop William Temple's reply to a questioner who challenged: "Well, of course, Arch-bishop, the point is that you believe what you believe because of the way you were brought up." To which the archbishop replied: "That is as it may be. But the fact remains that you believe I believe what I believe because of the way I was brought up, because of the way you were brought up."

In recent decades, several **cults**—which some social scientists prefer to call new religious movements—have gained much publicity: Sun Myung Moon's Unification Church, Jim Jones's People's Temple, David Koresh's Branch Davidians, and Marshall Applewhite's Heaven's Gate.

Sun Myung Moon's mixture of Christianity, anticommunism, and glorifica-tion of Moon himself as a new messiah attracted a worldwide following. In re-sponse to Moon's declaration, "What I wish must be your wish," many people committed themselves and their incomes to the Unification Church.

In 1978 in Guyana, 914 disciples of Jim Jones, who had followed him there from San Francisco, shocked the world when they died by following his order

cult (also called new religious movement)
A group typically characterized by (1) distinctive ritual and beliefs related to its devotion to a god or a person, (2) isolation from the surrounding "evil" culture, and (3) a charismatic leader. (A sect, by contrast, is a spinoff from a major religion.)

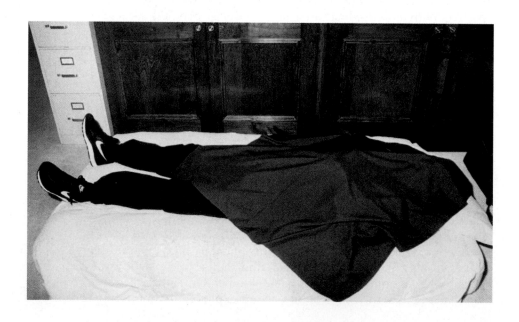

One of 37 suicide victims seeking heaven's gate.

to down a suicidal grape drink laced with tranquilizers, painkillers, and a lethal dose of cyanide.

In 1993, high-school dropout David Koresh used his talent for memorizing Scripture and mesmerizing people to seize control of a faction of a sect called the Branch Davidians. Over time, members were gradually relieved of their bank accounts and possessions. Koresh also persuaded the men to live celibately while he slept with their wives and daughters, and he convinced his 19 "wives" that they should bear his children. Under siege after a shootout that killed six members and four federal agents, Koresh told his followers they would soon die and go with him straight to heaven. Federal agents rammed the compound with tanks, hoping to inject tear gas, and, by the end of the assault, 86 people were consumed in a fire that engulfed the compound.

Marshall Applewhite was not similarly tempted to command sexual favors. Having been fired from two music teaching jobs for homosexual affairs with students, he sought sexless devotion by castration, as had 7 of the other 17 Heaven's Gate men who died with him (Chua-Eoan, 1997; Gardner, 1997). While in a psychiatric hospital in 1971, Applewhite had linked up with nurse and astrology dabbler Bonnie Lu Nettles, who gave the intense and charismatic Applewhite a cosmological vision of a route to "the next level." Preaching with passion, he persuaded his followers to renounce families, sex, drugs, and personal money with promises of a spaceship voyage to salvation.

How could these things happen? What persuaded these people to give such total allegiance? Shall we make dispositional explanations—by blaming the victims? Shall we dismiss them as gullible kooks or dumb weirdos? Or can familiar principles of conformity, compliance, dissonance, persuasion, and group influence explain their behavior—putting them on common ground with the rest of us who in our own ways are shaped by such forces?

Hundreds of thousands of people in recent years have been recruited by members of some 2,500 religious cults, but seldom through an abrupt decision. Copyright © The New Yorker Collection, 1982, Charles Addams, from cartoonbank.com. All Rights Reserved.

ATTITUDES FOLLOW BEHAVIOR

As Chapter 4 showed over and over again, people usually internalize commitments made voluntarily, publicly, and repeatedly. Cult leaders seem to know this.

Compliance breeds acceptance

New converts soon learn that membership is no trivial matter. They are quickly made active members of the team. Rituals within the cult community, and public canvassing and fund-raising, strengthen the initiates' identities as members. As those in social-psychological experiments come to believe in what they bear witness to (Aronson & Mills, 1959; Gerard & Mathewson, 1966), so cult initiates become committed advocates. The greater the personal commitment, the more the need to justify it.

"You go on home without me, Irene. I'm going to join this man's cult."

www.mhhe.com/myers8
When are we likely to change our behavior without really believing what we are doing? Visit the Online Learning Center for an interactivity on compliance.

The foot-in-the-door phenomenon

How are we induced to make commitments? Seldom by an abrupt, conscious decision. One does not just decide, "I'm through with mainstream religion. I'm gonna find a cult." Nor do cult recruiters approach people on the street with, "Hi. I'm a Moonie. Care to join us?" Rather, the recruitment strategy exploits the foot-in-the-door principle. Unification Church recruiters would invite people to a dinner and then to a weekend of warm fellowship and discussions of philosophies of life. At the weekend retreat, they would encourage the attenders to join them in songs, activities, and discussion. Potential converts were then urged to sign up for longer training retreats. Eventually the activities would become more arduous—soliciting contributions and attempting to convert others.

Jim Jones also used this foot-in-the-door technique. Psychologist Robert Ornstein (1991) recalls hearing Jones explain his recruitment successes. Unlike other street solicitors on behalf of the poor, Jones's operators would ask passersby merely to "help for just five minutes at work by folding and mailing a few envelopes." Having done so, Jones explained, "They came back for more. You know, once I get somebody, I can get them to do anything."

Once into the cult, monetary offerings were voluntary. Jones next inaugurated a required 10-percent-of-income contribution, which soon increased to 25 percent. Finally, he ordered members to turn over to him everything they owned. Workloads also became progressively more demanding. Former cult member Grace Stoen recalls the gradual progress:

> Nothing was ever done drastically. That's how Jim Jones got away with so much. You slowly gave up things and slowly had to put up with more, but it was always done very gradually. It was amazing, because you would sit up sometimes and say, wow, I really have given up a lot. I really am putting up with a lot. But he did it so slowly that you figured, I've made it this far, what the hell is the difference? (Conway & Siegelman, 1979, p. 236)

PERSUASIVE ELEMENTS

We can also analyze cult persuasion using the factors discussed in this chapter (and summarized in Figure 7–10): *Who* (the communicator) said *what* (the message) to *whom* (the audience)?

The communicator

Successful cults have a charismatic leader—someone who attracts and directs the members. As in experiments on persuasion, a credible communicator is someone the audience perceives as expert and trustworthy—for example, as "Father" Moon.

figure 7–10

Variables known to affect the impact of persuasive communications.

In real life, these variables may interact; the effect of one may depend on the level of another.

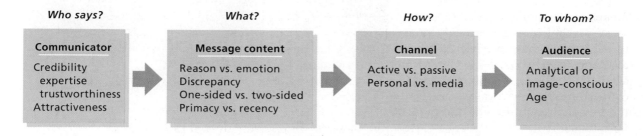

Who says?	What?	How?	To whom?

Communicator
Credibility
  expertise
  trustworthiness
Attractiveness
	Message content
	Reason vs. emotion
	Discrepancy
	One-sided vs. two-sided
	Primacy vs. recency
		Channel
		Active vs. passive
		Personal vs. media
			Audience
			Analytical or image-conscious
			Age

Jim Jones used "psychic readings" to establish his credibility. Newcomers were asked to identify themselves as they entered the church before services. Then one of his aides would quickly call the person's home and say, "Hi. We're doing a survey, and we'd like to ask you some questions." During the service, one ex-member recalled, Jones would call out the person's name and say

> Have you ever seen me before? Well, you live in such and such a place, your phone number is such and such, and in your living room you've got this, that, and the other, and on your sofa you've got such and such a pillow. . . . Now do you re-member me ever being in your house? (Conway & Siegelman, 1979, p. 234)

Trust is another aspect of credibility. Cult researcher Margaret Singer (1979) noted that middle-class Caucasian youths are more vulnerable to recruitment because they are more trusting. They lack the "street smarts" of lower-class youths (who know how to resist a hustle) and the wariness of upper-class youths (who have been warned of kidnappers since childhood). Many cult members have been recruited by friends or relatives, people they trust (Stark & Bainbridge, 1980).

The message

The vivid, emotional messages and the warmth and acceptance with which the group showers lonely or depressed people can be strikingly appealing: Trust the master, join the family; we have the answer, the "one way." The message echoes through channels as varied as lectures, small-group discussions, and direct so-cial pressure.

The audience

Recruits are often young—people under 25 and still at that comparatively open age before attitudes and values stabilize. Some, such as the followers of Jim Jones, are less-educated people who like the simplicity of the message and find it difficult to counterargue. But most are educated, middle-class people who, taken by the ideals, overlook the contradictions in those who profess selfless-ness and practice greed, who pretend concern and behave indifferently.

Potential converts are often at turning points in their lives, facing personal crises, or vacationing or living away from home. They have needs; the cult of-fers them an answer (Singer, 1979; Lofland & Stark, 1965). Gail Maeder joined Heaven's Gate after her T-shirt shop had failed. David Moore joined when he was 19, just out of high school, and searching for direction. Times of social and economic upheaval are especially conducive to someone who can make appar-ent simple sense out of the confusion (O'Dea, 1968; Sales, 1972).

GROUP EFFECTS

Cults also illustrate the next chapter's theme: the power of a group to shape members' views and behavior. The cult typically separates members from their previous social support systems and isolates them with other cultists. There may then occur what Rodney Stark and William Bainbridge (1980) call a "social implosion": External ties weaken until the group collapses inward socially, each person engaging only with other group members. Cut off from families and for-mer friends, they lose access to counterarguments. The group now offers iden-tity and defines reality. Because the cult frowns on or punishes disagreements, the apparent consensus helps eliminate any lingering doubts. Moreover, stress and emotional arousal narrow attention, making people "more susceptible to poorly supported arguments, social pressure, and the temptation to derogate nongroup members" (Baron, 2000).

Marshall Applewhite and Bonnie Nettles (who died of cancer in 1985) at first formed their own group of two, reinforcing each other's aberrant thinking—a phenomenon that psychiatrists call *folie à deux* (French for "insanity of two"). As others joined them, the group's social isolation facilitated more peculiar thinking. As Internet conspiracy theory discussion groups illustrate (Heaven's Gate was skilled in Internet recruiting), virtual groups can likewise foster paranoia.

Contrary to the idea that cults turn hapless people into mindless robots, these techniques—increasing behavioral commitments, persuasion, and group isolation—do not have unlimited power. The Unification Church has successfully recruited fewer than 1 in 10 people who attend its workshops (Ennis & Verrilli, 1989). Most who joined Heaven's Gate had left before that fateful day. David Koresh ruled with a mix of persuasion, intimidation, and violence. As Jim Jones made his demands more extreme, he, too, increasingly had to control people with intimidation. He used threats of harm to those who fled the community, beatings for noncompliance, and drugs to neutralize disagreeable members. By the end, he was as much an arm twister as a mind bender. Moreover, cult influence techniques are in some ways similar to techniques used by groups more familiar to us. Fraternity and sorority members have reported that the initial "love bombing" of potential cult recruits is not unlike their own "rush" period. Members lavish prospective pledges with attention and make them feel special. During the pledge period, new members are somewhat isolated, cut off from old friends who did not pledge. They spend time studying the history and rules of their new group. They suffer and commit time on its behalf. They are expected to comply with all its demands. The result is usually a committed new member.

Much the same is true of some therapeutic communities for recovering drug and alcohol abusers. Zealous self-help groups form a cohesive "social cocoon,"

Military training creates cohesion and commitment through some of the same tactics used by leaders of new religious movements, fraternities, and therapeutic communities.

have intense beliefs, and exert a profound influence on members' behavior (Galanter, 1989, 1990).

Another constructive use of persuasion is in counseling and psychotherapy, which social-counseling psychologist Stanley Strong views "as a branch of applied social psychology" (1978, p. 101). Like Strong, psychiatrist Jerome Frank (1974, 1982) recognized years ago that it takes persuasion to change self-defeating attitudes and behaviors. Frank noted that the psychotherapy setting, like cults and zealous self-help groups, provides (1) a supportive, confiding social relationship, (2) an offer of expertise and hope, (3) a special rationale or myth that explains one's difficulties and offers a new perspective, and (4) a set of rituals and learning experiences that promises a new sense of peace and happiness.

I chose the examples of fraternities, sororities, self-help groups, and psychotherapy not to disparage them but to illustrate two concluding observations. First, if we attribute new religious movements to the leader's mystical force or to the followers' peculiar weaknesses, we may delude ourselves into thinking we are immune to social control techniques. In truth, our own groups—and countless political leaders, educators, and other persuaders—successfully use many of these tactics on us. Between education and indoctrination, enlightenment and propaganda, conversion and coercion, therapy and mind control, there is but a blurry line.

Second, the fact that Jim Jones and other cult leaders abused the power of persuasion does not mean persuasion is intrinsically bad. Nuclear power enables us to light up homes or wipe out cities. Sexual power enables us to express and celebrate committed love or exploit people for selfish gratification. Persuasive power enables us to enlighten or deceive. Knowing that these powers can be harnessed for evil purposes should alert us, as scientists and citizens, to guard against their immoral use. But the powers themselves are neither inherently evil nor inherently good; how we use them determines whether their effect is destructive or constructive. Condemning persuasion because of deceit is like condemning eating because of gluttony.

Summing up

The successes of religious cults provide an opportunity to see powerful persuasion processes at work. It appears that their success has resulted from eliciting behavioral commitments (as described in Chapter 4), applying principles of effective persuasion (this chapter), and isolating members in like-minded groups (to be discussed in Chapter 8).

How can persuasion be resisted?

Having perused the "weapons of influence," we consider some tactics for resisting influence. How might we prepare people to resist unwanted persuasion?

Martial arts trainers devote as much time teaching defensive blocks, deflections, and parries as they do teaching attack. "On the social influence battlefield," note Brad Sagarin and his colleagues (2002), researchers have focused more on persuasive attack than on defense. Persuasion comes naturally, Daniel Gilbert and his colleagues (1990, 1993) report. It is easier to accept persuasive messages than to doubt them. To *understand* an assertion (say, that lead pencils are a health hazard) is to *believe* it—at least temporarily, until one actively undoes the initial, automatic acceptance. If a distracting event prevents the undoing, the acceptance lingers.

Still, blessed with logic, information, and motivation, we do resist falsehoods. If, because of an aura of credibility, the repair person's uniform and doctor's title have intimidated us into unquestioning agreement, we can rethink our habitual responses to authority. We can seek more information before committing time or money. We can question what we don't understand.

STRENGTHENING PERSONAL COMMITMENT

Chapter 6 presented another way to resist: Before encountering others' judgments, make a public commitment to your position. Having stood up for your convictions, you will become less susceptible (or should we say less "open"?) to what others have to say. In mock civil trials, straw polls of jurors can foster a hardening of expressed positions, leading to more deadlocks (Davis & others, 1993).

Challenging beliefs

How might we stimulate people to commit themselves? From his experiments, Charles Kiesler (1971) offered one possible way: Mildly attack their position. Kiesler found that when committed people were attacked strongly enough to cause them to react, but not so strongly as to overwhelm them, they became even more committed. Kiesler explained: "When you attack committed people and your attack is of inadequate strength, you drive them to even more extreme behaviors in defense of their previous commitment. Their commitment escalates, in a sense, because the number of acts consistent with their belief increases" (p. 88). Perhaps you can recall a time when this happened in an argument, as those involved escalated their rhetoric, committing themselves to increasingly extreme positions.

Developing counterarguments

There is a second reason a mild attack might build resistance. When someone attacks one of our cherished attitudes, we typically feel some irritation and contemplate counterarguments. Counterarguing helps people resist persuasion (Jacks & Cameron, 2003). Refute someone's persuasion, and know that you have done so, and you will feel more certain than ever (Tormala & Petty, 2002).

Like inoculations against disease, even weak arguments will prompt counterarguments, which are then available for a stronger attack. William McGuire (1964) documented this in a series of experiments. McGuire wondered: Could we inoculate people against persuasion much as we inoculate them against a virus? Is there such a thing as **attitude inoculation?** Could we take people raised in a "germ-free ideological environment"—people who hold some unquestioned belief—and stimulate their mental defenses? And would subjecting them to a small dose of belief-threatening material inoculate them against later persuasion?

That is what McGuire did. First, he found some cultural truisms, such as, "It's a good idea to brush your teeth after every meal if at all possible." He then showed that people were vulnerable to a massive, credible assault upon these truisms (for example, prestigious authorities were said to have discovered that too much toothbrushing can damage one's gums). If, however, before having

attitude inoculation
Exposing people to weak attacks upon their attitudes so that when stronger attacks come, they will have refutations available.

their belief attacked, they were "immunized" by first receiving a small challenge to their belief, *and* if they read or wrote an essay in refutation of this mild attack, then they were better able to resist the powerful attack. Inoculation works with values as well as truisms. After imagining refutations of a possible attack on their valuing of equality, Cardiff University students more effectively counterargued and resisted an actual challenge to their view (Bernard & others, 2003).

Robert Cialdini and his colleagues (2003) agree that appropriate counterarguments are a great way to resist persuasion but wondered how to bring them to mind in response to an opponents' ads, especially when the opponent (like most political incumbents) has a huge spending advantage. The answer, they suggest, is a "poison parasite" defense—one that combines a poison (strong counterarguments) with a parasite (retrieval cues that bring those arguments to mind when seeing the opponent's ads). In their studies, participants who viewed a familiar political ad were least persuaded by it when they had earlier seen counterarguments overlaid on a replica of the ad. Seeing the ad again thus also brought to mind the puncturing counterarguments. Antismoking ads have effectively done this, for example, by re-creating a "Marlboro Man" commercial set in the rugged outdoors but now showing a coughing, decrepit cowboy.

"The SLA . . . read me news items they clipped from the newspapers almost every day. Some of their stories were indisputable, sometimes I did not know what to believe. It was all very confusing. I realized that my life prior to my kidnapping had indeed been very sheltered; I had taken little or no interest in foreign affairs, politics, or economics."
—Patricia Campbell Hearst, *Every Secret Thing,* 1982

A "poison parasite" ad.

REAL-LIFE APPLICATIONS: INOCULATION PROGRAMS

Could attitude inoculation indeed prepare people to resist unwanted persuasion? Applied research on smoking prevention and consumer education offers encouraging answers.

Inoculating children against peer pressure to smoke

In a clear demonstration of how laboratory research findings can lead to practical applications, a research team led by Alfred McAlister (1980) had high school students "inoculate" seventh graders against peer pressures to smoke. The seventh graders were taught to respond to advertisements implying that liberated women smoke by saying, "She's not really liberated if she is hooked on tobacco." They also acted in role plays in which, after being called "chicken" for not taking a cigarette, they answered with statements like, "I'd be a real chicken if I smoked just to impress you." After several of these sessions during the seventh and eighth grades, the inoculated students were half as likely to begin smoking as were uninoculated students at another junior high school that had an identical parental smoking rate (Figure 7–11).

the story behind the research:
William McGuire on attitude inoculation

I confess to having felt like Mr. Clean when doing this immunization work because I was studying how to help people resist being manipulated. Then, after our research was published, an advertising executive called and said, "Very interesting, Professor: I was delighted to read about it." Somewhat righteously, I replied, "Very nice of you to say that Mr. Executive, but I'm really on the other side. You're trying to persuade people, and I'm trying to make them more resistant." "Oh, don't underrate yourself, Professor," he said. "We can use what you're doing to diminish the effect of our competitors' ads." And sure enough, it has become almost standard for advertisers to mention other brands and deflate their claims.

William McGuire
Yale University

Other research teams have confirmed that inoculation procedures, sometimes supplemented by other life skill training, reduce teen smoking (Botvin & others, 1995; Evans & others, 1984; Flay & others, 1985). Most newer efforts emphasize strategies for resisting social pressure. One study exposed sixth to eighth graders to antismoking films or to information about smoking, together with role plays of student-generated ways of refusing a cigarette (Hirschman & Leventhal, 1989). A year and a half later, 31 percent of those who watched the antismoking films had taken up smoking. Among those who role-played refusing, only 19 percent had begun smoking.

figure 7–11

The percentage of cigarette smokers at an "inoculated" junior high school was much less than at a matched control school using a more typical smoking education program. **Source:** Data from McAlister & others, 1980; Telch & others, 1981.

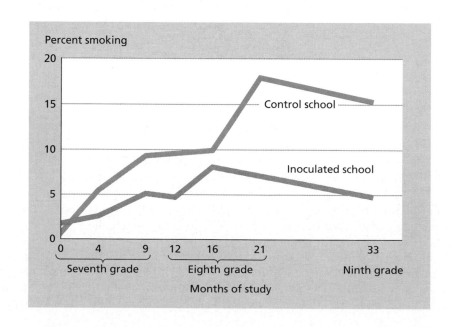

Antismoking and drug education programs apply other persuasion principles, too. They use attractive peers to communicate information. They trigger the students' own cognitive processing ("Here's something you might want to think about"). They get the students to make a public commitment (by making a rational decision about smoking and then announcing it, along with their reasoning, to their classmates). Some of these smoking-prevention programs require only two to six hours of class, using prepared printed materials or videotapes. Today any school district or teacher wishing to use the social-psychological approach to smoking prevention can do so easily, inexpensively, and with the hope of significant reductions in future smoking rates and associated health costs.

Inoculating children against the influence of advertising

Sweden, Italy, Greece, Belgium, Denmark, and Ireland all restrict advertising that targets children, and other European countries have been discussing doing the same (McGuire, 2002). In the United States, notes Robert Levine in *The Power of Persuasion: How We're Bought and Sold*, the average child sees over 10,000 commercials a year. "Two decades ago," he notes, "children drank twice as much milk as soda. Thanks to advertising, the ratio is now reversed" (2003, p. 16). Smokers often develop an "initial brand choice" in their teens, said a 1981 report from researchers at Philip Morris, a major player in the $11.2 billion spent annually on tobacco advertising and promotion (FTC, 2003). "Today's teenager is tomorrow's potential regular customer, and the overwhelming majority of smokers first begin to smoke while still in their teens" (Lichtblau, 2003).

In response, researchers have studied how to immunize young children against the effects of television commercials. This research was prompted partly by studies showing that children, especially those under 8 years old, (1) have trouble distinguishing commercials from programs and fail to grasp their persuasive intent, (2) trust television advertising rather indiscriminately, and (3) desire and badger their parents for advertised products (Adler & others, 1980; Feshbach, 1980; Palmer & Dorr, 1980). Children, it seems, are an advertiser's dream: gullible, vulnerable, an easy sell.

Armed with this data, citizens' groups have given the advertisers of such products a chewing out (Moody, 1980): "When a sophisticated advertiser spends millions to sell unsophisticated, trusting children an unhealthy product, this can only be called exploitation." In "Mothers' Statement to Advertisers" (Motherhood Project, 2001), a broad coalition of American women echoed this outrage:

> For us, our children are priceless gifts. For you, our children are customers, and childhood is a "market segment" to be exploited. . . . The line between *meeting* and *creating* consumer needs and desire is increasingly being crossed, as your battery of highly trained and creative experts study, analyze, persuade, and manipulate our children. . . . The driving messages are "You deserve a break today," "Have it your way," "Follow your instincts. Obey your thirst," "Just Do It," "No Boundaries," "Got the Urge?" These [exemplify] the dominant message of advertising and marketing: that life is about selfishness, instant gratification, and materialism.

On the other side are those who have commercial interests and claim that ads allow parents to teach their children consumer skills and, more important, finance children's television programs. In the United States, the Federal Trade Commission has been in the middle, pushed by research findings and political

"When it comes to targeting kid consumers, we at General Mills follow the Procter and Gamble model of 'cradle to grave.' . . . We believe in getting them early and having them for life."
—Wayne Chilicki, General Mills (quoted by Motherhood Project, 2001)

Children are the advertiser's dream. Researchers have therefore studied ways to inoculate children against the 20,000 or so ads they see each year, many as they are glued to a TV set.

pressures while trying to decide whether to place new constraints on TV ads for unhealthy foods and for R-rated movies aimed at underage youth.

Meanwhile, researchers have wondered whether children can be taught to resist deceptive ads. In one such effort, a team of investigators led by Norma Feshbach (1980; Cohen, 1980) gave small groups of Los-Angeles-area elementary school children three half-hour lessons in analyzing commercials. The children were inoculated by viewing ads and discussing them. For example, after viewing a toy ad, they were immediately given the toy and challenged to make it do what they had just seen in the commercial. Such experiences helped breed a more realistic understanding of commercials.

Consumer advocates worry that inoculation may be insufficient. Better to clean the air than to wear gas masks. When advertisers market products to children, then place them on lower store shelves where kids will see them, pick them up, and nag and whine until sometimes wearing the parent down, weary parents object. Thus, urges the "Mothers' Code for Advertisers," there should be no advertising in schools, no targeting children under 8, no product placements in movies and programs targeting children and adolescents, and no ads directed at children and adolescents "that promote an ethic of selfishness and a focus on instant gratification" (Motherhood Project, 2001).

IMPLICATIONS OF ATTITUDE INOCULATION

The best way to build resistance to brainwashing probably isn't stronger indoctrination into one's current beliefs. If parents are worried that their children might become members of a cult, they might better teach their children about the various cults and prepare them to counter persuasive appeals.

For the same reason, religious educators should be wary of creating a "germ-free ideological environment" in their churches and schools. An attack, if refuted, is more likely to solidify one's position than to undermine it, particularly if the threatening material can be examined with like-minded others. Cults apply this principle by forewarning members of how families and friends will attack the cult's beliefs. When the expected challenge comes, the member is armed with counterarguments.

Another implication is that, for the persuader, an ineffective appeal can be worse than none. Can you see why? Those who reject an appeal are inoculated against further appeals. Consider an experiment in which Susan Darley and Joel Cooper (1972) invited students to write essays advocating a strict dress code. Because this was against the students' own positions and the essays were to be published, all chose *not* to write the essay—even those offered money to do so. After turning down the money, they became even more extreme and confident in their anti-dress-code opinions. Having made an overt decision against the dress code, they became even more resistant to it. Those who have rejected initial appeals to quit smoking may likewise become immune to further appeals. Ineffective persuasion, by stimulating the listener's defenses, may be counterproductive. It may "harden the heart" against later appeals.

Summing up

How do people resist persuasion? A *prior public commitment* to one's own position, stimulated perhaps by a mild attack on the position, breeds resistance to later persuasion. A mild attack can also serve as an *inoculation,* stimulating one to develop counterarguments that will then be available if and when a strong attack comes. This implies, paradoxically, that one way to strengthen existing attitudes is to challenge them, though the challenge must not be so strong as to overwhelm them.

Personal Postscript: Being open but not naïve

As recipients of persuasion, our human task is to live in the land between gullibility and cynicism. Some people say that being persuadable is a weakness. "Think for yourself," we are urged. But is being closed to informational influence a virtue, or is it the mark of a fanatic? How can we live with humility and openness to others and yet be critical consumers of persuasive appeals?

To be open, we can assume that every person we meet is, in some ways, our superior. Each person I encounter has some expertise that exceeds my own and thus has something to teach me. As we connect, I hope to learn from this person and perhaps to be able to reciprocate by sharing my knowledge.

To be critical thinkers, we might take a cue from inoculation research. Do you want to build your resistance to persuasion without becoming closed to valid messages? Be an active listener and a critical thinker. Force yourself to counterargue. After hearing a political speech, discuss it with others. In other words, don't just listen; react. If the message cannot withstand careful analysis, so much the worse for it. If it can, its effect on you will be that much more enduring.

What do you think?

When have you been persuaded? Are you glad you were? If not, what might you have done to inoculate yourself?

Making the Social Connection

This chapter highlights Richard Petty's ideas about persuasion through his theory and research. We also reported Petty's ideas about dissonance in Chapter 4: Behavior and Attitudes. Go to the *SocialSense* CD-ROM to view Richard Petty on the central and peripheral routes to persuasion.

chapter 8

Group Influence

"Never doubt that a small group of thoughtful, committed citizens can change the world."

Anthropologist Margaret Mead

Tawna is nearing the end of her daily jog. Her mind prods her to keep going; her body begs her to walk the remaining six blocks. She compromises and does a slow jog home. The next day conditions are identical, except that two friends run with her. Tawna runs her route two minutes faster. She wonders, "Did I run better merely because Gail and José went along? Would I always run better if in a group?"

At almost every turn, we are involved in groups. Our world contains not only 6.4 billion individuals, but 200 nation-states, 4 million local communities, 20 million economic organizations, and hundreds of millions of other formal and informal groups—couples on dates, families, churches, housemates in bull sessions. How do these groups influence individuals?

Group interactions often have dramatic effects. Intellectual college students hang out with other intellectuals, and they strengthen one another's intellectual interests. Deviant youth hang out with other deviant youth, amplifying one another's antisocial tendencies. But how do these groups affect the attitudes of the people in the group? And what influences lead groups to smart and dumb decisions?

Individuals influence their groups. As the 1957 classic film *12 Angry Men* opens, 12 wary murder trial jurors file into the jury room. It is a hot day. The tired jurors are close to agreement and eager for a quick verdict convicting a teenage boy of knifing his father. But one maverick, played by Henry Fonda, refuses to vote guilty. As the heated deliberation proceeds, the jurors one by one change their verdicts until consensus is reached: "Not guilty." In real trials, a lone individual seldom sways the entire group. Yet history is made by minorities that sway majorities. What helps make a minority—or an effective leader—persuasive?

We will examine these intriguing phenomena of group influence one at a time. But first things first: What is a group and why do groups exist?

What is a group?

The answer to the question seems self-evident—until several people compare their definitions. Are jogging partners a group? Are airplane passengers a group? Is a group a set of people who identify with one another, who sense they belong together? Is a group those who share common goals and rely on one another? Does a group form when individuals become organized? When their relationships with one another continue over time? These are among the social psychological definitions of a group (McGrath, 1984).

Group dynamics expert Marvin Shaw (1981) argued that all groups have one thing in common: Their members interact. Therefore, he defines a **group** as two or more people who interact and influence one another. Moreover, notes Australian National University social psychologist John Turner (1987), groups perceive themselves as "us" in contrast to "them." So jogging companions are indeed a group. Groups may exist for a number of reasons—to meet a need to belong, to provide information, to supply rewards, to accomplish goals.

By Shaw's definition, students working individually in a computer room would not be a group. Although physically together, they are more a collection of individuals than an interacting group (each may, however, be part of an unseen group in a chat room). The distinction between collections of unrelated individuals in a computer lab and the more influential group behavior among interacting individuals sometimes blurs. People who are merely in one another's presence do sometimes influence one another. At a game, they may perceive themselves as "us" fans in contrast with "them" who root for the other team.

In this chapter we consider three examples of such collective influence: *social facilitation, social loafing,* and *deindividuation.* These three phenomena can occur with minimal interaction (in what we call "minimal group situations"). Then we consider three examples of social influence in interacting groups: *group polarization, groupthink,* and *minority influence.*

Social facilitation: How are we affected by the presence of others?

Let's begin with social psychology's most elementary question: Are we affected by the mere presence of another person? "Mere presence" means people are not

group
Two or more people who, for longer than a few moments, interact with and influence one another and perceive one another as "us."

*competing, do not reward or punish, and in fact do nothing except be present as a passive audience or as **co-actors**. Would the mere presence of others affect a person's jogging, eating, typing, or exam performance? The search for the answer is a scientific mystery story.*

THE MERE PRESENCE OF OTHERS

More than a century ago, Norman Triplett (1898), a psychologist interested in bicycle racing, noticed that cyclists' times were faster when racing together than when racing alone against the clock. Before he peddled his hunch (that others' presence boosts performance), Triplett conducted one of social psychology's first laboratory experiments. Children told to wind string on a fishing reel as rapidly as possible wound faster when they worked with co-actors than when they worked alone.

Ensuing experiments found that others' presence improves the speed with which people do simple multiplication problems and cross out designated letters. It also improves the accuracy with which people perform simple motor tasks, such as keeping a metal stick in contact with a dime-sized disk on a moving turntable (F. W. Allport, 1920; Dashiell, 1930; Travis, 1925). This **social facilitation** effect, also occurs with animals. In the presence of others of their species, ants excavate more sand, chickens eat more grain, and sexually active rat pairs mate more often (Bayer, 1929; Chen, 1937; Larsson, 1956).

But wait: Other studies revealed that on some tasks the presence of others *hinders* performance. In the presence of others, cockroaches, parakeets, and green finches learn mazes more slowly (Allee & Masure, 1936; Gates & Allee, 1933; Klopfer, 1958). This disruptive effect also occurs with people. Others' presence diminishes efficiency at learning non-sense syllables, completing a maze, and performing complex multiplication problems (Dashiell, 1930; Pessin, 1933; Pessin & Husband, 1933).

Saying that the presence of others sometimes facilitates performance and sometimes hinders it is about as satisfying as the typical Scottish weather forecast—predicting that it might be sunny but then again it might rain. By 1940, research activity in this area had ground to a halt, and it lay dormant for 25 years until awakened by the touch of a new idea.

Social psychologist Robert Zajonc (pronounced *Zy-ence*, rhymes with *science*) wondered whether these seemingly contradictory findings could be reconciled. As often happens at creative moments in science, Zajonc (1965) used one field of research to illuminate another. In this case the illumination came from a well-established principle in experimental psychology: Arousal enhances whatever response tendency is dominant. Increased arousal enhances performance on easy tasks for which the most likely—"dominant"—response is the correct one. People solve easy anagrams, such as *akec*,

co-actors
Co-participants working individually on a noncompetitive activity.

social facilitation
(1) Original meaning— the tendency of people to perform simple or well-learned tasks better when others are present. (2) Current meaning— the strengthening of dominant (prevalent, likely) responses in the presence of others.

Social facilitation: Do you ride faster when bicycling with others?

figure 8–1

The effects of social arousal.

Robert Zajonc reconciled apparently conflicting findings by proposing that arousal from others' presence strengthens dominant responses (the correct responses only on easy or well-learned tasks).

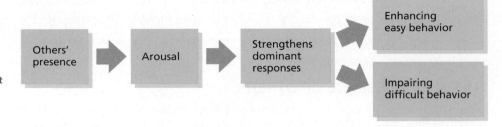

"Mere social contact begets . . . a stimulation of the animal spirits that heightens the efficiency of each individual workman."
—Karl Marx, *Das Kapital*, 1867

"Discovery consists of seeing what everybody has seen and thinking what nobody has thought."
—Albert von Szent-Gyorgyi, *The Scientist Speculates*, 1962

fastest when they are aroused. On complex tasks, for which the correct answer is not dominant, increased arousal promotes *incorrect* responding. On harder anagrams people do worse when anxious.

Could this principle solve the mystery of social facilitation? It seemed reasonable to assume what evidence now confirms—that others' presence will arouse or energize people (Mullen & others, 1997). (We can all recall feeling more tense or excited in front of an audience.) If social arousal facilitates dominant responses, it should *boost performance on easy tasks* and *hurt performance on difficult tasks*. Now the confusing results made sense. Winding fishing reels, doing simple multiplication problems, and eating were all easy tasks for which the responses were well learned or naturally dominant. Sure enough, having others around boosted performance. Learning new material, doing a maze, and solving complex math problems were more difficult tasks for which the correct responses were initially less probable. In these cases, the presence of others increased the number of *incorrect* responses on these tasks. The same general rule—*arousal facilitates dominant responses*—worked in both cases (see Figure 8–1). Suddenly, what had looked like contradictory results no longer seemed contradictory.

Zajonc's solution, so simple and elegant, left other social psychologists thinking what Thomas H. Huxley thought after first reading Darwin's *Origin of the Species*: "How extremely stupid not to have thought of that!" It seemed obvious—once Zajonc had pointed it out. Perhaps, however, the pieces appeared to merge so neatly only through the spectacles of hindsight. Would the solution survive direct experimental tests? After almost 300 studies, conducted with the help of more than 25,000 volunteers, the solution has survived (Bond & Titus, 1983; Guerin, 1993, 1999).

In various ways, later experiments confirmed that social arousal facilitates dominant responses, whether right or wrong. Peter Hunt and Joseph Hillery (1973) found that in others' presence, students took less time to learn a simple maze and more time to learn a complex one (just as the cockroaches do!). And James Michaels and his collaborators (1982) found that good pool players in a student union (who had made 71 percent of their shots while being unobtrusively observed) did even better (80 percent) when four observers came up to watch them play. Poor shooters (who had previously averaged 36 percent) did even worse (25 percent) when closely observed.

Athletes perform well-practiced skills, which helps explain why they often perform best when energized by the responses of a supportive crowd. Studies of more than 80,000 college and professional athletic events in Canada, the United States, and England reveal that home teams win about 6 in 10 games (somewhat fewer for baseball and football, somewhat more for basketball and

table 8–1   **Home advantage in major team sports**

Sport	Games Studied	Percentage of Home Games Won
baseball	135,665	54.3%
football	2,592	57.3
ice hockey	4,322	61.1
basketball	13,596	64.4
soccer	37,202	69.0

Source: Data from Courneya & Carron (1992). Baseball data from Schlenker & others (1995).

soccer—see Table 8–1). The home advantage may, however, also stem from the players' familiarity with their home environment, less travel fatigue, feelings of dominance derived from territorial control, or increased team identity when cheered by fans (Zillmann & Paulus, 1993).

CROWDING: THE PRESENCE OF MANY OTHERS

So people do respond to others' presence. But does the presence of observers really arouse people? In times of stress, a comrade can be comforting. But with others present, people perspire more, breathe faster, tense their muscles more, and have higher blood pressure and a faster heart rate (Geen & Gange, 1983; Moore & Baron, 1983). Even a supportive audience may elicit poorer performance on challenging tasks (Butler & Baumeister, 1998). Having your extended family at your first piano recital likely won't boost your performance.

The effect of other people increases with their number (Jackson & Latané, 1981; Knowles, 1983). Sometimes the arousal and self-conscious attention created by a large audience interferes even with well-learned, automatic behaviors, such as speaking. Given *extreme* pressure, we're vulnerable to choking. Stutterers tend to stutter more in front of larger audiences than when speaking to just one or two people (Mullen, 1986). College basketball players become slightly *less* accurate in their free-throw shooting when very highly aroused by a packed rather than a near empty fieldhouse (Sokoll & Mynatt, 1984).

Being *in* a crowd also intensifies positive or negative reactions. When they sit close together, friendly people are liked even more, and *un*friendly people are *dis*liked even more (Schiffenbauer & Schiavo, 1976; Storms & Thomas, 1977). In experiments with Columbia University students and with Ontario Science Center visitors, Jonathan Freedman and his co-workers (1979, 1980) had an accomplice listen to a humorous tape or watch a movie with other participants. When they all sat close together, the accomplice could more readily induce the individuals to laugh and clap. As theater directors and sports fans know, and as researchers have confirmed, a "good house" is a full house (Aiello & others, 1983; Worchel & Brown, 1984).

Perhaps you've noticed that a class of 35 students feels more warm and lively in a room that seats just 35 than when spread around a room that seats 100. This occurs partly because when others are close by, we are more likely to notice and join in their laughter or clapping. But crowding also enhances arousal, as Gary Evans (1979) found. He tested 10-person groups of University of Massachusetts

Heightened arousal in crowded homes also tends to increase stress. Crowding produces less distress in homes divided into many spaces, however, enabling people to withdraw in privacy (Evans & others, 1996, 2000).

A good house is a full house, as James Maas's Cornell University introductory psychology students experienced in this 2,000-seat auditorium. If the class had 100 students meeting in this large space, it would feel much less energized.

students, either in a room 20 by 30 feet or in one 8 by 12 feet. Compared with those in the large room, those densely packed had higher pulse rates and blood pressure (indicating arousal). On difficult tasks they made more errors, an effect of crowding replicated by Dinesh Nagar and Janak Pandey (1987) with university students in India. So, crowding enhances arousal, which facilitates dominant responses.

WHY ARE WE AROUSED IN THE PRESENCE OF OTHERS?

What you do well, you will be energized to do best in front of others (unless you become hyperaroused and self-conscious). What you find difficult may seem impossible in the same circumstances. What is it about other people that causes arousal? There is evidence to support at least three possible factors (Aiello & Douthitt, 2001): evaluation apprehension, distraction, and mere presence.

Evaluation apprehension

evaluation apprehension
Concern for how others are evaluating us.

Nickolas Cottrell surmised that observers make us apprehensive because we wonder how they are evaluating us. To test whether **evaluation apprehension** exists, Cottrell and his associates (1968) blindfolded observers, supposedly in preparation for a perception experiment. In contrast to the effect of the watching audience, the mere presence of these blindfolded people did *not* boost well-practiced responses.

Other experiments confirmed Cottrell's conclusion: The enhancement of dominant responses is strongest when people think they are being evaluated. In one experiment, joggers on a University of California at Santa Barbara jogging path sped up as they came upon a woman seated on the grass—*if* she was facing them rather than sitting with her back turned (Worringham & Messick, 1983).

Evaluation apprehension also helps explain

- Why people perform best when their co-actor is slightly superior (Seta, 1982)

- Why arousal lessens when a high-status group is diluted by adding people whose opinions don't matter to us (Seta & Seta, 1992)
- Why people who worry most about what others think are the ones most affected by their presence (Gastorf & others, 1980; Geen & Gange, 1983)
- Why social facilitation effects are greatest when the others are unfamiliar and hard to keep an eye on (Guerin & Innes, 1982)

The self-consciousness we feel when being evaluated can also interfere with behaviors that we perform best automatically (Mullen & Baumeister, 1987). If self-conscious basketball players analyze their body movements while shooting critical free throws, they are more likely to miss.

Driven by distraction

Glenn Sanders, Robert Baron, and Danny Moore (1978; Baron, 1986) carried evaluation apprehension a step further. They theorized that when we wonder how co-actors are doing or how an audience is reacting, we get distracted. This *conflict* between paying attention to others and paying attention to the task overloads our cognitive system, causing arousal. We are "driven by distraction." This response facilitation comes not just from the presence of another person but even from a nonhuman distraction, such as bursts of light (Sanders, 1981a, 1981b).

Mere presence

Zajonc, however, believes that the mere presence of others produces some arousal even without evaluation apprehension or arousing distraction. For example, people's color preferences are stronger when they make judgments with others present (Goldman, 1967). On such a task, there is no "good" or "right" answer for others to evaluate and thus no reason to be concerned with their reactions. Still, others' presence is energizing.

Recall that facilitation effects also occur with nonhuman animals. This hints at an innate social arousal mechanism common to much of the zoological world. (Animals probably are not consciously worrying about how other animals are evaluating them.) At the human level, most joggers are energized when jogging with someone else, even one who neither competes nor evaluates.

This is a good time to remind ourselves of the purpose of a theory. As we noted in Chapter 1, a good theory is a scientific shorthand: It simplifies and summarizes a variety of observations. Social facilitation theory does this well. It is a simple summary of many research findings. A good theory also offers clear predictions that (1) help confirm or modify the theory, (2) guide new exploration, and (3) suggest practical applications. Social facilitation theory has definitely generated the first two types of prediction: (1) The basics of the theory (that the presence of others is arousing and that this social arousal enhances dominant responses) have been confirmed, and (2) the theory has brought new life to a long dormant field of research.

Are there (3) some practical applications? We can make some educated guesses. As Figure 8–2 (see page 292) shows, many new office buildings have replaced private offices with large, open areas divided by low partitions. Might the resulting awareness of others' presence help boost the performance of well-learned tasks, but disrupt creative thinking on complex tasks? Can you think of other possible applications?

figure 8–2

In the "open-office plan"
people work in the
presence of others. How
might this affect worker
efficiency? **Source:** Photo
courtesy of Herman Miller Inc.

Summing up

Social psychology's most elementary
issue concerns the mere presence of
others. Some early experiments on
this question found that performance
improved with observers or co-actors
present. Others found that the presence of others can hurt performance.
Robert Zajonc reconciled these findings by applying a well-known
principle from experimental psychology: Arousal facilitates dominant
responses. Because the presence of
others is arousing, the presence of observers or co-actors boosts performance on easy tasks (for which the
correct response is dominant) and
hinders performance on difficult
tasks (for which incorrect responses
are dominant).

But why are we aroused by others'
presence? Experiments suggest that
the arousal stems partly from *evaluation apprehension* and partly from distraction—a conflict between paying
attention to others and concentrating
on the task. Other experiments, including some with animals, suggest
that the presence of others can be
arousing even when we are not evaluated or distracted.

Social loafing: Do individuals exert less effort in a group?

*In a team tug-of-war, will eight people on a side exert as much force as the sum
of their best efforts in individual tugs-of-war? If not, why not? And what level
of individual effort can we expect from members of work groups?*

Social facilitation usually occurs when people work toward individual goals
and when their efforts, whether winding fishing reels or solving math problems, can be individually evaluated. These situations parallel some everyday

figure 8–3

The rope-pulling apparatus.

People in the first position pulled less hard when they thought people behind them were also pulling.

Source: Data from Ingham, Levinger, Graves, & Peckham, 1974. Photo by Alan G. Ingham.

work situations, but not those in which people pool their efforts toward a *common* goal and where individuals are *not* accountable for their efforts. A team tug-of-war provides one such example. Organizational fund-raising—pooling candy sale proceeds to pay for the class trip—provides another. So does a class project where all get the same grade. On such "additive tasks"—tasks where the group's achievement depends on the sum of the individual efforts—will team spirit boost productivity? Will bricklayers lay bricks faster when working as a team than when working alone? One way to attack such questions is with laboratory simulations.

MANY HANDS MAKE LIGHT WORK

Nearly a century ago, French engineer Max Ringelmann (reported by Kravitz & Martin, 1986) found that the collective effort of tug-of-war teams was but half the sum of the individual efforts. This suggests, contrary to the presumption "in unity there is strength," that group members may actually be less motivated when performing additive tasks. Maybe, though, poor performance stemmed from poor coordination—people pulling a rope in slightly different directions at slightly different times. A group of Massachusetts researchers led by Alan Ingham (1974) cleverly eliminated this problem by making individuals think others were pulling with them, when in fact they were pulling alone. Blindfolded participants were assigned the first position in the apparatus shown in Figure 8–3 and told, "Pull as hard as you can." They pulled 18 percent harder when they knew they were pulling alone than when they believed that behind them two to five people were also pulling.

Researchers Bibb Latané, Kipling Williams, and Stephen Harkins (1979; Harkins & others, 1980) kept their ears open for other ways to investigate this phenomenon, which they labeled **social loafing.** They observed that the noise produced by six people shouting or clapping "as loud as you can" was less than three times that produced by one person alone. Like the tug-of-war task, however, noisemaking is vulnerable to group inefficiency. So Latané and his

www.mhhe.com/**myers8**
Visit the Online Learning Center for a scenario on social loafing.

social loafing
The tendency for people to exert less effort when they pool their efforts toward a common goal than when they are individually accountable.

figure 8–4

Effort decreases as group size increases.

A statistical digest of 49 studies, involving more than 4,000 participants, revealed that effort decreases (loafing increases) as the size of the group increases. Each dot represents the aggregate data from one of these studies. **Source:** From Williams, Jackson, & Karau, in *Social Dilemmas: Perspectives on Individuals and Groups*, edited by D. A. Schroeder, 1992. Praeger Publishers, an imprint of Greenwood Publishing Group, Inc., Westport, CT.

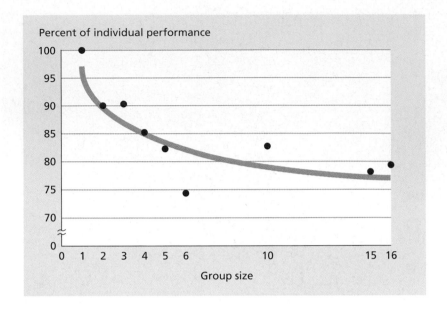

associates followed Ingham's example by leading their Ohio State University participants to believe others were shouting or clapping with them, when in fact they were doing so alone.

Their method was to blindfold six people, seat them in a semicircle, and have them put on headphones, over which they were blasted with the sound of people shouting or clapping. People could not hear their own shouting or clapping, much less that of others. On various trials they were instructed to shout or clap either alone or along with the group. People who were told about this experiment guessed the participants would shout louder when with others, because they would be less inhibited (Harkins, 1981). The actual result? Social loafing: When the participants believed five others were also either shouting or clapping, they produced one-third less noise than when they thought themselves alone. Social loafing occurred even when the participants were high school cheerleaders who believed themselves to be cheering together or alone (Hardy & Latané, 1986).

Curiously, those who clapped both alone and in groups did not view themselves as loafing; they perceived themselves as clapping equally in both situations. This parallels what happens when students work on group projects for a shared grade. Williams reports that all agree loafing occurs—but no one admits to doing the loafing.

John Sweeney (1973), a political scientist interested in the policy implications of social loafing, observed the phenomenon in an experiment at the University of Texas. Students pumped exercise bicycles more energetically (as measured by electrical output) when they knew they were being individually monitored than when they thought their output was being pooled with that of other riders. In the group condition, people were tempted to **free-ride** on the group effort.

free riders
People who benefit from the group but give little in return.

In this and 160 other studies (Karau & Williams, 1993, and Figure 8–4), we see a twist on one of the psychological forces that makes for social facilitation: evaluation apprehension. In the social loafing experiments, individuals believed they were evaluated only when they acted alone. The group situation

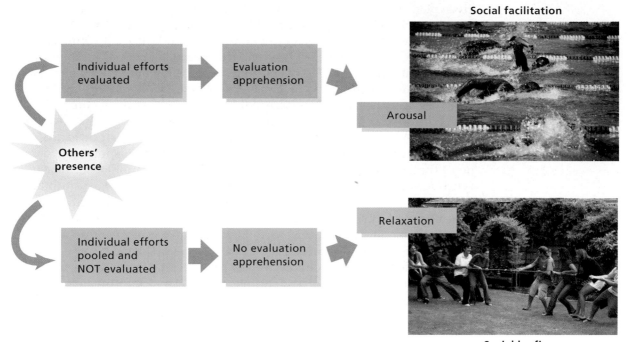

Social facilitation

Social loafing

figure 8–5

Social facilitation or social loafing?

When individuals cannot be evaluated or held accountable, loafing becomes more likely. An individual swimmer is evaluated on her ability to win the race. In tug of war, no single person on the team is held accountable, so any one member might relax or loaf.

(rope pulling, shouting, and so forth) *decreased* evaluation apprehension. When people are not accountable and cannot evaluate their own efforts, responsibility is diffused across all group members (Harkins & Jackson, 1985; Kerr & Bruun, 1981). By contrast, the social facilitation experiments *increased* exposure to evaluation. When made the center of attention, people self-consciously monitor their behavior (Mullen & Baumeister, 1987). So the principle is the same: When being observed *increases* evaluation concerns, social facilitation occurs; when being lost in a crowd *decreases* evaluation concerns, social loafing occurs (Figure 8–5).

To motivate group members, one strategy is to make individual performance identifiable. Some football coaches do this by filming and evaluating each player individually. Whether in a group or not, people exert more effort when their outputs are individually identifiable: University swim team members swim faster in intrasquad relay races when someone monitors and announces their individual times (Williams & others, 1989). Even without pay consequences, actual assembly line workers in one small experiment produced 16 percent more product when their individual output was identified (Faulkner & Williams, 1996).

SOCIAL LOAFING IN EVERYDAY LIFE

How widespread is social loafing? In the laboratory, the phenomenon occurs not only among people who are pulling ropes, cycling, shouting, and clapping but also among those who are pumping water or air, evaluating poems or editorials, producing ideas, typing, and detecting signals. Do these results generalize to everyday worker productivity?

On their collective farms under communism, Russian peasants worked one field one day, another field the next, with little direct responsibility for any given plot. For their own use, they were given small private plots. One analysis found that the private plots occupied 1 percent of the agricultural land, yet produced 27 percent of the Soviet farm output (H. Smith, 1976). In Hungary, private plots accounted for only 13 percent of the farmland but produced one-third of the output (Spivak, 1979). When China began allowing farmers to sell food grown in excess of that owed to the state, food production jumped 8 percent per year—2.5 times the annual increase in the preceding 26 years (Church, 1986).

In North America, workers who do not pay dues or volunteer time to their unions or professional associations nevertheless are usually happy to accept its benefits. So, too, are public television viewers who don't respond to their station's fund drives. This hints at another possible explanation of social loafing. When rewards are divided equally, regardless of how much one contributes to the group, any individual gets more reward per unit of effort by free-riding on the group. So people may be motivated to slack off when their efforts are not individually monitored and rewarded. Situations that welcome free riders can therefore be, in the words of one commune member, a "paradise for parasites."

In a pickle factory, for example, the key job is picking the right size dill pickle halves off the conveyor belt and stuffing them in jars. Unfortunately, workers are tempted to stuff any size pickle in, because their output is not identifiable (the jars go into a common hopper before reaching the quality-control section). Williams, Harkins, and Latané (1981) note that research on social loafing suggests "making individual production identifiable, and raises the question: 'How many pickles could a pickle packer pack if pickle packers were only paid for properly packed pickles?'"

But surely collective effort does not always lead to slacking off. Sometimes the goal is so compelling and maximum output from everyone is so essential that team spirit maintains or intensifies effort. In an Olympic crew race, will the individual rowers in an eight-person crew pull their oars with less effort than those in a one- or two-person crew?

Teamwork at the Charles River regatta in Boston. Social loafing occurs when people work in groups but without individual accountability—unless the task is challenging, appealing, or involving and the group members are friends.

The evidence assures us they will not. People in groups loaf less when the task is *challenging, appealing,* or *involving* (Karau & Williams, 1993). On challenging tasks, people may perceive their efforts as indispensable (Harkins & Petty, 1982; Kerr, 1983; Kerr & Bruun, 1983). When people see others in their group as unreliable or as unable to contribute much, they work harder (Plaks & Higgins, 2000; Williams & Karau, 1991). Adding incentives or challenging a group to strive for certain standards also promotes collective effort (Harkins & Szymanski, 1989; Shepperd & Wright, 1989). When groups believe high effort will enable performance that will bring rewards—their members will work hard (Shepperd & Taylor, 1999).

Groups also loaf less when their members are *friends* or identified with their group, rather than strangers (Davis & Greenlees, 1992; Karau & Williams, 1997; Worchel & others, 1998). Even just expecting to interact with someone again serves to increase effort on team projects (Groenenboom & others, 2001). Collaborate on a class project with others whom you will be seeing often and it is likely that you will feel more motivated than if you never expect to see them again. Latané notes that Israel's

communal kibbutz farms have actually outproduced Israel's noncollective farms (Leon, 1969). Cohesiveness intensifies effort. So will there be social loafing in group-centered cultures? To find out, Latané and his co-researchers (Gabrenya & others, 1985) headed for Asia, where they repeated their sound production experiments in Japan, Thailand, Taiwan, India, and Malaysia. Their findings? Social loafing was evident in all these countries, too.

Seventeen later studies in Asia reveal that people in collectivist cultures do, however, exhibit less social loafing than do people in individualist cultures (Karau & Williams, 1993; Kugihara, 1999). As we noted in Chapter 2, loyalty to family and work groups runs strong in collectivist cultures. Likewise, women (as Chapter 5 explained) tend to be less individualistic than men—and to exhibit less social loafing.

Some of these findings parallel those from studies of everyday work groups. When groups are given challenging objectives, when they are rewarded for group success, and when there is a spirit of commitment to the "team," group members work hard (Hackman, 1986). Keeping work groups small and forming them with equally competent people can also help members believe their contributions are indispensable (Comer, 1995). So while social loafing is a common occurrence when group members work collectively and without individual accountability, many hands need not always make light work.

Social facilitation researchers study people's performance on tasks where they can be evaluated individually. However, in many work situations people pool their efforts and work toward a common goal without individual accountability. Studies show that group members often work less hard when performing such "additive tasks." This finding parallels everyday situations where diffused responsibility tempts individual group members to free-ride on the group's effort.

Summing up

Deindividuation: When do people lose their sense of self in groups?

Group situations may cause people to lose self-awareness, with resulting loss of individuality and self-restraint. What circumstances trigger such "deindividuation"?

In April 2003, in the wake of American troops entering Iraqi's cities, looters—"liberated" from the scrutiny of Saddam Hussein's police—ran rampant. In "frenzied looting," hospitals lost beds. The National Library lost tens of thousands of old manuscripts and lay in smoldering ruins. Universities lost computers, chairs, even lightbulbs. The National Museum in Baghdad lost thousands of artifacts within 48 hours—most of what had previously been removed to safekeeping (Burns, 2003a, b; Lawler, 2003c). "Not since the Spanish conquistadors ravaged the Aztec and Inca cultures has so much been lost so quickly," reported *Science* (Lawler, 2003a). "They came in mobs: A group of 50 would come, then would go, and another would come," explained one university dean (Lawler, 2003b). Such reports had the rest of the world wondering: What happened to the looters' sense of morality? Why did such behavior erupt?

Apparently acting without their normal conscience, people looted Iraqi institutions after the toppling of Saddam Hussein's regime.

DOING TOGETHER WHAT WE WOULD NOT DO ALONE

Social facilitation experiments show that groups can arouse people. Social loafing experiments show that groups can diffuse responsibility. When arousal and diffused responsibility combine and normal inhibitions diminish, the results may be startling. People may commit acts that range from a mild lessening of restraint (throwing food in the dining hall, snarling at a referee, screaming during a rock concert) to impulsive self-gratification (group vandalism, orgies, thefts) to destructive social explosions (police brutality, riots, lynchings). In a 1967 incident, 200 University of Oklahoma students gathered to watch a disturbed fellow student threatening to jump from a tower. They began to chant "Jump. Jump. . . ." The student jumped to his death (UPI, 1967).

These unrestrained behaviors have something in common: They are somehow provoked by the power of a group. Groups can generate a sense of excitement, of being caught up in something bigger than one's self. It is harder to imagine a single rock fan screaming deliriously at a private rock concert, a single Oklahoma student trying to coax someone to suicide, or even a single police officer beating a defenseless motorist. In certain kinds of group situations, people are more likely to abandon normal restraints, to lose their sense of individual identity, to become responsive to group or crowd norms—in a word, to become what Leon Festinger, Albert Pepitone, and Theodore Newcomb (1952) labeled **deindividuated.** What circumstances elicit this psychological state?

Group size

deindividuation

Loss of self-awareness and evaluation apprehension; occurs in group situations that foster responsiveness to group norms, good or bad.

A group has the power not only to arouse its members but also to render them unidentifiable. The snarling crowd hides the snarling basketball fan. A lynch mob enables its members to believe they will not be prosecuted; they perceive the action as the *group's*. Looters, made faceless by the mob, are freed to loot. In an analysis of 21 instances in which crowds were present as someone threatened to jump from a building or bridge, Leon Mann (1981) found that when the crowd was small and exposed by daylight, people usually did not try to bait

figure 8–6

Anonymous women delivered more shock to helpless victims than did identifiable women.

the person. But when a large crowd or the cover of night gave people anonymity, the crowd usually baited and jeered.

Brian Mullen (1986) reports a similar effect of lynch mobs: The bigger the mob, the more its members lose self-awareness and become willing to commit atrocities, such as burning, lacerating, or dismembering the victim. In each of these examples, from sports crowds to lynch mobs, evaluation apprehension plummets. Because "everyone is doing it," all can attribute their behavior to the situation rather than to their own choices.

Philip Zimbardo (1970) speculated that the mere immensity of crowded cities produces anonymity and thus norms that permit vandalism. He purchased two 10-year-old cars and left them with the hoods up and license plates removed, one on a street near the old Bronx campus of New York University and one near the Stanford University campus in Palo Alto, a much smaller city. In New York the first auto strippers arrived within 10 minutes; they took the battery and radiator. After three days and 23 incidents of theft and vandalism (by neatly dressed White people), the car was reduced to a battered, useless hulk of metal. By contrast, the only person observed to touch the Palo Alto car in over a week was a passerby who lowered the hood when it began to rain.

Physical anonymity

How can we be sure that the crucial difference between the Bronx and Palo Alto is greater anonymity in the Bronx? We can't. But we can experiment with anonymity to see if it actually lessens inhibitions. Zimbardo (1970, 2002) got the idea for such an experiment from his undergraduate students, who questioned how good boys in William Golding's *Lord of the Flies* could so suddenly become monsters after painting their faces. To experiment with such anonymity, he dressed New York University women in identical white coats and hoods, rather like Ku Klux Klan members (Figure 8–6). Asked to deliver electric shocks to a woman, they pressed the shock button twice as long as did women who were visible and wearing large name tags.

The Internet offers similar anonymity. Millions of those who were aghast at the looting by the Baghdad mobs were on those very days anonymously

"A mob is a society of bodies voluntarily bereaving themselves of reason."

—Ralph Waldo Emerson, "Compensation," *Essays, First Series,* 1841

figure 8–7

Children were more likely to transgress by taking extra Halloween candy when in a group, when anonymous, and, especially, when deindividuated by the combination of group immersion and anonymity.

Source: Data from Diener & others, 1976.

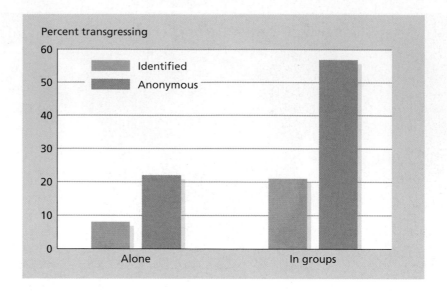

pirating music tracks using file-sharing software. With so many doing it, and with so little concern about being caught, downloading someone's copyright-protected property and then offloading it to an MP3 player just didn't seem terribly immoral. The anonymity offered by chat rooms, newsgroups, and listservs also has been observed to foster higher levels of hostile, uninhibited "flaming" behavior than observed in face-to-face conversations (Douglas & McGarty, 2001).

Testing the phenomenon on the streets, Patricia Ellison, John Govern, and their colleagues (1995) had a confederate driver stop at a red light and wait for 12 seconds whenever she was followed by a convertible or 4×4 vehicle. While enduring the wait, she recorded any horn-honking (a mild aggressive act) by the car behind. Compared with drivers of convertibles and 4×4s with the tops down, those who were relatively anonymous (with the tops up) honked one-third sooner, twice as often, and for nearly twice as long.

A research team led by Ed Diener (1976) cleverly demonstrated the effect both of being in a group *and* being physically anonymous. At Halloween, they observed 1,352 Seattle children trick-or-treating. As the children, either alone or in groups, approached 1 of 27 homes scattered throughout the city, an experimenter greeted them warmly, invited them to "take *one* of the candies," and then left the room. Hidden observers noted that children in groups were more than twice as likely to take extra candy as solo children. Also, those who were left anonymous were more than twice as likely to transgress as children who had been asked their names and where they lived. As Figure 8–7 shows, the transgression rate varied dramatically with the situation. When they were deindividuated by group immersion combined with anonymity, most children stole extra candy.

These experiments make me wonder about the effect of wearing uniforms. Preparing for battle, warriors in some tribal cultures (like rabid fans of some sports teams) depersonalize themselves with body and face paints or special masks. After the battle, some cultures kill, torture, or mutilate any remaining enemies; other cultures take prisoners alive. Robert Watson (1973) scrutinized

Soccer fans after a 1985 riot and the collapse of a wall that killed 39 people in Brussels. The soccer hooligans are often likable as individuals, reported one English journalist who ran with them for eight years, but demonic in a crowd (Buford, 1992).

anthropological files and discovered that the cultures with depersonalized warriors were also the cultures that brutalized their enemies. The uniformed Los Angeles police officers who beat Rodney King were angered and aroused by his defiant refusal to stop his car. They were enjoying one another's camaraderie and unaware that outsiders would view their actions. Thus, forgetting their normal standards, they were swept away by the situation.

In Northern Ireland, 206 of 500 violent attacks studied by Andrew Silke (2003) were conducted by attackers who wore masks, hoods, or other face disguises. Compared with undisguised attackers, these anonymous attackers inflicted more serious injuries, attacked more people, and committed more vandalism.

Does becoming physically anonymous *always* unleash our worst impulses? Fortunately, no. In all these situations, people were responding to clear antisocial cues. Robert Johnson and Leslie Downing (1979) point out that the Klan-like outfits worn by Zimbardo's participants may have encouraged hostility. In an experiment at the University of Georgia, women put on nurses' uniforms before deciding how much shock someone should receive. When those wearing the nurses' uniforms were made anonymous, they became *less* aggressive in administering shocks than when their names and personal identities were stressed. From their analysis of 60 deindividuation studies, Tom Postmes and Russell Spears (1998; Reicher & others, 1995) conclude that being anonymous makes one less self-conscious, more group-conscious, and more responsive to cues present in the situation, whether negative (Klan uniforms) or positive (nurses' uniforms). Given altruistic cues, deindividuated people even give more money (Spivey & Prentice-Dunn, 1990).

> "The use of self-control is like the use of brakes on a train. It is useful when you find yourself going in the wrong direction, but merely harmful when the direction is right."
> —Bertrand Russell, *Marriage and Morals*, 1929

Arousing and distracting activities

Aggressive outbursts by large groups often are preceded by minor actions that arouse and divert people's attention. Group shouting, chanting, clapping, or dancing serve both to hype people up and to reduce self-consciousness. One Moonie observer recalls how the "choo-choo" chant helped deindividuate:

All the brothers and sisters joined hands and chanted with increasing intensity, choo-choo-choo, Choo-choo-choo, CHOO-CHOO-CHOO! YEA! YEA! POWW!!!

The act made us a group, as though in some strange way we had all experienced something important together. The power of the choo-choo frightened me, but it made me feel more comfortable and there was something very relaxing about building up the energy and releasing it. (Zimbardo & others, 1977, p. 186)

Ed Diener's experiments (1976, 1979) have shown that activities such as throwing rocks and group singing can set the stage for more disinhibited behavior. There is a self-reinforcing pleasure in acting impulsively while observing others doing likewise. When we see others act as we are acting, we think they feel as we do, which reinforces our own feelings (Orive, 1984). Moreover, impulsive group action absorbs our attention. When we yell at the referee, we are not thinking about our values; we are reacting to the immediate situation. Later, when we stop to think about what we have done or said, we sometimes feel chagrined. Sometimes. At other times we seek deindividuating group experiences—dances, worship experiences, group encounters—where we can enjoy intense positive feelings and closeness to others.

"Attending a service in the Gothic cathedral, we have the sensation of being enclosed and steeped in an integral universe, and of losing a prickly sense of self in the community of worshipers."
—Yi-Fu Tuan, 1982

DIMINISHED SELF-AWARENESS

Group experiences that diminish self-consciousness tend to disconnect behavior from attitudes. Experiments by Ed Diener (1980) and Steven Prentice-Dunn and Ronald Rogers (1980, 1989) reveal that unself-conscious, deindividuated people are less restrained, less self-regulated, more likely to act without thinking about their own values, and more responsive to the situation. These findings complement and reinforce the experiments on *self-awareness* considered in Chapter 3.

Self-awareness is the opposite of deindividuation. Those made self-aware, by acting in front of a mirror or TV camera, exhibit *increased* self-control, and their actions more clearly reflect their attitudes. In front of a mirror, people taste-testing cream cheese varieties eat less of the high-fat variety (Sentyrz & Bushman, 1998). Perhaps dieters should put mirrors in the kitchen.

People made self-aware are also less likely to cheat (Beaman & others, 1979; Diener & Wallbom, 1976). So are those who generally have a strong sense of themselves as distinct and independent (Nadler & others, 1982). People who are self-conscious, or who are temporarily made so, exhibit greater consistency between their words outside a situation and their deeds in it. They also become more thoughtful and therefore less vulnerable to appeals that run counter to their values (Hutton & Baumeister, 1992).

Circumstances that decrease self-awareness, as alcohol consumption does, therefore increase deindividuation (Hull & others, 1983). And deindividuation decreases in circumstances that increase self-awareness: mirrors and cameras, small towns, bright lights, large name tags, undistracted quiet, individual clothes and houses (Ickes & others, 1978). When a teenager leaves for a party, a parent's parting advice could well be, "Have fun, and remember who you are." In other words, enjoy being with the group, but be self-aware; maintain your personal identity; don't become deindividuated.

Summing up

When high levels of social arousal combine with diffused responsibility, people may abandon their normal restraints and lose their sense of individuality. Such *deindividuation* is especially likely when, after being aroused and distracted, people feel anonymity while in a large group or wearing concealing clothing or costumes. The result is diminished self-awareness and self-restraint and increased responsiveness to the immediate situation, be it negative or positive.

Group polarization: Do groups intensify our opinions?

Many conflicts grow as people on both sides talk mostly with like-minded others. Does interaction with like-minded people amplify preexisting attitudes? If so, why?

Which effect—good or bad—does group interaction more often have? Police brutality and mob violence demonstrate its destructive potential. Yet support-group leaders, management consultants, and educational theorists proclaim its benefits, and social and religious movements urge their members to strengthen their identities by fellowship with like-minded others.

Studies of people in small groups have produced a principle that helps explain both bad and good outcomes: Group discussion often strengthens members' initial inclinations. The unfolding of this research on *group polarization* illustrates the process of inquiry—how an interesting discovery often leads researchers to hasty and erroneous conclusions, which ultimately get replaced with more accurate conclusions. This is one scientific mystery I can discuss first-hand, having been one of the detectives.

THE CASE OF THE "RISKY SHIFT"

A research literature of more than 300 studies began with a surprising finding by James Stoner (1961), then an MIT graduate student. For his master's thesis in industrial management, Stoner tested the commonly held belief that groups are more cautious than individuals. He posed decision dilemmas in which the participant's task was to advise imagined characters how much risk to take. Put yourself in the participant's shoes: What advice would you give the character in this situation?

> Helen is a writer who is said to have considerable creative talent but who so far has been earning a comfortable living by writing cheap westerns. Recently she has come up with an idea for a potentially significant novel. If it could be written and accepted, it might have considerable literary impact and be a big boost to her career. On the other hand, if she cannot work out her idea or if the novel is a flop, she will have expended considerable time and energy without remuneration.
>
> Imagine that you are advising Helen. Please check the *lowest* probability that you would consider acceptable for Helen to attempt to write the novel.
>
> Helen should attempt to write the novel if the chances that the novel will be a success are at least
>
> _____ 1 in 10   _____ 7 in 10
> _____ 2 in 10   _____ 8 in 10
> _____ 3 in 10   _____ 9 in 10
> _____ 4 in 10   _____ 10 in 10 (Place a check here if you think Helen
> _____ 5 in 10   should attempt the novel only if it is certain that the novel
> _____ 6 in 10   will be a success.)

After making your decision, guess what this book's average reader would advise.

Having marked their advice on a dozen such items, five or so individuals would then discuss and reach agreement on each item. How do you think the group decisions compared with the average decision before the discussions? Would the groups be likely to take greater risks, be more cautious, or stay the same?

To everyone's amazement, the group decisions were usually riskier. Dubbed the "risky shift phenomenon," this finding set off a wave of group risk-taking studies. These revealed that risky shift occurs not only when a group decides by consensus; after a brief discussion, individuals, too, will alter their decisions. What is more, researchers successfully repeated Stoner's finding with people of varying ages and occupations in a dozen nations.

During discussion, opinions converged. Curiously, however, the point toward which they converged was usually a lower (riskier) number than their initial average. Here was a delightful puzzle. The small risky shift effect was reliable, unexpected, and without any immediately obvious explanation. What group influences produce such an effect? And how widespread is it? Do discussions in juries, business committees, and military organizations also promote risk taking? Does this explain why teenage reckless driving, as measured by death rates, nearly doubles when a 16- or 17-year-old driver has two passengers rather than none (Chen & others, 2000)?

After several years of study, we discovered that the risky shift was not universal. We could write decision dilemmas on which people became more *cautious* after discussion. One of these featured "Roger," a young married man with two school-age children and a secure but low-paying job. Roger can afford life's necessities but few of its luxuries. He hears that the stock of a relatively unknown company may soon triple in value if its new product is favorably received or decline considerably if it does not sell. Roger has no savings. To invest in the company, he is considering selling his life insurance policy.

Can you see a general principle that predicts both the tendency to give riskier advice after discussing Helen's situation and more cautious advice after discussing Roger's?

If you are like most people, you would advise Helen to take a greater risk than Roger, even before talking with others. It turns out there is a strong tendency for discussion to accentuate these initial leanings.

DO GROUPS INTENSIFY OPINIONS?

Realizing that this group phenomenon was not a consistent shift to risk, we reconceived the phenomenon as a tendency for group discussion to *enhance* group members' initial leanings. This idea led investigators to propose what French researchers Serge Moscovici and Marisa Zavalloni (1969) called **group polarization:** *Discussion typically strengthens the average inclination of group members.*

Group polarization experiments

This new view of the changes induced by group discussion prompted experimenters to have people discuss attitude statements that most of them favored or

group polarization
Group-produced enhancement of members' preexisting tendencies; a strengthening of the members' average tendency, not a split within the group.

most of them opposed. Would talking in groups enhance their initial inclinations as it did with the decision dilemmas? In groups, would risk takers not only become riskier, but bigots become despisers, and givers become more philanthropic? That's what the group polarization hypothesis predicts (Figure 8–8).

Dozens of studies confirm group polarization.

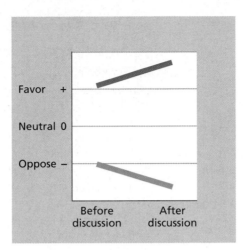

figure 8–8

Group polarization.

The group polarization hypothesis predicts that discussion will strengthen an attitude shared by group members.

- Moscovici and Zavalloni (1969) observed that discussion enhanced French students' initially positive attitude toward their president and negative attitude toward Americans.
- Mititoshi Isozaki (1984) found that Japanese university students gave more pronounced judgments of "guilty" after discussing a traffic case.
- Markus Brauer and his co-workers (2001) found that French students' dislike for certain other people was exacerbated after discussing their shared negative impressions.
- And Glen Whyte (1993) reported that groups exacerbate the "too much invested to quit" phenomenon that has cost many businesses huge sums of money. Canadian business students imagined themselves having to decide whether to invest more money in the hope of preventing losses in various failing projects (for example, whether to make a high-risk loan to protect an earlier investment). They exhibited the typical effect: Seventy-two percent reinvested money they would seldom have invested if they were considering it as a new investment on its own merits. When making the same decision in groups, 94 percent opted for reinvestment.

Another research strategy has been to pick issues on which opinions are divided and then isolate people who hold the same view. Does discussion with like-minded people strengthen shared views? Does it magnify the attitude gap that separates the two sides?

George Bishop and I wondered. So we set up groups of relatively prejudiced and unprejudiced high school students and asked them to respond—before and after discussion—to issues involving racial attitudes, such as property rights versus open housing (Myers & Bishop, 1970). We found that the discussions among like-minded students did indeed increase the initial gap between the two groups (Figure 8–9, see page 306).

Group polarization in everyday life

In everyday life people associate mostly with others whose attitudes are similar to their own (Chapter 11). (Look at your own circle of friends.) Does everyday group interaction with like-minded friends intensify shared attitudes? Do nerds become nerdier and jocks jockier?

figure 8–9

Discussion increased polarization between homogeneous groups of high- and low-prejudice high school students. Talking over racial issues increased prejudice in a high-prejudice group and decreased it in a low-prejudice group. **Source:** Data from Myers & Bishop, 1970.

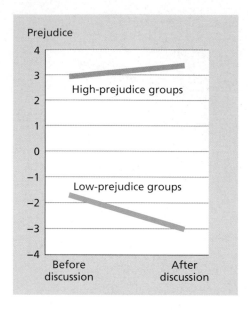

It happens. The self-segregation of boys into all-male groups and of girls into all-female groups accentuates over time their initially modest gender differences, notes Eleanor Maccoby (2002). Boys with boys become gradually more competitive and action oriented in their play and fictional fare, while girls with girls become more relationally oriented. On U.S. federal appellate court cases, "Republican-appointed judges tend to vote like Republicans and Democratic-appointed judges tend to vote like Democrats," David Schkade and Cass Sunstein (2003) have observed. But such tendencies are accentuated when among like-minded judges. "A Republican appointee sitting with two other Republicans votes far more conservatively than when the same judge sits with at least one Democratic appointee. A Democratic appointee, meanwhile, shows the same tendency in the opposite ideological direction."

Group polarization in schools.   Another real-life parallel to the laboratory phenomenon is what education researchers have called the "accentuation phenomenon": Over time, initial differences among groups of college students become accentuated. If the students at college X are initially more intellectual than the students at college Y, that gap is likely to grow during college. Likewise, compared with fraternity and sorority members, independents tend to have more liberal political attitudes, a difference that grows with time in college (Pascarella & Terenzini, 1991). Researchers believe this results partly from group members reinforcing shared inclinations.

Group polarization in communities.   Polarization also occurs in communities. During community conflicts, like-minded people associate increasingly with one another, amplifying their shared tendencies. Gang delinquency emerges from a process of mutual reinforcement within neighborhood gangs, whose members share attributes and hostilities (Cartwright, 1975). If, on your block, "a second out-of-control 15-year-old moves in," surmises David Lykken (1997), "the mischief they get into as a team is likely to be more than merely double what the first would do on his own. . . . A gang is more dangerous than the sum of its individual parts." Indeed, "unsupervised peer groups" are "the strongest predictor" of a neighborhood's crime victimization rate, report Bonita Veysey and Steven Messner (1999). Moreover, experimental interventions that group delinquent adolescents with other delinquents actually—no surprise to any group polarization researcher—increase the rate of problem behavior (Dishion & others, 1999).

From their analysis of terrorist organizations around the world, Clark McCauley and Mary Segal (1987; McCauley, 2002) note that terrorism does not erupt suddenly. Rather, it arises among people whose shared grievances bring

In two trials, South African courts reduced sentences after learning how social-psychological phenomena, including deindividuation and group polarization, led crowd members to commit murderous acts (Colman, 1991). Would you agree that courts should consider social-psychological phenomena as possible extenuating circumstances?

Animal gangs. The pack is more than the sum of the wolves.

them together. As they interact in isolation from moderating influences, they become progressively more extreme. The social amplifier brings the signal in stronger. The result is violent acts that the individuals, apart from the group, would never have committed.

For example, the 9/11 terrorists were bred by a long process that engaged the polarizing effect of the interaction among the like-minded. The process of becoming a terrorist, noted a National Research Council panel, isolates individuals from other belief systems, dehumanizes potential targets, and tolerates no dissent (Smelser & Mitchell, 2002). Ariel Merari (2002), an investigator of Middle Eastern and Sri Lankan suicide terrorism, believes the key to creating a terrorist suicide is the group process. "To the best of my knowledge, there has not been a single case of suicide terrorism which was done on a personal whim." Massacres are likewise group phenomena, enabled by the killers egging each other on (Zajonc, 2000).

Group polarization on the Internet.   E-mail and electronic chat rooms offer a potential new medium for group interaction. By the beginning of the new century, 85 percent of Canadian teens were using the Internet for an average of 9.3 hours weekly (TGM, 2000). Its countless virtual groups enable peacemakers and neo-Nazis, geeks and goths, conspiracy theorists, and cancer survivors to isolate themselves with one another and find support for their shared concerns, interests, and suspicions (Gerstenfeld, 2003; McKenna & Bargh, 1998, 2000; Sunstein, 2001). Without the nonverbal nuances of face-to-face contact, will such discussions produce group polarization? Will peacemakers become more pacifistic and militia members more terror prone? E-mail, Google, and chat rooms "make it much easier for small groups to rally like-minded people, crystallize diffuse hatreds and mobilize lethal force," observes Robert Wright (2003). As broadband spreads, Internet-spawned polarization will increase, he speculates. "Ever seen one of Osama bin Laden's recruiting videos? They're very effective, and they'll reach their targeted audience much more efficiently via broadband."

"The proliferation of media outlets and the segmentation of society have meant that it's much easier for people to hive themselves off into like-minded cliques. Some people live in towns where nobody likes President Bush. Others listen to radio networks where nobody likes Bill Clinton. In these communities, half-truths get circulated and exaggerated."
—David Brooks, "The Era of Distortion," 2004

focus on | group polarization

Shakespeare portrayed the polarizing power of the like-minded group in this dialogue of Julius Caesar's followers:

Antony: Kind souls, what weep you when you but behold Our Caesar's vesture wounded? Look you here. Here is himself, marr'd, as you see, with traitors.

    First Citizen: O piteous spectacle!

    Second Citizen: O noble Caesar!

    Third Citizen: O woeful day!

Fourth Citizen: O traitors, villains!

First Citizen: O most bloody sight!

Second Citizen: We will be revenged!

    All: Revenge! About! Seek! Burn! Fire! Kill! Slay! Let not a traitor live!

Source: From *Julius Caesar* by William Shakespeare, Act III, Scene ii, lines 199–209.

EXPLAINING POLARIZATION

Why do groups adopt stances that are more exaggerated than the average opinions of their individual members? Researchers hoped that solving the mystery of group polarization might provide some insights. Solving small puzzles sometimes provides clues for solving larger ones.

Among several proposed theories of group polarization, two survived scientific scrutiny. One deals with the arguments presented during a discussion, the other with how members of a group view themselves vis-à-vis the other members. The first idea is an example of what Chapter 6 called *informational influence* (influence that results from accepting evidence about reality). The second is an example of *normative influence* (influence based on a person's desire to be accepted or admired by others).

Informational influence

According to the best-supported explanation, group discussion elicits a pooling of ideas, most of which favor the dominant viewpoint. Ideas that were common knowledge to group members will often be brought up in discussion or, even if unmentioned, will jointly influence their discussion (Gigone & Hastie, 1993; Larson & others, 1994; Stasser, 1991). Other ideas may include persuasive arguments that some group members had not previously considered. When discussing Helen the writer, someone may say, "Helen should go for it, because she has little to lose. If her novel flops, she can always go back to writing cheap westerns." Such statements often entangle information about the person's *arguments* with cues concerning the person's *position* on the issue. But when people hear relevant arguments without learning the specific stands other people assume, they still shift their positions (Burnstein & Vinokur, 1977; Hinz & others, 1997). *Arguments*, in and of themselves, matter.

But there's more to attitude change than merely hearing someone else's arguments. *Active participation* in discussion produces more attitude change than does passive listening. Participants and observers hear the same ideas, but when participants express them in their own words, the verbal commitment magnifies the impact. The more group members repeat one another's ideas, the more they rehearse and validate them (Brauer & others, 1995). Just writing out one's ideas in preparation for an electronic discussion tends to polarize attitudes somewhat (Liu & Latané, 1998).

This illustrates a point made in Chapter 7. People's minds are not just blank tablets for persuaders to write upon; in central route persuasion, what people *think* in response to a message is crucial. Indeed, just thinking about an issue for a couple of minutes can strengthen opinions (Tesser & others, 1995). (Perhaps you can recall your feelings becoming polarized as you merely ruminated about someone you disliked, or liked.) Even just *expecting* to discuss an issue with an equally expert person holding an opposing view can motivate people to marshal their arguments and thus to adopt a more extreme position (Fitzpatrick & Eagly, 1981).

Normative influence

A second explanation of polarization involves comparison with others. As Leon Festinger (1954) argued in his influential theory of **social comparison,** we humans want to evaluate our opinions and abilities, something we can do by comparing our views with others'. We are most persuaded by people in our "reference groups"—groups we identify with (Abrams & others, 1990; Hogg & others, 1990). Moreover, wanting people to like us, we may express stronger opinions after discovering that others share our views.

social comparison
Evaluating one's opinions and abilities by comparing oneself to others.

Robert Baron and his colleagues (1996) explored the polarizing effect of having one's views socially corroborated. They asked University of Iowa dental clinic patients whether they considered the dental chair "comfortable" or "uncomfortable." Then some individuals heard the experimenter ask: "By the way, Dr. X, what did the last patient say?" The dentist always echoed whatever response the patient had just made. Finally, the patients rated the chair on a 150 to 250 scale. Compared with participants who had not heard their opinions corroborated, those who had gave decidedly more extreme ratings.

When we ask people (as I asked you earlier) to predict how others would respond to items such as the "Helen" dilemma, they typically exhibit pluralistic ignorance: They don't realize how much others support the socially preferred tendency (in this case, writing the novel). A typical person will advise writing the novel even if its chance of success is only 4 in 10 but will estimate that most other people would require 5 or 6 in 10. (This finding is reminiscent of the self-serving bias: People tend to view themselves as better-than-average embodiments of socially desirable traits and attitudes.) When the discussion begins, most people discover they are not outshining the others as they had supposed. In fact, some others are ahead of them, having taken an even stronger position for writing the novel. No longer restrained by a misperceived group norm, they are liberated to voice their preferences more strongly.

Perhaps you can recall a time when you and someone else wanted to go out, but each of you feared to make the first move, presuming the other probably did not have a reciprocal interest. Such **pluralistic ignorance** impedes the start-up of relationships (Vorauer & Ratner, 1996).

pluralistic ignorance
A false impression of what most other people are thinking, feeling, or responding.

Or perhaps you can recall a time when you and others were guarded and reserved in a group, until someone broke the ice and said, "Well, to be perfectly honest, I think . . ." Soon you were all surprised to discover strong support for your shared views. Sometimes when a professor asks if anyone has any questions, no one will respond, leading each student to infer that he or she is the

figure 8–10

On "risky" dilemma items (such as the case of Helen), mere exposure to others' judgments enhanced individuals' risk-prone tendencies. On "cautious" dilemma items (such as the case of Roger), exposure to others' judgments enhanced their cautiousness. **Source:** Data from Myers, 1978.

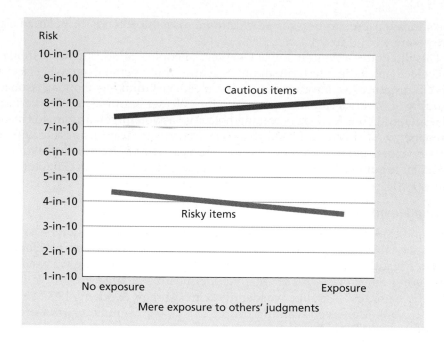

only one confused. All presume that fear of embarrassment explains their own silence, but that everyone else's silence means they understand the material.

Dale Miller and Cathy McFarland (1987) bottled this familiar phenomenon in a laboratory experiment. They asked people to read an incomprehensible article and to seek help if they ran into "any really serious problems in understanding the paper." Although none of the individuals sought help, they presumed *other* people would not be similarly restrained by fear of embarrassment. Thus, they wrongly inferred that people who didn't seek help didn't need any. To overcome such pluralistic ignorance, someone must break the ice and enable others to reveal and reinforce their shared reactions.

This social comparison theory prompted experiments that exposed people to others' positions but not to their arguments. This is roughly the experience we have when reading the results of an opinion poll or of exit polling on election day. When people learn others' positions—without prior commitment or discussion—will they adjust their responses to maintain a socially favorable position? As Figure 8–10 illustrates, they will. This comparison-based polarization is usually less than that produced by a lively discussion. Still, it's surprising that, instead of simply conforming to the group average, people often go it one better. Are people "one-upping" the observed norm to differentiate themselves from the group? Is this another example of our need to feel unique (Chapter 6)?

Group polarization research illustrates the complexity of social-psychological inquiry. As much as we like our explanations of a phenomenon to be simple, one explanation seldom accounts for all the data. Because people are complex, more than one factor frequently influences an outcome. In group discussions, persuasive arguments predominate on issues that have a factual element ("Is she guilty of the crime?"). Social comparison sways responses on value-laden judgments ("How long a sentence should she serve?") (Kaplan, 1989). On the many issues that have both factual and value-laden aspects, the two factors work together. Discovering that others share one's feelings (social comparison) unleashes arguments (informational influence) supporting what everyone secretly favors.

Potentially positive and negative results arise from group discussion. While trying to understand the curious finding that group discussion enhanced risk taking, investigators discovered that discussion actually tends to strengthen whatever is the initially dominant point of view, whether risky or cautious. In everyday situations, too, group interaction tends to intensify opinions. The *group polarization* phenomenon provided a window through which researchers could observe group influence. Experiments confirmed two group influences: *informational* and *normative.* The information gleaned from a discussion mostly favors the initially preferred alternative, thus reinforcing support for it. Moreover, people may go further out on the limb when, after comparing positions, they discover surprising support for their initial inclinations.

Summing up

Groupthink: Do groups hinder or assist good decisions?

When do group influences hinder good decisions? When do groups promote good decisions, and how can we lead groups to make optimal decisions?

Do the social-psychological phenomena we have been considering in these first eight chapters occur in sophisticated groups like corporate boards or the president's cabinet? Is there likely to be self-justification? Self-serving bias? A cohesive "we feeling" provoking conformity and rejection of dissent? Public commitment producing resistance to change? Group polarization? Social psychologist Irving Janis (1971, 1982) wondered whether such phenomena might help explain good and bad group decisions made by some twentieth-century American presidents and their advisers. To find out, he analyzed the decision-making procedures that led to several major fiascos:

- *Pearl Harbor.* In the weeks preceding the December 1941 Pearl Harbor attack that put the United States into World War II, military commanders in Hawaii received a steady stream of information about Japan's preparations for an attack on the United States somewhere in the Pacific. Then military intelligence lost radio contact with Japanese aircraft carriers, which had begun moving straight for Hawaii. Air reconnaissance could have spotted the carriers or at least provided a few minutes' warning. But complacent commanders decided against such precautions. The result: No alert was sounded until the attack on a virtually defenseless base was under way. The loss: 18 ships, 170 planes, and 2,400 lives.

- *The Bay of Pigs Invasion.* In 1961 President John Kennedy and his advisers tried to overthrow Fidel Castro by invading Cuba with 1,400 CIA-trained Cuban exiles. Nearly all the invaders were soon killed or captured, the United States was humiliated, and Cuba allied itself more closely with the former U.S.S.R. After learning the outcome, Kennedy wondered aloud, "How could we have been so stupid?"

• *The Vietnam War.* From 1964 to 1967 President Lyndon Johnson and his "Tuesday lunch group" of policy advisers escalated the war in Vietnam on the assumption that U.S. aerial bombardment, defoliation, and search-and-destroy missions would bring North Vietnam to the peace table with the appreciative support of the South Vietnamese populace. They continued the escalation despite warnings from government intelligence experts and nearly all U.S. allies. The resulting disaster cost more than 58,000 American and 1 million Vietnamese lives, polarized Americans, drove the president from office, and created huge budget deficits that helped fuel inflation in the 1970s.

groupthink
"The mode of thinking that persons engage in when concurrence-seeking becomes so dominant in a cohesive in-group that it tends to override realistic appraisal of alternative courses of action."—
Irving Janis (1971)

Janis believed these blunders were bred by the tendency of decision-making groups to suppress dissent in the interests of group harmony, a phenomenon he called **groupthink**. (See "The Story Behind the Research: Irving Janis on Groupthink.") In work groups, camaraderie boosts productivity (Mullen & Copper, 1994). Moreover, team spirit is good for morale. But when making decisions, close-knit groups may pay a price. Janis believed that the soil from which groupthink sprouts includes

• an amiable, *cohesive* group;
• relative *isolation* of the group from dissenting viewpoints;
• and a *directive leader* who signals what decision he or she favors.

When planning the ill-fated Bay of Pigs invasion, the newly elected President Kennedy and his advisers enjoyed a strong esprit de corps. Arguments critical of the plan were suppressed or excluded, and the president soon endorsed the invasion.

SYMPTOMS OF GROUPTHINK

From historical records and the memoirs of participants and observers, Janis identified eight groupthink symptoms. These symptoms are a collective form of

the story behind the research:
Irving Janis on groupthink

research

The idea of *groupthink* hit me while reading Arthur Schlesinger's account of how the Kennedy administration decided to invade the Bay of Pigs. At first, I was puzzled: How could bright, shrewd people like John F. Kennedy and his advisers be taken in by the CIA's stupid, patchwork plan? I began to wonder whether some kind of psychological contagion had interfered, such as social conformity or the concurrence-seeking that I had observed in cohesive small groups. Further study (initially aided by my daughter Charlotte's work on a high school term paper) convinced me that subtle group processes had hampered their carefully appraising the risks and debating the issues. When I then analyzed other U.S. foreign policy fiascos and the Watergate cover-up, I found the same detrimental group processes at work.

Irving Janis
(1918–1990)

dissonance reduction that surface as group members try to maintain their positive group feeling when facing a threat (Turner & others, 1992, 1994).

The first two groupthink symptoms lead group members to *overestimate their group's might and right.*

- *An illusion of invulnerability.* The groups Janis studied all developed an excessive optimism that blinded them to warnings of danger. Told that his forces had lost radio contact with the Japanese carriers, Admiral Kimmel, the chief naval officer at Pearl Harbor, joked that maybe the Japanese were about to round Honolulu's Diamond Head. They were, but Kimmel's laughing at the idea dismissed the very possibility of its being true.

- *Unquestioned belief in the group's morality.* Group members assume the inherent morality of their group and ignore ethical and moral issues. The Kennedy group knew that adviser Arthur Schlesinger, Jr., and Senator J. William Fulbright had moral reservations about invading a small, neighboring country. But the group never entertained or discussed these moral qualms.

Group members also become *closed-minded:*

- *Rationalization.* The groups discount challenges by collectively justifying their decisions. President Johnson's Tuesday lunch group spent far more time rationalizing (explaining and justifying) than reflecting upon and rethinking prior decisions to escalate. Each initiative became an action to defend and justify.

- *Stereotyped view of opponent.* Participants in these groupthink tanks consider their enemies too evil to negotiate with or too weak and unintelligent to defend themselves against the planned initiative. The Kennedy group convinced itself that Castro's military was so weak and his popular support so shallow that a single brigade could easily overturn his regime.

Finally, the group suffers from pressures toward *uniformity:*

- *Conformity pressure.* Group members rebuffed those who raised doubts about the group's assumption and plans, at times not by argument but by personal sarcasm. Once, when President Johnson's assistant Bill Moyers arrived at a meeting, the president derided him with, "Well, here comes Mr. Stop-the-Bombing." Faced with such ridicule, most people fall into line.

- *Self-censorship.* Since disagreements were often uncomfortable and the groups seemed in consensus, members withheld or discounted their misgivings. In the months following the Bay of Pigs invasion, Arthur Schlesinger (1965, p. 255) reproached himself "for having kept so silent during those crucial discussions in the Cabinet Room, though my feelings of guilt were tempered by the knowledge that a course of objection would have accomplished little save to gain me a name as a nuisance."

Self-censorship contributes to an illusion of unanimity.

"All those in favor say 'Aye'"
"Aye."   "Aye."   "Aye."
"Aye."   "Aye."

Groupthink on a Titanic scale. Despite four messages of possible icebergs ahead and the lookout person's unheeded plea for binoculars, Captain Edward Smith—a directive and respected leader—kept his ship sailing at full speed into the night. There was an illusion of invulnerability ("God Himself could not sink this ship," the captain had said). There was conformity pressure (crew mates chided the lookout for not being able to use his naked eye and dismissed his misgivings). And there was mindguarding (a Titanic telegraph operator failed to pass the last and most complete iceberg warning to Captain Smith).

People "are never so likely to settle a question rightly as when they discuss it freely."
—John Stuart Mill, *On Liberty*, 1859

• *Illusion of unanimity.* Self-censorship and pressure not to puncture the consensus create an illusion of unanimity. What is more, the apparent consensus confirms the group's decision. This appearance of consensus was evident in these three fiascos and in other fiascos before and since. Albert Speer (1971), an adviser to Adolf Hitler, described the atmosphere around Hitler as one where pressure to conform suppressed all deviation. The absence of dissent created an illusion of unanimity:

> In normal circumstances people who turn their backs on reality are soon set straight by the mockery and criticism of those around them, which makes them aware they have lost credibility. In the Third Reich there were no such correctives, especially for those who belonged to the upper stratum. On the contrary, every self-deception was multiplied as in a hall of distorting mirrors, becoming a repeatedly confirmed picture of a fantastical dream world which no longer bore any relationship to the grim outside world. In those mirrors I could see nothing but my own face reproduced many times over. No external factors disturbed the uniformity of hundreds of unchanging faces, all mine. (p. 379)

• *Mindguards.* Some members protect the group from information that would call into question the effectiveness or morality of its decisions. Before the Bay of Pigs invasion, Robert Kennedy took Schlesinger aside and told him, "Don't push it any further." Secretary of State Dean Rusk withheld diplomatic and intelligence experts' warnings against the invasion. They thus served as the president's "mindguards," protecting him from disagreeable facts rather than physical harm.

Groupthink symptoms can produce a failure to seek and discuss contrary information and alternative possibilities (Figure 8–11). When a leader promotes an idea and when a group insulates itself from dissenting views, groupthink may produce defective decisions (McCauley, 1989).

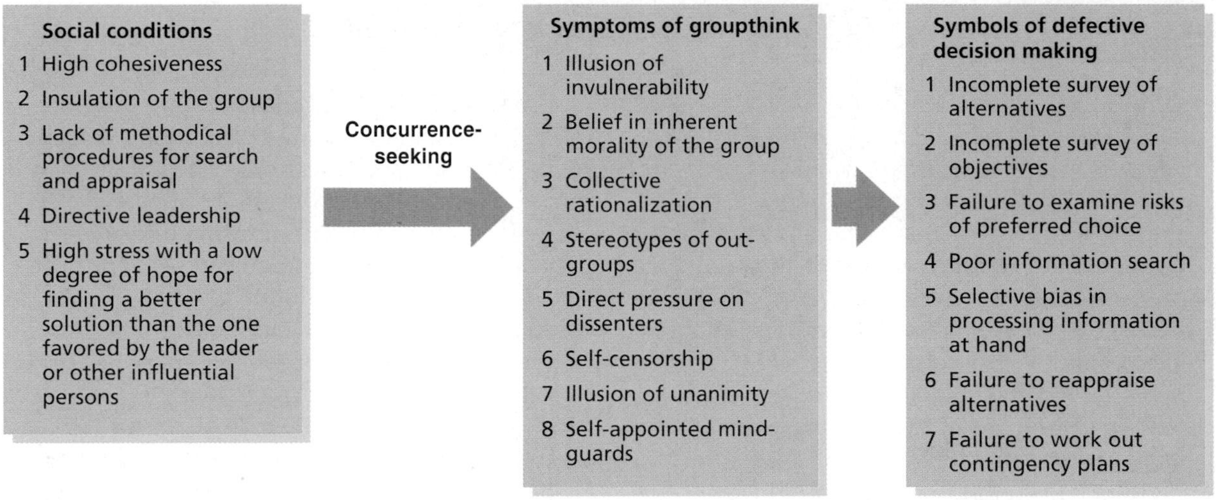

Social conditions		Symptoms of groupthink		Symbols of defective decision making
1 High cohesiveness 2 Insulation of the group 3 Lack of methodical procedures for search and appraisal 4 Directive leadership 5 High stress with a low degree of hope for finding a better solution than the one favored by the leader or other influential persons	Concurrence-seeking	1 Illusion of invulnerability 2 Belief in inherent morality of the group 3 Collective rationalization 4 Stereotypes of out-groups 5 Direct pressure on dissenters 6 Self-censorship 7 Illusion of unanimity 8 Self-appointed mind-guards		1 Incomplete survey of alternatives 2 Incomplete survey of objectives 3 Failure to examine risks of preferred choice 4 Poor information search 5 Selective bias in processing information at hand 6 Failure to reappraise alternatives 7 Failure to work out contingency plans

figure 8–11

Theoretical analysis of groupthink.

Source: Janis & Mann, 1977, p. 132.

British psychologists Ben Newell and David Lagnado (2003) believe groupthink symptoms may have also contributed to the Iraq war. They and others contended that both Saddam Hussein and George W. Bush surrounded themselves with like-minded advisers, intimidated opposing voices into silence, and received filtered information that mostly supported their assumptions—Iraq's expressed assumption that the invading force could be resisted and the United States' assumption that a successful invasion would be followed by a short, peaceful occupation and a soon-thriving democracy.

CRITIQUING GROUPTHINK

Although Janis's ideas and observations have received enormous attention, some researchers are skeptical (Fuller & Aldag, 1998; t'Hart, 1998). The evidence was retrospective, so Janis could pick supporting cases. Follow-up experiments suggested that

- Directive leadership is indeed associated with poorer decisions, sometimes because subordinates feel too weak or insecure to speak up (Granstrom & Stiwne, 1998; McCauley, 1998).
- Groups do prefer supporting over challenging information (Schulz-Hardt & others, 2000).
- When members look to a group for acceptance, approval, and social identity, they may suppress disagreeable thoughts (Hogg & Hains, 1998; Turner & Pratkanis, 1997).

Yet friendships need not breed groupthink (Esser, 1998; Mullen & others, 1994). Secure, highly cohesive groups (say, a married couple) can provide members with freedom to disagree. The norms of a cohesive group can favor consensus (which can lead to groupthink) or critical analysis, which prevents it (Postmes & others, 2001). When academic colleagues in a close-knit department share their draft manuscripts with one another they *want* critique: "Do what you can to save me from my own mistakes." In a free-spirited atmosphere, cohesion can enhance effective teamwork, too.

"Truth springs from argument amongst friends."
—Philosopher David Hume, 1711–1776

focus on   groupthink and the *Challenger* disaster

Groupthink was tragically evident in the decision process by which NASA decided to launch the space shuttle *Challenger* in January 1986 (Esser & Lindoerfer, 1989). Engineers at Morton Thiokol, which made the shuttle's rocket boosters, and at Rockwell International, which manufactured the orbiter, opposed the launch because of dangers posed to equipment by the subfreezing temperatures. The Thiokol engineers feared the cold would make the rubber seals between the rocket's four segments too brittle to contain the superhot gases. Several months before the doomed mission, the company's top expert had warned in a memo that it was a "jump ball" whether the seal would hold and that if it failed, "the result would be a catastrophe of the highest order" (Magnuson, 1986).

In a telephone discussion the night before the launch, the engineers argued their case with their uncertain managers and with NASA officials, who were eager to proceed with the already delayed launch. One Thiokol official later testified: "We got ourselves into the thought process that we were trying to find some way to prove to them [the booster] wouldn't work. We couldn't prove absolutely that it wouldn't work." The result was an *illusion of invulnerability.*

Conformity pressures also operated. One NASA official complained, "My God, Thiokol, when do you want me to launch, next April?" The top Thiokol executive declared, "We have to make a management decision," and then asked his engineering vice president to "take off his engineering hat and put on his management hat."

To create an *illusion of unanimity,* this executive then proceeded to poll only the management officials and ignore the engineers. The go-ahead decision made, one of the engineers belatedly pleaded with a NASA official to reconsider: "If anything happened to this launch," he said prophetically, "I sure wouldn't want to be the person that had to stand in front of a board of inquiry to explain why I launched."

Thanks, finally, to *mindguarding,* the top NASA executive who made the final decision never learned about the engineers' concerns, nor about the reservations of the Rockwell officials. Protected from disagreeable information, he confidently gave the go-ahead to launch the *Challenger* on its tragic flight.

In 2003, tragedy struck again after NASA removed five members of an expert panel that warned of safety troubles for its aging shuttle fleet (Broad & Hulse, 2002). NASA said it was only bringing in fresh blood, but some of the panelists said the agency was trying to suppress their criticisms, and that NASA was discounting their concerns, which, alas, gained credence when the *Columbia* disintegrated during its return to earth on February 1. The Columbia Accident Investigation Board (2003) concluded "that physical and organizational causes played an equal role in the *Columbia* accident—that the NASA organizational culture had as much to do with the accident as the foam that struck the Orbiter on ascent," and that organizational barriers "prevented effective communication of critical safety information and stifled professional differences of opinion."

Groupthink in action: the space shuttle Challenger *explosion, January 28, 1986.*

Moreover, when Philip Tetlock and his colleagues (1992) looked at a broader sample of historical episodes, it became clear that even good group procedures sometimes yield ill-fated decisions. As President Carter and his advisers plotted their humiliating attempt to rescue American hostages in Iran in 1980, they welcomed different views and realistically considered the perils. But for a helicopter problem the rescue might have succeeded. (Carter later reflected that had he sent in one more helicopter he would have been reelected president.) To reword Mister Rogers, sometimes good groups do bad things.

Reflecting on the critiques of groupthink, Paul Paulus (1998) reminds us of Leon Festinger's (1987) observation that only an untestable theory is unchanging. "If a theory is at all testable, it will not remain unchanged. It has to change. All theories are wrong." Thus, said Festinger, we shouldn't ask whether a theory is right or wrong, but rather "how much of the empirical realm can it handle and how must it be modified." Irving Janis, having tested and modified his own theory before his death in 1990, would surely have welcomed others continuing to reshape it. In science that is how we grope our way toward truth, by testing our ideas against reality, revising them, and then testing them some more.

PREVENTING GROUPTHINK

Flawed group dynamics help explain many failed decisions; sometimes too many cooks spoil the broth. However, given open leadership, a cohesive team spirit can improve decisions. Sometimes two or more heads are better than one.

In search of conditions that breed good decisions, Janis also analyzed two seemingly successful ventures: the Truman administration's formulation of the Marshall Plan for getting Europe back on its feet after World War II and the Kennedy administration's handling of the former U.S.S.R.'s attempts to install missile bases in Cuba in 1962. Janis's (1982) recommendations for preventing groupthink incorporate many of the effective group procedures used in both cases:

- Be impartial—do not endorse any position.
- Encourage critical evaluation; assign a "devil's advocate." Better yet, welcome the input of a genuine dissenter, which does even more to stimulate original thinking and to open a group to opposing views, report Charlan Nemeth and her colleagues (2001a, 2001b).
- Occasionally subdivide the group, then reunite to air differences.
- Welcome critiques from outside experts and associates.
- Before implementing, call a "second-chance" meeting to air any lingering doubts.

Some of these practical principles for improved group dynamics are now being taught to airline flight crews. Training programs, called crew resource management, developed from the realization that flight crew mistakes contribute to more than two-thirds of plane accidents. Having two or three people in the cockpit should increase the odds that someone will notice a problem or see its solution—if the information gets shared. Sometimes, however, groupthink pressures lead to conformity or self-censorship.

Robert Helmrich (1997), a social psychologist who studies flight crew performance, notes that flawed group dynamics were evident when an Air Florida plane lifted off from Washington's National Airport on a winter day in 1982. Ice

"There was a serious flaw in the decision-making process."
—Report of the Presidential Commission on the Space Shuttle *Challenger* Accident, 1986

Effective group dynamics enabled the crew of a disabled Denver to Chicago United flight to devise a technique for steering by adjusting relative power from its two remaining engines, enabling the survival of most passengers. Recognizing the importance of cockpit group dynamics, airlines now provide crew management training and seek pilots who are capable of functioning as team members.

in a sensor caused the speed indicators to read too high, leading the captain to apply too little power as the plane ascended:

> **First officer:** Ah, that's not right.
> **Captain:** Yes, it is, there's 80 [referring to speed].
> **First officer:** Nah, I don't think it's right. Ah, maybe it is.
> **Captain:** Hundred and twenty.
> **First officer:** I don't know.

It wasn't right, and the first officer's muting his concerns led to the plane's stalling and crashing into a Potomac River bridge, killing all but five people on board.

But in 1989, the three-person crew flying a United Airlines DC-10 flight from Denver to Chicago responded as a model team to imminent disaster. The crew, which had been trained in crew resource management, faced the disintegration of the center engine, severing lines to the rudder and ailerons needed to maneuver the plane. In the 34 minutes before crash landing just short of the Sioux City airport runway, the crew had to devise a strategy for bringing the plane under control, assessing damage, choosing a landing site, and preparing the crew and passengers for the crash. Minute-by-minute analysis of the cockpit conversation revealed intense interaction—31 communications per minute (one per second at its peak). In these minutes, the crew members recruited a fourth pilot who was flying as a passenger, prioritized their work, and kept one another aware of unfolding events and decisions. Junior crew members freely suggested alternatives and the captain responded with appropriate commands. Bursts of social conversation provided emotional support, enabling the crew to cope with the extreme stress, and to save the lives of 185 of the 296 people on board.

GROUP PROBLEM SOLVING

Under some conditions two or more heads *are* better than one. Patrick Laughlin and John Adamopoulos (1980, 1996; Laughlin & others, 2003)) have shown this with various intellectual tasks. Consider one of their analogy problems:

Assertion is to *disproved* as *action* is to
a. *hindered*
b. *opposed*
c. *illegal*
d. *precipitate*
e. *thwarted*

Most college students miss this question when answering alone, but answer correctly (thwarted) after discussion. Moreover, Laughlin finds that if but two members of a six-person group are initially correct, two-thirds of the time they convince all the others. If only one person is correct, this "minority of one" almost three-fourths of the time fails to convince the group.

"Two forecasters will come up with a forecast that is more accurate than either would have come up with working alone," reported Joel Myers (1997), president of the largest private forecasting service. Dell Warnick and Glenn Sanders (1980) and Verlin Hinsz (1990) confirmed that several heads can be better than one when they studied the accuracy of eyewitness reports of a videotaped crime or job interview. Groups of eyewitnesses gave accounts that were much more accurate than those provided by the average isolated individual. Several heads critiquing each other can also allow the group to avoid some forms of cognitive bias and produce some higher-quality ideas (McGlynn & others, 1995; Wright & others, 1990). None of us alone is as smart as all of us together.

Brainstorming with computer communication allows creative ideas to flow freely (Gallupe & others, 1994). But contrary to the popular idea that face-to-face brainstorming generates more creative ideas than do the same people working alone, researchers agree it isn't so (Paulus & others, 1995, 1997, 1998, 2000; Stroebe & Diehl, 1994). People *feel* more productive when generating ideas in groups (partly because people disproportionately credit themselves for the ideas that come out). But time and again researchers have found that people working alone usually will generate *more* good ideas than will the same people in a group. Large brainstorming groups are especially inefficient, causing some individuals to free-ride on others' efforts or to feel apprehensive about voicing oddball ideas. As John Watson and Francis Crick demonstrated in discovering DNA, challenging two-person conversations can more effectively engage creative thinking. Psychologists Daniel Kahneman and the late Amos Tversky similarly collaborated in their exploration of intuition and its influence on economic decision making (see Chapter 3 and "The Story Behind a Nobel Prize" on page 320).

However, Vincent Brown and Paul Paulus (2002) have identified three ways to enhance group brainstorming:

- *Combine group and solitary brainstorming.* Their data suggest using group brainstorming followed by solo brainstorming rather than the reverse order or either alone. With new categories primed by the group brainstorming, individuals' ideas can continue flowing without being impeded by the group context that only allows one person to speak at a time.

- *Have group members interact by writing.* Another way to take advantage of group priming, without being impeded by the one-at-a-time rule, is to have group members write and read, rather than speak and listen. Brown

the story behind a Nobel Prize:
research two minds are better than one

In the Spring of 1969, Amos Tversky, my younger colleague at the Hebrew University of Jerusalem, and I met over lunch and shared our own recurrent errors of judgment. From there were born our studies of human intuition.

I had enjoyed collaboration before, but this was magical. Amos was very smart, and also very funny. We could spend hours of solid work in continuous mirth. His work was always characterized by confidence and by a crisp elegance, and it was a joy to find those characteristics now attached to my ideas as well. As we were writing our first paper, I was conscious of how much better it was than the more hesitant piece I would have written by myself.

All our ideas were jointly owned. We did almost all the work on our joint projects while physically together, including the drafting of questionnaires and papers. Our principle was to discuss every disagreement until it had been resolved to our mutual satisfaction.

Some of the greatest joys of our collaboration—and probably much of its success—came from our ability to elaborate on each other's nascent thoughts: If I expressed a half-formed idea, I knew that Amos would be there to understand it, probably more clearly than I did, and that if it had merit, he would see it.

Amos and I shared the wonder of together owning a goose that could lay golden eggs—a joint mind that was better than our separate minds. We were a team, and we remained in that mode for well over a decade. The Nobel Prize was awarded for work that we produced during that period of intense collaboration.

Daniel Kahneman,
Princeton University,
Nobel Laureate, 2002

and Paulus describe this process of passing notes and adding ideas, which has everyone active at once, as "brainwriting."

- *Incorporate electronic brainstorming.* There is a potentially more efficient way to avoid the verbal traffic jams of traditional group brainstorming in larger groups: Let individuals produce and read ideas on networked computers.

Summing up

Analysis of the decisions that led to several international fiascos indicates that group desire for harmony can override realistic appraisal of contrary views. This is especially true when group members strongly desire unity, when they are isolated from opposing ideas, and when the leader signals what he or she wants from the group.

Symptomatic of this overriding concern for harmony, labeled *groupthink,* are (1) an illusion of invulnerability, (2) rationalization, (3) unquestioned belief in the group's morality, (4) stereotyped views of the opposition, (5) pressure to conform, (6) self-censorship of misgivings, (7) an illusion of unanimity, and (8) "mindguards" who protect the group from unpleasant information. Critics have noted that some aspects of Janis's groupthink model (such as directive leadership) seem more implicated in flawed decisions than others (such as cohesiveness).

Both in experiments and in actual history, however, groups sometimes decide wisely. These cases suggest remedies for groupthink. By seeking information from all sides and improving the evaluation of possible alternatives, a group can benefit from its members' combined insights.

The influence of the minority: How do individuals influence the group?

Groups influence individuals, but when—and how—do individuals influence their groups? What makes leadership—the power of individuals—effective?

Each chapter in this social influence unit concludes with a reminder of our power as individuals. We have seen that

- cultural situations mold us, but we also help create and choose these situations;
- pressures to conform sometimes overwhelm our better judgment, but blatant pressure can motivate us to assert our individuality and freedom;
- persuasive forces are indeed powerful, but we can resist persuasion by making public commitments and by anticipating persuasive appeals.

This chapter has emphasized group influences on the individual, so we conclude by seeing how individuals can influence their groups.

At the beginning of most social movements, a small minority will sometimes sway, and then even become, the majority. "All history," wrote Ralph Waldo Emerson, "is a record of the power of minorities, and of minorities of one." Think of Copernicus and Galileo, of Martin Luther King, Jr., of Susan B. Anthony. The American civil rights movement was ignited by the refusal of one African American woman, Rosa Parks, to relinquish her seat on a Montgomery, Alabama bus. Technological history has also been made by innovative minorities. As Robert Fulton developed his steamboat—"Fulton's Folly"—he endured constant derision: "Never did a single encouraging remark, a bright hope, a warm wish, cross my path" (Cantril & Bumstead, 1960).

What makes a minority persuasive? What might Arthur Schlesinger have done to get the Kennedy group to consider his doubts about the Bay of Pigs invasion? Experiments initiated by Serge Moscovici in Paris have identified several determinants of minority influence: consistency, self-confidence, and defection. Keep in mind that "minority influence" refers to minority *opinions*, not to ethnic minorities.

"If the single man plant himself indomitably on his instincts, and there abide, the huge world will come round to him."
—Ralph Waldo Emerson, *Nature, Address, and Lectures: The American Scholar*, 1849

CONSISTENCY

More influential than a minority that wavers is a minority that sticks to its position. Moscovici and his associates (1969, 1985) found that if a minority consistently judges blue slides as green, members of the majority will occasionally agree. But if the minority wavers, saying "blue" to one third of the blue slides and "green" to the rest, virtually no one in the majority will ever agree with "green."

Experiments show—and experience confirms—that nonconformity, especially persistent nonconformity, is often painful (Levine, 1989). That helps explain a *minority slowness effect*—a tendency for people with minority views to express them less quickly than do people in the majority (Bassili, 2003). If you set out to be Emerson's minority of one, prepare yourself for ridicule—especially when you argue an issue that's personally relevant to the majority and when the group wants to settle an issue by reaching consensus (Kameda & Sugimori, 1993; Kruglanski & Webster, 1991; Trost & others, 1992). People may attribute your dissent to psychological peculiarities (Papastamou & Mugny, 1990). When Charlan Nemeth (1979) planted a minority of two within a simulated jury and had them oppose the majority's opinions, the duo was inevitably disliked. Nevertheless, the majority acknowledged that the persistence of the two did more than anything else to make them rethink their positions.

In so doing, a minority may stimulate creative thinking (Martin, 1996; Mucchi-Faina & others, 1991; Peterson & Nemeth, 1996). With dissent from within one's own group, people take in more information, think about it in new ways, and often make better decisions. Believing that one need not win friends to influence people, Nemeth quotes Oscar Wilde: "We dislike arguments of any kind; they are always vulgar, and often convincing."

Some successful companies have recognized the creativity and innovation sometimes stimulated by minority perspectives, which may contribute new ideas and stimulate colleagues to think in fresh ways. 3M, which has been famed for valuing "respect for individual initiative," has welcomed employees spending time on wild ideas. The Post-it notes adhesive was a failed attempt by Spencer Silver to develop a super strong glue. Art Fry, after having trouble marking his church choir hymnal with pieces of paper, thought "What I need is a bookmark with Spence's adhesive along the edge." Even so, this was a minority view that eventually won over a skeptical marketing department (Nemeth, 1997).

SELF-CONFIDENCE

Consistency and persistence convey self-confidence. Furthermore, Nemeth and Joel Wachtler (1974) reported that any behavior by a minority that conveys self-confidence—for example, taking the head seat at the table—tends to raise self-doubts among the majority. By being firm and forceful, the minority's apparent self-assurance may prompt the majority to reconsider its position. This is especially so on matters of opinion rather than fact. In her research at Italy's University of Padova, Anne Maass and her colleagues (1996) report that minorities are less persuasive when answering a question of fact ("from which country does Italy import most of its raw oil?") than attitude ("from which country should Italy import most of its raw oil?").

DEFECTIONS FROM THE MAJORITY

A persistent minority punctures any illusion of unanimity. When a minority consistently doubts the majority wisdom, majority members become freer to express their own doubts and may even switch to the minority position. In research with University of Pittsburgh students, John Levine (1989) found that a

Defectors from a majority sometimes wield large influence. WorldCom employee Cynthia Cooper exposed the phony bookkeeping that covered the company's $3.8 billion losses. As an FBI staff attorney, Coleen Rowley helped reform the FBI after detailing its failures to respond to information that might have enabled heading off the 9/11 attacks. Enron's Sherron Watkins uncovered her company's improper accounting practices.

minority person who had defected from the majority was more persuasive than a consistent minority voice. In her jury-simulation experiments, Nemeth found that once defections begin, others often soon follow, initiating a snowball effect.

Are these factors that strengthen minority influence unique to minorities? Sharon Wolf and Bibb Latané (1985; Wolf, 1987) and Russell Clark (1995) believe not. They argue that the same social forces work for both majorities and minorities. Informational and normative influence fuels both group polarization and minority influence. And if consistency, self-confidence, and defections from the other side strengthen the minority, such variables also strengthen a majority. The social impact of any position depends on the strength, immediacy, and number of those who support it. Minorities have less influence than majorities simply because they are smaller.

Anne Maass and Russell Clark (1984, 1986) agree with Moscovici, however, that minorities are more likely to convert people to *accepting* their views. And from their analyses of how groups evolve over time, John Levine and Richard Moreland (1985) conclude that new recruits to a group exert a different type of minority influence than do longtime members. Newcomers exert influence through the attention they receive and the group awareness they trigger in the old-timers. Established members feel freer to dissent and to exert leadership.

There is a delightful irony in this new emphasis on how individuals can influence the group. Until recently, the idea that the minority could sway the majority was itself a minority view in social psychology. Nevertheless, by arguing consistently and forcefully, Moscovici, Nemeth, Maass, Clark, and others have convinced the majority of group influence researchers that minority influence is a phenomenon worthy of study. And the way that several of these minority influence researchers came by their interests should, perhaps, not surprise us. Anne Maass (1998) became interested in how minorities could effect social change after growing up in postwar Germany and hearing her grandmother's personal accounts of fascism. Charlan Nemeth (1999) developed her interest while she was a visiting professor in Europe "working with Henri Tajfel and Serge Moscovici. The three of us were 'outsiders'—I an American Roman Catholic female in Europe, they having survived World War II as Eastern European Jews. Sensitivity to the value and the struggles of the minority perspective came to dominate our work."

IS LEADERSHIP MINORITY INFLUENCE?

In 1910, the Norwegians and English engaged in an epic race to the South Pole. The Norwegians, effectively led by Roald Amundsen, made it. The English, ineptly led by Robert Falcon Scott, did not; Scott and three team members died. Amundsen illustrated the power of **leadership,** the process by which certain individuals mobilize and guide groups. The presidency of George W. Bush illustrates "the power of one," observes Michael Kinsley (2003). "Before Bush brought it up [there was] no popular passion" for the idea "that Saddam was a terrible threat and had to go. . . . You could call this many things, but one of them is leadership. If real leadership means leading people where they don't want to go, George W. Bush has shown himself to be a real leader."

Some leaders are formally appointed or elected; others emerge informally as the group interacts. What makes for good leadership often depends on the situation—the best person to lead the engineering team may not make the best leader of the sales force. Some people excel at **task leadership**—at organizing work, setting standards, and focusing on goal attainment. Others excel at **social leadership**—at building teamwork, mediating conflicts, and being supportive.

Task leaders often have a directive style—one that can work well if the leader is bright enough to give good orders (Fiedler, 1987). Being goal oriented, such leaders also keep the group's attention and effort focused on its mission. Experiments show that the combination of specific, challenging goals and periodic progress reports helps motivate high achievement (Locke & Latham, 1990).

Social leaders often have a democratic style—one that delegates authority, welcomes input from team members, and, as we have seen, helps prevent groupthink. Many experiments reveal that social leadership is good for morale. Group members usually feel more satisfied when they participate in making decisions (Spector, 1986; Vanderslice & others, 1987). Given control over their tasks, workers also become more motivated to achieve (Burger, 1987).

Given a chance to voice their opinions during a decision-making process, people respond more positively to its outcome (van den Bos & Spruijt, 2002). People who value good group feeling and take pride in achievement therefore thrive under democratic leadership, which can be seen in the move by many businesses toward participative management, a management style common in Sweden and Japan (Naylor, 1990; Sundstrom & others, 1990). Women more often than men have a democratic leadership style (Eagly & Johnson, 1990).

The once-popular "great person" theory of leadership—that all great leaders share certain traits—has fallen into disrepute. Effective leadership styles, we

leadership
The process by which certain group members motivate and guide the group.

task leadership
Leadership that organizes work, sets standards, and focuses on goals.

social leadership
Leadership that builds teamwork, mediates conflict, and offers support.

Participative management, illustrated in this "quality circle," requires democratic rather than autocratic leaders.

now know, vary with the situations. People who know what they are doing may resent task leadership, while those who don't may welcome it. Recently, however, social psychologists have again wondered if there might be qualities that mark a good leader in many situations (Hogan & others, 1994). British social psychologists Peter Smith and Monir Tayeb (1989) report that studies done in India, Taiwan, and Iran have found that the most effective supervisors in coal mines, banks, and government offices score high on tests of *both* task and social leadership. They are actively concerned with how work is progressing *and* sensitive to the needs of their subordinates.

Studies also reveal that many effective leaders of laboratory groups, work teams, and large corporations exhibit the behaviors that help make a minority view persuasive. Such leaders engender trust by *consistently* sticking to their goals. And they often exude a *self-confident* charisma that kindles the allegiance of their followers (Bennis, 1984; House & Singh, 1987). Charismatic leaders typically have a compelling *vision* of some desired state of affairs, an ability to *communicate* this to others in clear and simple language, and enough optimism and faith in their group to *inspire* others to follow. Not surprisingly, then, personality tests reveal that effective leaders tend to be outgoing, energetic, conscientious, agreeable, emotionally stable, and self-confident (Hogan & others, 1994).

To be sure, groups also influence their leaders. Sometimes those at the front of the herd have simply sensed where it is already heading. Political candidates know how to read the opinion polls. Someone who typifies the group's views is more likely to be selected as a leader; a leader who deviates too radically from the group's standards may be rejected (Hogg & others, 1998). Smart leaders usually remain with the majority and spend their influence prudently. In rare circumstances, the right traits matched with the right situation yield history-making greatness, notes Dean Keith Simonton (1994). To have a Winston Churchill or a Margaret Thatcher, a Thomas Jefferson or a Karl Marx, a Napoleon or an Adolph Hitler, an Abraham Lincoln or a Martin Luther King, Jr., takes the right person in the right place at the right time. When an apt combination of intelligence, skill, determination, self-confidence, and social charisma

www.mhhe.com/myers8
Visit the Online Learning Center for an interactivity on groups.

meets a rare opportunity, the result is sometimes a championship, a Nobel Prize, or a social revolution. Just ask Rosa Parks.

Summing up

If minority viewpoints never prevailed, history would be static and nothing would ever change. In experiments, a minority is most influential when it is consistent and persistent in its views, when its actions convey self-confidence, and after it begins to elicit some defections from the majority. Even if such factors do not persuade the majority to adopt the minority's views, they will increase the majority's self-doubts and prompt it to consider other alternatives, often leading to better, more creative decisions.

Through their task and social leadership, formal and informal group leaders exert disproportionate influence. Those who consistently press toward their goals and exude a self-confident charisma often engender trust and inspire others to follow.

Personal Postscript: Are groups bad for us?

A selective reading of this chapter could, I must admit, leave readers with the impression that, on balance, groups are bad. In groups we become more aroused, more stressed, more tense, more error-prone on complex tasks. Submerged in a group that gives us anonymity, we have a tendency to loaf or have our worst impulses unleashed by deindividuation. Police brutality, lynchings, gang destruction, and terrorism are all group phenomena. Discussion in groups often polarizes our views, enhancing mutual racism or hostility. It may also suppress dissent, creating a homogenized groupthink that produces disastrous decisions. No wonder we celebrate those individuals—minorities of one—who, alone against a group, have stood up for truth and justice. Groups, it seems, are ba-a-a-d.

All this is true, but it's only half the truth. The other half is that, as social animals, we are group-dwelling creatures. Like our distant ancestors, we depend on one another for sustenance, support, and security. Moreover, when our individual tendencies are positive, group interaction accentuates our best. In groups, runners run faster, audiences laugh louder, and givers become more generous. In self-help groups, people strengthen their resolve to stop drinking, lose weight, and study harder. In kindred-spirited groups, people expand their spiritual consciousness. "A devout communing on spiritual things sometimes greatly helps the health of the soul," observed fifteenth-century cleric Thomas a Kempis, especially when people of faith "meet and speak and commune together."

Depending on which tendency a group is magnifying or disinhibiting, groups can be very, very bad or very, very good. So we had best choose our group influences wisely and intentionally.

What do you think?

Think of a time when you were part of a "very, very good" group—a group with positive influence. Did the group benefit from effective leadership? Did it illustrate any principles of group influence discussed in this chapter of social facilitation, social loafing, deindividuation, group polarization, groupthink, or minority influence?

Making the Social Connection

In this chapter, we discussed group polarization and whether groups intensify opinions. This phenomenon will also be covered in Chapter 16 when we look at juries and how they make decisions. Can you think of other situations where group polarization might be in effect? Go to the *SocialSense* CD-ROM to view a clip about cliques and the influence of the group.

part three

Social Relations

Social psychology is the scientific study of how people think about, influence, and relate to one another. Having explored how we *think about* (Part One) and *influence* (Part Two) one another, we now consider how we *relate* to one another. Our feelings and actions toward people are sometimes negative, sometimes positive. Chapters 9, "Prejudice: Disliking Others," and 10, "Aggression: Hurting Others," examine the nastier aspects of human relations: Why do we dislike, even despise, one another? Why and when do we hurt one another? Then in Chapters 11, "Attraction and Intimacy: Liking and Loving Others," and 12, "Helping," we explore the nicer aspects: Why do we like or love particular people? When will we offer help to friends or strangers? Last, in Chapter 13, "Conflict and Peacemaking," we consider how social conflicts develop and how they can be justly and amicably resolved.

Every Body
Deserves
Respect

chapter 9

Prejudice: Disliking Others[1]

"Prejudice. A vagrant opinion without visible means of support."

Ambrose Bierce,
The Devil's
Dictionary, *1911*

Prejudices come in many forms—for our own group and against some other group: "northeastern liberals" or "southern hillbillies," against Arab "terrorists" or American "infidels," against people who are short or fat or homely.

The 9/11 attacks and their aftermath illustrate the power of hatred and prejudice:

"Our terrorism is against America. Our terrorism is a blessed terrorism."—Osama bin Laden in a video after the 9/11 attacks.

"If I see someone that comes in [an airport] that's got a diaper on his head and a fan belt wrapped around that diaper on his head, that guy needs to be pulled over."—U. S. Congressman John Cooksey in a radio interview after the 9/11 attacks.

---

[1] This eighth edition chapter was co-authored by Steven J. Spencer, associate professor and chair of the Social Psychology Department program at the University of Waterloo.

Dunagin's People

"I hate intolerance! Especially from **those** people!"

Shortly after 9/11, hostilities flared against people perceived to be of Arab descent. In suburban New York City, a man tried to run down a Pakistani woman while shouting that he was "doing this for my country" (Brown, 2001). In Denton, Texas, a mosque was firebombed (Thomson, 2001). At Boston University, a Middle Eastern student was stabbed, and at the University of Colorado, students spraypainted the library with "Arabs Go Home." These were not isolated events. The American-Arab Anti-Discrimination Committee catalogued more than 250 acts of violence against Arab American students on college campuses in the week following the 9/11 attacks (cnn.com, 2001). Negative views of Middle Eastern immigrants have persisted. In one U.S. survey six months after the 9/11 attacks, Pakistanis and Palestinians were rated as negatively as drug dealers (Fiske, 2002).

Other groups face profound prejudice too. When seeking love and employment, overweight people—especially overweight White women—face slim prospects. In correlational studies, overweight people marry less often, gain entry to less desirable jobs, and make less money. In experiments (in which some people are made to appear overweight) they are perceived as less attractive, intelligent, happy, self-disciplined, and successful (Gortmaker & others, 1993; Hebl & Heatherton, 1998; Pingitore & others, 1994). People have even denigrated those just standing or seated next to an obese person (Hebl & Mannix, 2003). Weight discrimination, in fact, notably exceeds race or gender discrimination and occurs at every employment stage—hiring, placement, promotion, compensation, discipline, and discharge (Roehling, 2000).

What is the nature and power of prejudice?

How is "prejudice" distinct from "stereotyping," "discrimination," "racism," and "sexism"? Are stereotypes necessarily false or malicious? What forms does prejudice assume today?

DEFINING PREJUDICE

prejudice
*A negative prejudgment
of a group and its
individual members.*

Prejudice, stereotyping, discrimination, racism, sexism—the terms often overlap. Let's clarify them. Each of the situations just described involved a negative evaluation of some group. And that is the essence of **prejudice:** a negative prejudgment of a group and its individual members. (Some prejudice definitions include *positive* prejudgments as well, but nearly all uses of "prejudice" refer to *negative* tendencies—or what Gordon Allport termed in his classic, *The Nature of Prejudice*, "an antipathy based upon a faulty and inflexible generalization"

[1954, p. 9].) Prejudice biases us against a person based on the person's perceived group.

Prejudice is an attitude. As we saw in Chapter 4, an attitude is a distinct combination of feelings, inclinations to act, and beliefs. This combination is the ABC of attitudes: *a*ffect (feelings), *b*ehavior tendency (inclination to act), and *c*ognition (beliefs). A prejudiced person might *dislike* those different from self and *behave* in a discriminatory manner, *believing* them ignorant and dangerous. Like many attitudes, prejudice is complex and may include a component of patronizing affection that serves to keep the target disadvantaged.

The negative evaluations that mark prejudice can stem from emotional associations, from the need to justify behavior, or from negative beliefs, called **stereotypes.** To stereotype is to generalize. To simplify the world, we generalize: The British are reserved. Americans are outgoing. Professors are absentminded. Here are some widely shared stereotypes uncovered in recent research:

- During the 1980s, women who assumed the title of "Ms." were seen as more assertive and ambitious than those who called themselves "Miss" or "Mrs." (Dion, 1987; Dion & Cota, 1991; Dion & Schuller, 1991). Now that "Ms." is more commonplace, the stereotype has shifted. Married women who keep their own surnames are seen as assertive and ambitious (Crawford & others, 1998; Etaugh & others, 1999).

- Public opinion surveys reveal that Europeans have definite ideas about other Europeans. They see Germans as relatively hardworking, the French as pleasure-loving, the British as cool and unexcitable, Italians as amorous, and the Dutch as reliable. (Coming from Willem Koomen and Michiel Bähler, 1996, at the University of Amsterdam, one expects these findings to be reliable.)

- Europeans also view southern Europeans as more emotional and less efficient than northern Europeans (Linssen & Hagendoorn, 1994). The stereotype of the southerner as more expressive even holds within countries: James Pennebaker and his colleagues (1996) report that across 20 Northern Hemisphere countries (but not in six Southern Hemisphere countries), southerners within a country are perceived as more expressive than northerners.

Such generalizations can be more or less true (and are not always negative). Southern countries in the Northern Hemisphere do have higher rates of violence. People living in the south in these countries do report being more expressive than those in the northern regions of their country. Teachers' stereotypes of achievement differences in students from different gender, ethnic, and class backgrounds tend to mirror reality (Madon & others, 1998). "Stereotypes," note Lee Jussim, Clark McCauley, and Yueh-Ting Lee (1995), "may be positive or negative, accurate or inaccurate." An accurate stereotype may even be desirable. We call it "sensitivity to diversity" or "cultural awareness in a multicultural world." To stereotype the British as more concerned about punctuality than Mexicans is to understand what to expect and how to act with minimal friction in each culture.

A problem with stereotypes arises when they are *overgeneralized* or just plain wrong. To presume that most American welfare clients are African American is to overgeneralize, because it just isn't so. University students' stereotypes of members of particular fraternities (as preferring foreign language courses to

stereotype
A belief about the personal attributes of a group of people. Stereotypes are sometimes overgeneralized, inaccurate, and resistant to new information.

Familiar stereotypes: "Heaven is a place with an American house, Chinese food, British police, a German car, and French art. Hell is a place with a Japanese house, Chinese police, British food, German art, and a French car."
—Anonymous, as reported by Yueh-Ting Lee (1996)

economics, or softball to tennis) contain a germ of truth but are overblown. Individuals within the stereotyped group vary more than expected (Brodt & Ross, 1998).

Prejudice is a negative *attitude*; **discrimination** is negative behavior. Discriminatory behavior often has its source in prejudicial attitudes (Dovidio & others, 1996). As Chapter 4 emphasized, however, attitudes and behavior are often loosely linked. Prejudiced attitudes need not breed hostile acts, nor does all oppression spring from prejudice. **Racism** and **sexism** are institutional practices that discriminate, even when there is no prejudicial intent. If word-of-mouth hiring practices in an all-White business have the effect of excluding potential non-White employees, the practice could be called racist—even if an employer intended no discrimination.

RACIAL PREJUDICE

In the context of the world, every race is a minority. Non-Hispanic Whites, for example, are only one-fifth of the world's people and will be one-eighth within another half-century. Thanks to mobility and migration during the past two centuries, the world's races now intermingle, in relations that are sometimes hostile, sometimes amiable.

To a molecular biologist, skin color is a trivial human characteristic, one controlled by a minuscule genetic difference between races. Moreover, nature doesn't cluster races in neatly defined categories. It is people, not nature, who sometimes label Tiger Woods "African American" (his ancestry is 25 percent African) or "Asian American" (he is also 25 percent Thai and 25 percent Chinese)—or even as Native American or Dutch (he is one-eighth each).

Most folks see prejudice—in other people. In a 1997 Gallup poll, White Americans estimated 44 percent of their peers to be high in prejudice ("5" or higher on a 10-point scale). How many gave themselves a high score? Just 14 percent (Whitman, 1998).

Is racial prejudice disappearing?

Which is right: the perceptions of bigotry around every corner, or the self-perceptions of little prejudice? And is racial prejudice becoming a thing of the past?

Racial attitudes can change very quickly. In 1942, most Americans agreed, "There should be separate sections for Negroes on streetcars and buses" (Hyman & Sheatsley, 1956). Today, the question would seem bizarre, because such blatant prejudice has nearly disappeared. In 1942, fewer than a third of all Whites (only 1 in 50 in the South) supported school integration; by 1980, support for it was 90 percent. Considering what a thin slice of history is covered by the years since 1942, or even since slavery was practiced, the changes are dramatic. In

discrimination
Unjustifiable negative behavior toward a group or its members.

racism
(1) An individual's prejudicial attitudes and discriminatory behavior toward people of a given race, or (2) institutional practices (even if not motivated by prejudice) that subordinate people of a given race.

sexism
(1) An individual's prejudicial attitudes and discriminatory behavior toward people of a given sex, or (2) institutional practices (even if not motivated by prejudice) that subordinate people of a given sex.

"I'm a 'Cablinasian.'" Tiger Woods, 1997 (describing his Caucasian, Black, Indian, and Asian ancestry)

Canada, too, acceptance of ethnic diversity and various immigrant groups has increased in recent decades (Berry & Kalin, 1995).

African Americans' attitudes also have changed since the 1940s, when Kenneth Clark and Mamie Clark (1947) demonstrated that many held anti-Black prejudices. In making its historic 1954 decision declaring segregated schools unconstitutional, the Supreme Court found it noteworthy that when the Clarks gave African American children a choice between Black dolls and White dolls, most chose the White. In studies from the 1950s through the 1970s, Black children were increasingly likely to prefer Black dolls. And adult Blacks came to view Blacks and Whites as similar in traits such as intelligence, laziness, and dependability (Jackman & Senter, 1981; Smedley & Bayton, 1978).

People of different races also now share many of the same attitudes and aspirations, notes Amitai Etzioni (1999). More than 9 in 10 Blacks and Whites say they could vote for a Black presidential candidate. More than 8 in 10 in both groups agree that "to graduate from high school, students should be required to understand the common history and ideas that tie all Americans together." Similar proportions in both groups seek "fair treatment for all, without prejudice or discrimination." And about 2 in 3 in both groups agree that moral and ethical standards have been in decline. Thanks to such shared ideals, notes Etzioni, the United States and most Western democracies have been spared the ethnic tribalism that has torn apart Kosovo and Rwanda.

Shall we conclude, then, that racial prejudice is extinct in countries such as the United States and Canada? Prejudice still appears among the 7,314 perpetrators of reported hate crime incidents during 2002 (FBI, 2002), and among the small proportion of Whites who, as Figure 9–1 shows, would not vote for a Black presidential candidate. Such people help explain why half of African

Psychologists usually capitalize Black and White to emphasize that these are socially applied race labels, not literal color labels for persons of African and European ancestry.

figure 9–1

Changing racial attitudes of White Americans from 1958 to 2003.

Source: Data from Gallup polls (gallup.com).

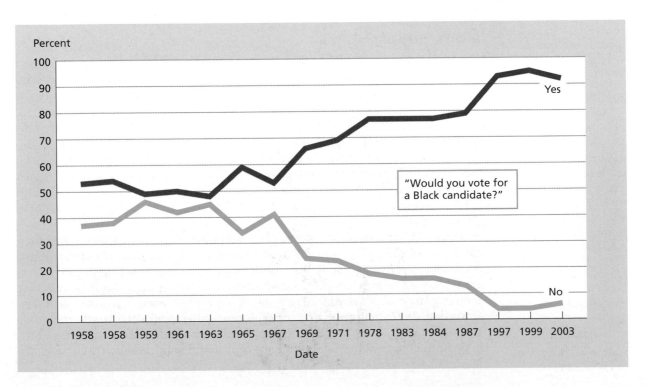

Although prejudice dies last in socially intimate contacts, interracial marriage has increased in most countries—for example, the number of interracial U.S. couples more than doubled between 1980 and 2000 (Bureau of the Census, 2002).

In several American states Black motorists have represented a minority of the drivers and speeders on interstate highways, yet they have been most often stopped and searched by state police (Lamberth, 1998; Staples, 1999a, 1999b). In one New Jersey Turnpike study, Blacks made up 13.5 percent of the car occupants, 15 percent of the speeders, and 35 percent of the drivers stopped.

Americans perceive themselves as having faced discrimination within the last 30 days—3 in 10 while shopping and 2 in 10 while dining out or at work (Gallup, 1997).

Questions concerning intimate interracial contacts still detect prejudice. "I would probably feel uncomfortable dancing with a Black person in a public place" detects more racial feeling in Whites than "I would probably feel uncomfortable riding a bus with a Black person." Many people who welcome diverse people as co-workers or classmates still socialize, date, and marry within their own race. This helps explain why, in a survey of students at 390 colleges and universities, 53 percent of African American students felt excluded from social activities (Hurtado & others, 1994). Such majority-minority relationships transcend race. On NBA basketball teams minority players (in this case, Whites) feel similarly detached from their group's socializing (Schoenfeld, 1995).

This phenomenon of *greatest prejudice in the most intimate social realms* seems universal. In India, people who accept the caste system will typically allow someone from a lower caste into their homes but would not consider marrying such a person (Sharma, 1981). In a national survey of Americans, 75 percent said they would "shop at a store owned by a homosexual," but only 39 percent would "see a homosexual doctor" (Henry, 1994).

Subtle forms of prejudice

Recall from Chapter 4 that when White students indicate racial attitudes and men indicate their sympathy for women's rights while hooked up to a supposed lie detector, they admit to prejudice. Other experiments have assessed people's *behavior* toward Blacks and Whites. As we will see in Chapter 13, Whites are equally helpful to any person in need—except when the needy person is remote (say, a wrong-number caller with an apparent Black accent who needs a message relayed). Likewise, when asked to use electric shocks to "teach" a task, White people give no more (if anything less) shock to a Black than to a White person—except when they are angered or when the recipient can't retaliate or know who did it (Crosby & others, 1980; Rogers & Prentice-Dunn, 1981).

Thus, prejudiced attitudes and discriminatory behavior surface when they can hide behind the screen of some other motive. In France, Britain, Germany, Australia, and the Netherlands, subtle prejudice (exaggerating ethnic differences, feeling less admiration and affection for immigrant minorities, rejecting them for supposedly nonracial reasons) is replacing blatant prejudice (Pedersen & Walker, 1997; Pettigrew, 1998). Some researchers call such subtle prejudice "modern racism" or "cultural racism." Modern prejudice often appears subtly, in our preferences for what is familiar, similar, and comfortable (Dovidio & others, 1992; Esses & others, 1993a).

On paper-and-pencil questionnaires, Janet Swim and her co-researchers (1995, 1997) have found a subtle ("modern") sexism that parallels subtle ("modern") racism. Both forms appear in denials of discrimination and in antagonism toward efforts to promote equality (as in "Blacks are getting too demanding in their push for equal rights").

We can also detect bias in behavior. That's what a research team led by Ian Ayres (1991) did. Team members visited 90 Chicago-area car dealers, using a uniform strategy to negotiate the lowest price on a new car that cost the dealer about $11,000. White males were given a final price that averaged $11,362; White females were given an average price of $11,504; Black males were given an average price of $11,783; and Black females were given an average price of $12,237. To test for possible labor market discrimination, M.I.T. researchers sent 5,000 résumés out in response to 1,300 varied employment ads (Bertrand & Mullainathan, 2003). Applicants randomly assigned White names (Emily, Greg) received one callback for every 10 résumés sent. Those given Black names (Lakisha, Jamal) received one callback for every 15 résumés sent.

Modern prejudice even appears as a race sensitivity that leads to exaggerated reactions to isolated minority persons—both overpraising their accomplishments and overcriticizing their mistakes (Fiske, 1989; Hart & Morry, 1997; Hass & others, 1991). It also appears as patronization. For example, Kent Harber (1998) gave White students at Stanford University a poorly written essay to evaluate. When the students thought that the writer was Black, they rated it *higher* than when they were led to think the author was White, and they rarely offered harsh criticisms. The evaluators, perhaps wanting to avoid the appearance of bias, patronized the Black essayists with less exacting standards. Such "inflated praise and insufficient criticism" may hinder minority student achievement, Harber noted.

John Dovidio, Kerry Kawakami, and Samuel Gaertner (2002) had White students interact with a White or a Black confederate. They found that the students' responses on racism scales predicted racial bias in what they said in the interaction. But their automatic emotional reactions to Blacks predicted their nonverbal behavior.

What challenges might interracial couples face? Go to the *SocialSense* CD-ROM to view a video clip.

Automatic prejudice

This sort of modern prejudice illustrates again our *dual attitude* system (Chapter 2). We can have differing explicit (conscious) and implicit (automatic) attitudes toward the same target. Thus we may retain from childhood a habitual, automatic fear or dislike of people for whom we now express respect and appreciation. Although explicit attitudes may change dramatically with education, implicit attitudes may linger, changing only as we form new habits through practice (Kawakami & others, 2000).

A raft of experiments by researchers at Yale University (Banaji & Bhaskar, 2000), Indiana University (Fazio & others, 1995), the University of Colorado (Wittenbrink & others, 1997), the University of Washington (Greenwald & others, 2000), and New York University (Bargh & Chartrand, 1999) have confirmed the phenomenon of automatic stereotyping and prejudice. These studies briefly flash words or faces that "prime" (automatically activate) stereotypes of some racial, gender, or age group. Without their awareness, the participants' activated stereotypes may then bias their behavior. Having been primed with images associated with African Americans, for example, they may then react with more

"Many [people] have confessed to me . . . that even though in their minds they no longer feel prejudice towards Blacks, they still feel squeamish when they shake hands with a Black. These feelings are left over from what they learned in their families as children."
—Thomas Pettigrew (1987, p. 20)

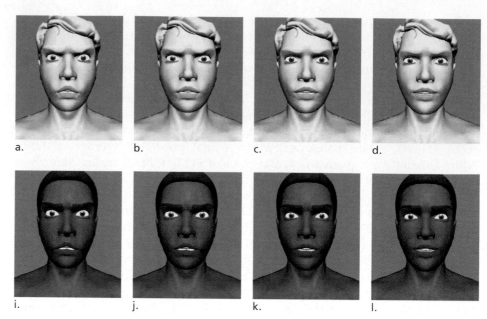

figure 9–2

Facing prejudice.

Where does the anger disappear? Kurt Hugenberg and Galen Bodenhausen showed university students a movie of faces morphing from angry to happy. Those who had scored as most prejudiced (on an implicit racial attitudes test) perceived anger lingering more in ambiguous Black than White faces.

Automatic prejudice. When Joshua Correll and his colleagues invited people to react quickly to people holding either a gun or a harmless object, race influenced perceptions and reactions.

hostility to an experimenter's annoying request. In clever experiments by Anthony Greenwald and his colleagues (1998, 2000), 9 in 10 White people took longer to identify pleasant words (such as *peace* and *paradise*) as "good" when associated with Black rather than White faces. The participants, mind you, typically expressed little or no prejudice, only an unconscious, unintended response. Moreover, report Kurt Hugenberg and Galen Bodenhausen (2003), the more strongly people exhibit such implicit prejudice, the readier they are to perceive anger in Black faces (Figure 9–2).

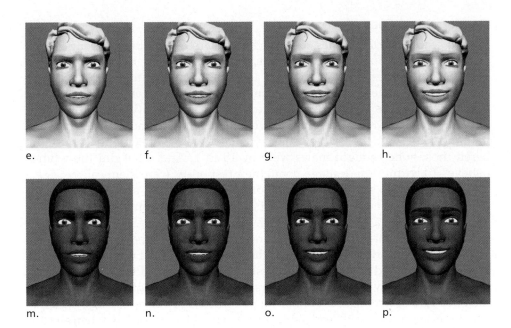

e.   f.   g.   h.

m.   n.   o.   p.

In separate experiments, Joshua Correll and his co-workers (2002) and Anthony Greenwald and his co-workers (2003) invited people to press buttons quickly to "shoot" or "not shoot" men who suddenly appeared on-screen holding either a gun or a harmless object such as a flashlight or bottle. The participants (both Blacks and Whites, in one of the studies) more often mistakenly shot targets who were Black. In a related series of studies, Keith Payne (2001), and Charles Judd and colleagues (2004), found that when primed with a Black rather than White face, people think guns: they more quickly recognize a gun and they more often mistake tools, such as a wrench, for a gun. These studies help explain why Amadou Diallo (a Black immigrant in New York City) was shot 41 times by police officers for removing his wallet from his back pocket.

Even the social scientists who study prejudice seem vulnerable to it, note Anthony Greenwald and Eric Schuh (1994). They analyzed biases in authors' citations of social science articles by people with selected non-Jewish names (Erickson, McBride, and so forth) and Jewish names (Goldstein, Siegel, and so forth). Their analysis of nearly 30,000 citations, including 17,000 citations of prejudice research, found something remarkable: Compared with Jewish authors, non-Jewish authors had 40 percent higher odds of citing non-Jewish names. (Greenwald and Schuh could not determine whether Jewish authors were overciting their Jewish colleagues, non-Jewish authors were overciting their non-Jewish colleagues, or both.)

GENDER PREJUDICE

How pervasive is prejudice against women? In Chapter 5, we examined gender-role norms—people's ideas about how women and men *ought* to behave. Here we consider gender *stereotypes*—people's beliefs about how women and men *do* behave. Norms are *pre*scriptive, stereotypes are *de*scriptive.

Gender stereotypes

From research on stereotypes, two conclusions are indisputable: Strong gender stereotypes exist, and, as often happens, members of the stereotyped group accept the stereotypes. Men and women agree that you *can* judge the book by its sexual cover. In one survey, Mary Jackman and Mary Senter (1981) found that gender stereotypes were much stronger than racial stereotypes. For example, only 22 percent of men thought the two sexes equally "emotional." Of the remaining 78 percent, those who believed females were more emotional outnumbered those who thought males were by 15 to 1. And what did the women believe? To within 1 percentage point, their responses were identical.

Consider, too, a study by Natalie Porter, Florence Geis, and Joyce Jennings Walstedt (1983). They showed students pictures of "a group of graduate students working as a team on a research project" (Figure 9–3). Then they gave them a test of "first impressions," asking them to guess who contributed most to the group. Ignoring the woman at the head of the table, each of the men in Figure 9–3 received more of the leadership choices than all three women combined! This stereotype of men as leaders was true not only of women as well as men but also of feminists as well as nonfeminists. Newer research reveals that behaviors associated with leadership are perceived less favorably when enacted by a woman (Eagly & Karau, 2000). Assertiveness can seem less becoming in a woman than in a man (making it harder for women to become and succeed as leaders). How pervasive are gender stereotypes? Very pervasive.

Remember that stereotypes are generalizations about a group of people and may be true, false, or overgeneralized from a kernel of truth. (They may also be self-fulfilling.) In Chapter 5, we noted that the average man and woman do differ somewhat in social connectedness, empathy, social power, aggressiveness, and sexual initiative (though not in intelligence). Do we then conclude that gender stereotypes are accurate? Sometimes stereotypes exaggerate differences. But

figure 9–3

Which one of these people would you guess is the group's strongest contributor? When shown this picture, college students usually guessed one of the two men, although those shown photos of same-sex groups most commonly guessed the person at the head of the table.

not always, observed Janet Swim (1994). She found that Pennsylvania State University students' stereotypes of men's and women's restlessness, nonverbal sensitivity, aggressiveness, and so forth were reasonable approximations of actual gender differences. Moreover, such stereotypes have persisted across time and culture. Averaging data from 27 countries, John Williams and his colleagues (1999, 2000) found that folks everywhere perceive women as more agreeable, men as more outgoing. The persistence and omnipresence of gender stereotypes leads some evolutionary psychologists to believe they reflect innate, stable reality (Lueptow & others, 1995).

Stereotypes (beliefs) are not prejudices (attitudes). Stereotypes may support prejudice. Yet one might believe, without prejudice, that men and women are "different yet equal." Let us therefore see how researchers probe for gender prejudice.

Gender attitudes

Judging from what people tell survey researchers, attitudes toward women have changed as rapidly as racial attitudes. In 1937, one-third of Americans said they would vote for a qualified woman whom their party nominated for president; by 2003, 87 percent said they would (Jones & Moore, 2003). In 1967, 56 percent of first-year American college students agreed that "the activities of married women are best confined to the home and family"; by 2002, only 22 percent agreed (Astin & others, 1987; Sax & others, 2002).

Alice Eagly and her associates (1991) and Geoffrey Haddock and Mark Zanna (1994) also report that people don't respond to women with gut-level negative emotions as they do to certain other groups. Most people like women more than men. They perceive women as more understanding, kind, and helpful. A *favorable* stereotype, which Eagly (1994) dubs the *women-are-wonderful effect*, results in a favorable attitude.

But gender attitudes often are ambivalent, report Peter Glick, Susan Fiske, and their colleagues (1996, 2000, 2001) from their surveys of 15,000 people in 19 nations. They frequently mix a *benevolent sexism* ("Women have a superior moral sensibility") with *hostile sexism* ("Once a man commits, she puts him on a tight leash").

There is good news for those who are upset by gender bias. One heavily publicized finding of prejudice against women came from a 1968 study in which Philip Goldberg gave women students at Connecticut College several short articles and asked them to judge the value of each. Sometimes a given article was attributed to a male author (for example, John T. McKay) and sometimes to a female author (for example, Joan T. McKay). In general, the articles received lower ratings when attributed to a female. The historic mark of oppression—self-deprecation—surfaced clearly: Women were prejudiced against women.

Eager to demonstrate the subtle reality of gender prejudice, I obtained Goldberg's materials and repeated the experiment for my own students' benefit. They (women and men) showed no such tendency to deprecate women's work. So Janet Swim, Eugene Borgida, Geoffrey Maruyama, and I (1989) searched the literature and corresponded with investigators to learn all we could about studies of gender bias in the evaluation of men's and women's work. To our surprise, the biases that occasionally surfaced were as often against men as women. But the most common result across 104 studies involving almost 20,000 people was *no difference*. On most comparisons, judgments of someone's work

"Women are wonderful primarily because they are [perceived as] so nice. [Men are] perceived as superior to women in agentic [competitive, dominant] attributes that are viewed as equipping people for success in paid work, especially in male-dominated occupations."
—Alice Eagly (1994)

"And just why do we always call <u>my</u> income the second income?"

Question: *"Misogyny" is the hatred of women. What is the corresponding word for the hatred of men?*
Answer: *In most dictionaries, no such word exists.*

In a 2000 survey of American women, 22 percent of those 65 and over said they had faced discrimination, as did 50 percent of those 28 to 34 (Hunt, 2000). Activity: Why the difference?

were unaffected by whether the work was attributed to a female or a male. Summarizing other studies of people's evaluations of women and men as leaders, professors, and so forth, Alice Eagly (1994) says, "Experiments have *not* demonstrated any *overall* tendency to devalue women's work."

Is gender bias fast becoming extinct in Western countries? Has the women's movement nearly completed its work? As with racial prejudice, blatant gender prejudice is dying, but subtle bias lives. The bogus-pipeline method, for example, exposes bias. As we noted in Chapter 4, men who believe an experimenter can read their true attitudes with a sensitive lie detector express less sympathy toward women's rights.

In the world beyond democratic Western countries, gender discrimination looms even larger:

- Two-thirds of the world's unschooled children are girls (United Nations, 1991).

- In Saudi Arabia, women are forbidden to drive (Beyer, 1990).

- Around the world, people tend to prefer having baby boys. In the United States in 1941, 38 percent of expectant parents said they preferred a boy if they could only have one child; 24 percent preferred a girl; and 23 percent said they didn't care. In 2003, the answers were virtually unchanged with 38 percent still preferring a boy (Lyons, 2003; Simmons, 2000). With the widespread use of ultrasound to determine the sex of a fetus and the growing availability of abortion, these preferences are affecting the number of boys and girls. The 2000 China census revealed 119 newborn boys for every 100 girls (Walfish, 2001). The 2001 India census reported that Punjab Province had 126 newborn boys for every 100 girls (Dugger, 2001). The net result is tens of millions of "missing women."

To conclude, overt prejudice against people of color and against women is far less common today than it was four decades ago. The same is true of prejudice against homosexual people. Nevertheless, techniques that are sensitive to subtle prejudice still detect widespread bias. And in parts of the world, gender prejudice is literally deadly. Therefore, we need to look carefully and closely at the social, emotional, and cognitive sources of prejudice.

Summing up

Stereotypes are *beliefs* about another group, beliefs that may be accurate, inaccurate, or overgeneralized but based on a kernel of truth. *Prejudice* is a prejudgmental negative *attitude*. Discrimination is unjustifiable negative *behavior*. *Racism* and *sexism* may refer to individuals' prejudicial attitudes or discriminatory behavior, or to oppressive institutional practices (even if not intentionally prejudicial).

Stereotypical beliefs, prejudicial attitudes, and discriminatory behavior have long poisoned human existence. Judging by what Americans have told survey researchers during the last four decades, their prejudice against Blacks and women has plunged. Nevertheless, subtle survey questions and indirect methods for assessing people's attitudes and behavior still reveal strong gender stereotypes and a fair amount of disguised racial and gender bias. Though less obvious, prejudice lurks.

What are the social sources of prejudice?

What social conditions breed prejudice? How does society maintain prejudice?

Prejudice springs from several sources. It may arise from differences in social status and people's desires to justify and maintain these differences. It may also be learned at our parent's knee as we are socialized about what differences matter between people. Finally, our social institutions may function to maintain and support prejudice. Consider first how prejudice can function to defend self-esteem and social position.

SOCIAL INEQUALITIES: UNEQUAL STATUS AND PREJUDICE

A principle to remember: *Unequal status breeds prejudice.* Masters view slaves as lazy, irresponsible, lacking ambition—as having just those traits that justify the slavery. Historians debate the forces that create unequal status. But once these inequalities exist, prejudice helps justify the economic and social superiority of those who have wealth and power. Tell me the economic relationship between two groups and I'll predict the intergroup attitudes. Stereotypes rationalize unequal status (Yzerbyt & others, 1997). Even temporary changes in status can affect prejudice. Jennifer Richeson and Nalini Ambady (2003) led White students to believe that they were interacting via computer with either a Black or a White partner as the partner's supervisor or subordinate. When the students interacted with a supposed Black partner, they were more likely to display automatic prejudice if they were the supervisor.

Real-life examples abound. Until recently, prejudice was greatest in regions where slavery was practiced. Nineteenth-century European politicians and

"Prejudice is never easy unless it can pass itself off for reason."
—William Hazlitt, (1778–1830), "On Prejudice"

writers justified imperial expansion by describing exploited colonized people as "inferior," "requiring protection," and a "burden" to be borne (G. W. Allport, 1958, pp. 204–205). Four decades ago, sociologist Helen Mayer Hacker (1951) noted how stereotypes of Blacks and women helped rationalize the inferior status of each: Many people thought both groups were mentally slow, emotional and primitive, and "contented" with their subordinate role. Blacks were "inferior"; women were "weak." Blacks were all right in their place; women's place was in the home.

As this hints, Peter Glick and Susan Fiske's distinction between "hostile" and "benevolent" sexism extends to other prejudices. We see other groups as competent or as likable, but usually not as both. We *respect* the competence of those high in status and *like* those who agreeably accept a lower status. In the United States, report Fiske and her colleagues (1999), Asians, Jews, Germans, nontraditional women, and assertive African Americans and gay men tend to be respected but not liked so well. Traditionally subordinate African Americans and Hispanics, traditional women, feminine gay men, and people with disabilities tend to be seen as less competent but liked for their emotional, spiritual, artistic, or athletic qualities.

In times of conflict, attitudes adjust easily to behavior. People often view enemies as subhuman and depersonalize them with labels. During World War II, the Japanese people became "the Japs." After the war was over, they became "the intelligent, hardworking Japanese." Attitudes are amazingly adaptable. As we have noted in previous chapters, cruel acts breed cruel attitudes.

Gender stereotypes, too, help rationalize gender roles. After studying these stereotypes worldwide, John Williams and Deborah Best (1990b) noted that if women provide most of the care to young children, it is reassuring to think women are naturally nurturant. If males run the businesses, hunt, and fight wars, it is comforting to suppose that men are aggressive, independent, and adventurous. In experiments, people perceive members of unknown groups as having traits that suit their roles (Hoffman & Hurst, 1990).

Some people notice and justify status differences. Those high in **social dominance orientation** tend to view people in terms of hierarchies. They like their social groups to be high status—they like to be on the top of the hierarchy.

"It is human nature to hate those whom we have injured."
—Tacitus, *Agricola*

social dominance orientation
A motivation to have one's group be dominant over other social groups.

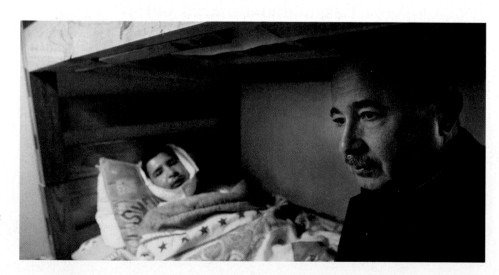

Racial prejudice often heightens during times of conflict, as after 9/11 when many Arab-Americans faced distrust or hostility. Here, an Arab-American father sits at the side of his son who was beaten by a mob.

Being in a dominant high-status position also tends to promote this orientation (Guimond & others, 2003). Jim Sidanius, Felicia Pratto, and their colleagues (Pratto & others, 1994; Sidanius & others, 1996; Sidanius & Pratto, 1999) argue that this desire to be on top leads people high in social dominance to embrace prejudice and to support political positions that justify prejudice. Indeed, people high in social dominance orientation often support policies that maintain hierarchies such as tax cuts for the well-off and oppose policies that undermine hierarchy, such as affirmative action. People high in social dominance orientation also prefer professions, such as politics and business, that increase their status and maintain hierarchies. They avoid jobs, such as social work, that undermine hierarchies. Status may breed prejudice, but some people seek it out and try to maintain this status more than others.

SOCIALIZATION

Prejudice springs from unequal status, and from other social sources, including our acquired values and attitudes.

The authoritarian personality

In the 1940s, University of California Berkeley researchers—two of whom had fled Nazi Germany—set out on an urgent research mission: to uncover the psychological roots of an anti-Semitism so poisonous that it caused the slaughter of millions of Jews and turned many millions of Europeans into indifferent spectators. In studies of American adults, Theodor Adorno and his colleagues (1950) discovered that hostility toward Jews often coexisted with hostility toward other minorities. Prejudice appeared to be less an attitude specific to one group than a way of thinking about those who are different. Moreover, these judgmental, **ethnocentric** people shared authoritarian tendencies—an intolerance for weakness, a punitive attitude, and a submissive respect for their ingroup's authorities, as reflected in their agreement with such statements as, "Obedience and respect for authority are the most important virtues children should learn."

ethnocentric
Believing in the superiority of one's own ethnic and cultural group, and having a corresponding disdain for all other groups.

As children, authoritarian people often faced harsh discipline. This supposedly led them to repress their hostilities and impulses and to "project" them onto outgroups. The insecurity of authoritarian children seemed to predispose them toward an excessive concern with power and status and an inflexible right-wrong way of thinking that made ambiguity difficult to tolerate. Such people therefore tended to be submissive to those with power over them and aggressive or punitive toward those beneath them.

Scholars criticized the research for focusing on right-wing authoritarianism and overlooking dogmatic authoritarianism of the left. Still, its main conclusion has survived: Authoritarian tendencies, sometimes reflected in ethnic tensions, surge during threatening times of economic recession and social upheaval (Doty & others, 1991; Sales, 1973). In contemporary Russia, individuals scoring high in authoritarianism have tended to support a return to Marxist-Leninist ideology and to oppose democratic reform (McFarland & others, 1992, 1996).

Moreover, contemporary studies of right-wing authoritarians by University of Manitoba psychologist Bob Altemeyer (1988, 1992) confirm that there *are* individuals whose fears and hostilities surface as prejudice. Feelings of moral superiority may go hand in hand with brutality toward perceived inferiors.

Different forms of prejudice—toward Blacks, gays and lesbians, women, old people, fat people, AIDS victims, the homeless—*do* tend to coexist in the same individuals (Bierly, 1985; Crandall, 1994; Peterson & others, 1993; Snyder & Ickes, 1985). As Altemeyer concludes, right-wing authoritarians tend to be "equal opportunity bigots."

Particularly striking are people high in social dominance orientation and authoritarian personality. Altemeyer (in press) reports that these "Double Highs" are, not surprisingly, "among the most prejudiced persons in our society." What is perhaps most surprising and more troubling is that they seem to display the worst qualities of each type of personality, striving for status often in manipulative ways while being dogmatic and ethnocentric. Altemeyer argues that although these people are relatively rare, they are predisposed to be leaders of hate groups.

Religion and prejudice

Those who benefit from social inequalities while avowing that "all are created equal" need to justify keeping things the way they are. What could be a more powerful justification than to believe God has ordained the existing social order? For all sorts of cruel deeds, noted William James, "Piety is the mask" (1902, p. 264).

In almost every country, leaders invoke religion to sanctify the present order. The use of religion to support injustice helps explain a consistent pair of findings concerning Christianity, North America's dominant religion: (1) Church members express more racial prejudice than nonmembers, and (2) those professing traditional or fundamentalist Christian beliefs express more prejudice than those professing less traditional beliefs (Altemeyer & Hunsberger, 1992; Batson & others, 1993; Woodberry & Smith, 1998).

Knowing the correlation between two variables—religion and prejudice—tells us nothing about their causal connection. There might be no connection at all. Perhaps people with less education are both more fundamentalist and more prejudiced. Perhaps prejudice causes religion, by leading people to create religious ideas to support their prejudices. Or perhaps religion causes prejudice, by leading people to believe that because all individuals possess free will, impoverished minorities have themselves to blame for their status.

If indeed religion causes prejudice, then more religious church members should also be more prejudiced. But three other findings consistently indicate otherwise.

- Among church members, faithful church attenders were, in 24 out of 26 comparisons, *less* prejudiced than occasional attenders (Batson & Ventis, 1982).

- Gordon Allport and Michael Ross (1967) found that those for whom religion is an end in itself (those who agree, for example, with the statement, "My religious beliefs are what really lie behind my whole approach to life") express *less* prejudice than those for whom religion is more a means to other ends (who agree, "A primary reason for my interest in religion is that my church is a congenial social activity"). And those who score highest on Gallup's "spiritual commitment" index are more welcoming of a person of another race moving in next door (Gallup & Jones, 1992).

- Protestant ministers and Roman Catholic priests gave more support to the civil rights movement than did laypeople (Fichter, 1968; Hadden,

1969). In Germany, 45 percent of clergy in 1934 had aligned themselves with the Confessing Church, which was organized to oppose the Nazi regime (Reed, 1989).

What, then, is the relationship between religion and prejudice? The answer we get depends on *how* we ask the question. If we define religiousness as church membership or willingness to agree at least superficially with traditional beliefs, then the more religious people are the more racially prejudiced. Bigots often rationalize bigotry with religion. If we assess depth of religious commitment in any of several other ways, however, then the very devout are less prejudiced—hence the religious roots of the modern civil rights movement, among whose leaders were many ministers and priests. As Gordon Allport concluded, "The role of religion is paradoxical. It makes prejudice and it unmakes prejudice" (1958, p. 413).

> "We have just enough religion to make us hate, but not enough to make us love one another."
> —Jonathan Swift, *Thoughts on Various Subjects*, 1706

Conformity

Once established, prejudice is maintained largely by inertia. If prejudice is socially accepted, many people will follow the path of least resistance and conform to the fashion. They will act not so much out of a need to hate as out of a need to be liked and accepted.

Thomas Pettigrew's (1958) studies of Whites in South Africa and the American South revealed that, during the 1950s, those who conformed most to other social norms were also most prejudiced; those who were less conforming mirrored less of the surrounding prejudice. The price of nonconformity was painfully clear to the ministers of Little Rock, Arkansas, where the U.S. Supreme Court's 1954 school desegregation decision was implemented. Most ministers favored integration but usually only privately; they feared that advocating it openly would lose them members and contributions (Campbell & Pettigrew, 1959). Or consider the Indiana steel workers and West Virginia coal miners of the same era. In the mills and the mines, the workers accepted integration. In the neighborhoods, the norm was rigid segregation (Minard, 1952; Reitzes, 1953). Prejudice was clearly *not* a manifestation of "sick" personalities but simply of the social norms.

Conformity also maintains gender prejudice. "If we have come to think that the nursery and the kitchen are the natural sphere of a woman," wrote George Bernard Shaw in an 1891 essay, "we have done so exactly as English children come to think that a cage is the natural sphere of a parrot—because they have never seen one anywhere else." Children who *have* seen women elsewhere—children of employed women—have less stereotyped views of men and women (Hoffman, 1977).

In all this, there is a message of hope. If prejudice is not deeply ingrained in personality, then as fashions change and new norms evolve, prejudice can diminish. And so it has.

INSTITUTIONAL SUPPORTS

Segregation is one way that social institutions (schools, government, the media) bolster prejudice. Political leaders may both reflect and reinforce prevailing attitudes. When Arkansas Governor Orville Faubus in 1957 barred the doors of Central High School in Little Rock to prevent integration, he was doing more than representing his constituents; he was legitimating their views.

Schools, too, reinforce dominant cultural attitudes. One analysis of stories in 134 children's readers written before 1970 found that male characters outnumbered female characters three to one (Women on Words and Images, 1972). Who was portrayed as showing initiative, bravery, and competence? Note the answer in this excerpt from the classic *Dick and Jane* children's reader: Jane, sprawled out on the sidewalk, her roller skates beside her, listens as Mark explains to his mother:

> "She cannot skate," said Mark.
> "I can help her.
> "I want to help her.
> "Look at her, Mother.
> "Just look at her.
> "She's just like a girl.
> "She gives up."

Not until the 1970s, when changing ideas about males and females brought new perceptions of such portrayals, was this blatant (to us) stereotyping widely noticed and changed.

Institutional supports for prejudice often go unnoticed. Usually, they are not deliberate attempts to oppress a group. More often, they simply reflect cultural assumptions, as when the one "flesh"-colored crayon in the Crayola box was pinkish white.

What contemporary examples of institutionalized biases still go unnoticed? Here is one that most of us failed to notice, although it was right before our eyes: By examining 1,750 photographs of people in magazines and newspapers, Dane Archer and his associates (1983) discovered that about two-thirds of the average male photo, but less than half of the average female photo, was devoted to the face. As Archer widened his search, he discovered that such "face-ism" is common. He found it in the periodicals of 11 other countries, in 920 portraits gathered from the artwork of six centuries, and in the amateur drawings of students at the University of California, Santa Cruz. Georgia Nigro and her colleagues (1988) confirmed the face-ism phenomenon in more magazines, including *Ms.*

The researchers suspect that the visual prominence given the faces of men and the bodies of women both reflects and perpetuates gender bias. In research in Germany, Norbert Schwarz and Eva Kurz (1989) confirmed that people whose faces are prominent in photos seem more intelligent and ambitious. But

Face-ism: Male photos in the media more often show just the face.

better a whole-body depiction than none at all. When Ruth Thibodeau (1989) examined the previous 42 years of *New Yorker* cartoons, she could find only a single instance in which an African American appeared in a cartoon unrelated to race. (Because so few widely distributed cartoons show diversity, it is much easier to depict diversity in this book's photos than in its cartoons.)

Films and television programs also embody and reinforce prevailing cultural attitudes. The muddle-headed, wide-eyed African American butlers and maids in 1930s movies helped perpetuate the stereotypes they reflected. Today most of us would find such images offensive, yet even a modern TV comedy skit of a crime-prone African American can later make another African American who is accused of assault seem more guilty (Ford, 1997). And violent rap music from Black artists leads both Black and White listeners to stereotype Blacks as having violent dispositions (Johnson & others, 2000).

Summing up

The social situation breeds and maintains prejudice in several ways. A group that enjoys social and economic superiority will often justify its standing with prejudicial beliefs. People are also brought up in ways that foster or reduce prejudice. The family, religious communities, and the broader society can sustain or reduce prejudices. Partly through inertia, social institutions also support prejudice.

What are the motivational sources of prejudice?

Prejudice may be bred by social situations, but motivation underlies both the hostilities of prejudice and the desire to be unbiased. Frustration can feed prejudice, as can the desire to see one's group as superior. But at times, people are also motivated to avoid prejudice.

FRUSTRATION AND AGGRESSION: THE SCAPEGOAT THEORY

As we will see in Chapter 10, pain and frustration (the blocking of a goal) often evoke hostility. When the cause of our frustration is intimidating or unknown, we often redirect our hostility. This phenomenon of "displaced aggression" may

"*And now at this point in the meeting I'd like to shift the blame away from me and onto someone else.*"

Scapegoats provide an outlet for frustrations and hostilities. Copyright © The New Yorker Collection, 1985, Michael Maslin, from cartoonbank.com. All Rights Reserved.

realistic group conflict theory
The theory that prejudice arises from competition between groups for scarce resources.

"Whoever is dissatisfied with himself is continually ready for revenge."
—Nietzsche, *The Gay Science,* 1882–1887

social identity
The "we" aspect of our self-concept; the part of our answer to "Who am I?" that comes from our group memberships.

have contributed to the lynchings of African Americans in the South after the Civil War. Between 1882 and 1930, more lynchings occurred in years when cotton prices were low and economic frustration was therefore presumably high (Hepworth & West, 1988; Hovland & Sears, 1940). Hate crimes seem not to have fluctuated with unemployment in recent decades (Green & others, 1998). However, when living standards are rising, societies tend to be more open to diversity and to antidiscrimination laws (Frank, 1999). Ethnic peace is easier to maintain during prosperous times.

Targets for this displaced aggression vary. Following their defeat in World War I and their country's subsequent economic chaos, many Germans saw Jews as villains. Long before Hitler came to power, one German leader explained: "The Jew is just convenient. . . . If there were no Jews, the anti-Semites would have to invent them" (quoted by G. W. Allport, 1958, p. 325). In earlier centuries people vented their fear and hostility on witches, whom they sometimes burned or drowned in public. Passions provoke prejudice.

One source of frustration is competition. When two groups compete for jobs, housing, or social prestige, one group's goal fulfillment can become the other group's frustration. Thus the **realistic group conflict theory** suggests that prejudice arises when groups compete for scarce resources (Esses & others, 1998). A corresponding ecological principle, Gause's law, states that maximum competition will exist between species with identical needs.

In western Europe, for example, some people agree, "Over the last five years people like yourself have been economically worse off than most [name of country's minority group]." These frustrated people express relatively high levels of blatant prejudice (Pettigrew & Meertens, 1995). In Canada, opposition to immigration since 1975 has gone up and down with the unemployment rate (Palmer, 1996). In America, the strongest anti-Black prejudice occurs among Whites who are closest to Blacks on the socioeconomic ladder (Greeley & Sheatsley, 1971; Pettigrew, 1978; Tumin, 1958). When interests clash, prejudice—for some people—pays.

SOCIAL IDENTITY THEORY: FEELING SUPERIOR TO OTHERS

Humans are a group-bound species. Our ancestral history prepares us to feed and protect ourselves—to live—in groups. Humans cheer for their groups, kill for their groups, die for their groups. Not surprisingly, we also define ourselves by our groups, note Australian social psychologists John Turner (1981, 1987, 1991, 2001), Michael Hogg (1992, 1996, 2003), and their colleagues. Self-concept—our sense of who we are—contains not just a *personal identity* (our sense of our personal attributes and attitudes) but a **social identity.** Fiona identifies herself as a woman, an Aussie, a Labourite, a University of New South Wales student, a member of the MacDonald family. We carry such social identities like playing cards, playing them when appropriate.

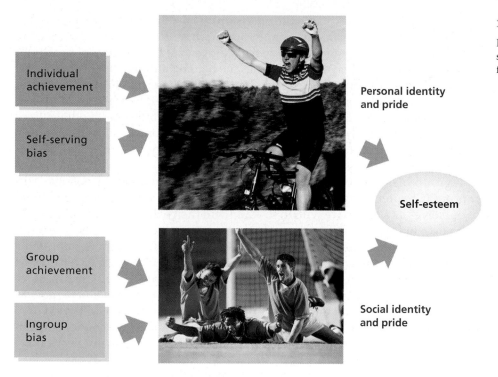

Individual achievement

Self-serving bias

Personal identity and pride

Group achievement

Ingroup bias

Social identity and pride

Self-esteem

figure 9–4
Personal identity and social identity together feed self-esteem.

Working with the late British social psychologist Henri Tajfel [pronounced TOSH-fel], Turner proposed *social identity theory.* Turner and Tajfel observed the following:

- *We categorize:* We find it useful to put people, ourselves included, into categories. To label someone as a Hindu, a Scot, or a bus driver is a shorthand way of saying some other things about the person.
- *We identify:* We associate ourselves with certain groups (our **ingroups**), and gain self-esteem by doing so.
- *We compare:* We contrast our groups with other groups (**outgroups**), with a favorable bias toward our own group.

We evaluate ourselves partly by our group memberships. Having a sense of "we-ness" strengthens our self-concepts. It *feels* good. We seek not only *respect* for ourselves but *pride* in our groups (Smith & Tyler, 1997). Moreover, seeing our groups as superior helps us feel even better. It's as if we all think, "I am an X [name your group]. X is good. Therefore, I am good."

Lacking a positive personal identity, people often seek self-esteem by identifying with a group. Thus, many youths find pride, power, and identity in gang affiliations. Many superpatriots define themselves by their national identities (Staub, 1997). And many people at loose ends find identity in their associations with new religious movements, self-help groups, or fraternal clubs (Figure 9–4).

Ingroup bias

The group definition of who you are—your race, religion, gender, academic major—implies a definition of who you are not. The circle that includes "us"

ingroup
"Us"—a group of people who share a sense of belonging, a feeling of common identity.

outgroup
"Them"—a group that people perceive as distinctively different from or apart from their ingroup.

"There is a tendency to define one's own group positively in order to evaluate oneself positively."
—John C. Turner (1984)

ingroup bias
The tendency to favor one's own group.

www.mhhe.com/**myers8**
Visit the Online Learning Center for an interactivity on prejudice.

(the ingroup) excludes "them" (the outgroup). Thus, the mere experience of being formed into groups may promote **ingroup bias.** Ask children, "Which are better, the children in your school or the children at [another school nearby]?" Virtually all will say their own school has the better children. For adults, too, the closer to home, the better things seem. More than 80 percent of both Whites and Blacks say race relations are generally good in their neighborhoods, but fewer than 60 percent see relations as generally good in the country as a whole (Sack & Elder, 2000). Merely sharing a birthday with someone creates enough of a bond to evoke heightened cooperation in a laboratory experiment (Miller & others, 1998).

Ingroup bias is one more example of the human quest for a positive self-concept (Chapter 2). We are so group conscious that given any excuse to think of ourselves as a group we will do so—and will then exhibit ingroup bias. Cluster people into groups defined by nothing more than their driver's license number's last digit, and they'll feel a certain kinship with their number mates. In a series of experiments, Tajfel and Michael Billig (1974; Tajfel, 1970, 1981, 1982) discovered how little it takes to provoke favoritism toward *us* and unfairness toward *them*. In one study, Tajfel and Billig had British teenagers evaluate modern abstract paintings and then told them that they and some others had favored the art of Paul Klee over that of Wassily Kandinsky. Finally, without ever meeting the other members of their group, the teens divided some money among members of both groups.

In this and other experiments, defining groups even in this trivial way produced ingroup favoritism. David Wilder (1981) summarized the typical result: "When given the opportunity to divide 15 points [worth money], subjects generally award 9 or 10 points to their own group and 5 or 6 points to the other group." This bias occurs with both sexes and with people of all ages and nationalities, though especially with people from individualist cultures (Gudykunst, 1989). (People in communal cultures identify more with all their peers and so treat everyone more the same.)

We also are more prone to ingroup bias when our group is small and lower in status relative to the outgroup (Ellemers & others, 1997; Mullen & others, 1992). When we're part of a small group surrounded by a larger group, we are also conscious of our group membership; when our ingroup is the majority, we think less about it. To be a foreign student, to be gay or lesbian, or to be of a minority race or gender at some social gathering is to feel one's social identity more keenly and to react accordingly.

Even forming conspicuous groups on *no* logical basis—say, merely by composing groups X and Y with the flip of a coin—will produce some ingroup bias (Billig & Tajfel, 1973; Brewer & Silver, 1978; Locksley & others, 1980). In Kurt Vonnegut's novel *Slapstick,* computers gave everyone a new middle name; all "Daffodil-11s" then felt unity with one another and distance from "Raspberry-13s." The self-serving bias (Chapter 2) rides again, enabling people to achieve a more positive social identity: "We" are better than "they," even when "we" and "they" are defined randomly!

Because of our social identifications, we conform to our group norms. We sacrifice ourselves for team, family, nation. We may dislike outgroups. The more important our social identity and the more strongly attached we feel to a group, the more we react prejudicially to threats from another group (Crocker & Luhtanen, 1990; Hinkle & others, 1992). Israeli historian and former Jerusalem

"Nationality is a sense of belonging and a sense of place—a pleasure in your history, in the peculiarities of your people's behaviour, in the music and the familiar sounds of the world around you. I don't think a particular culture is better. I just think it's a culture you are more at home with."
—Bill Wilson, Scottish Nationalist Party activist, 2003

deputy mayor Meron Benvenisti (1988) reported that among Jerusalem's Jews and Arabs, social identity is so central to self-concept that it constantly reminds them of who they are not. Thus, on the integrated street where he lived, his own children—to his dismay—"have not acquired a single Arab friend."

When our group has been successful, we can also make ourselves feel better by identifying more strongly with it. When queried after their football team's victory, college students frequently report "*We* won." When questioned after their team's defeat, students are more likely to say, "*They* lost." Basking in the reflected glory of a successful ingroup is strongest among those who have just experienced an ego blow, such as learning they did poorly on a "creativity test" (Cialdini & others, 1976). We can also bask in the reflected glory of a friend's achievement—except when the friend outperforms us on something pertinent to our identity (Tesser & others, 1988). If you think of yourself as an outstanding psychology student, you will likely take more pleasure in a friend's excellence in mathematics.

Ingroup bias is the favoring of one's own group. Such favoritism could reflect (1) liking for the ingroup, (2) dislike for the outgroup, or (3) both. If

Basking in reflected glory. After Jamaican-Canadian sprinter Ben Johnson won the Olympic 100-meter race, Canadian media described this victory by a "Canadian." After Johnson's gold medal was taken away due to steroid use, Canadian media then emphasized his "Jamaican" identity (Stelzl & Seligman, 2004).

"*Uh-oh! They seem to have loved it!*"

both, loyalty to one's group should produce a devaluing of other groups. Is that true? Does ethnic pride cause prejudice? Does a strong feminist identity lead feminists to dislike nonfeminists? Does loyalty to a particular fraternity or sorority lead its members to deprecate independents and members of other fraternities and sororities?

Experiments support both explanations. Outgroup stereotypes prosper when people feel keenly their ingroup identity, such as when they are with other ingroup members (Wilder & Shapiro, 1991). At a club meeting, we sense most strongly our differences from those in another club. When anticipating bias against our group, we more strongly disparage the outgroup (Vivian & Berkowitz, 1993).

Yet ingroup bias results as much or more from perceiving that one's own group is good (Brewer, 1979) as from a sense that other groups are bad (Rosenbaum & Holtz, 1985). So it seems that positive feelings for our own groups need not be mirrored by equally strong negative feelings for outgroups. Devotion to one's own race, religion, and social group sometimes does predispose a person to devalue other races, religions, and social groups. But the sequence is not automatic. Indeed, a multicultural rather than a color-blind perspective does not lead to sharper perception of group differences, note Christopher Wolsko and others (2000) from their research with university students. But some of the stereotypes bred by multiculturalism are favorable to the outgroup. For psychological and social health, they say, we need to acknowledge simultaneously our individual uniqueness, our group identity, and our common humanity.

Need for status, self-regard, and belonging

Status is relative: To perceive ourselves as having status, we need people below us. Thus one psychological benefit of prejudice, or of any status system, is a feeling of superiority. Most of us can recall a time when we took secret satisfaction

Father, Mother, and
   Me, sister and
   Auntie say
All the people like us
   are We, and every
   one else is They.
And They live over
   the sea, While We
   live over the way.
But would you
   believe it? They
   look upon We
As only a sort of
   They!
—Rudyard Kipling, 1926
(quoted by Mullen, 1991)

The curse of cliques? Did the tendency of high school students to form ingroups and disparage outgroups—jocks, preppies, goths, geeks—contribute to a tribal atmosphere that helped form the context for recent school massacres, here at Colorado's Columbine High School, or elsewhere?

in another's failure—perhaps seeing a brother or sister punished or a classmate failing a test. In Europe and North America, prejudice is often greater among those low or slipping on the socioeconomic ladder and among those whose positive self-image is being threatened (Lemyre & Smith, 1985; Pettigrew & others, 1998; Thompson & Crocker, 1985). In one study, members of lower-status sororities were more disparaging of other sororities than were members of higher-status sororities (Crocker & others, 1987). Perhaps people whose status is secure have less need to feel superior.

But other factors associated with low status could also account for prejudice. Imagine yourself as one of the Arizona State University students who took part in an experiment by Robert Cialdini and Kenneth Richardson (1980). You are walking alone across campus. Someone approaches you and asks your help with a five-minute survey. You agree. After the researcher gives you a brief "creativity test," he deflates you with the news that "you have scored relatively low on the test." The researcher then completes the survey by asking you some evaluative questions about either your school or its traditional rival, the University of Arizona. Would your feelings of failure affect your ratings of either school? Compared with those in a control group whose self-esteem was not threatened, the students who experienced failure gave higher ratings to their own school and lower ratings to their rival. Apparently, asserting one's social identity by boasting about one's own group and denigrating outgroups can boost one's ego.

James Meindl and Melvin Lerner (1984) found that a humiliating experience—accidentally knocking over a stack of someone's important computer cards—provoked English-speaking Canadian students to express increased hostility toward French-speaking Canadians. And Teresa Amabile and Ann Glazebrook (1982) found that Dartmouth College men who were made to feel insecure judged others' work more harshly.

In study after study, thinking about your own mortality—by writing a short essay on dying and the emotions aroused by thinking about death—also provokes enough insecurity to intensify ingroup favoritism and outgroup prejudice (Greenberg & others, 1990, 1994; Harmon-Jones & others, 1996; Schimel & others 1999; Solomon & others, 2000). Among Whites, thinking about death can even promote liking for racists who argue for their group's superiority (Greenberg & others, in press). With death on their minds, people exhibit "terror management" by derogating those who further arouse their anxiety by challenging their worldviews. When people are already feeling vulnerable about their mortality, prejudice helps bolster a threatened belief system. The news is not all bad, however. Thinking about death can also lead people to pursue communal feelings such as togetherness and altruism (McGregor & others, 2001).

All this suggests that a man who doubts his own strength and independence might, by proclaiming women to be pitifully weak and dependent, boost his masculine image. Indeed, when Joel Grube, Randy Kleinhesselink, and Kathleen Kearney (1982) had Washington State University men view young

"It's not enough that we succeed. Cats must also fail."

women's videotaped job interviews, men with low self-acceptance disliked strong, nontraditional women. Men with high self-acceptance preferred them. Experiments confirm the connection between self-image and prejudice: Affirm people and they will evaluate an outgroup more positively; threaten their self-esteem and they will restore it by denigrating an outgroup (Fein & Spencer, 1997; Spencer & others, 1998).

A despised outgroup serves yet another need: the need to belong to an ingroup. As we will see in Chapter 13, the perception of a common enemy unites a group. School spirit is seldom so strong as when the game is with the archrival. The sense of comradeship among workers is often highest when they all feel a common antagonism toward management. To solidify the Nazi hold over Germany, Hitler used the "Jewish menace." Despised outgroups can strengthen the ingroup. When the need to belong is met, people become more accepting of outgroups, report Mario Mikulincer and Phillip Shaver (2001). They subliminally primed some Israeli students with words that fostered a sense of belonging (*love, support, hug*) and others with neutral words. The students then read an essay that was supposedly written either by a fellow Jewish student or an Arab student. When primed with neutral words, the Israeli students evaluated the supposed Israeli student's essay as superior to the supposed Arab student's essay. When primed with a sense of belonging, this bias disappeared.

MOTIVATION TO AVOID PREJUDICE

Motivations not only lead people to be prejudiced, they also lead people to avoid prejudice. Although most of us don't want to be prejudiced, a prejudice habit lingers. Patricia Devine and her colleagues (1989, 2000) report that people low and high in prejudice sometimes have similar automatic prejudicial responses.

Try as we might to suppress unwanted thoughts—thoughts about food, thoughts about romance with a friend's partner, judgmental thoughts about another group—they sometimes refuse to go away (Macrae & others, 1994; Wegner & Erber, 1992). This is especially so for older adults, who lose some of their ability to inhibit unwanted thoughts and therefore to suppress old stereotypes (von Hippel & others, 2000). The result for all of us: Unwanted (dissonant) thoughts and feelings often persist. Breaking the prejudice habit is not easy.

In real life, encountering a minority person may trigger a similar knee-jerk stereotype. Those with accepting and those with disapproving attitudes toward homosexuals may both feel uncomfortable sitting with a gay male on a bus seat (Monteith, 1993). Encountering an unfamiliar Black male, people—even those who pride themselves on not being prejudiced—may respond warily. In one experiment by E. J. Vanman and colleagues (1990), White people viewed slides of White and Black people, imagined themselves interacting with them, and rated their probable liking of the person. Although the participants saw themselves liking the Black more than the White persons, their facial muscles told a different story. Instruments revealed that when a Black face appeared, there tended to be more activity in frowning than smiling muscles. An emotion processing center in the brain also becomes more active as a person views an unfamiliar person of another race (Hart & others, 2000).

On a brighter note, researchers who study stereotyping contend that prejudicial reactions are not inevitable (Crandall & Eshelman, 2003; Kunda & Spencer, 2003). The motivation to avoid prejudice can lead people to modify their thoughts and actions. Aware of the gap between how they *should* feel and how they *do* feel, self-conscious people will feel guilt and try to inhibit their prejudicial response (Bodenhausen & Macrae, 1998; Macrae & others, 1998; Zuwerink & others, 1996). Even automatic prejudices subside, notes Devine and her colleagues (in press), when people's motivation to avoid prejudice is internal (because prejudice is wrong) rather than external (because they don't want others to think badly of them).

The moral: Overcoming what Devine calls "the prejudice habit" isn't easy. If you find yourself reacting with knee-jerk presumptions or feelings, don't despair; that's not unusual. It's what you do with that awareness that matters. Do you let those feelings hijack your behavior? Or do you compensate by monitoring and correcting your behavior in future situations?

<table>
<tr><td>

People's motivations impact prejudice. Frustration breeds hostility, which people sometimes vent on scapegoats and sometimes express more directly against competing groups. People also are motivated to view themselves and their groups as superior to other groups. Even trivial group memberships lead people to favor their group over others. A threat to self-image heightens such ingroup favoritism, as does the need to belong. On a more positive note, the motivation to avoid prejudice can lead people to break the prejudice habit.

</td><td>

Summing up

</td></tr>
</table>

What are the cognitive sources of prejudice?

To understand stereotyping and prejudice, it also helps to remember how our minds work. How does the way we think about the world, and simplify it, influence our stereotypes? And how do our stereotypes affect our judgments?

Much of the explanation of prejudice so far could have been written in the 1960s—but not what follows. This new look at prejudice, fueled in the 1990s by more than 2,100 articles on stereotyping, applies the new research on social thinking. The basic point is this: Stereotyped beliefs and prejudiced attitudes exist not only because of social conditioning and because they enable people to displace hostilities, but also as by-products of normal thinking processes. Many stereotypes spring less from malice of the heart than the machinery of the mind. Like perceptual illusions, which are by-products of our knack for interpreting the world, stereotypes can be by-products of how we simplify our complex worlds.

CATEGORIZATION: CLASSIFYING PEOPLE INTO GROUPS

One way we simplify our environment is to *categorize*—to organize the world by clustering objects into groups (Macrae & Bodenhausen, 2000). A biologist classifies plants and animals. A human classifies people. Having done so, we think about them more easily. If persons in a group share some similarities—if most MENSA members are smart, most basketball players are tall—knowing their group memberships can provide useful information with minimal effort (Macrae & others, 1994). Stereotypes sometimes offer "a beneficial ratio of information gained to effort expended" (Sherman & others, 1998). Customs inspectors and airplane antihijack personnel are therefore given "profiles" of suspicious individuals (Kraut & Poe, 1980).

Spontaneous categorization

We find it especially easy and efficient to rely on stereotypes when

- pressed for time (Kaplan & others, 1993),
- preoccupied (Gilbert & Hixon, 1991),
- tired (Bodenhausen, 1990),
- emotionally aroused (Esses & others, 1993b; Stroessner & Mackie, 1993), and
- too young to appreciate diversity (Biernat, 1991).

Ethnicity and sex are, in our current world, powerful ways of categorizing people. Imagine Tom, a 45-year-old, African American New Orleans real estate agent. I suspect that your image of "Black male" predominates over the categories "middle-aged," "businessperson," and "American southerner." Moreover, when shown pictures of Black or White individuals, our brains respond differently, beginning within about one-tenth of a second (Ito & Urland, 2003).

Experiments expose our spontaneous categorization of people by race. Much as we organize what is actually a color continuum into what we perceive as distinct colors, so we cannot resist categorizing people into groups. We label people of widely varying ancestry as simply "Black" or "White," as if such categories were black and white. When individuals view different people making statements, they often forget who said what, yet they remember the race of the person who made each statement (Hewstone & others, 1991; Stroessner & others, 1990; Taylor & others, 1978). By itself, such categorization is not prejudice, but it does provide a foundation for prejudice.

In fact, it's necessary for prejudice. Social identity theory implies that those who feel their social identity keenly will concern themselves with correctly categorizing people as *us* or *them*. To test this prediction, Jim Blascovich and his co-researchers (1997) compared racially prejudiced people (who feel their racial identity keenly) with nonprejudiced people—who proved equally speedy at classifying white, black, and gray ovals. But how much time did each group take to categorize *people* by race? Especially when shown faces whose race was somewhat ambiguous (Figure 9–5), prejudiced people took longer, with more apparent concern for classifying people as either us (one's own race) or them (another race). Prejudice requires racial categorization.

figure 9–5

Racial categorization.

Quickly: What race is this person? Less prejudiced people respond more quickly, with less apparent concern with possibly misclassifying someone (as if thinking, "who cares?").

Perceived similarities and differences

Picture the following objects: apples, chairs, pencils.

There is a strong tendency to see objects within a group as being more uniform than they really are. Were your apples all red? Your chairs all straight-backed? Your pencils all yellow? Once we classify two days in the same month, they seem more alike, temperature-wise, than the same interval across months. People guess the eight-day average temperature difference between, say, November 15 and 23 to be less than the eight-day difference between November 30 and December 8 (Krueger & Clement, 1994).

It's the same with people. Once we assign people to groups—athletes, drama majors, math professors—we are likely to exaggerate the similarities within the groups and the differences between them (S. E. Taylor, 1981; Wilder, 1978). Mere division into groups can create an **outgroup homogeneity effect**—a sense that *they* are "all alike" and different from "us" and "our" group (Ostrom & Sedikides, 1992). Because we generally like people we think are similar to us and dislike those we perceive as different, the natural result is ingroup bias (Byrne & Wong, 1962; Rokeach & Mezei, 1966; Stein & others, 1965).

The mere fact of a group decision can also lead outsiders to overestimate a group's unanimity. If a conservative wins a national election by a slim majority, observers infer "the people have turned conservative." If a liberal won by a similarly slim margin, voter attitudes would hardly have differed, but observers would now attribute a "liberal mood" to the country. Whether a decision is made by majority rule or by a designated group executive, people tend to presume that it reflects the entire group's attitudes, observe Scott Allison and his co-workers (1985 to 1996). In the 1994 U.S. elections, Republicans captured the Congress with 53 percent of the votes (in an election in which most adults did not vote)—producing what commentators interpreted as a "revolution," a "landslide," a "sea change" in American politics. Even the 2000 U.S. presidential election, a virtual draw, was interpreted by some as a repudiation of losing candidate, Al Gore, who actually received more votes.

When the group is our own, we are more likely to see diversity:

- Many non-Europeans see the Swiss as a fairly homogeneous people. But to the people of Switzerland, the Swiss are diverse, encompassing French-, German-, and Italian-speaking groups.
- Many Anglo-Americans lump "Latinos" together. Mexican Americans, Cuban Americans, and Puerto Ricans see important differences (Huddy & Virtanen, 1995).
- Sorority sisters perceive the members of any other sorority as less diverse than the mix in their own (Park & Rothbart, 1982).

In general, the greater our familiarity with a social group, the more we see its diversity (Brown & Wootton-Millward, 1993; Linville & others, 1989). The less our familiarity, the more we stereotype. Also, the smaller and less powerful the group, the less we attend to them and the more we stereotype (Fiske, 1993; Mullen & Hu, 1989). To those in power, we pay attention.

Perhaps you have noticed: *They*—the members of any racial group other than your own—even *look* alike. Many of us can recall embarrassing ourselves by confusing two people of another racial group, prompting the person we've misnamed to say, "You think we all look alike." Experiments by John Brigham, June Chance, Alvin Goldstein, and Roy Malpass in the United States and by Hayden Ellis in Scotland reveal that people of other races do in fact *seem* to look more alike than do people of one's own race (Chance & Goldstein, 1981, 1996; Ellis, 1981; Meissner & Brigham, 2001). When White students are shown faces of a

outgroup homogeneity effect
Perception of outgroup members as more similar to one another than are ingroup members. Thus "they are alike; we are diverse."

"Women are more like each other than men [are]."
—Lord (not Lady) Chesterfield

figure 9–6

The own-race bias.
White subjects more accurately recognize the faces of Whites than of Blacks; Black subjects more accurately recognize the faces of Blacks than of Whites. **Source:** From P. G. Devine and R. S. Malpass, 1985.

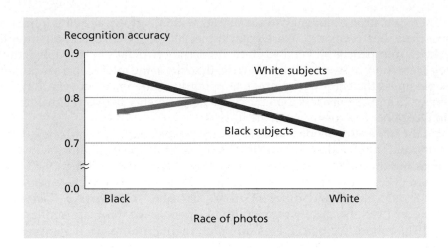

own-race bias
The tendency for people to more accurately recognize faces of their own race.

few White and a few Black individuals and then asked to pick these individuals out of a photographic lineup, they show an **own-race bias.** They more accurately recognize the White faces than the Black, and they often falsely recognize Black faces never before seen.

As Figure 9–6 illustrates, Blacks more easily recognize another Black than they do a White (Bothwell & others, 1989). And Hispanics more readily recognize another Hispanic whom they saw a couple of hours earlier than they do an Anglo (Platz & Hosch, 1988).

It's true outside the laboratory as well, as Daniel Wright and his colleagues (2001) found after either a Black or a White researcher approached Black and White people in South African and English shopping malls. When later asked to identify the researcher from lineups, people better recognized those of their own race. It's not that we cannot perceive differences among faces of another race. Rather, when looking at a face from another racial group we often attend, first, to race ("that man is Black") rather than to individual features. When viewing someone of our own race, we are less race conscious and more attentive to individual details (Levin, 2000).

Follow-up research also reveals an "own-age bias": People more accurately recognize people similar to their own age (Wright & Stroud, 2002).

DISTINCTIVENESS: PERCEIVING PEOPLE WHO STAND OUT

Other ways we perceive our worlds also breed stereotypes. Distinctive people and vivid or extreme occurrences often capture attention and distort judgments.

Distinctive people

Have you ever found yourself in a situation where you were the only person of your gender, race, or nationality? If so, your difference from the others probably made you more noticeable and the object of more attention. A Black in an otherwise White group, a man in an otherwise female group, or a woman in an otherwise male group seems more prominent and influential and to have exaggerated good and bad qualities (Crocker & McGraw, 1984; S. E. Taylor & others, 1979). When someone in a group is made salient (conspicuous), we tend to see that person as causing whatever happens (Taylor & Fiske, 1978). If we are positioned to look at Joe, an average group member, Joe will seem to have a greater than average influence on the group. People who capture our attention seem more responsible for what happens.

Have you noticed that people also define you by your most distinctive traits and behaviors? Tell people about someone who is a skydiver and a tennis player, report Lori Nelson and Dale Miller (1995), and they will think of the person as a skydiver. Asked to choose a gift book for the person, they will pick a skydiving book over a tennis book. A person who has both a pet snake and a pet dog is seen more as a snake owner than a dog owner. People also take note of those who violate expectations (Bettencourt & others, 1997). "Like a flower blooming in winter, intellect is more readily noticed where it is not expected," reflected Stephen Carter (1993, p. 54) on his experience as an African American intellectual. Such perceived distinctiveness makes it easier for highly capable job applicants from low-status groups to get noticed, though they also must work harder to prove that their abilities are genuine (Biernat & Kobrynowicz, 1997).

Ellen Langer and Lois Imber (1980) cleverly demonstrated the attention paid to distinctive people. They asked Harvard students to watch a video of a man reading. The students paid closer attention when they were led to think he was out of the ordinary—a cancer patient, a homosexual, or a millionaire. They detected characteristics that other viewers

Distinctive people, such as Houston Rockets 7'6" player Yao Ming, draw attention.

ignored, and their evaluation of him was more extreme. Those who thought the man was a cancer patient noticed distinctive facial characteristics and bodily movements and thus perceived him to be much more "different from most people" than did the other viewers. The extra attention we pay to distinctive people creates an illusion that they differ from others more than they really do. If people thought you had the IQ of a genius, they would probably notice things about you that otherwise would pass unnoticed.

When surrounded by Whites, Blacks sometimes detect people reacting to their distinctiveness. Many report being stared or glared at, being subject to insensitive comments, and receiving bad service (Swim & others, 1998). Sometimes we misperceive others as reacting to our distinctiveness. At Dartmouth College, researchers Robert Kleck and Angelo Strenta (1980) discovered this when they led college women to feel disfigured. The women thought the purpose of the experiment was to assess how someone would react to a facial scar created with theatrical makeup; the scar was on the right cheek, running from the ear to the mouth. Actually, the purpose was to see how the women themselves, when made to feel deviant, would perceive others' behavior toward them. After applying the makeup, the experimenter gave each woman a small hand mirror so she could see the authentic-looking scar. When she put the mirror down, he then applied some "moisturizer" to "keep the makeup from cracking." What the "moisturizer" really did was remove the scar.

The scene that followed was poignant. A young woman, feeling terribly self-conscious about her supposedly disfigured face, talked with another woman who sees no such disfigurement and knows nothing of what has gone on before. If you have ever felt similarly self-conscious—perhaps about a physical handicap, acne, even just a bad hair day—then perhaps you can sympathize with the self-conscious woman. Compared with women who were led to believe their conversational partners merely thought they had an allergy, the "disfigured" women became acutely sensitive to how their partners were looking at them. They rated their partners as more tense, distant, and patronizing. In fact, observers who later analyzed videotapes of how the partners treated "disfigured" persons could find no such differences in treatment. Self-conscious about being different, the "disfigured" women misinterpreted mannerisms and comments they would otherwise not have noticed.

Self-conscious interactions between a majority and minority person can therefore feel tense even when both are well intentioned (Devine & others, 1996). Tom, who is known to be gay, meets Bill, who is straight. Tolerant Bill wants to respond without prejudice. But feeling unsure of himself, he holds back a bit. Tom, expecting negative attitudes from most people, misreads Bill's hesitancy as hostility and responds with a seeming chip on his shoulder.

Anyone can experience this phenomenon. Majority group members (Manitoba White people in one study) often have beliefs—"meta-stereotypes"—about how minorities stereotype them (Vorauer & others, 1998). Even relatively unprejudiced Canadian Whites, Israeli Jews, or American Christians may sense that outgroup minorities stereotype them as prejudiced, arrogant, or patronizing. If George worries that Gamal perceives him as "your typical educated racist," he may be on guard when talking with Gamal.

People vary in *stigma consciousness*—in how likely they are to expect that others will stereotype them. Gays and lesbians, for example, differ in how much they suppose others "interpret all my behaviors" in terms of their homosexuality (Pinel, 1999). Seeing oneself as a victim of pervasive prejudice has its ups and downs (Branscombe & others, 1999; Dion, 1998). The downside is that those who perceive themselves as frequent victims live with the stress of stereotype threats and presumed antagonism and therefore experience lower well-being. While living in Europe, stigma-conscious Americans—people who perceive

www.mhhe.com/myers8
Visit the Online Learning Center for a scenario on stereotypes.

Self-consciousness about being different affects how we interpret others' behavior.

Europeans as resenting Americans—live more fretfully than those who feel accepted.

The upside is that perceptions of prejudice buffer individual self-esteem. If someone is nasty, "Well, it's not directed at me personally." Moreover, perceived prejudice and discrimination enhance our feelings of social identity and prepare us to join in collective social action.

Vivid cases

Our minds also use distinctive cases as a shortcut to judging groups. Are Blacks good athletes? "Well, there's Venus and Serena Williams and Shaquille O'Neal. Yeah, I'd say so." Note the thought processes at work here: Given limited experience with a particular social group, we recall examples of it and generalize from those (Sherman, 1996). Moreover, encountering exemplars of negative stereotypes (say, a hostile Black) can prime such stereotypes, leading us to minimize contact with the group (Hendersen-King & Nisbett, 1996).

Generalizing from single cases can cause problems. Vivid instances, though more available in memory, are seldom representative of the larger group. Exceptional athletes, though distinctive and memorable, are not the best basis for judging the distribution of athletic talent among an entire group.

Those in a numerical minority, being more distinctive, also may be numerically overestimated by the majority. What proportion of your country's population would you say is Muslim? People in non-Muslim countries often overestimate this proportion. In the United States, for example, less than 0.5 percent declared themselves Muslim in a 2002 Gallup survey (Strausberg, 2003). (See Figure 9–7.)

Or consider a 1990 Gallup poll report that the average American greatly overestimated the U.S. Black population and Hispanic populations (Figure 9–7). A 2002 Gallup poll found the average American thinking 21 percent of men were gay and 22 percent of women were lesbian (Robinson, 2002). Repeated surveys suggest that about 3 or 4 percent of men and 1 or 2 percent of women have a same-sex orientation (National Center for Health Statistics, 1991; Smith, 1998, Tarmann, 2002).

Myron Rothbart and his colleagues (1978) showed how distinctive cases also fuel stereotypes. They had University of Oregon students view 50 slides, each of which stated a man's height. For one group of students, 10 of the men were slightly over 6 feet (up to 6 feet, 4 inches). For other students, these 10 men were

figure 9–7
Overestimating minority populations.

Source: 1990 Gallup Poll (Gates, 1993).

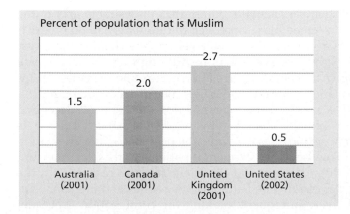

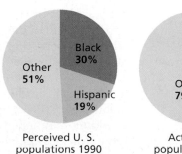

Perceived U. S. populations 1990

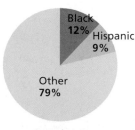

Actual U. S. populations 1990

well over 6 feet (up to 6 feet, 11 inches). When asked later how many of the men were over 6 feet, those given the moderately tall examples recalled 5 percent too many. Those given the extremely tall examples recalled 50 percent too many. In a follow-up experiment, students read descriptions of the actions of 50 men, 10 of whom had committed either nonviolent crimes, such as forgery, or violent crimes, such as rape. Of those shown the list with the violent crimes, most overestimated the number of criminal acts.

The attention-getting power of distinctive, extreme cases helps explain why middle-class people so greatly exaggerate the dissimilarities between themselves and the underclass. The less we know about a group, the more we are influenced by a few vivid cases (Quattrone & Jones, 1980). Contrary to stereotypes of "welfare queens" driving Cadillacs, people living in poverty generally share the aspirations of the middle class and would rather provide for themselves than accept public assistance (Cook & Curtin, 1987).

Distinctive events

Stereotypes assume a correlation between group membership and individuals' characteristics ("Italians are emotional," "Jews are shrewd," "Accountants are perfectionists"). Even under the best of conditions, our attentiveness to unusual occurrences can create illusory correlations. Because we are sensitive to distinctive events, the co-occurrence of two such events is especially noticeable—more noticeable than each of the times the unusual events do not occur together. Thus Rupert Brown and Amanda Smith (1989) found that British faculty members overestimated the number of (relatively rare, though noticeable) female senior faculty at their university.

David Hamilton and Robert Gifford (1976) demonstrated illusory correlation in a classic experiment. They showed students slides on which various people, members of "Group A" or "Group B," were said to have done something desirable or undesirable. For example, "John, a member of Group A, visited a sick friend in the hospital." Twice as many statements described members of Group A as Group B, but both groups did nine desirable acts for every four undesirable behaviors. Since both Group B and the undesirable acts were less frequent, their co-occurrence—for example, "Allen, a member of Group B, dented the fender of a parked car and didn't leave his name"—was an unusual combination that caught people's attention. The students therefore overestimated the frequency with which the "minority" group (B) acted undesirably, and they judged Group B more harshly.

Remember, Group B members actually committed undesirable acts in the same proportion as Group A members. Moreover, the students had no preexisting biases for or against Group B, and they received the information more systematically than daily experience ever offers it. Although researchers debate why it happens, they agree that illusory correlation occurs and provides yet another source for the formation of racial stereotypes (Berndsen & others, 2002).

The mass media reflect and feed this phenomenon. When a self-described homosexual murders or sexually abuses someone, homosexuality often gets mentioned. When a heterosexual does the same, the person's sexual orientation is seldom mentioned. Likewise, when ex-mental patients Mark Chapman and John Hinckley, Jr., shot John Lennon and President Reagan, respectively, the assailants' mental histories commanded attention. Assassins and mental hospitalization are both relatively infrequent, making the combination especially newsworthy. Such reporting adds to the illusion of a large correlation between (1) violent tendencies and (2) homosexuality or mental hospitalization.

Unlike the students who judged Groups A and B, we often have preexisting biases. David Hamilton's further research with Terrence Rose (1980) reveals that our preexisting stereotypes can lead us to "see" correlations that aren't there. The researchers had University of California Santa Barbara students read sentences in which various adjectives described the members of different occupational groups ("Doug, an accountant, is timid and thoughtful"). In actuality, each occupation was described equally often by each adjective; accountants, doctors, and salespeople were equally often timid, wealthy, and talkative. The students, however, *thought* they had more often read descriptions of timid accountants, wealthy doctors, and talkative salespeople. Their stereotyping led them to perceive correlations that weren't there, thus helping to perpetuate the stereotypes. To believe is to see.

ATTRIBUTION: IS IT A JUST WORLD?

In explaining others' actions, we frequently commit what Chapter 3 called the fundamental attribution error: We attribute their behavior so much to their inner dispositions that we discount important situational forces. The error occurs partly because our attention focuses on the persons, not the situation. A person's race or sex is vivid and gets attention; the situational forces working upon that person are usually less visible. Slavery was often overlooked as an explanation for slave behavior; the behavior was instead attributed to the slaves' own nature. Until recently, the same was true of how we explained the perceived differences between women and men. Because gender-role constraints were hard to see, we attributed men's and women's behavior solely to their innate dispositions. The more people assume that human traits are fixed dispositions, the stronger are their stereotypes (Levy & others, 1998).

Group-serving bias

Thomas Pettigrew (1979, 1980) showed how attribution errors bias people's explanations of group members' behaviors. We grant members of our own group the benefit of the doubt: "She donated because she has a good heart; he refused because he had to under the circumstances." When explaining acts by members of other groups, we more often assume the worst: "He donated to gain favor; she refused because she's selfish." Hence, as we noted earlier in this chapter, the shove that Whites perceive as mere "horsing around" when done by another White becomes a "violent gesture" when done by a Black.

Positive behavior by outgroup members is more often dismissed. It may be seen as a "special case" ("He is certainly bright and hardworking—not at all like other . . ."), as owing to luck or some special advantage ("She probably got admitted just because her med school had to fill its quota for women applicants"), as demanded by the situation ("Under the circumstances, what could the cheap Scot do but pay the whole check?"), or as attributable to extra effort ("Asian students get better grades because they're so compulsive"). Disadvantaged groups and groups that stress modesty (such as the Chinese) exhibit less of this **group-serving bias** (Fletcher & Ward, 1989; Heine & Lehman, 1997; Jackson & others, 1993).

The group-serving bias can subtly color our language. A team of University of Padova (Italy) researchers led by Anne Maass (1995, 1999) has found that

group-serving bias
Explaining away outgroup members' positive behaviors; also attributing negative behaviors to their dispositions (while excusing such behavior by one's own group).

table 9–1 **How self-enhancing social identities support stereotypes**

	Ingroup	Outgroup
Attitude	Favoritism	Denigration
Perceptions	Heterogeneity (we differ)	Homogeneity (they're alike)
Attributions for negative behavior	To situations	To dispositions

positive behaviors by another ingroup member are often described as general dispositions (for example, "Lucy is helpful"). When performed by an outgroup member, the same behavior is often described as a specific, isolated act ("Maria opened the door for the man with the cane"). With negative behavior, the specificity reverses: "Joe shoved her" versus "Juan was aggressive." Maass calls this group-serving bias the *linguistic intergroup bias*.

Earlier we noted that blaming the victim can justify the blamer's own superior status (Table 9–1). Blaming occurs as people attribute an outgroup's failures to its members' flawed dispositions, notes Miles Hewstone (1990): "They fail because they're stupid; we fail because we didn't try." If women, Blacks, or Jews have been abused, they must somehow have brought it on themselves. When the British made a group of German civilians walk through the Bergen-Belsen concentration camp at the close of World War II, one German responded: "What terrible criminals these prisoners must have been to receive such treatment."

The just-world phenomenon

In a series of experiments conducted at the Universities of Waterloo and Kentucky, Melvin Lerner and his colleagues (Lerner & Miller, 1978; Lerner, 1980) discovered that merely *observing* another innocent person being victimized is enough to make the victim seem less worthy. Imagine that you, along with some others, are participating in one of Lerner's studies—supposedly on the perception of emotional cues (Lerner & Simmons, 1966). One of the participants, a confederate, is selected by lottery to perform a memory task. This person receives painful shocks whenever she gives a wrong answer. You and the others note her emotional responses.

After watching the victim receive these apparently painful shocks, the experimenter asks you to evaluate her. How would you respond? With compassionate sympathy? We might expect so. As Ralph Waldo Emerson wrote, "The martyr cannot be dishonored." On the contrary, the experiments revealed that martyrs can be dishonored. When observers were powerless to alter the victim's fate, they often rejected and devalued the victim. Juvenal, the Roman satirist, anticipated these results: "The Roman mob follows after Fortune . . . and hates those who have been condemned."

Linda Carli and her colleagues (1989, 1999) report that this **just-world phenomenon** colors our impressions of rape victims. Carli had people read detailed descriptions of interactions between a man and a woman. For example, a woman and her boss meet for dinner, go to his home, and each have a glass of wine. Some read a scenario that has a happy ending: "Then he led me to the couch. He held my hand and asked me to marry him." In hindsight, people find the ending unsurprising and admire the man's and woman's character traits.

just-world phenomenon
The tendency of people to believe the world is just and that people therefore get what they deserve and deserve what they get.

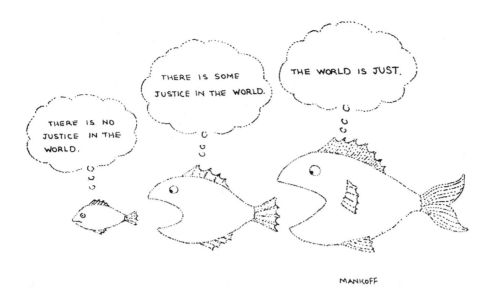

The just-world phenomenon.

Others read the same scenario with a different ending: "But then he became very rough and pushed me onto the couch. He held me down on the couch and raped me." Given this ending, people see it as inevitable and blame the woman for behavior that seems faultless in the first scenario.

Lerner (1980) noted that such disparaging of hapless victims results from the human need to believe that, "I am a just person living in a just world, a world where people get what they deserve." From early childhood, he argues, we are taught that good is rewarded and evil punished. Hard work and virtue pay dividends; laziness and immorality do not. From this it is but a short leap to assuming that those who flourish must be good and those who suffer must deserve their fate.

The classic illustration is the Old Testament story of Job, a good person who suffers terrible misfortune. Job's friends surmise that, this being a just world, Job must have done something wicked to elicit such terrible suffering. Like Job's friends, Americans by better than a two-to-one margin agree, "Most people who don't get ahead should not blame the system, they have only themselves to blame" (Morin, 1998). Opposition to affirmative action programs that redress past discrimination therefore grows not only from prejudice but also from perceiving affirmative action as violating norms of justice and fairness (Bobocel & others, 1998).

This line of research suggests that people are indifferent to social injustice not because they have no concern for justice but because they see no injustice. Those who assume a just world believe that rape victims must have behaved seductively (Borgida & Brekke, 1985), that battered spouses must have provoked their beatings (Summers & Feldman, 1984), that poor people don't deserve better (Furnham & Gunter, 1984), and that sick people are responsible for their illnesses (Gruman & Sloan, 1983). Such beliefs enable successful people to reassure themselves that they, too, deserve what they have. The wealthy and healthy can see their own good fortune, and others' misfortune, as justly deserved. Linking good fortune with virtue and misfortune with moral failure enables the fortunate to feel pride and to avoid responsibility for the unfortunate.

People loathe a loser even when the loser's misfortune quite obviously stems from mere bad luck. People *know* that gambling outcomes are just good or bad luck and should not affect their evaluations of the gambler. Still, they can't resist playing Monday-morning quarterback—judging people by their results. Ignoring the fact that reasonable decisions can bring bad results, they judge losers as less competent (Baron & Hershey, 1988). Lawyers and stock market speculators may similarly judge themselves by their outcomes, becoming smug after successes and self-reproachful after failures. Talent and initiative are not unrelated to success. But the just-world assumption discounts the uncontrollable factors that can derail one's best efforts.

Summing up

A fresh look at prejudice in recent research shows how the stereotyping that underlies prejudice is a by-product of our thinking—our ways of simplifying the world. First, clustering people into categories exaggerates the uniformity within a group and the differences between groups. Second, a distinctive individual, such as a lone minority person, has a compelling quality. Such persons make us aware of differences that would otherwise go unnoticed. The occurrence of two distinctive events—perhaps a minority person committing an unusual crime—helps create an *illusory correlation* between people and behavior. Third, attributing others' behavior to their dispositions can lead to the *group-serving bias*: assigning outgroup members' negative behavior to their natural character while explaining away their positive behaviors. Blaming the victim also results from the common presumption that because this is a just world, people get what they deserve.

What are the consequences of prejudice?

Beyond the causes of prejudice, it is important to examine its consequences. Stereotypes can be self-perpetuating—their existence can prevent their change. Stereotypes can also create their own reality. Even if they are initially untrue, their existence can make them become true. The negative allegations of prejudice can also undermine people's performance and affect how people interpret discrimination.

SELF-PERPETUATING STEREOTYPES

Prejudice is prejudgment. Prejudgments are inevitable: None of us is a dispassionate bookkeeper of social happenings, tallying evidence for and against our biases. Our prejudgments guide our attention, our interpretations, and our memories.

Whenever a member of a group behaves as expected, we duly note the fact; our prior belief is confirmed. When a member of a group behaves inconsistently with our expectation, we may interpret or explain away the behavior as due to special circumstances (Crocker & others, 1983). The contrast to a stereotype can also make someone seem exceptional. Telling some people that "Mary played basketball" and others that "Mark played basketball" may make Mary seem more athletic than Mark (Biernat, 2003). Stereotypes therefore influence how we

When people violate our stereotypes, we salvage the stereotype by splitting off a new subgroup stereotype, such as "senior Olympians."

construe someone's behavior (Kunda & Sherman-Williams, 1993, Sanbonmatsu & others, 1994; Stangor & McMillan, 1992).

Perhaps you, too, can recall a time when, try as you might, you could not overcome someone's opinion of you, a time when no matter what you did you were misinterpreted. Misinterpretations are likely when someone *expects* an unpleasant encounter with you (Wilder & Shapiro, 1989). William Ickes and his colleagues (1982) demonstrated this in an experiment with pairs of college-age men. As the men arrived, the experimenters falsely forewarned one member of each pair that the other person was "one of the unfriendliest people I've talked to lately." The two were then introduced and left alone together for five minutes. Students in another condition of the experiment were led to think the other participant was exceptionally friendly.

Those in both conditions were friendly to the new acquaintance. In fact, those who expected him to be *un*friendly went out of their way to be friendly, and their smiles and other friendly behaviors elicited a warm response. But unlike the positively biased students, those expecting an unfriendly person attributed this reciprocal friendliness to their own "kid-gloves" treatment of him. They afterward expressed more mistrust and dislike for the person and rated his behavior as less friendly. Despite their partner's actual friendliness, the negative bias induced these students to "see" hostilities lurking beneath his "forced smiles." They would never have seen it if they hadn't believed it.

"Labels act like shrieking sirens, deafening us to all finer discriminations that we might otherwise perceive."
—Gordon Allport, *The Nature of Prejudice*, 1954

We do notice information that is strikingly inconsistent with a stereotype, but even this information has less impact than might be expected. When we focus on an atypical example, we can salvage the stereotype by splitting off a new category (Brewer, 1988; Hewstone, 1994; Kunda & Oleson, 1995, 1997). The positive image that British schoolchildren form of their friendly school police officers (whom they perceive as a special category) doesn't improve their image of police officers in general (Hewstone & others, 1992). This **subtyping** putting people who deviate into a different class of people—helps maintain the stereotype that police officers are unfriendly and dangerous. A different way to accommodate the inconsistent information is to recognize that the stereotype does not apply for everyone in the category. Homeowners who have desirable Black neighbors can form a new and different stereotype of "professional, middle-class Blacks." This **subgrouping**—forming a subgroup stereotype—tends to lead to modest change in the stereotype as the stereotype becomes more differentiated (Richards & Hewstone, 2001). Subtypes are exceptions to the group; subgroups are acknowledged as a part of the overall group.

DISCRIMINATION'S IMPACT: THE SELF-FULFILLING PROPHECY

Attitudes may coincide with the social hierarchy not only as a rationalization for it but also because discrimination affects its victims. "One's reputation," wrote Gordon Allport, "cannot be hammered, hammered, hammered into one's head without doing something to one's character" (1958, p. 139). If we could snap our fingers and end all discrimination, it would be naive then to say, "The tough times are all over, folks! You can now put on suits or dresses and be attaché-carrying executives and professionals." When the oppression ends, its effects linger, like a societal hangover.

In *The Nature of Prejudice*, Allport catalogued 15 possible effects of victimization. Allport believed these reactions were reducible to two basic types—those that involve blaming oneself (withdrawal, self-hate, aggression against one's own group) and those that involve blaming external causes (fighting back, suspiciousness, increased group pride). If the net results are negative—say, higher rates of crime—people can use them to justify the discrimination that helps maintain them: "If we let those people in our nice neighborhood, property values will plummet."

Does discrimination affect its victims in this way? We must be careful not to overstate the point. The soul and style of Black culture is for many a proud heritage, not just a response to victimization (Jones, 2003). Thus, while White youth are learning to de-emphasize ethnic differences and avoid stereotypes, African American youth "are increasingly taking pride in their ethnicity and positively valuing ethnic differences," noted Charles Judd and his co-researchers (1995). Cultural differences need not imply social deficits.

Nevertheless, social beliefs *can* be self-confirming, as demonstrated in a clever pair of experiments by Carl Word, Mark Zanna, and Joel Cooper (1974). In the first experiment, Princeton University White men interviewed White and Black research assistants posing as job applicants. When the applicant was Black, the interviewers sat farther away, ended the interview 25 percent sooner, and made 50 percent more speech errors than when the applicant was White. Imagine being interviewed by someone who sat at a distance, stammered, and ended the interview rather quickly. Would it affect your performance or your feelings about the interviewer?

subtyping
Accommodating groups of individuals who deviate from one's stereotype by thinking of them as a special category of people with different properties.

subgrouping
Accommodating groups of individuals who deviate from one's stereotype by forming a new stereotype about this subset of the group.

"It is understandable that the suppressed people should develop an intense hostility towards a culture whose existence they make possible by their work, but in whose wealth they have too small a share."
—Sigmund Freud, *The Future of an Illusion*, 1927

To find out, the researchers conducted a second experiment in which trained interviewers treated students as the interviewers in the first experiment had treated either the White or Black applicants. When videotapes of the interviews were later rated, those who were treated like the Blacks in the first experiment seemed more nervous and less effective. Moreover, the interviewees could themselves sense a difference; those treated as were the Blacks judged their interviewers to be less adequate and less friendly. The experimenters concluded part of "the 'problem' of Black performance resides . . . within the interaction setting itself." As with other self-fulfilling prophecies (recall Chapter 3), prejudice affects its targets (Swim & Stangor, 1998).

"If we foresee evil in our fellow man, we tend to provoke it; if good, we elicit it."
—Gordon Allport, *The Nature of Prejudice*, 1958

STEREOTYPE THREAT

Placed in a situation where others expect you to perform poorly, your anxiety may cause you to confirm the belief. I am a short guy in my early 60s. When I join a pickup basketball game with bigger, younger players, I often suspect that they expect me to be a detriment to their team and that tends to undermine my confidence and performance. Claude Steele and his colleagues call this phenomenon **stereotype threat**—a self-confirming apprehension that one will be evaluated based on a negative stereotype (Steele, 1997; Steele & others, 2002).

stereotype threat
A disruptive concern, when facing a negative stereotype, that one will be evaluated based on a negative stereotype. Unlike self-fulfilling prophecies that hammer one's reputation into one's self-concept, stereotype threat situations have immediate effects.

In several experiments, Steven Spencer, Steele, and Diane Quinn (1999) gave a very difficult math test to men and women students who had similar math backgrounds. When told that there were *no* gender differences on the test and no evaluation of any group stereotype, the women's performance consistently equaled the men's. Told that there *was* a gender difference, the women dramatically confirmed the stereotype (Figure 9–8). Frustrated by the extremely difficult test questions, they apparently felt added apprehension, which undermined their performances.

The media can provoke stereotype threat. Paul Davies and his colleagues (2002) had women and men watch a series of commercials expecting that they would be tested for their memory of details. For half the participants, the

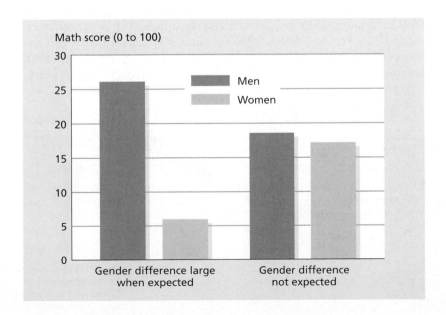

figure 9–8

Stereotype vulnerability and women's math performance.
Steven Spencer, Claude Steele, and Diane Quinn (1999) gave equally capable men and women a difficult math test. When participants were led to believe there were gender differences on the test, women scored lower than men. When the threat of confirming the stereotype was removed (when gender differences were not expected), women did just as well as men.

Why do non-White students tend to underachieve? Go to the *SocialSense* CD-ROM to view a video clip on Claude Steele's stereotype threat.

"Math class is tough!"
—"Teen talk" Barbie doll (later removed from the market)

figure 9–9

Stereotype threat.

Threat from facing a negative stereotype can produce performance deficits and disidentification.

commercials contained only neutral stimuli; for the other half, some of the commercials contained images of "air-headed" women. After seeing the stereotypic images, women not only performed worse than men on a math test, they also reported less interest in obtaining a math or science major or entering a math or science career.

Might racial stereotypes be similarly self-fulfilling? Steele and Joshua Aronson (1995) confirmed that they are when giving difficult verbal abilities tests to Whites and Blacks. Blacks underperformed Whites only when taking the tests under conditions high in stereotype threat. Jeff Stone and his colleagues (1999) report that stereotype threat affects athletic performance, too. Blacks did worse than usual when a golf task was framed as a test of "sports intelligence," and Whites did worse when it was a test of "natural athletic ability." "When people are reminded of a negative stereotype about themselves—'White men can't jump' or 'Black men can't think'—it can adversely affect performance," Stone (2000) surmised.

If you tell students they are at risk of failure (as is often suggested by minority support programs), the stereotype may erode their performance, says Steele (1997), and cause them to "disidentify" with school and seek self-esteem elsewhere (Figure 9–9). Indeed, as African American students move from eighth to tenth grade, there is a weakening connection between their school performance and self-esteem (Osborne, 1995). Moreover, students led to think they have benefited from gender- or race-based preferences in gaining admission to a college or an academic group tend to underperform those who are led to feel competent (Brown & others, 2000). Better, therefore, to challenge students to believe in their potential, observes Steele. In another of his research team's experiments, Black students responded well to criticism of their writing when also told, "I wouldn't go to the trouble of giving you this feedback if I didn't think, based on what I've read in your letter, that you are capable of meeting the higher standard that I mentioned" (Cohen & others, 1999).

But how does stereotype threat undermine performance? One rout is cognitive. Stereotype threat is distracting: The effort it takes to dismiss its allegations increases mental demands and decreases working memory (Croizet & others, 2004; Schmader & Johns, 2003; Steele & others, 2002). Another effect is motivational: Worrying about mistakes under stereotype threat can impair a person's performance (Keller & Dauenheimer, 2003; Seibt & Forster, 2004), and the physiological arousal that accompanies stereotype threat can impair

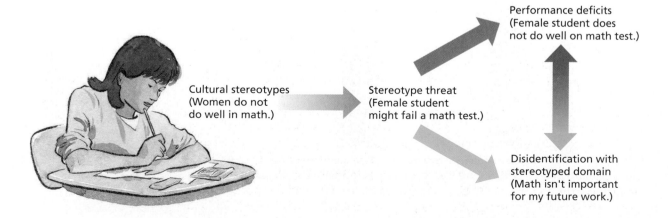

the story behind the research:
Claude Steele on stereotype threat

During a committee meeting on campus diversity at the University of Michigan in the late 1980's, I noticed an interesting fact: at every level of entering SAT score, minority students were getting lower college grades than their non-minority counterparts. Soon, Steven Spencer, Joshua Aronson and I found that this was a national phenomenon; it happened at most colleges and it happened to other groups whose abilities were negatively stereotyped, such as women in advanced math classes. This underperformance wasn't caused by group differences in preparation. It happened at all levels of preparation (as measured by SATs).

Eventually, we produced this underperformance in the laboratory by simply having motivated people perform a difficult task in a domain where their group was negatively stereotyped. We also found that we could eliminate this underperformance by making the same task irrelevant to the stereotype, by removing the "stereotype threat," as we had come to call it. This latter finding spawned more research: figuring out how to reduce stereotype threat and its ill effects. Through this work, we have gained an appreciation for two big things: first, the importance of life context in shaping psychological functioning, and second, the importance of social identities like age, race, and gender in shaping that context.

Claude Steele

performance on hard tests (O'Brien & Crandall, 2003; Ben-Zeev, Fein & Inzlicht, 2004). (Recall from Chapter 8, Group Influence, that arousal from others; presence tends to strengthen performance on easy tasks and disrupt performance on hard tasks.)

If stereotype threats can disrupt performance, could *positive* stereotypes enhance it? Margaret Shih, Todd Pittinsky, and Nalini Ambady (1999) confirmed this possibility. When Asian American females were asked biographical questions that reminded them of their gender identity before taking a math test, their performance plunged (compared with a control group). When similarly reminded of their Asian identity, their performance rose. Negative stereotypes disrupt performance, and positive stereotypes, it seems, facilitate performance.

DO STEREOTYPES BIAS JUDGMENTS OF INDIVIDUALS?

Yes, stereotypes bias judgments, but here is good news: *People often evaluate individuals more positively than the groups they compose* (Miller & Felicio, 1990). Anne Locksley, Eugene Borgida, and Nancy Brekke have found that once someone knows a person, "Stereotypes may have minimal, if any, impact on judgments about that person" (Borgida & others, 1981; Locksley & others, 1980, 1982). They discovered this by giving University of Minnesota students anecdotal information about recent incidents in the life of "Nancy." In a supposed transcript of a telephone conversation, Nancy told a friend how she responded to three different situations (for example, being harassed by a seedy character while shopping). Some of the students read transcripts portraying Nancy responding assertively (telling the seedy character to leave); others read a report of passive responses (simply ignoring the character until he finally drifts away). Still other students received the same information, except that the person was named "Paul" instead of Nancy. A day later the students predicted how Nancy (or Paul) would respond to other situations.

Did knowing the person's gender have any effect on these predictions? None at all. Expectations of the person's assertiveness were influenced solely by what the students had learned about that individual the day before. Even their judgments of masculinity and femininity were unaffected by knowing the person's gender. Gender stereotypes had been left on the shelf; the students evaluated Nancy and Paul as individuals.

The explanation for this finding is implied by an important principle discussed in Chapter 3. Given (1) general (base-rate) information about a group and (2) trivial but vivid information about a particular group member, the vivid information usually overwhelms the effect of the general information. This is especially so when the person doesn't fit our image of the typical group member (Fein & Hilton, 1992; Lord & others, 1991). For example, imagine yourself being told how *most* people in a conformity experiment actually behaved and then viewing a brief interview with one of the supposed participants. Would you react like the typical viewer—by guessing the person's behavior from the interview, ignoring the base-rate information on how most people actually behaved?

People often believe such stereotypes, yet ignore them when given vivid, anecdotal information. Thus, many people believe "politicians are crooks" but "our Senator Jones has integrity." (No wonder people have such a low opinion of politicians yet usually reelect their own representatives.)

These findings resolve a puzzling set of findings considered early in this chapter. We know that gender stereotypes (1) are strong yet (2) have little effect on people's judgments of work attributed to a man or a woman. Now we see why. People may have strong gender stereotypes, yet ignore them when judging a particular individual.

Strong stereotypes matter

However, *strong* and seemingly relevant stereotypes do color our judgments of individuals (Krueger & Rothbart, 1988). When Thomas Nelson, Monica Biernat, and Melvin Manis (1990) had students estimate the heights of individually pictured men and women, they judged the individual men as taller—even when their heights were equal, even when they were told that in this sample sex didn't predict height, and even when they were offered cash rewards for accuracy.

In a follow-up study, Nelson, Michele Acker, and Manis (1996) showed University of Michigan students photos of other students from the university's engineering and nursing schools, along with descriptions of each student's interests. Even when informed that the sample contained an equal number of males and females from each school, the same description was judged more likely to come from a nursing student when attached to a female face. Thus, even when a strong gender stereotype is known to be irrelevant, it has an irresistible force.

Stereotypes bias interpretations and memories

Stereotypes also color how we interpret events, note David Dunning and David Sherman (1997). If people are told, "Some felt the politician's statements were untrue," they will infer that the politician was lying. If told, "Some felt the physicist's statements were untrue," they infer only that the physicist was mistaken. When told two people had an altercation, people perceive it as a fistfight if told it involved two lumberjacks, but as a verbal spat if told it involved two marriage counselors. A person concerned about her physical condition seems vain if she is a model but health conscious if she is a triathlete. Indeed, individuals will often later "recognize" false descriptions of an event that fit their stereotype-influenced interpretations. As a prison guides and constrains its inmates, conclude Dunning and Sherman, the "cognitive prison" of our stereotypes guides and constrains our impressions.

Sometimes we make judgments, or begin interacting with someone, with little to go on but our stereotype. In such cases stereotypes can strongly bias our interpretations and memories of people. For example, Charles Bond and his colleagues (1988) found that, after getting to know their patients, White psychiatric nurses put Black and White patients in physical restraints equally often. But they restrained *incoming* Black patients more often than their White counterparts. With little else to go on, stereotypes mattered.

Such bias can also operate more subtly. In an experiment by John Darley and Paget Gross (1983), Princeton University students viewed a videotape of a fourth-grade girl, Hannah. The tape depicted her either in a depressed urban neighborhood, supposedly the child of lower-class parents, or in an affluent suburban setting, the child of professional parents. Asked to guess Hannah's ability level in various subjects, both groups of viewers refused to use Hannah's class background to prejudge her ability level; each group rated her ability level at her grade level. Other students also viewed a second videotape, showing Hannah taking an oral achievement test in which she got some questions right and some wrong.

Those who had previously been introduced to upper-class Hannah judged her answers as showing high ability and later recalled her getting most questions right; those who had met lower-class Hannah judged her ability as below grade level and recalled her missing almost half the questions. But remember: The second videotape was *identical* for both groups. So we see that, when stereotypes are strong and the information about someone is ambiguous

People sometimes maintain general prejudices (such as against gays and lesbians) without applying their prejudice to particular individuals whom they know and respect, such as Ellen DeGeneres and Elton John.

(unlike the cases of Nancy and Paul), stereotypes can *subtly* bias our judgments of individuals.

Finally, we evaluate people more extremely when their behavior violates our stereotypes (Bettencourt & others, 1997). A woman who rebukes someone cutting in front of her in a movie line ("Shouldn't you go to the end of the line?") may seem more assertive than a man who reacts similarly (Manis & others, 1988). Aided by the testimony of social psychologist Susan Fiske and her colleagues (1991), the U.S. Supreme Court saw such stereotyping at work when Price Waterhouse, one of the nation's top accounting firms, denied Ann Hopkins's promotion to partner. Among the 88 candidates for promotion, Hopkins, the only woman, was number one in the amount of business she brought in to the company and, by all accounts, was hardworking and exacting. By other accounts, she needed a "course at charm school," where she could learn to "walk more femininely, talk more femininely, dress more femininely. . . ." After reflecting on the case and on stereotyping research, the Supreme Court in 1989 decided that encouraging men to be aggressive, but not women, is to act "on the basis of gender":

> We sit not to determine whether Ms. Hopkins is nice, but to decide whether the partners reacted negatively to her personality because she is a woman. . . . An employer who objects to aggressiveness in women but whose positions require this trait places women in an intolerable Catch 22: out of a job if they behave aggressively and out of a job if they don't.

Summing up

Prejudice and stereotyping has important consequences, especially when strongly held, when judging unknown individuals, and when deciding policies regarding whole groups. Once formed, stereotypes tend to perpetuate themselves and resist change. They also create their own realities through self-fulfilling prophecies. Prejudice can also undermine people's performance through stereotype threat, by making people apprehensive that others will view them stereotypically.

Personal Postscript: Can we reduce prejudice?

Social psychologists have been more successful in explaining prejudice than in alleviating it. Because prejudice results from many interrelated factors, there is no simple remedy. Nevertheless, we can now anticipate techniques for reducing prejudice (discussed further in chapters to come): If unequal status breeds prejudice, then we can seek to create cooperative, equal-status relationships. If prejudice often rationalizes discriminatory behavior, then we can mandate nondiscrimination. If social institutions support prejudice, then we can pull out those supports (for example, persuade the media to model interracial harmony). If outgroups seem more unlike one's own group than they really are, then we can make efforts to personalize their members. If automatic prejudices lead us to engage in behaviors that make us feel guilty, then we can use this guilt to motivate us to break the prejudice habit.

Since the end of World War II in 1945 a number of these antidotes have been applied, and racial and gender prejudices have indeed diminished. Social-psychological research also has helped break down discriminatory barriers.

"We risked a lot by testifying on Ann Hopkins's behalf, no doubt about it," Susan Fiske (1999) later wrote.

> As far as we knew, no one had ever introduced the social psychology of stereotyping in a gender case before. . . . If we succeeded, we would get the latest stereotyping research out of the dusty journals and into the muddy trenches of legal debate, where it might be useful. If we failed, we might hurt the client, slander social psychology, and damage my reputation as a scientist. At the time I had no idea that the testimony would eventually make it successfully through the Supreme Court.

It now remains to be seen whether, during the next century, progress will continue . . . or whether, as could easily happen in a time of increasing population and diminishing resources, antagonisms will again erupt into open hostility.

What do you think?

Describe an incident where you have observed or experienced racial or gender prejudice. What was the source of the prejudice? The motivation? What might be done to diminish this type of prejudice?

Making the Social Connection

Claude Steele's work on stereotype threat is only one of his contributions to social psychology. In Chapter 4, for example, we considered his work on self-affirmation. Have you ever been concerned that you were being stereotyped? Go to the *SocialSense* CD-ROM to view Steele's discussion of what research tells us about stereotyping's impact on its targets.

chapter 10

Aggression: Hurting Others

"Our behavior toward each other is the strangest, most unpredictable, and most unaccountable of all the phenomena with which we are obliged to live. In all of nature, there is nothing so threatening to humanity as humanity itself."

Lewis Thomas (1981)

although Woody Allen's tongue-in-cheek prediction that "by 1990 kidnapping will be the dominant mode of social interaction" went unfulfilled, the years since have hardly been serene. The horror of 9/11 may have been the most dramatic violence, but in terms of human lives, it was not the most catastrophic. About the same time, the human carnage from tribal warfare in the Congo was claiming an estimated 3 million lives, some hacked to death with machetes, many others dying of starvation and disease after fleeing in terror from their villages (Sengupta, 2003). Neighboring Rwandans, where some 750,000 people—including half the Tutsi population—were slaughtered in the genocidal summer of 1994, understood this human capacity for carnage (Staub, 1999).

Such hatred and destruction is hardly peculiar to the post-2000 Middle Eastern and African worlds. Worldwide, more than $2 billion per day is spent on arms and armies—$2 billion that could feed, educate, and protect the environment of the world's impoverished millions. During the last century, some 250 wars killed 110 million people, enough to populate a "nation of the dead" with more than the combined population of France, Belgium, the Netherlands,

figure 10–1

The bloodiest century.

Twentieth-century humanity was the most educated, and homicidal, in history (data from Renner, 1999). Adding in genocides and human-made famines, there were approximately 182 million "deaths by mass unpleasantness" (White, 2000).

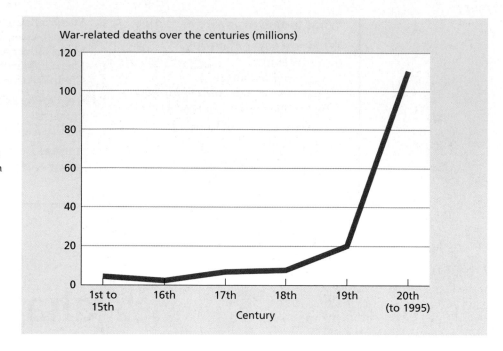

War-related deaths over the centuries (millions)

"Every gun that is made, every warship launched, every rocket fired signifies, in the final sense, a theft from those who hunger and are not fed, those who are cold and are not clothed."

—President Dwight Eisenhower, Speech to the American Society of Newspaper Editors, 1953

"Is there any way of delivering mankind from the menace of war?"

—Albert Einstein, letter to Sigmund Freud, 1932

Denmark, Finland, Norway, and Sweden (Figure 10–1). The tolls came not only from the world wars, but also from genocides, including the 1915 to 1923 genocide of Armenians by the Ottoman Empire, the 1971 Pakistani genocide of 3 million Bangladeshis, and the 1.5 million Cambodians murdered in a reign of terror starting in 1975 (Sternberg, 2003). As Hitler's genocide of millions of Jews, Stalin's genocide of millions of Russians, Mao's genocide of millions of Chinese, and the early Americans' genocide of millions of Native Americans makes plain, the human potential for extraordinary cruelty crosses the globe.

Are we like the mythical Minotaur, half human, half beast? What explains that midsummer day in 1941 when the non-Jewish half of the Polish town of Jebwabne murdered the other half in a macabre frenzy of violence, leaving only a dozen or so survivors among the 1,600 Jews (Gross, 2001)? What explains this propensity for hurt?

- Is aggression biologically predisposed, or do we learn it?
- What circumstances prompt hostile outbursts?
- Do the media influence aggression?
- How might we reduce aggression?

In this chapter, these are our questions. First, however, we need to clarify the term "aggression."

What is aggression?

The original Thugs, members of a criminal fraternity in northern India, were aggressing when between 1550 and 1850 they strangled more than 2 million people and claimed to do so in the service of a goddess. But people also use "aggressive" to describe a dynamic salesperson. Social psychologists distinguish such self-assured, energetic, go-getting behavior from behavior that hurts, harms, or destroys. The former is assertiveness, the latter aggression.

A nineteenth-century engraving of Spanish warriors conquering Montezuma's Aztec empire.

Chapter 5 defines **aggression** as physical or verbal behavior intended to hurt someone. This excludes auto accidents, dental treatments, sidewalk collisions, and assisted suicide. It includes slaps, direct insults, even gossipy "digs," and by having people decide how much to hurt someone, such as how much electric shock to impose.

This definition covers two distinct types of aggression. Animals exhibit *social* aggression, characterized by displays of rage, and *silent* aggression, as when a predator stalks its prey. Social and silent aggression involve separate brain regions. In humans, psychologists label the two types "hostile" and "instrumental" aggression. **Hostile aggression** springs from anger, its goal is to injure. **Instrumental aggression** aims to hurt only as a means to some other end.

Most terrorism is instrumental aggression. "What nearly all suicide terrorist campaigns have in common is a specific secular and strategic goal," concludes Robert Pape (2003) after studying all suicide bombings from 1980 to 2001. That goal is "to compel liberal democracies to withdraw military forces from territory that the terrorists consider to be their homeland." In 2003, American and British leaders justified attacking Iraq not as a hostile effort to kill Iraqis, but as an instrumental act of liberation and of self-defense against presumed weapons of mass destruction. Hostile aggression is "hot"; instrumental aggression is "cool."

Most murders are hostile. Approximately half erupt from arguments, while others result from romantic triangles or

aggression
Physical or verbal behavior intended to hurt someone.

hostile aggression
Aggression driven by anger and performed as an end in itself (also called affective aggression).

instrumental aggression
Aggression that is a means to some other end.

"Of course, we'll never actually *use* it against a potential enemy, but it will allow us to negotiate from a position of strength."

Humanity has armed its capacity for destruction without comparably arming its capacity for the inhibition of aggression.
Reprinted with permission of General Media Magazines.

brawls while under the influence of alcohol or narcotics (Ash, 1999). Such murders are impulsive, emotional outbursts—which helps explain why data from 110 nations show that enforcing the death penalty has not resulted in fewer homicides (Costanzo, 1998; Wilkes, 1987). Some murders and many other violent acts of retribution and sexual coercion, however, are instrumental (Felson, 2000). Most of Chicago's more than 1,000 mob murders after 1919 were cool and calculated.

What are some theories of aggression?

In analyzing causes of hostile and instrumental aggression, social psychologists have focused on three big ideas: (1) There is a biologically rooted aggressive drive; (2) aggression is a natural response to frustration; and (3) aggressive behavior is learned.

AGGRESSION AS BIOLOGY

Philosophers have debated whether our human nature is fundamentally that of a benign, contented, "noble savage" or that of a brute. The first view, argued by the eighteenth-century French philosopher Jean-Jacques Rousseau (1712–1778), blames society, not human nature, for social evils. The second idea, associated with the English philosopher Thomas Hobbes (1588–1679), sees society's laws as necessary to restrain and control the human brute. In the twentieth century, the "brutish" view—that aggressive drive is inborn and thus inevitable—was argued by Sigmund Freud in Vienna and Konrad Lorenz in Germany.

Instinct theory and evolutionary psychology

Freud speculated that human aggression springs from a self-destructive impulse. It redirects toward others the energy of a primitive death urge (which, loosely speaking, he called the "death instinct"). Lorenz, an animal behavior expert, saw aggression as adaptive rather than self-destructive. Both agreed that aggressive energy is **instinctual** (unlearned and universal). If not discharged, it supposedly builds up until it explodes or until an appropriate stimulus "releases" it, like a mouse releasing a mousetrap. Although Lorenz (1976) also argued that we have innate mechanisms for inhibiting aggression (such as making ourselves defenseless), he feared the implications of arming our "fighting instinct" without arming our inhibitions. The imbalanced focus on releasing aggressive tendencies helps explain why more people were killed in twentieth-century wars than in all prior wars.

instinctive behavior
An innate, unlearned behavior pattern exhibited by all members of a species.

The idea that aggression is an instinct collapsed as the list of supposed human instincts grew to include nearly every conceivable human behavior. Nearly 6,000 supposed instincts were enumerated in one 1924 survey of social science books (Barash, 1979). The social scientists had tried to *explain* social behavior by *naming* it. It's tempting to play this explaining-by-naming game: "Why do sheep stay together?" "Because of their herd instinct." "How do you know they have a herd instinct?" "Just look at them: They're always together!"

Instinct theory also fails to account for the variations in aggressiveness from person to person and culture to culture. How would a shared human instinct for aggression explain the difference between the peaceful Iroquois before White invaders came and the hostile Iroquois after the invasion (Hornstein,

1976)? Although aggression *is* biologically influenced, the human propensity to aggress seems not to qualify as instinctive behavior.

Our distant ancestors nevertheless sometimes found aggression adaptive, note evolutionary psychologists David Buss and Todd Shackelford (1997). Aggressive behavior was a strategy for gaining resources, defending against attack, intimidating or eliminating male rivals for females, and deterring mates from sexual infidelity. In some preindustrial societies, being a good warrior made for higher status and reproductive opportunities (Roach, 1998). The adaptive value of aggression, Buss and Shackelford believe, helps explain the relatively high levels of male-male aggression across human history. "This does not imply . . . that men have an 'aggression instinct' in the sense of some pent-up energy that must be released. Rather, men have inherited from their successful ancestors psychological mechanisms" that improve their odds of contributing their genes to future generations.

Neural influences

Because aggression is a complex behavior, no one spot in the brain controls it. But researchers have found neural systems in both animals and humans that facilitate aggression. When the scientists activate these areas in the brain, hostility increases; when they deactivate them, hostility decreases. Docile animals can thus be provoked into rage, and raging animals into submission.

In one experiment, researchers placed an electrode in an aggression-inhibiting area of a domineering monkey's brain. A smaller monkey, given a button that activated the electrode, learned to push it every time the tyrant monkey became intimidating. Brain activation works with humans, too. After receiving painless electrical stimulation in her amygdala (a part of the brain core), one woman became enraged and smashed her guitar against the wall, barely missing her psychiatrist's head (Moyer, 1976, 1983).

So, are violent people's brains in some way abnormal? To find out, Adrian Raine and his colleagues (1998, 2000) used brain scans to measure brain activity in murderers and to measure the amount of gray matter in men with antisocial conduct disorder. They found that the prefrontal cortex, which acts like an emergency brake on deeper brain areas involved in aggressive behavior, was 14 percent less active than normal in nonabused murderers and 15 percent smaller in the antisocial men. As other studies of murderers and death-row inmates confirm, abnormal brains can contribute to abnormally aggressive behavior (Davidson & others, 2000; Lewis, 1998; Pincus, 2001). Did the brain abnormality by itself predispose violence? Possibly not, but for some violent people it likely is a factor (Davidson & others, 2000).

Genetic influences

Heredity influences the neural system's sensitivity to aggressive cues. It has long been known that animals can be bred for aggressiveness. Sometimes this is done for practical purposes (the breeding of fighting cocks). Sometimes, breeding is done for research. Finnish psychologist Kirsti Lagerspetz (1979) took normal albino mice and bred the most aggressive ones together and the least aggressive ones. After repeating the procedure for 26 generations, she had one set of fierce mice and one set of placid mice.

Aggressiveness varies among primates and humans (Asher, 1987; Olweus, 1979). Our temperaments—how intense and reactive we are—are partly

Genes predispose the pit bull's aggressiveness.

brought with us into the world, influenced by our sympathetic nervous system's reactivity (Kagan, 1989). A person's temperament, observed in infancy, usually endures (Larsen & Diener, 1987; Wilson & Matheny, 1986). A fearless, impulsive, temper-prone child is at risk for adolescent violent behavior (American Psychological Association, 1993). A child who is nonaggressive at age 8 will very likely still be a nonaggressive person at age 48 (Huesmann & others, 2003). Thus, identical twins, when asked separately, are more likely than fraternal twins to agree on whether they have "a violent temper" or have gotten in fights (Rushton & others, 1986; Rowe & others, 1999). Half of identical twins of convicted criminals (but only one in five fraternal twins) also have criminal records (Raine, 1993).

Long-term studies following several hundred New Zealand children reveal that the recipe for aggressive behavior combines a gene that alters neurotransmitter balance with childhood maltreatment (Caspi & others, 2002; Moffitt & others, 2003). Neither "bad" genes nor a "bad" environment alone predispose later aggressiveness and antisocial behavior; rather, genes predispose some children to be more sensitive and responsive to maltreatment. Nature and nurture interact.

Biochemical influences

Blood chemistry also influences neural sensitivity to aggressive stimulation. Both laboratory experiments and police data indicate that when people are provoked, alcohol unleashes aggression (Bushman, 1993; Taylor & Chermack, 1993; Testa, 2002). Violent people are more likely (1) to drink, and (2) to become aggressive when intoxicated (White & others, 1993). Consider:

- In experiments, intoxicated people administer stronger shocks and feel angrier when thinking back on relationship conflicts (MacDonald & others, 2000).
- Surveys of rapists reveal that slightly over half had been drinking before committing their offenses. In a recent survey of nearly 90,000 students at 171 colleges and universities, four in five students experiencing unwanted intercourse acknowledged consuming alcohol or drugs beforehand (Pressley & others, 1997). So also, presumably, did most of their assailants.
- In 65 percent of homicides and 55 percent of in-home fights and assaults, the assailant and/or the victim had been drinking (American

Psychological Association, 1993).

- If spouse-battering alcoholics cease their problem drinking after treatment, their violent behavior typically ceases (Murphy & O'Farrell, 1996).

Alcohol and sexual assault. "Ordinary men who drank too much," was the New York Times *description of the mob that openly assaulted some 50 women attending a June 2000 NYC parade. "Stoked with booze, they worked up from hooting at women, to grabbing them, to drenching them with water and pulling off their tops and pants" (Staples, 2000).*

Alcohol enhances aggressiveness by reducing people's self-awareness and by reducing their ability to consider consequences (Hull & Bond, 1986; Ito & others, 1996; Steele & Southwick, 1985). Alcohol deindividuates, and it disinhibits.

Aggressiveness also correlates with the male sex hormone, testosterone. Hormonal influences appear much stronger in lower animals than in humans. But drugs that diminish testosterone levels in violent human males will subdue their aggressive tendencies. When beeped with electronic pagers, very high testosterone individuals report feeling slightly more restless and tense (Dabbs & others, 1997). They also exhibit more impulsivity and irritability and lower frustration tolerance (Harris, 1999).

After people reach age 25, their testosterone levels and rates of violent crime decrease together. Testosterone levels tend to be higher among prisoners convicted of planned and unprovoked violent crimes than of nonviolent crimes (Dabbs, 1992; Dabbs & others, 1995, 1997, 2001). And among the normal range of teen boys and adult men, those with high testosterone levels are more prone to delinquency, hard drug use, and aggressive responses to provocation (Archer, 1991; Dabbs & Morris, 1990; Olweus & others, 1988). Testosterone, says James Dabbs (2000), "is a small molecule with large effects." Injecting a man with testosterone won't automatically make him aggressive, yet men with low testosterone are somewhat less likely to react aggressively when provoked (Geen, 1998). Testosterone is roughly like battery power. Only if the battery levels are very low will things noticeably slow down.

Another culprit often found at the scene of violence is low levels of the neurotransmitter serotonin, for which the impulse-controlling frontal lobes have many receptors. In both primates and humans, low serotonin is often found among violence-prone children and adults (Bernhardt, 1997; Mehlman, 1994; Wright, 1995). Moreover, lowering people's serotonin levels in the laboratory increases their response to aversive events and willingness to deliver supposed electric shocks.

It is important to remember that the traffic between testosterone, serotonin, and behavior flows both ways. Testosterone, for example, may facilitate dominance and aggressiveness, but dominating or defeating behavior also boosts testosterone levels (Mazur & Booth, 1998). After a World Cup soccer match or a big basketball game between archrivals, testosterone levels rise in the winning fans and fall in the losing fans (Bernhardt & others, 1998). People shunted low on the socioeconomic ladder tend to have low serotonin. Evolutionary

"We could avoid two-thirds of all crime simply by putting all able-bodied young men in cryogenic sleep from the age of 12 through 28."
—David Lykken, *The Antisocial Personalities*, 1995

Some violent sex offenders, wishing to free themselves of persistent, damaging impulses and to reduce their prison terms, have requested castration. Should their requests be granted? If so, and if they are deemed no longer at risk to commit sexual violence, should their prison terms be reduced or eliminated?

psychologists have suggested that may be nature's response—preparing them to take risks that may advance their interests (Wright, 1995).

So, neural, genetic, and biochemical influences predispose some people to react aggressively to conflict and provocation. But is aggression so much a part of human nature that it makes peace unattainable? The American Psychological Association and the International Council of Psychologists have joined other organizations in endorsing a statement on violence developed by scientists from a dozen nations (Adams, 1991): "It is scientifically incorrect [to say that] war or any other violent behavior is genetically programmed into our human nature [or that] war is caused by 'instinct' or any single motivation." Thus there are, as we will see, ways to reduce human aggression.

AGGRESSION AS A RESPONSE TO FRUSTRATION

It is a warm evening. Tired and thirsty after two hours of studying, you borrow some change from a friend and head for the nearest soft-drink machine. As the machine devours the change, you can almost taste the cold, refreshing cola. But when you push the button, nothing happens. You push it again. Then you flip the coin return button. Still nothing. Again, you hit the buttons. You slam them. And finally you shake and whack the machine. You stomp back to your studies, empty-handed and shortchanged. Should your roommate beware? Are you now more likely to say or do something hurtful?

frustration-aggression theory
The theory that frustration triggers a readiness to aggress.

One of the first psychological theories of aggression, the popular **frustration-aggression theory,** answered yes. "Frustration always leads to some form of aggression," said John Dollard and his colleagues (1939, p. 1). **Frustration** is anything (such as the malfunctioning vending machine) that blocks our attaining a goal. Frustration grows when our motivation to achieve a goal is very strong, when we expected gratification, and when the blocking is complete. When Rupert Brown and his colleagues (2001) surveyed British ferry passengers heading to France, they found much higher aggressive attitudes on a day when French fishing boats blockaded the port, preventing their travel. Blocked from obtaining their goal, the passengers became more likely (in responding to various vignettes) to agree with an insult toward a French person who had spilled coffee and with the boycott of a French patisserie that was threatening the livelihood of a local village baker.

frustration
The blocking of goal-directed behavior.

displacement
The redirection of aggression to a target other than the source of the frustration. Generally, the new target is a safer or more socially acceptable target.

As Figure 10–2 suggests, the aggressive energy need not explode directly against its source. We learn to inhibit direct retaliation, especially when others might disapprove or punish; instead, we *displace* our hostilities to safer targets. **Displacement** occurs in the old anecdote about a man who, humiliated by his boss, berates his wife, who yells at their son, who kicks the dog, which bites the mail carrier. In experiments and in real life, however, displaced aggression is most likely when the target shares some similarity to the instigator and does some minor irritating act that unleashes the displaced aggression (Marcus-Newhall & others, 2000; Miller & others, 2003; Pedersen & others, 2000). When a person is harboring anger from a prior provocation, even a trivial offense—one that would normally produce no response—may elicit an explosive overreaction.

Various commentators have observed that the understandably intense American anger over 9/11 contributed to the eagerness to attack Iraq. Americans were looking for an outlet for their rage and found one in an evil tyrant,

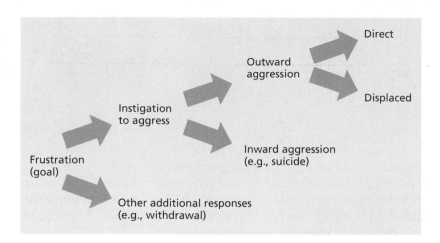

figure 10–2
The classic frustration-aggression theory.
Frustration creates a motive to aggress. Fear of punishment or disapproval for aggressing against the source of frustration may cause the aggressive drive to be displaced against some other target or even redirected against oneself.
Source: Based on Dollard & others, 1939, and Miller, 1941.

Saddam Hussein, who was once their ally. "The 'real reason' for this war," noted Thomas Friedman (2003), "was that after 9/11 America needed to hit someone in the Arab-Muslim world. . . . We hit Saddam for one simple reason: because we could, and because he deserved it, and because he was right in the heart of that world." One of the war's advocates, Vice President Richard Cheney (2003), seemed to concur. When asked why most others in the world disagreed with America's launching war, he replied "They didn't experience 9/11."

Frustration-aggression theory revised

Laboratory tests of the frustration-aggression theory produced mixed results: Sometimes frustration increased aggressiveness, sometimes not. For example, if the frustration was understandable—if, as in one experiment, a confederate disrupted a group's problem solving because his hearing aid malfunctioned (rather than just because he paid no attention)—then frustration led to irritation, not aggression (Burnstein & Worchel, 1962).

Leonard Berkowitz (1978, 1989) realized that the original theory overstated the frustration-aggression connection, so he revised it. Berkowitz theorized that frustration produces *anger*, an emotional readiness to aggress. Anger arises when someone who frustrates us could have chosen to act otherwise (Averill, 1983; Weiner, 1981). A frustrated person is especially likely to lash out when aggressive cues pull the cork, releasing bottled-up anger (Figure 10–3). Sometimes the cork will blow without such cues. But, as we will see, cues associated with aggression amplify aggression (Carlson & others, 1990).

Is frustration the same as deprivation?

Picture someone feeling extremely frustrated—economically, sexually, or politically.

Frustration-triggered aggression sometimes appears as road rage.

Note that frustration-aggression theory *is designed to explain hostile aggression, not instrumental aggression.*

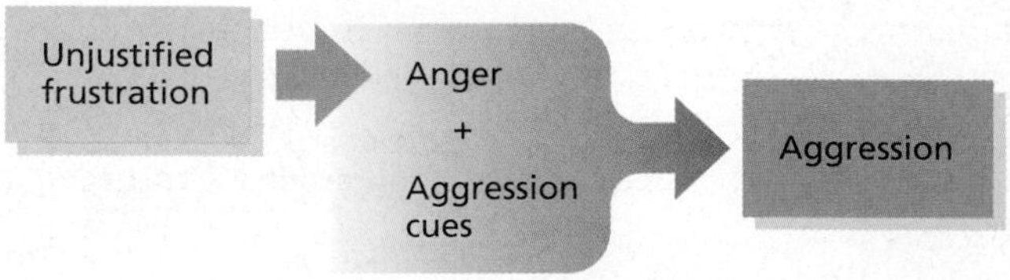

figure 10–3

A simplified synopsis of Leonard Berkowitz's revised frustration-aggression theory.

Unjustified frustration → Anger + Aggression cues → Aggression

"I would say a person is deprived if he lacks a goal object people generally regard as attractive or desirable, but is frustrated only when he had been anticipating the pleasure to be gotten from this object and then cannot fulfill this expectation."
—Leonard Berkowitz (1972)

"Evils which are patiently endured when they seem inevitable become intolerable when once the idea of escape from them is suggested."
—Alexis de Tocqueville, 1856

My hunch is that you are imagining someone economically, sexually, or politically *deprived*. And with good reason: When communities experience job layoffs, violence rates rise (Catalano & others, 1997). As American unemployment declined sharply during the late 1990s, so did violent crime. As it rose again in the early twenty-first century, so did violent crime.

But frustration may be unrelated to deprivation. The most sexually frustrated people are probably not celibate. The most economically frustrated people are probably not the impoverished residents of Jamaican shantytowns. When economic misery was everywhere during the 1930s depression, violent crime was not notably high. As the 1969 National Commission on the Causes and Prevention of Violence concluded, economic advancement may even increase frustration and escalate violence. Likewise, Palestinian suicide bombers have not been the most deprived of Palestinians. Like Northern Ireland's IRA, Italy's Red Brigades, and Germany's Bader-Meinhof gang, they are mostly middle class (Krueger & Maleckova, 2003; Pettigrew, 2003). So, too, were the 9/11 terrorists, who were professionally trained and world-traveled. Collective humiliation and antagonism feed terrorism far more than does absolute deprivation. Let's pause to see why.

Just before a 1967 Detroit riot, in which 43 people were killed and 683 structures burned, Michigan's governor boasted to the media about his state's leadership in civil rights legislation and about the $367 million in federal aid pumped into Detroit during the five preceding years. No sooner were his words broadcast than a large African American Detroit neighborhood exploded into last century's worst U.S. civil disorder.

People were stunned. Why Detroit? Although things were still bad there relative to the affluence of the White populace, there were greater injustices elsewhere. The National Advisory Commission on Civil Disorders, established to answer the question, concluded that one immediate psychological cause was the frustration of expectations fueled by the legislative and judicial civil rights victories of the 1960s. When there occurs a "revolution of rising expectations," as happened in Detroit and elsewhere, frustrations may escalate, even while conditions improve.

The principle works everywhere. The political scientist–social psychologist team of Ivo and Rosaline Feierabend (1968, 1972) applied the frustration-aggression theory in a study of political instability within 84 nations. When people in rapidly modernizing nations become urbanized and literacy is improved, they become more aware of material possibilities. Since affluence usually diffuses slowly, however, the increasing gap between people's aspirations and their achievements intensified frustration. Even as deprivation diminished, frustration and political aggression escalated. Expectation outstripped reality.

The point is not that deprivation and social injustice are irrelevant to social unrest, but that *frustration arises from the gap between expectations and attainments.* When your expectations are fulfilled by your attainments, and when your desires are reachable at your income, you feel satisfied rather than frustrated (Solberg & others, 2002).

Relative deprivation

Frustration is often compounded when we compare ourselves with others. Workers' feelings of well-being depend on whether their compensation compares favorably with others in their line of work (Yuchtman, 1976). A raise in salary for a city's police officers, while temporarily lifting their morale, may deflate that of the firefighters.

Such feelings, called **relative deprivation,** predict the reactions to perceived inequities by minority groups (Kawakami & Dion, 1993, 1995). Relative deprivation also explains why happiness tends to be lower and crime rates higher in communities and nations with large income inequality (Hagerty, 2000; Kawachi & others, 1999). And it explains why East Germans revolted against their communist regime: They had a higher standard of living than some Western European countries, but a frustratingly lower one than their West German neighbors (Baron & others, 1992).

The term *relative deprivation* was coined by researchers studying the satisfaction felt by American soldiers in World War II (Merton & Kitt, 1950; Stouffer & others, 1949). Ironically, those in the air corps felt *more* frustrated about their own rate of promotion than those in the military police, for whom promotions were slower. The air corps' promotion rate was rapid, and most air corps personnel probably perceived themselves as better than the average air corps member (the self-serving bias). Thus, their aspirations soared higher than their achievements. The result? Frustration.

One possible source of such frustration today is the affluence depicted in television programs and commercials. In cultures where television is a universal appliance, it helps turn absolute deprivation (lacking what others have) into relative deprivation (feeling deprived). Karen Hennigan and her co-workers (1982) analyzed crime rates in American cities around the time television was introduced. In 34 cities where television ownership became widespread in 1951, the 1951 larceny theft rate (for crimes such as shoplifting and bicycle stealing) took an observable jump. In 34 other cities, where a government freeze had delayed the introduction of television until 1955, a similar jump in the theft rate occurred—in 1955.

relative deprivation
The perception that one is less well off than others to whom one compares oneself.

"A house may be large or small; as long as the surrounding houses are equally small, it satisfies all social demands for a dwelling. But let a palace arise beside the little house, and it shrinks from a little house into a hut."
—Karl Marx

"Women's discontent increases in exact proportion to her development."
—Elizabeth Cady Stanton, 1815–1902, American suffragist

AGGRESSION AS LEARNED SOCIAL BEHAVIOR

Theories of aggression based on instinct and frustration assume that hostile urges erupt from inner emotions, which naturally "push" aggression from within. Social psychologists contend that learning also "pulls" aggression out of us.

The rewards of aggression

By experience and by observing others, we learn that aggression often pays. Experiments have transformed animals from docile creatures into ferocious fighters. Severe defeats, on the other hand, create submissiveness (Ginsburg & Allee, 1942; Kahn, 1951; Scott & Marston, 1953).

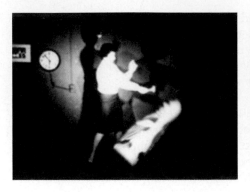

Monkey see, monkey do. In Bandura's famous experiment, children exposed to an adult's aggression against a Bobo doll were likely to reproduce the observed aggression.

SS

What are the characteristics of children who bully? Go to the *SocialSense* CD-ROM to view a clip on bullying.

People, too, can learn the rewards of aggression. A child whose aggressive acts successfully intimidate other children will likely become increasingly aggressive (Patterson & others, 1967). Aggressive hockey players—the ones sent most often to the penalty box for rough play—score more goals than nonaggressive players (McCarthy & Kelly, 1978a, 1978b). Canadian teenage hockey players whose fathers applaud physically aggressive play show the most aggressive attitudes and style of play (Ennis & Zanna, 1991). In these cases, aggression is instrumental in achieving certain rewards.

Collective violence can also pay. After the 1967 Detroit riot, the Ford Motor Company accelerated its efforts to hire minority workers, prompting comedian Dick Gregory to joke, "Last summer the fire got too close to the Ford plant. Don't scorch the Mustangs, baby."

The same is true of terrorist acts, which enable powerless people to garner widespread attention. "Kill one, frighten ten thousand," asserts an ancient Chinese proverb. Deprived of what Margaret Thatcher called "the oxygen of publicity," terrorism would surely diminish, concluded Jeffrey Rubin (1986). It's like the 1970s incidents of naked spectators "streaking" onto football fields for a few seconds of television exposure. Once the networks decided to ignore the incidents, the phenomenon ended.

Observational learning

social learning theory
The theory that we learn social behavior by observing and imitating and by being rewarded and punished.

Albert Bandura (1997) proposed a **social learning theory** of aggression. He believes that we learn aggression not only by experiencing its payoffs but also by observing others. As with most social behaviors, we acquire aggression by watching others act and noting the consequences.

Picture this scene from one of Bandura's experiments (Bandura & others, 1961). A Stanford nursery school child is put to work on an interesting art activity. An adult is in another part of the room, where there are Tinker Toys, a mallet, and a big, inflated "Bobo" doll. After a minute of working with the Tinker Toys, the adult gets up and for almost 10 minutes attacks the inflated doll. She pounds it with the mallet, kicks it, and throws it, while yelling, "Sock him in the nose. . . . Knock him down. . . . Kick him."

After observing this outburst, the child goes to a different room with many very attractive toys. But after two minutes the experimenter interrupts, saying these are her best toys and she must "save them for the other children." The frustrated child now goes into another room with various toys for aggressive and nonaggressive play, two of which are a Bobo doll and a mallet.

Seldom did children who were not exposed to the aggressive adult model display any aggressive play or talk. Although frustrated, they nevertheless played calmly. Those who had observed the aggressive adult were many times more likely to pick up the mallet and lash out at the doll. Watching the adult's aggressive behavior lowered their inhibitions. Moreover, the children often reproduced the model's acts and said her words. Observing aggressive behavior had both lowered their inhibitions and taught them ways to aggress.

Bandura (1979) believes that everyday life exposes us to aggressive models in the family, the subculture, and the mass media.

The family.   Physically aggressive children tend to have had physically punitive parents, who disciplined them by modeling aggression with screaming, slapping, and beating—(Patterson & others, 1982). These parents often had parents who were physically punitive (Bandura & Walters, 1959; Straus & Gelles, 1980). Although most abused children do not become criminals or abusive parents, 30 percent do later abuse their own children—four times the general population rate (Kaufman & Zigler, 1987; Widom, 1989). Violence often begets violence.

Family influence also appears in higher violence rates in cultures and in families with absentee fathers (Triandis, 1994). The U.S. Bureau of Justice Statistics reports that the minority of juveniles who did not grow up with two parents has accounted for 70 percent of juveniles in detention (Beck & others, 1988). From such data, David Lykken (2000) has computed that American children reared without fathers are about seven times more likely to be abused, to drop out of school, to become runaways, to become unmarried teenage parents, and to commit violent crimes. Two-parent families differ not only in increased care and positive discipline by fathers, they also have less poverty, more educational achievement, and fewer uprootings. But the father absence effect is mediated by more than increased poverty. The correlation between parental absence (usually father absence) and violence holds across races, income levels, education, and locations (Staub, 1996; Zill, 1988). Moreover, in one British study that has followed more than 10,000 children for 33 years since birth, children's risk of problems increased following a parental breakup (Cherlin & others, 1998).

The correlation also appears over time. In the United States of 1960, barely more than 1 in 10 children did not live with two parents and only 16,000 juveniles were arrested for violent crime. In 2000, 3 in 10 children did not live with two parents, and a similar-sized juvenile population produced more than 100,000 arrests for violent crime. The point is not that children from father-absent homes are likely to become delinquent or violent (nurtured by a caring mother and extended family, most such children thrive). And the point is also not that father absence is the only plausible explanation of the correlation. The point is simply that where and when fathers are absent, the violence risk increases. The situation, it seems, matters.

The culture.   The social environment outside the home also provides models. In communities where "macho" images are admired, aggression is readily transmitted to new generations (Cartwright, 1975; Short, 1969). The violent subculture of teenage gangs, for instance, provides its junior members with aggressive models.

The broader the culture also matters. Show me a man from a nondemocratic culture that is economically underdeveloped, that has great economic

figure 10–4

The social learning view of aggression.

The emotional arousal stemming from an aversive experience motivates aggression. Whether aggression or some other response actually occurs depends on what consequences we have learned to expect.

Source: Based on Bandura, 1979, 1997.

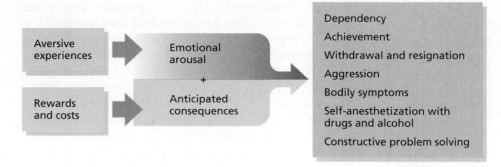

inequality, and that prepares men to be warriors and has engaged in war, and I will show you someone who is likely to be predisposed to support and engage in aggressive behavior (Bond, 2003). Show us someone from a culture that values honor and we will also show you someone with an aggressive mind-set, add Richard Nisbett (1990, 1993) and Dov Cohen (1996, 1998). Within the United States, they report, the sober, cooperative White folk who settled New England and the Middle Atlantic region produced a different culture than the swashbuckling, honor-preserving White folk (many of them my Scots-Irish ancestral cousins) who settled much of the South. The former were farmer-artisans; the latter, more aggressive hunters and herders. To the present, American cities and areas populated by southerners have much higher White homicide rates than those populated by northerners. For example, the Texas Panhandle (whose settlers came from the Upper South) has White homicide rates four times that of Nebraska (whose settlers came from the East, Midwest, and Europe). In the Texas Panhandle even towns with low poverty rates have much higher homicide rates than Nebraska towns with high poverty rates.

It's not violence in general that southerners are more likely to advocate, but, report Nisbett & Cohen (1996), violence that protects one's property and honor, and violence that punishes. "A man has a right to kill to defend his home," agree 18 percent of White nonsouthern men and 36 percent of White southern men. White southern men are twice as likely as rural midwestern White men to report having guns for protection. Southerners more strongly support wars and favor spanking (thus modeling violence in social relations). And people in "honor cultures," such as Brazil, express more sympathy for a husband's violent response to the humiliation of his wife's infidelity (Vandello & Cohen, 2003).

People learn aggressive responses both by experience and by observing aggressive models. But when will aggressive responses actually occur? Bandura (1979) contended that aggressive acts are motivated by a variety of aversive experiences—frustration, pain, insults (Figure 10–4). Such experiences arouse us emotionally. But whether we act aggressively depends on the consequences we anticipate. Aggression is most likely when we are aroused and it seems safe and rewarding to aggress.

Summing up

Aggression manifests itself in two forms: *hostile aggression,* which springs from emotions such as anger and intends to injure, and *instrumental aggression,* which is a means to some other end.

There are three broad theories of aggression. The *instinct* view, most commonly associated with Sigmund Freud and Konrad Lorenz, contended that aggressive energy will accumulate from within, like water accumulating behind a dam. Although the available evidence offers little support for this view, aggression is biologically influenced by heredity, blood chemistry, and the brain.

According to the second view, *frustration* causes anger and hostility. Given aggressive cues, this anger may provoke aggression. Frustration stems not from deprivation itself but from the gap between expectations and achievements.

The *social learning* view presents aggression as learned behavior. By experience and by observing others' success, we sometimes learn that aggression pays. Social learning enables family, subcultural, and media influences on aggression.

What are some influences on aggression?

Under what conditions do we aggress? The factors tugging at our trigger include aversive incidents, arousal, the media, and the group context.

AVERSIVE INCIDENTS

The recipe for aggression often includes some type of aversive experience: pain, uncomfortable heat, an attack, or overcrowding.

Pain

Researcher Nathan Azrin wanted to know if switching off foot shocks would reinforce two rats' positive interactions with each other. Azrin planned to turn on the shock and then, once the rats approached each other, cut off the pain. To his great surprise, the experiment proved impossible. As soon as the rats felt pain, they attacked each other, before the experimenter could switch off the shock. The greater the shock (and pain), the more violent the attack.

Is this true of rats alone? The researchers found that with a wide variety of species, the cruelty the animals imposed on each other matched zap for zap the cruelty imposed on them. As Azrin (1967) explained, the pain-attack response occurred

> in many different strains of rats. Then we found that shock produced attack when pairs of the following species were caged together: some kinds of mice, hamsters, opossums, raccoons, marmosets, foxes, nutria, cats, snapping turtles, squirrel monkeys, ferrets, red squirrels, bantam roosters, alligators, crayfish, amphiuma (an amphibian), and several species of snakes including the boa constrictor, rattlesnake, brown rat-snake, cottonmouth, copperhead, and black snake. The shock-attack reaction was clearly present in many very different kinds of creatures. In all the species in which shock produced attack it was fast and consistent, in the same "push-button" manner as with the rats.

The animals were not choosy about their targets. They would attack animals of their own species and also those of a different species, or stuffed dolls, or even tennis balls.

The researchers also varied the source of pain. They found that not just shocks induced attack; intense heat and "psychological pain"—for example, suddenly not rewarding hungry pigeons that have been trained to expect a grain reward after pecking at a disk—brought the same reaction as shocks. This "psychological pain" is, of course, frustration.

Today's ethical guidelines restrict researchers' use of painful stimuli.

Pain attack. Frustrated after losing the first two rounds of his 1997 heavyweight championship fight with Evander Holyfield, and feeling pain from an accidental head butt, Mike Tyson reacts by biting off part of Holyfield's ear.

Pain heightens aggressiveness in humans, also. Many of us can recall such a reaction after stubbing a toe or suffering a headache. Leonard Berkowitz and his associates demonstrated this by having University of Wisconsin students hold one hand in lukewarm water or painfully cold water. Those whose hands were submerged in the cold water reported feeling more irritable and more annoyed, and they were more willing to blast another person with unpleasant noise. In view of such results, Berkowitz (1983, 1989, 1998) proposed that aversive stimulation rather than frustration is the basic trigger of hostile aggression. Frustration is certainly one important type of unpleasantness. But any aversive event, whether a dashed expectation, a personal insult, or physical pain, can incite an emotional outburst. Even the torment of a depressed state increases the likelihood of hostile aggressive behavior.

Heat

People have theorized for centuries about the effect of climate on human action. Hippocrates (ca. 460–377 B.C.), comparing the civilized Greece of his day to the savagery in what is now Germany and Switzerland, believed the cause to be northern Europe's harsh climate. Later, the English attributed their "superior" culture to *England's* ideal climate. French thinkers proclaimed the same for France. Because climate remains steady while cultural traits change, the climate theory of culture obviously has limited validity.

Temporary climate variations, however, can affect behavior. Offensive odors, cigarette smoke, and air pollution have all been linked with aggressive behavior (Rotton & Frey, 1985). But the most-studied environmental irritant is heat. William Griffitt (1970; Griffitt & Veitch, 1971) found that compared with students who answered questionnaires in a room with a normal temperature, those who did so in an uncomfortably hot room (over 90°F) reported feeling more tired and aggressive and expressed more hostility toward a stranger. Follow-up experiments revealed that heat also triggers retaliative actions (Bell, 1980; Rule & others, 1987).

Does uncomfortable heat increase aggression in the real world as well as in the laboratory? Consider:

"I pray thee, good Mercutio, let's retire; The day is hot, the Capulets abroad, And, if we meet, we shall not 'scape a brawl, For now, these hot days, is the mad blood stirring."
—Shakespeare, *Romeo and Juliet*

- In heat-stricken Phoenix, Arizona, drivers without air conditioning have been more likely to honk at a stalled car (Kenrick & MacFarlane, 1986).
- During the 1986 to 1988 major league baseball seasons, the number of batters hit by a pitch was two-thirds greater for games played above 90°F than for games played below 80°F (Reifman & others, 1991). Pitchers weren't wilder on hot days—they had no more walks and wild pitches. They just clobbered more batters.
- The riots occurring in 79 U.S. cities between 1967 and 1971 were more likely on hot than on cool days.

Los Angeles, May 1993.
Riots are more likely during
hot summer weather.

- Studies in six cities have found that when the weather is hot, violent crimes are more likely (Anderson & Anderson, 1984; Cohn, 1993; Cotton, 1981, 1986; Harries & Stadler, 1988; Rotton & Frey, 1985).
- Across the Northern Hemisphere, not only do hotter days have more violent crimes, so do hotter seasons of the year, hotter summers, hotter years, hotter cities, and hotter regions (Anderson & Anderson, 1998, 2000). If a 4-degree Fahrenheit (about 2°C) global warming occurs, Anderson and his colleagues project that the United States alone would annually see at least 50,000 more serious assaults.

Do these real-world findings show that heat discomfort directly fuels aggressiveness? Although the conclusion appears plausible, these *correlations* between temperature and aggression don't prove it. People certainly could be more irritable in hot, sticky weather. And in the laboratory, hot temperatures do increase arousal and hostile thoughts and feelings (Anderson & others, 1999). There may be other contributing factors, however. Maybe hot summer evenings drive people into the streets. There, other group influence factors may well take over.

Attacks

Being attacked or insulted by another is especially conducive to aggression. Several experiments, including one at Osaka University by Kennichi Ohbuchi and Toshihiro Kambara (1985), confirm that intentional attacks breed retaliatory attacks. In most of these experiments, one person competes with another in a reaction-time contest. After each test trial, the winner chooses how much shock to give the loser. Actually, each person is playing a programmed opponent, who steadily escalates the amount of shock. Do the real participants respond charitably? Hardly. Extracting "an eye for an eye" is the more likely response.

AROUSAL

So far we have seen that various aversive stimulations can arouse anger. Do other types of arousal, such as those that accompany exercise or sexual excitement, have a similar effect? Imagine that Tawna, having just finished a stimulating short run, comes home to discover that her date for the evening has called and left word that he has made other plans. Will Tawna more likely explode in fury after her run than if she discovered the same message after awakening from a nap? Or, having just exercised, will her aggressive tendencies be exorcised? To discover an answer, consider how we interpret and label our bodily states.

In a famous experiment, Stanley Schachter and Jerome Singer (1962) found we can experience an aroused bodily state in different ways. They aroused University of Minnesota men by injecting adrenaline. The drug produced body flushing, heart palpitation, and more rapid breathing. When forewarned that the drug would produce these effects, the men felt little emotion, even when waiting with either a hostile or a euphoric person. Of course, they could readily attribute their bodily sensations to the drug. Schachter and Singer led another group of men to believe the drug produced no such side effects. Then they, too, were placed in the company of a hostile or euphoric person. How did they feel and act? They were angered when with the hostile person, amused when with the person who was euphoric. The seeming principle: *A given state of bodily arousal feeds one emotion or another, depending on how the person interprets and labels the arousal.*

Other experiments indicate that arousal is not as emotionally undifferentiated as Schachter believed. Yet being physically stirred up does intensify just about any emotion (Reisenzein, 1983). For example, Paul Biner (1991) reports that people find radio static unpleasant, *especially* when they are aroused by bright lighting. And Dolf Zillmann (1988), Jennings Bryant, and their collaborators found that people who have just pumped an exercise bike or watched a film of a Beatles rock concert find it easy to misattribute their arousal to a provocation. They then retaliate with heightened aggression. Although common sense might lead us to assume that Tawna's run would have drained her aggressive tensions, enabling her to accept bad news calmly, these studies show that arousal feeds emotions.

Sexual arousal and other forms of arousal, such as anger, can therefore amplify one another (Zillmann, 1989). Love is never so passionate as after a fight or a fright. In the laboratory, erotic stimuli are more arousing to people who have just been frightened. Similarly, the arousal of a roller-coaster ride may spill over into romantic feeling for one's partner.

A frustrating, hot, or insulting situation heightens arousal. When it does, the arousal, combined with hostile thoughts and feelings, may form a recipe for aggressive behavior (Figure 10–5).

AGGRESSION CUES

As we noted earlier, violence is most likely when aggressive cues pull the cork, releasing pent-up anger. Leonard Berkowitz (1968, 1981, 1995) and others have found that the sight of a weapon is such a cue, especially when perceived as an instrument of violence rather than recreation. In one experiment, children who had just played with toy guns became more willing to knock down another child's blocks. In another, angered University of Wisconsin men gave more electric shocks to their tormenter when a rifle and a revolver (supposedly left over from a previous experiment) were nearby than when badminton rackets had been left behind (Berkowitz & LePage, 1967). Guns prime hostile thoughts and

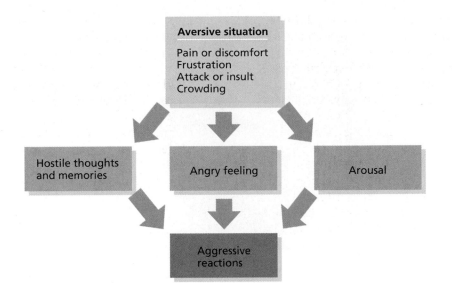

figure 10–5

Elements of hostile aggression.

An aversive situation can trigger aggression by provoking hostile cognitions, hostile feelings, and arousal. These reactions make us more likely to perceive harmful intent and to react aggressively. **Source:** Simplified from Anderson, Deuser, and DeNeve, 1995.

punitive judgments (Anderson & others, 1998; Dienstbier & others, 1998). What's within sight is within mind. Thus, Berkowitz was not surprised that half of all U.S. murders are committed with handguns and that handguns in homes are far more likely to kill household members than intruders. "Guns not only permit violence," he reported, "they can stimulate it as well. The finger pulls the trigger, but the trigger may also be pulling the finger."

Berkowitz is further unsurprised that countries that ban handguns have lower murder rates. Compared with the United States, Britain has one-fourth as many people and one-sixteenth as many murders. The United States has 10,000 handgun homicides a year; Australia has about a dozen, Britain two dozen, and Canada 100. When Washington, D.C., adopted a law restricting handgun possession, the numbers of gun-related murders and suicides each abruptly dropped about 25 percent. No changes occurred in other methods of murder and suicide, nor did adjacent areas outside the reach of this law experience any such declines (Loftin & others, 1991).

Researchers also have examined risks of violence in homes with and without guns. This is controversial research, because such homes may differ in many ways. One study sponsored by the Centers for Disease Control compared gun owners and nonowners of the same gender, race, age, and neighborhood. The ironic and tragic result was that those who kept a gun in the home (often for protection) were 2.7 times more likely to be murdered—nearly always by a family member or close acquaintance (Kellermann, 1993, 1997). Another study found a fivefold increased risk of suicide in homes with guns (Taubes, 1992). A newer national study found the link between guns and homicide or suicide to be somewhat less. Compared with others of the same gender, age, and race, people with guns at home were 41 percent more likely to be homicide victims and 3.4 times more likely to die of suicide (Wiebe, 2003). A gun in the home has often meant the difference between a fight and a funeral, or between suffering and suicide.

Guns not only serve as aggression cues, they also put psychological distance between aggressor and victim. As Milgram's obedience studies taught us,

www.mhhe.com/myers8
Visit the Online Learning Center for a scenario on aggression cues.

figure 10–6

Weapons used to commit murder in the United States in 2002.

Source: FBI Uniform Crime Reports.

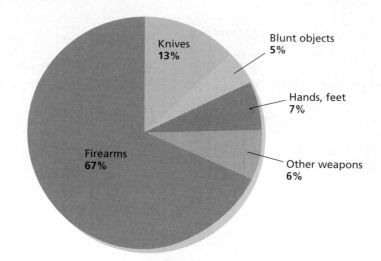

remoteness from the victim facilitates cruelty. A knife can kill someone, but a knife attack is more difficult than pulling a trigger from a distance (Figure 10–6).

MEDIA INFLUENCES: PORNOGRAPHY AND SEXUAL VIOLENCE

The increase in violent crime reported between 1960 and the early 1990s, especially among juveniles, prompts us to wonder: Why the change? What social forces have caused the mushrooming violence?

Alcohol contributes to aggression, but alcohol use has not dramatically changed since 1960. Other biological factors (testosterone, genes, neurotransmitters) also influence aggression but cannot explain the large cultural changes. Might the surging violence instead be fueled by the growth in individualism and materialism? By the growing gap between the powerful rich and the powerless poor? By the decline in two-parent families and the increase in absent fathers? By the media's increasing modeling of violence and unrestrained sexuality? The last question arises because increased rates of violence and sexual coercion have coincided with increases in media mayhem and sexual suggestion. Is the historical correlation a coincidence? To find out, researchers have explored the social consequences of pornography (which *Webster's* defines as erotic depictions intended to excite sexual arousal) and the effects of modeling violence in movies and on television.

In the United States, pornography has become a bigger business than professional football, basketball, and baseball combined, thanks to some $10 billion a year spent on the industry's cable and satellite networks, on its theaters and pay-per-view movies, on in-room hotel movies, phone sex, and sex magazines, and on the estimated 400,000 for-profit websites (National Research Council, 2002; Rich, 2001; Schlosser, 2003). In one survey of university students, 57 percent of men and 35 percent of women reported having sought out sex-related websites, though only 6 percent of men and 1 percent of women did so "frequently" (Banfield & McCabe, 2001).

Social-psychological research on pornography has focused mostly on depictions of sexual violence. A typical sexually violent episode finds a man forcing himself upon a woman. She at first resists and tries to fight off her attacker. Gradually she becomes sexually aroused, and her resistance melts. By the end she is in ecstasy, pleading for more. We have all viewed or read nonpornographic versions of this sequence: She resists, he persists. Dashing man grabs and forcibly kisses protesting woman. Within moments, the arms that were pushing him away are clutching him tight, her resistance overwhelmed by her unleashed passion. In *Gone With the Wind*, Scarlett O'Hara is carried to bed protesting and kicking and wakes up singing.

Social psychologists report that viewing such fictional scenes of a man overpowering and arousing a woman can distort one's perceptions of how women actually respond to sexual coercion and increase men's aggression against women, at least in laboratory settings.

Distorted perceptions of sexual reality

Does viewing sexual violence reinforce the "rape myth"—that some women would welcome sexual assault—that "no doesn't really mean no"? To find out, Neil Malamuth and James Check (1981) showed University of Manitoba men either two nonsexual movies or two movies depicting a man sexually overcoming a woman. A week later, when surveyed by a different experimenter, those who saw the films with mild sexual violence were more accepting of violence against women. Other studies confirm that exposure to pornography increases acceptance of the rape myth (Oddone-Paolucci & others, 2000). For example, while spending three evenings watching sexually violent movies, male viewers in an experiment by Charles Mullin and Daniel Linz (1995) also became progressively less bothered by the raping and slashing. Compared with others not exposed to the films, they also, three days later, expressed less sympathy for domestic violence victims, and they rated the victims' injuries as less severe. In fact, said researchers Edward Donnerstein, Daniel Linz, and Steven Penrod (1987), what better way for an evil character to get people to react calmly to the torture and mutilation of women than to show a gradually escalating series of such films?

Note that the sexual message (that many women enjoy being "taken") was subtle and unlikely to elicit counterarguing. Given frequent media images of women's resistance melting in the arms of a forceful man, we shouldn't be surprised that even women often believe that some *other* woman might enjoy being sexually overpowered—though virtually none think it of themselves (Malamuth & others, 1980). "Me turned on by an overpowering man? Not on your life!"

Aggression against women

Evidence also suggests that pornography contributes to men's actual aggression toward women. Correlational studies raise that possibility. John Court (1985) noted that across the world, as pornography became more widely available during the 1960s and 1970s, the rate of reported rapes sharply increased—except in countries and areas where pornography was controlled. (The examples that counter this trend, such as Japan, where violent pornography is available but the rape rate is low, remind us that other factors are also important.) In Hawaii, the number of reported rapes rose ninefold between 1960 and 1974, dropped when restraints on pornography were temporarily imposed, and rose again when the restraints were lifted.

In another correlational study, Larry Baron and Murray Straus (1984) discovered that the sales of sexually explicit magazines (such as *Hustler* and *Playboy*) in the 50 states correlated with state rape rates, even after controlling for other

"Pornography that portrays sexual aggression as pleasurable for the victim increases the acceptance of the use of coercion in sexual relations."

—Social science consensus at Surgeon General's Workshop on Pornography and Public Health (Koop, 1987)

Did Ted Bundy's (1989) comments on the eve of his execution for a series of rape-murders acknowledge pornography's toll or make it a handy excuse?: "The most damaging kinds of pornography [involve] sexual violence. Like an addiction, you keep craving something that is harder, harder, something which, which gives you a greater sense of excitement. Until you reach a point where the pornography only goes so far, you reach that jumping off point where you begin to wonder if maybe actually doing it would give you that which is beyond just reading it or looking at it."

factors, such as the percentage of young males in each state. Alaska ranked first in sex magazine sales and first in rape. Nevada was second on both measures.

When interviewed, Canadian and American sexual offenders commonly acknowledge pornography use. For example, William Marshall (1989) reported that Ontario rapists and child molesters used pornography much more than men who were not sexual offenders. An FBI study also reported considerable exposure to pornography among serial killers, as did the Los Angeles Police Department among most child sex abusers (Bennett, 1991; Ressler & others, 1988).

Although limited to the sorts of short-term behaviors that can be studied in the laboratory, controlled experiments reveal what correlational studies cannot—cause and effect. A consensus statement by 21 leading social scientists summed up the results: "Exposure to violent pornography increases punitive behavior toward women" (Koop, 1987). One of these social scientists, Edward Donnerstein (1980), had shown 120 University of Wisconsin men a neutral, an erotic, or an aggressive-erotic (rape) film. Then, the men, supposedly as part of another experiment, "taught" a male or female confederate some nonsense syllables by choosing how much shock to administer for incorrect answers. The men who had watched the rape film administered markedly stronger shocks (Figure 10–7), especially when angered and with a female victim.

If the ethics of conducting such experiments trouble you, rest assured that these researchers appreciate the controversial and powerful experience they are giving participants. Only after giving their knowing consent do people participate. Moreover, after the experiment, researchers effectively debunk any myths the films communicated (Check & Malamuth, 1984).

Repeated exposure to erotic films featuring quick, uncommitted sex also tends to

- *decrease attraction for one's partner,*
- *increase acceptance of extramarital sex and of women's sexual submission to men, and*
- *increase men's perceiving women in sexual terms.*

(Source: See Myers, 2000)

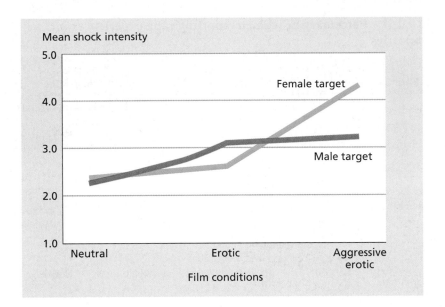

figure 10–7

After viewing an aggressive-erotic film, college men delivered stronger shocks than before, especially to a woman. **Source:** Data from Donnerstein, 1980.

Justification for this experimentation is not only scientific but also humanitarian:

- In one careful national survey, 22 percent of women reported having been forced by a man to do something sexual (Laumann & others, 1994).

- In another, 18 percent of women reported an experience that met the definition of rape (Tjaden & Thoennes, 2000). Six times in seven the perpetrator was someone they knew.

- In surveys of 6,200 college students nationwide and 2,200 Ohio working women, Mary Koss and her colleagues (1988, 1990, 1993) found that 28 percent of the women reported an experience that met the legal definition of rape or attempted rape (although most, having been overcome on a date or by an acquaintance, didn't label it as rape; women's "scripts" for rape usually involve violence by a stranger [Kahn & others, 1994]).

- Surveys in other industrialized countries offer similar results (Table 10–1, see page 402). Three in four stranger rapes and nearly all acquaintance rapes went unreported to police. Thus, the known rape rate *greatly* underestimates the actual rape rate.

Eight different surveys have asked college males whether there was any chance they would rape a woman "if you could be assured that no one would know and that you could in no way be punished" (Stille & others, 1987). A disturbing proportion—about one-third—admit to at least a slim possibility of doing so. Compared with men who indicate no possibility of raping, these men are more like convicted rapists in their belief in rape myths, in their being sexually aroused by rape depictions, and in their behaving aggressively toward women—in both laboratory and dating situations. Such aggression is greatest among those who have formed the sort of rape-supportive attitudes that pornography cultivates (Figure 10–8, see page 402).

"Pornography is the theory and rape the practice."
—Robin Morgan (1980, p. 139)

table 10–1   Percentage of women reporting rape experiences in five countries

Country	Sample of Women	Completed and Attempted Rape
Canada	National sample at 95 colleges and universities	23% rape or sexual assault
Germany	Berlin late adolescents	17% criminal sexual violence
New Zealand	Convenience sample of psychology students	25%
United Kingdom	Convenience sample at 22 universities	19%
United States	Representative sample at 32 colleges and universities	28%
Seoul, Korea	Adult women	22%

Source: Studies reported by Koss, Heise, and Russo (1994) and Krahé (1998)

Media awareness education

As most Germans quietly tolerated the degrading anti-Semitic images that fed the Holocaust, so most people today tolerate media images of women that feed sexual harassment, abuse, and rape. So, should portrayals that demean or violate women be restrained?

In the contest of individual versus collective rights, people in most Western nations side with individual rights. As an alternative to censorship, many psychologists favor "media awareness training." Recall that pornography researchers have successfully resensitized and educated participants to women's actual responses to sexual violence. Could educators similarly promote critical viewing skills? By sensitizing people to the view of women that predominates in pornography and to issues of sexual harassment and violence, it should be possible to counter the myth that women enjoy being coerced. "Our utopian and perhaps naive hope," say Edward Donnerstein, Daniel Linz, and Steven Penrod (1987, p. 196), "is that in the end the truth revealed through good science will prevail and the public will be convinced that these images not only demean those portrayed but also those who view them."

Is such a hope naive? Consider: Without banning cigarettes, the number of U.S. smokers dropped from 42 percent in 1965 to 23 percent in the early twenty-first century. Without censoring racism, once-common media images of African Americans as childlike, superstitious buffoons have nearly disappeared. As public consciousness changed, script writers, producers, and media executives decided that exploitative images of minorities were not good. More recently

figure 10–8

Sexually aggressive men.

Men who sexually coerce women often combine a history of impersonal sex with hostile masculinity, reports Neil Malamuth (1996, 2003).

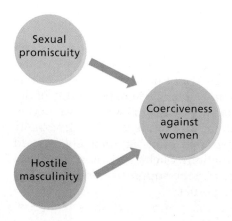

they have decided that drugs are not glamorous, as many films and songs from the 1960s and 1970s implied, but dangerous—and high school seniors' marijuana use during the previous month has dropped from 37 percent in 1979 to 12 percent in 1992, before rebounding to 23 percent in 1996 as the cultural anti-drug voice softened and drug use became reglamorized in some music and films (Johnston & others, 1996). Will we one day look back with embarrassment on the time when movies entertained people with scenes of exploitation, mutilation, and sexual coercion?

MEDIA INFLUENCES: TELEVISION

We have seen that watching an aggressive model can unleash children's aggressive urges and teach them new ways to aggress. And we have seen that after viewing sexual violence, many angry men will act more violently toward women. Does television have any similar effects?

Consider these few facts about watching television. In 1945, the Gallup poll asked Americans, "Do you know what television is?" (Gallup, 1972, p. 551). Today, in much of the industrialized world, nearly all households (99.2 percent in Australia, for example) have a TV set, more than have telephones (Trewin, 2001). Most homes have more than one set, which helps explain why parents' reports of what their children watch correlate minimally with children's reports of what they watch (Donnerstein, 1998). With MTV in 140 countries and CNN spanning the globe, television is creating a global pop culture (Gundersen, 2001).

In the average home, the set is on seven hours a day, with individual household members averaging three to four hours which means that someone living to age 80 would have spent a decade watching television. Women watch more than men, non-Whites more than Whites, preschoolers and retired people more than those in school or working, and the less educated more than the highly educated (Comstock & Scharrer, 1999). For the most part, these facts about Americans' viewing habits also characterize Europeans, Australians, and Japanese (Murray & Kippax, 1979).

During all those hours, what social behaviors are modeled? From 1994 to 1997, bleary-eyed employees of the National Television Violence Study (1997) analyzed some 10,000 programs from the major networks and cable channels. Their findings? Six in 10 programs contained violence ("physically compelling action that threatens to hurt or kill, or actual hurting or killing"). During fistfights, people who went down usually shook it off and came back stronger—unlike most real fistfights that last one punch (often resulting in a broken jaw or hand). In 73 percent of violent scenes, the aggressors went unpunished. In 58 percent, the victim was not shown to experience pain. In children's programs, only 5 percent of violence was shown to have any long-term consequences; two-thirds depicted violence as funny.

What does it add up to? All told, television beams its electromagnetic waves into children's eyeballs for more growing-up hours than they spend in school. More hours, in fact, than they spend in any other waking activity. By the end of elementary school, the average child views some 8,000 TV murders and 100,000 other violent acts (Huston & others, 1992). Reflecting on his 22 years of cruelty counting, media researcher George Gerbner (1994) lamented: "Humankind has had more bloodthirsty eras but none as filled with *images* of violence as the present. We are awash in a tide of violent representations the world has never

"What we're trying to do is raise the level of awareness of violence against women and pornography to at least the level of awareness of racist and Ku Klux Klan literature."
—Gloria Steinem (1988)

seen . . . drenching every home with graphic scenes of expertly choreographed brutality."

Does prime-time crime stimulate the behavior it depicts? Or, as viewers vicariously participate in aggressive acts, do the shows drain off aggressive energy? The latter idea, a variation on the **catharsis** hypothesis, maintains that watching violent drama enables people to release their pent-up hostilities. Defenders of the media cite this theory frequently and remind us that violence predates television. In an imaginary debate with one of television's critics, the medium's defender might argue, "Television played no role in the genocides of Jews and Native Americans. Television just reflects and caters to our tastes." "Agreed," responds the critic, "but it's also true that during America's TV age, reported violent crime increased several times faster than the population rate. Surely you don't mean the popular arts are mere passive reflections, without any power to influence public consciousness, or that advertisers' belief in the medium's power is an illusion." The defender replies: "The violence epidemic results from many factors. TV may even reduce aggression by keeping people off the streets and by offering them a harmless opportunity to vent their aggression."

Studies of television viewing and aggression aim to identify effects more subtle and pervasive than the occasional "copycat" murders that capture public attention. They ask: How does television affect viewers' *behavior* and viewers' *thinking*?

Television's effects on behavior

Do viewers imitate violent models? Examples abound of people reenacting television crimes. In one survey of 208 prison convicts, 9 of 10 admitted that they learned new criminal tricks by watching crime programs. Four out of 10 said they had attempted specific crimes seen on television (*TV Guide*, 1977).

Correlating TV viewing and behavior.   Crime stories are not scientific evidence. Researchers therefore use correlational and experimental studies to examine the effects of viewing violence. One technique, commonly used with schoolchildren, asks whether their TV watching predicts their aggressiveness. To some extent it does. The more violent the content of the child's TV viewing, the more aggressive the child (Eron, 1987; Turner & others, 1986). The relationship is modest but consistently found in North America, Europe, and Australia.

So can we conclude that a diet of violent TV fuels aggression? Perhaps you are already thinking that because this is a correlational study, the cause-effect relation could also work in the opposite direction. Maybe aggressive children prefer aggressive programs. Or maybe some underlying third factor, such as lower intelligence, predisposes some children both to prefer aggressive programs and to act aggressively.

Researchers have developed two ways to test these alternative explanations. They test the "hidden third factor" explanation by statistically pulling out the influence of some of these possible factors. For example, William Belson (1978; Muson, 1978) studied 1,565 London boys. Compared with those who watched little violence, those who watched a great deal (especially realistic rather than cartoon violence) admitted to 50 percent more violent acts during the preceding six months (for example, "I busted the telephone in a telephone box"). Belson also examined 22 likely third factors, such as family size. The heavy and light

---

catharsis
Emotional release. The catharsis view of aggression is that aggressive drive is reduced when one "releases" aggressive energy, either by acting aggressively or by fantasizing aggression.

"One of television's great contributions is that it brought murder back into the home where it belongs. Seeing a murder on television can be good therapy. It can help work off one's antagonisms."
—Alfred Hitchcock

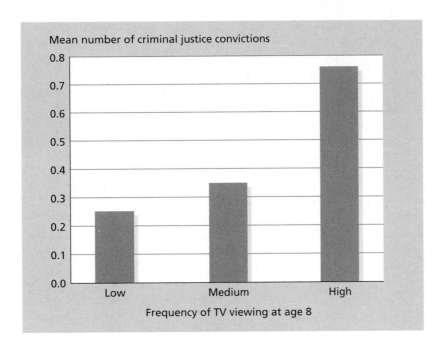

figure 10–9

Children's television viewing and later criminal activity.

Violence viewing at age 8 was a predictor of a serious criminal offense by age 30. **Source:** Data from Eron and Huesmann (1984).

viewers still differed after equating them with respect to potential third factors. So Belson surmised that the heavy viewers were indeed more violent *because* of their TV exposure.

Similarly, Leonard Eron and Rowell Huesmann (1980, 1985) found that violence viewing among 875 8-year-olds correlated with aggressiveness even after statistically pulling out several obvious possible third factors. Moreover, when they restudied these individuals as 19-year-olds, they discovered that viewing violence at age 8 modestly predicted aggressiveness at age 19, but that aggressiveness at age 8 did *not* predict viewing violence at age 19. Aggression followed viewing, not the reverse. Moreover, by age 30, the children who had watched the most violence had become adults who were more likely to have been convicted of a crime (Figure 10–9).

Huesmann and his colleagues (1984, 2003) confirmed these findings in follow-up studies of Chicago-area youngsters. Boys who as 8-year-olds had been in the top 20 percent of violence watchers were, 15 years later, twice as likely as others to acknowledge pushing, grabbing, or shoving their wives, and their violence-viewing female counterparts were twice as likely, as young women, to have thrown something at their husbands.

Adolescent viewing also clues us to future adult behaviors, as Jeffrey Johnson and his co-workers (2002) found when they followed more than 700 lives through time. Among 14-year-olds who watched less than an hour of TV daily, 6 percent were involved in aggressive acts (such as assault, robbery, or threats of injury) at ages 16 to 22, as were five times as many—29 percent—of those who had watched more than three hours a day.

Sharp-eyed students may wonder if these correlations result from higher levels of aggression among those who were already aggressive when first observed, or who are less intelligent and educated. (Less educated and intelligent people do watch more television.) But when both the Huesmann and Johnson research teams controlled for such factors, the differences persisted.

From Funny Times, February 1994. Reprinted with permission.

" I TOLD YOU THE KIDS WERE WATCHING TOO MUCH TELEVISION. "

Another fact to ponder: Where television goes, increased violence follows. Even murder rates increase when and where television comes. In Canada and the United States, the homicide rate doubled between 1957 and 1974 as violent television spread. In census regions where television came later, the homicide rate jumped later, too. In White South Africa, where television was not introduced until 1975, a similar near doubling of the homicide rate did not begin until after 1975 (Centerwall, 1989). And in a closely studied rural Canadian town where television came late, playground aggression doubled soon after (Williams, 1986).

Notice that these studies illustrate how researchers are now using correlational findings to *suggest* cause and effect. Yet an infinite number of possible third factors could be creating a merely coincidental relation between viewing violence and aggression. Fortunately, the experimental method can control these extraneous factors. If we randomly assign some children to watch a violent film and others a nonviolent film, any later aggression difference between the two groups will be due to the only factor that distinguishes them: what they watched.

TV viewing experiments.   The trailblazing experiments by Albert Bandura and Richard Walters (1963) sometimes had young children view the adult pounding the inflated doll on film instead of observing it live—with much the same effect. Then Leonard Berkowitz and Russell Geen (1966) found that angered college students who viewed a violent film acted more aggressively than did similarly angered students who viewed nonaggressive films. These laboratory experiments, coupled with growing public concern, were sufficient to prompt the U.S. Surgeon General to commission 50 new research studies during the early 1970s. By and large, these studies, and more than 100 later ones, confirmed that viewing violence amplifies aggression (Anderson & Bushman, 2002; Bushman & Anderson, 2001).

For example, research teams led by Ross Parke (1977) in the United States and Jacques Leyens (1975) in Belgium showed institutionalized American and

"Then shall we simply allow our children to listen to any story anyone happens to make up, and so receive into their minds ideas often the very opposite of those we shall think they ought to have when they are grown up?"

—Plato, *The Republic,* 360 B.C.E.

Belgian delinquent boys a series of either aggressive or nonaggressive commercial films. Their consistent finding: "Exposure to movie violence . . . led to an increase in viewer aggression." Compared with the week preceding the film series, physical attacks increased sharply in cottages where boys were viewing violent films. Dolf Zillmann and James Weaver (1999) similarly exposed men and women, on four consecutive days, to violent or nonviolent feature films. When participating in a different project on the fifth day, those exposed to the violent films were more hostile to the research assistant.

The aggression provoked in these experiments is not assault and battery; it's more on the scale of a shove in the lunch line, a cruel comment, a threatening gesture. Nevertheless, the convergence of evidence is striking. "The irrefutable conclusion," said a 1993 American Psychological Association youth violence commission, is "that viewing violence increases violence." This is especially so among people with aggressive tendencies (Bushman, 1995). The violence viewing effect also is strongest when an attractive person commits justified, realistic violence that goes unpunished and that shows no pain or harm (Donnerstein, 1998).

All in all, conclude researchers Brad Bushman and Craig Anderson (2001), violence-viewing's effect on aggression surpasses the effect of passive smoking on lung cancer, calcium intake on bone mass, and homework on academic achievement. As with smoking and cancer, not everyone shows the effect—other factors matter as well. The cumulative long-term effects are what's worrisome, and corporate interests pooh-pooh the evidence. But the evidence is now "overwhelming," say Bushman and Anderson: "Exposure to media violence causes significant increases in aggression." The research base is large, the methods diverse, and the overall findings consistent, echo a National Institute of Mental Health task force of leading media violence researchers (Anderson & others, in press). "Our in-depth review . . . reveals unequivocal evidence that exposure to media violence can increase the likelihood of aggressive and violent behavior in both immediate and long-term contexts."

Given the convergence of correlational and experimental evidence, researchers have explored *why* viewing violence has this effect. Consider three possibilities (Geen & Thomas, 1986). One is that it is not the violent content that causes social violence but the *arousal* it produces (Mueller & others, 1983; Zillmann, 1989). As we noted earlier, arousal tends to spill over: One type of arousal energizes other behaviors.

Other research shows that viewing violence *disinhibits*. In Bandura's experiment, the adult's punching of the Bobo doll seemed to make these outbursts legitimate and to lower the children's inhibitions. Viewing violence primes the viewer for aggressive behavior by activating violence-related thoughts (Berkowitz, 1984; Bushman & Geen, 1990; Josephson, 1987). Listening to music with sexually violent lyrics seems to have a similar effect (Barongan & Hall, 1995; Johnson & others, 1995; Pritchard, 1998).

Media portrayals also evoke *imitation*. The children in Bandura's experiments reenacted the specific behaviors they had witnessed. The commercial television industry is hard-pressed to dispute that television leads viewers to imitate what they have seen: Its advertisers model consumption. Are media executives right, however, to argue that TV merely holds a mirror to a violent society? That art imitates life? And that the "reel" world therefore shows us the real world? Actually, on TV programs, acts of assault have outnumbered affectionate acts four to one. In other ways as well, television models an unreal world (Table 10–2).

"High exposure to media violence is a major contributing cause of the high rate of violence in modern U.S. society."
—Social psychologist Craig A. Anderson, testifying to the U.S. Senate Commerce, Science, and Transportation Committee, March 21, 2000

table 10–2   America's television world versus the real world

How closely does prime-time network television drama mirror the world around us? Compare the percentages of people and behaviors on TV dramas with those in the real world. Television may reflect culture's mythology, but it distorts the reality.

Item Viewed	Seen on Television (%)	In the Real World (%)
Female	33	51
Married	10	61
Blue collar	25	67
Having a religious affiliation	6	88
Implied intercourse partners unmarried	85	unknown
Beverages consumed: percentage alcoholic	45	16
Murder as percentage of crimes on reality-based police shows	50	0.2

From an analysis of nearly 35,000 television characters since 1969 by George Gerbner (1993; Gerbner & others, 1986). TV sex data from Fernandez-Collado & others (1978). TV religion data from Skill & others (1994); actual religion data from Saad & McAneny (1994)—percent for whom religion is fairly or very important. Alcohol data from NCTV (1988). Percentage of sex acts that occur among unmarried partners is surely a fraction of that depicted on TV, given that most adults are married, that frequency of intercourse is higher among the married than among singles, and that extramarital sex is rarer than commonly believed (Greeley, 1991; Laumann & others, 1994). Murder data from Oliver (1994).

One TV critic estimated that if real people were murdered at the rate of TV characters, the population would be killed off in 50 days (Medved, 1995).

But there is good news here, too. If the ways of relating and problem solving modeled on television do trigger imitation, especially among young viewers, then modeling **prosocial behavior** should be socially beneficial. Chapter 12 contains good news: Television's subtle influence can indeed teach children positive lessons in behavior.

prosocial behavior
Positive, constructive, helpful social behavior; the opposite of antisocial behavior.

Television's effects on thinking

We have focused on television's effect on behavior. Researchers have also examined the cognitive effects of viewing violence: Does prolonged viewing desensitize us to cruelty? Does it distort perceptions of reality? Does it prime aggressive thoughts?

Desensitization.   Repeat an emotion-arousing stimulus, like an obscene word, over and over. What happens? From introductory psychology you may recall that the emotional response will "extinguish." After witnessing thousands of acts of cruelty, there is good reason to expect a similar emotional numbing. The most common response might well become, "Doesn't bother me at all." Such a response is precisely what Victor Cline and his colleagues (1973) observed when they measured the physiological arousal of 121 Utah boys who watched a brutal boxing match. Compared with boys who watched little television, the responses of those who watched habitually were more a shrug than a concern.

Of course, these boys might differ in ways other than television viewing. But in experiments on the effects of viewing sexual violence, similar desensitization—a sort of psychic numbness—occurs among young men who view slasher films. Moreover, experiments by Ronald Drabman and Margaret Thomas (1974, 1975, 1976) confirmed that such viewing breeds a more blasé reaction when later viewing the film of a brawl or when actually observing two children fighting.

In one survey of 5,456 middle-school students, exposure to movies with brutality was widespread (Sargent & others, 2002). Two-thirds had seen *Scream*. Such viewing patterns help explain why, despite the portrayals of extreme violence (or should we say *because* of it) Gallup youth surveys show that the percentage of 13- to 17-year-olds feeling there was too much movie violence has declined, from 42 percent in 1977 to 27 percent in 2003. As movies have become more sexually explicit, teen concern about sex in the movies has similarly declined. Today's teens "appear to have become considerably more desensitized to graphic depictions of violence and sex than their parents were at their age," concludes Gallup researcher Josephine Mazzuca (2002).

(Dan Perkins/THIS MODERN WORLD)

People who watch many hours of television see the world as a dangerous place. Reprinted with permission of Dan Perkins.

Altered perceptions. Does television's fictional world also mold our conceptions of the real world? George Gerbner and his University of Pennsylvania associates (1979, 1994) suspected this is television's most potent effect. Their surveys of both adolescents and adults show that heavy viewers (four hours a day or more) are more likely than light viewers (two hours or fewer) to exaggerate the frequency of violence in the world around them and to fear being personally assaulted. Similar feelings of vulnerability have been expressed by South African women after viewing violence against women (Reid & Finchilescu, 1995). A national survey of American 7- to 11-year-old children found that heavy viewers were more likely than light viewers to admit fears "that somebody bad might get into your house" or that "when you go outside, somebody might hurt you" (Peterson & Zill, 1981).

Cognitive priming. Finally, new evidence reveals that watching violent videos primes networks of aggressive-related ideas (Bushman, 1998). After viewing violence, people offer more hostile explanations for others' behavior (was the shove intentional?). They interpret spoken homonyms with the more aggressive meaning (interpreting "punch" as a hit rather than a drink). And they recognize aggressive words more quickly.

Perhaps television's biggest effect relates not to its quality but its quantity. Compared with more active recreation, TV watching sucks people's energy and

"The more fully that any given generation was exposed to television in its formative years, the lower its civic engagement [its rate of voting, joining, meeting, giving, and volunteering]."
—Robert Putnam, *Bowling Alone*, 2000

dampens their moods (Kubey & Csikszentmihaly, 2002). Moreover, TV annually replaces in people's lives a thousand or more hours of other activities. If, like most others, you have spent a thousand-plus hours per year watching TV, think how you might have used that time if there were no television. What difference would that have made in who you are today? In seeking to explain the post-1960 decline in civic activities and organizational memberships, Robert Putnam (2000) reported that every added hour a day spent watching TV competes with civic participation. Television steals time from club meetings, volunteering, church activity, and political engagement.

MEDIA INFLUENCES: VIDEO GAMES

"The scientific debate over *whether* media violence has an effect is basically over," contend Douglas Gentile and Craig Anderson (2003). Researchers are now shifting their attention to video games, which have exploded in popularity and are exploding with increasing brutality. Educational research shows that "video games are excellent teaching tools," note Gentile and Anderson. "If health video games can successfully teach health behaviors, and flight simulator video games can teach people how to fly, then what should we expect violent murder-simulating games to teach?"

The games kids play

"We had an internal rule that we wouldn't allow violence against people."
—Nolan Bushnell, Atari founder

In 2002, the video game industry celebrated its 30th birthday. Since the first video game in 1972 we have moved, as the timeline in Table 10–3 shows, from electronic Ping-Pong to splatter games (Anderson, 2004; Gentile & Anderson, 2003).

table 10–3 **The history of video game violence**

1972	*Pong*, the first commercial video game, introduced.
1976	*Death Race*, the first violent video game, invites players to drive a car over running stick figures.
1977	Atari console video game era begins. Contains (by today's standards) modest violence, such as blowing up alien spaceships.
1985	Nintendo era begins. Offers moderate violence, such as throwing fireballs in *Super Mario Brothers* games.
1992	*Wolfenstein 3D* offers first-person shooter game, enabling player to see action as if one was holding the gun, moving in realistic three-dimensional world, and seeing blood and gore.
1993	*Mortal Kombat* and successor games offer fights to the death; the most graphically violent versions sell millions.
1995	Sony Playstation era begins, with new graphics displaying more vivid violence.
2000	*Soldier of Fortune* displays realistic gore, as when shooting someone in the arm rips the arm from its socket and exposes bone, sinew, and blood.
2002	*Grand Theft Auto: Vice City* and its predecessors abandon boundaries of civilized behavior, enabling players to shoot cops, beat women to death with baseball bats, and have sex with and kill prostitutes.

These mass murder simulators are not obscure games. By the turn of the century, some 200 million games a year were being purchased, and the average 2- to 17-year-old was playing video games seven hours a week. In one survey of fourth graders, 59 percent of girls and 73 percent of boys reported their favorite games as violent ones (Anderson, 2003, 2004). Games rated "M" (mature) are supposedly intended for sale only to those 17 and older but often get marketed to those younger. The Federal Trade Commission found that in four out of five attempts, underage children could easily purchase them (Pereira, 2003).

Effects of the games kids play

Concerns about violent video games heightened after teen assassins in Kentucky, Arkansas, and Colorado enacted the horrific violence they had so often played on-screen. People wondered: When youth role-play attacking and dismembering people, do they learn anything that stays with them?

Most smokers don't die of heart disease. Most abused children don't become abusive. And most people who spend hundreds of hours rehearsing human slaughter live gentle lives. This enables video game defenders, like tobacco and TV interests, to say their products are harmless. "There is absolutely no evidence, none, that playing a violent game leads to aggressive behavior," contended Doug Lowenstein (2000), president of the Interactive Digital Software Association. Gentile and Anderson nevertheless offer some reasons why violent game playing *might* have a more toxic effect than watching violent television. With game playing, players

- identify with, and play the role of, a violent character.
- actively rehearse violence, not just passively watch it.
- engage in the whole sequence of enacting violence—selecting victims, acquiring weapons and ammunition, stalking the victim, aiming the weapon, pulling the trigger.
- are engaged with continual violence and threats of attack.
- repeat violent behaviors over and over.
- are rewarded for effective aggression.

For such reasons, military organizations often prepare soldiers to fire in combat (which many in World War II reportedly were hesitant to do) by engaging them with attack simulation games.

But what does the available research actually find? Craig Anderson (2003, 2004; Anderson & others, in press) offers statistical digests of three dozen available studies that reveal five consistent effects. Playing violent video games, more than playing nonviolent games

- *increases arousal*—heart rate and blood pressure rise.
- *increases aggressive thinking*—for example, Brad Bushman and Anderson (2002) found that after playing games such as *Duke Nukem* and *Mortal Kombat,* university students became more likely to guess that a man whose car was just rear-ended would respond aggressively, by using abusive language, kicking out a window, or starting a fight. Anderson and his colleagues (2003) find that violent music lyrics also prime aggressive thinking, making students more likely to complete "h_t" as "hit" rather than "hat."

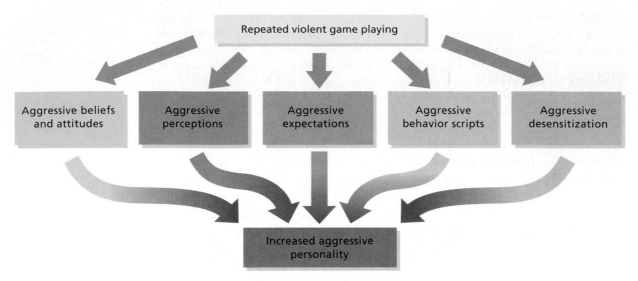

figure 10–10

Violent video game influences on aggressive tendencies.

Source: Adapted from Craig A. Anderson and Brad J. Bushman (2001).

- *increases aggressive feelings*—frustration levels rise, as does expressed hostility.
- *increases aggressive behaviors*—after violent game play, children and youth play more aggressively with their peers, get into more arguments with their teachers, and participate in more fights. The effect occurs inside and outside of the laboratory, across self-reports, teacher reports, and parent reports, and for reasons illustrated in Figure 10–10.
- *decreases prosocial behaviors*—after violent video game playing, people become slower to help a person whimpering in the hallway outside and slower to offer help to peers.

Moreover, the more violent the games played, the bigger the effects. Video games *have* become more violent, which helps explain why newer studies find the biggest effects. Although much remains to be learned, these studies indicate that, contrary to the catharsis hypothesis, practicing violence breeds rather than releases violence.

As a concerned scientist, Anderson (2003, 2004) therefore encourages parents to discover what their kids are ingesting and to ensure that their media diet, as least in their own home, is healthy. Parents may not be able to control what their child watches, plays, and eats in someone else's home, but they can oversee consumption in their own home and provide increased time for alternative activities. Networking with other parents can build a kid-friendly neighborhood. And schools can help by providing media awareness education.

GROUP INFLUENCES

We have considered what provokes *individuals* to aggress. If frustrations, insults, and aggressive models heighten the aggressive tendencies of isolated people, then such factors are likely to prompt the same reaction in groups. As a riot begins, aggressive acts often spread rapidly after the "trigger" example of one antagonistic person. Seeing looters freely helping themselves to TV sets, normally law-abiding bystanders may drop their moral inhibitions and imitate.

the story behind the research:
Craig Anderson on video game violence

Understanding the clearly harmful effects being documented by TV/film violence researchers, I was disturbed as I noticed the increasing violence in video games. With one of my graduate students, Karen Dill, I therefore began correlational and experimental investigations that intersected with growing public concern and led to my testifying before a U.S. Senate subcommittee and consulting for a wide array of government and public policy groups, including parent and child advocacy organizations.

Although it is gratifying to see one's research have a positive impact, the video game industry has gone to great lengths to dismiss the research, much as 30 years ago cigarette manufacturers ridiculed basic medical research by asking how many Marlboros a lab rat had to smoke before contracting cancer. I also get some pretty nasty mail from gamers, and the volume of requests for information led me to offer resources and answers at www. psychology.iastate.edu/faculty/caa.

Many people believe that the best way to enhance understanding of a complicated topic is to find people who will give opposite views and give each "side" equal time. Media violence news stories typically give equal time to industry representatives and their preferred "experts" along with reassuring words from a carefree 14-year-old, which can leave the impression that we know less than we do. If all the experts in a given area agree, does this idea of "fairness" and "balance" make sense? Or should we expect that legitimate experts will have published peer-reviewed original research articles on the issue at hand?

Craig A. Anderson,
Iowa State University

Groups can amplify aggressive reactions partly by diffusing responsibility. Decisions to attack in war typically are made by strategists remote from the front lines. They give orders, but others carry them out. Does such distancing make it easier to recommend aggression?

Jacquelin Gaebelein and Anthony Mander (1978) simulated this situation in the laboratory. They asked their University of North Carolina Greensboro students to *shock* someone or to *advise* someone how much shock to administer. When the recipient was innocent of any provocation, as are most victims of mass aggression, the front-line participants gave less shock than recommended by the advisers, who felt less directly responsible for any hurt.

Diffusion of responsibility increases not only with distance but with numbers. (Recall from Chapter 8 the phenomenon of deindividuation.) Brian Mullen (1986) analyzed information from 60 lynchings occurring between 1899 and 1946 and made an interesting discovery: The greater the number of people in a lynch mob, the more vicious the murder and mutilation.

Through social "contagion," groups magnify aggressive tendencies, much as they polarize other tendencies. Examples are youth gangs, soccer fans, rapacious soldiers, urban rioters, and what Scandinavians call "mobbing"—schoolchildren in groups repeatedly harassing or attacking an insecure, weak

Social contagion. When 17 juvenile, orphaned male bull elephants were relocated during the mid-1990s to a South African park, they became an out-of-control adolescent gang and killed 40 white rhinoceros. In 1998, concerned park officials relocated six older, stronger bull elephants into their midst. The result: The rampaging soon quieted down (Slotow & others, 2000). One of these dominant bulls, at left, faces down several of the juveniles.

"The worst barbarity of war is that it forces men collectively to commit acts against which individually they would revolt with their whole being."
—Ellen Key, *War, Peace, and the Future,* 1916

schoolmate (Lagerspetz & others, 1982). Mobbing is a group activity. One bully alone rarely taunts or attacks.

Youths sharing antisocial tendencies and lacking close family bonds and expectations of academic success may find social identity in a gang. As group identity develops, conformity pressures and de-individuation increase (Staub, 1996). Self-identity diminishes as members give themselves over to the group, often feeling a satisfying oneness with the others. The frequent result is social contagion—group-fed arousal, disinhibition, and polarization. Until gang members marry out, age out, get a job, go to prison, or die, explained gang expert Arnold Goldstein (1994), they hang out. They define their turf, display their colors, challenge rivals, and sometimes commit delinquent acts and fight over drugs, territory, honor, girls, or insults.

The twentieth-century massacres that claimed over 150 million lives were "not the sums of individual actions," notes Robert Zajonc (2000). *"Genocide is not the plural of homicide."* Massacres are *social* phenomena fed by "moral impera-tives"—a collective mentality (including images, rhetoric, and ideology) that mobilizes a group or a culture for extraordinary actions. The massacres of Rwanda's Tutsis, of Europe's Jews, and of America's native population were collective phenomena requiring widespread support, organization, and partici-pation. Rwanda's Hutu government and business leaders bought and distrib-uted 2 million Chinese machetes "for but one purpose."

Experiments in Israel by Yoram Jaffe and Yoel Yinon (1983) confirm that groups can amplify aggressive tendencies. In one, university men angered by a supposed fellow participant retaliated with decisions to give much stronger shocks when in groups than when alone. In another experiment (Jaffe & others, 1981), people decided, either alone or in groups, how much punishing shock to give someone for incorrect answers on an ESP task. As Figure 10–11 shows, in-dividuals gave progressively more of the assumed shock as the experiment pro-ceeded, and group decision making magnified this individual tendency. When circumstances provoke an individual's aggressive reaction, the addition of group interaction will often amplify it.

Aggression studies provide an apt opportunity to ask how well social psy-chology's laboratory findings generalize to everyday life. Do the circumstances that trigger someone to deliver electric shock really tell us anything about the circumstances that trigger verbal abuse or a punch in the face? Craig Anderson and Brad Bushman (1997; Bushman & Anderson, 1998) note that social psy-chologists have studied aggression in both the laboratory and everyday worlds, and the findings are strikingly consistent. In both contexts, increased aggression is predicted by the following:

- Male actors
- Aggressive or Type A personalities
- Alcohol use
- Violence viewing

- Anonymity
- Provocation
- The presence of weapons
- Group interaction

The laboratory allows us to test and revise theories under controlled condi-tions. Real-world events inspire ideas and provide the venue for applying our

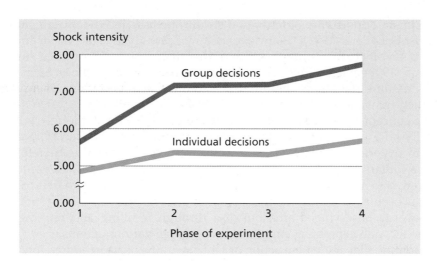

figure 10–11
Group-enhanced aggression.
When individuals chose how much shock to administer as punishment for wrong answers, they escalated the shock level as the experiment proceeded. Group decision making further polarized this tendency. **Source:** Data from Jaffe & others, 1981.

theories. Aggression research illustrates that an interplay between studies in the controlled lab and the complex real world advances psychology's contribution to human welfare. Hunches gained from everyday experience inspire theories, which stimulate laboratory research, which then deepens our understanding and our ability to apply psychology to real problems.

Summing up

Aversive experiences include not only frustrations but also discomfort, pain, and personal attacks, both physical and verbal. Arousal from almost any source, even physical exercise or sexual stimulation, can be transformed into anger.

Television portrays considerable violence. Correlational and experimental studies converge on the conclusion that viewing violence (1) breeds a modest increase in *aggressive behavior*, especially in people who are provoked, and (2) *desensitizes* viewers to aggression and alters their *perceptions* of reality. These two findings parallel the results of research on the effects of viewing violent pornography, which can increase men's aggression against women and distort their perceptions of women's responses to sexual coercion. Repeatedly playing violent video games may even more greatly increase aggressive thinking, feelings, and behavior.

Much aggression is committed by groups. Circumstances that provoke individuals may also provoke groups. By diffusing responsibility and polarizing actions, group situations amplify aggressive reactions.

How can aggression be reduced?

We have examined instinct, frustration-aggression, and social learning theories of aggression, and we have scrutinized influences on aggression. How, then, can we reduce aggression? Do theory and research suggest ways to control aggression?

CATHARSIS?

"Youngsters should be taught to vent their anger." So advised Ann Landers (1969). If a person "bottles up his rage, we have to find an outlet. We have to give him an opportunity of letting off steam." So asserted the prominent psychiatrist Fritz Perls (1973). "Some expression of prejudice . . . lets off steam . . . it can siphon off conflict through words, rather than actions." So argued Andrew Sullivan (1999) in a *New York Times Magazine* article on hate crimes. Such statements assume the "hydraulic model"—accumulated aggressive energy, like dammed-up water, needs a release.

The concept of catharsis is usually credited to Aristotle. Although Aristotle actually said nothing about aggression, he did argue that we can purge emotions by experiencing them and that viewing the classic tragedies therefore enabled a catharsis ("purgation") of pity and fear. To have an emotion excited, he believed, is to have that emotion released (Butcher, 1951). The catharsis hypothesis has been extended to include the emotional release supposedly obtained not only by observing drama but also through recalling and reliving past events, through expressing emotions, and through various actions.

Assuming that aggressive action or fantasy drains pent-up aggression, some therapists and group leaders encourage people to ventilate suppressed aggression by acting it out—by whopping one another with foam bats or beating a bed with a tennis racket while screaming. If led to believe that catharsis effectively vents emotions, people will react more aggressively to an insult as a way to improve their mood (Bushman & others, 2001). Some psychologists, believing that catharsis is therapeutic, advise parents to encourage children's release of emotional tension through aggressive play. Actually, notes researcher Brad Bushman (2002), "Venting to reduce anger is like using gasoline to put out a fire."

Many lay people have also bought the catharsis idea, as reflected in their nearly two-to-one agreement with the statement, "Sexual materials provide an outlet for bottled-up impulses" (Niemi & others, 1989). But then other national surveys reveal that most Americans also agree, "Sexual materials lead people to commit rape." So is the catharsis approach valid or not?

"It is time to put a bullet, once and for all, through the heart of the catharsis hypothesis. The belief that observing violence (or 'ventilating it') gets rid of hostilities has virtually never been supported by research."
—Carol Tavris (1988, p. 194)

If viewing erotica provides an outlet for sexual impulses, places with high consumption of sex magazines should have low rape rates. After viewing erotica people should experience diminished sexual desire and men should be less likely to view and treat women as sexual objects. But studies show the opposites are true (Kelley & others, 1989; McKenzie-Mohr & Zanna, 1990). Sexually explicit videos are an aphrodisiac; they feed sexual fantasies that fuel a variety of sexual behaviors.

The near consensus among social psychologists is that contrary to what Freud, Lorenz, and their followers supposed, catharsis also fails to occur with violence (Geen & Quanty, 1977). For example, Robert Arms and his associates report that Canadian and American spectators of football, wrestling, and hockey games exhibit *more* hostility after viewing the event than before (Arms & others, 1979; Goldstein & Arms, 1971; Russell, 1983). Not even war seems to purge aggressive feelings. After a war, a nation's murder rate tends to jump (Archer & Gartner, 1976).

In laboratory tests of catharsis, Brad Bushman (2002) invited angered participants to hit a punching bag while either ruminating about the person who angered them or thinking about becoming physically fit. A third group did not hit the punching bag. Then, when given a chance to administer loud blasts of noise to the person who angered them, people in the punching bag plus rumination condition felt angrier and were most aggressive. Doing nothing at all more effectively reduced aggression than "blowing off steam."

In some real-life experiments, too, aggressing has led to heightened aggression. Ebbe Ebbesen and his co-researchers (1975) interviewed 100 engineers and technicians shortly after they were angered by layoff notices. Some were asked questions that gave them an opportunity to express hostility against their employer or supervisors—for example, "What instances can you think of where the company has not been fair with you?" Afterward, they answered a questionnaire assessing attitudes toward the company and the supervisors. Did the previous opportunity to "vent" or "drain off" their hostility reduce it? To the contrary, their hostility increased. Expressing hostility bred more hostility.

Sound familiar? Recall from Chapter 4 that cruel acts beget cruel attitudes. Furthermore, as we noted in analyzing Stanley Milgram's obedience experiments, little aggressive acts can breed their own justification. People derogate their victims, rationalizing further aggression. Even if retaliation sometimes (in the short run) reduces tension, in the long run it reduces inhibitions. Even when provoked people hit a punching bag *believing* it will be cathartic, the effect is the opposite—leading them to exhibit *more* cruelty, report Bushman and his colleagues (1999, 2000, 2001). "It's like the old joke," reflected Bushman (1999). "How do you get to Carnegie Hall? Practice, practice, practice. How do you become a very angry person? The answer is the same. Practice, practice, practice."

Should we therefore bottle up anger and aggressive urges? Silent sulking is hardly more effective, because it allows us to continue reciting our grievances as we conduct conversations in our head. Fortunately, there are nonaggressive ways to express our feelings and to inform others how their behavior affects us. Across cultures, those who reframe accusatory "you" messages as "I" messages— "I'm angry," or, "When you leave dirty dishes I get irritated"—communicate their feelings in a way that better enables the other person to make a positive response (Kubany & others, 1995). We can be assertive without being aggressive.

> "He who gives way to violent gestures will increase his rage."
> —Charles Darwin, *The Expression of Emotion in Man and Animals*, 1872

A SOCIAL LEARNING APPROACH

If aggressive behavior is learned, then there is hope for its control. Let us briefly review factors that influence aggression and speculate how to counteract them.

Aversive experiences such as frustrated expectations and personal attacks predispose hostile aggression. So it is wise to refrain from planting false, unreachable expectations in people's minds. Anticipated rewards and costs influence instrumental aggression. This suggests that we should reward cooperative, nonaggressive behavior. In experiments, children become less aggressive when caregivers ignore their aggressive behavior and reinforce their nonaggressive behavior (Hamblin & others, 1969). Punishing the aggressor is less consistently effective. Threatened punishment deters aggression only under ideal conditions when the punishment is strong, prompt, and sure; when it is combined with reward for the desired behavior; and when the recipient is not angry (R. A. Baron, 1977). Lacking such deterrence, aggression may erupt. This was evident in 1969 when the Montreal police force went on a 16-hour strike, in 1992 when helicopter TV coverage of the Los Angeles riot showed areas abandoned by police. In both cases, looting and destruction erupted until the police returned, and in 2003 when Iraq was overrun by looters during the post-Saddam police vacuum.

But there are limits to punishment's effectiveness. Most mortal aggression is impulsive, hot aggression—the result of an argument, an insult, or an attack. Thus, we must *prevent* aggression before it happens. We must teach

focus on | a clinical researcher looks at catharsis

John Bradshaw, in his best-seller *Homecoming: Reclaiming and Championing Your Inner Child*, details several of his imaginative techniques: asking forgiveness of your inner child, divorcing your parent and finding a new one (like Jesus), stroking your inner child, writing your childhood history. These techniques go by the name *catharsis*, that is, emotional engagement in past trauma-laden events. Catharsis is magnificent to experience and impressive to behold. Weeping, raging at parents long dead, hugging the wounded little boy who was once you are all stirring. You have to be made of stone not to be moved to tears. For hours afterward, you may feel cleansed and at peace—perhaps for the first time in years. Awakening, beginning again, and new departures all beckon.

Catharsis, as a therapeutic technique, has been around for more than a hundred years. It used to be a mainstay of psychoanalytic treatment, but no longer. Its main appeal is its afterglow. Its main drawback is that there is no evidence that it works. When you measure how much people like doing it, you hear high praise. When you measure whether anything changes, catharsis fares badly.

Source: From Martin E. P. Seligman, *What You Can Change and What You Can't: The Complete Guide to Successful Self-Improvement*, Alfred A. Knopf, 1994, pp. 238–239.

nonaggressive conflict-resolution strategies. If mortal aggression were cool and instrumental we could hope that waiting till it happens and severely punishing the criminal afterward would deter such acts. In that world, states that impose the death penalty might have a lower murder rate than states without the death penalty. But in our world of hot homicide, that is not so (Costanzo, 1998).

Physical punishment can also have negative side effects. Punishment is aversive stimulation; it models the behavior it seeks to prevent. And it is coercive (recall that we seldom internalize actions coerced with strong external justifications). These are reasons violent teenagers and child-abusing parents so often come from homes where discipline took the form of harsh physical punishment.

To foster a gentler world, we could model and reward sensitivity and cooperation from an early age, perhaps by training parents how to discipline without violence. Training programs encourage parents to reinforce desirable behaviors and to frame statements positively ("When you finish cleaning your room you can go play," rather than, "If you don't clean your room, you're grounded"). One "aggression-replacement program" has reduced rearrest rates of juvenile offenders and gang members by teaching the youths and their parents communication skills, training them to control anger, and raising their level of moral reasoning (Goldstein & others, 1998).

If observing aggressive models lowers inhibitions and elicits imitation, then we might also reduce brutal, dehumanizing portrayals in films and on television—steps comparable to those already taken to reduce racist and sexist portrayals. We can also inoculate children against the effects of media violence. Wondering if the TV networks would ever "face the facts and change their programming," Eron and Huesmann (1984) taught 170 Oak Park, Illinois, children that television portrays the world unrealistically, that aggression is less common and less effective than TV suggests, and that aggressive behavior is undesirable.

(Drawing upon attitude research, Eron and Huesmann encouraged children to draw these inferences themselves and to attribute their expressed criticisms of television to their own convictions.) When restudied two years later, these children were less influenced by TV violence than were untrained children. In a more recent study, Stanford University used 18 classroom lessons to persuade children to simply reduce their TV watching and video game playing (Robinson & others, 2001). They reduced their TV viewing by a third—and the children's aggressive behavior at school dropped 25 percent compared with children in a control school.

Aggressive stimuli also trigger aggression. This suggests reducing the availability of weapons such as handguns. Jamaica in 1974 implemented a sweeping anticrime program that included strict gun control and censorship of gun scenes from television and movies (Diener & Crandall, 1979). In the following year, robberies dropped 25 percent, nonfatal shootings 37 percent. In Sweden, the toy industry has discontinued the sale of war toys. The Swedish Information Service (1980) states the national attitude: "Playing at war means learning to settle disputes by violent means."

Suggestions such as these can help us minimize aggression. But given the complexity of aggression's causes and the difficulty of controlling them, who can feel the optimism expressed by Andrew Carnegie's forecast that, in the twentieth century, "To kill a man will be considered as disgusting as we in this day consider it disgusting to eat one." Since Carnegie uttered those words in 1900, some 200 million human beings have been killed. It is a sad irony that although today we understand human aggression better than ever before, humanity's inhumanity endures. Nevertheless, cultures can change. "The Vikings slaughtered and plundered," notes Natalie Angier, "Their descendants in Sweden haven't fought a war in nearly 200 years."

www.mhhe.com/**myers8**
Visit the Online Learning Center for an interactivity on aggression.

Summing up

How can we minimize aggression? Contrary to the catharsis hypothesis, expressing aggression more often breeds than reduces further aggression. The social learning approach suggests controlling aggression by counteracting the factors that provoke it—by reducing aversive stimulation, by rewarding and modeling nonaggression, and by eliciting reactions incompatible with aggression.

Personal Postscript: Reforming a violent culture

In 1960 the United States (apologies to readers elsewhere, but we Americans do have a special problem with violence) had 3.3 police officers for every reported violent crime. In 1993 we had 3.5 crimes for every police officer (Walinsky, 1995). Since then, the crime rate has lessened, thanks partly to our incarceration of six times as many people today as in 1960 and to a temporary drop in the population of 15- to 25-year-old males. Still, on my small campus, which required no campus police in 1960, we now employ six full-time and seven part-time officers, and we offer a nightly shuttle service to transport students around campus.

Americans' ideas for protecting ourselves abound:

- Buy a gun for self-protection. (We have . . . 211 million guns. . . which puts one at tripled risk of being murdered, often by a family member, and at fivefold increased risk of suicide [Taubes, 1992]. More sensible would be following the safer nations' policies of domestic disarmament.)
- Build more prisons. (We have, but until very recently crime continued to escalate. Moreover, the social and fiscal costs of incarcerating 2 million people, mostly men, are enormous.)
- Impose a "three strikes and you're out" requirement of lifetime incarceration for those convicted of three violent crimes. (But are we really ready to pay for all the new prisons—and prison hospitals and nursing homes—we would need to house and care for senescent former muggers?)
- Deter brutal crime and eliminate the worst offenders as Iran and Iraq do—by executing the offenders. To show that killing people is wrong— kill people who kill people. (But nearly all the cities and states with the dozen highest violent-crime rates already have the death penalty. Because most homicide is impulsive or under the influence of drugs or alcohol, murderers rarely calculate consequences.)

What matters more than a punishment's severity is its certainty. The National Research Council (1993) reports that a 50 percent increase in the probability of apprehension and incarceration reduces subsequent crime twice as much as does doubling incarceration duration. Even so, former FBI director Louis Freeh (1993) was skeptical that tougher or swifter punishment is the ultimate answer: "The frightening level of lawlessness which has come upon us like a plague is more than a law enforcement problem. The crime and disorder which flow from hopeless poverty, unloved children, and drug abuse can't be solved merely by bottomless prisons, mandatory sentencing, and more police." Reacting to crime after it happens is the social equivalent of Band-Aids on cancer.

An alternative approach is suggested by a story about the rescue of a drowning person from a rushing river. Having successfully administered first aid, the rescuer spots another struggling person and pulls her out, too. After a half dozen repetitions, the rescuer suddenly turns and starts running away while the river sweeps yet another floundering person into view. "Aren't you going to rescue that fellow?" asks a bystander. "Heck no," the rescuer shouts. "I'm going upstream to find out what's pushing all these people in."

To be sure, we need police, prisons, and social workers, all of whom help us deal with the social pathologies that plague us. It's fine to swat the mosquitoes, but better if we can drain the swamps—by revisioning our culture, challenging the social toxins that corrupt youth, and renewing the moral roots of character.

What do you think?

What forms of violence are commonplace in your community (your home or campus)? What punishments or repercussions are there for this violence? Are the punishments satisfactory? Are they deterring violence in your community? Based on the information in this chapter, discuss the nature of the violence and which theory of aggression most likely applies. What influenced this aggression? How might this type of aggression be reduced in your community?

Making the Social Connection

In this chapter we briefly considered David Buss's ideas about the evolutionary psychology of aggression. From Chapter 5, you may recall David Buss's ideas about evolution, gender, and mating preferences. In Chapter 11, we will encounter Buss's application of evolutionary psychology to physical attractiveness. Are there commonalities between mating strategies in humans and in animals? Go to the *SocialSense* CD-ROM to view a brief clip of Buss discussing evolutionary psychology.

chapter 11

Attraction and Intimacy: Liking and Loving Others

"I get by with a little help from my friends."

John Lennon and Paul McCartney, Sgt. Pepper's Lonely Hearts Club Band, *1967*

need to belong
A motivation to bond with others in relationships that provide ongoing, positive interactions.

Our lifelong dependence on one another puts relationships at the core of our existence. In the beginning there was attraction—the attraction between a particular man and a particular woman to which we each owe our existence. Aristotle called humans "the social animal." Indeed, we have an intense **need to belong**—to connect with others in enduring, close relationships.

Social psychologists Roy Baumeister and Mark Leary (1995) illustrate the power of social attractions bred by our need to belong.

- For our ancestors, mutual attachments enabled group survival. When hunting game or erecting shelter, 10 hands were better than 2.

- For a woman and a man, the bonds of love can lead to children, whose survival chances are boosted by the nurturing of two bonded parents who support each other.

- For children and their caregivers, social attachments enhance survival. Unexplainably separated from each other, parent and toddler may each panic, until reunited in a tight embrace. Reared under extreme neglect or in institutions without belonging to anybody, children become pathetic, anxious creatures.

- For people everywhere, actual and hoped-for close relationships preoccupy thinking and color emotions. Finding a supportive soul mate in whom we can confide, we feel accepted and prized. Falling in love, we feel irrepressible joy. Longing for acceptance and love, we spend billions on cosmetics, clothes, and diets.

- Exiled, imprisoned, or in solitary confinement, people ache for their own people and places. Rejected, we are at risk for depression (Nolan & others, 2003). Time goes slower and life seems more meaningless (Twenge & others, 2003).

- For the jilted, the widowed, and the sojourner in a strange place, the loss of social bonds triggers pain, loneliness, or withdrawal. Losing a soul-mate relationship, adults feel jealous, distraught, or bereaved, as well as more mindful of death and the fragility of life.

- Reminders of death in turn heighten our need to belong, to be with others and hold close those we love (Mikulincer & others, 2003; Wisman & Koole, 2003). Facing the terror of 9/11, millions of Americans called and connected with loved ones. Likewise, the shocking death of a classmate, co-worker, or family member brings people together, their differences no longer mattering.

We are, indeed, social animals. We need to belong. As Chapter 14 confirms, when we do belong—when we feel supported by close, intimate relationships—we tend to be healthier and happier.

At Australia's University of New South Wales, Kipling Williams (2002) explored what happens when our need to belong is thwarted by *ostracism* (acts of excluding or ignoring). Humans in all cultures, whether in schools, workplaces, or homes, use ostracism to regulate social behavior. So what is it like to be shunned—to be avoided, met with averted eyes, or given the silent treatment? People (women especially) respond to ostracism with depressed mood, anxiety, hurt feelings, efforts to restore relationship, and eventual withdrawal. The silent treatment is "emotional abuse" and "a terrible, terrible weapon to use" say those who have experienced it from a family member or co-worker. In experiments, people who are left out of a simple game of ball tossing feel deflated and stressed.

Sometimes deflation turns nasty. In several studies, Jean Twenge and her collaborators (2001, 2002; Baumeister & others, 2002) gave some people an experience of being socially included. Others experienced exclusion: They were either told (based on a personality test) that they "were likely to end up alone later in life" or that others whom they'd met didn't want them in their group. Those led to feel excluded became not only more likely to engage in self-defeating behaviors, such as underperforming on an aptitude test, they also became more likely to disparage or deliver a blast of noise to someone who had insulted them. If a small laboratory experience could produce such aggression, noted the

A recipe for violence: an unstable disposition plus ostracism. Mark Leary, Robin Kowalski, and their colleagues (2003) report that in all but 2 of 15 school shootings from 1995 to 2001, such as by Eric Harris and Dylan Klebold at Columbine High School, the assailants had suffered ostracism, bullying, or romantic rejection.

researchers, one wonders what aggressive tendencies "might arise from a series of important rejections or chronic exclusion."

Williams and his colleagues (2000) were surprised to discover that even "cyberostracism" by faceless people whom one will never meet takes a toll. (Perhaps you have experienced this when feeling ignored in a chat room or when your e-mail is not answered.) The researchers had 1,486 participants from 62 countries play a web-based game of throwing a flying disc with two others (actually computer-generated fellow players). Those ostracized by the other players experienced poorer moods and became more likely to conform to others' wrong judgments on a subsequent perceptual task. They also, in a follow-up experiment, exhibited heightened activity in a brain cortex area that also is activated in response to physical pain (Figure 11–1). Ostracism, it seems, is a real pain.

Williams and four of his colleagues (2000) even found ostracism stressful when each of them was ignored for an agreed-upon day by the unresponsive four others. Contrary to their expectations that this would be a laughter-filled

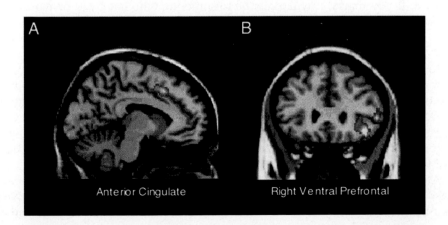

figure 11–1

The pain of rejection.

Naomi Eisenberger, Matthew Lieberman, and Kipling Williams (2003) report that social ostracism evokes a brain response similar to that triggered by physical pain.

Close relationships with friends and family contribute to health and happiness.

"I cannot tell how my ankles bend, nor whence the cause of my faintest wish, Nor the cause of the friendship I emit, nor the cause of the friendship I take again."
—Walt Whitman, *Song of Myself*, 1855

role-playing game, the simulated ostracism disrupted work, interfered with pleasant social functioning, and "caused temporary concern, anxiety, paranoia, and general fragility of spirit." To thwart our deep need to belong is to unsettle our life.

What leads to friendship and attraction?

What factors nurture liking and loving? Let's start with those that help initiate attraction: proximity, physical attractiveness, similarity, and feeling liked.

What predisposes one person to like, or to love, another? Few questions about human nature arouse greater interest. The ways affections flourish and fade form the stuff and fluff of soap operas, popular music, novels, and much of our everyday conversation. Long before I knew there was a field such as social psychology, I had memorized Dale Carnegie's recipe for *How to Win Friends and Influence People*.

So much has been written about liking and loving that almost every conceivable explanation—and its opposite—has already been proposed. For most people—and for you—what factors nurture liking and loving? Does absence make the heart grow fonder? Or is someone who is out of sight also out of mind? Is it likes that attract? Or opposites? How much do good looks matter? What has fostered your close relationships? Let's start with those factors that help a friendship begin and then consider those that sustain and deepen a relationship, thus satisfying our need to belong.

PROXIMITY

proximity
Geographical nearness. Proximity (more precisely, "functional distance") powerfully predicts liking.

One powerful predictor of whether any two people are friends is sheer **proximity.** Proximity can also breed hostility; most assaults and murders involve people living close together. But far more often, proximity kindles liking. Though it may seem trivial to those pondering the mysterious origins of romantic love, sociologists have found that most people marry someone who lives in the same neighborhood, or works at the same company or job, or sits in the same class (Bossard, 1932; Burr, 1973; Clarke, 1952; Katz & Hill, 1958). Look around. If you marry, it will likely be to someone who has lived or worked or studied within walking distance.

Interaction

Actually, it is not geographic distance that is critical but "functional distance"— how often people's paths cross. We frequently become friends with those who use the same entrances, parking lots, and recreation areas. Randomly assigned college roommates, who of course can hardly avoid frequent interaction, are far more likely to become good friends than enemies (Newcomb, 1961). Such interaction enables people to explore their similarities, to sense one another's liking, and to perceive themselves as a social unit (Arkin & Burger, 1980).

At my college the men and women once lived on opposite sides of the campus. They understandably bemoaned the lack of cross-sex friendships. Now that they occupy different areas of the same dormitories and share common

Feeling close to those close by. People often become attached to, and sometimes fall in love with, familiar co-workers.

sidewalks, lounges, and laundry facilities, friendships between men and women are far more frequent. So if you're new in town and want to make friends, try to get an apartment near the mailboxes, a desk near the coffeepot, a parking spot near the main buildings. Such is the architecture of friendship.

The chance nature of such contacts helps explain a surprising finding. Consider: If you had an identical twin who became engaged to someone, wouldn't you (being in so many ways similar to your twin) expect to share your twin's attraction to this person? But no, report researchers David Lykken and Auke Tellegen (1993); only half of identical twins recall really liking their twin's selection, and only 5 percent said, "I could have fallen for my twin's fiancée." Romantic love is often rather like ducklings' imprinting, surmised Lykken and Tellegen. With repeated exposure to someone, our infatuation may fix on almost anyone who has roughly similar characteristics and who reciprocates our affection.

Why does proximity breed liking? One factor is availability; obviously there are fewer opportunities to get to know someone who attends a different school or lives in another town. But there is more to it than that. Most people like their roommates, or those one door away, better than those two doors away. Those just a few doors away, or even a floor below, hardly live at an inconvenient distance. Moreover, those close by are potential enemies as well as friends. So why does proximity encourage affection more often than animosity?

> "When I'm not near the one I love, I love the one I'm near."
> —E. Y. Harburg, *Finian's Rainbow,* London: Chappell Music, 1947

Anticipation of interaction

Already we have noted that proximity enables people to discover commonalities and exchange rewards. What is more, merely *anticipating* interaction boosts liking. John Darley and Ellen Berscheid (1967) discovered this when they gave University of Minnesota women ambiguous information about two other women, one of whom they expected to talk with intimately. Asked how much they liked each one, the women preferred the person they expected to meet. Expecting to date someone similarly boosts liking (Berscheid & others, 1976). Even voters on the losing side of an election will find their opinions of the winning candidate—whom they are now stuck with—rising (Gilbert & others, 1998).

The phenomenon is adaptive. Anticipatory liking—expecting that someone will be pleasant and compatible—increases the chance of forming a rewarding relationship (Knight & Vallacher, 1981; Klein & Kunda, 1992; Miller & Marks, 1982). And how good that we are biased to like those we often see. Our lives are filled with relationships with people whom we may not have chosen but with whom we need to have continuing interactions—roommates, siblings, grandparents, teachers, classmates, co-workers. Liking such people is surely conducive to better relationships with them, which in turn makes for happier, more productive living.

Mere exposure

mere-exposure effect
The tendency for novel stimuli to be liked more or rated more positively after the rater has been repeatedly exposed to them.

Proximity leads to liking not only because it enables interaction and anticipatory liking, but also for another reason: More than 200 experiments reveal that, contrary to an old proverb, familiarity does not foster contempt. Rather it breeds fondness (Bornstein, 1989, 1999). **Mere exposure** to all sorts of novel stimuli—nonsense syllables, Chinese characters, musical selections, faces—boosts people's ratings of them. Do the supposed Turkish words *nansoma*, *saricik*, and *afworbu* mean something better or something worse than the words *iktitaf*, *biwojni*, and *kadirga*? University of Michigan students tested by Robert Zajonc (1968, 1970) preferred whichever of these words they had seen most frequently. The more times they had seen a meaningless word or a Chinese ideograph, the more likely they were to say it meant something good (Figure 11–2). This, I have found, makes a nifty class demonstration. Periodically flash certain

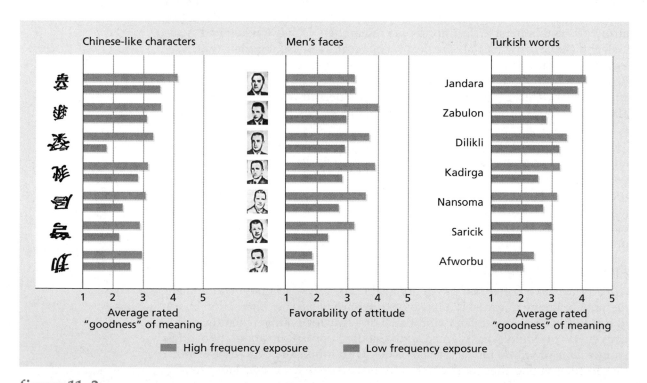

figure 11–2

The mere-exposure effect.

Students rated stimuli—a sample of which is shown here—more positively after being shown them repeatedly. **Source:** From Zajonc, 1968.

nonsense words on a screen. By the end of the semester, students will rate those "words" more positively than other nonsense words they have never before seen.

Or consider: What are your favorite letters of the alphabet? People of differing nationalities, languages, and ages prefer the letters appearing in their own names and those that frequently appear in their own languages (Hoorens & others, 1990, 1993; Kitayama & Karasawa, 1997; Nuttin, 1987). French students rate capital *W*, the least frequent letter in French, as their least favorite letter. Japanese students not only prefer letters from their names, but numbers corresponding to their birth dates. This "name letter effect" reflects more than mere exposure, however—see "Focus on: Liking Things Associated with Oneself" on page 430.

The mere-exposure effect violates the commonsense prediction of boredom—*decreased* interest in—repeatedly heard music or tasted foods (Kahneman & Snell, 1992). Unless the repetitions are incessant ("Even the best song becomes tiresome if heard too often," says a Korean proverb), liking usually increases. When completed in 1889, the Eiffel Tower in Paris was mocked as grotesque (Harrison, 1977). Today it is the beloved symbol of Paris.

Such changes make one wonder about initial reactions to new things. Do visitors to the Louvre in Paris really adore the *Mona Lisa*, or are they simply delighted to find a familiar face? It might be both: To know her is to like her. Eddie Harmon-Jones and John Allen (2001) explored this phenomenon experimentally. When they showed someone a woman's face, the person's cheek (smiling) muscle typically became more active with repeated viewings. Mere exposure breeds pleasant feelings.

Zajonc and his co-workers, William Kunst-Wilson and Richard Moreland, reported that exposure leads to liking even when people don't know that they have been exposed (Kunst-Wilson & Zajonc, 1980; Moreland & Zajonc, 1977; Wilson, 1979). In fact, mere exposure has an even stronger effect when people receive stimuli without awareness (Bornstein & D'Agostino, 1992). In one experiment, women students using headphones listened in one ear to a prose passage. They also repeated the words out loud and compared them with a written version to check for errors. Meanwhile, brief, novel melodies played in the other ear. This procedure focused attention on the verbal material and away from the tunes. Later, when the women heard the tunes interspersed among similar ones not previously played, they did not recognize them. Nevertheless, they *liked best* the tunes they had previously heard.

Note that conscious judgments about the stimuli in these experiments provided fewer clues to what people had heard or seen than did their instant feelings. You can probably recall immediately liking or disliking something or someone without consciously knowing why. Zajonc (1980) argues that *emotions are often more instantaneous than thinking*. Zajonc's rather astonishing idea—that emotions are semi-independent of thinking ("affect may precede cognition")—has found support in recent brain research. Emotion and cognition are enabled by distinct brain regions. Lesion a monkey's amygdala (an emotion-related structure) and its emotional responses will be impaired but its cognitive functions will be intact. Lesion its hippocampus (a memory-related structure) and its cognition will be impaired but its emotional responses remain intact (Zola-Morgan & others, 1991).

The mere-exposure effect has "enormous adaptive significance," notes Zajonc (1998). It is a "hardwired" phenomenon that predisposes our attractions and attachments. It helped our ancestors categorize things and people as either

focus on   liking things associated with oneself

We humans love to feel good about ourselves, and generally we do. Not only are we prone to self-serving bias (Chapter 2), we exhibit what Brett Pelham, Matthew Mirenberg, and John Jones (2002) call *implicit egotism:* We like what we associate with ourselves. This includes the letters of our name, but also the people, places, and things that we unconsciously connect with ourselves (Jones & others, 2002; Koole & others, 2001).

Such preferences appear to subtly influence major life decisions, including our locations and careers, report Pelham and his colleagues. Philadelphia, being larger than Jacksonville, has 2.2 times as many men named Jack. But it has 10.4 times as many people named Philip. Likewise, Virginia Beach has a disproportionate number of people named Virginia.

Does this merely reflect the influence of one's place when naming one's baby? Are people in Georgia, for example, more likely to name their babies George or Georgia? That may be so, but it doesn't explain why states tend to have a relative excess of people whose *last* names are similar to the state names. California, for example, has a disproportionate number of people whose names begin with Cali (as in Califano). Likewise, major Canadian cities tend to have larger-than-expected numbers of people whose last names overlap with the city names. Toronto has a marked excess of people whose names begin with Tor.

Moreover, women named "Georgia" are disproportionately likely to *move* to Georgia, as do Virginias to Virginia. Such mobility could help explain why St. Louis has a 49 percent excess (relative to the national proportion) of men named Louis, and why people named Hill, Park, Beach, Lake, or Rock are disproportionately likely to live in cities with names such as Park City that include their names. "People are attracted to places that resemble their names," surmise Pelham, Mirenberg, and Jones.

Weirder yet—I am not making this up—people seem to prefer careers related to their names. Across the United States, Jerry, Dennis, and Walter are equally popular names (0.42 percent of people carry each of these names). Yet America's dentists are almost twice as likely to be named Dennis as Jerry or Walter. There also are 2.5 times as many dentists named Denise as there are with the equally popular names, Beverly or Tammy. People named George or Geoffrey are overrepresented among geoscientists (geologists, geophysicists, and geochemists). And in the 2000 presidential campaign, people with last names beginning with B and G were more likely to contribute to the campaigns of Bush and Gore, respectively.

Reading about implicit egotism–based preferences gives me pause: Has this anything to do with why I enjoyed that trip to Fort Myers? Why I've written about moods, the media, and marriage? Why I collaborated with Professor Murdoch?

familiar and safe, or unfamiliar and possibly dangerous. The mere-exposure effect colors our evaluations of others: We like familiar people (Swap, 1977). Of course, the phenomenon's darker side is, as we noted in Chapter 9, our wariness of the unfamiliar—which may explain the primitive, automatic prejudice people often feel when confronting those who are different. Fearful or prejudicial feelings are not always expressions of stereotyped beliefs; sometimes the beliefs arise later as justifications for intuitive feelings.

We even like ourselves better when we are the way we're used to seeing ourselves. In a delightful experiment, Theodore Mita, Marshall Dermer, and Jeffrey Knight (1977) photographed women students at the University of Wisconsin-

The mere-exposure effect. If he is like most of us, Canadian prime minister Paul Martin may prefer his familiar mirror-image (left), which he sees each morning while brushing his teeth, to his actual image (right).

Milwaukee and later showed each one her actual picture along with a mirror image of it. Asked which picture they liked better, most preferred the mirror image—the image they were used to seeing. (No wonder our photographs never look quite right.) When close friends of the women were shown the same two pictures, they preferred the true picture—the image *they* were used to seeing.

Advertisers and politicians exploit this phenomenon. When people have no strong feelings about a product or a candidate, repetition alone can increase sales or votes (McCullough & Ostrom, 1974; Winter, 1973). After endless repetition of a commercial, shoppers often have an unthinking, automatic, favorable response to the product. If candidates are relatively unknown, those with the most media exposure usually win (Patterson, 1980; Schaffner & others, 1981). Political strategists who understand the mere-exposure effect have replaced reasoned argument with brief ads that hammer home a candidate's name and sound-bite message.

The respected chief of the Washington State Supreme Court, Keith Callow, learned this lesson when in 1990 he lost to a nominal opponent, Charles Johnson. Johnson, an unknown attorney who handled minor criminal cases and divorces, filed for the seat on the principle that judges "need to be challenged." Neither man campaigned, and the media ignored the race. On election day, the two candidates' names appeared without any identification—just one name next to the other. The result: a 53 percent to 47 percent Johnson victory. "There are a lot more Johnsons out there than Callows," offered the ousted judge afterward to a stunned legal community. Indeed, the state's largest newspaper counted 27 Charlie Johnsons in its local phone book. There was Charles Johnson, the local judge. And, in a nearby city, there was television anchorman Charles Johnson, whose broadcasts were seen on statewide cable TV. Forced to choose between two unknown names, many voters preferred the comfortable, familiar name of Charlie Johnson.

"We should look to the mind, and not to the outward appearances."
—Aesop, *Fables*

"Personal beauty is a greater recommendation than any letter of introduction."
—Aristotle, *Diogenes Laertius*

PHYSICAL ATTRACTIVENESS

What do (or did) you look for in a potential date? Sincerity? Good looks? Character? Humor? Conversational ability? Sophisticated, intelligent people are unconcerned with such superficial qualities as good looks; they know "beauty is only skin deep" and "you can't judge a book by its cover." At least they know that's how they *ought* to feel. As Cicero counseled, "Resist appearance."

The belief that looks matter little may be another instance of how we deny real influences upon us, for there is now a file cabinet full of research studies showing that appearance *does* matter. The consistency and pervasiveness of this effect is disconcerting. Good looks are a great asset.

Attractiveness and dating

Like it or not, a young woman's physical attractiveness is a moderately good predictor of how frequently she dates. A young man's attractiveness is slightly less a predictor of how frequently he dates (Berscheid & others, 1971; Krebs & Adinolfi, 1975; Reis & others, 1980, 1982; Walster & others, 1966). Moreover, women more than men say they would prefer a mate who's homely and warm over one who's attractive and cold (Fletcher & others, 2003). Does this imply, as many have surmised, that women are better at following Cicero's advice? Or does it merely reflect the fact that men more often do the inviting? If women were to indicate their preferences among various men, would looks be as important to them as to men? Philosopher Bertrand Russell (1930, p. 139) thought not: "On the whole women tend to love men for their character while men tend to love women for their appearance."

To see whether men are indeed more influenced by looks, researchers have provided male and female students with information about someone of the other sex, including a picture of the person. Or they have briefly introduced a man and a woman and later asked each about their interest in dating the other. In such experiments, men do put somewhat more value on opposite-sex physical attractiveness, as they do in opinion polls (Figure 11–3) (Feingold, 1990, 1991; Sprecher & others, 1994). Perhaps sensing this, women worry more about

figure 11–3

What women and men report finding most attractive.

Source: Fox News/Opinion Dynamics Poll of registered voters, 1999.

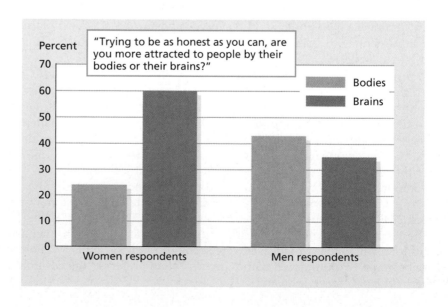

Percent

"Trying to be as honest as you can, are you more attracted to people by their bodies or their brains?"

Bodies
Brains

Women respondents   Men respondents

their appearance and constitute nearly 90 percent of cosmetic surgery patients (ASAPS, 2003). But women, too, respond to a man's looks.

In one ambitious study, Elaine Hatfield and her co-workers (1966) matched 752 University of Minnesota first-year students for a "Welcome Week" computer dance. The researchers gave each student personality and aptitude tests but then matched the couples randomly. On the night of the dance, the couples danced and talked for two and one-half hours and then took a brief intermission to evaluate their dates.

Attractiveness and dating. For Internet dating customers, looks are part of what is offered and sought.

How well did the personality and aptitude tests predict attraction? Did people like someone better who was high in self-esteem, or low in anxiety, or different from themselves in outgoingness? The researchers examined a long list of possibilities. But so far as they could determine, only one thing mattered: how physically attractive the person was (as previously rated by the researchers). The more attractive a woman was, the more the man liked her and wanted to date her again. And the more attractive the man was, the more the woman liked him and wanted to date him again. Pretty pleases.

The matching phenomenon

Not everyone can end up paired with someone stunningly attractive. So how do people pair off? Judging from research by Bernard Murstein (1986) and others, they pair off with people who are about as attractive as they are. Several studies have found a strong correspondence between the attractiveness of husbands and wives, of dating partners, and even of those within particular fraternities (Feingold, 1988). People tend to select as friends and especially to marry those who are a "good match" not only to their level of intelligence but also to their level of attractiveness.

Experiments confirm this **matching phenomenon.** When choosing whom to approach, knowing the other is free to say yes or no, people often approach someone whose attractiveness roughly matches (or not too greatly exceeds) their own (Berscheid & others, 1971; Huston, 1973; Stroebe & others, 1971). Good physical matches may also be conducive to good relationships, as Gregory White (1980) found in a study of UCLA dating couples. Those who were most similar in physical attractiveness were most likely, nine months later, to have fallen more deeply in love.

So who might we expect to be most closely matched for attractiveness—married couples or couples casually dating? White found, as have other researchers, that married couples are better matched.

Perhaps this research prompts you to think of happy couples who are not equally attractive. In such cases, the less attractive person often has compensating qualities. Each partner brings assets to the social marketplace, and the value

"If you would marry wisely, marry your equal."
—Ovid, 43 B.C.–A.D. 17

matching phenomenon
The tendency for men and women to choose as partners those who are a "good match" in attractiveness and other traits.

Dilbert   ## Scott Adams

DILBERT reprinted by permission of United Feature Syndicate, Inc.

"Love is often nothing but a favorable exchange between two people who get the most of what they can expect, considering their value on the personality market."

—Erich Fromm, *The Sane Society,* 1955

of the respective assets creates an equitable match. Personal advertisements exhibit this exchange of assets (Cicerello & Sheehan, 1995; Koestner & Wheeler, 1988; Rajecki & others, 1991). Men typically offer wealth or status and seek youth and attractiveness; women more often do the reverse: "Attractive, bright woman, 26, slender, seeks warm, professional male." Men who advertise their income and education, and women who advertise their youth and looks, receive more responses to their ads (Baize & Schroeder, 1995). The asset-matching process helps explain why beautiful young women often marry older men of higher social status (Elder, 1969).

The physical-attractiveness stereotype

Does the attractiveness effect spring entirely from sexual attractiveness? Clearly not, as Vicky Houston and Ray Bull (1994) discovered when they used a makeup artist to give an accomplice an apparently scarred, bruised, or birthmarked face. When riding on a Glasgow commuter rail line, people of both sexes avoided sitting next to the accomplice when she appeared facially disfigured. Moreover, much as adults are biased toward attractive adults, young children are biased toward attractive children (Dion, 1973; Dion & Berscheid, 1974; Langlois & others, 2000). To judge from how long they gaze at someone, even babies prefer attractive faces (Langlois & others, 1987). At three months, infants have not yet been brainwashed by *Baywatch* or *The Bachelor*.

Adults show a similar bias when judging children. Margaret Clifford and Elaine Hatfield (Clifford & Walster, 1973) gave Missouri fifth-grade teachers identical information about a boy or girl, but with the photograph of an attractive or unattractive child attached. The teachers perceived the attractive child as more intelligent and successful in school. Think of yourself as a playground supervisor having to discipline an unruly child. Might you, like the women studied by Karen Dion (1972), show less warmth and tact to an unattractive child? The sad truth is that most of us assume what we might call a "Bart Simpson effect"—that homely children are less able and socially competent than their beautiful peers.

What is more, we assume that beautiful people possess certain desirable traits. Other things being equal, we guess beautiful people are happier, sexually warmer, and more outgoing, intelligent, and successful—though not more

Asset matching. High-status Paul McCartney (60) and beautiful bride Heather Mills (34).

honest or concerned for others (Eagly & others, 1991; Feingold, 1992b; Jackson & others, 1995). In collectivist Korea, honesty and concern for others are highly valued and *are* traits people associate with attractiveness (Wheeler & Kim, 1997).

Added together, the findings define a **physical-attractiveness stereotype:** What is beautiful is good. Children learn the stereotype quite early. Snow White and Cinderella are beautiful—and kind. The witch and the stepsisters are ugly—and wicked. "If you want to be loved by somebody who isn't already in your family, it doesn't hurt to be beautiful," surmised one 8-year-old girl. Or as one kindergarten girl put it when asked what it means to be pretty, "It's like to be a princess. Everybody loves you" (Dion, 1979). Think Princess Diana.

If physical attractiveness is this important, then permanently changing people's attractiveness should change the way others react to them. But is it ethical to alter someone's looks? Such manipulations are performed millions of times a year by plastic surgeons and orthodontists. With teeth and nose straightened, hair replaced and dyed, face lifted, fat liposuctioned, and breasts enlarged, lifted, or reduced, can a self-dissatisfied person now find happiness? Despite spending much more on cosmetics and body alterations than in 1970, the proportion of women unhappy with their appearance has *increased* (Feingold & Mazzella, 1998).

To examine the effect of such alterations, Michael Kalick (1977) had Harvard students rate their impressions of eight women based on profile photographs taken before or after cosmetic surgery. Not only did they judge the women as more physically attractive after the surgery but also as kinder, more sensitive, more sexually warm and responsive, more likable, and so on. Ellen Berscheid (1981) noted that although such cosmetic improvements can boost self-image, they can also be temporarily disturbing:

> Most of us—at least those of us who have *not* experienced swift alterations of our physical appearance—can continue to believe that our physical attractiveness level plays a minor role in how we are treated by others. It is harder, however, for those

physical-attractiveness stereotype
The presumption that physically attractive people possess other socially desirable traits as well: What is beautiful is good.

"Even virtue is fairer in a fair body."
—Virgil, *Aeneid*

who have actually experienced swift changes in appearance to continue to deny and to minimize the influence of physical attractiveness in their own lives—and the fact of it may be disturbing, even when the changes are for the better.

To say that attractiveness is important, other things being equal, is not to say that physical appearance always outranks other qualities. Some people more than others judge people by their looks (Livingston, 2001). Moreover, attractiveness probably most affects first impressions. But first impressions are important—and are becoming more so as societies become increasingly mobile and urbanized and as contacts with people become more fleeting (Berscheid, 1981).

Though interviewers may deny it, attractiveness and grooming affect first impressions in job interviews (Cash & Janda, 1984; Mack & Rainey, 1990; Marvelle & Green, 1980). This helps explain why attractive people have more prestigious jobs and make more money (Umberson & Hughes, 1987). Patricia Roszell and her colleagues (1990) looked at the attractiveness of a national sample of Canadians whom interviewers had rated on a 1 (homely) to 5 (strikingly attractive) scale. They found that for each additional scale unit of rated attractiveness, people earned, on average, an additional $1,988 annually. Irene Hanson Frieze and her associates (1991) did the same analysis with 737 MBA graduates after rating them on a similar 1 to 5 scale using student picture book photos. For each additional scale unit of rated attractiveness, men earned an added $2,600 and women earned an added $2,150.

Do beautiful people indeed have desirable traits? Or was Leo Tolstoy correct when he wrote that it's "a strange illusion . . . to suppose that beauty is goodness"? There is some truth to the stereotype. Attractive children and young adults are somewhat more relaxed, outgoing, and socially polished (Feingold, 1992b; Langlois & others, 2000). William Goldman and Philip Lewis (1977) demonstrated this by having 60 University of Georgia men call and talk for five minutes with each of three women students. Afterward the men and women rated the most attractive of their unseen telephone partners as somewhat more socially skillful and likable. Physically attractive individuals tend also to be more popular, more outgoing, and more gender typed (more traditionally masculine if male, more feminine if female) (Langlois & others, 1996).

These small average differences between attractive and unattractive people probably result from self-fulfilling prophecies. Attractive people are valued and favored, and so many develop more social self-confidence. (Recall from Chapter 2 an experiment in which men evoked a warm response from unseen women they *thought* were attractive.) By this analysis, what's crucial to your social skill is not how you look but how people treat you and how you feel about yourself—whether you accept yourself, like yourself, feel comfortable with yourself.

Despite all the advantages of being beautiful, attraction researchers Elaine Hatfield and Susan Sprecher (1986) report there is also an ugly truth about beauty. Exceptionally attractive people may suffer unwelcome sexual advances and resentment from those of their own sex. They may be unsure whether others are responding to their performance, inner qualities, or just to their looks, which in time will fade (Satterfield & Muehlenhard, 1997). Moreover, if they can coast on their looks, they may be less motivated to develop themselves in other ways. Ellen Berscheid wonders whether we might still be lighting our houses

the story behind the research:
Ellen Berscheid on attractiveness

I vividly remember the afternoon I began to appreciate the far-reaching implications of physical attractiveness. Graduate student Karen Dion (now a professor at the University of Toronto) learned that some researchers at our Institute of Child Development had collected popularity ratings from nursery school children and taken a photo of each child. Although teachers and caregivers of children had persuaded us that "all children are beautiful" and no physical-attractiveness discriminations could be made, Dion suggested we instruct some people to rate each child's looks and correlate these with popularity. After doing so, we realized our long shot had hit home: Attractive children were popular children. Indeed, the effect was far more potent than we and others had assumed, with a host of implications that investigators are still tracing.

Ellen Berscheid
University of Minnesota

with candles if Charles Steinmetz, the homely and exceptionally short genius of electricity, had instead been subjected to the social enticements experienced by a Denzel Washington.

Who is attractive?

I have described attractiveness as if it were an objective quality like height, which some people have more of, some less. Strictly speaking, attractiveness is whatever the people of any given place and time find attractive. This, of course, varies. The beauty standards by which Miss Universe is judged hardly apply even to the whole planet. People in various places and times have pierced noses, lengthened necks, dyed hair, painted skin, gorged themselves to become voluptuous, starved to become thin, and bound themselves with leather garments to make their breasts seem small and used silicone and padded bras to make them seem big.

Despite such variations, there remains "strong agreement both within and across cultures about who is and who is not attractive," notes Judith Langlois and her colleagues (2000). People's agreement about others' attractiveness is especially high when men rate women, and less so for men rating men (Marcus & Miller, 2003).

To be really attractive is, ironically, to be perfectly average. Research teams led by Judith Langlois and Lorri Roggman (1990, 1994) at the University of Texas and Anthony Little and David Perrett (2002), working with Ian Penton-Voak at the University of St. Andrews, have digitized multiple faces and averaged them using a computer. Inevitably, people find the composite faces more appealing than almost all the actual faces.

Computer-averaged faces also tend to be perfectly symmetrical—another characteristic of strikingly attractive and reproductively successful people (Gangestad & Thornhill, 1997; Mealey & others, 1999; Shackelford & Larsen, 1997). Research teams led by Gillian Rhodes (1999) and by Ian Penton-Voak

figure 11–4

What of these faces do you find most attractive?

Biopsychologist Victor Johnston (2000) created the face on the left by averaging 16 female Caucasian faces. Then he subtly exaggerated the ways in which female faces differ from male faces to create a feminized hyperfemale face, which most people find the more attractive.

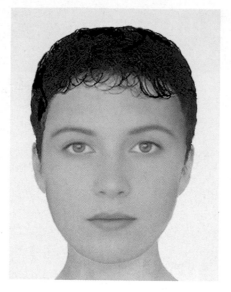 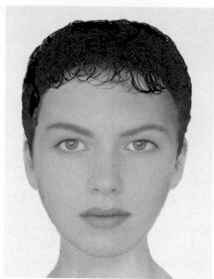

(2001) have shown that if you could merge either half of your face with its mirror image—thus forming a perfectly symmetrical new face—you would boost your looks a tad. Averaging a number of such symmetrical faces produces an even better looking face. So, in some respects, perfectly average is quite attractive. It's even true for dogs, birds, and wristwatches, report Jamin Halberstadt and Rhodes (2000). For example, what people perceive as your average dog they also rate as attractive.

Perfectly average is quite attractive. And what's attractive therefore feels more familiar than what's atypical and unattractive, observes Benoît Monin (2003). But even more attractive is a modest caricature of attractive features. Thus, for computer-generated female faces, the fairest of them all tends to be hyperfemale, with slightly smaller than average lower jaw, fuller lips, and larger eyes (Figure 11–4).

Evolution and attraction.   Psychologists working from the evolutionary perspective explain these gender differences in terms of reproductive strategy (Chapter 5). They assume that beauty signals biologically important information: health, youth, and fertility. Over time, men who preferred fertile-looking women outreproduced those who were as happy to mate with prepubescent or postmenopausal females. They also assume evolution predisposes women to favor male traits that signify an ability to provide and protect resources. That, David Buss (1989) believes, explains why the males he studied in 37 cultures—from Australia to Zambia—did indeed prefer female characteristics that signify reproductive capacity. And it explains why physically attractive females tend to marry high-status males and why men compete with such determination to display status by achieving fame and fortune. In screening potential mates, report Norman Li and his fellow researchers (2002), men require a modicum of physical attractiveness, women require status and resources, and both welcome kindness and intelligence.

Evolutionary psychologists have also explored men's and women's response to other cues to reproductive success. Judging from yesterday's Stone Age

"I love power because it attracts women."
—Henry Kissinger

figurines to today's centerfolds and beauty pageant winners, men everywhere have felt most attracted to women whose waists are 30 percent narrower than their hips—a shape associated with peak sexual fertility (Singh, 1993, 1995a; Singh & Young, 1995; Streeter & McBurney, 2003). Circumstances that reduce a woman's fertility—malnutrition, pregnancy, menopause—also change her shape.

When judging males as potential marriage partners, women, too, prefer a waist-to-hip ratio suggesting health and vigor and during ovulation show heightened preference for men with masculinized features (Gangestad & others, 2003; Macrae & others, 2002). This makes evolutionary sense, notes Jared Diamond (1996): A muscular hunk was more likely than a scrawny fellow to gather food, build houses, and defeat rivals. But today's women prefer even more those with high incomes (Singh, 1995b).

So, in every culture the beauty business is a big and growing business. Asians, Britains, Germans, and Americans are all seeking cosmetic surgery in rapidly increasing numbers (Wall, 2002). In the United States, for example, cosmetic procedures such as liposuction, breast augmentation, and Botox injections rose 228 percent between 1997 and 2002 (ASAPS, 2003). Beverly Hills now has

"My eggs, your sperm . . . sounds like a plan."

Evolutionary psychologists study reproductive strategies more subtle than this.
Copyright © David Sipress. Reprinted by permission of David Sipress.

Extreme makeover (as illustrated by former President Clinton's accuser, Paula Jones). If you imperfectly meet your culture's beauty standard, you can accept yourself, imperfections and all. Or you can paralyze wrinkle-causing muscles, suck away fat, and reshape your nose with a makeover. Question: Where would you draw the line between appropriate self-improvement and self-indulgent vanity? To what extent should we accept ourselves versus change our (unacceptable) selves? Would you support shaping up by losing weight? Acne treatments? Braces to align crooked teeth? A chin tuck? A nose job? Breast enlargement? An extreme makeover?

MAXINE by Marian Henley

Maxine!Comix © Marian Henley. Reprinted by permission of the artist.

"Women in the 50's vacuumed. Women in the 00's *are* vacuumed. Our Hoovers have turned on us!"

—*New York Times* columnist Maureen Dowd on liposuction (January 19, 2000)

twice as many plastic surgeons as pediatricians (*People*, 2003). Modern, affluent people with cracked or discolored teeth fix them. More and more, so do people with wrinkles and flab.

We are, evolutionary psychologists suggest, driven by primal attractions. Like eating and breathing, attraction and mating are too important to leave to the whims of culture.

Social comparison.   Although our mating psychology has biological wisdom, attraction is not all hardwired. What's attractive to you also depends on your comparison standards.

Douglas Kenrick and Sara Gutierres (1980) had male confederates interrupt Montana State University men in their dormitory rooms and explain, "We have a friend coming to town this week and we want to fix him up with a date, but we can't decide whether to fix him up with her or not, so we decided to conduct a survey. . . . We want you to give us your vote on how attractive you think she is . . . on a scale of 1 to 7." Shown a picture of an average young woman, those who had just been watching *Charlie's Angels,* a television show featuring three beautiful women, rated her less attractive than those who hadn't.

Laboratory experiments confirm this "contrast effect." To men who have recently been gazing at centerfolds, average women or even their own wives tend to seem less attractive (Kenrick & others, 1989). Viewing pornographic films simulating passionate sex similarly decreases satisfaction with one's own partner (Zillmann, 1989). Being sexually aroused may *temporarily* make a person of the other sex seem more attractive. But the lingering effect of exposure to perfect "10s," or of unrealistic sexual depictions, is to make one's own partner seem less appealing—more like a "6" than an "8."

It works the same way with our self-perceptions. After viewing a super-attractive person of the same gender, people feel *less* attractive than after viewing a homely person (Brown & others, 1992; Thornton & Maurice, 1997). This appears especially true for women. Men's self-rated desirability is also deflated by exposure to more dominant, successful men. Thanks to modern media, we may see in an hour "dozens of individuals who are more attractive and more successful than any of our ancestors would have seen in a year, or even a lifetime," note Sara Gutierres and her co-researchers (1999). Such extraordinary

"Love is only a dirty trick played on us to achieve a continuation of the species."

—Novelist W. Somerset Maugham, 1874–1965

Standards of beauty differ from culture to culture. Yet some people are considered attractive throughout most of the world.

comparison standards trick us into devaluing our potential mates and ourselves and spending billions and billions on cosmetics, diet aids, and plastic surgery.

The attractiveness of those we love.   Let's conclude our discussion of attractiveness on an upbeat note. First, a 17-year-old girl's facial attractiveness is a surprisingly weak predictor of her attractiveness at ages 30 and 50. Sometimes an average-looking adolescent, especially one with a warm, attractive personality, becomes a quite attractive middle-aged adult (Zebrowitz & others, 1993, 1998).

Second, not only do we perceive attractive people as likable, we also perceive likable people as attractive. Perhaps you can recall individuals who, as you grew to like them, became more attractive. Their physical imperfections were no longer so noticeable. Alan Gross and Christine Crofton (1977) had students view someone's photograph after reading a favorable or unfavorable description of the person's personality. Those portrayed as warm, helpful, and considerate also *looked* more attractive. Discovering someone's similarities to us also makes the person seem more attractive (Beaman & Klentz, 1983; Klentz & others, 1987).

Moreover, love sees loveliness: The more in love a woman is with a man, the more physically attractive she finds him (Price & others, 1974). And the more in love people are, the less attractive they find all others of the opposite sex (Johnson & Rusbult, 1989; Simpson & others, 1990). "The grass may be greener on the other side," note Rowland Miller and Jeffry Simpson (1990), "but happy gardeners are less likely to notice." To paraphrase Benjamin Franklin, when Jill's in love, she finds Jack more handsome than his friends.

"Do I love you because you are beautiful, or are you beautiful because I love you?"
—Prince Charming, in Rodgers & Hammerstein's *Cinderella*

Warm and likable people seem more attractive.
Copyright © Dan Piraro. Reprinted with special permission of King Features Syndicate.

Henry James's description of novelist George Eliot (the pen name of Mary Ann Evans): "She is magnificently ugly— deliciously hideous. She has a low forehead, a dull grey eye, a vast pendulous nose, a huge mouth, fully of uneven teeth, and a chin and jaw-bone qui n'en finissent pas. . . . Now in this vast ugliness resides a most powerful beauty which, in a very few minutes, steals forth and charms the mind, so that you end as I ended, in falling in love with her."

"Can two walk together except they be agreed?"
—Amos 3:3

SIMILARITY VERSUS COMPLEMENTARITY

From our discussion so far, one might surmise Leo Tolstoy was entirely correct: "Love depends . . . on frequent meetings, and on the style in which the hair is done up, and on the color and cut of the dress." As people get to know one another, however, other factors influence whether acquaintance develops into friendship.

Do birds of a feather flock together?

Of this much we may be sure: Birds that flock together are of a feather. Friends, engaged couples, and spouses are far more likely than people randomly paired to share common attitudes, beliefs, and values. Furthermore, the greater the similarity between husband and wife, the happier they are and the less likely they are to divorce (Byrne, 1971; Caspi & Herbener, 1990). Such correlational findings are intriguing. But cause and effect remain an enigma. Does similarity lead to liking? Or does liking lead to similarity?

Likeness begets liking.   To discern cause and effect, we experiment. Imagine that at a campus party Laura gets involved in a long discussion of politics, religion, and personal likes and dislikes with Les and Larry. She and Les discover they agree on almost everything, she and Larry on few things. Afterward, she reflects: "Les is really intelligent . . . and so likable . . . hope we meet again." In experiments, Donn Byrne (1971) and his colleagues captured the essence of Laura's experience. Over and over again, they found that the more similar someone's attitudes are to your own, the more likable you will find the person.

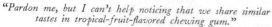
"Pardon me, but I can't help noticing that we share similar tastes in tropical-fruit-flavored chewing gum."

Likeness produces liking not only for college students but also for children and the elderly, for people of various occupations, and for those in various cultures.

This is especially so for those satisfied with themselves (Klohnen & Mendelsohn, 1998). If you like yourself, you are likely to partner with someone like yourself.

The likeness-leads-to-liking effect has been tested in real-life situations by noting who comes to like whom.

- At the University of Michigan, Theodore Newcomb (1961) studied two groups of 17 unacquainted male transfer students. After 13 weeks of boardinghouse life, those whose agreement was initially highest were most likely to have formed close friendships. One group of friends was composed of five liberal arts students, each a political liberal with strong intellectual interests. Another was made up of three conservative veterans who were all enrolled in the engineering college.

- William Griffitt and Russell Veitch (1974) compressed the getting-to-know-you process by confining 13 unacquainted men in a fallout shelter. (The men were paid volunteers.) Knowing the men's opinions on various issues, the researchers could predict with better-than-chance accuracy those each man would most like and most dislike.

- At two of Hong Kong's universities, Royce Lee and Michael Bond (1996) found that roommate friendships flourished over a six-month period when roommates shared values and personality traits, but more so when they perceived their roommates as similar. As so often happens, reality matters, but perception matters more.

- People like not only those who think as they do, but also those who act as they do. Subtle mimicry fosters fondness. Have you noticed that when someone nods their head as you do and echoes your thoughts, you feel a certain rapport and liking? That's a common experience, report Rick van Baaren and his colleagues (2003a, 2003b), and one result is higher tips for Dutch restaurant servers who mimic their customers by merely repeating their order. Moreover, people who are primed to affiliate with someone become more likely to mimic—for example, to unwittingly shake their foot or touch their face when the other does. Mimicry increases rapport, note Jessica Lakin and Tanya Chartrand (2003), and desire for rapport increases mimicry.

- When Peter Buston and Stephen Emlen (2003) surveyed nearly 1,000 college-age people, they found that the desire for similar mates far outweighed the desire for beautiful mates. Attractive people sought attractive mates. Wealthy people wanted mates with money. Family-oriented people desired family-oriented mates.

"And they are friends who have come to regard the same things as good and the same things as evil, they who are friends of the same people, and they who are the enemies of the same people. . . . We like those who resemble us, and are engaged in the same pursuits."
—Aristotle, *Rhetoric*

The matching phenomenon. Attractive people, such as Jennifer Aniston and husband Brad Pitt, value attractiveness in others and seek well-matched mates.

"Actually, Lou, I think it was more than just my being in the right place at the right time. I think it was my being the right race, the right religion, the right sex, the right socioeconomic group, having the right accent, the right clothes, going to the right schools . . ."

The most appealing people are those most like us.

So similarity breeds content. Birds of a feather *do* flock together. Surely you have noticed this upon discovering a special someone who shares your ideas, values, and desires, a soul mate who likes the same music, the same activities, even the same foods you do.

Dissimilarity breeds dislike.   We have a bias—the false consensus bias—toward assuming that others share our attitudes. When we discover that someone has dissimilar attitudes, we may dislike the person. People in one political party often are not so much fond of fellow party members as they are disdainful of the opposition (Rosenbaum, 1986; Hoyle, 1993).

In general, dissimilar attitudes depress liking more than similar attitudes enhance it (Singh & others, 1999, 2000). Within their own groups, where they expect similarity, people find it especially hard to like someone with dissimilar views (Chen & Kenrick, 2002). That perhaps explains why dating partners and roommates become more similar over time in their emotional responses to events and in their attitudes (Anderson & others, 2003; Davis & Rusbult, 2001). "Attitude alignment" helps promote and sustain close relationships, a phenomenon that can lead partners to overestimate their attitude similarities (Kenny & Acitelli, 2001; Murray & others, 2002). After four decades of life together, my wife and I think pretty much alike, although perhaps not quite as much alike as we each suppose. Although we're aware of our occasional differences from our close friends and partners, some "false consensus" tendency can help sustain our sense of being true kindred spirits.

Whether people perceive those of another race as similar or dissimilar influences their racial attitudes. Wherever one group of people regards another as "other"—as creatures who speak differently, live differently, think differently— the potential for oppression is high. In fact, except for intimate relationships such as dating, the perception of like minds seems more important for attraction than like skins. Most Whites have expressed more liking for, and willingness to work with, a like-minded Black than a dissimilarly minded White (Insko & others, 1983; Rokeach, 1968). The more that Whites presume that Blacks support their values, the more positive their racial attitudes (Biernat & others, 1996). Likewise, the more Montreal residents perceive a Canadian ethnic group as similar to themselves, the more willing they are to associate with its members (Osbeck & others, 1996).

"Cultural racism" persists, argues James Jones (1988, 2003, 2004), because cultural differences are a fact of life. Black culture tends to be present-oriented, spontaneously expressive, spiritual, and emotionally driven. White culture tends to be more future-oriented, materialistic, and achievement-driven. Rather than trying to eliminate such differences, says Jones, we might better appreciate what they "contribute to the cultural fabric of a multicultural society." There are situations in which expressiveness is advantageous and situations in which future orientation is advantageous. Each culture has much to learn from the other. In countries such as Canada, Britain, and the United States, where migration

and different birthrates make for growing diversity, educating people to respect and enjoy those who differ is a major challenge. Given increasing cultural diversity and given our natural wariness of differences, this may in fact be the major social challenge of our time.

Do opposites attract?

Are we not also attracted to people who in some ways *differ* from ourselves, in ways that complement our own characteristics? Researchers have explored this question by comparing not only friends' and spouses' attitudes and beliefs but also their ages, religions, races, smoking behaviors, economic levels, educations, height, intelligence, and appearance. In all these ways and more, similarity still prevails (Buss, 1985; Kandel, 1978). Smart birds flock together. So do rich birds, Protestant birds, tall birds, pretty birds.

Still we resist: Are we not attracted to people whose needs and personalities complement our own? Would a sadist and a masochist find true love? Even the *Reader's Digest* has told us that "opposites attract. . . . Socializers pair with loners, novelty-lovers with those who dislike change, free spenders with scrimpers, risk-takers with the very cautious" (Jacoby, 1986). Sociologist Robert Winch (1958) reasoned that the needs of an outgoing and domineering person would naturally complement those of someone who is shy and submissive. The logic seems compelling, and most of us can think of couples who view their differences as complementary: "My husband and I are perfect for each other. I'm Aquarius—a decisive person. He's Libra—can't make decisions. But he's always happy to go along with arrangements I make."

Given the idea's persuasiveness, the inability of researchers to confirm it is astonishing. For example, most people feel attracted to expressive, outgoing people (Friedman & others, 1988). Would this be especially so when one is down in the dumps? Do depressed people seek those whose gaiety will cheer them up? To the contrary, it is *non*depressed people who most prefer the company of happy people (Locke & Horowitz, 1990; Rosenblatt & Greenberg, 1988, 1991; Wenzlaff & Prohaska, 1989). When you're feeling blue, another's bubbly personality can be aggravating. The contrast effect that makes average people

www.mhhe.com/myers8
Visit the Online Learning Center for a scenario on love.

feel homely in the company of beautiful people also makes sad people more conscious of their misery in the company of cheerful people.

complementarity
The popularly supposed tendency, in a relationship between two people, for each to complete what is missing in the other.

Some **complementarity** may evolve as a relationship progresses (even a relationship between two identical twins). Yet people seem slightly more prone to like and to marry those whose needs and personalities are *similar* (Botwin & others, 1997; Buss, 1984; Fishbein & Thelen, 1981a, 1981b; Nias, 1979). Perhaps one day we will discover some ways (other than heterosexuality) in which differences commonly breed liking. Dominance/submissiveness may be one such way (Dryer & Horowitz, 1997). And we tend not to feel attracted to those who show our own worst traits (Schimel & others, 2000). But researcher David Buss (1985) doubts complementarity: "The tendency of opposites to marry, or mate . . . has never been reliably demonstrated, with the single exception of sex."

LIKING THOSE WHO LIKE US

Liking is usually mutual. Proximity and attractiveness influence our initial attraction to someone, and similarity influences longer-term attraction as well. If we have a deep need to belong and to feel liked and accepted, would we not also take a liking to those who like us? Are the best friendships mutual admiration societies? Indeed, one person's liking for another does predict the other's liking in return (Kenny & Nasby, 1980).

"The average man is more interested in a woman who is interested in him than he is in a woman with beautiful legs."
—Actress Marlene Dietrich (1901–1992)

But does one person's liking another *cause* the other to return the appreciation? People's reports of how they fell in love suggest yes (Aron & others, 1989). Discovering that an appealing someone really likes you seems to awaken romantic feelings. Experiments confirm it: Those told that certain others like or admire them usually feel a reciprocal affection (Berscheid & Walster, 1978).

And consider this finding by Ellen Berscheid and her colleagues (1969): Students like another student who says eight positive things about them better than one who says seven positive things and one negative thing. We are sensitive to the slightest hint of criticism. Writer Larry L. King speaks for many in noting, "I have discovered over the years that good reviews strangely fail to make the author feel as good as bad reviews make him feel bad." Whether we are judging ourselves or others, negative information carries more weight because, being less usual, it grabs more attention (Yzerbyt & Leyens, 1991). People's votes are more influenced by their impressions of presidential candidates' weaknesses than by their impressions of strengths (Klein, 1991), a phenomenon that has not been lost on those who design negative campaigns. It's a general rule of life, note Roy Baumeister and his colleagues (2001): Bad is stronger than good (see "Focus on: Bad Is Stronger Than Good").

That we like those we perceive as liking us was recognized long ago. Observers from the ancient philosopher Hecato ("If you wish to be loved, love") to Ralph Waldo Emerson ("The only way to have a friend is to be one") to

"Well—and I'm not just saying this because you're my husband—it stinks."

Dale Carnegie ("Dole out praise lavishly") anticipated the findings. What they did not anticipate was the precise conditions under which the principle works.

Attribution

As we've seen, flattery *will* get you somewhere. But not everywhere. If praise clearly violates what we know is true—if someone says, "Your hair looks great," when we haven't washed it in days—we may lose respect for the flatterer and wonder whether the compliment springs from ulterior motives (Shrauger,

> "If 60,000 people tell me they loved a show, then one walks past and says it sucked, that's the comment I'll hear."
> —Musician Dave Matthews, 2000

focus on | bad is stronger than good

Dissimilar attitudes, we have noted, turn us off to others more than similar attitudes turn us on. And others' criticism captures our attention and affects our emotion more than does their praise. Roy Baumeister, Ellen Bratslavsky, Catrin Finkenauer, and Kathleen Vohs (2001) say this is just the tip of an iceberg: "In everyday life, bad events have stronger and more lasting consequences than comparable good events." Consider:

- Destructive acts harm close relationships more than constructive acts build them. (Cruel words linger beyond kind words.)
- Bad moods affect our thinking and memory more than good moods. (Despite our natural optimism, it's easier to think of past bad emotional events than good ones.)
- There are more words for negative than positive emotions, and people asked to think of emotion words mostly come up with negative words. (*Sadness, anger,* and *fear* are the three most common.)
- Single bad events (traumas) have more lasting effects than single very good events. (A single rape produces harm that the most euphoric romantic experience cannot offset. A death triggers more search for meaning than does a birth.)
- Routine bad events receive more attention and trigger more rumination than do routine good events. (Losing money upsets people more than gaining the same money makes them happy.)
- Very bad family environments override the genetic influence on intelligence more than

do very good family environments. (Bad parents can make their genetically bright children less intelligent; good parents have more trouble making unintelligent children smarter.)
- A bad reputation is easier to acquire, and harder to shed, than a good one. (A single act of lying can destroy one's reputation for integrity.)
- Bad health decreases happiness more than good health increases it. (Pain produces misery far more than comfort produces joy.)

The power of the bad prepares us to deal with threats and protects us from death and disability. For survival, bad can be badder than good is good. The importance of the bad is one likely reason why the first century of psychology focused so much more on the bad than the good. Since 1887 *Psychological Abstracts* (a guide to psychology's literature) included 11,195 articles mentioning anger, 73,223 mentioning anxiety, and 90,169 mentioning depression. For every 18 articles on these topics, only one dealt with the positive emotions of joy (1,205), life satisfaction (4,585), or happiness (4,100). Similarly, "fear" (23,153 articles) has triumphed over "courage" (904). But the strength of the bad is "perhaps the best reason for a positive psychology movement," Baumeister and his colleagues surmise. To overcome the strength of individual bad events, "human life needs far more good than bad."

1975). Thus we often perceive criticism to be more sincere than praise (Coleman & others, 1987).

Laboratory experiments reveal something we've noted in previous chapters: Our reactions depend on our attributions. Do we attribute the flattery to **ingratiation**—to a self-serving strategy? Is the person trying to get us to buy something, to acquiesce sexually, to do a favor? If so, both the flatterer and the praise lose appeal (Gordon, 1996; Jones, 1964). But if there is no apparent ulterior motive, then we warmly receive both flattery and flatterer.

How we explain our own actions also matters. Clive Seligman, Russell Fazio, and Mark Zanna (1980) paid undergraduate dating couples to indicate "why you go out with your girlfriend/boyfriend." They asked some to rank seven intrinsic reasons, such as "I go with _____ because we always have a good time together" and "because we share the same interests and concerns." Others ranked possible extrinsic reasons: "because my friends think more highly of me since I began seeing her/him" and "because she/he knows a lot of important people." Asked later to respond to a "Love Scale," those whose attention had been drawn to possible extrinsic reasons for their relationships expressed less love for their partners and saw marriage as a less likely possibility than did those made aware of possible intrinsic reasons. (Sensitive to ethical concerns, the researchers debriefed all the participants afterward and confirmed that the experiment had no long-term effects on the participants' relationships.)

Self-esteem and attraction

Elaine Hatfield (Walster, 1965) wondered if another's approval is especially rewarding after we have been deprived of approval, much as eating is most rewarding after fasting. To test this idea, she gave some Stanford University women either very favorable or very unfavorable analyses of their personalities, affirming some and wounding others. Then she asked them to evaluate several people, including an attractive male confederate who just before the experiment had struck up a warm conversation with each woman and had asked each for a date. (Not one turned him down.) Which women do you suppose most liked the man? It was those whose self-esteem had been temporarily shattered and who were presumably hungry for social approval. (After this experiment Hatfield spent almost an hour explaining the experiment and talking with each woman. She reports that in the end, none remained disturbed by the temporary ego blow or the broken date.)

This helps explain why people sometimes fall passionately in love on the rebound, after an ego-bruising rejection. Unfortunately, however, low-self-esteem individuals tend to underestimate their partner's appreciation for them. They also reciprocate with less generous views of their partner and therefore feel less happy with the relationship (Murray & others, 2000). If you feel down about yourself, you will likely feel pessimistic about your relationships. Feel good about yourself and you're more likely to feel confident of your dating partner or spouse's regard.

Gaining another's esteem

If approval that comes after disapproval is powerfully rewarding, then would we most like someone who liked us after initially disliking us? Or would we most like someone who liked us from the start (and therefore gave us more total approval)? Dick is in a small discussion class with his roommate's cousin, Jan.

ingratiation
The use of strategies, such as flattery, by which people seek to gain another's favor.

After the first week of classes, Dick learns via his "pipeline" that Jan thinks him rather shallow. As the semester progresses, he learns that Jan's opinion of him is steadily rising; gradually she comes to view him as bright, thoughtful, and charming. Would Dick like Jan more if she had thought well of him from the beginning? If Dick is simply counting the number of approving comments he receives, then the answer will be yes. But if, after her initial disapproval, Jan's rewards become more potent, Dick then might like her better than if she had been consistently affirming.

To see which is most often true, Elliot Aronson and Darwyn Linder (1965) captured the essence of Dick's experience in a clever experiment. They "allowed" 80 University of Minnesota women to overhear a sequence of evaluations of themselves by another woman. Some women heard consistently positive things about themselves, some consistently negative. Others heard evaluations that changed either from negative to positive (like Jan's evaluations of Dick) or from positive to negative. In this and other experiments, the target person was especially well liked when the individual experienced a *gain* in the other's esteem, especially when the gain occurred gradually and reversed the earlier criticism (Aronson & Mettee, 1974; Clore & others, 1975). Perhaps Jan's nice words have more credibility coming after her not-so-nice words. Or perhaps after being withheld, they are especially gratifying.

> "Hatred which is entirely conquered by love passes into love, and love on that account is greater than if it had not been preceded by hatred."
> —Benedict Spinoza, *Ethics*

Aronson speculated that constant approval can lose value. When a husband says for the five-hundredth time, "Gee, honey, you look great," the words carry far less impact than were he now to say, "Gee, honey, you don't look good in that dress." A loved one you've doted on is hard to reward but easy to hurt. This suggests that an open, honest relationship—one where people enjoy one another's esteem and acceptance yet are honest—is more likely to offer continuing rewards than one dulled by the suppression of unpleasant emotions, one in which people try only, as Dale Carnegie advised, to "lavish praise." Aronson (1988) put it this way:

> As a relationship ripens toward greater intimacy, what becomes increasingly important is authenticity—our ability to give up trying to make a good impression and begin to reveal things about ourselves that are honest even if unsavory. . . . If two people are genuinely fond of each other, they will have a more satisfying and exciting relationship over a longer period of time if they are able to express both positive and negative feelings than if they are completely "nice" to each other at all times. (p. 323)

> "It takes your enemy and your friend, working together, to hurt you to the heart; the enemy to slander you and the friend to get the news to you."
> —Mark Twain, *Pudd'nhead Wilson's New Calendar*, 1897

In most social interactions, we self-censor our negative feelings. Thus, note William Swann and his colleagues (1991), some people receive no corrective feedback. Living in a world of pleasant illusion, they continue to act in ways that alienate their would-be friends. A true friend is one who can let us in on bad news.

Although honest, someone who really loves us will also tend to see us through rose-colored glasses. When Sandra Murray and her co-workers (1996, 1997) studied dating and married couples, they found that the happiest (and those who became happier with time) were those who idealized one another, who even saw their partners more positively than their partners saw themselves. When we're in love, we're biased to find those we love not only physically attractive, but socially attractive as well. Moreover, the most satisfied married couples tend to approach problems without immediately criticizing

> "No one is perfect until you fall in love with them."
> —Andy Rooney

their partners and fault-finding (Karney & Bradbury, 1997). Honesty has its place in a good relationship, but so does a presumption of the other's basic goodness.

RELATIONSHIP REWARDS

Asked why they are friends with someone or why they were attracted to their partners, most people can readily answer. "I like Carol because she's warm, witty, and well-read." What this explanation leaves out—and what social psychologists believe is most important—is ourselves. Attraction involves the one who is attracted as well as the attractor. Thus a more psychologically accurate answer might be, "I like Carol because of how I feel when I'm with her." We are attracted to those we find it satisfying and gratifying to be with. Attraction is in the eye (and brain) of the beholder.

The point can be expressed as a simple **reward theory of attraction:** Those who reward us, or whom we associate with rewards, we like. If a relationship gives us more rewards than costs, we will like it and will wish it to continue. This will be especially true if the relationship is more profitable than alternative relationships (Burgess & Huston, 1979; Kelley, 1979; Rusbult, 1980). Mutual attraction flourishes when each meets the other's unmet needs. In his 1665 book of *Maxims*, La Rochefoucauld conjectured, "Friendship is a scheme for the mutual exchange of personal advantages and favors whereby self-esteem may profit."

We not only like people who are rewarding to be with; we also, according to the second version of the reward principle, like those we *associate* with good feelings. According to theorists Donn Byrne and Gerald Clore (1970), Albert Lott and Bernice Lott (1974), and Jan DeHouwer and colleagues (2001), conditioning creates positive feelings toward things and people linked with rewarding events. When, after a strenuous week, we relax in front of a fire, enjoying good food, drink, and music, we will likely feel a special warmth toward those around us. We are less likely to take a liking to someone we meet while suffering a splitting headache.

Pawel Lewicki (1985) tested this liking-by-association principle. In one experiment, University of Warsaw students were virtually 50-50 in choosing which of two pictured women (A or B in Figure 11–5) looked friendlier. Other students, having interacted with a warm, friendly experimenter who resembled woman A, chose woman A, by a six-to-one margin. In a follow-up study, the experimenter acted *un*friendly toward half the participants. When these individuals later had to turn in their data to one of two women, they nearly always *avoided* the one who resembled the experimenter. (Perhaps you can recall a time when you reacted positively or negatively to someone who reminded you of someone else.)

Other experiments confirm this phenomenon of liking—and disliking—by association. In one, college students who evaluated strangers in a pleasant room liked them better than those who evaluated them in an uncomfortably hot room (Griffitt, 1970). In another, people evaluated photographs of other people while in either an elegant, sumptuously furnished room or in a shabby, dirty room (Maslow & Mintz, 1956). Again, the good feelings evoked by the elegant surroundings transferred to the people being rated. Elaine Hatfield and William Walster (1978) found a practical tip in these research studies: "Romantic dinners, trips to the theatre, evenings at home together, and vacations never

reward theory of attraction
The theory that we like those whose behavior is rewarding to us or whom we associate with rewarding events.

Experimenter   Person A   Person B

figure 11–5

Liking by association.

After interacting with a friendly experimenter, people preferred someone who looked like her (Person A) to one who didn't (Person B). After interacting with an unfriendly experimenter, people avoided the woman who resembled her (Lewicki, 1985).

stop being important. . . . If your relationship is to survive, it's important that you *both* continue to associate your relationship with good things."

This simple theory of attraction—we like those who reward us and those we associate with rewards—helps us understand why people everywhere feel attracted to those who are warm, trustworthy, and responsive (Fletcher & others, 1999; Regan, 1998; Wojciszke & others, 1998). The reward theory also helps explain some of the influences on attraction:

- *Proximity* is rewarding. It costs less time and effort to receive friendship's benefits with someone who lives or works close by.

- We like *attractive* people because we perceive that they offer other desirable traits and because we benefit by associating with them.

- If others have *similar* opinions, we feel rewarded because we presume that they like us in return. Moreover, those who share our views help validate them. We especially like people if we have successfully

Our liking and disliking of people is influenced by the events with which they are associated. © Mell Lazarus. By permission of Mell Lazarus and Creators Syndicate, Inc.

converted them to our way of thinking (Lombardo & others, 1972; Riordan, 1980; Sigall, 1970).

- We like to be liked and love to be loved. Thus, liking is usually mutual. We like those who like us.

Summing up

We have examined four powerful influences upon liking and friendship. The best predictor of whether any two people are friends is their sheer *proximity* to one another. Proximity is conducive to repeated exposure and interaction, which enables us to discover similarities and to feel one another's liking.

A second determinant of initial attraction is *physical attractiveness*. Both in laboratory studies and in field experiments involving blind dates, college students tend to prefer attractive people. In everyday life, however, people tend actually to choose and marry someone whose attractiveness roughly matches their own (or someone who, if less attractive, has other compensating qualities). Positive attributions about attractive people define a physical-attractiveness stereotype—an assumption that what is beautiful is good.

Liking for another is greatly aided by *similarity* of attitudes, beliefs, and values. Likeness leads to liking; opposites rarely attract. We are also likely to develop friendships with people who *like us*.

A simple principle helps explain these influences on our attractions to one another: We like people whose behavior we find rewarding or whom we have associated with rewarding events.

What is love?

What is this thing called "love"? Can passionate love endure? If not, what can replace it?

"Love is nature's way of giving a reason to be living."
—Paul Webster, "Love Is a Many Splendored Thing"

Loving is more complex than liking and thus more difficult to measure, more perplexing to study. People yearn for it, live for it, die for it. Yet only in the last few years has loving become a serious topic in social psychology.

Most attraction researchers have studied what is most easily studied—responses during brief encounters between strangers. The influences on our initial liking of another—proximity, attractiveness, similarity, being liked, and other rewarding traits—also influence our long-term, close relationships. The impressions that dating couples quickly form of each other therefore provide a clue to their long-term future (Berg, 1984; Berg & McQuinn, 1986). Indeed, if North American romances flourished *randomly*, without regard to proximity and similarity, then most Catholics (being a minority) would marry Protestants, most Blacks would marry Whites, and college graduates would be as apt to marry high school dropouts as fellow graduates.

So first impressions are important. Nevertheless, long-term loving is not merely an intensification of initial liking. Social psychologists have therefore shifted their attention from the mild attraction experienced during first encounters to the study of enduring, close relationships.

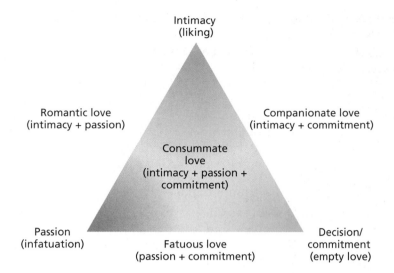

figure 11–6
Robert Sternberg's (1988) conception of kinds of loving as combinations of three basic components of love.

PASSIONATE LOVE

The first step in scientifically studying romantic love, as in studying any variable, is to decide how to define and measure it. We have ways to measure aggression, altruism, prejudice, and liking—but how do we measure love?

"How do I love thee? Let me count the ways" wrote Elizabeth Barrett Browning. Social scientists have counted various ways. Psychologist Robert Sternberg (1998) views love as a triangle, whose three sides (of varying lengths) are passion, intimacy, and commitment (Figure 11–6). Drawing from ancient philosophy and literature, sociologist John Alan Lee (1988) and psychologists Clyde Hendrick and Susan Hendrick (1993, 2003) identify three primary love styles— *eros* (self-disclosing passion), *ludus* (uncommitted game playing), and *storge* (friendship)—which, like the primary colors, combine to form secondary love styles. Some love styles, notably eros and storge, predict high relationship satisfaction; others, such as ludus, predict low satisfaction.

Some elements are common to all loving relationships: mutual understanding, giving and receiving support, enjoying the loved one's company. Some elements are distinctive. If we experience passionate love, we express it physically, we expect the relationship to be exclusive, and we are intensely fascinated with our partner. You can see it in our eyes. Zick Rubin confirmed this. He administered a love scale to hundreds of University of Michigan dating couples. Later, from behind a one-way mirror in a laboratory waiting room, he clocked eye contact among "weak-love" and "strong-love" couples. His result will not surprise you: The strong-love couples gave themselves away by gazing long into one another's eyes. When talking, Gian Gonzaga and others (2001) have observed, they also nod their head, smile naturally, and lean forward.

Passionate love is emotional, exciting, intense. Elaine Hatfield (1988) defined it as *"a state of intense longing for union with another"* (p. 193). If reciprocated, one feels fulfilled and joyous; if not, one feels empty or despairing. Like other forms of emotional excitement, passionate love involves a roller coaster of elation and gloom, tingling exhilaration and dejected misery. "We are never so defenseless against suffering as when we love," said Freud. Passionate love preoccupies the

passionate love
A state of intense longing for union with another. Passionate lovers are absorbed in one another, feel ecstatic at attaining their partner's love, and are disconsolate on losing it.

Researchers report that sustained eye contact, nodding and smiling are indicators of passionate love.

two-factor theory of emotion
Arousal × its label = emotion.

"The 'adrenaline' associated with a wide variety of highs can spill over and make passion more passionate. (Sort of a 'Better loving through chemistry' phenomenon.)"
—Elaine Hatfield and Richard Rapson (1987)

lover with thoughts of the other—as Robert Graves put it, "Listening for a knock; waiting for a sign."

Passionate love is what you feel when you not only love someone, you are "in love" with him or her. As Sarah Meyers and Ellen Berscheid (1997) note, we understand that someone who says, "I love you, but I'm not in love with you" means to say, "I like you. I care about you. I think you're marvelous. But I don't feel sexually attracted to you." I feel *storge* (friendship love) but not *eros* (passion).

A theory of passionate love

To explain passionate love, Hatfield notes that a given state of arousal can be steered into any of several emotions, depending on how we attribute the arousal. An emotion involves both body and mind—both arousal and how we interpret and label the arousal. Imagine yourself with pounding heart and trembling hands: Are you experiencing fear, anxiety, joy? Physiologically, one emotion is quite similar to another. You may therefore experience the arousal as joy if you are in a euphoric situation, anger if your environment is hostile, and passionate love if the situation is romantic. In this view, passionate love is the psychological experience of being biologically aroused by someone we find attractive.

If indeed passion is a revved-up state that's labeled "love," then whatever revs one up should intensify feelings of love. In several experiments, college men aroused sexually by reading or viewing erotic materials had a heightened response to a woman—for example, by scoring much higher on a love scale when describing their girlfriend (Carducci & others, 1978; Dermer & Pyszczynski, 1978; Stephan & others, 1971). Proponents of the **two-factor theory of emotion,** developed by Stanley Schachter and Jerome Singer (1962), argue that when the revved-up men responded to a woman, they easily misattributed some of their arousal to her.

According to this theory, being aroused by *any* source should intensify passionate feelings—providing the mind is free to attribute some of the arousal to a romantic stimulus. In a dramatic demonstration of this phenomenon, Donald Dutton and Arthur Aron (1974) had an attractive young woman approach individual young men as they crossed a narrow, wobbly, 450-foot-long suspension walkway hanging 230 feet above British Columbia's rocky Capilano River. The woman asked each man to help her fill out a class questionnaire. When he had finished, she scribbled her name and phone number and invited him to call if he wanted to hear more about the project. Most accepted the phone number, and half who did so called. By contrast, men approached by the woman on a low, solid bridge, and men approached on the high bridge by a *male* interviewer, rarely called. Once again, physical arousal accentuated romantic responses.

Scary movies, roller-coaster rides, and physical exercise have the same effect, especially to those we find attractive (Foster & others, 1998; White & Kight,

1984). The effect holds true with married couples, too. Those who do exciting things together report the best relationships. And after doing an arousing rather than a mundane laboratory task (roughly the equivalent of a three-legged race on their hands and knees), couples also reported higher satisfaction with their overall relationship (Aron & others, 2000). Adrenaline makes the heart grow fonder.

Variations in love: Culture and gender

There is always a temptation to assume that most others share our feelings and ideas. We as-

"When in doubt, Sis, you've got to listen to your heart. If it's going thump, thump, thump, slow and steady, you've got the wrong guy."

sume, for example, that love is a precondition for marriage. Most cultures— 89 percent in one analysis of 166 cultures—do have a concept of romantic love, as reflected in flirtation or couples running off together (Jankowiak & Fischer, 1992). But in some cultures, notably those practicing arranged marriages, love tends to follow rather than to precede marriage. Until recently in North America, marital choices, especially those by women, were strongly influenced by considerations of economic security, family background, and professional status.

Do males and females differ in how they experience passionate love? Studies of men and women falling in and out of love reveal some surprises. Most people, including the writer of the following letter to a newspaper advice columnist, suppose that women fall in love more readily:

> Dear Dr. Brothers:
> Do you think it's effeminate for a 19-year-old guy to fall in love so hard it's like the whole world's turned around? I think I'm really crazy because this has happened several times now and love just seems to hit me on the head from nowhere. . . . My father says this is the way girls fall in love and that it doesn't happen this way with guys—at least it's not supposed to. I can't change how I am in this way but it kind of worries me.—P.T. (quoted by Dion & Dion, 1985)

P.T. would be reassured by the repeated finding that it is actually *men* who tend to fall more readily in love (Dion & Dion, 1985; Peplau & Gordon, 1985). Men also seem to fall out of love more slowly and are less likely than women to break up a premarital romance. Women in love, however, are typically as emotionally involved as their partners, or more so. They are more likely to report feeling euphoric and "giddy and carefree," as if they were "floating on a cloud." Women are also somewhat more likely than men to focus on the intimacy of the friendship and on their concern for their partner. Men are more likely than women to think about the playful and physical aspects of the relationship (Hendrick & Hendrick, 1995).

Unlike passionate love, companionate love can last a lifetime.

COMPANIONATE LOVE

Although passionate love burns hot, it inevitably simmers down. The longer a relationship endures, the fewer its emotional ups and downs (Berscheid & others, 1989). The high of romance may be sustained for a few months, even a couple of years. But as we noted in the discussion of adaptation (Chapter 10), no high lasts forever. "When you're in love it's the most glorious two-and-a-half days of your life," jests comedian Richard Lewis. The novelty, the intense absorption in the other, the thrill of the romance, the giddy "floating on a cloud" feeling, fades. After two years of marriage, spouses express affection about half as often as when they were newlyweds (Huston & Chorost, 1994). About four years after marriage, the divorce rate peaks in cultures worldwide (Fisher, 1994). If a close relationship is to endure, it will settle to a steadier but still warm afterglow that Hatfield calls **companionate love.**

Unlike the wild emotions of passionate love, companionate love is lower key; it's a deep, affectionate attachment. And it is just as real. Nisa, a !Kung San woman of the African Kalahari Desert, explains: "When two people are first together, their hearts are on fire and their passion is very great. After a while, the fire cools and that's how it stays. They continue to love each other, but it's in a different way—warm and dependable" (Shostak, 1981).

It won't surprise those who know the rock song "Addicted to Love" to find out that the flow and ebb of romantic love follows the pattern of addictions to coffee, alcohol, and other drugs. At first, a drug gives a big kick, perhaps a high. With repetition, opponent emotions gain strength and tolerance develops. An amount that once was highly stimulating no longer gives a thrill. Stopping the substance, however, does not return you to where you started. Rather, it triggers withdrawal symptoms—malaise, depression, the blahs. The same often happens in love. The passionate high is fated to become lukewarm. The no-longer-romantic relationship becomes taken for granted—until it ends. Then the jilted lover, the widower, the divorcee, are surprised at how empty life now seems without the person they long ago stopped feeling passionately attached to.

companionate love
The affection we feel for those with whom our lives are deeply intertwined.

"When two people are under the influence of the most violent, most insane, most delusive, and most transient of passions, they are required to swear that they will remain in that excited, abnormal, and exhausting condition continuously until death do them part."
—George Bernard Shaw

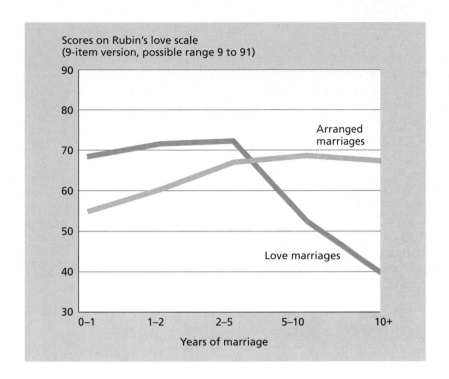

figure 11–7
Romantic love between partners in arranged or love marriages in Jaipur, India.
Source: Data from Gupta & Singh, 1982.

Having focused on what was not working, they stopped noticing what was (Carlson & Hatfield, 1992).

The cooling of passionate love over time and the growing importance of other factors, such as shared values, can be seen in the feelings of those who enter arranged versus love-based marriages in India. Usha Gupta and Pushpa Singh (1982) asked 50 couples in Jaipur, India, to complete a love scale. They found that those who married for love reported diminishing feelings of love if they had been married more than five years. By contrast, those in arranged marriages reported *more* love if they were not newlyweds (Figure 11–7). Other studies provide a mixed picture of arranged marriages confirming Gupta and Singh's finding of successful arranged marriages in India, but observing that Chinese and Japanese women were happier if they chose their mates (Blood, 1967; Xu & Whyte, 1990; Yelsma & Athappily, 1988).

The cooling of intense romantic love often triggers a period of disillusion, especially among those who regard that romantic love as essential both for a marriage and for its continuation. Jeffry Simpson, Bruce Campbell, and Ellen Berscheid (1986) suspect "the sharp rise in the divorce rate in the past two decades is linked, at least in part, to the growing importance of intense positive emotional experiences (e.g., romantic love) in people's lives, experiences that may be particularly difficult to sustain over time." Compared with North Americans, Asians tend to focus less on personal feelings and more on the practical aspects of social attachments (Dion & Dion, 1988; Sprecher & others, 1994, 2002). Thus, they are less vulnerable to disillusionment. Asians are also less prone to the self-focused individualism that in the long run can undermine a relationship and lead to divorce (Dion & Dion, 1991, 1996; Triandis & others, 1988).

The decline in intense mutual fascination may be natural and adaptive for species survival. The result of passionate love frequently is children, whose

How is companionate love defined? Go to the *SocialSense* CD-ROM to view a brief video clip on companionate love in late adulthood.

"Grow old with me! The best is yet to be."
—Robert Browning

survival is aided by the parents' waning obsession with each other (Kenrick & Trost, 1987). Nevertheless, for those married more than 20 years, some of the lost romantic feeling is often renewed as the family nest empties and the parents are once again free to focus their attention on each other (Hatfield & Sprecher, 1986). "No man or woman really knows what love is until they have been married a quarter of a century," said Mark Twain. If the relationship has been intimate and mutually rewarding, companionate love rooted in a rich history of shared experiences deepens.

Summing up
Occasionally, acquaintance develops not just into friendship but into *passionate* love. Such love is often a bewildering confusion of ecstasy and anxiety, elation and pain. The two-factor theory of emotion suggests that in a romantic context arousal from any source, even painful experiences, can be steered into passion. In the best of relationships, the initial romantic high settles to a steadier, more affectionate relationship called *companionate* love.

What enables close relationships?

What factors influence the ups and downs of our close relationships? We consider several factors: attachment styles, equity, and self-disclosure.

ATTACHMENT

Love is less an experience of choice than of biological imperative. We are, in our roots, social creatures, destined to bond with others. Our need to belong is adaptive, as we noted at this chapter's beginning. Cooperation promoted our species' survival. In solo combat, our ancestors were not the toughest predators, but as hunter-gatherers, and in fending off predators, they gained strength from numbers. Because group dwellers survived and reproduced, we today carry genes that predispose such bonds.

Our infant dependency strengthens our human bonds. Soon after birth we exhibit various social responses—love, fear, anger. But the first and greatest of these is love. As babies, we almost immediately prefer familiar faces and voices. We coo and smile when our parents give us attention. By eight months, we crawl toward mother or father and typically let out a wail when separated from them. Reunited, we cling. By keeping infants close to their caregivers, social attachment serves as a powerful survival impulse.

Deprived of familiar attachments, sometimes under conditions of extreme neglect, children may become withdrawn, frightened, silent. After studying the mental health of homeless children for the World Health Organization, psychiatrist John Bowlby (1980, p. 442) reflected, "Intimate attachments to other human beings are the hub around which a person's life revolves. . . . From these intimate attachments [people draw] strength and enjoyment of life."

Researchers have compared the nature of attachment and love in various close relationships—between parents and children, between friends, and between spouses or lovers (Davis, 1985; Maxwell, 1985; Sternberg & Grajek, 1984). Some elements are common to all loving attachments: mutual understanding, giving and receiving support, valuing and enjoying being with the loved one.

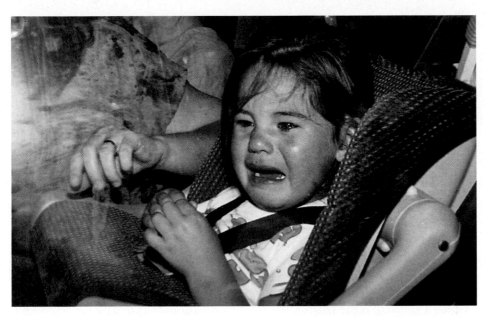

Attachment, especially to caretakers, is a powerful survival impulse. In August 1993, after an emotional custody battle, a distraught 2½-year-old "Baby Jessica" is wrenched from the only family she has known, to be returned to her biological parents.

Passionate love is, however, spiced with some added features: physical affection, an expectation of exclusiveness, and an intense fascination with the loved one.

Passionate love is not just for lovers. Phillip Shaver and his co-workers (1988) note that year-old infants display a passionate attachment to their parents. Much like young adult lovers, they welcome physical affection, feel distress when separated, express intense affection when reunited, and take great pleasure in the significant other's attention and approval. Knowing that infants vary in their styles of relating to caregivers, Shaver and Cindy Hazan (1993, 1994) wondered whether infant attachment styles might carry over to adult relationships.

Attachment styles

About 7 in 10 infants, and nearly that many adults, exhibit **secure attachment** (Baldwin & others, 1996; Jones & Cunningham, 1996; Mickelson & others, 1997). When placed as infants in a strange situation (usually a laboratory playroom), they play comfortably in their mother's presence, happily exploring this strange environment. If she leaves, they get distressed; when she returns, they run to her, hold her, then relax and return to exploring and playing (Ainsworth, 1973, 1979). This trusting attachment style, many researchers believe, forms a working model of intimacy—a blueprint for one's adult intimate relationships. Secure adults find it easy to get close to others and don't fret about getting too dependent or being abandoned. As lovers, they enjoy sexuality within the context of a secure, committed relationship. And their relationships tend to be satisfying and enduring (Feeney, 1996; Feeney & Noller, 1990; Simpson & others, 1992).

About 2 in 10 infants and adults exhibit **avoidant attachment.** Although internally aroused, avoidant infants reveal little distress during separation or clinging upon reunion. Avoiding closeness, these adults tend to be less invested in relationships and more likely to leave them. They also are more likely to

secure attachment
Attachments rooted in trust and marked by intimacy.

avoidant attachment
Relationship style marked by dismissive detachment.

engage in one-night stands of sex without love. Kim Bartholomew and Leonard Horowitz (1991) note that avoidance individuals may be either *fearful* ("I am uncomfortable getting close to others") or *dismissing* ("It is very important to me to feel independent and self-sufficient").

Some 1 in 10 infants and adults exhibit the anxiousness and ambivalence that mark **insecure attachment.** In the strange situation, they are more likely to cling anxiously to their mother. If she leaves, they cry; when she returns, they may be indifferent or hostile. As adults, anxious-ambivalent individuals are less trusting, and therefore more possessive and jealous. They may break up repeatedly with the same person. When discussing conflicts, they get emotional and often angry (Cassidy, 2000; Simpson & others, 1996). When pregnant and perceiving anger or little support from their husbands, they are more at risk for depression six months after the birth than are more secure women (Simpson & others, 2003.)

Some researchers attribute these varying attachment styles to parental responsiveness. Cindy Hazan (2004) sums up the idea: "Early attachment experiences form the basis of *internal working models* or characteristic ways of thinking about relationships." Thus, sensitive, responsive mothers—mothers who engender a sense of basic trust in the world's reliability—typically have securely attached infants, observed Mary Ainsworth (1979) and Erik Erikson (1963). And youths who have experienced nurturant and involved parenting tend later to have warm and supportive relationships with their romantic partners (Conger & others, 2000). Other researchers believe attachment styles may reflect inherited temperament (Harris, 1998). Regardless, early attachment styles do seem to lay a foundation for future relationships.

EQUITY

If both partners in a relationship pursue their personal desires willy-nilly, the friendship will die. Therefore, our society teaches us to exchange rewards by what Elaine Hatfield, William Walster, and Ellen Berscheid (1978) have called an **equity** principle of attraction: What you and your partner get out of a relationship should be proportional to what you each put into it. If two people receive equal outcomes, they should contribute equally; otherwise one or the other will feel it is unfair. If both feel their outcomes correspond to the assets and efforts each contributes, then both perceive equity.

Strangers and casual acquaintances maintain equity by exchanging benefits: You lend me your class notes; later, I'll lend you mine. I invite you to my party; you invite me to yours. Those in an enduring relationship, including roommates and those in love, do not feel bound to trade similar benefits—notes for notes, parties for parties (Berg, 1984). They feel freer to maintain equity by exchanging a variety of benefits ("When you drop by to lend me your notes, why don't you stay for dinner?") and eventually to stop keeping track of who owes whom.

Long-term equity

Is it crass to suppose that friendship and love are rooted in an equitable exchange of rewards? Don't we sometimes give in response to a loved one's need, without expecting any sort of return? Indeed, those involved in an equitable, long-term relationship are unconcerned with short-term equity. Margaret Clark and Judson Mills (1979, 1993; Clark, 1984, 1986) argue that people even take

insecure attachment
attachments marked by anxiety, ambivalence, and possessiveness.

equity
A condition in which the outcomes people receive from a relationship are proportional to what they contribute to it. Note: Equitable outcomes needn't always be equal outcomes.

"Love is the most subtle kind of self-interest."
—Holbrook Johnson

pains to *avoid* calculating any exchange benefits. When we help a good friend, we do not want instant repayment. If someone has us for dinner, we wait before reciprocating, lest the person attribute the motive for our return invitation to be merely paying off a social debt. True friends tune into one another's needs even when reciprocation is impossible (Clark & others, 1986, 1989). As people observe their partners sacrificing self-interest, their sense of trust grows (Wieselquist & others, 1999). One clue that an acquaintance is becoming a close friend is that the person shares when sharing is unexpected (Miller & others, 1989). Happily married people tend *not* to keep score of how much they are giving and getting (Buunk & Van Yperen, 1991).

In experiments with University of Maryland students, Clark and Mills confirmed that *not* being calculating is a mark of friendship. Tit-for-tat exchanges boosted people's liking when the relationship was relatively formal but *diminished* liking when the two sought friendship. Clark and Mills surmise that marriage contracts in which each partner specifies what is expected from the other are more likely to undermine than to enhance love. Only when the other's positive behavior is voluntary can we attribute it to love.

Still, the long-term equity principle explains why people usually bring equal assets to romantic relationships. Recall that often they are matched for attractiveness, status, and so forth. If they are mismatched in one area, such as attractiveness, they tend to be mismatched in some other area, such as status. But in total assets, they are an equitable match. No one says, and few even think, "I'll trade you my good looks for your big income." But especially in relationships that last, equity is the rule.

Perceived equity and satisfaction

Those in an equitable relationship are more content (Fletcher & others, 1987; Hatfield & others, 1985; Van Yperen & Buunk, 1990). Those who perceive their relationship as inequitable feel discomfort: The one who has the better deal may feel guilty and the one who senses a raw deal may feel strong irritation. (Given the self-serving bias—most husbands perceive themselves as contributing more

Perceived inequity—thinking one contributes more to a relationship and receives less than one's spouse—predicts marital distress and dissatisfaction.

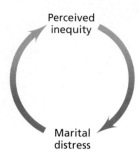

figure 11–8

Perceived inequities trigger marital distress, which fosters the perception of inequities.

Source: Adapted from Grote & Clark, 2001.

housework than their wives credit them for—the person who is "overbene-fited" is less sensitive to the inequity.)

Robert Schafer and Patricia Keith (1980) surveyed several hundred married couples of all ages, noting those who felt their marriages were somewhat unfair because one spouse contributed too little to the cooking, housekeeping, parenting, or providing. Inequity took its toll: Those who perceived inequity also felt more distressed and depressed. During the child-rearing years, when wives often feel underbenefited and husbands overbenefited, marital satisfaction tends to dip. During the honeymoon and empty-nest stages, spouses are more likely to perceive equity and to feel satisfaction with their marriages (Feeney & others, 1994). When both partners freely give and receive, and make decisions together, the odds of sustained, satisfying love are good.

Perceived inequity triggers marital distress, agree Nancy Grote and Margaret Clark (2001) from their tracking of married couples over time. But they report that the traffic between inequity and distress runs both ways: Marital distress exacerbates the perception of unfairness (Figure 11-8). When we become upset in a relationship, we also become more likely to see it as a raw deal in which we're giving more than receiving.

SELF-DISCLOSURE

Deep, companionate relationships are intimate. They enable us to be known as we truly are and to feel accepted. We discover this delicious experience in a good marriage or a close friendship—a relationship where trust displaces anxiety and where we are free to open ourselves without fear of losing the other's affection (Holmes & Rempel, 1989). Such relationships are characterized by what the late Sidney Jourard called **self-disclosure** (Derlega & others, 1993). As a relationship grows, self-disclosing partners reveal more and more of themselves to each other; their knowledge of each other penetrates to deeper and deeper levels until it reaches an appropriate depth.

Research studies find that most of us enjoy this intimacy. We feel pleased when a normally reserved person says that something about us "made me feel like opening up" and shares confidential information (Archer & Cook, 1986; D. Taylor & others, 1981). It's gratifying to be singled out for another's disclosure. Not only do we like those who disclose, we disclose to those whom we like. And after disclosing to them, we like them more (Collins & Miller, 1994). Lacking opportunities for intimacy, we experience the pain of loneliness (Berg & Peplau, 1982; Solano & others, 1982).

Experiments have probed both the *causes* and the *effects* of self-disclosure. When are people most willing to disclose intimate information concerning "what you like and don't like about yourself" or "what you're most ashamed and most proud of"? And what effects do such revelations have on those who reveal and receive them?

We disclose more when distressed—when angry or anxious (Stiles & others, 1992). We disclose more to those with whom we anticipate further interaction (Shaffer & others, 1996). And we disclose more if we have a secure attachment style (Keelan & others, 1998). But the most reliable finding is the **disclosure reciprocity** effect: Disclosure begets disclosure (Berg, 1987; Miller, 1990; Reis & Shaver, 1988). We reveal more to those who have been open with us. But intimacy is seldom instant. (If it is, the person may seem indiscreet and unstable.)

self-disclosure
Revealing intimate aspects of oneself to others.

disclosure reciprocity
The tendency for one person's intimacy of self-disclosure to match that of a conversational partner.

That Certain Someone, Inc.
INTRODUCTION SERVICE
● MEMBERSHIP ...
● STRICT CONFIDENTIALITY
● COMPUTERIZED ...
● ALL INQUIRI...
... GUARANTEED

"My preference is for someone who's afraid of closeness, like me."

Appropriate intimacy progresses like a dance: I reveal a little, you reveal a little—but not too much. You then reveal more, and I reciprocate.

For those in love, deepening intimacy is exciting. "Rising intimacy will create a strong sense of passion," note Roy Baumeister and Ellen Bratslavsky (1999). When intimacy is stable, passion is less. This helps explain why those who remarry after the loss of a spouse tend to begin the new marriage with an increased frequency of sex, and why passion often rides highest when intimacy is restored following severe conflict. "Passion and friendship [are] the two major predictors for relationship satisfaction," observe love researchers Susan Hendrick and Clyde Hendrick (1997). As it happens, the two can ride together: Deepening friendship feeds passion.

Some people—most of them women—are especially skilled "openers"; they easily elicit intimate disclosures from others, even from those who normally don't reveal very much of themselves (Miller & others, 1983; Pegalis & others, 1994; Shaffer & others, 1996). Such people tend to be good listeners. During conversation they maintain attentive facial expressions and appear to be comfortably enjoying themselves (Purvis & others, 1984). They may also express interest by uttering supportive phrases while their conversational partner is speaking. They are what psychologist Carl Rogers (1980) called "growth-promoting" listeners—people who are *genuine* in revealing their own feelings, who are *accepting* of others' feelings, and who are *empathic,* sensitive, reflective listeners.

What are the effects of such self-disclosure? Jourard (1964) argued that dropping our masks, letting ourselves be known as we are, nurtures love. He presumed that it is gratifying to open up to another and then to receive the trust another implies by being open with us. For example, having an intimate friend with whom we can discuss threats to our self-image seems to help us survive such stresses (Swann & Predmore, 1985). A true friendship is a special relationship that helps us cope with our other relationships. "When I am with my

"What is a Friend? I will tell you. It is a person with whom you dare to be yourself."
—Frank Crane, *A Definition of Friendship*

figure 11–9

Love: An overlapping of selves—you become part of me, I part of you.

In A. L. Weber and J. H. Weber, *Perspective on Close Relationships.* Copyright © 1994 by Allyn & Bacon. Reprinted by permission.

Source: From Aron & Aron, 1994.

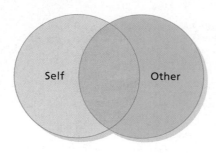

friend," reflected the Roman playwright Seneca, "methinks I am alone, and as much at liberty to speak anything as to think it." At its best, marriage is such a friendship, sealed by commitment.

Intimate self-disclosure is one also of companionate love's delights. Dating and married couples who most reveal themselves to one another express most satisfaction with their relationship and are more likely to endure in it (Berg & McQuinn, 1986; Hendrick & others, 1988; Sprecher, 1987). Married partners who mostly strongly agree that "I try to share my most intimate thoughts and feelings with my partner" tend to have the most satisfying marriages (Sanderson & Cantor, 2001). In a Gallup national marriage survey, 75 percent of those who prayed with their spouses (and 57 percent of those who didn't) reported their marriages as very happy (Greeley, 1991). Among believers, shared prayer from the heart is a humbling, intimate, soulful exposure. Those who pray together also more often say they discuss their marriages together, respect their spouses, and rate their spouses as skilled lovers.

Researchers have also found that women are often more willing to disclose their fears and weaknesses than are men (Cunningham, 1981). As Kate Millett (1975) put it, "Women express, men repress." Nevertheless, men today, particularly men with egalitarian gender-role attitudes, seem increasingly willing to reveal intimate feelings and to enjoy the satisfactions that accompany a relationship of mutual trust and self-disclosure. And that, say Arthur Aron and Elaine Aron (1994), is the essence of love—two selves connecting, disclosing, and identifying with each other; two selves, each retaining their individuality, yet sharing activities, delighting in similarities, and mutually supporting (Figure 11–9).

That being so, might we cultivate closeness by experiences that mirror the escalating closeness of budding friendships? The Arons and their collaborators (1997) wondered. So they paired volunteer students for 45 minutes with another student whom they didn't know. For the first 15 minutes, they shared thoughts on a list of personal, but low-intimacy topics such as, "When did you last sing to yourself?" The next 15 minutes were spent on more intimate topics such as, "What is your most treasured memory?" The last 15 minutes invited even more self-disclosure, with questions such as: "Complete this sentence: 'I wish I had someone with whom I could share . . .'" and "When did you last cry in front of another person? By yourself?"

Compared with control participants who spent the 45 minutes in small talk ("What was your high school like?" "What is your favorite holiday?"), those who experienced the escalating self-disclosure ended the hour feeling remarkably close to their conversation partners—in fact, "closer than the closest relationship in the lives of 30 percent of similar students," reported the researchers. These relationships surely were not yet marked by the loyalty and commitment of true friendship. Nevertheless, the experiment provides a striking demonstration of how readily a sense of closeness to others can grow, given open self-disclosure—which can also occur via the Internet (see "Focus on: Does the Internet Create Intimacy or Isolation?").

focus on | does the Internet create intimacy or isolation?

As a reader of this college text, you are almost surely one of the world's 600 million people (as of 2003) with Internet access. It took the telephone seven decades to go from 1 percent to 75 percent penetration of North American households. Internet access reached 75 percent penetration about seven years (Putnam, 2000). You and soon a billion others enjoy e-mail, Web surfing, and perhaps participating in listservs, news groups, or chat rooms.

What do you think: Is computer-mediated communication within virtual communities a poor substitute for in-person relationships? Or is it a wonderful way to widen our social circles? Does the Internet do more to connect people or to drain time from face-to-face relationships? Consider the emerging debate.

Point: The Internet, like the printing press and telephone, expands communication, and communication enables relationships. Printing reduced face-to-face storytelling and the telephone reduced face-to-face chats, but both enable us to reach and be reached by people without limitations of time and distance. Social relations involve networking, and the Net is the ultimate network. It enables efficient networking with family, friends, and kindred spirits—including people we otherwise never would have found, be they fellow MS patients, St. Nicholas collectors, or Harry Potter fans.

Counterpoint: True, but computer communication is impoverished. It lacks the nuances of eye-to-eye contact punctuated with nonverbal cues and physical touches. Except for simple emoticons—such as a :-) for an unnuanced smile—electronic messages are devoid of gestures, facial expressions, and tones of voice. No wonder it's so easy to misread them. The absence of expressive e-motion makes for ambiguous emotion.

For example, vocal nuances can signal whether a statement is serious, kidding, or sarcastic. Research by Justin Kruger and his colleagues (1999) shows that communicators often think their "just kidding" intent is equally clear, whether e-mailed or spoken, when it isn't

when e-mailed. Thanks also to one's anonymity in virtual discussions, the occasional result is a hostile "flame war."

The Internet, like television, diverts time from real relationships. Internet romances are not the developmental equivalent of real dating. Cybersex is artificial intimacy. Individualized web-based entertainment displaces getting together for bridge. Such artificiality and isolation is regrettable, because our ancestral history predisposes our needing real-time relationships, replete with smirks and smiles. No wonder that a Stanford University survey found that 25 percent of more than 4,000 adults surveyed reported that their time online had reduced time spent in person and on the phone with family and friends (Nie & Erbring, 2000).

Point: But most folks don't perceive the Internet to be isolating. Another national survey found that "Internet users in general—and online women in particular—believe that their use of e-mail has strengthened their relationships and increased their contact with relatives and friends" (Pew, 2000). Internet use may displace in-person intimacy, but it also displaces television watching. If one-click cyber-shopping is bad for your local bookstore, it frees time for relationships. Telecommuting does the same, enabling people to work from home and to have time for their families.

Why say that computer-formed relationships are unreal? On the Internet your looks and location cease to matter. Your appearance, age, and race don't deter people from relating to you based on what's more genuinely important—your shared interests and values. In workplace and professional networks, computer-mediated discussions are less influenced by status and are therefore more candid and equally participatory. Computer-mediated communication fosters more spontaneous self-disclosure than face-to-face conversation (Joinson, 2001).

By 2003, online dating sites were receiving 45 million visits per month (Harmon, 2003).

(Continued on page 466)

focus on   *(continued)*

Americans alone, in the first half of 2003, spent $214 million on Internet dating sites—almost triple their spending in all of 2001 (Egan, 2003).

Most Internet flirtations go nowhere. "Everyone I know who has tried online dating . . . agrees that we loathe spending (wasting?) hours gabbing to someone and then meeting him and realizing that he is a creep," observed one Toronto woman (Dicum, 2003). But friendships and romantic relationships that form on the Internet are *more* likely to last for at least two years, report Katelyn McKenna and John Bargh, and their colleagues (Bargh & others, 2002; McKenna & Bargh, 1998, 2000; McKenna & others, 2002). In one experiment, they found that people disclosed more, with greater honesty and less posturing, when they met people online. They also felt more liking for people whom they conversed with online for 20 minutes than for those met for the same time face-to-face. This was even true when they unknowingly met the *same* person in both contexts. People surveyed similarly feel that Internet friendships are as real, important, and close as offline relationships.

Counterpoint: The Internet allows people to be who they really are, but also to feign who they really aren't, sometimes in the interests of sexual exploitation. Internet sexual media, like other forms of pornography, likely serve to distort people's perceptions of sexual reality, decrease the attractiveness of their real-life partner, prime men to perceive women in sexual terms, make sexual coercion seem more trivial, provide mental scripts for how to act in sexual situations, increase arousal, and lead to disinhibition and imitation of loveless sexual behaviors.

Finally, suggests Robert Putnam (2000), the social benefits of computer-mediated communication are constrained by two other realities:

The "digital divide" accentuates social and educational inequalities between the haves and have nots. While "cyberbalkanization" enables BMW 2002 owners to network, it also, as noted in Chapter 8, enables White supremacists to find each other. The digital divide may be remedied with lowering prices and increasing public access locations. The balkanization is intrinsic to the medium.

As the debate over the Internet's social consequences continues, "the most important question," says Putnam (p. 180), will be "not what the Internet will do to us, but what we will do with it? . . . How can we harness this promising technology for thickening community ties? How can we develop the technology to enhance social presence, social feedback, and social cues? How can we use the prospect of fast, cheap communication to enhance the now fraying fabric of our real communities?"

"*I loved your E-mail, but I thought you'd be older.*"

The Internet allows people to feign who they really aren't.

From infancy to old age, attachments are central to human life. Secure attachments, as in an enduring marriage, mark happy lives.

One reward of companionate love is the opportunity for intimate self-disclosure, a state achieved gradually as each partner reciprocates the other's increasing openness. Companionate love is most likely to endure when both partners feel the partnership is equitable, with both perceiving themselves receiving from the relationship in proportion to what they contribute to it.

Summing up

How do relationships end?

Often love dies. What factors predict marital dissolution? How do couples typically detach or renew their relationships?

In 1971, a man wrote a love poem to his bride, slipped it into a bottle, and dropped it into the Pacific Ocean between Seattle and Hawaii. A decade later, a jogger found it on a Guam beach:

> If, by the time this letter reaches you, I am old and gray, I know that our love will be as fresh as it is today.
> It may take a week or it may take years for this note to find you. . . . If this should never reach you, it will still be written in my heart that I will go to extreme means to prove my love for you. Your husband, Bob.

The woman to whom the love note was addressed was reached by phone. When the note was read to her she burst out laughing. And the more she heard, the harder she laughed. "We're divorced," she finally said, and slammed down the phone.

So it often goes. Comparing their unsatisfying relationship with the support and affection they imagine are available elsewhere, people are divorcing more often—at double the 1960 rate. Roughly half of American marriages and 40 percent of Canadian marriages now end in divorce. Enduring relationships are rooted in enduring love and satisfaction, but also in inattention to possible alternative partners, fear of the termination cost, and a sense of moral obligation (Adams & Jones, 1997; Miller, 1997). As economic and social barriers to divorce weakened during the 1960s and 1970s, thanks partly to women's increasing employment, divorce rates rose. "We are living longer, but loving more briefly," quips Os Guiness (1993, p. 309).

Britain's royal House of Windsor knows well the hazards of modern marriage. The fairy-tale marriages of Princess Margaret, Princess Anne, Prince Charles, and Prince Andrew all crumbled, smiles replaced with stony stares. Shortly after her 1986 marriage to Prince Andrew, Sarah Ferguson gushed, "I love his wit, his charm, his looks. I worship him." Andrew reciprocated her euphoria: "She is the best thing in my life." Six years later, Andrew, having decided her friends were "philistines," and Sarah, having derided Andrew's boorish behavior as "terribly gauche," called it quits (*Time*, 1992).

DIVORCE

Divorce rates have varied widely by country, ranging from .01 percent of the population annually in Bolivia, the Philippines, and Spain to 4.7 percent in the world's most divorce-prone country, the United States. To predict a culture's divorce rates, it helps to know its values (Triandis, 1994). Individualistic cultures (where love is a feeling and people ask, "What does my heart say?") have more divorce than do communal cultures (where love entails obligation and people ask, "What will other people say?"). Individualists marry "for as long as we both shall love," collectivists more often for life. Individualists expect more passion and personal fulfillment in a marriage, which puts greater pressure on the relationship (Dion & Dion, 1993). "Keeping romance alive" was rated as important to a good marriage by 78 percent of American women surveyed and 29 percent of Japanese women (*American Enterprise,* 1992).

Even in Western society, however, those who enter relationships with a long-term orientation and an intention to persist do experience healthier, less turbulent, and more durable partnerships (Arriaga, 2001; Arriaga & Agnew, 2001). Those whose commitment to a union outlasts the desire that gave birth to it will often endure times of conflict and unhappiness. One national survey found that 86 percent of those who were unhappily married but who stayed with the marriage were, when reinterviewed five years later, now mostly "very" or "quite" happy with their marriages (Popenoe, 2002). By contrast, "narcissists"—those more focused on their own desires and image—enter relationships with less commitment and less likelihood of long-term relational success (Campbell & Foster, 2002).

Risk of divorce also depends on who marries whom (Fergusson & others, 1984; Myers, 2000; Tzeng, 1992). People usually stay married if they

- married after age 20.
- both grew up in stable, two-parent homes.
- dated for a long while before marriage.

"Don't you understand? I love you! I need you! I want to spend the rest of my vacation with you!"

- are well and similarly educated.
- enjoy a stable income from a good job.
- live in a small town or on a farm.
- did not cohabit or become pregnant before marriage.
- are religiously committed.
- are of similar age, faith, and education.

None of these predictors, by itself, is essential to a stable marriage. But if none of these things is true for someone, marital breakdown is an almost sure bet. If all are true, they are very likely to stay together until death. The English perhaps had it right, several centuries ago, when presuming that the temporary intoxication of passionate love was a foolish basis for permanent marital decisions. Better, they felt, to choose a mate based on stable friendship and compatible backgrounds, interests, habits, and values (Stone, 1977).

THE DETACHMENT PROCESS

Severing bonds produces a predictable sequence of agitated preoccupation with the lost partner, followed by deep sadness and, eventually, the beginnings of emotional detachment and a return to normal living (Hazan & Shaver, 1994). Even newly separated couples who have long ago ceased feeling affection are often surprised at their desire to be near the former partner. Deep and long-standing attachments seldom break quickly; detaching is a process, not an event.

Among dating couples, the closer and longer the relationship and the fewer the available alternatives, the more painful the breakup (Simpson, 1987). Surprisingly, Roy Baumeister and Sara Wotman (1992) report that, months or years later, people recall more pain over spurning someone's love than over having been spurned. Their distress arises from guilt over hurting someone, from upset over the heartbroken lover's persistence, or from uncertainty over how to respond. Among married couples, breakup has additional costs: shocked parents and friends, guilt over broken vows, possibly restricted parental rights. Still, each year millions of couples are willing to pay such costs to extricate themselves from what they perceive as the greater costs of continuing a painful, unrewarding relationship. Such costs include, in one study of 328 married couples, a tenfold increase in depression symptoms when a marriage is marked by discord rather than satisfaction (O'Leary & others, 1994).

When relationships suffer, those without better alternatives or who feel invested in a relationship (through time, energy, mutual friends, possessions, and perhaps children) will seek alternatives to exiting the relationship. Caryl Rusbult and her colleagues (1986, 1987, 1998) have explored three ways of coping with a failing relationship (Table 11–1, see page 470). Some people exhibit *loyalty*—by waiting for conditions to improve. The problems are too painful to speak of and the risks of separation are too great, so the loyal partner perseveres, hoping the good old days will return. Others (especially men) exhibit *neglect;* they ignore the partner and allow the relationship to deteriorate.

"Passionate love is in many ways an altered state of consciousness. . . . In many states today, there are laws that a person must not be in an intoxicated condition when marrying. . . . But passionate love is a kind of intoxication."
—Roy Baumeister, *Meanings of Life,* 1991

table 11–1   **Responses to relationship distress**

	Passive	Active
Constructive	*Loyalty:* Await improvement	*Voice:* Seek to improve relationships
Destructive	*Neglect:* Ignore the partner	*Exit:* End the relationship

Source: Rusbult & others, 1986, 1987, 1998, 2001.

When painful dissatisfactions are ignored, an insidious emotional uncoupling ensues as the partners talk less and begin redefining their lives without each other. Still others will *voice* their concerns and take active steps to improve the relationship by discussing problems, seeking advice, and attempting to change.

Study after study—in fact, 115 studies of 45,000 couples—reveal that unhappy couples disagree, command, criticize, and put down. Happy couples more often agree, approve, assent, and laugh (Karney & Bradbury, 1995; Noller & Fitzpatrick, 1990). After observing 2,000 couples, John Gottman (1994, 1998) noted that healthy marriages were not necessarily devoid of conflict. Rather, they were marked by an ability to reconcile differences and to overbalance criticism with affection. In successful marriages, positive interactions (smiling, touching, complimenting, laughing) outnumbered negative interactions (sarcasm, disapproval, insults) by at least a five-to-one ratio.

Gottman and his colleagues also followed 130 newlywed couples for six years. When husbands accepted their wives' criticisms (perhaps responding to "stop interrupting me" with "Sorry, what were you saying?"), the marriages usually survived. When they responded with defensive belligerence ("I wouldn't have to interrupt if I could get a word in edgewise"), divorce was more likely. It's not distress and arguments that predict divorce, add Ted Huston and colleagues (2001) from their following of newlyweds through time. (Most newlyweds experience conflict.) Rather, it's coldness, disillusionment, and hopelessness that predicts a dim marital future. This is especially so, observed William Swann and his associates (2003), when inhibited men are coupled with critical women (violating traditional gender expectations).

Successful couples have learned, sometimes aided by communication training, to restrain the cancerous put-downs and gut-level reactions, to fight fair (by stating feelings without insulting), and to depersonalize conflict with comments like, "I know it's not your fault" (Markman & others, 1988; Notarius & Markman, 1993; Yovetich & Rusbult, 1994). Would unhappy relationships get better if the partners agreed to *act* more as happy couples do—by complaining and criticizing less? By affirming and agreeing more? By setting times aside to voice their concerns? By praying or playing together daily? As attitudes trail behaviors, do affections trail actions?

Joan Kellerman, James Lewis, and James Laird (1989) wondered. They knew that among couples passionately in love, eye gazing is typically prolonged and mutual (Rubin, 1973). Would intimate eye gazing similarly stir feelings between those not in love (much as 45 minutes of escalating self-disclosure evoked feelings of closeness among those unacquainted students)? To find out, they asked unacquainted male-female pairs to gaze intently for two minutes either at each other's hands or in each other's eyes. When they separated, the eye gazers reported a tingle of attraction and affection toward each other. Simulating love had begun to stir it.

By enacting and expressing love, researcher Robert Sternberg (1988) believes the passion of initial romance can evolve into enduring love:

"Living happily ever after" need not be a myth, but if it is to be a reality, the happiness must be based upon different configurations of mutual feelings at various times in a relationship. Couples who expect their passion to last forever, or their intimacy to remain unchallenged, are in for disappointment. . . . We must constantly work at understanding, building, and rebuilding our loving relationships. Relationships are constructions, and they decay over time if they are not maintained and improved. We cannot expect a relationship simply to take care of itself, any more than we can expect that of a building. Rather, we must take responsibility for making our relationships the best they can be.

Summing up

Often love does not endure. As divorce rates rose, researchers discerned predictors of marital dissolution. These include an individualistic culture that values feelings over commitment and predictors such as the couple's age, education, values, and similarity. Researchers are also identifying the process through which couples either detach or rebuild their relationships. And they are identifying the positive and nondefensive communication styles that mark healthy, stable marriages.

Personal Postscript: Making love

Two facts of contemporary life seem beyond dispute: First, *close, enduring relationships are hallmarks of a happy life.* In National Opinion Research Center surveys of 40,605 Americans since 1972, 40 percent of married adults, 22 percent of those never married, 19 percent of the divorced, and 16 percent of the separated declared their lives "very happy." Similar results come from national surveys in Canada and Europe (Inglehart, 1990).

Second, *close, enduring relationships are in decline.* Compared with several decades ago, people today more often move, live alone, divorce, and have a succession of relationships.

Given the psychological ingredients of marital happiness—kindred minds, social and sexual intimacy, equitable giving and receiving of emotional and material resources—it does, however, become possible to contest the French saying, "Love makes the time pass and time makes love pass." But it takes effort to stem love's decay. It takes effort to carve out time each day to talk over the day's happenings. It takes effort to forgo nagging and bickering and instead to disclose and hear each other's hurts, concerns, and dreams. It takes effort to make a relationship into "a classless utopia of social equality" (Sarnoff & Sarnoff, 1989), in which both partners freely give and receive, share decision making, and enjoy life together.

By "minding" our close relationships, sustained satisfaction is possible, note John Harvey and Julia Omarzu (1997). Australian relationships researcher Patricia Noller (1996) concurs: "Mature love . . . love that sustains marriage and family as it creates an environment in which individual family members can grow...is sustained by beliefs that love involves acknowledging and accepting differences and weaknesses; that love involves an internal decision to love another person and a long-term commitment to maintain that love; and finally that love is controllable and needs to be nurtured and nourished by the lovers."

For those who commit themselves to creating an equitable, intimate, mutually supportive relationship there may come the security, and the joy, of enduring, companionate love. When someone "loves you for a long, long time," explained the wise, old Skin Horse to the Velveteen Rabbit,

> "not just to play with, but REALLY loves you, then you become Real."
> "Does it hurt?" asked the Rabbit.
> "Sometimes," said the Skin Horse, for he was always truthful. "When you are Real you don't mind being hurt."
> "Does it happen all at once, like being wound up," he asked, "or bit by bit?"
> "It doesn't happen all at once," said the Skin Horse. "You become. It takes a long time. That's why it doesn't often happen to people who break easily, or have sharp edges, or who have to be carefully kept. Generally, by the time you are Real, most of your hair has been loved off, and your eyes drop out and you get loose in the joints and very shabby. But these things don't matter at all, because once you are Real you can't be ugly, except to people who don't understand."

What do you think?

Reflect on your style of attachment. Would you describe yourself as secure, insecure, avoidant? What changes would you like to make, if any, in your attachment style?

Making the Social Connection

As we began this chapter on attraction and intimacy, we considered Kipling Williams's research on ostracism. This is the same Kipling Williams whose research on social loafing we encountered in Chapter 8 on group influence. This chapter highlights relationships, including research by Rusbult and Sternberg on the ending of relationships. Chapter 2 noted research by Dr. Emery on married couples' unrealistic optimism about their chances of divorcing. What research has been done on trends in divorce? Go to the *SocialSense* CD-ROM to view Dr. Emery speaking about ending relationships and divorce.

chapter 12

Helping

hearing the rumble of an approaching New York subway train, Everett Sanderson leapt down onto the tracks and raced toward the approaching headlights to rescue Michelle De Jesus, a 4-year-old who had fallen from the platform. Three seconds before the train would have run her over, Sanderson flung Michelle into the crowd above. As the train roared in, he himself failed in his first effort to jump back to the platform. At the last instant, bystanders pulled him to safety (Young, 1977).

In another strikingly heroic and caring act, Otis Gaither, a 23-year-old African American construction worker, saw flames spewing from a mobile home one night in 1997. So he smashed through the door and pulled out Larry Leroy Whitten, 44, and then revived the White man with mouth-to-mouth resuscitation, ignoring the Confederate battle flag fluttering overhead. Hailed for his race-blind heroism, Gaither said, "I don't deserve the attention. Someone would do the same for me" (*Time*, 1997).

On a hillside in Jerusalem, hundreds of trees form the Garden of the Righteous Among the Nations. Beneath each tree is a plaque with the name of a European Christian who gave refuge to one or more Jews during the Nazi Holocaust. These "righteous Gentiles" knew that if the refugees were discovered, Nazi policy dictated that both host and refugee would suffer a common

The Wall of Honor in the Garden of the Righteous, Jerusalem, honors more than 16,000 rescuers as "Righteous Among the Nations." Most were humble people who saw their own behavior as mere common decency (Rochat & Modigliani, 1995).

fate. Many did (Hellman, 1980; Wiesel, 1985). Countless more rescuers remain nameless. For every Jew who survived the war in Nazi territory, dozens of people often acted heroically. Orchestra conductor Konrad Latte, one of 2,000 Jews who lived out the war in Berlin, was saved by the heroism of 50 Germans who served as his protectors (Schneider, 2000).

On 9/11 and in the days that followed, one coordinated act of evil triggered innumerable acts of kindness. Multitudes of people overwhelmed blood banks, food banks, and clothing banks, hoping to give something from their hearts that spoke to the hearts and needs of those devastated. Some were self-sacrificially altruistic. After the World Trade Center's North Tower was struck, Ed Emery gathered five Fiduciary Trust colleagues on the South Tower's 90th floor, escorted them down 12 floors, got them on a packed express elevator, let the door close in front of him, and then headed back up to the 97th floor, hoping to evacuate six more colleagues who were backing up the computers. Alas, when moments later his own building was struck beneath him, his fate was sealed. Nearby, his colleague Edward McNally was thinking of how, in his last moments, he could help his loved ones. As the floor began buckling, he called his wife, Liz, and recited life insurance work policies and bonuses. "He said I meant the world to him, and he loved me," Mrs. McNally later recalled as they seemingly exchanged their final goodbyes (*New York Times*, 2002). But her phone rang one more time. McNally sheepishly reported he had booked them a trip to Rome for her 40th birthday. "Liz, you have to cancel that."

Less dramatic acts of comforting, caring, and compassion abound: Without asking anything in return, people offer directions, donate money, give blood, volunteer time.

- Why, and when, will people help?
- Who will help?
- What can be done to lessen indifference and increase helping?

These are this chapter's primary questions.

altruism
A motive to increase another's welfare without conscious regard for one's self-interests.

Altruism is selfishness in reverse. An altruistic person is concerned and helpful even when no benefits are offered or expected in return. Jesus' parable of the Good Samaritan provides the classic illustration:

A man was going down from Jerusalem to Jericho, and fell into the hands of robbers, who stripped him, beat him, and went away, leaving him half dead. Now by chance a priest was going down that road; and when he saw him, he passed by on the other side. So likewise a Levite, when he came to the place and saw him, passed by on the other side. But a Samaritan while traveling came near him; and when he saw him, he was moved with pity. He went to him and bandaged his wounds, having poured oil and wine on them. Then he put him on his own animal, brought him to an inn, and took care of him. The next day he took out two denarii, gave them to the innkeeper, and said, "Take care of him; and when I come back, I will repay you whatever more you spend." (Luke 10:30–35)

The Samaritan illustrates altruism. Filled with compassion, he is motivated to give a stranger time, energy, and money while expecting neither repayment nor appreciation.

Good Samaritan, Fernand *Schultz-Wettel*

Why do we help?

To study helping acts, social psychologists examine the conditions under which people perform such deeds. Before looking at what the experiments reveal, let's consider what might motivate helping.

GAINING REWARDS, AVOIDING PUNISHMENT

Several theories of helping agree that, in the long run, helping behavior benefits the giver as well as the receiver. One explanation assumes that human interactions are guided by a "social economics." We exchange not only material goods and money but also social goods—love, services, information, status (Foa & Foa, 1975). In doing so, we use a "minimax" strategy—minimize costs, maximize rewards. **Social-exchange theory** does not contend that we consciously monitor costs and rewards, only that such considerations predict our behavior.

Suppose your campus is having a blood drive and someone asks you to participate. Might you not weigh the *costs* of donating (needle prick, time, fatigue) versus those of not donating (guilt, disapproval)? Might you not also weigh the *benefits* of donating (feeling good about helping someone, free refreshments) versus those of not donating (saving the time, discomfort, and anxiety)? According to social-exchange theory—supported by studies of Wisconsin blood donors by Jane Allyn Piliavin and her research team (1982, 2003)—such subtle calculations precede decisions to help or not. As if needing an excuse for their compassion, people will donate more money to a charity when offered a product, such as candy or candles. Even when they don't want (and would never go buy) the product, it defines a social exchange (Holmes & others, 1997).

social-exchange theory
The theory that human interactions are transactions that aim to maximize one's rewards and minimize one's costs.

Social exchange

Rewards that motivate helping may be external or internal. When businesses donate money to improve their corporate images or when someone offers

"Hey, there's Sara, padding her college–entrance résumé!"

another a ride hoping to receive appreciation or friendship, the reward is external. We give to get. Thus we are most eager to help someone attractive to us, someone whose approval we desire (Krebs, 1970; Unger, 1979).

Helping also increases our sense of self-worth. Nearly all blood donors in Jane Piliavin's research agreed that giving blood "makes you feel good about yourself" and "gives you a feeling of self-satisfaction." Indeed, "Give blood," advises an old Red Cross poster. "All you'll feel is good." This helps explain why people far from home will do kindnesses to strangers whom they will never see again.

The positive effect of helping on feelings of self-worth are one explanation for why so many people do well after doing good. One month-long study of 85 couples found that giving emotional support to one's partner was positive for the giver; giving support boosted the giver's mood (Gleason & others, 2003). Piliavin (2003) and Susan Andersen (1998) point to dozens of studies showing that youth engaged in community service projects, school-based "service learning," or tutoring children develop social skills and positive social values. They are at markedly less risk for delinquency, pregnancy, and school dropout and are more likely to become engaged citizens. Volunteering likewise benefits the morale and even the health of adults. Those who do good tend to do well.

This cost-benefit analysis can seem demeaning. In defense of the theory, however, is it not a credit to humanity that helping can be inherently rewarding? That much of our behavior is not antisocial but "prosocial"? That we can find fulfillment in the giving of love? How much worse if we gained pleasure only by serving ourselves.

"True," some readers may reply. "Still, reward theories imply that a helpful act is never truly altruistic—that we merely call it 'altruistic' when its rewards

"Men do not value a
good deed unless it
brings a reward."
—Ovid, *Epistulae ex Ponto*

are inconspicuous. If we help the screaming woman so we can gain social approval, relieve our distress, prevent guilt, or boost our self-image, is it really altruistic?" This argument is reminiscent of B. F. Skinner's (1971) analysis of helping. We credit people for their good deeds, said Skinner, only when we can't explain them. We attribute their behavior to their inner dispositions only when we lack external explanations. When the external causes are obvious, we credit the causes, not the person.

There is, however, a weakness in reward theory. It easily degenerates into explaining-by-naming. If someone volunteers for the Big Sister tutor program, it is tempting to "explain" her compassionate action by the satisfaction it brings her. But such after-the-fact naming of rewards creates a circular explanation: "Why did she volunteer?" "Because of the inner rewards." "How do you know there are inner rewards?" "Why else would she have volunteered?" Because of this flaw, **egoism**—the idea that self-interest motivates all behavior—has fallen into disrepute among researchers. Egoism's ultimate goal is increasing one's own welfare; altruism's ultimate goal is increasing another's welfare.

To escape the circularity, we must define the rewards and costs independently of the helping behavior. If social approval motivates helping, then in experiments we should find that when approval follows helping, helping increases. And it does (Staub, 1978).

Internal rewards

So far, we have mostly considered the external rewards of helping. We also need to consider internal factors, such as the helper's emotional state or personal traits.

The benefits of helping include internal self-rewards. Near someone in distress, we may feel distress. A woman's scream outside your window arouses and distresses you. If you cannot reduce your arousal by interpreting the scream as a playful shriek, then you may investigate or give aid, thereby reducing your distress (Piliavin & Piliavin, 1973). Dennis Krebs (1975) found that Harvard University men whose physiological responses and self-reports revealed the most arousal in response to another's distress also gave the most help to the person.

Guilt. Distress is not the only negative emotion we act to reduce. Throughout recorded history, guilt has been a painful emotion, so painful that we will act in ways that avoid guilt feelings. As Everett Sanderson remarked after saving the child who fell from the subway platform, "If I hadn't tried to save that little girl, if I had just stood there like the others, I would have died inside. I would have been no good to myself from then on."

Cultures have institutionalized ways to relieve guilt: animal and human sacrifices, offerings of grain and money, penitent behavior, confession, denial. In ancient Israel, the sins of the people were periodically laid on a "scapegoat" animal that was then led into the wilderness to carry away the people's guilt.

To examine the consequences of guilt, social psychologists have induced people to transgress: to lie, to deliver shock, to knock over a table loaded with alphabetized cards, to break a machine, to cheat. Afterward, the guilt-laden participants may be offered a way to relieve their guilt: by confessing, by disparaging the one harmed, or by doing a good deed to offset the bad one. The results are remarkably consistent: People will do whatever can be done to expunge the guilt, relieve their bad feelings, and restore their self-image.

"For it is in giving that we receive."
—Saint Francis of Assisi, 1181–1226

egoism
A motive (supposedly underlying all behavior) to increase one's own welfare. The opposite of altruism, which aims to increase another's welfare.

Dennis Krebs (1999) reports that "my interest in altruism has been fueled by the generosity of those who helped me overcome my past." A 14-year-old student leader-turned-outcast upon moving from Vancouver, B.C. to California, Krebs's repeated bouts with the law landed him in juvenile detention homes and then jail, from which he escaped. After making his way back to British Columbia, he got admitted to university, graduated at the top of his class, and was accepted for doctoral study at Harvard. Owning up to his past, he turned himself in, suffered the ensuing publicity, and with support from many people, was pardoned and later became a Harvard professor and chair of psychology at Simon Fraser University. "I disclose this history," says Krebs, "as a way of encouraging people with two strikes against them to remain in the game."

Picture yourself as a participant in one such experiment conducted with Mississippi State University students by David McMillen and James Austin (1971). You and another student, each seeking to earn credit toward a course requirement, arrive for the experiment. Soon after, a confederate enters, portraying himself as a previous participant looking for a lost book. He strikes up a conversation in which he mentions that the experiment involves taking a multiple-choice test, for which most of the correct answers are "B." After the accomplice departs, the experimenter arrives, explains the experiment and then asks, "Have either of you been in this experiment before or heard anything about it?"

Would you lie? The behavior of those who have gone before you in this experiment—100 percent of whom told the little lie—suggests that you would. After you have taken the test (without receiving any feedback on it), the experimenter says: "You are free to leave. However, if you have some spare time, I could use your help in scoring some questionnaires." Assuming you have told the lie, do you think you would now be more willing to volunteer some time? Judging from the results, the answer again is yes. On average, those who had not been induced to lie volunteered only two minutes of time. Those who had lied were apparently eager to redeem their self-images; on average they offered a whopping 63 minutes. One moral of this experiment was well expressed by a 7-year-old girl, who, in one of our own experiments, wrote: "Don't Lie or youl Live with gilt" (and you will feel a need to relieve it).

Our eagerness to do good after doing bad reflects both our need to reduce *private* guilt and restore a shaken self-image and our desire to reclaim a positive *public* image. We are more likely to redeem ourselves with helpful behavior when other people know about our misdeeds (Carlsmith & Gross, 1969). But even when our guilt is private, we act to reduce it. Dennis Regan and his associates (1972) demonstrated this in a New York shopping center. They led women to think they had broken a camera. A few moments later a confederate, carrying a shopping bag with candy spilling out, crossed paths with each woman. Compared with women not put on the guilt trip—only 15 percent of whom bothered to alert the confederate to the spillage—nearly four times as many of the guilt-laden women did so. The guilt-laden women had no need to redeem themselves in the confederate's eyes. Their helpfulness instead offered relief from their private guilt feelings. It redeemed their self-images. Other ways of relieving guilt—as by confession—reduce guilt-induced helping (Carlsmith & others, 1968).

All in all, guilt leads to much good. By motivating people to confess, apologize, help, and avoid repeated harm, it boosts sensitivity and sustains close relationships.

Negative mood.   If guilt increases helping, do other negative feelings do the same? If, while depressed over a bad grade, you saw someone spill papers on the sidewalk, would you be more likely than usual to help? Or less likely?

At first glance, the results are confusing. Putting people in a negative mood (by having them read or think about something sad) sometimes increases helping, sometimes decreases it. But if we look closely, we find order amid the confusion. First, the studies in which negative mood decreased helping usually involved children (Isen & others, 1973; Kenrick & others, 1979; Moore & others, 1973); those that found increased helping usually involved adults (Aderman & Berkowitz, 1970; Apsler, 1975; Cialdini & others, 1973; Cialdini & Kenrick, 1976). Why do you suppose a negative mood affects children and adults differently?

Robert Cialdini, Douglas Kenrick, and Donald Baumann (1981; Baumann & others, 1981) surmise that altruism is self-gratifying for adults. It carries its own inner rewards. Blood donors feel better about themselves for having donated. Students who've helped pick up dropped materials feel better about themselves after helping (Williamson & Clark, 1989). Thus, when an adult is in a guilty, a sad, or an otherwise negative mood, a helpful deed (or any other mood-improving experience) helps neutralize the bad feelings.

Why doesn't this work with children? Cialdini, Kenrick, and Baumann argue that helping is not similarly rewarding for children. When reading stories, young children view unhelpful characters as happier than helpful ones; as children grow older, their views reverse (Perry & others, 1986). Although young children exhibit empathy, they do not take much pleasure in being helpful; such behavior results from *socialization*.

Schoolchildren packing toy donations for the needy. As children mature, they usually come to take pleasure in being helpful to others.

To test their belief, Cialdini and his colleagues had children in early elementary school, late elementary school, and high school reminisce about sad or neutral experiences. Then they were given a chance to donate prize coupons privately to other children (Cialdini & Kenrick, 1976). When sad, the youngest children donated slightly less, the middle groups donated slightly more, and the teenage group donated significantly more. Only the teenagers seemed to find generosity a self-gratifying technique for cheering themselves up.

As the researchers note, these results are consistent with the view that we are born selfish. Such results are also consistent with the view that helping grows naturally with age as children come to see things from another person's point of view (Bar-Tal, 1982; Rushton, 1976; Underwood & Moore, 1982). At first, helping is a response to material rewards, then to social rewards, and finally to self-rewards, suggest Cialdini and his colleagues.

Exceptions to the feel bad–do good scenario.   Among well-socialized adults, should we always expect to find the "feel bad–do good" phenomenon? No. In a previous chapter, we saw that one negative mood, anger, produces anything but compassion. Another exception is profound grief. People who suffer the loss of a spouse or a child, whether through death or separation, often undergo a period of intense self-preoccupation, which restrains giving to others (Aderman & Berkowitz, 1983; Gibbons & Wicklund, 1982).

In a powerful laboratory simulation of self-focused grief, William Thompson, Claudia Cowan, and David Rosenhan (1980) had Stanford University students listen privately to a taped description of a person (whom they were to imagine was their best friend of the other sex) dying of cancer. The experiment focused some students' attention on their own worry and grief:

> He (she) could die and you would lose him, never be able to talk to him again. Or worse, he could die slowly. You would know every minute could be your last time together. For months you would have to be cheerful for him while you were sad. You would have to watch him die in pieces, until the last piece finally went, and you would be alone.

For others, it focused their attention on the friend:

> He spends his time lying in bed, waiting those interminable hours, just waiting and hoping for something to happen. Anything. He tells you that it's not knowing that is the hardest.

The researchers report that regardless of which tape the participants heard, they were profoundly moved and sobered by the experience, yet not the least regretful of participating (although some participants who in a control condition listened to a boring tape were regretful). Did their moods affect their helpfulness? When immediately thereafter they were given a chance to help a graduate student with her research anonymously, 25 percent of those whose attention had been self-focused helped. Of those whose attention was other-focused, 83 percent helped. The two groups were equally touched, but only the other-focused participants found helping someone especially rewarding. In short, the feel bad–do good effect occurs with people whose attention is on others, people for whom altruism is therefore rewarding (Barnett & others, 1980; McMillen & others, 1977). If they are not self-preoccupied by depression or grief, sad people are sensitive, helpful people.

Feel good, do good. Are happy people unhelpful? Quite the contrary. There are few more consistent findings in psychology: Happy people are helpful people. This effect occurs with both children and adults, regardless of whether the good mood comes from a success, from thinking happy thoughts, or from any of several other positive experiences (Salovey & others, 1991). One woman recalled her experience after falling in love:

> At the office, I could hardly keep from shouting out how deliriously happy I felt. The work was easy; things that had annoyed me on previous occasions were taken in stride. And I had strong impulses to help others; I wanted to share my joy. When Mary's typewriter broke down, I virtually sprang to my feet to assist. Mary! My former "enemy"! (Tennov, 1979, p. 22)

"It's curious how, when you're in love, you yearn to go about doing acts of kindness to everybody."
—P. G. Wodehouse, *The Mating Season*, 1949

In experiments on happiness and helpfulness, the person who is helped may be someone seeking a donation, an experimenter seeking help with paperwork, or a woman who drops papers. Here are two examples.

In Opole, Poland, Dariusz Dolinski and Richard Nawrat (1998) found that a positive mood of relief can dramatically boost helping. Imagine yourself as one of their unwitting subjects. After illegally parking your car for a few moments, you return to discover what looks like a ticket under your windshield wiper (where parking tickets are placed). Groaning inwardly, you pick up the apparent ticket, and then are much relieved to discover it is only an ad (or a blood drive appeal). Moments later, a university student approaches you and asks you to spend 15 minutes answering questions—to "help me complete my MA thesis." Would your positive, relieved mood make you more likely to help?

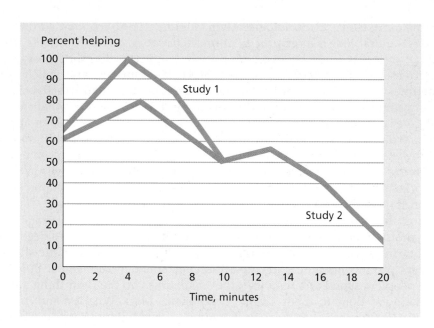

figure 12–1

Percentage of those willing to relay a phone message 0 to 20 minutes after receiving a free sample.

Of control subjects who did not receive a gift, only 10 percent helped. **Source:** Data from Isen & others, 1976.

Indeed, 62 percent of people whose fear had just turned to relief agreed willingly. This was nearly double the number who did so when no ticketlike paper was left or when it was left on the car door (not a place for a ticket).

In another experiment, Alice Isen, Margaret Clark, and Mark Schwartz (1976) had a confederate call people who had received a free sample of stationery 0 to 20 minutes earlier. The confederate said she had used her last dime to dial this (supposedly wrong) number and asked each person to relay a message by phone. As Figure 12–1 shows, the individuals' willingness to relay the phone message rose during the five minutes afterward. Then, as the good mood wore off, helpfulness dropped.

If sad people are sometimes extra helpful, how can it be that happy people are also helpful? Experiments reveal that several factors are at work (Carlson & others, 1988). Helping softens a bad mood and sustains a good mood. A positive mood is, in turn, conducive to positive thoughts and positive self-esteem, which predispose us to positive behavior (Berkowitz, 1987; Cunningham & others, 1990; Isen & others, 1978). In a good mood—after being given a gift or while feeling the warm glow of success—people are more likely to have positive thoughts and associations with being helpful. Positive thinkers are likely to be positive actors.

Social norms

Often we help others not because we have calculated consciously that such behavior is in our self-interest but because of a subtler form of self-interest: because something tells us we *ought* to. We ought to help a new neighbor move in. We ought to return the wallet we found. We ought to protect our combat buddies from harm. Norms (as you may recall from Chapter 5) are social expectations. They *prescribe* proper behavior, the *oughts* of our lives. Researchers studying helping behavior have identified two social norms that motivate altruism: the reciprocity norm and the social-responsibility norm.

reciprocity norm
An expectation that people will help, not hurt, those who have helped them.

"If you don't go to somebody's funeral, they won't come to yours."
—Yogi Berra

The reciprocity norm.   Sociologist Alvin Gouldner (1960) contended that one universal moral code is a **reciprocity norm:** *To those who help us, we should return help, not harm.* Gouldner believed this norm is as universal as the incest taboo. We "invest" in others and expect dividends. Mail surveys and solicitations sometimes include a little gift of money or individualized address labels, assuming some people will reciprocate the favor. Politicians know that the one who gives a favor can later expect a favor. The reciprocity norm even applies with marriage. At times, one may give more than one receives. But in the long run, the exchange should balance out. In all such interactions, to receive without giving in return violates the reciprocity norm. Reciprocity within social networks helps define the "social capital"—the supportive connections, information flow, trust, and cooperative actions—that keep a community healthy. Keeping an eye on each other's homes is social capital in action.

The norm operates most effectively as people respond publicly to deeds earlier done to them. In laboratory games as in everyday life, fleeting one-shot encounters produce greater selfishness than sustained relationships. But even when people respond anonymously, they sometimes do the right thing and repay the good done to them. In one experiment, Mark Whatley and his colleagues (1999) found that more university students willingly made a pledge to the charity of someone who had previously bought them some candy (Figure 12–2).

When people cannot reciprocate, they may feel threatened and demeaned by accepting aid. Thus, proud, high-self-esteem people are often reluctant to seek help (Nadler & Fisher, 1986). Receiving unsolicited help can take one's self-esteem down a notch (Schneider & others, 1996; Shell & Eisenberg, 1992). Studies show this can happen to beneficiaries of affirmative action, especially when affirmative action fails to affirm the person's competence and chances for future success (Pratkanis & Turner, 1996).

figure 12–2

Private and public reciprocation of a favor.

People were more willing to pledge to an experimental confederate's charity if the confederate had done a small favor for them earlier, especially when their reciprocation was made known to the confederate. **Source:** From Whatley & others, 1999.

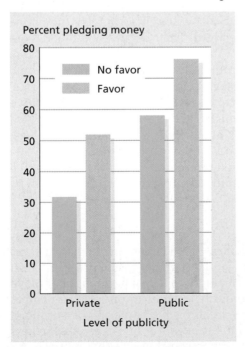

The social-responsibility norm.   The reciprocity norm reminds us to balance giving and receiving in social relations. If the only norm were reciprocity, however, the Samaritan would not have been the Good Samaritan. In the parable, Jesus obviously had something more humanitarian in mind, something explicit in another of his teachings: "If you love those who love you [the reciprocity norm], what right have you to claim any credit? . . . I say to you, love your enemies" (Matthew 5:46, 44).

With people who clearly are dependent and unable to reciprocate—children, the severely impoverished and disabled, and others perceived as unable to return as much as they receive—another social norm motivates

As flood waters rise, the social responsibility norm engages help.

our helping. The **social-responsibility norm** is the belief that people should help those who need help, without regard to future exchanges (Berkowitz, 1972b; Schwartz, 1975). The norm motivates people to retrieve a dropped book for a person on crutches, for example. In India, a relatively collectivist culture, people support the social-responsibility norm more strongly than in the individualist West (Baron & Miller, 2000). They voice an obligation to help even when the need is not life-threatening or the needy person—perhaps a stranger needing a bone marrow transplant—is outside their family circle.

Experiments show that even when helpers remain anonymous and have no expectation of any reward, they often help needy people (Shotland & Stebbins, 1983). However, they usually apply the social-responsibility norm selectively to those whose need appears not to be due to their own negligence. Especially among political conservatives (Skitka & Tetlock, 1993), the norm seems to be: Give people what they deserve. If they are victims of circumstance, like natural disaster, then by all means be generous. If they seem to have created their own problems, by laziness, immorality, or lack of foresight, then, the norm suggests, they should get what they deserve. Responses are thus closely tied to *attributions*. If we attribute the need to an uncontrollable predicament, we help. If we attribute the need to the person's choices, fairness does not require us to help; we say it's the person's own fault (Weiner, 1980).

Imagine yourself as one of the University of Wisconsin students in a study by Richard Barnes, William Ickes, and Robert Kidd (1979). You receive a call from "Tony Freeman," who explains that he is in your introductory psychology class. He says that he needs help for the upcoming exam and that he has gotten your name from the class roster. "I don't know. I just don't seem to take good notes in there," Tony explains. "I know I can, but sometimes I just don't feel like it, so most of the notes I have aren't very good to study with." How sympathetic would you feel toward Tony? How much of a sacrifice would you make to lend

social-responsibility norm
An expectation that people will help those dependent on them.

"A language's syntax and vocabulary are not determined by our biological nature (otherwise, there could not be a multitude of tongues), but are products of human culture. Likewise, moral norms are not determined by biological processes, but by cultural traditions and principles that are products of human history."
—Evolutionary biologist Francisco Ayala, *The Difference of Being Human*, 1995

When the Titanic sank, 70 percent of the females and 20 percent of the males survived. The chances of survival were 2.5 times better for a first- than a third-class passenger. Yet, thanks to gender norms for altruism, the survival odds were better for third-class passengers who were women (47 percent) than for first-class passengers who were men (31 percent).

him your notes? If you are like the students in this experiment, you would probably be much less inclined to help than if Tony had just explained that his troubles were beyond his control.

The social-responsibility norm compels us to help those most in need and those most deserving. Grocery store shoppers are more willing to give change to a woman who wants to buy milk than to one who wants to buy cookie dough (Bickman & Kamzan, 1973).

Gender and helping norms.   If, indeed, perception of another's need strongly determines one's willingness to help, will women, if perceived as less competent and more dependent, receive more help than men? This is indeed the case. Alice Eagly and Maureen Crowley (1986) located 35 studies that compared help received by male or female victims. (Virtually all the studies involved short-term encounters with strangers in need—the very situations in which people expect males to be chivalrous, note Eagly and Crowley.)

Men offered more help when the persons in need were females. Women offered help equally to males and females. Several experiments have found that women with disabled cars (for example, with a flat tire) get many more offers of help than men (Penner & others, 1973; Pomazal & Clore, 1973; West & others, 1975). Similarly, solo female hitchhikers receive far more offers of help than solo males or couples (Pomazal & Clore, 1973; M. Snyder & others, 1974). Of course, men's chivalry toward lone women may be motivated by something other than altruism. Not surprisingly, men more frequently help attractive than unattractive women (Mims & others, 1975; Stroufe & others, 1977; West & Brown, 1975).

Women not only receive more offers of help in certain situations, they also seek more help. They are twice as likely to seek medical and psychiatric help. They are the majority of callers to radio counseling programs and clients of college counseling centers. They more often welcome help from friends. Arie

Nadler (1991), a Tel Aviv University expert on help seeking, attributes this to gender differences in independence versus interdependence (Chapter 5).

EVOLUTIONARY PSYCHOLOGY

The third explanation of helping comes from evolutionary theory. As you may recall from Chapters 5 and 11, evolutionary psychology contends that the essence of life is gene survival. Our genes drive us in ways that have maximized their chance of survival. When our ancestors died, their genes lived on, predisposing us to behave in ways that will spread them into the future.

As suggested by the title of Richard Dawkins's (1976) popular book, *The Selfish Gene*, evolutionary psychology offers a humbling human image—one that psychologist Donald Campbell (1975a, 1975b) called a biological reaffirmation of a deep, self-serving "original sin." Genes that predispose individuals to self-sacrifice in the interests of strangers' welfare would not survive in the evolutionary competition. Genetic selfishness should, however, predispose us toward two specific types of selfless or even self-sacrificial helping: kin protection and reciprocity.

Kin protection

Our genes dispose us to care for relatives. Thus one form of self-sacrifice that *would* increase gene survival is devotion to one's children. Parents who put their children's welfare ahead of their own are more likely to pass their genes on than parents who neglect their children. As evolutionary psychologist David Barash (1979, p. 153) wrote, "Genes help themselves by being nice to themselves, even if they are enclosed in different bodies." Genetic egoism (at the biological level) fosters parental altruism (at the psychological level). Although evolution favors self-sacrifice for one's children, children have less at stake in the survival of their parents' genes. Thus, parents are generally more devoted to their children than their children are to them.

Other relatives share genes in proportion to their biological closeness. You share one-half your genes with your brothers and sisters, one-eighth with your cousins. **Kin selection**—favoritism toward those who share our genes—led the evolutionary biologist J. B. S. Haldane to jest that while he would not give up his life for his brother, he would sacrifice himself for *three* brothers—or for nine cousins. Haldane would not have been surprised that genetically identical twins are noticeably more mutually supportive than fraternal twins (Segal, 1984). In one laboratory game experiment, identical twins were half again as likely to cooperate with their twin for a shared gain when playing for money (Segal & Hershberger, 1999).

The point is not that we calculate genetic relatedness before helping but that nature (as well as culture) programs us to care about close relatives. The Carnegie medal for heroism is seldom awarded for saving an immediate family member. When Carlos Rogers of the Toronto Raptors NBA basketball team volunteered to end his career and donate a kidney to his sister (who died before she received it), people applauded his self-sacrificial love. But such acts for close kin are not totally unexpected. What we do not expect (and therefore honor) is the altruism of those who, like our subway hero Everett Sanderson (page 475), risk themselves to save a stranger.

We share common genes with many besides our relatives. Blue-eyed people share particular genes with other blue-eyed people. How do we detect the

Fallen heroes do not have children. If self-sacrifice results in fewer descendants, the genes that allow heroes to be created can be expected to disappear gradually from the population."
—E. O. Wilson, *On Human Nature*, 1978

kin selection
The idea that evolution has selected altruism toward one's close relatives to enhance the survival of mutually shared genes.

people in which copies of our genes occur most abundantly? As the blue-eyes example suggests, one clue lies in physical similarities. Also, in evolutionary history, genes were shared more with neighbors than with foreigners. Are we therefore biologically biased to be more helpful to those similar to us and toward those who live near us? In the aftermath of natural disasters and other life-and-death situations, the order of who gets helped would not surprise an evolutionary psychologist: the young before the old, family members before friends, neighbors before strangers (Burnstein & others, 1994; Form & Nosow, 1958).

Some evolutionary psychologists note that kin selection predisposes ethnic in-group favoritism—the root of countless historical and contemporary conflicts (Rushton, 1991). E. O. Wilson (1978) noted that kin selection is "the enemy of civilization. If human beings are to a large extent guided . . . to favor their own relatives and tribe, only a limited amount of global harmony is possible" (p. 167).

Reciprocity

Genetic self-interest also predicts reciprocity. An organism helps another, biologist Robert Trivers argues, because it expects help in return (Binham, 1980). The giver expects later to be the getter, whereas failure to reciprocate gets punished. The cheat, the turncoat, and the traitor are universally despised.

Reciprocity works best in small, isolated groups, groups in which one will often see the people for whom one does favors. If a vampire bat has gone a day or two without food—it can't go much more than 60 hours without starving to death—it asks a well-fed nestmate to regurgitate food for a meal (Wilkinson, 1990). The donor bat does so willingly, losing fewer hours till starvation than the recipient gains. But such favors occur only among familiar nestmates who share in the give-and-take. Those who always take and never give, and those who have no relationship with the donor bat, go hungry.

For similar reasons, reciprocity is stronger in rural villages than in big cities. Small schools, towns, churches, work teams, and dorms are all conducive to a community spirit in which people care for one another. Compared with people in small-town or rural environments, those in big cities are less willing to relay a phone message, less likely to mail "lost" letters, less cooperative with survey interviewers, less helpful to a lost child, and less willing to do small favors (Hedge & Yousif, 1992; Steblay, 1987).

If individual self-interest inevitably wins in genetic competition, then why will we help strangers? Why will we help those whose limited resources or abilities preclude their reciprocating? And what causes soldiers to throw themselves on grenades? One answer, initially favored by Darwin (then discounted by selfish gene theorists but now back again) is group selection: When groups are in competition, groups of mutually supportive altruists outlast groups of nonaltruists (Krebs, 1998; McAndrew, 2002; Sober & Wilson, 1998).

Donald Campbell (1975) offered another basis for unreciprocated altruism: Human societies evolved ethical and religious rules that serve as brakes on the biological bias toward self-interest. Commandments such as "love your neighbor" admonish us to balance self-concern with concern for the group, and so contribute to the survival of the group. Richard Dawkins (1976) offered a similar conclusion: "Let us try to *teach* generosity and altruism, because we are born selfish. Let us understand what our selfish genes are up to, because we may

"Just as nature is said to abhor a vacuum, so it abhors true altruism. Society, on the other hand, adores it."
—Evolutionary psychologist David Barash, "The Conflicting Pressures of Selfishness and Altruism," 2003

table 12–1   **Comparing theories of altruism**

Theory	Level of Explanation	How Is Altruism Explained?	
		Externally Rewarded Helping	Intrinsic Helping
Social-exchange	Psychological	External rewards for helping	Distress→inner rewards for helping
Social norms	Sociological	Reciprocity norm	Social-responsibility norm
Evolutionary	Biological	Reciprocity	Kin selection

then at least have the chance to upset their designs, something no other species has ever aspired to" (p. 3).

COMPARING AND EVALUATING THEORIES OF HELPING

By now you have perhaps noticed similarities among the social-exchange, social norm, and evolutionary views of altruism. As Table 12–1 shows, each proposes two types of prosocial behavior: a tit-for-tat reciprocal exchange and a more unconditional helpfulness. They do so at three complementary levels of explanation. If the evolutionary view is correct, then our genetic predispositions *should* manifest themselves in psychological and sociological phenomena.

Each theory appeals to logic. Yet each is vulnerable to charges of being speculative and after the fact. When we start with a known effect (the give-and-take of everyday life) and explain it by conjecturing a social-exchange process, a "reciprocity norm," or an evolutionary origin, we might merely be explaining-by-naming. The argument that a behavior occurs because of its survival function is hard to disprove. With hindsight, it's easy to think it had to be that way. If we can explain *any* conceivable behavior after the fact as the result of a social exchange, a norm, or natural selection, then we cannot disprove the theories. Each theory's task is therefore to generate predictions that enable us to test it.

An effective theory also provides a coherent scheme for summarizing a variety of observations. On this criterion, these three altruism theories get higher marks. Each offers us a broad perspective that illuminates both enduring commitments and spontaneous help.

GENUINE ALTRUISM

Are lifesaving heroes, everyday blood donors, and Peace Corps volunteers ever motivated by an ultimate goal of selfless concern for another, perhaps mixed with other motives? Or is their ultimate goal solely some form of self-benefit, such as gaining a reward, avoiding punishment and guilt, or relieving distress?

Abraham Lincoln illustrated the philosophical issue in a conversation with another passenger in a horse-drawn coach. After Lincoln argued that selfishness prompts all good deeds, he noticed a sow making a terrible noise. Her piglets had gotten into a marshy pond and were in danger of drowning. Lincoln called the coach to a halt, jumped out, ran back, and lifted the little pigs to safety. Upon his return, his companion remarked, "Now, Abe, where does selfishness come in on this little episode?" "Why, bless your soul, Ed, that was the very essence of selfishness. I should have had no peace of mind all day had I gone and left that suffering old sow worrying over those pigs. I did it to get peace of

"Are you all right, Mister? Is there anything I can do?"

"Young man, you're the only one who bothered to stop! I'm a millionaire and I'm going to give you five thousand dollars!"

We never know what benefits may come from helping someone in distress. Copyright © The New Yorker Collection, 1972, Barney Tobey, from cartoonbank.com. All Rights Reserved.

empathy
An emotion evoked by sympathy for another.

mind, don't you see?" (Sharp, cited by Batson & others, 1986). Until recently, psychologists would have sided with Lincoln.

However, psychologist Daniel Batson (2001) theorizes that our willingness to help is influenced by both self-serving and selfless considerations (Figure 12–3). Distress over someone's suffering motivates us to relieve our upset, either by escaping the distressing situation (like the priest and Levite) or by helping (like the Samaritan). But especially when we feel attached to someone, report Batson and his colleagues, we also feel **empathy.** Loving parents suffer when their children suffer and rejoice over their children's joys—an empathy lacking in child abusers and other perpetrators of cruelty (Miller & Eisenberg, 1988). We also feel empathy for those with whom we identify. In September 1997, millions of people who never came within 50 miles of England's Princess Diana (but who felt as if they knew her after hundreds of tabloid stories and 44 *People* magazine cover articles) wept for her and her motherless sons (after shedding no tears for the nearly 1 million faceless Rwandans murdered or having died in squalid refugee camps since 1994).

When we feel empathy, we focus not so much on our own distress as on the sufferer. Genuine sympathy and compassion motivate us to help the person for his or her own sake. Such empathy comes naturally. Even day-old infants cry more when they hear another infant cry (Hoffman, 1981). In hospital nurseries, one baby's crying sometimes evokes a chorus of crying. To some, this suggests that we are hardwired for empathy.

Often distress and empathy together motivate responses to a crisis. In 1983, people watched on television as an Australian bushfire wiped out hundreds of homes near Melbourne. Afterward, Paul Amato (1986) studied donations of money and goods. He found that those who felt angry or indifferent gave less

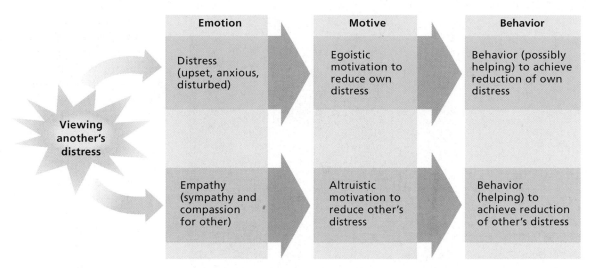

figure 12–3

Egoistic and altruistic routes to helping.

Viewing another's distress can evoke a mixture of self-focused distress and other-focused empathy. Researchers agree that distress triggers egoistic motives. But they debate whether empathy can trigger a pure altruistic motive. **Source:** Adapted from Batson, Fultz, & Schoenrade, 1987.

than those who felt either distressed (shocked and sickened) or empathic (sympathetic and worried for the victims).

To separate egoistic distress reduction from empathy-based altruism, Batson's research group conducted studies that aroused feelings of empathy and varied ease of escape. Then the researchers noted whether the aroused people would reduce their own distress by escaping the situation or whether they would go out of their way to aid the person. The results were consistent: With their empathy aroused, people usually helped.

In one of these experiments, Batson and his associates (1981) had University of Kansas women observe a young woman suffering while she supposedly received electric shocks. During a pause in the experiment, the obviously upset victim explained to the experimenter that a childhood fall against an electric fence left her acutely sensitive to shocks. The experimenter suggested that perhaps the observer (the actual participant in this experiment) might trade places and take the remaining shocks for her. Previously, half of these actual participants had been led to believe the suffering person was a kindred spirit on matters of values and interests (thus arousing their empathy). Some also were led to believe that their part in the experiment was completed, so that in any case they were done observing the woman's suffering. Nevertheless, their empathy aroused, virtually all willingly offered to substitute for the victim.

Is this genuine altruism? Mark Schaller and Robert Cialdini (1988) doubted it. Feeling empathy for a sufferer makes one sad, they noted. In one of their experiments, they led people to believe that their sadness was going to be relieved by a different sort of mood-boosting experience—listening to a comedy tape. Under such conditions, people who felt empathy were not especially helpful. Schaller and Cialdini concluded that if we feel empathy but know that something else will make us feel better, we aren't so likely to help.

Other findings suggest that genuine altruism may exist:

• Empathy produces helping even toward members of rival groups, though only when people believe the other will receive the needed help (Batson & others, 1997).

Might genuine empathy motivate a Peace Corps worker's explaining dental hygiene to Ecuadorian children? Daniel Batson believes it does.

"The measure of our character is what we would do if we were never found out."
—Paraphrased from Thomas Macaulay

- With their empathy aroused, people will help even when they believe no one will know about their helping. Their concern continues until someone *has* helped (Fultz & others, 1986). If their efforts to help are unsuccessful, they feel bad even if the failure is not their fault (Batson & Weeks, 1996).

- People will sometimes persist in wanting to help a suffering person even when they believe their own distressed mood has been temporarily maintained by a "mood-fixing" drug (Schroeder & others, 1988).

So everyone agrees that some helpful acts are either obviously egoistic (done to gain external rewards or avoid punishment) or subtly egoistic (done to gain internal rewards or relieve inner distress). Is there a third type of helpfulness—a genuine altruism that aims simply to increase another's welfare (producing happiness for oneself merely as a by-product)? Is empathy-based helping a source of such altruism? Cialdini (1991) and his colleagues Mark Schaller and Jim Fultz have doubted it. They note that no experiment rules out all possible egoistic explanations for helpfulness.

But after 25 experiments testing egoism versus altruistic empathy, Batson (2001) and others (Dovidio, 1991; Staub, 1991) believe that sometimes people do focus on others' welfare, not on their own. Batson, a former philosophy and theology student, had begun his research feeling "excited to think that if we could ascertain whether people's concerned reactions were genuine, and not simply a subtle form of selfishness, then we could shed new light on a basic issue regarding human nature" (1999a). Two decades later he believes he has his answer. Genuine "empathy-induced altruism is part of human nature" (1999b). And that, says Batson, raises the hope—confirmed by research—that inducing empathy might improve attitudes toward stigmatized people—people with AIDS, the homeless, the imprisoned, and other minorities (See "Focus on: The Benefit—and the Costs—of Empathy-Induced Altruism").

During the Vietnam War, 63 soldiers received Medals of Honor for using their bodies to shield their buddies from exploding devices (Hunt, 1990). Most were in close-knit combat groups. Most threw themselves on live hand

focus on   the benefits—and the costs—of empathy-induced altruism

People do most of what they do, including much of what they do for others, for their own benefit, acknowledges University of Kansas altruism researcher Daniel Batson and his colleagues (2004). But egoism is not the whole story of helping, they believe; there is also a genuine altruism rooted in empathy, in feelings of sympathy and compassion for others' welfare. We are supremely social creatures. There is good news in that:

Empathy-induced altruism

- *produces sensitive helping.* Where there is empathy, it's not just the thought that counts, it's alleviating the other's suffering.

- *inhibits aggression.* Show Batson someone who feels empathy for a target of potential aggression and he'll show you someone who's unlikely to favor attack, someone who's as likely to forgive as to harbor anger. In general, women report more empathic feelings than men, and they are less likely to support war and other forms of aggression (Jones, 2003).

- *increases cooperation.* In laboratory experiments, Batson and Nadia Ahmad found that people in potential conflict are more trusting and cooperative when they feel empathy for the other. Personalizing an out-group, by getting to know people in it, helps people understand their perspective.

- *improves attitudes toward stigmatized groups.* Take others' perspective, allow yourself to feel what they feel, and you may become more supportive of others like them (the homeless, those with AIDS, or even convicted criminals).

But empathy-induced altruism comes with liabilities, notes the Batson group. It

- *can be harmful.* People who risk their lives on behalf of others sometimes lose them. People who seek to do good can also do harm, sometimes by unintentionally humiliating or demotivating the recipient.

- *can't address all needs.* It's easier to feel empathy for a needy individual than, say, for Mother Earth, whose environment is being stripped and warmed at the peril of our descendants.

- *burns out.* Feeling others' pain is painful, which may cause us to avoid situations that evoke our empathy, or to experience "burnout" or "compassion fatigue."

- *can feed favoritism, injustice, and indifference to the larger common good.* Empathy, being particular, produces partiality—toward a single child or family or pet. Moral principles, being universal, produce concern for unseen others as well. Empathy-based estate planning focuses inheritances on particular loved ones. Morality-based estate planning is more inclusive. With their empathy for someone aroused, people will violate their own standards of fairness and justice by giving that person favored treatment (Batson & others, 1997, 1999). Ironically, empathy-induced altruism can therefore "pose a powerful threat to the common good [by leading] me to narrow my focus of concern to those for whom I especially care—the needing friend—and in so doing to lose sight of the bleeding crowd." No wonder charity so often stays close to home.

grenades. In doing so, 59 sacrificed their lives. Unlike other altruists, such as the 50,000 Gentiles now believed to have rescued 200,000 Jews from the Nazis, these soldiers had no time to reflect on the shame of cowardice or the eternal rewards of self-sacrifice. Yet something drove them to act.

Summing up

Three theories explain helping behavior by suggesting its external and internal rewards. The *social-exchange theory* assumes that helping, like other social behaviors, is motivated by a desire to minimize costs and maximize rewards. The rewards can be internal. After transgressing, people often become more willing to offer help, apparently hoping to relieve guilt or to restore self- image. Sad people also tend to be helpful. This feel bad–do good effect is not found in young children, however, suggesting that the inner rewards of helping are a product of later socialization. Finally, there is a striking feel good–do good effect: Happy people are helpful people.

Social norms also mandate helping. The *reciprocity norm* stimulates us to return help, not harm, to those who have helped us. The *social-responsibility norm* beckons us to help needy people, even if they cannot reciprocate, so long as they are deserving. Women in crisis, partly because they may be seen as more needy, receive more offers of help than men, especially from men.

Evolutionary psychology assumes two types of helping: *devotion to kin* and *reciprocity*. Most evolutionary psychologists, however, believe that the genes of selfish individuals are more likely to survive than the genes of self-sacrificing individuals and that society must therefore teach helping.

In addition to helping that is motivated by external and internal rewards, and the evading of punishment or distress, there appears also to be a genuine, empathy-based altruism. With their empathy aroused, many people are motivated to assist others in need or distress, even when their helping is anonymous or their own mood will be unaffected.

When will we help?

What circumstances prompt people to help, or not to help? How and why is helping influenced by the number and behavior of other bystanders? By mood states? By traits and values?

On March 13, 1964, bar manager Kitty Genovese was set upon by a knife-wielding attacker as she returned to her Queens, New York, apartment house at 3:00 A.M. Her screams of terror and pleas for help—"Oh my God, he stabbed me! Please help me! Please help me!"—aroused 38 of her neighbors. Many came to their windows and caught fleeting glimpses as the attacker left and returned to attack again. Not until her attacker finally departed did anyone call the police. Soon after, she died.

Why had Genovese's neighbors not come to her aid? Were they callous? Indifferent? Apathetic? If so, there are many such people.

- Andrew Mormille was knifed in the stomach as he rode the subway home. After his attackers left the car, 11 other riders watched the young man bleed to death.
- Eleanor Bradley tripped and broke her leg while shopping. Dazed and in pain, she pleaded for help. For 40 minutes, the stream of shoppers simply parted and flowed around her. Finally, a cab driver helped her to a doctor (Darley & Latané, 1968).

- As more than a million locals and tourists mingled in the warm sun during and after a June 2000 parade alongside New York's Central Park, a pack of alcohol-fueled young men became sexually aggressive—groping, and in some cases stripping, 60 individual women. In the days that followed, media attention focused on the mob psychology behind this sexual aggression and on police inaction (at least two victims had approached nearby police, who failed to respond). But what about the thousands of milling people? Why did they tolerate this? Among the many bystanders with cell phones, why did not one person call the police (Dateline, 2000)?

Bystander inaction. What influences our interpretations of a scene such as this, and our decisions to help or not to help?

What is shocking is not that in these cases some people failed to help, but that in each of these groups (of 38, 11, 40, hundreds, and thousands) almost 100 percent of those involved failed to respond. Why? In the same or similar situations, would you or I react as they did?

Social psychologists were curious and concerned about bystanders' lack of involvement during such events as the Kitty Genovese murder. So they undertook experiments to identify when people will help in an emergency. Then they broadened the question to, Who is likely to help in nonemergencies—by such deeds as giving money, donating blood, or contributing time? Let's examine these experiments by looking first at the *circumstances* that enhance helpfulness and then at the characteristics of the *people* who help.

NUMBER OF BYSTANDERS

Bystander passivity during emergencies has prompted social commentators to lament people's "alienation," "apathy," "indifference," and "unconscious sadistic impulses." By attributing the nonintervention to the bystanders' dispositions, we can reassure ourselves that, as caring people, we would have helped. But were the bystanders such inhuman characters?

Social psychologists Bibb Latané and John Darley (1970) were unconvinced. They staged ingenious emergencies and found that a single situational factor— the presence of other bystanders—greatly decreased intervention. By 1980, four dozen experiments had compared help given by bystanders who perceived themselves to be either alone or with others. In about 90 percent of these comparisons, involving nearly 6,000 people, lone bystanders were more likely to help (Latané & Nida, 1981).

Sometimes, the victim was actually less likely to get help when many people were around. When Latané, James Dabbs (1975), and 145 collaborators "accidentally" dropped coins or pencils during 1,497 elevator rides, they were helped 40 percent of the time when one other person was on the elevator and less than 20 percent of the time when there were six passengers.

Why do other bystanders sometimes inhibit helping? Latané and Darley surmised that as the number of bystanders increases, any given bystander is less likely to *notice* the incident, less likely to *interpret* the incident as a problem or emergency, and less likely to *assume responsibility* for taking action (Figure 12–4).

figure 12–4

Latané and Darley's decision tree.

Only one path up the tree leads to helping. At each fork of the path, the presence of other bystanders may divert a person down a branch toward not helping. **Source:** Adapted from Darley & Latané, 1968.

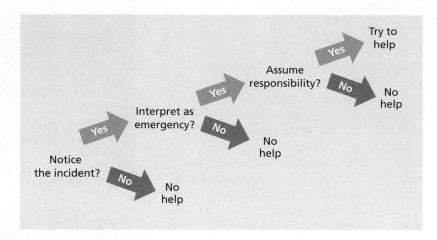

When is a person most likely to help another person? Go to the *SocialSense* CD-ROM to view a video clip on the bystander effect.

Noticing

Twenty minutes after Eleanor Bradley has fallen and broken her leg on a crowded city sidewalk, you come along. Your eyes are on the backs of the pedestrians in front of you (it is bad manners to stare at those you pass) and your private thoughts are on the day's events. Would you therefore be less likely to notice the injured woman than if the sidewalk were virtually deserted?

To find out, Latané and Darley (1968) had Columbia University men fill out a questionnaire in a room, either by themselves or with two strangers. While they were working (and being observed through a one-way mirror), there was a staged emergency: Smoke poured into the room through a wall vent. Solitary students, who often glanced idly about the room while working, noticed the smoke almost immediately—usually in less than five seconds. Those in groups kept their eyes on their work. It typically took them about 20 seconds to notice the smoke.

Interpreting

Once we notice an ambiguous event, we must interpret it. Put yourself in the room filling with smoke. Though worried, you don't want to embarrass

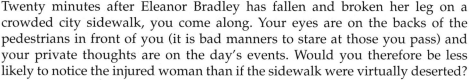

the story behind the research:
research John M. Darley on bystander reactions

Shocked by the Kitty Genovese murder, Bibb Latané and I met over dinner and began to analyze the bystanders' reactions. Being social psychologists, we thought not about the personality flaws of the "apathetic" individuals, but rather about how anyone in that situation might react as did these people. By the time we finished our dinner, we had formulated several factors that together could lead to the surprising result: no one helping. Then we set about

conducting experiments that isolated each factor and demonstrated its importance in an emergency situation.

John M. Darley, Princeton University

yourself by appearing flustered. You glance at the others. They look calm, in-different. Assuming everything must be okay, you shrug it off and go back to work. Then one of the others notices the smoke and, noting your apparent un-concern, reacts similarly. This is yet another example of informational influence (Chapter 6). Each person uses others' behavior as clues to reality.

The misinterpretations are fed by what Thomas Gilovich, Kenneth Savitsky, and Victoria Husted Medvec (1998) call an *illusion of transparency*—a tendency to overestimate others' ability to "read" our internal states. In their experiments, people facing an emergency presumed their concern was more visible than it was. More than we usually suppose, our disgust, our deceit, and our alarm is opaque. Keenly aware of our emotions, we presume they leak out and that oth-ers see right through us. Sometimes others do read our emotions, but often we keep our cool quite effectively. The result is what Chapter 8 called "pluralistic ignorance"—ignorance that others are thinking and feeling what we are. In emergencies, each person may think, "I'm very concerned," but perceive others as calm—"so maybe it's not an emergency."

So it happened in Latané and Darley's experiment. When those working alone noticed the smoke, they usually hesitated a moment, then got up, walked over to the vent, felt, sniffed, and waved at the smoke, hesitated again, and then went to report it. In dramatic contrast, those in groups of three did not move. Among the 24 men in eight groups, only one person reported the smoke within the first four minutes (Figure 12–5). By the end of the six-minute experiment, the smoke was so thick it was obscuring the men's vision and they were rub-bing their eyes and coughing. Still, in only three of the eight groups did even a single person leave to report the problem.

Equally interesting, the group's passivity affected its members' interpreta-tions. What caused the smoke? "A leak in the air conditioning." "Chemistry labs in the building." "Steam pipes." "Truth gas." Not one said, "Fire." The group members, by serving as nonresponsive models, influenced one another's inter-pretation of the situation.

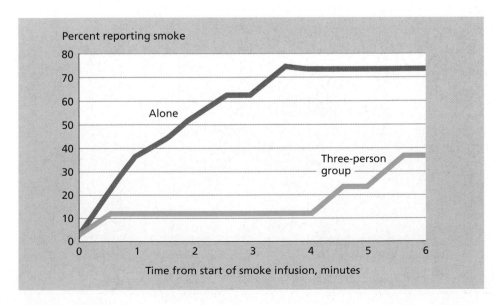

figure 12–5

The smoke-filled room experiment.

Smoke pouring into the testing room was much more likely to be reported by individuals working alone than by three-person groups. **Source:** Data from Darley & Latané, 1968.

This experimental dilemma parallels dilemmas we all face. Are the shrieks outside merely playful antics or the desperate screams of someone being assaulted? Is the boys' scuffling a friendly tussle or a vicious fight? Is the person slumped in the doorway sleeping, high on drugs, or seriously ill, perhaps in a diabetic coma? That surely was the question confronting those who passed by Sidney Brookins (AP, 1993). Brookins, who had suffered a concussion when beaten, died after lying near the door to a Minneapolis apartment house for two days. That may also have been the question for those who in 2003 watched Brandon Vedas overdose and die online. As his life ebbed, his audience, which was left to wonder whether he was putting on an act, failed to decipher available clues to his whereabouts and to contact police (Nichols, 2003).

bystander effect
The finding that a person is less likely to provide help when there are other bystanders.

Unlike the smoke-filled-room experiment, each of these everyday situations involves another in desperate need. To see if the same **bystander effect** occurs in such situations, Latané and Judith Rodin (1969) staged an experiment around a woman in distress. A female researcher set Columbia University men to work on a questionnaire and then left through a curtained doorway to work in an adjacent office. Four minutes later she could be heard (from a tape recorder) climbing on a chair to reach some papers. This was followed by a scream and a loud crash as the chair collapsed and she fell to the floor. "Oh, my God, my foot . . . I . . . I . . . can't move it," she sobbed. "Oh . . . my ankle . . . I . . . can't get this . . . thing . . . off me." Only after two minutes of moaning did she manage to make it out her office door.

Seventy percent of those who were alone when they overheard the "accident" came into the room or called out to offer help. Among pairs of strangers confronting the emergency, only 40 percent of the time did either person offer help. Those who did nothing apparently interpreted the situation as a nonemergency. "A mild sprain," said some. "I didn't want to embarrass her," explained others. This again demonstrates the bystander effect. As the number of people known to be aware of an emergency increases, any given person becomes *less* likely to help. For the victim, there is no safety in numbers.

Interpretations matter. Is this man locked out of his car or is he a burglar? Our answer affects how we respond.

People's interpretations also affect their reactions to street crimes. In staging physical fights between a man and a woman, Lance Shotland and Margaret Straw (1976) found that bystanders intervened 65 percent of the time when the woman shouted, "Get away from me; I don't know you," but only 19 percent of the time when she shouted, "Get away from me; I don't know why I ever married you." Assumed spouse abuse, it seems, just doesn't trigger as much intervention as stranger abuse.

Harold Takooshian and Herzel Bodinger (1982) suspected that bystanders' interpretations could also affect their reactions to burglaries. When they staged hundreds of car burglaries in 18 cities (using a coat hanger to gain access to a valuable object, such as a TV set or fur coat), they were astonished. Fewer than 1 in 10 people walking by questioned their activity. Many noticed and even stopped to stare, snicker, or offer help. Some apparently interpreted the "burglar" as the car's owner.

Assuming responsibility

Failing to notice and misinterpretation are not the bystander effect's only cause. Takooshian and Bodinger report that even when a shabby 14-year-old was the "burglar," when someone simultaneously broke into two adjacent cars, or when onlookers saw a different person breaking into the car than had just gotten out of it, there still was virtually no intervention by New Yorkers. And what about those times when an emergency is obvious? Those who saw and heard Kitty Genovese's pleas for help correctly interpreted what was happening. But the lights and silhouetted figures in neighboring windows told them that others were also watching. This diffused the responsibility for action.

Responsibility diffusion. The nine paparazzi photographers on the scene immediately after the Princess Diana car accident all had cell phones. With one exception, none called for help. Their almost unanimous explanation was that they assumed "someone else" had already called (Sancton, 1997).

Few of us have observed a murder. But all of us have at times been slower to react to a need when others were present. Passing a stranded motorist on a highway, we are less likely to offer help than on a country road. To explore bystander inaction in clear emergencies, Darley and Latané (1968) simulated the Genovese drama. They placed people in separate rooms from which the participants would hear a victim crying for help. To create this situation, Darley and Latané asked some New York University students to discuss their problems with university life over a laboratory intercom. The researchers told the students that to guarantee their anonymity, no one would be visible, nor would the experimenter eavesdrop. During the ensuing discussion, when the experimenter turned his microphone on, the participants heard one person lapse into a seizure. With increasing intensity and speech difficulty, he pleaded for someone to help.

Of those led to believe there were no other listeners, 85 percent left their room to seek help. Of those who believed four others also overheard the victim, only 31 percent went for help. Were those who didn't respond apathetic and indifferent? When the experimenter came in to end the experiment, she did not find this response. Most immediately expressed concern. Many had

www.mhhe.com/**myers8**
Visit the Online Learning Center for a scenario on helping.

trembling hands and sweating palms. They believed an emergency had occurred but were undecided whether to act.

After the smoke-filled room, the woman-in-distress, and the seizure experiments, Latané and Darley asked the participants whether the presence of others had influenced them. We know the others had a dramatic effect. Yet the participants almost invariably denied the influence. They typically replied, "I was aware of the others, but I would have reacted just the same if they weren't there." This response reinforces a familiar point: *We often do not know why we do what we do.* That is why experiments are revealing. A survey of uninvolved bystanders following a real emergency would have left the bystander effect hidden.

Further experiments revealed situations in which others' presence sometimes does *not* inhibit people from offering help. Irving Piliavin and his colleagues (1969) staged an emergency in a laboratory on wheels, the unwitting participants being 4,450 riders of New York's subway. On each of 103 occasions, a confederate entered a subway car and stood in the center next to a pole. After the train pulled out of the station, he staggered, then collapsed. When the victim carried a cane, one or more bystanders almost always offered help promptly. Even when the victim carried a bottle and smelled of liquor, he was often offered prompt aid—especially when several male bystanders were close by. Why? Did the presence of other passengers provide a sense of security to those who helped? Was it because the situation was unambiguous and because others' responses were apparent? (The passengers couldn't help noticing and realizing what was happening.)

Even just imagining others' presence (for example, imagining strangers in a theater) diminishes people's helping and giving (Garcia & others, 2002).

To test this latter possibility, Linda Solomon, Henry Solomon, and Ronald Stone (1978) conducted experiments in which New Yorkers either saw and heard someone's distress, as in the subway experiment, or only heard it, as in the woman-in-distress experiment (leaving the situation more open to interpretation). When the emergencies were very clear, those in groups were only slightly less likely to help than were those alone. When the emergencies were somewhat ambiguous, however, the people in groups were far less likely to help than were solitary bystanders.

New Yorkers, like other urbanites, are seldom alone in public places, which helps account for why city people often are less helpful than country people. "Compassion fatigue" and "sensory overload" from encountering so many people in need further restrain helping in large cities across the world (Yousif & Korte, 1995). Fatigue and overload help explain what happened when Robert LeVine and colleagues (1994) approached several thousand people in 36 U.S. cities, dropping an unnoticed pen, asking for change, simulating a blind person needing help at a corner, and so forth. The bigger and more densely populated the city, the less likely people were to help. Levine and his collaborators (2001, 2003) found that willingness to help strangers also varies around the world (Figure 12–6). People in economically advanced countries tended to offer *less* help to strangers, and those in cultures marked by amiable and agreeable "simpatia" (in Spanish) or "simpatico" (in Portuguese) were *more* helpful.

In Thirty-Eight Witnesses, *A. M. Rosenthal reflects on the Kitty Genovese murder and asks how far away one must be from a known murder to be absolved of responsibility. A block? A mile? A thousand miles?*

Nations, too, have often been bystanders to catastrophes, even to genocide. As 800,000 people were murdered in Rwanda, we all stood by. "With many potential actors, each feels less responsible," notes Ervin Staub (1997). "It's not our responsibility," say the leaders of unaffected nations. Psychologist Peter Suedfeld (2000)—like Staub, a Holocaust survivor—notes that the diffusion of

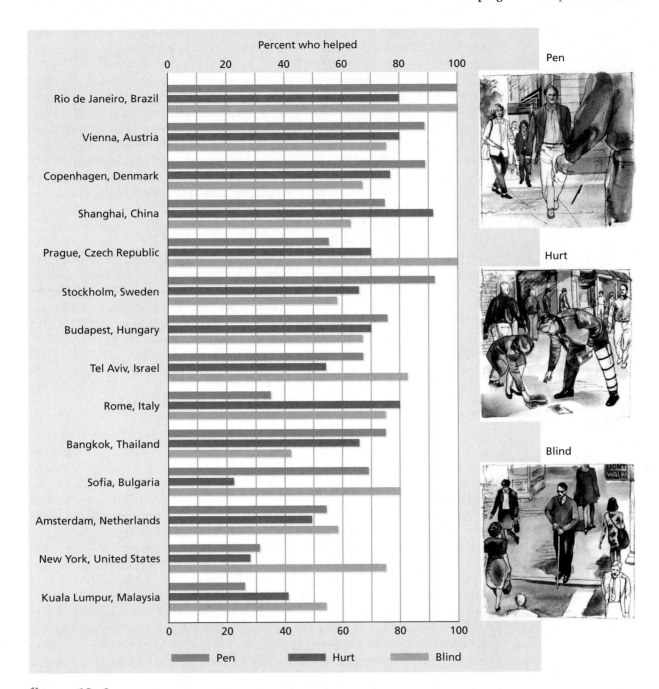

figure 12–6

A world of difference in helping strangers.

To compare helping in different cities and cultures, Robert Levine and his collaborators would "accidentally" drop a pen, drop magazines while limping with an apparently injured leg, or feign blindness when approaching an intersection as the light turned green. Those dropping a pen in Rio were, for example, four times more likely to be helped than those doing so in New York City or Kuala Lumpur. (This is a sample of data from 14 countries.) **Source:** Adapted from R. V. Levine (2003). The kindness of strangers. *American Scientist*, 91, 226–233.

responsibility also helps explain "why the vast majority of European citizens stood idly by during the persecution, removal, and killing of their Jewish compatriots."

In Piliavin's subway experiment, the passengers sat face-to-face, allowing them to see the alarm on one another's faces. To explore the effect of facial communication, Darley, Allan Teger, and Lawrence Lewis (1973) had people working either face-to-face or back-to-back when they heard a crash in the adjacent room as several metal screens fell on a workman. Unlike those working alone, who almost always offered help, pairs working back-to-back seldom offered help. A person working face-to-face with a partner could notice the other's facial expression and know that the person had also observed the event. Apparently, this led both people to interpret the situation as an emergency and to feel some responsibility to act, for these pairs were virtually as likely to give aid as were those working alone.

Finally, all the experiments we have considered involved groups of strangers. Imagine yourself facing any of these emergencies with a group of friends. Would your acquaintance with the other bystanders make a difference? Experiments conducted in two Israeli cities and at the University of Illinois at Chicago suggest that it would (Rutkowski & others, 1983; Yinon & others, 1982). Cohesive groups are *less* inhibited about helping than are solitary individuals. To summarize: The presence of other bystanders inhibits helping especially *if* the emergency is *ambiguous* and the other bystanders are *strangers* who *cannot easily read one another's reactions.*

Revisiting research ethics

These experiments raise again the issue of research ethics. Is it right to force hundreds of subway riders to witness someone's apparent collapse? Were the researchers in the seizure experiment ethical when they forced people to decide whether to abort the discussion to report the problem? Would you object to being in such a study? Note that it would have been impossible to get your "informed consent"; doing so would have destroyed the cover for the experiment.

In defense of the researchers, they were always careful to debrief the laboratory participants. After explaining the seizure experiment, probably the most stressful, the experimenter gave the participants a questionnaire. One hundred percent said the deception was justified and that they would be willing to take part in similar experiments in the future. None reported feeling angry at the experimenter. Other researchers confirm that the overwhelming majority of participants in such experiments say that their participation was both instructive and ethically justified (Schwartz & Gottlieb, 1981). In field experiments, such as the one in the subway car, an accomplice assisted the victim if no one else did, thus reassuring bystanders that the problem was being dealt with.

Remember that the social psychologist has a twofold ethical obligation: to protect the participants and to enhance human welfare by discovering influences upon human behavior. Such discoveries can alert us to unwanted influences and show us how we might exert positive influences. The ethical principle seems to be: After protecting participants' welfare, social psychologists fulfill their responsibility to society by doing such research.

HELPING WHEN SOMEONE ELSE DOES

If aggressive models can heighten aggression (Chapter 10) and if unresponsive models can heighten nonresponding, then will helpful models promote helping? Imagine hearing a crash followed by sobs and moans. If another by-stander said, "Uh oh. This is an emergency! We've got to do something," would it stimulate others to help?

The evidence is clear: Prosocial models do promote altruism. Some examples:

- James Bryan and Mary Ann Test (1967) found that Los Angeles drivers were more likely to offer help to a female driver with a flat tire if a quarter mile earlier they witnessed someone helping another woman change a tire.
- In another experiment, Bryan and Test observed that New Jersey Christmas shoppers were more likely to drop money in a Salvation Army kettle if they had just seen someone else do the same.
- Philippe Rushton and Anne Campbell (1977) found British adults more willing to donate blood if they were approached after observing a confederate consent to donating.
- A glimpse of extraordinary human kindness and charity—such as I gave you in the examples of heroic altruism at this chapter's outset—often triggers what Jonathan Haidt (2003) calls *elevation*, "a distinctive feeling in the chest of warmth and expansion" that may provoke chills, tears, and throat clenching and that often inspires people to become more self-giving.

Models sometimes, however, contradict in practice what they preach. Parents may tell their children, "Do as I say, not as I do." Experiments show that children learn moral judgments both from what they hear preached and what they see practiced (Rice & Grusec, 1975; Rushton, 1975). When exposed to hypocrites, they imitate: They do what the model does and say what the model says.

"We are, in truth, more than half what we are by imitation. The great point is, to choose good models and to study them with care."
—Lord Chesterfield, *Letters,* January 18, 1750

TIME PRESSURES

Darley and Batson (1973) discerned another determinant of helping in the Good Samaritan parable. The priest and the Levite were both busy, important people, probably hurrying to their duties. The lowly Samaritan surely was less pressed for time. To see whether people in a hurry would behave as the priest and Levite did, Darley and Batson cleverly staged the situation described in the parable.

After collecting their thoughts prior to recording a brief extemporaneous talk (which, for half the participants, was on the Good Samaritan parable), Princeton Theological Seminary students were directed to a recording studio in an adjacent building. En route, they passed a man sitting slumped in a doorway, head down, coughing and groaning. Some of the students had been sent off nonchalantly: "It will be a few minutes before they're ready for you, but you might as well head on over." Of these, almost two-thirds stopped to offer help. Others were told, "Oh, you're late. They were expecting you a few minutes ago . . . so you'd better hurry." Of these, only 10 percent offered help.

Reflecting on these findings, Darley and Batson remarked:

A person not in a hurry may stop and offer help to a person in distress. A person in a hurry is likely to keep going. Ironically, he is likely to keep going even if he is hurrying to speak on the parable of the Good Samaritan, thus inadvertently confirming the point of the parable. (Indeed, on several occasions, a seminary student going to give his talk on the parable of the Good Samaritan literally stepped over the victim as he hurried on his way!)

Are we being unfair to the seminary students, who were, after all, hurrying to *help* the experimenter? Perhaps they keenly felt the social-responsibility norm but found it pulling them two ways—toward the experimenter and toward the victim. In another enactment of the Good Samaritan situation, Batson and his associates (1978) directed 40 University of Kansas students to an experiment in another building. Half were told they were late; half knew they had plenty of time. Half of each of these groups thought their participation was vitally important to the experimenter; half thought it was not essential. The results: Those leisurely on their way to an unimportant appointment usually stopped to help. But people seldom stopped to help if, like the White Rabbit in *Alice's Adventures in Wonderland,* they were late for a very important date.

Can we conclude that those who were rushed were callous? Did the seminarians notice the victim's distress and then consciously choose to ignore it? No. Harried, preoccupied, rushing to help the experimenter, they simply did not take time to tune in to the person in need. As social psychologists have so often observed, behavior was influenced more by context than conviction.

SIMILARITY

Because similarity is conducive to liking (Chapter 11), and liking is conducive to helping, we are more empathic and helpful toward those *similar* to us (Miller & others, 2001). The similarity bias applies to both dress and beliefs. Tim Emswiller and his fellow researchers (1971) had confederates, dressed either conservatively or in counterculture garb, approach "conservative" and "hip" Purdue University students seeking a dime for a phone call. Fewer than half the students did the favor for those dressed differently from themselves. Two-thirds did so for those dressed similarly. Likewise, Scottish shoppers in a more anti-gay era were less willing to make change for someone if the person wore a T-shirt with a pro-gay slogan (Gray & others, 1991).

No face is more familiar than one's own. That explains why, when Lisa De-Bruine (2002) had McMaster University students play an interactive game with a supposed other player, they were more trusting and generous when the other person's pictured face had some features of their own face morphed into it (Figure 12–7). In me I trust. Even just sharing a birthday, a first name, or a fingerprint pattern leads people to respond more to a request for help (Burger & others, 2004).

figure 12–7

Similarity breeds cooperation.

Lisa DeBruine (2002) morphed participants' faces (left) with strangers' faces (right) to make the composite center faces— toward whom the participants were more generous than toward the stranger.

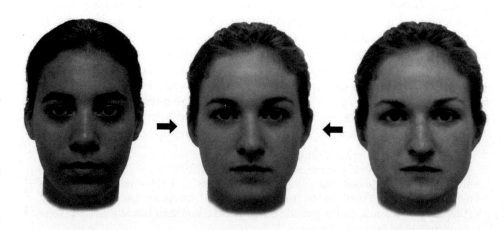

Does the similarity bias extend to race? During the 1970s, researchers explored this question with confusing results:

- Some studies found a same-race bias (Benson & others, 1976; Clark, 1974; Franklin, 1974; Gaertner, 1973; Gaertner & Bickman, 1971; Sissons, 1981).
- Others found no bias (Gaertner, 1975; Lerner & Frank, 1974; Wilson & Donnerstein, 1979; Wispe & Freshley, 1971).
- Still others—especially those involving face-to-face situations—found a bias toward helping those of a different race (Dutton, 1971, 1973; Dutton & Lake, 1973; Katz & others, 1975).

Is there a general rule that resolves these seemingly contradictory findings?

Few people want to appear prejudiced. Perhaps, then, people favor their own race but keep this bias secret to preserve a positive image. If so, the same-race bias should appear only when people can attribute failure to help to nonrace factors. This is what happened in experiments by Samuel Gaertner and John Dovidio (1977, 1986). For example, University of Delaware White women were less willing to help a Black than a White woman in distress *if* their responsibility could be diffused among the bystanders ("I didn't help the Black woman because there were others who could"). When there were no other bystanders, the women were equally helpful to the Black and the White women. The rule seems to be: When norms for appropriate behavior are well defined, Whites don't discriminate; when norms are ambiguous or conflicting, racial similarity may bias responses.

For me, the laboratory came to life recently as I walked from a dinner meeting in Washington, D.C., to my hotel. On a deserted sidewalk, a well-dressed, distraught-seeming man about my age approached me and begged for a dollar. He explained that he had just come over from London and, after visiting the Holocaust Museum, had accidentally left his wallet in a taxi. So here he was, stranded and needing a $24 taxi fare to a friend's home in suburban D.C.

"So how's one dollar going to get you there?" I asked.

"I asked people for more, but no one would help me," he nearly sobbed, "so I thought maybe if I asked for less I could collect taxi fare."

"But why not take the Metro?" I challenged.

"It stops about five miles from Greenbriar, where I need to go," he explained. "Oh my, how am I ever going to get there? If you could help me out, I will mail you back the money on Monday."

Here I was, as if a participant in an on-the-street altruism experiment. Having grown up in a city, and as a frequent visitor to New York and Chicago, I am accustomed to panhandling and have never rewarded it. But I also consider myself a caring person. Moreover, this fellow was unlike any panhandler I had ever met. He was dressed sharply. He was intelligent. He had a convincing story. And he looked like me! If he's lying, he's a slimeball, I said to myself, and giving him money would be stupid, naive, and rewarding slimeballism. If he's a truth-teller and I turn my back on him, I'm a slimeball.

He had asked for $1. I gave him $30, along with my name and address, which he took gratefully, and disappeared into the night.

As I walked on, I began to realize—correctly as it turned out—that I had been a patsy. Having lived in Britain, why had I not tested his knowledge of England? Why had I not taken him to a phone booth to call his friend? Why had I at least not offered to pay a taxi driver and send him on his way, rather than give him the money? And why, after a lifetime of resisting scams, had I succumbed to this one?

Sheepishly, because I like to think myself not influenced by ethnic stereotypes, I had to admit that it was not only his socially skilled, personal approach but also the mere fact of his similarity to me.

Who will help?

We have considered internal influences on the decision to help (such as guilt and mood) and external influences as well (such as social norms, number of bystanders, time pressures, and similarity). We also need to consider the helpers' dispositions, including, for example, their personality traits and religious values.

PERSONALITY TRAITS

Surely some traits must distinguish the Mother Teresa types. Faced with identical situations, some people will respond helpfully, others won't bother. Who are the likely helpers?

For many years social psychologists were unable to discover a single personality trait that predicted helping with anything close to the predictive power of the situation, guilt, and mood factors. Modest relationships were found between helping and certain personality variables, such as a need for social approval. But by and large, the personality tests were unable to identify the helpers. Studies of rescuers of Jews in Nazi Europe reveal a similar conclusion: Although the social context clearly influenced willingness to help, there was no definable set of altruistic personality traits (Darley, 1995).

If that has a familiar ring, it could be from a similar conclusion by conformity researchers (Chapter 6): Conformity, too, seemed more influenced by the situation than by measurable personality traits. Perhaps, though, you recall from Chapter 2 that who we are does affect what we do. Attitude and trait measures seldom predict a *specific* act, which is what most experiments on altruism measure (in contrast to the lifelong altruism of a Mother Teresa). But they predict average behavior across many situations more accurately.

Personality researchers have responded to the challenge. First, they have found *individual differences* in helpfulness and shown that these differences persist over time and are noticed by one's peers (Hampson, 1984; Penner, 2002; Rushton & others, 1981). Some people are reliably more helpful. Second, researchers are gathering clues to the *network of traits* that predispose a person to helpfulness. Those high in positive emotionality, empathy, and self-efficacy are most likely to be concerned and helpful (Bierhoff & others, 1991; Eisenberg & others, 1991; Krueger & others, 2001). Third, personality influences how particular people react to *particular situations* (Carlo & others, 1991; Romer & others, 1986; Wilson & Petruska, 1984). Those high in self-monitoring are attuned to others' expectations and are therefore helpful *if* they think helpfulness will be socially rewarded (White & Gerstein, 1987). Others' opinions matter less to internally guided, low self-monitoring people.

This interaction of person and situation also appears in the 172 studies that have compared the helpfulness of nearly 50,000 male and female individuals.

"There are . . . reasons why personality should be rather unimportant in determining people's reactions to the emergency. For one thing, the situational forces affecting a person's decision are so strong."
—Bibb Latané and John Darley (1970, p. 115)

After analyzing these results, Alice Eagly and Maureen Crowley (1986) reported that, when faced with potentially dangerous situations in which strangers need help (such as with a flat tire or a fall in a subway), men more often help. (Eagly and Crowley also report that among 6,767 individuals who have received the Carnegie medal for heroism in saving human life, 90 percent have been men.) But in safer situations, such as volunteering to help with an experiment or spend time with children with developmental disabilities, women are slightly more likely to help. Thus, the gender difference interacts with (depends on) the situation. And Eagly and Crowley guessed that if researchers were to study caring behavior in long-term, close relationships rather than in short-term encounters with strangers, they would discover that women are significantly more helpful. Indeed, report Darren George and his collaborators (1998), women respond to a friend's problems with greater empathy and more time spent helping.

RELIGIOUS FAITH

With Nazi submarines sinking ships faster than the Allied forces could replace them, the troop ship SS *Dorchester* steamed out of New York harbor with 902 men headed for Greenland (Elliott, 1989; Parachin, 1992). Among those leaving anxious families behind were four chaplains, Methodist preacher George Fox, Rabbi Alexander Goode, Catholic priest John Washington, and Reformed Church minister Clark Poling. Some 150 miles from their destination, submarine *U-456* caught the *Dorchester* in its cross hairs. Within moments of the torpedo's impact, stunned men were pouring out of their bunks as the ship began listing. With power cut off, the escort vessels, unaware of the unfolding tragedy, pushed on in the darkness. On board, chaos reigned as panicky men came up from the hold without life jackets and leapt into overcrowded lifeboats.

As the four chaplains arrived on the steeply sloping deck, they began guiding the men to their boat stations. They opened a storage locker, distributed life jackets, and coaxed the men over the side. When Petty Officer John Mahoney turned back to retrieve his gloves, Rabbi Goode responded, "Never mind. I have two pairs." Only later did Mahoney realize that the Rabbi was not conveniently carrying an extra pair; he was giving up his own.

In the icy, oil-smeared water, Private William Bednar heard the chaplains preaching courage and found the strength to swim out from under the ship until he reached a life raft. Still on board, Grady Clark watched in awe as the chaplains handed out the last life jacket and then, with ultimate selflessness, gave away their own. As Clark slipped into the waters, he looked back at an unforgettable sight: The four chaplains were standing—their arms linked—praying, in Latin, Hebrew, and English. Other men joined them in a huddle as the *Dorchester* slid beneath the sea. "It was the finest thing I have ever seen or hope to see this side of heaven," said John Ladd, another of the 230 survivors.

Does the chaplains' heroic example rightly imply that faith promotes courage and caring? Most studies of helping explore spontaneous acts. Confronted with a minor emergency, intrinsically religious people are only slightly more responsive (Trimble, 1993). Researchers are also now exploring planned helping—the sort of sustained helping provided by AIDS volunteers, Big Brother and Big Sister helpers, and supporters of campus service organizations. It is when making intentional choices about long-term helping that religious faith better predicts altruism.

The four chaplains' ultimate selflessness inspired this painting, which hangs in Valley Forge, Pennsylvania's Chapel of the Four Chaplains.

From their analyses of why people volunteer, as when befriending AIDS patients, Mark Snyder, Allen Omoto, and Gil Clary (Clary & Snyder, 1993, 1995; Clary & others, 1998, 1999) have discerned six motivations. Some are rooted in rewards—seeking to join a group, gain approval, enhance job prospects, reduce guilt, learn skills, or boost self-esteem. Others help to act upon their religious or humanitarian values and concern for others.

In studies of college students and the general public, those religiously committed have reported volunteering more hours, for example, as tutors, relief workers, and campaigners for social justice than have the religiously uncommitted (Benson & others, 1980; Hansen & others, 1995; Penner, 2002). Among the 12 percent of Americans whom George Gallup (1984) classified as "highly spiritually committed," 46 percent said they were currently working among the poor, the infirm, or the elderly—many more than the 22 percent among those "highly uncommitted" (Figure 12–8). In a follow-up Gallup survey (Colasanto, 1989), charitable and social service volunteering was reported by 28 percent of those who rated religion "not very important" in their lives and by 50 percent of those who rated it "very important." In another Gallup survey, 37 percent of those attending church yearly or less, and 76 percent of those attending weekly, reported thinking at least a "fair amount" about "responsibility to the poor" (Wuthnow, 1994).

Moreover, Sam Levenson's jest—"When it comes to giving, some people stop at nothing"—is seldom true of church and synagogue members. In a Gallup survey, Americans who said they never attended church or synagogue reported giving away 1.1 percent of their incomes (Hodgkinson & others, 1990).

"Religion is the mother of philanthropy."
—Frank Emerson Andrews, *Attitudes Toward Giving,* 1953

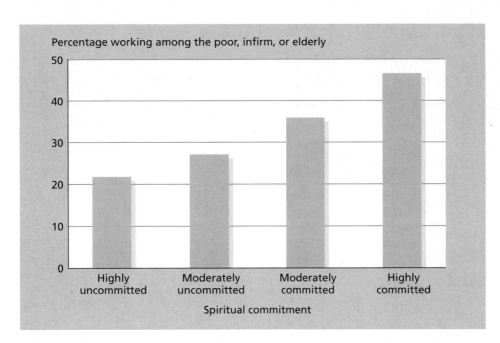

Percentage working among the poor, infirm, or elderly

Spiritual commitment

figure 12–8

Religion and long-term altruism.

Those whom George Gallup (1984) classified as "highly spiritually committed" were more likely to report working among the needy. **Source:** Simplified from Anderson, Deuser, and DeNeve, 1995.

Weekly attenders were two and a half times as generous. This 24 percent of the population gave 48 percent of all charitable contributions. The other three-quarters of Americans give the remaining half. Follow-up 1990 and 1992 Gallup surveys and a 2001 Independent Sector survey confirmed the faith and philanthropy correlation (Hodgkinson & Weitzman, 1990, 1992).

Do the religious links with planned helping extend similarly to other communal organizations? Robert Putnam (2000) analyzed national survey data from 22 types of organizations, including hobby clubs, professional associations, self-help groups, and service clubs. "It was membership in religious groups," he reports, "that was most closely associated with other forms of civic involvement, like voting, jury service, community projects, talking with neighbors, and giving to charity" (p. 67).

Summing up

Several situational influences work to inhibit or to encourage altruism. As the number of bystanders at an emergency increases, any given bystander is (1) less likely to notice the incident, (2) less likely to interpret it as an emergency, and (3) less likely to assume responsibility.

When are people most likely to help? (1) After observing someone else helping and (2) when not hurried. Personal influences such as mood also matter.

In contrast to altruism's potent situational and mood determinants, personality test scores have served as only modest predictors of helping. However, new evidence indicates that some people are consistently more helpful than others and that the effect of personality or gender may depend on the situation. Religious faith predicts long-term altruism, as reflected in volunteerism and charitable contributions.

How can we increase helping?

To increase helping, can we reverse the factors that inhibit helping? Or can we teach norms of helping and socialize people to see themselves as helpful?

As social scientists, our goal is to understand human behavior, thus also suggesting ways to improve it. We therefore wonder how we might apply insights from research to increase helping.

UNDOING THE RESTRAINTS ON HELPING

One way to promote altruism is to reverse those factors that inhibit it. Given that hurried, preoccupied people are less likely to help, can we think of ways to encourage them to slow down and turn their attention outward? If the presence of others diminishes each bystander's sense of responsibility, how can we enhance responsibility?

Reduce ambiguity, increasing responsibility

If Latané and Darley's decision tree (refer back to Figure 12–4) describes the dilemmas bystanders face, then assisting people to interpret an incident correctly and to assume responsibility should increase their involvement. Leonard Bickman and his colleagues (1975, 1977, 1979) tested this presumption in a series of experiments on crime reporting. In each, supermarket or bookstore shoppers witnessed a shoplifting. Some witnesses had seen signs that attempted to sensitize them to shoplifting and to inform them how to report it, but the signs had little effect. Other witnesses heard a bystander interpret the incident: "Say, look at her. She's shoplifting. She put that into her purse." (The bystander then left to look for a lost child.) Still others heard this person add, "We saw it. We should report it. It's our responsibility." Both comments substantially boosted reporting of the crime.

The potency of personal influence is no longer in doubt. Robert Foss (1978) surveyed several hundred blood donors and found that neophyte donors, unlike veterans, were usually there at someone's personal invitation. Leonard Jason and his collaborators (1984) confirmed that personal appeals for blood donation are much more effective than posters and media announcements—if the personal appeals come from friends. Nonverbal appeals can also be effective when they are personalized. Mark Snyder and his co-workers (1974; Omoto & Snyder, 2002) have found that hitchhikers doubled the number of ride offers by looking drivers straight in the eye and that most AIDS volunteers got involved via someone's personal influence. A personal approach, as my panhandler knew, makes one feel less anonymous, more responsible.

Henry Solomon and Linda Solomon (1978; Solomon & others, 1981) explored ways to reduce anonymity. They found that bystanders who had identified themselves to one another—by name, age, and so forth—were more likely to offer aid to a sick person than were anonymous bystanders. Similarly, when a female experimenter caught the eye of another shopper and gave her a warm smile prior to stepping on an elevator, that shopper was far more likely than other shoppers to offer help when the experimenter later said, "Damn. I've left my glasses. Can anyone tell me what floor the umbrellas are on?" Even a trivial momentary conversation with someone ("Excuse me, aren't you Suzie Spear's sister?" "No, I'm not") dramatically increased the person's later helpfulness.

Helpfulness also increases when one expects to meet the victim and other witnesses again. Using a laboratory intercom system, Jody Gottlieb and Charles Carver (1980) led University of Miami students to believe they were discussing problems of college living with other students. (Actually, the other discussants were tape-recorded.) When one of the supposed fellow discussants had a choking fit and cried out for help, she was helped most quickly by those who believed they would soon be meeting the discussants face-to-face. In short, anything that personalizes bystanders—a personal request, eye contact, stating one's name, anticipation of interaction—increases willingness to help.

Personal treatment makes bystanders more self-aware and therefore more attuned to their own altruistic ideals. Recall from earlier chapters that people made self-aware by acting in front of a mirror or TV camera exhibit increased consistency between attitudes and actions. By contrast, "deindividuated" people are less responsible. Thus, circumstances that promote self-awareness—name tags, being watched and evaluated, undistracted quiet—should also increase helping. Shelley Duval, Virginia Duval, and Robert Neely (1979) confirmed this. They showed some University of Southern California women their own images on a TV screen or had them complete biographical questionnaires just before giving them a chance to contribute time and money to people in need. Those made self-aware contributed more. Similarly, pedestrians who have just had their pictures taken by someone became more likely to help another pedestrian pick up dropped envelopes (Hoover & others, 1983). Self-aware people more often put their ideals into practice.

Guilt and concern for self-image

Earlier we noted that people who feel guilty will act to reduce guilt and restore their self-worth. Can heightening people's awareness of their transgressions therefore increase desire to help? A Reed College research team led by Richard Katzev (1978) wondered. So when visitors to the Portland Art Museum disobeyed a "Please do not touch" sign, experimenters reprimanded some of them: "Please don't touch the objects. If everyone touches them, they will deteriorate." Likewise, when visitors to the Portland Zoo fed unauthorized food to the bears, some of them were admonished with, "Hey, don't feed unauthorized food to the animals. Don't you know it could hurt them?" In both cases, 58 percent of the now guilt-laden individuals shortly thereafter offered help to another experimenter who had "accidentally" dropped something. Of those not reprimanded, only one-third helped.

People also care about their public images. When Robert Cialdini and his colleagues (1975) asked some of their Arizona State University students to chaperone delinquent children on a zoo trip, only 32 percent agreed to do so. With other students the questioner first made a very large request—that the students commit two years as volunteer counselors to delinquent children. After getting the **door-in-the-face** in response to this request (all refused), the questioner then counteroffered with the chaperoning request, saying, in effect, "OK, if you won't do that, would you do just this much?" With this technique, nearly twice as many—56 percent—agreed to help.

Cialdini and David Schroeder (1976) offer another practical way to trigger concern for self-image: Ask for a contribution so small that it's hard to say no without feeling like a Scrooge. Cialdini (1995) discovered this when a United Way canvasser came to his door. As she solicited his contribution, he

door-in-the-face technique
A strategy for gaining a concession. After someone first turns down a large request (the door-in-the-face), the same requester counteroffers with a more reasonable request.

Door-in-the-face technique.
Reprinted with special
permission of King Features
Syndicate.

was mentally preparing his refusal—until she said magic words that demolished his financial excuse: "Even a penny will help." "I had been neatly finessed into compliance," recalled Cialdini. "And there was another interesting feature of our exchange as well. When I stopped coughing (I really had choked on my attempted rejection), I gave her not the penny she had mentioned but the amount I usually allot to legitimate charity solicitors. At that, she thanked me, smiled innocently, and moved on." Was Cialdini's response atypical? To find out, he and Schroeder had a solicitor approach suburbanites. When the solicitor said, "I'm collecting money for the American Cancer Society," 29 percent contributed an average of $1.44 each. When the solicitor added, "Even a penny will help," 50 percent contributed an average of $1.54 each. When James Weyant (1984) repeated this experiment, he found similar results: The "even a penny will help" boosted the number contributing from 39 to 57 percent. And when 6,000 people were solicited by mail for the American Cancer Society, those asked for small amounts were more likely to give—and gave no less on average—than those asked for larger amounts (Weyant & Smith, 1987). When approaching previous donors, bigger requests (within reason) do elicit bigger donations (Doob & McLaughlin, 1989). But with door-to-door solicitation, there is more success with requests for small contributions, which are difficult to turn down and still allow the person to maintain an altruistic self-image.

Labeling people as helpful can also strengthen a helpful self-image. After they had made charitable contributions, Robert Kraut (1973) told some Connecticut women, "You are a generous person." Two weeks later, these women were more willing than those not so labeled to contribute to a different charity.

SOCIALIZING ALTRUISM

If we can learn altruism, then how might we socialize it? Here are four ways (Figure 12–9).

Teaching moral inclusion

moral exclusion
The perception of certain individuals or groups as outside the boundary within which one applies moral values and rules of fairness. Moral inclusion is regarding others as within one's circle of moral concern.

Rescuers of Jews in Nazi Europe, leaders of the American antislavery movement, and medical missionaries shared at least one thing in common: They included people who differed from them within the human circle to which their moral values and rules of justice applied. These people were *morally inclusive,* as illustrated by one rescuer who faked a pregnancy on behalf of a pregnant hidden Jew—thus including the soon-to-be-born child within the circle of her own children's identities (Fogelman, 1994).

Moral exclusion—omitting certain people (and animals) from one's circle of moral concern—has the opposite effect. It justifies all sorts of harm, from

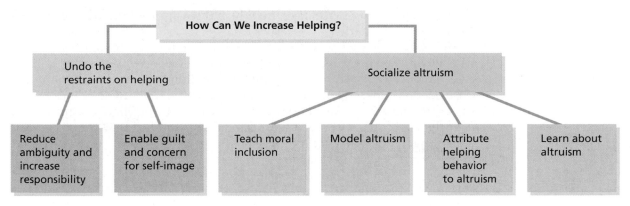

figure 12–9
Practical ways to increase helping.

discrimination to genocide (Opotow, 1990; Staub, in press; Tyler & Lind, 1990). Exploitation or cruelty becomes acceptable, even appropriate, toward those people we regard as undeserving or as nonpersons (and also toward animals outside one's circle of concern). The Nazis excluded Jews from their moral community. Anyone who participates in enslavement, death squads, or torture practices a similar exclusion. To a lesser extent, moral exclusion describes those of us who concentrate our concerns, favors, and financial inheritance upon "our people" (for example, our children) to the exclusion of others.

A first step toward socializing altruism is therefore to counter the natural in-group bias favoring kin and tribe by broadening the range of people whose well-being concerns us. Daniel Batson (1983) notes how religious teachings do this. They extend the reach of kin-linked altruism by urging "brotherly and sisterly" love toward all "children of God" in the whole human "family." If everyone is part of our family, then everyone has a moral claim on us. The boundaries between "we" and "they" fade. Inviting advantaged people to put themselves in others' shoes, to imagine how they feel, also helps (Batson & others, 2003). To "do unto others as you would have them do unto you" one must take the others' perspective.

"We consider humankind our family."
—Parliament of the World Religions, *Towards a Global Ethic,* 1993

Modeling altruism

Earlier we noted that seeing unresponsive bystanders makes us less likely to help. People reared by extremely punitive parents, as were many delinquents, chronic criminals, and Nazi mass murderers, also show much less of the empathy and principled caring that typifies altruists.

If we see or read about someone helping, we are more likely to offer assistance. It's better, find Robert Cialdini and his co-workers (2003), *not* to publicize rampant tax cheating, littering, and teen drinking, and instead to emphasize—to define a norm of—people's widespread honesty, cleanliness, and abstinence. In one experiment, they asked visitors not to remove petrified wood from along the paths of the Petrified Forest National Park. Some were also told that "past visitors have removed the petrified wood." Other people who were told that "past visitors have left the petrified wood" in order to preserve the park were much less likely to pick up samples placed along a path. Perhaps norms for generosity could also be cultivated by simply including a new line on tax forms that requires people to compute—and thus to know—their annual donations as a percentage of income (Ayres & Nalebuff, 2003). People know and sometimes discuss their tipping percentage, for which there are well-defined norms, but usually not their charity.

Modeling effects were also apparent within the families of European Christians who risked their lives to rescue Jews in the 1930s and 1940s and of 1950s civil rights activists. In both cases these exceptional altruists had warm and close relationships with at least one parent who was, similarly, a strong "moralist" or committed to humanitarian causes (London, 1970; Oliner & Oliner, 1988; Rosenhan, 1970). Their families—and often their friends and churches—had taught them the norm of helping and caring for others. This "prosocial value orientation" led them to include people from other groups in their circle of moral concern and to feel responsible for others' welfare, noted Ervin Staub (1989, 1991, 1992).

Staub (1999) knows of what he speaks: "As a young Jewish child in Budapest I survived the Holocaust, the destruction of most European Jews by Nazi Germany and its allies. My life was saved by a Christian woman who repeatedly endangered her life to help me and my family, and by Raoul Wallenberg, the Swede who came to Budapest and with courage, brilliance, and complete commitment saved the lives of tens of thousands of Jews destined for the gas chambers. These two heroes were not passive bystanders, and my work is one of the ways for me not to be one." (See "Focus on: Behavior and Attitudes among Rescuers of Jews.")

Do television's positive models promote helping, much as its aggressive portrayals promote aggression? Prosocial TV models have actually had even greater effects than antisocial models. Susan Hearold (1986) statistically combined 108 comparisons of prosocial programs with neutral programs or no program. She found that, on average, "If the viewer watched prosocial programs instead of neutral programs, he would [at least temporarily] be elevated from the 50th to the 74th percentile in prosocial behavior—typically altruism."

In one such study, researchers Lynette Friedrich and Aletha Stein (1973; Stein & Friedrich, 1972) showed preschool children *Mister Rogers' Neighborhood* episodes each day for four weeks as part of their nursery school program. (*Mister Rogers'* aims to enhance young children's social and emotional development.) During this viewing period, children from less educated homes became more cooperative, helpful, and likely to state their feelings. In a follow-up study, kindergartners who viewed four *Mister Rogers'* programs were able to state its prosocial content, both on a test and in puppet play (Friedrich & Stein, 1975; also Coates & others, 1976).

Attributing helpful behavior to altruistic motives

Another clue to socializing altruism comes from research on what Chapter 4 called the **overjustification effect:** When the justification for an act is more than sufficient, the person may attribute the act to the extrinsic justification rather than to an inner motive. Rewarding people for doing what they would do anyway therefore undermines intrinsic motivation. We can state the principle positively: By providing people with just enough justification to prompt a good deed (weaning them from bribes and threats when possible), we may increase their pleasure in doing such deeds on their own.

Daniel Batson and his associates (1978, 1979) put the overjustification phenomenon to work. In several experiments, they found that University of Kansas students felt most altruistic after they agreed to help someone without payment

"Children can learn to be altruistic, friendly and self-controlled by looking at television programs depicting such behavior patterns."
—National Institute of Mental Health, *Television and Behavior,* 1982

overjustification effect
Undermining intrinsic motivation by bribing people to do what they already like doing; they may then see their action as externally controlled rather than intrinsically appealing.

focus on | behavior and attitudes among rescuers of Jews

Goodness, like evil, often evolves in small steps. The Gentiles who saved Jews often began with a small commitment—to hide someone for a day or two. Having taken that step, they began to see themselves differently, as people who help. Then they became more intensely involved. Given control of a confiscated Jewish-owned factory, Oskar Schindler began by doing small favors for his Jewish workers, who were earning him handsome profits. Gradually, he took greater and greater risks to protect them. He got permission to set up workers' housing next to the factory. He rescued individuals separated from their families and reunited loved ones. Finally, as the Russians advanced, he saved some 1,200 Jews by setting up a fake factory in his hometown and taking along his entire group of "skilled workers" to staff it.

Others, like Raoul Wallenberg, began by agreeing to a personal request for help and ended up repeatedly risking their lives. Wallenberg became Swedish ambassador to Hungary, where he saved tens of thousands of Hungarian Jews from extermination at Auschwitz. One of those given protective identity papers was six-year-old Ervin Staub, now a University of Massachusetts social psychologist whose experience set him on a lifelong mission to understand why some people perpetrate evil, some stand by, and some help.

Munich, 1948. Oskar Schindler with some of the Jews he saved from the Nazis during World War II.
Source: Rappoport & Kren, 1993.

or implied social pressure. When pay had been offered or social pressures were present, people felt less altruistic after helping.

In another experiment, the researchers led students to attribute a helpful act to compliance ("I guess we really don't have a choice") or to compassion ("The guy really needs help"). Later, when the students were asked to volunteer their time to a local service agency, 25 percent of those who had been led to perceive their previous helpfulness as mere compliance now volunteered; of those led to see themselves as compassionate, 60 percent volunteered. The moral? When people wonder, "Why am I helping?" it's best if the circumstances enable them to answer, "Because help was needed, and I am a caring, giving, helpful person."

Although rewards undermine intrinsic motivation when they function as controlling bribes, an unanticipated compliment can make people feel competent and worthy. When Joe is coerced with, "If you quit being chicken and give blood, we'll win the fraternity prize for most donations," he isn't likely to attribute his donation to altruism. When Jocelyn is rewarded with, "That's terrific that you'd choose to take an hour out of such a busy week to give blood," she's more likely to walk away with an altruistic self-image—and thus to contribute again (Piliavin & others, 1982; Thomas & Batson, 1981; Thomas & others, 1981).

To predispose more people to help in situations where most don't, it can also pay to induce a tentative positive commitment, from which people may infer their own helpfulness. Delia Cioffi and Randy Garner (1998) observed that only about 5 percent of students responded to a campus blood drive after receiving an e-mail announcement a week ahead. They asked other students to reply to the announcement with a yes, "if you think you probably will donate." Of these, 29 percent did reply and the actual donation rate was 8 percent. They asked a third group to reply with a no if they did *not* anticipate donating. Now 71 percent implied they might give (by not replying). Imagine yourself in this third group. Might you have decided not to say no because, after all, you *are* a caring person so there's a chance you might give? And might that thought have opened you to persuasion as you encountered campus posters and flyers during the ensuing week? That apparently is what happened, because 12 percent of these students—more than twice the normal rate—showed up to offer their blood.

Inferring that one is a helpful person seems also to have happened when Dariusz Dolinski (2000) stopped pedestrians on the streets of Wroclaw, Poland, and asked them for directions to a nonexistent "Zubrzyckiego Street" or to an illegible address. Everyone tried unsuccessfully to help. After doing so, about two-thirds (twice the number of those not given the opportunity to try to help) agreed when asked by someone 100 meters farther down the road to watch their heavy bag or bicycle for five minutes. On a larger scale, "service learning" and volunteer programs woven into a school curriculum have been shown to increase later citizen involvement, social responsibility, cooperation, and leadership (Andersen, 1998; Putnam, 2000). Attitudes follow behavior. Helpful actions therefore promote the self-perception that one is caring and helpful, which in turn promotes further helping.

Learning about altruism

Researchers have found another way to boost altruism, one that provides a happy conclusion to this chapter. Some social psychologists worry that, as people become more aware of social psychology's findings, their behavior may change, thus invalidating the findings (Gergen, 1982). Will learning about the factors that inhibit altruism reduce their influence? Sometimes, such "enlightenment" is not our problem but one of our goals.

Experiments with University of Montana students by Arthur Beaman and his colleagues (1978) revealed that once people understand why the presence of bystanders inhibits helping, they become more likely to help in group situations. The researchers used a lecture to inform some students how bystander inaction can affect the interpretation of an emergency and feelings of responsibility. Other students heard either a different lecture or no lecture at all. Two weeks later, as part of a different experiment in a different location, the participants found themselves walking (with an unresponsive confederate) past someone slumped over or past a person sprawled beneath a bicycle. Of those who had not heard the helping lecture, a fourth paused to offer help; twice as many of those "enlightened" did so.

Having read this chapter, you, too, perhaps have changed. As you come to understand what influences people's responses, will your attitudes and your behavior be the same?

Research suggests that we can enhance helpfulness in two ways. First, we can reverse those factors that inhibit helping. We can take steps to reduce the ambiguity of an emergency situation to make a personal appeal, and to increase feelings of responsibility. We can even use reprimands or the door-in-the face technique to evoke guilt feelings or a concern for self-image. Second, we can teach altruism. Research into television's portrayals of prosocial models shows the medium's power to teach positive behavior. Children who view helpful behavior tend to act helpfully.

If we want to coax altruistic behavior from people, we should remember the overjustification effect: When we coerce good deeds, intrinsic love of the activity often diminishes. If we provide people with enough justification for them to decide to do good, but not much more, they will attribute their behavior to their own altruistic motivation and henceforth be more willing to help. Learning about altruism, as you have just done, can also prepare people to perceive and respond to others' needs.

Summing up

PS Personal Postscript: Taking social psychology into life

Those of us who research, teach, and write about social psychology do so believing that our work matters. It engages humanly significant phenomena. Studying social psychology can therefore expand our thinking and prepare us to live and act with greater awareness and compassion, or so we presume.

How good it feels, then, when students and former students confirm our presumptions with stories of how they have related social psychology to their lives. Shortly before I wrote the last paragraph, a former student, now living in Washington, D.C., stopped by. She mentioned that she recently found herself part of a stream of pedestrians striding past a man lying unconscious on the sidewalk. "It took my mind back to our social psych class and the accounts of why people fail to help in such situations. Then I thought, 'Well, if I just walk by, too, who's going to help him?'" So she made a call to an emergency help number and waited with the victim—and other bystanders who now joined her—until help arrived.

What do you think?

In the last week, have you noticed someone who needed help? Did you, or someone, help the person or not? If the person was helped, what prompted the help? Could you discern any rewards for helping? Any influence of other bystanders? Of time pressures? Of personal traits?

Making the Social Connection

As part of this chapter's exploration of helping, we engaged John Darley's classic research on the bystander effect. The chapter on prejudice (Chapter 9) introduced Darley's work on how stereotypes can subtly bias our judgments of individuals. Why does the presence of others inhibit people's helping? Go to the *SocialSense* CD-ROM to see Darley describe his research.

chapter 13

Conflict and Peacemaking

"If you want peace, work for justice."

Pope Paul VI

conflict
A perceived incompatibility of actions or goals.

There is a speech that has been spoken in many languages by the leaders of many countries. It goes like this: "The intentions of our country are entirely peaceful. Yet, we are also aware that other nations, with their new weapons, threaten us. Thus we must defend ourselves against attack. By so doing, we shall protect our way of life and preserve the peace" (Richardson, 1960). Almost every nation claims concern only for peace but, mistrusting other nations, arms itself in self-defense. The result is a world that has been spending $2 billion per day on arms and armies while hundreds of millions die of malnutrition and untreated disease.

The elements of such **conflict** (a perceived incompatibility of actions or goals) are similar at all levels, from nations in an arms race, to conflicted Middle Easterners, to corporate executives and workers disputing salaries, to a feuding married couple. Whether their perceptions are accurate or inaccurate, people in conflict sense that one side's gain is the other's loss. "We want peace and security." "So do we, but you threaten us." "We want more pay." "We can't afford to give it to you." "I'd like the music off." "I'd like it on."

As civil rights leaders know, creatively managed conflicts can have constructive outcomes.

A relationship or an organization without conflict is probably apathetic. Conflict signifies involvement, commitment, and caring. If conflict is understood, if recognized, it can end oppression and stimulate renewed and improved human relations. Without conflict, people seldom face and resolve their problems.

Peace, in its most positive sense, is more than the suppression of open conflict, more than a tense, fragile, surface calmness. Peace is the outcome of a creatively managed conflict. Peace is the parties reconciling their perceived differences and reaching genuine accord. "We got our increased pay. You got your increased profit. Now each of us is helping the other achieve our aspirations."

In this chapter, we explore conflict and peacemaking by asking:

- What social situations feed conflict?
- How do misperceptions fuel conflict?
- Does contact with the other side reduce conflict?
- When do cooperation, communication, and mediation enable reconciliation?

What creates conflict?

Social-psychological studies have identified several ingredients of conflict. What's striking (and what simplifies our task) is that these ingredients are common to all levels of social conflict, whether international, intergroup, or interpersonal.

SOCIAL DILEMMAS

Several of the problems that most threaten our human future—nuclear arms, global warming, overpopulation, natural resource depletion—arise as various parties pursue their self-interests, ironically, to their collective detriment. Anyone can think, "It would cost me a lot to buy expensive pollution controls. Besides, by itself my pollution is trivial." Many others reason similarly, and the result is unclean air and water.

In some societies individuals benefit by having many children who, they assume, can assist with the family tasks and provide security in the parents' old age. But when most families have many children, the result is the collective devastation of overpopulation. Choices that are individually rewarding become collectively punishing. We therefore have an urgent dilemma: How can we reconcile the right of individuals to pursue their personal interests with communal well-being?

To isolate and illustrate this dilemma, social psychologists have used laboratory games that expose the heart of many real social conflicts. By showing us how well-meaning people become trapped in mutually destructive behavior, they illuminate some fascinating, yet troubling, paradoxes.

"Social psychologists who study conflict are in much the same position as the astronomers," noted conflict researcher Morton Deutsch (1999). "We cannot conduct true experiments with large-scale social events. But we can identify the conceptual similarities between the large scale and the small, as the astronomers have between the planets and Newton's apple. That is why the games people play as subjects in our laboratory may advance our understanding of war, peace, and social justice."

Consider two examples: the Prisoners' Dilemma and the Tragedy of the Commons.

The Prisoners' Dilemma

One dilemma derives from an anecdote concerning two suspects questioned separately by the district attorney (DA) (Rapoport, 1960). They are jointly guilty; however, the DA has only enough evidence to convict them of a lesser offense. So the DA creates an incentive for each to confess privately:

- If one confesses and the other doesn't, the DA will grant the confessor immunity (and will use the confession to convict the other of a maximum offense).
- If both confess, each will receive a moderate sentence.
- If neither confesses, each will receive a light sentence.

The matrix of Figure 13–1 (see page 522) summarizes the choices. Faced with such a dilemma, would you confess?

To minimize their own sentences, many would confess, despite the fact that mutual confession elicits more severe sentences than mutual nonconfession. Note from the matrix that no matter what the other prisoner decides, each is better off confessing. If the other also confesses, one then gets a moderate sentence instead of a severe one. If the other does not confess, one goes free. Of course, each prisoner understands this. Hence, the social trap.

In some 2,000 studies (Dawes, 1991), university students have faced variations of the Prisoners' Dilemma with the outcomes not being prison terms but chips, money, or course points. As Figure 13–2 (see page 522) illustrates, on any given decision, a person is better off defecting (because such behavior exploits the other's cooperation or protects against the other's exploitation). However—and here's the rub—by not cooperating, both parties end up far worse off than if they had trusted each other and thus had gained a joint profit. This dilemma often traps each one in a maddening predicament in which both realize they *could* mutually profit. But unable to communicate and mistrusting one another, they become "locked in" to not cooperating.

In such dilemmas, the unbridled pursuit of self-interest can be detrimental to all. This was the case during the arms race between the United States and the

figure 13–1

The Classic Prisoners' Dilemma.

In each box, the number above the diagonal is prisoner A's outcome. Thus, if both prisoners confess, both get five years. If neither confesses, each gets a year. If one confesses, that prisoner is set free in exchange for evidence used to convict the other of a crime bringing a 10-year sentence. If you were one of the prisoners, unable to communicate with your fellow prisoner, would you confess?

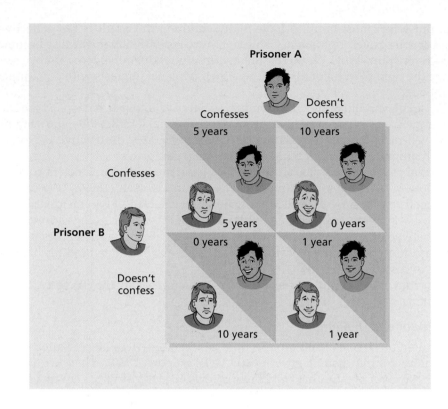

figure 13–2

Laboratory version of the Prisoners' Dilemma.

The numbers represent some reward, such as money. In each box, the number above the diagonal lines is the outcome for person A. Unlike the classic Prisoners' Dilemma (a one-shot decision), most laboratory versions involve repeated plays.

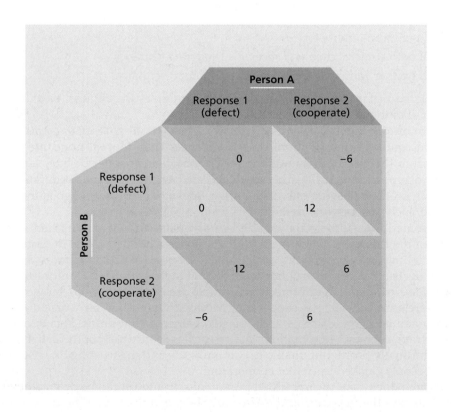

former Soviet Union after 1945. An observer from another planet would likely consider the military policy of "mutually assured destruction," as its acronym implies, MAD. As U.S. President Dwight D. Eisenhower lamented,

> Every gun that is made, every warship launched, every rocket fired signifies, in the final sense, a theft from those who hunger and are not fed, those who are cold and are not clothed. This world in arms is not spending money alone. It is spending the sweat of its laborers, the genius of its scientists, the hopes of its children. . . . This is not a way of life, at all, in any true sense. Under the cloud of threatening war, it is humanity hanging from a cross of iron.

It may occasionally be true that maintaining a balance of terror helps prevent war that might occur if one nation could easily exploit another's weaknesses. But neither the historical record nor the psychological evidence we will consider supports the idea that threatening an enemy with big sticks, such as nuclear weapons, deters war (Lebow & Stein, 1987). More wars were fought during the heavily armed 1980s than in any previous decade in history (Sivard, 1991). Moreover, the people of all nations would surely be more secure if there were no weapons threat and if military spending were available for productive purposes. And consider the irony of countries where people demand the right to own guns for personal security—and end up collectively less secure than those in countries where people are not armed.

It's easy to say all this, but the dilemma faced by national leaders—and by college students in laboratory simulations of the arms race dilemma—is that one-sided disarmament makes one vulnerable to attack or blackmail. In the laboratory, those who adopt an unconditionally cooperative strategy often get exploited (Oskamp, 1971; Reychler, 1979; Shure & others, 1965). So, alas, the arms spending continues.

"When multiplied by 2, a national policy of Peace Through Strength leads inevitably to an arms race."
—George Levinger (1987)

The Tragedy of the Commons

Many social dilemmas involve more than two parties. Global warming stems from deforestation and from the carbon dioxide emitted by cars, furnaces, and coal-fired power plants. Each gas-guzzling SUV contributes infinitesimally to the problem, and the harm each does is diffused over many people. To model such social predicaments, researchers have developed laboratory dilemmas that involve multiple people.

A metaphor for the insidious nature of social dilemmas is what ecologist Garrett Hardin (1968) called the **Tragedy of the Commons.** He derived the name from the centrally located pasture in old English towns, but the "commons" can be air, water, whales, cookies, or any shared and limited resource. If all use the resource in moderation, it may replenish itself as rapidly as it's harvested. The grass will grow, the whales will reproduce, and the cookie jar gets restocked. If not, there occurs a tragedy of the commons.

Imagine 100 farmers surrounding a commons capable of sustaining 100 cows. When each grazes one cow, the common feeding ground is optimally used. But then someone reasons, "If I put a second cow in the pasture, I'll double my output, minus the mere 1 percent overgrazing." So this farmer adds a second cow. So do each of the other farmers. The inevitable result? The Tragedy of the Commons—a mud field.

Many real predicaments parallel this story. Internet congestion occurs as individuals, seeking to maximize their own gain, surf the Web, filling its pipelines

Tragedy of the Commons
The "commons" is any shared resource, including air, water, energy sources, and food supplies. The tragedy occurs when individuals consume more than their share, with the cost of their doing so dispersed among all, causing the ultimate collapse—the tragedy—of the commons.

with graphical information (Huberman & Lukose, 1997). Likewise, environmental pollution is the sum of many minor pollutions, each of which benefits the individual polluters much more than they could benefit themselves (and the environment) if they stopped polluting. We litter public places—dorm lounges, parks, zoos—while keeping our personal spaces clean. We deplete our natural resources because the immediate personal benefits of, say, taking a long, hot shower outweigh the seemingly inconsequential costs. Whalers knew others would exploit the whales if they didn't and that taking a few whales would hardly diminish the species. Therein lies the tragedy. Everybody's business (conservation) becomes nobody's business.

Is such individualism uniquely American? Kaori Sato (1987) gave students in a more collective culture, Japan, opportunities to harvest—for actual money—trees from a simulated forest. When the students shared equally the costs of planting the forest, the result was like those in Western cultures. More than half the trees were harvested before they had grown to the most profitable size.

Sato's forest reminds me of the cookie jar in our home. What we *should* have done is conserve cookies during the interval between weekly restockings, so that each day we could each munch two or three. Lacking regulation and fearing that other family members would soon deplete the resource, what we actually did was maximize our individual cookie consumption by downing one after the other. The result: Within 24 hours the cookie glut would often end, the jar sitting empty.

When resources are not partitioned, people often consume more than they realize (Herlocker & others, 1997). As a bowl of mashed potatoes is passed around a table of 10, it's likely that more people will scoop out a disproportionate share than when a platter of 10 chicken drumsticks is passed.

The Prisoners' Dilemma and the Tragedy of the Commons games have several similar features. First, both tempt people to explain their own behavior situationally ("I had to protect myself against exploitation by my opponent") and to explain their partners' behavior dispositionally ("she was greedy," "he was untrustworthy"). Most never realize that their counterparts are viewing them with the same fundamental attribution error (Gifford & Hine, 1997; Hine & Gifford, 1996).

Second, motives often change. At first, people are eager to make some easy money, then to minimize their losses, and finally to save face and avoid defeat (Brockner & others, 1982; Teger, 1980). These shifting motives are strikingly similar to the shifting motives during the buildup of the 1960s Vietnam War. At first, President Johnson's speeches expressed concern for democracy, freedom, and justice. As the conflict escalated, his concern became protecting America's honor and avoiding the national humiliation of losing a war.

non-zero-sum games
Games in which outcomes need not sum to zero. With cooperation, both can win; with competition, both can lose. (Also called mixed-motive situations.)

Third, most real-life conflicts, like the Prisoners' Dilemma and the Tragedy of the Commons, are **non-zero-sum games.** The two sides' profits and losses need not add up to zero. Both can win; both can lose. Each game pits the immediate interests of individuals against the well-being of the group. Each is a diabolical social trap that shows how, even when individuals behave "rationally," harm can result. No malicious person planned for the earth's atmosphere to be warmed by a blanket of carbon dioxide.

Not all self-serving behavior leads to collective doom. In a plentiful commons—as in the world of the eighteenth-century capitalist economist Adam Smith (1776, p. 18)—individuals who seek to maximize their own profit may

When, after their 1980–1988 war, more than a million casualties, and ruined economies, Iran and Iraq finally laid down their arms, the border over which they had fought was exactly the same as when they started.
STEVE BENSON reprinted by permission of United Feature Syndicate, Inc.

also give the community what it needs: "It is not from the benevolence of the butcher, the brewer, or the baker, that we expect our dinner," he observed, "but from their regard to their own interest."

Resolving social dilemmas

In those situations that are indeed social traps, how can we induce people to cooperate for their mutual betterment? Research with the laboratory dilemmas reveals several ways (Gifford & Hine, 1997).

Regulation.   Reflecting on the Tragedy of the Commons, Garrett Hardin (1968) wrote, "Ruin is the destination to which all men rush, each pursuing his own best interest in a society that believes in the freedom of the commons. Freedom in a commons brings ruin to all." Consider this: If taxes were entirely voluntary, how many would pay their full share? Surely, many would not, which is why modern societies do not depend on charity to pay for schools, parks, and social and military security.

We also develop laws and regulations for our common good. An International Whaling Commission sets an agreed-upon "harvest" that enables whales to regenerate. The United States and the former Soviet Union mutually commit themselves to an Atmospheric Test Ban Treaty that reduces radiation in our common air. When enforced, environmental regulations equalize the burden for all; no steel company need fear that other companies will gain a competitive advantage by disregarding their environmental responsibilities.

In everyday life, regulation has costs—costs of administering and enforcing the regulations, costs of diminished personal freedom. A volatile political question thus arises: At what point does a regulation's cost exceed its benefits?

Small is beautiful.   There is another way to resolve social dilemmas: Make the group small. In a small commons, each person feels more responsible and

Small is cooperative. On the isle of Muck, off Scotland's west coast, Constable Lawrence MacEwan has had an easy time policing the island's residents, currently numbering 33. Over his 40 years on the job, there has never been a single crime (Scottish Life, 2001).

effective (Kerr, 1989). As a group grows larger, people more often think, "I couldn't have made a difference anyway"—a common excuse for noncooperation (Kerr & Kaufman-Gilliland, 1997). In small groups, people also feel more identified with a group's success. Anything else that enhances group identity will also increase cooperation. Even just a few minutes of discussion or just believing that one shares similarities with others in the group can increase "we feeling" and cooperation (Brewer, 1987; Orbell & others, 1988).

In small rather than large groups, individuals are also more likely to take no more than their equal share of available resources (Allison & others, 1992). On the Pacific Northwest island where I grew up, our small neighborhood shared a communal water supply. On hot summer days when the reservoir ran low, a light came on, signaling our 15 families to conserve. Recognizing our responsibility to one another, and feeling like our conservation really mattered, each of us conserved. Never did the reservoir run dry.

"For that which is common to the greatest number has the least care bestowed upon it."
—Aristotle

In a much larger commons—say, a city—voluntary conservation is less successful. Because the harm one does diffuses across many others, each individual can rationalize away personal accountability. Some political theorists and social psychologists therefore argue that, where feasible, the commons should be divided into smaller territories (Edney, 1980). In his 1902 *Mutual Aid*, the Russian revolutionary Pyotr Kropotkin set down a vision of small communities rather than central government making consensus decisions for the benefit of all (Gould, 1988).

Communication.   To escape a social trap, people must communicate. In the laboratory, group communication sometimes degenerates into threats and name calling (Deutsch & Krauss, 1960). More often, communication enables people to cooperate (Bornstein & others, 1988, 1989). Discussing the dilemma forges a group identity, which enhances concern for everyone's welfare. It devises group norms and consensus expectations and puts pressure on members to follow them. Especially when people are face-to-face, it enables them to commit themselves to cooperation (Bouas & Komorita, 1996; Drolet & Morris, 2000; Kerr & others, 1994, 1997; Pruitt, 1998).

A clever experiment by Robyn Dawes (1980, 1994) illustrates. Imagine that an experimenter offered you and six strangers each a choice: You could each have $6. Or you could give it to the others, knowing that the experimenter would double your gift and allocate $2 to each of the strangers. No one will be told whether you chose to give or keep. So if all seven cooperate and give, everyone pockets $12. If you alone keep the $6 and the others give, you pocket $18. If you give and the others keep, you pocket nothing. Clearly, cooperation is mutually advantageous, but it requires sacrifice, trust, and risk. Dawes found that, without discussion, about 30 percent of people gave; with discussion, about 80 percent gave.

Open, clear, forthright communication reduces mistrust. Without communication, those who expect others not to cooperate will usually refuse to cooperate themselves (Messé & Sivacek, 1979; Pruitt & Kimmel, 1977). One who mistrusts almost has to be uncooperative (to protect against exploitation). Noncooperation, in turn, feeds further mistrust ("What else could I do? It's a dog-eat-dog world"). In experiments, communication reduces mistrust, enabling people to reach agreements that lead to their common betterment.

Changing the payoffs.   Cooperation rises when experimenters change the payoff matrix to make cooperation more rewarding and exploitation less rewarding (Komorita & Barth, 1985; Pruitt & Rubin, 1986). Changing payoffs also helps resolve actual dilemmas. In some cities, freeways clog and skies smog because people prefer the convenience of driving themselves directly to work. Each knows that one more car does not add noticeably to the congestion and pollution. To alter the personal cost-benefit calculations, many cities now give carpoolers incentives, such as designated freeway lanes or reduced tolls.

Appeals to altruistic norms.   In Chapter 12, we saw how increasing people's feelings of responsibility for others boosts altruism. So, will appeals to altruistic motives prompt people to act for the common good?

The evidence is mixed. On the one hand, just *knowing* the dire consequences of noncooperation has little effect on cooperation. In laboratory games, people realize that their self-serving choices are mutually destructive, yet they continue to make them. Outside the laboratory, warnings of doom and appeals to conserve have brought little response. Shortly after taking office in 1976, President Carter declared that America's response to the energy crisis should be "the moral equivalent of war" and urged conservation. The following summer, Americans consumed more gasoline than ever before. At the beginning of this new century, people knew that global warming was under way—and were buying gas-slurping SUVs in record numbers. As attitudes sometimes fail to influence behavior, so *knowing* the good does not necessarily lead to *doing* the good.

"My own belief is that Russian and Chinese behavior is as much influenced by suspicion of our intentions as ours is by suspicion of theirs. This would mean that we have great influence on their behavior—that, by treating them as hostile, we assure their hostility."
—U.S. Senator J. William Fulbright (1971)

To change behavior, many cities have changed the payoff matrix. Fast carpool-only lanes increase the benefits of carpooling and the costs of driving alone.

Still, most people do adhere to norms of social responsibility, reciprocity, equity, and keeping one's commitments (Kerr, 1992). The problem is how to tap such feelings. One way is through the influence of a charismatic, self-giving leader who inspires others to cooperate (De Cremer, 2002). Another way is by defining situations in ways that imply cooperative norms. Lee Ross and Andrew Ward (1996) invited Stanford dormitory advisers to nominate male students whom they thought especially likely to cooperate and to defect while playing a Prisoners' Dilemma game. In reality, the two groups of students were equally likely to cooperate. What affected cooperation dramatically was whether the researchers labeled the simulation the "Wall Street Game" (in which case one-third of the participants cooperated) or the "Community Game" (with two-thirds cooperating).

Communication can also tap altruistic norms. When permitted to communicate, participants in laboratory games frequently appeal to the social-responsibility norm: "If you defect on the rest of us, you're going to have to live with it for the rest of your life" (Dawes & others, 1977). Noting this, researcher Robyn Dawes (1980) and his associates gave people a short sermon about group benefits, exploitation, and ethics. Then the people played a dilemma game. The appeal worked: People were convinced to forgo immediate personal gain for the common good. (Recall, too, from Chapter 12, the disproportionate volunteerism and charitable contributions by people who regularly hear sermons in churches and synagogues.)

Could such appeals work in large-scale dilemmas? Jeffery Scott Mio and his colleagues (1993) found that, after reading about the commons dilemma (as you have), theater patrons littered less than patrons who read about voting. Moreover, when cooperation obviously serves the public good, one can usefully appeal to the social-responsibility norm (Lynn & Oldenquist, 1986). When, for example, people believe public transportation can save time, they will be more likely to use it if they also believe it reduces pollution (Van Vugt & others, 1996). In the struggle for civil rights, many marchers willingly agreed, for the sake of the larger group, to suffer harassment, beatings, and jail. In wartime, people make great personal sacrifices for the good of their group. As Winston Churchill said of the Battle of Britain, the actions of the Royal Air Force pilots were genuinely altruistic: A great many people owed a great deal to those who flew into battle knowing there was a high probability—70 percent for those on a standard tour of duty—they would not return (Levinson, 1950).

To summarize, we can minimize destructive entrapment in social dilemmas by establishing rules that regulate self-serving behavior, by keeping groups small, by enabling people to communicate, by changing payoffs to make cooperation more rewarding, and by invoking altruistic norms.

COMPETITION

Hostilities often arise when groups compete for scarce jobs, housing, or resources. When interests clash, conflict erupts—a phenomenon described by "realistic group conflict theory." The effects of competition for space, jobs, and political power helped fuel the Northern Ireland conflict, where since 1969 hostilities between the ruling Protestant majority and the Catholic minority have claimed more than 3,200 lives. (A comparable population proportion would number 515,000 in the United States, 107,000 in Britain, 57,000 in Canada, and 36,000 in Australia.)

"Never in the field of human conflict was so much owed by so many to so few."

—Sir Winston Churchill, House of Commons, August 20, 1940

Competition accentuates perceived differences. When put in competition with others, their attitudes seem more different (Holtz & Miller, 2001). But does competition by itself provoke hostile conflict? To find out, Craig Anderson and Melissa Morrow (1995) had people alternate with someone else playing Nintendo's Super Mario Brothers. Half played as competition (comparing points), half as cooperation (combining points). Given the competitive mind-set, people unnecessarily killed (by stomping or fireballing) 61 percent more of the game creatures. Competition primed aggression.

Will competition also trigger destructive behavior under more realistic circumstances? To experiment, we could randomly divide people into two groups, have the groups compete for a scarce resource, and note what happens. This is precisely what Muzafer Sherif (1966) and his colleagues did in a dramatic series of experiments with typical 11- and 12-year-old boys. The inspiration for these experiments dated back to Sherif's witnessing, as a teenager, Greek troops invading his Turkish province in 1919.

> They started killing people right and left. [That] made a great impression on me. There and then I became interested in understanding why these things were happening among human beings. . . . I wanted to learn whatever science or specialization was needed to understand this intergroup savagery. (quoted by Aron & Aron, 1989, p. 131)

After studying the social roots of savagery, Sherif introduced the seeming essentials into several three-week summer camping experiences. In one such study, he divided 22 unacquainted Oklahoma City boys into two groups, took them to a Boy Scout camp in separate buses, and settled them in bunkhouses about a half-mile apart at Oklahoma's Robber's Cave State Park. For most of the first week, they were unaware of the other group's existence. By cooperating in various activities—preparing meals, camping out, fixing up a swimming hole, building a rope bridge—each group soon became close-knit. They gave themselves names: "Rattlers" and "Eagles." Typifying the good feeling, a sign appeared in one cabin: "Home Sweet Home."

Group identity thus established, the stage was set for the conflict. Toward the end of the first week, the Rattlers "discovered the Eagles on 'our' baseball field." When the camp staff then proposed a tournament of competitive activities between the two groups (baseball games, tugs-of-war, cabin inspections, treasure hunts, and so forth), both groups responded enthusiastically. This was win-lose competition. The spoils (medals, knives) would all go to the tournament victor.

The result? The camp gradually degenerated into open warfare. It was like a scene from William Golding's novel *Lord of the Flies*, which depicts the social disintegration of boys marooned on an island. In Sherif's study, the conflict began with each side calling the other names during the competitive activities. Soon it escalated to dining hall "garbage wars," flag burnings, cabin ransackings, even fistfights. Asked to describe the other group, the boys said "they" were "sneaky," "smart alecks," "stinkers," while referring to their own group as "brave," "tough," "friendly."

The win-lose competition had produced intense conflict, negative images of the outgroup, and strong ingroup cohesiveness and pride. Group polarization no doubt exacerbated the conflict. In experiments, groups behave more competitively than individuals in competition-fostering situations (Wildschut & others, 2003).

Little known fact: How did Sherif unobtrusively observe the boys without inhibiting their behavior? He became the camp maintenance man (Williams, 2002).

Competition kindles conflict. Here, in the Sherif's Robber's Cave experiment, one group of boys raids the bunkhouse of another.

All this occurred without any cultural, physical, or economic differences between the two groups and with boys who were their communities' "cream of the crop." Sherif noted that, had we visited the camp at this point, we would have concluded these "were wicked, disturbed, and vicious bunches of youngsters" (1966, p. 85). Actually, their evil behavior was triggered by an evil situation. Competition breeds such conflict, later research has shown, especially when (a) people perceive that resources such as money, jobs, or power are limited and available on a non-zero-sum basis (others' gain is one's loss), and (b) a distinct outgroup stands out as a potential competitor (Esses & others, in press). Thus, those who see immigrants as competing for their own jobs will tend to express negative attitudes toward immigrants and immigration.

Fortunately, as we will see, Sherif not only made strangers into enemies; he then made the enemies into friends.

PERCEIVED INJUSTICE

"That's unfair!" "What a ripoff!" "We deserve better!" Such comments typify conflicts bred by perceived injustice. But what is "justice"? According to some social-psychological theorists, people perceive justice as equity—the distribution of rewards in proportion to individuals' contributions (Walster & others, 1978). If you and I have a relationship (employer-employee, teacher-student, husband-wife, colleague-colleague), it is equitable if

$$\frac{\text{My outcomes}}{\text{My inputs}} = \frac{\text{Your outcomes}}{\text{Your inputs}}$$

If you contribute more and benefit less than I do, you will feel exploited and irritated; I may feel exploitative and guilty. Chances are, though, that you more than I will be sensitive to the inequity (Greenberg, 1986; Messick & Sentis, 1979). In experiments, people often don't demand a distribution that favors themselves or their group. But they do gladly accept and rationalize receiving a big piece of the pie (Diekmann & others, 1997). Latisha might not demand an above-average bonus, yet she may easily justify one when someone else decides in her favor.

We may agree with the equity principle's definition of justice yet disagree on whether our relationship is equitable. If two people are colleagues, what will

What might a lesbian couple perceive as unfair in their relationship? Go to the *SocialSense* CD-ROM to view a video clip.

"Do unto others 20% better than you would expect them to do unto you, to correct for subjective error."
—Linus Pauling (1962)

table 13–1   Gallup polls reveal increased perceptions of gender inequality

All things considered, who has a better life in this country—men or women?

	1972	1993
Men	29%	60%
Women	35%	21%
Same	30%	15%
No opinion	6%	5%

Source: Roper Center for Public Opinion Research, 1997.

each consider a relevant input? The one who is older may favor basing pay on seniority, the other on current productivity. Given such a disagreement, whose definition is likely to prevail? More often than not, those with social power convince themselves and others that they deserve what they're getting (Mikula, 1984). This has been called a "golden" rule: Whoever has the gold makes the rules.

Knowing that one's group has overbenefited can trigger collective guilt, much as individuals can feel guilt when receiving what's undeserved. To restore a sense of justice, such collective guilt can motivate an apology or an offer of compensation (Mallet & Swim, 2003). However, the exploiter can also relieve guilt by devaluing others' inputs. As we noted in Chapter 9, those who inflict harm may blame the victim and thus maintain their belief in a just world.

And how do those who are exploited react? Elaine Hatfield, William Walster, and Ellen Berscheid (1978) detected three possibilities. They can accept and justify their inferior position ("We're poor but we're happy"). They can demand compensation, perhaps by harassing, embarrassing, even cheating their exploiter. If all else fails, they may try to restore equity by retaliating.

An interesting implication of equity theory—an implication that has been confirmed experimentally—is that the more competent and worthy people feel (the more they value their inputs), the more they will feel underbenefitted and thus eager to retaliate (Ross & others, 1971). Intense social protests generally come from those who, perhaps after being educated, believe themselves worthy of more than they are receiving.

Since 1970 professional opportunities for women have increased significantly. Ironically, though understandably to an equity theorist, so have people's feelings that women's status is *in*equitable (Table 13–1). So long as women compared their opportunities and earnings with those of other women, they felt generally satisfied—as they did with their disproportionate share of family labor (Jackson, 1989; Major, 1989, 1993). Now that women are more likely to see themselves as men's equals, their sense of relative deprivation has grown (Desmarais & Curtis, 2001). If secretarial work and truck driving have "comparable worth" (for the skills required), then they deserve comparable pay; that's equity, say advocates of gender equality (Lowe & Wittig, 1989).

Critics argue that equity is not the only conceivable definition of justice. (Pause a moment: Can you imagine any other?) Edward Sampson (1975) says equity theorists wrongly assume that the economic principles that guide

"Awards should be 'according to merit'; for all people agree that what is just in distribution must be according to merit in some sense, though they do not all specify the same sort of merit."
—Aristotle

Western, capitalist nations are universal. Some noncapitalist cultures define justice not as equity but as *equality* or even *fulfillment of need*: "From each according to his abilities, to each according to his needs" (Karl Marx). When rewards are distributed to those within one's group, people socialized under the influence of collectivist cultures, such as China and India, likewise favor equality or need more than do individualistic Americans (Hui & others, 1991; Leung & Bond, 1984; Murphy-Berman & others, 1984).

In collectivist, age-respecting Japan, pay is less often based on productivity, more often on seniority (Kitayama & Markus, 2000). In individualistic America, 53 percent of people surveyed favored basing pay on performance, as did only 32 percent in Britain and 26 percent in Spain. And should government reduce income differences or guarantee incomes? Yes, said 39 percent of Americans, 48 percent of Canadians, and 65 percent of Britishers (Brown, 1995). Even within individualistic cultures, criteria other than equity sometimes define justice (Deutsch, 1985). In a family or an altruistic institution, the criterion may be need. In a friendship, it may be equality. In a competitive relationship, the winner may take all.

How universal, then, is the tendency to define justice as equity? And on what basis *should* rewards be distributed? Merit? Equality? Need? Some combination of these? Political philosopher John Rawls (1971) invites us to consider a future in which our own place on the economic ladder was unknown. Which standard of justice would we prefer? Gregory Mitchell and his colleagues (1993) report that American University students want some reward for productivity, but also enough priority placed on equality to meet their own needs, should they find themselves at the bottom.

MISPERCEPTION

Recall that conflict is a *perceived* incompatibility of actions or goals. Many conflicts contain but a small core of truly incompatible goals; the bigger problem is the misperceptions of the other's motives and goals. The Eagles and the Rattlers did indeed have some genuinely incompatible aims. But their perceptions subjectively magnified their differences (Figure 13–3).

In earlier chapters we considered the seeds of such misperception. The *self-serving bias* leads individuals and groups to accept credit for their good deeds and shuck responsibility for bad deeds, without according others the same benefit of the doubt. A tendency to *self-justify* further inclines people to deny the wrong of their evil acts that cannot be shucked off. Thanks to the *fundamental attribution error*, each side sees the other's hostility as reflecting an evil disposition. One then filters the information and interprets it to fit one's *preconceptions*. Groups frequently *polarize* these self-serving, self-justifying, biasing tendencies. One symptom of *groupthink* is the tendency to perceive one's own group as moral and strong, the opposition as evil and weak. Terrorist acts that are despicable brutality to most people are "holy war" to others. Indeed, the mere fact of being in a

"Solutions to the distribution problem are nontrivial. Children fight, colleagues complain, group members resign, tempers flare, and nations battle over issues of fairness. As parents, employers, teachers, and presidents know, the most frequent response to an allocation decision is 'not fair.'"
—Arnold Kahn & William Gaeddert (1985)

figure 13–3

Many conflicts contain a core of truly incompatible goals surrounded by a larger exterior of misperceptions.

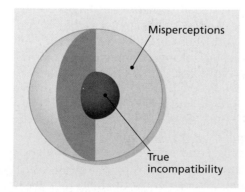

Misperceptions

True incompatibility

group triggers an *ingroup bias*. And negative *stereotypes*, once formed, are often resistant to contradictory evidence.

So it should not surprise us, though it should sober us, to discover that people in conflict—people everywhere—form distorted images of one another. Wherever in the world you live, was it not true that when your country was last at war it clothed itself in moral virtue? It prepared for war by demonizing the enemy? And its people accepted their government's case for war and rallied 'round its flag? Show social psychologists Ervin Staub and Daniel Bar-Tal (2003) a group in intractable conflict and they will show you a group that

- sees its own goals as supremely important.
- takes pride in "us" and intensely devalues "them."
- believes itself victimized.
- elevates patriotism, solidarity, and loyalty to group's needs.
- celebrates self-sacrifice and suppresses criticism.

Although one side to a conflict may indeed be acting with greater moral virtue, the point is that enemy images are fairly predictable. Even the types of misperception are intriguingly predictable.

> "Aggression breeds patriotism, and patriotism curbs dissent."
> —Maureen Dowd, "The Iceman Cometh," 2003

Mirror-image perceptions

To a striking degree, the misperceptions of those in conflict are mutual. People in conflict attribute similar virtues to themselves and vices to the other. When American psychologist Urie Bronfenbrenner (1961) visited the former Soviet Union in 1960 and conversed with many ordinary citizens in Russian, he was astonished to hear them saying the same things about America that Americans were saying about Russia. The Russians said that the U.S. government was militarily aggressive; that it exploited and deluded the American people; that in diplomacy it was not to be trusted. "Slowly and painfully, it forced itself upon one that the Russians' distorted picture of us was curiously similar to our view of them—a mirror image."

Analyses of American and Russian perceptions by psychologists (Tobin & Eagles, 1992; White, 1984) and political scientists (Jervis, 1985) revealed that mirror-image perceptions persisted into the 1980s. The same action (patrolling the other's coast with submarines, selling arms to smaller nations) seemed more hostile when *they* did it.

Mirror-image perceptions also fueled the arms race. Political statements revealed that people in both nations (1) preferred mutual disarmament to all other outcomes, (2) wanted above all not to disarm while the other side armed, but (3) perceived the other side as preferring to achieve military superiority (Plous, 1985, 1993; Table 13–2, see page 534). Thus, though both nations claimed to prefer disarmament, both felt compelled to arm themselves.

When the two sides have clashing perceptions, at least one of the two is misperceiving the other. And when such misperceptions exist, noted Bronfenbrenner, "It is a psychological phenomenon without parallel in the gravity of its consequences . . . for *it is characteristic of such images that they are self-confirming.*" If A expects B to be hostile, A may treat B in such a way that B fulfills A's expectations, thus beginning a vicious circle. Morton Deutsch (1986) explained:

> You hear the false rumor that a friend is saying nasty things about you; you snub him; he then badmouths you, confirming your expectation. Similarly, if the

table 13–2   **Mirror-image perceptions that fed the arms race**

Assumption	Sample Statement by the U.S. President	Sample Statement by the Soviet General Secretary
1: "We prefer mutual disarmament."	"We want more than anything else to join with them in reducing the number of weapons." (*New York Times*, 6/15/84)	"We do not strive . . . for military superiority over them; we want termination, not continuation of the arms race." (*New York Times*, 3/12/85)
2: "We must avoid disarming while the other side arms."	"We refuse to become weaker while potential adversaries remain committed to their imperialist adventures." (*New York Times*, 6/18/82)	"Our country does not seek [nuclear] superiority, but it also will not allow superiority to be gained over it." (*Pravda*, 4/9/84)
3: "Unlike us, the other side aims for military superiority."	"For the [former] Soviet leaders peace is not the real issue; rather, the issue is the attempt to spread their dominance using military power." (*New York Times*, 6/28/84)	"The main obstacle—and the entire course of the Geneva talks is persuasive evidence of this—is the attempts by the U.S. and its allies to achieve military superiority." (*Pravda*, 1/3/84)

Adapted from Scott Plous (1985, 1993).

mirror-image perceptions
Reciprocal views of one another often held by parties in conflict; for example, each may view itself as moral and peace-loving and the other as evil and aggressive.

policymakers of East and West believe that war is likely and either attempts to increase its military security vis-à-vis the other, the other's response will justify the initial move.

Negative **mirror-image perceptions** have been an obstacle to peace in many places:

- Both sides of the Arab-Israeli conflict insisted that "we" are motivated by our need to protect our security and our territory, while "they" want to obliterate us and gobble up our land. "We" are the indigenous people here, "they" are the invaders. "We" are the victims, "they" are the

Self-confirming, mirror-image perceptions are a hallmark of intense conflict, as in the former Yugoslavia.

Mirror-image perceptions fuel conflict. In the 2000 U.S. presidential election recount in Florida, each side's supporters said, "We only want a fair and accurate ballot count. The other side is trying to steal the election."

aggressors" (Heradstveit, 1979; Rouhana & Bar-Tal, 1998). Given such intense mistrust, negotiation is difficult.

- At Northern Ireland's University of Ulster, J. A. Hunter and his colleagues (1991) showed Catholic and Protestant students videos of a Protestant attack at a Catholic funeral and a Catholic attack at a Protestant funeral. Most students attributed the other side's attack to "bloodthirsty" motives but its own side's attack to retaliation or self-defense.

- As the United States and Iraq prepared for war, each repeatedly spoke of the other as "evil." To George W. Bush, Saddam Hussein was a "murderous tyrant" and "madman" who was threatening the civilized world with weapons of mass destruction. To Iraq's government, the Bush government was a "gang of evil" that "threatens the world with their evil schemes and lusts for Middle Eastern oil" (Zajonc, 2003).

Such conflicts, notes Philip Zimbardo (2004), engage "a two-category world—of good people, like US, and of bad people, like THEM." Opposing sides in a conflict tend to exaggerate their differences, note David Sherman, Leif Nelson, and Lee Ross (2003). On issues such as abortion, immigration, and affirmative action, proponents aren't as liberal and opponents aren't as conservative as their adversaries suppose. To resolve conflicts, it helps to understand the other's mind. But it isn't easy, notes Robert Wright (2003): "Putting yourself in the shoes of people who do things you find abhorrent may be the hardest moral exercise there is."

Destructive mirror-image perceptions also operate in conflicts between small groups and between individuals. As we saw in the dilemma games, both parties may say, "We want to cooperate. But their refusal to cooperate forces us to react defensively." In a study of executives, Kenneth Thomas and Louis Pondy (1977) uncovered such attributions. Asked to describe a significant recent conflict, only 12 percent felt the other party was cooperative; 74 percent perceived themselves as cooperative. The executives explained that they had "suggested," "informed," and "recommended," while their antagonist had "demanded," "disagreed with everything I said," and "refused."

Group conflicts are often fueled by an illusion that the enemy's top leaders are evil but their people, though controlled and manipulated, are pro-us. This

"A successful war on terrorism demands an understanding of how so much of the world has come to dislike America. When people who are born with the same human nature as you and I grow up to commit suicide bombings—or applaud them—there must be a reason."

—Robert Wright, "Two Years Later, a Thousand Years Ago," 2003

evil leader–good people perception characterized Americans' and Russians' views of each other during the cold war. The United States entered the Vietnam War believing that in areas dominated by the Communist Vietcong "terrorists," many of the people were allies-in-waiting. As suppressed information later revealed, these beliefs were mere wishful thinking. In 2003, the United States began the Iraq war presuming the existence of "a vast underground network that would rise in support of coalition forces to assist security and law enforcement" (Phillips, 2003). Alas, the network didn't materialize, and the resulting postwar security vacuum enabled looting, sabotage, and persistent attacks on American forces.

> "The American people are good, but the leaders are bad."
> —Baghdad grocer Adul Gesan after 1998 American bombing of Iraq

Another type of mirror-image perception is each side's exaggeration of the other's position. People with opposing views on issues such as abortion, capital punishment, and government budget cuts often differ less than they suppose. Each side overestimates the extremity of the other's views. And each presumes that "our" beliefs follow from the facts while "their" ideology dictates their interpretation of facts (Keltner & Robinson, 1996; Robinson & others, 1995). From such exaggerated perceptions arise culture wars. Ralph White (1996, 1998) reports that the Serbs started the war in Bosnia partly out of an exaggerated fear of the relatively secularized Bosnian Muslims, whose beliefs they wrongly associated with Middle Eastern Islamic fundamentalism and fanatical terrorism.

Simplistic thinking

When tension rises—as happens during an international crisis—rational thinking becomes more difficult (Janis, 1989). Views of the enemy become more simplistic and stereotyped, and seat-of-the-pants judgments become more likely. Experiments by Peter Carnevale and Tahira Probst (1998) show that even the mere expectation of conflict can serve to freeze thinking and impede creative problem solving. Social psychologist Philip Tetlock (1988) observed inflexible thinking when he analyzed the complexity of Russian and American rhetoric since 1945. During the Berlin blockade, the Korean War, and the Russian invasion of Afghanistan, political statements became simplified into stark, good-versus-bad terms. At other times—notably after Mikhail Gorbachev became the Soviet general secretary (Figure 13–4)—political statements acknowledged that each country's motives are complex.

Researchers have also analyzed political rhetoric preceding the outset of major wars, surprise military attacks, Middle Eastern conflicts, and revolutions (Conway & others, 2001). In nearly every case, attacking leaders displayed increasingly simplistic we-are-good/they-are-bad thinking immediately prior to their aggressive action. But shifts *away* from simplistic rhetoric typically preceded new U.S.-Russian agreements, reported Tetlock. His optimism was confirmed when President Reagan in 1988 traveled to Moscow to sign the American-Russian intermediate-range nuclear force (INF) treaty, and then Gorbachev visited New York and told the United Nations that he would remove 500,000 Soviet troops from Eastern Europe:

> I would like to believe that our hopes will be matched by our joint effort to put an end to an era of wars, confrontation and regional conflicts, to aggressions against nature, to the terror of hunger and poverty as well as to political terrorism. This is our common goal and we can only reach it together.

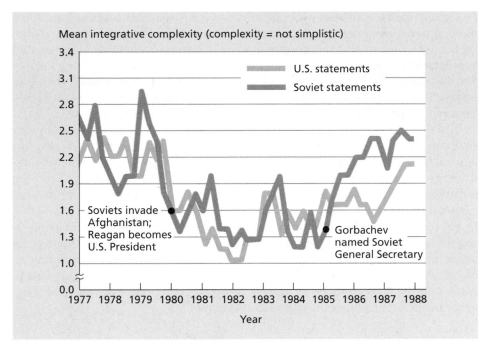

figure 13–4
Complexity of official U.S. and Soviet policy statements, 1977–1986.

Source: From Tetlock, 1988.

Shifting perceptions

If misperceptions accompany conflict, then they should appear and disappear as conflicts wax and wane. They do, with startling regularity. The same processes that create the enemy's image can reverse that image when the enemy becomes an ally. Thus the "bloodthirsty, cruel, treacherous, buck-toothed little Japs" of World War II soon became—in North American minds (Gallup, 1972) and in the media—our "intelligent, hardworking, self-disciplined, resourceful allies."

Shifting perceptions. The United States, once Iraq's friend and arms supplier, became Iraq's enemy, and then after the war sought to be its friend again.

The Germans, who after two world wars were hated, then admired, and then again hated, were once again admired—apparently no longer plagued by what earlier was presumed to be cruelty in their national character. So long as Iraq was attacking Iran, even while using chemical weapons and massacring its own Kurds, many nations supported it. Our enemy's enemy is our friend. When Iraq ended its war with Iran and invaded oil-rich Kuwait, Iraq's behavior suddenly became "barbaric." Images of our enemies change with amazing ease.

The extent of misperceptions during conflict provides a chilling reminder that people need not be insane or abnormally evil to form these distorted images of their antagonists. When we experience conflict with another nation, another group, or simply a roommate or parent, we readily misperceive our own motives and actions as wholly good and the other's as totally evil. Our antagonists usually form a mirror-image perception of us.

So, trapped in a social dilemma, competing for scarce resources, or perceiving injustice, the conflict continues until something enables both parties to peel away their misperceptions and work at reconciling their actual differences. Good advice, then, is this: When in conflict, do not assume that the other fails to share your values and morality. Rather, compare perceptions, assuming that the other is likely perceiving the situation differently.

Summing up

Whenever two people, two groups, or two nations interact, their perceived needs and goals may conflict. Many social problems arise as people pursue individual self-interest, to their collective detriment. Two laboratory games, the Prisoners' Dilemma and the Tragedy of the Commons, capture this clash of individual versus communal well-being. In real life, as in laboratory experiments, we can avoid such traps by establishing rules that regulate self-serving behavior; by keeping social groups small so people feel responsibility for one another; by enabling communication, thus reducing mistrust; by changing payoffs to make cooperation more rewarding; and by invoking altruistic norms.

When people compete for scarce resources, human relations often sink into prejudice and hostility. In his famous experiments, Muzafer Sherif found that win-lose competition quickly made strangers into enemies, triggering outright warfare even among normally upstanding boys.

Conflicts also arise when people feel unjustly treated. According to equity theory, people define justice as the distribution of rewards in proportion to one's contributions. Conflicts occur when people disagree on the extent of their contributions and thus on the equity of their outcomes.

Conflicts frequently contain a small core of truly incompatible goals, surrounded by a thick layer of misperceptions of the adversary's motives and goals. Often, conflicting parties have mirror-image perceptions. When both sides believe, "We are peace-loving—they are hostile," each may treat the other in ways that provoke confirmation of its expectations. International conflicts are sometimes also fed by an evil leader–good people illusion.

How can peace be achieved?

Although toxic forces can breed destructive conflict, we can harness other forces to bring conflict to a constructive resolution. What are these ingredients of peace and harmony?

We have seen how conflicts are ignited by social traps, competition, perceived injustices, and misperceptions. Although the picture is grim, it is not hopeless. Sometimes closed fists become open arms as hostilities evolve into friendship. Social psychologists have focused on four strategies for helping enemies become comrades. We can remember these as the four Cs of peacemaking: contact, cooperation, communication, conciliation.

CONTACT

Might putting two conflicting individuals or groups into close contact enable them to know and like each other? We have seen why it might not: In Chapter 3, we saw how negative expectations can bias judgments and create self-fulfilling prophecies. When tensions run high, contacts may foster fights.

But we also saw, in Chapter 11, that proximity—and the accompanying interaction, anticipation of interaction, and mere exposure—boosts liking. In Chapter 4, we noted how blatant racial prejudice declined following desegregation, showing that "attitudes follow behavior." If this social-psychological principle now seems obvious, remember: That's how things usually seem once you know them. To the U.S. Supreme Court in 1896, the idea that desegregated behavior might influence racial attitudes was anything but obvious. What seemed obvious at the time was, "Legislation is powerless to eradicate racial instincts" (*Plessy v. Ferguson*).

During the last 30 years in the United States, segregation and prejudice have diminished together. Was interracial contact the *cause* of these improved attitudes? Were those who actually experienced desegregation affected by it?

Does desegregation improve racial attitudes?

School desegregation has produced measurable benefits, such as leading more Blacks to attend and succeed in college (Stephan, 1988). Does desegregation of schools, neighborhoods, and workplaces also produce favorable *social* results? The evidence is mixed.

On the one hand, many studies conducted during and shortly after the desegregation following World War II found Whites' attitudes toward Blacks improving markedly. Whether the people were department store clerks and customers, merchant marines, government workers, police officers, neighbors, or students, racial contact led to diminished prejudice (Amir, 1969; Pettigrew, 1969). For example, near the end of World War II, the U.S. Army partially desegregated some of its rifle companies (Stouffer & others, 1949). When asked their opinions of such desegregation, 11 percent of the White soldiers in segregated companies approved. Of those in desegregated companies, 60 percent approved.

When Morton Deutsch and Mary Collins (1951) took advantage of a made-to-order natural experiment, they observed similar results. In accord with state law, New York City desegregated its public housing units; it assigned families to apartments without regard to race. In a similar development across the river in Newark, Blacks and Whites were assigned to separate buildings. When surveyed, White women in the desegregated development were far more likely to favor interracial housing and to say their attitudes toward Blacks had improved. Exaggerated stereotypes had wilted in the face of reality. As one woman put it, "I've really come to like it. I see they're just as human as we are."

Contact predicts tolerant attitudes in nonracial realms as well. In a painstakingly complete analysis, Linda Tropp and Thomas Pettigrew (2004)

"We know more about war than we do about peace—more about killing than we know about living."
—General Omar Bradley, 1893–1981, former U. S. Army Chief of Staff

assembled data from 515 studies of 250,513 people in 38 nations. In 94 percent of studies, *increased contact predicted decreased prejudice.* The correlation holds not only for interracial contacts, but also contacts with the elderly, psychiatric patients, gays, and children with disabilities, notes Miles Hewstone (2003).

Findings such as these influenced the Supreme Court's 1954 decision to desegregate U.S. schools and helped fuel the civil rights movement of the 1960s (Pettigrew, 1986). Yet studies of the effects of school desegregation have been less encouraging. After reviewing all the available studies, Walter Stephan (1986) concluded that racial attitudes had been little affected by desegregation. For Blacks, the more noticeable consequence of desegregated schooling was their increased likelihood of attending integrated (or predominantly White) colleges, living in integrated neighborhoods, and working in integrated settings.

Likewise, many student exchange programs have had less-than-hoped-for positive effects on student attitudes toward their host countries. For example, when eager American students study in France, often living with other Americans as they do so, their stereotypes of the French tend not to improve (Stroebe & others, 1988). Contact also failed to allay the loathing of Rwandan Tutsis by their Hutu neighbors or to eliminate the sexism of many men living in constant contact with women. People may more easily despise the homosexuals or immigrants whom they have never knowingly met, but they can also scorn people they see often.

So sometimes desegregation improves racial attitudes; sometimes it doesn't. Such disagreements excite the scientist's detective spirit. What explains the difference? So far, we've been lumping all kinds of desegregation together. Actual desegregation occurs in many ways and under vastly different conditions.

When does desegregation improve racial attitudes?

Might the frequency of interracial contact be a factor? Indeed it seems to be. Researchers have gone into dozens of desegregated schools and observed with whom children of a given race eat, talk , and loiter. Race influences contact. Whites disproportionately associate with Whites, Blacks with Blacks (Schofield, 1982, 1986). The same self-imposed segregation was evident in a South African desegregated beach, as John Dixon and Kevin Durrheim (2003) discovered when they recorded the location of Black, White, and Indian beachgoers one midsummer (December 30th) afternoon (Figure 13–5). Efforts to facilitate contact sometimes help, but sometimes fall flat. "We had one day when some of the Protestant schools came over," explained one Catholic youngster after a Northern Ireland school exchange (Cairns & Hewstone, 2002). "It was supposed to be like . . . mixing, but there was very little mixing. It wasn't because we didn't want to; it was just really awkward."

Friendship.   In contrast, the more encouraging older studies of store clerks, soldiers, and housing project neighbors involved considerable interracial contact, more than enough to reduce the anxiety that marks initial intergroup contact. Other studies involving prolonged, personal contact—between Black and White prison inmates and between Black and White girls in an interracial summer camp—show similar benefits (Clore & others, 1978; Foley, 1976). Among American students who have studied in Germany or Britain, the more their contact with host country people, the more positive their attitudes (Stangor & others, 1996). In experiments, those who form *friendships* with outgroup members

figure 13–5
Desegregation needn't mean contact.
After this Scottburgh, South Africa, beach became "open" and desegregated in the new South Africa, Blacks (represented by red circles), Whites (blue circles), and Indians (yellow circles) tended to cluster with their own race. **Source:** From Dixon & Durrheim, 2003.

develop more positive attitudes toward the outgroup (Pettigrew & Tropp, 2000; Wright & others, 1997). It's not just head knowledge of other people that matters, it's the *emotional* ties that form with intimate friendships and that serve to reduce anxiety (Hewstone, 2003; Pettigrew & Tropp, 2000).

But "group salience" also matters. If you forever think of that friend solely as an individual, your affective ties may not generalize to other members of the friend's group (Miller, 2002). Ideally, then, we should form trusting friendships across group lines, but also recognize that the friend represents those in another group—with whom we turn out to have much in common.

We will be most likely to befriend people if their outgroup identity is initially minimized—if we see them as essentially like us rather than feeling threatened by their being different. If our liking for our new friends is to generalize to others, their group identity must at some point become salient. So, to reduce prejudice and conflict, we had best initially minimize group diversity, then acknowledge it, then transcend it.

Surveys of nearly 4,000 Europeans reveal that friendship is a key to successful contact: If you have a minority-group friend, you become much more likely to express sympathy and support for the friend's group, and even somewhat more support for immigration by that group. It's true of West Germans' attitudes toward Turks, French people's attitudes toward Asians and North Africans, Netherlanders' attitudes toward Surinamers and Turks, and Britishers' attitudes toward West Indians and Asians (Brown & others, 1999; Hamberger & Hewstone, 1997; Pettigrew, 1997). Likewise, antigay feeling is lower among people who know gays personally (Herek, 1993). Additional studies of attitudes toward the elderly, the mentally ill, AIDS patients, and those with disabilities confirm that contact often predicts positive attitudes (Pettigrew, 1998).

Equal-status contact.   The social psychologists who advocated desegregation never claimed that contact of *any* sort would improve attitudes. They expected poor results when contacts were competitive, unsupported by authorities, and

www.mhhe.com/myers8
Visit the Online Learning Center for a scenario on racial tensions.

unequal (Pettigrew, 1988; Stephan, 1987). Before 1954, many prejudiced Whites had frequent contacts with Blacks—as shoeshine men and domestic workers. As we saw in Chapter 9, such unequal contacts breed attitudes that merely justify the continuation of inequality. So it's important that the contact be **equal-status contact,** like that between the store clerks, the soldiers, the neighbors, the prisoners, and the summer campers.

equal-status contact
Contact on an equal basis. Just as a relationship between people of unequal status breeds attitudes consistent with their relationship, so do relationships between those of equal status. Thus, to reduce prejudice, interracial contact should be between persons equal in status.

The contact in desegregated schools was often unequal. White students were often more active, more influential, more successful (Cohen, 1980a; Riordan & Ruggiero, 1980). When a seventh-grade Black girl from an academically inferior school is dropped suddenly into a predominantly White middle-class junior high school with White middle-class teachers who expect less of her, she is likely to be perceived, by her classmates and by herself, as having lower academic status.

In colleges and universities, informal interactions enabled by classroom ethnic diversity pay dividends for all students, report University of Michigan researcher Patricia Gurin and colleagues from national collegiate surveys (2002). Such interactions tend to be intellectually growth-promoting and to foster greater acceptance of difference as compatible with societal unity—findings that informed the U.S. Supreme Court's 2003 decision—that racial diversity is a compelling interest of higher education and may be a criterion in admissions.

COOPERATION

Although equal-status contact can help, it is sometimes not enough. It didn't help when Muzafer Sherif stopped the Eagles versus Rattlers competition and brought the groups together for noncompetitive activities, such as watching movies, shooting off fireworks, and eating. By this time, their hostility was so strong that mere contact only provided opportunities for taunts and attacks. When an Eagle was bumped by a Rattler, his fellow Eagles urged him to "brush off the dirt." Obviously, desegregating the two groups had hardly promoted their social integration.

Shared predicaments trigger cooperation, as these Wal-Mart workers on strike in Germany demonstrate.

Given entrenched hostility, what can a peacemaker do? Think back to the successful and unsuccessful desegregation efforts. The army's racial mixing of rifle companies not only brought Blacks and Whites into equal-status contact but also made them interdependent. Together, they were fighting a common enemy, striving toward a shared goal.

Does this suggest a second factor that predicts whether the effect of desegregation will be favorable? Does competitive contact divide and *cooperative* contact unite? Consider what happens to people who together face a common predicament.

Common external threats build cohesiveness

Together with others, have you ever been victimized by the weather; harassed as part of your initiation into a group; punished by a teacher; or persecuted and ridiculed because of your social, racial, or religious identity? If so, you may recall feeling close to those with whom you shared the predicament. Perhaps previous social barriers were dropped as you helped one another dig out of the snow or struggled to cope with your common enemy.

Such friendliness is common among those who experience a shared threat. John Lanzetta (1955) observed this when he put four-man groups of naval ROTC cadets to work on problem-solving tasks and then began informing them over a loudspeaker that their answers were wrong, their productivity inexcusably low, their thinking stupid. Other groups did not receive this harassment. Lanzetta observed that the group members under duress became friendlier to one another, more cooperative, less argumentative, less competitive. They were in it together. And the result was a cohesive spirit.

Having a common enemy unified the groups of competing boys in Sherif's camping experiments—and in many subsequent experiments (Dion, 1979). Times of interracial strife similarly heighten group pride. For Chinese university students in Toronto, facing discrimination heightens a sense of kinship with other Chinese (Pak & others, 1991). Just being reminded of an outgroup (say, a rival school) heightens people's responsiveness to their own group (Wilder & Shapiro, 1984). When keenly conscious of who "they" are, we also know who "we" are.

During wartimes against a well-defined external threat, we-feeling soars. The membership of civic organizations mushrooms (Putnam, 2000). Citizens unite behind their leader and support their troops. This was dramatically evident after the catastrophe of 9/11 and the threats of further terrorist attacks. In New York City, "old racial antagonisms have dissolved," reported the *New York Times,* at least for a while (Sengupta, 2001). "I just thought of myself as Black," said 18-year-old Louis Johnson, reflecting on life before 9/11. "But now I feel like I'm an American, more than ever." One sampling of conversation on 9/11, and another of New York Mayor Giuliani's press conferences before and after 9/11, found a doubled rate of the word "we" (Liehr & others, in press; Pennebaker & Lay, 2002).

George W. Bush's job performance ratings reflected this threat-bred spirit of unity. Just before 9/11, a mere 51 percent of Americans approved of his presidential performance. Just after, an exceptional 90 percent approved. In the public eye, the mediocre president of 9/10 had become the exalted president of 10/10—"our leader" in the fight against "those who hate us." Thereafter, his ratings gradually declined but then jumped again as the war against Iraq began (Figure 13–6, page 546). When Sheldon Solomon and his colleagues (2004) asked American students to reflect on the events of 9/11 (rather than on an upcoming exam), they become more likely to agree that "I endorse the actions of President Bush and the members of his administration who have taken bold action in Iraq."

Leaders may even *create* a threatening external enemy as a technique for building group cohesiveness. George Orwell's novel *1984* illustrates the tactic: The leader of the protagonist nation uses border conflicts with the other two major powers to lessen internal strife. From time to time the enemy shifts, but there is always an enemy. Indeed, the nation seems to *need* an enemy. For the world, for a nation, for a group, having a common enemy is powerfully unifying.

Simultaneous external threats were also breeding unity elsewhere in the world. Suicide bombers in Israel rallied partisan Jews behind Prime Minister Ariel Sharon and his government, while the Israeli Defense Force killing of

"I couldn't help but say to [Mr. Gorbachev], just think how easy his task and mine might be in these meetings that we held if suddenly there was a threat to this world from some other species from another planet. [We'd] find out once and for all that we really are all human beings here on this earth together."
—Ronald Reagan, December 4, 1985, speech

focus on   why do we care who wins?

Why, for sports fans everywhere, does it matter who wins? Why does it matter to New Yorkers whether two dozen of George Steinbrenner's multimillionaire temporary employees, most born in other states or countries, win the World Series? During the annual NCAA basketball "March Madness," why do perfectly normal adults become insanely supportive of their team, and depressed when it loses? And why for that penultimate sporting event, World Cup Football, do soccer fans worldwide dream of their country victorious?

Theory and evidence indicate that the roots of rivalry run deep. There's something primal at work when the crowd erupts as the two rivals take the floor. There's something tribal at work during the ensuing two hours of passion,

all in response to the ups and downs of a mere orange leather sphere. Our ancestors, living in a world where neighboring tribes occasionally raided and pillaged one another's camps, knew that there was safety in solidarity (those who didn't band together left fewer descendants). Whether hunting, defending, or attacking, 10 hands were better than 2. Dividing the world into "us" and "them" entails significant costs, such as racism and war, but also provides the benefits of communal solidarity. To identify us and them, our ancestors—not so far removed from today's rabid fans—dressed or painted themselves in group-specific costumes and colors.

As social animals, we live in groups, cheer on our groups, kill for our groups, die for our

Group identity feeds, and is fed by, competition.

Palestinians and destruction of their property united Muslim factions in their animosity toward Sharon (Pettigrew, 2003). And after the United States attacked Iraq, Pew Research Center (2003) polls of Indonesian and Jordanian Muslims found rising anti-Americanism. The 53 percent of Jordanians who expressed a positive view of Americans in the summer of 2002 plummeted to 18 percent shortly after the war. "Before the war, I would have said that if Osama (bin Laden) was responsible for the two towers, we would not be proud of it," said

groups. We also define ourselves by our groups. Our self-concept—our sense of who we are—consists not only of our personal attributes and attitudes, but also of our social identity. Our social identities—our knowing who "we" are—strengthens self-concept and pride, especially when perceiving that "we" are superior. Lacking a positive identity, many youths find pride, power, and identity in gangs. Many superpatriots define themselves by their national identities. Many cheeseheads find added identity in their association with the Green Bay Packers.

The group definition of who we *are* also implies who we are *not*. Many social psychological experiments reveal that being formed into groups—even arbitrary groups—promotes "in-group bias." Ask children, "Who are better, the children in your school or the children at [another nearby school]?" Virtually all will say their own school has better children. Cluster people into groups defined by nothing more than their birth date or even the last digit of their driver's license and they'll feel a certain kinship with their number mates, and will show them favoritism. So strong is our group consciousness that "we" seem better than "they" even when "we" and "they" are defined randomly.

As post September 11th America illustrates, group solidarity soars when people face a common enemy. As Muzafer Sherif's Robber's Camp experiment vividly demonstrated, competition creates enemies. Fueled by competition and unleashed by the anonymity of a crowd, passions can culminate in sport's worst moments—fans taunting opponents, screaming at umpires, even pelting referees with beer bottles.

Group identification soars further with success. Fans find self-respect by their personal achievements, but also, in at least small measure, by their association with the victorious athletes when their team wins. Queried after a big football victory, university students commonly report that "*we* won." They bask in reflected glory, note Robert Cialdini and his colleagues (1976). Asked the outcome after a defeat, students more often reply that "*they* lost."

Ironically, we often reserve our most intense passions for rivals most similar to us. Freud long ago recognized that animosities formed around small differences. "Of two neighbouring towns, each is the other's most jealous rival; every little canton looks down upon the others with contempt. Closely related races keep one another at arm's length; the South German cannot endure the North German, the Englishman casts every kind of aspersion upon the Scot, the Spaniard despises the Portuguese." Cubs and White Sox fans nod knowingly.

As an occasional resident of Scotland, I've witnessed many examples of *The Xenophobe's Guide to the Scots* observation—that Scots divide non-Scots "into two main groups: (1) The English; (2) The Rest." As rabid Cubs fans are happy if either the Cubs win *or* the White Sox lose, so rabid fans of Scottish soccer rejoice in either a Scotland victory or an England defeat. "Phew! They Lost," rejoiced one Scottish tabloid front-page headline after England's 1996 Euro Cup defeat—by Germany, no less.

one Syrian 21-year-old Islamic law student. "But if he did it now we would be proud of him" (Rubin, 2003).

Superordinate goals foster cooperation

Closely related to the unifying power of an external threat is the unifying power of **superordinate goals,** goals that unite all in a group and require cooperative effort. To promote harmony among his warring campers, Sherif introduced

superordinate goal
A shared goal that necessitates cooperative effort; a goal that overrides people's differences from one another.

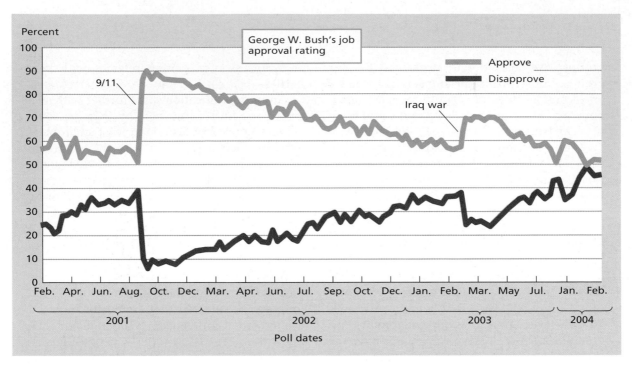

Percent

George W. Bush's job approval rating

— Approve
— Disapprove

9/11

Iraq war

Feb. Apr. Jun. Aug. Oct. Dec. Mar. Apr. Jun. Jul. Sep. Oct. Dec. Jan. Feb. Mar. May Jul. Jan. Feb.

2001   2002   2003   2004

Poll dates

figure 13–6

External threats breed internal unity.

As the ups and downs of President George Bush's approval ratings illustrate, national conflicts mold public attitudes (Gallup, 2003).

such goals. He created a problem with the camp water supply, necessitating both groups' cooperation to restore the water. Given an opportunity to rent a movie, one expensive enough to require the joint resources of both groups, they again cooperated. When a truck "broke down" on a camping trip, a staff member casually left the tug-of-war rope nearby, prompting one boy to suggest that they all pull the truck to get it started. When it started, a backslapping celebration ensued over their victorious "tug-of-war against the truck."

After working together to achieve such superordinate goals, the boys ate together and enjoyed themselves around a campfire. Friendships sprouted across group lines. Hostilities plummeted (Figure 13–7). On the last day, the boys decided to travel home together on one bus. During the trip they no longer sat by groups. As the bus approached Oklahoma City and home, they, as one, spontaneously sang "Oklahoma" and then bade their friends farewell. With isolation and competition, Sherif made strangers into bitter enemies. With superordinate goals, he made enemies into friends.

Are Sherif's experiments mere child's play? Or can pulling together to achieve superordinate goals be similarly beneficial with adults in conflict? Robert Blake and Jane Mouton (1979) wondered. So in a series of two-week experiments involving more than 1,000 executives in 150 different groups, they recreated the essential features of the situation experienced by the Rattlers and Eagles. Each group first engaged in activities by itself, then competed with another group, and then cooperated with the other group in working toward jointly chosen superordinate goals. Their results provided "unequivocal evidence that adult reactions parallel those of Sherif's younger subjects."

Extending these findings, Samuel Gaertner, John Dovidio, and their collaborators (1993, 2000) report that working cooperatively has especially favorable effects under conditions that lead people to define a new, inclusive group that

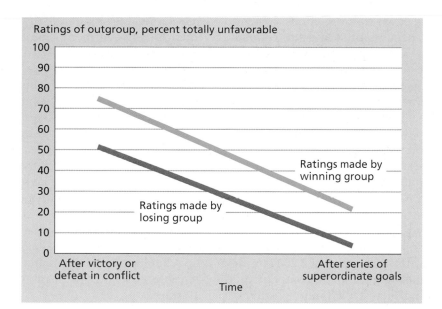

figure 13–7

After competition, the Eagles and Rattlers rated each other unfavorably. After they worked cooperatively to achieve superordinate goals, hostility dropped sharply.
Source: Data from Sherif, 1966, p. 84.

dissolves their former subgroups. Old feelings of bias against another group diminish when members of the two groups sit alternately around a table (rather than on opposite sides), give their new group a single name, and then work together under conditions that foster a good mood. "Us" and "them" become "we." To combat Germany, Italy, and Japan during World War II, the United States and the former USSR, along with other nations, formed one united group named the Allies. So long as the superordinate goal of defeating a common enemy lasted, so did supportive U.S. attitudes toward the Russians.

The cooperative efforts by Rattlers and Eagles ended in success. Would the same harmony have emerged if the water had remained off, the movie unaffordable, the truck still stalled? Likely not. In experiments with University of Virginia students, Stephen Worchel and his associates (1977, 1978, 1980) confirmed that *successful* cooperation between two groups boosts their attraction for one another. If previously conflicting groups *fail* in a cooperative effort, however, *and* if conditions allow them to attribute their failure to each other, the conflict may worsen. Sherif's groups were already feeling hostile to one another. Thus, failure to raise sufficient funds for the movie might have been attributed to the one group's "stinginess" and "selfishness." This would have exacerbated rather than alleviated their conflict.

Promoting "common ingroup identity." The banning of gang colors and the common European practice of school uniforms—an increasing trend in the United States, as well—aim to change "us" and "them" to "we."

Cooperative learning improves racial attitudes

So far we have noted the apparently meager social benefits of typical school desegregation (especially if unaccompanied by the emotional bonds of friendship and by equal-status relationships). And we have noted the apparently dramatic social benefits of successful, cooperative contacts between members of rival groups. Could putting these two findings together suggest a constructive alternative to traditional desegregation practices? Several independent research teams speculated yes. Each wondered whether, without compromising academic achievement, we could promote interracial friendships by replacing competitive learning situations with cooperative ones. Given the diversity of their methods—all involving students on integrated study teams, sometimes in competition with other teams—the results are striking and very heartening.

Are students who participate in existing cooperative activities, such as interracial athletic teams and class projects, less prejudiced? Robert Slavin and Nancy Madden (1979) analyzed survey data from 2,400 students in 71 American high schools and found encouraging results. Those of different races who play and work together are more likely to report having friends of another race and to express positive racial attitudes. Charles Green and his colleagues (1988) confirmed this in a study of 3,200 Florida middle-school students. Compared with students at traditional, competitive schools, those at schools with interracial learning "teams" had more positive racial attitudes.

From this correlational finding, can we conclude that cooperative interracial activity improves racial attitudes? Again, the way to find out is to experiment. Randomly designate some students, but not others, to work together in racially mixed groups. Slavin (1985, 2003) and his colleagues divided classes into interracial teams, each composed of four or five students from all achievement levels. Team members sat together, studied a variety of subjects together, and at the end of each week competed with the other teams in a class tournament. All members contributed to the team score by doing well, sometimes by competing with other students whose recent achievements were similar to their own, sometimes by competing with their own previous scores. Everyone had a chance to succeed. Moreover, team members were motivated to help one another prepare for the weekly tournament—by drilling each other on fractions, spelling, or historical events—whatever was the next event. Rather than

Interracial cooperation—on athletic teams, in class projects and extracurricular activities—melts differences and improves racial attitudes. White teen athletes who play cooperative team sports (such as basketball) with Black teammates express more liking and support for Blacks than do their counterparts involved in individual sports (such as wrestling) (Brown & others, 2003).

isolating students from one another, team competition brought them into closer contact and drew out mutual support.

Another research team, led by Elliot Aronson (1978, 2000, 2002; Aronson & Gonzalez, 1988), elicited similar group cooperation with a "jigsaw" technique. In experiments in Texas and California elementary schools, the researchers assigned children to racially and academically diverse six-member groups. The subject was then divided into six parts, with each student becoming the expert on his or her part. In a unit on Chile, one student might be the expert on Chile's history, another on its geography, another on its culture. First, the various "historians," "geographers," and so forth got together to master their material. Then they returned to the home groups to teach it to their classmates. Each group member held, so to speak, a piece of the jigsaw. The self-confident students therefore had to listen to and learn from the reticent students, who in turn soon realized they had something important to offer their peers. Other research teams—led by David Johnson and Roger Johnson (1987, 1994, 2000) at the University of Minnesota, Elizabeth Cohen (1980) at Stanford University, Shlomo Sharan and Yael Sharan (1976, 1994) at Tel Aviv University, and Stuart Cook (1985) at the University of Colorado—have devised additional methods for cooperative learning.

From all this research—818 studies by one count (Druckman & Bjork, 1994)— what can we conclude? With cooperative learning, students learn not only the material but other lessons as well. Cooperative learning, say Slavin and Cooper (1999), promotes "the academic achievement of all students while simultaneously improving intergroup relations among students of different racial and ethnic backgrounds." Aronson reported that "children in the interdependent, jigsaw classrooms grow to like each other better, develop a greater liking for school, and develop greater self-esteem than children in traditional classrooms" (1980, p. 232).

"This was truly an exciting event. My students and I had found a way to make desegregation work the way it was intended to work!"
—Elliot Aronson, "Drifting My Own Way," 2003

Cooperation and peace. Researchers have identified more than 40 peaceful societies—societies where people live with no, or virtually no, recorded instances of violence. An analysis of 25 of these societies, including the Amish shown here, reveals that most base their worldviews on cooperation rather than competition (Bonta, 1997).

focus on | Branch Rickey, Jackie Robinson, and the integration of baseball

Jackie Robinson and Branch Rickey

On April 10, 1947, 19 words that forever changed the face of baseball would also put social-psychological principles to the test. In the sixth inning of a Brooklyn Dodgers exhibition game with their top minor league club, the Montreal Royals' radio announcer Red Barber read a statement from Dodger president Branch Rickey: "The Brooklyn Dodgers today purchased the contract of Jackie Roosevelt Robinson from the Montreal Royals. He will report immediately." Five days later, Robinson

became the first African American since 1887 to play major league baseball. In the fall, Dodger fans realized their dreams of going to the World Series. Robinson, after enduring racial taunts, beanballs, and spikes, was voted *Sporting News* rookie of the year and in a poll finished second to Bing Crosby as the most popular man in America. Baseball's racial barrier was forever broken.

Motivated by both his Methodist morality and a drive for baseball success, Rickey had been planning the move for some time, report social psychologists Anthony Pratkanis and Marlene Turner (1994a, b). Three years earlier, Rickey had been asked by the sociologist-chair of the Mayor's Committee on Unity to desegregate his team. His response was to ask for time (so the hiring would not be attributed to pressure) and for advice on how best to do it. In 1945, Rickey was the only owner voting against keeping Blacks out of baseball. In 1947 he made his move using these principles identified by Pratkanis and Turner:

- *Create a perception that change is inevitable.* Leave little possibility that protest or resistance can turn back the clock. The

Cross-racial friendships also begin to blossom. The exam scores of minority students improve (perhaps because academic achievement is now peer-supported). After the experiments are over, many teachers continue using cooperative learning (D. W. Johnson & others, 1981; Slavin, 1990). "It is clear," wrote race-relations expert John McConahay (1981), that cooperative learning "is the most effective practice for improving race relations in desegregated schools that we know of to date."

Should we have "known it all along"? At the time of the 1954 Supreme Court decision, Gordon Allport spoke for many social psychologists in predicting, "Prejudice . . . may be reduced by equal status contact between majority and minority groups in the pursuit of common goals" (1954, p. 281). Cooperative learning experiments confirmed Allport's insight, making Robert Slavin and his colleagues (1985, 2003) optimistic: "Thirty years after Allport laid out the basic principles operationalized in cooperative learning methods, we finally have practical, proven methods for implementing contact theory in the desegregated classroom. . . . Research on cooperative learning is one of the greatest success stories in the history of educational research."

announcer Red Barber, a traditional southerner, recalled that in 1945 Rickey took him to lunch and explained very slowly and strongly that his scouts were searching for "the first black player I can put on the white Dodgers. I don't know who he is or where he is, but, he is coming." An angered Barber at first intended to quit, but in time decided to accept the inevitable and keep the world's "best sports announcing job." Rickey was equally matter-of-fact with the players in 1947, offering to trade any player who didn't want to play with Robinson.

- *Establish equal-status contact with a superordinate goal.* One sociologist explained to Rickey that when relationships focus on an overarching goal, such as winning the pennant, "the people involved would adjust appropriately." One of the players initially opposed later helped Robinson with his hitting, explaining, "When you're on a team, you got to pull together to win."
- *Puncture the norm of prejudice.* Rickey led the way, but others helped. Team leader, shortstop Pee Wee Reese, a southerner, set a pattern of sitting and eating with Robinson.

One day in Cincinnati, as the crowd was hurling slurs—"get the nigger off the field"—Reese left his shortstop position, walked over to Robinson at first base, smiled and spoke to him, and then—with a hushed crowd watching—put his arm around Robinson's shoulder.

- *Cut short the spiral of violence by practicing nonviolence.* Rickey, wanting "a ballplayer with guts enough not to fight back," role-played for Robinson the kind of insults and dirty play he would experience and gained Robinson's commitment not to return violence with violence. When Robinson was taunted and spiked, he left the responses to his teammates. Team cohesion was thereby increased.

Robinson and Bob Feller later became the first players in baseball history elected to the Hall of Fame in their first year of eligibility. As he received the award, Robinson asked three persons to stand beside him: his mother, Mallie; his wife, Rachel; and his friend, Branch Rickey.

So, cooperative, equal-status contacts exert a positive influence on boy campers, industrial executives, college students, and schoolchildren. Does the principle extend to all levels of human relations? Are families unified by pulling together to farm the land, restore an old house, or sail a sloop? Are communal identities forged by barn raisings, group singing, or cheering on the football team? Is international understanding bred by international collaboration in science and space, by joint efforts to feed the world and conserve resources, by friendly personal contacts between people of different nations? Indications are that the answer to all these questions is yes (Brewer & Miller, 1988; Desforges & others, 1991, 1997; Deutsch, 1985, 1994). Thus an important challenge facing our divided world is to identify and agree on our superordinate goals and to structure cooperative efforts to achieve them.

Group and superordinate identities

In everyday life, we often reconcile multiple identities (Gaertner & others, 2000, 2001; Hewstone & Greenland, 2000; Huo & others, 1996). We acknowledge our subgroup identity (as parent or child) and then transcend it (sensing our

table 13–3   **Ethnic and cultural identity**

Identification with Majority Group	Identification with Ethnic Group	
	Strong	**Weak**
strong	bicultural	assimilated
weak	separated	marginal

"Most of us have overlapping identities which unite us with very different groups. We *can* love what we are, without hating what—and who—we are *not*. We can thrive in our own tradition, even as we learn from others, and come to respect their teachings."
—Kofi Annan, Nobel Peace Prize Lecture, 2001

superordinate identity as a family). Blended families and corporate mergers leave us mindful of who we were, and who we are. Pride in our ethnic heritage can complement our larger communal or national identity. Subgroup identity and social cohesion can co-exist (Brewer, 2000; Crisp & Hewstone, 1999, 2000).

But in ethnically diverse cultures, how do people balance their ethnic identities with their national identities? They may have what identity researcher Jean Phinney (1990) calls a "bicultural" identity, one that identifies both with the ethnic culture and the larger culture. Ethnically conscious Asians living in England may also feel strongly British (Hutnik, 1985). French Canadians who identify with their ethnic roots may or may not also feel strongly Canadian (Driedger, 1975). Hispanic Americans who retain a strong sense of their "Cubanness" (or of their Mexican or Puerto Rican heritage) may feel strongly American (Roger & others, 1991). As W. E. B. DuBois (1903, p. 17) explained in *The Souls of Black Folk*, "The American Negro [longs] . . . to be both a Negro and an American."

With time, identification with a new culture often grows. Former East and West Germans come to see themselves as "German" (Kessler & Mummendey, 2001). Second-generation Chinese immigrants to Australia and the United States feel their Chinese identity somewhat less keenly, and their new national identity more strongly, than do immigrants who were born in China (Rosenthal & Feldman, 1992). Often, however, the *grand*children of immigrants feel more comfortable identifying with their ethnicity (Triandis, 1994).

Researchers have wondered whether pride in one's group competes with identification with the larger culture. As we noted in Chapter 9, we evaluate ourselves partly in terms of our group memberships. Seeing our own group (our school, our employer, our family, our race, our nation) as good helps us feel good about ourselves. A positive ethnic identity can therefore contribute to positive self-esteem. So can a positive mainstream culture identity. "Marginal" people, who have neither an ethnic nor a mainstream identity (Table 13–3), often have low self-esteem. Bicultural people, who affirm both identities, typically have a strongly positive self-concept (Phinney, 1990). Often, they alternate between their two cultures, adapting their language and behavior to whichever group they are with (LaFromboise & others, 1993).

Taken to an extreme, group pride becomes destructive tribalism. Preoccupation with diversity may counter the sense of unity that facilitates conflict resolution (Mayton & others, 1996). By seeking to understand, appreciate, and protect all people, universalists such as Gandhi, Martin Luther King, Jr., and Nelson Mandela advocate peaceful routes to justice.

By forging unifying ideals, immigrant countries such as the United States, Canada, and Australia have avoided ethnic wars. In these countries, Irish and

Italians, Swedes and Scots, Asians and Africans seldom kill in defense of their ethnic identities. Nevertheless, even the immigrant nations struggle between separation and wholeness, between people's pride in their distinct heritage and unity as one nation, between acknowledging the reality of diversity and questing for shared values. The ideal of *community incorporating diversity* forms the United States motto: *E pluribus unum*. Out of many, one.

COMMUNICATION

Conflicting parties have other ways to resolve their differences. When husband and wife, or labor and management, or nation X and nation Y disagree, they can **bargain** with one another directly. They can ask a third party to **mediate** by making suggestions and facilitating their negotiations. Or they can **arbitrate** by submitting their disagreement to someone who will study the issues and impose a settlement.

A difficult balancing act. These ethnically conscious French Canadians—supporting Bill 101 "live French in Quebec"—may or may not also feel strongly Canadian. As countries become more ethnically diverse, people debate how we can build societies that are both plural and unified.

bargaining
Seeking an agreement to a conflict through direct negotiation between parties.

mediation
An attempt by a neutral third party to resolve a conflict by facilitating communication and offering suggestions.

arbitration
Resolution of a conflict by a neutral third party who studies both sides and imposes a settlement.

Bargaining

If you want to buy or sell a new car, are you better off adopting a tough bargaining stance—opening with an extreme offer so that splitting the difference will yield a favorable result? Or are you better off beginning with a sincere "good-faith" offer?

Experiments suggest no simple answer. On the one hand, those who demand more will often get more. Robert Cialdini, Leonard Bickman, and John Cacioppo (1979) provide a typical result: In a control condition, they approached various Chevrolet dealers and asked the price of a new Monte Carlo sports coupe with designated options. In an experimental condition, they approached other dealers and first struck a tougher bargaining stance, asking for and rejecting a price on a *different* car ("I need a lower price than that. That's a lot"). When they then asked the price of the Monte Carlo, exactly as in the control condition, they received offers that averaged some $200 lower.

Tough bargaining may lower the other party's expectations, making the other side willing to settle for less (Yukl, 1974). But toughness can sometimes backfire. Many a conflict is not over a pie of fixed size but over a pie that shrinks if the conflict continues. Yet often negotiators fail to realize their common interests, and about 20 percent of the time negotiate "lose-lose" agreements that are mutually costly (Thompson & Hrebec, 1996).

Delayed agreements can be costly. When a strike is prolonged, both labor and management lose. Being tough can also diminish the chances of actually reaching an agreement. If the other party responds with an equally extreme stance, both may be locked into positions from which neither can back down without losing face. In the weeks before the 1991 Persian Gulf War, President Bush threatened, in the full glare of publicity, to "kick Saddam's ass." Saddam Hussein, no less macho, threatened to make "infidel" Americans "swim in their own blood." After such belligerent statements, it was difficult for each side to evade war and save face. If face-saving had been implemented, perhaps negotiations could have averted war.

Mediation

A third-party mediator may offer suggestions that enable conflicting parties to make concessions and still save face (Pruitt, 1998). If my concession can be attributed to a mediator, who is gaining an equal concession from my antagonist, then neither of us will be viewed as weakly caving in to the other's demands.

Turning win-lose into win-win.   Mediators also help resolve conflicts by facilitating constructive communication. Their first task is to help the parties rethink the conflict and gain information about others' interests (Thompson, 1998). Typically, people on both sides have a competitive "win-lose" orientation: They are successful if their opponent is unhappy with the result, and unsuccessful if their opponent is pleased (Thompson & others, 1995). The mediator aims to replace this win-lose orientation with a cooperative "win-win" orientation, by prodding both sides to set aside their conflicting demands and instead to think about each other's underlying needs, interests, and goals. In experiments, Leigh Thompson (1990a, 1990b) found that, with experience, negotiators become better able to make mutually beneficial trade-offs and thus to achieve win-win resolutions.

A classic story of such a resolution concerns the two sisters who quarreled over an orange (Follett, 1940). Finally they compromised and split the orange in half, whereupon one sister squeezed her half for juice while the other used the peel to make a cake. In experiments at the State University of New York at Buffalo, Dean Pruitt and his associates induced bargainers to search for **integrative agreements** (Johnson & Johnson, 2003; Pruitt & Lewis, 1975, 1977). If the sisters had agreed to split the orange, giving one sister all the juice and the other all the peel, they would have hit on such an agreement, one that integrates both parties' interests. Compared with compromises, in which each party sacrifices something important, integrative agreements are more enduring. Because they are mutually rewarding, they also lead to better ongoing relationships (Pruitt, 1986).

Unraveling misperceptions with controlled communications.   Communication often helps reduce self-fulfilling misperceptions. Perhaps you can recall experiences similar to that of this college student:

> Often, after a prolonged period of little communication, I perceive Martha's silence as a sign of her dislike for me. She, in turn, thinks that my quietness is a result of my being mad at her. My silence induces her silence, which makes me even more silent . . . until this snowballing effect is broken by some occurrence that makes it

integrative agreements
Win-win agreements that reconcile both parties' interests to their mutual benefit.

necessary for us to interact. And the communication then unravels all the misinterpretations we had made about one another.

The outcome of such conflicts often depends on *how* people communicate their feelings to one another. Roger Knudson and his colleagues (1980) invited married couples to come to the University of Illinois psychology laboratory and relive, through role playing, one of their past conflicts. Before, during, and after their conversation (which often generated as much emotion as the actual previous conflict), the couples were observed closely and questioned. Couples who evaded the issue—by failing to make their positions clear or failing to acknowledge their spouse's position—left with the illusion that they were more in harmony and agreement than they really were. Often, they came to believe they now agreed more when actually they agreed less. In contrast, those who engaged the issue—by making their positions clear and by taking one another's views into account—achieved more actual agreement and gained more accurate information about one another's perceptions. That helps explain why couples who communicate their concerns directly and openly are usually happily married (Grush & Glidden, 1987).

Such findings have triggered new programs that train couples and children how to manage conflicts constructively (Horowitz and Boardman, 1994). If managed constructively, conflict provides opportunities for reconciliation and more genuine harmony. Psychologists Ian Gotlib and Catherine Colby (1988) offer advice on how to avoid destructive quarrels and how to have good quarrels (see Table 13–4). Children, for example, learn that conflict is normal, that people can learn to get along with those who are different, that most disputes can be resolved with two winners, and that nonviolent communication strategies are an alternative to a world of bullies and victims. This "violence prevention curriculum . . . is not about passivity," notes Deborah Prothrow-Stith (1991, p. 183). "It

table 13–4   **How to fight constructively**

Do Not	Do
• apologize prematurely.	• fight privately away from children.
• evade the argument, give the silent treatment, or walk out on it.	• clearly define the issue and repeat the other's arguments in your own words.
• use your intimate knowledge of the other person to hit below the belt and humiliate.	• divulge your positive and negative feelings.
• bring in unrelated issues.	• welcome feedback about your behavior.
• feign agreement while harboring resentment.	• clarify where you agree and disagree and what matters most to each of you.
• tell the other party how she or he is feeling.	• ask questions that help the other find words to express the concern.
• attack indirectly by criticizing someone or something the other person values.	• wait for spontaneous explosions to subside, without retaliating.
• undermine the other by intensifying their insecurity or threatening disaster.	• offer positive suggestions for mutual improvement.

Communication facilitators work to break down barriers, as in this diversity training exercise for teenagers.

is about using anger not to hurt oneself or one's peers, but to change the world."

David Johnson and Roger Johnson (1995, 2000, 2003) put first- through ninth-grade children through about a dozen hours of conflict resolution training in six schools, with very heartening results. Before the training, most students were involved in daily conflicts—put-downs and teasing, playground turn-taking conflicts, conflicts over possessions—conflicts that nearly always also resulted in a winner and a loser. After training, the children more often found win-win solutions, better mediated friends' conflicts, and retained and applied their new skills in and out of school throughout the school year. When implemented with a whole student body, the result is a more peaceful student community and increased academic achievement.

Conflict researchers report that a key factor is *trust* (Ross & Ward, 1995). If you believe the other person is well intentioned, you are then more likely to divulge your needs and concerns. Lacking trust, you may fear that being open will give the other party information that might be used against you.

When the two parties mistrust each other and communicate unproductively, a third-party mediator—a marriage counselor, a labor mediator, a diplomat—sometimes helps. Often the mediator is someone trusted by both sides. In the 1980s it took an Algerian Muslim to mediate the conflict between Iran and Iraq, and the Pope to resolve a geographical dispute between Argentina and Chile (Carnevale & Choi, 2000).

After coaxing the conflicting parties to rethink their perceived win-lose conflict, the mediator often has each party identify and rank its goals. When goals are compatible, the ranking procedure makes it easier for each to concede on less important goals so that both achieve their chief goals (Erickson & others,

1974; Schulz & Pruitt, 1978). South Africa achieved internal peace when Black and White South Africans granted each other's top priorities—replacing apartheid with majority rule and safeguarding the security, welfare, and rights of Whites (Kelman, 1998).

Once labor and management both believe that management's goal of higher productivity and profit is compatible with labor's goal of better wages and working conditions, they can begin to work for an integrative win-win solution. If workers will forgo benefits that are moderately beneficial to them but very costly to management (perhaps company-provided dental care), and if management will forgo moderately valuable arrangements that workers very much resent (perhaps inflexibility of working hours), then both sides may gain (Ross & Ward, 1995). Rather than seeing itself as making a concession, each side can see the negotiation as an effort to exchange bargaining chips for things more valued.

When the parties then convene to communicate directly, they are usually *not* set loose in the hope that, eyeball to eyeball, the conflict will resolve itself. In the midst of a threatening, stressful conflict, emotions often disrupt the ability to understand the other party's point of view. Communication may become most difficult just when it is most needed (Tetlock, 1985). The mediator will therefore often structure the encounter to help each party understand and feel understood by the other. The mediator may ask the conflicting parties to restrict their arguments to statements of fact, including statements of how they feel and how they respond when the other acts in a given way: "I enjoy music. But when you play it loud, I find it hard to concentrate. That makes me crabby." Also, the mediator may ask people to reverse roles and argue the other's position or to imagine and explain what the other person is experiencing. (Experiments show that inducing empathy decreases stereotyping and increases cooperation—Batson & Moran, 1999; Galinsky & Muskowitz, 2000.) Or the mediator may have them restate one another's positions before replying with their own: "My turning up the stereo bugs you."

Neutral third parties may also suggest mutually agreeable proposals that would be dismissed—"reactively devalued"—if offered by either side. Constance Stillinger and her colleagues (1991) found that a nuclear disarmament proposal that Americans dismissed when attributed to the former Soviet Union seemed more acceptable when attributed to a neutral third party. Likewise, people will often reactively devalue a concession offered by an adversary ("they must not value it"); the same concession may seem more than a token gesture when suggested by a third party.

These peacemaking principles—based partly on laboratory experiments, partly on practical experience—have helped mediate both international and industrial conflicts (Blake & Mouton, 1962, 1979; Fisher, 1994; Wehr, 1979). One small team of Arab and Jewish Americans, led by social psychologist Herbert Kelman (1997), has conducted workshops bringing together influential Arabs and Israelis. Another social psychologist team, led by Ervin Staub and Laurie Ann Pearlman (2004), worked in Rwanda between 1999 and 2003 by training facilitators and journalists to understand and write about Rwanda's traumas in ways that promote healing and reconciliation. Using methods such as those we've considered, Kelman and colleagues counter misperceptions and have participants seek creative solutions for their common good. Isolated, the participants are free to speak directly to their adversaries without fear that their constituents are second-guessing what they are saying. The result? Those from both sides typically come to understand the other's perspective and how the other side responds to their own group's actions.

Arbitration

Some conflicts are so intractable, the underlying interests so divergent, that a mutually satisfactory resolution is unattainable. In Bosnia and Kosovo, both Serbs and Muslims could not have jurisdiction over the same homelands. In a divorce dispute over custody of a child, both parents cannot enjoy full custody. In these and many other cases (disputes over tenants' repair bills, athletes' wages, and national territories), a third-party mediator may—or may not—help resolve the conflict.

If not, the parties may turn to *arbitration* by having the mediator or another third party *impose* a settlement. Disputants usually prefer to settle their differences without arbitration, so they retain control over the outcome. Neil McGillicuddy and others (1987) observed this preference in an experiment involving disputants coming to a dispute settlement center. When people knew they would face an arbitrated settlement if mediation failed, they tried harder to resolve the problem, exhibited less hostility, and thus were more likely to reach agreement.

In cases where differences seem large and irreconcilable, the prospect of arbitration may cause the disputants to freeze their positions, hoping to gain an advantage when the arbitrator chooses a compromise. To combat this tendency, some disputes, such as those involving salaries of individual baseball players, are settled with "final-offer arbitration" in which the third party chooses one of the two final offers. Final-offer arbitration motivates each party to make a reasonable proposal.

Typically, however, the final offer is not as reasonable as it would be if each party, free of self-serving bias, saw its own proposal through others' eyes. Negotiation researchers report that most disputants are made stubborn by "optimistic overconfidence" (Kahneman & Tversky, 1995). Successful mediation is hindered when, as often happens, both parties believe they have a two-thirds chance of winning a final-offer arbitration (Bazerman, 1986, 1990).

CONCILIATION

Sometimes tension and suspicion run so high that communication, much less resolution, becomes all but impossible. Each party may threaten, coerce, or retaliate against the other. Unfortunately, such acts tend to be reciprocated, escalating the conflict. So, would a strategy of appeasing the other party by being unconditionally cooperative produce a satisfying result? Often not. In laboratory games, those who are 100 percent cooperative often get exploited. Politically, a one-sided pacifism is usually out of the question anyway.

GRIT

Social psychologist Charles Osgood (1962, 1980) advocated a third alternative, one that is conciliatory, yet strong enough to discourage exploitation. Osgood called it "graduated and reciprocated initiatives in tension reduction." He nicknamed it **GRIT,** a label that suggests the determination it requires. GRIT aims to

"In the research on the effects of mediation, one finding stands out: The worse the state of the parties' relationship is with one another, the dimmer the prospects that mediation will be successful."
—Kenneth Kressel & Dean Pruitt (1985)

GRIT
Acronym for "graduated and reciprocated initiatives in tension reduction"—a strategy designed to de-escalate international tensions.

reverse the "conflict spiral" by triggering reciprocal de-escalation. To do so, it draws upon social-psychological concepts, such as the norm of reciprocity and the attribution of motives.

GRIT requires one side to initiate a few small de-escalatory actions, after *announcing a conciliatory intent.* The initiator states its desire to reduce tension, declares each conciliatory act prior to making it, and invites the adversary to reciprocate. Such announcements create a framework that helps the adversary correctly interpret what otherwise might be seen as weak or tricky actions. They also bring public pressure on the adversary to follow the reciprocity norm.

Next, the initiator establishes credibility and genuineness by carrying out, exactly as announced, several verifiable *conciliatory acts.* This intensifies the pressure to reciprocate. Making conciliatory acts diverse—perhaps offering medical information, closing a military base, and lifting a trade ban—keeps the initiator from making a significant sacrifice in any one area and leaves the adversary freer to choose its own means of reciprocation. If the adversary reciprocates voluntarily, its own conciliatory behavior may soften its attitudes.

GRIT *is* conciliatory. But it is not "surrender on the installment plan." The remaining aspects of the plan protect each side's self-interest by *maintaining retaliatory capability.* The initial conciliatory steps entail some small risk but do not jeopardize either one's security; rather, they are calculated to begin edging both sides down the tension ladder. If one side takes an aggressive action, the other side reciprocates in kind, making clear it will not tolerate exploitation. Yet the reciprocal act is not an overresponse that would reescalate the conflict. If the adversary offers its own conciliatory acts, these, too, are matched or even slightly exceeded. Morton Deutsch (1993) captures the spirit of GRIT in advising negotiators to be " 'firm, fair, and friendly': *firm* in resisting intimidation, exploitation, and dirty tricks; *fair* in holding to one's moral principles and not reciprocating the other's immoral behavior despite his or her provocations; and *friendly* in the sense that one is willing to initiate and reciprocate cooperation."

Does GRIT really work? In laboratory dilemma games a successful strategy has proved to be simple "tit-for-tat," which similarly begins with a cooperative opening play and thereafter matches the other party's last response (Axelrod & Dion, 1988; Parks & Rumble, 2001; Van Lange & Visser, 1999). Although initially friendly, tit-for-tat immediately punishes noncooperation but also immediately forgives wayward opponents who again cooperate. In a lengthy series of experiments at Ohio University, Svenn Lindskold and his associates (1976 to 1988) found "strong support for the various steps in the GRIT proposal." In laboratory games, announcing cooperative intent *does* boost cooperation. Repeated conciliatory acts *do* breed greater trust (although self-serving biases often make one's own acts seem more conciliatory and less hostile than those of the adversary). Maintaining an equality of power *does* protect against exploitation.

Lindskold was not contending that the world of the laboratory experiment mirrors the more complex world of everyday life. Rather, experiments enable us to formulate and verify powerful theoretical principles, such as the reciprocity

"Don't worry, dear—it's just a *peace* offensive."

People perceive that they respond more favorably to conciliation, but that others might be responsive to coercion. BALOO reprinted by permission of Cartoon Features Syndicate.

"Perhaps the best policy in the nuclear age is to speak softly and carry a small- to medium-sized stick."
—Richard Ned Lebow & Janice Stein (1987)

"I am not suggesting that principles of individual behavior can be applied to the behavior of nations in any direct, simpleminded fashion. What I am trying to suggest is that such principles may provide us with hunches about international behavior that can be tested against experience in the larger arena."
—Charles E. Osgood (1966)

norm and the self-serving bias. As Lindskold (1981) noted, "It is the theories, not the individual experiments, that are used to interpret the world."

Real-world applications

www.mhhe.com/**myers8**
Visit the Online Learning Center for an interactivity on common mistakes in negotiation.

GRIT-like strategies have occasionally been tried outside the laboratory, with promising results. During the Berlin crisis of the early 1960s, U.S. and Russian tanks faced one another barrel to barrel. The crisis was defused when the Americans pulled back their tanks step by step. At each step, the Russians reciprocated. Small concessions by Israel and Egypt (for example, Israel allowing Egypt to open up the Suez Canal, Egypt allowing ships bound for Israel to pass through) helped reduce tension to a point where the negotiations became possible (Rubin, 1981).

To many, the most significant attempt at GRIT was the so-called Kennedy experiment (Etzioni, 1967). On June 10, 1963, President Kennedy gave a major speech, "A Strategy for Peace." He noted that "Our problems are man-made . . . and can be solved by man," and then announced his first conciliatory act: The United States was stopping all atmospheric nuclear tests and would not resume them unless another country did. In the former Soviet Union, Kennedy's speech was published in full. Five days later Premier Khrushchev reciprocated, announcing he had halted production of strategic bombers. There soon followed further reciprocal gestures: The United States agreed to sell wheat to Russia, the Russians agreed to a "hot line" between the two countries, and the two countries soon achieved a test-ban treaty. For a time, these conciliatory initiatives warmed relations between the two countries.

Might conciliatory efforts also help reduce tension between individuals? There is every reason to expect so. When a relationship is strained and communication nonexistent, it sometimes takes only a conciliatory gesture—a soft answer, a warm smile, a gentle touch—for both parties to begin easing down the tension ladder, to a rung where contact, cooperation, and communication again become possible.

Summing up

Although conflicts are readily kindled and fueled by social dilemmas, competition, and misperceptions, some equally powerful forces, such as *contact, cooperation, communication,* and *conciliation,* can transform hostility into harmony.

Might putting people into close contact reduce their hostilities? Despite some encouraging early studies, other studies show that, in schools, mere desegregation has little effect upon racial attitudes. But when contact encourages emotional ties with individuals identified with an out-group and when it is structured to convey *equal status,* hostilities often lessen.

Contacts are especially beneficial when people work together to overcome a common threat or to achieve a superordinate goal. Taking their cue from experiments on *cooperative contact,* several research teams have replaced competitive classroom learning situations with opportunities for cooperative learning, with heartening results.

Conflicting parties can also seek to resolve their differences by bargaining either directly or through a *third-party mediator*. Third-party mediators can help by prodding the antagonists to replace their competitive win-lose view of their conflict with a more cooperative win-win orientation. Mediators can also structure communications that will peel away misperceptions and increase mutual understanding and trust. When a negotiated settlement is not reached, the conflicting parties may defer the outcome to an *arbitrator*, who either dictates a settlement or selects one of the two final offers.

Sometimes tensions run so high that genuine communication is impossible. In such cases, small concilia-tory gestures by one party may elicit reciprocal conciliatory acts by the other party. One such conciliatory strategy, *GRIT* (graduated and reciprocated initiatives in tension reduction), aims to alleviate tense international situations.

Those who mediate tense labor-management and international conflicts sometimes use another peacemaking strategy. They instruct the participants, as this chapter instructed you, in the dynamics of conflict and peacemaking in the hope that understanding can help us establish and enjoy peaceful, rewarding relationships.

Personal Postscript: Conflict between individual and communal rights

Many social conflicts are a contest between individual and collective rights. One person's right to own handguns conflicts with a neighborhood's right to safe streets. One person's right to smoke conflicts with others' rights to a smoke-free environment. One industrialist's right to do unregulated business conflicts with a community's right to clean air.

Hoping to blend the best of individualist and collectivist values, some social scientists—myself included—are now exploring a communitarian synthesis that aims to balance individual rights with the collective right to communal well-being. Communitarians welcome incentives for individual initiative and appreciate why Marxist economies have crumbled. "If I were, let's say, in Albania at this moment," said communitarian sociologist Amitai Etzioni (1991), "I probably would argue that there's too much community and not enough individual rights." But communitarians also question the other extreme—the rugged individualism and self-indulgence of the 1960s ("Do your own thing"), the 1970s (the "Me decade"), the 1980s ("Greed is good"), and the 1990s ("Follow your bliss"). Unrestrained personal freedom, they say, destroys a culture's social fabric; unrestrained commercial freedom, they add, plunders our shared environment. Echoing the French Revolutionists, their motto might well be "liberty, equality, *and* fraternity."

During the last half-century, Western individualism has intensified. Parents have become more likely to prize independence and self-reliance in their children, and less concerned with obedience (Alwin, 1990; Remley, 1988). Clothing and grooming styles have become more diverse, personal freedoms have

"This is the age of the individual."
—President Ronald Reagan, Address on Wall Street, 1982

"There is no society. There are only individuals and their families."
—Prime Minister Margaret Thatcher, after her third election

increased, and common values have waned (Putnam, 2000; Schlesinger, 1991). Accompanying this growing individualism was, until very recently, not only increased depression but other indicators of social recession—marked increases in most Western countries in rates of divorce, teen suicide, juvenile violence, and children living apart from fathers.

Some words of caution: Such trends have multiple causes. The mere correlation over time between increased individualism and social decay does not prove cause and effect. Also, communitarians are not advocating a nostalgia trip—a return, for example, to the more restrictive and unequal gender roles of the 1950s. Rather, they propose a middle ground between the individualism of the West and the collectivism of the East, between the macho independence traditionally associated with males and the caregiving connectedness traditionally associated with females, between concerns for individual rights and for communal well-being, between liberty and fraternity, between me-thinking and we-thinking.

As with luggage searches at airports, smoking bans on planes, and sobriety checkpoints and speed limits on highways, societies are accepting some adjustments to individual rights in order to protect the public good. Environmental restraints on individual freedoms (to pollute, to whale, to deforest) similarly exchange certain short-term liberties for long-term communal gain. Some individualists warn that such constraints on individual liberties may plunge us down a slippery slope leading to the loss of more important liberties. If today we let them search our luggage, tomorrow they'll be knocking down the doors of our houses. If today we censor cigarette ads or pornography on television, tomorrow they'll be removing books from our libraries. If today we ban handguns, tomorrow they'll take our hunting rifles. In protecting the interests of the majority do we risk suppressing the basic rights of minorities? Communitarians reply that if we don't balance concern for individual rights with concern for our collective well-being, we risk worse civic disorder, which in turn *will* fuel cries for an autocratic crackdown.

This much is sure: As the conflict between individual and collective rights continues, cross-cultural and gender scholarship can illuminate alternative cultural values and make visible our own assumed values.

What do you think?

Have you encountered a situation where your individual rights were constrained by community rights (for example, by a leash law that prevented letting your dog run free in a park)? And can you identify a situation where others' exercising their liberty (for example, to play music loud) disrupted the well-being of you and others? How might lines be drawn that appropriately balance individual and communal rights?

Making the Social Connection

SS This chapter described Elliot Aronson's work on the jigsaw technique of cooperative learning—a seemingly effective technique for effective learning and social integration. Did you connect Aronson to the text's earlier descriptions of his work on mundane realism (Chapter 1), persuasion (Chapter 7), and approval and attraction (Chapter 11)? Why is the jigsaw approach successful? Go to the *SocialSense* CD-ROM to view Aronson explaining how the jigsaw classroom works.

part four

Applying Social Psychology

Throughout this book, I linked laboratory (research) and life by relating social psychology's principles and findings to everyday happenings. Now, we conclude by recalling a number of these principles and applying them in three practical contexts. Chapter 14, "Social Psychology in the Clinic," applies social psychology to evaluating and promoting mental and physical health. Chapter 15, "Social Psychology in Court," explores social thinking and social influences as individual jurors, as well as groups, make judgments. Chapter 16, "Social Psychology and the Sustainable Future," asks what social-psychological principles might contribute to help avert an ecological nightmare, triggered by increasing population, consumption, and global warming.

chapter 14

Social Psychology in the Clinic

"Life does not consist mainly, or even largely, of facts and happenings. It consists mainly of the storm of thoughts that are forever blowing through one's mind."

—Mark Twain, 1835–1910

clinical psychology
The study, assessment, and treatment of people with psychological difficulties.

if you are a typical college student, you may occasionally feel mildly depressed. Perhaps you have at times felt dissatisfied with your life, discouraged about the future, sad, lacking appetite and energy, unable to concentrate, perhaps even wondering if life is worth it. Maybe disappointing grades have seemed to jeopardize your career goals. Perhaps the breakup of a relationship has left you in despair. At such times, your self-focused brooding only worsens your feelings. For some 10 percent of men and nearly twice that many women, life's down times are not just temporary blue moods but one or more major depressive episodes that last for weeks without any obvious cause.

Among the many thriving areas of applied social psychology is one that relates social psychology's concepts to depression, to other problems such as loneliness, anxiety, and physical illness, and now to happiness and well-being. This bridge-building research between social psychology and **clinical psychology** seeks answers to four important questions:

- As laypeople or as professional psychologists, how can we improve our judgments and predictions about others?

- How can the ways in which we think about self and others feed problems such as depression, loneliness, anxiety, and ill health?

- How might these maladaptive thought patterns be reversed?
- What part do close, supportive relationships play in health and happiness?

In this chapter we explore some answers.

What biases clinical judgments?

Do the influences on our social judgment discussed in Chapters 2 through 4 also affect clinicians' judgments of clients? If so, what biases should clinicians (and their clients) be wary of?

A parole board talks with a convicted rapist and ponders whether to release him. A clinical psychologist ponders whether her patient is seriously suicidal. A physician notes a patient's symptoms and surmises the likelihood of cancer. A school social worker ponders whether a child's overheard threat was a macho joke, a onetime outburst, or a signal indicating a potential school assassin.

Each of these professionals must decide whether to make their judgments subjectively or objectively. Should they follow their intuitions? Should they listen to their gut instincts, their hunches, their inner wisdom? Or should they rely on the wisdom embedded in formulas, statistical analyses, and computerized predictions?

In the contest between heart and head, most clinicians vote with their hearts. They listen to the whispers from their experience, a still small voice that clues them. They prefer not to let cold calculations decide the futures of warm human beings. As Figure 14–1 indicates, they are far more likely than nonclinical (and more research-oriented) psychologists to welcome nonscientific "ways of knowing." Feelings trump formulas.

Clinical judgments are also *social* judgments and thus vulnerable to illusory correlations, overconfidence bred by hindsight, and self-confirming diagnoses (Maddux, 1993). Let's see why alerting mental health workers to how people

"To free a man of error is to give, not to take away. Knowledge that a thing is false is a truth."
—Arthur Schopenhauer, 1788–1860

figure 14–1
Clinical intuition.
When Narina Nunez, Debra Ann Poole, and Amina Memon (in press) surveyed a national sample of clinical and nonclinical psychologists, they discovered "two cultures"—one mostly skeptical of "alternative ways of knowing," the other mostly accepting.
Source: From Nunez, Poole, & Memon, in press.

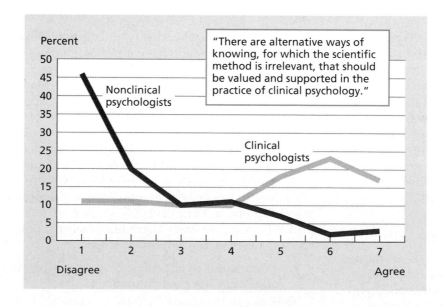

Percent

"There are alternative ways of knowing, for which the scientific method is irrelevant, that should be valued and supported in the practice of clinical psychology."

Nonclinical psychologists

Clinical psychologists

Disagree   Agree

form impressions (and *mis*impressions) might help avert serious misjudgments (McFall, 1991, 2000).

ILLUSORY CORRELATIONS

Consider the following court transcript in which a seemingly confident psychologist (PSY) is being questioned by an attorney (ATT):

ATT: You asked the defendant to draw a human figure?

PSY: Yes.

ATT: And this is the figure he drew for you? What does it indicate to you about his personality?

PSY: You will note this is a rear view of a male. This is very rare, statistically. It indicates hiding guilt feelings, or turning away from reality.

ATT: And this drawing of a female figure, does it indicate anything to you; and, if so, what?

PSY: It indicates hostility toward women on the part of the subject. The pose, the hands on the hips, the hard-looking face, the stern expression.

ATT: Anything else?

PSY: The size of the ears indicates a paranoid outlook, or hallucinations. Also, the absence of feet indicates feelings of insecurity. (Jeffery, 1964)

The assumption here, as in so many clinical judgments, is that test results reveal something important. Do they? There is a simple way to find out. Have one clinician administer and interpret the test. Have another clinician assess the same person's symptoms. Repeat this process with many people. The proof is in the pudding: Are test outcomes in fact correlated with reported symptoms? Some tests are indeed predictive. Others, such as the preceding Draw-a-Person test, have correlations far weaker than their users suppose (Lilienfeld & others, 2000). Why, then, do clinicians continue to express confidence in uninformative or ambiguous tests?

Pioneering experiments by Loren Chapman and Jean Chapman (1969, 1971) helped us see why. They invited both college students and professional clinicians to study some test performances and diagnoses. If the students or clinicians *expected* a particular association they generally *perceived* it, regardless of whether the data were supportive. For example, clinicians who believed that suspicious people draw peculiar eyes on the Draw-a-Person test perceived such a relationship—even when shown cases in which suspicious people drew peculiar eyes less often than nonsuspicious people. Believing that a relationship existed between two things, they were more likely to notice confirming instances. To believe is to see.

In fairness to clinicians, illusory thinking also occurs among political analysts, historians, sportscasters, personnel directors, stockbrokers, and many other professionals, including the research psychologists who point them out. As a researcher, I have often been unaware of the shortcomings of my theoretical analyses. I so eagerly presume that my idea of truth is *the* truth that, no matter how hard I try, I cannot see my own error. This is evident in the editorial review process that precedes any research publication. During the last 30 years, I have read dozens of reviews of my own manuscripts and have been a reviewer for dozens of others. My experience is that it is far easier to spot someone else's sloppy thinking than to perceive one's own.

www.mhhe.com/myers8
Visit the Online Learning Center for an interactivity on illusory correlations: "Does a relationship exist, or not?"

"No one can see his own errors."
—Psalms 19:12

20/20 hindsight. Kurt Cobain, member of the rock group Nirvana, *whose songs often expressed depressed, suicidal thinking. Should others have used such signs to predict or prevent his suicide?*

HINDSIGHT AND OVERCONFIDENCE

If someone we know commits suicide, how do we react? One common reaction is to think that we, or those close to the person, should have been able to predict and therefore to prevent the suicide: "We should have known!" In hindsight, we can see the suicidal signs and the pleas for help. One experiment gave people a description of a depressed person who later committed suicide. Compared with those not informed of the suicide, those told the person committed suicide were more likely to say they "would have expected" it (Goggin & Range, 1985). Moreover, those told of the suicide viewed the victim's family more negatively. After a tragedy, the I-should-have-known-it-all-along phenomenon can leave family, friends, and therapists feeling guilty.

David Rosenhan (1973) and seven associates provided a striking example of potential error in after-the-fact explanations. To test mental health workers' clinical insights, they each made an appointment with a different mental hospital admissions office and complained of "hearing voices." Apart from giving false names and vocations, they reported their life histories and emotional states honestly and exhibited no further symptoms. Most were diagnosed as schizophrenic and remained hospitalized for two to three weeks. Hospital clinicians then searched for early incidents in the pseudopatients' life histories and hospital behavior that "confirmed" and "explained" the diagnosis. Rosenhan tells of one pseudopatient who truthfully explained to the interviewer that he had a close relationship with his mother but was rather remote from his father during his early childhood. During adolescence and beyond, however, his father became a close friend, while his relationship with his mother cooled. His present relationship with his wife was characteristically close and warm. Apart from occasional angry exchanges, friction was minimal. The children had rarely been spanked.

The interviewer, "knowing" the person suffered from schizophrenia, explained the problem this way:

> This white 39-year-old male . . . manifests a long history of considerable ambivalence in close relationships, which begins in early childhood. A warm relationship with his mother cools during his adolescence. A distant relationship to his father is described as becoming very intense. Affective stability is absent. His attempts to control emotionality with his wife and children are punctuated by angry outbursts and, in the case of the children, spankings. And while he says that he has several good friends, one senses considerable ambivalence embedded in those relationships also.

Rosenhan later told some staff members (who had heard about his controversial experiment but doubted such mistakes could occur in their hospital) that during the next three months one or more pseudopatients would seek admission to their hospital. After the three months, he asked the staff to guess which of the 193 patients admitted during that time were really pseudopatients. Of the

193 new patients, 41 were accused by at least one staff member of being pseudopatients. Actually, there were none.

SELF-CONFIRMING DIAGNOSES

So far we've seen that mental health workers sometimes perceive illusory correlations and that hindsight explanations are often questionable. A third problem with clinical judgment is that people may also supply information that fulfills clinicians' expectations. In a clever series of experiments at the University of Minnesota, Mark Snyder (1984), in collaboration with William Swann and others, gave interviewers some hypotheses to test concerning individuals' traits. To get a feel for their experiments, imagine yourself on a blind date with someone who has been told that you are an uninhibited, outgoing person. To see whether this is true, your date slips questions into the conversation, such as, "Have you ever done anything crazy in front of other people?" As you answer such questions, will your date meet a different "you" than if you were probed for instances when you were shy and retiring?

Snyder and Swann found that people often test for a trait by looking for information that confirms it. If they are trying to find out if someone is an extravert, they often solicit instances of extraversion ("What would you do if you wanted to liven things up at a party?"). Testing for introversion, they are more likely to ask, "What factors make it hard for you to really open up to people?" In response, those probed for extraversion seem more sociable, and those probed for introversion seem more shy. Our assumptions help create the kind of people we expect to see.

At Indiana University, Russell Fazio and his colleagues (1981) reproduced this finding and also discovered that those asked the "extraverted questions" later perceived themselves as actually more outgoing than those asked the introverted questions. Moreover, they really became noticeably more outgoing. An accomplice of the experimenter later met each participant in a waiting room and 70 percent of the time guessed correctly from the person's behavior which condition the person had come from. Likewise, the framing of questions asked of an alleged rape victim—"Did you dance with Peter?" versus "Did Peter dance with you?"—can subtly influence who is perceived as responsible (Semin & De Poot, 1997).

When given the structured list of questions to choose from, even experienced psychotherapists, when testing for extraversion, prefer extraverted questions that trigger extraverted behavior among their interviewees (Copeland & Snyder, 1995; Dallas & Baron, 1985; Snyder & Thomsen, 1988). Even when making up their own questions, interviewers' expectations may influence their questioning if they have definite preexisting ideas (Devine & others, 1990; Hodgins & Zuckerman, 1993; Swann & Giuliano, 1987). In the clinic as in the laboratory, strong beliefs may generate their own confirmation.

Confirmation bias also appears when people evaluate themselves. Consider for a moment: Are you happy with your social life? Zva Kunda and colleagues (1993) put this question to students at the University of Waterloo and elsewhere. The students searched their memories for confirming instances and thus ended up feeling happier than students asked, "Are you unhappy with your social life?" Seek and you shall find.

In other experiments, Snyder and his colleagues (1982) tried to get people to search for behaviors that would *disconfirm* the trait they were testing. In one

"As is your sort of mind,
So is your sort of search:
You'll find
What you desire."
—Robert Browning, 1812–1889

experiment, they told the interviewers, "It is relevant and informative to find out ways in which the person . . . may not be like the stereotype." In another experiment Snyder (1981a) offered "$25 to the person who develops the set of questions that tell the most about . . . the interviewee." Still, confirmation bias persisted: People resisted choosing "introverted" questions when testing for extraversion.

Based on Snyder's experiments, can you see why the behaviors of people undergoing psychotherapy come to fit the theories of their therapists (Whitman & others, 1963)? When Harold Renaud and Floyd Estess (1961) conducted life-history interviews of 100 healthy, successful adult men, they were startled to discover that their subjects' childhood experiences were loaded with "traumatic events," tense relations with certain people, and bad decisions by their parents—the very factors usually used to explain psychiatric problems. When Freudian therapists go fishing for traumas in early childhood experiences, they often find their hunches confirmed. Thus, surmises Snyder (1981a):

> The psychiatrist who believes (erroneously) that adult gay males had bad childhood relationships with their mothers may meticulously probe for recalled (or fabricated) signs of tension between their gay clients and their mothers, but neglect to so carefully interrogate their heterosexual clients about their maternal relationships. No doubt, any individual could recall some friction with his or her mother, however minor or isolated the incidents.

Might therapists' search for hunch-confirming information explain many "recovered memories"? Books such as Ellen Bass and Laura Davis's (1994) *The Courage to Heal* suggest that survivors of child sex abuse are likely to experience feelings of depression, shame, unworthiness, perfectionism, and powerlessness. When patients present such symptoms (which may actually result from many causes), some therapists will search actively for evidence that confirms their suspicions of sex abuse (Harris, 1994; Loftus, 2000; Loftus & Ketcham, 1994; Poole & others, 1995). The therapist may explain that "people who've been abused often have your symptoms, so you probably were abused." If the patient cannot remember any abuse, the therapist may use hypnosis, guided imagery, or dream interpretation in hopes of recovering confirming information. Such confirmation-seeking tactics have led some clients to create memories for events that never happened.

CLINICAL VERSUS STATISTICAL PREDICTION

"A very bright young man who is likely to succeed in life. He is intelligent enough to achieve lofty goals as long as he stays on task and remains motivated."

—Probation officer's clinical intuition in response to Eric Harris's "homicidal thoughts"—two and a half months before he committed the Columbine High School massacre

Given these hindsight- and diagnosis-confirming tendencies, it will come as no surprise that most clinicians and interviewers express more confidence in their intuitive assessments than in statistical data (such as using past grades and aptitude scores to predict success in graduate or professional school). Yet when researchers pit statistical prediction against intuitive prediction, the statistics usually win. Statistical predictions are indeed unreliable, but human intuition—even expert intuition—is even more unreliable (Faust & Ziskin, 1988; Meehl, 1954; Swets & others, 2000).

Three decades after demonstrating the superiority of statistical over intuitive prediction, Paul Meehl (1986) found the evidence stronger than ever:

> There is no controversy in social science which shows [so many] studies coming out so uniformly in the same direction as this one . . . When you are pushing 90 investigations, predicting everything from the outcome of football games to the

diagnosis of liver disease and when you can hardly come up with a half dozen studies showing even a weak tendency in favor of the clinician, it is time to draw a practical conclusion.

Consider examples of this provocative research:

- In *House of Cards: Psychology and Psychotherapy Built on Myth*, Robyn Dawes (1994) reports that during the 1970s the University of Texas Medical School at Houston admitted 150 students annually, based on interviewers' ratings of their 800 most qualified candidates. When the legislature suddenly required them to admit 50 more students, they admitted the only ones still available—those to whom the interviewers had given low ratings. So what was the difference in performance between the two groups? Nil. The top-rated 150 and bottom 50 each had 82 percent of their group receive the M.D. and similar proportions receive honors. Even after the first year of residency, both groups were doing equally well. The unavoidable conclusion: Some people just interview better than others.

- A research team from Canada's Ministry of the Solicitor General combined data from 64 samples of more than 25,000 mentally disordered criminal offenders. What best predicted risk of future offense? As in studies with other types of offenders, it was past criminal activity. What was among the *least* accurate predictors of future criminality? A clinician's judgment (Bonta & others, 1998).

- In an all-encompassing digest ("meta-analysis") of 134 studies predicting human behavior or making psychological or medical diagnoses and prognoses, a University of Minnesota research team reached a similar conclusion (Grove & others, 2000). In only eight of the studies, which were mostly conducted in medical, mental health, or education settings, did clinical prediction surpass "mechanical" (statistical) prediction. In eight times as many (63 studies), statistical prediction fared better (the rest were a virtual draw). Ah, but would clinicians fare differently when given the opportunity for a firsthand clinical interview? Yes, report the researchers: Allowed interviews, the clinicians fared substantially *worse*. "It is fair to say that 'the ball is in the clinicians' court,'" the researchers concluded. "Given the overall deficit in clinicians' accuracy relative to mechanical prediction, the burden falls on advocates of clinical prediction to show that clinicians' predictions are more [accurate or cost-effective]."

What if we combined statistical prediction with clinical intuition? What if we gave professional clinicians the statistical prediction of someone's future academic performance or risk of parole violation or suicide and asked them to refine or improve on the prediction? Alas, in the few studies where this has been done, prediction was better if the "improvements" were ignored (Dawes, 1994).

Why then do so many clinicians continue to interpret Rorschach inkblot tests and offer intuitive predictions about parolees, suicide risks, and likelihood of child abuse? Partly out of sheer ignorance, says Meehl, but also partly out of "mistaken conceptions of ethics":

If I try to forecast something important about a college student, or a criminal, or a depressed patient by inefficient rather than efficient means, meanwhile charging

"The effect of Meehl's work on clinical practice in the mental health area can be summed up in a single word: Zilch. He was honored, elected to the presidency of [the American Psychological Association] at a very young age in 1962, recently elected to the National Academy of Sciences, and ignored."
—Robyn M. Dawes (1989)

When a parole board meets to decide prisoner releases, its members would do best to consider statistical predictors of risk rather than their own impressions.

this person or the taxpayer 10 times as much money as I would need to achieve greater predictive accuracy, that is not a sound ethical practice. That it feels better, warmer, and cuddlier to me as predictor is a shabby excuse indeed.

Such words are shocking. Do Meehl and the other researchers underestimate our intuition? To see why their findings are apparently true, consider the assessment of human potential by graduate admissions interviewers. Dawes (1976) explained why statistical prediction is so often superior to an interviewer's intuition when predicting certain outcomes such as graduate school success:

> What makes us think that we can do a better job of selection by interviewing (students) for a half hour, than we can by adding together relevant (standardized) variables, such as undergraduate GPA, GRE score, and perhaps ratings of letters of recommendation? The most reasonable explanation to me lies in our overevaluation of our cognitive capacity. And it is really cognitive conceit. Consider, for example, what goes into a GPA. Because for most graduate applicants it is based on at least 3½ years of undergraduate study, it is a composite measure arising from a minimum of 28 courses and possibly, with the popularity of the quarter system, as many as 50 . . . Yet you and I, looking at a folder or interviewing someone for a half hour, are supposed to be able to form a better impression than one based on 3½ years of the cumulative evaluations of 20–40 different professors . . . Finally, if we do wish to ignore GPA, it appears that the only reason for doing so is believing that the candidate is particularly brilliant even though his or her record may not show it. What better evidence for such brilliance can we have than a score on a carefully devised aptitude test? Do we really think we are better equipped to assess such aptitude than is the Educational Testing Service, whatever its faults?

IMPLICATIONS

Professional clinicians are "vulnerable to insidious errors and biases," concludes James Maddux (1993). They

- are frequently the victims of illusory correlation;
- are too readily convinced of their own after-the-fact analyses;
- often fail to appreciate that erroneous diagnoses can be self-confirming; and
- often overestimate the predictive powers of their clinical intuition.

"'I beseech ye in the bowels of Christ, think that ye may be mistaken.' I shall like to have that written over the portals of every church, every school, and every courthouse, and, may I say, of every legislative body in the United States."
—Judge Learned Hand, 1951, echoing Oliver Cromwell's 1650 plea to the Church of Scotland

The implications for mental health workers are more easily stated than practiced: Be mindful that clients' verbal agreement with what you say does not prove its validity. Beware of the tendency to see relationships that you expect to see or that are supported by striking examples readily available in your memory. Rely on your notes more than your memory. Recognize that hindsight is seductive: It can lead you to feel overconfident and sometimes to judge yourself too harshly for not hav-

When evaluating clients, mental health workers, like all of us, are vulnerable to cognitive illusions.

ing foreseen outcomes. Guard against the tendency to ask questions that assume your preconceptions are correct; consider opposing ideas and test them, too (Garb, 1994).

Research on illusory thinking has implications not only for mental health workers but for all psychologists. What Lewis Thomas (1978) said of biology may as justly be said of psychology:

> The solidest piece of scientific truth I know of, the one thing about which I feel totally confident, is that we are profoundly ignorant about nature. Indeed, I regard this as the major discovery of the past 100 years of biology . . . It is this sudden confrontation with the depth and scope of ignorance that represents the most significant contribution of 20th century science to the human intellect. We are, at last, facing up to it. In earlier times, we either pretended to understand how things worked or ignored the problem, or simply made up stories to fill the gaps.

Psychology has crept only a little way across the edge of insight into our human condition. Ignorant of their ignorance, some psychologists invent theories to fill gaps in their understanding. Intuitive observation seems to support these theories, even if they are mutually contradictory. Research on illusory thinking therefore leads us to a new humility: It reminds research psychologists why they must test their preconceptions before presenting them as truth. To seek the hard facts, even if they threaten cherished illusions, is the goal of every science.

I am *not* arguing that the scientific method can answer all human questions. There are questions that it cannot address and ways of knowing that it cannot capture. But science *is* one means for examining claims about nature, human nature included. Propositions that imply observable results are best evaluated by systematic observation and experiment—which is the whole point of social psychology. We also need inventive genius, or we may test only trivialities. But whatever unique and enduring insights psychology can offer will be hammered out by research psychologists sorting through competing claims. Science always involves an interplay between intuition and rigorous test, between creative hunch and skepticism.

"One thing I have learned in a long life: that all our science, measured against reality, is primitive and childlike and yet it is the most precious thing we have."
—Albert Einstein, in B. Hoffman & H. Dukes, *Albert Einstein: Creator and Rebel*, 1973

"Science is the great antidote to the poison of enthusiasm and superstition."
—Adam Smith, *Wealth of Nations*, 1776

focus on   a physician's view

Reading this book helps me understand the human behaviors I observe in my work as a cancer specialist and as medical director of a large staff of physicians. A few examples:

Reviews of medical records illustrate the "I-knew-it-all-along phenomenon." Physician reviewers who assess the medical records of their colleagues often believe, in hindsight, that problems such as cancer or appendicitis should clearly have been recognized and treated much more quickly. Once you know the correct diagnosis, it's easy to look back and interpret the early symptoms accordingly.

For many physicians I have known, the intrinsic motives behind their entering the profession—to help people, to be scientifically stimulated—soon become "overjustified" by the high pay. Before long, the joy is lost. The extrinsic rewards become the reason to practice, and the physician, having lost the altruistic motives, works to increase "success," measured in income.

"Self-serving bias" is ever present. We physicians gladly accept personal credit when things go well. When they don't—when the patient is misdiagnosed or doesn't get well or dies—we attribute the failure elsewhere. We were given inadequate information or the case was ill-fated from the beginning.

I also observe many examples of "belief perseverance." Even when presented with the documented facts about, say, how AIDS is transmitted, people will strangely persist in wrongly believing that it is just a "gay" disease or that they should fear catching it from mosquito bites. It makes me wonder: How can I more effectively persuade people of what they need to know and act upon?

Indeed, as I observe medical attitudes and decision making I feel myself submerged in a giant practical laboratory of social psychology. To understand the goings-on around me, I find social psychological insights invaluable and would strongly advise premed students to study the field.

Burton F. VanderLaan,
Chicago, Illinois

Summing up   As psychiatrists and clinical psychologists diagnose and treat their clients, they may perceive *illusory correlations*. *Hindsight* explanations of people's difficulties are sometimes too easy. Indeed, after-the-fact explaining can breed overconfidence in clinical judgment. When interacting with clients, erroneous diagnoses are sometimes *self-confirming*, because interviewers tend to seek and recall information that verifies what they are looking for.

Research on the errors that so easily creep into intuitive judgments illustrates the need for rigorous testing of intuitive conclusions. The scientific method cannot answer all questions and is itself vulnerable to bias. Thankfully, however, it can help us sift truth from falsehood.

What cognitive processes accompany behavior problems?

One of psychology's most intriguing research frontiers concerns the cognitive processes that accompany psychological disorders. What are the memories, attributions, and expectations of depressed, lonely, shy, or illness-prone people?

DEPRESSION

As we all know from experience, depressed people are negative thinkers. They view life through dark-colored glasses. With seriously depressed people—those who are feeling worthless, lethargic, uninterested in friends and family, and unable to sleep or eat normally—the negative thinking becomes self-defeating. Their intensely pessimistic outlook leads them to magnify bad experiences and minimize good ones. A depressed young woman illustrates, "The real me is worthless and inadequate. I can't move forward with my work because I become frozen with doubt" (Burns, 1980, p. 29).

Distortion or realism?

Are all depressed people unrealistically negative? To find out, Lauren Alloy and Lyn Abramson (1979) studied college students who were either mildly depressed or not depressed. They had the students observe whether their pressing a button was linked with a light coming on. Surprisingly, the depressed students were quite accurate in estimating their degree of control. It was the nondepressives whose judgments were distorted, who exaggerated the extent of their control.

This surprising phenomenon of **depressive realism,** nicknamed the "sadder-but-wiser effect," shows up in various judgments of one's control or skill (Ackermann & DeRubeis, 1991; Alloy & others, 1990). Shelley Taylor (1989, p. 214) explains:

> Normal people exaggerate how competent and well liked they are. Depressed people do not. Normal people remember their past behavior with a rosy glow. Depressed people [unless severely depressed] are more evenhanded in recalling their successes and failures. Normal people describe themselves primarily positively. Depressed people describe both their positive and negative qualities. Normal people take credit for successful outcomes and tend to deny responsibility for failure. Depressed people accept responsibility for both success and failure. Normal people exaggerate the control they have over what goes on around them. Depressed people are less vulnerable to the illusion of control. Normal people believe to an unrealistic degree that the future holds a bounty of good things and few bad things. Depressed people are more realistic in their perceptions of the future. In fact, on virtually every point on which normal people show enhanced self-regard, illusions of control, and unrealistic visions of the future, depressed people fail to show the same biases. "Sadder but wiser" does indeed appear to apply to depression.

Underlying the thinking of depressed people are their attributions of responsibility. Consider: If you fail an exam and blame yourself, you may conclude that you are stupid or lazy and feel depressed. If you attribute the failure to an unfair exam or to other circumstances beyond your control, you may feel angry. In over 100 studies involving 15,000 subjects, depressed people have been more likely than nondepressed people to exhibit a negative **explanatory style** (Sweeney & others, 1986; Peterson & Steen, 2002, and Figure 14–2, see page 578). They are more likely to attribute failure and setbacks to causes that are *stable* ("It's going to last forever"), *global* ("It's going to affect everything I do"), and *internal* ("It's all my fault"). The result of this pessimistic, overgeneralized, self-blaming thinking, say Abramson and her colleagues (1989), is a depressing sense of hopelessness.

"Life is the art of being well deceived."
—William Hazlitt, 1778–1830

depressive realism
The tendency of mildly depressed people to make accurate rather than self-serving judgments, attributions, and predictions.

www.mhhe.com/myers8
Visit the Online Learning Center for a scenario on depression and explanatory style.

explanatory style
One's habitual way of explaining life events. A negative, pessimistic, depressive explanatory style attributes failure to stable, global, and internal causes.

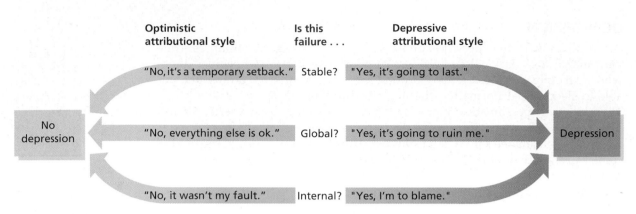

Optimistic attributional style	Is this failure . . .	Depressive attributional style
"No, it's a temporary setback."	Stable?	"Yes, it's going to last."
"No, everything else is ok."	Global?	"Yes, it's going to ruin me."
"No, it wasn't my fault."	Internal?	"Yes, I'm to blame."

figure 14–2

Depressive explanatory style.

Depression is linked with a negative, pessimistic way of explaining and interpreting failures.

Is negative thinking a cause or a result of depression?

The cognitive accompaniments of depression raise a chicken-and-egg question: Do depressed moods cause negative thinking, or does negative thinking cause depression?

Depressed moods cause negative thinking.   As we saw in Chapter 3, our moods definitely color our thinking. When we *feel* happy, we *think* happy. We see and

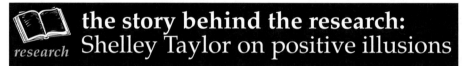

the story behind the research:
Shelley Taylor on positive illusions

Some years ago, I was conducting interviews with people who had cancer for a study on adjustment to intensely stressful events. I was surprised to learn that, for some people, the cancer experience actually seemed to have brought benefits, as well as the expected liabilities. Many people told me that they thought they were better people for the experience, they felt they were better adjusted to cancer than other people, they believed that they could exert control over their cancer in the future, and they believed their futures would be cancer-free, even when we knew from their medical histories that their cancers were likely to recur.

As a result, I became fascinated by how people can construe even the worst of situations as good, and I've studied these "positive illusions" ever since. Through our research, we learned quickly that you don't have to experience a trauma to demonstrate positive illusions. Most people, including the majority of college students, think of themselves as somewhat better than average, as more in control of the circumstances around them than may actually be true, and as likely to experience more positive future outcomes in life than may be realistic. These illusions are not a sign of maladjustment, quite the contrary. Good mental health may depend on the ability to see things as somewhat better than they are and to find benefits even when things seem most bleak.

Shelley Taylor, UCLA

recall a good world. But let our mood turn gloomy, and our thoughts switch to a different track. Off come the rose-colored glasses; on come the dark glasses. Now the bad mood primes our recollections of negative events (Bower, 1987; Johnson & Magaro, 1987). Our relationships seem to sour, our self-images dive, our hopes for the future dim, people's behavior seems more sinister (Brown & Taylor, 1986; Mayer & Salovey, 1987). As depression increases, memories and expectations plummet; when depression lifts, thinking brightens (Barnett & Gotlib, 1988; Kuiper & Higgins, 1985). Thus, *currently* depressed people recall their parents as having been rejecting and punitive. But *formerly* depressed people recall their parents in the same positive terms as do never-depressed people (Lewinsohn & Rosenbaum, 1987). (When you hear depressed people trashing their parents, remember: Moods modify memories.)

Edward Hirt and his colleagues (1992) demonstrated, in a study of Indiana University basketball fans, that even a temporary bad mood induced by defeat can darken our thinking. After the fans were either depressed by watching their team lose or elated by a victory, the researchers asked them to predict the team's future performance, and their own. After a loss, people offered bleaker assessments not only of the team's future but also of their own likely performance at throwing darts, solving anagrams, and getting a date. When things aren't going our way, it may seem as though they never will.

A depressed mood also affects behavior. The person who is withdrawn, glum, and complaining does not elicit joy and warmth in others. Stephen Strack and James Coyne (1983) found that depressed people were realistic in thinking that others didn't appreciate their behavior. Their pessimism and bad moods trigger social rejection (Carver & others, 1994). Depressed behavior can also trigger reciprocal depression in others. College students who have depressed roommates tend to become a little depressed themselves (Burchill & Stiles, 1988; Joiner, 1994; Sanislow & others, 1989). In dating couples, too, depression is often contagious (Katz & others, 1999).

Depressed people are at risk for being divorced, fired, or shunned, thus magnifying their depression (Coyne & others, 1991; Gotlib & Lee, 1989; Sacco & Dunn, 1990). They may also seek out those whose unfavorable views of them verify, and further magnify, their low self-images (Lineham, 1997; Swann & others, 1991). One experiment gave people a choice between reading a favorable assessment of their personality by one graduate student or an unfavorable assessment by another student. Twenty-five percent of high-self-esteem people and 82 percent of depressed people elected to see the unfavorable feedback (Giesler & others, 1996).

Being depressed has cognitive and behavioral effects. Does it also have cognitive origins?

Negative thinking causes depressed moods.   Depression is natural when experiencing severe stress—losing a job, getting divorced or rejected, suffering physical trauma—anything that disrupts our sense of who we are and why we are worthy human beings (Hamilton & others, 1993; Kendler & others, 1993). Such brooding can be adaptive; insights gained during times of depressed inactivity may later result in better strategies for interacting with the world. But depression-prone people respond to bad events with self-focused rumination and self-blame (Mor & Winquist, 2002; Pyszczynski & others, 1991). Their self-esteem fluctuates more rapidly up with boosts and down with threats (Butler & others, 1994).

"To the man who is enthusiastic and optimistic, if what is to come should be pleasant, it seems both likely to come about and likely to be good, while to the indifferent or depressed man it seems the opposite."
—Aristotle, *The Art of Rhetoric*

Stresses challenge some people and defeat others. Researchers have sought to understand the "explanatory style" that makes some people more vulnerable to depression.

Why are some people so affected by *minor* stresses? Evidence suggests that when stress-induced rumination is filtered through a negative explanatory style, the frequent outcome is depression (Robinson & Alloy, 2003). Colin Sacks and Daphne Bugental (1987) asked some young women to get acquainted with a stranger who sometimes acted cold and unfriendly, creating an awkward social situation. Unlike optimistic women, those with a pessimistic explanatory style—who characteristically offer stable, global, and internal attributions for bad events—reacted to the social failure by feeling depressed. Moreover, they then behaved more antagonistically toward the next people they met. Their negative thinking led to a negative mood response, which then led to negative behavior.

Outside the laboratory, studies of children, teenagers, and adults confirm that those with the pessimistic explanatory style are more likely to become depressed when bad things happen. One study monitored university students every six weeks for two and a half years (Alloy & others, 1999). Only 1 percent of those who began college with optimistic thinking styles had a first depressive episode, but 17 percent of those with pessimistic thinking styles did. "A recipe for severe depression is preexisting pessimism encountering failure," notes Martin Seligman (1991, p. 78). Moreover, patients who end therapy no longer feeling depressed but retaining a negative explanatory style tend to relapse as bad events occur (Seligman, 1992). If those with a more optimistic explanatory style relapse, they often recover quickly (Metalsky & others, 1993; Needles & Abramson, 1990).

Researcher Peter Lewinsohn and his colleagues (1985) have assembled these findings into a coherent psychological understanding of depression. In their view, the negative self-image, attributions, and expectations of a depressed person are an essential link in a vicious cycle that is triggered by negative experience—perhaps academic or vocational failure or family conflict or social rejection (Figure 14–3). In those vulnerable to depression, such stresses trigger brooding, self-focused, self-blaming thoughts (Pyszczynski & others, 1991; Wood & others, 1990a, 1990b). Such ruminations create a depressed mood that alters drastically the way a person thinks and acts, which then fuels further negative experiences, self-blame, and depressed mood. In experiments, mildly depressed people's moods brighten when a task diverts their attention to something external (Nix & others, 1995). (Happiness seems best pursued by focusing not on oneself but beyond oneself.)

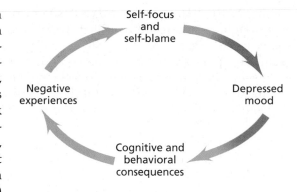

figure 14–3
The vicious cycle of depression.

Depression is therefore *both* a cause and a consequence of negative cognitions.

Martin Seligman (1991, 1998, 2002) believes that self-focus and self-blame help explain the near-epidemic levels of depression in the Western world today. In North America, for example, young adults today are three times as likely as their grandparents to have suffered depression—despite their grandparents' greater years at risk (Cross-National Collaborative Group, 1992; Swindle & others, 2000). Seligman believes that the decline of religion and family, plus the growth of individualism, breeds hopelessness and self-blame when things don't go well. Failed courses, careers, and marriages produce despair when we stand alone, with nothing and no one to fall back on. If, as a macho *Fortune* ad declared, you can "make it on your own," on "your own drive, your own guts, your own energy, your own ambition," then whose fault is it if you *don't* make it? In non-Western cultures, where close-knit relationships and cooperation are the norm, major depression is less common and less tied to guilt and self-blame over perceived personal failure. In Japan, for example, depressed people instead tend to report feeling shame over letting down their family or co-workers (Draguns, 1990).

These insights into the thinking style linked with depression have prompted social psychologists to study thinking patterns associated with other problems. How do those who are plagued with excessive loneliness, shyness, or substance abuse view themselves? How well do they recall their successes and their failures? To what do they attribute their ups and downs? Where is their attention focused—on themselves or on others?

LONELINESS

If depression is the common cold of psychological disorders, then loneliness is the headache. Loneliness, whether chronic or temporary, is a painful awareness that our social relationships are less numerous or meaningful than we desire. Jenny de Jong-Gierveld (1987) observed in her study of Dutch adults that unmarried and unattached people are more likely to feel lonely. This prompted her to speculate that the modern emphasis on individual fulfillment and the depreciation of marriage and family life may be "loneliness-provoking" (as well as depression-provoking). Job-related mobility also makes for fewer long-term family and social ties and increased loneliness (Dill & Anderson, 1999).

Feeling lonely and excluded

But loneliness need not coincide with aloneness. One can feel lonely in the middle of a party. "In America, there is loneliness but no solitude," lamented Mary

What is the significance of time alone on adolescent emotions? Go to the *SocialSense* CD-ROM to view a video clip on adolescent loneliness.

Pipher (2002). "There are crowds but no community." In Los Angeles, observed her daughter, "There are 10 million people around me but nobody knows my name." And one can be utterly alone—as I am while writing these words in the solitude of an isolated turret office at a British university 5,000 miles from home—without feeling lonely. To feel lonely is to feel excluded from a group, unloved by those around you, unable to share your private concerns, or different and alienated from those in your surroundings (Beck & Young, 1978; Davis & Franzoi, 1986).

Adolescents more than adults experience loneliness. When beeped by an electronic pager at various times during a week and asked to record what they were doing and how they felt, adolescents more often than adults reported feeling lonely when alone (Larsen & others, 1982). Males and females feel lonely under somewhat different circumstances—males when isolated from group interaction, females when deprived of close one-to-one relationships (Berg & McQuinn, 1988; Stokes & Levin, 1986). Men's relationships, it is said, tend to be side-by-side; women's relationships tend to be face-to-face. But for all people, including those recently widowed, the loss of a person with whom one has been attached can produce unavoidable feelings of loneliness (Stroebe & others, 1996).

Perceiving others negatively

Like depressed people, chronically lonely people seem caught in a vicious cycle of self-defeating social cognitions and social behaviors. They have some of the negative explanatory style of the depressed; they perceive their interactions as making a poor impression, blame themselves for their poor social relationships, and see most things as beyond their control (Anderson & others, 1994; Christensen & Kashy, 1998; Snodgrass, 1987). Moreover, they perceive others in negative ways. When paired with a stranger of the same gender or with a first-year college roommate, lonely students are more likely to perceive the other person negatively (Jones & others, 1981; Wittenberg & Reis, 1986). As Figure 14–4 illustrates, loneliness, depression, and shyness sometimes feed one another.

These negative views may both reflect and color the lonely person's experience. Believing in their social unworthiness and feeling pessimistic about others inhibit lonely people from acting to reduce their loneliness. Lonely people often find it hard to introduce themselves, make phone calls, and participate in groups (Rook, 1984; Spitzberg & Hurt, 1987; Nurmi & others, 1996, 1997). Being slow to self-disclose, they disdain those who disclose too much too soon (Rotenberg, 1997). They tend to be self-conscious and low in self-esteem (Check & Melchior, 1990; Vaux, 1988). When talking with a stranger, they spend more time talking about themselves and take less interest in their conversational partners than do nonlonely people (Jones & others, 1982). After such conversations, the new acquaintances often come away with more negative impressions of the lonely people (Jones & others, 1983).

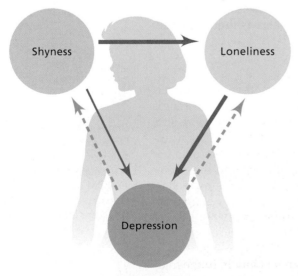

figure 14–4

The interplay of chronic shyness, loneliness, and depression.

Solid arrows indicate primary cause-effect direction, as summarized by Jody Dill and Craig Anderson (1998).

Close relationships and a positive explanatory style help protect people from feelings of loneliness.

ANXIETY

Being interviewed for a much-wanted job, dating someone for the first time, stepping into a roomful of strangers, performing before an important audience, or (the most common phobia) giving a speech can make almost anyone feel anxious. Some people, especially those who are shy or easily embarrassed, feel anxious in almost any situation in which they might be evaluated. For these people, anxiety is more a trait than a temporary state.

Doubting our ability in social situations

What causes us to feel anxious in social situations? Why are some people shackled in the prison of their own shyness? Barry Schlenker and Mark Leary (1982b, 1985; Leary & Kowalski, 1995) answer these questions by applying self-presentation theory. As you may recall from Chapters 2 and 4, self-presentation theory assumes that we are eager to present ourselves in ways that make a good impression. The implications for social anxiety are straightforward: *We feel anxious when we are motivated to impress others but doubt our ability to do so.* This simple principle helps explain a variety of research findings, each of which may ring true in your own experience. We feel most anxious when we are

- with powerful, high-status people—people whose impressions of us matter;
- in an evaluative context, such as when making a first impression on the parents of one's fiancé;
- self-conscious (as shy people often are) and our attention is focused on ourselves and how we are coming across;
- focused on something central to our self-image, as when a college professor presents ideas before peers at a professional convention; or

- in novel or unstructured situations, such as a first school dance or first formal dinner, where we are unsure of the social rules.

The natural tendency in all such situations is to be cautiously self-protective: to talk less; to avoid topics that reveal one's ignorance; to be guarded about oneself; to be unassertive, agreeable, and smiling. Ironically, such anxious concern with making a good impression often makes a bad impression (Broome & Wegner, 1994; Meleshko & Alden, 1993). With time, however, shy people often become well liked. They are less egotistical and their modesty, sensitivity, and discretion wears well (Gough & Thorne, 1986; Paulhus & Morgan, 1997; Shepperd & others, 1995).

Overpersonalizing situations

Shyness is a form of social anxiety characterized by self-consciousness and worry about what others think (Anderson & Harvey, 1988; Asendorpf, 1987; Carver & Scheier, 1986). Compared with unshy people, shy, self-conscious people (whose numbers include many adolescents) see incidental events as somehow relevant to themselves (Fenigstein, 1984; Fenigstein & Vanable, 1992). Shown someone they think is interviewing them live (actually a videotaped interviewer), they perceive the interviewer as less accepting and interested in them (Pozo & others, 1991).

Shy, anxious people also overpersonalize situations, a tendency that breeds anxious concern and, in extreme cases, paranoia. They also overestimate the extent to which other people are watching and evaluating them. If their hair won't comb right or they have a facial blemish, they assume everyone else notices and judges them accordingly. Shy people may even be conscious of their self-consciousness. They wish they could stop worrying about blushing, about what others are thinking, or about what to say next.

When a person is eager to impress important people, social anxiety is natural.

To reduce social anxiety, some people turn to alcohol. Alcohol lowers anxiety as it reduces self-consciousness (Hull & Young, 1983). Thus, chronically self-conscious people are especially likely to drink following a failure. If recovering from alcoholism, they are more likely than those low in self-consciousness to relapse when they again experience stress or failure.

Symptoms as diverse as anxiety and alcohol abuse can also serve a self-handicapping function. Labeling oneself as anxious, shy, depressed, or under the influence of alcohol can provide an excuse for failure (Snyder & Smith, 1986). Behind a barricade of symptoms, the person's ego stands secure. "Why don't I date? Because I'm shy, so people don't easily get to know the real me." The symptom is an unconscious strategic ploy to explain away negative outcomes.

What if we were to remove the need for such a ploy by providing people with a handy alternative explanation for their anxiety and therefore for possible failure? Would a shy person no longer need to be shy? That is precisely what Susan Brodt and Philip Zimbardo (1981) found when they brought shy and not-shy college women to the laboratory and had them converse with a handsome male who posed as another participant. Before the conversation, the women were cooped up in a small chamber and blasted with loud noise. Some of the shy women (but not others) were told that the noise would leave them with a pounding heart, a common symptom of social anxiety. Thus when these women later talked with the man, they could attribute their pounding hearts and any conversational difficulties to the noise, not to their shyness or social inadequacy. Compared with the shy women who were not given this handy explanation for their pounding hearts, these women were no longer so shy. They talked fluently once the conversation got going and asked questions of the man. In fact, unlike the other shy women (whom the man could easily spot as shy), these women were to him indistinguishable from the not-shy women.

ILLNESS

In the industrialized world, at least half of all deaths are linked with behavior— with consuming cigarettes, alcohol, drugs, and harmful foods; with reactions to stress; with lack of exercise and not following a doctor's orders. Efforts to study and change these behavioral contributions to illness helped create a new interdisciplinary field called **behavioral medicine.** Psychology's contribution to this interdisciplinary science is its subfield, **health psychology.** Its numbers include many of the estimated 3,900 psychologists working in Canadian and U.S. medical schools (Williams & Kohut, 1999). Health psychologists study how people respond to illness symptoms and how emotions and explanations influence health.

behavioral medicine
An interdisciplinary field that integrates and applies behavioral and medical knowledge about health and disease.

health psychology
Provides psychology's contribution to behavioral medicine by studying the psychological roots of health and illness.

Reactions to illness

How do people decide whether they are ill? How do they explain their symptoms? What influences their willingness to seek and follow treatment?

Noticing symptoms.   Chances are you have recently experienced at least one of these physical complaints: headache, stomachache, nasal congestion, sore muscles, ringing in the ears, excess perspiration, cold hands, racing heart, dizziness, stiff joints, and diarrhea or constipation (Pennebaker, 1982). Such symptoms require interpretation. Are they meaningless? Or are you coming down with something? Hardly a week goes by without our playing doctor by self-diagnosing the significance of some symptom.

Noticing and interpreting our body's signals is like noticing and interpreting how our car is running. Unless the signals are loud and clear, we often miss them. Most of us cannot tell whether a car needs an oil change merely by listening to its engine. Similarly, most of us are not astute judges of our heart rate, blood-sugar level, or blood pressure. People guess their blood pressure based on how they feel, which often is unrelated to their actual blood pressure (Baumann & Leventhal, 1985). Furthermore, the early signs of many illnesses, including cancer and heart disease, are subtle and easy to miss. Half or more of heart attack victims die before seeking and receiving medical help (Friedman & DiMatteo, 1989).

Explaining symptoms: Am I sick?   With more serious aches and pains, the questions become more specific—and more critical. Does the small cyst match our idea of a malignant lump? Is the stomachache bad enough to be appendicitis? Is the pain in the chest area merely—as many heart attack victims suppose—a muscle spasm? What factors influence how we explain symptoms?

Once we notice symptoms, we interpret them using familiar disease schemas (Bishop, 1991). In medical schools, this can have amusing results. As part of their training, medical students learn the symptoms associated with various diseases. Because they also experience various symptoms, they sometimes attribute their symptoms to recently learned disease schemas. ("Maybe this wheeze is the beginning of pneumonia.") As you may have discovered, psychology students are prone to this same effect as they read about psychological disorders.

Socially constructed disorders.   The commonness and ambiguity of mild symptoms opens the door to social suggestion. On April 13, 1989, some 2,000 spectators assembled in the Santa Monica Civic Auditorium in California to enjoy music performances by 600 secondary school students. Shortly after the program began, the nervous students began complaining to one another of headaches, dizziness, stomachaches, and nausea. Eventually 247 became ill, forcing evacuation of the auditorium. A fire department treatment operation was set up on the lawn outside. Later investigation revealed nothing—no diagnosable illnesses and no environmental problems. The symptoms subsided quickly and were not shared by the audience. The instant epidemic, it seemed, was socially constructed (Small & others, 1991).

Might people also socially construct an everyday ailment? Might people form the idea that their everyday symptoms match those of an ailment they've heard about, and then use it to explain such symptoms? That, researchers Pamela Kato and Diane Ruble (1992) maintain, helps explain why many women believe they are more depressed, tense, and irritable during the two or three days before menstruation. As we saw in Chapter 4, illusory correlations occur when people notice and remember instances that confirm their beliefs and do not notice instances that contradict them. Thus, a woman who feels tense the day before her period is due may attribute the tension to the so-called premenstrual syndrome (PMS). But if the woman feels similarly tense a week later or does not feel tense the day her next period is about to start, she may be less likely to notice and remember these disconfirming instances.

Many researchers now believe that some women do indeed experience not only menstrual discomfort but also premenstrual tension (Hurt & others, 1992; Richardson, 1990; Schmidt & others, 1998). Thus, the American Psychiatric Association included a severe form of PMS (called *premenstrual dysphoric disorder*) in *DSM-IV*. They did so despite objections from the American Psychological Association and from the Psychiatric Association's Committee on Women, which maintain that women's menstrual cycle problems should not be pathologized as a psychiatric disorder (DeAngelis, 1993).

Several studies have engaged Canadian and Australian women in keeping daily mood diaries (Hardie, 1997; and see Figure 14–5). Although many women *recall* feeling out of sorts just before their last period, their own day-to-day self-reports often reveal little emotional fluctuation across the menstrual cycle. Moreover, women who *say* they suffer PMS don't differ in mood fluctuations from those who don't. In one study, those who reported severe premenstrual symptoms differed only slightly from other women in actual day-to-day reports

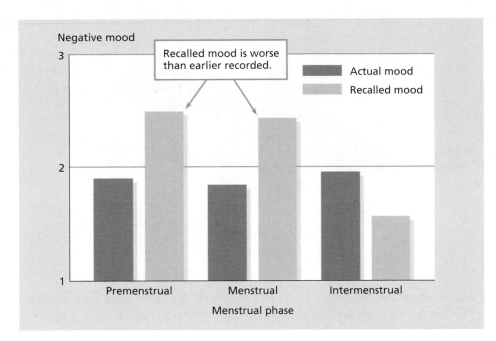

figure 14–5

Menstruation, actual mood, and recalled mood.

Cathy McFarland and her colleagues (1989) found that Ontario women's daily mood reports did not vary across their menstrual cycle. Yet they *recalled* that their moods were generally worse just before and during menstruation and better at other times of the cycle.

throughout their menstrual cycles (Gallant & others, 1992). And contrary to the presumptions of some employers, women's physical and mental skills do not fluctuate noticeably with their menstrual cycles. Leta Hollingworth discovered this in her 1914 doctoral dissertation (using women's daily reports rather than their recollections). Many others since then have confirmed her finding (Rosenberg, 1984; Sommer, 1992).

Moreover, PMS complaints vary with culture but not with any known biological differences among women. All this is just what one would expect from a socially constructed disorder, say critics (Richardson, 1993; Rodin, 1992; Usher, 1992). With so many everyday symptoms on PMS checklists—lethargy, sadness, irritability, headaches, insomnia (or sleepiness), disinterest in sex (or heightened interest in sex)—"who wouldn't have 'PMS'?" asked Carol Tavris (1992).

Do I need treatment?   Once people notice a symptom and interpret it as possibly serious, several factors influence their decision to seek medical care. People more often seek treatment if they believe their symptoms have a physical rather than a psychological cause (Bishop, 1987). They may delay seeking help, however, if they feel embarrassed, if they think the likely benefits of medical attention won't justify the cost and inconvenience, or if they want to avoid a possibly devastating diagnosis.

The U.S. National Center for Health Statistics reports a gender difference in decisions to seek medical treatment: Women report more symptoms, use more prescription and nonprescription drugs, and visit physicians 40 percent more often. Women also visit psychotherapists 50 percent more often (Olfson & Pincus, 1994).

Are women more often sick? Apparently not. In fact, men may be more disease-prone. Among other problems, men have higher rates of hypertension, ulcers, and cancer, as well as shorter life expectancies. So why are women more likely to see a doctor? Perhaps women are more attentive to their internal states.

"When a man can't explain a woman's actions, the first thing he thinks about is the condition of her uterus."
—Clare Boothe Luce, *Slam the Door Softly,* 1970

figure 14–6

Stress-caused negative emotions may have various effects on health. This is especially so for depressed or anger-prone people.

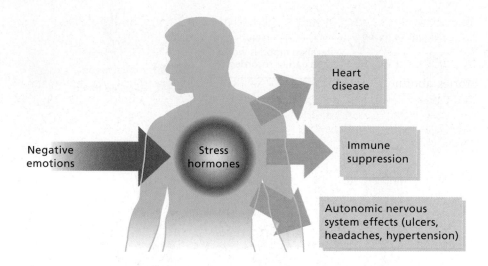

Perhaps they are less reluctant to admit "weakness" and seek help (Bishop, 1984). Or perhaps women simply feel freer to make time for a doctor's appointment (Marcus & Siegel, 1982).

Patients are more willing to follow treatment instructions when they have warm relationships with their doctors, when they help plan their treatment, and when options are framed attractively. People are more likely to elect an operation when given "a 40 percent chance of surviving" than when given "a 60 percent chance of not surviving" (Rothman & Salovey, 1997; Wilson & others, 1987). Such "gain-framed" messages also persuade more people to use sunscreen, disdain cigarettes, and get HIV tests (Detweiler & others, 1999; Schneider & others, 2000; Salovey & others, 2002). Better to tell people that "sunscreen maintains healthy, young-looking skin" than to tell them that "not using sunscreen decreases your chances of healthy, young-looking skin."

Emotions and illness

Do our emotions predict our susceptibility to heart disease, stroke, cancer, and other ailments (Figure 14–6)? Consider the following.

Heart disease has been linked with a competitive, impatient, and—the aspect that matters—*anger-prone* personality (Smith & Ruiz, 2002; Williams, 1993). Under stress, reactive, anger-prone "Type A" people secrete more of the stress hormones believed to accelerate the buildup of plaque on the walls of the heart's arteries.

Depression also increases the risk of various ailments. Mildly depressed people are more vulnerable to heart disease, even after controlling for differences in smoking and other disease-related factors (Anda & others, 1993). The year after a heart attack, depressed people have a doubled risk of further heart problems (Frasure-Smith & others, 1995, 1999). The toxicity of negative emotions contributes to the high rate of depression and anxiety among chronically ill people (Cohen & Rodriguez, 1995).

When George Vaillant (1997) followed a group of male Harvard alums from midlife into old age he witnessed the effect of distress and negative emotion. Of those whom at age 52 he classified as "squares" (having never abused alcohol, used tranquilizers, or seen a psychiatrist), only 5 percent had died by age 75. Of those classified as "distressed" (who had abused alcohol and either used tranquilizers or seen a psychiatrist), 38 percent had died.

Optimism and health

Stories abound of people who take a sudden turn for the worse when something makes them lose hope, or who suddenly improve when hope is renewed. As cancer attacks the liver of nine-year-old Jeff, his doctors fear the worst. But Jeff remains optimistic. He is determined to grow up to be a cancer research scientist. One day Jeff is elated. A specialist who has taken a long-distance interest in his case is planning to stop off while on a cross-country trip. There is so much Jeff wants to tell the doctor and to show him from the diary he has kept since he got sick. On the anticipated day, fog blankets his city. The doctor's plane is diverted to another city, from which the doctor flies on to his final destination. Hearing the news, Jeff cries quietly. The next morning, pneumonia and fever have developed, and Jeff lies listless. By evening he is in a coma. The next afternoon he dies (Visintainer & Seligman, 1983).

Understanding the links between attitudes and disease requires more than dramatic true stories. If hopelessness coincides with cancer, we are left to wonder: Does cancer breed hopelessness, or does hopelessness also hinder resistance to cancer? To resolve this chicken-and-egg riddle, researchers have (1) experimentally created hopelessness by subjecting organisms to uncontrollable stresses and (2) correlated the hopeless explanatory style with future illnesses.

Stress and illness.   The clearest indication of the effects of hopelessness—what Chapter 2 labels *learned helplessness*—comes from experiments that subject animals to mild but uncontrollable electric shocks, loud noises, or crowding. Such experiences do not cause diseases such as cancer, but they do lower the body's resistance. Rats injected with live cancer cells more often develop and die of tumors if they also receive inescapable shocks than if they receive escapable shocks or no shocks. Moreover, compared with juvenile rats given controllable shocks, those given uncontrollable shocks are twice as likely in adulthood to develop tumors if given cancer cells and another round of shocks (Visintainer & Seligman, 1985). Animals that have learned helplessness react more passively, and blood tests reveal a weakened immune response.

It's a big leap from rats to humans. But a growing body of evidence reveals that people who undergo highly stressful experiences become more vulnerable to disease. Sustained stress directs energy from the immune system, leaving us more vulnerable to infections and malignancy (Cohen, 2002). The death of a spouse, the stress of a space flight landing, even the strain of an exam week have all been associated with depressed immune defenses (Jemmott & Locke, 1984).

Consider:

- A temporary stress magnified the severity of symptoms experienced by volunteers who were knowingly infected with a cold virus (Dixon, 1986).
- Newlywed couples who became angry while discussing problems suffered more immune system suppression the next day (Kiecolt-Glaser & others, 1993).
- A large Swedish study found that, compared with unstressed workers, those with a history of workplace stress had 5.5 times greater risk of

colon cancer (Courtney & others, 1993). The cancer difference was not attributable to differences in age, smoking, drinking, or physical traits.

- Compared with nonprocrastinating students, carefree procrastinators reported lower stress and illness early in a semester but higher stress and illness late in the term. Overall, the self-defeating procrastinators also were sicker and got lower grades (Tice & Baumeister, 1997).

Explanatory style and illness. If uncontrollable stress affects health, depresses immune functioning, and generates a passive, hopeless resignation, then will people who exhibit such pessimism be more vulnerable to illness? Several studies have confirmed that a pessimistic style of explaining bad events (saying, "It's my responsibility, it's going to last, and it's going to undermine everything") makes illness more likely. Christopher Peterson and Martin Seligman (1987) studied the press quotations of 94 members of baseball's Hall of Fame and gauged how often they offered pessimistic (stable, global, internal) explanations for bad events, such as losing big games. Those who routinely did so tended to die at somewhat younger ages. Optimists—who offered stable, global, and internal explanations for good events—usually outlived the pessimists.

Michael Scheier and Charles Carver (1992) similarly report that optimists (who agree, for example, that "I usually expect the best") are less often bothered by various illnesses and recover faster from coronary bypass surgery. They also cope with physical adversity more actively and effectively and with greater happiness (Affleck & others, 2000; Aspinwall & Taylor, 1997; Scheier & others, 2000).

Other studies have followed lives through time. In one study, reported by Peterson and his colleagues (1988), introductory psychology students who offered optimistic explanations for bad events suffered fewer colds, sore throats, and flus a year later. In another, Harvard graduates who expressed the most optimism in 1946 were the healthiest when restudied 34 years later. In yet another, Catholic nuns who expressed the most positive feelings at an average age of 22 outlived their more dour counterparts by an average seven years over the

The Delany sisters, both over 100, attributed their longevity to a positive outlook on life.

ensuing half century and more (Danner & others, 2001). Healthy behaviors—exercise, good nutrition, not drinking to excess—are an essential contributor to the longevity of many optimists (Peterson & Bossio, 2000).

From their own studies, researchers Howard Tennen and Glenn Affleck (1987) agree that a positive, hopeful explanatory style is generally good medicine. The healing power of positive belief is evident in the well-known *placebo effect*, referring to the healing power of *believing* that one is getting an effective treatment. (If you *think* a treatment is going to be effective, it just may be—even if it's actually inert.) Tennen and Affleck also remind us that every silver lining has a cloud. Optimists may see themselves as invulnerable and thus fail to take sensible precautions. (Those who smoke hazardous high-tar cigarettes optimistically underestimate the risks involved [Segerstrom & others, 1993].) And when things go wrong in a big way—when the optimist encounters a devastating illness—adversity can be shattering. Optimism *is* good for health. But remember: Even optimists have a mortality rate of 100 percent.

"You are dust, and to dust you shall return."
—Genesis 3:19

Summing up

Social psychologists are actively exploring the attributions and expectations of depressed, lonely, socially anxious, and physically ill people. Depressed people have a *negative explanatory style*. Compared with nondepressed people, they engage in more self-blame, they interpret and recall events in a more negative light, and they are less hopeful about the future. Despite their more negative judgments, mildly depressed people in laboratory tests tend to be surprisingly realistic.

Depressed thinking has consequences for the depressed person's behavior, which in turn helps maintain a self-defeating cycle. Much the same can be said of those who suffer chronic loneliness and states of social anxiety, such as extreme shyness.

The mushrooming field of health psychology is exploring how people decide they are ill, how they explain their symptoms, and when they seek and follow treatment. It also is exploring the effects of negative emotions and the links among illness, stress, and a pessimistic explanatory style.

What are some social-psychological approaches to treatment?

We have considered patterns of thinking that are linked with problems in living, ranging from serious depression to extreme shyness to physical illness. Do these maladaptive thought patterns suggest any treatments?

There is no social-psychological therapy. But therapy is a social encounter, and social psychologists have suggested how their principles might be integrated into existing treatment techniques (Forsyth & Leary, 1997; Strong & others, 1992). Consider three approaches.

INDUCING INTERNAL CHANGE THROUGH EXTERNAL BEHAVIOR

In Chapter 4, we reviewed a broad range of evidence for a simple but powerful principle: Our actions affect our attitudes. The roles we play, the things we say and do, and the decisions we make influence who we are.

Consistent with this attitudes-follow-behavior principle, several psychotherapy techniques prescribe action. Behavior therapists try to shape behavior and assume that inner dispositions will tag along after the behavior changes. Assertiveness training employs the foot-in-the-door procedure. The individual first role-plays assertiveness in a supportive context, then gradually becomes assertive in everyday life. Rational-emotive therapy assumes that we generate our own emotions; clients receive "homework" assignments to talk and act in new ways that will generate new emotions: Challenge that overbearing relative. Stop telling yourself you're an unattractive person and ask someone out. Self-help groups subtly induce participants to behave in new ways in front of the group—to express anger, cry, act with high self-esteem, express positive feelings. All these techniques share a common assumption: If we cannot directly control our feelings by sheer willpower, we can influence them indirectly through our behavior.

Experiments confirm that what we say about ourselves can affect how we feel. In one experiment, students were induced to write self-laudatory essays (Mirels & McPeek, 1977). These students, more than others who wrote essays about a current social issue, later expressed higher self-esteem when rating themselves privately for a different experimenter. In several more experiments, Edward Jones and his associates (1981; Rhodewalt & Agustsdottir, 1986) influenced students to present themselves to an interviewer in either self-enhancing or self-deprecating ways. Again, the public displays—whether upbeat or downbeat—carried over to later private responses on a test of actual self-esteem. Saying is believing, even when we talk about ourselves. This was especially true when the students were made to feel responsible for how they presented themselves.

The importance of perceived choice was apparent in an experiment by Pamela Mendonca and Sharon Brehm (1983). They invited one group of overweight children who were about to begin a weight-loss program to choose the treatment they preferred. Then they reminded them periodically that they had chosen their treatment. Other children who simultaneously experienced the same eight-week program were given no choice. Those who felt responsible for their treatment had lost more weight both at the end of the eight weeks and three months later.

When choice and personal responsibility is yoked to a high level of effort, the impact is even greater, report Danny Axsom and Joel Cooper (1985; Axsom, 1989). They put women who wanted to lose weight through some supposedly (but not actually) therapeutic tasks, such as making perceptual judgments. Those who committed the most effort to the tasks lost the most weight. This result is especially evident when the commitment is freely chosen. So, the most therapeutic commitments are both uncoerced and effortful.

BREAKING VICIOUS CYCLES

If depression, loneliness, and social anxiety maintain themselves through a vicious cycle of negative experiences, negative thinking, and self-defeating behavior, it should be possible to break the cycle at any of several points—by changing the environment, by training the person to behave more constructively, by reversing negative thinking. And it is. Several different therapy methods help free people from depression's vicious cycle.

Social skills training

Depression, loneliness, and shyness are not just problems in someone's mind. To be around a depressed person for any length of time can be irritating and depressing. As lonely and shy people suspect, they may indeed come across poorly in social situations. In these cases, social skills training may help. By observing and then practicing new behaviors in safe situations, the person may develop the confidence to behave more effectively in other situations.

As the person begins to enjoy the rewards of behaving more skillfully, a more positive self-perception develops. Frances Haemmerlie and Robert Montgomery (1982, 1984, 1986) demonstrated this in several heartwarming studies with shy, anxious college students. Those who are inexperienced and nervous around those of the other sex may say to themselves, "I don't date much, so I must be socially inadequate, so I shouldn't try reaching out to anyone." To reverse this negative sequence, Haemmerlie and Montgomery enticed such students into pleasant interactions with people of the other sex.

In one experiment, college men completed social anxiety questionnaires and then came to the laboratory on two different days. Each day they enjoyed 12-minute conversations with each of six young women. The men thought the women were also participants. Actually, the women were confederates who had been asked to carry on a natural, positive, friendly conversation with each of the men.

The effect of these two and a half hours of conversation was remarkable. As one participant wrote afterward, "I had never met so many girls that I could have a good conversation with. After a few girls, my confidence grew to the point where I didn't notice being nervous like I once did." Such comments were supported by a variety of measures. Unlike men in a control condition, those who experienced the conversations reported considerably less female-related anxiety when retested one week and six months later. Placed alone in a room with an attractive female stranger, they also became much more likely to start a conversation. Outside the laboratory they actually began occasional dating.

Haemmerlie and Montgomery note that not only did all this occur without any counseling but it may very well have occurred *because* there was no

Social skills training: When shy, anxious people observe, then rehearse, then try out more assertive behaviors in real situations, their social skills often improve.

counseling. Having behaved successfully on their own, the men could now perceive themselves as socially competent. Although seven months later the researchers did debrief the participants, by that time the men had presumably enjoyed enough social success to maintain their internal attributions for success. "Nothing succeeds like success," concluded Haemmerlie (1987)—"as long as there are no external factors present that the client can use as an excuse for that success!"

Explanatory style therapy

The vicious cycles that maintain depression, loneliness, and shyness can be broken by social skills training, by positive experiences that alter self-perceptions, *and* by changing negative thought patterns. Some people have social skills, but their experiences with hypercritical friends and family have convinced them they do not. For such people it may be enough to help them reverse their negative beliefs about themselves and their futures. Among the cognitive therapies with this aim is an *explanatory style therapy* proposed by social psychologists (Abramson, 1988; Gillham & others, 2000a, b; Greenberg & others, 1992).

One such program taught depressed college students to change their typical attributions. Mary Anne Layden (1982) first explained the advantages of making attributions more like those of the typical nondepressed person (by accepting credit for successes and seeing how circumstances can make things go wrong). After assigning a variety of tasks, she helped the students see how they typically interpreted success and failure. Then came the treatment phase: Layden instructed them to keep a diary of daily successes and failures, noting how they contributed to their own successes and noting external reasons for their failures. When retested after a month of this attributional retraining and compared with an untreated control group, their self-esteem had risen and their attributional style had become more positive. The more their explanatory style improved, the more their depression lifted. By changing their attributions, they had changed their emotions.

MAINTAINING CHANGE THROUGH INTERNAL ATTRIBUTIONS FOR SUCCESS

Two of the principles considered so far—that internal change may follow behavior change and that changed self-perceptions and self-attributions can help break a vicious cycle—converge on a corollary principle: Once improvement is achieved, it endures best if people attribute it to factors under their own control rather than to a treatment program.

As a rule, coercive techniques trigger the most drastic and immediate behavior changes (Brehm & Smith, 1986). By making the unwanted behavior extremely costly or embarrassing and the healthier behavior extremely rewarding, a therapist may achieve quick and dramatic results. The problem, as 30 years of social-psychological research reminds us, is that coerced changes in behavior soon wane.

Consider the experience of Martha, who is concerned with her mild obesity and frustrated with her inability to do anything about it. Martha is considering several different commercial weight-control programs. Each claims it achieves the best results. She chooses one and is ordered onto a strict 1,200-calorie-a-day diet. Moreover, she is required to record and report her calorie intake each day and to come in once a week and be weighed so she and her instructor can know precisely how she is doing. Confident of the program's value and not wanting to embarrass herself, Martha adheres to the program and is delighted to find the unwanted pounds gradually disappearing. "This unique program really does work!" Martha tells herself as she reaches her target weight.

Sadly, however, after graduating from the program, Martha's experience repeats that of most weight-control graduates (Jeffery & others, 2000): She regains the lost weight. On the street, she sees her instructor approaching. Embarrassed, she moves to the other side of the sidewalk and looks away. Alas, she is recognized by the instructor, who warmly invites her back into "the program." Admitting that the program achieved good results for her the first time, Martha grants her need of it and agrees to return, beginning a second round of yo-yo dieting.

Martha's experience typifies that of the participants in several weight-control experiments, including one by Janet Sonne and Dean Janoff (1979). Half the participants were led, like Martha, to attribute their changed eating behavior to the program. The others were led to credit their own efforts. Both groups lost weight during the program. But when reweighed 11 weeks later, those in the self-control condition had maintained the weight loss best. These people, like those in the shy-man-meets-women study described earlier, illustrate the benefits of self-efficacy. Having learned to cope successfully and believing that *they did it*, they felt more confident and were more effective.

Having emphasized what changed behavior and thought patterns can accomplish, we do well to remind ourselves of their limits. Social skills training and positive thinking cannot transform us into consistent winners who are loved and admired by everyone. Furthermore, temporary depression, loneliness, and shyness are perfectly appropriate responses to profoundly sad events. It is when such feelings exist chronically and without any discernible cause that there is reason for concern and a need to change the self-defeating thoughts and behaviors.

USING THERAPY AS SOCIAL INFLUENCE

Psychologists more and more accept the idea that social influence—one person affecting another—is at the heart of therapy. Stanley Strong (1991) offers a prototypical example: A thirtyish woman comes to a therapist complaining of depression. The therapist gently probes her feelings and her situation. She explains her helplessness and her husband's demands. Although admiring her devotion, the therapist helps her see how she takes responsibility for her husband's problems. She protests. But the therapist persists. In time, she grants that her husband may not be as fragile as she presumed. She begins to see how she can respect both her husband and herself. With the therapist, she plans strategies for each new week. At the end of a long stream of reciprocal influences between therapist and client, she emerges no longer depressed and with new ways of behaving.

Early analyses of psychotherapeutic influence focused on how therapists establish credible expertise and trustworthiness and how their credibility enhances their influence (Strong, 1968). More recent analyses have focused less on the therapist than on how the interaction affects the client's thinking (Cacioppo & others, 1991; McNeill & Stoltenberg, 1988; Neimeyer & others, 1991). Peripheral cues, such as therapist credibility, may open the door for ideas that the therapist can now get the client to think about. But the thoughtful central route to persuasion provides the most enduring attitude and behavior change. Therapists should therefore aim not to elicit a client's superficial agreement with their expert judgment but to change the client's own thinking.

Fortunately, most clients entering therapy are motivated to take the central route, to think deeply about their problems under the therapist's guidance. The therapist's task is to offer arguments and raise questions calculated to elicit favorable thoughts. The therapist's insights matter less than the thoughts they evoke in the client. The therapist needs to put things in ways that a client can hear and understand, ways that will prompt agreement rather than counterargument, and that will allow time and space for the client to reflect. Questions such as "How do you respond to what I just said?" can stimulate the client's thinking.

Martin Heesacker (1989) illustrates with the case of Dave, a 35-year-old male graduate student. Having seen what Dave denied—an underlying substance abuse problem—the counselor drew on his knowledge of Dave, an intellectual person who liked hard evidence, in persuading him to accept the diagnosis and join a treatment-support group. The counselor said, "OK, if my diagnosis is wrong, I'll be glad to change it. But let's go through a list of the characteristics of a substance abuser to check out my accuracy." The counselor then went through each criterion slowly, giving Dave time to think about each point. As he finished, Dave sat back and exclaimed, "I don't believe it: I'm a damned alcoholic."

In an experiment, John Ernst and Heesacker (1993) showed the effectiveness of escorting participants in an assertion training workshop through the central route to persuasion. Some participants experienced the typical assertiveness workshop by learning and rehearsing concepts of assertiveness. Others learned the same concepts but also volunteered a time when they hurt themselves by being unassertive. Then they heard arguments that Ernst and Heesacker knew were likely to trigger favorable thoughts (for example, "By failing to assert yourself, you train others to mistreat you"). At the workshop's end, Ernst and Heesacker asked the people to stop and reflect on how they now felt about all they had learned. Compared with those in the first group, those who went through the thought-evoking workshop left the experience with more favorable attitudes and intentions regarding assertiveness. Moreover, their roommates noticed greater assertiveness during the ensuing two weeks.

In his 1620 *Pensées*, the philosopher Pascal foresaw this principle: "People are usually more convinced by reasons they discover themselves than by those found by others." It's a principle worth remembering.

Summing up

Among the social-psychological principles that may be usefully applied in treatment are these three: (1) Changes in external behavior can trigger internal change. (2) A self-defeating cycle of negative attitudes and behaviors can be broken by training more skillful behavior, by positive experiences that alter self-perceptions, and by changing negative thought patterns. (3) Improved states are best maintained after treatment if people attribute their improvement to internal factors under their continued control rather than to the treatment program itself.

Mental health workers also are recognizing that changing clients' attitudes and behaviors requires persuasion. Therapists, aided by their image as expert, trustworthy communicators, aim to stimulate healthier thinking by offering cogent arguments and raising questions.

How do social relationships support health and well-being?

There is one other major topic in the social psychology of mental and physical well-being. Supportive close relationships—feeling liked, affirmed, and encouraged by intimate friends and family—predict both health and happiness.

Our relationships are fraught with stress. "Hell is others," wrote Jean-Paul Sartre. When Peter Warr and Roy Payne (1982) asked a representative sample of British adults what, if anything, had emotionally strained them the day before, "family" was their most frequent answer. And stress, as we have seen, aggravates health problems such as coronary heart disease, hypertension, and suppression of our disease-fighting immune system.

Still, on balance, close relationships contribute less to illness than to health and happiness. Asked what prompted yesterday's times of pleasure, the same British sample, by an even larger margin, again answered "family." Close relationships provide our greatest heartaches, but also our greatest joys.

CLOSE RELATIONSHIPS AND HEALTH

Eight massive investigations, each interviewing thousands of people across several years, have reached a common conclusion: Close relationships predict health (Berkman, 1995; Ryff & Singer, 2000). Health risks are greater among lonely people, who often experience more stress, sleep less well, and commit suicide more often (Cacioppo & others, 2002a, b; 2003). Compared with those with few social ties, those who have close relationships with friends, kin, or other members of close-knit religious or community organizations are less likely to die prematurely. Outgoing, affectionate, relationship-oriented people not only have more friends, they are less susceptible to experimentally injected cold viruses (see Figure 14–7, Cohen & others, 1997, 2003). Moreover, in one five-year study of 423 elderly married couples, those who *gave* the most social

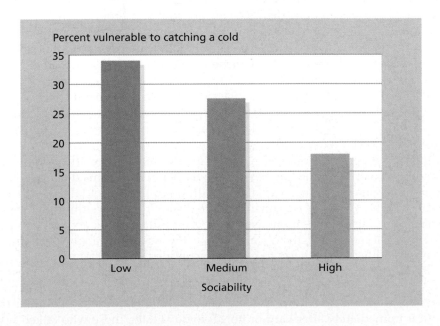

figure 14–7

Rate of colds by sociability.

After a cold virus injection, highly sociable people were less vulnerable to catching colds. **Source:** From Cohen & others, 2003.

support (from rides and errands for friends and neighbors to emotional support of their spouse) enjoyed greater longevity, even after controlling for age, sex, initial health, and economic status (Brown & others, 2003). It is, it seems, better to give than only to receive.

Losing social ties heightens the risk of disease.

- A Finnish study of 96,000 widowed people found their risk of death doubled in the week following their partner's death (Kaprio & others, 1987).
- A National Academy of Sciences study reveals that those who are recently widowed become more vulnerable to disease and death (Dohrenwend & others, 1982).
- A study of 30,000 men revealed that when a marriage ends, men drink and smoke more and eat fewer vegetables and more fried foods (Eng & others, 2001).

Confiding and health

So there is a link between social support and health. Why? Perhaps those who enjoy close relationships eat better, exercise more, and smoke and drink less. Perhaps friends and family help bolster our self-esteem. Perhaps a supportive network helps us evaluate and overcome stressful events (Taylor & others, 1997). In more than 80 studies, social support has been linked with better functioning cardiovascular and immune systems (Uchino & others, 1996). Thus, when we are wounded by someone's dislike or the loss of a job, a friend's advice, help, and reassurance may indeed be good medicine (Cutrona, 1986; Rook, 1987). Even when the problem isn't mentioned, friends provide us with distraction and a sense that, come what may, we're accepted, liked, and respected.

"Friendship is a
sovereign antidote
against all calamities."
—Seneca, 5 B.C.–A.D. 65

We may confide painful feelings with someone we consider a close friend. In one study, James Pennebaker and Robin O'Heeron (1984) contacted the surviving spouses of suicide or car accident victims. Those who bore their grief alone had more health problems than those who expressed it openly. When Pennebaker (1990) surveyed more than 700 college women, he found 1 in 12 reported a traumatic sexual experience in childhood. Compared with women who had experienced nonsexual traumas, such as parental death or divorce, the sexually abused women reported more headaches, stomach ailments, and other health problems, *especially if they had kept their secret to themselves.*

To isolate the confiding, confessional side of close relationships, Pennebaker asked the bereaved spouses to relate the upsetting events that had been preying on their minds. Those they first asked to describe a trivial event were physically tense. They stayed tense until they confided their troubles. Then they relaxed. Writing about personal traumas in a diary also seems to help. When volunteers in another experiment did so, they had fewer health problems during the next six months. One participant explained, "Although I have not talked with anyone about what I wrote, I was finally able to deal with it, work through the pain instead of trying to block it out. Now it doesn't hurt to think about it." Even if it's only "talking to my diary," and even if the writing is about one's future dreams and life goals, it helps to be able to confide (King, 2001).

Other experiments confirm the benefits of engaging rather than suppressing stressful experiences. In one, Stephen Lepore and his colleagues (2000) had students view a stressful slide show and video on the Holocaust and either talk about it immediately afterward or not. Two days later, those who talked were experiencing less stress and fewer intrusive thoughts. Even mentally revisiting a recent problem that was still "stressing you out"—vividly recalling the incident and associated feelings—served to boost active coping and mood (Rivkin & Taylor, 1999).

Poverty, inequality, and health

We have seen connections between health and the feelings of control that accompany a positive explanatory style. And we have seen connections between health and social support. Feelings of control and support together with health care and nutrition factors help explain why economic status correlates with longevity. Recall from Chapter 1 the study of old Glasgow, Scotland, grave markers: Those with the costliest, highest pillars (indicating affluence) tended to live the longest (Carroll & others, 1994). Still today, in Scotland, the United States, and Canada, poorer people are at greater risk for premature death. Poverty predicts perishing. To be poor is to be at risk for increased stress, negative emotions, and a toxic environment (Adler & Snibbe, 2003; Gallo & Matthews, 2003). Even among primates, those with the least control—at the bottom of the social pecking order—are most vulnerable when exposed to a coldlike virus (Cohen & others, 1997).

People also die younger in regions with great income inequality (Kawachi & others, 1999; Lynch & others, 1998; Marmot & Wilkinson, 1999). People in Britain and the United States have larger income disparities and lower life expectancies than people in Japan and Sweden. Where inequality has grown over the last decade, as in Eastern Europe and Russia, life expectancy has been at the falling end of the teeter-totter.

Is inequality merely an indicator of poverty? The mixed evidence indicates that poverty matters, but that inequality matters, too. John Lynch and his colleagues (1998, 2000) report that people at every income level are at greater risk of early death if they live in a community with great income inequality.

CLOSE RELATIONSHIPS AND HAPPINESS

Confiding painful feelings is good not only for the body but for the soul as well. That's the conclusion of studies showing that people are happier when supported by a network of friends and family.

Some studies, summarized in Chapter 2, compare people in a competitive, individualistic culture, such as the United States, Canada, and Australia, with those in collectivist cultures, such as Japan and many developing countries. Individualistic cultures offer independence, privacy, and pride in personal achievements. The tighter social bonds of collectivist cultures offer protection from loneliness, alienation, divorce, and stress-related diseases. Even within an individualistic country, those who have a relatively group-centered approach to life report greater life satisfaction than do individualists (Bettencourt & Dorr, 1997).

"Woe to him who is alone when he falls and has not another to lift him up."
—Ecclesiastes 4:10b

Friendships and happiness

Other studies compare individuals with few or many close relationships. Being attached to friends with whom we can share intimate thoughts has two effects, observed the seventeenth-century philosopher Francis Bacon. "It redoubleth joys, and cutteth griefs in half." So it seems from answers to a question asked of Americans by the National Opinion Research Center (Burt, 1986): "Looking over the last six months, who are the people with whom you discussed matters important to you?" Compared with those who could name no such intimate, those who named five or more such friends were 60 percent more likely to feel "very happy."

Other findings confirm the importance of social networks. Across the life span, friendships foster self-esteem and well-being (Hartup & Stevens, 1997). For example,

- The happiest university students are those who feel satisfied with their love life (Emmons & others, 1983).

- Those who enjoy close relationships cope better with various stresses, including bereavement, rape, job loss, and illness (Abbey & Andrews, 1985; Perlman & Rook, 1987).

- Among 800 alumni of Hobart and William Smith Colleges surveyed by Wesley Perkins, those with "Yuppie values"—those who preferred a high income and occupational success and prestige to having very close friends and a close marriage—were twice as likely as their former classmates to describe themselves as "fairly" or "very" unhappy (Perkins, 1991).

- When asked "What is necessary for your happiness?" or "What is it that makes your life meaningful?," most people mention—before anything else—satisfying close relationships with family, friends, or romantic partners (Berscheid, 1985; Berscheid & Peplau, 1983). Happiness hits close to home.

> "The sun looks down on nothing half so good as a household laughing together over a meal."
> —C. S. Lewis, "Membership," 1949

Marital attachment and happiness

For more than 9 in 10 people worldwide, one eventual example of a close relationship has been marriage. Does marriage correlate positively with happiness? Or is there more happiness in the pleasure-seeking single life than in the "bondage," "chains," and "yoke" of marriage?

A mountain of data reveal that most people are happier attached than unattached. Survey after survey of many tens of thousands of Europeans and Americans has produced a consistent result: Compared with those single or widowed, and especially compared with those divorced or separated, married people report being happier and more satisfied with life (Gove & others, 1990; Inglehart, 1990). In representative surveys of 42,000 Americans since 1972, for example, 22 percent of never-married adults, but 40 percent of married adults, have reported being "very happy" (NORC, 2003). This marriage-happiness link occurs across ethnic groups (Parker & others, 1995). Moreover, satisfaction with marriage predicts overall happiness much better than does satisfaction with job, finances, or community (Lane, 1998). And among the nonmarried, rates of suicide and depression run higher (Stack, 1992; and see Figure 14–8). Indeed, there are few stronger predictors of happiness than a close, nurturing, equitable, intimate, lifelong companionship with one's best friend.

Is marriage, as is so often supposed, more strongly associated with men's happiness than women's? Given women's greater contribution to household work and to supportive nurturing, we might expect so. The married versus never-married happiness gap, however, is only slightly greater among men than women. In European surveys and in a statistical digest of 93 other studies, the marital happiness gap is virtually identical for men and women (Inglehart, 1990; Wood & others, 1989). Although a bad marriage is often more depressing to a woman than to a man, the myth that single women are happier than married women can be laid to rest. Throughout the Western world, married

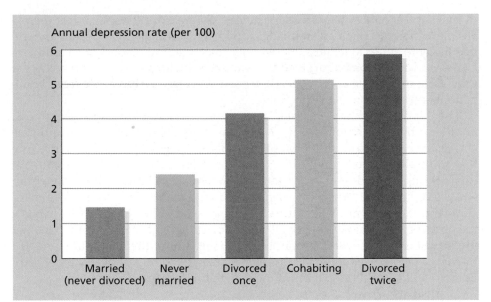

Annual depression rate (per 100)

figure 14–8

Marital status and depression.

A National Institute of Mental Health survey of psychological disorders found depression rates two to four times greater for adults not married.

Source: Data from Robins & Regier, 1991, p. 72.

people of both sexes report more happiness than those never married, divorced, or separated.

More important than being married, however, is the marriage's quality. People who say their marriages are satisfying—who find themselves still in love with their partners—rarely report being unhappy, discontented with life, or depressed. Fortunately, most married people *do* declare their marriages happy ones. In the United States, almost two-thirds say their marriages are "very happy." Three out of four say their spouses are their best friends. Four out of five people say they would marry the same people again. As a consequence, most such people feel quite happy with life as a whole.

Why are married people generally happier? Does marriage promote happiness, or is it the other way around—does happiness promote marriage? Are happy people more appealing as marriage partners? Do grouchy or depressed people more often stay single or suffer divorce? Certainly, happy people are more fun to be with. They are also more outgoing, trusting, compassionate, and focused on others (Myers, 1993). Unhappy people, as we have noted, are more often socially rejected. Depression often triggers marital stress, which deepens the depression (Davila & others, 1997). So, positive, happy people more readily form happy relationships.

But "the prevailing opinion of researchers," reports University of Oslo sociologist Arne Mastekaasa (1995), is that the marriage-happiness connection is "mainly due" to the beneficial effects of marriage. Put on your thinking cap: If the happiest people marry sooner and more often, then as people age (and progressively less happy people move into marriage), the average happiness of both married and never-married people should decline. (The older, less happy newlyweds would pull down the average happiness of married people, and the unmarried group would be more and more left with the unhappy people.) But the data do not support this prediction. This suggests that marital intimacy does—for most people—pay emotional dividends. A Rutgers University team that followed 1,380 New Jersey adults over 15 years concurs (Horwitz & others, 1997). The tendency for married people to be less depressed occurs even after controlling for premarital happiness.

Marriage enhances happiness for at least two reasons. First, married people are more likely to enjoy an enduring, supportive, intimate relationship and are less likely to suffer loneliness. No wonder male medical students in a study by UCLA's Robert Coombs survived medical school with less stress and anxiety if they were married (Coombs, 1991). A good marriage gives each partner a dependable companion, a lover, a friend.

There is a second, more prosaic, reason why marriage promotes happiness, or at least buffers us from misery. Marriage offers the roles of spouse and parent, which can provide additional sources of self-esteem (Crosby, 1987). It is true that multiple roles can multiply stress. Our circuits can and do overload. Yet each role also provides rewards, status, avenues to enrichment, and escape from stress faced in other parts of one's life. A self with many identities is like a mansion with many rooms. When fire struck one wing of Windsor Castle, most of the castle still remained for royals and tourists to enjoy. When our personal identity stands on several legs, it, too, holds up under the loss of any one. If I mess up at work, well, I can tell myself I'm still a good husband and father, and, in the final analysis, these parts of me are what matter most.

Summing up

Health and happiness are influenced not only by social cognition but also by social relations. People who enjoy close, supportive relationships are at less risk for illness and premature death. Such relationships help people cope with stress, especially by enabling people to confide their intimate emotions.

Close relationships also foster happiness. People who have intimate, long-term attachments with friends and family members cope better with loss and report greater happiness. Compared with unmarried adults, those married, for example, are much more likely to report being very happy and are at less risk for depression. This appears due both to the greater social success of happy people and to the well-being engendered by a supportive life companion.

PS Personal Postscript: Enhancing happiness

Several years ago I wrote a book, *The Pursuit of Happiness,* that reported key findings from new research studies of happiness. When the editors wanted to subtitle the book, *What Makes People Happy?,* I cautioned them: That's not a question this or any book can answer. What we have learned is simply what correlates with—and therefore predicts—happiness. Thus, the book's revised subtitle: *Who is Happy—and Why?*

Nevertheless, in 400 subsequent media interviews concerning happiness, the most frequent question has been, "What can people do to be happy?" Without claiming any easy formula for health and happiness, I assembled 10 research-based points to ponder:

1. *Realize that enduring happiness doesn't come from "making it."* People adapt to changing circumstances—even to wealth or a disability. Thus wealth is like health: Its utter absence breeds misery, but having it (or any circumstance we long for) doesn't guarantee happiness.

2. *Take control of your time.* Happy people feel in control of their lives, often aided by mastering their use of time. It helps to set goals and break them into daily aims. Although we often overestimate how much we will accomplish in any given day (leaving us frustrated), we generally

underestimate how much we can accomplish in a year, given just a little progress every day.

3. *Act happy.* We can sometimes act ourselves into a frame of mind. Manipulated into a smiling expression, people feel better; when they scowl, the whole world seems to scowl back. So put on a happy face. Talk *as if* you feel positive self-esteem, are optimistic, and are outgoing. Going through the motions can trigger the emotions.

4. *Seek work and leisure that engages your skills.* Happy people often are in a zone called "flow"—absorbed in a task that challenges them without overwhelming them. The most expensive forms of leisure (sitting on a yacht) often provide less flow experience than gardening, socializing, or craft work.

5. *Join the "movement" movement.* An avalanche of research reveals that aerobic exercise not only promotes health and energy, it also is an antidote for mild depression and anxiety. Sound minds reside in sound bodies. Off your duffs, couch potatoes.

6. *Give your body the sleep it wants.* Happy people live active, vigorous lives yet reserve time for renewing sleep and solitude. Many people suffer from a sleep debt, with resulting fatigue, diminished alertness, and gloomy moods.

7. *Give priority to close relationships.* Intimate friendships with those who care deeply about you can help you weather difficult times. Confiding is good for soul and body. Resolve to nurture your closest relationships: to *not* take those closest to you for granted, to display to them the sort of kindness that you display to others, to affirm them, to play together and share together. To rejuvenate your affections, resolve in such ways to *act* lovingly.

8. *Focus beyond the self.* Reach out to those in need. Happiness increases helpfulness (those who feel good do good). But doing good also makes one feel good.

9. *Keep a gratitude journal.* Those who pause each day to reflect on some positive aspect of their lives (their health, friends, family, freedom, education, senses, natural surroundings, and so on) experience heightened well-being.

10. *Nurture your spiritual self.* For many people, faith provides a support community, a reason to focus beyond self, and a sense of purpose and hope. Study after study finds that actively religious people are happier and that they cope better with crises.

What do you think?

Reflect for a minute on your own happiness. Are you happy? What relationships contribute to your happiness? Explain how these relationships support your well-being. Which of the items on this list of 10 do you already incorporate into your life? How might you incorporate the others?

Making the Social Connection

SS This chapter described negative thinking and whether it is a cause or a result of depression. We also addressed moods in the section "Mood and Judgment" in Chapter 3: Social Beliefs and Judgments. What are some causes of depression? Go to the *SocialSense* CD-ROM to view a description of theories on depression and its treatments.

chapter 15

Social Psychology in Court

"A courtroom is a battleground where lawyers compete for the minds of jurors."

James Randi, 1999

It was the most publicized criminal case in human history: Football hero, actor, and broadcaster O. J. Simpson was accused of brutally murdering his estranged wife and a male acquaintance. The evidence was compelling, the prosecution argued. Simpson's behavior fit a longstanding pattern of spouse abuse and threats of violence. Blood tests confirmed that his blood was at the crime scene and his victims' blood was on his glove, his car, even on a sock in his bedroom. His travels the night of the murder and his fleeing when his arrest was imminent fit the crime.

Simpson's defense attorneys argued that racial prejudice may have motivated the officer who allegedly found the bloody glove at Simpson's estate. Moreover, they said, Simpson could not receive a fair trial. Would the jurors—10 of whom were women—be kindly disposed to a man alleged to have abused and murdered a woman? And how likely was it that jurors could heed the judge's instructions to ignore prejudicial pretrial publicity?

The case raised other questions that have been examined in social-psychological experiments:

- There were no eyewitnesses to this crime. How influential is eyewitness testimony? How trustworthy are eyewitness recollections? What makes a credible witness?
- Simpson was handsome, beloved, rich, and famous. Can jurors ignore, as they should, a defendant's attractiveness and social status?
- How well do jurors comprehend important information, such as statistical probabilities involved in DNA blood tests?
- The jury in the criminal case was composed mostly of women and Blacks, but it also included two men, one Hispanic, and two non-Hispanic Whites. In the follow-up civil trial, in which Simpson was sued for damages, the jury had nine Whites. Do jurors' characteristics bias their verdicts? If so, can lawyers use the jury selection process to stack a jury in their favor?
- In cases such as this, a 12-member jury deliberates before delivering a verdict. During deliberations, how do jurors influence one another? Can a minority win over the majority? Do 12-member juries reach the same decisions as 6-member juries?

Such questions fascinate lawyers, judges, and defendants. And they are questions to which social psychology can suggest answers, as law schools have recognized by hiring professors of "law and social science" and as trial lawyers have recognized when hiring psychological consultants.

We can think of a courtroom as a miniature social world, one that magnifies everyday social processes with major consequences for those involved. In criminal cases, psychological factors may influence decisions involving arrest, interrogation, prosecution, plea bargaining, sentencing, and parole. Of criminal cases disposed of in U.S. district courts, four in five never come to trial (U.S. Department of Justice, 1980). Much of the trial lawyer's work therefore "is not persuasion in the courtroom but bargaining in the conference room" (Saks & Hastie, 1978, pp. 119–120). Even in the conference room, decisions are made based on speculation about what a jury or judge might do.

Whether a case reaches a jury verdict or not, the social dynamics of the courtroom matter. Let's therefore consider two sets of factors that have been heavily researched: (1) eyewitness testimony and its influence on judgments of a defendant and (2) characteristics of jurors as individuals and as a group.

How reliable is eyewitness testimony?

As the courtroom drama unfolds, jurors hear testimony, form impressions of the defendant, listen to

"What are you—some kind of justice freak?"

instructions from the judge, and render a verdict. Let's take these steps one at a time, starting with eyewitness testimony.

THE POWER OF PERSUASIVE EYEWITNESSES

In Chapter 3 we noted that vivid anecdotes and personal testimonies can be powerfully persuasive, often more so than compelling but abstract information. There's no better way to end an argument than to say, "I saw it with my own eyes!" Seeing is believing.

At the University of Washington, Elizabeth Loftus (1974, 1979) found that those who had "seen" were indeed believed, even when their testimony was shown to be useless. When students were presented with a hypothetical robbery-murder case with circumstantial evidence but no eyewitness testimony, only 18 percent voted for conviction. Other students received the same information but with the addition of a single eyewitness. Now, knowing that someone had declared, "That's the one!" 72 percent voted for conviction. For a third group, the defense attorney discredited this testimony (the witness had 20/400 vision and was not wearing glasses). Did this discrediting reduce the effect of the testimony? In this case, not much: Sixty-eight percent still voted for conviction.

Later experiments revealed that discrediting may reduce somewhat the number of guilty votes (Whitley, 1987). But unless contradicted by another eyewitness, a vivid eyewitness account is difficult to erase from jurors' minds (Leippe, 1985). That helps explain why, compared with criminal cases lacking eyewitness testimony (such as the O. J. case), those that have eyewitness testimony are more likely to produce convictions (Visher, 1987).

Can't jurors spot erroneous testimony? To find out, Gary Wells, R. C. L. Lindsay, and their colleagues staged hundreds of eyewitnessed thefts of a University of Alberta calculator. Afterward, they asked each eyewitness to identify the culprit from a photo lineup. Other people, acting as jurors, observed the eyewitnesses being questioned and then evaluated their testimony. Are incorrect eyewitnesses believed less often than those who are accurate? As it happened, both correct and incorrect eyewitnesses were believed 80 percent of the time (Wells & others, 1979). This led the researchers to speculate that "human observers have absolutely no ability to discern eyewitnesses who have mistakenly identified an innocent person" (Wells & others, 1980).

In a follow-up experiment, Lindsay, Wells, and Carolyn Rumpel (1981) staged the theft under conditions that sometimes allowed witnesses a good, long look at the thief and sometimes didn't. The jurors believed the witnesses more when conditions were good. But even when conditions were so poor that two-thirds of the witnesses had actually misidentified an innocent person, 62 percent of the jurors still usually believed the witnesses.

Wells and Michael Leippe (1981) also have found that jurors are more skeptical of eyewitnesses whose memory for trivial details is poor—though

"As it turned out, my battery of lawyers was no match for their battery of eyewitnesses."

James Newsome

Dennis Emerson

The innocent James Newsome mistakenly identified by eyewitnesses, and the actual culprit.

"Certitude is not the test of certainty."
—Oliver Wendell Holmes, *Collected Legal Papers*

Eyewitness recall of detail is sometimes impressive. When John Yuille and Judith Cutshall (1986) studied accounts of a midafternoon murder on a busy Burnaby, British Columbia, street, they found that eyewitnesses' recall for detail was 80 percent accurate.

these tend to be the most *accurate* witnesses. Jurors think a witness who can remember that there were three pictures hanging in the room must have "really been paying attention" (Bell & Loftus, 1988, 1989). Actually, those who pay attention to details are less likely to pay attention to the culprit's face.

The persuasive power of three eyewitnesses sent Chicagoan James Newsome, who had never been arrested before, to prison on a life sentence for supposedly gunning down a convenience store owner. Fifteen years later he was released, after fingerprint technology revealed the real culprit to be Dennis Emerson, a career criminal who was three inches taller and had longer hair (*Chicago Tribune*, 2002).

WHEN EYES DECEIVE

Is eyewitness testimony often inaccurate? Stories abound of innocent people who have wasted years in prison because of the testimony of eyewitnesses who were sincerely wrong (Brandon & Davies, 1973). Seventy years ago, Yale law professor Edwin Borchard (1932) documented 65 convictions of people whose innocence was later proven. Most resulted from mistaken identifications, and some were saved from execution by a whisker. At the turn of the millennium, DNA testing had exonerated more than 100 who had been convicted of crimes they did not commit, more than 75 percent of whom were victims of mistaken eyewitness identifications (Wells & Olson, 2003). Another analysis estimated that 0.5 percent of 1.5 million American criminal convictions each year err, with roughly 4,500 of these 7,500 wrongful convictions based on mistaken identification (Cutler & Penrod, 1995). (See Focus on: Eyewitness Testimony.)

To assess the accuracy of eyewitness recollections, we need to learn their overall rates of "hits" and "misses." One way to gather such information is to stage crimes comparable to those in everyday life and then solicit eyewitness reports.

This has been done many times, sometimes with disconcerting results. For example, at the California State University–Hayward, 141 students witnessed an "assault" on a professor. Seven weeks later, when Robert Buckhout (1974) asked them to identify the assailant from a group of six photographs, 60 percent chose an innocent person. No wonder eyewitnesses to actual crimes sometimes disagree about what they saw. Later studies have confirmed that eyewitnesses often are more confident than correct. For example, Brian Bornstein and Douglas Zickafoose (1999) found that students felt, on average, 74 percent sure of their later recollections of a classroom visitor, but were only 55 percent correct.

Of course, some witnesses are more confident than others. Wells and his colleagues report (2002) that it's the confident witnesses whom jurors find most believable. In the convictions overturned by DNA evidence, the eyewitnesses proved persuasive because of their great but mistaken confidence in their identifications of the perpetrator. So it is disconcerting that, unless conditions are very favorable, as when the culprit is very distinctive-looking, the certainty of witnesses often bears only a modest relation to their accuracy. Intuitive confidence does correlate with accuracy when there is great variation in how long witnesses view the culprit—those who view longer are both more accurate and more confident (Lindsay & others, 1998; Wells & others, 2002). Yet some people—whether right or wrong—chronically express themselves more assertively. And that, says Michael Leippe (1994), explains why mistaken eyewitnesses are so often persuasive.

focus on | eyewitness testimony

In 1984, I was a 22-year-old college student with a perfect GPA and a bright future. One dark night someone broke into my apartment, put a knife to my throat, and raped me.

During my ordeal I was determined that if, by the grace of God, I should live, I was going to make sure that my rapist was caught and punished. My mind quickly separated me from my body and began recording every detail of my attacker. I carefully studied his face: noting his hairline, his brow, his chin. I listened hard to his voice, his speech, his words. I looked for scars, for tattoos, for anything that would help me identify him. Then, after what seemed like an eternity, and in a brief moment when my rapist let down his guard, I fled from my apartment in the early morning wrapped only in a blanket. I had survived.

Later that day I began the painstaking process of trying to bring my attacker to justice. For hours I sat with a police artist and meticulously looked through books filled with hundreds of noses, eyes, eyebrows, hairlines, nostrils, and lips—reliving the attack again and again in the minute details that together made up his composite sketch. The next day the newspaper carried my rapist's image on the front page. There was a lead. The case had its first suspect. Several days later I sat before a series of photographs and picked out my attacker. I got him. I knew he was the man. I was completely confident. I was sure.

When the case went to trial six months later, I took the witness stand, put my hand on the Bible, and swore to "tell the whole truth and nothing but the truth." Based on my eyewitness testimony Ronald Junior Cotton was sentenced to prison for life. Ronald Cotton was never going to see the light of day again. Ronald Cotton would never rape another woman again.

During a 1987 retrial hearing the defense brought forward another inmate, Bobby Poole, who had bragged of raping me. In court, he denied raping me. When asked if I had ever seen this man, I emphatically answered that I had never seen him before in my life. Another vic-

Jennifer Thompson talks with Ronald Cotton after his release.

tim agreed. Ronald Cotton was resentenced to two life sentences with no chance for parole.

In 1995, 11 years after I had first identified Ronald Cotton as my rapist, I was asked if I would consent to a blood sample so that DNA tests could be run on evidence from the rape. I agreed because I knew that Ronald Cotton had raped me and DNA was only going to confirm that. That test would put to rest any future appeals brought on Cotton's behalf.

I will never forget the day I learned the DNA results. I stood in my kitchen as the detective and district attorney told me: "Ronald Cotton didn't rape you. It was Bobby Poole." Their words struck me like a thunderbolt. The man I was convinced I never saw before in my life was the man who held a knife to my throat, who hurt me, who raped me, who crushed my spirit, who robbed me of my soul. The man I was positive did all those things and whose face continued to haunt me at night was innocent.

Ronald Cotton was released from prison after serving 11 years, becoming the first convicted felon in North Carolina exonerated through DNA testing. Bobby Poole, serving a life sentence of his own and dying of cancer, confessed to the rapes without remorse.

(Continued on page 610)

focus on   *(continued)*

Ronald Cotton and I now shared something in the brutal crime that had pitted us against each other for years—we were both victims. My part in his conviction, though, filled me with guilt and shame. We were the same age, so I knew what he had missed during those 11 years in prison. I had had the opportunity to move on and begin to heal. To graduate from college. To find trust and love in marriage. To find self-confidence in work. And to find the hope of a bright future in the gifts of my beautiful children. Ronald Cotton, on the other hand, spent those years alone defending him-self from the violence that punctuated his life in prison.

Sometime after Ronald Cotton's release I requested a meeting through our attorneys so that I might say I was sorry and seek his forgiveness. In the end, Ron and I finally found total freedom through forgiveness. I will forever look back now through our unlikely friendship, thankful that in Ron's case of mistaken identity, I wasn't dead wrong.

Jennifer Thompson, North Carolina, USA

This finding would surely come as a surprise to members of the 1972 U.S. Supreme Court. In a judgment that established the position of the U.S. judiciary system regarding eyewitness identifications, the Court, we now realize, goofed. It declared that among the factors to be considered in determining accuracy is "the level of certainty demonstrated by the witness" (Wells & Murray, 1983).

Errors sneak into our perceptions and our memories because our minds are not videotape machines. People are quite good at recognizing a pictured face when later shown the same picture alongside a new face. But University of Stirling face researcher Vicki Bruce (1998) was surprised to discover that subtle differences in views, expressions, or lighting "are hard for human vision to deal with." We construct our memories based partly on what we perceived at the time and partly on our expectations, beliefs, and current knowledge (Figures 15–1 and 15–2).

figure 15–1

Sometimes believing is seeing.

Cultural expectations affect perceiving, remembering, and reporting. In a 1947 experiment on rumor transmission, Gordon Allport and Leo Postman showed people this picture of a White man holding a razor blade and then had them tell a second person about it, who then told a third person, and so on. After six tellings, the razor blade in the White man's hand usually shifted to the Black man's. **Source:** Allport, G. W. and L. Postman (1947,1975). Figure from *The Psychology of Rumor* by Gordon W. Allport and Leo Postman, copyright © 1947 and renewed 1975 by Holt, Rinehart and Winston, reproduced by permission of the publisher. Illustration by Graphic Presentation Services.

THE MISINFORMATION EFFECT

Elizabeth Loftus and her associates (1978) provided a dramatic demonstration of memory construction. They showed University of Washington students 30 slides depicting successive stages of an automobile-pedestrian accident. One critical slide showed a red Datsun stopped at a stop sign or a yield sign.

figure 15–2

Expectations affect perception.

Is the drawing on the far right a face or figure?

Source: From Fisher, 1968, adapted by Loftus, 1979. Drawing by Anne Canevari Green.

figure 15–3

The misinformation effect.

When shown one of these two pictures and then asked a question suggesting the sign from the other photo, most people later "remembered" seeing the sign they had never actually seen. **Source:** From Loftus, Miller, & Burns, 1978. Photos courtesy of Elizabeth Loftus.

Afterward they asked half the students, among other questions, "Did another car pass the red Datsun while it was stopped at the stop sign?" They asked the other half the same question, but with the words "stop sign" replaced by "yield sign." Later, all viewed both slides in Figure 15–3 and recalled which one they had seen previously. Those who had been asked the question consistent with what they had seen were 75 percent correct. Those previously asked the misleading question were only 41 percent correct; more often than not, they denied seeing what they had actually seen and instead "remembered" the picture they had never seen!

misinformation effect

Incorporating "misinformation" into one's memory of the event after receiving misleading information about it.

In other studies of this **misinformation effect** (remembering misleading information), Loftus (1979a, 1979b, 2001) found that after suggestive questions witnesses may believe that a red light was actually green or that a robber had a mustache when he didn't. When questioning eyewitnesses, police and attorneys commonly ask questions framed by their own understanding of what happened. So it is troubling to discover how easily witnesses incorporate misleading information into their memories, especially when they believe the questioner is well informed and when suggestive questions are repeated (Smith & Ellsworth, 1987; Zaragoza & Mitchell, 1996).

It also is troubling to realize that false memories feel and look like real memories. They can be as persuasive as real memories—convincingly sincere, yet sincerely wrong. This is true of young children (who are especially susceptible to misinformation) as well as adults. Stephen Ceci and Maggie Bruck (1993a,b, 1995) demonstrated children's suggestibility by telling children, once a week for 10 weeks, "Think real hard, and tell me if this ever happened to you." For example, "Can you remember going to the hospital with the mousetrap on your finger?" Remarkably, when then interviewed by a new adult who asked the same question, 58 percent of preschoolers produced false and often detailed stories about the fictitious event. One boy explained that his brother had pushed him into a basement woodpile, where his finger got stuck in the trap. "And then we went to the hospital, and my mommy, daddy, and Colin drove me there, to the hospital in our van, because it was far away. And the doctor put a bandage on this finger."

Given such vivid stories, professional psychologists were often fooled. They could not reliably separate real from false memories—nor could the children. Told the incident never actually happened, some protested. "But it really did happen. I remember it!" For Bruck and Ceci (1999), such findings raise the possibility of false accusations, as in alleged child sex abuse cases where children's memories may have been contaminated by repeated suggestive questioning and where there is no corroborating evidence.

RETELLING

Retelling events commits people to their recollections, accurate or not. An accurate retelling helps them later resist misleading suggestions (Bregman & McAllister, 1982). Other times, the more we retell a story, the more we convince ourselves of a falsehood. Wells, Ferguson, and Lindsay (1981) demonstrated this by having eyewitnesses to a staged theft rehearse their answers to questions before taking the witness stand. Doing so increased the confidence of those who were wrong and thus made jurors who heard their false testimony more likely to convict the innocent person.

In Chapter 4 we noted that we often adjust what we say to please our listeners and, having done so, come to believe the altered message. Imagine witnessing an argument that erupts into a fight in which one person injures the other. Afterward, the injured party sues. Before the trial, a smooth lawyer for one of the two parties interviews you. Might you slightly adjust your testimony, giving a version of the fight that supports this lawyer's client? If you did so, might your later recollections in court be similarly slanted?

Blair Sheppard and Neil Vidmar (1980) report that the answer to both questions is yes. At the University of Western Ontario, they had some students serve as witnesses to a fight and others as lawyers and judges. When interviewed by lawyers for the defendant, the witnesses later gave the judge testimony that was more favorable to the defendant. In a follow-up experiment, Vidmar and Nancy Laird (1983) noted that witnesses did not omit important facts from their testimony; they just changed their tone of voice and choice of words depending on whether they thought they were witnesses for the defendant or for the plaintiff.

www.mhhe.com/myers8
Visit the Online Learning Center for an interactivity on the misinformation effect. "Seeing is believing."

How accurate is the testimony of a child? Go to the *SocialSense* CD-ROM to view a video clip.

Even this was enough to bias the impressions of those who heard the testimony. So it's not only suggestive questions that can distort eyewitness recollections but also their own retellings, which may be adjusted subtly to suit their audience.

FEEDBACK TO WITNESSES

Eyewitness to a crime on viewing a lineup: "Oh, my God . . . I don't know . . . It's one of those two . . . but I don't know . . . Oh, man . . . the guy a little bit taller than number two . . . It's one of those two, but I don't know. . . ."
Months later at trial: "You were positive it was number two? It wasn't a maybe?"
Eyewitness's answer: "There was no maybe about it . . . I was absolutely positive." (*Missouri v. Hutching,* 1994, reported by Wells & Bradfield, 1998).

What explains witnesses misrecalling their original uncertainty? Gary Wells and Amy Bradfield (1998, 1999) wondered. Research had shown that one's confidence gains a boost from learning that another witness has fingered the same person, from being asked the same question repeatedly, and from preparing for cross-examination (Lüüs & Wells, 1994; Shaw, 1996; Wells & others, 1981). Might the lineup interviewer's feedback also influence not just confidence but recollections of earlier confidence ("I knew it all along")?

To find out, Wells and Bradfield conducted two experiments in which 352 Iowa State University students viewed a grainy security camera video of a man entering a store. Moments later, off camera, he murders a security guard. The students then viewed the photo spread from the actual criminal case, minus the gunman's photo, and were asked to identify the gunman. All 352 students made a false identification, following which the experimenter gave confirming feedback ("Good. You identified the actual suspect"), disconfirming feedback ("Actually, the suspect was number _____"), or no feedback. Finally, all were later asked, "At the time that you identified the person in the photo spread, how certain were you that the person you identified from the photos was the gunman that you saw in the video?" (from 1, not at all certain, to 7, totally certain).

The experiment produced two striking results: First, the effect of the experimenter's casual comment was huge. In the confirming feedback condition, 58 percent of the eyewitnesses rated their certainty as 6 or 7 when making their initial judgments—4 times the 14 percent who said the same in the no-feedback condition and 11 times the 5 percent in the disconfirming condition. We shouldn't be surprised that witnesses' postfeedback confidence would be raised by confirming feedback, but these were ratings of their remembered *pre*feedback confidence.

It wasn't obvious to the participants that their judgments were affected, for the second rather amazing finding is that, when asked if the feedback had influenced their answers, 58 percent said no. Moreover, as a group, those who felt uninfluenced were no less so than those who said they were (Figure 15–4).

The lesson runs deeper than jury research. Once again we see why we need social-psychological research. As social psychologists have so often found—recall Milgram's obedience experiments—simply asking people how they would act, or asking what explains their actions, sometimes gives us wrong answers. Benjamin Franklin was right: "There are three things extremely hard, Steel, a Diamond, and to know one's self." That is why we need to do not only surveys that ask people to explain themselves, but experiments in which we see what they actually do.

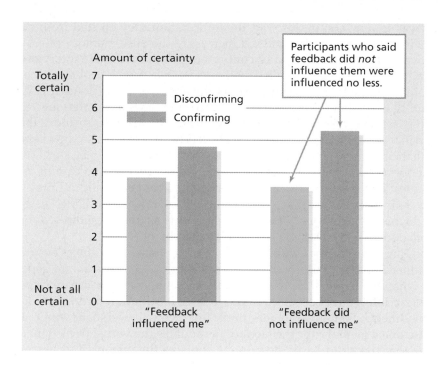

Amount of certainty

Totally certain

Participants who said feedback did *not* influence them were influenced no less.

Disconfirming
Confirming

"Feedback influenced me"   "Feedback did not influence me"

Not at all certain

figure 15–4

Recalled certainty of eyewitnesses' false identification after receiving confirming or disconfirming feedback (Experiment 2).

Note that participants who said feedback did *not* influence them were influenced no less. **Source:** Data from Wells & Bradfield, 1998.

REDUCING ERROR

Given these error-prone tendencies, what constructive steps can be taken to increase the accuracy of eyewitnesses and jurors? Former U.S. Attorney General Janet Reno wondered, as had Canada's Law Reform Commission a decade earlier, and invited Gary Wells to share suggestions. Afterward, the Department of Justice convened a panel of researchers, attorneys, and law enforcement officers to hammer out a law enforcement guide (Technical Group, 1999; Wells & others, 2000). Their suggestions parallel many of those from a recent Canadian review of eyewitness identification procedures (Yarmey, 2003a). They include ways to train police interviewers and administer lineups.

Train police interviewers

When Ronald Fisher and his co-workers (1987) examined tape-recorded interviews of eyewitnesses conducted by experienced Florida police detectives, they found a typical pattern. Following an open-ended beginning ("Tell me what you recall"), the detectives would occasionally interrupt with follow-up questions, including questions eliciting terse answers ("How tall was he?"). The new guide book says interviews should begin by allowing eyewitnesses to offer their own unprompted recollections.

The recollections will be most complete if the interviewer jogs the memory by first guiding people to reconstruct the setting. Have them visualize the scene and what they were thinking and feeling at the time. Even showing pictures of the setting—of, say, the store checkout lane with a clerk standing where she was robbed—can promote accurate recall (Cutler & Penrod, 1988). After giving witnesses ample, uninterrupted time to report everything that comes to mind, the interviewer then jogs their memory with evocative questions ("Was there anything unusual about the voice? Was there anything unusual about the person's appearance or clothing?"). When Fisher and his colleagues (1989, 1994) trained

"Witnesses probably ought to be taking a more realistic oath: "Do you swear to tell the truth, the whole truth, or whatever it is you think you remember?"
—Elizabeth F. Loftus, "Memory in Canadian Courts of Law," 2003

detectives to question in this way, the information they elicited from eyewitnesses increased 50 percent without increasing the false memory rate. A later statistical summary of 42 studies confirmed that the cognitive interview substantially increases details recalled, with no loss in accuracy (Kohnken & others, 1999). In response to such results, most police agencies in North America and all of them in England and Wales have adopted this "cognitive interview" procedure (Geiselman, 1996; Kebbell & others, 1999). The FBI now includes the procedure in its training program (Bower, 1997). (The procedure also shows promise for enhancing information gathered in oral histories and medical surveys.)

Interviewers on memory reconnaissance missions must be careful to keep their questions free of hidden assumptions. Loftus and Guido Zanni (1975) found that questions such as, "Did you see the broken headlight?" triggered twice as many "memories" of nonexistent events as did questions without the hidden assumption: "Did you see a broken headlight?"

Flooding eyewitnesses with an array of mug shots also reduces accuracy in later identifying the culprit (Brigham & Cairns, 1988). Errors are especially likely when the witness has to stop, think, and analytically compare faces. Verbally describing a robber's face disrupts later recognition of it from a photographic lineup. Some researchers think this "verbal overshadowing" occurs because one's memory for the face accommodates the verbal depiction; others believe that the word-based description replaces the unconscious perception, or makes it inaccessible (Fallshore & Schooler, 1995; Meissner & others, 2001; Schooler, 2002).

Lineup fairness? From the suspect's perspective a lineup is fair, note John Brigham, David Ready, and Stacy Spier (1990), when "the other lineup members are reasonably similar in general appearance to the suspect."

Accurate identifications tend to be automatic and effortless. The right face just pops out (Dunning & Stern, 1994). In recent studies by David Dunning and Scott Perretta (2002), eyewitnesses who make their identifications in less than 10 to 12 seconds were nearly 90 percent accurate; those taking longer were roughly 50 percent accurate.

Minimize false lineup identifications

The case of Ron Shatford illustrates how the composition of a police lineup can promote misidentification (Doob & Kirshenbaum, 1973). After a suburban Toronto department store robbery, the cashier involved could only recall that the culprit was not wearing a tie and was "very neatly dressed and rather good looking." When police put the good-looking Shatford in a lineup with 11 unattractive men, all of whom wore ties, the cashier readily identified him as the culprit. Only after he had served 15 months of a long sentence did another person confess, allowing Shatford to be retried and found not guilty.

Gary Wells (1984, 1993) and the *Eyewitness Evidence* guide report that one way to reduce misidentifications is to remind witnesses that the person they saw may or may not be in the lineup. Alternatively, give eyewitnesses a "blank" lineup that contains no suspects and screen out those who make false identifications. Those who do not

THE FAR SIDE® BY GARY LARSON

© 1985 FarWorks, Inc. All Rights Reserved/Dist. by Creators Syndicate

The Far Side® by Gary Larson © 1985 FarWorks, Inc. All Rights Reserved. Used with permission.

"*That's* him! *That's* the one! ... I'd recognize that silly little hat anywhere!"

make such errors turn out to be more accurate when they later face the actual lineup.

Dozens of studies in Europe, North America, Australia, and South Africa show that mistakes also subside when witnesses simply make individual yes or no judgments in response to a *sequence* of people (Lindsay & Wells, 1985; Steblay & others, 2001). A simultaneous lineup tempts people to pick the person who, among the lineup members, most resembles the perpetrator. Witnesses viewing just one suspect at a time are just as likely to make accurate identifications and much less likely to make false ones. If witnesses view a group of photos or people simultaneously, they are more likely to choose whoever most resembles the culprit.

These no-cost procedures make police lineups more like good experiments. They contain a *control group* (a no-suspect lineup or a lineup in which mock witnesses try to guess the suspect based merely on a general description). They have an experimenter who is *blind* to the hypothesis (an officer who doesn't know which person is the suspect). Questions are *scripted and neutral*, so they don't subtly demand a particular response (the procedure doesn't imply the culprit is in the lineup). And they prohibit confidence-inflating post-lineup comments ("you got him") prior to trial testimony. Such procedures greatly reduce the natural human confirmation bias (having an idea and seeking confirming evidence).

www.mhhe.com/**myers8**
Visit the Online Learning Center for a scenario on eyewitnesses.

Although procedures such as double-blind testing are common in psychological science, they are still uncommon in criminal procedures (Wells & Olson, 2003). But their time may be coming. New Jersey's attorney general has mandated statewide blind testing, to avoid steering witnesses toward suspects, and sequential lineups, to minimize simply comparing people and choosing the person who most resembles the one they saw commit a crime (Kolata & Peterson, 2001; Wells & others, 2002). Police might also use a new procedure tested by Sean Pryke, Rod Lindsay, and colleagues (2004). They invited students to identify a prior class visitor from multiple lineups that separately presented face, body, and voice samples. Their finding: An eyewitness who consistently identified the same suspect—by face, by body, and by voice—was nearly always an accurate eyewitness.

Educate jurors

Do jurors evaluate eyewitness testimony rationally? Do they understand how the circumstances of a lineup determine its reliability? Do they know whether to take an eyewitness's self-confidence into account? Do they realize how memory can be influenced—by earlier misleading questions, by stress at the time of the incident, by the interval between the event and the questioning, by whether the suspect is the same or a different race, by whether recall of other details is sharp or hazy? Studies in Canada, Great Britain, and the United States reveal that jurors fail to fully appreciate most of these factors, all of which are known to influence eyewitness testimony (Cutler & others, 1988; Devenport & others, 2002; Noon & Hollin, 1987; Wells & Turtle, 1987; Yarmey, 2003a,b).

To educate jurors, experts now are asked frequently (usually by defense attorneys) to testify about eyewitness testimony. Their aim is to offer jurors the sort of information you have been reading about to help them evaluate the testimony of both prosecution and defense witnesses. Table 15–1 (see page 618), drawn from a survey of 64 researchers on eyewitness testimony, lists some of the most agreed-upon phenomena.

table 15–1 **Influences on eyewitness testimony**

Phenomenon	Eyewitness Experts Agreeing*
Question wording. An eyewitness's testimony about an event can be affected by how the questions put to that eyewitness are worded.	98%
Lineup instructions. Police instructions can affect an eyewitness's willingness to make an identification.	98%
Confidence malleability. An eyewitness's confidence can be influenced by factors that are unrelated to identification accuracy.	95%
Mug-shot-induced bias. Exposure to mug shots of a suspect increases the likelihood that the witness will later choose that suspect in a lineup.	95%
Postevent information. Eyewitnesses' testimony about an event often reflects not only what they actually saw but information they obtained later on.	94%
Attitudes and expectations. An eyewitness's perception and memory of an event may be affected by his or her attitudes and expectations.	92%
Cross-race bias. Eyewitnesses are more accurate when identifying members of their own race than members of other races.	90%
Accuracy versus confidence. An eyewitness's confidence is not a good predictor of his or her identification accuracy.	87%

*"This phenomenon is reliable enough for psychologists to present it in courtroom testimony."
Source: From S. M. Kassin, V. A. Tubb, H. M. Hosch, & A. Memon (2001).

Taught the conditions under which eyewitness accounts are trustworthy, jurors become more discerning (Cutler & others, 1989; Devenport & others, 2002; Wells, 1986). Moreover, attorneys and judges are recognizing the importance of some of these factors when deciding when to ask for or permit suppression of lineup evidence (Stinson & others, 1996, 1997).

Summing up Courtroom procedures have been on trial in hundreds of recent experiments, because social psychologists believe that the courtroom offers a natural context for studying how people form judgments and that social psychology's principles and methods can shed new light on important judicial issues.

Experiments reveal that both witnesses and jurors readily succumb to an illusion that a given witness's mental-recording equipment functions free of significant error. But as witnesses construct and rehearse memories of what they have observed, errors creep in. Research suggests ways to lessen such error, both in eyewitness reports and in jurors' use of such reports.

What other factors influence juror judgments?

Are the defendant's attractiveness and similarity to jurors likely to bias them? How faithfully do jurors follow judges' instructions?

THE DEFENDANT'S CHARACTERISTICS

According to the famed trial lawyer Clarence Darrow (1933), jurors seldom convict a person they like or acquit one they dislike. He argued that the main job of the trial lawyer is to make a jury like the defendant. Was he right? And is it true, as Darrow also said, that "facts regarding the crime are relatively unimportant"?

Darrow overstated the case. One study of more than 3,500 criminal cases and 4,000 civil cases found that four times in five the judge agreed with the jury's decision (Kalven & Zeisel, 1966). Although both may have been wrong, the evidence usually is clear enough that jurors can set aside their biases, focus on the facts, and agree on a verdict (Saks & Hastie, 1978; Visher, 1987). Facts do matter.

Nevertheless, when jurors are asked to make social judgments—would this defendant intentionally commit *this* offense?—facts are not all that matter. As we noted in Chapter 7, communicators are more persuasive if they seem credible and attractive. Jurors cannot help forming impressions of the defendant. Can they put these impressions aside and decide the case based on the facts alone?

To judge from the more lenient treatment often received by high-status defendants (McGillis, 1979), it seems that some cultural bias lingers. But actual cases vary in so many ways—in the type of crime, in the status, age, gender, and race of the defendant—that it's hard to isolate the factors that influence jurors. So experimenters have controlled such factors by giving mock jurors the same basic facts of a case while varying, say, the defendant's attractiveness or similarity to the jurors.

Other things being equal, people often judge physically appealing defendants more leniently.

Physical attractiveness

In Chapter 11, we noted a physical attractiveness stereotype: Beautiful people seem like good people. Michael Efran (1974) wondered whether this stereotype would bias students' judgments of someone accused of cheating. He asked some of his University of Toronto students whether attractiveness should affect presumption of guilt. They answered, "No, it shouldn't." But did it? Yes. When Efran gave other students a description of the case with a photograph of either an attractive or an unattractive defendant, they judged the most attractive as least guilty and recommended that person for the least punishment.

Other experimenters have confirmed that when the evidence is meager or ambiguous, justice is not blind to a defendant's looks (Mazzella & Feingold, 1994). Diane Berry and Leslie Zebrowitz-McArthur (1988) discovered this when they asked people to judge the guilt of baby-faced and mature-faced defendants. Baby-faced adults (people with large, round eyes and small chins) seemed more naive and were found guilty more often of crimes of mere negligence but less often of intentional criminal acts. If convicted, unattractive people also strike people as

THE FAR SIDE®   BY GARY LARSON

© 1980 FarWorks, Inc. All Rights Reserved/Dist. by Creators Syndicate

"And so I ask the jury—is that the face of a mass murderer?"

figure 15–5

Attractiveness and legal judgments.

Texas Gulf Coast judges set higher bails and fines for less attractive defendants. **Source:** Data from Downs & Lyons, 1991.

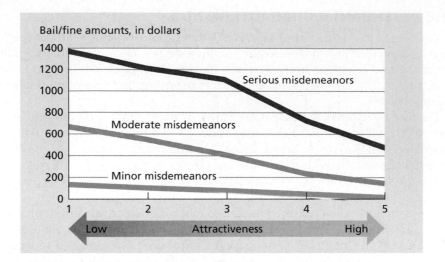

more dangerous, especially if they are sexual offenders (Esses & Webster, 1988). O. J.'s being, as one prospective juror put it, "a hunk of a fellow," probably did not hurt his cause.

In a mammoth experiment conducted with BBC Television, Richard Wiseman (1998) showed viewers evidence about a burglary, with but one variation. Some viewers saw the defendant played by an actor that fit what a panel of 100 people judged as the stereotypical criminal—unattractive, crooked nose, small eyes. Among 64,000 people phoning in their verdict, 41 percent judged him guilty. British viewers elsewhere saw an attractive, baby-faced defendant with large blue eyes. Only 31 percent found him guilty.

To see if these findings extend to the real world, Chris Downs and Phillip Lyons (1991) asked police escorts to rate the physical attractiveness of 1,742 defendants appearing before 40 Texas judges in misdemeanor cases. Whether the misdemeanor was serious (such as forgery), moderate (such as harassment), or minor (such as public intoxication), the judges set higher bails and fines for less attractive defendants (Figure 15–5). What explains this dramatic effect? Are unattractive people also lower in status? Are they indeed more likely to flee or to commit crime, as the judges perhaps suppose? Or do judges simply ignore the Roman statesman Cicero's advice: "The final good and the supreme duty of the wise man is to resist appearance."

Similarity to the jurors

If Clarence Darrow was even partly right in his declaration that liking or disliking a defendant colors judgments, then other factors that influence liking should also matter. Among such influences is the principle, noted in Chapter 11, that likeness (similarity) leads to liking. When people pretend they are jurors, they are indeed more sympathetic to a defendant who shares their attitudes, religion, race, or (in cases of sexual assault) gender (Selby & others, 1977; Towson & Zanna, 1983; Ugwuegbu, 1979).

Some examples:

- When Paul Amato (1979) had Australian students read evidence concerning a left- or right-wing person accused of a politically motivated burglary, they judged the defendant less guilty if his or her political views were similar to their own.

- When Cookie Stephan and Walter Stephan (1986) had English-speaking people judge someone accused of assault, they were more likely to think the person not guilty if the defendant's testimony was in English, rather than translated from Spanish or Thai.

"You look like this sketch of someone who's thinking about committing a crime."

- When a defendant's race fits a crime stereotype—say, a White defendant charged with embezzlement or a Black defendant charged with auto theft—mock jurors offer more negative verdicts and punishments (Jones & Kaplan, 2003; Mazzella & Feingold, 1994). Whites who espouse nonprejudiced views are more likely to demonstrate racial bias in trials where race issues are not blatant (Sommers & Ellsworth, 2000, 2001).

- In actual capital cases, reports Craig Haney (1991), data "show that Blacks are overpunished as defendants or undervalued as victims, or both." One analysis of 80,000 criminal convictions during 1992 and 1993 found that U.S. federal judges—only 5 percent of whom were Black—sentenced Blacks to 10 percent longer sentences than Whites when comparing cases with the same seriousness and criminal history (Associated Press, 1995). Likewise, Blacks who kill Whites are more often sentenced to death than Whites who kill Blacks (Butterfield, 2001).

There were differences within each race in perceptions of Simpson's guilt or innocence. White women whose identity focused on gender were especially likely to think Simpson guilty. African Americans for whom race was central to their identity were especially likely to think him innocent (Fairchild & Cowan, 1997; Newman & others, 1997).

So it seems we are more sympathetic toward a defendant with whom we can identify. If we think we wouldn't have committed that criminal act, we may assume that someone like us is also unlikely to have done it. That helps explain why, in acquaintance rape trials, men more often than women judge the defendant not guilty (Fischer, 1997). That also helps explain why a national survey before the O. J. Simpson trial got under way found that 77 percent of Whites, but only 45 percent of Blacks, saw the case against him as at least "fairly strong" (Smolowe, 1994). And it helps explain the riotous outrage that followed the initial acquittal (by a jury with no Blacks) of the White officers who clubbed African American Rodney King. People debated: If an unarmed White man had been arrested after a car chase by four Black officers, who were videotaped beating him mercilessly, would the same jury have acquitted them?

Ideally, jurors would leave their biases outside the courtroom and begin a trial with open minds. So implies the Sixth Amendment to the U.S. Constitution: "The accused shall

"Surely not guilty. Next case."

enjoy the right to a speedy and public trial by impartial jury." In its concern for objectivity, the judicial system is similar to science. Both scientists and jurors are supposed to sift and weigh the evidence. Both the courts and science have rules about what evidence is relevant. Both keep careful records and assume that others given the same evidence would decide similarly.

When the evidence is clear and individuals focus on it (as when they reread and debate the meaning of testimony), their biases are indeed minimal (Kaplan & Schersching, 1980). The quality of the evidence matters more than the prejudices of the individual jurors.

THE JUDGE'S INSTRUCTIONS

In the courtroom, judges instruct jurors to ignore biasing information. All of us can recall courtroom dramas in which an attorney exclaimed, "Your honor, I object!" whereupon the judge sustained the objection and ordered the jury to ignore the other attorney's suggestive question or the witness's remark.

Nearly all states in the United States now have "rape shield" statutes that prohibit or limit testimony concerning the victim's prior sexual activity. Such testimony, though irrelevant to the case at hand, tends to make jurors more sympathetic to the accused rapist's claim that the woman consented to sexual relations (Borgida, 1981; Cann & others, 1979). If such reliable, illegal, or prejudicial testimony is nevertheless slipped in by the defense or blurted out by a witness, will jurors follow a judge's instruction to ignore it? And is it enough for the judge to remind jurors, "The issue is not whether you like or dislike the defendant but whether the defendant committed the offense"?

Very possibly not. Several experimenters report that jurors show concern for due process (Fleming & others, 1999), but that it is sometimes hard for jurors to ignore inadmissible evidence, such as the defendant's previous convictions. In one study, Stanley Sue, Ronald Smith, and Cathy Caldwell (1973) gave University of Washington students a description of a grocery store robbery-murder and a summary of the prosecution's case and the defense's case. When the prosecution's case was weak, no one judged the defendant guilty. When a tape recording of an incriminating phone call made by the defendant was added to the weak case, about one-third judged the person guilty. The judge's instructions that the tape was not legal evidence and should be ignored did nothing to erase the effect of the damaging testimony.

Indeed, Sharon Wolf and David Montgomery (1977) found that a judge's order to ignore testimony—"It must play no role in your consideration of the case. You have no choice but to disregard it"—can even boomerang, adding to the testimony's impact. Perhaps such statements create **reactance** in the jurors. Or perhaps they sensitize jurors to the inadmissible testimony, as when I warn you not to look at your nose as you finish this sentence. Judges can more easily strike inadmissible testimony from the court records than from the jurors' minds. As trial lawyers sometimes say, "You can't unring a bell." This is especially so with emotional information (Edwards & Bryan, 1997). When jurors are told vividly about a defendant's record ("hacking up a woman"), a judge's instructions to ignore are more likely to boomerang than when the inadmissible information is less emotional ("assault with a deadly weapon"). Even if jurors later claim to have ignored the inadmissible information, it may alter how they construe other information.

reactance
A motive to protect or restore one's sense of freedom. Reactance arises when someone threatens our freedom of action.

Pretrial publicity is also hard for jurors to ignore, especially in studies with real jurors and serious crimes (Steblay & others, 1999). In one massive experiment, Geoffrey Kramer and his colleagues (1990) exposed nearly 800 mock jurors (most from actual jury rolls) to incriminating news reports about the past convictions of a man accused of robbing a supermarket. After the jurors viewed a videotaped reenactment of the trial, they either did or did not hear the judge's instructions to disregard the pretrial publicity. The effect of the judicial admonition was nil. People whose opinions are biased by such publicity typically deny its effect on them, and this denial makes it hard to eliminate biased jurors (Moran & Cutler, 1991). In experiments, even getting mock jurors to pledge their impartiality and their willingness to disregard prior information has not eliminated the pretrial publicity effect (Dexter & others, 1992). O. J. Simpson's attorneys, it seems, had reason to worry about the massive pretrial publicity. And the trial judge had reason to order jurors not to view pertinent media publicity and to isolate them during the trial.

Will jurors clear their minds of pretrial publicity that might bias their evaluation of evidence? Although jurors will deny being biased, experiments have shown otherwise.

Judges can hope, with some support from available research, that during deliberation, jurors who bring up inadmissible evidence will be chastened for doing so, and that jury group verdicts may therefore be less influenced by such evidence (London & Nunez, 2000). To minimize the effects of inadmissible testimony, judges also can forewarn jurors that certain types of evidence, such as a rape victim's sexual history, are irrelevant. Once jurors form impressions based on such evidence, a judge's admonitions have much less effect (Borgida & White, 1980; Kassin & Wrightsman, 1979). Thus, reports Vicki Smith (1991), a pretrial training session pays dividends. Teaching jurors legal procedures and standards of proof improves their understanding of the trial procedure and their willingness to withhold judgment until after they have heard all the trial information.

Better yet, judges could cut inadmissible testimony before the jurors hear it—by videotaping testimonies and removing the inadmissible parts. Live and videotaped testimonies have much the same impact as do live and videotaped lineups (Cutler & others, 1989; Miller & Fontes, 1979). Perhaps courtrooms of the future will have life-size television monitors. Critics object that the procedure prevents jurors from observing how the defendant and others react to the witness. Proponents argue that videotaping not only enables the judge to edit out inadmissible testimony but also speeds up the trial and allows witnesses to talk about crucial events before memories fade.

It is not easy for jurors to erase inadmissible testimony from memory.

"The jury will disregard the witness's last remarks."

OTHER ISSUES

We have considered three courtroom factors—eyewitness testimony, the defendant's characteristics, and the judge's instructions. Researchers are also studying the influence of other factors. For example, at Michigan State University, Norbert Kerr and his colleagues (1978, 1981, 1982) have studied these issues: Does a severe potential punishment (for example, a death penalty) make jurors less willing to convict—and was it therefore strategic for the Los Angeles prosecutors not to seek the death penalty for O. J. Simpson? Do experienced jurors' judgments differ from those of novice jurors? Are defendants judged more harshly when the *victim* is attractive or has suffered greatly? Kerr's research suggests that the answer to all three questions is yes.

Experiments by Mark Alicke and Teresa Davis (1989) and by Michael Enzle and Wendy Hawkins (1992) show that jurors' judgments of blame and punishment can be affected by the victim's characteristics—even when the defendant is unaware of such. Consider the 1984 case of the "subway vigilante" Bernard Goetz. When four teens approached Goetz for $5 on a New York subway, the frightened Goetz pulled out a loaded gun and shot each of them, leaving one partly paralyzed. When Goetz was charged with attempted homicide, there was an outcry of public support for him based partly on the disclosure that the youths had extensive criminal records and that three of them were carrying concealed, sharpened screwdrivers. Although Goetz didn't know any of this, he was acquitted of the attempted homicide charge and convicted only of illegal firearm possession.

Summing up

The facts of a case are usually compelling enough that jurors can lay aside their biases and render a fair judgment. When the evidence is ambiguous, however, jurors are more likely to interpret it with their preconceived biases and to feel sympathetic to a defendant who is attractive or similar to themselves.

When jurors are exposed to damaging pretrial publicity or to inadmissible evidence, will they follow a judge's instruction to ignore it? In simulated trials, the judge's orders were sometimes followed, but often, especially when the judge's admonition came *after* an impression was made, they were not. Researchers have also explored the influence of other factors, such as the victim's characteristics.

What influences the individual juror?

Verdicts depend on what happens in the courtroom—the eyewitness testimonies, the defendant's characteristics, the judge's instructions. But verdicts also depend on how the individual jurors process information.

Courtroom influences on "the average juror" are worth pondering. But no juror is the average juror; each carries into the courthouse individual attitudes and personalities. And when they deliberate, jurors influence one another. So two key questions are (1) how are verdicts influenced by individual jurors' dispositions? and (2) how are verdicts influenced by jurors' group deliberation?

JUROR COMPREHENSION

To gain insight into juror comprehension, Nancy Pennington and Reid Hastie (1993) had mock jurors, sampled from courthouse jury pools, view reenactments of actual trials. In making their decisions, the jurors first constructed a story that made sense of all the evidence. After observing one murder trial, for example, some jurors concluded that a quarrel made the defendant angry, triggering him to get a knife, search for the decedent, and stab him to death. Others surmised that the frightened defendant picked up a knife that he used to defend himself when he later encountered the decedent. When jurors begin deliberating, they are often surprised to discover that others have constructed different

Effective prosecutors offer jurors plausible stories.

stories. This implies—and research confirms—that jurors are best persuaded when attorneys present evidence in narrative fashion—a story. In felony cases, where the national conviction rate is 80 percent, the prosecution case more often than the defense case follows a narrative structure.

Understanding instructions

Next, the jurors must grasp the judge's instructions concerning the available verdict categories. For these instructions to be effective, jurors must first understand them. Study after study has found that many people do not understand the standard legalese of

"Your Honor, we're going to go with the prosecution's spin."

Faced with an incomprehensibly complex accounting of Imelda Marcos's alleged thefts of public money, jurors fell back on their intuitive assessments of the seemingly devout and sincere woman and found her not guilty.

judicial instructions. Depending on the type of case, a jury may be told that the standard of proof is a "preponderance of the evidence," "clear and convincing evidence," or "beyond a reasonable doubt." Such statements may have one meaning for the legal community and different meanings in the minds of jurors (Kagehiro, 1990). In one study of Nevada criminal instructions, viewers of videotaped instructions could answer only 15 percent of 89 questions posed to them about what they had heard (Elwork & others, 1982).

A judge may also remind jurors to avoid premature conclusions as they weigh each new item of presented evidence. But research with both college students and mock jurors chosen from actual prospective jury pools shows that warm-blooded human beings do have premature leanings, and these leanings do influence how they interpret new information (Carlson & Russo, 2001).

After observing actual cases and later interviewing the jurors, Stephen Adler (1994) found "lots of sincere, serious people who—for a variety of reasons— were missing key points, focusing on irrelevant issues, succumbing to barely recognized prejudices, failing to see through the cheapest appeals to sympathy or hate, and generally botching the job."

In the trial of Imelda Marcos, who was charged with transferring hundreds of millions of dollars of Philippine money into American banks for her own use, lawyers eliminated anyone who was aware of her role in her husband's dictatorship. Ill-equipped to follow the complex money transactions, the uninformed people who made it onto the jury fell back on sympathy for Imelda, whom they would see dressed in black, clutching her rosaries, and wiping away tears (Adler, 1994).

Jurors may be further confused if the criteria change as proceedings move from the trial phase determining guilt or innocence into the penalty phase (Luginbuhl, 1992). In North Carolina, for example, jurors are to convict only if there is "proof beyond a reasonable doubt." But a "preponderance of the evidence" is sufficient when judging whether mitigating circumstances, such as an abusive childhood, should preclude a death sentence.

Finally, jurors must compare their explanation with the verdict categories. When using the judge's definition of justifiable self-defense, for example, jurors must decide whether "pinned against a wall" matches their understanding of the required circumstance "unable to escape." Often a judge's abstract, jargon-filled definition of verdict categories loses in the competition with the jurors' own mental images of these crimes. Vicki Smith (1991) reports that, regardless of the judge's definition, if a defendant's actions match jurors' images of "vandalism," "assault," or "robbery," they will find the person guilty.

Understanding statistical information

Tests on blood found at the scene where O. J. Simpson's ex-wife and her fellow victim were murdered revealed bloodstains that matched Simpson's mix of blood proteins, but not the victims'. Learning that only 1 in 200 people share this blood type, some people assumed the chances were 99.5 percent that Simpson was the culprit. But 1 in 200 means the culprit could be any one of at least 40,000 people in the Los Angeles area, noted the defense. Faced with such arguments, three in five people will discount the relevance of the blood-type evidence, report William Thompson and Edward Schumann (1987). Actually, both attorneys were wrong. The evidence is relevant because few of the other 40,000 people can reasonably be considered suspects. But the 99.5 percent argument ignores the fact that the defendant was charged partly because his blood type matched.

When a more precise DNA match with Simpson's blood was found, prosecutors contended that the chance of such a match was 1 in 170 million, while the defense showed that experts disagreed about the reliability of DNA testing. But Gary Wells (1992) and Keith Niedermeier and colleagues (1999) report that even when people (including experienced trial judges) understand naked statistical probabilities, they may be unpersuaded. Told that 80 percent of the tires of the Blue Bus Co. but only 20 percent of the alternative Grey Bus Co. match the tracks of a bus that killed a dog, people seldom convict the Blue Co. The naked numbers allow a plausible alternative scenario—that the accident was caused by one of 20 percent of Grey buses. Told that an eyewitness identified the bus as blue, people usually will convict, even if the eyewitness was shown to be only 80 percent accurate in making such identifications. The plausible alternative scenario in the first case creates a psychological difference between saying there is an 80 percent chance that something is true and saying that something is true based on 80 percent reliable evidence.

Naked numbers, it seems, must be supported by a convincing story. Thus, reports Wells, one Toronto mother lost a paternity suit seeking child support from her child's alleged father despite a blood test showing a 99.8 percent probability that the man was her child's father. She lost after the man took the stand and persuasively denied the allegation.

Increasing jurors' understanding

Understanding how jurors misconstrue judicial instructions and statistical information is a first step toward better decisions. A next step might be giving jurors access to transcripts rather than forcing them to rely on their memories in processing complex information (Bourgeois & others, 1993). A further step would be devising and testing clearer, more effective ways to present information—a task on which several social psychologists are currently at work. For example, when a judge quantifies the required standard of proof (as, say, 51, 71, or 91 percent certainty), jurors understand and respond appropriately (Kagehiro, 1990).

And surely there must be a simpler way to tell jurors, as required by the Illinois Death Penalty Act, not to impose the death sentence in murder cases when there are justifying circumstances: "If you do not unanimously find from your consideration of all the evidence that there are no mitigating factors sufficient to preclude imposition of a death sentence, then you should sign the verdict requiring the court to impose a sentence other than death" (Diamond, 1993).

Alan Dershowitz, an O. J. Simpson defense attorney, argued to the media that only 1 in 1,000 men who abuse their wives later murder them. More relevant, replied critics, is the probability that a husband is guilty given that (a) he abused his wife, and (b) his wife was murdered. From available data, Jon Merz and Jonathan Caulkins (1995) calculated that probability as .81.

When jurors are given instructions rewritten into simple language, they are less susceptible to the judge's biases (Halverson & others, 1997).

Phoebe Ellsworth and Robert Mauro (1998) sum up the dismal conclusions of jury researchers: "Legal instructions are typically delivered in a manner likely to frustrate the most conscientious attempts at understanding. . . . The language is technical and . . . no attempt is made either to assess jurors' mistaken preconceptions about the law or to provide any kind of useful education."

JURY SELECTION

Given the variations among individual jurors, can trial lawyers use the jury selection process to stack juries in their favor? Legal folklore suggests that sometimes they can. One president of the Association of Trial Lawyers of America boldly proclaimed, "Trial attorneys are acutely attuned to the nuances of human behavior, which enables them to detect the minutest traces of bias or inability to reach an appropriate decision" (Bigam, 1977).

Mindful that people's assessments of others are error-prone, social psychologists doubt that attorneys come equipped with fine-tuned social Geiger counters. In some 6,000 American trials a year, consultants—some of them social scientists in the American Society of Trial Consultants—help lawyers pick juries and plot strategy (Gavzer, 1997; Miller, 2001). In several celebrated trials, survey researchers have used "scientific jury selection" to help attorneys weed out those likely to be unsympathetic. One famous trial involved two of President Nixon's former cabinet members, conservatives John Mitchell and Maurice Stans. A survey revealed that from the defense's viewpoint the worst possible juror was "a liberal, Jewish, Democrat who reads the *New York Times* or the *Post*, listens to Walter Cronkite, is interested in political affairs, and is well-informed about Watergate" (Zeisel & Diamond, 1976). Of the first nine trials, relying on "scientific" selection methods, the defense won seven (Hans & Vidmar, 1981; Wrightsman, 1978). (However, we can't know how many of these nine would have been won anyway, without scientific juror selection.)

Many trial attorneys have now used scientific jury selection to identify questions they can use to exclude those biased against their clients, and most report satisfaction with the results (Gayoso & others, 1991; Moran & others, 1994). Most jurors, when asked by a judge to "raise your hand if you've read anything about this case that would prejudice you," don't directly acknowledge their preconceptions. It takes further questioning to reveal them. For example, if the judge allows an attorney to check prospective jurors' attitudes toward drugs, the attorney can often guess their verdicts in a drug-trafficking case (Moran & others, 1990). Likewise, people who acknowledge they "don't put much faith in the testimony of psychiatrists" are less likely to accept an insanity defense (Cutler & others, 1992).

Individuals react differently to specific features of a case. Racial prejudice becomes relevant in racially charged cases; gender seems linked with verdicts only in rape and battered woman cases; belief in personal responsibility versus corporate responsibility relates to personal injury awards in suits against businesses (Ellsworth & Mauro, 1998).

> "Beware of the Lutherans, especially the Scandinavians; they are almost always sure to convict."
> —Clarence Darrow, "How to Pick a Jury," 1936

O. J. Simpson attorneys in the criminal trial also used a jury selection consultant—and won (Lafferty, 1994). Meeting the press after the not-guilty verdict, Simpson's attorney immediately thanked the jury selection consultant.

Despite the excitement—and ethical concern—about scientific jury selection, experiments reveal that attitudes and personal characteristics don't always predict verdicts. There are "no magic questions to be asked of prospective jurors, not even a guarantee that a particular survey will detect useful attitude-behavior or personality-behavior relationships," caution Steven Penrod and Brian Cutler (1987). Researchers Michael Saks and Reid Hastie (1978) agree: "The studies are unanimous in showing that evidence is a substantially more potent determinant of jurors' verdicts than the individual characteristics of jurors" (p. 68). "The best conclusion is that there are cases where jury-selection consultants can make a difference but such cases are few and far between," add Neil Kressel and Dorit Kressel (2002). In courtrooms, jurors' public pledge of fairness and the judge's instruction to "be fair" strongly commit most jurors to the norm of fairness.

In experiments, it's when the evidence is ambiguous that jurors' personalities and general attitudes have an effect. Moreover, note Gary Moran and his co-researchers, if scientific jury selection can even slightly surpass your attorney's hunches about a juror's leanings, wouldn't you welcome the help in a vital case?

Still, variations in the situation, especially in the evidence, are what matter most. Saks and Hastie conclude that, "What this implies about human behavior, on juries or off, is that while we are unique individuals, our differences are vastly overshadowed by our similarities. Moreover, the range of situations we are likely to encounter is far more varied than the range of human beings who will encounter them" (p. 69).

"DEATH-QUALIFIED" JURORS

A *close* case can, however, be decided by who gets selected for the jury. In criminal cases, people who do not oppose the death penalty—and who therefore are eligible to serve when a death sentence is possible—are more prone to favor the prosecution, to feel that courts coddle criminals, and to oppose protecting the constitutional rights of defendants (Bersoff, 1987). Simply put, those who favor the death penalty are more concerned with crime control and less concerned with due process of law. When a court dismisses potential jurors who have moral scruples against the death penalty—something O. J. Simpson's prosecutors chose not to do—it constructs a jury that is more likely to vote guilty.

On this issue, social scientists are in "virtual unanimity . . . about the biasing effects of death qualification," reports Craig Haney (1993). The research record is "unified," reports Phoebe Ellsworth (1985, p. 46): "Defendants in capital-punishment cases do assume the extra handicap of juries predisposed to find them guilty." What is more, conviction-prone jurors tend also to be more authoritarian—more rigid, punitive, closed to mitigating circumstances, and contemptuous of those of lower status (Gerbasi & others, 1977; Luginbuhl & Middendorf, 1988; Moran & Comfort, 1982, 1986; Werner & others, 1982).

Because the legal system operates on tradition and precedent, such research findings only slowly alter judicial practice. In 1986, the U.S. Supreme Court, in a split decision, overturned a lower-court ruling that "death-qualified" jurors are indeed a biased sample. Ellsworth (1989) believes the Court in this case disregarded the compelling and consistent evidence partly because of its "ideological commitment to capital punishment" and partly because of the havoc that would result if the convictions of thousands of people on death row had to be

"The kind of juror who would be unperturbed by the prospect of sending a man to his death . . . is the kind of juror who would too readily ignore the presumption of the defendant's innocence, accept the prosecution's version of the facts, and return a verdict of guilty."
Witherspoon v. Illinois, 1968

Guilty. Jury selection criteria may yield conviction-prone jurors. Copyright © The New Yorker Collection, 2002, Nick Downes, from cartoonbank.com. All Rights Reserved.

Average homicide rate per 100,000

- *for entire United States: 9*
- *for death-penalty states: 9.3*

Source: Scientific American, *February, 2001*

reconsidered. The solution, should the Court ever wish to adopt it for future cases, is to convene separate juries to (a) decide guilt in capital murder cases, and, given a guilty verdict, to (b) hear additional evidence on factors motivating the murder and to decide between death or imprisonment.

But a deeper issue is at stake here: whether the death penalty itself falls under the U.S. Constitution's ban on "cruel and unusual punishment." Other countries assume so. As readers in Canada, Australia, New Zealand, Western Europe, and most of South America know, their countries prohibit capital punishment. There, as in the United States, public attitudes tend to support whatever is the prevailing practice (Costanzo, 1997). But American pro-capital punishment attitudes seem to be softening. After reaching 80 percent in 1994, support fell to 70 percent in 2002 (Jones, 2003). After 13 men in Illinois's death row were exonerated by new evidence, Governor George Ryan declared a moratorium on executions (Johnson, 2000).

In wrestling with the punishment, U.S. courts have considered whether courts inflict the penalty arbitrarily, whether they apply it with racial bias, and whether legal killing deters illegal killing. The social science answers to these questions are clear, note social psychologists Mark Costanzo (1997) and Craig Haney and Deana Logan (1994). Consider the deterrence issue. States with a death penalty do not have lower homicide rates. Homicide rates have not dropped when states have initiated the death penalty, and they have not risen when states have abandoned it. When committing a crime of passion, people don't pause to calculate the consequences (which include life in prison without parole as another potent deterrent). Moreover, the death penalty is applied inconsistently (in Texas 40 times as often as in New York). And it is applied more often with poor defendants, who often receive a weak defense (*Economist*, 2000). Nevertheless, the Supreme Court has determined that admitting only death-qualified jurors provides a representative jury of one's peers and that "the death penalty undoubtedly is a significant deterrent."

Humanitarian considerations aside, say the appalled social scientists, what is the rationale for clinging to cherished assumptions and intuitions in the face of contradictory evidence? Why not put our cultural ideas to the test? If they find support, so much the better for them. If they crash against a wall of contradictory evidence, so much the worse for them. Such are the ideals of critical thinking that fuel both psychological science and civil democracy.

Summing up

What matters is what happens not only in the courtroom but also within and among the jurors themselves.

In forming their judgments, individual jurors (1) construct a story that explains the evidence, (2) consider the judge's instructions, and (3) compare their understandings with the possible verdicts. In a close case, the jurors' own characteristics can influence their verdicts. Jurors who favor capital punishment or who are highly authoritarian appear more likely to convict certain types of defendants. Nevertheless, what matters most is not the jurors' personalities and general attitudes but rather the situation they must react to.

How do group influences affect juries?

What influences how individual jurors' prejudgments coalesce into a group decision?

Imagine a jury that has just finished a trial and has entered the jury room to begin its deliberations. Researchers Harry Kalven and Hans Zeisel (1966) reported that chances are about two in three that the jurors will *not* agree initially on a verdict. Yet, after discussion, 95 percent emerge with a consensus. Obviously, group influence has occurred.

In the United States, 300,000 times a year small groups sampled from the 3 million people called for jury duty convene to seek a group decision (Kagehiro, 1990). Are they and juries elsewhere subject to the social influences that mold other decision groups—to patterns of majority and minority influence, to group polarization, to groupthink? Let's start with a simple question: If we knew the jurors' initial leanings, could we predict their verdict?

The law prohibits observation of actual juries. So researchers simulate the jury process by presenting a case to mock juries and having them deliberate as a real jury would. In a series of such studies at the University of Illinois, James Davis, Robert Holt, Norbert Kerr, and Garold Stasser tested various mathematical schemes for predicting group decisions, including decisions by mock juries (Davis & others, 1975, 1977, 1989; Kerr & others, 1976). Will some mathematical combination of initial decisions predict the final group decision? Davis and his colleagues found that the scheme that predicts best varies according to the nature of the case. But in several experiments, a "two-thirds-majority" scheme fared best: The group verdict was usually the alternative favored by at least two-thirds of the jurors at the outset. Without such a majority, a hung jury was likely.

Likewise, in Kalven and Zeisel's survey of juries, 9 in 10 reached the verdict favored by the majority on the first ballot. Although you or I might fantasize about someday being the courageous lone juror who sways the majority, the fact is it seldom happens.

MINORITY INFLUENCE

Seldom, yet sometimes, what was initially a minority opinion prevails. A typical 12-person jury is like a typical small college class: The three quietest people rarely talk and the three most vocal people contribute more than half the talking (Hastie & others, 1983). In the Mitchell-Stans trial, the four jurors who favored acquittal persisted, were vocal, and eventually prevailed. From the research on minority influence, we know that jurors in the minority will be most persuasive when they are consistent, persistent, and self-confident. This is especially so if they can begin to trigger some defections from the majority (Gordijn & others, 2002; Kerr, 1981).

Ironically, the most influential minority juror in the Mitchell-Stans trial, Andrew Choa, was a well-educated *New York Times* reader—someone who did not fit the survey profile of a juror sympathetic to the defense. But Choa was also a dedicated supporter of Richard Nixon and a bank vice president who ingratiated himself with the other jurors through various favors, such as taking them to movies in his bank's private auditorium (Zeisel & Diamond, 1976). Choa also illustrates a common finding from jury experiments: High-status male jurors tend to be most influential (Gerbasi & others, 1977).

GROUP POLARIZATION

Jury deliberation shifts people's opinions in other intriguing ways as well. In experiments, deliberation often magnifies initial sentiments. For example, Robert Bray and Audrey Noble (1978) had University of Kentucky students listen to a 30-minute tape of a murder trial. Then, assuming the defendant was found guilty, they recommended a prison sentence. Groups of high authoritarians initially recommended strong punishments (56 years) and after deliberation were even more punitive (68 years). The low-authoritarian groups were initially more lenient (38 years) and after deliberation became more so (29 years).

Confirmation that group polarization can occur in juries comes from an ambitious study in which Reid Hastie, Steven Penrod, and Nancy Pennington (1983) put together 69 twelve-person juries from Massachusetts citizens on jury duty. Each jury was shown a reenactment of an actual murder case, with roles played by an experienced judge and actual attorneys. Then they were given unlimited time to deliberate the case in a jury room. As Figure 15–6 shows, the evidence was incriminating: Four out of five jurors voted guilty before

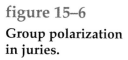

figure 15–6

Group polarization in juries.

In highly realistic simulations of a murder trial, 828 Massachusetts jurors stated their initial verdict preferences, then deliberated the case for periods ranging from three hours to five days. Deliberation strengthened initial tendencies, which favored the prosecution.

Source: From Hastie & others, 1983.

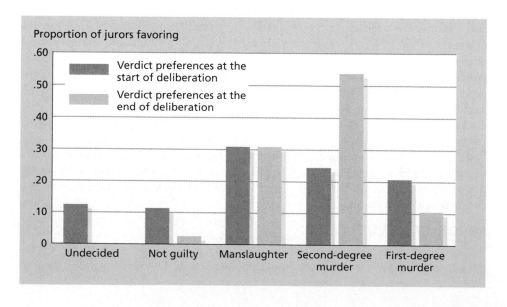

Proportion of jurors favoring

Verdict preferences at the start of deliberation

Verdict preferences at the end of deliberation

Undecided   Not guilty   Manslaughter   Second-degree murder   First-degree murder

deliberation, but felt unsure enough that a weak verdict of manslaughter was their most popular preference. After deliberation, nearly all agreed the accused was guilty, and most now preferred a stronger verdict—second-degree murder. Through deliberation, their initial leanings had grown stronger.

LENIENCY

In many experiments, one other curious effect of deliberation has surfaced: Especially when the evidence is not highly incriminating, deliberating jurors often become more lenient (MacCoun & Kerr, 1988). This qualifies the "two-thirds-majority-rules" finding, for if even a bare majority initially favors *acquittal*, it usually will prevail (Stasser & others, 1981). Moreover, a minority that favors acquittal stands a better chance of prevailing than one that favors conviction (Tindale & others, 1990).

Once again, a survey of actual juries confirms the laboratory results. Kalven and Zeisel (1966) report that, in those cases where the majority does not prevail, it usually shifts to acquittal (as in the Mitchell-Stans trial). When a judge disagrees with the jury's decision, it is usually because the jury acquits someone the judge would have convicted.

Might "informational influence" (stemming from others' persuasive arguments) account for the increased leniency? The "innocent-unless-proved-guilty" and "proof-beyond-a-reasonable-doubt" rules put the burden of proof on those who favor conviction. Perhaps this makes evidence of the defendant's innocence more persuasive. Or perhaps "normative influence" creates the leniency effect, as jurors who view themselves as fair-minded confront other jurors who are even more concerned with protecting a possibly innocent defendant.

"It is better that ten guilty persons escape than one innocent suffer."
—William Blackstone, 1769

ARE TWELVE HEADS BETTER THAN ONE?

In Chapter 8 we saw that on thought problems where there is an objective right answer, group judgments surpass those by most individuals. Does the same hold true in juries? When deliberating, jurors exert normative pressure by trying to shift others' judgments by the sheer weight of their own. But they also share information, thus enlarging one another's knowledge of the case. So does informational influence produce superior collective judgment?

The evidence, though meager, is partially encouraging. Groups recall information from a trial better than do their individual members (Vollrath & others, 1989). Deliberation sometimes cancels out certain biases and draws jurors' attention away from their own prejudgments and to the evidence. Twelve heads can be, it seems, better than one.

ARE SIX HEADS AS GOOD AS TWELVE?

In keeping with their British heritage, juries in the United States and Canada have traditionally been composed of 12 people whose task is to reach consensus—a unanimous verdict. However, in several cases appealed during the early 1970s, the U.S. Supreme Court declared that in civil cases and state criminal cases not potentially involving a death penalty, courts could use 6-person juries. Moreover, the Court affirmed a state's right to allow less than unanimous verdicts, even upholding one Louisiana conviction based on a 9 to 3 vote (Tanke & Tanke, 1979). There is no reason to suppose, argued the Court, that smaller juries, or juries not required to reach consensus, will deliberate or decide differently from the traditional jury.

The Court's assumptions triggered an avalanche of criticism from both legal scholars and social psychologists (Saks, 1974, 1996). Some criticisms were matters of simple statistics. For example, if 10 percent of a community's total jury pool is Black, then 72 percent of 12-member juries but only 47 percent of 6-member juries may be expected to have at least one Black person. So smaller juries are less likely to reflect a community's diversity. And if, in a given case, one-sixth of the jurors initially favor acquittal, that would be a single individual in a 6-member jury and 2 people in a 12-member jury. The Court assumed that, psychologically, the two situations would be identical. But as you may recall from our discussion of conformity, resisting group pressure is far more difficult for a minority of one than for a minority of two. Psychologically speaking, a jury split 10 to 2 is not equivalent to a jury split 5 to 1. Not surprisingly, then, 12-person juries are twice as likely as 6-person juries to have hung verdicts (Ellsworth & Mauro, 1998, Saks & Marti, 1997).

Other criticisms were based on experiments by James Davis and others (1975), Charlan Nemeth (1977), and Michael Saks (1977, 1996). In these mock jury experiments, the overall distribution of verdicts from small or nonunanimous juries did not differ much from the verdicts pronounced by unanimous 12-member juries (although verdicts from the smaller juries were more unpredictable—for example, more variable when awarding damages). There are, however, greater effects on deliberation. A smaller jury has the advantage of greater and more evenly balanced participation per juror. Nicolas Fay, Simon Garrod, and Jean Carletta (2000) note the benefits of smaller groups from their studies with Glasgow University students. Compared with deliberations in larger 10-person groups, dominant individuals in smaller groups have a less disproportionate impact; with more dialogue and less monologue, shared consensus more often emerges.

Larger juries, as we've seen, do have important advantages, however. Jury researcher Michael Saks (1998) sums them up: "Larger juries are more likely than smaller juries to contain members of minority groups, more accurately recall trial testimony, give more time to deliberation, hang more often, and appear more likely to reach 'correct' verdicts."

In 1978, after some of these studies were reported, the Supreme Court rejected Georgia's 5-member juries (although it still retains the 6-member jury). Announcing the Court's decision, Justice Harry Blackmun drew upon both the logical and the experimental data to argue that 5-person juries would be less representative, less reliable, less accurate (Grofman, 1980). Ironically, many of these data actually involved comparisons of 6- versus 12-member juries, and thus also argued against the 6-member jury. But having made and defended a public commitment to the 6-member jury, the Court was not convinced that the same arguments applied (Tanke & Tanke, 1979).

From lab to life: Simulated and real juries

Perhaps while reading this chapter, you have wondered what some critics (Tapp, 1980; Vidmar, 1979) have wondered: Isn't there an enormous gulf between college students discussing a hypothetical case and real jurors deliberating a real person's fate? Indeed there is. It is one thing to ponder a pretend decision, given minimal information, and quite another to agonize over the complexities and profound consequences of an actual case. So Reid Hastie,

Hung juries are rarely a problem. Among 59,511 U.S. federal court criminal trials during one recent 13-year period, 2.5 percent ended in a hung jury, as did a mere 0.6 percent of 67,992 federal civil trials (Saks, 1998).

"We have considered [the social science studies] carefully because they provide the only basis, besides judicial hunch, for a decision about whether smaller and smaller juries will be able to fulfill the purposes and functions of the Sixth Amendment."
—Justice Harry Blackmun, *Ballew v. Georgia*, 1978

Martin Kaplan, James Davis, Eugene Borgida, and others have asked their participants, who sometimes are drawn from actual juror pools, to view enactments of actual trials. The enactments are so realistic that sometimes participants forget the trial they are watching on television is staged (Thompson & others, 1981).

Student mock jurors become engaged, too. "As I eavesdropped on the mock juries," recalls researcher Norbert Kerr (1999), "I became fascinated by the jurors' insightful arguments, their mix of amazing recollections and memory fabrications, their prejudices, their attempts to persuade or coerce, and their occasional courage in standing alone. Here brought to life before me were so many of the psychological processes I had been studying! Although our student jurors understood they were only simulating a real trial, they really cared about reaching a fair verdict."

The U.S. Supreme Court (1986) debated the usefulness of jury research in its decision regarding the use of "death-qualified" jurors in capital punishment cases. Defendants have a constitutional "right to a fair trial and an impartial jury whose composition is not biased toward the prosecution." The dissenting judges argued that this right is violated when jurors include only those who accept the death penalty. Their argument, they said, was based chiefly on "the essential unanimity of the results obtained by researchers using diverse subjects and varied methodologies." The majority of the judges, however, declared their "serious doubts about the value of these studies in predicting the behavior of actual jurors." The dissenting judges replied that the courts have not allowed experiments with actual juries; thus "defendants claiming prejudice from death

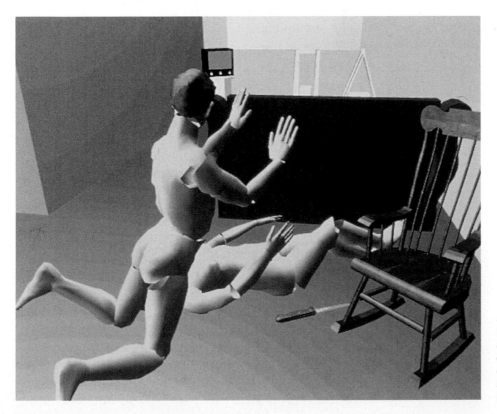

Attorneys are using new technology to present crime stories in ways jurors can easily grasp, as in this computer simulation of a homicide generated on the basis of forensic evidence.

qualification should not be denied recourse to the only available means of proving their case."

Researchers also defend the laboratory simulations by noting that the laboratory offers a practical, inexpensive method of studying important issues under controlled conditions (Bray & Kerr, 1982; Dillehay & Nietzel, 1980; Kerr & others, 1979). As researchers have begun testing them in more realistic situations, findings from the laboratory studies have often held up quite well. No one contends that the simplified world of the jury experiment mirrors the complex world of the real courtroom. Rather, the experiments help us formulate theories with which we interpret the complex world.

Come to think of it, are these jury simulations any different from social psychology's other experiments, all of which create simplified versions of complex realities? By varying just one or two factors at a time in this simulated reality, the experimenter pinpoints how changes in one or two aspects of a situation can affect us. And that is the essence of social psychology's experimental method.

Summing up

Juries are groups, and they are swayed by the same influences that bear upon other types of groups—persuasive arguments, patterns of majority and minority influence, group polarization, information exchange. Researchers have also examined and questioned the assumptions underlying several recent U.S. Supreme Court decisions permitting smaller juries and nonunanimous juries.

Simulated juries are not real juries, so we must be cautious in generalizing research findings to actual courtrooms. Yet, like all experiments in social psychology, laboratory jury experiments help us formulate theories and principles that we can use to interpret the more complex world of everyday life.

Personal Postscript: Thinking smart with psychological science

An intellectually fashionable idea, sometimes called "postmodernism," contends that truth is socially constructed; knowledge always reflects the cultures that form it. Indeed, as we have often noted in this book, we do often follow our hunches, our biases, our cultural bent. Social scientists are not immune to confirmation bias, belief perseverance, overconfidence, and the biasing power of preconceptions. Our preconceived ideas and values guide our theory development, our interpretations, our topics of choice, and our language.

Being mindful of hidden values within psychological science should motivate us to clean the cloudy spectacles through which we view the world. Mindful of our vulnerability to bias and error, we can steer between the two extremes—of being naive about a value-laden psychology that pretends to be value-neutral, or being tempted to an unrestrained subjectivism that dismisses evidence as nothing but collected biases. In the spirit of humility, we can put testable ideas to the test. If we think capital punishment does (or does not) deter crime more than other available punishments, we can utter our personal opinions, as has the U.S. Supreme Court. Or we can ask whether states with a death penalty have lower homicide rates, whether their rates have dropped after instituting the death penalty, and whether they have risen when abandoning the penalty.

As we have seen, the Court considered pertinent social science evidence when disallowing five-member juries and ending school desegregation. But it has discounted research when offering opinions as to whether the death penalty deters crime, whether society views execution as what the U.S. Constitution prohibits ("cruel and unusual punishment"), whether courts inflict the penalty arbitrarily, whether they apply it with racial bias, and whether potential jurors selected by virtue of their accepting capital punishment are biased toward conviction.

As the Court's deciding the 2000 presidential election illustrated—with the more conservative judges forming a five to four majority in favoring the side of the more conservative George Bush—beliefs and values do guide the perceptions of judges as well as scientists and laypeople. And that is why we need to think smarter—to rein in our hunches and biases by testing them against available evidence. If our beliefs find support, so much the better for them. If not, so much the worse for them. That's the humble spirit that underlies both psychological science and everyday critical thinking.

What do you think?

If you were chosen as a juror in a murder case, what biases might you bring to the courtroom? (Do you believe in capital punishment? If so, might you, like others, be more conviction-prone? Might you more likely convict a man than a woman, or a person who differs from you rather than looks and thinks like you?) In what ways do you need to "think smarter," to rein in your biases by testing them against reliable evidence?

Making the Social Connection

This chapter discussed the accuracy of our memories, specifically the memories of eyewitnesses of a crime. Chapter 3: Social Beliefs and Judgments describes how we construct memories. Think about how the accuracy of our memory connects to other topics in social psychology. Do our memories deceive us? Go to the *SocialSense* CD-ROM to learn about memory and how our eyes can deceive us.

chapter 16

Social Psychology and the Sustainable Future[1]

"It was the best of times, it was the worst of times,
  it was the age of wisdom, it was the age of foolishness,
  it was the epoch of belief, it was the epoch of incredulity,
  it was the season of Light, it was the season of Darkness,
  it was the spring of hope, it was the winter of despair,
  we had everything before us, we had nothing before us,
  we were all going direct to Heaven,
  we were all going direct the other way."

Charles Dickens
A Tale of Two Cities

---

[1] Parts of this chapter are adapted and updated from, *The American Paradox: Spiritual Hunger in an Age of Plenty* (by David G. Myers. Yale University Press, 2000), where further information about materialism and wealth, inequality, and well-being may be found.

as the world entered this millennium, good news was bursting from all around:

- Although world population had doubled since 1960, food production had tripled and food was cheaper than ever before.
- Inflation—the "cruelest tax"—was at a 30-year low, interest rates had plunged, and stock markets, even after the recent recession, were at previously undreamed of heights.
- The prices of cars, air travel, petrol, and hamburgers were at record inflation-adjusted lows. The half-gallon of milk that cost the average American 39 minutes of work in 1919 now required only 7 minutes.
- Heavy drinking rates, hard liquor consumption, and drunken driving fatalities were declining.
- New drugs were shrinking our tumors and enlarging our sexual potency.

Compare life today with "the good old days" of a century ago

- no indoor plumbing;
- children laboring in mines, families often broken by death, and no social safety net underneath the poor;
- most people's education limited, women facing restricted opportunities, and minorities shunned;
- less electricity generated each year than we now consume in a day;
- trivial infections sometimes taking a life and with people fearing the two leading causes of death—tuberculosis and pneumonia.

In 1999, Joyce and Paul Bowler—a couple with a keen interest in past lifestyles—were selected from among 450 applicants to Britain's Channel 4 network to spend three months with four of their children living the middle-class life of 1900 (which at the time must have seemed like a cup of tea compared with working-class life). After just a week of rising at 5:30 each morning; preparing food as the Victorians did; wearing corsets; shampooing with a mixture of egg, lemon, borax, and camphor; and playing parlor games by gaslight at night, they were "close to calling it quits." The Bowlers endured. But the realities of 1900s life lacked the romantic appeal of Victorian movies.

Small wonder, noted economist Paul Krugman (2000). "On sheer material grounds one would almost surely prefer to be poor today than upper middle class a century ago." Today's working class enjoy luxuries—electricity, hot running water, flush toilets, television, and transportation—unknown to royalty of centuries past. These are, indeed, the best of times. In less developed countries, people are aware of this good life and clamoring to share in it.

Our best of times have, as we will see, confronted us with a global ecological crisis. After examining the environmental price of today's consumption, we will consider social psychology's perspective on materialism and wealth and on steps we might take toward a sustainable future.

What is the global crisis and what can be done about it?

Because of increased population and consumption, we have overshot the earth's long-term carrying capacity. A sustainable future therefore will require controlled population, increased efficiency and productivity, and moderated consumption.

Alas, this good news is but half the story. In gatherings hosted by the United Nations, Britain's Royal Society, and the U.S. National Academy of Sciences, world scientific leaders note that we have overshot the earth's ecological carrying capacity. We are now spending our environmental capital, not just living off the interest (Heap & Kent, 2000; Oskamp, 2000). With population destined to double again and consumption rising, we are hurtling toward an ecological holocaust.

OVERSHOOTING THE EARTH'S CARRYING CAPACITY

More than 200 years ago, Robert Malthus foresaw that surging population would exceed the earth's carrying capacity. Thanks to advancing technology and agriculture, Malthus's prediction of population outrunning food supply has not yet come true. Not yet. But consider the following.

World population will increase

The good news: Birthrates are falling. In more than 40 countries, fertility rates have dropped to replacement levels (2.1 children per woman) or below. The bad news: In developing nations, birthrates have fallen too little to preclude rapid population growth. And even when replacement level birthrates are reached, populations continue to grow because of the wave of people reaching their childbearing years. As Figure 16–1 shows, it took 100 years after 1830 for the world to gain its second billion people, 30 more years to gain its third billion, 15 years to gain its fourth billion, and 12 years to gain its fifth and sixth billions. If the world, especially its poorer countries such as Pakistan and India, seems crowded now, watch out: Demographers expect world population to gain its

"We must find new ways to provide for a human society that presently has outstripped the limits of global sustainability."

—Peter H. Raven, Presidential address to the American Association for the Advancement of Science, 2002

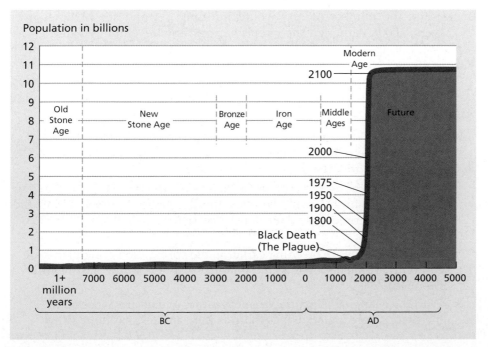

figure 16–1

World population growth through history.

Source: Population Reference Bureau; and United Nations, *World Population Projections to 2100* (1998).

Mount Kilimanjaro, 1979 (left) before and 1999 (right) after late-twentieth-century global warming and deforestation surrounding the mountain.

seventh, eighth, and ninth billion within the lifetimes of most people reading this book.

Such growth obviously cannot continue indefinitely. Exploding population has already meant impoverishment, malnutrition, and illness for half the world, notes Stuart Oskamp (2003). "If we don't control human population growth voluntarily, it will eventually be controlled coercively. The death rate *will* catch up with the birth rate—either through starvation and famines, diseases (e.g., AIDS, which is already ravaging Africa), or by wars and genocide."

Economic growth is increasing consumption

The earth is being assaulted by a double whammy—more people consuming more of its resources. In 1950, the earth carried 2.5 billion people and 50 million cars. Today it has more than 6 billion people and ten times as many cars. If world economic growth enabled all countries to match Americans' present car ownership, the number of cars would multiply yet another 13 times over (N. Myers, 2000). Although that won't happen, the developing countries are rapidly adopting the automobile. Asians now buy more new cars than Western Europeans and North Americans together (Heap & Kent, 2000).

These cars, along with the burning of coal and oil to generate electricity and heat homes, produce greenhouse gases that contribute to global warming (Hileman, 1999). Consider these cold facts about global warming:

- Nine of the 10 warmest years (since recording began in 1861) have occurred since 1990. The three hottest were between 1998 and 2003, reports the World Meteorological Association.
- In the Arctic, the air temperature is increasing, the permafrost is thawing, the trees and shrubs are invading the tundra, the icecaps are melting, the glaciers are shrinking, and the sea is encroaching on villages (Sturm & others, 2003).
- Elsewhere, birds are breeding earlier in the spring, flowering plants are climbing Alpine mountains, and butterflies are migrating northward (Kennedy, 2002).
- With the changing climate, extreme weather events are expected to increase. As precipitation falls more as rain, and less as snow, rainy

"One day fairly soon we will all go belly up like guppies in a neglected fishbowl. I suggest an epitaph for the whole planet: . . . 'We could have saved it, but we were too darn cheap and lazy.'"
—Kurt Vonnegut, "Notes from My Bed of Gloom," 1990

seasons may produce more floods and dry seasons may offer less melting snow and glaciers to feed rivers. In 2003, reports the World Meteorological Organization, Western Europe experienced its hottest weather ever, with 14,802 heat-related deaths in France alone. May 2003 (the warmest May in world history) brought the United States 562 tornados, easily breaking the previous monthly record of 399.

If global warming is occurring, if it is a potential weapon of mass destruction, and if, as most scientists presume, it results primarily from human-produced greenhouse gases, then why is global warming not a hotter topic? Why, ask environmentalists, do we spend more than $100 billion to protect ourselves against Iraq's presumed weapons of mass destruction but not against more likely and globally consequential ones?

And why do only 28 percent of Americans worry a "great deal" about global warming? Is it, as Gallup researcher Lydia Saad (2003) believes, because on a chilly winter day " 'global warming' may sound, well, appealing"? Might people be more concerned about averting "global heating"? Recall from earlier chapters that labels matter. Whether we call those resisting the foreign occupation of their country "terrorists," "the guerrilla resistance," or "freedom fighters" colors our attitudes. Whether we describe someone who responds to others as "conforming" or as "sensitive" and "open" shapes our perceptions. Language shapes thought.

Most of the world's original forest cover has been taken down, and what remains in the tropics is being cleared for agriculture, livestock grazing, logging, and settlements. With deforestation comes diminished absorption of

"Call this an iceberg? When I was a kid we wouldn't have called this an iceberg!"

"Most of the observed warming over the last 50 years is likely to have been due to the increase in greenhouse gas concentrations."
—The United Nations–sponsored Intergovernmental Panel on Climate Change, 2001

Consuming our capital. Overfishing of North Atlantic cod, partly by factory fishing trawlers from other countries, left Newfoundland's fishing industry high and dry during much of the 1990s. A fishing ban aimed to give stocks some time to begin recovering.

greenhouse gases and sometimes flooding, soil erosion, changing rainfall and temperature, and the decimation of many animal species. At the present rate of habitat destruction, estimates biologist Peter Raven (2002), extinction may await "two-thirds of all species on Earth by the end of this century."

A growing population's appetite for fish, together with ecosystem destruction, has lead to decreasing annual catches in 11 of 15 major oceanic fishing areas and in 7 in 10 major fish species (McGinn, 1998; Karavellas, 2000). Due in part to overfishing, stocks of wild salmon, Atlantic cod, haddock, herring, and other species have suffered major depletion

Who is most responsible for global warming and resource depletion? The uncomfortable fact is that it's those of us in countries where this book is most likely to be read. Despite variations among industrialized countries—in the Netherlands 30 percent of urban trips are made on bicycle, as are 1 percent in the United States—industrialization everywhere has been ecologically toxic. Recent statements by the United Nations (and jointly by London's Royal Society with the U.S. National Academy of Sciences) offer examples (Heap & Kent, 2000; N. Myers, 2000):

- Bangladesh's population is growing 2.4 million per year, Britain's about 100,000 per year. But carbon dioxide emissions per person are 50 times greater in Britain. Thus the 100,000 new Brits each year account for double the emissions of the 2.4 million new people in Bangladesh.

- Since 1950 the world's richest fifth have doubled their per person meat and timber consumption, while the poorest fifth have hardly increased their consumption.

- The richest fifth now account for 87 percent of the world's vehicles and consume 85 percent of all paper, while the poorest fifth consume 1 percent.

The bottom line: The earth seems capable of permanently supporting but two billion people consuming as do today's Western Europeans and North Americans (Pimentel & others, 1999; Willey, 1999). One calculation, using the UN's statistics, estimates "ecological footprints"—how much biologically productive space people in different nations require to produce what they consume and to absorb their waste (Wackernagel, 2000). The average Canadian requires somewhat more than 10 soccer fields. The average American 30 percent more than this, the average Britisher, Swiss, and German about 30 percent less. Everyone's consuming like today's Americans and Canadians would require the natural resources of three earths. However, those in developing countries consume less, so the world has only been overshooting its carrying capacity since about 1980 (Figure 16–2).

With population beyond six billion and the less developed nations understandably working toward greater prosperity, the need for sustainable consumption has taken on "urgency and global significance" (Heap & Kent, 2000). It's not just that consumption levels among rich nations *should* decline, notes Norman Myers (2000), they *will* decline "because the Earth cannot indefinitely support the present consumption," let alone increased future consumption (p. 13). On the current trajectory, say ecologists, we are headed toward what Chapter 13 called the tragedy of the commons.

"We will not do anything that harms our economy, because first things first are the people who live in America."
—President George W. Bush, 2001, explaining his decision to abandon the Kyoto global warming treaty negotiated by more than 100 nations.

"If one wants to be a world leader, one must know how to look after the entire earth and not only American industry."
—Response by Romano Prodi, 2001, President, European Union Commission

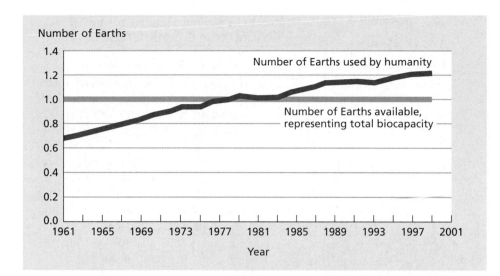

figure 16–2
The ecological overshoot.
The human demand for things such as land, timber, fish, and fuels is increasingly exceeding the earth's regenerative capacity. If allowance is also made for protecting nonhuman species, the usage line would be higher. **Source:** *Proceedings of the National Academy of Sciences* (Wackernagel & others, 2002).

Rather than continuing to steal from our descendants, can we work toward more sustainable development and consumption? Recognizing that the problems involve human behavior—it is we who drive gas-slurping sport utility vehicles, eat grain-slurping beef, and operate tree-slurping deforestation machines—how can social psychology help? Let's consider some possible solutions.

ENABLING SUSTAINABLE LIFESTYLES

So, what shall we do? Eat, drink, and be merry for tomorrow is doom? Behave as have so many participants in prisoners' dilemma games, by pursing self-interest to our collective detriment? ("Heck, on a global scale, my consumption is infinitesimal; it provides me pleasure at but a nominal cost to the world.") Wring our hands and vow never to bring children into a hurting world? Must fertility plus prosperity produce calamity?

Those more optimistic about the future see two routes to sustainable lifestyles: (a) increasing technological efficiency and agricultural productivity, and (b) moderating consumption and decreasing population.

Smaller families, bigger houses. In 1966, 22 percent of new American houses had more than 2,000 square feet; in 2001, 56 percent did.

© Ken Avidor. Reprinted with permission.

Increasing efficiency and productivity

One route to a sustainable future is through improving ecotechnologies. Already we have replaced many incandescent bulbs with cool fluorescent bulbs, replaced printed and delivered letters and catalogs with e-mail and e-commerce, and developed environmentally friendlier cars. Today's middle-aged adults drive cars that get twice the mileage and produce a twentieth the pollution of their first cars.

Plausible future technologies include diodes that emit light for 20 years without bulbs; ultrasound washing machines that consume no water, heat, or soap; reusable and compostable plastics; cars running on fuel cells that combine hydrogen and oxygen and produce water exhaust; extralight materials stronger than steel; and roofs and roads that double as solar energy collectors (N. Myers, 2000). Moreover, the spread of technological innovation is accelerating. In the

United States, electricity was embraced by one-fourth of people in 46 years, the telephone in 35 years, television in 26 years, the personal computer in 16 years, the Internet in 7 years (United Nations, 1998).

Agriculture is also undergoing a revolution. Controversial genetic modification and less controversial plant hybrids have increased yields. They have also produced blight-resistant potatoes, more nutritious rice, increased drought and salinity resistance, and resistance to insects, viruses, and bacteria.

Although it will take time to evaluate the safety and viability of these technological and agricultural innovations, increased efficiency and productivity will surely be one route to the sustainable future. Given the speed of innovation—who could have imagined today's world a century ago?—the future will surely bring solutions that we aren't yet imagining. Surely, say the optimists, the future will bring increased material well-being for more people requiring many fewer raw materials and much less polluting waste.

Reducing consumption

The second route to a sustainable future is through reduced consumption. Instead of more people consuming and polluting more, a stable population will need to consume and pollute less.

Thanks to family planning efforts, the world's population growth rate has decelerated, especially in developed nations. Where food security has improved and women have become educated and empowered, birthrates have fallen. But even if birthrates everywhere instantly fell to replacement levels, the lingering momentum of population growth, fed by the bulge of younger humans, would continue for years to come.

Given that we have already overshot the earth's carrying capacity, individual consumption must also moderate. With our material appetites continually swelling—as people seek more CDs, more air conditioning, more holiday travel—what can be done to moderate consumption?

One way is through public policies that harness the motivating power of incentives. As a general rule, what we tax we get less of, what we reward we get more of. If our highways are jammed and our air polluted, we can create fast lanes that reward carpooling and penalize driving solo. We can build bike lanes and subsidize mass transportation, thus encouraging alternatives to cars. We can tax petrol heavily, as in Europe, and reward recycling with a refundable deposit on soda cans and bottles (see "Focus on: Creating Incentives to Conserve").

Robert Frank (1999), an economist well versed in social psychology, suggests how a socially responsible market economy might reward achievement while promoting more sustainable consumption. He proposes a progressive consumption tax that encourages savings and investment while increasing the price on

In early 21st century America, SUVs and pickup trucks—which were slightly more than half of new auto sales—were exempt from pollution emission and fuel efficiency standards required of other new cars (Easterbrook, 2003).

"You just parked on a Saturn."

focus on   creating incentives to conserve

This August 2000 letter to the *Scotsman*—written in a European country where people pay more than 30 pounds (some 45 American dollars) for a ten-gallon fill-up (three-fourths taxes) applauds the use of tax and reward policies to motivate more sustainable petrol consumption:

> Despite having to drive the national average 12,000 miles a year to earn less than the average income of £18,000 a year, I applaud the rising costs of private motoring. For one thing, it seems likely that less tax on fuel means more tax elsewhere, and so any saving is illusory.
>
> Taxes on fuel are cheap to collect, proportionate and cannot easily be cheated.

> Only the most ill-informed motorist remains unaware of the part played by fossil fuels in global warming. And only the most selfish motorist doesn't care about his/her contribution to such an unbalancing of nature as typified by the present global run of bizarre seasons, weathers and rising sea levels.
>
> If people choose to live far from work, to drive fast, to drive thirsty cars, to neglect local shops or to allow public transport to go into a decline, then they must bear those costs.

Tim Flinn, St. Andrews

nonessential luxury goods, such as the $18,500 Range Rover child's toy car. His proposal is simple: Tax people not on what they earn but on what they spend—which is their earnings minus their savings and perhaps their charity. The tax could be made progressive with ample exemptions for dependents and higher tax rates for the big spenders. Frank argues that a progressive consumption tax (beginning, say, with a 20 percent tax rate on annual consumption beyond $30,000 for a family of four and rising to 70 percent for consumption over $500,000) promises to moderate consumption. People who would have bought a BMW may now adjust, with no less happiness, down to a Mazda.

Such policies would direct the power of self-interest in more earth-friendly directions, but their enactment requires political acts supported by public attitudes. If the Royal Society, National Academy, and UN's scientific experts are right to state that we have already overshot the earth's carrying capacity, then public and political sentiments will eventually change as the atmosphere heats and competition for scare resources increases. Is there any reason to hope that public consciousness might also change in the short run—that late-twentieth-century individualism and materialism might in the early twenty-first century give way to more communal values?

As the swiftly changing attitudes accompanying the 1960s civil rights movement and 1970s women's movement testify (see Chapter 9), public consciousness can indeed change in the blink of a historical eye. In the United States, the social landscape dramatically changed between 1960 and the early 1990s, with doubled divorce, tripled teen suicide, quadrupled juvenile violence, a quintupled prison population, and a sextupled proportion of babies born to unmarried parents. Post-1960 American life has also been marked by rising individualism and a free fall in communal engagement. Compared with 1960, today's middle-aged and young adults, as Robert Putnam (2000) documents, are more often *Bowling Alone* (and voting, visiting, entertaining, carpooling, trusting, joining, meeting, neighboring, volunteering, and giving proportionately less). In response to these realities, a blossoming turn-of-the-century social ecology movement is promoting communal "we" thinking, character education in schools, and the renewal of marriage and coparenting—and taking heart that teen suicide, violence, and pregnancy are now subsiding and volunteerism is now rising. Voilà, for better or worse, *cultures can change.* So, is there reason to hope that materialistic appetites might soon lessen?

Summing up

These are good times. Never have we lived healthier, longer, or with more prosperity, human rights, and technological advances. Yet scientific leaders report that we are imperiled by a global crisis. Exploding population and increasing consumption have together exceeded the earth's carrying capacity. With 10 times the cars on earth as half a century ago, and increasing burning of oil and coal to produce heat and electricity, greenhouse gases are collecting and the planet is warming. The bottom line: the earth cannot support today's consumption by those in the rich nations, much less further increases in consumption. Concerned scientists and citizens are therefore pondering how humanity might prepare for a sustainable future. How might we increase technological efficiency and agricultural productivity? How can we create incentives and change actions and attitudes to control population and moderate consumption? Attending to concepts in social psychology that address our attitudes and our behaviors may help. Rapid cultural change has happened in the last 40 years, and in response to the global crisis it can happen again.

What is the social psychology of materialism and wealth?

What might social psychology contribute to our understanding of changing materialism? To what extent do money and consumption buy happiness? And why do materialism and economic growth not bring enduringly greater satisfaction?

Does money buy happiness? Few of us would answer yes. But ask a different question—"Would a *little* more money make you a *little* happier?"—and many of us will smirk and nod. There is, we believe, some connection between wealth and well-being. That belief feeds what Juliet Schor (1998) calls the "cycle of work and spend"—working more to buy more.

INCREASED MATERIALISM

Materialism—the valuing of money and possessions—abounds when people feel insecure, unsafe, and impoverished, contends psychologist Tim Kasser (2002). When feeling insecure, people often gain a temporary mood lift by acquiring new things. Alas, the satisfaction is short-lived.

Materialism also abounds in modern Western cultures. Although the earth asks that we live more lightly upon it, materialism has surged, most clearly in the United States. According to one Gallup poll (1990), 1 in 2 women, 2 in 3 men, and 4 in 5 people earning more than $75,000 a year would like to be rich. Think of it as today's American dream: life, liberty, and the purchase of happiness.

figure 16–3

Changing materialism, from annual surveys of more than 200,000 entering U.S. collegians (total sample nearly 7 million students).

Source: Data from Dey, Astin, & Korn, 1991, and subsequent annual reports.

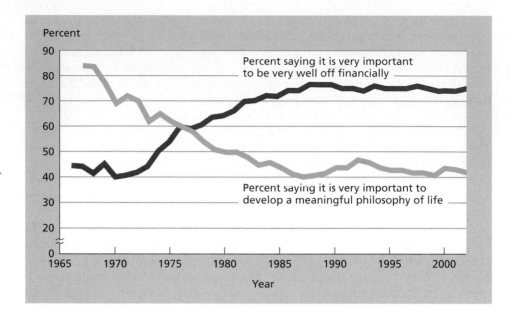

Such materialism surged during the 1970s and 1980s. The most dramatic evidence comes from the UCLA/American Council on Education annual survey of nearly a quarter million entering collegians. Those agreeing that a "very important" reason for their going to college was "to make more money" rose from one to two in 1971 to nearly three in four in 2000. And the proportion considering it "very important or essential" that they become "very well-off financially" rose from 39 percent in 1970 to 75 percent in 2003 (Figure 16–3). These proportions virtually flip-flopped with those who considered it very important to "develop a meaningful philosophy of life." Materialism was up, spirituality down.

What a change in values. Among 19 listed objectives, new American collegians now rank becoming "very well-off financially" number one. This has outranked not only developing a life philosophy but also "becoming an authority in my own field," "helping others in difficulty," and "raising a family."

Collegians are not alone in their materialism. Robert Frank reports that, with more people having more money to spend, "luxury fever" has struck. Late 1990s spending on luxury goods was growing four times as fast as overall spending. Thousand dollar-a-night suites at the Palm Beach Four Seasons Hotel were booked months ahead for weddings, as were $5,000-a-night suites at Aspen. America's 5,000 hundred-foot yachts are double the number of a decade ago and may cost more than $10,000 per hour of use. Cars costing more than $30,000 (in 1996 dollars) have shot up in the last decade from 7 to 12 percent of vehicles sold.

"Whoever said money can't buy happiness isn't spending it right."
—Lexus advertisement

WEALTH AND WELL-BEING

Does unsustainable consumption indeed enable "the good life"? Does being well-off produce—or at least correlate with—psychological well-being? Would people be happier if they could exchange a simple lifestyle for one with palatial surroundings, Alps ski vacations, and executive class travel? Would you be happier if you won a publishers' sweepstakes and could choose from its suggested indulgences: a 40-foot yacht, deluxe motor home, designer wardrobe,

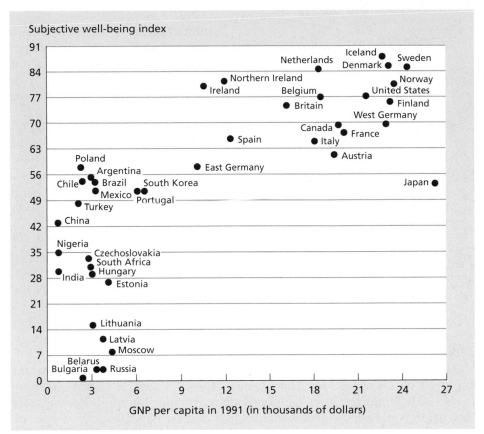

figure 16–4

National wealth and well-being, from World Bank data and the 1990–1991 World Values Survey.
Subjective well-being index combines happiness and life satisfaction (average of percentage describing themselves as (a) "very happy" or "happy" minus percentage "not very happy" or "unhappy", and as (b) 7 or above minus 4 or below on a 10-point life satisfaction scale). **Source:** From Ronald Inglehart, 1997, p. 62.

luxury car, and private housekeeper? Social psychological theory and evidence offer some answers.

Are rich countries happier?

As Ed Diener (2000) reports, there is some tendency for wealthy nations to have more satisfied people. The Swiss and Scandinavians, for instance, are generally prosperous and satisfied. In poor nations, people more often lack assured food and housing. Moreover, comparing themselves with the abundance of the rich may accentuate their felt poverty. Nevertheless, among nations with more than $8,000 GNP per person, the correlation between national wealth and well-being evaporates (Figure 16–4). Better (so far as happiness and life satisfaction go) to be Irish than Bulgarian. But whether one has the income of the typical Irish, Belgian, Norwegian, or American hardly matters. Indeed, the Irish during the 1980s reported consistently greater life satisfaction than the doubly wealthy but less satisfied West Germans (Inglehart, 1990). Ed Diener and his colleagues (1995), however, note that national wealth is associated with civil rights, literacy, and the number of continuous years of democracy. For a clearer look at money and happiness, researchers have asked whether, across individuals and over time, people's well-being rises with their wealth.

Are rich people happier?

In poor countries such as India, where low income more often threatens basic human needs, being relatively well-off does predict greater well-being (Argyle,

"But on the positive side, money can't buy happiness—so who cares?"

www.mhhe.com/myers8
Visit the Online Learning Center for an interactivity on measuring materialism and happiness.

It was later reported that some of Frank Capaci's old friends were no longer talking to him, that he had bought a shredder to dispose of unwanted mail, and had temporarily gone into hiding (Annin, 1999).

1999). Psychologically as well as materially, it is better to be high caste than low. But in affluent countries, where most can afford life's necessities, affluence matters surprisingly little. In the United States, Canada, and Europe, the correlation between income and personal happiness, noted Ronald Inglehart (1990, p. 242), "is surprisingly weak (indeed, virtually negligible)." Happiness tends to be lower among the very poor. But once comfortable, more money provides diminishing returns. Summarizing his own studies of happiness, David Lykken (1999, p. 17) observes, "People who go to work in their overalls and on the bus are just as happy, on the average, as those in suits who drive to work in their own Mercedes."

Even very rich people—for example, the *Forbes* 100 wealthiest Americans surveyed by Diener, Jeffrey Horwitz, and Robert Emmons (1985)—have reported only slightly greater happiness than average. Although having more than enough money to buy many things they don't need and hardly care about, 4 in 5 of the 49 superrich responding to the survey agreed that "money can increase OR decrease happiness, depending on how it is used." And some were indeed unhappy. One fabulously wealthy man could never remember being happy. One woman reported that money could not undo misery caused by her children's problems. When sailing on the *Titanic*, even first class cannot get you where you want to go.

Does economic growth improve human morale?

Over time, does happiness rise with affluence? Are Frank and Shirley Mae Capaci enduringly happier for having in 1998 won the $195 million Powerball lottery? Likely not as much as they initially supposed. A recent windfall from a lottery, an inheritance, or a surging economy does boost happiness (Diener & Oishi, 2000; Gardner & Oswald, 2001). Yet lottery winners typically gain only a temporary jolt of joy from their winnings (Brickman & others, 1978; Argyle, 1986). Although delighted to have won, the euphoria eventually fades. Likewise, those whose incomes have increased over the previous decade are not happier than those whose income has not increased (Diener & others, 1993). As Richard Ryan (1999) notes, such satisfactions have "a short half-life."

If enduring personal happiness generally does not rise with personal affluence, does collective happiness float upward with a rising economic tide? Are Americans happier today than in 1940, when two out of five homes lacked a shower or bathtub, heat often meant feeding a furnace wood or coal, and 35 percent of homes had no toilet (Bureau of the Census, 1994)? Or consider 1957, the year in which economist John Galbraith was describing the United

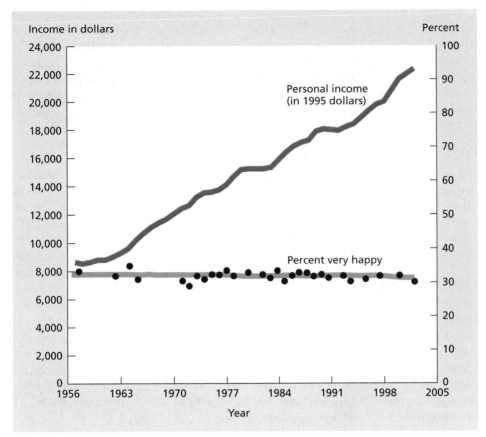

figure 16–5

Has economic growth advanced human morale? While inflation-adjusted income has risen, self-reported happiness has not. **Source:** Happiness data from General Social Surveys, National Opinion Research Center, University of Chicago. Income data from Bureau of the Census (1975) and *Economic Indicators.*

States as *The Affluent Society.* Americans' per person income, expressed in to-day's dollars, was about $9,000. Today, it is more than $20,000. Compared with 1957, Americans are therefore "the doubly affluent society"—with double what money buys. Not everyone has experienced the surging affluence—the rising tide has lifted the yachts faster than the dinghies—and large income disparity is a marker for unhealthy communities. Yet nearly all boats have risen somewhat. Americans today own twice as many cars per person, eat out more than twice as often, and commonly enjoy microwave ovens, big-screen color TVs, home computers, and air conditioning. Much the same is true for people in other in-dustrialized nations.

So, believing that it is "very important" to be very well-off financially, and having seen their affluence ratchet upward little by little over four decades, are Americans now happier?

They are not. As Figure 16–5 indicates, those reporting themselves "very happy" has, if anything, declined slightly between 1957 and 2002, from 35 to 30 percent. Twice as rich and no happier. Meanwhile, depression rates have soared, especially among youth and young adults (Seligman, 1989; Klerman & Wiessman, 1989; Cross-National Collaborative Group, 1992). Compared with their grandparents, today's young adults have grown up with much more affluence, slightly less happiness, and much greater risk of depression and assorted social pathologies.

It is hard to avoid a startling conclusion: Our becoming much better off over the last four decades has not been accompanied by one iota of increased subjective well-being. The same is true of the European countries and Japan, reports Richard Easterlin (1995). In Britain, for example, sharp increases in the percentage of households with cars, central heating, and telephones have not been accompanied by increased happiness. The conclusion is startling because it challenges modern materialism: *Economic growth in affluent countries has provided no apparent boost to human morale.*

WHY MATERIALISM FAILS TO SATISFY

What experiences produce happiness? Go to the *SocialSense* CD-ROM to view a video clip about satisfying life events.

It is striking that economic growth in affluent countries has failed to satisfy. It is further striking that individuals who strive most for wealth tend to live with lower well-being, a finding that "comes through very strongly in every culture I've looked at," reports Richard Ryan (1999). His collaborator, Tim Kasser (2000, 2002), concludes from their studies that those who instead strive for "intimacy, personal growth, and contribution to the community" experience a higher quality of life. Kasser and Ryan's (1993, 1996) research (together with Peter Schmuck [2000] in Germany) echoes an earlier finding by H. W. Perkins (1991): Among 800 college alumni surveyed, those with "Yuppie values"—who preferred a high income and occupational success and prestige to having very close friends and a close marriage—were twice as likely as their former classmates to describe themselves as "fairly" or "very" *un*happy. Another study recontacted 13,000 college alums. Those who had modest incomes—despite 20 years earlier having rated "being very well-off financially" as very important or essential—were less happy than other modest income people who had earlier espoused less materialism (Nickerson & others, 2003).

Pause a moment and think: What is the single most personally satisfying event that you experienced in the last month? Kennon Sheldon and his colleagues (2001) put that question (and similar questions about the last week and semester) to samples of university students. Then they asked them to rate the extent to which 10 different needs were met by the satisfying event. The students rated self-esteem, relatedness (feeling connected with others), and autonomy (feeling in control) as the emotional needs that most strongly accompanied the satisfying event. At the bottom of the list of factors predicting satisfaction was money and luxury.

People who identify themselves with expensive possessions experience fewer positive moods, report Emily Solberg, Ed Diener, and Michael Robinson (2003). Such materialists tend to report a relatively large gap between what they want and what they have, and to enjoy fewer close, fulfilling relationships. Especially unhappy are those who desire money to overcome self-doubt and to surpass others, rather than to enhance family security, enjoy freedom, and be charitable (Srivastava & others, 2001). Diener and Martin Seligman (2002) also report that *very* happy university students are marked not by their money but by their "rich and satisfying close relationships." The challenge for healthy nations, then, is to foster improving standards of living without encouraging a materialism and consumerism that displaces the deep need to belong.

"Why do you spend your money for that which is not bread, and your labor for that which does not satisfy?"
—Isaiah 55:2

We know these ecological and personal perils of materialism . . . sort of. In a nationally representative survey, Princeton sociologist Robert Wuthnow (1994) found that 89 percent of more than 2,000 American participants believed, "Our society is much too materialistic." *Other* people are too materialistic, that is. For

84 percent also wished they had more money, and 78 percent said it was "very or fairly important" to have "a beautiful home, a new car and other nice things."

So why are we not happier after getting that beautiful home and new car? Why do 41 percent of Americans—up from 13 percent in 1973—regard automobile air-conditioning as "a necessity" (Schor, 1998)? And how do yesterday's luxuries—CD sound systems, color television, high-speed Internet access—so quickly become today's necessities and tomorrow's relics? (Our family's first desktop computer, with information loaded from a cassette tape, seemed remarkable, until we got that speedier hard-drive machine, which itself became poky once we got a Pentium chip, which has since become frustratingly anemic.)

Two principles drive this psychology of consumption. The first is our human capacity for adaptation. The second is our penchant for social comparison.

The adaptation-level phenomenon

The **adaptation-level phenomenon** implies that feelings of success and failure, satisfaction and dissatisfaction, are relative to prior achievements. If our current achievements fall below what we previously accomplished, we feel dissatisfied, frustrated; if they rise above that level, we feel successful, satisfied.

If we continue to achieve, however, we soon adapt to success. What formerly felt good registers as neutral, and what formerly felt neutral now feels like deprivation. This helps explain why, despite the rapid increase in real income during the past several decades, the average person is no happier.

Most of us have experienced the adaptation-level phenomenon. More consumer goods, academic achievement, or social prestige provide an initial surge of pleasure. Yet all too soon the feeling wanes. Then we need an even higher level to give us another surge of pleasure. "Even as we contemplate our satisfaction with a given accomplishment, the satisfaction fades," noted Philip Brickman and Donald Campbell (1971), "to be replaced finally by a new indifference and a new level of striving."

As you may recall from Chapter 2, we underestimate our adaptive capacity. People have difficulty predicting the intensity and duration of their future emotions, a phenomenon called "durability bias" (Wilson & Gilbert, 2003). The elation from getting what we want—riches, top exam scores, the Chicago Cubs winning the World Series—evaporates more rapidly than we expect. We also sometimes "miswant." When first-year university students predicted their satisfaction with various housing possibilities shortly before entering their school's housing lottery, they focused on physical features. "I'll be happiest in a beautiful and well-located dorm," many students seemed to think. But they were

adaptation-level phenomenon
The tendency to adapt to a given level of stimulation and thus to notice and react to changes from that level.

Parkinson's second law: Expenditures rise to meet income.

Could Lucy ever experience enough "ups"? Not according to the adaptation-level phenomenon. PEANUTS reprinted by permission of United Features Syndicate, Inc.

"O.K., if you can't see your way to giving me a pay raise, how about giving Parkerson a pay cut?"

Social comparisons foster feelings. Copyright © The New Yorker Collection, 2001, Barbara Smaller from cartoonbank.com. All Rights Reserved.

Evolutionary psychologists reason that men seek to accumulate and display more resources than other men for the same reason peacocks compete in tail displays: to compete for female attention.

upward social comparison
Comparing with others who are better, or better off, may trigger feelings of relative deprivation.

wrong. When contacted a year later, it was the social features, such as sense of community, that predicted happiness, report Elizabeth Dunn and her colleagues (2003). When focused on the short term and forgetting how quickly we adapt, we may think that the material features of our world predispose our happiness. Actually, report Leaf Van Boven and Thomas Gilovich (2003) from their surveys and experiments, positive *experiences* (often social experiences) leave us happier. The best things in life are not things.

Social comparison

Much of life is about comparison, a point made by the joke about two hikers who meet a bear. One reaches into his backpack and pulls out a pair of sneakers. "Why bother putting those on?" asks the other. "You can't outrun a bear." "I don't have to outrun the bear," answers the first. "I just have to outrun you."

Happiness, too, is relative not only to our past experience but also to our comparisons with others (Lyubomirsky, 2001). Whether we feel good or bad depends on with whom we're comparing ourselves. We are slow-witted or clumsy only when others are smart or agile. When one baseball player signs for $10 million a year, his $7 million teammate may now feel dissatisfied. "Human judgment is comparative," notes comparison researcher Thomas Mussweiler (2003).

Further feeding our luxury fever is the tendency to compare upward: As we climb the ladder of success or affluence, we mostly compare ourselves with peers who are at or above our current level. Those living in communities with unequal incomes that are skewed by a very rich class tend to feel less satisfied as they compare upward. The rich-poor gap has grown, observes Michael Hagerty (2000), and this helps explain why rising affluence has not produced increased happiness. In general, people are happier when incomes are more equal and there are fewer people markedly above them.

The frequent result of **upward social comparison** is what Chapter 10 called *relative deprivation*. Television watching, for example, creates feelings of relative deprivation, making us aware that others have something we lack. The more people watch TV dramas and compare their lifestyles with the relatively wealthy, the more their own material desires escalate and the less satisfied they are (Schor, 1998).

How can social psychology help to create a sustainable future?

Will our human tendencies to adapt to new pleasures and compare with others fuel a continually spiraling materialism and consumerism? Or might materialism give way to a simpler "postmaterialism"? Is mere knowledge unlikely to be persuasive, much as knowing the perils of smoking fails to liberate a nicotine addict? Or can educating people about the modest connections between wealth and well-being contribute to a sustainable future?

ADJUSTING ADAPTATIONS AND COMPARISONS

The adaptation-level and social comparison phenomena have a thought-provoking implication: Seeking satisfaction through material achievement requires continually expanding affluence merely to *maintain* satisfaction. "Poverty," said Plato, "consists not in the decrease of one's possessions, but in the increase of one's greed."

Fortunately, adaptation also can enable us to adjust downward, should we choose or need to simplify our lives. If our buying power shrinks, initially we feel some pain. But eventually we adapt to the new reality. In the aftermath of the 1970s gas price hikes, North Americans managed to reduce substantially their "need" for large, gas-slurping cars. Robert Frank (1996) experienced adaptation to a simpler lifestyle when

> As a young man fresh out of college, I served as a Peace Corps Volunteer in rural Nepal. My one-room house had no electricity, no heat, no indoor toilet, no running water. The local diet offered little variety and virtually no meat. . . . Yet, although my living conditions in Nepal were a bit startling at first, the most salient feature of my experience was how quickly they came to seem normal. Within a matter of weeks, I lost all sense of impoverishment. Indeed, my $40 monthly stipend was more than most others had in my village, and with it I experienced a feeling of prosperity that I have recaptured only in recent years.

As New Zealand psychologist Richard Kammann (1983) realized two decades ago, "Objective life circumstances have a negligible role to play in a theory of happiness." People living where everyone lived in 4,000-square-foot houses would likely be no happier than those living where everyone had 2,000-square-foot houses.

Even victims of paralyzing accidents, the blind, and other people with severe handicaps usually cope with courageous resilience. They adapt to their disabilities and achieve normal or near-normal levels of life satisfaction (Brickman & others, 1978; Chwalisz & others, 1988; Schulz & Decker, 1985). Victims of tragic accidents surely wish they were able-bodied, and many of us envy those who have won a lottery. Yet, after a period of adjustment, the astonishing fact is that none of these three groups differs appreciably from the others in moment-to-moment happiness. Human beings have an enormous capacity to adapt.

Psychology's contribution to a sustainable future will come partly through its insights into adaptation and social comparison. Experiences that lower our comparison standards can cool luxury fever and renew contentment. To feel better, compare with those worse off—those feeling more pain, those in worse relationships, those with less (Affleck & others, 2000; Buunk & others, 2001; Locke, 2003). An experiment by Marshall Dermer and his colleagues (1979) illustrates the positive power of **downward social comparisons.** They put University of Wisconsin–Milwaukee women through some imaginative exercises in deprivation. After viewing depictions of how grim life was in Milwaukee in 1900, or after imagining and then writing about being burned and disfigured, the women expressed greater satisfaction with their own lives. In another experiment, Jennifer Crocker and Lisa Gallo (1985) found that those who five

"All our wants, beyond those which a very moderate income will supply, are purely imaginary."
—Henry St. John, *Letter to Swift*, 1719

"However great the discrepancies between men's lots, there is always a certain balance of joy and sorrow which equalizes all."
—La Rochefoucauld, *Maxims*, 1665

downward social comparison
Comparing with others who are worse, or worse off, may trigger improved feelings about oneself.

times completed the sentence "I'm glad I'm not a . . ." afterward felt less depressed and more satisfied with life than did those who had completed sentences beginning "I wish I were a . . .".

People seem to understand intuitively the benefits of downward comparisons. Those facing personal threat often search for a silver lining and boost their self-esteem by comparing with the less fortunate (Gibbons & others, 2002; Reis & others, 1993; Taylor, 1989). Realizing that others have it worse helps us count our blessings and realize that maybe we don't need all that "stuff." "I cried because I had no shoes," says a Persian proverb, "until I met a man who had no feet."

POSTMATERIALIST ATTITUDES AND BEHAVIOR

In Chapter 4 we noted that behavior is influenced by attitudes, but also by other external influences, and that attitudes often follow behavior. More earth-friendly behavior will, therefore, arise from multiple sources—from public policies that give incentive for conservation, from persuasive appeals that elicit commitments to specific behaviors, and from changing "me" thinking to "we" thinking and present thinking to future thinking (McKenzie-Mohr, 2000; Stern, 2000; Winter, 2000). Education—this chapter's aim—also has a place, by offering information that counters to what George Howard (2000) calls "Killer Thoughts for a World With Limits." (See "Focus on: Lethal Thoughts for a World with Limits.")

As we have seen, the late twentieth century was marked by increasing materialism and consumption, most notably in the United States. Asked by Roper pollsters to identify what makes "the good life," 38 percent of Americans in 1975, and 63 percent in 1996, chose "a lot of money" (Putnam, 2000). "I cannot afford to buy everything I really need," agree 39 percent of Americans earning $75,000 to $100,000 per year (Schor, 1998).

However, there are signs that a shift to postmaterialist values is under way as people

- confront the realities of population growth, climate change, and habitat and species destruction;
- realize that wealth striving marks less happy lives;

focus on   lethal thoughts for a world with limits

1. *Consumption will produce happiness.* "I'll be happy when we get that vacation home."
2. *Discount the future.* "The future will take care of itself. My life is now."
3. *Growth is good.* "More is better."
4. *Greed is good.* "We should all get as much as we can."
5. *Paying less is better than paying more.* "Don't tax gas to induce conservation—I want cheap gas."
6. *If it ain't broke yet, don't fix it.* "Global warming projections may err."

Adapted from George S. Howard (2000), "Adapting Human Lifestyles for the 21st Century," *American Psychologist 55*, 509–515.

- appreciate that economic growth in affluent countries has not bred contentment.

Striving for wealth has often produced stacks of unplayed CDs, closets full of seldom-worn clothes, garages with luxury cars, all without endowing a good life. We have bigger houses and more broken homes, higher incomes and more troubled youth, more mental health professionals and more people needing their services. As conspicuous consumption was a social status marker in the last century, will it become gauche in this new century?

Ronald Inglehart (1990), a social scientist who follows values surveys across the Western world, was one of the first to discern the beginnings of a decline in materialist values. In Europe and North America, he has seen signs of a new generation maturing with decreasing concern for economic growth and strong defense, and with increasing concern for personal relationships, the integrity of nature, and the meaning of life.

Pollster George Gallup, Jr. (1998) believes the desire to connect to things larger than self is growing: "One of two dominant trends in society today [along with a search for deeper, more meaningful relationships] is the search for spiritual moorings." From 1994 to late 1998, reported Gallup (1998), the percentage of Americans feeling a need to "experience spiritual growth" rose from 58 to 82 percent. Accompanying this contemporary spirituality is often a concern for humanity's "stewardship" of the earth.

"If the world is to change for the better it must have a change in human consciousness." [We must discover] "a deeper sense of responsibility toward the world, which means responsibility toward something higher than self."
—Czech poet-president Vaclav Havel, 1990

Research on enhancing quality of life

Social psychology also contributes to a sustainable future through its studies of the good life. If materialism does not enhance quality of life, what does?

- *Close, supportive relationships.* As we saw in Chapter 11, our deep need to belong is satisfied by close, supportive relationships. Those supported by intimate friendships or a committed marriage are much likelier to declare themselves "very happy."
- *Faith communities* are often a source of such connections, as well as of meaning and hope. That helps explain a finding from National Opinion Research Center surveys of 42,000 Americans since 1972: 26 percent of those rarely or never attending religious services declared themselves very happy, as did 47 percent of those attending multiple times weekly.
- *Positive traits.* Optimism, self-esteem, perceived control, and extraversion also mark happy experiences and happy lives.
- *Flow.* Work and leisure experiences that engage one's skills also mark happy lives. Between the anxiety of being overwhelmed and stressed, and the apathy of being underwhelmed and bored, notes Mihaly Csikszentmihalyi (1990, 1999), lies a zone in which people experience *flow*, an optimal state in which, absorbed in an activity, we lose consciousness of self and time. When their experience is sampled using electronic pagers, people report greatest enjoyment not when mindlessly passive, but when unself-consciously absorbed in a mindful challenge. In fact, the less expensive (and generally more involving) a leisure activity, the *happier* people are while doing it. Most people are happier gardening than power boating, talking to friends than watching TV. Low-consumption recreations prove most satisfying.

"Better is a dinner with herbs where love is than a fatted calf with hatred."
—Proverbs 15:17

That is good news indeed. Those things that make for the genuinely good life—close relationships, a hope-filled faith, positive traits, engaging activity—are enduringly sustainable. And that is an idea close to the heart of Jigme Singye Wangchuk, King of Bhutan. "Gross national happiness is more important than gross national product," he believes. Writing from Bhutan's Center of Bhutan Studies, Sander Tideman (2003) explains: "Gross National Happiness . . . aims to promote real progress and sustainability by measuring the quality of life, rather than the mere sum of production and consumption."

Summing up

Do materialism and consumption pay emotional dividends? To judge from the expressed values of college students and the "luxury fever" that marked late-twentieth-century America, Americans—and to a lesser extent people in other Western countries—live in a materialistic age.

Does wealth indeed advance well-being? People in rich nations do report greater happiness and life satisfaction than those in poor nations (though with diminishing returns as one moves from moderately to very wealthy countries). Are rich people within a country happier than working-class people? Somewhat, though again more and more money

provides diminishing returns (as evident in studies of the superrich and of lottery winners). Does economic growth over time make people happier? Not at all, it seems from the slight decline in self-reported happiness and the increasing rate of depression during the post-1960 years of increasing affluence.

Two principles help explain why materialism fails to satisfy: the adaptation-level phenomenon and social comparison. When incomes and consumption rise, we soon adapt. And comparing with others we may find our relative position unchanged.

℘ Personal Postscript: How does one live responsibly in the modern world?

We must recognize that . . . we are one human family and one Earth community with a common destiny. We must join together to bring forth a sustainable global society founded on respect for nature, universal human rights, economic justice, and a culture of peace. Towards this end, it is imperative that we, the peoples of the Earth, declare our responsibility to one another, to the greater community of life, and to future generations.
—Preamble, The Earth Charter, www.earthcharter.org

Reading and writing about population growth, global warming, materialism, consumption, adaptation, comparison, and sustainability provokes my reflection: Am I part of the answer or part of the problem? I can talk a good line. But do I walk my own talk?

If I'm to be honest, my record is mixed.

I ride a bike to work year-round. But I also flew 80,000 miles last year on fuel-guzzling jets.

We have insulated our 105-year-old home, installed an efficient furnace, and turned the winter daytime thermostat down to 67. But having grown up in a cool summer climate, I can't imagine living without my air-conditioning on sweltering summer days.

To control CO_2 production, I routinely turn off lights and the computer monitor when away from my office and have planted trees around my house. But I've helped finance South American deforestation with the imported beef I've scarfed and the lattés I've sipped.

I applauded in 1973 when the United States established an energy-conserving 55 mph national maximum speed limit and was disappointed when it was abandoned in 1995. But now that the highway around my town is back up to 70 mph I drive no less than 70 mph—even with (blush) no other cars in sight.

We recycle all our home paper, cans, and bottles. But each week we receive enough mail, newspapers, and periodicals to fill a three-cubic-foot paper recycling bin.

Not bad, I tell myself. But it's hardly a bold response to the looming crisis. Our great-great-grandchildren will not thrive on this planet were all of today's six-plus billion humans (much less all of tomorrow's nine billion) to demand a similar-sized ecological footprint.

So how does one participate in the modern world, welcoming its beauties and conveniences, yet remain mindful of our environmental legacy? Even the leaders of the simpler living movement—who also flew gas-guzzling jets to the three conferences we attended together in splendid surroundings—struggle with how to live responsibly in the modern world.

Beyond our personal choices, we face difficult social and political issues. How might a market economy mix incentives for prosperity with restraints that preserve a habitable planet? To what extent can we depend on technological innovations, such as alternative energy sources, to reduce our ecological footprints? And in the meantime, to what extent does the superordinate goal of preserving the earth for our grandchildren call us to limit our own liberties— our freedom to drive, burn, and dump whatever we wish?

What do you think?

What regulations do you favor or oppose? Higher fuel-efficiency requirements for cars and trucks? Auto pollution checks? Leaf burning bans to reduce smog? If you live in a country where high fuel taxes motivate people's driving small fuel-efficient cars, do you wish you could have the much lower fuel taxes and cheaper petrol that enable Americans to drive big cars? If you are an American, would you favor higher gasoline and oil taxes to help conserve resources and restrain global heating?

How likely is it that humanity will be able to restrain global warming and resource depletion? If the biologist E. O. Wilson (2002) is right to speculate that humans evolved to commit themselves only to their small piece of geography, their own kin, and their own time, can we hope that our species will exhibit "extended altruism" by caring for our distant descendants? Will today's status objects, such as a 10 mpg Hummer, be tomorrow's relics of shame? Will today's envied "lifestyles of the rich and famous" become gauche in a future where sustainability becomes necessity? Or will people's concern for themselves and for displaying the symbols of success always trump their concerns for their unseen great-grandchildren?

"The great dilemma of environmental reasoning stems from this conflict between short-term and long-term values."
—E. O. Wilson, *The Future of Life*, 2002

Making the Social Connection

SS   This chapter states that depression rates have soared among youth and young adults even though they have grown up with more affluence than their grandparents. In Chapter 14 we discussed whether negative thinking causes depression or vice versa.

In Chapter 2 on the self and Chapter 8 on group influence, we introduced social comparison—evaluating ourselves by comparing ourselves to others. This idea resurfaces in this chapter as we discuss what makes us happy. Often, comparing ourselves to others does not encourage happiness. (My neighbor has a better car than I do.)

Indeed, there is another connection between creating a sustainable future and social psychology. This chapter mentions that the frequent result of upward comparison is called relative deprivation, a concept you may recall from Chapter 10.

Epilogue

If you have read this entire book, your introduction to social psychology is complete. In the Preface I offered my hope that this book "would be at once solidly scientific and warmly human, factually rigorous and intellectually provocative." You, not I, are the judge of whether that goal has been achieved. But I can tell you that giving away the discipline has been a joy for me as your author. If receiving my gift has brought you any measure of pleasure, stimulation, and enrichment, then my joy is compounded.

A knowledge of social psychology, I do believe, has the power to restrain intuition with critical thinking, illusion with understanding, and judgmentalism with compassion. In these 16 chapters, we have assembled social psychology's insights into belief and persuasion, love and hate, conformity and independence. We have glimpsed incomplete answers to intriguing questions: How do our attitudes feed and get fed by our actions? What leads people sometimes to hurt and sometimes to help one another? What kindles social conflict, and how can we transform closed fists into helping hands? Answering such questions expands our minds. And, "once expanded to the dimensions of a larger idea," noted Oliver Wendell Holmes, the mind "never returns to its original size." Such has been my experience, and perhaps yours, as you, through this and other courses, become an educated person.

WHAT DO YOU THINK?

Take a few minutes to reflect on this book and your course in social psychology. Make a list of three or four ideas that struck you. What surprised you? What, if anything, has affected you or the way you intend to live?

David G. Myers

davidmyers.org

glossary

A

acceptance conformity that involves both acting and believing in accord with social pressure.

adaptation-level phenomenon the tendency to adapt to a given level of stimulation and thus to notice and react to changes from that level.

aggression physical or verbal behavior intended to hurt someone. In laboratory experiments, this might mean delivering electric shocks or saying something likely to hurt another's feelings.

altruism a motive to increase another's welfare without conscious regard for one's self-interests.

arbitration resolution of a conflict by a neutral third party who studies both sides and imposes a settlement.

attitude a favorable or unfavorable evaluative reaction toward something or someone, exhibited in one's beliefs, feelings, or intended behavior.

attitude inoculation exposing people to weak attacks upon their attitudes so that when stronger attacks come, they will have refutations available.

attractiveness having qualities that appeal to an audience. An appealing communicator (often someone similar to the audience) is most persuasive on matters of subjective preference.

attribution theory the theory of how people explain others' behavior; for example, by attributing it either to internal dispositions (enduring traits, motives, and attitudes) or to external situations.

autokinetic phenomenon self (*auto*) motion (*kinetic*). The apparent movement of a stationary point of light in the dark.

automatic processing "implicit" or intuitive thinking that is effortless, habitual, and without awareness.

availability heuristic a cognitive rule that judges the likelihood of things in terms of their availability in memory. If instances of something come readily to mind, we presume it to be commonplace.

avoidant attachment relationship style marked by dismissive detachment.

B

bargaining seeking an agreement to a conflict through direct negotiation between parties.

behavioral confirmation a type of self-fulfilling prophecy whereby people's social expectations lead them to act in ways that cause others to confirm their expectations.

behavioral medicine an interdisciplinary field that integrates and applies behavioral and medical knowledge about health and disease.

belief perserverance persistence of one's initial conceptions, as when the basis for one's belief is discredited but an explanation of why the belief might be true survives.

bogus pipeline a procedure that fools people into disclosing their attitudes. Participants are first convinced that a machine can use their psychological responses to measure their private attitudes. Then they are asked to predict the machine's reading, thus revealing their attitudes.

bystander effect the finding that a person is less likely to provide help when there are other bystanders.

C

catharsis emotional release. The catharsis view of aggression is that aggressive drive is reduced when one "releases" aggressive energy, either by acting aggressively or by fantasizing aggression.

central route to persuasion occurs when interested people focus on the arguments and respond with favorable thoughts.

channel of communication the way the message is delivered—whether face to face, in writing, on film, or in some other way.

clinical psychology the study, assessment, and treatment of people with psychological difficulties.

co-actors co-participants working individually on a noncompetitive activity.

cognitive dissonance tension that arises when one is simultaneously aware of two inconsistent cognitions. For example, dissonance may occur when we realize that we have, with little justification, acted contrary to our attitudes or made a decision favoring one alternative despite reasons favoring another.

cohesiveness a "we feeling"; the extent to which members of a group are bound together, such as by attraction for one another.

collectivism giving priority to the goals of one's groups (often one's extended family or work group) and defining one's identity accordingly.

companionate love the affection we feel for those with whom our lives are deeply intertwined.

complementarity the popularly supposed tendency, in a relationship between two people, for each to complete what is missing in the other.

compliance conformity that involves publicly acting in accord with an implied or explicit request while privately disagreeing.

confederate an accomplice of the experimenter.

confirmation bias a tendency to search for information that confirms one's preconceptions.

conflict a perceived incompatibility of actions or goals.

conformity a change in behavior or belief to accord with others.

controlled processing "explicit" thinking that is deliberate, reflective, and conscious.

correlational research the study of the naturally occurring relationships among variables.

counterfactual thinking imagining alternative scenarios and outcomes that might have happened, but didn't.

credibility believability. A credible communicator is perceived as both expert and trustworthy.

cult (also called a new religious movement) a group typically characterized by (1) distinctive ritual and beliefs related to its devotion to a god or a person, (2) isolation from the surrounding "evil" culture, and (3) a charismatic leader. (A sect, by contrast, is a spinoff from a major religion.)

culture the enduring behaviors, ideas, attitudes, and traditions shared by a large group of people and transmitted from one generation to the next.

D

debriefing in social psychology, the postexperimental explanation of a study to its participants. Debriefing usually discloses any deception and often queries participants regarding their understandings and feelings.

deception occurs in research when participants are misinformed or misled about the study's methods and purposes.

deindividuation loss of self-awareness and evaluation apprehension; occurs in group situations that foster responsiveness to group norms, good or bad.

demand characteristics cues in an experiment that tell the participant what behavior is expected.

dependent variable the variable being measured, so-called because it may depend on manipulations of the independent variable.

depressive realism the tendency of mildly depressed people to make accurate rather than self-serving judgments, attributions, and predictions.

disclosure reciprocity the tendency for one person's intimacy of self-disclosure to match that of a conversational partner.

discrimination unjustifiable negative behavior toward a group or its members.

displacement the redirection of aggression to a target other than the source of the frustration. Generally, the new target is a safer or more socially acceptable target.

dispositional attribution attributing behavior to the person's disposition and traits.

door-in-the-face technique a strategy for gaining a concession. After someone first turns down a large request (the door-in-the-face), the same requester counteroffers with a more reasonable request.

downward social comparison comparing with others who are worse, or worse off, may trigger improved feelings about oneself.

dual attitudes differing implicit (automatic) and explicit (consciously controlled) attitudes toward the same object. Verbalized explicit attitudes may change with education and persuasion; implicit attitudes change slowly, with practice that forms new habits.

E

egoism a motive (supposedly underlying all behavior) to increase one's own welfare. The opposite of altruism, which aims to increase another's welfare.

empathy the vicarious experience of another's feelings; putting oneself in another's shoes. An emotion evoked by sympathy for another.

equal-status contact contact on an equal basis. Just as a relationship between people of unequal status breeds attitudes consistent with their relationship, so do relationships between those of equal status. Thus, to reduce prejudice, interracial contact should be between persons equal in status.

equity a condition in which the outcomes people receive from a relationship are proportional to what they contribute to it. Note: Equitable outcomes needn't always be equal outcomes.

ethnocentric believing in the superiority of one's own ethnic and cultural group, and having a corresponding disdain for all other groups.

evaluation apprehension concern for how others are evaluating us.

evolutionary psychology the study of the evolution of behavior using principles of natural selection.

experimental realism degree to which an experiment absorbs and involves its participants.

experimental research studies that seek clues to cause-effect relationships by manipulating one or more factors (independent variables) while controlling others (holding them constant).

explanatory style one's habitual way of explaining life events. A negative, pessimistic, depressive explanatory style attributes failures to stable, global, and internal causes.

F

false consensus effect the tendency to overestimate the commonality of one's opinions and one's undesirable or unsuccessful behaviors.

false uniqueness effect the tendency to underestimate the commonality of one's abilities and one's desirable or successful behaviors.

field research research done in natural, real-life settings outside the laboratory.

foot-in-the-door phenomenon the tendency for people who have first agreed to a small request to comply later with a larger request.

free riders people who benefit from the group but give little in return.

frustration the blocking of goal-directed behavior.

frustration aggression theory the theory that frustration triggers a readiness to aggress.

fundamental attribution error the tendency for observers to underestimate situational influences and overestimate dispositional influences upon others' behavior. (Also called *correspondence bias*, because we so often see behavior as corresponding to a disposition.)

G

gender in psychology, the characteristics, whether biological or socially influenced, by which people define male and female.

gender role a set of behavior expectations (norms) for males and females.

GRIT acronym for "graduated and reciprocated initiatives in tension reduction"—a strategy designed to de-escalate international tensions.

group two or more people who, for longer than a few moments, interact with and influence one another and perceive one another as "us."

group polarization group-produced enhancement of members' preexisting tendencies; a strengthening of the members' *average* tendency, not a split within the group.

group-serving bias explaining away outgroup members' positive behaviors; also attributing negative behaviors to their dispositions (while excusing such behavior by one's own group).

groupthink "The mode of thinking that persons engage in when concurrence-seeking becomes so dominant in a cohesive in-group that it tends to override realistic appraisal of alternative courses of action."—Irving Janis (1971).

H

health psychology provides psychology's contribution to behavioral medicine by studying the psychological roots of health and illness.

heuristic a thinking strategy that enables quick, efficient judgments.

hindsight bias the tendency to exaggerate, *after* learning an outcome, one's ability to have foreseen how something turned out. Also known as the *I-knew-it-all-along phenomenon*.

hostile aggression aggression driven by anger and performed as an end in itself (also called affective aggression).

hypothesis a testable proposition that describes a relationship that may exist between events.

I

illusion of control perception of uncontrollable events as subject to one's control or as more controllable than they are.

illusion of transparency the illusion that our concealed emotions leak out and can be easily read by others.

illusory correlation perception of a relationship where none exists, or perception of a stronger relationship than actually exists.

independent variable the experimental factor that a researcher manipulates.

individualism the concept of giving priority to one's own goals over group goals and defining one's identity in terms of personal attributes rather than group identifications.

informational influence conformity occurring when people accept evidence about reality provided by other people.

informed consent an ethical principle requiring that research participants be told enough to enable them to choose whether they wish to participate.

ingratiation the use of strategies, such as flattery, by which people seek to gain another's favor.

ingroup "us"—a group of people who share a sense of belonging, a feeling of common identity.

ingroup bias the tendency to favor one's own group.

insecure attachment attachments marked by anxiety, ambivalence, and possessiveness.

instinctive behavior an innate, unlearned behavior pattern exhibited by all members of a species.

instrumental aggression aggression that is a means to some other end.

insufficient justification effect reduction of dissonance by internally justifying one's behavior when external justification is "insufficient."

integrative agreements win-win agreements that reconcile both parties' interests to their mutual benefit.

interaction the effect of one factor (such as biology) depends on another factor (such as environment).

J

just-world phenomenon the tendency of people to believe the world is just and that people therefore get what they deserve and deserve what they get.

K

kin selection the idea that evolution has selected altruism toward one's close relatives to enhance the survival of mutually shared genes.

L

leadership the process by which certain group members motivate and guide the group.

learned helplessness the hopelessness and resignation learned when a human or animal perceives no control over repeated bad events.

locus of control the extent to which people perceive outcomes as internally controllable by their own efforts and actions or as externally controlled by chance or outside forces.

low-ball technique a tactic for getting people to agree to something. People who agree to an initial request will often still comply when the requester ups the ante. People who receive only the costly request are less likely to comply with it.

M

matching phenomenon   the tendency for men and women to choose as partners those who are a "good match" in attractiveness and other traits.

mediation   an attempt by a neutral third party to resolve a conflict by facilitating communication and offering suggestions.

mere-exposure effect   the tendency for novel stimuli to be liked more or rated more positively after the rater has been repeatedly exposed to them.

mirror-image perceptions   reciprocal views of one another often held by parties in conflict; for example, each may view itself as moral and peace-loving and the other as evil and aggressive.

misinformation effect   incorporating "misinformation" into one's memory of the event, after witnessing an event and receiving misleading information about it.

moral exclusion   the perception of certain individuals or groups as outside the boundary within which one applies moral values and rules of fairness. Moral inclusion is regarding others as within one's circle of moral concern.

mundane realism   degree to which an experiment is superficially similar to everyday situations.

N

natural selection   the evolutionary process by which nature selects traits that best enable organisms to survive and reproduce in particular environmental niches.

naturalistic fallacy   the error of defining what is good in terms of what is observable. For example: What's typical is normal; what's normal is good.

need for cognition   the motivation to think and analyze. Assessed by agreement with items such as "the notion of thinking abstractly is displeasing to me" and disagreement with items such as "I only think as hard as I have to."

need to belong   a motivation to bond with others in relationships that provide ongoing, positive interactions.

non-zero-sum games   games in which outcomes need not sum to zero. With cooperation, both can win; with competition, both can lose. (Also called *mixed-motive situations*.)

normative influence   conformity based on a person's desire to fulfill others' expectations, often to gain acceptance.

norms   rules for accepted and expected behavior. Norms *prescribe* "proper" behavior. (In a different sense of the word, norms also *describe* what most others do—what is *normal*.)

O

obedience   acting in accord with a direct order.

outgroup   "them"—a group that people perceive as distinctively different from or apart from their ingroup.

outgroup homogeneity effect   perception of outgroup members as more similar to one another than are ingroup members. Thus "they are alike; we are diverse."

overconfidence phenomenon   the tendency to be more confident than correct—to overestimate the accuracy of one's beliefs.

overjustification effect   the result of bribing people to do what they already like doing; they may then see their actions as externally controlled rather than intrinsically appealing.

own-race bias   the tendency for people to more accurately recognize faces of their own race.

P

passionate love   a state of intense longing for union with another. Passionate lovers are absorbed in one another, feel ecstatic at attaining their partner's love, and are disconsolate on losing it.

peripheral route to persuasion   occurs when people are influenced by incidental cues, such as a speaker's attractiveness.

personal space   the buffer zone we like to maintain around our bodies. Its size depends on our familiarity with whoever is near us.

persuasion   the process by which a message induces change in beliefs, attitudes, or behaviors.

physical-attractiveness stereotype   the presumption that physically attractive people possess other socially desirable traits as well: What is beautiful is good.

pluralistic ignorance   a false impression of how other people are thinking, feeling, or responding.

possible selves   images of what we dream of or dread becoming in the future.

prejudice   a negative prejudgment of a group and its individual members.

primacy effect   other things being equal, information presented first usually has the most influence.

priming   activating particular associations in memory.

prosocial behavior   positive, constructive, helpful social behavior; the opposite of antisocial behavior.

proximity   geographical nearness. Proximity (more precisely, "functional distance") powerfully predicts liking.

R

racism   (1) an individual's prejudicial attitudes and discriminatory behavior toward people of a given race, or (2) institutional practices (even if not motivated by prejudice) that subordinate people of a given race.

random assignment   the process of assigning participants to the conditions of an experiment such that all persons have the same chance of being in a given condition. (Note the distinction between random *assignment* in experiments and random *sampling* in surveys. Random assignment helps us infer cause and effect. Random sampling helps us generalize to a population.)

random sample   survey procedure in which every person in the population being studied has an equal chance of inclusion.

reactance   a motive to protect or restore one's sense of freedom. Reactance arises when someone threatens our freedom of action.

realistic group conflict theory   the theory that prejudice arises from competition between groups for scarce resources.

recency effect   information presented last sometimes has the most influence. Recency effects are less common than primacy effects.

reciprocity norm   an expectation that people will help, not hurt, those who have helped them.

regression toward the average   the statistical tendency for extreme scores or extreme behavior to return toward one's average.

relative deprivation   the perception that one is less well off than others to whom one compares oneself.

representativeness heuristic   the tendency to presume, sometimes despite contrary odds, that someone or something belongs to a particular group if resembling (representing) a typical member.

reward theory of attraction   the theory that we like those whose behavior is rewarding to us or whom we associate with rewarding events.

role   a set of norms that defines how people in a given social position ought to behave.

S

secure attachment   attachments rooted in trust and marked by intimacy.

self-affirmation theory   a theory that (a) people often experience a self-image threat after engaging in an undesirable behavior; and that (b) they can compensate by affirming another aspect of the self. Threaten people's self-concept in one domain and they will compensate by either refocusing or by doing good deeds in some other domain.

self-awareness   a self-conscious state in which attention focuses on oneself. It makes people more sensitive to their own attitudes and dispositions.

self-concept   a person's answers to the question "Who am I?"

self-disclosure   revealing intimate aspects of oneself to others.

self-efficacy   a sense that one is competent and effective, distinguished from self-esteem, one's sense of self-worth. A bombardier might feel high self-efficacy and low self-esteem.

self-esteem   a person's overall self-evaluation or sense of self-worth.

self-fulfilling prophecy   a belief that leads to its own fulfillment.

self-handicapping protecting one's self-image with behaviors that create a handy excuse for later failure.

self-monitoring being attuned to the way one presents oneself in social situations and adjusting one's performance to create the desired impression.

self-perception theory the theory that when we are unsure of our attitudes, we infer them much as would someone observing us, by looking at our behavior and the circumstances under which it occurs.

self-presentation the act of expressing oneself and behaving in ways designed to create a favorable impression or an impression that corresponds to one's ideals.

self-reference effect the tendency to process efficiently and remember well information related to oneself.

self-schema beliefs about self that organize and guide the processing of self-relevant information.

self-serving bias the tendency to perceive oneself favorably.

sexism (1) an individual's prejudicial attitudes and discriminatory behavior toward people of a given sex, or (2) institutional practices (even if not motivated by prejudice) that subordinate people of a given sex.

situational attribution attributing behavior to the environment.

sleeper effect a delayed impact of a message occurs when an initially discounted message becomes effective, as we remember the message but forget the reason for discounting it.

social comparison evaluating one's abilities and opinions by comparing oneself to others.

social dominance orientation a motivation to have one's group be dominant over other social groups.

social-exchange theory the theory that human interactions are transactions that aim to maximize one's rewards and minimize one's costs.

social facilitation (1) original meaning—the tendency of people to perform simple or well-learned tasks better when others are present; (2) current meaning—strengthening of dominant (prevalent, likely) responses owing to the presence of others.

social identity the "we" aspect of our self-concept. The part of our answer to "Who am I?" that comes from our group memberships.

social leadership leadership that builds teamwork, mediates conflict, and offers support.

social learning theory the theory that we learn social behavior by observing and imitating and by being rewarded and punished.

social loafing the tendency for people to exert less effort when they pool their efforts toward a common goal than when they are individually accountable.

social psychology the scientific study of how people think about, influence, and relate to one another.

social representations socially shared beliefs—widely held ideas and values, including our assumptions and cultural ideologies. Our social representations help us make sense of our world.

social responsibility norm an expectation that people will help those dependent on them.

spotlight effect the belief that others are paying more attention to one's appearance and behavior than they really are.

stereotype a belief about the personal attributes of a group of people. Stereotypes are sometimes overgeneralized, inaccurate, and resistant to new information.

stereotype threat a disruptive concern, when facing a negative stereotype, that one will be evaluated based on a negative stereotype. Unlike self-fulfilling prophecies that hammer one's reputation into one's self-concept, stereotype threat situations have immediate effects.

subgrouping accommodating groups of individuals who deviate from one's stereotype by forming a new stereotype about this subset of the group.

subtyping accommodating groups of individuals who deviate from one's stereotype by thinking of them as a special category of people with different properties.

superordinate goal a shared goal that necessitates cooperative effort; a goal that overrides people's differences from one another.

T

task leadership leadership that organizes work, sets standards, and focuses on goals.

theory an integrated set of principles that explains and predicts observed events.

Tragedy of the Commons the "commons" is any shared resource, including air, water, energy sources, and food supplies. The tragedy occurs when individuals consume more than their share, with the cost of their doing so dispersed among all, causing the ultimate collapse—the tragedy—of the commons.

two-factor theory of emotion arousal × label = emotion.

two-step flow of communication the process by which media influence often occurs through opinion leaders, who in turn influence others.

U

upward social comparison comparing with others who are better, or better off, may trigger feelings of relative deprivation.

references

Abbey, A. (1987). Misperceptions of friendly behavior as sexual interest: A survey of naturally occurring incidents. *Psychology of Women Quarterly*, **11**, 173–194. (p. 85)

Abbey, A. (1991). Misperception as an antecedent of acquaintance rape: A consequence of ambiguity in communication between women and men. In A. Parrot (Ed.), *Acquaintance rape*. New York: John Wiley. (p. 85)

Abbey, A., & Andrews, F. M. (1985). Modeling the psychological determinants of life quality. *Social Indicators Research*, **16**, 1–34. (p. 600)

Abbey, A., McAuslan, P., & Ross, L. T. (1998). Sexual assault perpetration by college men: The role of alcohol, misperception of sexual intent, and sexual beliefs and experiences. *Journal of Social and Clinical Psychology*, **17**, 167–195. (p. 85)

Abelson, R. (1972). Are attitudes necessary? In B. T. King & E. McGinnies (Eds.), *Attitudes, conflict and social change*. New York: Academic Press. (p. 135)

Abelson, R. P., Kinder, D. R., Peters, M. D., & Fiske, S. T. (1982). Affective and semantic components in political person perception. *Journal of Personality and Social Psychology*, **42**, 619–630. (p. 256)

Abrams, D. (1991). AIDS: What young people believe and what they do. Paper presented at the British Association for the Advancement of Science conference. (p. 71)

Abrams, D., Wetherell, M., Cochrane, S., Hogg, M. A., & Turner, J. C. (1990). Knowing what to think by knowing who you are: Self-categorization and the nature of norm formation, conformity and group polarization. *British Journal of Social Psychology*, **29**, 97–119. (p. 309)

Abramson, L. Y. (Ed.). (1988). *Social cognition and clinical psychology: A synthesis*. New York: Guilford. (p. 594)

Abramson, L. Y., Metalsky, G. I., & Alloy, L. B. (1989). Hopelessness depression: A theory-based subtype. *Psychological Review*, **96**, 358–372. (p. 577)

Acitelli, L. K., & Antonucci, T. C. (1994). Gender differences in the link between marital support and satisfaction in older couples. *Journal of Personality and Social Psychology*, **67**, 688–698. (p. 183)

Ackermann, R., & DeRubeis, R. J. (1991). Is depressive realism real? *Clinical Psychology Review*, **11**, 565–584. (p. 577)

Adair, J. G., Dushenko, T. W., & Lindsay, R. C. L. (1985). Ethical regulations and their impact on research practice. *American Psychologist*, **40**, 59–72. (p. 28)

Adams, D. (Ed.) (1991). *The Seville statement on violence: Preparing the ground for the constructing of peace*. UNESCO. (p. 386)

Adams, J. M., & Jones, W. H. (1997). The conceptualization of marital commitment: An integrative analysis. *Journal of Personality and Social Psychology*, **72**, 1177–1196. (p. 467)

Addis, M. E., & Mahalik, J. R. (2003). Men, masculinity, and the contexts of help seeking. *American Psychologist*, **58**, 5–14. (p. 182)

Aderman, D., & Berkowitz, L. (1970). Observational set, empathy, and helping. *Journal of Personality and Social Psychology*, **14**, 141–148. (p. 480)

Aderman, D., & Berkowitz, L. (1983). Self-concern and the unwillingness to be helpful. *Social Psychology Quarterly*, **46**, 293–301. (p. 481)

Adler, N. E., Boyce, T., Chesney, M. A., Cohen, S., Folkman, S., Kahn, R. L., & Syme, S. L. (1993). Socioeconomic inequalities in health: No easy solution. *Journal of the American Medical Association*, **269**, 3140–3145. (p. 23)

Adler, N. E., & Snibbe, A. C. (2003). The role of psychosocial processes in explaining the gradient between socioeconomic status and health. *Current Directions in Psychological Science*, **12**, 119–123. (p. 599)

Adler, R. P., Lesser, G. S., Meringoff, L. K., Robertson, T. S., & Ward, S. (1980). *The effects of television advertising on children*. Lexington, MA: Lexington Books. (p. 281)

Adler, S. J. (1994). *The jury*. New York: Times Books. (p. 626)

Adorno, T., Frenkel-Brunswik, E., Levinson, D., & Sanford, R. N. (1950). *The authoritarian personality*, New York: Harper. (p. 345)

Affleck, G., Tennen, H., & Apter, A. (2000). Optimism, pessimism, and daily life with chronic illness. In E. C. Chang (Ed.), *Optimism and pessimism*. Washington, DC: APA Books. (pp. 590, 657)

Agostinelli, G., Sherman, S. J., Presson, C. C., & Chassin, L. (1992). Self-protection and self-enhancement biases in estimates of population prevalence. *Personality and Social Psychology Bulletin*, **18**, 631–642. (pp. 63)

Agres, S. J. (1987). Rational, emotional and mixed appeals in advertising: Impact on recall and persuasion. Paper presented at the American Psychological Association convention. (Available from Lowe Marschalk, Inc., 1345 Avenue of the Americas, New York, NY, 10105.) (p. 256)

Aiello, J. R., & Douthitt, E. Z. (2001). Social facilitation from Triplett to electronic performance monitoring. *Group Dynamics: Theory, Research, and Practice*, **5**, 163–180. (p. 290)

Aiello, J. R., Thompson, D. E., & Brodzinsky, D. M. (1983). How funny is crowding anyway? Effects of room size, group size, and the introduction of humor. *Basic and Applied Social Psychology*, **4**, 193–207. (p. 289)

Ainsworth, M. D. S. (1973). The development of infant-mother attachment. In B. Caldwell &

H. Ricciuti (Eds.), *Review of child development research* (Vol. 3). Chicago: University of Chicago Press. (p. 459)

Ainsworth, M. D. S. (1979). Infant-mother attachment. *American Psychologist, 34,* 932–937. (p. 459)

Ajzen, I. (1982). On behaving in accordance with one's attitudes. In M. P. Zanna, E. T. Higgins, & C. P. Herman (Eds.). *Consistency in social behavior: The Ontario Symposium,* vol. 2. Hillside, NJ: Erlbaum. (p. 138)

Ajzen, I. (2002). Perceived behavioral control, self-efficacy, locus of control, and the theory of planned behavior. *Journal of Applied Social Psychology, 32,* 665–683. (p. 138)

Ajzen, I., & Fishbein, M. (1977). Attitude-behavior relations: A theoretical analysis and review of empirical research. *Psychological Bulletin, 84,* 888–918. (pp. 138)

Albarracin, D., Johnson, B. T., Fishbein, M., & Muellerleile, P. A. (2001). Theories of reasoned action and planned behavior as models of condom use: A meta-analysis. *Psychological Bulletin, 127,* 142–161. (p. 138)

Albee, G. (1979, June 19). Politics, power, prevention, and social change. Keynote address to Vermont Conference on Primary Prevention of Psychopathology. (p. 204)

Alicke, M. D., & Davis, T. L. (1989). The role of *a posteriori* victim information in judgments of blame and sanction. *Journal of Experimental Social Psychology, 25,* 362–377. (p. 624)

Allee, W. C., & Masure, R. M. (1936). A comparison of maze behavior in paired and isolated shell-parakeets (*Melopsittacus undulatus Shaw*) in a two-alley problem box. *Journal of Comparative Psychology, 22,* 131–155. (p. 287)

Allen, V. L., & Levine, J. M. (1969). Consensus and conformity. *Journal of Experimental Social Psychology, 5,* 389–399. (p. 229)

Allen, V. L., & Wilder, D. A. (1980). Impact of group consensus and social support on stimulus meaning: Mediation of conformity by cognitive restructuring. *Journal of Personality and Social Psychology, 39,* 1116–1124. (p. 235)

Allison, S. T., Beggan, J. K., McDonald, R. A., & Rettew, M. L. (1995). The belief in majority determination of group decision outcomes. *Basic and Applied Social Psychology, 16,* 367–382. (p. 359)

Allison, S. T., Jordan, M. R., & Yeatts, C. E. (1992). A cluster-analytic approach toward identifying the structure and content of human decision making. *Human Relations, 45,* 49–72. (p. 359)

Allison, S. T., Mackie, D. M., & Messick, D. M. (1996). Outcome biases in social perception: Implications for dispositional inference, attitude change, stereotyping, and social behavior. *Advances in Experimental Social Psychology, 28,* 53–93. (p. 359)

Allison, S. T., Mackie, D. M., Muller, M. M., & Worth, L. T. (1993). Sequential correspondence biases and perceptions of change: The Castro studies revisited. *Personality and Social Psychology Bulletin, 19,* 151–157. (pp. 88, 359)

Allison, S. T., McQueen, L. R., & Schaerfl, L. M. (1992). Social decision making processes and the equal partitionment of shared resources. *Journal of Experimental Social Psychology, 28,* 23–42. (pp. 114, 359, 526)

Allison, S. T., & Messick, D. M. (1985). The group attribution error. *Journal of Experimental Social Psychology, 21,* 563–579. (p. 359)

Allison, S. T., & Messick, D. M. (1987). From individual inputs to group outputs, and back again: Group processes and inferences about members. In C. Hendrick (Ed.), *Group processes: Review of personality and social psychology,* Vol. 8. Newbury Park, CA: Sage. (p. 359)

Allison, S. T., Messick, D. M., & Goethals, G. R. (1989). On being better but not smarter than others: The Muhammad Ali effect. *Social Cognition, 7,* 275–296. (pp. 69, 359)

Allison, S. T., Worth, L. T., & King, M. W. C. (1990). Group decisions as social inference heuristics. *Journal of Personality and Social Psychology, 58,* 801–811. (p. 359)

Alloy, L. B., & Abramson, L. Y. (1979). Judgment of contingency in depressed and nondepressed students: Sadder but wiser? *Journal of Experimental Psychology: General, 108,* 441–485. (p. 577)

Alloy, L. B., Abramson, L. Y., Whitehouse, W. G., Hogan, M. E., Tashman, N. A., Steinberg, D. L., Rose, D. T., & Donovan, P. (1999). Depressogenic cognitive styles: Predictive validity, information processing and personality characteristics, and developmental origins. *Behaviour Research and Therapy, 37,* 503–531. (p. 580)

Alloy, L. B., Albright, J. S., Abramson, L. Y., & Dykman, B. M. (1990). Depressive realism and nondepressive optimistic illusions: The role of the self. In R. E. Ingram (Ed.), *Contemporary psychological approaches to depression: Theory, research and treatment.* New York: Plenum. (p. 577)

Allport, F. H. (1920). The influence of the group upon association and thought. *Journal of Experimental Psychology, 3,* 159–182. (p. 287)

Allport, G. (1954). *The nature of prejudice.* Cambridge, MA: Addison-Wesley. (pp. 332–333, 369, 550)

Allport, G. W. (1958). *The nature of prejudice* (abridged). Garden City, NY: Anchor Books. (pp. 343–344, 347, 350, 370, 371)

Allport, G. W., & Ross, J. M. (1967). Personal religious orientation and prejudice. *Journal of Personality and Social Psychology, 5,* 432–443. (p. 346)

Altemeyer, B. (1988). *Enemies of freedom: Understanding right-wing authoritarianism.* San Francisco: Jossey-Bass. (pp. 345–346)

Altemeyer, B. (1992). Six studies of right-wing authoritarianism among American state legislators. Unpublished manuscript, University of Manitoba. (pp. 345–346)

Altemeyer, B., & Hunsberger, B. (1992). Authoritarianism, religious fundamentalism, quest, and prejudice. *International Journal for the Psychology of Religion, 2,* 113–133. (p. 346)

Altemeyer, R. (in press). Highly dominating, highly authoritarian personalities. *Journal of Social Psychology.* (p. 346)

Altman, I., & Vinsel, A. M. (1978). Personal space: An analysis of E. T. Hall's proxemics framework. In I. Altman & J. Wohlwill (Eds.), *Human behavior and the environment*. New York: Plenum Press. (p. 175)

Alwin, D. F. (1990). Historical changes in parental orientations to children. In N. Mandell (Ed.), *Sociological studies of child development*, Vol. 3. Greenwich, CT: JAI Press. (p. 561)

Alwin, D. F., Cohen, R. L., & Newcomb, T. M. (1991). *Political attitudes over the life span: The Bennington women after fifty years*. Madison, WI: University of Wisconsin Press. (p. 268)

Amabile, T. M., & Glazebrook, A. H. (1982). A negativity bias in interpersonal evaluation. *Journal of Experimental Social Psychology, 18*, 1–22. (p. 355)

Amato, P. R. (1979). Juror-defendant similarity and the assessment of guilt in politically motivated crimes. *Australian Journal of Psychology, 31*, 79–88. (p. 620)

Amato, P. R. (1986). Emotional arousal and helping behavior in a real-life emergency. *Journal of Applied Social Psychology, 16*, 633–641. (pp. 490–491)

Ambady, N., & Rosenthal, R. (1992). Thin slices of expressive behavior as predictors of interpersonal consequences: A meta-analysis. *Psychological Bulletin, 111*, 256–274. (p. 123)

Ambady, N., & Rosenthal, R. (1993). Half a minute: Predicting teacher evaluations from thin slices of nonverbal behavior and physical attractiveness. *Journal of Personality and Social Psychology, 64*, 431–441. (p. 123)

American Enterprise (1992, January/February). Women, men, marriages & ministers. P. 106. (p. 468)

American Psychological Association (1993). *Violence and youth: Psychology's response. Vol I: Summary report of the American Psychological Assocation Commission on Violence and Youth*. Washington, DC: Public Interest Directorate, American Psychological Association. (pp. 384–385)

American Psychological Association (2002). *Ethical principles of psychologists and code of conduct 2002*. Washington, DC: APA (www.apa.org/ethics/code2002.html). (p. 32)

Amir, Y. (1969). Contact hypothesis in ethnic relations. *Psychological Bulletin, 71*, 319–342. (p. 539)

Anda, R., Williamson, D., Jones, D., Macera, C., Eaker, E., Glassman, A., & Marks, J. (1993). Depressed affect, hopelessness, and the risk of ischemic heart disease in a cohort of U.S. adults. *Epidemiology, 4*, 285–294. (p. 588)

Andersen, S. M. (1998). Service Learning: A National Strategy for Youth Development. A Position Paper issued by the Task Force on Education Policy. Washington, DC: Institute for Communitarian Policy Studies, George Washington University. (pp. 478, 516)

Andersen, S. M., & Chen, S. (2002). The relational self: An interpersonal social-cognitive theory. *Psychological Review, 109*, 619–645. (p. 41)

Anderson, C. A. (1982). Inoculation and counter-explanation: Debiasing techniques in the perseverance of social theories. *Social Cognition, 1*, 126–139. (p. 102)

Anderson, C. A. (1999). Attributional style, depression, and loneliness: A cross-cultural comparison of American and Chinese students. *Personality and Social Psychology Bulletin, 25*, 482–499. (p. 80)

Anderson, C. A. (2003). Video games and aggressive behavior. In D. Ravitch and J. P. Viteritti (Eds.), *Kids stuff: Marking violence and vulgarity in the popular culture*. Baltimore, MD: Johns Hopkins University Press. (pp. 411, 412)

Anderson, C. A. (2004). An update on the effects of violent video games. *Journal of Adolescence, 27*, 113–122. (p. 410)

Anderson, C. A., & Anderson, D. C. (1984). Ambient temperature and violent crime: Tests of the linear and curvilinear hypotheses. *Journal of Personality and Social Psychology, 46*, 91–97. (p. 395)

Anderson, C. A., & Anderson, K. B. (1998). Temperature and aggression: Paradox, controversy, and a (fairly) clear picture. In R. G. Geen & E. Donnerstein (Eds.), *Human aggression: Theories, research, and implications for social policy*. San Diego, CA: Academic Press. (p. 395)

Anderson, C. A., Anderson, K. B., Dorr, N., DeNeve, K. M., & Flanagan, M. (2000). Temperature and aggression. In M. P. Zanna (Ed.), *Advances in Experimental Social Psychology*. San Diego, CA: Academic Press. (p. 395)

Anderson, C. A., Benjamin, A. J., Jr., & Bartholow, B. D. (1998). Does the gun pull the trigger? Automatic priming effects of weapon pictures and weapon names. *Psychological Science, 9*, 308–314. (pp. 396–397)

Anderson, C. A., Berkowitz, L., Donnerstein, E., Huesmann, R. L., Johnson, J., Linz, D., Malamuth, N., & Wartella, E. (in press). The influence of media violence on youth. *Psychological Science in the Public Interest*. (p. 407)

Anderson, C. A., & Bushman, B. J. (1997). External validity of "trivial" experiments: The case of laboratory aggression. *Review of General Psychology, 1*, 19–41. (p. 414)

Anderson, C. A., & Bushman, B. J. (2001). Effects of violent video games on aggressive behavior, aggressive cognition, aggressive affect, physiological arousal, and prosocial behavior: A meta-analytic review of the scientific literature. *Psychological Science, 12*, 353–359. (p. 412)

Anderson, C. A., & Bushman, B. J. (2002). Media violence and the American public revisited. *American Psychologist, 57*, 448–450. (p. 406)

Anderson, C. A., Carnagey, N. L., & Eubanks, J. (2003). Exposure to violent media: The effects of songs with violent lyrics on aggressive thoughts and feelings. *Journal of Personality and Social Psychology, 84*, 960–971. (p. 411)

Anderson, C. A., Carnagey, N. L., Flanagan, M., Benjamin, A. J., Eubanks, J., & Valentine, J. C. (in press). Violent video games: Specific effects of violent content on aggressive thoughts and behavior. *Advances in Experimental Social Psychology*. (p. 411)

Anderson, C. A., Deuser, W. E., & DeNeve, K. M. (1995). Hot temperatures, hostile affect, hostile cognition, and arousal: Tests of a general model of affective aggression.

Personality and Social Psychology Bulletin, 21, 434–448. (pp. 397, 509)

Anderson, C. A., & Harvey, R. J. (1988). Discriminating between problems in living: An examination of measures of depression, loneliness, shyness, and social anxiety. *Journal of Social and Clinical Psychology, 6,* 482–491. (p. 584)

Anderson, C. A., Horowitz, L. M., & French, R. D. (1983). Attributional style of lonely and depressed people. *Journal of Personality and Social Psychology, 45,* 127–136. (p. 75)

Anderson, C. A., Lepper, M. R., & Ross, L. (1980). Perseverance of social theories: The role of explanation in the persistence of discredited information. *Journal of Personality and Social Psychology, 39,* 1037–1049. (p. 102)

Anderson, C. A., Lindsay, J. J., & Bushman, B. J. (1999). Research in the psychological laboratory: Truth or triviality? *Current Directions in Psychological Science, 8,* 3–9. (pp. 33, 395)

Anderson, C. A., Miller, R. S., Riger, A. L., Dill, J. C., & Sedikides, C. (1994). Behavioral and characterological attributional styles as predictors of depression and loneliness: Review, refinement, and test. *Journal of Personality and Social Psychology, 66,* 549–558. (p. 582)

Anderson, C. A., & Morrow, M. (1995). Competitive aggression without interaction: Effects of competitive versus cooperative instructions on aggressive behavior in video games. *Personality and Social Psychology Bulletin, 21,* 1020–1031. (p. 529)

Anderson, C. A., & Sechler, E. S. (1986). Effects of explanation and counterexplanation on the development and use of social theories. *Journal of Personality and Social Psychology, 50,* 24–34. (p. 102)

Anderson, C., Keltner, D., & John, O. P. (2003). Emotional convergence between people over time. *Journal of Personality and Social Psychology, 84,* 1054–1068. (p. 444)

Anderson, K. J., & Leaper, C. (1998). Meta-analyses of gender effects on conversational interruption: Who, what, when, where, and how. *Sex Roles, 39,* 225–252. (p. 186)

Angier, N. (2003, November 11). Is war our biological destiny? *New York Times* (www.nytimes.com). (p. 419)

Annin, P. (1999, April 19). Big money, big trouble. *Newsweek,* p. 59. (p. 652)

Antill, J. K. (1983). Sex role complementarity versus similarity in married couples. *Journal of Personality and Social Psychology, 45,* 145–155. (p. 185)

AP (1993, June 10). Walking past a dying man. *New York Times* (via Associated Press). (p. 498)

Apsler, R. (1975). Effects of embarrassment on behavior toward others. *Journal of Personality and Social Psychology, 32,* 145–153. (p. 480)

Archer, D., & Gartner, R. (1976). Violent acts and violent times: A comparative approach to postwar homicide rates. *American Sociological Review, 41,* 937–963. (p. 416)

Archer, D., Iritani, B., Kimes, D. B., & Barrios, M. (1983). Face-ism: Five studies of sex differences in facial prominence. *Journal of Personality and Social Psychology, 45,* 725–735. (p. 348)

Archer, J. (1991). The influence of testosterone on human aggression. *British Journal of Psychology, 82,* 1–28. (p. 385)

Archer, J. (2000). Sex differences in aggression between heterosexual partners: A meta-analytic review. *Psychological Bulletin, 126,* 651–680. (pp. 187–188)

Archer, J. (2002). Sex differences in physically aggressive acts between heterosexual partners: A meta-analytic review. *Aggression and Violent Behavior, 7,* 313–351. (pp. 187–188)

Archer, R. L., & Cook, C. E. (1986). Personalistic self-disclosure and attraction: Basis for relationship or scarce resource. *Social Psychology Quarterly, 49,* 268–272. (p. 462)

Arendt, H. (1963). *Eichmann in Jerusalem: A report on the banality of evil.* New York: Viking Press. (p. 226)

Argyle, M. (1986). *The psychology of happiness.* London: Methuen. (p. 652)

Argyle, M. (1999). Causes and correlates of happiness. In D. Kahneman, E. Diener, and N. Schwartz (Eds.), *Foundations of hedonic psychology: Scientific perspectives on enjoyment and suffering.* New York: Russell Sage Foundation. (pp. 651–652)

Argyle, M., & Henderson M. (1985). *The anatomy of relationships.* London: Heinemann. (p. 175)

Argyle, M., Shimoda, K., & Little, B. (1978). Variance due to persons and situations in England and Japan. *British Journal of Social and Clinical Psychology, 17,* 335–337. (p. 203)

Arkes, H. R. (1990). Some practical judgment/decision making research. Paper presented at the American Psychological Association convention. (p. 264)

Arkin, R. M., Appleman, A., & Burger, J. M. (1980). Social anxiety, self-presentation, and the self-serving bias in causal attribution. *Journal of Personality and Social Psychology, 38,* 23–35. (p. 79)

Arkin, R. M., & Baumgardner, A. H. (1985). Self-handicapping. In J. H. Harvey & C. Weary (Eds.), *Attribution: Basic issues and applications.* New York: Academic Press. (p. 79)

Arkin, R. M., & Burger, J. M. (1980). Effects of unit relation tendencies on interpersonal attraction. *Social Psychology Quarterly, 43,* 380–391. (p. 426)

Arkin, R. M., Cooper, H., & Kolditz, T. (1980). A statistical review of the literature concerning the self-serving attribution bias in interpersonal influence situations. *Journal of Personality, 48,* 435–448. (p. 69)

Arkin, R. M., Lake, E. A., & Baumgardner, A. H. (1986). Shyness and self-presentation. In W. H. Jones, J. M. Cheek, & S. R. Briggs (Eds.), *Shyness: Perspectives on research and treatment.* New York: Plenum. (p. 78)

Arkin, R. M., & Maruyama, G. M. (1979). Attribution, affect, and college exam performance. *Journal of Educational Psychology, 71,* 85–93. (p. 68)

Armitage, C. J., & Conner, M. (2001). Efficacy of the theory of planned behaviour: A meta-analytic review. *British Journal of Social Psychology, 40,* 471–499. (p. 138)

Armor, D. A., & Taylor, S. E. (1996). Situated optimism: Specific outcome expectancies and self-regulation. In M. P. Zanna (Ed.), *Advances in experimental social psychology,* vol. 30. San Diego, CA: Academic Press. (p. 71)

Arms, R. L., Russell, G. W., & Sandilands, M. L. (1979). Effects on the hostility of spectators of viewing aggressive sports. *Social Psychology Quarterly, 42,* 275–279. (p. 416)

Aron, A., & Aron, E. (1989). *The heart of social psychology,* 2nd ed. Lexington, MA: Lexington Books. (pp. 213, 529)

Aron, A., & Aron, E. N. (1994). Love. In A. L. Weber & J. H. Harvey (Eds.), *Perspective on close relationships.* Boston: Allyn & Bacon. (p. 464)

Aron, A., Dutton, D. G., Aron, E. N., & Iverson, A. (1989). Experiences of falling in love. *Journal of Social and Personal Relationships, 6,* 243–257. (p. 446)

Aron, A., Melinat, E., Aron, E. N., Vallone, R. D., & Bator, R. J. (1997). The experimental generation of interpersonal closeness: A procedure and some preliminary findings. *Personality and Social Psychology Bulletin, 23,* 363–377. (p. 464)

Aron, A., Norman, C. C., Aron, E. N., McKenna, C., & Heyman, R. E. (2000). Couples' shared participation in novel and arousing activities and experienced relationship quality. *Journal of Personality and Social Psychology, 78,* 273–284. (p. 455)

Aronson, E. (1988). *The social animal.* New York: Freeman. (p. 449)

Aronson, E. (1997). Bring the family address to American Psychological Society annual convention, reported in *APS Observer,* July/August, pp. 17, 34, 35. (p. 258)

Aronson, E. (2000). *Nobody left to hate: Teaching compassion after Columbine.* New York: Freeman/Worth. (p. 549)

Aronson, E. (2002). Building empathy, compassion, and achievement in the jigsaw classroom. In J. Aronson (Ed.), *Improving academic achievement: Impact of psychological factors on education.* San Diego, CA: Academic Press. (p. 549)

Aronson, E., Blaney, N., Stephan, C., Sikes, J., & Snapp, M. (1978). *The jigsaw classroom.* Beverly Hills, CA: Sage Publications. (p. 549)

Aronson, E., Brewer, M., & Carlsmith, J. M. (1985). Experimentation in social psychology. In G. Lindzey & E. Aronson (Eds.), *Handbook of social psychology,* vol. 1. Hillsdale, NJ: Erlbaum. (p. 31)

Aronson, E., & Gonzalez, A. (1988). Desegregation, jigsaw, and the Mexican-American experience. In P. A. Katz & D. Taylor (Eds.), *Towards the elimination of racism: Profiles in controversy.* New York: Plenum. (p. 549)

Aronson, E., & Linder, D. (1965). Gain and loss of esteem as determinants of interpersonal attractiveness. *Journal of Experimental Social Psychology, 1,* 156–171. (p. 449)

Aronson, E., & Mettee, D. R. (1974). Affective reactions to appraisal from others. *Foundations of interpersonal attraction.* New York: Academic Press. (p. 449)

Aronson, E., & Mills, J. (1959). The effect of severity of initiation on liking for a group. *Journal of Abnormal and Social Psychology, 59,* 177–181. (p. 273)

Aronson, E., Turner, J. A., & Carlsmith, J. M. (1963). Communicator credibility and communicator discrepancy as determinants of opinion change. *Journal of Abnormal and Social Psychology, 67,* 31–36. (pp. 259, 260)

Arriaga, X. B. (2001). The ups and downs of dating: Fluctuations in satisfaction in newly formed romantic relationships. *Journal of Personality and Social Psychology, 80,* 754–765. (p. 468)

Arriaga, X. B., & Agnew, C. R. (2001). Being committed: Affective, cognitive, and conative components of relationship commitment. *Personality and Social Psychology Bulletin, 27,* 1190–1203. (p. 468)

ASAPS (2003). Statistics 2002. The American Society for Aesthetic Plastic Surgery (www.surgery.org). (pp. 432–433, 439)

Asch, S. E. (1946). Forming impressions of personality. *Journal of Abnormal and Social Psychology, 41,* 258–290. (p. 262)

Asch, S. E. (1955, November). Opinions and social pressure. *Scientific American,* pp. 31–35. (pp. 213–214, 229, 230)

Asendorpf, J. B. (1987). Videotape reconstruction of emotions and cognitions related to shyness. *Journal of Personality and Social Psychology, 53,* 541–549. (p. 584)

Ash, R. (1999). *The top 10 of everything 2000.* New York: DK Publishing. (p. 382)

Asher, J. (1987, April). Born to be shy? *Psychology Today,* pp. 56–64. (p. 382)

Aspinwall, L. G., & Taylor, S. E. (1997). A stitch in time: Self-regulation and proactive coping. *Psychological Bulletin, 121,* 417–436. (p. 590)

Associated Press (1995, September 25). Blacks are given tougher sentences, analysis shows. *Grand Rapids Press,* p. A3. (p. 621)

Astin, A. W. (1972). *Four critical years.* San Francisco: Jossey-Bass. (p. 265)

Astin, A. W., Green, K. C., Korn, W. S., & Schalit, M. (1987). *The American freshman: National norms for Fall 1987.* Los Angeles: Higher Education Research Institute, UCLA. *(b)* (pp. 197, 341)

Augoustinos, M., & Innes, J. M. (1990). Towards an integration of social representations and social schema theory. *British Journal of Social Psychology, 29,* 213–231. (p. 14)

Averill, J. R. (1983). Studies on anger and aggression: Implications for theories of emotion. *American Psychologist, 38,* 1145–1160. (p. 387)

Axelrod, R., & Dion, D. (1988). The further evolution of cooperation. *Science, 242,* 1385–1390. (p. 559)

Axsom, D. (1989). Cognitive dissonance and behavior change in psychotherapy. *Journal of Experimental Social Psychology, 25,* 234–252. (p. 592)

Axsom, D., & Cooper, J. (1985). Cognitive dissonance and psychotherapy: The role of effort justification in inducing weight loss. *Journal of Experimental Social Psychology, 21,* 149–160. (p. 592)

Axsom, D., Yates, S., & Chaiken, S. (1987). Audience response as a heuristic cue in persuasion. *Journal of Personality and Social Psychology, 53,* 30–40. (p. 269)

Ayres, I. (1991). Fair driving: Gender and race discrimination in retail car negotiations. *Harvard Law Review, 104,* 817–872. (p. 337)

Ayres, I., & Nalebuff, B. (2003, April 15). Charity begins at Schedule A. *New York Times* (www.nytimes.com). (p. 513)

Azrin, N. H. (1967, May). Pain and aggression. *Psychology Today,* pp. 27–33. (p. 393)

Babad, E., Bernieri, F., & Rosenthal, R. (1991). Students as judges of teachers' verbal and nonverbal behavior. *American Educational Research Journal,* **28,** 211–234. (p. 123)

Babad, E., Hills, M., & O'Driscoll, M. (1992). Factors influencing wishful thinking and predictions of election outcomes. *Basic and Applied Social Psychology,* **13,** 461–476. (p. 72)

Bachman, J. G., Johnston, L. D., O'Malley, P. M., & Humphrey, R. N. (1988). Explaining the recent decline in marijuana use: Differentiating the effects of perceived risks, disapproval, and general lifestyle factors. *Journal of Health and Social Behavior,* **29,** 92–112. (p. 252)

Bachman, J. G., & O'Malley, P. M. (1977). Self-esteem in young men: A longitudinal analysis of the impact of educational and occupational attainment. *Journal of Personality and Social Psychology,* **35,** 365–380. (p. 24)

Bailey, J. M., Gaulin, S., Agyei, Y., & Gladue, B. A. (1994). Effects of gender and sexual orientation on evolutionary relevant aspects of human mating psychology. *Journal of Personality and Social Psychology,* **66,** 1081–1093. (p. 188)

Bailey, J. M., Kirk, K. M., Zhu, G., Dunne, M. P., & Martin, N. G. (2000). Do individual differences in sociosexuality represent genetic or environmentally contingent strategies? Evidence from the Australian Twin Registry. *Journal of Personality and Social Psychology,* **78,** 537–545. (p. 188)

Baize, H. R., Jr., & Schroeder, J. E. (1995). Personality and mate selection in personal ads: Evolutionary preferences in a public mate selection process. *Journal of Social Behavior and Personality,* **10,** 517–536. (p. 434)

Baker, L. A., & Emery, R. E. (1993). When every relationship is above average: Perceptions and expectations of divorce at the time of marriage. *Law and Human Behavior,* **17,** 439–450. (p. 71)

Baldwin, M. W., Keelan, J. P. R., Fehr, B., Enns, V., Koh-Rangarajoo, E. (1996). Social-cognitive conceptualization of attachment working models: Availability and accessibility effects. *Journal of Personality and Social Psychology,* **71,** 94–109. (p. 459)

Banaji, M. R. & Bhaskar, R. (2000). Implicit stereotypes and memory: The bounded rationality of social beliefs. In D. L. Schacter & E. Scarry (Eds.), *Memory, brain, and belief.* Cambridge, MA: Harvard University Press. (p. 337)

Bandura, A. (1979). The social learning perspective: Mechanisms of aggression. In H. Toch (Ed.), *Psychology of crime and criminal justice.* New York: Holt, Rinehart & Winston. (pp. 391, 392)

Bandura, A. (1997). *Self-efficacy: The exercise of control.* New York: Freeman. (pp. 57, 390, 392)

Bandura, A. (2000). Social cognitive theory: An agentic perspective. *Annual Review of Psychology,* **52,** 1–26. (p. 57)

Bandura, A., Pastorelli, C., Barbaranelli, C., & Caprara, G. V. (1999). Self-efficacy pathways to childhood depression. *Journal of Personality and Social Psychology,* **76,** 258–269. (p. 57)

Bandura, A., Ross, D., & Ross, S. A. (1961). Transmission of aggression through imitation of aggressive models. *Journal of Abnormal and Social Psychology,* **63,** 575–582. (p. 390)

Bandura, A., & Walters, R. H. (1959). *Adolescent aggression.* New York: Ronald Press. (p. 391)

Bandura, A., & Walters, R. H. (1963). *Social learning and personality development.* New York: Holt, Rinehart and Winston. (p. 406)

Banfield, S. & McCabe, M. P. (2001). Extra relationship involvement among women: Are they different from men? *Archives of Sexual Behavior,* **30,** 119–142. (p. 398)

Banks, S. M., Salovey, P., Greener, S., Rothman, A. J., Moyer, A., Beauvais, J., & Epel, E. (1995). The effects of message framing on mammography utilization. *Health Psychology,* **14,** 178–184. (p. 258)

Barash, D. (1979). *The whisperings within.* New York: Harper & Row. (pp. 382, 487)

Barash, D. P. (2003, November 7). Unreason's seductive charms. *Chronicle of Higher Education* (www.chronicle.com/free/v50/i11/11b00601.htm). (p. 171)

Barber, B. M., & Odean, T. (2001). The Internet and the investor. *Journal of Economic Perspectives,* **15,** 41–54. (p. 117)

Barber, N. (2000). On the relationship between country sex ratios and teen pregnancy rates: A replication. *Cross-Cultural Research,* **34,** 327–333. (pp. 188–189)

Bargh, J. A. (1994). The four horsemen of automaticity: Awareness, intention, efficiency, and control in social cognition. In R. S. Wyer & T. K. Srull (Eds.), *Handbook of social cognition,* 2nd ed. (Vol. 1). Hillsdale, NJ: Erlbaum. (p. 107)

Bargh, J. A. (1997). The automaticity of everyday life. In R. S. Wyer, Jr. (Ed.), *Advances in Social Cognition,* **Vol. 10.** Mahwah, NJ: Erlbaum. (pp. 107, 108)

Bargh, J. A., & Chartrand, T. L. (1999). The unbearable automaticity of being. *American Psychologist,* **54,** 462–479. (pp. 105, 106–107, 337)

Bargh, J. A., McKenna, K. Y. A., & Fitzsimons, G. M. (2002). Can you see the real me? Activation and expression of the "true self" on the Internet. *Journal of Social Issues,* **58,** 33–48. (p. 466)

Bargh, J. A., & Raymond, P. (1995). The naive misuse of power: Nonconscious sources of sexual harassment. *Journal of Social Issues,* **51,** 85–96. (p. 85)

Barnes, R. D., Ickes, W., & Kidd, R. F. (1979). Effects of the perceived intentionality and stability of another's dependency on helping behavior. *Personality and Social Psychology Bulletin,* **5,** 367–372. (p. 485)

Barnett, M. A., King, L. M., Howard, J. A., & Melton, E. M. (1980). Experiencing negative affect about self or other: Effects on helping behavior in children and adults. Paper presented at the Midwestern Psychological Association convention. (p. 482)

Barnett, P. A., & Gotlib, I. H. (1988). Psychosocial functioning and depression: Distinguishing among antecedents, concomitants, and consequences. *Psychological Bulletin, 104*, 97–126. (p. 579)

Baron, J., & Hershey, J. C. (1988). Outcome bias in decision evaluation. *Journal of Personality and Social Psychology, 54*, 569–579. (p. 368)

Baron, J., & Miller, J. G. (2000). Limiting the scope of moral obligations to help: A cross-cultural investigation. *Journal of Cross-Cultural Psychology, 31*, 703–725. (p. 485)

Baron, L., & Straus, M. A. (1984). Sexual stratification, pornography, and rape in the United States. In N. M. Malamuth & E. Donnerstein (Eds.), *Pornography and sexual aggression.* New York: Academic Press. (pp. 399–400)

Baron, R. A. (1977). *Human aggression.* New York: Plenum Press. (p. 417)

Baron, R. S. (1986). Distraction-conflict theory: Progress and problems. In L. Berkowitz (Ed.), *Advances in experimental social psychology,* Orlando, FL: Academic Press. (p. 291)

Baron, R. S. (2000). Arousal, capacity, and intense indoctrination. *Personality and Social Psychology Review, 4*, 238–254. (pp. 275–276)

Baron, R. S., David, J. P., Inman, M., & Brunsman, B. M. (1997). Why listeners hear less than they are told: Attentional load and the teller-listener extremity effect. *Journal of Personality and Social Psychology, 72*, 826–838. (p. 94)

Baron, R. S., Hoppe, S. I., Kao, C. F., Brunsman, B., Linneweh, B., & Rogers, D. (1996). Social corroboration and opinion extremity. *Journal of Experimental Social Psychology, 32*, 537–560. (p. 309)

Baron, R. S., Kerr, N. L., & Miller, N. (1992). *Group process, group decision, group action.* Pacific Grove, CA: Brooks/Cole. (p. 389)

Barongan, C., & Hall, G. C. N. (1995). The influence of misogynous rap music on sexual aggression against women. *Psychology of Women Quarterly, 19*, 195–207. (p. 407)

Barrett, L. F., Lane, R. D., Sechrest, L., Schwartz, G. E. (2000). Sex differences in emotional awareness. *Personality & Social Psychology Bulletin, 26*, 1027–1035. (p. 185)

Barry, D. (1995, January). Bored Stiff. *Funny Times,* p. 5. (p. 189)

Barry, D. (1998). *Dave Barry Turns 50.* New York: Crown. (p. 70)

Bar-Tal, D. (1982). Sequential development of helping behavior: A cognitive-learning approach. *Development Review, 2*(2), 101–124. (p. 481)

Bartholomew, K., & Horowitz, L. (1991). Attachment styles among young adults: A test of a four-category model. *Journal of Personality and Social Psychology, 61*, 226–244. (p. 460)

Bartholomew, R. E., & Goode, E. (2000, May/June). Mass delusions and hysterias: Highlights from the past millennium. *Skeptical Inquirer,* pp. 20–28. (p. 212)

Barzun, J. (1975). *Simple and direct.* New York: Harper & Row, pp. 173–174. (p. 164)

Bass, E., & Davis, L. (1994). *The courage to heal.* New York: Harper & Row. (p. 572)

Bassili, J. N. (2003). The minority slowness effect: Subtle inhibitions in the expression of views not shared by others. *Journal of Personality and Social Psychology, 84*, 261–276. (p. 322)

Batson, C. D. (1983). Sociobiology and the role of religion in promoting prosocial behavior: An alternative view. *Journal of Personality and Social Psychology, 45*, 1380–1385. (p. 513)

Batson, C. D. (1999a). Behind the scenes. In D. G. Myers, *Social psychology,* 6th edition. New York: McGraw-Hill. (p. 492)

Batson, C. D. (1999b). Addressing the altruism question experimentally. Paper presented at a Templeton Foundation/Fetzer Institute Symposium on Empathy, Altruism, and Agape, Cambridge, MA. (p. 492)

Batson, C. D. (2001). Addressing the altruism question experimentally. In S. G. Post, L. B. Underwood, J. P. Schloss, & W. B. Hurlbut (Eds.), *Altruism and altruistic love: Science, philosophy, and religion in dialogue.*

New York: Oxford University Press. (pp. 490, 492)

Batson, C. D., Ahmad, N., & Stocks, E. L. (2004). Benefits and liabilities of empathy-induced altruism. In A. G. Miller (Ed.), *The social psychology of good and evil.* New York: Guilford Publications. (p. 493)

Batson, C. D., Ahmad, N., Yin, J., Bedell, S. J., Johnson, J. W., Templin, C. M., & Whiteside, A. (1999). Two threats to the common good: Self-interested egoism and empathy-induced altruism. *Personality and Social Psychology Bulletin, 25*, 3–16. (p. 493)

Batson, C. D., Bolen, M. H., Cross, J. A., & Neuringer-Benefiel, H. E. (1986). Where is the altruism in the altruistic personality? *Journal of Personality and Social Psychology, 50*, 212–220. (p. 490)

Batson, C. D., Cochran, P. J., Biederman, M. F., Blosser, J. L., Ryan, M. J., & Vogt, B. (1978). Failure to help when in a hurry: Callousness or conflict? *Personality and Social Psychology Bulletin, 4*, 97–101. (p. 504)

Batson, C. D., Coke, J. S., Jasnoski, M. L., & Hanson, M. (1978). Buying kindness: Effect of an extrinsic incentive for helping on perceived altruism. *Personality and Social Psychology Bulletin, 4*, 86–91. (pp. 514–515)

Batson, C. D., Duncan, B. D., Ackerman, P., Buckley, T., & Birch, K. (1981). Is empathic emotion a source of altruistic motivation? *Journal of Personality and Social Psychology, 40*, 290–302. (p. 491)

Batson, C. D., Fultz, J., & Schoenrade, P. A. (1987). Distress and empathy: Two qualitatively distinct vicarious emotions with different motivational consequences. *Journal of Personality, 55*, 19–40. (p. 491)

Batson, C. D., Harris, A. C., McCaul, K. D., Davis, M., & Schmidt, T. (1979). Compassion or compliance: Alternative dispositional attributions for one's helping behavior. *Social Psychology Quarterly, 42*, 405–409. (pp. 514–515)

Batson, C. D., Klein, T. R., Highberger, L., & Shaw, L. L. (1997). Immorality from empathy-induced altruism: When compassion and justice conflict. *Journal of Personality* and *Social Psychology*, **68**, 1042–1058. (p. 491)

Batson, C. D., Kobrynowicz, D., Dinnerstein, J. L., Kampf, H. C., & Wilson, A. D. (1997). In a very different voice: Unmasking moral hypocrisy. *Journal of Personality and Social Psychology*, **72**, 1335–1348. (p. 135)

Batson, C. D., Lishner, D. A., Carpenter, A., Dulin, L., Harjusola-Webb, S., Stocks, E. L., Gale, S., Hassan, O., & Sampat, B. (2003). ". . . As you would have them do unto you": Does imagining yourself in the other's place stimulate moral action? *Personality and Social Psychology Bulletin*, **29**, 1190–1201. (p. 513)

Batson, C. D., & Moran, T. (1999). Empathy-induced altruism in a prisoner's dilemma. *European Journal of Social Psychology*, **29**, 909–924. (p. 557)

Batson, C. D., Sager, K., Garst, E., Kang, M., Rubchinsky, K., & Dawson, K. (1997). Is empathy-induced helping due to self-other merging? *Journal of Personality and Social Psychology*, **73**, 495–509. (p. 493)

Batson, C. D., Schoenrade, P., & Ventis, W. L. (1993). *Religion and the individual: A social-psychological perspective.* New York: Oxford University Press. (p. 346)

Batson, C. D., Sympson, S. C., Hindman, J. L., Decruz, P., Todd, R. M., Jennings, G., & Burris, C. T. (1996). "I'be been there, too": Effect on empathy of prior experience with a need. *Personality and Social Psychology Bulletin*, **22**, 474–482. (p. 184)

Batson, C. D., & Thompson, E. R. (2001). Why don't moral people act morally? Motivational considerations. *Current Directions in Psychological Science*, **10**, 54–57. (p. 135)

Batson, C. D., Thompson, E. R., & Chen, H. (2002). Moral hypocrisy: Addressing some alternatives. *Journal of Personality and Social Psychology*, **83**, 330–339. (p. 135)

Batson, C. D., Thompson, E. R., Seuferling, G., Whitney, H., & Strongman, J. A. (1999). Moral hypocrisy: Appearing moral to oneself without being so. *Journal of Personality and Social Psychology*, **77**, 525–537. (p. 139)

Batson, C. D., & Ventis, W. L. (1982). *The religious experience: A social psychological perspective.* New York: Oxford University Press. (p. 346)

Batson, C. D., & Weeks, J. L. (1996). Mood effects of unsuccessful helping: Another test of the empathy-altruism hypothesis. *Personality and Social Psychology Bulletin*, **22**, 148–157. (p. 492)

Baumann, D. J., Cialdini, R. B., & Kenrick, D. T. (1981). Altruism as hedonism: Helping and self-gratification as equivalent responses. *Journal of Personality and Social Psychology*, **40**, 1039–1046. (p. 481)

Baumann, L. J., & Leventhal, H. (1985). "I can tell when my blood pressure is up, can't I?" *Health Psychology*, **4**, 203–218. (p. 585)

Baumeister, R. F. (1991). *Meanings of life.* New York: Guilford. (p. 469)

Baumeister, R. F., & Bratslavsky, E. (1999). Passion, intimacy, and time: Passionate love as a function of change in intimacy. *Personality and Social Psychology Review*, **3**, 49–67. (p. 463)

Baumeister, R. F., Bratslavsky, E., Finkenauer, C., & Vohs, D. K. (2001). Bad is stronger than good. *Review of General Psychology*, **5**, 323–370. (pp. 446, 447)

Baumeister, R. F., Bratslavsky, E., Muraven, M., & Tice, D. M. (1998). Ego depletion: Is the active self a limited resource? *Journal of Personality and Social Psychology*, **74**, 1252–1265. (p. 57)

Baumeister, R. F., Campbell, J. D., Krueger, J. I., & Vohs, K. D. (2003). Does high self-esteem cause better performance, interpersonal success, happiness, or healthier lifestyles? *Psychological Science in the Public Interest*, **4** (1), 1–44. (pp. 23, 62, 64, 65)

Baumeister, R. F., Catanese, K. R., & Vohs, K. D. (2001). Is there a gender difference in strength of sex drive? Theoretical views, conceptual distinctions, and a review of relevant evidence. *Personality and Social Psychology Review*, **5**, 242–273. (pp. 188, 446)

Baumeister, R. F., Catanese, K. R., & Wallace, H. M. (2002). Conquest by force: A narcissistic reactance theory of rape and sexual coercion. *Review of General Psychology*, **6**, 92–135. (p. 239)

Baumeister, R. F., Chesner, S. P., Senders, P. S., & Tice, D. M. (1988). Who's in charge here? Group leaders do lend help in emergencies. *Personality and Social Psychology Bulletin*, **14**, 17–22. (p. 89)

Baumeister, R. F., & Exline, J. J. (2000). Self-control, morality, and human strength. *Journal of Social and Clinical Psychology*, **19**, 29–42. (p. 57)

Baumeister, R. F., & Ilko, S. A. (1995). Shallow gratitude: Public and private acknowledgement of external help in accounts of success. *Basic and Applied Social Psychology*, **16**, 191–209. (p. 78)

Baumeister, R. F., & Leary, M. R. (1995). The need to belong: Desire for interpersonal attachment as a fundamental human motivation. *Psychological Bulletin*, **117**, 497–529. (p. 423)

Baumeister, R. F., Muraven, M., & Tice, D. M. (2000). Ego depletion: A resource model of volition, self-regulation, and controlled processing. *Social Cognition*, **18**, 130–150. (p. 57)

Baumeister, R. F., & Scher, S. J. (1988). Self-defeating behavior patterns among normal individuals: Review and analysis of common self-destructive tendencies. *Psychological Bulletin*, **104**, 3–22. (p. 78)

Baumeister, R. F., Smart, L., & Boden, J. (1996). The dark side of high self-esteem. *Psychological Review*. (p. 65)

Baumeister, R. F., Twenge, J. M., & Nuss, C. K. (2002). Effects of social exclusion on cognitive processes: Anticipated aloneness reduces intelligent thought. *Journal of Personality and Social Psychology*, **83**, 817–827. (p. 424)

Baumeister, R. F., & Vohs, K. (in press). Sexual economics: Sex as female resource for social exchange in heterosexual interactions. *Personality and Social Psychology Bulletin*. (pp. 188–189)

Baumeister, R. F., & Wotman, S. R. (1992). *Breaking hearts: The two sides of unrequited love.* New York: Guilford. (p. 469)

Baumgardner, A. H., & Brownlee, E. A. (1987). Strategic failure in social interaction: Evidence for expectancy disconfirmation process. *Journal of Personality and Social Psychology, 52,* 525–535. (p. 79)

Baumgardner, A. H., Kaufman, C. M., & Levy, P. E. (1989). Regulating affect interpersonally: When low esteem leads to greater enhancement. *Journal of Personality and Social Psychology, 56,* 907–921. (p. 66)

Baumhart, R. (1968). *An honest profit.* New York: Holt, Rinehart & Winston. (p. 70)

Baxter, T. L., & Goldberg, L. R. (1987). Perceived behavioral consistency underlying trait attributions to oneself and another: An extension of the actor-observer effect. *Personality and Social Psychology Bulletin, 13,* 437–447. (p. 94)

Bayer, E. (1929). Beitrage zur zeikomponenten theorie des hungers. *Zeitschrift fur Psychologie, 112,* 1–54. (p. 287)

Bazerman, M. H. (1986, June). Why negotiations go wrong. *Psychology Today,* pp. 54–58. (p. 558)

Bazerman, M. H. (1990). *Judgment in managerial decision making,* 2nd ed. New York: Wiley. (p. 558)

Beaman, A. L., Barnes, P. J., Klentz, B., & McQuirk, B. (1978). Increasing helping rates through information dissemination: Teaching pays. *Personality and Social Psychology Bulletin, 4,* 406–411. (p. 516)

Beaman, A. L., & Klentz, B. (1983). The supposed physical attractiveness bias against supporters of the women's movement: A meta-analysis. *Personality and Social Psychology Bulletin, 9,* 544–550. (p. 441)

Beaman, A. L., Klentz, B., Diener, E., & Svanum, S. (1979). Self-awareness and transgression in children: Two field studies. *Journal of Personality and Social Psychology, 37,* 1835–1846. (p. 302)

Bearman, P. S., & Brueckner, H. (2001). Promising the future: Virginity pledges and first intercourse. *American Journal of Sociology, 106,* 859–912. (p. 233)

Beauregard, K. S., & Dunning, D. (1998). Turning up the contrast: Self-enhancement motives prompt egocentric contrast effects in social

judgments. *Journal of Personality and Social Psychology, 74,* 606–621. (p. 74)

Beauvois, J. L., & Dubois, N. (1988). The norm of internality in the explanation of psychological events. *European Journal of Social Psychology, 18,* 299–316. (p. 96)

Beck, A. J., Kline, S. A., & Greenfeld, L. A. (1988). Survey of youth in custody, 1987. U.S. Department of Justice, Bureau of Justice Statistics Special Report. (p. 391)

Beck, A. T., & Young, J. E. (1978, September). College blues. *Psychology Today,* pp. 80–92. (p. 582)

Bell, B. E., & Loftus, E. F. (1988). Degree of detail of eyewitness testimony and mock juror judgments. *Journal of Applied Social Psychology, 18,* 1171–1192. (p. 608)

Bell, B. E., & Loftus, E. F. (1989). Trivial persuasion in the courtroom: The power of (a few) minor details. *Journal of Personality and Social Psychology, 56,* 669–679. (p. 608)

Bell, P. A. (1980). Effects of heat, noise, and provocation on retaliatory evaluative behavior. *Journal of Social Psychology, 110,* 97–100. (p. 394)

Bellah, R. N. (1995/1996, Winter). Community properly understood: A defense of 'democratic communitarianism.' *The Responsive Community,* pp. 49–54. (p. 242)

Belson, W. A. (1978). *Television violence and the adolescent boy.* Westmead, England: Saxon House, Teakfield Ltd. (pp. 404–405)

Bem, D. J. (1972). Self-perception theory. In L. Berkowitz (Ed.), *Advances in experimental social psychology.* Vol. 6. New York: Academic Press. (pp. 156, 161)

Bem, D. J., & McConnell, H. K. (1970). Testing the self-perception explanation of dissonance phenomena: On the salience of premanipulation attitudes. *Journal of Personality and Social Psychology, 14,* 23–31. (p. 103)

Bennett, R. (1991, February). Pornography and extrafamilial child sexual abuse: Examining the relationship. Unpublished manuscript, Los Angeles Police Department Sexually Exploited Child Unit. (p. 400)

Bennis, W. (1984). Transformative power and leadership. In T. J. Sergiovani & J. E. Corbally (Eds.), *Leadership and organizational culture.* Urbana: University of Illinois Press. (p. 325)

Benson, P. L., Dehority, J., Garman, L., Hanson, E., Hochschwender, M., Lebold, C., Rohr, R., & Sullivan, J. (1980). Intrapersonal correlates of nonspontaneous helping behavior. *Journal of Social Psychology, 110,* 87–95. (p. 508)

Benson, P. L., Karabenick, S. A., & Lerner, R. M. (1976). Pretty pleases: The effects of physical attractiveness, race, and sex on receiving help. *Journal of Experimental Social Psychology, 12,* 409–415. (p. 505)

Benvenisti, M. (1988, October 16). Growing up in Jerusalem. *New York Times Magazine,* pp. 34–37. (pp. 352–353)

Ben-Zeev, T., Fein, S., & Inzlicht, M. (2004). Arousal and stereotype threat. *Journal of Experimental Social Psychology.* (p. 373)

Berenbaum, S. A., & Hines, M. (1992). Early androgens are related to childhood sex-typed toy preferences. *Psychological Science, 3,* 203–206. (p. 192)

Berg, J. H. (1984). Development of friendship between roommates. *Journal of Personality and Social Psychology, 46,* 346–356. (pp. 452, 460)

Berg, J. H. (1987). Responsiveness and self-disclosure. In V. J. Derlega & J. H. Berg (Eds.), *Self-disclosure: Theory, research, and therapy.* New York: Plenum. (p. 462)

Berg, J. H., & McQuinn, R. D. (1986). Attraction and exchange in continuing and noncontinuing dating relationships. *Journal of Personality and Social Psychology, 50,* 942–952. (pp. 452, 464)

Berg, J. H., & McQuinn, R. D. (1988). Loneliness and aspects of social support networks. Unpublished manuscript, University of Mississippi. (p. 582)

Berg, J. H., & Peplau, L. A. (1982). Loneliness: The relationship of self-disclosure and androgyny. *Personality and Social Psychology Bulletin, 8,* 624–630. (p. 462)

Berglas, S., & Jones, E. E. (1978). Drug choice as a self-handicapping strategy in response to noncontingent success. *Journal of Personality and Social Psychology, 36*, 405–417. (p. 78)

Berkman, L. F. (1995). The role of social relations in health promotion. *Psychosomatic Medicine, 57*, 245–254. (p. 597)

Berkowitz, L. (1954). Group standards, cohesiveness, and productivity. *Human Relations, 7*, 509–519. (p. 231)

Berkowitz, L. (1968, September). Impulse, aggression and the gun. *Psychology Today*, pp. 18–22. (p. 396)

Berkowitz, L. (1972). Frustrations, comparisons, and other sources of emotional arousal as contributors to social unrest. *Journal of Social Issues, 28*, 77–91. *(a)* (p. 388)

Berkowitz, L. (1972). Social norms, feelings, and other factors affecting helping and altruism. In L. Berkowitz (Ed.), *Advances in experimental social psychology* (Vol. 6). New York: Academic Press. *(b)* (p. 485)

Berkowitz, L. (1978). Whatever happened to the frustration-aggression hypothesis? *American Behavioral Scientists, 21*, 691–708. (p. 387)

Berkowitz, L. (1981, June). How guns control us. *Psychology Today*, pp. 11–12. (p. 396)

Berkowitz, L. (1983). Aversively stimulated aggression: Some parallels and differences in research with animals and humans. *American Psychologist, 38*, 1135–1144. (p. 394)

Berkowitz, L. (1984). Some effects of thoughts on anti- and prosocial influences of media events: A cognitive-neoassociation analysis, *Psychological Bulletin, 95*, 410–427. (p. 407)

Berkowitz, L. (1987). Mood, self-awareness, and willingness to help. *Journal of Personality and Social Psychology, 52*, 721–729. (p. 483)

Berkowitz, L. (1989). Frustration-aggression hypothesis: Examination and reformulation. *Psychological Bulletin, 106*, 59–73. (pp. 387, 394)

Berkowitz, L. (1995). A career on aggression. In G. G. Brannigan & M. R. Merrens (Eds.), *The social psychologists:*

Research adventures. New York: McGraw-Hill. (p. 396)

Berkowitz, L. (1998). Affective aggression: The role of stress, pain, and negative affect. In R. G. Geen & E. Donnerstein (Eds.), *Human aggression: Theories, research, and implications for social policy.* San Diego, CA: Academic Press. (p. 394)

Berkowitz, L., & Geen, R. G. (1966). Film violence and the cue properties of available targets. *Journal of Personality and Social Psychology, 3*, 525–530. (p. 406)

Berkowitz, L., & LePage, A. (1967). Weapons as aggression-eliciting stimuli. *Journal of Personality and Social Psychology, 7*, 202–207. (p. 396)

Bernard, J. (1976). *Sex differences: An overview.* New York: MSS Modular Publications. (p. 182)

Bernard, M. M., Maio, G. R., & Olson, J. M. (2003). The vulnerability of values to attack: Inoculation of values and value-relevant attitudes. *Personality and Social Psychology Bulletin, 29*, 63–75. (p. 279)

Berndsen, M., Spears, R., & van der Plight, J. (1996). Illusory correlation and attitude-based vested interest. *European Journal of Social Psychology, 26*, 247–264. (p. 117)

Berndsen, M., Spears, R., van der Plight, J., & McGarty, C. (2002). Illusory correlation and stereotype formation: Making sense of group differences and cognitive biases. In C. McGarty, V. Y. Yzerbyt, & R. Spears (Eds.), *Stereotypes as explanations: The formation of meaningful beliefs about social groups.* New York: Cambridge University Press. (p. 364)

Bernhardt, P. C. (1997). Influences of serotonin and testosterone in aggression and dominance: Convergence with social psychology. *Current Directions in Psychology, 6*, 44–48. (p. 385)

Bernhardt, P. C., Dabbs, J. M., Jr., Fielden, J. A., & Lutter, C. D. (1998). Testosterone changes during vicarious experiences of winning and losing among fans at sporting events. *Physiology and Behavior, 65*, 59–62. (p. 385)

Bernieri, F. J., Davis, J. M., Rosenthal, R., & others. (1994, June).

Interactional synchrony and rapport: Measuring synchrony in displays devoid of sound and facial affect. *Personality & Social Psychology Bulletin, 20*, 303–311. (p. 158)

Berry, D. S., & Zebrowitz-McArthur, L. (1988). What's in a face: Facial maturity and the attribution of legal responsibility. *Personality and Social Psychology Bulletin, 14*, 23–33. (p. 619)

Berry, J. W., & Kalin, R. (1995). Multicultural and ethnic attitudes in Canada: An overview of the 1991 national survey. *Canadian Journal of Behavioural Science, 27*, 301–320. (pp. 334–335)

Berscheid, E. (1981). An overview of the psychological effects of physical attractiveness and some comments upon the psychological effects of knowledge of the effects of physical attractiveness. In W. Lucker, K. Ribbens, & J. A. McNamera (Eds.), *Logical aspects of facial form (craniofacial growth series).* Ann Arbor: University of Michigan Press. (pp. 435–436)

Berscheid, E. (1985). Interpersonal attraction. In G. Lindzey & E. Aronson (Eds.), *The handbook of social psychology.* New York: Random House. (p. 600)

Berscheid, E. (1999). The greening of relationship science. *American Psychologist, 54*, 260–266. (p. 93)

Berscheid, E., Boye, D., & Walster (Hatfield), E. (1968). Retaliation as a means of restoring equity. *Journal of Personality and Social Psychology, 10*, 370–376. (p. 146)

Berscheid, E., Dion, K., Walster (Hatfield), E., & Walster, G. W. (1971). Physical attractiveness and dating choice: A test of the matching hypothesis. *Journal of Experimental Social Psychology, 7*, 173–189. (pp. 432, 433)

Berscheid, E., Graziano, W., Monson, T., & Dermer, M. (1976). Outcome dependency: Attention, attribution, and attraction. *Journal of Personality and Social Psychology, 34*, 978–989. (p. 427)

Berscheid, E., & Peplau, L. A. (1983). The emerging science of relationships. In Kelley, H. H., Berscheid, E., Christensen, A., Harvey, J. H., Huston, T. L., Levinger, G., McClintock, E., Peplau, L. A. & Peterson, D. R. (Eds.),

Close relationships. New York: Freeman. (p. 600)

Berscheid, E., Snyder, M., & Omoto, A. M. (1989). Issues in studying close relationships: Conceptualizing and measuring closeness. In C. Hendrick (Ed.), *Review of personality and social psychology*, Vol. 10. Newbury Park, CA: Sage. (p. 456)

Berscheid, E., & Walster (Hatfield), E. (1978). *Interpersonal attraction*. Reading, MA: Addison-Wesley. (p. 446)

Berscheid, E., Walster, G. W., & Hatfield (was Walster), E. (1969). Effects of accuracy and positivity of evaluation on liking for the evaluator. Unpublished manuscript. Summarized by E. Berscheid and E. Walster (Hatfield) (1978), *Interpersonal attraction*. Reading, MA: Addison-Wesley. (p. 446)

Bersoff, D. N. (1987). Social science data and the Supreme Court: Lockhart as a case in point. *American Psychologist, 42,* 52–58. (p. 629)

Bertrand, M., & Mullainathan, S. (2003). Are Emily and Greg more employable than Lakisha and Jamal? A field experiment on labor market discrimination. Massachusetts Institute of Technology, Department of Economics, Working Paper 03-22. (p. 337)

Bettencourt, A., & Dorr, N. (1997). Collective self-esteem as a mediator of the relationship between allocentrism and subjective well-being. *Personality and Social Psychology Bulletin, 23,* 955–965. (p. 599)

Bettencourt, B. A., Dill, K. E., Greathouse, S. A., Charlton, K., & Mulholland, A. (1997). Evaluations of ingroup and outgroup members: The role of category-based expectancy violation. *Journal of Experimental Social Psychology, 33,* 244–275. (pp. 361, 376)

Bettencourt, B. A., & Miller, N. (1996). Gender differences in aggression as a function of provocation: A meta-analysis. *Psychological Bulletin, 119,* 422–447. (p. 187)

Beyer, L. (1990, Fall issue on women). Life behind the veil. *Time,* p. 37. (p. 342)

Bianchi, S. M., Milkie, M. A., Sayer, L. C., & Robinson, J. P. (2000). Is anyone doing the housework? Trends in the gender division of household labor. *Social Forces, 79,* 191–228. (pp. 195, 198)

Bickman, L. (1975). Bystander intervention in a crime: The effect of a mass-media campaign. *Journal of Applied Social Psychology, 5,* 296–302. (p. 510)

Bickman, L. (1979). Interpersonal influence and the reporting of a crime. *Personality and Social Psychology Bulletin, 5,* 32–35. (p. 510)

Bickman, L., & Green, S. K. (1977). Situational cues and crime reporting: Do signs make a difference? *Journal of Applied Social Psychology, 7,* 1–18. (p. 510)

Bickman, L., & Kamzan, M. (1973). The effect of race and need on helping behavior. *Journal of Social Psychology, 89,* 73–77. (p. 486)

Bierbrauer, G. (1979). Why did he do it? Attribution of obedience and the phenomenon of dispositional bias. *European Journal of Social Psychology 9,* 67–84. (p. 226)

Bierhoff, H. W., Klein, R., & Kramp, P. (1991). Evidence for the altruistic personality from data on accident research. *Journal of Personality, 59,* 263–280. (p. 506)

Bierly, M. M. (1985). Prejudice toward contemporary outgroups as a generalized attitude. *Journal of Applied Social Psychology, 15,* 189–199. (pp. 345–346)

Biernat, M. (1991). Gender stereotypes and the relationship between masculinity and femininity: A developmental analysis. *Journal of Personality and Social Psychology, 61,* 351–365. (p. 358)

Biernat, M. (2003). Toward a broader view of social stereotyping. *American Psychologist, 58,* 1019–1027. (p. 368)

Biernat, M., & Kobrynowicz, D. (1997). Gender- and race-based standards of competence: Lower minimum standards but higher ability standards for devalued groups. *Journal of Personality and Social Psychology, 72,* 544–557. (p. 361)

Biernat, M., Vescio, T. K., & Green, M. L. (1996). Selective self-stereotyping. *Journal of Personality and Social Psychology, 71,* 1194–1209. (p. 76)

Biernat, M., Vescio, T. K., & Theno, S. A. (1996). Violating American values: A "Value congruence" approach to understanding outgroup attitudes. *Journal of Experimental Social Psychology, 32,* 387–410. (p. 444)

Biernat, M., & Wortman, C. B. (1991). Sharing of home responsibilities between professionally employed women and their husbands. *Journal of Personality and Social Psychology, 60,* 844–860. (p. 195)

Bigam, R. G. (1977, March). Voir dire: The attorney's job. *Trial 13,* p. 3. Cited by G. Bermant & J. Shepard in "The voir dire examination, juror challenges, and adversary advocacy." In B. D. Sales (Ed.), *Perspectives in law and psychology (Vol. II): The trial process.* New York: Plenum Press, 1981. (p. 628)

Billig, M., & Tajfel, H. (1973). Social categorization and similarity in intergroup behaviour. *European Journal of Social Psychology, 3,* 27–52. (p. 352)

Biner, P. M. (1991). Effects of lighting-induced arousal on the magnitude of goal valence. *Personality and Social Psychology Bulletin, 17,* 219–226. (p. 396)

Binham, R. (1980, March–April). Trivers in Jamaica. *Science, 80,* pp. 57–67. (p. 488)

Bird, C. E. (1999). Gender, household labor, and psychological distress: The impact of the amount and division of housework. *Journal of Health & Social Behavior, 40,* 32–45. (p. 67)

Bishop, G. D. (1984). Gender, role, and illness behavior in a military population. *Health Psychology, 3,* 519–534. (p. 588)

Bishop, G. D. (1987). Lay conceptions of physical symptoms. *Journal of Applied Social Psychology, 17,* 127–146. (p. 587)

Bishop, G. D. (1991). Understanding the understanding of illness: Lay disease representations. In J. A. Skelton & R. T. Croyle (Eds.), *Mental representation in health and illness.* New York: Springer-Verlag. (p. 586)

Björkqvist, K. (1994). Sex differences in physical, verbal, and indirect aggression: A review of recent research. *Sex Roles, 30,* 177–188. (p. 187)

Blackburn, R. T., Pellino, G. R., Boberg, A., & O'Connell, C. (1980). Are instructional improvement programs off target? *Current Issues in Higher Education*, **1**, 31–48. (p. 76)

Blake, R. R., & Mouton, J. S. (1962). The intergroup dynamics of win-lose conflict and problem-solving collaboration in union-management relations. In M. Sherif (Ed.), *Intergroup relations and leadership.* New York: Wiley. (p. 557)

Blake, R. R., & Mouton, J. S. (1979). Intergroup problem solving in organizations: From theory to practice. In W. G. Austin and S. Worchel (Eds.), *The social psychology of intergroup relations.* Monterey, CA: Brooks/Cole. (pp. 546, 557)

Blanchard, F. A., & Cook, S. W. (1976). Effects of helping a less competent member of a cooperating interracial group on the development of interpersonal attraction. *Journal of Personality and Social Psychology*, **34**, 1245–1255. (p. 148)

Blank, H., Fischer, V., & Erdfelder, E. (2003). Hindsight bias in political elections. *Memory*, **11**, 491–504. (p. 104)

Blanton, H., Pelham, B. W., DeHart, T., & Carvallo, M. (2001). Overconfidence as dissonance reduction. *Journal of Experimental Social Psychology*, **37**, 373–385. (p. 155)

Blascovich, J., Wyer, N. A., Swart, L. A., & Kibler, J. L. (1997). Racism and racial categorization. *Journal of Personality and Social Psychology*, **72**, 1364–1372. (p. 358)

Blass, T. (1990). Psychological approaches to the Holocaust: Review and evaluation. Paper presented to the American Psychological Association convention. (p. 236)

Blass, T. (1991). Understanding behavior in the Milgram obedience experiment: The role of personality, situations, and their interactions. *Journal of Personality and Social Psychology*, **60**, 398–413. (p. 218)

Blass, T. (1996). Stanley Milgram: A life of inventiveness and controversy. In G. A. Kimble, C. A. Boneau, & M. Wertheimer (Eds.). *Portraits of pioneers in psychology*, Vol. II. Washington, DC: American Psychological Association. (p. 237)

Blass, T. (2000). The Milgram paradigm after 35 years: Some things we now know about obedience to authority. In T. Blass (Ed.), *Obedience to authority: Current perspectives on the Milgram paradigm.* Mahwah, NJ: Erlbaum. (p. 237)

Block J., & Funder, D. C. (1986). Social roles and social perception: Individual differences in attribution and error. *Journal of Personality and Social Psychology*, **51**, 1200–1207. (p. 90)

Blood, R. O., Jr. (1967). *Love match and arranged marriage.* New York: Free Press. (p. 457)

Blundell, W. E. (1986). *Storyteller step by step: A guide to better feature writing.* New York: Dow Jones. Cited by S. H. Stocking & P. H. Gross (1989), *How do journalists think? A proposal for the study of cognitive bias in newsmaking.* Bloomington, IN: ERIC Clearinghouse on Reading and Communication Skills, Smith Research Center, Indiana University. (p. 128)

Bobocel, D. R., Hing, L. S. S., Davey, L. M., Stanley, D. J., & Zanna, M. P. (1998). Justice-based opposition to social policies: Is it genuine? *Journal of Personality and Social Psychology*, **75**, 653–669. (p. 367)

Bodenhausen, G. V. (1990). Stereotypes as judgmental heuristics: Evidence of circadian variations in discrimination. *Psychological Science*, **1**, 319–322. (p. 358)

Bodenhausen, G. V. (1993). Emotions, arousal, and stereotypic judgments: A heuristic model of affect and stereotyping. In D. M. Mackie & D. L. Hamilton (Eds.), *Affect, cognition, and stereotyping: Interactive processes in group perception.* San Diego, CA: Academic Press. (p. 257)

Bodenhausen, G. V., & Macrae, C. N. (1998). Stereotype activation and inhibition. In R. S. Wyer, Jr., *Stereotype activation and inhibition: Advances in social cognition*, vol. 11. Mahwah, NJ: Erlbaum. (p. 357)

Bodenhausen, G. V., Sheppard, L. A., & Kramer, G. F. (1994). Negative affect and social judgment: The differential impact of anger and sadness. *European Journal of Social Psychology*, **24**, 45–62. (p. 120)

Boggiano, A. K., Barrett, M., Weiher, A. W., McClelland, G. H., & Lusk, C. M. (1987). Use of the maximal-operant principle to motivate children's intrinsic interest. *Journal of Personality and Social Psychology*, **53**, 866–879. (p. 159)

Boggiano, A. K., Harackiewicz, J. M., Bessette, J. M., & Main, D. S. (1985). Increasing children's interest through performance-contingent reward. *Social Cognition*, **3**, 400–411. (p. 159)

Boggiano, A. K., & Ruble, D. N. (1985). Children's responses to evaluative feedback. In R. Schwarzer (Ed.), *Self-related cognitions in anxiety and motivation.* Hillsdale, NJ: Erlbaum. (p. 160)

Bohner, G., Bless, H., Schwarz, N., & Strack, F. (1988). What triggers causal attributions? The impact of valence and subjective probability. *European Journal of Social Psychology*, **18**, 335–345. (p. 84)

Bond, C. F., Jr., DiCandia, C. G., & MacKinnon, J. R. (1988). Responses to violence in a psychiatric setting: The role of patient's race. *Personality and Social Psychology Bulletin*, **14**, 448–458. (p. 375)

Bond, C. F., Jr., & Titus, L. J. (1983). Social facilitation: A meta-analysis of 241 studies. *Psychological Bulletin*, **94**, 265–292. (p. 288)

Bond, M. H. (2004). Culture and aggression: From context to coercion. *Personality and Social Psychology Review*, **8**, 62–78. (pp. 391–392)

Bond, R., & Smith, P. B. (1996). Culture and conformity: A meta-analysis of studies using Asch's (1952b, 1956) line judgment task. *Psychological Bulletin*, **119**, 111–137. (p. 237)

Boninger, D. S., Gleicher, F., & Strathman, A. (1994). Counterfactual thinking: From what might have been to what may be. *Journal of Personality and Social Psychology*, **67**, 297–307. (p. 115)

Bonta, B. D. (1997). Cooperation and competition in peaceful societies. *Psychological Bulletin*, **121**, 299–320. (p. 549)

Bonta, J., Law, M., & Hanson, K. (1998). The prediction of criminal and violent recidivism among mentally disordered offenders: A meta-analysis.

Psychological Bulletin, **123**, 123–142. (p. 573)

Borchard, E. M. (1932). *Convicting the innocent: Errors of criminal justice.* New Haven, CT: Yale University Press. Cited by E. R. Hilgard & E. F. Loftus (1979) "Effective interrogation of the eyewitness." *International Journal of Clinical and Experimental Hypnosis*, **17**, 342–359. (p. 608)

Borgida, E. (1981). Legal reform of rape laws. In L. Bickman (Ed.), *Applied social psychology annual.* Vol. 2. Beverly Hills, CA: Sage Publications, pp. 211–241. (p. 622)

Borgida, E., & Brekke, N. (1985). Psycholegal research on rape trials. In A. W. Burgess (Ed.), *Rape and sexual assault: A research handbook.* New York: Garland. (p. 367)

Borgida, E., Locksley, A., & Brekke, N. (1981). Social stereotypes and social judgment. In N. Cantor & J. Kihlstrom (Eds.), *Cognition, social interaction, and personality.* Hillsdale, NJ: Lawrence Erlbaum. (p. 373)

Borgida, E., & White, P. (1980). Judgmental bias and legal reform. Unpublished manuscript, University of Minnesota. (p. 623)

Bornstein, B. H., & Zicafoose, D. J. (1999). "I know I know it, I know I saw it": The stability of the confidence-accuracy relationship across domains. *Journal of Experimental Psychology: Applied*, **5**, 76–88. (p. 608)

Bornstein, G., & Rapoport, A. (1988). Intergroup competition for the provision of step-level public goods: Effects of preplay communication. *European Journal of Social Psychology*, **18**, 125–142. (p. 526)

Bornstein, G., Rapoport, A., Kerpel, L., & Katz, T. (1989). Within- and between-group communication in intergroup competition for public goods. *Journal of Experimental Social Psychology*, **25**, 422–436. (p. 526)

Bornstein, R. F. (1989). Exposure and affect: Overview and meta-analysis of research, 1968–1987. *Psychological Bulletin*, **106**, 265–289. (p. 428)

Bornstein, R. F. (1999). Source amnesia, misattribution, and the power of unconscious perceptions and memories. *Psychoanalytic Psychology*, **16**, 155–178. (p. 428)

Bornstein, R. F., & D'Agostino, P. R. (1992). Stimulus recognition and the mere exposure effect. *Journal of Personality and Social Psychology*, **63**, 545–552. (p. 429)

Bossard, J. H. S. (1932). Residential propinquity as a factor in marriage selection. *American Journal of Sociology*, **38**, 219–224. (p. 426)

Bothwell, R. K., Brigham, J. C., & Malpass, R. S. (1989). Cross-racial identification. *Personality and Social Psychology Bulletin*, **15**, 19–25. (p. 360)

Botvin, G. J., Schinke, S., & Orlandi, M. A. (1995). School-based health promotion: Substance abuse and sexual behavior. *Applied & Preventive Psychology*, **4**, 167–184. (p. 280)

Botwin, M. D., Buss, D. M., & Shackelford, T. K. (1997). Personality and mate preferences: Five factors in mate selection and marital satisfaction. *Journal of Personality*, **65**, 107–136. (p. 446)

Bouas, K. S., & Komorita, S. S. (1996). Group discussion and cooperation in social dilemmas. *Personality and Social Psychology Bulletin*, **22**, 1144–1150. (p. 526)

Bourgeois, M. J., Horowitz, I. A., & Lee, L. F. (1993). Effects of technicality and access to trial transcripts on verdicts and information processing in a civil trial. *Personality and Social Psychology Bulletin*, **19**, 219–226. (p. 627)

Bowen, E. (1988, April 4). What ever became of Honest Abe? *Time.* (p. 5)

Bower, B. (1997). Thanks for the memories: Scientists evaluate interviewing tactics for boosting eyewitness recall. *Science*, **151**, 246–247. (p. 616)

Bower, G. H. (1986). Prime time in cognitive psychology. In P. Eelen (Ed.), *Cognitive research and behavior therapy: Beyond the conditioning paradigm.* Amsterdam: North Holland Publishers. (p. 105)

Bower, G. H. (1987). Commentary on mood and memory. *Behavioral Research and Therapy*, **25**, 443–455. (pp. 119, 579)

Bowlby, J. (1980). *Loss, sadness and depression. Vol. III of Attachment and loss.* London: Basic Books. (p. 458)

Boyatzis, C. J., Matillo, G. M., & Nesbitt, K. M. (1995). Effects of the "Mighty Morphin Power Rangers" on children's aggression with peers. *Child Study Journal*, **25**, 45–55. (p. 29)

Bradley, W., & Mannell, R. C. (1984). Sensitivity of intrinsic motivation to reward procedure instructions. *Personality and Social Psychology Bulletin*, **10**, 426–431. (p. 160)

Brandon, R., & Davies, C. (1973). *Wrongful imprisonment: Mistaken convictions and their consequences.* Hamden, CT: Archon Books. (p. 608)

Branscombe, N. R., Schmitt, M. T., & Harvey, R. D. (1999). Perceiving pervasive discrimination among African Americans: Implications for group identification and well-being. *Journal of Personality and Social Psychology*, **77**, 135–149. (p. 362)

Brauer, M., Judd, C. M., & Gliner, M. D. (1995). The effects of repeated expressions on attitude polarization during group discussions. *Journal of Personality and Social Psychology*, **68**, 1014–1029. (p. 308)

Brauer, M., Judd, C. M., & Jacquelin, V. (2001). The communication of social stereotypes: The effects of group discussion and information distribution on stereotypic appraisals. *Journal of Personality and Social Psychology*, **81**, 463–475. (p. 305)

Bray, R. M., & Kerr, N. L. (1982). Methodological considerations in the study of the psychology of the courtroom. In N. L. Kerr & R. M. Bray (Eds.), *The psychology of the courtroom.* Orlando, FL: Academic Press. (p. 636)

Bray, R. M., & Noble, A. M. (1978). Authoritarianism and decisions of mock juries: Evidence of jury bias and group polarization. *Journal of Personality and Social Psychology*, **36**, 1424–1430. (p. 632)

Bregman, N. J., & McAllister, H. A. (1982). Eyewitness testimony: The role of commitment in increasing reliability. *Social Psychology Quarterly*, **45**, 181–184. (p. 613)

Brehm, J. W. (1956). Post-decision changes in desirability of alternatives. *Journal of Abnormal Social Psychology*, **52**, 384–389. (p. 155)

Brehm, J. W. (1999). Would the real dissonance theory please stand up? American Psychological Society convention, 1999. (p. 163)

Brehm, S., & Brehm, J. W. (1981). *Psychological reactance: A theory of freedom and control.* New York: Academic Press. (p. 238)

Brehm, S. S., & Smith, T. W. (1986). Social psychological approaches to psychotherapy and behavior change. In S. L. Garfield & A. E. Bergin (Eds.), *Handbook of psychotherapy and behavior change,* 3rd ed. New York: Wiley. (p. 594)

Brenner, S. N., & Molander, E. A. (1977). Is the ethics of business changing? *Harvard Business Review,* January–February, pp. 57–71. (p. 70)

Brewer, M. B. (1979). In-group bias in the minimal intergroup situation: A cognitive-motivational analysis. *Psychological Bulletin,* **86,** 307–324. (p. 354)

Brewer, M. B. (1987). Collective decisions. *Social Science,* **72,** 140–143. (p. 526)

Brewer, M. B. (1988). A dual process model of impression formation. In T. Srull & R. Wyer (Eds.), *Advances in social cognition,* Vol. 1. Hillsdale, NJ: Erlbaum. (p. 370)

Brewer, M. B. (2000). Reducing prejudice through cross-categorization: Effects of multiple social identities. In S. Oskamp (Ed.), *Reducing prejudice and discrimination.* Mahwah, NJ: Erlbaum, 2000. (p. 552)

Brewer, M. B., & Miller, N. (1988). Contact and cooperation: When do they work? In P. A. Katz & D. Taylor (Eds.), *Towards the elimination of racism: Profiles in controversy.* New York: Plenum. (p. 551)

Brewer, M. B., & Silver, M. (1978). In-group bias as a function of task characteristics. *European Journal of Social Psychology,* **8,** 393–400. (p. 352)

Brickman, P. (1978). Is it real? In J. Harvey, W. Ickes, & R. Kidd (Eds.), *New directions in attribution research.* Vol. 2. Hillsdale, NJ: Erlbaum. (p. 179)

Brickman, P., & Campbell, D. T. (1971). Hedonic relativism and planning the good society. In M. H. Appley (Ed.), *Adaptation-level theory.* New York: Academic Press. (p. 655)

Brickman, P., Coates, D. & Janoff-Bulman, R. J. (1978). Lottery winners and accident victims: Is happiness relative? *Journal of Personality and Social Psychology,* **36,** 917–927. (pp. 652, 657)

Brigham, J. C., & Cairns, D. L. (1988). The effect of mugshot inspections on eyewitness identification accuracy. *Journal of Applied Social Psychology,* **18,** 1394–1410. (p. 616)

Brigham, J. C., Ready, D. J., & Spier, S. A. (1990). Standards for evaluating the fairness of photograph lineups. *Basic and Applied Social Psychology,* **11,** 149–163. (p. 616)

Briñol, P., & Petty, R. E. (2003). Overt head movements and persuasion: A self-validation analysis. *Journal of Personality and Social Psychology,* **84,** 1123–1139. (p. 158)

British Psychological Society (2000). *Code of conduct, ethical principles and guidelines.* Leicester, England: British Psychological Society (www.bps.org.uk/documents/Code.pdf). (p. 32)

Broad, W. J., & Hulse, C. (2003, February 3). NASA dismissed advisers who warned about safety. *New York Times* (www.nytimes.com). (p. 316)

Brock, T. C. (1965). Communicator-recipient similarity and decision change. *Journal of Personality and Social Psychology,* **1,** 650–654. (p. 254)

Brockner, J., & Hulton, A. J. B. (1978). How to reverse the vicious cycle of low self-esteem: The importance of attentional focus. *Journal of Experimental Social Psychology,* **14,** 564–578. (p. 44)

Brockner, J., Rubin, J. Z., Fine, J., Hamilton, T. P., Thomas, B., & Turetsky, B. (1982). Factors affecting entrapment in escalating conflicts: The importance of timing. *Journal of Research in Personality,* **16,** 247–266. (p. 524)

Brodt, S. E., & Ross, L. D. (1998). The role of stereotyping in overconfident social prediction. *Social Cognition,* **16,** 228–252. (p. 334)

Brodt, S. E., & Zimbardo, P. G. (1981). Modifying shyness-related social behavior through symptom misattribution. *Journal of Personality and Social Psychology,* **41,** 437–449. (p. 585)

Bronfenbrenner, U. (1961). The mirror image in Soviet-American relations. *Journal of Social Issues,* **17**(3), 45–56. (p. 533)

Broome, A., & Wegner, D. M. (1994). Some positive effects of releasing socially anxious people from the need to please. Paper presented to the American Psychological Society convention. (p. 584)

Brown, D. E. (1991). *Human universals.* New York: McGraw-Hill. (p. 170)

Brown, D. E. (2000). Human universals and their implications. In N. Roughley (Ed.), *Being humans: Anthropological universality and particularity in transdisciplinary perspectives.* New York: Walter de Gruyter. (p. 170)

Brown, H. J., Jr. (1990). *P.S. I love you.* Nashville, TN: Rutledge Hill. (pp. 70–71)

Brown, J. (2001, September 13). Anti-Arab passions sweep the U.S. Salon.com (www.salon.com/news/feature/2001/09/13/backlash/print.html) (p. 332)

Brown, J. D. (1986). Evaluations of self and others: Self-enhancement biases in social judgments. *Social Cognition,* **4,** 353–376. (p. 75)

Brown, J. D. (1991). Accuracy and bias in self-knowledge: Can knowing the truth be hazardous to your health? In C. R. Snyder & D. F. Forsyth (Eds.), *Handbook of social and clinical psychology: The health perspective.* New York: Pergamon Press. (p. 44)

Brown, J. D. (2003). The self-enhancement motive in collectivistic cultures: The rumors of my death have been greatly exaggerated. *Journal of Cross-Cultural Psychology,* **34,** 603–605. (p. 80)

Brown, J. D., Collins, R. L., & Schmidt, G. W. (1988). Self-esteem and direct versus indirect forms of self-enhancement. *Journal of Personality and Social Psychology,* **55,** 445–453. (p. 75)

Brown, J. D., & Dutton, K. A. (1994). From the top down: Self-esteem and self-evaluation. Unpublished manuscript, University of Washington. (p. 63)

Brown, J. D., & Gallagher, F. M. (1992). Coming to terms with failure: Private self-enhancement and public self-effacement. *Journal of Experimental Social Psychology,* **28,** 3–22. (p. 63)

Brown, J. D., & Kobayashi, C. (2002). Self-enhancement in Japan and America. *Asian Journal of Social Psychology, 5,* 145–167. (p. 80)

Brown, J. D., & Kobayashi, C. (2003). Culture and the self-enhancement bias. *Journal of Cross-Cultural Psychology, 34,* 492–495. (p. 80)

Brown, J. D., & Kobayashi, C. (2003). Motivation and manifestation: Cross-cultural expression of the self-enhancement motive. *Asian Journal of Social Psychology, 6,* 85–88. (p. 80)

Brown, J. D., Novick, N. J., Lord, K. A., & Richards, J. M. (1992). When Gulliver travels: Social context, psychological closeness, and self-appraisals. *Journal of Personality and Social Psychology, 62,* 717–727. (p. 440)

Brown, J. D., & Rogers, R. J. (1991). Self-serving attributions: The role of physiological arousal. *Personality and Social Psychology Bulletin, 17,* 501–506. (p. 63)

Brown, J. D., & Taylor, S. E. (1986). Affect and the processing of personal information: Evidence for mood-activated self-schemata. *Journal of Experimental Social Psychology, 22,* 436–452. (pp. 119, 579)

Brown, K. T., Brown, T. N., Jackson, J. S., Sellers, R. M., & Manuel, W. J. (2003). Teammates on and off the field? Contact with Black teammates and the racial attitudes of White student athletes. *Journal of Applied Social Psychology, 33,* 1379–1403. (p. 548)

Brown, P. A. (1995, April 9). Survey shows Americans are different (reporting on Roper Center for Public Opinion Research study). Scripps Howard News Service, *Grand Rapids Press,* p. A10. (p. 532)

Brown, R. (1965). *Social psychology.* New York: Free Press. (pp. 176, 177)

Brown, R., Maras, P., Masser, B., Vivian, J., & Hewstone, M. (2001). Life on the ocean wave: Testing some intergroup hypotheses in a naturalistic setting. *Group Processes and Intergroup Relations, 4,* 81–97. (p. 386)

Brown, R., & Smith, A. (1989). Perceptions of and by minority groups: The case of women in academia. *European Journal of Social Psychology, 19,* 61–75. (p. 364)

Brown, R., Vivian, J., & Hewstone, M. (1999). Changing attitudes through intergroup contact: The effects of group membership salience. *European Journal of Social Psychology, 29,* 741–764. (p. 541)

Brown, R., & Wootton-Millward, L. (1993). Perceptions of group homogeneity during group formation and change. *Social Cognition, 11,* 126–149. (p. 359)

Brown, R. P., Charnsangavej, T., Keough, K. A., Newman, M. L., & Rentfrom, P. J. (2000). Putting the "affirm" into affirmative action: Preferential selection and academic performance. *Journal of Personality and Social Psychology, 79,* 736–747. (p. 372)

Brown, S. L., Nesse, R. M., Vinokur, A. D., & Smith, D. M. (2003). Providing social support may be more beneficial than receiving it. *Psychological Science, 14,* 320–327. (pp. 597–598)

Brown, V. R., & Paulus, P. B. (2002). Making group brainstorming more effective: Recommendations from an associative memory perspective. *Current Directions in Psychological Science, 11,* 208–212. (pp. 319–320)

Browning, C. (1992). *Ordinary men: Reserve police battalion 101 and the final solution in Poland.* New York: HarperCollins. (p. 226)

Bruce, V. (1998, July). Identifying people caught on video. *The Psychologist,* pp. 331–335. (p. 610)

Bruck, C. (1976, April). Zimbardo: Solving the maze. *Human Behavior,* pp. 25–31. (p. 236)

Bruck, M., & Ceci, S. J. (1999). The suggestibility of children's memory. *Annual Review of Psychology, 50,* 419–439. (p. 613)

Bryan, J. H., & Test, M. A. (1967). Models and helping: Naturalistic studies in aiding behavior. *Journal of Personality and Social Psychology, 6,* 400–407. (p. 503)

Buckhout, R. (1974, December). Eyewitness testimony. *Scientific American,* pp. 23–31. (p. 608)

Buehler, R., & Griffin, D. (1994). Change of meaning effects in conformity and dissent: Observing construal processes over time. *Journal of Personality and Social Psychology, 67,* 984–996. (p. 235)

Buehler, R., & Griffin, D. (2003). Planning, personality, and prediction: The role of future focus in optimistic time predictions. *Organizational Behavior and Human Decision Processes, 92,* 80–90. (p. 110)

Buehler, R., Griffin, D., & Ross, M. (1994). Exploring the "planning fallacy": When people underestimate their task completion times. *Journal of Personality and Social Psychology, 67,* 366–381. (p. 110)

Buehler, R., Griffin, D., & Ross, M. (2002). Inside the planning fallacy: The causes and consequences of optimistic time predictions. In T. Gilovich, D. Griffin, & D. Kahneman (Eds.), *Heuristics and biases: The psychology of intuitive judgment.* Cambridge: Cambridge University Press. (p. 110)

Buford, B. (1992). *Among the thugs.* New York: Norton. (p. 301)

Bundy, T. (1989, January 25). Interview with James Dobson. *Detroit Free Press,* 1A, 5A. (p. 400)

Burchill, S. A. L., & Stiles, W. B. (1988). Interactions of depressed college students with their roommates: Not necessarily negative. *Journal of Personality and Social Psychology, 55,* 410–419. (p. 579)

Bureau of the Census (1975). *Historical abstract of the United States: Colonial times to 1970.* Washington, DC: Superintendent of Documents. (p. 653)

Bureau of the Census (1993, May 4). Voting survey, reported by Associated Press. (p. 104)

Bureau of the Census (1994). *Tracking the American dream.* Summarized by the Associated Press (*Grand Rapids Press,* September 13, 1994, p. A4). (p. 652)

Bureau of the Census (1998). *Statistical abstract of the United States 1996* (Table 1223). Washington, DC: Superintendent of Documents. (p. 642)

Bureau of the Census (1999). *Statistical abstract of the United States 1996* (Table 65). Washington, DC: Superintendent of Documents. (p. 197)

Bureau of the Census (2002). *Statistical abstract of the United States 2002.*

Washington, DC: Superintendent of Documents. (p. 336)

Burger, J. M. (1987). Increased performance with increased personal control: A self-presentation interpretation. *Journal of Experimental Social Psychology, 23,* 350–360. (p. 324)

Burger, J. M. (1991). Changes in attributions over time: The ephemeral fundamental attribution error. *Social Cognition, 9,* 182–193. (p. 93)

Burger, J. M., & Burns, L. (1988). The illusion of unique invulnerability and the use of effective contraception. *Personality and Social Psychology Bulletin, 14,* 264–270. (p. 71)

Burger, J. M., & Caldwell, D. F. (2003). The effects of monetary incentives and labeling on the foot-in-the-door effect: Evidence for a self-perception process. *Basic and Applied Social Psychology, 25,* 235–241. (p. 157)

Burger, J. M., & Guadagno, R. E. (2003). Self-concept clarity and the foot-in-the-door procedure. *Basic and Applied Social Psychology, 25,* 79–86. (p. 145)

Burger, J. M., Messian, N., Patel, S., del Prade, A., & Anderson, C. (2004). What a coincidence! The effects of incidental similarity on compliance. *Personality and Social Psychology Bulletin, 30,* 35–43. (pp. 230, 504)

Burger, J. M., & Palmer, M. L. (1991). Changes in and generalization of unrealistic optimism following experiences with stressful events: Reactions to the 1989 California earthquake. *Personality and Social Psychology Bulletin, 18,* 39–43. (p. 71)

Burger, J. M., & Pavelich, J. L. (1994). Attributions for presidential elections: The situational shift over time. *Basic and Applied Social Psychology, 15,* 359–371. (p. 93)

Burger, J. M., Soroka, S., Gonzago, K., Murphy, E., Somervell, E. (2001). The effect of fleeting attraction on compliance to requests. *Personality and Social Psychology Bulletin, 27,* 1578–1586. (p. 253)

Burgess, R. L., & Huston, T. L. (Eds.) (1979). *Social exchange in developing relationships.* New York: Academic Press. (p. 450)

Burkholder, R. (2003, February 14). Unwilling coalition? Majorities in

Britain, Canada oppose military action in Iraq. *Gallup Poll Tuesday Briefing* (www.gallup.com/poll). (pp. 245–246)

Burn, S. M. (1992). Locus of control, attributions, and helplessness in the homeless. *Journal of Applied Social Psychology, 22,* 1161–1174. (p. 61)

Burns, D. D. (1980). *Feeling good: The new mood therapy.* New York: Signet. (p. 577)

Burns, J. F. (2003a, April 13). Pillagers strip Iraqi museum of its treasure. *New York Times* (www.nytimes.com). (p. 297)

Burns, J. F. (2003b, April 14). Baghdad residents begin a long climb to an ordered city. *New York Times* (www.nytimes.com). (p. 297)

Burnstein, E., Crandall, R., & Kitayama, S. (1994). Some neo-Darwinian decision rules for altruism: Weighing cues for inclusive fitness as a function of the biological importance of the decision. *Journal of Personality and Social Psychology, 67,* 773–789. (p. 488)

Burnstein, E., & Vinokur, A. (1977). Persuasive argumentation and social comparison as determinants of attitude polarization. *Journal of Experimental Social Psychology, 13,* 315–332. (p. 308)

Burnstein, E., & Worchel, P. (1962). Arbitrariness of frustration and its consequences for aggression in a social situation. *Journal of Personality, 30,* 528–540. (p. 387)

Burr, W. R. (1973). *Theory construction and the sociology of the family.* New York: Wiley. (p. 426)

Burros, M. (1988, February 24). Women: Out of the house but not out of the kitchen. *New York Times.* (p. 67)

Burt, R. S. (1986). Strangers, friends and happiness. *GSS Technical Report No. 72.* Chicago: National Opinion Research Center, University of Chicago. (pp. 599–600)

Bushman, B. J. (1993). Human aggression while under the influence of alcohol and other drugs: An integrative research review. *Current Directions in Psychological Science, 2,* 148–152. (p. 384)

Bushman, B. J. (1995). Moderating role of trait aggressiveness in the effects of

violent media on aggression. *Journal of Personality and Social Psychology, 69,* 950–960. (p. 407)

Bushman, B. J. (1998). Priming effects of media violence on the accessibility of aggressive constructs in memory. *Personality and Social Psychology Bulletin, 24,* 537–545. (p. 409)

Bushman, B. J. (2002). Does venting anger feed or extinguish the flame? Catharsis, rumination, distraction, anger, and aggressive responding. *Personality and Social Psychology Bulletin, 28,* 724–731. (p. 416)

Bushman, B. J., & Anderson, C. A. (1998). Methodology in the study of aggression: Integrating experimental and nonexperimental findings. In R. Geen & E. Donnerstein (Eds.), *Human aggression: Theories, research and implications for policy.* San Diego, CA: Academic Press (p. 414)

Bushman, B. J., & Anderson, C. A. (2001). Media violence and the American public: Scientific facts versus media misinformation. *American Psychologist, 56,* 477–489. (pp. 406, 407)

Bushman, B. J., & Anderson, C. A. (2002). Violent video games and hostile expectations: A test of the general aggression model. *Personality and Social Psychology Bulletin, 28,* 1679–1686. (p. 411)

Bushman, B. J., & Baumeister, R. (1998). Threatened egotism, narcissism, self-esteem, and direct and displaced aggression: Does self-love or self-hate lead to violence? *Journal of Personality and Social Psychology, 75,* 219–229. (pp. 64–65)

Bushman, B. J., Baumeister, R. F., & Phillips, C. M. (2000). Do people aggress to improve their mood? Catharsis beliefs, affect regulation opportunity, and aggressive responding. *Journal of Personality and Social Psychology.* (p. 417)

Bushman, B. J., Baumeister, R. F., & Phillips, C. M. (2001). Do people aggress to improve their mood? Catharsis beliefs, affect regulation opportunity, and aggressive responding. *Journal of Personality and Social Psychology, 81,* 17–32. (pp. 416, 417)

Bushman, B. J., Baumeister, R. F., & Stack, A. D. (1999). Catharsis, aggression, and persuasive influence: Self-fulfilling or self-defeating prophecies? *Journal of Personality and Social Psychology, 76*, 367–376. (p. 417)

Bushman, B. J., & Geen, R. G. (1990). Role of cognitive-emotional mediators and individual differences in the effects of media violence on aggression. *Journal of Personality and Social Psychology, 58*, 156–163. (p. 407)

Buss, D. M. (1984). Toward a psychology of person-environment (PE) correlation: The role of spouse selection. *Journal of Personality and Social Psychology, 47*, 361–377. (p. 446)

Buss, D. M. (1985). Human mate selection. *American Scientist, 73*, 47–51. (pp. 445, 446)

Buss, D. M. (1989). Sex differences in human mate preferences: Evolutionary hypotheses tested in 37 cultures. *Behavioral and Brain Sciences, 12*, 1–49. (p. 438)

Buss, D. M. (1994a). *The evolution of desire: Strategies of human mating.* New York: Basic Books. (pp. 191–192)

Buss, D. M. (1994b). The strategies of human mating. *American Scientist, 82*, 238–249. (p. 192)

Buss, D. M. (1995a). Evolutionary psychology: A new paradigm for psychological science. *Psychological Inquiry, 6*, 1–30. (pp. 191, 194)

Buss, D. M. (1995b). Psychological sex differences: Origins through sexual selection. *American Psychologist, 50*, 164–168. (p. 190)

Buss, D. M. (1999). Behind the scenes. In D. G. Myers, *Social psychology,* 6th edition. New York: McGraw-Hill. (pp. 191–192)

Buss, D. M., & Shackelford, T. K. (1997). Human aggression in evolutionary psychological perspective. *Clinical Psychology Review, 17*, 605–619. (p. 383)

Buston, P. M., & Emlen, S. T. (2003). Cognitive processes underlying human mate choice: The relationship between self-perception and mate preference in Western society. *Proceedings of the National Academy of Sciences, 100*, 8805–8810. (p. 443)

Butcher, S. H. (1951). *Aristotle's theory of poetry and fine art.* New York: Dover Publications. (p. 416)

Butler, A. C., Hokanson, J. E., & Flynn, H. A. (1994). A comparison of self-esteem liability and low trait self-esteem as vulnerability factors for depression. *Journal of Personality and Social Psychology, 66*, 166–177. (p. 579)

Butler, J. L., & Baumeister, R. F. (1998). The trouble with friendly faces: Skilled performance with a supportive audience. *Journal of Personality and Social Psychology, 75*, 1213–1230. (p. 289)

Butterfield, F. (2001, April 20). Victims' race affects decisions on killers' sentence, study finds. *New York Times,* p. A10. (p. 621)

Buunk, B. P., Oldersma, F. L., & de Dreu, C. K. W. (2001). Enhancing satisfaction through downward comparison: The role of relational discontent and individual differences in social comparison orientation. *Journal of Experimental Social Psychology, 37*, 452–467. (p. 657)

Buunk, B. P., & van der Eijnden, R. J. J. M. (1997). Perceived prevalence, perceived superiority, and relationship satisfaction: Most relationships are good, but ours is the best. *Personality and Social Psychology Bulletin, 23*, 219–228. (p. 76)

Buunk, B. P., & Van Yperen, N. W. (1991). Referential comparisons, relational comparisons, and exchange orientation: Their relation to marital satisfaction. *Personality and Social Psychology Bulletin, 17*, 709–717. (p. 461)

Byrne, D. (1971). *The attraction paradigm.* New York: Academic Press. (p. 442)

Byrne, D., & Clore, G. L. (1970). A reinforcement model of evaluative responses. *Personality: An International Journal, 1*, 103–128. (p. 450)

Byrne, D., & Wong, T. J. (1962). Racial prejudice, interpersonal attraction, and assumed dissimilarity of attitudes. *Journal of Abnormal and Social Psychology, 65*, 246–253. (p. 359)

Byrnes, J. P., Miller, D. C., & Schafer, W. D. (1999). Gender differences in risk taking: A meta-analysis. *Psychological Bulletin, 125*, 367–383. (p. 186)

Bytwerk, R. L. (1976). Julius Streicher and the impact of *Der Stürmer. Wiener Library Bulletin, 29*, 41–46. (p. 245)

Bytwerk, R. L., & Brooks, R. D. (1980). Julius Streicher and the rhetorical foundations of the holocaust. Paper presented to the Central States Speech Association convention. (p. 259)

Cacioppo, J. T., Claiborn, C. D., Petty, R. E., & Heesacker, M. (1991). General framework for the study of attitude change in psychotherapy. In C. R. Snyder & D. R. Forsyth (Eds.), *Handbook of social and clinical psychology.* New York: Pergamon. (p. 595)

Cacioppo, J. T., Hawkley, L. C. Crawford, L. E., Ernst, J. M., Burleson, M. H., Kowalewski, R. B., Malarkey, W. B., Van Cauter, E., & Bernston, G. G. (2002b). Loneliness and health: Potential mechanisms. *Psychosomatic Medicine, 64*, 407–417. (p. 597)

Cacioppo, J. T., Hawkley, L. C., & Bernston, G. G. (2003). The anatomy of loneliness. *Current Directions in Psychological Science, 12*, 71–74. (p. 597)

Cacioppo, J. T., Hawkley, L. C., Bernston, G. G., Ernst, J. M., Gibbs, A. C., Stickgold, R., & Hobson, J. A. (2002a). Do lonely days invade the nights? Potential social modulation of sleep efficiency. *Psychological Science, 13*, 384–387. (p. 597)

Cacioppo, J. T., & Petty, R. E. (1981). Electromyograms as measures of extent and affectivity of information processing. *American Psychologist, 36*, 441–456. (p. 136)

Cacioppo, J. T., & Petty, R. E. (1986). Social processes. In M. G. H. Coles, E. Donchin, & S. W. Porges (Eds.), *Psychophysiology.* New York: Guilford Press. (p. 162)

Cacioppo, J. T., Petty, R. E., Feinstein, J. A., & Jarvis, W. B. G. (1996). Dispositional differences in cognitive motivation: The life and times of individuals varying in need for cognition. *Psychological Bulletin, 119*, 197–253. (pp. 256, 269)

Cacioppo, J. T., Petty, R. E., & Morris, K. J. (1983). Effects of need for cognition on message evaluation, recall, and persuasion. *Journal of Personality and Social Psychology, 45*, 805–818. (p. 256)

Cacioppo, J. T., Priester, J. R., & Bernston, G. G. (1993). Rudimentary determinants of attitudes. II: Arm flexion and extension have differential effects on attitudes. *Journal of Personality and Social Psychology, 65,* 5–17. (pp. 158–159)

Cacioppo, J. T., Uchino, B. N., Crites, S. L., Snydersmith, M. A., Smith, G., Berntson, G. G., & Lang, P. J. (1991). Relationship between facial expressiveness and sympathetic activation in emotion: A critical review, with emphasis on modeling underlying mechanisms and individual differences. *Journal of Personality and Social Psychology, 62,* 110–128. (p. 158)

Cairns, E., & Hewstone, M. (2002). The impact of peacemaking in Northern Ireland on intergroup behavior. In S. Gabi & B. Nevo (Eds.), *Peace education: The concept, principles, and practices around the world.* Mahwah, NJ: Erlbaum. (p. 540)

Campbell, D. T. (1975). The conflict between social and biological evolution and the concept of original sin. *Zygon, 10,* 234–249. *(a)* (p. 487)

Campbell, E. Q., & Pettigrew, T. F. (1959). Racial and moral crisis: The role of Little Rock ministers. *American Journal of Sociology, 64,* 509–516. (p. 347)

Campbell, W. K., & Foster, C. A. (2002). Narcissism and commitment in romantic relationships: An investment model analysis. *Personality and Social Psychology Bulletin, 28,* 484–495. (p. 468)

Campbell, W. K., & Sedikides, C. (1999). Self-threat magnifies the self-serving bias: A meta-analytic integration. *Review of General Psychology, 3,* 23–43. (p. 67)

Canadian Centre on Substance Abuse (1997). *Canadian profile: Alcohol, tobacco, and other drugs.* Ottawa: Canadian Centre on Substance Abuse. (p. 239)

Canadian Psychological Association (2000). *Canadian code of ethics for psychologists.* Ottawa: Canadian Psychological Association (www.cpa.ca/ethics2000.html). (p. 32)

Cann, A., Calhoun, L. G., & Selby, J. W. (1979). Attributing responsibility to the victim of rape: Influence of information regarding past sexual experience. *Human Relations, 32,* 57–67. (p. 622)

Cantril, H., & Bumstead, C. H. (1960). *Reflections on the human venture.* New York: New York University Press. (p. 321)

Carducci, B. J., Cosby, P. C., & Ward, D. D. (1978). Sexual arousal and interpersonal evaluations. *Journal of Experimental Social Psychology, 14,* 449–457. (p. 454)

Carli, L. L. (1991). Gender, status, and influence. In E. J. Lawler & B. Markovsky (Ed.), *Advances in group processes: Theory and research,* vol. 8. Greenwich, CT: JAI Press. (p. 186)

Carli, L. L. (1999). Cognitive reconstruction, hindsight, and reactions to victims and perpetrators. *Personality and Social Psychology Bulletin, 25,* 966–979. (pp. 366–367)

Carli, L. L., & Leonard, J. B. (1989). The effect of hindsight on victim derogation. *Journal of Social and Clinical Psychology, 8,* 331–343. (pp. 366–367)

Carlo, G., Eisenberg, N., Troyer, D., Switzer, G., & Speer, A. L. (1991). The altruistic personality: In what contexts is it apparent? *Journal of Personality and Social Psychology, 61,* 450–458. (p. 506)

Carlsmith, J. M., & Gross, A. E. (1969). Some effects of guilt on compliance. *Journal of Personality and Social Psychology, 11,* 232–239. (p. 480)

Carlsmith, J. M., Ellsworth, P., & Whiteside, J. (1968). Guilt, confession and compliance. Unpublished manuscript, Stanford University. Cited by J. L. Freeman, D. O. Sears, & J. M. Carlsmith in *Social psychology.* Englewood Cliffs, NJ: Prentice-Hall, 1970, pp. 275–276. (p. 480)

Carlson, J., & Hatfield, E. (1992). *The psychology of emotion.* Fort Worth, TX: Holt, Rinehart & Winston. (p. 457)

Carlson, K. A., & Russo, J. E. (2001). Biased interpretation of evidence by mock jurors. *Journal of Experimental Psychology: Applied, 7,* 91–103. (p. 626)

Carlson, M., Charlin, V., & Miller, N. (1988). Positive mood and helping behavior: A test of six hypotheses. *Journal of Personality and Social Psychology, 55,* 211–229. (p. 483)

Carlson, M., Marcus-Newhall, A., & Miller, N. (1990). Effects of situational aggression cues: A quantitative review. *Journal of Personality and Social Psychology, 58,* 622–633. (p. 387)

Carlston, D. E., & Shovar, N. (1983). Effects of performance attributions on others' perceptions of the attributor. *Journal of Personality and Social Psychology, 44,* 515–525. (p. 80)

Carnevale, P. J., & Choi, D-W. (2000). Culture in the mediation of international disputes. *International Journal of Psychology, 35,* 105–110. (p. 556)

Carnevale, P. J., & Probst, T. M. (1998). Social values and social conflict in creative problem solving and categorization. *Journal of Personality and Social Psychology, 74,* 1300–1309. (p. 536)

Carroll, D., Davey Smith, G., & Bennett, P. (1994, March). Health and socio-economic status. *The Psychologist,* pp. 122–125. (pp. 22, 599)

Carter, S. L. (1993). *Reflections of an affirmative action baby.* New York: Basic Books. (p. 361)

Cartwright, D. S. (1975). The nature of gangs. In D. S. Cartwright, B. Tomson, & H. Schwartz (Eds.), *Gang delinquency.* Monterey, CA: Brooks/Cole. (pp. 306, 391)

Carver, C. S., Kus, L. A., & Scheier, M. F. (1994). Effect of good versus bad mood and optimistic versus pessimistic outlook on social acceptance versus rejection. *Journal of Social and Clinical Psychology, 13,* 138–151. (p. 579)

Carver, C. S., & Scheier, M. F. (1978). Self-focusing effects of dispositional self-consciousness, mirror presence, and audience presence. *Journal of Personality and Social Psychology, 36,* 324–332. (pp. 93–94)

Carver, C. S., & Scheier, M. F. (1981). *Attention and self-regulation.* New York: Springer-Verlag. (p. 139)

Carver, C. S., & Scheier, M. F. (1986). Analyzing shyness: A specific application of broader self-regulatory principles. In W. H. Jones, J. M. Cheek, & S. R. Briggs (Eds.), *Shyness: Perspectives on research and treatment.* New York: Plenum. (p. 584)

Cash, T. F., & Janda, L. H. (1984, December). The eye of the beholder. *Psychology Today*, pp. 46–52. (p. 436)

Caspi, A., & Herbener, E. S. (1990). Continuity and change: Assortative marriage and the consistency of personality in adulthood. *Journal of Personality and Social Psychology, 58*, 250–258. (p. 442)

Caspi, A., McClay, J., Moffitt, T., Mill, J., Martin, J., Craig, I. W., Taylor, A., & Poulton, R. (2002). Role of genotype in the cycle of violence in maltreated children. *Science, 297*, 851–854. (p. 384)

Cassidy, J. (2000). Adult romantic attachments: A developmental perspective on individual differences. *Review of General Psychology Special Issue: Adult attachment, 4*, 111–131. (p. 460)

Catalano, R., Novaco, R., & McConnell, W. (1997). A model of the net effect of job loss on violence. *Journal of Personality and Social Psychology, 72*, 1440–1447. (p. 388)

Ceci, S. J., & Bruck, M. (1993). Child witnesses: Translating research into policy. *Social Policy Report* (Society for Research in Child Development), *7*(3), 1–30. (p. 613)

Ceci, S. J., & Bruck, M. (1993). Suggestibility of the child witness: A historical review and synthesis. *Psychological Bulletin, 113*, 403–439. (p. 613)

Ceci, S. J., & Bruck, M. (1995). *Jeopardy in the courtroom: A scientific analysis of children's testimony*. Washington, DC: American Psychological Association. (p. 613)

Centerwall, B. S. (1989). Exposure to television as a risk factor for violence. *American Journal of Epidemiology, 129*, 643–652. (p. 406)

Chaiken, S. (1979). Communicator physical attractiveness and persuasion. *Journal of Personality and Social Psychology, 37*, 1387–1397. (p. 254)

Chaiken, S. (1980). Heuristic versus systematic information processing and the use of source versus message cues in persuasion. *Journal of Personality and Social Psychology, 39*, 752–766. (p. 256)

Chaiken, S., & Eagly, A. H. (1976). Communication modality as a determinant of message persuasiveness and message comprehensibility. *Journal of Personality and Social Psychology, 34*, 605–614. (p. 266)

Chaiken, S., & Eagly, A. H. (1978). Communication modality as a determinant of message persuasiveness and message comprehensibility. *Journal of Personality and Social Psychology, 34*, 605–614. (p. 267)

Chaiken, S., & Eagly, A. H. (1983). Communication modality as a determinant of persuasion: The role of communicator salience. *Journal of Personality and Social Psychology, 45*, 241–256. (p. 266)

Chaiken, S., & Maheswaran, D. (1994). Neuristic processing can bias systematic processing: Effects of source credibility, argument ambiguity, and task importance on attitude judgment. *Journal of Personality and Social Psychology, 66*, 460–473. (p. 249)

Chance, J. E., & Goldstein, A. G. (1981). Depth of processing in response to own- and other-race faces. *Personality and Social Psychology Bulletin, 7*, 475–480. (p. 359)

Chance, J. E., Goldstein, A. G. (1996). The other-race effect and eyewitness identification. In *Psychological issues in eyewitness identification*, (Sporer, S. L., Ed.). Mahwah, NJ: Lawrence Erlbaum Associates, Inc. 153–176. (p. 359)

Chapman, L. J., & Chapman, J. P. (1969). Genesis of popular but erroneous psychodiagnostic observations. *Journal of Abnormal Psychology, 74*, 272–280. (p. 569)

Chapman, L. J., & Chapman, J. P. (1971, November). Test results are what you think they are. *Psychology Today*, pp. 18–22, 106–107. (p. 569)

Chartrand, T. L., & Bargh, J. A. (1999). The chameleon effect: The perception-behavior link and social interaction. *Journal of Personality and Social Psychology, 76*, 893–910. (p. 211)

Check, J., & Malamuth, N. (1984). Can there be positive effects of participation in pornography experiments? *Journal of Sex Research, 20*, 14–31. (p. 400)

Check, J. M., & Melchior, L. A. (1990). Shyness, self-esteem, and self-consciousness. In H. Leitenberg (Ed.), *Handbook of social and evaluation anxiety*. New York: Plenum. (p. 582)

Chen, F. F., & Kenrick, D. T. (2002). Repulsion or attraction? Group membership and assumed attitude similarity. *Journal of Personality and Social Psychology, 83*, 111–125. (p. 444)

Chen, H. C., Reardon, R., & Rea, C. (1992). Forewarning of content and involvement: Consequences for persuasion and resistance to persuasion. *Journal of Experimental Social Psychology, 28*, 523–541. (p. 269)

Chen, L-H., Baker, S. P., Braver, E. R., & Li, G. (2000). Carrying passengers as a risk factor for crashes fatal to 16- and 17-year-old drivers. *Journal of the American Medical Association, 283*, 1578–1582. (p. 304)

Chen, S. C. (1937). Social modification of the activity of ants in nest-building. *Physiological Zoology, 10*, 420–436. (p. 287)

Cheney, R. (2003, March 16). Comments on Face the Nation, CBS News. (p. 387)

Cherlin, A. J., Chase-Lansdale, P. L., & McRae, C. (1998). Effects of parental divorce on mental health throughout the life course. *American Sociological Review, 63*, 239–249. (p. 391)

Chicago Tribune (2002, September 30). When believing isn't seeing. *Chicago Tribune* (www.chicagotribune.com). (p. 608)

Chodorow, N. J. (1978). *The reproduction of mother: Psychoanalysis and the sociology of gender*. Berkeley, CA: University of California Press. (p. 182)

Chodorow, N. J. (1989). *Feminism and psychoanalytic theory*. New Haven, CT: Yale University Press. (p. 182)

Choi, I., & Choi, Y. (2002). Culture and self-concept flexibility. *Personality & Social Psychology Bulletin, 28*, 1508–1517. (p. 48)

Choi, I., Nisbett, R. E., & Norenzayan, A. (1999). Causal attribution across cultures: Variation and universality. *Psychological Bulletin, 125*, 47–63. (p. 95)

Christensen, P. N., & Kashy, D. A. (1998). Perceptions of and by lonely people in initial social interaction. *Personality and Social Psychology Bulletin, 24*, 322–329. (p. 582)

Chua-Eoan, H. (1997, April 7). Imprisoned by his own passions. *Time*, pp. 40–42. (p. 273)

Church, G. J. (1986, January 6). China. *Time*, pp. 6–19. (p. 296)

Chwalisz, K., Diener, E., & Gallagher, D. (1988). Autonomic arousal feedback and emotional experience: Evidence from the spinal cord injured. *Journal of Personality and Social Psychology, 54*, 820–828. (p. 657)

CIA (2002, February). *Chiefs of state and cabinet members of foreign governments* (www.msad.state.mn.us/ onlinecareerfair/human/ Bethlockard.htm). (p. 185)

Cialdini, R. B. (1984). *Influence: How and why people agree to things.* New York: William Morrow. (p. 156)

Cialdini, R. B. (1988). *Influence: Science and practice.* Glenview, IL: Scott, Foresman/Little, Brown. (pp. 146, 150)

Cialdini, R. B. (1991). Altruism or egoism? That is (still) the question. *Psychological Inquiry, 2*, 124–126. (p. 492)

Cialdini, R. B. (1995). A full-cycle approach to social psychology. In G. G. Brannigan & M. R. Merrens (Eds.), *The social psychologists: Research adventures.* New York: McGraw-Hill. (pp. 511–512)

Cialdini. R. B. (2000). *Influence: Science and practice*, 4th edition. Boston: Allyn & Bacon. (p. 254)

Cialdini, R. B. (2003). Crafting normative messages. *Current Directions in Psychological Science, 12*, 105–109.

Cialdini, R. B., Bickman, L., & Cacioppo, J. T. (1979). An example of consumeristic social psychology: Bargaining tough in the new car showroom. *Journal of Applied Social Psychology, 9*, 115–126. (p. 553)

Cialdini, R. B., Borden, R. J., Thorne, A., Walker, M. R., Freeman, S., & Sloan, L. R. (1976). Basking in reflected glory: Three (football) field studies. *Journal of Personality and Social Psychology, 39*, 406–415. (pp. 353, 545)

Cialdini, R. B., Cacioppo, J. T., Bassett, R., & Miller, J. A. (1978). Lowball procedure for producing compliance: Commitment then cost. *Journal of Personality and Social Psychology, 36*, 463–476. (pp. 145–146)

Cialdini, R. B., Darby, B. L., & Vincent, J. E. (1973). Transgression and altruism: A case for hedonism. *Journal of Experimental Social Psychology, 9*, 502–516. (p. 480)

Cialdini, R. B., Demaine, L. J., Barrett, D. W., Sagarin, B. J., & Rhoads, K. L. V. (2003). The poison parasite defense: A strategy for sapping a stronger opponent's persuasive strength. Unpublished manuscript, Arizona State University. (pp. 279, 513)

Cialdini, R. B., & Kenrick, D. T. (1976). Altruism as hedonism: A social development perspective on the relationship of negative mood state and helping. *Journal of Personality and Social Psychology, 34*, 907–914. (pp. 480, 481)

Cialdini, R. B., Kenrick, D. T., & Baumann, D. J. (1981). Effects of mood on prosocial behavior in children and adults. In N. Eisenberg-Berg (Ed.), *The development of prosocial behavior.* New York: Academic Press. (p. 481)

Cialdini, R. B., & Richardson, K. D. (1980). Two indirect tactics of image management: Basking and blasting. *Journal of Personality and Social Psychology, 39*, 406–415. (p. 355)

Cialdini, R. B., & Schroeder, D. A. (1976). Increasing compliance by legitimizing paltry contributions: When even a penny helps. *Journal of Personality and Social Psychology, 34*, 599–604. (pp. 511–512)

Cialdini, R. B., Vincent, J. E., Lewis, S. K., Catalan, J., Wheeler, D., & Danby, B. L. (1975). Reciprocal concessions procedure for inducing compliance: The door-in-the-face technique. *Journal of Personality and Social Psychology, 31*, 206–215. (p. 511)

Cialdini, R. B., Wosinska, W., Dabul, A. J., Whetstone-Dion, R., & Heszen, I. (1998). When social role salience leads to social role rejection: Modest self-presentation among women and men in two cultures. *Personality and Social Psychology Bulletin, 24*, 473–481. (p. 238)

Cicerello, A., & Sheehan, E. P. (1995). Personal advertisements: A content analysis. *Journal of Social Behavior and Personality, 10*, 751–756. (p. 434)

Cinnirella, M. (1997). Towards a European identity? Interactions between the national and European social identities manifested by university students in Britain and Italy. *British Journal of Social Psychology, 36*, 19–31. (p. 43)

Cioffi, D., & Garner, R. (1998). The effect of response options on decisions and subsequent behavior: Sometimes inaction is better. *Personality and Social Psychology Bulletin, 24*, 463–472. (p. 516)

Clancy, S. M., & Dollinger, S. J. (1993). Photographic depictions of the self: Gender and age differences in social connectedness. *Sex Roles, 29*, 477–495. (p. 183)

Clark, K., & Clark, M. (1947). Racial identification and preference in Negro children. In T. M. Newcomb & E. L. Hartley (Eds.), *Readings in social psychology.* New York: Holt. (p. 335)

Clark, M. S. (1984). Record keeping in two types of relationships. *Journal of Personality and Social Psychology, 47*, 549–557. (pp. 460–461)

Clark, M. S. (1986). Evidence for the effectiveness of manipulations of desire for communal versus exchange relationships. *Personality and Social Psychology Bulletin, 12*, 414–425. (pp. 460–461)

Clark, M. S., & Bennett, M. E. (1992). Research on relationships: Implications for mental health. In D. Ruble, P. Costanzo (Ed.), *The social psychology of mental health.* New York: Guilford. (p. 64)

Clark, M. S., & Mills, J. (1979). Interpersonal attraction in exchange and communal relationships. *Journal of Personality and Social Psychology, 37*, 12–24. (pp. 460–461)

Clark, M. S., & Mills, J. (1993). The difference between communal and exchange relationships: What it is and is not. *Personality and Social Psychology Bulletin, 19*, 684–691. (pp. 460–461)

Clark, M. S., Mills, J., & Corcoran, D. (1989). Keeping track of needs and inputs of friends and strangers.

Personality and Social Psychology Bulletin, **15**, 533–542. (p. 461)

Clark, M. S., Mills, J., & Powell, M. C. (1986). Keeping track of needs in communal and exchange relationships. *Journal of Personality and Social Psychology*, **51**, 333–338. (p. 461)

Clark, R. D., III. (1974). Effects of sex and race on helping behavior in a nonreactive setting. *Representative Research in Social Psychology*, **5**, 1–6. (p. 505)

Clark, R. D., III. (1995). A few parallels between group polarization and minority influence. In S. Moscovici, H. Mucchi-Faina, & A. Maass (Eds.), *Minority influence*. Chicago: Nelson-Hall. (p. 323)

Clark, R. D., III., & Maass, S. A. (1988). The role of social categorization and perceived source credibility in minority influence. *European Journal of Social Psychology*, **18**, 381–394. (p. 230)

Clarke, A. C. (1952). An examination of the operation of residual propinquity as a factor in mate selection. *American Sociological Review*, **27**, 17–22. (p. 426)

Clarke, V. (2003, March 25). Quoted in Street fighting: A volatile enemy. *Wall Street Journal*, p. A1, A13. (p. 175)

Clary, E. G., & Snyder, M. (1993). Persuasive communications strategies for recruiting volunteers. In D. R. Young, R. M. Hollister, & V. A. Hodgkinson (Eds.), *Governing, leading, and managing nonprofit organizations*. San Francisco: Jossey-Bass. (p. 508)

Clary, E. G., & Snyder, M. (1995). Motivations for volunteering and giving: A functional approach. In C. H. Hamilton & W. E. Ilchman (Eds.), *Cultures of giving II: How heritage, gender, wealth, and values influence philanthropy*. Bloomington, IN: Indiana University Center on Philanthropy. (p. 508)

Clary, E. G., & Snyder, M. (1999). The motivations to volunteer: Theoretical and practical considerations. *Current Directions in Psychological Science*, **8**, 156–159. (p. 508)

Clary, E. G., Snyder, M., Ridge, R. D., Copeland, J., Stukas, A. A., Haugen, J., & Miene, P. (1998). Understanding and assessing the motivations of volunteers: A functional approach. *Journal of*

Personality and Social Psychology, **74**, 1516–1531. (p. 508)

Cleghorn, R. (1980, October 31). ABC News, meet the Literary Digest. *Detroit Free Press*. (p. 26)

Clifford, M. M., & Walster, E. H. (1973). The effect of physical attractiveness on teacher expectation. *Sociology of Education*, **46**, 248–258. (p. 434)

Cline, V. B., Croft, R. G., & Courrier, S. (1973). Desensitization of children to television violence. *Journal of Personality and Social Psychology*, **27**, 360–365. (p. 408)

Clore, G. L., Bray, R. M., Itkin, S. M., & Murphy, P. (1978). Interracial attitudes and behavior at a summer camp. *Journal of Personality and Social Psychology*, **36**, 107–116. (p. 540)

Clore, G. L., Wiggins, N. H., & Itkin, G. (1975). Gain and loss in attraction: Attributions from nonverbal behavior. *Journal of Personality and Social Psychology*, **31**, 706–712. (p. 449)

cnn.com (2001, September 17). Hate crimes reports up in wake of terrorist attacks. cnn.com/U.S. (www.cnn.com/2001/US/09/16/gen.hate.crimes/) (p. 332)

Coates, B., Pusser, H. E., & Goodman, I. (1976). The influence of "Sesame Street" and "Mister Rogers' Neighborhood" on children's social behavior in the preschool. *Child Development*, **47**, 138–144. (p. 514)

Coats, E. J., & Feldman, R. S. (1996). Gender differences in nonverbal correlates of social status. *Personality and Social Psychology Bulletin*, **22**, 1014–1022. (p. 185)

Codol, J.-P. (1976). On the so-called superior conformity of the self behavior: Twenty experimental investigations. *European Journal of Social Psychology*, **5**, 457–501. (pp. 76, 80)

Cohen, D. (1996). Law, social policy, and violence: The impact of regional cultures. *Journal of Personality and Social Psychology*, **70**, 961–978. (p. 392)

Cohen, D. (1998). Culture, social organization, and patterns of violence. *Journal of Personality and Social Psychology*, **75**, 408–419. (p. 392)

Cohen, E. G. (1980). Design and redesign of the desegregated school:

Problems of status, power and conflict. In W. G. Stephan & J. R. Feagin (Eds.), *School desegregation: Past, present, and future*. New York: Plenum Press. *(a)* (p. 549)

Cohen, E. G. (1980). A multi-ability approach to the integrated classroom. Paper presented at the American Psychological Association convention. (p. 542)

Cohen, G. L., Steele, C. M., & Ross, L. D. (1999). The mentor's dilemma: Providing critical feedback across the racial divide. *Personality and Social Psychology Bulletin*, **25**, 1302–1318. (p. 372)

Cohen, M., & Davis, N. (1981). *Medication errors: Causes and prevention*. Philadelphia: G. F. Stickley Co. Cited by R. B. Cialdini (1989). Agents of influence: Bunglers, smugglers, and sleuths. Paper presented at the American Psychological Association convention. (p. 221)

Cohen, S. (1980). Training to understand TV advertising: Effects and some policy implications. Paper presented at the American Psychological Association convention. (p. 282)

Cohen, S. (2002). Psychosocial stress, social networks, and susceptibility to infection. In H. G. Koenig & H. J. Cohen (Eds.), *The link between religion and health: Psychoneuroimmunology and the faith factor*. New York: Oxford University Press. (p. 589)

Cohen, S., Doyle, W. J., Skoner, D. P., Rabin, B. S., & Gwaltney, J. M., Jr. (1997). Social ties and susceptibility to the common cold. *Journal of the American Medical Association*, **277**, 1940–1944. (p. 597)

Cohen, S., Doyle, W. J., Turner, R., Alper, C. M., & Skoner, D. P. (2003). Sociability and susceptibility to the common cold. *Psychological Science*, **14**, 389–395. (p. 597)

Cohen, S., Line, S., Manuck, S. B., Rabin, B. S., Heise, E. R., & Kaplan, J. R. (1997). Chronic social stress, social status, and susceptibility to upper respiratory infections in nonhuman primates. *Psychosomatic Medicine*, **59**, 213–221. (p. 599)

Cohen, S., & Rodriguez, M. S. (1995). Pathways linking affective disturbances and physical disorders. *Health Psychology, 14*, 374–380. (p. 588)

Cohn, E. G. (1993). The prediction of police calls for service: The influence of weather and temporal variables on rape and domestic violence. *Environmental Psychology, 13*, 71–83. (p. 395)

Colasanto, D. (1989, November). Americans show commitment to helping those in need. *Gallup Report,* No. 290, pp. 17–24. (p. 508)

Coleman, L. M., Jussim, L., & Abraham, J. (1987). Students' reactions to teachers' evaluations: The unique impact of negative feedback. *Journal of Applied Social Psychology, 17*, 1051–1070. (p. 448)

Collins, N. L., & Miller, L. C. (1994). Self-disclosure and liking: A meta-analytic review. *Psychological Bulletin, 116*, 457–475. (p. 462)

Colman, A. M. (1991). Crowd psychology in South African murder trials. *American Psychologist, 46*, 1071–1079. See also, A. M. Colman (1991), Psychological evidence in South African murder trials. *The Psychologist, 14*, 482–486. (p. 306)

Columbia Accident Investigation Board (2003, August). Volume 1. Washington, DC: National Aeronautics and Space Administration and the Government Printing Office. (p. 316)

Comer, D. R. (1995). A model of social loafing in real work group. *Human Relations, 48*, 647–667. (p. 297)

Comstock, G., & Scharrer, E. (1999). *Television: What's on, who's watching and what it means.* San Diego, CA: Academic Press. (p. 403)

Conger, R. D., Cui, M., Bryant, C. M., & Elder, G. H. (2000). Competence in early adult romantic relationships: A developmental perspective on family influences. *Journal of Personality and Social Psychology, 79*, 224–237. (p. 460)

Contrada, R. J., Ashmore, R. D., Gary, M. L., Coups, E., Egeth, J. D., Sewell, A., Ewell, K., Goyal, T. M., & Chasse, V. (2000). Ethnicity-related sources of stress and their effects on well-being. *Current Directions in Psychological Science, 9*, 136–139. (p. 231)

Conway, F., & Siegelman, J. (1979). *Snapping: America's epidemic of sudden personality change.* New York: Delta Books. (pp. 274, 275)

Conway, L. G., III., Suedfeld, P., & Tetlock, P. E. (2001). Integrative complexity and political decisions that lead to war or peace. In D. J. Christie, R. V. Wagner, & D. Winter (Eds.), *Peace, conflict, and violence: Peace psychology for the 21st century.* Englewood Cliffs, NY: Prentice-Hall. (p. 536)

Conway, M., & Ross, M. (1985). Remembering one's own past: The construction of personal histories. In R. Sorrentino & E. T. Higgins (Eds.) *Handbook of motivation and cognition.* New York: Guilford. (p. 205)

Conway, M., & Ross, M. (1986). Remembering one's own past: The construction of personal histories. In R. Sorrentino & E. T. Higgins (Eds.), *Handbook of motivation and cognition.* New York: Guilford. (p. 105)

Cook, S. W. (1985). Experimenting on social issues: The case of school desegregation. *American Psychologist, 40*, 452–460. (p. 549)

Cook, T. D., & Curtin, T. R. (1987). The mainstream and the underclass: Why are the differences so salient and the similarities so unobtrusive? In J. C. Masters & W. P. Smith (Eds.), *Social comparison, social justice, and relative deprivation: Theoretical, empirical, and policy perspectives.* Hillsdale, NJ: Erlbaum. (p. 364)

Cook, T. D., & Flay, B. R. (1978). The persistence of experimentally induced attitude change. In L. Berkowitz (Ed.), *Advances in experimental social psychology.* Vol. 11. New York: Academic Press. (pp. 251–252)

Cooley, C. H. (1902). *Human nature and the social order.* New York: Schocken Books. (p. 45)

Coombs, R. H. (1991, January). Marital status and personal well-being: A literature review. *Family Relations, 40*, 97–102. (p. 602)

Cooper, H. (1983). Teacher expectation effects. In L. Bickman (Ed.), *Applied social psychology annual*, Vol. 4. Beverly Hills, CA: Sage. (p. 123)

Cooper, J. (1999). Unwanted consequences and the self: In search of the motivation for dissonance

reduction. In E. Harmon-Jones & J. Mills (Eds.), *Cognitive dissonance: Progress on a pivotal theory in social psychology.* Washington, DC: American Psychological Association. (p. 162)

Copeland, J., & Snyder, M. (1995). When counselors confirm: A functional analysis. *Personality and Social Psychology Bulletin, 21*, 1210–1221. (p. 571)

Correll, J., Park, B., Judd, C. M., & Wittenbrink, B. (2002). The police officer's dilemma: Using ethnicity to disambiguate potentially threatening individuals. *Journal of Personality and Social Psychology, 83*, 1314–1329. (pp. 338–339)

Costanzo, M. (1997). *Just revenge: Costs and consequences of the death penalty.* New York: St. Martin's. (p. 630)

Costanzo, M. (1998). *Just revenge.* New York: St. Martin's. (pp. 382, 418)

Cota, A. A., & Dion, K. L. (1986). Salience of gender and sex composition of ad hoc groups: An experimental test of distinctiveness theory. *Journal of Personality and Social Psychology, 50*, 770–776. (p. 240)

Cotton, J. L. (1981). Ambient temperature and violent crime. Paper presented at the Midwestern Psychological Association convention. (p. 395)

Cotton, J. L. (1986). Ambient temperature and violent crime. *Journal of Applied Social Psychology, 16*, 786–801. (p. 395)

Cottrell, N. B., Wack, D. L., Sekerak, G. J., & Rittle, R. M. (1968). Social facilitation of dominant responses by the presence of an audience and the mere presence of others. *Journal of Personality and Social Psychology, 9*, 245–250. (p. 290)

Courneya, K. S., & Carron, A. V. (1992). The home advantage in sport competitions: A literature review. *Journal of Sport and Exercise Psychology, 14*, 13–27. (p. 289)

Court, J. H. (1985). Sex and violence: A ripple effect. In N. M. Malamuth & E. Donnerstein (Eds.), *Pornography and sexual aggression.* New York: Academic Press. (p. 399)

Courtney, J. G., Longnecker, M. P., Theorell, T., & de Verdier, M. G.

(1993). Stressful life events and the risk of colorectal cancer. *Epidemiology, 4,* 407–414. (pp. 589–590)

Cousins, N. (1978, September 16). The taxpayers revolt: Act two. *Saturday Review,* p. 56. (p. 130)

Coyne, J. C., Burchill, S. A. L., & Stiles, W. B. (1991). In C. R. Snyder & D. O. Forsyth (Eds.), *Handbook of social and clinical psychology: The health perspective.* New York: Pergamon. (p. 579)

Crabb, P. B., & Bielawski, D. (1994). The social representation of material culture and gender in children's books. *Sex Roles, 30,* 6979. (p. 195)

Crabtree, S. (2002, January 22). Gender roles reflected in teen tech use. *Gallup Tuesday Briefing* (www.gallup.com). (p. 182)

Crandall, C. S. (1988). Social contagion of binge eating. *Journal of Personality and Social Psychology, 55,* 588–598. (pp. 230–231)

Crandall, C. S. (1994). Prejudice against fat people: Ideology and self-interest. *Journal of Personality and Social Psychology, 66,* 882–894. (pp. 345–346)

Crandall, C. S., & Eshleman, A. (2003). A justification–suppression model of the expression and experience of prejudice. *Psychological Bulletin, 129,* 414–446. (p. 356)

Crano, W. D., & Mellon, P. M. (1978). Causal influence of teachers' expectations on children's academic performance: A cross-legged panel analysis. *Journal of Educational Psychology, 70,* 39–49. (p. 121)

Crawford, M., Stark, A. C., & Renner, C. H. (1998). The meaning of Ms.: Social assimilation of a gender concept. *Psychology of Women Quarterly, 22,* 197–208. (p. 333)

Crawford, T. J. (1974). Sermons on racial tolerance and the parish neighborhood context. *Journal of Applied Social Psychology, 4,* 1–23. (pp. 263–264)

Crisp, R. J., & Hewstone, M. (1999). Differential evaluation of crossed category groups: Patterns, processes, and reducing intergroup bias. *Group Processes & Intergroup Relations, 2,* 307–333. (p. 552)

Crisp, R. J., & Hewstone, M. (2000). Multiple categorization and social identity. In D. Capozza & R. Brown (Eds.), *Social identity theory: Trends in theory and research.* Beverly Hills, CA: Sage. (p. 552)

Crocker, J. (1981). Judgment of covariation by social perceivers. *Psychological Bulletin, 90,* 272–292. (p. 117)

Crocker, J. (1994, October 14). Who cares what they think? Reflected and deflected appraisal. Presentation to the Society of Experimental Social Psychology meeting. (p. 49)

Crocker, J. (2002). The costs of seeking self-esteem. *Journal of Social Issues, 58,* 597–615. (p. 66)

Crocker, J., & Gallo, L. (1985). The self-enhancing effect of downward comparison. Paper presented at the American Psychological Association convention. (pp. 657–658)

Crocker, J., Hannah, D. B., & Weber, R. (1983). Personal memory and causal attributions. *Journal of Personality and Social Psychology, 44,* 55–56. (p. 368)

Crocker, J., & Luhtanen, R. (1990). Collective self-esteem and ingroup bias. *Journal of Personality and Social Psychology, 58,* 60–67. (p. 352)

Crocker, J., & Luhtanen, R. (2003). Level of self-esteem and contingencies of self-worth: Unique effects on academic, social, and financial problems in college students. *Personality and Social Psychology Bulletin, 29,* 701–712. (p. 66)

Crocker, J., & McGraw, K. M. (1984). What's good for the goose is not good for the gander: Solo status as an obstacle to occupational achievement for males and females. *American Behavioral Scientist, 27,* 357–370. (p. 360)

Crocker, J., & Park, L. E. (2004). The costly pursuit of self-esteem. *Psychological Bulletin, 130,* 392–414. (p. 66)

Crocker, J., Thompson, L. L., McGraw, K. M., & Ingerman, C. (1987). Downward comparison, prejudice, and evaluations of others: Effects of self-esteem and threat. *Journal of Personality and Social Psychology, 52,* 907–916. (p. 355)

Crocker, J., & Wolfe, C. (2001). Contingencies of self-worth. *Psychological Review.* (p. 62)

Croizet, J. C., Despres, G., Gauzins, M. E., Huguet, P., Leyens, J. P., & Meot, A. (2004). Stereotype threat undermines intellectual performance by triggering a disruptive mental load. *Personality and Social Psychology Bulletin, 30,* 721–731. (p. 372)

Crosby, F., Bromley, S., & Saxe, L. (1980). Recent unobtrusive studies of black and white discrimination and prejudice: A literature review. *Psychological Bulletin, 87,* 546–563. (p. 336)

Crosby, F. J. (Ed.) (1987). *Spouse, parent, worker: On gender and multiple roles.* New Haven, CT: Yale University Press. (p. 602)

Cross, P. (1977). Not *can* but *will* college teaching be improved? *New Directions for Higher Education,* Spring, No. 17, pp. 1–15. (p. 76)

Cross, S. E., Liao, M-H., & Josephs, R. (1992). A cross-cultural test of the self-evaluation maintenance model. Paper presented at the American Psychological Association convention. (p. 48)

Crossen, C. (1993). *Tainted truth: The manipulation of face in America.* New York: Simon & Schuster. (p. 28)

Cross-National Collaborative Group (1992). The changing rate of major depression. *Journal of the American Medical Association, 268,* 3098–3105. (pp. 581, 653)

Croxton, J. S., Eddy, T., & Morrow, N. (1984). Memory biases in the reconstruction of interpersonal encounters. *Journal of Social and Clinical Psychology, 2,* 348–354. (pp. 96, 105)

Croxton, J. S., & Miller, A. G. (1987). Behavioral disconfirmation and the observer bias. *Journal of Social Behavior and Personality, 2,* 145–152. (p. 96)

Croyle, R. T., & Cooper, J. (1983). Dissonance arousal: Physiological evidence. *Journal of Personality and Social Psychology, 45,* 782–791. (p. 162)

Csikszentmihalyi, M. (1990). *Flow: The psychology of optimal experience.* New York: Harper & Row. (p. 659)

Csikszentmihalyi, M. (1999). If we are so rich, why aren't we happy?

American Psychologist, 54, 821–827. (p. 659)

Cunningham, J. D. (1981). Self-disclosure intimacy: Sex, sex-of-target, cross-national, and generational differences. *Personality and Social Psychology Bulletin, 7*, 314–319. (p. 464)

Cunningham, M. R., Shaffer, D. R., Barbee, A. P., Wolff, P. L., & Kelley, D. J. (1990). Separate processes in the relation of elation and depression to helping: Social versus personal concerns. *Journal of Experimental Social Psychology, 26*, 13–33. (p. 483)

Cutler, B. L., Moran, G., & Narvy, D. J. (1992). Jury selection in insanity defense cases. *Journal of Research in Personality, 26*, 165–182. (p. 628)

Cutler, B. L., & Penrod, S. D. (1988). Context reinstatement and eyewitness identification. In G. M. Davies & D. M. Thomson (Eds.), *Context reinstatement and eyewitness identification*. New York: Wiley. *(a)* (p. 617)

Cutler, B. L., & Penrod, S. D. (1988). Improving the reliability of eyewitness identification: Lineup construction and presentation. *Journal of Applied Psychology, 73*, 281–290. *(b)* (p. 615)

Cutler, B. L., & Penrod, S. D. (1995). Mistaken identification: The eyewitness, psychology, and the law. New York: Cambridge University Press. (p. 608)

Cutler, B. L., Penrod, S. D., & Dexter, H. R. (1989). The eyewitness, the expert psychologist and the jury. *Law and Human Behavior, 13*, 311–332. (pp. 618, 623)

Cutrona, C. E. (1986). Behavioral manifestations of social support: A microanalytic investigation. *Journal of Personality and Social Psychology, 51*, 201–208. (p. 598)

Dabbs, J. M., Jr. (1992). Testosterone measurements in social and clinical psychology. *Journal of Social and Clinical Psychology, 11*, 302–321. (p. 385)

Dabbs, J. M., Jr. (2000). Heroes, rogues, and lovers: Testosterone and behavior. New York: McGraw-Hill. (pp. 193, 385)

Dabbs, J. M., Jr., Carr, T. S., Frady, R. L., & Riad, J. K. (1995). Testosterone, crime, and misbehavior among 692 male prison inmates. *Personality and Individual Differences, 18*, 627–633. (p. 385)

Dabbs, J. M., Jr. & Janis, I. L. (1965). Why does eating while reading facilitate opinion change? An experimental inquiry. *Journal of Experimental Social Psychology, 1*, 133–144. (p. 256)

Dabbs, J. M., Jr., & Morris, R. (1990). Testosterone, social class, and antisocial behavior in a sample of 4,462 men. *Psychological Science, 1*, 209–211. (p. 382)

Dabbs, J. M., Jr., Riad, J. K., & Chance, S. E. (2001). Testosterone and ruthless homicide. *Personality and Individual Differences, 31*, 599–603. (p. 385)

Dabbs, J. M., Jr., Strong, R., & Milun, R. (1997). Exploring the mind of testosterone: A beeper study. *Journal of Research in Personality, 31*, 577–588. (p. 385)

Dallas, M. E. W., & Baron, R. S. (1985). Do psychotherapists use a confirmatory strategy during interviewing? *Journal of Social and Clinical Psychology, 3*, 106–122. (p. 571)

Damon, W. (1995). *Greater Expectations: Overcoming the Culture of Indulgence in America's Homes and Schools*. New York: Free Press. (p. 23)

Danner, D. D., Snowdon, D. A., & Friesen, W. V. (2001). Positive emotions in early life and longevity: Findings from the Nun Study. *Journal of Personality and Social Psychology, 80*, 804–813. (pp. 590–591)

Darley, J. (1996). How organizations socialize individuals into evil-doing. In D. Messick and Ann Tenbrunsel (Eds.), *Codes of conduct: Behavioral research into business ethics*. New York: Russell Sage. (p. 225)

Darley, J. M. (1995). Book review essay. *Political Psychology*. (p. 506)

Darley, J. M., & Batson, C. D. (1973). From Jerusalem to Jericho: A study of situational and dispositional variables in helping behavior. *Journal of Personality and Social Psychology, 27*, 100–108. (p. 503)

Darley, J. M., & Berscheid, E. (1967). Increased liking as a result of the anticipation of personal contact. *Human Relations, 20*, 29–40. (p. 427)

Darley, J. M., & Gross, P. H. (1983). A hypothesis-confirming bias in labelling effects. *Journal of Personality and Social Psychology, 44*, 20–33. (p. 375)

Darley, J. M., & Latané, B. (1968). Bystander intervention in emergencies: Diffusion of responsibility. *Journal of Personality and Social Psychology, 8*, 377–383. (pp. 494, 496, 497, 499–500)

Darley, J. M., Teger, A. I., & Lewis, L. D. (1973). Do groups always inhibit individuals' response to potential emergencies? *Journal of Personality and Social Psychology, 26*, 395–399. (p. 502)

Darley, S., & Cooper, J. (1972). Cognitive consequences of forced noncompliance. *Journal of Personality and Social Psychology, 24*, 321–326. (p. 283)

Darrow, C. (1933), cited by E. H. Sutherland & D. R. Cressy, *Principles of criminology*. Philadelphia: Lippincott, 1966, p. 442. (pp. 619, 628)

Darwin, C. (1859/1988). *The origin of species*. Vol. 15 of *The Works of Charles Darwin*, edited by P. H. Barrett & R. B. Freeman. New York: New York University Press. (p. 171)

Das, E. H. H. J., de Wit, J. B. F., & Stroebe, W. (2003). Fear appeals motivate acceptance of action recommendations: Evidence for a positive bias in the processing of persuasive messages. *Personality and Social Psychology Bulletin, 29*, 650–664. (p. 258)

Dashiell, J. F. (1930). An experimental analysis of some group effects. *Journal of Abnormal and Social Psychology, 25*, 190–199. (p. 287)

Dateline (2000, June 20). Dateline NBC. New York: NBC. (p. 495)

Davidson, R. J., Putnam, K. M., & Larson, C. L. (2000). Dysfunction in the neural circuitry of emotion regulation—A possible prelude to violence. *Science, 289*, 591–594. (p. 383)

Davies, M. F. (1997). Belief persistence after evidential discrediting: The impact of generated versus provided explanations on the likelihood of discredited outcomes. *Journal of Experimental Social Psychology, 33*, 561–578. (p. 102)

Davies, P. G., Spencer, S. J., Quinn, D. M., & Gerhardstein, R. (2002). Consuming images: How television commercials that elicit stereotype threat can restrain women academically and professionally. *Personality and Social Psychology Bulletin, 28*, 1615–1628. (pp. 371–372)

Davila, J., Bradbury, T. N., Cohan, C. L., & Tochluk, S. (1997). Marital functioning and depressive symptoms: Evidence for a stress generation model. *Journal of Personality and Social Psychology, 73*, 849–861. (p. 601)

Davis, B. M., & Gilbert, L. A. (1989). Effect of dispositional and situational influences on women's dominance expression in mixed-sex dyads. *Journal of Personality and Social Psychology, 57*, 294–300. (p. 186)

Davis, C. G., Lehman, D. R., Silver, R. C., Wortman, C. B., & Ellard, J. H. (1996). Self-blame following a traumatic event: The role of perceived avoidability. *Personality and Social Psychology Bulletin, 22*, 557–567. (p. 116)

Davis, C. G., Lehman, D. R., Wortman, C. B., Silver, R. C., & Thompson, S. C. (1995). The undoing of traumatic life events. *Personality and Social Psychology Bulletin, 21*, 109–124. (p. 116)

Davis, J. H., Kameda, T., Parks, C., Stasson, M., & Zimmerman, S. (1989). Some social mechanics of group decision making: The distribution of opinion, polling sequence, and implications for consensus. *Journal of Personality and Social Psychology, 57*, 1000–1012. (p. 631)

Davis, J. H., Kerr, N. L., Atkin, R. S., Holt, R., & Meek, D. (1975). The decision processes of 6- and 12-person mock juries assigned unanimous and two-thirds majority rules. *Journal of Personality and Social Psychology, 32*, 1–14. (pp. 631, 634)

Davis, J. H., Kerr, N. L., Strasser, G., Meek, D., & Holt, R. (1977). Victim consequences, sentence severity, and decision process in mock juries. *Organizational Behavior and Human Performance, 18*, 346–365. (p. 631)

Davis, J. H., Stasson, M. F., Parks, C. D., Hulbert, L., Kameda, T., Zimmerman, S. K., & Ono, K. (1993). Quantitative decisions by groups and individuals: Voting procedures and monetary awards by mock civil juries. *Journal of Experimental Social Psychology, 29*, 326–346. (p. 278)

Davis, J. L., & Rusbult, C. E. (2001). Attitude alignment in close relationships. *Journal of Personality and Social Psychology, 81*, 65–84. (p. 444)

Davis, K. E. (1985, February). Near and dear: Friendship and love compared. *Psychology Today*, pp. 22–30. (p. 458)

Davis, K. E., & Jones, E. E. (1960). Changes in interpersonal perception as a means of reducing cognitive dissonance. *Journal of Abnormal and Social Psychology, 61*, 402–410. (p. 146)

Davis, L., & Greenlees, C. (1992). Social loafing revisited: Factors that mitigate—and reverse—performance loss. Paper presented at the Southwestern Psychological Association convention. (p. 296)

Davis, M. H. (1979). The case for attributional egotism. Paper presented at the American Psychological Association convention. (p. 69)

Davis, M. H., & Franzoi, S. L. (1986). Adolescent loneliness, self-disclosure, and private self-consciousness: A longitudinal investigation. *Journal of Personality and Social Psychology, 51*, 595–608. (p. 582)

Davis, M. H., & Stephan, W. G. (1980). Attributions for exam performance. *Journal of Applied Social Psychology, 10*, 235–248. (p. 68)

Dawes, R. (1998, October). The social usefulness of self-esteem: A skeptical view. *Harvard Mental Health Letter*, pp. 4–5. (p. 64)

Dawes, R. M. (1980). Social dilemmas. *Annual Review of Psychology, 31*, 169–193. (pp. 527, 528)

Dawes, R. M. (1980). You can't systematize human judgment: Dyslexia. In R. A. Shweder (Ed.), *New directions for methodology of social and behavioral science: Fallible judgment in behavioral research*. San Francisco: Jossey-Bass. (p. 129)

Dawes, R. M. (1989, January). Resignation letter to the American Psychological Association. *APS Observer*, pp. 14–15. (p. 573)

Dawes, R. M. (1990). The potential nonfalsity of the false consensus effect. In R. M. Hogarth (Ed.), *Insights in decision making: A tribute to Hillel J. Einhorn*. Chicago: University of Chicago Press. (p. 73)

Dawes, R. M. (1991). Social dilemmas, economic self-interest, and evolutionary theory. In D. R. Brown & J. E. Keith Smith (Eds.), *Frontiers of mathematical psychology: Essays in honor of Clyde Coombs*. New York: Springer-Verlag. (p. 521)

Dawes, R. M. (1994). *House of cards: Psychology and psychotherapy built on myth*. New York: Free Press. (pp. 23, 64, 65, 527, 573–574)

Dawes, R. M., McTavish, J., & Shaklee, H. (1977). Behavior, communication, and assumptions about other people's behavior in a commons dilemma situation. *Journal of Personality and Social Psychology, 35*, 1–11. (p. 528)

Dawkins, R. (1976). *The selfish gene*. New York: Oxford University Press. (pp. 487, 488–489)

Dawson, N. V., Arkes, H. R., Siciliano, C., Blinkhorn, R., Lakshmanan, M., & Petrelli, M. (1988). Hindsight bias: An impediment to accurate probability estimation in clinicopathologic conferences. *Medical Decision Making, 8*, 259–264. (p. 20)

De Cremer, D. (2002). Charismatic leadership and cooperation in social dilemmas: A matter of transforming motives? *Journal of Applied Social Psychology, 32*, 997–1016. (p. 528)

De Houwer, J., Thomas, S., & Baeyens, F. (2001). Associative learning of likes and dislikes: A review of 25 years of research on human evaluative conditioning. *Psychological Bulletin, 127*, 853–869. (p. 450)

de Jong-Gierveld, J. (1987). Developing and testing a model of loneliness. *Journal of Personality and Social Psychology, 53*, 119–128. (p. 581)

de Vries, N. K., & Van Knippenberg, A. (1987). Biased and unbiased self-evaluations of ability: The effects of further testing. *British Journal of Social Psychology, 26*, 9–15. (p. 80)

DeAngelis, T. (1993, September). Controversial diagnosis is voted into latest DSM. *Monitor*, pp. 32–33. (p. 586)

Deaux, K., & LaFrance, M. (1998). Gender. In D. Gilbert, S. Fiske, and

G. Lindzey (Eds.), *The handbook of social psychology*, 4th edition. Hillsdale, NJ: Erlbaum. (pp. 186–187)

DeBruine, L. M. (2002). Facial resemblance enhances trust. *Proceedings of the Royal Society of London,* **269**, 1307–1312. (p. 504)

Deci, E. L., & Ryan, R. M. (1985). *Intrinsic motivation and self-determination in human behavior.* New York: Plenum. (p. 161)

Deci, E. L., & Ryan, R. M. (1987). The support of autonomy and the control of behavior. *Journal of Personality and Social Psychology,* **53**, 1024–1037. (p. 60)

Deci, E. L., & Ryan, R. M. (1991). A motivational approach to self: Integration in personality. In R. Dienstbier (Ed.) Vol. 38. Perspectives on motivation (pp. 237–288), Lincoln: University of Nebraska Press. *Nebraska Symposium on Motivation.* (pp. 159, 161)

Deci, E. L., & Ryan, R. M. (1997). Behaviorists in search of the null: Revisiting the undermining of intrinsic motivation by extrinsic rewards. Unpublished manuscript, University of Rochester. (p. 159)

Delgado, J. (1973). In M. Pines, *The brain changers.* New York: Harcourt Brace Jovanovich. (p. 140)

della Cava, M. R. (2003, April 2). Iraq gets sympathetic press around the world. *USA Today* (www.usatoday.com). (p. 246)

Dembroski, T. M., Lasater, T. M., & Ramirez, A. (1978). Communicator similarity, fear arousing communications, and compliance with health care recommendations. *Journal of Applied Social Psychology,* **8**, 254–269. (p. 254)

DePaulo, B. M., Charlton, K., Cooper, H., Lindsay, J. J., & Muhlenbruck, L. (1997). The accuracy-confidence correlation in the detection of deception. *Personality and Social Psychology Review,* **1**, 346–357. (p. 110)

Derlega, V., Metts, S., Petronio, S., & Margulis, S. T. (1993). *Self-disclosure.* Newbury Park, CA: Sage. (p. 462)

Dermer, M., & Pyszczynski, T. A. (1978). Effects of erotica upon men's loving and liking responses for women they love. *Journal of Personality and Social Psychology,* **36**, 1302–1309. (p. 454)

Dermer, M., Cohen, S. J., Jacobsen, E., & Anderson, E. A. (1979). Evaluative judgments of aspects of life as a function of vicarious exposure to hedonic extremes. *Journal of Personality and Social Psychology,* **37**, 247–260. (p. 657)

Desforges, D. M., Lord, C. G., Pugh, M. A., Sia, T. L., Scarberry, N. C., & Ratcliff, C. D. (1997). Role of group representativeness in the generalization part of the contact hypothesis. *Basic and Applied Social Psychology,* **19**, 183–204. (p. 551)

Desforges, D. M., Lord, C. G., Ramsey, S. L., Mason, J. A., Van Leeuwen, M. D., West, S. C., & Lepper, M. R. (1991). Effects of structured cooperative contact on changing negative attitudes toward stigmatized social groups. *Journal of Personality and Social Psychology,* **60**, 531–544. (p. 551)

Desmarais, S., & Curtis, J. (2001). Gender and perceived income entitlement among full-time workers: Analyses for Canadian national samples, 1984 and 1994. *Basic and Applied Social Psychology,* **23**, 157–168. (p. 531)

DeSteno, D. A., & Salovey, P. (1996). Jealousy and the characteristics of one's rival: A self-evaluation maintenance perspective. *Personality and Social Psychology Bulletin,* **22**, 920–932. (p. 64)

Detweiler, J. B., Bedell, B. T., Salovey, P., Pronin, E., & Rothman, A. J. (1999). Message framing and sunscreen use: Gain-framed messages motivate beach-goers. *Health Psychology,* **18**, 189–196. (p. 588)

Deutsch, M. (1985). *Distributive justice: A social psychological perspective.* New Haven, CT: Yale University Press. (pp. 532, 551)

Deutsch, M. (1986). Folie à deux: A psychological perspective on Soviet-American relations. In M. P. Kearns (Ed.), *Persistent patterns and emergent structures in a waving century.* New York: Praeger. (p. 533–534)

Deutsch, M. (1993). Educating for a peaceful world. *American Psychologist,* **48**, 510–517. (p. 559)

Deutsch, M. (1994). Constructive conflict resolution: Principles, training, and research. *Journal of Social Issues,* **50**, 13–32. (p. 551)

Deutsch, M. (1999). Behind the scenes. In D. G. Myers, *Social psychology*, 6th edition. New York: McGraw-Hill, 519. (p. 521)

Deutsch, M., & Collins, M. E. (1951). *Interracial housing: A psychological evaluation of a social experiment.* Minneapolis: University of Minnesota Press. (p. 539)

Deutsch, M., & Gerard, H. B. (1955). A study of normative and informational social influence upon individual judgment. *Journal of Abnormal and Social Psychology,* **51**, 629–636. (pp. 232, 234)

Deutsch, M., & Krauss, R. M. (1960). The effect of threat upon interpersonal bargaining. *Journal of Abnormal and Social Psychology,* **61**, 181–189. (p. 526)

Devenport, J. L., Stinson, V., Cutler, B. L., & Kravitz, D. A. (2002). How effective are the cross-examination and expert testimony safeguards? Jurors' perceptions of the suggestiveness and fairness of biased lineup procedures. *Journal of Applied Psychology,* **87**, 1042–1054. (pp. 617, 618)

Devine, P. G. (1989). Stereotypes and prejudice: Their automatic and controlled components. *Journal of Personality and Social Psychology,* **56**, 5–18. (p. 356)

Devine, P. G., Brodish, A. B., & Vance, S. L. (2004). Self-regulatory processes in interracial interactions: The role of internal and external motivation to respond without prejudice. In J. P. Forgas, K. D. Williams, & W. von Hippel (Eds.), *Social motivation: Conscious and unconscious processes.* New York: Cambridge University Press. (p. 357)

Devine, P. G., Evett, S. R., & Vasquez-Suson, K. A. (1996). Exploring the interpersonal dynamics of intergroup contact. In R. Sorrentino & E. T. Higgins (Eds.), *Handbook of motivation and cognition: The interpersonal content,* vol. 3. New York: Guilford. (p. 362)

Devine, P. G., Hirt, E. R., & Gehrke, E. M. (1990). Diagnostic and confirmation strategies in trait hypothesis testing. *Journal of*

Personality and Social Psychology, **58**, 952–963. (p. 571)

Devine, P. G., & Malpass, R. S. (1985). Orienting strategies in differential face recognition. *Personality and Social Psychology Bulletin*, **11**, 33–40. (p. 360)

Devine, P. G., Plant, E. A., & Buswell, B. N. (2000). Breaking the prejudice habit: Progress and obstacles. In S. Oskamp (Ed.), *Reducing prejudice and discrimination.* Mahwah, NJ: Erlbaum, 2000. (p. 356)

Devos-Comby, L., & Salovey, P. (2002). Applying persuasion strategies to alter HIV-relevant thoughts and behavior. *Review of General Psychology*, **6**, 287–304. (pp. 258, 259)

Dexter, H. R., Cutler, B. L., & Moran, G. (1992). A test of voir dire as a remedy for the prejudicial effects of pretrial publicity. *Journal of Applied Social Psychology*, **22**, 819–832. (p. 623)

Dey, E. L., Astin, A. W., & Korn, W. S. (1991). *The American freshman: Twenty-five year trends.* Los Angeles: Higher Education Research Institute, UCLA. (p. 650)

Diamond, J. (1996, December). The best ways to sell sex. *Discover*, pp. 78–86. (p. 439)

Diamond, S. S. (1993). Instructing on death: Psychologists, juries, and judges. *American Psychologist*, **48**, 423–434. (p. 627)

Dicum, J. (2003, November 11). Letter to the editor. *New York Times*, p. A20. (p. 466)

Diekman, A. B., McDonald, M., & Gardner, W. L. (2000). Love means never having to be careful: The relationship between reading romance novels and safe sex behavior. *Psychology of Women Quarterly*, **24**, 179–188. (p. 114)

Diekmann, K. A., Samuels, S. M., Ross, L., & Bazerman, M. H. (1997). Self-interest and fairness in problems of resource allocation: Allocators versus recipients. *Journal of Personality and Social Psychology*, **72**, 1061–1074. (pp. 68, 530)

Diener, E. (1976). Effects of prior destructive behavior, anonymity, and group presence on deindividuation and aggression. *Journal of Personality and Social Psychology*, **33**, 497–507. (pp. 300, 302)

Diener, E. (1979). Deindividuation, self-awareness, and disinhibition. *Journal of Personality and Social Psychology*, **37**, 1160–1171. (p. 302)

Diener, E. (1980). Deindividuation: The absence of self-awareness and self-regulation in group members. In P. Paulus (Ed.), *The psychology of group influence.* Hillsdale, NJ: Erlbaum. (p. 302)

Diener, E. (2000). Subjective well-being: The science of happiness, and some policy implications. *American Psychologist*, **55**, 34–43. (p. 651)

Diener, E., & Crandall, R. (1979). An evaluation of the Jamaican anticrime program. *Journal of Applied Social Psychology*, **9**, 135–146. (p. 419)

Diener, E., Diener, M., & Diener, C. (1995). Factors predicting the subjective well-being of nations. *Journal of Personality and Social Psychology*, **69**, 851–864. (p. 651)

Diener, E., Horwitz, J., & Emmons, R. A. (1985). Happiness of the very wealthy. *Social Indicators*, **16**, 263–274. (p. 652)

Diener, E., & Oishi, S. (2000). Money and happiness: Income and subjective well-being across nations. In E. Diener & E. M. Suh (Eds.), *Subjective well-being across cultures.* Cambridge, MA: MIT Press. (p. 652)

Diener, E., Sandvik, E., Seidlitz, L., & Diener, M. (1993). The relationship between income and subjective well-being: Relative or absolute? *Social Indicators Research*, **28**, 195–223. (p. 652)

Diener, E. & Seligman, M. E. P. (2002). Very happy people. *Psychological Science*, **13**, 81–84. (p. 654)

Diener, E., & Wallbom, M. (1976). Effects of self-awareness on antinormative behavior. *Journal of Research in Personality*, **10**, 107–111. (pp. 139, 300, 302)

Dienstbier, R. A., Roesch, S. C., Mizumoto, A., Hemenover, S. H., Lott, R. C., & Carlo, G. (1998). Effects of weapons on guilt judgments and sentencing recommendations for criminals. *Basic and Applied Social Psychology*, **20**, 93–102. (pp. 396–397)

Dill, J. C., & Anderson, C.A. (1999). Loneliness, shyness, and depression: The etiology and interrelationships of everyday problems in living. In T. Joiner and J. C. Coyne (Eds.) *The interactional nature of depression: Advances in interpersonal approaches.* Washington, DC: American Psychological Association. (pp. 581, 582)

Dillehay, R. C., & Nietzel, M. T. (1980). Constructing a science of jury behavior. In L. Wheeler (Ed.), *Review of personality and social psychology* (Vol. 1). Beverly Hills, CA: Sage Publications. (p. 637)

Dindia, K., & Allen, M. (1992). Sex differences in self-disclosure: A meta-analysis. *Psychological Bulletin*, **112**, 106–124. (pp. 182–183)

Dion, K. K. (1972). Physical attractiveness and evaluations of children's transgressions. *Journal of Personality and Social Psychology*, **24**, 207–213. (p. 434)

Dion, K. K. (1973). Young children's stereotyping of facial attractiveness. *Developmental Psychology*, **9**, 183–188. (p. 434)

Dion, K. K., & Berscheid, E. (1974). Physical attractiveness and peer perception among children. *Sociometry*, **37**, 1–12. (p. 434)

Dion, K. K., & Dion, K. L. (1985). Personality, gender, and the phenomenology of romantic love. In P. R. Shaver (Ed.), *Review of personality and social psychology*, vol. 6. Beverly Hills, CA: Sage. (p. 455)

Dion, K. K., & Dion, K. L. (1991). Psychological individualism and romantic love. *Journal of Social Behavior and Personality*, **6**, 17–33. (p. 457)

Dion, K. K., & Dion, K. L. (1993). Individualistic and collectivistic perspectives on gender and the cultural context of love and intimacy. *Journal of Social Issues*, **49**, 53–69. (p. 468)

Dion, K. K., & Dion, K. L. (1996). Cultural perspectives on romantic love. *Personal Relationships*, **3**, 5–17. (p. 457)

Dion, K. K., & Stein, S. (1978). Physical attractiveness and interpersonal influence. *Journal of Experimental Social Psychology*, **14**, 97–109. (p. 254)

Dion, K. L. (1979). Intergroup conflict and intragroup cohesiveness. In W. G. Austin, & S. Worchel (Eds.), *The social psychology of intergroup relations.* Monterey, CA: Brooks/Cole. (p. 543)

Dion, K. L. (1987). What's in a title? The Ms. stereotype and images of women's titles of address. *Psychology of Women Quarterly,* **11,** 21–36. (p. 333)

Dion, K. L. (1998). The social psychology of perceived prejudice and discrimination. Colloquium presentation, Carleton University. (p. 362)

Dion, K. L., & Cota, A. A. (1991). The Ms. stereotype: Its domain and the role of explicitness in title preference. *Psychology of Women Quarterly,* **15,** 403–410. (p. 333)

Dion, K. L., & Dion, K. K. (1988). Romantic love: Individual and cultural perspectives. In R. J. Sternberg & M. L. Barnes (Eds.), *The psychology of love.* New Haven, CT: Yale University Press. (p. 457)

Dion, K. L., & Schuller, R. A. (1991). The Ms. stereotype: Its generality and its relation to managerial and marital status stereotypes. *Canadian Journal of Behavioural Science,* **23,** 25–40. (p. 333)

Dishion, T. J., McCord, J., & Poulin, F. (1999). When interventions harm: Peer groups and problem behavior. *American Psychologist,* **54,** 755–764. (p. 306)

Ditto, P. H., Scepansky, J. A., Munro, G. D., Apanovitch, A. M., & Lockhart, L. K. (1997). Motivated sensitivity to preference-inconsistent information. Unpublished manuscript, Kent State University. (p. 88)

Dixon, B. (1986, April). Dangerous thoughts: How we think and feel can make us sick. *Science 86,* pp. 63–66. (p. 589)

Dixon, J., & Durrheim, K. (2003). Contact and the ecology of racial division: Some varieties of informal segregation. *British Journal of Social Psychology,* **42,** 1–23. (pp. 540–541)

Dohrenwend, B., Pearlin, L., Clayton, P., Hamburg, B., Dohrenwend, B. P., Riley, M., & Rose, R. (1982). Report on stress and life events. In G. R. Elliott & C. Eisdorfer (Eds.), *Stress and human health: Analysis and implications of*

research (A study by the Institute of Medicine/National Academy of Sciences). New York: Springer. (p. 598)

Dolinski, D. (2000). On inferring one's beliefs from one's attempt and consequences for subsequent compliance. *Journal of Personality and Social Psychology,* **78,** 260–272. (p. 516)

Dolinski, D., & Nawrat, R. (1998). "Fear-then-relief" procedure for producing compliance: Beware when the danger is over. *Journal of Experimental Social Psychology,* **34,** 27–50. (p. 482)

Dollard, J., Doob, L., Miller, N., Mowrer, O. H., & Sears, R. R. (1939). *Frustration and aggression.* New Haven, CT: Yale University Press. (pp. 386–387)

Dolnik, L., Case, T. I., & Williams, K. D. (2003). Stealing thunder as a courtroom tactic revisited: Processes and boundaries. *Law and Human Behavior,* **27,** 265–285. (p. 268)

Donnerstein, E. (1980). Aggressive erotica and violence against women. *Journal of Personality and Social Psychology,* **39,** 269–277. (pp. 400–401)

Donnerstein, E. (1998). Why do we have those new ratings on television. Invited address to the National Institute on the Teaching of Psychology. (pp. 403, 407)

Donnerstein, E., Linz, D., & Penrod, S. (1987). *The question of pornography.* London: Free Press. (pp. 399, 402)

Doob, A. N., & Kirshenbaum, H. M. (1973). Bias in police lineups—partial remembering. *Journal of Police Science and Administration,* **1,** 287–293. (p. 616)

Doob, A. N., & McLaughlin, D. S. (1989). Ask and you shall be given: Request size and donations to a good cause. *Journal of Applied Social Psychology,* **19,** 1049–1056. (p. 512)

Doob, A. N., & Roberts, J. (1988). Public attitudes toward sentencing in Canada. In N. Walker & M. Hough (Eds.), *Sentencing and the public.* London: Gower. (p. 114)

Doty, R. M., Peterson, B. E., & Winter, D. G. (1991). Threat and authoritarianism in the United States, 1978–1987. *Journal of Personality and Social Psychology,* **61,** 629–640. (p. 345)

Douglas, K. M., & McGarty, C. (2001). Identifiability and self-presentation: Computer-mediated communication and intergroup interaction. *British Journal of Social Psychology,* **40,** 399–416. (p. 300)

Douglass, F. (1845/1960). *Narrative of the life of Frederick Douglass, an American slave: Written by himself.* (B. Quarles, Ed.). Cambridge, MA: Harvard University Press. (p. 142)

Dovidio, J. F. (1991). The empathy-altruism hypothesis: Paradigm and promise. *Psychological Inquiry,* **2,** 126–128. (p. 492)

Dovidio, J. R., Brigham, J. C., Johnson, B. T., & Gaertner, S. L. (1996). Stereotyping, prejudice, and discrimination: Another look. In N. Macrae, M. Hewstone, & C. Stangor (Eds.), *Stereotypes and stereotyping.* New York: Guilford. (p. 334)

Dovidio, J. F., Gaertner, S. L., Anastasio, P. A., & Sanitioso, R. (1992). Cognitive and motivational bases of bias: Implications of aversive racism for attitudes toward Hispanics. In S. Knouse, P. Rosenfeld, & A. Culbertson (Eds.), *Hispanics in the workplace.* Newbury Park, CA: Sage. (p. 336)

Dovidio, J. F., Kawakami, K., & Gaertner, S. L. (2002). Implicit and explicit prejudice and interracial interactions. *Journal of Personality and Social Psychology,* **82,** 62–68. (p. 337)

Downs, A. C., & Lyons, P. M. (1991). Natural observations of the links between attractiveness and initial legal judgments. *Personality and Social Psychology Bulletin,* **17,** 541–547. (p. 620)

Drabman, R. S., & Thomas, M. H. (1974). Does media violence increase children's toleration of real-life aggression? *Developmental Psychology,* **10,** 418–421. (p. 409)

Drabman, R. S., & Thomas, M. H. (1975). Does TV violence breed indifference? *Journal of Communications,* **25**(4), 86–89. (p. 409)

Drabman, R. S., & Thomas, M. H. (1976). Does watching violence on television cause apathy? *Pediatrics,* **57,** 329–331. (p. 409)

Draguns, J. G. (1990). Normal and abnormal behavior in cross-cultural perspective: Specifying the nature of their relationship. *Nebraska Symposium on Motivation 1989, 37,* 235–277. (p. 581)

Driedger, L. (1975). In search of cultural identity factors: A comparison of ethnic students. *Canadian Review of Sociology and Anthropology, 12,* 150–161. (p. 552)

Driskell, J. E., & Mullen, B. (1990). Status, expectations, and behavior: A meta-analytic review and test of the theory. *Personality and Social Psychology Bulletin, 16,* 541–553. (p. 231)

Drolet, A. L., & Morris, M. W. (2000). Rapport in conflict resolution: Accounting for how face-to-face contact fosters mutual cooperation in mixed-motive conflicts. *Journal of Experimental Social Psychology, 36,* 26–50. (p. 526)

Druckman, D., & Bjork, R. A. (Eds.). (1994). Cooperative learning. Chapter 5 in *Learning, remembering, believing: Enhancing human performance.* Washington, DC: National Academy Press. (p. 549)

Dryer, D. C., & Horowitz, L. M. (1997). When do opposites attract? Interpersonal complementarity versus similarity. *Journal of Personality and Social Psychology, 72,* 592–603. (p. 446)

DuBois, W. E. B. (1903/1961). *The souls of black folk.* Greenwich, CT: Fawcett Books. (p. 552)

Duck, J. M., Hogg, M. A., & Terry, D. J. (1995). Me, us and them: political identification and the third-person effect in the 1993 Australian federal election. *European Journal of Social Psychology, 25,* 195–215. (p. 264)

Duffy, M. (2003, June 9). Weapons of mass disappearance. *Time,* pp. 28–33. (pp. 152, 246)

Dugger, C. W. (2001, April 22). Abortion in India spurred by sex text skew the ratio against girls. *The New York Times.* Late edition, p. 12. (p. 342)

Dunn, E. W., Wilson, T. D., & Gilbert, D. T. (2003). Location, location, location: The misprediction of satisfaction in housing lotteries. *Personality and Social Psychology Bulletin, 29,* 1421–1432. (p. 656)

Dunning, D. (1995). Trait importance and modifiability as factors influencing self-assessment and self-enhancement motives. *Personality and Social Psychology Bulletin, 21,* 1297–1306. (p. 74)

Dunning, D. (1999). A newer look: Motivated social cognition and the schematic representation of social concepts. *Psychological Inquiry, 10,* 1–11. (p. 63)

Dunning, D., Griffin, D. W., Milojkovic, J. D., & Ross, L. (1990). The overconfidence effect in social prediction. *Journal of Personality and Social Psychology, 58,* 568–581. (pp. 109–110)

Dunning, D., & Hayes, A. F. (1996). Evidence for egocentric comparison in social judgment. *Journal of Personality and Social Psychology, 71,* 213–229. (p. 42)

Dunning, D., Meyerowitz, J. A., & Holzberg, A. D. (1989). Ambiguity and self-evaluation. *Journal of Personality and Social Psychology, 57,* 1082–1090. (p. 69)

Dunning, D., Perie, M., & Story, A. L. (1991). Self-serving prototypes of social categories. *Journal of Personality and Social Psychology, 61,* 957–968. (p. 69)

Dunning, D., & Perretta, S. (2002). Automaticity and eyewitness accuracy: A 10- to 12-second rule for distinguishing accurate from inaccurate positive identifications. *Journal of Applied Psychology, 87,* 951–962. (p. 616)

Dunning, D., & Sherman, D. A. (1997). Stereotypes and tacit inference. *Journal of Personality and Social Psychology, 73,* 459–471. (pp. 374–375)

Dunning, D., & Stern, L. B. (1994). Distinguishing accurate from inaccurate eyewitness identifications via inquiries about decision processes. *Journal of Personality and Social Psychology, 67,* 818–835. (p. 616)

Dutton, D. G. (1971). Reactions of restauranteurs to blacks and whites violating restaurant dress regulations. *Canadian Journal of Behavioural Science, 3,* 298–302. (p. 505)

Dutton, D. G. (1973). Reverse discrimination: The relationship of amount of perceived discrimination toward a minority group and the behavior of majority group members. *Canadian Journal of Behavioural Science, 5,* 34–45. (p. 505)

Dutton, D. G., & Aron, A. P. (1974). Some evidence for heightened sexual attraction under conditions of high anxiety. *Journal of Personality and Social Psychology, 30,* 510–517. (pp. 51, 454)

Dutton, D. G., & Lake, R. A. (1973). Threat of own prejudice and reverse discrimination in interracial situations. *Journal of Personality and Social Psychology, 28,* 94–100. (p. 505)

Duval, S., Duval, V. H., & Neely, R. (1979). Self-focus, felt responsibility, and helping behavior. *Journal of Personality and Social Psychology, 37,* 1769–1778. (p. 511)

Duval, S., & Wicklund, R. A. (1972). *A theory of objective self-awareness.* New York: Academic Press. (p. 93)

Eagly, A. H. (1987). Sex differences in social behavior: A social-role interpretation. Hillsdale, NJ: Erlbaum. (pp. 182–183, 201)

Eagly, A. H. (1994). Are people prejudiced against women? Donald Campbell Award invited address, American Psychological Association convention. (pp. 182, 341, 342)

Eagly, A. H. (1995). The science and politics of comparing women and men. *American Psychologist, 50,* 145–158. (p. 182)

Eagly, A. H., Ashmore, R. D., Makhijani, M. G., & Longo, L. C. (1991). What is beautiful is good, but . . .: A meta-analytic review of research on the physical attractiveness stereotype. *Psychological Bulletin, 110,* 109–128. (pp. 434–435)

Eagly, A. H., & Chaiken, S. (1993). *The psychology of attitudes.* San Diego, CA: Harcourt Brace Jovanovich. (p. 248)

Eagly, A. H., & Chaiken, S. (1998). Attitude structure and function. In D. Gilbert, S. Fiske, and G. Lindzey (Eds.), *The handbook of social psychology,* 4th edition. New York: McGraw-Hill. (p. 248)

Eagly, A. H., & Crowley, M. (1986). Gender and helping behavior: A meta-analytic review of the social psychological literature. *Psychological Bulletin, 100,* 283–308. (pp. 183, 486, 507)

Eagly, A. H., Diekman, A. B., Schneider, M., & Kulesa, P. (2003). Experimental tests of an attitudinal theory of the gender gap in voting. *Personality and Social Psychology Bulletin, 29,* 1245–1258. (pp. 185–186)

Eagly, A. H., Johannesen-Schmidt, M. C., & van Engen, M. L. (2003). Transformational, transactional, and laissez-faire leadership styles: A meta-analysis comparing women and men. *Psychological Bulletin, 129,* 569–591. (pp. 185, 186)

Eagly, A. H., & Johnson, B. T. (1990). Gender and leadership style: A meta-analysis. *Psychological Bulletin, 108,* 233–256. (pp. 186, 324)

Eagly, A. H., & Karau, S. J. (2000). Few women at the top: Is prejudice a cause? Unpublished manuscript, Northwestern University. (p. 340)

Eagly, A. H., Makhijani, M. G., & Klonsky, B. G. (1992). Gender and the evaluation of leaders: A meta-analysis. *Psychological Bulletin, 111,* 3–22. (p. 186)

Eagly, A. H., Mladinic, A., & Otto, S. (1991). Are women evaluated more favorably than men? *Psychology of Women Quarterly, 15,* 203–216. (p. 341)

Eagly, A. H., & Wood, W. (1991). Explaining sex differences in social behavior: A meta-analytic perspective. *Personality and Social Psychology Bulletin, 17,* 306–315. (p. 201)

Eagly, A. H., & Wood, W. (1999). The origins of sex differences in human behavior: Evolved dispositions versus social roles. *American Psychologist, 54,* 408–423. (pp. 201–202)

Eagly, A. H., Wood, W., & Chaiken, S. (1978). Casual inferences about communicators and their effect on opinion change. *Journal of Personality and Social Psychology, 36,* 424–435. (p. 252–253)

Easterbrook, G. (2003). *The progress paradox: How life gets better while people feel worse.* New York: Random House. (p. 647)

Easterlin, R. (1995). Will raising the incomes of all increase the happiness of all? *Journal of Economic Behavior and Organization, 27,* 35–47. (p. 654)

Ebbesen, E. B., Duncan, B., & Konecni, V. J. (1975). Effects of content of verbal aggression on future verbal aggression: A field experiment. *Journal of Experimental Social Psychology, 11,* 192–204. (p. 417)

Economist (2000, June 10). America's death-penalty lottery. *The Economist.* (p. 630)

Edney, J. J. (1980). The commons problem: Alternative perspectives. *American Psychologist, 35,* 131–150. (p. 526)

Edwards, C. P. (1991). Behavioral sex differences in children of diverse cultures: The case of nurturance to infants. In M. Pereira & L. Fairbanks (Eds.), *Juveniles: Comparative socioecology.* Oxford: Oxford University Press. (p. 195)

Edwards, E., & Smith, E. E. (1996). A disconfirmation bias in the evaluation of arguments. *Journal of Personality and Social Psychology, 71,* 5–24. (p. 100)

Edwards, K. (1990). The interplay of affect and cognition in attitude formation and change. *Journal of Personality and Social Psychology, 59,* 202–216. (p. 256)

Edwards, K., & Bryan, T. S. (1997). Judgmental biases produced by instructions to disregard: The (paradoxical) case of emotional information. *Personality and Social Psychology Bulletin, 23,* 849–864. (p. 622)

Efran, M. G. (1974). The effect of physical appearance on the judgment of guilt, interpersonal attraction, and severity of recommended punishment in a simulated jury task. *Journal of Research in Personality, 8,* 45–54. (p. 619)

Egan, J. (2003, November 23). Love in the time of no time. *New York Times* (www.nytimes.com). (p. 466)

Ehrlich, P., & Feldman, M. (2003). Genes and cultures: What creates our behavioral phenome? *Current Anthropology, 44,* 87–95. (p. 193)

Eibach, R. P., Libby, L. K., & Gilovich, T. D. (2003). When change in the self is mistaken for change in the world. *Journal of Personality and Social Psychology, 84,* 917–931. (p. 73)

Einon, D. (1994). Are men more promiscuous than women? *Ethology and Sociobiology, 15,* 131–143. (p. 193)

Eisenberg, N., & Lennon, R. (1983). Sex differences in empathy and related capacities. *Psychological Bulletin, 94,* 100–131. (p. 184)

Eisenberg, N., Fabes, R. A., Schaller, M., Miller, P., Carlo, G., Poulin, R., Shea, C., & Shell, R. (1991). Personality and socialization correlates of vicarious emotional responding. *Journal of Personality and Social Psychology, 61,* 459–470. (p. 506)

Eisenberger, N. I., Lieberman, M. D., & Williams, K. D. (2003). Does rejection hurt? An fMRI study of social exclusion. *Science, 302,* 290–292. (p. 425)

Eisenberger, R., & Rhoades, L. (2001). Incremental effects of reward on creativity. *Journal of Personality and Social Psychology, 81,* 728–741. (p. 160)

Eisenberger, R., Rhoades, L., & Cameron, J. (1999). Does pay for performance increase or decrease perceived self-determination and intrinsic motivation? *Journal of Personality and Social Psychology, 77,* 1026–1040. (p. 160)

Eiser, J. R., Sutton, S. R., & Wober, M. (1979). Smoking, seat-belts, and beliefs about health. *Addictive Behaviors, 4,* 331–338. (p. 151)

Elder, G. H., Jr. (1969). Appearance and education in marriage mobility. *American Sociological Review, 34,* 519–533. (p. 434)

Eldersveld, S. J., & Dodge, R. W. (1954). Personal contact or mail propaganda? An experiment in voting turnout and attitude change. In D. Katz, D. Cartwright, S. Eldersveld, & A. M. Lee (Eds.), *Public opinion and propaganda.* New York: Dryden Press. (p. 265)

Ellemers, N., Van Rijswijk, W., Roefs, M., & Simons, C. (1997). Bias in intergroup perceptions: Balancing group identity with social reality. *Personality and Social Psychology Bulletin, 23,* 186–198. (p. 352)

Elliott, L. (1989, June). Legend of the four chaplains. *Reader's Digest,* pp. 66–70. (p. 507)

Ellis, B. J., & Symons, D. (1990). Sex difference in sexual fantasy: An evolutionary psychological approach. *Journal of Sex Research, 27,* 490–521. (p. 189)

Ellis, H. D. (1981). Theoretical aspects of face recognition. In G. H. Davies, H. D. Ellis, & J. Shepherd (Eds.), *Perceiving and remembering faces.* London: Academic Press. (p. 359)

Ellison, P. A., Govern, J. M., Petri, H. L., & Figler, M. H. (1995). Anonymity and aggressive driving behavior: A field study. *Journal of Social Behavior and Personality, 10,* 265–272. (p. 300)

Ellsworth, P. (1985, July). Juries on trial. *Psychology Today,* pp. 44–46. (p. 629)

Ellsworth, P. (1989, March 6). Supreme Court ignores social science research on capital punishment. Quoted by *Behavior Today,* pp. 7–8. (p. 629)

Ellsworth, P. C., & Mauro, R. (1998). Psychology and law. In D. Gilbert, S. T. Fiske, & G. Lindzey (Eds.), *Handbook of social psychology,* 4th ed. New York: McGraw-Hill. (pp. 628, 634)

Ellyson, S. L., Dovidio, J. F., & Brown, C. E. (1991). The look of power: Gender differences and similarities in visual dominance behavior. In C. Ridgeway (Ed.), *Gender and interaction: The role of microstructures in inequality.* New York: Springer-Verlag. (p. 186)

Elms, A. C. (1995). Obedience in retrospect. *Journal of Social Issues, 51,* 21–31. (p. 218)

Elwork, A., Sales, B. D., & Alfini, J. J. (1982). *Making jury instructions understandable.* Charlottesville, VA: The Michie Co. (p. 626)

Emmons, R. A., Larsen, R. J., Levine, S., & Diener, E. (1983). Factors predicting satisfaction judgments: A comparative examination. Paper presented at the Midwestern Psychological Association. (p. 600)

Emswiller, T., Deaux, K., & Willits, J. E. (1971). Similarity, sex, and requests for small favors. *Journal of Applied Social Psychology, 1,* 284–291. (p. 504)

Eng, P. M., Kawachi, I., Fitzmaurice, G., & Rimm, E. B. (2001). Effects of marital transitions on changes in dietary and other health behaviors in men. Paper presented to the American Psychosomatic Society meeting. (p. 598)

Engs, R., & Hanson, D. J. (1989). Reactance theory: A test with collegiate drinking. *Psychological Reports, 64,* 1083–1086. (p. 239)

Ennis, B. J., & Verrilli, D. B., Jr. (1989). Motion for leave to file brief amicus curiae and brief of Society for the Scientific Study of Religion, American Sociological Association, and others. U.S. Supreme Court Case No. 88–1600, Holy Spirit Association for the Unification of World Christianity, *et al.,* v. David Molko and Tracy Leal. On petition for write of certiorari to the Supreme Court of California. Washington, DC: Jenner & Block, 21 Dupont Circle NW. (p. 276)

Ennis, R., & Zanna, M. P. (1991). Hockey assault: Constitutive versus normative violations. Paper presented at the Canadian Psychological Association convention. (p. 390)

Enzle, M. E., & Hawkins, W. L. (1992). A priori actor negligence mediates a posteriori outcome. *Journal of Experimental Social Psychology, 28*(2), 169–185. (p. 624)

Epley, N., & Dunning, D. (2000). Feeling 'holier than thou': Are self-serving assessments produced by errors in self- or other prediction? *Journal of Personality and Social Psychology 79,* 861–875. (p. 53)

Epley, N., & Huff, C. (1998). Suspicion, affective response, and educational benefit as a result of deception in psychology research. *Personality and Social Psychology Bulletin, 24,* 759–768. (p. 32)

Epstein, S. (1980). The stability of behavior: II. Implications for psychological research. *American Psychologist, 35,* 790–806. (p. 236)

Epstein, S., & Feist, G. J. (1988). Relation between self- and other-acceptance and its moderation by identification. *Journal of Personality and Social Psychology, 54,* 309–315. (p. 66)

Erickson, B., Holmes, J. G., Frey, R., Walker, L., & Thibaut, J. (1974). Functions of a third party in the resolution of conflict: The role of a judge in pretrial conferences. *Journal of Personality and Social Psychology, 30,* 296–306. (pp. 556–557)

Erickson, B., Lind, E. A. Johnson, B. C., & O'Barr, W. M. (1978). Speech style and impression formation in a court setting: The effects of powerful and powerless speech. *Journal of Experimental Social Psychology, 14,* 266–279. (p. 252)

Erikson, E. H. (1963). *Childhood and society.* New York: Norton. (p. 460)

Ernst, J. M., & Heesacker, M. (1993). Application of the elaboration likelihood model of attitude change to assertion training. *Journal of Counseling Psychology, 40,* 37–45. (p. 596)

Eron, L. D. (1987). The development of aggressive behavior from the perspective of a developing behaviorism. *American Psychologist, 42,* 425–442. (p. 404)

Eron, L. D., & Huesmann, L. R. (1980). Adolescent aggression and television. *Annals of the New York Academy of Sciences, 347,* 319–331. (p. 405)

Eron, L. D., & Huesmann, L. R. (1984). The control of aggressive behavior by changes in attitudes, values, and the conditions of learning. In R. J. Blanchard & C. Blanchard (Eds.), *Advances in the study of aggression,* vol. 1. Orlando, FL: Academic Press. (pp. 405, 418–419)

Eron, L. D., & Huesmann, L. R. (1985). The role of television in the development of prosocial and antisocial behavior. In D. Olweus, M. Radke-Yarrow, and J. Block (Eds.), *Development of antisocial and prosocial behavior.* Orlando, FL: Academic Press. (p. 405)

Esser, J. K. (1998, February–March). Alive and well after 25 years. A review of groupthink research. *Organizational Behavior and Human Decision Processes, 73,* 116–141. (p. 315)

Esser, J. K., & Lindoerfer, J. S. (1989). Groupthink and the space shuttle Challenger accident: Toward a quantitative case analysis. *Journal of Behavioral Decision Making, 2,* 167–177. (p. 316)

Esses, V. M., Dovidio, J. F., Danso, H. A., Jackson, L. M., & Semenya, A. (2004). Historical and modern perspectives on group competition. In C. S. Crandall & M. Schaller (Eds.), *The social psychology of prejudice: Historical perspectives.* Seattle, WA: Lewinian Press. (p. 530)

Esses, V. M., Haddock, G., & Zanna, M. P. (1993a). Values, stereotypes, and emotions as determinants of intergroup attitudes. In D. Mackie & D. Hamilton (Eds.), *Affect, cognition and stereotyping: Interactive processes in intergroup perception.* San Diego, CA: Academic Press. (p. 336)

Esses, V. M., Haddock, G., & Zanna, M. P. (1993b). The role of mood in the expression of intergroup stereotypes. In M. P. Zanna & J. M. Olson (Eds.), *The psychology of prejudice: The Ontario symposium,* vol. 7. Hillsdale, NJ: Erlbaum. (p. 358)

Esses, V. M., Jackson, L. M., & Armstrong, T. L. (1998). Intergroup competition and attitudes toward immigrants and immigration: An instrumental model of group conflict. *Journal of Social Issues,* 54, 699–724. (p. 350)

Esses, V. M., & Webster, C. D. (1988). Physical attractiveness, dangerousness, and the Canadian criminal code. *Journal of Applied Social Psychology,* 18, 1017–1031. (pp. 619–620)

Etaugh, C. E., Bridges, J. S., Cummings-Hill, M., & Cohen, J. (1999). "Names can never hurt me": The effects of surname use on perceptions of married women. *Psychology of Women Quarterly,* 23, 819–823. (p. 333)

Etzioni, A. (1967). The Kennedy experiment. *The Western Political Quarterly,* 20, 361–380. (p. 560)

Etzioni, A. (1972, June 3). Human beings are not very easy to change after all. *Saturday Review,* 45–47. (p. 136)

Etzioni, A. (1991, May–June). The community in an age of individualism (interview). *The Futurist,* pp. 35–39. (p. 561)

Etzioni, A. (1993). *The spirit of community.* New York: Crown. (p. 242)

Etzioni, A. (1999). The monochrome society. *The Public Interest,* 137 (Fall), 42–55. (p. 335)

Evans, G. W. (1979). Behavioral and physiological consequences of crowding in humans. *Journal of Applied Social Psychology,* 9, 27–46. (pp. 289–290)

Evans, G. W., Lepore, S. J., & Allen, K. M. (2000). Cross-cultural differences in tolerance for crowding: Fact or fiction? *Journal of Personality and Social Psychology,* 79, 204–210. (p. 289)

Evans, G. W., Lepore, S. J., & Schroeder, A. (1996). The role of interior design elements in human responses to crowding. *Journal of Personality and Social Psychology,* 70, 41–46. (p. 289)

Evans, R. I., Smith, C. K., & Raines, B. E. (1984). Deterring cigarette smoking in adolescents: A psycho-social-behavioral analysis of an intervention strategy. In A. Baum, J. Singer, & S. Taylor (Eds.), *Handbook of psychology and health: Social psychological aspects of health,* vol. 4, Hillsdale, NJ: Erlbaum. (p. 280)

Exline, J. J., & Lobel, M. (1999). The perils of outperformance: Sensitivity about being the target of a threatening upward comparison. *Psychological Bulletin,* 125, 307–337. (p. 78)

Fabrigar, L. R., & Petty, R. E. (1999). The role of the affective and cognitive bases of attitudes in susceptibility to affectively and cognitively based persuasion. *Personality and Social Psychology Bulletin,* 25, 363–381. (p. 256)

Fairchild, H. H., & Cowan, G. (1997). The O. J. Simpson trial: Challenges to science and society. *Journal of Social Issues,* 53, 583–591. (p. 621)

Falbo, T., Poston, D. L., Jr., Triscari, R. S., & Zhang, X. (1997). Self-enhancing illusions among Chinese schoolchildren. *Journal of Cross-Cultural Psychology,* 28, 172–191. (p. 80)

Fallshore, M., & Schooler, J. W. (1995). Verbal vulnerability of perceptual expertise. *Journal of Experimental Psychology: Learning, Memory, and Cognition,* 21, 1608–1623. (p. 616)

Farquhar, J. W., Maccoby, N., Wood, P. D., Alexander, J. K., Breitrose, H., Brown, B. W., Jr., Haskell, W. L., McAlister, A. L., Meyer, A. J., Nash, J. D., & Stern, M. P. (1977, June 4). Community education for cardiovascular health. *Lancet,* 1192–1195. (p. 265)

Farwell, L., & Weiner, B. (2000). Bleeding hearts and the heartless: Popular perceptions of liberal and conservative ideologies. *Personality and Social Psychology Bulletin,* 26, 845–852. (p. 95)

Faulkner, S. L., & Williams, K. D. (1996). A study of social loafing in industry. Paper presented to the Midwestern Psychological Association convention. (p. 295)

Faust, D., & Ziskin, J. (1988). The expert witness in psychology and psychiatry. *Science,* 241, 31–35. (p. 572)

Fay, N., Garrod, S., & Carletta, J. (2000). Group discussion as interactive dialogue or as serial monologue: The influence of group size. *Psychological Science,* 11, 481–486. (p. 634)

Fazio, R. (1987). Self-perception theory: A current perspective. In M. P. Zanna, J. M. Olson, & C. P. Herman (Eds.), *Social influence: The Ontario symposium,* vol. 5. Hillsdale, NJ: Erlbaum. (p. 163)

Fazio, R. H., Effrein, E. A., & Falender, V. J. (1981). Self-perceptions following social interaction. *Journal of Personality and Social Psychology,* 41, 232–242. (p. 571)

Fazio, R. H., Jackson, J. R., Dunton, B. C., & Williams, C. J. (1995). Variability in automatic activation as an unobtrusive measure of racial attitudes: A bona fide pipeline? *Journal of Personality and Social Psychology,* 69, 1013–1027. (p. 337)

Fazio, R. H., Zanna, M. P., & Cooper, J. (1977). Dissonance versus self-perception: An integrative view of each theory's proper domain of application. *Journal of Experimental Social Psychology,* 13, 464–479. (p. 163)

Fazio, R. H., Zanna, M. P., & Cooper, J. (1979). On the relationship of data to theory: A reply to Ronis and Greenwald. *Journal of Experimental Social Psychology,* 15, 70–76. (p. 163)

FBI (2001). *Uniform crime reports for the United States.* Washington, DC: Federal Bureau of Investigation. (p. 187)

FBI (2003). *Hate Crime Statistics, 2002.* www.fbi.gov/ucr/ucr.htm (p. 335)

Feather, N. T. (1983). Causal attributions for good and bad outcomes in achievement and affiliation situations. *Australian Journal of Psychology,* 35, 37–48. *(b)* (p. 80)

Feeney, J., Peterson, C., & Noller, P. (1994). Equity and marital satisfaction over the family life cycle. *Personality Relationships,* 1, 83–99. (p. 462)

Feeney, J. A. (1996). Attachment, caregiving, and marital satisfaction. *Personal Relationships, 3*, 401–416. (p. 459)

Feeney, J. A., & Noller, P. (1990). Attachment style as a predictor of adult romantic relationships. *Journal of Personality and Social Psychology, 58*, 281–291. (p. 459)

Feierabend, I., & Feierabend, R. (1968, May). Conflict, crisis, and collision: A study of international stability. *Psychology Today*, pp. 26–32, 69–70. (p. 388)

Feierabend, I., & Feierabend, R. (1972). Systemic conditions of political aggression: An application of frustration-aggression theory. In I. K. Feierabend, R. L. Feierabend, & T. R. Gurr (Eds.), *Anger, violence, and politics: Theories and research*. Englewood Cliffs, NJ: Prentice Hall. (p. 388)

Fein, S., & Hilton, J. L. (1992). Attitudes toward groups and behavioral intentions toward individual group members: The impact of nondiagnostic information. *Journal of Experimental Social Psychology, 28*, 101–124. (p. 374)

Fein, S., & Spencer, S. J. (1997). Prejudice as self-image maintenance: Affirming the self through derogating others. *Journal of Personality and Social Psychology, 73*, 31–44. (p. 356)

Feingold, A. (1988). Matching for attractiveness in romantic partners and same-sex friends: A meta-analysis and theoretical critique. *Psychological Bulletin, 104*, 226–235. (p. 433)

Feingold, A. (1990). Gender differences in effects of physical attractiveness on romantic attraction: A comparison across five research paradigms. *Journal of Personality and Social Psychology, 59*, 981–993. (p. 432)

Feingold, A. (1991). Sex differences in the effects of similarity and physical attractiveness on opposite-sex attraction. *Basic and Applied Social Psychology, 12*, 357–367. (p. 432)

Feingold, A. (1992). Gender differences in mate selection preferences: A test of the parental investment model. *Psychological Bulletin, 112*, 125–139. (p. 191–192)

Feingold, A. (1992). Good-looking people are not what we think.

Psychological Bulletin, 111, 304–341. (pp. 435, 436)

Feingold, A., & Mazzella, R. (1998). Gender differences in body image are increasing. *Psychological Science, 9*, 190–195. (p. 435)

Feldman, R. S., & Prohaska, T. (1979). The student as Pygmalion: Effect of student expectation on the teacher. *Journal of Educational Psychology, 71*, 485–493. (p. 123)

Feldman, R. S., & Theiss, A. J. (1982). The teacher and student as Pygmalions: Joint effects of teacher and student expectations. *Journal of Educational Psychology, 74*, 217–223. (p. 123)

Felson, R. B. (1984). The effect of self-appraisals of ability on academic performance. *Journal of Personality and Social Psychology, 47*, 944–952. (p. 44)

Felson, R. B. (2000). A social psychological approach to interpersonal aggression. In V. B. Van Hasselt & M. Hersen (Eds.), *Aggression and violence: An introductory text*. Boston: Allyn & Bacon. (p. 382)

Fenigstein, A. (1984). Self-consciousness and the overperception of self as a target. *Journal of Personality and Social Psychology, 47*, 860–870. (pp. 42, 584)

Fenigstein, A., & Carver, C. S. (1978). Self-focusing effects of heartbeat feedback. *Journal of Personality and Social Psychology, 36*, 1241–1250. (p. 93)

Fenigstein, A., & Vanable, P. A. (1992). Paranoia and self-consciousness. *Journal of Personality and Social Psychology, 62*, 129–138. (p. 584)

Fergusson, D. M., Horwood, L. J., & Shannon, F. T. (1984). A proportional hazards model of family breakdown. *Journal of Marriage and the Family, 46*, 539–549. (pp. 468–469)

Fernandez-Collado, C., & Greenberg, B. S., with Korzenny, F., & Atkin, C. K. (1978). Sexual intimacy and drug use in TV series. *Journal of Communication, 28*(3), 30–37. (p. 408)

Feshbach, N. D. (1980). The child as "psychologist" and "economist": Two curricula. Paper presented at the American Psychological Association convention. (p. 282)

Feshbach, S. (1980). Television advertising and children: Policy issues

and alternatives. Paper presented at the American Psychological Association convention. (p. 281)

Festinger, L. (1954). A theory of social comparison processes. *Human Relations, 7*, 117–140. (pp. 44, 309)

Festinger, L. (1957). *A theory of cognitive dissonance*. Stanford, CA: Stanford University Press. (p. 151)

Festinger, L. (1987). Reflections on cognitive dissonance theory: 30 years later. Paper presented at the American Psychological Association convention. (p. 317)

Festinger, L., & Carlsmith, J. M. (1959). Cognitive consequences of forced compliance. *Journal of Abnormal and Social Psychology, 58*, 203–210. (pp. 152–153, 154)

Festinger, L., & Maccoby, N. (1964). On resistance to persuasive communications. *Journal of Abnormal and Social Psychology, 68*, 359–366. (p. 269)

Festinger, L., Pepitone, A., & Newcomb, T. (1952). Some consequences of deindividuation in a group. *Journal of Abnormal and Social Psychology, 47*, 382–389. (p. 298)

Feynman, R. (1967). *The character of physical law*. Cambridge, MA: MIT Press. (pp. 161–162)

Fichter, J. (1968). *America's forgotten priests: What are they saying?* New York: Harper. (pp. 346–347)

Fiebert, M. S. (1990). Men, women and housework: The Roshomon effect. *Men's Studies Review, 8*, 6. (p. 67)

Fiedler, F. E. (1987, September). When to lead, when to stand back. *Psychology Today*, pp. 26–27. (p. 324)

Fiedler, K., Semin, G. R., & Koppetsch, C. (1991). Language use and attributional biases in close personal relationships. *Personality and Social Psychology Bulletin, 17*, 147–155. (p. 90)

Fincham, F. D., & Jaspars, J. M. (1980). Attribution of responsibility: From man the scientist to man as lawyer. In L. Berkowitz (Ed.), *Advances in experimental social psychology* (Vol. 13). New York: Academic Press. (p. 91)

Findley, M. J., & Cooper, H. M. (1983). Locus of control and academic achievement: A literature review. *Journal of Personality and Social Psychology*, **44**, 419–427. (p. 59)

Fineberg, H. V. (1988). Education to prevent AIDS: Prospects and obstacles. *Science, ***239**, 592–596. (p. 258)

Fischer, G. J. (1997). Gender effects on individual verdicts and on mock jury verdicts in a simulated acquaintance rape trial. *Sex Roles*, **36**, 491–501. (p. 621)

Fischhoff, B. (1982). Debiasing. In D. Kahneman, P. Slovic, & A. Tversky (Eds.), *Judgment under uncertainty: Heuristics and biases.* New York: Cambridge University Press. (p. 112)

Fischhoff, B., & Bar-Hillel, M. (1984). Diagnosticity and the base rate effect. *Memory and Cognition*, **12**, 402–410. (p. 113)

Fishbein, D., & Thelen, M. H. (1981). Husband-wife similarity and marital satisfaction: A different approach. Paper presented at the Midwestern Psychological Association convention. *(a)* (p. 446)

Fishbein, D., & Thelen, M. H. (1981). Psychological factors in mate selection and marital satisfaction: A review (Ms. 2374). *Catalog of Selected Documents in Psychology*, **11**, 84. *(b)* (p. 446)

Fishbein, M., & Ajzen, I. (1974). Attitudes toward objects as predictive of single and multiple behavioral criteria. *Psychological Review*, **81**, 59–74. (p. 137)

Fisher, H. (1994, April). The nature of romantic love. *Journal of NIH Research*, pp. 59–64. (p. 456)

Fisher, G. H. (1968). Ambiguity of form: Old and new. *Perception and Psychophysics*, **4**, 189–192. (p. 611)

Fisher, R. J. (1994). Generic principles for resolving intergroup conflict. *Journal of Social Issues*, **50**, 47–66. (p. 557)

Fisher, R. P., Geiselman, R. E., & Amador, M. (1989). Field test of the cognitive interview: Enhancing the recollection of actual victims and witnesses of crime. *Journal of Applied Psychology*, **74**, 722–727. (pp. 615–616)

Fisher, R. P., Geiselman, R. E., & Raymond, D. S. (1987). Critical analysis of police interview techniques. *Journal of Police Science and Administration*, **15**, 177–185. (p. 615)

Fisher, R. P., McCauley, M. R., & Geiselman, R. E. (1994). Improving eyewitness testimony with the Cognitive Interview. In D. F. Ross, J. D. Read, & M. P. Toglia (Eds.), *Adult eyewitness testimony: Current trends and developments*. Cambridge, England: Cambridge University Press. (pp. 615–616)

Fiske, A. P., Kitayama, S., Markus, H. R., & Nisbett, R. E. (1998). The cultural matrix of social psychology. In D. Gilbert, S. Fiske, and G. Lindzey (Eds.), *The handbook of social psychology*, 4th edition. Hillsdale, NJ: Erlbaum. (p. 172)

Fiske, S. T. (1989). Interdependence and stereotyping: From the laboratory to the Supreme Court (and back). Invited address, American Psychological Association convention. (p. 337)

Fiske, S. T. (1992). Thinking is for doing: Portraits of social cognition from Daguerrotype to Laserphoto. *Journal of Personality and Social Psychology*, **63**, 877–889. (pp. 129, 171)

Fiske, S. T. (1993). Controlling other people: The impact of power on stereotyping. *American Psychologist*, **48**, 621–628. (p. 359)

Fiske, S. T. (1999). Behind the scenes. In D. G. Myers, *Social psychology*, 6th edition. New York: McGraw-Hill. (p. 377)

Fiske, S. T. (2002, June). Envy, contempt, pity, and pride: Dangerous intergroup emotions on September 11th. Talk given at the APS symposium "Psychological Science perspectives on September 11th." (p. 332)

Fiske, S. T., Bersoff, D. N., Borgida, E., Deaux, K., & Heilman, M. E. (1991). Social science research on trial: The use of sex stereotyping research in *Price Waterhouse v. Hopkins*. *American Psychologist*, **46**, 1049–1060. (p. 376)

Fiske, S. T., Xu, J., Cuddy, A. C., & Glick, P. (1999). (Dis)respecting versus (Dis)liking: Status and interdependence predict ambivalent stereotypes of competence and warmth. *Journal of Social Issues*, **55**, 473–489. (p. 344)

Fitzpatrick, A. R., & Eagly, A. H. (1981). Anticipatory belief polarization as a function of the expertise of a discussion partner. *Personality and Social Psychology Bulletin*, **1**, 636–642. (p. 309)

Flay, B. R., Ryan, K. B., Best, J. A., Brown, K. S., Kersell, M. W., d'Avernas, J. R., & Zanna, M. P. (1985). Are social-psychological smoking prevention programs effective? The Waterloo study. *Journal of Behavioral Medicine*, **8**, 37–59. (p. 280)

Fleming, M. A., Wegener, D. T., & Petty, R. E. (1999). Procedural and legal motivations to correct for perceived judicial biases. *Journal of Experimental Social Psychology*, **35**, 186–203. (p. 622)

Fletcher, G. J. O., Danilovics, P., Fernandez, G., Peterson, D., & Reeder, G. D. (1986). Attributional complexity: An individual differences measure. *Journal of Personality and Social Psychology*, **51**, 875–884. (p. 98)

Fletcher, G. J. O., Fincham, F. D., Cramer, L., & Heron, N. (1987). The role of attributions in the development of dating relationships. *Journal of Personality and Social Psychology*, **53**, 481–489. (p. 461)

Fletcher, G. J. O., Simpson, J. A., Thomas, G., & Giles, L. (1999). Ideals in intimate relationships. *Journal of Personality and Social Psychology*, **76**, 72–89. (p. 451)

Fletcher, G. J. O., Tither, J. M., O'Loughlin, C., Friesen, M., & Overall, N. (2003). Warm and homely or cold and beautiful? Sex differences in trading off traits in mate selection. Paper presented to the Society for Personality and Social Psychology meeting, Los Angeles. (p. 432)

Fletcher, G. J. O., & Ward, C. (1989). Attribution theory and processes: A cross-cultural perspective. In M. H. Bond (Ed.), *The cross-cultural challenge to social psychology*. Newbury Park, CA: Sage. (p. 365)

Foa, U. G., & Foa, E. B. (1975). *Resource theory of social exchange*. Morristown, NJ: General Learning Press. (p. 477)

Fogelman, E. (1994). *Conscience and courage: Rescuers of Jews during the Holocaust*. New York: Doubleday Anchor. (p. 512)

Foley, L. A. (1976). Personality and situational influences on changes in prejudice: A replication of Cook's railroad game in a prison setting. *Journal of Personality and Social Psychology, 34,* 846–856. (p. 540)

Follett, M. P. (1940). Constructive conflict. In H. C. Metcalf & L. Urwick (Eds.), *Dynamic administration: The collected papers of Mary Parker Follett.* New York: Harper. (p. 554)

Ford, T. E. (1997). Effects of stereotypical television portrayals of African-Americans on person perception. *Social Psychology Quarterly, 60,* 266–278. (p. 349)

Forgas, J. P. (1994). The role of emotion in social judgments: An introductory review and an Affect Infusion Model (AIM). *European Journal of Social Psychology, 24,* 1–24. (p. 120)

Forgas, J. P. (1995). Mood and judgment: The affect infusion model (AIM). *Psychological Bulletin, 117,* 39–66. (p. 120)

Forgas, J. P. (1999). Behind the scenes. In D. G. Myers, *Social psychology,* 6th edition. New York: McGraw-Hill. (p. 119)

Forgas, J. P., Bower, G. H., & Krantz, S. E. (1984). The influence of mood on perceptions of social interactions. *Journal of Experimental Social Psychology, 20,* 497–513. (p. 120)

Forgas, J. P., & Moylan, S. (1987). After the movies: Transient mood and social judgments. *Personality and Social Psychology Bulletin, 13,* 467–477. (p. 119)

Form, W. H., & Nosow, S. (1958). *Community in disaster.* New York: Harper. (p. 488)

Forsyth, D. R., & Leary, M. R. (1997). Achieving the goals of the scientist-practitioner model: The seven interfaces of social and counseling psychology. *The Counseling Psychologist, 25,* 180–200. (p. 591)

Foss, R. D. (1978). The role of social influence in blood donation. Paper presented at the American Psychological Association convention. (p. 510)

Foster, C. A., Witcher, B. S., Campbell, W. K., & Green, J. D. (1998). Arousal and attraction: Evidence for automatic and controlled processes. *Journal of Personality and Social Psychology, 74,* 86–101. (p. 454)

Frank, J. D. (1974). *Persuasion and healing: A comparative study of psychotherapy.* New York: Schocken. (p. 277)

Frank, J. D. (1982). Therapeutic components shared by all psychotherapies. In J. H. Harvey & M. M. Parks (Eds.), *The master lecture series: Vol. 1. Psychotherapy research and behavior change.* Washington, DC: American Psychological Association. (p. 277)

Frank, M. G., & Gilovich, T. (1989). Effect of memory perspective on retrospective causal attributions. *Journal of Personality and Social Psychology, 57,* 399–403. (p. 92)

Frank, R. (1999). *Luxury fever: Why money fails to satisfy in an era of excess.* New York: The Free Press. (pp. 350, 647–648)

Frank, R. H. (1996). The empty wealth of nations. Unpublished manuscript, Johnson Graduate School of Management, Cornell University. (p. 657)

Frankel, A., & Snyder, M. L. (1987). Egotism among the depressed: When self-protection becomes self-handicapping. Paper presented at the American Psychological Association convention. (p. 79)

Franklin, B. J. (1974). Victim characteristics and helping behavior in a rural southern setting. *Journal of Social Psychology, 93,* 93–100. (p. 505)

Frasure-Smith, N., Lesperance, F., Juneau, M., Talajic, M., & Bourassa, M. G. (1999). Gender, depression, and one-year prognosis after myocardial infarction. *Psychosomatic Medicine, 61,* 26–37. (p. 588)

Frasure-Smith, N., Lesperance, F., & Talajic, M. (1995). The impact of negative emotions on prognosis following myocardial infarction: Is it more than depression? *Health Psychology, 14,* 388–398. (p. 588)

Freedman, J. L., & Fraser, S. C. (1966). Compliance without pressure: The foot-in-the-door technique. *Journal of Personality and Social Psychology, 4,* 195–202. (p. 144)

Freedman, J. L., & Perlick, D. (1979). Crowding, contagion, and laughter. *Journal of Experimental Social Psychology, 15,* 295–303. (p. 289)

Freedman, J. L., & Sears, D. O. (1965). Warning, distraction, and resistance to influence. *Journal of Personality and Social Psychology, 1,* 262–266. (p. 268)

Freedman, J. S. (1965). Long-term behavioral effects of cognitive dissonance. *Journal of Experimental Social Psychology, 1,* 145–155. (p. 147)

Freeh, L. (1993, September 1). Inaugural address as FBI director. (p. 420)

Freeman, M. A. (1997). Demographic correlates of individualism and collectivism: A study of social values in Sri Lanka. *Journal of Cross-Cultural Psychology, 28,* 321–341. (p. 46)

French, J. R. P. (1968). The conceptualization and the measurement of mental health in terms of self-identity theory. In S. B. Sells (Ed.), The definition and measurement of mental health. Washington, DC: Department of Health, Education, and Welfare. (Cited by M. Rosenberg, 1979, *Conceiving the self.* New York: Basic Books.) (p. 70)

Friedman, H. S., & DiMatteo, M. R. (1989). *Health psychology.* Englewood Cliffs, NJ: Prentice-Hall. (p. 585)

Friedman, H. S., Riggio, R. E., & Casella, D. F. (1988). Nonverbal skill, personal charisma, and initial attraction. *Personality and Social Psychology Bulletin, 14,* 203–211. (p. 445)

Friedman, T. L. (2003, April 9). Hold your applause. *New York Times* (www.nytimes.com). (p. 387)

Friedman, T. L. (2003, June 4). Because we could. *New York Times* (www.nytimes.com). (p. 246)

Friedrich, J. (1996). On seeing oneself as less self-serving than others: The ultimate self-serving bias? *Teaching of Psychology, 23,* 107–109. (pp. 76–77)

Friedrich, L. K., & Stein, A. H. (1973). Aggressive and prosocial television programs and the natural behavior of preschool children. *Monographs of the Society of Research in Child Development, 38* (4, Serial No. 151). (p. 514)

Friedrich, L. K., & Stein, A. H. (1975). Prosocial television and young children: The effects of verbal labeling and role playing on learning and behavior. *Child Development, 46,* 27–38. (p. 514)

Frieze, I. H., Olson, J. E., & Russell, J. (1991). Attractiveness and income for men and women in management. *Journal of Applied Social Psychology*, **21**, 1039–1057. (p. 436)

Froming, W. J., Walker, G. R., & Lopyan, K. J. (1982). Public and private self-awareness: When personal attitudes conflict with societal expectations. *Journal of Experimental Social Psychology*, **18**, 476–487. (p. 139)

FTC (2003, June 12). Federal Trade Commission cigarette report for 2001 (www.ftc.gov/opa/2003/06/2001cigrpt.htm). (p. 281)

Fuller, S. R., & Aldag, R. J. (1998). Organizational Tonypandy: Lessons from a quarter century of the groupthink phenomenon. *Organizational Behavior and Human Decision Processes*, **73**, 163–185. (p. 315)

Fultz, J., Batson, C. D., Fortenbach, V. A., McCarthy, P. M., & Varney, L. L. (1986). Social evaluation and the empathy-altruism hypothesis. *Journal of Personality and Social Psychology*, **50**, 761–769. (p. 492)

Funder, D. C. (1987). Errors and mistakes: Evaluating the accuracy of social judgment. *Psychological Bulletin*, **101**, 75–90. (p. 127)

Furnham, A. (1982). Explanations for unemployment in Britain. *European Journal of Social Psychology*, **12**, 335–352. (p. 96)

Furnham, A., & Gunter. B. (1984). Just world beliefs and attitudes towards the poor. *British Journal of Social Psychology*, **23**, 265–269. (p. 367)

Gabrenya, W. K., Jr., Wang, Y.-E., & Latané, B. (1985). Social loafing on an optimizing task: Cross-cultural differences among Chinese and Americans. *Journal of Cross-Cultural Psychology*, **16**, 223–242. (p. 297)

Gabriel, S., & Gardner, W. L. (1999). Are there "his" and "hers" types of interdependence? The implications of gender differences in collective versus relational interdependence for affect, behavior, and cognition. *Journal of Personality and Social Psychology*, **77**, 642–655. (p. 182)

Gaebelein, J. W., & Mander, A. (1978). Consequences for targets of aggression as a function of aggressor and instigator roles: Three experiments. *Personality and Social Psychology Bulletin*, **4**, 465–468. (p. 413)

Gaertner, L., Sedikides, C., & Graetz, K. (1999). In search of self-definition: Motivational primacy of the individual self, motivational primacy of the collective self, or contextual primacy? *Journal of Personality and Social Psychology*, **76**, 5–18. (p. 49)

Gaertner, S. L. (1973). Helping behavior and racial discrimination among liberals and conservatives. *Journal of Personality and Social Psychology*, **25**, 335–341. (p. 505)

Gaertner, S. L. (1975). The role of racial attitudes in helping behavior. *Journal of Social Psychology*, **97**, 95–101. (p. 505)

Gaertner, S. L., & Bickman, L. (1971). Effects of race on the elicitation of helping behavior. *Journal of Personality and Social Psychology*, **20**, 218–222. (p. 505)

Gaertner, S. L., & Dovidio, J. F. (1977). The subtlety of white racism, arousal, and helping behavior. *Journal of Personality and Social Psychology*, **35**, 691–707. (p. 505)

Gaertner, S. L., & Dovidio, J. F. (1986). The aversive form of racism. In J. F. Dovidio & S. L. Gaertner (Eds.), *Prejudice, discrimination, and racism*. Orlando, FL: Academic Press. (p. 505)

Gaertner, S. L., Dovidio, J. F., Anastasio, P. A., Bachman, B. A., & Rust, M. C. (1993). The Common Ingroup Identity Model: Recategorization and the reduction of intergroup bias. In W. Stroebe & M. Hewstone (Eds.), *European Review of Social Psychology*, vol. 4. London: Wiley. (pp. 546–547)

Gaertner, S. L., Dovidio, J. F., Nier, J. A., Banker, B. S., Ward, C. M., Houlette, M., & Loux, S. (2000). The common ingroup identity model for reducing intergroup bias: Progress and challenges. In D. Capozza & R. Brown (Eds.), *Social identity processes: Trends in theory and research*. London: Sage. (pp. 546–547, 551)

Gaertner, S. L., Mann, J., Murrell, A., & Dovidio, J. F. (2001). Reducing intergroup bias: The benefits of recategorization. In M. A. Hogg & D. Abrams (Eds.), *Intergroup relations: Essential readings*. Philadelphia, PA: Psychology Press. (p. 551)

Galanter, M. (1989). *Cults: Faith, healing, and coercion*. New York: Oxford University Press. (pp. 276–277)

Galanter, M. (1990). Cults and zealous self-help movements: A psychiatric perspective. *American Journal of Psychiatry*, **147**, 543–551. (pp. 276–277)

Galinsky, A. D., & Moskowitz, G. B. (2000). Perspective-taking: Decreasing stereotype expression, stereotype accessibility, and in-group favoritism. *Journal of Personality and Social Psychology*, **78**, 708–724. (p. 557)

Galizio, M., & Hendrick, C. (1972). Effect of musical accompaniment on attitude: The guitar as a prop for persuasion. *Journal of Applied Social Psychology*, **2**, 350–359. (p. 256)

Gallant, S. J., Popiel, D. A., Hoffman, D. M., Chakraborty, P. K., and Hamilton, J. A. (1992). Using daily ratings to confirm premenstrual syndrome/late luteal phase disorder. Part I. Effects of demand characteristics and expectations. *Psychosomatic Medicine*, **54**, 149–166. (pp. 586–587)

Gallo, L. C., & Matthews, K. A. (2003). Understanding the association between socioeconomic status and physical health: Do negative emotions play a role? *Psychological Bulletin*, **129**, 10–51. (p. 599)

Gallup, G., Jr. (1984, March). Religion in America. *The Gallup Report*, Report No. 222. (p. 509)

Gallup, G. H. (1972). *The Gallup poll: Public opinion 1935–1971*. (Vol. 3). New York: Random House, pp. 551, 1716. (pp. 403, 537)

Gallup, G. H., Jr. (1998, December). Remarkable surge of interest in spiritual growth noted as next century approaches. *Emerging Trends*, p. 1. (p. 659)

Gallup, G. H., Jr., & Jones, T. (1992). *The saints among us*. Harrisburg, PA: Morehouse. (p. 346)

Gallup, G. H., Jr., & Lindsay, D. M. (1999). *Surveying the religious landscape: Trends in U.S. beliefs*. Harrisburg, PA: Morehouse Publishing. (p. 172)

Gallup Organization (1990). April 19–22 survey reported in *American Enterprise*, September/October, 1990, p. 92. (p. 190)

Gallup Organization (2003). Bush job approval rating www.gallup.com. (p. 546)

Gallup Organization (2003, July 8). American public opinion about Iraq. Gallup Poll News Service (www.gallup.com). (p. 152)

Gallup Organization (2003, June 10). American public opinion about Iraq. Gallup Poll News Service (www.gallup.com/poll/focus/sr030610.asp). (pp. 152, 246)

Gallup Organization (2003, March 29). The gender gap: Have you cried because of the war? *Gallup Tuesday Briefing* www.gallup.com/poll/pollinsights. (p. 184)

Gallup Poll (1990, July). Reported by G. Gallup, Jr., & F. Newport, Americans widely disagree on what constitutes "rich." *Gallup Poll Monthly*, pp. 28–36. (p. 649)

Gallup Poll (1997). Black/White relations in the U.S. http://www.gallup.com/poll/special/race/rcrls.htm (pp. 70, 335–336)

Gallupe, R. B., Cooper, W. H., Grise, M. L., & Bastianutti, L. M. (1994). Blocking electronic brainstorms. *Journal of Applied Psychology*, **79**, 77–86. (p. 319)

Gangestad, S. W., Simpson, J. A., & Cousins, A. J. (2004). Women's preferences for male behavioral displays change across the menstrual cycle. *Psychological Science*, **15**, 203–207. (p. 439)

Gangestad, S. W., & Snyder, M. (2000). Self-monitoring: Appraisal and reappraisal. *Psychological Bulletin*, **126**, 530–555. (p. 79)

Gangestad, S. W., & Thornhill, R. (1997). Human sexual selection and developmental stability. In J. A. Simpson & D. T. Kenrick (Eds.), *Evolutionary social psychology*. Mahwah, NJ: Erlbaum. (p. 437)

Garb, H. N. (1994). Judgment research: Implications for clinical practice and testimony in court. *Applied and Preventive Psychology*, **3**, 173–183. (p. 575)

Garcia, S. M., Weaver, K., Moskowitz, G. B., & Darley, J. M. (2002). Crowded minds: The implicit bystander effect.

Journal of Personality and Social Psychology, **83**, 843–853. (p. 500)

Gardner, J., & Oswald, A. (2001). Does money buy happiness? A longitudinal study using data on windfalls. Working paper, Department of Economics, Cambridge University. (p. 652)

Gardner, M. (1997, July/August). Heaven's Gate: The UFO cult of Bo and Peep. *Skeptical Inquirer*, pp. 15–17. (p. 273)

Garry, M., Manning, C. G., Loftus, E. F., & Sherman, S. J. (1996). Imagination inflation: Imagining a childhood event inflates confidence that it occurred. *Psychonomic Bulletin & Review*, **3**, 208–214. (p. 103)

Gastorf, J. W., Suls, J., & Sanders, G. S. (1980). Type A coronary-prone behavior pattern and social facilitation. *Journal of Personality and Social Psychology*, **8**, 773–780. (p. 291)

Gates, D. (1993, March 29). White male paranoia. *Newsweek*, pp. 48–53. (p. 363)

Gates, M. F., & Allee, W. C. (1933). Conditioned behavior of isolated and grouped cockroaches on a simple maze. *Journal of Comparative Psychology*, **15**, 331–358. (p. 287)

Gavanski, I., & Hoffman, C. (1987). Awareness of influences on one's own judgments: The roles of covariation detection and attention to the judgment process. *Journal of Personality and Social Psychology*, **52**, 453–463. (p. 51)

Gavzer, B. (1997, January 5). Are trial consultants good for justice? *Parade*, p. 20. (p. 628)

Gawande, A. (2002). *Complications: A surgeon's notes on an imperfect science.* New York: Metropolitan Books, Holt and Company. (p. 70)

Gayoso, A., Cutler, B. L., & Moran, G. (1991). Assessing the value of social scientists as trial consultants: A consumer research approach. Unpublished manuscript, Florida International University. (p. 628)

Gazzaniga, M. S. (1985). *The social brain: Discovering the networks of the mind.* New York: Basic Books. (p. 140)

Gazzaniga, M. S. (1992). *Nature's mind: The biological roots of thinking, emotions,*

sexuality, language, and intelligence. New York: Basic Books. (p. 109)

Geen, R. G. (1998). Aggression and antisocial behavior. In D. Gilbert, S. Fiske, & G. Lindzey (Eds.), *Handbook of social psychology*, 4th ed. New York: McGraw-Hill. (p. 385)

Geen, R. G., & Gange, J. J. (1983). Social facilitation: Drive theory and beyond. In H. H. Blumberg, A. P. Hare, V. Kent, & M. Davies (Eds.), *Small groups and social interaction*, Vol. 1. London: Wiley. (pp. 289, 291)

Geen, R. G., & Quanty, M. B. (1977). The catharsis of aggression: An evaluation of a hypothesis. In L. Berkowitz (Ed.), *Advances in experimental social psychology* (Vol. 10). New York: Academic Press. (p. 416)

Geen, R. G., & Thomas, S. L. (1986). The immediate effects of media violence on behavior. *Journal of Social Issues*, **42**(3), 7–28. (p. 407)

Geers, A. L., Handley, I. M., & McLarney, A. R. (2003). Discerning the role of optimism in persuasion: The valence-enhancement hypothesis. *Journal of Personality and Social Psychology*, **85**, 554–565. (p. 261)

Geiselman, R. E. (1996, May 14). On the use and efficacy of the cognitive interview: Commentary on Memon & Stevenage on witness memory. *Psycoloquy.96.7.11.witness-memory.2.geiselman* (from psyc@phoenix.princeton.edu@ukacr1.bitnet). (p. 616)

Gentile, D. A., & Anderson, C. A. (2003). Violent video games: The newest media violence hazard. In D. A. Gentile (Ed.), *Media violence and children.* Westport, CT: Ablex. (p. 410)

George, D., Carroll, P., Kersnick, R., & Calderon, K. (1998). Gender-related patterns of helping among friends. *Psychology of Women Quarterly*, **22**, 685–704. (p. 507)

Gerard, H. B. (1999). A social psychologist examines his past and looks to the future. In A. Rodrigues & R. Levine (Eds.), *Reflections on 100 years of experimental social psychology.* New York: Basic Books. (p. 234)

Gerard, H. B., & Mathewson, G. C. (1966). The effects of severity of initiation on liking for a group: A replication. *Journal of Experimental Social Psychology, 2*, 278–287. (p. 273)

Gerard, H. B., Wilhelmy, R. A., & Conolley, E. S. (1968). Conformity and group size. *Journal of Personality and Social Psychology, 8*, 79–82. (p. 228)

Gerbasi, K. C., Zuckerman, M., & Reis, H. T. (1977). Justice needs a new blindfold: A review of mock jury research. *Psychological Bulletin, 84*, 323–345. (pp. 629, 632)

Gerbner, G. (1993, June). Women and minorities on television: A study in casting and fate. A report to the Screen Actors Guild and the American Federation of Radio and Television Artists. (p. 408)

Gerbner, G. (1994). The politics of media violence: Some reflections. In C. Hamelink & O. Linne (Eds.), *Mass communication research: On problems and policies.* Norwood, NJ: Ablex. (pp. 403–404, 409)

Gerbner, G., Gross, L., Morgan, M., & Signorielli, N. (1986). Living with television: The dynamics of the cultivation process. In J. Bryant & D. Zillman (Eds.), *Perspectives on media effects.* Hillsdale, NJ: Erlbaum. (p. 408)

Gerbner, G., Gross, L., Signorielli, N., Morgan, M., & Jackson-Beeck, M. (1979). The demonstration of power: Violence profile No. 10. *Journal of Communication, 29*, 177–196. (p. 409)

Gergen, K. E. (1982). *Toward transformation in social knowledge.* New York: Springer-Verlag. (p. 516)

Gerrig, R. J. & Prentice, D. A. (1991, September). The representation of fictional information. *Psychological Science, 2*, 336–340. (p. 114)

Gerstenfeld, P. B., Grant, D. R., & Chiang, C-P. (2003). Hate online: A content analysis of extremist Internet sites. *Analyses of Social Issues and Public Policy, 3*, 29–44. (p. 307)

Gibbons, F. X. (1978). Sexual standards and reactions to pornography: Enhancing behavioral consistency through self-focused attention. *Journal of Personality and Social Psychology, 36*, 976–987. (p. 139)

Gibbons, F. X., Lane, D. J., Gerrard, M., Reis-Bergan, M., Lautrup, C. L., Pexa, N. A., & Blanton, H. (2002). Comparison-level preferences after performance: Is downward comparison theory still useful? *Journal of Personality and Social Psychology, 83*, 865–880. (p. 658)

Gibbons, F. X., & Wicklund, R. A. (1982). Self-focused attention and helping behavior. *Journal of Personality and Social Psychology, 43*, 462–474. (p. 481)

Gibson, B., & Sachau, D. (2000). Sandbagging as a self-presentational strategy: Claiming to be less than you are. *Personality and Social Psychology Bulletin, 26*, 56–70. (p. 78)

Gibson, B., & Sanbonmatsu, D. M. (2004). Optimism, pessimism, and gambling: The downside of optimism. *Personality and Social Psychology Bulletin, 30*, 149–160. (p. 71)

Giesler, R. B., Josephs, R. A., & Swann, W. B., Jr. (1996). Self-verification in clinical depression: The desire for negative evaluation. *Journal of Abnormal Psychology, 105*, 358–368. (p. 579)

Gifford, R., & Hine, D. W. (1997). "I'm cooperative, but you're greedy": Some cognitive tendencies in a commons dilemma. *Canadian Journal of Behavioural Science, 29*, 257–265. (p. 524)

Gifford, R., & Hine, D. W. (1997). Toward cooperation in commons dilemmas. *Canadian Journal of Behavioural Science, 29*, 167–179. (p. 525)

Gigerenzer, G., Todd, P. M. (1999). *Simple heuristics that make us smart.* New York: Oxford. (pp. 108, 129)

Gigone, D., & Hastie, R. (1993). The common knowledge effect: Information sharing and group judgment. *Journal of Personality and Social Psychology, 65*, 959–974. (p. 308)

Gilbert, D. T., & Ebert, J. E. J. (2002). Decisions and revisions: The affective forecasting of escapable outcomes. Unpublished manuscript, Harvard University. (pp. 53, 61)

Gilbert, D. T., Giesler, R. B., & Morris, K. A. (1995). When comparisons arise. *Journal of Personality and Social Psychology, 69*, 227–236. (p. 44)

Gilbert, D. T., & Hixon, J. G. (1991). The trouble of thinking: Activation and application of stereotypic beliefs. *Journal of Personality and Social Psychology, 60*, 509–517. (p. 358)

Gilbert, D. T., & Jones, E. E. (1986). Perceiver-induced constraint: Interpretations of self-generated reality. *Journal of Personality and Social Psychology, 50*, 269–280. (p. 89)

Gilbert, D. T., Krull, D. S., & Malone, P. S. (1990). Unbelieving the unbelievable: Some problems in the rejection of false information. *Journal of Personality and Social Psychology, 59*, 601–613. (p. 277)

Gilbert, D. T., Lieberman, M. D., Morewedge, C. K., & Wilson, T. D. (2004). The peculiar longevity of things not so bad. *Psychological Science, 15*, 14–19. (p. 55)

Gilbert, D. T., & Malone, P. S. (1995). The correspondence bias. *Psychological Bulletin, 117*, 21–38. (pp. 85–86, 96)

Gilbert, D. T., McNulty, S. E., Giuliano, T. A., & Benson, J. E. (1992). Blurry words and fuzzy deeds: The attribution of obscure behavior. *Journal of Personality and Social Psychology, 62*, 18–25. (p. 96)

Gilbert, D. T., Pelham, B. W., & Krull, D. S. (1988). On cognitive busyness: When person perceivers meet persons perceived. *Journal of Personality and Social Psychology, 54*, 733–740. (p. 96)

Gilbert, D. T., Pinel, E. C., Wilson, T. D., Blumberg, S. J., & Wheatley, T. P. (1998). Immune neglect: A source of durability bias in affective forecasting. *Journal of Personality and Social Psychology, 75*, 617–638. (pp. 54, 427)

Gilbert, D. T., Tafarodi, R. W., & Malone, P. S. (1993). You can't not believe everything you read. *Journal of Personality and Social Psychology, 65*, 221–233. (p. 277)

Gilbert, D. T., & Wilson, T. D. (2000). Miswanting: Some problems in the forecasting of future affective states. In J. Forgas (Ed.), *Feeling and thinking: The role of affect in social cognition.* Cambridge: Cambridge University Press. (pp. 53–54)

Gillham, J. E., Shatte, A. J., Reivich, K. J., & Seligman, M. E. P. (2000). Optimism, pessimism, and explanatory style. In E. C. Chang (Ed.), *Optimism and pessimism.* Washington, DC: APA Books. (p. 594)

Gilligan, C. (1982). *In a different voice: Psychological theory and women's development.* Cambridge, MA: Harvard University Press. (p. 182)

Gilligan, C., Lyons, N. P., & Hanmer, T. J. (Eds.) (1990). *Making connections: The relational worlds of adolescent girls at Emma Willard School.* Cambridge, MA: Harvard University Press. (p. 182)

Gillis, J. S., & Avis, W. E. (1980). The male-taller norm in mate selection. *Personality and Social Psychology Bulletin,* 6, 396–401. (p. 200)

Gilmor, T. M., & Reid, D. W. (1979). Locus of control and causal attribution for positive and negative outcomes on university examinations. *Journal of Research in Personality,* 13, 154–160. (p. 68)

Gilovich, T. (1987). Secondhand information and social judgment. *Journal of Experimental Social Psychology,* 23, 59–74. (p. 94)

Gilovich, T., & Douglas, C. (1986). Biased evaluations of randomly determined gambling outcomes. *Journal of Experimental Social Psychology,* 22, 228–241. (p. 117)

Gilovich, T., & Eibach, R. (2001). The fundamental attribution error where it really counts. *Psychological Inquiry,* 12, 23–26. (p. 97)

Gilovich, T., Kerr, M., & Medvec, V. H. (1993). Effect of temporal perspective on subjective confidence. *Journal of Personality and Social Psychology,* 64, 552–560. (p. 110)

Gilovich, T., & Medvec, V. H. (1994). The temporal pattern to the experience of regret. *Journal of Personality and Social Psychology,* 67, 357–365. (p. 116)

Gilovich, T., Medvec, V. H., & Savitsky, K. (2000). The spotlight effect in social judgment: An egocentric bias in estimates of the salience of one's own actions and appearance. *Journal of Personality and Social Psychology,* 78, 211–222. (p. 40)

Gilovich, T., Savitsky, K., & Medvec, V. H. (1998). The illusion of transparency: Biased assessments of others' ability to read one's emotional states. *Journal of Personality and Social Psychology,* 75, 332–346. (pp. 40, 497)

Gilovich, T., Wang, R. F., Regan, D., & Nishina, S. (2003). Regrets of action and inaction across cultures. *Journal of Cross-Cultural Psychology,* 34, 61–71. (p. 116)

Giner-Sorolla, R., Garcia, M. T., & Bargh, J. (1999). The automatic evaluation of pictures. *Social Cognition,* 17, 79–96. (p. 107)

Ginsburg, B., & Allee, W. C. (1942). Some effects of conditioning on social dominance and subordination in inbred strains of mice. *Physiological Zoology,* 15, 485–506. (p. 389)

Gladwell, M. (2003, March 10). Connecting the dots: The paradoxes of intelligence reform. *The New Yorker,* pp. 83–88. (p. 19)

Glass, D. C. (1964). Changes in liking as a means of reducing cognitive discrepancies between self-esteem and aggression. *Journal of Personality,* 32, 531–549. (p. 146)

Gleason, M. E. J., Iida, M., Bolger, N., & Shrout, P. E. (2003). Daily supportive equity in close relationships. *Personality and Social Psychology Bulletin,* 29, 1036–1045. (p. 478)

Glenn, N. D. (1980). Aging and attitudinal stability. In O. G. Brim, Jr., & J. Kagan (Eds.), *Constancy and change in human development.* Cambridge, MA: Harvard University Press. (p. 267)

Glenn, N. D. (1981). Personal communication. (p. 267)

Glick, P., Fiske, S. J. & 29 others (2000). Beyond prejudice as simple antipathy: Hostile and benevolent sexism across cultures. *Journal of Personality and Social Psychology,* 79, 763–775. (p. 341)

Glick, P., & Fiske, S. T. (1996). The ambivalent sexism inventory: Differentiating hostile and benevolent sexism. *Journal of Personality and Social Psychology,* 70, 491–512. (p. 341)

Glick, P., & Susan, S. T. (2001). An ambivalent alliance: Hostile and benevolent sexism as complementary justifications for gender inequality. *American Psychologist,* 56, 109–118. (p. 341)

Goethals, G. R., Messick, D. M., & Allison, S. T. (1991). The uniqueness bias: Studies of constructive social comparison. In J. Suls & T. A. Wills (Eds.), *Social comparison: Contemporary theory and research.* Hillsdale, NJ: Erlbaum. (p. 73)

Goethals, G. R., & Nelson, E. R. (1973). Similarity in the influence process: The belief-value distinction. *Journal of Personality and Social Psychology,* 25, 117–122. (p. 254)

Goggin, W. C., & Range, L. M. (1985). The disadvantages of hindsight in the perception of suicide. *Journal of Social and Clinical Psychology,* 3, 232–237. (p. 570)

Goldhagen, D. J. (1996). *Hitler's willing executioners.* New York: Knopf. (p. 245)

Goldman, J. (1967). A comparison of sensory modality preference of children and adults. Dissertation: Thesis (Ph.D.). Ferkauf Graduate School of Humanities and Social Sciences, Yeshiva University. (p. 291)

Goldman, W., & Lewis, P. (1977). Beautiful is good: Evidence that the physically attractive are more socially skillful. *Journal of Experimental Social Psychology,* 13, 125–130. (p. 436)

Goldsmith, C. (2003, March 25). World media turn wary eye on U.S. *Wall Street Journal,* p. A12. (p. 246)

Goldstein, A. P. (1994). Delinquent gangs. In A. P. Goldstein, B. Harootunian, and J. C. Conoley (Eds.), *Student aggression: Prevention, control, and replacement.* New York: Guilford. (p. 414)

Goldstein, A. P., Glick, B., & Gibbs, J. C. (1998). Aggression replacement training: A comprehensive intervention for aggressive youth (rev. ed.). Champaign, IL: Research Press. (p. 418)

Goldstein, J. H., & Arms, R. L. (1971). Effects of observing athletic contests on hostility. *Sociometry,* 34, 83–90. (p. 416)

Gonzaga, G., Keltner, D., Londahl, E. A., & Smith, M. D. (2001). Love and the commitment problem in romantic relations and friendship. *Journal of Personality and Social Psychology,* 81, 247–262. (p. 453)

Goodhart, D. E. (1986). The effects of positive and negative thinking on performance in an achievement situation. *Journal of Personality and Social Psychology,* 51, 117–124. (p. 72)

Gordijn, E. H., De Vries, N. K., & De Dreu, C. K. W. (2002). Minority influence on focal and related attitudes: Change in size, attributions and information processing. *Personality and Social Psychology Bulletin, 28*, 1315–1326. (p. 632)

Gordon, R. A. (1996). Impact of ingratiation on judgments and evaluations: A meta-analytic investigation. *Journal of Personality and Social Psychology, 71*, 54–70. (p. 448)

Gortmaker, S. L., Must, A., Perrin, J. M., Sobol, A. M., & Dietz, W. H. (1993). Social and economic consequences of overweight in adolescence and young adulthood. *New England Journal of Medicine, 329*, 1008–1012. (pp. 28, 332)

Gotlib, I. H., & Colby, C. A. (1988). How to have a good quarrel. In P. Marsh (Ed.), *Eye to eye: How people interact.* Topsfield, MA: Salem House. (p. 555)

Gotlib, I. H., & Lee, C. M. (1989). The social functioning of depressed patients: A longitudinal assessment. *Journal of Social and Clinical Psychology, 8*, 223–237. (p. 579)

Gottlieb, J., & Carver, C. S. (1980). Anticipation of future interaction and the bystander effect. *Journal of Experimental Social Psychology, 16*, 253–260. (p. 511)

Gottman, J. (with N. Silver) (1994). *Why marriages succeed or fail.* New York: Simon & Schuster. (p. 470)

Gottman, J. M. (1998). Psychology and the study of marital processes. *Annual Review of Psychology, 49*, 169–197. (p. 470)

Gough, H. G., & Thorne, A. (1986). Positive, negative, and balanced shyness. In W. H. Jones, J. M. Cheek, & S. R. Briggs (Eds.), *Shyness: Perspectives on Research and Treatment.* New York: Plenum. (p. 584)

Gough, S. (2003, November 3). My journey so far. www.nakedwalk.alivewww.co.uk/about_me.htm (p. 224)

Gould, M. S., & Shaffer, D. (1986). The impact of suicide in television movies: Evidence of imitation. *New England Journal of Medicine, 315*, 690–694. (p. 213)

Gould, R., Brounstein, P. J., & Sigall, H. (1977). Attributing ability to an opponent: Public aggrandizement and private denigration. *Sociometry, 40*, 254–261. (pp. 77–78)

Gould, S. J. (1988, July). Kropotkin was no crackpot. *Natural History*, pp. 12–21. (p. 526)

Gould, S. J. (1997, October 20). Quoted by J. M. Nash, Evolutionary pop star. *Time*, p. 92. (p. 193)

Gouldner, A. W. (1960). The norm of reciprocity: A preliminary statement. *American Sociological Review, 25*, 161–178. (p. 484)

Gove, W. R., Style, C. B., & Hughes, M. (1990). The effect of marriage on the well-being of adults: A theoretical analysis. *Journal of Family Issues, 11*, 4–35. (p. 600)

Graham, S., Weiner, B., & Zucker, G.S. (1997). An attributional analysis of punishment goals and public reactions to O. J. Simpson. *Personality and Social Psychology Bulletin, 23*, 331–346. (p. 91)

Granstrom, K., & Stiwne, D. (1998). A bipolar model of groupthink: An expansion of Janis's concept. *Small Group Research, 29*, 32–56. (p. 315)

Gray, C., Russell, P., & Blockley, S. (1991). The effects upon helping behaviour of wearing pro-gay identification. *British Journal of Social Psychology, 30*, 171–178. (p. 504)

Gray, J. D., & Silver, R. C. (1990). Opposite sides of the same coin: Former spouses' divergent perspectives in coping with their divorce. *Journal of Personality and Social Psychology, 59*, 1180–1191. (p. 68)

Graziano, W. G., Jensen-Campbell, L. A., & Finch, J. F. (1997). The self as a mediator between personality and adjustment. *Journal of Personality and Social Psychology, 73*, 392–404. (p. 57)

Greeley, A. M. (1991). *Faithful attraction.* New York: Tor Books. (pp. 408, 464)

Greeley, A. M., & Sheatsley, P. B. (1971). Attitudes toward racial integration. *Scientific American, 225*(6), 13–19. (pp. 148, 350)

Green, C. W., Adams, A. M., & Turner, C. W. (1988). Development and validation of the school interracial climate scale. *American Journal of Community Psychology, 16*, 241–259. (p. 548)

Green, D. P., Glaser, J., & Rich, A. (1998). From lynching to gay bashing: The elusive connection between economic conditions and hate crime. *Journal of Personality and Social Psychology, 75*, 82–92. (p. 350)

Green, M. C., Strange, J. J., & Brock, T. C. (Eds.) (2002). *Narrative impact: Social and cognitive foundations.* Mahwah, NJ: Erlbaum. (p. 114)

Greenberg, J. (1986). Differential intolerance for inequity from organizational and individual agents. *Journal of Applied Social Psychology, 16*, 191–196. (p. 530)

Greenberg, J., Pyszczynski, T., Burling, J., & Tibbs, K. (1992). Depression, self-focused attention, and the self-serving attributional bias. *Personality and Individual Differences, 13*, 959–965. (p. 594)

Greenberg, J., Pyszczynski, T., Solomon, S., Rosenblatt, A., Veeder, M., Kirkland, S., & Lyon, D. (1990). Evidence for terror management theory II: The effects of mortality salience on reactions to those who threaten or bolster the cultural worldview. *Journal of Personality and Social Psychology, 58*, 308–318. (p. 355)

Greenberg, J., Pyszczynski, T., Solomon, S., Simon, L., & Breus, M. (1994). Role of consciousness and accessibility of death-related thoughts in mortality salience effects. *Journal of Personality and Social Psychology, 67*, 627–637. (p. 355)

Greenberg, J., Schimel, J., & Martins, A. (in press). *Motivation and Emotion.* (p. 355)

Greenberg, J., Solomon, S., & Pyszczynski, T. (1997). Terror management theory of self-esteem and cultural worldviews: Empirical assessments and conceptual refinements. *Advances in Experimental Social Psychology, 29*, 61–142. (p. 75)

Greenwald, A. G. (1975). On the inconclusiveness of crucial cognitive tests of dissonance versus self-perception theories. *Journal of Experimental Social Psychology, 11*, 490–499. (p. 161)

Greenwald, A. G. (1980). The totalitarian ego: Fabrication and revision of personal history. *American Psychologist, 35*, 603–618. (p. 104)

Greenwald, A. G. (1992). New look 3: Unconscious cognition reclaimed. *American Psychologist, 47,* 766–779. (p. 109)

Greenwald, A. G., & Banaji, M. R. (1995). Implicit social cognition: Attitudes, self-esteem, and stereotypes. *Psychological Review, 102,* 4–27. (p. 107)

Greenwald, A. G., Banaji, M. R., Rudman, L. A., Farnham, S. D., Nosek, B. A., & Mellott, D. S. (2002). A unified theory of implicit attitudes, stereotypes, self-esteem, and self-concept. *Psychological Bulletin, 109,* 3–25. (p. 136)

Greenwald, A. G., Banaji, M. R., Rudman, L. A., Farnham, S. D., Nosek, B. A., & Rosier, M. (2000). Prologue to a unified theory of attitudes, stereotypes, and self-concept. In J. P. Forgas (Ed.), *Feeling and thinking: The role of affect in social cognition and behavior.* New York: Cambridge University Press. (pp. 337, 338)

Greenwald, A. G., Carnot, C. G., Beach, R., & Young, B. (1987). Increasing voting behavior by asking people if they expect to vote. *Journal of Applied Psychology, 72,* 315–318. (p. 144)

Greenwald, A. G., McGhee, D. E., Schwartz, J. L. K. (1998). Measuring individual differences in implicit cognition: The implicit association test. *Journal of Personality and Social Psychology, 74,* 1464–1480. (pp. 337–338)

Greenwald, A. G., Nosek, B. A., & Banaji, M. R. (2003). Understanding and using the implicit association test: I. An improved scoring algorithm. *Journal of Personality and Social Psychology, 85,* 197–216. (pp. 136, 339)

Greenwald, A. G., & Schuh, E. S. (1994). An ethnic bias in scientific citations. *European Journal of Social Psychology, 24,* 623–639. (p. 339)

Griffin, B. Q., Combs, A. L., Land, M. L., & Combs, N. N. (1983). Attribution of success and failure in college performance. *Journal of Psychology, 114,* 259–266. (p. 68)

Griffitt, W. (1970). Environmental effects on interpersonal affective behavior. Ambient effective temperature and attraction. *Journal of Personality and Social Psychology, 15,* 240–244. (pp. 394, 450)

Griffitt, W. (1987). Females, males, and sexual responses. In K. Kelley (Ed.), *Females, males, and sexuality: Theories and research.* Albany: State University of New York Press. (p. 188)

Griffitt, W., & Veitch, R. (1971). Hot and crowded: Influences of population density and temperature on interpersonal affective behavior. *Journal of Personality and Social Psychology, 17,* 92–98. (p. 394)

Griffitt, W., & Veitch, R. (1974). Preacquaintance attitude similarity and attraction revisited: Ten days in a fallout shelter. *Sociometry, 37,* 163–173. (p. 443)

Groenenboom, A., Wilke, H. A. M., & Wit, A. P. (2001). Will we be working together again? The impact of future interdependence on group members' task motivation. *European Journal of Social Psychology, 31,* 369–378. (p. 296)

Grofman, B. (1980). The slippery slope: Jury size and jury verdict requirements—legal and social science approaches. In B. H. Raven (Ed.), *Policy studies review annual* (Vol. 4). Beverly Hills, CA: Sage Publications. (p. 634)

Gross, A. E., & Crofton, C. (1977). What is good is beautiful. *Sociometry, 40,* 85–90. (p. 441)

Gross, J. T. (2001). *Neighbors: The destruction of the Jewish community in Jedwabne, Poland.* Princeton, NJ: Princeton University Press. (p. 380)

Gross, S. R., & Miller, N. (1997). The "Golden Section" and bias in perceptions of social consensus. *Personality and Social Psychology Review, 1,* 241–271. (p. 73)

Grossman, M., & Wood, W. (1993). Sex differences in intensity of emotional experience: A social role interpretation. *Journal of Personality and Social Psychology, 65,* 1010–1022. (p. 184)

Grote, N. K., & Clark, M. S. (2001). Perceiving unfairness in the family: Cause or consequence of marital distress? *Journal of Personality and Social Psychology, 80,* 281–293. (p. 462)

Grove, J. R., Hanrahan, S. J., & McInman, A. (1991). Success/failure bias in attributions across involvement categories in sport. *Personality and Social Psychology Bulletin, 17,* 93–97. (p. 67)

Grove, W. M., Zald, D. H., Lebow, B. S., Snitz, B. E., & Nelson, C. (2000). Clinical versus mechanical prediction: A meta-analysis. *Psychological Assessment, 12,* 19–30. (p. 573)

Grube, J. W., Kleinhesselink, R. R., & Kearney, K. A. (1982). Male self-acceptance and attraction toward women. *Personality and Social Psychology Bulletin, 8,* 107–112. (pp. 355–356)

Gruder, C. L. (1977). Choice of comparison persons in evaluating oneself. In J. M. Suls & R. L. Miller (Eds.), *Social comparison processes.* Washington, DC: Hemisphere Publishing. (p. 44)

Gruder, C. L., Cook, T. D., Hennigan, K. M., Flay, B., Alessis, C., & Kalamaj, J. (1978). Empirical tests of the absolute sleeper effect predicted from the discounting cue hypothesis. *Journal of Personality and Social Psychology, 36,* 1061–1074. (pp. 251–252)

Gruman, J. C., & Sloan, R. P. (1983). Disease as justice: Perceptions of the victims of physical illness. *Basic and Applied Social Psychology, 4,* 39–46. (p. 367)

Grunberger, R. (1971). *The 12-year-Reich: A social history of Nazi Germany 1933–1945.* New York: Holt, Rinehart & Winston. (p. 149)

Grush, J. E. (1980). Impact of candidate expenditures, regionality, and prior outcomes on the 1976 Democratic presidential primaries. *Journal of Personality and Social Psychology, 38,* 337–347. (p. 264)

Grush, J. E., & Glidden, M. V. (1987). Power and satisfaction among distressed and nondistressed couples. Paper presented at the Midwestern Psychological Association convention. (p. 555)

Gudykunst, W. B. (1989). Culture and intergroup processes. In M. H. Bond (Ed.), *The cross-cultural challenge to social psychology.* Newbury Park, CA: Sage. (p. 352)

Guéguen, N., & Jacob, C. (2001). Fund-raising on the Web: The effect of an electronic foot-in-the-door on donation. *CyberPsychology and Behavior,* **4,** 705–709. (p. 145)

Guerin, B. (1993). *Social facilitation.* Paris: Cambridge University Press. (p. 288)

Guerin, B. (1994). What do people think about the risks of driving? Implications for traffic safety interventions. *Journal of Applied Social Psychology,* **24,** 994–1021. (p. 70)

Guerin, B. (1999). Social behaviors as determined by different arrangements of social consequences: Social loafing, social facilitation, deindividuation, and a modified social loafing. *The Psychological Record,* **49,** 565–578. (p. 288)

Guerin, B., & Innes, J. M. (1982). Social facilitation and social monitoring: A new look at Zajonc's mere presence hypothesis. *British Journal of Social Psychology,* **21,** 7–18. (p. 291)

Guimond, S., Dambrun, N., Michinov, N., & Duarte, S. (2003). Does social dominance generate prejudice? Integrating individual and contextual determinants of intergroup cognitions. *Journal of Personality and Social Psychology,* **84,** 697–721. (p. 345)

Guiness, O. (1993). *The American hour: A time of reckoning and the once and future role of faith.* New York: Free Press. (p. 467)

Gundersen, E. (2001, August 1). MTV is a many splintered thing. *USA Today,* p. 1D. (p. 403)

Gupta, U., & Singh, P. (1982). Exploratory study of love and liking and type of marriages. *Indian Journal of Applied Psychology,* **19,** 92–97. (p. 457)

Gurin, P., Dey, E. L., Hurtado, S., & Gurin, G. (2002). Diversity and higher education: Theory and impact on educational outcomes. *Harvard Educational Review,* **72,** 330–366. (p. 542)

Gutierres, S. E., Kenrick, D. T., & Partch, J. J. (1999). Beauty, dominance, and the mating game: Contrast effects in self-assessment reflect gender differences in mate selection. *Journal of Personality and Social Psychology,* **25,** 1126–1134. (p. 440)

Gutmann, D. (1977). The cross-cultural perspective: Notes toward a comparative psychology of aging. In J. E. Birren & K. Warner Schaie (Eds.), *Handbook of the psychology of aging.* New York: Van Nostrand Reinhold. (p. 193)

Hacker, H. M. (1951). Women as a minority group. *Social Forces,* **30,** 60–69. (p. 344)

Hackman, J. R. (1986). The design of work teams. In J. Lorsch (Ed.), *Handbook of organizational behavior.* Englewood Cliffs, NJ: Prentice-Hall. (p. 297)

Hadden, J. K. (1969). *The gathering storm in the churches.* Garden City, NY: Doubleday. (pp. 346–347)

Haddock, G., & Zanna, M. P. (1994). Preferring "housewives" to "feminists." *Psychology of Women Quarterly,* **18,** 25–52. (pp. 182, 341)

Haemmerlie, F. M. (1987). Creating adaptive illusions in counseling and therapy using a self-perception theory perspective. Paper presented at the Midwestern Psychological Association, Chicago. (p. 594)

Haemmerlie, F. M., & Montgomery, R. L. (1982). Self-perception theory and unobtrusively biased interactions: A treatment for heterosocial anxiety. *Journal of Counseling Psychology,* **29,** 362–370. (pp. 593–594)

Haemmerlie, F. M., & Montgomery, R. L. (1984). Purposefully biased interventions: Reducing heterosocial anxiety through self-perception theory. *Journal of Personality and Social Psychology,* **47,** 900–908. (pp. 593–594)

Haemmerlie, F. M., & Montgomery, R. L. (1986). Self-perception theory and the treatment of shyness. In W. H. Jones, J. M. Cheek, & S. R. Briggs (Eds.), *A sourcebook on shyness: Research and treatment.* New York: Plenum. (pp. 593–594)

Hafner, H., & Schmidtke, A. (1989). Do televised fictional suicide models produce suicides? In D. R. Pfeffer (Ed.), *Suicide among youth: Perspectives on risk and prevention.* Washington, DC: American Psychiatric Press. (p. 213)

Hagerty, M. R. (2000). Social comparisons of income in one's community: Evidence from national surveys of income and happiness. *Journal of Personality and Social Psychology,* **78,** 764–771. (pp. 389, 656)

Hagiwara, S. (1983). Role of self-based and sample-based consensus estimates as mediators of responsibility judgments for automobile accidents. *Japanese Psychological Research,* **25,** 16–28. (p. 80)

Haidt, J. (2003). The moral emotions. In R. J. Davidson (Ed.). *Handbook of affective sciences.* Oxford: Oxford University Press. (p. 503)

Halberstadt, A. G., & Saitta, M. B. (1987). Gender, nonverbal behavior, and perceived dominance: A test of the theory. *Journal of Personality and Social Psychology,* **53,** 257–272. (pp. 183–184)

Halberstadt, J., & Rhodes, G. (2000). The attractiveness of nonface averages: Implications for an evolutionary explanation of the attractiveness of average faces. *Psychological Science,* **11,** 285–289. (p. 438)

Hall, J. A. (1984). *Nonverbal sex differences: Communication accuracy and expressive style.* Baltimore: Johns Hopkins University Press. (pp. 184–185, 187)

Hall, T. (1985, June 25). The unconverted: Smoking of cigarettes seems to be becoming a lower-class habit. *Wall Street Journal,* pp. 1, 25. (p. 104)

Hallahan, M., Lee, F., & Herzog, T. (1997). It's not just whether you win or lose, it's also where you play the game: A naturalistic, cross-cultural examination of the positivity bias. *Journal of Cross-Cultural Psychology,* **28,** 768–778. (p. 80)

Halverson, A. M., Hallahan, M., Hart, A. J., & Rosenthal, R. (1997). Reducing the biasing effects of judges' nonverbal behavior with simplified jury instruction. *Journal of Applied Psychology,* **82,** 590–598. (p. 628)

Hamberger, J., & Hewstone, M. (1997). Inter-ethnic contact as a predictor of blatant and subtle prejudice: Tests of a model in four West European nations. *British Journal of Social Psychology,* **36,** 173–190. (p. 541)

Hamblin, R. L., Buckholdt, D., Bushell, D., Ellis, D., & Feritor, D. (1969). Changing the game from get the teacher to learn. *Transaction,* January, pp. 20–25, 28–31. (p. 417)

Hamilton, D. L., & Gifford, R. K. (1976). Illusory correlation in interpersonal perception: A cognitive basis of stereotypic judgments. *Journal of Experimental Social Psychology*, **12**, 392–407. (p. 364)

Hamilton, D. L., & Rose, T. L. (1980). Illusory correlation and the maintenance of stereotypic beliefs. *Journal of Personality and Social Psychology*, **39**, 832–845. (p. 365)

Hamilton, V. L., Hoffman, W. S., Broman, C. L., & Rauma, D. (1993). Unemployment, distress, and coping: A panel study of autoworkers. *Journal of Personality and Social Psychology*, **65**, 234–247. (p. 579)

Hampson, R. B. (1984). Adolescent prosocial behavior: Peer-group and situational factors associated with helping. *Journal of Personality and Social Psychology*, **46**, 153–162. (p. 506)

Haney, C. (1991). The fourteenth amendment and symbolic legality: Let them eat due process. *Law and Human Behavior*, **15**, 183–204. (p. 621)

Haney, C. (1993). Psychology and legal change. *Law and Human Behavior*, **17**, 371–398. (p. 629)

Haney, C., & Logan, D. D. (1994). Broken promise: The Supreme Court's response to social science research on capital punishment. *Journal of Social Issues*, **50**, 75–101. (p. 630)

Haney, C., & Zimbardo, P. (1998). The past and future of U.S. prison policy: Twenty-five years after the Stanford Prison Experiment. *American Psychologist*, **53**, 709–727. (p. 141)

Hans, V. P., & Vidmar, N. (1981). Jury selection. In N. L. Kerr & R. M. Bray (Eds.), *The psychology of the courtroom*. New York: Academic Press. (p. 628)

Hansen, D. E., Vandenberg, B., & Patterson, M. L. (1995). The effects of religious orientation on spontaneous and nonspontaneous helping behaviors. *Personality and Individual Differences*, **19**, 101–104. (p. 508)

Harber, K. D. (1998), Feedback to minorities: Evidence of a positive bias. *Journal of Personality and Social Psychology*, **74**, 622–628. (p. 337)

Hardie, E. A. (1997). Prevalence and predictors of cyclic and noncyclic affective change. *Psychology of Women Quarterly*, **21**, 299–314. (p. 586)

Hardin, G. (1968). The tragedy of the commons. *Science*, **162**, 1243–1248. (pp. 523, 525)

Hardy, C., & Latané, B. (1986). Social loafing on a cheering task. *Social Science*, **71**, 165–172. (p. 294)

Haritos-Fatouros, M. (1988). The official torturer: A learning model for obedience to the authority of violence. *Journal of Applied Social Psychology*, **18**, 1107–1120. (p. 224)

Haritos-Fatouros, M. (2002). *Psychological origins of institutionalized torture*. New York: Routledge. (p. 224)

Harkins, S. G. (1981). Effects of task difficulty and task responsibility on social loafing. Presentation to the First International Conference on Social Processes in Small Groups, Kill Devil Hills, North Carolina. (p. 294)

Harkins, S. G., & Jackson, J. M. (1985). The role of evaluation in eliminating social loafing. *Personality and Social Psychology Bulletin*, **11**, 457–465. (p. 295)

Harkins, S. G., Latané, B., & Williams, K. (1980). Social loafing: Allocating effort or taking it easy? *Journal of Experimental Social Psychology*, **16**, 457–465. (p. 293)

Harkins, S. G., & Petty, R. E. (1981). Effects of source magnification of cognitive effort on attitudes: An information-processing view. *Journal of Personality and Social Psychology*, **40**, 401–413. (p. 269)

Harkins, S. G., & Petty, R. E. (1982). Effects of task difficulty and task uniqueness on social loafing. *Journal of Personality and Social Psychology*, **43**, 1214–1229. (p. 296)

Harkins, S. G., & Petty, R. E. (1987). Information utility and the multiple source effect. *Journal of Personality and Social Psychology*, **52**, 260–268. (p. 269)

Harkins, S. G., & Szymanski, K. (1989). Social loafing and group evaluation. *Journal of Personality and Social Psychology*, **56**, 934–941. (p. 296)

Harmon, A. (2003, June 29). Online dating sheds its stigma as Losers.com. *New York Times* (www.nytimes.com). (p. 465)

Harmon-Jones, E. (2000). Cognitive dissonance and experienced negative affect: Evidence that dissonance increases experienced negative affect even in the absence of aversive consequences. *Personality and Social Psychology Bulletin*, **26**, 1490–1501. (p. 163)

Harmon-Jones, E., & Allen, J. J. B. (2001). The role of affect in the mere exposure effect: Evidence from psychophysiological and individual differences approaches. *Personality and Social Psychology Bulletin*, **27**, 889–898. (p. 429)

Harmon-Jones, E., Brehm, J. W., Greenberg, J., Simon, L., & Nelson, D. E. (1996). Evidence that the production of aversive consequences is not necessary to create cognitive dissonance. *Journal of Personality and Social Psychology*, **70**, 5–16. (p. 163)

Harmon-Jones, E., Greenberg, J., Solomon, S., & Simon, L. (1996). The effects of mortality salience on intergroup bias between minimal groups. *European Journal of Social Psychology*, **26**, 677–681. (p. 355)

Harries, K. D., & Stadler, S. J. (1988). Heat and violence: New findings from Dallas field data, 1980–1981. *Journal of Applied Social Psychology*, **18**, 129–138. (p. 395)

Harris, J. A. (1999). Review and methodological considerations in research on testosterone and aggression. *Aggression and Violent Behavior*, **4**, 273–291. (p. 385)

Harris, J. R. (1998). *The nurture assumption*. New York: Free Press. (pp. 181, 198, 460)

Harris, M. J. (1994). Self-fulfilling prophecies in the clinical context: Review and implications for clinical practice. *Applied & Preventive Psychology*, **3**, 145–158. (p. 572)

Harris, M. J., & Rosenthal, R. (1985). Mediation of interpersonal expectancy effects: 31 meta-analyses. *Psychological Bulletin*, **97**, 363–386. (p. 123)

Harris, M. J., & Rosenthal, R. (1986). Four factors in the mediation of teacher expectancy effects. In R. S. Feldman (Ed.), *The social psychology of education*. New York: Cambridge University Press. (p. 123)

Harrison, A. A. (1977). Mere exposure. In L. Berkowitz (Ed.), *Advances in experimental social psychology* (Vol. 10).

New York: Academic Press, pp. 39–83. (p. 429)

Hart, A. J., & Morry, M. M. (1997). Trait inferences based on racial and behavioral cues. *Basic and Applied Social Psychology, 19,* 33–48. (p. 337)

Hart, A. J., Whalen, P. J., Shin, L. M., & others. (2000, August). Differential response in the human amygdala to racial outgroup vs. ingroup face stimuli. *Neuroreport: For Rapid Communication of Neuroscience Research, 11,* 2351–2355. (p. 336)

Hartlage, S., Alloy, A. B., Vazquez, C., & Dykman, B. (1993). Automatic and effortful processing in depression. *Psychological Bulletin, 113,* 247–278. (p. 120)

Hartup, W. W., & Stevens, N. (1997). Friendships and adaptation in the life course. *Psychological Bulletin, 121,* 355–370. (p. 600)

Harvey, J. H., & Omarzu, J. (1997). Minding the close relationship. *Personality and Social Psychology Review, 1,* 224–240. (p. 472)

Harvey, J. H., Town, J. P., & Yarkin, K. L. (1981). How fundamental is the fundamental attribution error? *Journal of Personality and Social Psychology, 40,* 346–349. (p. 95)

Haselton, M. G., & Buss, D. M. (2000). Error management theory: A new perspective on biases in cross-sex mind reading. *Journal of Personality and Social Psychology, 78,* 81–91. (p. 129)

Hass, R. G., Katz, I., Rizzo, N., Bailey, J., & Eisenstadt, D. (1991). Cross-racial appraisal as related to attitude ambivalence and cognitive complexity. *Personality and Social Psychology Bulletin, 17,* 83–92. (p. 337)

Hastie, R., Penrod, S. D., & Pennington, N. (1983). *Inside the jury.* Cambridge, MA: Harvard University Press. (pp. 631–632)

Hastorf, A., & Cantril, H. (1954). They saw a game: A case study. *Journal of Abnormal and Social Psychology, 49,* 129–134. (p. 14)

Hatfield, E. (1988). Passionate and compassionate love. In R. J. Sternberg & M. L. Barnes (Eds.), *The psychology of love.* New Haven, CT: Yale University Press. (p. 453)

Hatfield (Walster), E., Aronson, V., Abrahams, D., & Rottman, L. (1966). Importance of physical attractiveness in dating behavior. *Journal of Personality and Social Psychology, 4,* 508–516. (p. 433)

Hatfield, E., Cacioppo, J. T., & Rapson, R. (1992). The logic of emotion: Emotional contagion. In M. S. Clark (Ed.), *Review of Personality and Social Psychology.* Newbury Park, CA: Sage. (p. 158)

Hatfield, E., & Rapson, R. L. (1987). Passionate love: New directions in research. In W. H. Jones & D. Perlman (Eds.), *Advances in personal relationships,* Vol. 1. Greenwich, CT: JAI Press. (p. 454)

Hatfield, E., & Sprecher, S. (1986). *Mirror, mirror: The importance of looks in everyday life.* Albany, NY: SUNY Press. (pp. 436, 458)

Hatfield, E., Traupmann, J., Sprecher, S., Utne, M., & Hay, J. (1985). Equity and intimate relations: Recent research. In W. Ickes (Ed.), *Compatible and incompatible relationships.* New York: Springer-Verlag. (p. 461)

Hatfield (Walster), E., Walster, G. W., & Berscheid, E. (1978). *Equity: Theory and research.* Boston: Allyn and Bacon. (pp. 450–451, 460, 531)

Haugtvedt, C. P., & Wegener, D. T. (1994). Message order effects in persuasion: An attitude strength perspective. *Journal of Consumer Research, 21,* 205–218. (p. 262)

Hazan, C. (2004). Intimate attachment/capacity to love and be loved. In C. Peterson & M. E. P. Seligman (Eds.), *The values in action classification of strengths and virtues.* Washington, DC: American Psychological Association. (p. 460)

Hazan, C., & Shaver, P. R. (1994). Attachment as an organizational framework for research on close relationships. *Psychological Inquiry, 5,* 1–22. (p. 469)

Headey, B., & Wearing, A. (1987). The sense of relative superiority–central to well-being. *Social Indicators Research, 20,* 497–516. (p. 70)

Heap, B., & Kent, J. (Eds.) (2000). *Towards sustainable consumption: A European perspective.* London: The Royal Society. (pp. 641, 642, 644)

Hearold, S. (1986). A synthesis of 1043 effects of television on social behavior. In G. Comstock (Ed.), *Public communication and behavior,* Vol. 1. Orlando, FL: Academic Press. (p. 514)

Heatherton, T. F. & Vohs, K. D. (2000). Personality processes and individual differences—interpersonal evaluations following threats to self: role of self-esteem. *Journal of Personality and Social Psychology, 78,* 725–736. (pp. 64–65)

Hebl, M. R., & Heatherton, T. F. (1998). The stigma of obesity in women: The difference is black and white. *Personality and Social Psychology Bulletin, 24,* 417–426. (p. 332)

Hebl, M. R., & Mannix, L. M. (2003). The weight of obesity in evaluating others: A mere proximity effect. *Personality and Social Psychology Bulletin, 29,* 28–38. (p. 332)

Hedge, A., & Yousif, Y. H. (1992). Effects of urban size, urgency, and cost on helpfulness: A cross-cultural comparison between the United Kingdom and the Sudan. *Journal of Cross-Cultural Psychology, 23,* 107–115. (p. 488)

Heesacker, M. (1989). Counseling and the elaboration likelihood model of attitude change. In J. F. Cruz, R. A. Goncalves, & P. P. Machado (Eds.), *Psychology and education: Investigations and interventions.* (Proceedings of the International Conference on Interventions in Psychology and Education, Porto, Portugal, July, 1987.) Porto, Portugal : Portugese Psychological Association. (p. 596)

Heider, F. (1958). *The psychology of interpersonal relations.* New York: Wiley. (p. 86)

Heilman, M. E. (1976). Oppositional behavior as a function of influence attempt intensity and retaliation threat. *Journal of Personality and Social Psychology, 33,* 574–578. (p. 239)

Heine, S. J., Kitayama, S., Lehman, D. R., Takata, T., Ide, E., Leung, C., & Matsumoto, H. (2001). Divergent consequences of success and failure in Japan and North America: An investigation of self-improving motivations and malleable selves.

Journal of Personality and Social Psychology, 81, 599–615. (p. 45)

Heine, S. J., & Lehman, D. R. (1997). Culture, dissonance, and self-affirmation. *Personality and Social Psychology Bulletin, 23*, 389–400. (p. 163)

Heine, S. J., & Lehman, D. R. (1997). The cultural construction of self-enhancement: An examination of group-serving biases. *Journal of Personality and Social Psychology, 72*, 1268–1283. (p. 365)

Heine, S. J., Lehman, D. R., Markus, H. R., & Kitayama, S. (1999). Is there a universal need for positive self-regard? *Psychological Review, 106*, 766–794. (pp. 46, 49)

Heine, S. J., Takata, T., & Lehman, D. R. (2000). Beyond self-presentation: Evidence for self-criticism among Japanese. *Personality and Social Psychology Bulletin, 26*, 71–78. (p. 80)

Hellman, P. (1980). *Avenue of the righteous of nations.* New York: Atheneum. (pp. 475–476)

Helmrich, R. L. (1997, May). Managing human error in aviation. *Scientific American*, pp. 62–67. (pp. 317–318)

Hemsley, G. D., & Doob, A. N. (1978). The effect of looking behavior on perceptions of a communicator's credibility. *Journal of Applied Social Psychology, 8*, 136–144. (p. 252)

Henderson-King, E. I., & Nisbett, R. E. (1996). Anti-black prejudice as a function of exposure to the negative behavior of a single black person. *Journal of Personality and Social Psychology, 71*, 654–664. (p. 363)

Hendrick, C., & Hendrick, S. (1993). *Romantic love.* Newbury Park, CA: Sage. (p. 453)

Hendrick, C., & Hendrick, S. (2003). Romantic love: Measuring Cupid's arrow. In S. J. Lopez & C. R. Snyder (Eds.), *Positive psychological assessment: A handbook of models and measures.* Washington, DC: American Psychological Association. (p. 453)

Hendrick, S. S., & Hendrick, C. (1995). Gender differences and similarities in sex and love. *Personal Relationships, 2*, 55–65. (p. 455)

Hendrick, S. S., & Hendrick, C. (1997). Love and satisfaction. In R. J. Sternberg & M. Hojjat (Eds.), *Satisfaction in close relationships.* New York: Guilford Publications. (p. 463)

Hendrick, S. S., Hendrick, C., & Adler, N. L. (1988). Romantic relationships: Love, satisfaction, and staying together. *Journal of Personality and Social Psychology, 54*, 980–988. (p. 464)

Henley, N. (1977). *Body politics: Power, sex, and nonverbal communication.* Englewood Cliffs, NJ: Prentice-Hall. (p. 187)

Hennigan, K. M., Del Rosario, M. L., Health, L., Cook, T. D., Wharton, J. D., & Calder, B. J. (1982). Impact of the introduction of television on crime in the United States: Empirical findings and theoretical implications. *Journal of Personality and Social Psychology, 42*, 461–477. (p. 389)

Henry, W. A., III. (1994, June 27). Pride and prejudice. *Time*, pp. 54–59. (p. 336)

Henslin, M. (1967). Craps and magic. *American Journal of Sociology, 73*, 316–330. (p. 117)

Hepworth, J. T., & West, S. G. (1988). Lynchings and the economy: A time-series reanalysis of Hovland and Sears (1940). *Journal of Personality and Social Psychology, 55*, 239–247. (p. 350)

Heradstveit, D. (1979). *The Arab-Israeli conflict: Psychological obstacles to peace* (Vol. 28). Oslo, Norway: Universitetsforlaget. Distributed by Columbia University Press. Reviewed by R. K. White, *Contemporary Psychology*, 1980, *25*, 11–12. (p. 534–535)

Herek, G. (1993). Interpersonal contact and heterosexuals' attitudes toward gay men: Results from a national survey. *Journal of Sex Research, 30*, 239–244. (p. 541)

Herlocker, C. E., Allison, S. T., Foubert, J. D., & Beggan, J. K. (1997). Intended and unintended overconsumption of physical, spatial, and temporal resources. *Journal of Personality and Social Psychology, 73*, 992–1004. (p. 524)

Herman, C. P., Roth, D. A., & Polivy, J. (2003). Effects of the presence of others on food intake: A normative interpretation. *Psychological Bulletin, 129*, 873–886. (p. 287)

Hewstone, M. (1990). The 'ultimate attribution error'? A review of the literature on intergroup causal attribution. *European Journal of Social Psychology, 20*, 311–335. (p. 366)

Hewstone, M. (1994). Revision and change of stereotypic beliefs: In search of the elusive subtyping model. In S. Stroebe & M. Hewstone (Eds.), *European review of social psychology*, vol. 5. Chichester, England: Wiley. (p. 370)

Hewstone, M. (2003). Intergroup contact: Panacea for prejudice? *The Psychologist, 16*, 352–355. (pp. 540, 541)

Hewstone, M., & Fincham, F. (1996). Attribution theory and research: Basic issues and applications. In M. Hewstone, W. Stroebe, and G. M. Stephenson (Eds.), *Introduction to social psychology: A European perspective.* Oxford, England: Blackwell. (p. 85)

Hewstone, M., & Greenland, K. (2000). Intergroup conflict. Unpublished manuscript, Cardiff University. (p. 551)

Hewstone, M., Hantzi, A., & Johnston, L. (1991). Social categorisation and person memory: The pervasiveness of race as an organizing principle. *European Journal of Social Psychology, 21*, 517–528. (p. 358)

Hewstone, M., Hopkins, N., & Routh, D. A. (1992). Cognitive models of stereotype change: Generalization and subtyping in young people's views of the police. *European Journal of Social Psychology, 22*, 219–234. (p. 370)

Higbee, K. L., Millard, R. J., & Folkman, J. R. (1982). Social psychology research during the 1970s: Predominance of experimentation and college students. *Personality and Social Psychology Bulletin, 8*, 180–183. (p. 28)

Higgins, E. T., & Bargh, J. A. (1987). Social cognition and social perception. *Annual Review of Psychology, 38*, 369–425. (p. 42)

Higgins, E. T., & McCann, C. D. (1984). Social encoding and subsequent attitudes, impressions and memory: "Context-driven" and motivational aspects of processing. *Journal of Personality and Social Psychology, 47*, 26–39. (p. 143)

Higgins, E. T., & Rholes, W. S. (1978). Saying is believing: Effects of message modification on memory and liking for the person described. *Journal of*

Experimental Social Psychology, **14**, 363–378. (p. 143)

Higgins, E. T., Rholes, W. S., & Jones, C. R. (1977). Category accessibility and impression formation. *Journal of Experimental Social Psychology*, **13**, 141–154. (p. 106)

Hileman, B. (1999, August 9). Case grows for climate change. *Chemical and Engineering News*, pp. 16–23. (p. 642)

Hill, T., Smith, N. D., & Lewicki, P. (1989). The development of self-image bias: A real-world demonstration. *Personality and Social Psychology Bulletin*, **15**, 205–211. (pp. 69–70)

Hilton, J. L. & Darley, J. M. (1985). Constructing other persons: A limit on the effect. *Journal of Experimental Social Psychology*, **21**, 1–18. (pp. 125–126)

Hilton, J. L., & von Hippel, W. (1990). The role of consistency in the judgment of stereotype-relevant behaviors. *Personality and Social Psychology Bulletin*, **16**, 430–448. (p. 99)

Hine, D. W., & Gifford, R. (1996). Attributions about self and others in commons dilemmas. *European Journal of Social Psychology*, **26**, 429–445. (p. 524)

Hines, M., & Green, R. (1991). Human hormonal and neural correlates of sex-typed behaviors. *Review of Psychiatry*, **10**, 536–555. (p. 192)

Hinkle, S., Brown, R., & Ely, P. G. (1992). Social identity theory processes: Some limitations and limiting conditions. *Revista de Psicologia Social*, 99–111. (p. 352)

Hinsz, V. B. (1990). Cognitive and consensus processes in group recognition memory performance. *Journal of Personality and Social Psychology*, **59**, 705–718. (p. 319)

Hinsz, V. B., Tindale, R. S., & Vollrath, D. A. (1997). The emerging conceptualization of groups as information processors. *Psychological Bulletin*, **121**, 43–64. (p. 308)

Hirschman, R. S., & Leventhal, H. (1989). Preventing smoking behavior in school children: An initial test of a cognitive-development program. *Journal of Applied Social Psychology*, **19**, 559–583. (p. 280)

Hirt, E. R. (1990). Do I see only what I expect? Evidence for an expectancy-guided retrieval model. *Journal of Personality and Social Psychology*, **58**, 937–951. (p. 103)

Hirt, E. R., & Markman, K. D. (1995). Multiple explanation: A consider-an-alternative strategy for debiasing judgments. *Journal of Personality and Social Psychology*, **69**, 1069–1088. (p. 102)

Hirt, E. R., Zillmann, D., Erickson, G. A., & Kennedy, C. (1992). Costs and benefits of allegiance: Changes in fans' self-ascribed competencies after team victory versus defeat. *Journal of Personality and Social Psychology*, **63**, 724–738. (p. 579)

Hobden, K. L., & Olson, J. M. (1994). From jest to antipathy: Disparagement humor as a source of dissonance-motivated attitude change. *Basic and Applied Social Psychology*, **15**, 239–249. (p. 153)

Hodgins, H. S., & Zuckerman, M. (1993). Beyond selecting information: Biases in spontaneous questions and resultant conclusions. *Journal of Experimental Social Psychology*, **29**, 387–407. (p. 571)

Hodgkinson, V. A., & Weitzman, M. S. (1992). *Giving and volunteering in the United States*. Washington, DC: Independent Sector. (p. 509)

Hodgkinson, V. A., Weitzman, M. S., & Kirsch, A. D. (1990). From commitment to action: How religious involvement affects giving and volunteering. In R. Wuthnow, V. A. Hodgkinson & Associates (Eds.), *Faith and philanthropy in America: Exploring the role of religion in America's voluntary sector*. San Francisco: Jossey-Bass. (pp. 508, 509)

Hoffman, C., & Hurst, N. (1990). Gender stereotypes: Perception or rationalization? *Journal of Personality and Social Psychology*, **58**, 197–208. (p. 394)

Hoffman, L. W. (1977). Changes in family roles, socialization, and sex differences. *American Psychologist*, **32**, 644–657. (p. 347)

Hoffman, M. L. (1981). Is altruism part of human nature? *Journal of Personality and Social Psychology*, **40**, 121–137. (p. 490)

Hoffrage, U., Hertwig, R., & Gigerenzer, G. (2000, May). Hindsight bias: A by-product of knowledge updating? *Journal of Experimental Psychology: Learning, Memory, and Cognition*, **26**, 566–581. (p. 17)

Hofling, C. K., Brotzman, E., Dairymple, S., Graves, N., & Pierce, C. M. (1966). An experimental study in nurse-physician relationships. *Journal of Nervous and Mental Disease*, **143**, 171–180. (p. 220)

Hogan, R., Curphy, G. J., & Hogan, J. (1994). What we know about leadership: Effectiveness and personality. *American Psychologist*, **49**, 493–504. (p. 325)

Hogg, M. A. (1992). *The social psychology of group cohesiveness: From attraction to social identity*. London: Harvester Wheatsheaf. (p. 350)

Hogg, M. A. (1996). Intragroup processes, group structure and social identity. In W. P. Robinson (Ed.), *Social groups and identities: Developing the legacy of Henri Tajfel*. Oxford: Butterworth Heinemann. (p. 350)

Hogg, M. A. (2001). A social identity theory of leadership. *Personality and Social Psychology Review*, **5**, 184–200. (p. 231)

Hogg, M. A. (2003). Social identity. In M. R. Leary & J. P. Tangey (Eds.), *Handbook of self and identity*. New York: Guilford Press. (p. 350)

Hogg, M. A., & Hains, S. C. (1998). Friendship and group identification: A new look at the role of cohesiveness in groupthink. *European Journal of Social Psychology*, **28**, 323–341. (p. 315)

Hogg, M. A., Hains, S. C., & Mason, I. (1998). Identification and leadership in small groups: Salience, frame of reference, and leader stereotypicality effects on leader evaluations. *Journal of Personality and Social Psychology*, **75**, 1248–1263. (p. 325)

Hogg, M. A., Turner, J. C., & Davidson, B. (1990). Polarized norms and social frames of reference: A test of the self-categorization theory of group polarization. *Basic and Applied Social Psychology*, **11**, 77–100. (p. 309)

Holland, R. W., Meertens, R. M., & Van Vugt, M. (2002). Dissonance on the road: Self-esteem as a moderator of internal and external self-justification strategies. *Personality and Social*

Psychology Bulletin, **28**, 1712–1724. (p. 162)

Hollander, E. P. (1958). Conformity, status, and idiosyncrasy credit. *Psychological Review,* **65**, 117–127. (p. 234)

Holmberg, D., & Holmes, J. G. (1994). Reconstruction of relationship memories: A mental models approach. In N. Schwarz & S. Sudman (Eds.), *Autobiographical memory and the validity of retrospective reports.* New York: Springer-Verlag. (p. 104)

Holmes, J. G., Miller, D. T., & Lerner, M. J. (1997). Committing altruism under the cloak of self-interest: The exchange fiction. Unpublished manuscript, University of Waterloo. (p. 477)

Holmes, J. G., & Rempel, J. K. (1989). Trust in close relationships. In C. Hendrick (Ed.), *Review of personality and social psychology,* Vol. 10. Newbury Park, CA: Sage. (p. 462)

Holtgraves, T. (1997). Styles of language use: Individual and cultural variability in conversational indirectness. *Journal of Personality and Social Psychology,* **73**, 624–637. (p. 48)

Holtz, R., & Miller, N. (2001). Intergroup competition, attitudinal projection, and opinion certainty: Capitalizing on conflict. *Group Processes and Intergroup Relations,* **4**, 61–73. (p. 529)

Holtzworth, A., & Jacobson, N. S. (1988). An attributional approach to marital dysfunction and therapy. In J. E. Maddux, C. D. Stoltenberg, & R. Rosenwein (Eds.), *Social processes in clinical and counseling psychology.* New York: Springer-Verlag. (p. 84)

Holtzworth-Munroe, A., & Jacobson, N. S. (1985). Causal attributions of married couples: When do they search for causes? What do they conclude when they do? *Journal of Personality and Social Psychology,* **48**, 1398–1412. (p. 84)

Hoorens, V. (1993). Self-enhancement and superiority biases in social comparison. In W. Stroebe & M. Hewstone (Eds.), *European review of social psychology,* vol. 4. Chichester, England: Wiley. (p. 70)

Hoorens, V. (1995). Self-favoring biases, self-presentation and the self-other

asymmetry in social comparison. *Journal of Personality,* **63**, 793–819. (p. 70)

Hoorens, V., & Nuttin, J. M. (1993). Overvaluation of own attributes: Mere ownership or subjective frequency? *Social Cognition,* **11**, 177–200. (p. 429)

Hoorens, V., Nuttin, J. M., Herman, I. E., & Pavakanun, U. (1990). Mastery pleasure versus mere ownership: A quasi-experimental cross-cultural and cross-alphabetical test of the name letter effect. *European Journal of Social Psychology,* **20**, 181–205. (p. 429)

Hoover, C. W., Wood, E. E., & Knowles, E. S. (1983). Forms of social awareness and helping. *Journal of Experimental Social Psychology,* **19**, 577–590. (p. 511)

Hooykaas, R. (1972). *Religion and the rise of modern science.* Grand Rapids, MI: Eerdmans. (p. 130)

Horgan, T. G., Mast, M. S., Hall, J. A., & Carter, J. D. (2004). Gender differences in memory for the appearance of others. *Personality and Social Psychology Bulletin,* **30**, 185–196. (p. 185)

Hormuth, S. E. (1986). Lack of effort as a result of self-focused attention: An attributional ambiguity analysis. *European Journal of Social Psychology,* **16**, 181–192. (p. 79)

Hornstein, H. (1976). *Cruelty and kindness.* Englewood Cliffs, NJ: Prentice-Hall. (pp. 382–383)

Horowitz, S. V., & Boardman, S. K. (1994). Managing conflict: Policy and research implications. *Journal of Social Issues,* **50**, 197–211. (p. 555)

Horwitz, A. V., White, H. R., Howell-White, S. (1997). Becoming married and mental health: A longitudinal study of a cohort of young adults. *Journal of Marriage and the Family,* **58**, 895–907. (p. 601)

Höss, R. (1959). *Commandant at Auschwitz: Autobiography.* London: Weidenfeld and Nicolson. (pp. 91–92)

House, R. J., & Singh, J. V. (1987). Organizational behavior: Some new directions for I/O psychology. *Annual Review of Psychology,* **38**, 669–718. (p. 325)

Houston, V., & Bull, R. (1994). Do people avoid sitting next to someone who is facially disfigured? *European*

Journal of Social Psychology, **24**, 279–284. (p. 434)

Hovland, C. I., Lumsdaine, A. A., & Sheffield, F. D. (1949). *Experiments on mass communication. Studies in social psychology in World War II* (Vol. III). Princeton, NJ: Princeton University Press. (pp. 247–248, 256, 260–261)

Hovland, C. I., & Sears, R. (1940). Minor studies of aggression: Correlation of lynchings with economic indices. *Journal of Psychology,* **9**, 301–310. (p. 350)

Howard, D. J. (1997). Familiar phrases as peripheral persuasion cues. *Journal of Experimental Social Psychology,* **33**, 231–243. (p. 249)

Hoyle, R. H. (1993). Interpersonal attraction in the absence of explicit attitudinal information. *Social Cognition,* **11**, 309–320. (p. 444)

Huberman, B., & Lukose, R. (1997). Social dilemmas and internet congestion. *Science,* **277**, 535–537. (pp. 523–524)

Huddy, L., & Virtanen, S. (1995). Subgroup differentiation and subgroup bias among Latinos as a function of familiarity and positive distinctiveness. *Journal of Personality and Social Psychology,* **68**, 97–108. (p. 359)

Huesmann, L. R. (2003). Gender differences in the continuity of aggression from childhood to adulthood: Evidence from some recent longitudinal studies. In S. Fein, A. Goethals, and M. Sandstrom (Eds.). *Gender and aggression: The 2001 G. Stanley Hall symposium.* Mahwah, NJ: Erlbaum, in press. (p. 305)

Huesmann, L. R., Lagerspetz, K., & Eron, L. D. (1984). Intervening variables in the TV violence-aggression relation: Evidence from two countries. *Developmental Psychology,* **20**, 746–775. (p. 405)

Huesmann, L. R., Moise-Titus, J., Podolski, C-L., & Eron, L. D. (2003). Longitudinal relations between children's exposure to TV violence and their aggressive and violent behavior in young adulthood: 1977–1992. *Developmental Psychology,* **39**, 201–222. (p. 384)

Hugenberg, K. & Bodenhausen, G. V. (2003). Facing prejudice: Implicit prejudice and the perception of facial threat. *Psychological Science, 14*, 640–643. (p. 338)

Hui, C. H., Triandis, H. C., & Yee, C. (1991). Cultural differences in reward allocation: Is collectivism the explanation? *British Journal of Social Psychology, 30*, 145–157. (p. 532)

Hull, J. G., & Bond, C. F., Jr. (1986). Social and behavioral consequences of alcohol consumption and expectancy: A meta-analysis. *Psychological Bulletin, 99*, 347–360. (p. 385)

Hull, J. G., Levenson, R. W., Young, R. D., & Sher, K. J. (1983). Self-awareness-reducing effects of alcohol consumption. *Journal of Personality and Social Psychology, 44*, 461–473. (p. 302)

Hull, J. G., & Young, R. D. (1983). The self-awareness-reducing effects of alcohol consumption: Evidence and implications. In J. Suls & A. G. Greenwald (Eds.), *Psychological perspectives on the self*, Vol. 2. Hillsdale, NJ: Erlbaum. (p. 584)

Humphrey, R. (1985). How work roles influence perception: Structural-cognitive processes and organizational behavior. *American Sociological Review, 50*, 242–252. (p. 179)

Hunt, A. R. (2000, June 22). Major progress, inequities cross 3 generations. *Wall Street Journal*, pp. A9, A14. (pp. 197, 342)

Hunt, M. (1990). *The compassionate beast: What science is discovering about the humane side of human kind.* New York: William Morrow. (pp. 184, 492–493)

Hunt, M. (1993). *The story of psychology.* New York: Doubleday. (p. 58)

Hunt, P. J., & Hillery, J. M. (1973). Social facilitation in a location setting: An examination of the effects over learning trials. *Journal of Experimental Social Psychology, 9*, 563–571. (p. 288)

Hunter, J. A., Stringer, M., & Watson, R. P. (1991). Intergroup violence and intergroup attributions. *British Journal of Social Psychology, 30*, 261–266. (p. 535)

Hunter, J. D. (2002, June 21–22). "To change the world." Paper presented to the Board of Directors of The Trinity Forum, Denver, Colorado. (p. 246)

Huo, Y. J., Smith, H. J., Tyler, T. R., & Lind, E. A. (1996). Superordinate identification, subgroup identification, and justice concerns: Is separatism the problem; is assimilation the answer? *Psychological Science, 7*, 40–45. (p. 551)

Hurt, S. W., Schnurr, P. P., Severino, S. K., Freeman, E. W., Gise, L. H., Rivera-Tovar, A., & Steege, J. F. (1992). Late luteal phase dysphoric disorder in 670 women evaluated for premenstrual complaints. *American Journal of Psychiatry, 149*, 525–530. (p. 586)

Hurtado, S., Dey, E. L., & Trevino, J. G. (1994). Exclusion or self-segregation? Interaction across racial/ethnic groups on college campuses. Paper presented at the American Educational Research Association annual meeting. (p. 336)

Huston, A. C., Donnerstein, E., Fairchild, H., Feshbach, N. D., Katz, P. A., & Murray, J. P. (1992). *Big world, small screen: The role of television in American society.* Lincoln: University of Nebraska Press. (p. 403)

Huston, T. L. (1973). Ambiguity of acceptance, social desirability, and dating choice. *Journal of Experimental Social Psychology, 9*, 32–42. (p. 433)

Huston, T. L., & Chorost, A. F. (1994). Behavioral buffers on the effect of negativity on marital satisfaction: A longitudinal study. *Personal Relationships, 1*, 223–239. (p. 456)

Huston, T. L., Niehuis, S., & Smith, S. E. (2001). The early marital roots of conjugal distress and divorce. *Current Directions in Psychological Science, 10*, 116–119. (p. 470)

Hutnik, N. (1985). Aspects of identity in a multi-ethnic society. *New Community, 12*, 298–309. (p. 552)

Hutton, D. G., & Baumeister, R. F. (1992). Self-awareness and attitude change: Seeing oneself on the central route to persuasion. *Personality and Social Psychology Bulletin, 18*, 68–75. (p. 302)

Hyman, H. H., & Sheatsley, P. B. (1956 & 1964). Attitudes toward desegregation. *Scientific American, 195*(6), 35–39, and *211*(1), 16–23. (p. 334)

Hyman, I. E., Jr., Husband, T. H., & Billings, F. J. (1995). False memories of childhood experiences. *Applied Cognitive Psychology, 9*, 181–197. (p. 103)

Hyman, I. E., Jr., & Pentland, J. (1996). The role of mental imagery in the creation of false childhood memories. *Journal of Memory and Language, 35*, 101–117. (p. 103)

Hyman, R. (1981). Cold reading: How to convince strangers that you know all about them. In K. Frazier (Ed.), *Paranormal borderlands of science.* Buffalo, NY: Prometheus Books. (p. 143)

Ickes, B. (1980). On disconfirming our perceptions of others. Paper presented at the American Psychological Association convention. (p. 94)

Ickes, W. (1993). Traditional gender roles: Do they make, and then break, our relationships? *Journal of Social Issues, 49*, 7185. (p. 195)

Ickes, W. (2003). Everyday mind reading: Understanding what others think and feel. Buffalo, NY: Prometheus Books. (p. 185)

Ickes, W., Layden, M. A., & Barnes, R. D. (1978). Objective self-awareness and individuation: An empirical link. *Journal of Personality, 46*, 146–161. (p. 302)

Ickes, W., Patterson, M. L., Rajecki, D. W., & Tanford, S. (1982). Behavioral and cognitive consequences of reciprocal versus compensatory responses to preinteraction expectancies. *Social Cognition, 1*, 160–190. (pp. 236, 369)

Ickes, W., Snyder, M., & Garcia, S. (1997). Personality influences on the choice of situations. In R. Hogan, J. Johnson, & S. Briggs (Eds.), *Handbook of Personality Psychology.* San Diego, CA: Academic Press. (p. 203)

Idson, L. C., & Mischel, W. (2001). The personality of familiar and significant people: The lay perceiver as a social-cognitive theorist. *Journal of Personality and Social Psychology, 80*, 585–596. (p. 94)

ILO (1997, December 11). Women's progress in workforce improving worldwide, but occupation segregation still rife. International Labor Association press release (www.ilo.org/public/english/bureau/inf/pr/1997/35.htm) (p. 196)

Imai, Y. (1994). Effects of influencing attempts on the perceptions of powerholders and the powerless.

Journal of Social Behavior and Personality, 9, 455–468. (p. 68)

Independent Sector (2002). *Faith and philanthropy: The connection between charitable behavior and giving to religion.* Washington, DC: Independent Sector. (p. 509)

Ingham, A. G., Levinger, G., Graves, J., & Peckham, V. (1974). The Ringelmann effect: Studies of group size and group performance. *Journal of Experimental Social Psychology, 10,* 371–384. (pp. 293–294)

Inglehart, M. R., Markus, H., & Brown, D. R. (1989). The effects of possible selves on academic achievement—a panel study. In J. P. Forgas & J. M. Innes (Eds.), *Recent advances in social psychology: An international perspective.* North-Holland: Elsevier Science Publishers. (p. 42)

Inglehart, R. (1990). *Culture shift in advanced industrial society.* Princeton, NJ: Princeton University Press. (pp. 471, 600, 651, 652, 659)

Inglehart, R. (1997). *Modernization and postmodernization.* Princeton, NJ: Princeton University Press. (p. 651)

Insko, C. A., Nacoste, R. W., & Moe, J. L. (1983). Belief congruence and racial discrimination: Review of the evidence and critical evaluation. *European Journal of Social Psychology, 13,* 153–174. (p. 444)

IPU (2002, April 10). Women in national parliaments. Inter-Parliamentary Union (www.ipu.org/wmn-e/world.htm). (p. 185)

Isen, A. M., Clark, M., & Schwartz, M. F. (1976). Duration of the effect of good mood on helping: Footprints on the sands of time. *Journal of Personality and Social Psychology, 34,* 385–393. (p. 483)

Isen, A. M., Horn, N., & Rosenhan, D. L. (1973). Effects of success and failure on children's generosity. *Journal of Personality and Social Psychology, 27,* 239–247. (p. 480)

Isen, A. M., & Means, B. (1983). The influence of positive affect on decision-making strategy. *Social Cognition, 2,* 28–31. (p. 119)

Isen, A. M., Shalker, T. E., Clark, M., & Karp, L. (1978). Affect, accessibility of material in memory, and behavior: A cognitive loop. *Journal of Personality and Social Psychology, 36,* 1–12. (p. 483)

Isozaki, M. (1984). The effect of discussion on polarization of judgments. *Japanese Psychological Research, 26,* 187–193. (p. 305)

ISR Newsletter (1975). Institute for Social Research, University of Michigan, 3(4), 4–7. (p. 148)

Ito, T. A., Miller, N., & Pollock, V. E. (1996). Alcohol and aggression: A meta-analysis on the moderating effects of inhibitory cues, triggering events, and self-focused attention. *Psychological Bulletin, 120,* 60–82. (p. 385)

Ito, T. A., & Urland, G. R. (2003). Race and gender on the brain: Electrocortical measures of attention to the race and gender of multiply categorizable individuals. *Journal of Personality and Social Psychology, 85,* 616–626. (p. 358)

Iyengar, S. S., & Lepper, M. R. (2000). When choice is demotivating: Can one desire too much of a good thing? *Journal of Personality and Social Psychology, 79,* 995–1006. (p. 61)

Iyer, P. (1993, Fall). The global village finally arrives. *Time,* pp. 86–87. (p. 173)

Jackman, M. R., & Senter, M. S. (1981). Beliefs about race, gender, and social class different, therefore unequal: Beliefs about trait differences between groups of unequal status. In D. J. Treiman & R. V. Robinson (Eds.), *Research in stratification and mobility* (Vol. 2). Greenwich, CT: JAI Press. (pp. 335, 340)

Jacks, J. Z., & Cameron, K. A. (2003). Strategies for resisting persuasion. *Basic and Applied Social Psychology, 25,* 145–161. (p. 278)

Jackson, J. M., & Latané, B. (1981). All alone in front of all those people: Stage fright as a function of number and type of co-performers and audience. *Journal of Personality and Social Psychology, 40,* 73–85. (p. 289)

Jackson, J. W., Kirby, D., Barnes, L, & Shepard, L. (1993). Institutional racism and pluralistic ignorance: A cross-national comparison. In M. Wievorka (Ed.), *Racisme et modernite.* Paris: Editions la Découverte. (p. 365)

Jackson, L. A. (1989). Relative deprivation and the gender wage gap. *Journal of Social Issues, 45*(4), 117–133. (p. 531)

Jackson, L. A., Hunter, J. E., & Hodge, C. N. (1995). Physical attractiveness and intellectual competence: A meta-analytic review. *Social Psychology Quarterly, 58,* 108–123. (p. 435)

Jacobs, R. C., & Campbell, D. T. (1961). The perpetuation of an arbitrary tradition through several generations of a laboratory microculture. *Journal of Abnormal and Social Psychology, 62,* 649–658. (p. 210)

Jacoby, S. (1986, December). When opposites attract. *Reader's Digest,* pp. 95–98. (p. 445)

Jaffe, Y., Shapir, N., & Yinon, Y. (1981). Aggression and its escalation. *Journal of Cross-Cultural Psychology, 12,* 21–36. (pp. 414–415)

Jaffe, Y., & Yinon, Y. (1983). Collective aggression: The group-individual paradigm in the study of collective antisocial behavior. In H. H. Blumberg, A. P. Hare, V. Kent, & M. Davies (Eds.), *Small groups and social interaction,* Vol. 1. Cambridge: Wiley. (p. 414)

Jain, U. (1990). Social perspectives on causal attribution. In G. Misra (Ed.), *Applied social psychology in India.* New Delhi: Sage. (p. 80)

James, W. (1890, reprinted 1950). *The principles of psychology,* vol. 2. New York: Dover Publications. (pp. 78, 158)

James, W. (1899). Talks to teachers on psychology: And to students on some of life's ideals. New York: Holt, 1922, p. 33. Cited by W. J. McKeachie, Psychology in America's bicentennial year. *American Psychologist, 31,* 819–833. (p. 165)

James, W. (1902, reprinted 1958). *The varieties of religious experience.* New York: Mentor Books. (p. 346)

Jamieson, D. W., Lydon, J. E., Stewart, G., & Zanna, M. P. (1987). Pygmalion revisited: New evidence for student expectancy effects in the classroom. *Journal of Educational Psychology, 79,* 461–466. (p. 123)

Janes, L. M., & Olson, J. M. (2000). Jeer pressure: The behavioral effects of observing ridicule of others.

Personality and Social Psychology Bulletin, **26**, 474–485. (p. 234)

Janis, I. L. (1971, November). Groupthink. *Psychology Today*, pp. 43–46. (pp. 311–313)

Janis, I. L. (1982). Counteracting the adverse effects of concurrence-seeking in policy-planning groups: Theory and research perspectives. In H. Brandstatter, J. H. Davis, & G. Stocker-Kreichgauer (Eds.), *Group decision making*. New York: Academic Press. (pp. 311–313, 317)

Janis, I. L. (1989). Crucial decisions: Leadership in policymaking and crisis management. New York: Free Press. (p. 536)

Janis, I. L., Kaye, D., & Kirschner, P. (1965). Facilitating effects of eating while reading on responsiveness to persuasive communications. *Journal of Personality and Social Psychology*, **1**, 181–186. (p. 256)

Janis, I. L., & Mann, L. (1977). *Decision-making: A psychological analysis of conflict, choice and commitment*. New York: Free Press. (p. 315)

Jankowiak, W. R., & Fischer, E. F. (1992). A cross-cultural perspective on romantic love. *Ethnology*, **31**, 149–155. (p. 455)

Jason, L. A., Rose, T., Ferrari, J. R., & Barone, R. (1984). Personal versus impersonal methods for recruiting blood donations. *Journal of Social Psychology*, **123**, 139–140. (p. 510)

Jeffery, R. (1964). The psychologist as an expert witness on the issue of insanity. *American Psychologist*, **19**, 838–843. (p. 569)

Jeffery, R. W., Drewnowski, A., Epstein, L. H., Stunkard, A. J., Wilson, G. T., Wing, R. R., & Hill, D. R. (2000). Long-term maintenance of weight loss: Current status. *Health Psychology*, **19**, No. 1 (Supplement), 5–16. (p. 595)

Jelalian, E., & Miller, A. G. (1984). The perseverance of beliefs: Conceptual perspectives and research developments. *Journal of Social and Clinical Psychology*, **2**, 25–56. (p. 102)

Jellison, J. M., & Green, J. (1981). A self-presentation approach to the fundamental attribution error: The norm of internality. *Journal of*

Personality and Social Psychology, **40**, 643–649. (p. 94)

Jemmott, J. B., III., & Gonzalez, E. (1989). Social status, the status distribution, and performance in small groups. *Journal of Applied Social Psychology*, **19**, 584–598. (p. 179)

Jemmott, J. B., III., & Locke, S. E. (1984). Psychosocial factors, immunologic mediation, and human susceptibility to infectious diseases: How much do we know? *Psychological Bulletin*, **95**, 78–108. (p. 589)

Jennings, D. L., Amabile, T. M., & Ross, L. (1982). Informal covariation assessment: Data-based vs theory-based judgments. In D. Kahneman, P. Slovic, & A. Tversky (Eds.), *Judgment under uncertainty: Heuristics and biases*. New York: Cambridge University Press. (p. 117)

Jervis, R. (1985). Perceiving and coping with threat: Psychological perspectives. In R. Jervis, R. N. Lebow, & J. Stein (Eds.), *Psychology and deterrence*. Baltimore: Johns Hopkins University Press. (pp. 100, 533)

John, O. P., & Srivastava, S. (1999). The Big Five trait taxonomy: History, measurement, and theoretical perspectives. In L. A. Pervin & O. P. John (Eds.), *Handbook of personality: Theory and research*. New York: Guilford. (p. 175)

Johnson, B. T., & Eagly, A. H. (1989). Effects of involvement on persuasion: A meta-analysis. *Psychological Bulletin*, **106**, 290–314. (p. 247)

Johnson, B. T., & Eagly, A. H. (1990). Involvement and persuasion: Types, traditions, and the evidence. *Psychological Bulletin*, **107**, 375–384. (p. 269)

Johnson, C. B., Stockdale, M. S., & Saal, F. E. (1991). Persistence of men's misperceptions of friendly cues across a variety of interpersonal encounters. *Psychology of Women Quarterly*, **15**, 463–475. (p. 85)

Johnson, D. (2000, February 1). Illinois, citing faulty verdicts, bars executions. *New York Times* (www.nytimes.com). (p. 630)

Johnson, D. J., & Rusbult, C. E. (1989). Resisting temptation: Devaluation of alternative partners as a means of maintaining commitment in close

relationships. *Journal of Personality and Social Psychology*, **57**, 967–980. (p. 441)

Johnson, D. W., & Johnson, R. T. (1987). *Learning together and alone: Cooperative, competitive, and individualistic learning*, 2nd ed. Englewood Cliffs, NJ: Prentice-Hall. (p. 549)

Johnson, D. W., & Johnson, R. T. (1994). Constructive conflict in the schools. *Journal of Social Issues*, **50**, 117–137. (p. 549)

Johnson, D. W., & Johnson, R. T. (1995). Teaching students to be peacemakers: Results of five years of research. *Peace and Conflict: Journal of Peace Psychology*, **1**, 417–438. (p. 556)

Johnson, D. W., & Johnson, R. T. (2000). The three Cs of reducing prejudice and discrimination. In S. Oskamp (Ed.), *Reducing prejudice and discrimination*. Mahwah, NJ: Erlbaum, 2000. (pp. 549, 556)

Johnson, D. W., & Johnson, R. T. (2003). Field testing integrative negotiations. *Peace and Conflict*, **9**, 39–68. (pp. 554, 556)

Johnson, D. W., Maruyama, G., Johnson, R., Nelson, D., & Skon, L. (1981). Effects of cooperative, competitive, and individualistic goal structures on achievement: A meta-analysis. *Psychological Bulletin*, **89**, 47–62. (p. 550)

Johnson, E. J., & Tversky, A. (1983). Affect, generalization, and the perception of risk. *Journal of Personality and Social Psychology*, **45**, 20–31. (p. 119)

Johnson, J. D., Jackson, L. A., & Gatto, L. (1995). Violent Attitudes and Deferred Academic Aspirations: Deleterious Effects of Exposure to Rap Music. *Basic and Applied Social Psychology*, **16**, 27–41. (p. 407)

Johnson, J. D., Trawalter, S., & Dovidio, J. F. (2000). Converging interracial consequences of exposure to violent rap music on stereotypical attributions of Blacks. *Journal of Experimental Social Psychology*, **36**, 233–251. (p. 349)

Johnson, J. G., Cohen, P., Smailes, E. M., Kasen, S., & Brook, J. S. (2002). Television viewing and aggressive behavior during adolescence and adulthood. *Science*, **295**, 2468–2471. (p. 405)

Johnson, J. T., Jemmott, J. B., III, & Pettigrew, T. F. (1984). Causal attribution and dispositional inference: Evidence of inconsistent judgments. *Journal of Experimental Social Psychology, 20,* 567–585. (p. 96)

Johnson, M. H., & Magaro, P. A. (1987). Effects of mood and severity on memory processes in depression and mania. *Psychological Bulletin, 101,* 28–40. (pp. 119, 579)

Johnson, P. (1988, November 25–27). Hearst seeks pardon. *USA Today,* p. 3A. (p. 179)

Johnson, R. D., & Downing, L. L. (1979). Deindividuation and valence of cues: Effects of prosocial and antisocial behavior. *Journal of Personality and Social Psychology, 37,* 1532–1538. (p. 301)

Johnson, R. W., Kelly, R. J., & LeBlanc, B. A. (1995). Motivational basis of dissonance: Aversive consequences or inconsistency. *Personality and Social Psychology Bulletin, 21,* 850–855. (p. 163)

Johnston, L., O'Malley, P. M., & Bachman, J. G. (1996). *National survey results on drug use from the Monitoring the Future study, 1975–1995.* Rockville, MD: National Institute on Drug Abuse, U. S. Dept. of Health and Human Services, Public Health Service, National Institutes of Health, Washington, DC. (p. 403)

Johnston, V. (2000). Female facial beauty: The fertility hypothesis. *Pragmatics & Cognition, 8,* 107–122. (p. 438)

Joiner, T. E., Jr. (1994). Contagious depression: Existence, specificity to depressed symptoms, and the role of reassurance seeking. *Journal of Personality and Social Psychology, 67,* 287–296. (p. 579)

Joiner, T. E., Jr. (1999). The clustering and contagion of suicide. *Current Directions in Psychological Science, 8,* 89–92. (p. 213)

Joinson, A. N. (2001). Self-disclosure in computer-mediated communication: The role of self-awareness and visual anonymity. *European Journal of Social Psychology, 31,* 177–192. (p. 465)

Jonas, K. (1992). Modelling and suicide: A test of the Werther effect. *British Journal of Social Psychology, 31,* 295–306. (p. 213)

Jones, C. S., & Kaplan, M. F. (2003). The effects of racially stereotypical crimes on juror decision-making and information-processing strategies. *Basic and Applied Social Psychology, 25,* 1–13. (p. 621)

Jones, E. E. (1964). *Ingratiation.* New York: Appleton-Century-Crofts. (p. 448)

Jones, E. E. (1976). How do people perceive the causes of behavior? *American Scientist, 64,* 300–305. (p. 91)

Jones, E. E., & Davis, K. E. (1965). From acts to dispositions: The attribution process in person perception. In L. Berkowitz (Ed.), *Advances in experimental social psychology* (Vol. 2). New York: Academic Press. (pp. 86–87)

Jones, E. E., & Harris, V. A. (1967). The attribution of attitudes. *Journal of Experimental Social Psychology, 3,* 2–24. (p. 88)

Jones, E. E., & Nisbett, R. E. (1971). *The actor and the observer: Divergent perceptions of the cases of behavior.* Morristown, NJ: General Learning Press. (p. 91)

Jones, E. E., Rhodewalt, F., Berglas, S., & Skelton, J. A. (1981). Effects of strategic self-presentation on subsequent self-esteem. *Journal of Personality and Social Psychology, 41,* 407–421. (pp. 582, 592)

Jones, E. E., Rock, L., Shaver, K. G., Goethals, G. R., & Ward, L. M. (1968). Pattern of performance and ability attribution: An unexpected primacy effect. *Journal of Personality and Social Psychology, 10,* 317–340. (p. 262)

Jones, E. E., & Sigall, H. (1971). The bogus pipeline: A new paradigm for measuring affect and attitude. *Psychological Bulletin, 76,* 349–364. (p. 137)

Jones, J. M. (2004). TRIOS: A model for coping with the universal context of racism? In G. Philogène (Ed.), *Racial identity in context: The legacy of Kenneth B. Clark.* Washington, DC: American Psychological Association. (p. 444)

Jones, J. M. (1988). Piercing the veil: Bi-cultural strategies for coping with prejudice and racism. Invited address at the national conference, "Opening Doors: An Appraisal of Race Relations in America," University of Alabama, June 11. (p. 444)

Jones, J. M. (2003). TRIOS: A psychological theory of the African legacy in American culture. *Journal of Social Issues, 59,* 217–242. (pp. 370, 444)

Jones, J. M. (2003, March 12). Plurality of Americans believe death penalty not imposed often enough: Basic support for death penalty at 70%. The Gallup Organization (www.gallup.com). (p. 246)

Jones, J. M. (2003, March 28). Blacks showing decided opposition to war. *Gallup Poll News Service* (www.gallup.com). (p. 493)

Jones, J. M. (2003, May 19). Support for the death penalty remains high at 74%. Gallup News Service (www.gallup.com). (p. 630)

Jones, J. M., & Moore, D. W. (2003, June 17). Generational differences in support for a woman president. The Gallup Organization (www.gallup.com). (p. 341)

Jones, J. T., & Cunningham, J. D. (1996). Attachment styles and other predictors of relationship satisfaction in dating couples. *Personal Relationships, 3,* 387–399. (p. 459)

Jones, J. T., Pelham, B. W., & Mirenberg, M. C. (2002). Name letter preferences are not merely mere exposure: Implicit egotism as self-regulation. *Journal of Experimental Social Psychology, 38,* 170–177. (p. 430)

Jones, R. A., & Brehm, J. W. (1970). Persuasiveness of one- and two-sided communications as a function of awareness there are two sides. *Journal of Experimental Social Psychology, 6,* 47–56. (p. 261)

Jones, T. F. & 7 others (2000). Mass psychogenic illness attributed to toxic exposure at a high school. *New England Journal of Medicine, 342,* 96–100. (p. 212)

Jones, W. H., Carpenter, B. N., & Quintana, D. (1985). Personality and interpersonal predictors of loneliness in two cultures. *Journal of Personality and Social Psychology, 48,* 1503–1511. (p. 33)

Jones, W. H., Hobbs, S. A., & Hockenbury, D. (1982). Loneliness and social skill deficits. *Journal of Personality and Social Psychology, 42*, 682–689. (p. 582)

Jones, W. H., Sansone, C., & Helm, B. (1983). Loneliness and interpersonal judgments. *Personality and Social Psychology Bulletin, 9*, 437–441. (p. 582)

Jordan, C. H., Spencer, S. J., Zanna, M. P., Hoshino-Browne, E., & Correll, J. (2003). Secure and defensive high self-esteem. *Journal of Personality and Social Psychology, 85*, 969–978. (p. 66)

Josephson, W. L. (1987). Television violence and children's aggression: Testing the priming, social script, and disinhibition predictions. *Journal of Personality and Social Psychology, 53*, 882–890. (p. 407)

Jourard, S. M. (1964), *The transparent self*. Princeton, NJ: Van Nostrand. (p. 463)

Jourden, F. J., & Heath, C. (1996). The evaluation gap in performance perceptions: Illusory perceptions of groups and individuals. *Journal of Applied Psychology, 81*, 369–379. (p. 76)

Judd, C. M., Blair, I. V., & Chapleau, K. M. (2004). Automatic stereotypes vs. automatic prejudice: Sorting out the possibilities in the Payne (2001) weapon paradigm. *Journal of Experimental Social Psychology, 40*, 75–81. (p. 339)

Judd, C. M., Park, B., Ryan, C. S., Brauer, M., & Kraus, S. (1995). Stereotypes and ethnocentrism: Diverging interethnic perceptions of African American and White American youth. *Journal of Personality and Social Psychology, 69*, 460–481. (p. 370)

Jussim, L. (1986). Self-fulfilling prophecies: A theoretical and integrative review. *Psychological Review, 93*, 429–445. (p. 123)

Jussim, L. (1993). Accuracy in interpersonal expectations: A reflection-construction analysis of current and classic research. *Journal of Personality, 61*, 637–668. (p. 125)

Jussim, L., Eccles, J., & Madon, S. (1996). Social perception, social stereotypes, and teacher expectations: Accuracy and the quest for the powerful self-fulfilling prophecy. *Advances in Experimental Social Psychology*. (p. 121)

Jussim, L., McCauley, C. R., & Lee, Y-T. (1995). Introduction: Why study stereotype accuracy and inaccuracy? In Y. T. Lee, L. Jussim, & C. R. McCauley (Eds.), *Stereotypes accuracy: Toward appreciating group differences*. Washington, DC: American Psychological Association. (p. 333)

Kagan, J. (1989). Temperamental contributions to social behavior. *American Psychologist, 44*, 668–674. (pp. 383–384)

Kagehiro, D. K. (1990). Defining the standard of proof in jury instructions. *Psychological Science, 1*, 194–200. (pp. 626, 627, 631)

Kahan, T. L., & Johnson, M. K. (1992). Self effects in memory for person information. *Social Cognition, 10*, 30–50. (p. 42)

Kahle, L. R., & Berman, J. (1979). Attitudes cause behaviors: A cross-lagged panel analysis. *Journal of Personality and Social Psychology, 37*, 315–321. (p. 137)

Kahn, A. S., & Gaeddert, W. P. (1985). From theories of equity to theories of justice. In V. W. O'Leary, R. K. Unger, & B. S. Wallston (Eds.), *Women, gender, and social psychology*. Hillsdale, NJ: Erlbaum. (p. 532)

Kahn, A. S., Mathie, V. A., & Torgler, C. (1994). Rape scripts and rape acknowledgment. *Psychology of Women Quarterly, 18*, 53–66. (p. 401)

Kahn, M. W. (1951). The effect of severe defeat at various age levels on the aggressive behavior of mice. *Journal of Genetic Psychology, 79*, 117–130. (p. 389)

Kahneman, D., & Miller, D. T. (1986). Norm theory: Comparing reality to its alternatives. *Psychological Review, 93*, 75–88. (p. 116)

Kahneman, D., & Snell, J. (1992). Predicting a changing taste: Do people know what they will like? *Journal of Behavioral Decision Making, 5*, 187–200. (p. 429)

Kahneman, D., & Tversky, A. (1979). Intuitive prediction: Biases and corrective procedures. *Management Science, 12*, 313–327. (p. 109)

Kahneman, D., & Tversky, A. (1995). Conflict resolution: A cognitive perspective. In K. Arrow, R. Mnookin, L. Ross, A. Tversky, & R. Wilson (Eds.), *Barriers to the negotiated resolution of conflict*. New York: Norton. (p. 558)

Kalick, S. M. (1977). *Plastic surgery, physical appearance, and person perception*. Unpublished doctoral dissertation, Harvard University. Cited by E. Berscheid in, An overview of the psychological effects of physical attractiveness and some comments upon the psychological effects of knowledge of the effects of physical attractiveness. In W. Lucker, K. Ribbens, & J. A. McNamera (Eds.), *Logical aspects of facial form* (craniofacial growth series). Ann Arbor: University of Michigan Press, 1981. (pp. 435–436)

Kalin, R., & Berry, J. W. (1995). Ethnic and civic self-identity in Canada: Analyses of 1974 and 1991 national surveys. *Canadian Ethnic Studies, 27*, 1–15. (p. 43)

Kalven, H., Jr., & Zeisel, H. (1966). *The American jury*. Chicago: University of Chicago Press. (pp. 619, 631, 633)

Kameda, T., & Sugimori, S. (1993). Psychological entrapment in group decision making: An assigned decision rule and a groupthink phenomenon. *Journal of Personality and Social Psychology, 65*, 282–292. (p. 322)

Kammann, R. (1983). Objective circumstances, life satisfactions, and sense of well-being: Consistencies across time and place. *New Zealand Journal of Psychology, 12*, 14–22. (p. 657)

Kammer, D. (1982). Differences in trait ascriptions to self and friend: Unconfounding intensity from variability. *Psychological Reports, 51*, 99–102. (p. 94)

Kanagawa, C., Cross, S. E., & Markus, H. R. (2001). "Who am I?" The cultural psychology of the conceptual self. *Personality and Social Psychology Bulletin, 27*, 90–103. (p. 46)

Kandel, D. B. (1978). Similarity in real-life adolescent friendship pairs. *Journal of Personality and Social Psychology, 36*, 306–312. (p. 445)

Kanekar, S., & Nazareth, A. (1988). Attributed rape victim's fault as a function of her attractiveness, physical hurt, and emotional disturbance. *Social Behaviour, 3*, 37–40. (p. 85)

Kaplan, J. (1995, March 4–10). Why kids need heroes. *TV Guide*, pp. 25–30. (p. 404)

Kaplan, M. F. (1989). Task, situational, and personal determinants of influence processes in group decision making. In E. J. Lawler (Ed.), *Advances in group processes* (vol. 6). Greenwich, CT: JAI Press. (p. 310)

Kaplan, M. F., & Schersching, C. (1980). Reducing juror bias: An experimental approach. In P. D. Lipsitt & B. D. Sales (Eds.), *New directions in psycholegal research*. New York: Van Nostrand Reinhold, pp. 149–170. (p. 622)

Kaplan, M. F., Wanshula, L. T., & Zanna, M. P. (1993). Time pressure and information integration in social judgment: The effect of need for structure. In O. Svenson & J. Maule (Eds.), *Time pressure and stress in human judgment and decision making*. Cambridge: Cambridge University Press. (p. 358)

Kaprio, J., Koskenvuo, M., & Rita, H. (1987). Mortality after bereavement: A propsective study of 95,647 widowed persons. *American Journal of Public Health, 77*, 283–287. (p. 598)

Karau, S. J., & Williams, K. D. (1993). Social loafing: A meta-analytic review and theoretical integration. *Journal of Personality and Social Psychology, 65*, 681–706. (pp. 294, 296, 297)

Karau, S. J., & Williams, K. D. (1997). The effects of group cohesiveness on social loafing and compensation. *Group Dynamics: Theory, Research, and Practice, 1*, 156–168. (p. 296)

Karavellas, D. (2000). Sustainable consumption and fisheries. In B. Heap and J. Kent (Eds.), *Towards sustainable consumption: A European perspective*. London: The Royal Society. (p. 644)

Karney, B. R., & Bradbury, T. N. (1995). The longitudinal course of marital quality and stability: A review of theory, method, and research. *Psychological Bulletin, 118*, 3–34. (p. 470)

Karney, B. R., & Bradbury, T. N. (1997). Neuroticism, marital interaction, and the trajectory of marital satisfaction. *Journal of Personality and Social Psychology, 72*, 1075–1092. (pp. 449–450)

Kashima, E. S., & Kashima, Y. (1998). Culture and language: the case of cultural dimensions and personal pronoun use. *Journal of Cross-Cultural Psychology, 29*, 461–486. (p. 46)

Kashima, Y., & Kashima, E. S. (2003). Individualism, GNP, climate, and pronoun drop: Is individualism determined by affluence and climate, or does language use play a role? *Journal of Cross-Cultural Psychology, 34*, 125–134. (p. 46)

Kasser, T. (2000). Two versions of the american dream: Which goals and values make for a high quality of life? In E. Diener and D. Rahtz (Eds.), *Advances in quality of life: Theory and research*. Dordrecht, Netherlands: Kluwer. (p. 654)

Kasser, T. (2002). *The high price of materialism*. Cambridge, MA: MIT Press. (pp. 649, 654)

Kasser, T., & Ryan, R. (1996). Further examining the American dream: Differential correlates of intrinsic and extrinsic goals. *Personality and Social Psychology Bulletin, 22*, 280–287. (p. 654)

Kasser, T., & Ryan, R. M. (1993). A dark side of the American dream: Correlates of financial success as a central life aspiration. *Journal of Personality and Social Psychology, 65*, 410–422. (p. 654)

Kassin, S. M., Goldstein, C. C., & Savitsky, K. (2003). Behavioral confirmation in the interrogation room: On the dangers of presuming guilt. *Law and Human Behavior, 27*, 187–203. (p. 124)

Kassin, S. M., Tubb, V. A., Hosch, H. M., & Memon, A. (2001). On the "general acceptance" of eyewitness testimony research: A new survey of the experts. *American Psychologist, 56*, 405–416. (p. 618)

Kassin, S. M., & Wrightsman, L. S. (1979). On the requirements of proof: The timing of judicial instruction and mock juror verdicts. *Journal of Personality and Social Psychology, 37*, 1877–1887. (p. 623)

Kato, P. S., & Ruble, D. N. (1992). Toward an understanding of women's experience of menstrual cycle symptoms. In V. Adesso, D. Reddy, & R. Fleming (Eds.), *Psychological*

perspectives on women's health. Washington, DC: Hemisphere. (p. 586)

Katz, A. M., & Hill, R. (1958). Residential propinquity and marital selection: A review of theory, method, and fact. *Marriage and Family Living, 20*, 237–335. (p. 426)

Katz, E. (1957). The two-step flow of communication: An up-to-date report on a hypothesis. *Public Opinion Quarterly, 21*, 61–78. (pp. 265–266)

Katz, I., Cohen, S., & Glass, D. (1975). Some determinants of cross-racial helping behavior. *Journal of Personality and Social Psychology, 32*, 964–970. (p. 505)

Katz, J., Beach, S. R. H., & Joiner, T. E., Jr. (1999). Contagious depression in dating couples. *Journal of Social and Clinical Psychology, 18*, 1–13. (p. 579)

Katzev, R., Edelsack, L., Steinmetz, G., & Walker, T. (1978). The effect of reprimanding transgressions on subsequent helping behavior: Two field experiments. *Personality and Social Psychology Bulletin, 4*, 126–129. (p. 511)

Katzev, R., & Wang, T. (1994). Can commitment change behavior? A case study of environmental actions. *Journal of Social Behavior and Personality, 9*, 13–26. (p. 233)

Kaufman, J., & Zigler, E. (1987). Do abused children become abusive parents? *American Journal of Orthopsychiatry, 57*, 186–192. (p. 391)

Kawachi, I., Kennedy, B. P., & Wilkinson, R. G. (1999). Crime: Social disorganization and relative deprivation. *Social Science and Medicine, 48*, 719–731. (p. 389)

Kawachi, I., Kennedy, B. P., Wilkinson, R. G., & Kawachi, K. W. (Eds.) (1999). *Society and population health reader: Income inequality and health*. New York: New Press. (p. 599)

Kawakami, K., & Dion, K. L. (1993). The impact of salient self-identities on relative deprivation and action intentions. *European Journal of Social Psychology, 23*, 525–540. (p. 389)

Kawakami, K., & Dion, K. L. (1995). Social identity and affect as determinants of collective action: Toward an integration of relative deprivation and social identity theories. *Theory and Psychology*, **5**, 551–577. (p. 389)

Kawakami, K., Dovidio, J. F., Moll, J., Hermsen, S., & Russin, A. (2000). Just say no (to stereotyping): Effects of training in the negation of stereotypic associations on stereotype activation. *Journal of Personality and Social Psychology*, **78**, 871–888. (p. 337)

Keating, J. P., & Brock, T. C. (1974). Acceptance of persuasion and the inhibition of counterargumentation under various distraction tasks. *Journal of Experimental Social Psychology*, **10**, 301–309. (p. 269)

Kebbell, M. R., Milne, R., & Wagstaff, G. F. (1999). The cognitive interview: A survey of its forensic effectiveness. *Psychology, Crime, and Law*, **5**, 101–115. (p. 616)

Keelan, J. P. R., Dion, K. K., & Dion, K. L. (1998, January). Attachment style and relationship satisfaction: Test of a self-disclosure explanation. *Canadian Journal of Behavioural Science*, **30**, 24–35. (p. 462)

Keller, J., & Dauenheimer, D. (2003). Stereotype threat in the classroom: Dejection mediates the disrupting threat effect on women's math performance. *Personality and Social Psychology Bulletin*, **29**, 371–381. (p. 372)

Kellerman, J., Lewis, J., & Laird, J. D. (1989). Looking and loving: The effects of mutual gaze on feelings of romantic love. *Journal of Research in Personality*, **23**, 145–161. (p. 471)

Kellermann, A. L. (1997). Comment: Gunsmoke–changing public attitudes toward smoking and firearms. *American Journal of Public Health*, **87**, 910–912. (p. 397)

Kellermann, A. L. & 9 others (1993). Gun ownership as a risk factor for homicide in the home. *New England Journal of Medicine*, **329**, 1984–1991. (p. 397)

Kelley, H. H. (1973). The process of causal attribution. *American Psychologist*, **28**, 107–128. (p. 87)

Kelley, H. H. (1979). *Personal relationships: Their structures and processes*. Hillsdale, NJ: Erlbaum. (p. 450)

Kelley, H. H., & Stahelski, A. J. (1970). The social interaction basis of cooperators' and competitors' beliefs about others. *Journal of Personality and Social Psychology*, **16**, 66–91. (p. 124)

Kelley, K., Dawson, L., & Musialowski, D. M. (1989). Three faces of sexual explicitness: The good, the bad, and the useful. In D. Zillmann & J. Bryant (Eds.), *Pornography: Research advances and policy considerations*. Hillsdale, NJ: Erlbaum. (p. 416)

Kelman, H. C. (1997). Group processes in the resolution of international conflicts: Experiences from the Israeli-Palestinian case. *American Psychologist*, **52**, 212–220. (p. 557)

Kelman, H. C. (1998). Building a sustainable peace: The limits of pragmatism in the Israeli-Palestinian negotiations. Address to the American Psychological Association convention. (p. 557)

Keltner, D., & Robinson, R. J. (1996). Extremism, power, and the imagined basis of social conflict. *Current Directions in Psychological Science*, **5**, 101–105. (p. 536)

Kendler, K. S., Neale, M., Kessler, R., Heath, A., & Eaves, L. (1993). A twin study of recent life events and difficulties. *Archives of General Psychiatry*, **50**, 789–796. (p. 579)

Kennedy, D. (2002). POTUS and the fish. *Science*, **297**, 477. (p. 642)

Kennedy, J. F. (1956). *Profiles in courage*. New York: Harper. (p. 234)

Kenny, D. A. (1994). *Interpersonal perception: A social relations analysis*. Storrs, CT: Guilford Press. (p. 53)

Kenny, D. A., & Acitelli, L. K. (2001). Accuracy and bias in the perception of the partner in a close relationship. *Journal of Personality and Social Psychology*, **80**, 439–448. (p. 444)

Kenny, D. A., & Nasby, W. (1980). Splitting the reciprocity correlation. *Journal of Personality and Social Psychology*, **38**, 249–256. (p. 446)

Kenrick, D. T. (1987). Gender, genes, and the social environment: A biosocial interactionist perspective. In P. Shaver & C. Hendrick (Eds.), *Sex and gender: Review of personality and social psychology*, vol. 7. Beverly Hills, CA: Sage. (pp. 190, 194)

Kenrick, D. T., Baumann, D. J., & Cialdini, R. B. (1979). A step in the socialization of altruism as hedonism: Effects of negative mood on children's generosity under public and private conditions. *Journal of Personality and Social Psychology*, **37**, 747–755. (p. 480)

Kenrick, D. T., & Gutierres, S. E. (1980). Contrast effects and judgments of physical attractiveness: When beauty becomes a social problem. *Journal of Personality and Social Psychology*, **38**, 131–140. (p. 440)

Kenrick, D. T., Gutierres, S. E., & Goldberg, L. L. (1989). Influence of popular erotica on judgments of strangers and mates. *Journal of Experimental Social Psychology*, **25**, 159–167. (p. 440)

Kenrick, D. T., & Keefe, R. C. (1992). Age preferences in mates reflect sex differences in reproductive strategies. *Behavioral and Brain Sciences*, **15**, 75–133. (p. 192)

Kenrick, D. T., & MacFarlane, S. W. (1986). Ambient temperature and horn-honking: A field study of the heat/aggression relationship. *Environment and Behavior*, **18**, 179–191. (p. 394)

Kenrick, D. T., & Trost, M. R. (1987). A biosocial theory of heterosexual relationships. In K. Kelly (Ed.), *Females, males, and sexuality*. Albany: State University of New York Press. (pp. 457–458)

Kernis, M. H. (2003). High self-esteem: A differentiated perspective. In E. C. Chang & L. J. Sanna (Eds.), *Virtue, vice, and personality: The complexity of behavior*. Washington, DC: APA Books. (p. 66)

Kerr, N. (1999). Behind the scenes. In D. G. Myers, *Social psychology*, 6th edition. New York: McGraw-Hill. (p. 635)

Kerr, N. L. (1978). Beautiful and blameless: Effects of victim attractiveness and responsibility on mock jurors' verdicts. *Journal of Personality and Social Psychology*, **4**, 479–482. *(a)* (p. 624)

Kerr, N. L. (1978). Severity of prescribed penalty and mock jurors' verdicts. *Journal of Personality and Social Psychology*, **36**, 1431–1442. *(b)* (p. 624)

Kerr, N. L. (1981). Effects of prior juror experience on juror behavior. *Basic and Applied Social Psychology, 2,* 175–193. (pp. 624, 632)

Kerr, N. L. (1981). Social transition schemes: Charting the group's road to agreement. *Journal of Personality and Social Psychology, 41,* 684–702. (p. 632)

Kerr, N. L. (1983). Motivation losses in small groups: A social dilemma analysis. *Journal of Personality and Social Psychology, 45,* 819–828. (p. 296)

Kerr, N. L. (1989). Illusions of efficacy: The effects of group size on perceived efficacy in social dilemmas. *Journal of Experimental Social Psychology, 25,* 287–313. (pp. 525–526)

Kerr, N. L. (1992). Norms in social dilemmas. In D. Schroeder (Ed.), *Social dilemmas: Psychological perspectives.* New York: Praeger. (p. 528)

Kerr, N. L., Atkin, R. S., Stasser, G., Meek, D., Holt, R. W., & Davis, J. H. (1976). Guilt beyond a reasonable doubt: Effects of concept definition and assigned decision rule on the judgments of mock jurors. *Journal of Personality and Social Psychology, 34,* 282–294. (p. 631)

Kerr, N. L., & Bruun, S. E. (1981). Ringelmann revisited: Alternative explanations for the social loafing effect. *Personality and Social Psychology Bulletin, 7,* 224–231. (p. 295)

Kerr, N. L., & Bruun, S. E. (1983). Dispensibility of member effort and group motivation losses: Free-rider effects. *Journal of Personality and Social Psychology, 44,* 78–94. (p. 296)

Kerr, N. L., Garst, J., Lewandowski, D. A., & Harris, S. E. (1997). That still, small voice: Commitment to cooperate as an internalized versus a social norm. *Personality and Social Psychology Bulletin, 23,* 1300–1311. (p. 526)

Kerr, N. L., Harmon, D. L., & Graves, J. K. (1982). Independence of multiple verdicts by jurors and juries. *Journal of Applied Social Psychology, 12,* 12–29. (pp. 186, 624)

Kerr, N. L., & Kaufman-Gilliland, C. M. (1994). Communication, commitment, and cooperation in social dilemmas. *Journal of Personality and Social Psychology, 66,* 513–529. (p. 526)

Kerr, N. L. & Kaufman-Gilliland, C. M. (1997). ". . . and besides, I probably couldn't have made a difference anyway": Justification of social dilemma defection via perceived self-inefficacy. *Journal of Experimental Social Psychology, 33,* 211–230. (p. 526)

Kerr, N. L., & MacCoun, R. J. (1985). The effects of jury size and polling method on the process and product of jury deliberation. *Journal of Personality and Social Psychology, 48,* 349–363. (pp. 232–233)

Kerr, N. L., Nerenz, D., & Herrick, D. (1979). Role playing and the study of jury behavior. *Sociological Methods and Research, 7,* 337–355. (p. 636)

Kessler, T., & Mummendey, A. (2001). Is there any scapegoat around? Determinants of intergroup conflicts at different categorization levels. *Journal of Personality and Social Psychology, 81,* 1090–1102. (p. 552)

Kidd, J. B., & Morgan, J. R. (1969). A predictive information system for management. *Operational Research Quarterly, 20,* 149–170. (p. 76)

Kiecolt-Glaser, J. K., Malarkey, W. B., Chee, M., Newton, T., Cacioppo, J. T., Mao, H-Y., & Glaser, R. (1993). Negative behavior during marital conflict is associated with immunological down-regulation. *Psychosomatic Medicine, 55,* 395–409. (p. 589)

Kiesler, C. A. (1971). *The psychology of commitment: Experiments linking behavior to belief.* New York: Academic Press. (p. 278)

Kihlstrom, J. F. (1994). The social construction of memory. Address to the American Psychological Society convention. (p. 103)

Kihlstrom, J. F., & Cantor, N. (1984). Mental representations of the self. In L. Berkowitz (Ed.), *Advances in experimental social psychology,* vol. 17. New York: Academic Press. (p. 41)

Kim, H., & Markus, H. R. (1999). Deviance of uniqueness, harmony or conformity? A cultural analysis. *Journal of Personality and Social Psychology, 77,* 785–800. (pp. 48–49)

Kimmel, A. J. (1998). In defense of deception. *American Psychologist, 53,* 803–805. (p. 32)

Kinder, D. R., & Sears, D. O. (1985). Public opinion and political action. In G. Lindzey & E. Aronson (Eds.), *The handbook of social psychology,* 3rd ed. New York: Random House. (pp. 100, 264)

King, L. A. (2001). The health benefits of writing about life goals. *Personality and Social Psychology Bulletin, 27,* 798–807. (p. 598)

Kingdon, J. W. (1967). Politicians' beliefs about voters. *The American Political Science Review, 61,* 137–145. (p. 67)

Kinnier, R. T., & Metha, A. T. (1989). Regrets and priorities at three stages of life. *Counseling and Values, 33,* 182–193. (p. 116)

Kinsley, M. (2003, April 21). The power of one. *Time,* p. 86. (p. 324)

Kitayama, S. (1996). The mutual constitution of culture and the self: Implications for emotion. Paper presented to the American Psychological Society convention. (p. 45)

Kitayama, S., & Karasawa, M. (1997). Implicit self-esteem in Japan: Name letters and birthday numbers. *Personality and Social Psychology Bulletin, 23,* 736–742. (p. 429)

Kitayama, S., & Markus, H. R. (1995). Culture and self: Implications for internationalizing psychology. In N. R. Godlberger & J. B. Veroff (Eds.), *The culture and psychology reader.* New York: New York University Press. (p. 46)

Kitayama, S., & Markus, H. R. (2000). The pursuit of happiness and the realization of sympathy: Cultural patterns of self, social relations, and well-being. In E. Diener & E. M. Suh (Eds.), *Subjective well-being across cultures.* Cambridge, MA: MIT Press. (pp. 49, 532)

Kitayama, S., Duffy, S., Kawamura, T., & Larsen, J. T. (2003). Perceiving an object and its context in different cultures: A cultural look at new look. *Psychological Science, 14,* 201–206. (p. 47)

Kitayama, S., Snibbe, A. C., Markus, H. R., & Suzuki, T. (2004). Is there any "free" choice? Self and dissonance in two cultures. *Psychological Science,* in press. (p. 163)

Kite, M. E. (2001). Changing times, changing gender roles: Who do we want women and men to be? In R. K. Unger (Ed.), *Handbook of the psychology of women and gender.* New York: Wiley. (p. 195)

Klaas, E. T. (1978). Psychological effects of immoral actions: The experimental evidence. *Psychological Bulletin, 85,* 756–771. (p. 143)

Kleck, R. E., & Strenta, A. (1980). Perceptions of the impact of negatively valued physical characteristics on social interaction. *Journal of Personality and Social Psychology, 39,* 861–873. (p. 361)

Klein, I., & Snyder, M. (2003). Stereotypes and behavioral confirmation: From interpersonal to intergroup perspectives. *Advances in Experimental Social Psychology, 35,* 153–235. (p. 125)

Klein, J. G. (1991). Negative effects in impression formation: A test in the political arena. *Personality and Social Psychology Bulletin, 17,* 412–418. (p. 446)

Klein, O., Snyder, M., & Livingston, R. W. (in press). Prejudice on the stage. *British Journal of Social Psychology.* (p. 80)

Klein, W. M., & Kunda, Z. (1992). Motivated person perception: Constructing justifications for desired beliefs. *Journal of Experimental Social Psychology, 28,* 145–168. (p. 428)

Kleinke, C. L. (1977). Compliance to requests made by gazing and touching experimenters in field settings. *Journal of Experimental Social Psychology, 13,* 218–223. (p. 220)

Kleinke, C. L., Peterson, T. R., & Rutledge, R. R. (1998). Effects of self-generated facial expressions on mood. *Journal of Personality and Social Psychology, 74,* 272–279. (p. 157)

Klentz, B., Beaman, A. L., Mapelli, S. D., & Ullrich, J. R. (1987). Perceived physical attractiveness of supporters and nonsupporters of the women's movement: An attitude-similarity-mediated error (AS-ME). *Personality and Social Psychology Bulletin, 13,* 513–523. (p. 441)

Klerman, G. L., & Weissman, M. M. (1989). Increasing rates of depression. *Journal of the American Medical Association, 261,* 2229–2235. (p. 653)

Klohnen, E. C., & Mendelsohn, G. A. (1998). Partner selection for personality characteristics: A couple-centered approach. *Personality and Social Psychology Bulletin, 24,* 268–278. (p. 443)

Klopfer, P. H. (1958). Influence of social interaction on learning rates in birds. *Science, 128,* 903. (p. 287)

Knight, G. P., Fabes, R. A., & Higgins, D. A. (1996). Concerns about drawing causal inferences from meta-analyses: An example in the study of gender differences in aggression. *Psychological Bulletin, 119,* 410–421. (p. 187)

Knight, J. A., & Vallacher, R. R. (1981). Interpersonal engagement in social perception: The consequences of getting into the action. *Journal of Personality and Social Psychology, 40,* 990–999. (p. 428)

Knight, P. A., & Weiss, H. M. (1980). Benefits of suffering: Communicator suffering, benefitting, and influence. Paper presented at the American Psychological Association convention. (p. 253)

Knowles, E. S. (1983). Social physics and the effects of others: Tests of the effects of audience size and distance on social judgment and behavior. *Journal of Personality and Social Psychology, 45,* 1263–1279. (p. 289)

Knox, R. E., & Inkster, J. A. (1968). Postdecision dissonance at post-time. *Journal of Personality and Social Psychology, 8,* 319–323. (p. 155)

Knudson, R. M., Sommers, A. A., & Golding, S. L. (1980). Interpersonal perception and mode of resolution in marital conflict. *Journal of Personality and Social Psychology, 38,* 751–763. (p. 555)

Koehler, D. J. (1991). Explanation, imagination, and confidence in judgment. *Psychological Bulletin, 110,* 499–519. (p. 112)

Koestner, R. F. (1993). False consensus effects for the 1992 Canadian referendum. Paper presented at the American Psychological Association. (p. 72)

Koestner, R., & Wheeler, L. (1988). Self-presentation in personal advertisements: The influence of implicit notions of attraction and role expectations. *Journal of Social and Personal Relationships, 5,* 149–160. (p. 434)

Kohnken, G., Milne, R., Memon, A., & Bull, R. (1999). The cognitive interview: A meta-analysis. *Psychology, Crime, and Law, 5,* 3–27. (p. 616)

Kolata, G., & Peterson, I. (2001, July 21). New way to insure eyewitnesses can ID the right bad guy. *New York Times* (www.nytimes.com). (p. 617)

Komorita, S. S., & Barth, J. M. (1985). Components of reward in social dilemmas. *Journal of Personality and Social Psychology, 48,* 364–373. (p. 527)

Konrad, A. M., Ritchie, J. E., Jr., Lieb, P., & Corrigall, E. (2000). Sex differences and similarities in job attribute preferences: A meta-analysis. *Psychological Bulletin, 126,* 593–641. (p. 183)

Koole, S. L., Dijksterhuis, A., & van Knippenberg, A. (2001). What's in a name? Implicit self-esteem and the automatic self. *Journal of Personality and Social Psychology, 80,* 669–685. (p. 430)

Koomen, W., & Bahler, M. (1996). National stereotypes: Common representations and ingroup favouritism. *European Journal of Social Psychology, 26,* 325–331. (p. 333)

Koomen, W., & Dijker, A. J. (1997). Ingroup and outgroup stereotypes and selective processing. *European Journal of Social Psychology, 27,* 589–601. (p. 174)

Koop, C. E. (1987). Report of the Surgeon General's workshop on pornography and public health. *American Psychologist, 42,* 944–945. (pp. 399, 400)

Koop, C. E. (1997, June 22). Quoted by J. Fisher and J. Schwartz, Trying to snuff out the tobacco culture. *Washington Post,* pp. A1, A3. (p. 134)

Koppel, M., Argamon, S., & Shimoni, A. R. (2002). Automatically categorizing written texts by author gender. *Literary and Linguistic Computing, 17,* 401–412. (p. 186)

Koriat, A., Lichtenstein, S., & Fischhoff, B. (1980). Reasons for confidence. *Journal of Experimental*

Social Psychology: Human Learning and Memory, **6**, 107–118. (p. 112)

Korn, J. H., & Nicks, S. D. (1993). The rise and decline of deception in social psychology. Poster presented at the American Psychological Society convention. (p. 31)

Koss, M. P. (1990, August 29). Rape incidence: A review and assessment of the data. Testimony on behalf of the American Psychological Association before the U.S. Senate Judiciary Committee. (p. 401)

Koss, M. P. (1993). Rape: Scope, impact, interventions, and public policy responses. *American Psychologist, 48,* 1062–1069. (p. 401)

Koss, M. P., Dinero, T. E., Seibel, C. A., & Cox, S. L. (1988). Stranger and acquaintance rape. *Psychology of Women*, **12**, 1–24. (p. 401)

Koss, M. P., Heise, L., & Russo, N. F. (1994). The global health burden of rape. *Psychology of Women Quarterly,* **18**, 509–537. (p. 402)

Krackow, A., & Blass, T. (1995). When nurses obey or defy inappropriate physician orders: Attributional differences. *Journal of Social Behavior and Personality*, **10**, 585–594. (p. 221)

Krahé, B. (1998). Sexual aggression among adolescents: Prevalence and predictors in a German sample. *Psychology of Women Quarterly*, **22**, 537–554. (p. 401)

Kramer, G. P., Kerr, N. L., & Carroll, J. S. (1990). Pretrial publicity, judicial remedies, and jury bias. *Law and Human Behavior*, **14**, 409–438. (p. 623)

Kraus, S. J. (1995). Attitudes and the prediction of behavior: A meta-analysis of the empirical literature. *Personality and Social Psychology Bulletin*, **21**, 58–75. (pp. 136, 139)

Kraut, R. E. (1973). Effects of social labeling on giving to charity. *Journal of Experimental Social Psychology*, **9**, 551–562. (p. 512)

Kraut, R. E., & Poe, D. (1980). Behavioral roots of person perception: The deception judgments of customs inspectors and laymen. *Journal of Personality and Social Psychology*, **39**, 784–798. (pp. 357–358)

Kravitz, D. A., & Martin, B. (1986). Ringelmann rediscovered: The original

article. *Journal of Personality and Social Psychology*, **50**, 936–941. (p. 293)

Krebs, D. (1970). Altruism—An examination of the concept and a review of the literature. *Psychological Bulletin*, **73**, 258–302. (p. 478)

Krebs, D. (1975). Empathy and altruism. *Journal of Personality and Social Psychology*, **32**, 1134–1146. (p. 479)

Krebs, D. (1999). Behind the scenes. In D. G. Myers, *Social psychology*, 6th edition. New York: McGraw-Hill. (p. 477)

Krebs, D. L. (1998). The evolution of moral behaviors. In C. Crawford & D. L. Krebs (Eds.), *Handbook of evolutionary psychology: Ideas, issues, and applications*. Mahwah, NJ: Erlbaum. (p. 488)

Krebs, D., & Adinolfi, A. A. (1975). Physical attractiveness, social relations, and personality style. *Journal of Personality and Social Psychology*, **31**, 245–253. (p. 432)

Kressel, K., & Pruitt, D. G. (1985). Themes in the mediation of social conflict. *Journal of Social Issues*, **41**, 179–198. (p. 558)

Kressel, N. J., & Kressel, D. F. (2002). *Stack and sway: The new science of jury consulting*. Boulder, CO: Westview Press. (p. 629)

Kroger, R. O., & Wood, L. A. (1992). Are the rules of address universal? IV: Comparison of Chinese, Korean, Greek, and German usage. *Journal of Cross-Cultural Psychology*, **23**, 148–162. (p. 176)

Krosnick, J. A., & Alwin, D. F. (1989). Aging and susceptibility to attitude change. *Journal of Personality and Social Psychology*, **57**, 416–425. (p. 268)

Krosnick, J. A., & Schuman, H. (1988). Attitude intensity, importance, and certainty and susceptibility to response effects. *Journal of Personality and Social Psychology*, **54**, 940–952. (p. 26)

Krueger, A. B., & Maleckova, J. (2003, June 6). Seeking the roots of terrorism. *The Chronicle Review* (www.chronicle.com). (p. 388)

Krueger, J. (1996). Personal beliefs and cultural stereotypes about racial characteristics. *Journal of Personality*

and *Social Psychology*, **71**, 536–548. (p. 73)

Krueger, J. (1998b). On the perception of social consensus. *Advances in Experimental Social Psychology*, **30**, 163–240. (p. 73)

Krueger, J. I., & Funder, D. C. (2003a). Towards a balanced social psychology: Causes, consequences and cures for the problem-seeking approach to social behavior and cognition. *Behavioral and Brain Sciences*, in press. (p. 127)

Krueger, J. I., & Funder, D. C. (2003b). Social psychology: A field in search of a center. *Behavioral and Brain Sciences*, in press. (p. 127)

Krueger, J., & Clement, R. W. (1994). Memory-based judgments about multiple categories: A revision and extension of Tajfel's accentuation theory. *Journal of Personality and Social Psychology*, **67**, 35–47. (p. 359)

Krueger, J., & Clement, R. W. (1994). The truly false consensus effect: An ineradicable and egocentric bias in social perception. *Journal of Personality and Social Psychology*, **67**, 596–610. (p. 72)

Krueger, J., & Clement, R. W. (1997). Estimates of social consensus by majorities and minorities: The case for social projection. *Personality and Social Psychology Review*, **1**, 299–313. (p. 73)

Krueger, J., & Rothbart, M. (1988). Use of categorical and individuating information in making inferences about personality. *Journal of Personality and Social Psychology*, **55**, 187–195. (p. 374)

Krueger, R. F., Hicks, B. M., & McGue, M. (2001). Altruism and antisocial behavior: Independent tendencies, unique personality correlates, distinct etiologies. *Psychological Science*, **12**, 397–402. (p. 506)

Kruger, J., & Dunning, D. (1999). Unskilled and unaware of it: How difficulties in recognizing one's own incompetence lead to inflated self-assessments. *Journal of Personality and Social Psychology*, **77**, 1121–1134. (p. 110)

Kruger, J., & Gilovich, T. (1999). "I cynicism" in everyday theories of responsibility assessment: On biased assumptions of bias. *Journal of Personality and Social Psychology*, **76**, 743–753. (p. 68)

Kruger, J., Epley, N., & Gilovich, T. (1999). Egocentrism over email. Paper presented to the American Psychological Society meeting. (p. 465)

Kruglanski, A. W., & Ajzen, I. (1983). Bias and error in human judgment. *European Journal of Social Psychology*, **13**, 1–44. (p. 127)

Kruglanski, A. W., & Webster, D. M. (1991). Group members' reactions to opinion deviates and conformists at varying degrees of proximity to decision deadline and of environmental noise. *Journal of Personality and Social Psychology*, **61**, 212–225. (p. 322)

Krugman, P. (2000, June 18). Turn of the century. *New York Times* (www.nytimes.com). (p. 640)

Krugman, P. (2003, February 18). Behind the great divide. *New York Times* (www.nytimes.com). (p. 246)

Krull, D. S., Loy, M. H-M., Lin, J., Wang, C-F., Chen, S., & Zhao, X. (1999). The fundamental attribution error: Correspondence bias in individualist and collectivist cultures. *Personality and Social Psychology Bulletin*, **25**, 1208–1219. (p. 95)

Kubany, E. S., Bauer, G. B., Pangilinan, M. E., Muroka, M. Y., & Enriquez, V. G. (1995). Impact of labeled anger and blame in intimate relationships. *Journal of Cross-Cultural Psychology*, **26**, 65–83. (p. 417)

Kubey, R., & Csikszentmihalyi, M. (2002, February). Television addiction is no mere metaphor. *Scientific American*, **286**, 74–82. (pp. 409–410)

Kugihara, N. (1999). Gender and social loafing in Japan. *Journal of Social Psychology*, **139**, 516–526. (p. 297)

Kuhn, D., & Lao, J. (1996). Effects of evidence on attitudes: Is polarization the norm? *Psychological Science*, **7**, 115–120. (p. 100)

Kuiper, N. A., & Higgins, E. T. (1985). Social cognition and depression: A general integrative perspective. *Social Cognition*, **3**, 1–15. (p. 579)

Kuiper, N. A., & Rogers, T. B. (1979). Encoding of personal information: Self-other differences. *Journal of Personality and Social Psychology*, **37**, 499–514. (p. 42)

Kull, S. (2003, June 4). Quoted in Many Americans unaware WMD have not been found. Program on International Policy Attitudes (http://pipa.org/whatsnew/html/new_6_04_03.html). (pp. 151–152)

Kunda, Z. & Spencer, S. J. (2003). When do stereotypes come to mind and when do they color judgment? A goal-based theoretical framework for stereotype activation and application. *Psychological Bulletin*, **129**, 522–544. (p. 356)

Kunda, Z. (1990). The case for motivated reasoning. *Psychological Bulletin*, **108**, 480–498. (p. 63)

Kunda, Z., & Oleson, K. C. (1995). Maintaining stereotypes in the face of disconfirmation: Constructing grounds for subtyping deviants. *Journal of Personality and Social Psychology*, **68**, 565–579. (p. 370)

Kunda, Z., & Oleson, K. C. (1997). When exceptions prove the rule: How extremity of deviance determines the impact of deviant examples on stereotypes. *Journal of Personality and Social Psychology*, **72**, 965–979. (p. 370)

Kunda, Z., & Sherman-Williams, B. (1993). Stereotypes and the construal of individuating information. *Personality and Social Psychology Bulletin*, **19**, 90–99. (pp. 368–369)

Kunda, Z., Fong, G. T., Sanitioso, R., & Reber, E. (1993). Directional questions direct self-conceptions. *Journal of Experimental Social Psychology*, **29**, 63–86. (p. 571)

Kunst-Wilson, W. R., & Zajonc, R. B. (1980). Affective discrimination of stimuli that cannot be recognized. *Science*, **207**, 557–558. (p. 429)

Kwan, V. S. Y., Bond, M. H., & Singelis, T. M. (1997). *Journal of Personality and Social Psychology*, **73**, 1038–1051. (p. 49)

La Rochefoucauld, F. (1665). Maxims. (p. 180)

Lafferty, E. (1994, November 14). Now, a jury of his peers. *Time*, p. 64. (p. 628)

LaFrance, M. (1985). Does your smile reveal your status? *Social Science News Letter*, **70** (Spring), 15–18. (pp. 183–184)

LaFrance, M., Hecht, M. A., & Paluck, E. L. (2003). The contingent smile: A meta-analysis of sex differences in smiling. *Psychological Bulletin*, **129**, 305–334. (p. 183)

LaFromboise, T., Coleman, H. L. K., & Gerton, J. (1993). Psychological impact of biculturalism: Evidence and theory. *Psychological Bulletin*, **114**, 395–412. (p. 552)

Lagerspetz, K. (1979). Modification of aggressiveness in mice. In S. Feshbach & A. Fraczek (Eds.), *Aggression and behavior change*. New York: Praeger. (p. 383)

Lagerspetz, K. M. J., Bjorkqvist, K., Berts, M., & King, E. (1982). Group aggression among school children in three schools. *Scandinavian Journal of Psychology*, **23**, 45–52. (p. 414)

Laird, J. D. (1974). Self-attribution of emotion: The effects of expressive behavior on the quality of emotional experience. *Journal of Personality and Social Psychology*, **29**, 475–486. (p. 157)

Laird, J. D. (1984). The real role of facial response in the experience of emotion: A reply to Tourangeau and Ellsworth, and others. *Journal of Personality and Social Psychology*, **47**, 909–917. (p. 157)

Lakin, J. L., & Chartrand, T. L. (2003). Using nonconscious behavioral mimicry to create affiliation and rapport. *Psychological Science*, **14**, 334–339. (p. 443)

Lalancette, M-F., & Standing, L. (1990). Asch fails again. *Social Behavior and Personality*, **18**, 7–12. (p. 237)

Lalonde, R. N. (1992). The dynamics of group differentiation in the face of defeat. *Personality and Social Psychology Bulletin*, **18**, 336–342. (p. 67)

Lamal, P. A. (1979). College student common beliefs about psychology. *Teaching of Psychology*, **6**, 155–158. (p. 103)

Lamberth, J. (1998, August 6). Driving while black: A statistician proves that prejudice still rules the road. *Washington Post*, p. C1. (p. 336)

Landers, A. (1969, April 8). Syndicated newspaper column. April 8, 1969. Cited by L. Berkowitz in, The case for bottling up rage. *Psychology Today*, September, 1973, pp. 24–31. (pp. 415–416)

Landers, A. (1985, August). Is affection more important than sex? *Reader's Digest*, pp. 44–46. (p. 25)

Landers, S. (1988, July). Sex, drugs 'n' rock: Relation not causal. *APA Monitor*, p. 40. (p. 23)

Lane, R. E. (1998). Searching for lost companions in the groves of the market. In D. Kahneman, E. Diener, & N. Schwarz (Eds.), *Understanding well-being: Scientific perspectives on enjoyment and suffering.* New York: Russell Sage Foundation. (p. 600)

Laner, M. R., & Ventrone, N. A. (1998). Egalitarian daters/traditionalist dates. *Journal of Family Issues*, **19**, 468–477. (p. 186)

Laner, M. R., & Ventrone, N. A. (2000). Dating scripts revised. *Journal of Family Issues*, **21**, 488–500. (p. 186)

Langer, E. J. (1977). The psychology of chance. *Journal for the Theory of Social Behavior*, **7**, 185–208. (p. 117)

Langer, E. J., & Benevento, A. (1978). Self-induced dependence. *Journal of Personality and Social Psychology*, **36**, 886–893. (p. 179)

Langer, E. J., & Imber, L. (1980). The role of mindlessness in the perception of deviance. *Journal of Personality and Social Psychology*, **39**, 360–367. (p. 361)

Langer, E. J., & Rodin, J. (1976). The effects of choice and enhanced personal responsibility for the aged: A field experiment in an institutional setting. *Journal of Personality and Social Psychology*, **334**, 191–198. (p. 60)

Langer, E. J., & Roth, J. (1975). Heads I win, tails it's chance: The illusion of control as a function of the sequence of outcomes in a purely chance task. *Journal of Personality and Social Psychology*, **32**, 951–955. (p. 262)

Langer, E. J., Janis, I. L., & Wofer, J. A. (1975). Reduction of psychological stress in surgical patients. *Journal of Experimental Social Psychology*, **11**, 155–165. (p. 60)

Langlois, J. H., & Roggman, L. A. (1990). Attractive faces are only average. *Psychological Science*, **1**, 115–121. (p. 437)

Langlois, J. H., Kalakanis, L., Rubenstein, A. J., Larson, A., Hallam, M., & Smoot, M. (2000). Maxims or myths of beauty? A meta-analytic and theoretical review. *Psychological Bulletin*, **126**, 390–423. (pp. 434, 436, 437)

Langlois, J. H., Roggman, L. A., & Musselman, L. (1994). What is average and what is not average about attractive faces? *Psychological Science*, **5**, 214–220. (p. 437)

Langlois, J. H., Roggman, L. A., Casey, R. J., Ritter, J. M., Rieser-Danner, L. A., & Jenkins, V. Y. (1987). Infant preferences for attractive faces: Rudiments of a stereotype? *Developmental Psychology*, **23**, 363–369. (p. 434)

Langlois, J., Kalakanis, L., Rubenstein, A., Larson, A., Hallam, M., & Smoot, M. (1996). Maxims and myths of beauty: A meta-analytic and theoretical review. Paper presented to the American Psychological Society convention. (p. 436)

Lanzetta, J. T. (1955). Group behavior under stress. *Human Relations*, **8**, 29–53. (p. 543)

Larsen, K. (1974). Conformity in the Asch experiment. *Journal of Social Psychology*, **94**, 303–304. (p. 237)

Larsen, K. S. (1990). The Asch conformity experiment: Replication and transhistorical comparisons. *Journal of Social Behavior and Personality*, **5**(4), 163–168. (p. 237)

Larsen, R. J., & Diener, E. (1987). Affect intensity as an individual difference characteristic: A review. *Journal of Research in Personality*, **21**, 1–39. (p. 384)

Larsen, R. J., Csikszentmihalyi, N., & Graef, R. (1982). Time alone in daily experience: Loneliness or renewal? In L. A. Peplau & D. Perlman (Eds.), *Loneliness: A sourcebook of current theory, research and therapy.* New York: Wiley. (p. 582)

Larson, J. R., Jr., Foster-Fishman, P. G., & Keys, C. B. (1994). Discussion of shared and unshared information in decision-making groups. *Journal of Personality and Social Psychology*, **67**, 446–461. (p. 308)

Larsson, K. (1956). *Conditioning and sexual behavior in the male albino rat.* Stockholm: Almqvist & Wiksell. (p. 287)

Larwood, L. (1978). Swine flu: A field study of self-serving biases. *Journal of Applied Social Psychology*, **18**, 283–289. (p. 70)

Larwood, L., & Whittaker, W. (1977). Managerial myopia: Self-serving biases in organizational planning. *Journal of Applied Psychology*, **62**, 194–198. (p. 76)

Lassiter, G. D., & Dudley, K. A. (1991). The *a priori* value of basic research: The case of videotaped confessions. *Journal of Social Behavior and Personality*, **6**, 7–16. (p. 92)

Lassiter, G. D., & Irvine, A. A. (1986). Videotaped confessions: The impact of camera point of view on judgments of coercion. *Journal of Applied Social Psychology*, **16**, 268–276. (p. 92)

Lassiter, G. D., & Munhall, P. J. (2001). The genius effect: Evidence for a nonmotivational interpretation. *Journal of Experimental Social Psychology*, **37**, 349–355. (p. 70)

Lassiter, G. D., Geers, A. L., Handley, I. M., Weiland, P. E., & Munhall, P. J. (2002). Videotaped interrogations and confessions: A simple change in camera perspective alters verdicts in simulated trials. *Journal of Applied Psychology*, **87**, 867–874. (p. 92)

Lassiter, G. D., Geers, A. L., Munhall, P. J., Handley, I. M., & Beers, M. J. (in press). Videotaped confessions: Is guilt in the eye of the camera? *Advances in Experimental Social Psychology.* (pp. 92)

Latané, B., & Dabbs, J. M., Jr. (1975). Sex, group size and helping in three cities. *Sociometry*, **38**, 180–194. (p. 495)

Latané, B., & Darley, J. M. (1968). Group inhibition of bystander intervention in emergencies. *Journal of Personality and Social Psychology*, **10**, 215–221. (p. 496)

Latané, B., & Darley, J. M. (1970). *The unresponsive bystander: Why doesn't he help?* New York: Appleton-Century-Crofts. (pp. 495, 506)

Latané, B., & Nida, S. (1981). Ten years of research on group size and helping. *Psychological Bulletin*, **89**, 308–324. (p. 495)

Latané, B., & Rodin, J. (1969). A lady in distress: Inhibiting effects of friends and strangers on bystander intervention. *Journal of Experimental Social Psychology, 5*, 189–202. (p. 498)

Latané, B., Williams, K., & Harkins. S. (1979). Many hands make light the work: The causes and consequences of social loafing. *Journal of Personality and Social Psychology, 37*, 822–832. (pp. 293–294)

Laughlin, P. R. (1996). Group decision making and collective induction. In E. H. Witte & J. H. Davis (Eds.), *Understanding group behavior: Consensual action by small groups.* Mahwah, NJ: Erlbaum. (pp. 318–319)

Laughlin, P. R., & Adamopoulos, J. (1980). Social combination processes and individual learning for six-person cooperative groups on an intellective task. *Journal of Personality and Social Psychology, 38*, 941–947. (pp. 318–319)

Laughlin, P. R., Zander, M. L., Knievel, E. M., & Tan, T. K. (2003). Groups perform better than the best individuals on letters-to-numbers problems: Informative equations and effective strategies. *Journal of Personality and Social Psychology, 85*, 684–694. (pp. 318–319)

Laumann, E. O., Gagnon, J. H., Michael, R. T., & Michaels, S. (1994). *The social organization of sexuality: Sexual practices in the United States.* Chicago: University of Chicago Press. (pp. 85, 188, 401, 408)

Lawler, A. (2003c). Mayhem in Mesopotamia. *Science, 301*, 582–588. (p. 297)

Lawler, A. (2003a). Ten millennia of culture pilfered amid Baghdad chaos. *Science, 300*, 402–403. (p. 297)

Lawler, A. (2003b). Iraq's shattered universities. *Science, 300*, 1490–1491. (p. 297)

Layden, M. A. (1982). Attributional therapy. In C. Antaki & C. Brewin (Eds.), *Attributions and psychological change: Applications of attributional theories to clinical and educational practice.* London: Academic Press. (p. 594)

Lazarsfeld, P. F. (1949). *The American soldier—an expository review. Public Opinion Quarterly, 13*, 377–404. (p. 17)

Leary, M. (1994). *Self-presentation: Impression management and interpersonal behavior.* Pacific Grove, CA: Brooks/Cole. (p. 151)

Leary, M. R. (1998). The social and psychological importance of self-esteem. In R. M. Kowalski & M. R. Leary (Eds.), *The social psychology of emotional and behavioral problems.* Washington, DC: American Psychological Association. (pp. 23, 45, 64)

Leary, M. R. (1999). Making sense of self-esteem. *Current Directions in Psychology, 8*, 32–35. (p. 64)

Leary, M. R. (2001). Social anxiety as an early warning system: A refinement and extension of the self-presentation theory of social anxiety. In S. G. Hofmann & P. M. DiBartolo (Eds.), *From social anxiety to social phobia: Multiple perspectives.* Needham Heights, MA: Allyn & Bacon. (p. 151)

Leary, M. R., & Buttermore, N. R. (2003). The evolution of the human self: Tracing the natural history of self-awareness. *Journal for the Theory of Social Behaviour, 33*, 365–404. (p. 41)

Leary, M. R., & Kowalski, R. M. (1995). *Social anxiety.* New York: Guilford. (p. 583)

Leary, M. R., Kowalski, R. M., Smith, L., & Phillips, S. (2003). Teasing, rejection, and violence: Case studies of the school shootings. *Aggressive Behavior, 29*, 202–214. (p. 425)

Leary, M. R., Nezlek, J. B., Radford-Davenport, D., Martin, J., & McMullen, A. (1994). Self-presentation in everyday interactions: Effects of target familiarity and gender composition. *Journal of Personality and Social Psychology, 67*, 664–673. (p. 79)

Leary, M. R., Tchvidjian, L. R., & Kraxberger, B. E. (1994). Self-presentation can be hazardous to your health: Impression management and health risk. *Health Psychology, 13*, 461–470. (p. 79)

Lebow, R. N., & Stein, J. G. (1987). Beyond deterrence. *Journal of Social Issues, 43*(4), 5–71. (pp. 523, 559)

LeDoux, J. (1994, June). Emotion, memory and the brain. *Scientific American*, pp. 50–57. (p. 107)

LeDoux, J. (1996). *The emotional brain: The mysterious underpinnings of emotional life.* New York: Simon & Schuster. (pp. 107, 108)

Lee, F., Hallahan, M., & Herzog, T. (1996). Explaining real-life events: How culture and domain shape attributions. *Personality and Social Psychology Bulletin, 22*, 732–741. (p. 95)

Lee, J. A. (1988). Love-styles. In R. J. Sternberg & M. L. Barnes (Eds.), *The psychology of love.* New Haven, CT: Yale University Press. (p. 453)

Lee, R. Y-P., & Bond, M. H. (1996). How friendship develops out of personality and values: A study of interpersonal attraction in Chinese culture. Unpublished manuscript, Chinese University of Hong Kong. (p. 443)

Lee, Y-T. (1996, June 29). Quoted by B. Bower, Fighting stereotype stigma. *Science News* (www.sciencenews.org). (p. 333)

Lefcourt, H. M. (1982). *Locus of control: Current trends in theory and research.* Hillsdale, NJ: Erlbaum. (p. 59)

Lefebvre, L. M. (1979). Causal attributions for basketball outcomes by players and coaches. *Psychological Belgica, 19*, 109–115. (p. 80)

Legrain, P. (2003, May 9). Cultural globalization is not Americanization. *Chronicle of Higher Education* (www.chronicle.com/free). (p. 173)

Lehman, D. R., Lempert, R. O., & Nisbett, R. E. (1988). The effects of graduate training on reasoning: Formal discipline and thinking about everyday-life events. *American Psychologist, 43*, 431–442. (p. 129)

Leippe, M. R. (1985). The influence of eyewitness nonidentification on mock-jurors. *Journal of Applied Social Psychology, 15*, 656–672. (p. 607)

Leippe, M. R. (1994). The appraisal of eyewitness testimony. In D. F. Ross, J. D. Read, & M. P. Toglia (Eds.), *Adult eyewitness testimony: Current trends and developments.* New York: Cambridge. (p. 608)

Leippe, M. R., & Eisenstadt, D. (1994). Generalization of dissonance reduction: Decreasing prejudice through induced compliance. *Journal of Personality and Social Psychology, 67*, 395–413. (p. 153)

Leippe, M. R., & Elkin, R. A. (1987). Dissonance reduction strategies and accountability to self and others: Ruminations and some initial research. Presentation to the Fifth International Conference on Affect, Motivation, and Cognition, Nags Head Conference Center. (pp. 153, 269)

Lemyre, L., & Smith, P. M. (1985). Intergroup discrimination and self-esteem in the minimal group paradigm. *Journal of Personality and Social Psychology, 49,* 660–670. (p. 355)

Leon, D. (1969). *The Kibbutz: A new way of life.* London: Pergamon Press. Cited by B. Latané, K. Williams, & S. Harkins (1979), Many hands make light the work: The causes and consequences of social loafing. *Journal of Personality and Social Psychology,* 1979, *37,* 822–832. (pp. 296–297)

Lepore, S. J., Ragan, J. D., & Jones, S. (2000). Talking facilitates cognitive-emotional processes of adaptation to an acute stressor. *Journal of Personality and Social Psychology, 78,* 499–508. (pp. 598–599)

Lepper, M. R., & Greene, D. (Eds.) (1979). *The hidden costs of reward.* Hillsdale, NJ: Erlbaum. (p. 159)

Lerner, M. J. (1980). *The belief in a just world: A fundamental delusion.* New York: Plenum. (pp. 366, 367)

Lerner, M. J., & Miller, D. T. (1978). Just world research and the attribution process: Looking back and ahead. *Psychological Bulletin, 85,* 1030–1051. (p. 366)

Lerner, M. J., & Simmons, C. H. (1966). Observer's reaction to the "innocent victim": Compassion or rejection? *Journal of Personality and Social Psychology, 4,* 203–210. (p. 366)

Lerner, M. J., Somers, D. G., Reid, D., Chiriboga, D., & Tierney, M. (1991). Adult children as caregivers: Egocentric biases in judgments of sibling contributions. *The Gerontologist, 31,* 746–755. (p. 70)

Lerner, R. M., & Frank, P. (1974). Relation of race and sex to supermarket helping behavior. *Journal of Social Psychology, 94,* 201–203. (p. 505)

Leung, K., & Bond, M. H. (1984). The impact of cultural collectivism on reward allocation. *Journal of Personality and Social Psychology, 47,* 793–804. (p. 532)

Leung, K., & Bond, M. H. (2004). Social axioms: A model of social beliefs in multi-cultural perspective. *Advances in Experimental Social Psychology,* in press. (pp. 175–176)

Leventhal, H. (1970). Findings and theory in the study of fear communications. In L. Berkowitz (Ed.), *Advances in experimental social psychology* (Vol. 5). New York: Academic Press. (p. 258)

Levin, D. T. (2000). Race as a visual feature: Using visual search and perceptual discrimination tasks to understand face categories and the cross-race recognition deficit. *Journal of Experimental Psychology: General, 129,* 559–574. (p. 360)

Levine, G. M., Halberstadt, J. B., & Goldstone, R. L. (1996). Reasoning and the weighting of attributes in attitude judgments. *Journal of Personality and Social Psychology, 70,* 230–240. (p. 56)

Levine, J. M. (1989). Reaction to opinion deviance in small groups. In P. Paulus (Ed.), *Psychology of group influence: New perspectives.* Hillsdale, NJ: Erlbaum. (pp. 322–323)

Levine, J. M., & Moreland, R. L. (1985). Innovation and socialization in small groups. In S. Moscovici, G. Mugny, & E. Van Avermaet (Eds.), *Perspectives on minority influence.* Cambridge: Cambridge University Press. (p. 323)

Levine, R. (2003). *The power of persuasion: How we're bought and sold.* New York: Wiley. (p. 281)

Levine, R. V. (2001). Cross-cultural differences in helping strangers. *Journal of Cross-Cultural Psychology, 32,* 543–560. (pp. 500–501)

Levine, R. V. (2003). The kindness of strangers. *American Scientist, 91,* 226–233. (pp. 70, 500)

Levinger, G. (1987). The limits of deterrence: An introduction. *Journal of Social Issues, 43*(4), 1–4. (p. 523)

Levinson, H. (1950). *The science of chance: From probability to statistics.* New York: Rinehart. (p. 528)

Levy, B. (1996). Improving memory in old age through implicit self-stereotyping. *Journal of Personality and Social Psychology, 71,* 1092–1107. (p. 58)

Levy, S. R., Stroessner, S. J., & Dweck, C. S. (1998). Stereotype formation and endorsement: The role of implicit theories. *Journal of Personality and Social Psychology, 74,* 1421–1436. (p. 365)

Levy-Leboyer, C. (1988). Success and failure in applying psychology. *American Psychologist, 43,* 779–785. (p. 258)

Lewicki, P. (1985). Nonconscious biasing effects of single instances on subsequent judgments. *Journal of Personality and Social Psychology, 48,* 563–574. (pp. 450–451)

Lewin, K. (1936). *A dynamic theory of personality.* New York: McGraw-Hill. (p. 236)

Lewinsohn, P. M., & Rosenbaum, M. (1987). Recall of parental behavior by acute depressives, remitted depressives, and nondepressives. *Journal of Personality and Social Psychology, 52,* 611–619. (p. 579)

Lewinsohn, P. M., Hoberman, H., Teri, L., & Hautziner, M. (1985). An integrative theory of depression. In S. Reiss & R. Bootzin (Eds.), *Theoretical issues in behavior therapy.* New York: Academic Press. (p. 580)

Lewis, C. S. (1952). *Mere Christianity.* New York: Macmillan. (pp. 51, 156)

Lewis, C. S. (1974). *The horse and his boy.* New York: Collier Books. (p. 155)

Lewis, D. O. (1998). *Guilty by reason of insanity.* London: Arrow. (p. 383)

Leyens, J-P., Camino, L., Parke, R. D., & Berkowitz, L. (1975). Effects of movie violence on aggression in a field setting as a function of group dominance and cohesion. *Journal of Personality and Social Psychology, 32,* 346–360. (pp. 406–407)

Li, N. P., Bailey, J. M., Kenrick, D. T., & Linsenmeier, J. A. W. (2002). The necessities and luxuries of mate preferences: Testing the tradeoffs. *Journal of Personality and Social Psychology, 82,* 947–955. (p. 438)

Liberman, A., & Chaiken, S. (1992). Defensive processing of personally relevant health messages. *Personality and Social Psychology Bulletin, 18,* 669–679. (p. 259)

Lichtblau, E. (2003, March 18). U.S. seeks $289 billion in cigarette makers' profits. *New York Times* (www.nytimes.com). (p. 281)

Lichtenstein, S., & Fischhoff, B. (1980). Training for calibration. *Organizational Behavior and Human Performance*, **26**, 149–171. (p. 112)

Lickliter, R., & Honeycutt, H. (2003). Developmental dynamics: Toward a biologically plausible evolutionary psychology. *Psychological Bulletin*, **129**, 819–835. (p. 172)

Lieberman, M. D., Ochsner, K. N., Gilbert, D. T., & Schacter, D. L. (2001). Do amnesics exhibit cognitive dissonance reduction? The role of explicit memory and attention in attitude change. *Psychological Science*, **12**, 135–140. (p. 163)

Liebrand, W. B. G., Messick, D. M., & Wolters, F. J. M. (1986). Why we are fairer than others: A cross-cultural replication and extension. *Journal of Experimental Social Psychology*, **22**, 590–604. (pp. 80–81)

Liehr, P., Mehl, M. R., Summers, L. C., & Pennebaker, J. W. (in press). Connecting with others in the midst of stressful upheaval on September 11, 2001. *Applied Nursing Research*. (p. 543)

Lilienfeld, S. O., Wood, J. M., & Garb, H. N. (2000). The scientific status of projective techniques. *Psychological Science in the Public Interest*, **1**, 27–66. (p. 569)

Lindsay, D. S., Read, J. D., & Sharma, K. (1998). Accuracy and confidence in person identification: The relationship is strong when witnessing conditions vary widely. *Psychological Science*, **9**, 215–218. (p. 608)

Lindsay, R. C. L., & Wells, G. L. (1985). Improving eyewitness identifications from lineups: Simultaneous versus sequential lineup presentation. *Journal of Applied Psychology*, **70**, 556–564. (p. 617)

Lindsay, R. C. L., Wells, G. L., & Rumpel, C. H. (1981). Can people detect eyewitness-identification accuracy within and across situations? *Journal of Applied Psychology*, **66**, 79–89. (p. 607)

Lindskold, S. (1978). Trust development, the GRIT proposal, and the effects of conciliatory acts on conflict and cooperation. *Psychological Bulletin*, **85**, 772–793. (p. 559)

Lindskold, S. (1979). Conciliation with simultaneous or sequential interaction: Variations in trustworthiness and vulnerability in the prisoner's dilemma. *Journal of Conflict Resolution*, **27**, 704–714. (p. 559)

Lindskold, S. (1979). Managing conflict through announced conciliatory initiatives backed with retaliatory capability. In W. G. Austin and S. Worchel (Eds.), *The social psychology of intergroup relations*. Monterey, CA: Brooks/Cole. (p. 559)

Lindskold, S. (1981). The laboratory evaluation of GRIT: Trust, cooperation, aversion to using conciliation. Paper presented at the American Association for the Advancement of Science convention. (pp. 559, 560)

Lindskold, S. (1983). Cooperators, competitors, and response to GRIT. *Journal of Conflict Resolution*, **27**, 521–532. (p. 559)

Lindskold, S., & Aronoff, J. R. (1980). Conciliatory strategies and relative power. *Journal of Experimental Social Psychology*, **16**, 187–198. (p. 559)

Lindskold, S., & Collins, M. G. (1978). Inducing cooperation by groups and individuals. *Journal of Conflict Resolution*, **22**, 679–690. (p. 559)

Lindskold, S., & Finch, M. L. (1981). Styles of announcing conciliation. *Journal of Conflict Resolution*, **25**, 145–155. (p. 559)

Lindskold, S., & Han, G. (1988). GRIT as a foundation for integrative bargaining. *Personality and Social Psychology Bulletin*, **14**, 335–345. (p. 559)

Lindskold, S., Bennett, R., & Wayner, M. (1976). Retaliation level as a foundation for subsequent conciliation. *Behavioral Science*, **21**, 13–18. (p. 559)

Lindskold, S., Betz, B., & Walters, P. S. (1986). Transforming competitive or cooperative climate. *Journal of Conflict Resolution*, **30**, 99–114. (p. 559)

Lindskold, S., Han, G., & Betz, B. (1986). Repeated persuasion in interpersonal conflict. *Journal of Personality and Social Psychology*, **51**, 1183–1188. *(b)* (p. 559)

Lindskold, S., Han, G., & Betz, B. (1986). The essential elements of communication in the GRIT strategy. *Personality and Social Psychology Bulletin*, **12**, 179–186. *(a)* (p. 559)

Lindskold, S., Walters, P. S., Koutsourais, H., & Shayo, R. (1981). Cooperators, competitors, and response to GRIT. Unpublished manuscript, Ohio University. (p. 559)

Lineham, M. M. (1997). Self-verification and drug abusers: Implications for treatment. *Psychological Science*, **8**, 181–184. (p. 579)

Linssen, H., & Hagendoorn, L. (1994). Social and geographical factors in the explanation of the content of European nationality stereotypes. *British Journal of Social Psychology*, **33**, 165–182. (p. 333)

Linville, P. W., Gischer, W. G., & Salovey, P. (1989). Perceived distributions of the characteristics of in-group and out-group members: Empirical evidence and a computer simulation. *Journal of Personality and Social Psychology*, **57**, 165–188. (p. 359)

Lipsitz, A., Kallmeyer, K., Ferguson, M., & Abas, A. (1989). Counting on blood donors: Increasing the impact of reminder calls. *Journal of Applied Social Psychology*, **19**, 1057–1067. (p. 144)

Little, A., & Perrett, D. (2002). Putting beauty back in the eye of the beholder. *The Psychologist*, **15**, 28–32. (p. 437)

Liu, J. H., & Latané, B. (1998). Extremitization of attitudes: Does thought- and discussion-induced polarization cumulate? *Basic and Applied Social Psychology*, **20**, 103–110. (pp. 308–309)

Livingston, R. W. (2001). What you see is what you get: Systematic variability in perceptual-based social judgment. *Personality and Social Psychology Bulletin*, **27**, 1086–1096. (p. 436)

Locke, E. A., & Latham, G. P. (1990). Work motivation and satisfaction: Light at the end of the tunnel. *Psychological Science*, **1**, 240–246. (p. 324)

Locke, K. D. (2003). Status and solidarity in social comparison: Agentic and communal values and vertical and horizontal directions.

Journal of Personality and Social Psychology, 84, 619–631. (p. 657)

Locke, K. D., & Horowitz, L. M. (1990). Satisfaction in interpersonal interactions as a function of similarity in level of dysphoria. *Journal of Personality and Social Psychology, 58*, 823–831. (p. 445)

Locksley, A., Borgida, E., Brekke, N., & Hepburn, C. (1980). Sex stereotypes and social judgment. *Journal of Personality and Social Psychology, 39*, 821–831. (p. 373)

Locksley, A., Hepburn, C., & Ortiz, V. (1982). Social stereotypes and judgments of individuals: An instance of the base-rate fallacy. *Journal of Experimental Social Psychology, 18*, 23–42. (p. 373)

Locksley, A., Ortiz, V., & Hepburn, C. (1980). Social categorization and discriminatory behavior: Extinguishing the minimal intergroup discrimination effect. *Journal of Personality and Social Psychology, 39*, 773–783. (p. 352)

Lockwood, P. (2002). Could it happen to you? Predicting the impact of downward comparisons on the self. *Journal of Personality and Social Psychology, 87*, 343–358. (p. 44)

Loewenstein, G., & Schkade, D. (1999). Wouldn't it be nice? Predicting future feelings. In D. Kahneman, E. Diener, & N. Schwarz (Eds.), *Understanding well-being: Scientific perspectives on enjoyment and suffering.* New York: Russell Sage Foundation, pp. 85–105. (p. 53)

Lofland, J., & Stark, R. (1965). Becoming a worldsaver: A theory of conversion to a deviant perspective. *American Sociological Review, 30*, 862–864. (p. 275)

Loftin, C., McDowall, D., Wiersema, B., & Cottey, T. J. (1991). Effects of restrictive licensing of handguns on homicide and suicide in the District of Columbia. *New England Journal of Medicine, 325*, 1615–1620. (p. 397)

Loftus, E. F. (1974, December). Reconstructing memory: The incredible eyewitness. *Psychology Today*, pp. 117–119. (p. 607)

Loftus, E. F. (1979). *Eyewitness testimony.* Cambridge, MA: Harvard University Press. *(a)* (pp. 607, 611)

Loftus, E. F. (1979). The malleability of human memory. *American Scientist, 67*, 312–320. *(b)* (pp. 607, 611)

Loftus, E. F. (1993). The reality of repressed memory. *American Psychologist, 48*, 518–537. (p. 105)

Loftus, E. F. (2000). Remembering what never happened. In E. Tulving (Ed.), *Memory, consciousness, and the brain.* Philadelphia, PA: Psychology Press/Taylor & Francis. (p. 572)

Loftus, E. F. (2001, November). Imagining the past. *The Psychologist, 14*, 584–587. (p. 612)

Loftus, E. F., & Klinger, M. R. (1992). Is the unconscious smart or dumb? *American Psychologist, 47*, 761–765. (p. 108–109)

Loftus, E. F., & Pickrell, J. (1995). The formation of false memories. *Psychiatric Annals, 25*, 720–725. (p. 103)

Loftus, E. F., & Zanni, G. (1975). Eyewitness testimony: The influence of the wording in a question. *Bulletin of the Psychonomic Society, 5*, 86–88. (p. 616)

Loftus, E. F., Donders, K., Hoffman, H. G., & others. (1989, September). Creating new memories that are quickly accessed and confidently held. *Memory & Cognition, 17*, 607–616. (p. 105)

Loftus, E. F., Miller, D. G., & Burns, H. J. (1978). Semantic integration of verbal information into a visual memory. *Journal of Experimental Social Psychology: Human Learning and Memory, 4*, 19–31. (pp. 611–612)

Loftus, E., & Ketcham, K. (1994). *The myth of repressed memory.* New York: St. Martin's Press. (p. 572)

Lombardo, J. P., Weiss, R. F., & Buchanan, W. (1972). Reinforcing and attracting functions of yielding. *Journal of Personality and Social Psychology, 21*, 359–368. (pp. 451–452)

London, K., & Nunez, N. (2000). The effect of jury deliberations on jurors' propensity to disregard inadmissable evidence. *Journal of Applied Psychology, 85*, 932–939. (p. 623)

London, P. (1970). The rescuers: Motivational hypotheses about Christians who saved Jews from the Nazis. In J. Macaulay & L. Berkowitz (Eds.), *Altruism and helping behavior.* New York: Academic Press. (p. 514)

Lonner, W. J. (1980). The search for psychological universals. In H. C. Triandis & W. W. Lambert (Eds.), *Handbook of cross-cultural psychology* (vol. 1). Boston: Allyn and Bacon. (p. 175)

Lonner, W. J. (1989). The introductory psychology text and cross-cultural psychology: Beyond Ekman, Whorf, and biased I.Q. tests. In D. Keats, D. R. Munro & L. Mann (Eds.), *Heterogeneity in cross-cultural psychology.* (p. 180)

Lord, C. G., Desforges, D. M., Ramsey, S. L., Trezza, G. R., & Lepper, M. R. (1991). Typicality effects in attitude-behavior consistency: Effects of category discrimination and category knowledge. *Journal of Experimental Social Psychology, 27*, 550–575. (p. 374)

Lord, C. G., Lepper, M. R., & Preston, E. (1984). Considering the opposite: A corrective strategy for social judgment. *Journal of Personality and Social Psychology, 47*, 1231–1243. (p. 102)

Lord, C. G., Ross, L., & Lepper, M. (1979). Biased assimilation and attitude polarization: The effects of prior theories on subsequently considered evidence. *Journal of Personality and Social Psychology, 37*, 2098–2109. (p. 100)

Lorenz, K. (1976). *On aggression.* New York: Bantam Books. (p. 382)

Losch, M. E., & Cacioppo, J. T. (1990). Cognitive dissonance may enhance sympathetic tonus, but attitudes are changed to reduce negative affect rather than arousal. *Journal of Experimental Social Psychology, 26*, 289–304. (p. 162)

Lott, A. J., & Lott, B. E. (1961). Group cohesiveness, communication level, and conformity. *Journal of Abnormal and Social Psychology, 62*, 408–412. (p. 231)

Lott, A. J., & Lott, B. E. (1974). The role of reward in the formation of positive interpersonal attitudes. In T. Huston (Ed.), *Foundations of interpersonal attraction.* New York: Academic Press. (p. 450)

Lovett, F. (1997). Thinking about values (report of December 13, 1996 *Wall Street Journal* national survey). *The Responsive Community, 7*(2), 87. (p. 70)

Lowe, R. H., & Wittig, M. A. (1989). Comparable worth: Individual, interpersonal, and structural considerations. *Journal of Social Issues*, **45**, 223–246. (p. 531)

Lowenstein, D. (2000 May 20). Interview. *The World*. www.cnn.com/TRANSCRIPTS/0005/20/stc.00.html (p. 411)

Lowenthal, M. F., Thurnher, M., Chiriboga, D., Beefon, D., Gigy, L., Lurie, E., Pierce, R., Spence, D., & Weiss, L. (1975). *Four stages of life*. San Francisco: Jossey-Bass. (p. 193)

Loy, J. W., & Andrews, D. S. (1981). They also saw a game: A replication of a case study. *Replications in Social Psychology*, **1**(2), 45–59. (p. 14)

Lueptow, L. B., Garovich, L., & Lueptow, M. B. (1995). The persistence of gender stereotypes in the face of changing sex roles: Evidence contrary to the sociocultural model. *Ethology and Sociobiology*, **16**, 509–530. (p. 341)

Luginbuhl, J. (1992). Comprehension of judges' instructions in the penalty phase of a capital trial: Focus on mitigating circumstances. *Law and Human Behavior*, **16**, 203–218. (p. 626)

Luginbuhl, J., & Middendorf, K. (1988). Death penalty beliefs and jurors' responses to aggravating and mitigating circumstances in capital trials. *Law and Human Behavior*, **12**, 263–281. (p. 629)

Lumsdaine, A. A., & Janis, I. L. (1953). Resistance to "counter-propaganda" produced by one-sided and two-sided "propaganda" presentations. *Public Opinion Quarterly*, **17**, 311–318. (p. 261)

Lumsden, A., Zanna, M. P., & Darley, J. M. (1980). When a newscaster presents counter-additional information: Education or propaganda? Paper presented to the Canadian Psychological Association annual convention. (p. 247)

Luntz, F. (2003, June 10). Quoted by T. Raum, "Bush insists banned weapons will be found." Associated Press (story.news.yahoo.com). (p. 152)

Lüüs, C. A. E., & Wells, G. L. (1994). Determinants of eyewitness confidence. In D. F. Ross, J. D. Read, & M. P. Toglia (Eds.), *Adult eyewitness testimony: Current trends and developments*, pp. 348–362. New York: Cambridge University Press. (p. 614)

Lüüs, C. A. E., & Wells, G. L. (1994). Eyewitness identification confidence. In D. F. Ross, J. D. Read, & M. P. Toglia (Eds.), *Adult eyewitness testimony: Current trends and developments*. Cambridge, England: Cambridge University Press. (p. 614)

Lydon, J., & Dunkel-Schetter, C. (1994). Seeing is committing: A longitudinal study of bolstering commitment in amniocenesis patients. *Personality and Social Psychology Bulletin*, **20**, 218–227. (p. 219)

Lykken, D. T. (1997). The American crime factory. *Psychological Inquiry*, **8**, 261–270. (p. 306)

Lykken, D. T. (1999). *Happiness*. New York: Golden Books. (p. 652)

Lykken, D. T. (2000, Spring). Psychology and the criminal justice system: A reply to Haney and Zimbardo. *The General Psychologist*, **35**, 11–15. (p. 391)

Lykken, D. T., & Tellegen, A. (1993). Is human mating adventitious or the result of lawful choice? A twin study of mate selection. *Journal of Personality and Social Psychology*, **65**, 56–68. (p. 427)

Lynch, B. S., & Bonnie, R. J. (1994). Toward a youth-centered prevention policy. In B. S. Lynch and R. J. Bonnie (Eds.), *Growing up tobacco free: Preventing nicotine addiction in children and youths*. Washington, DC: National Academy Press. (p. 54)

Lynch, J. W., Kaplan, G. A., Pamuk, E. R., Cohen, R. D., Heck, K. E., Balfour, J. L., & Yen, I. H. (1998). Income inequality and mortality in metropolitan areas of the United States. *American Journal of Public Health*, **88**, 1074–1080. (p. 599)

Lynch, J. W., Smith, G. D., Kaplan, G. A., & House, J. S. (2000). Income inequality and health: A neo-material interpretation. *British Medical Journal*, **320**, 1200–1204. (p. 599)

Lynn, M., & Oldenquist, A. (1986). Egoistic and nonegoistic motives in social dilemmas. *American Psychologist*, **41**, 529–534. (p. 528)

Lyons, L. (2003, September 23). Oh, boy: Americans still prefer sons. *Gallup Poll Tuesday Briefing* (www.gallup.com). (p. 342)

Lyubomirsky, S. (2001). Why are some people happier than others? The role of cognitive and motivational processes in well-being. *American Psychologist*, **56**, 239–249. (p. 656)

Ma, V., & Schoeneman, T. J. (1997). Individualism versus collectivism: A comparison of Kenyan and American self-concepts. *Basic and Applied Social Psychology*, **19**, 261–273. (p. 46)

Maass, A. (1998). Personal communication from Universita degli Studi di Padova. (p. 324)

Maass, A. (1999). Linguistic intergroup bias: Stereotype perpetuation through language. In M. P. Zanna (Ed.), *Advances in Experimental Social Psychology*, **31**, 79–121. (pp. 365–366)

Maass, A., & Clark, R. D., III. (1984). Hidden impact of minorities: Fifteen years of minority influence research. *Psychological Bulletin*, **95**, 428–450. (p. 323)

Maass, A., & Clark, R. D., III. (1986). Conversion theory and simultaneous majority/minority influence: Can reactance offer an alternative explanation? *European Journal of Social Psychology*, **16**, 305–309. (p. 323)

Maass, A., Milesi, A., Zabbini, S., & Stahlberg, D. (1995). Linguistic intergroup bias: Differential expectancies or in-group protection? *Journal of Personality and Social Psychology*, **68**, 116–126. (pp. 365–366)

Maass, A., Volparo, C., & Mucchi-Faina, A. (1996). Social influence and the verifiability of the issue under discussion: Attitudinal versus objective items. *British Journal of Social Psychology*, **35**, 15–26. (p. 322)

Maccoby, E. E. (2002). Gender and group process: A developmental perspective. *Current Directions in Psychological Science*, **11**, 54–58. (pp. 182, 306)

Maccoby, N. (1980). Promoting positive health behaviors in adults. In L. A. Bond & J. C. Rosen (Eds.), *Competence and coping during adulthood*. Hanover, NH: University Press of New England. (pp. 265, 266)

Maccoby, N., & Alexander, J. (1980). Use of media in lifestyle programs. In

P. O. Davidson & S. M. Davidson (Eds.). *Behavioral medicine: Changing health lifestyles.* New York: Brunner/Mazel. (p. 265)

MacCoun, R. J., & Kerr, N. L. (1988). Asymmetric influence in mock jury deliberation: Jurors' bias for leniency. *Journal of Personality and Social Psychology, 54,* 21–33. (p. 633)

MacDonald, G., Zanna, M. P., & Holmes, J. G. (2000). An experimental test of the role of alcohol in relationship conflict. *Journal of Experimental Social Psychology, 36,* 182–193. (p. 384)

MacDonald, T. K., & Ross, M. (1997). Assessing the accuracy of predictions about dating relationships: How and why do lovers' predictions differ from those made by observers? Unpublished manuscript, University of Lethbridge. (p. 52)

Mack, D., & Rainey, D. (1990). Female applicants' grooming and personnel selection. *Journal of Social Behavior and Personality, 5,* 399–407. (p. 436)

MacKay, J. L. (1980). Selfhood: Comment on Brewster Smith. *American Psychologist, 35,* 106–107. (p. 60)

MacLeod, C., & Campbell, L. (1992). Memory accessibility and probability judgments: An experimental evaluation of the availability heuristic. *Journal of Personality and Social Psychology, 63,* 890–902. (p. 114)

Macrae, C. N., Alnwick, M. A., Milne, A. B., & Schloerscheidt, A. M. (2002). Person perception across the menstrual cycle: Hormonal influences on social-cognitive functioning. *Psychological Science, 13,* 532–536. (p. 439)

Macrae, C. N., & Bodenhausen, G. V. (2000). Social cognition: Thinking categorically about others. *Annual Review of Psychology, 51,* 93–120. (p. 357)

Macrae, C. N., Bodenhausen, G. V., & Milne, A. B. (1998). Saying no to unwanted thoughts: Self-focus and the regulation of mental life. *Journal of Personality and Social Psychology, 74,* 578–590. (p. 337)

Macrae, C. N., Bodenhausen, G. V., Milne, A. B., & Jetten, J. (1994). Out of mind but back in sight: Stereotypes on the rebound. *Journal of Personality and Social Psychology, 67,* 808–817. (p. 357)

Macrae, C. N., & Johnston, L. (1998). Help, I need somebody: Automatic action and inaction. *Social Cognition, 16,* 400–417. (p. 107)

Macrae, C. N., Stangor, C., & Milne, A. B. (1994). Activating social stereotypes: A functional analysis. *Journal of Experimental Social Psychology, 30,* 370–389. (p. 357)

Maddux, J. E. (1993). The mythology of psychopathology: A social cognitive view of deviance, difference, and disorder. *The General Psychologist, 29*(2), 34–45. (pp. 568–569, 574)

Maddux, J. E., & Gosselin, J. T. (2003). Self-efficacy. In M. R. Leary, & J. P. Tangney (Eds.), *Handbook of self and identity.* New York: Guilford. (p. 57)

Maddux, J. E., & Rogers, R. W. (1983). Protection motivation and self-efficacy: A revised theory of fear appeals and attitude change. *Journal of Experimental Social Psychology, 19,* 469–479. (p. 258)

Madon, S., Jussim, L., & Eccles, J. (1997). In search of the powerful self-fulfilling prophecy. *Journal of Personality and Social Psychology, 72,* 791–809. (p. 123)

Madon, S., Jussim, L., Keiper, S., Eccles, J., Smith, A., & Palumbo, P. (1998). The accuracy and power of sex, social class, and ethnic stereotypes: A naturalistic study in person perception. *Personality and Social Psychology Bulletin, 24,* 1304–1318. (p. 333)

Mae, L., & Carlston, D. E. (1999). Spontaneous trait transference to familiar communicators: Is a little knowledge a dangerous thing? *Journal of Personality and Social Psychology, 77,* 233–246. (p. 101)

Magnuson, E. (1986, March 10). "A serious deficiency": The Rogers Commission faults NASA's "flawed" decision-making process. *Time,* pp. 40–42, international ed. (p. 316)

Major, B. (1989). Gender differences in comparisons and entitlement: Implications for comparable worth. *Journal of Social Issues, 45,* 99–116. (p. 531)

Major, B. (1993). Gender, entitlement, and the distribution of family labor. *Journal of Social Issues, 49,* 141–159. (p. 531)

Major, B., Kaiser, C. R., & McCoy, S. K. (2003). It's not my fault: When and why attributions to prejudice protect self-esteem. *Personality and Social Psychology Bulletin, 29,* 772–781. (p. 68)

Malamuth, N. M. (1996). The confluence model of sexual aggression. In D. M. Buss & N. M. Malamuth (Eds.), *Sex, power, conflict: Evolutionary and feminist perspectives.* New York: Oxford University Press. (p. 402)

Malamuth, N. M. (2003). Criminal and noncriminal sexual aggressors: Integrating psychopathy in a hierarchical-mediational confluence model. In R. A. Prentky, E. Janus, & M. Seto (Eds.), *Sexually coercive behavior: Understanding and management.* New York: Annals of the New York Academy of Sciences. (p. 402)

Malamuth, N. M., & Brown, L. M. (1994). Sexually aggressive men's perceptions of women's communications: Testing three explanations. *Journal of Personality and Social Psychology, 67,* 699–712. (p. 85)

Malamuth, N. M., & Check, J. V. P. (1981). The effects of media exposure on acceptance of violence against women: A field experiment. *Journal of Research in Personality, 15,* 436–446. (p. 399)

Malamuth, N. M., Haber, S., Feshbach, S., & others. (1980, March). *Journal of Research in Personality, 14,* 121–137. (p. 399)

Malkiel, B. G. (1999). *A random walk down Wall Street,* revised edition. New York: Norton. (p. 111)

Mallett, R. K., & Swim, J. K. (2003). Collective guilt in the United States: Predicting support for social policies that alleviate social injustice. In N. Branscombe & B. Doosje (Eds.), *Collective guilt: International perspectives.* New York: Cambridge University Press. (p. 531)

Manis, M., Cornell, S. D., & Moore, J. C. (1974). Transmission of attitude-relevant information through a communication chain. *Journal of*

Personality and Social Psychology, 30, 81–94. (pp. 142–143)

Manis, M., Nelson, T. E., & Shedler, J. (1988). Stereotypes and social judgment: Extremity, assimilation, and contrast. *Journal of Personality and Social Psychology, 55,* 28–36. (p. 376)

Mann, L. (1981). The baiting crowd in episodes of threatened suicide. *Journal of Personality and Social Psychology, 41,* 703–709. (pp. 298–299)

Marcus, A. C., & Siegel, J. M. (1982). Sex differences in the use of physician services: A preliminary test of the fixed role hypothesis. *Journal of Health and Social Behavior, 23,* 186–197. (p. 588)

Marcus, D. K., & Miller, R. S. (2003). Sex differences in judgments of physical attractiveness: A social relations analysis. *Personality and Social Psychology Bulletin, 29,* 325–335. (p. 437)

Marcus, S. (1974). Review of *Obedience to authority.* New York Times Book Review, January 13, pp. 1–2. (p. 218)

Marcus-Newhall, A., Pedersen, W. C., Carlson, M., & Miller, N. (2000). Displaced aggression is alive and well: A meta-analytic review. *Journal of Personality and Social Psychology, 78,* 670–689. (p. 386)

Markey, P. M., Wells, S. M., & Markey, C. N. (2002). In S. P. Shohov (Ed.), *Advances in Psychology Research, 9,* 94–113. Huntington, NY: Nova Science. (pp. 144–145)

Markman, H. J., Floyd, F. J., Stanley, S. M., & Storaasli, R. D. (1988). Prevention of marital distress: A longitudinal investigation. *Journal of Consulting and Clinical Psychology, 56,* 210–217. (p. 470)

Markman, K. D., & McMullen, M. N. (2003). A reflection and evaluation model of comparative thinking. *Personality and Social Psychology Review, 7,* 244–267. (p. 116)

Marks, G., & Miller, N. (1987). Ten years of research on the false-consensus effect: An empirical and theoretical review. *Psychological Bulletin, 102,* 72–90. (p. 72)

Markus, H. R., & Kitayama, S. (1994). A collective fear of the collective: Implications for selves and theories of selves. *Personality and Social Psychology Bulletin, 20,* 568–579. (p. 208)

Markus, H., & Kitayama, S. (1991). Culture and the self: Implications for cognition, emotion, and motivation. *Psychological Review, 98,* 224–253. (p. 48)

Markus, H., & Nurius, P. (1986). Possible selves. *American Psychologist, 41,* 954–969. (p. 42)

Markus, H., & Wurf, E. (1987). The dynamic self-concept: A social psychological perspective. *Annual Review of Psychology, 38,* 299–337. (p. 41)

Marmot, M. G., & Wilkinson, R. G. (Eds.) (1999). *Social determinants of health.* Oxford: Oxford University Press. (p. 599)

Marsh, H. W., Kong, C-K., & Hau, K-T. (2000). Longitudinal multilevel models of the big-fish-little-pond effect on academic self-concept: Counterbalancing contrast and reflected-glory effects in Hong Kong schools. *Journal of Personality and Social Psychology, 78,* 337–349. (p. 44)

Marsh, H. W., & Young, A. S. (1997). Causal effects of academic self-concept on academic achievement: Structural equation models of longitudinal data. *Journal of Educational Psychology, 89,* 41–54. (p. 44)

Marshall, R. (1997). Variances in levels of individualism across two cultures and three social classes. *Journal of Cross-Cultural Psychology, 28,* 490–495. (p. 46)

Marshall, W. L. (1989). Pornography and sex offenders. In D. Zillmann & J. Bryant (Eds.), *Pornography: Research advances and policy considerations.* Hillsdale, NJ: Erlbaum. (p. 400)

Martin, R. (1996). Minority influence and argument generation. *British Journal of Social Psychology, 35,* 91–103. (p. 322)

Marty, M. (1988, December 1). Graceful prose: Your good deed for the day. *Context,* p. 2. (p. 34)

Maruyama, G., Rubin, R. A., & Kingbury, G. (1981). Self-esteem and educational achievement: Independent constructs with a common cause? *Journal of Personality and Social Psychology, 40,* 962–975. (p. 24)

Marvelle, K., & Green, S. (1980). Physical attractiveness and sex bias in hiring decisions for two types of jobs. *Journal of the National Association of Women Deans, Administrators, and Counselors, 44*(1), 3–6. (p. 436)

Marx, G. (1960). *Groucho and me.* New York: Dell. (p. 66)

Maslow, A. H., & Mintz, N. L. (1956). Effects of esthetic surroundings: I. Initial effects of three esthetic conditions upon perceiving "energy" and "well-being" in faces. *Journal of Psychology, 41,* 247–254. (p. 450)

Mastekaasa, A. (1995). Age variations in the suicide rates and self-reported subjective well-being of married and never married persons. *Journal of Community & Applied Social Psychology, 5,* 21–39. (p. 601)

Masuda, T., & Kitayama, S. (in press). Perceiver-induced constraint and attitude attribution in Japan and the U.S.: A case for culture-dependence of correspondence bias. *Journal of Experimental Social Psychology,* in press. (p. 95)

Matheson, K., Cole, B., & Majka, K. (2003). Dissidence from within: Examining the effects of intergroup context on group members' reactions to attitudinal opposition. *Journal of Experimental Social Psychology, 39,* 161–169. (p. 234)

Matheson, K., & Dursun, S. (2001). Social identity precursors to the hostile media phenomenon: Partisan perceptions of coverage of the Bosnian conflict. *Group Processes and Intergroup Relations, 4,* 116–125. (p. 99)

Maxwell, G. M. (1985). Behaviour of lovers: Measuring the closeness of relationships. *Journal of Personality and Social Psychology, 2,* 215–238. (p. 458)

Mayer, J. D., & Salovey, P. (1987). Personality moderates the interaction of mood and cognition. In K. Fiedler & J. Forgas (Eds.), *Affect, cognition, and social behavior.* Toronto: Hogrefe. (pp. 119, 579)

Mayton, D. M., II, Diessner, R., & Granby, C. D. (1996). Nonviolence and human values: Empirical support for theoretical relations. *Peace and Conflict: Journal of Peace Psychology, 2,* 245–253. (p. 552)

Mazur, A., & Booth, A. (1998). Testosterone and dominance in men. *Behavioral and Brain Sciences, 21,* 353–363. (p. 385)

Mazzella, R., & Feingold, A. (1994). The effects of physical attractiveness, race, socioeconomic status, and gender of defendants and victims on judgments of mock jurors: A meta-analysis. *Journal of Applied Social Psychology, 24,* 1315–1344. (pp. 619, 621)

Mazzuca, J. (2002, August 20). Teens shrug off movie sex and violence. *Gallup Tuesday Briefing* (www.gallup.com). (p. 409)

McAlister, A., Perry, C., Killen, J., Slinkard, L. A., & Maccoby, N. (1980). Pilot study of smoking, alcohol and drug abuse prevention. *American Journal of Public Health, 70,* 719–721. (pp. 279–280)

McAndrew, F. T. (1981). Pattern of performance and attributions of ability and gender. *Journal of Personality and Social Psychology, 7,* 583–587. (p. 262)

McAndrew, F. T. (2002). New evolutionary perspectives on altruism: Multilevel-selection and costly-signaling theories. *Current Directions in Psychological Science, 11,* 79–82. (p. 488)

McCann, C. D., & Hancock, R. D. (1983). Self-monitoring in communicative interactions: Social cognitive consequences of goal-directed message modification. *Journal of Experimental Social Psychology, 19,* 109–121. (pp. 79–80)

McCarrey, M., Edwards, H. P., & Rozario, W. (1982). Ego-relevant feedback, affect, and self-serving attributional bias. *Personality and Social Psychology Bulletin, 8,* 189–194. (p. 74)

McCarthy, J. F., & Kelly, B. R. (1978). Aggressive behavior and its effect on performance over time in ice hockey athletes: An archival study. *International Journal of Sport Psychology, 9,* 90–96. *(a)* (p. 390)

McCarthy, J. F., & Kelly, B. R. (1978). Aggression, performance variables, and anger self-report in ice hockey players. *Journal of Psychology, 99,* 97–101. *(b)* (p. 390)

McCauley, C. (1989). The nature of social influence in groupthink: Compliance and internalization.

Journal of Personality and Social Psychology, 57, 250–260. (p. 314)

McCauley, C. (1998). Group dynamics in Janis's theory of groupthink: Backward and forward. *Organizational Behavior and Human Decision Processes, 73,* 142–163. (p. 315)

McCauley, C. R. (2002). Psychological issues in understanding terrorism and the response to terrorism. In C. E. Stout (Ed.), *The psychology of terrorism, Vol. 3.* Westport, CT: Praeger/Greenwood. (pp. 306–307)

McCauley, C. R., & Segal, M. E. (1987). Social psychology of terrorist groups. In C. Hendrick (Ed.), *Group processes and intergroup relations: Review of personality and social psychology,* Vol. 9. Newbury Park, CA: Sage. (pp. 306–307)

McClure, J. (1998). Discounting causes of behavior: Are two reasons better than one? *Journal of Personality and Social Psychology, 74,* 7–20. (p. 87)

McConahay, J. B. (1981). Reducing racial prejudice in desegregated schools. In W. D. Hawley (Ed.), *Effective school desegregation.* Beverly Hills, CA: Sage. (p. 550)

McCrae, R. R., & Costa, P. T., Jr. (1999). A five-factor theory of personality. In L. A. Pervin & O. P. John (Eds.), *Handbook of personality: Theory and research.* New York: Guilford. (p. 175)

McCullough, J. L., & Ostrom, T. M. (1974). Repetition of highly similar messages and attitude change. *Journal of Applied Psychology, 59,* 395–397. (p. 431)

McFall, R. M. (1991). Manifesto for a science of clinical psychology. *The Clinical Psychologist, 44,* 75–88. (p. 569)

McFall, R. M. (2000). Elaborate reflections on a simple manifesto. *Applied and Preventive Psychology, 9,* 5–21. (p. 569)

McFarland, C., & Ross, M. (1985). The relation between current impressions and memories of self and dating partners. Unpublished manuscript, University of Waterloo. (p. 104)

McFarland, C., Ross, M., & DeCourville, N. (1989). Women's theories of menstruation and biases in recall of menstrual symptoms. *Journal*

of Personality and Social Psychology, 57, 522–531. (p. 587)

McFarland, S. G., Ageyev, V. S., & Abalakina-Paap, M. A. (1992). Authoritarianism in the former Soviet Union. *Journal of Personality and Social Psychology, 63,* 1004–1010. (p. 345)

McFarland, S. G., Ageyev, V. S., & Djintcharadze, N. (1996). Russian authoritarianism two years after communism. *Personality and Social Psychology Bulletin, 22,* 210–217. (p. 345)

McGillicuddy, N. B., Welton, G. L., & Pruitt, D. G. (1987). Third-party intervention: A field experiment comparing three different models. *Journal of Personality and Social Psychology, 53,* 104–112. (p. 558)

McGillis, D. (1979). Biases and jury decision making. In I. H. Frieze, D. Bar-Tal, & J. S. Carroll, *New approaches to social problems.* San Francisco: Jossey-Bass. (p. 619)

McGinn, A. P. (1998, June 20). Hidden forces mask crisis in world fisheries. Worldwatch Institute (www.worldwatch.org). (p. 644)

McGlone, M. S., & Tofighbakhsh, J. (2000). Birds of a feather flock conjointly (?): Rhyme as reason in aphorisms. *Psychological Science, 11,* 424–428. (p. 264)

McGlynn, R. P., Tubbs, D. D., & Holzhausen, K. G. (1995). Hypothesis generation in groups constrained by evidence. *Journal of Experimental Social Psychology, 31,* 64–81. (p. 319)

McGrath, J. E. (1984). *Groups: Interaction and performance.* Englewood Cliffs, NJ: Prentice-Hall. (p. 286)

McGregor, I., Newby-Clark, I. R., & Zanna, M. P. (1998). Epistemic discomfort is moderated by simultaneous accessibility of inconsistent elements. In E. Harmon-Jones and J. Mills (Eds.), *Cognitive dissonance theory 40 years later: A revival with revisions and controversies.* Washington, DC: American Psychological Association. (p. 163)

McGregor, I., Zanna, M. P., Holmes, J. G., & Spencer, S. J. (2001). Conviction in the face of uncertainty: Going to extremes and being oneself. *Journal of Personality and Social Psychology, 80,* 472–478. (p. 355)

McGuire, A. (2002, August 19). Charity calls for debate on adverts aimed at children. *The Herald* (Scotland), p. 4. (p. 281)

McGuire, W. J. (1964). Inducing resistance to persuasion: Some contemporary approaches. In L. Berkowitz (Ed.), *Advances in experimental social psychology* (Vol. 1). New York: Academic Press. (p. 278)

McGuire, W. J. (1986). The myth of massive media impact: Savagings and salvagings. In G. Comstock (Ed.), *Public communication and behavior*, Vol. 1. Orlando, FL: Academic Press. (p. 264)

McGuire, W. J., & McGuire, C. V. (1986). Differences in conceptualizing self versus conceptualizing other people as manifested in contrasting verb types used in natural speech. *Journal of Personality and Social Psychology*, **51**, 1135–1143. (p. 90)

McGuire, W. J., McGuire, C. V., & Winton, W. (1979). Effects of household sex composition on the salience of one's gender in the spontaneous self-concept. *Journal of Experimental Social Psychology*, **15**, 77–90. (p. 240)

McGuire, W. J., McGuire, C. V., Child, P., & Fujioka, T. (1978). Salience of ethnicity in the spontaneous self-concept as a function of one's ethnic distinctiveness in the social environment. *Journal of Personality and Social Psychology*, **36**, 511–520. (p. 240)

McGuire, W. J., & Padawer-Singer, A. (1978). Trait salience in the spontaneous self-concept. *Journal of Personality and Social Psychology*, **33**, 743–754. (p. 240)

McKelvie, S. J. (1995). Bias in the estimated frequency of names. *Perceptual and Motor Skills*, **81**, 1331–1338. (p. 114)

McKelvie, S. J. (1997). The availability heuristic: Effects of fame and gender on the estimated frequency of male and female names. *Journal of Social Psychology*, **137**, 63–78. (p. 114)

McKenna, F. P., & Myers, L. B. (1997). Illusory self-assessments—Can they be reduced? *British Journal of Psychology*, **88**, 39–51. (p. 70)

McKenna, K. Y. A., & Bargh, J. A. (1998). Coming out in the age of the Internet: Identity demarginalization through virtual group participation. *Journal of Personality and Social Psychology*, **75**, 681–694. (pp. 307, 466)

McKenna, K. Y. A., & Bargh, J. A. (2000). Plan 9 from cyberspace: The implications of the Internet for personality and social psychology. *Personality and Social Psychology Review*, **4**, 57–75. (pp. 307, 466)

McKenna, K. Y. A., Green, A. S., & Gleason, M. E. J. (2002). What's the big attraction? Relationship formation on the Internet. *Journal of Social Issues*, **58**, 9–31. (p. 466)

McKenzie-Mohr, D. (2000). Fostering sustainable behavior through community-based social marketing. *American Psychologist*, **55**, 531–537. (p. 658)

McKenzie-Mohr, D., & Zanna, M. P. (1990). Treating women as sexual objects: Look to the (gender schematic) male who has viewed pornography. *Personality and Social Psychology Bulletin*, **16**, 296–308. (p. 416)

McMillen, D. L., & Austin, J. B. (1971). Effect of positive feedback on compliance following transgression. *Psychonomic Science*, **24**, 59–61. (p. 480)

McMillen, D. L., Sanders, D. Y., & Solomon, G. S. (1977). Self-esteem, attentiveness, and helping behavior. *Journal of Personality and Social Psychology*, **3**, 257–261. (p. 482)

McNeill, B. W., & Stoltenberg, C. D. (1988). A test of the elaboration likelihood model for therapy. *Cognitive Therapy and Research*, **12**, 69–79. (p. 595)

Mead, G. H. (1934). *Mind, self, and society*. Chicago: University of Chicago Press. (p. 45)

Mealey, L., Bridgstock, R., & Townsend, G. C. (1999). Symmetry and perceived facial attractiveness: A monozygotic co-twin comparison. *Journal of Personality and Social Psychology*, **76**, 151–158. (p. 437)

Medalia, N. Z., & Larsen, O. N. (1958). Diffusion and belief in collective delusion: The Seattle windshield pitting epidemic. *American Sociological Review*, **23**, 180–186. (p. 211)

Medvec, V. H., Madey, S. F., & Gilovich, T. (1995). When less is more: Counterfactual thinking and satisfaction among Olympic medalists. *Journal of Personality and Social Psychology*, **69**, 603–610. (p. 115)

Medvec, V. H., & Savitsky, K. (1997). When doing better means feeling worse: The effects of categorical cutoff points on counterfactual thinking and satisfaction. *Journal of Personality and Social Psychology*, **72**, 1284–1296. (p. 115)

Meech, P., & Kilborn, R. (1992). Media and identity in a stateless nation: The case of Scotland. *Media, Culture and Society*, **14**, 245–259. (p. 43)

Meehl, P. E. (1954). *Clinical vs. statistical prediction: A theoretical analysis and a review of evidence*. Minneapolis: University of Minnesota Press. (pp. 572–574)

Mehl, M. R., & Pennebaker, J. W. (2003). The sounds of social life: A psychometric analysis of students' daily social environments and natural conversations. *Journal of Personality and Social Psychology*, **84**, 857–870. (p. 8)

Mehlman, P. T. & 7 others (1994). Low CSF 5-HIAA concentrations and severe aggression and impaired impulse control in nonhuman primates. *American Journal of Psychiatry*, **151**, 1485–1491. (p. 385)

Meindl, J. R., & Lerner, M. J. (1984). Exacerbation of extreme responses to an out-group. *Journal of Personality and Social Psychology*, **47**, 71–84. (p. 355)

Meissner, C. A., & Brigham, J. C. (2001). Thirty years of investigating the own-race bias in memory for faces: A meta-analytic review. *Psychology, Public Policy, & Law*, **7**, 3–35. (p. 359)

Meissner, C. A., Brigham, J. C., & Kelley, C. M. (2001). The influence of retrieval processes in verbal overshadowing. *Memory and Cognition*, **29**, 176–186. (p. 616)

Meleshko, K. G. A., & Alden, L. E. (1993). Anxiety and self-disclosure: Toward a motivational model. *Journal of Personality and Social Psychology*, **64**, 1000–1009. (p. 584)

Mellers, B., Hertwig, R., & Kahneman, D. (2001). Do frequency representations eliminate conjunction effects: An exercise in adversarial collaboration. *Psychological Science, 12*, 269–275. (p. 113)

Mendonca, P. J., & Brehm, S. S. (1983). Effects of choice on behavioral treatment of overweight children. *Journal of Social and Clinical Psychology, 1*, 343–358. (p. 592)

Menon, T., Morris, M. W., Chiu, C-Y., Hong, Y-Y. (1999). Culture and the construal of agency: Attribution to individual versus group dispositions. *Journal of Personality & Social Psychology, 76*, 701–717. (p. 95)

Merari, A. (2002). Explaining suicidal terrorism: Theories versus empirical evidence. Invited address to the American Psychological Association. (p. 307)

Merton, R. K. (1938; reprinted 1970). *Science, technology and society in seventeenth-century England.* New York: Fertig. (p. 130)

Merton, R. K. (1948). The self-fulfilling prophecy. *Antioch Review, 8*, 193–210. (p. 121)

Merton, R. K., & Kitt, A. S. (1950). Contributions to the theory of reference group behavior. In R. K. Merton & P. F. Lazarsfeld (Eds.), *Continuities in social research: Studies in the scope and method of the American soldier.* Glencoe, IL: Free Press. (p. 389)

Merz, J. F. & Caulkins, J. P. (1995). Propensity to abuse—propensity to murder? *Chance, 8*, 14. (p. 627)

Messé, L. A., & Sivacek, J. M. (1979). Predictions of others' responses in a mixed-motive game: Self-justification or false consensus? *Journal of Personality and Social Psychology, 37*, 602–607. (p. 527)

Messé, L. A., Kerr, N. L., & Sattler, D. N. (1992). "But some animals are more equal than others": The supervisor as a privileged status in group contexts. In S. Worchel, W. Wood, & J. Simpson (Eds.) *Group process and productivity.* Newbury Park, CA: Sage. (p. 179)

Messick, D. M., & Sentis, K. P. (1979). Fairness and preference. *Journal of Experimental Social Psychology, 15*, 418–434. (p. 530)

Metalsky, G. I., Joiner, T. E., Jr., Hardin, T. S., & Abramson, L. Y. (1993). Depressive reactions to failure in a naturalistic setting: A test of the hopelessness and self-esteem theories of depression. *Journal of Abnormal Psychology, 102*, 101–109. (p. 580)

Meyers, S. A., & Berscheid, E. (1997). The language of love: The difference a preposition makes. *Personality and Social Psychology Bulletin, 23*, 347–362. (p. 454)

Michaels, J. W., Blommel, J. M., Brocato, R. M., Linkous, R. A., & Rowe, J. S. (1982). social facilitation and inhibition in a natural setting. *Replications in Social Psychology, 2*, 21–24. (p. 288)

Mickelson, K. D., Kessler, R. C., & Shaver, P. R. (1997). Adult attachment in a nationally representative sample. *Journal of Personality and Social Psychology, 73*, 1092–1106. (p. 459)

Mikula, G. (1984). Justice and fairness in interpersonal relations: Thoughts and suggestions. In H. Taijfel (Ed.), *The social dimension: European developments in social psychology*, Vol. 1, Cambridge: Cambridge University Press. (p. 531)

Mikulincer, M., Florian, V., & Hirschberger, G. (2003). The existential function of close relationships: Introducing death into the science of love. *Personality and Social Psychology Review, 7*, 20–40. (p. 424)

Mikulincer, M., & Shaver, P. R. (2001). Attachment theory and intergroup bias: Evidence that priming the secure base schema attenuates negative reactions to out-groups. *Journal of Personality and Social Psychology, 81*, 97–115. (p. 356)

Milgram, A. (2000). My personal view of Stanley Milgram. In T. Blass (Ed.), *Obedience to authority: Current perspectives on the Milgram paradigm.* Mahwah, NJ: Erlbaum. (p. 217)

Milgram, S. (1961, December). Nationality and conformity. *Scientific American*, December, pp. 45–51. (p. 237)

Milgram, S. (1965). Some conditions of obedience and disobedience to authority. *Human Relations, 18*, 57–76. (pp. 215–217)

Milgram, S. (1974). *Obedience to authority.* New York: Harper and Row. (pp. 5, 215–217, 223, 226–227, 231, 236)

Milgram, S., Bickman, L., & Berkowitz, L. (1969). Note on the drawing power of crowds of different size. *Journal of Personality and Social Psychology, 13*, 79–82. (p. 229)

Milgram, S., & Sabini, J. (1983). On maintaining social norms: A field experiment in the subway. In H. H. Blumberg, A. P. Hare, V. Kent, and M. Davies (Eds.), *Small groups and social interaction*, Vol. 1. London: Wiley. (p. 225)

Millar, M. G., & Millar, K. U. (1996). Effects of message anxiety on disease detection and health promotion behaviors. *Basic and Applied Social Psychology, 18*, 61–74. (p. 258)

Millar, M. G., & Tesser, A. (1992). The role of beliefs and feelings in guiding behavior: The mismatch model. In L. Martin & A. Tesser (Eds.), *The construction of social judgment.* Hillsdale NJ: Erlbaum. (p. 56)

Miller, A. G. (1986). *The obedience experiments: A case study of controversy in social science.* New York: Praeger. (p. 218)

Miller, A. G. (2004). What can the Milgram obedience experiments tell us about the Holocaust? Generalizing from the social psychological laboratory. In A. G. Miller (Ed.), *The social psychology of good and evil.* New York: Guilford. (p. 222)

Miller, A. G., Ashton, W., & Mishal, M. (1990). Beliefs concerning the features of constrained behavior: A basis for the fundamental attribution error. *Journal of Personality and Social Psychology, 59*, 635–650. (p. 88)

Miller, A. G., Gillen, G., Schenker, C., & Radlove, S. (1973). Perception of obedience to authority. *Proceedings of the 81st annual convention of the American Psychological Association, 8*, 127–128. (p. 226)

Miller, C. E., & Anderson, P. D. (1979). Group decision rules and the rejection of deviates. *Social Psychology Quarterly, 42*, 354–363. (p. 234)

Miller, C. T., & Felicio, D. M. (1990). Person-positivity bias: Are individuals liked better than groups? *Journal of Experimental Social Psychology, 26*, 408–420. (p. 373)

Miller, D. T., Downs, J. S., & Prentice, D. A. (1998). Minimal conditions for the creation of a unit relationship: The social bond between birthdaymates. *European Journal of Social Psychology*, **28**, 475. (p. 352)

Miller, D. T., & McFarland, C. (1987). Pluralistic ignorance: When similarity is interpreted as dissimilarity. *Journal of Personality and Social Psychology*, **53**, 298–305. (p. 310)

Miller, D. W. (2001, November 23). Jury consulting on trial. *Chronicle of Higher Education*, pp. A15, A16. (p. 628)

Miller, G. R., & Fontes, N. E. (1979). *Videotape on trial: A view from the jury box*. Beverly Hills, CA: Sage Publications. (p. 623)

Miller, J. B. (1986). *Toward a new psychology of women*, 2nd ed. Boston: Beacon Press. (p. 182)

Miller, J. G. (1984). Culture and the development of everyday social explanation. *Journal of Personality and Social Psychology*, **46**, 961–978. (p. 95)

Miller, K. I., & Monge, P. R. (1986). Participation, satisfaction, and productivity: A meta-analytic review. *Academy of Management Journal*, **29**, 727–753. (p. 61)

Miller, L. C. (1990). Intimacy and liking: Mutual influence and the role of unique relationships. *Journal of Personality and Social Psychology*, **59**, 50–60. (p. 462)

Miller, L. C., Berg, J. H., & Archer, R. L. (1983). Openers: Individuals who elicit intimate self-disclosure. *Journal of Personality and Social Psychology*, **44**, 1234–1244. (p. 463)

Miller, L. C., Berg, J. H., & Rugs, D. (1989). Selectivity and sharing: Needs and norms in developing friendships. Unpublished manuscript, Scripps College. (p. 461)

Miller, L. E., & Grush, J. E. (1986). Individual differences in attitudinal versus normative determination of behavior. *Journal of Experimental Social Psychology*, **22**, 190–202. (p. 139)

Miller, N. (2002). Personalization and the promise of contact theory. *Journal of Social Issues*, **58**, 387–410. (p. 541)

Miller, N., & Campbell, D. T. (1959). Recency and primacy in persuasion as a function of the timing of speeches and measurements. *Journal of Abnormal and Social Psychology*, **59**, 1–9. (p. 262)

Miller, N., & Marks, G. (1982). Assumed similarity between self and other: Effect of expectation of future interaction with that other. *Social Psychology Quarterly*, **45**, 100–105. (p. 428)

Miller, N., Maruyama, G., Beaber, R. J., & Valone, K. (1976). Speed of speech and persuasion. *Journal of Personality and Social Psychology*, **34**, 615–624. (p. 253)

Miller, N., Pedersen, W. C., Earleywine, M., & Pollock, V. F. (2003). A theoretical model of triggered displaced aggression. *Personality and Social Psychology Review*, **7**, 75–97. (p. 386)

Miller, N. E. (1941). The frustration-aggression hypothesis. *Psychological Review*, **48**, 337–342. (p. 387)

Miller, P. A., & Eisenberg, N. (1988). The relation of empathy to aggressive and externalizing/antisocial behavior. *Psychological Bulletin*, **103**, 324–344. (p. 490)

Miller, P. A., Kozu, J., & Davis, A. C. (2001). Social influence, empathy, and prosocial behavior in cross-cultural perspective. In W. Wosinska, R. B. Cialdini, D. W. Barrett, & J. Reykowski (Eds.), *The practice of social influence in multiple cultures*. Mahwah, NJ: Erlbaum. (p. 504)

Miller, P. C., Lefcourt, H. M., Holmes, J. G., Ware, E. E., & Saley, W. E. (1986). Marital locus of control and marital problem solving. *Journal of Personality and Social Psychology*, **51**, 161–169. (p. 59)

Miller, R. L., Brickman, P., & Bolen, D. (1975). Attribution versus persuasion as a means for modifying behavior. *Journal of Personality and Social Psychology*, **31**, 430–441. (p. 125)

Miller, R. S. (1997). Inattentive and contented: Relationship commitment and attention to alternatives. *Journal of Personality and Social Psychology*, **73**, 758–766. (p. 467)

Miller, R. S., & Schlenker, B. R. (1985). Egotism in group members: Public and private attributions of responsibility for group performance. *Social Psychology Quarterly*, **48**, 85–89. (p. 80)

Miller, R. S., & Simpson, J. A. (1990). Relationship satisfaction and

attentiveness to alternatives. Paper presented at the American Psychological Association convention. (p. 441)

Millett, K. (1975). The shame is over. *Ms.*, January, pp. 26–29. (p. 464)

Mims, P. R., Hartnett, J. J., & Nay, W. R. (1975). Interpersonal attraction and help volunteering as a function of physical attractiveness. *Journal of Psychology*, **89**, 125–131. (p. 486)

Minard, R. D. (1952). Race relationships in the Pocohontas coal field. *Journal of Social Issues*, **8**(1), 29–44. (p. 347)

Mio, J. S., Thompson, S. C., & Givens, G. H. (1993). The commons dilemma as a metaphor: Memory, influence, and implications for environmental conservation. *Metaphor and Symbolic Activity*, **8**, 23–42. (p. 528)

Mirels, H. L., & McPeek, R. W. (1977). Self-advocacy and self-esteem. *Journal of Consulting and Clinical Psychology*, **45**, 1132–1138. (p. 592)

Mischel, W. (1968). *Personality and assessment*. New York: Wiley. (pp. 136, 235)

Mita, T. H., Dermer, M., & Knight, J. (1977). Reversed facial images and the mere-exposure hypothesis. *Journal of Personality and Social Psychology*, **35**, 597–601. (pp. 430–431)

Mitchell, G., Tetlock, P. E., Mellers, B. A., & Ordonez, L. D. (1993). Judgments of social justice: Compromises between equality and efficiency. *Journal of Personality and Social Psychology*, **65**, 629–639. (p. 532)

Mitchell, T. R., & Thompson, L. (1994). A theory of temporal adjustments of the evaluation of events: Rosy prospection and rosy retrospection. In C. Stubbart, J. Porac, & J. Meindl (Eds.), *Advances in managerial cognition and organizational information processing*. Greenwich, CT: JAI Press. (p. 103)

Mitchell, T. R., Thompson, L., Peterson, E., & Cronk, R. (1997). Temporal adjustments in the evaluation of events: The "rosy view." *Journal of Experimental Social Psychology*, **33**, 421–448. (p. 103)

Moffitt, T., Caspi, A., Sugden, K., Taylor, A., Craig, I. W., Harrington, H., McClay, J., Mill, J.,

Martin, J., Braithwaite, A., Poulton, R. (2003). Influence of life stress on depression: Moderation by a polymorphism in the 5-HTT gene. *Science, 301*, 386–389. (p. 384)

Monin, B. (2003). The warm glow heuristic: When liking leads to familiarity. *Journal of Personality and Social Psychology, 85*, 1035–1048. (p. 438)

Monin, B., & Norton, M. I. (2003). Perceptions of a fluid consensus: Uniqueness bias, false consensus, false polarization, and pluralistic ignorance in a water conservation crisis. *Personality and Social Psychology, 29*, 559–567. (p. 72)

Monson, T. C., Hesley, J. W., & Chernick, L. (1982). Specifying when personality traits can and cannot predict behavior: An alternative to abandoning the attempt to predict single-act criteria. *Journal of Personality and Social Psychology, 43*, 385–399. (p. 236)

Monson, T. C., & Snyder, M. (1977). Actors, observers, and the attribution process: Toward a reconceptualization. *Journal of Experimental Social Psychology, 13*, 89–111. (p. 96)

Monteith, M. J. (1993). Self-regulation of prejudiced responses: Implications for progress in prejudice-reduction efforts. *Journal of Personality and Social Psychology, 65*, 469–485. (p. 356)

Moody, K. (1980). *Growing up on television: The TV effect.* New York: Times Books. (p. 281)

Moore, B. S., Underwood, B., & Rosenhan, D. L. (1973). Affect and altruism. *Developmental Psychology, 8*, 99–104. (p. 480)

Moore, D. L., & Baron, R. S. (1983). Social facilitation: A physiological analysis. In J. T. Cacioppo & R. Petty (Eds.), *Social psychophysiology.* New York: Guilford Press. (p. 289)

Moore, D. W. (2004, January 6). A constitutional amendment to ban gay marriages. *Gallup Poll Tuesday Briefing* (www.gallup.com). (p. 27)

Moore, D. W. (2003, March 11). Half of young people expect to strike it rich: But expectations fall rapidly with age. Gallup News Service (www.gallup.com/poll/releases/pr030311.asp). (p. 71)

Moore, D. W. (2003, March 18). Public approves of Bush ultimatum by more than 2-to-1 margin. Gallup News Service (www.gallup.com). (pp. 245–246)

Mor, N., & Winquist, J. (2002). Self-focused attention and negative affect: A meta-analysis. *Psychological Bulletin, 128*, 638–662. (p. 579)

Moran, G., & Comfort, J. C. (1982). Scientific juror selection: Sex as a moderator of demographic and personality predictors of impaneled felony juror behavior. *Journal of Personality and Social Psychology, 43*, 1052–1063. (p. 629)

Moran, G., & Comfort, J. C. (1986). Neither "tentative" nor "fragmentary": Verdict preference of impaneled felony jurors as a function of attitude toward capital punishment. *Journal of Applied Psychology, 71*, 146–155. (p. 629)

Moran, G., & Cutler, B. L. (1991). The prejudicial impact of pretrial publicity. *Journal of Applied Social Psychology, 21*, 345–367. (p. 623)

Moran, G., Cutler, B. L., & De Lisa, A. (1994). Attitudes toward tort reform, scientific jury selection, and juror bias: Verdict inclination in criminal and civil trials. *Law and Psychology Review, 18*, 309–328. (p. 628)

Moran, G., Cutler, B. L., & Loftus, E. F. (1990). Jury selection in major controlled substance trials: The need for extended voir dire. *Forensic Reports, 3*, 331–348. (p. 628)

Moreland, R. L., & Zajonc, R. B. (1977). Is stimulus recognition a necessary condition for the occurrence of exposure effects? *Journal of Personality and Social Psychology, 35*, 191–199. (p. 429)

Morier, D., & Seroy, C. (1994). The effect of interpersonal expectancies on men's self-presentation of gender role attitudes to women. *Sex Roles, 31*, 493–504. (p. 196)

Morin, R. (1998). *Washington Post/Henry J. Kaiser Family Foundation/Harvard University Studies of Political Values.* Washington, DC: *Washington Post.* (p. 367)

Morris, W. N., & Miller, R. S. (1975). The effects of consensus-breaking and consensus-preempting partners on

reduction of conformity. *Journal of Experimental Social Psychology, 11*, 215–223. (p. 229)

Morrow, L. (1983, August 1). All the hazards and threats of success. *Time*, pp. 20–25. (p. 208)

Moscovici, S. (1985). Social influence and conformity. In G. Lindzey & E. Aronson (Eds.), *The handbook of social psychology*, 3rd ed. Hillsdale, NJ: Erlbaum. (pp. 321–322)

Moscovici, S. (1988). Notes towards a description of social representations. *European Journal of Social Psychology, 18*, 211–250. (p. 14)

Moscovici, S., Lage, S., & Naffrechoux, M. (1969). Influence of a consistent minority on the responses of a majority in a color perception task. *Sociometry, 32*, 365–380. (pp. 321–322)

Moscovici, S., & Zavalloni, M. (1969). The group as a polarizer of attitudes. *Journal of Personality and Social Psychology, 12*, 124–135. (pp. 304, 305)

Moskowitz, D. S., Suh, E. J., & Desaulniers, J. (1994). Situational influences on gender differences in agency and communion. *Journal of Personality and Social Psychology, 66*, 753–761. (p. 202)

Motherhood Project (2001, May 2). Watch out for children: A mothers' statement to advertisers. Institute for American Values (www.watchoutforchildren.org). (pp. 281, 282)

Moyer, K. E. (1976). *The psychobiology of aggression.* New York: Harper & Row. (p. 383)

Moyer, K. E. (1983). The physiology of motivation: Aggression as a model. In C. J. Scheier & A. M. Rogers (Eds.), *G. Stanley Hall Lecture Series* (Vol. 3). Washington, DC: American Psychological Association. (p. 383)

Moynihan, D. P. (1979). Social science and the courts. *Public Interest, 54*, 12–31. (p. 13)

Mucchi-Faina, A., Maass, A., & Volpato, C. (1991). Social influence: The role of originality. *European Journal of Social Psychology, 21*, 183–197. (p. 322)

Muehlenhard, C. L. (1988). Misinterpreted dating behaviors and the risk of date rape. *Journal of Social and Clinical Psychology, 6,* 20–37. (p. 85)

Mueller, C. W., Donnerstein, E., & Hallam, J. (1983). Violent films and prosocial behavior. *Personality and Social Psychology Bulletin, 9,* 83–89. (p. 407)

Muldoon, O. (2003). On home ground. *Psychologist, 16* (http://www.bps.org.uk/publications/thepsychologist/0703news.pdf). (p. 142)

Mullen, B. (1986). Atrocity as a function of lynch mob composition: A self-attention perspective. *Personality and Social Psychology Bulletin, 12,* 187–197. *(a)* (pp. 299, 413)

Mullen, B. (1986). Stuttering, audience size, and the other-total ratio: A self-attention perspective. *Journal of Applied Social Psychology, 16,* 139–149. *(b)* (p. 289)

Mullen, B., Anthony, T., Salas, E., & Driskell, J. E. (1994). Group cohesiveness and quality of decision making: An integration of tests of the groupthink hypothesis. *Small Group Research, 25,* 189–204. (p. 315)

Mullen, B., & Baumeister, R. F. (1987). Group effects on self-attention and performance: Social loafing, social facilitation, and social impairment. In C. Hendrick (Ed.), *Group processes and intergroup relations: Review of personality and social psychology,* Vol. 9. Newbury Park, CA: Sage. (p. 295)

Mullen, B., Brown, R., & Smith, C. (1992). Ingroup bias as a function of salience, relevance, and status: An integration. *European Journal of Social Psychology, 22,* 103–122. (p. 352)

Mullen, B., Bryant, B., & Driskell, J. E. (1997). Presence of others and arousal: An integration. *Group Dynamics: Theory, Research, and Practice, 1,* 52–64. (p. 288)

Mullen, B., & Copper, C. (1994). The relation between group cohesiveness and performance: An integration. *Psychological Bulletin, 115,* 210–227. (p. 311)

Mullen, B., Copper, C., & Driskell, J. E. (1990). Jaywalking as a function of model behavior. *Personality and Social Psychology Bulletin, 16,* 320–330. (p. 231)

Mullen, B., & Goethals, G. R. (1990). Social projection, actual consensus and valence. *British Journal of Social Psychology, 29,* 279–282. (p. 72)

Mullen, B., & Hu, L. (1989). Perceptions of ingroup and outgroup variability: A meta-analytic integration. *Basic and Applied Social Psychology, 10,* 233–252. (p. 359)

Mullen, B., & Riordan, C. A. (1988). Self-serving attributions for performance in naturalistic settings: A meta-analytic review. *Journal of Applied Social Psychology, 18,* 3–22. (p. 67)

Muller, S., & Johnson, B. T. (1990). Fear and persuasion: A linear relationship? Paper presented to the Eastern Psychological Association convention. (p. 257)

Mullin, C. R., & Linz, D. (1995). Desensitization and resensitization to violence against women: Effects of exposure to sexually violent films on judgments of domestic violence victims. *Journal of Personality and Social Psychology, 69,* 449–459. (p. 399)

Munro, G. D., & Ditto, P. H. (1997). Biased assimilation, attitude polarization, and affect in reactions to stereotype-relevant scientific information. *Personality and Social Psychology Bulletin, 23,* 636–653. (p. 100)

Munro, G. D., Ditto, P. H., Lockhart, L. K., Fagerlin, A., Gready, M., & Peterson, E. (1997). Biased assimilation of sociopolitical arguments: Evaluating the 1996 U.S. Presidential debate. Unpublished manuscript, Hope College. (p. 100)

Muraven, M., Tice, D. M., & Baumeister, R. F. (1998). Self-control as a limited resource: Regulatory depletion patterns. *Journal of Personality and Social Psychology, 74,* 774–790. (p. 57)

Murphy, C. (1990, June). New findings: Hold on to your hat. *The Atlantic,* pp. 22–23. (pp. 17, 19)

Murphy, C. M., & O'Farrell, T. J. (1996). Marital violence among alcoholics. *Current Directions in Psychological Science, 5,* 183–187. (p. 385)

Murphy-Berman, V., Berman, J. J., Singh, P., Pachauri, A., & Kumar, P. (1984). Factors affecting allocation to needy and meritorious recipients: A cross-cultural comparison. *Journal of Personality and Social Psychology, 46,* 1267–1272. (p. 532)

Murphy-Berman, V., & Sharma, R. (1986). Testing the assumptions of attribution theory in India. *Journal of Social Psychology, 126,* 607–616. (p. 80)

Murray, J. P., & Kippax, S. (1979). From the early window to the late night show: International trends in the study of television's impact on children and adults. In L. Berkowitz (Ed.), *Advances in experimental social psychology,* vol. 12. New York: Academic Press. (p. 403)

Murray, S. L., Gellavia, G. M., Rose, P., & Griffin, D. W. (2003). Once hurt, twice hurtful: How perceived regard regulates daily marital interactions. *Journal of Personality and Social Psychology, 84,* 126–147. (p. 124)

Murray, S. L., & Holmes, J. G. (1997). A leap of faith? Positive illusions in romantic relationships. *Personality and Social Psychology Bulletin, 23,* 586–604. (p. 449)

Murray, S. L., Holmes, J. G., Gellavia, G., Griffin, D. W., & Dolderman, D. (2002). Kindred spirits? The benefits of egocentrism in close relationships. *Journal of Personality and Social Psychology, 82,* 563–581. (pp. 66, 444)

Murray, S. L., Holmes, J. G., & Griffin, D. W. (1996). The benefits of positive illusions: Idealization and the construction of satisfaction in close relationships. *Journal of Personality and Social Psychology, 70,* 79–98. (p. 449)

Murray, S. L., Holmes, J. G., & Griffin, D. W. (1996). The self-fulfilling nature of positive illusions in romantic relationships: Love is not blind, but prescient. *Journal of Personality and Social Psychology, 71,* 1155–1180. (p. 124)

Murray, S. L., Holmes, J. G., & Griffin, D. W. (2000). Self-esteem and the quest for felt security: How perceived regard regulates attachment processes. *Journal of Personality and Social Psychology, 78,* 478–498. (pp. 124, 448)

Murray, S. L., Holmes, J. G., MacDonald, G., & Ellsworth, P. C. (1998). Through the looking glass darkly? When self-doubts turn into relationship insecurities. *Journal of*

Personality and Social Psychology, 75, 1459–1480. (p. 66)

Murray, S. L., Rose, P., Bellavia, G. M., Holmes, J. G., & Kusche, A. G. (2002). When rejection stings: How self-esteem constrains relationship-enhancement processes. *Journal of Personality and Social Psychology, 83,* 556–573. (p. 74)

Murstein, B. L. (1986). *Paths to marriage.* Newbury Park, CA: Sage. (p. 433)

Muson, G. (1978). Teenage violence and the telly. *Psychology Today,* March, pp. 50–54. (pp. 404–405)

Musser, L. M., & Graziano, W. F. (1991). Behavioral confirmation in children's interaction with peers. *Basic and Applied Social Psychology, 12,* 441–456. (p. 179)

Mussweiler, T. (2003). Comparison processes in social judgment: Mechanisms and consequences. *Psychological Review, 110,* 472–489. (p. 656)

Myers, D. G. (1978). Polarizing effects of social comparison. *Journal of Experimental Social Psychology, 14,* 554–563. (p. 310)

Myers, D. G. (1993). *The pursuit of happiness.* New York: Avon. (pp. 119, 601)

Myers, D. G. (2000). *The American paradox: Spiritual hunger in an age of plenty.* New Haven, CT: Yale University Press. (pp. 61, 400, 468–469)

Myers, D. G. (2000). The funds, friends, and faith of happy people. *American Psychologist, 55,* 56–67. (p. 119)

Myers, D. G., & Bishop, G. D. (1970). Discussion effects on racial attitudes. *Science, 169,* 778–789. (pp. 305–306)

Myers, J. N. (1997, December). Quoted by S. A. Boot, Where the weather reigns. *World Traveler,* pp. 86, 88, 91, 124. (p. 319)

Myers, N. (2000). Sustainable consumption: The meta-problem. In B. Heap & J. Kent (Eds.), *Towards sustainable consumption: A European perspective.* London: The Royal Society. (pp. 642, 644, 646)

Nadler, A. (1991). Help-seeking behavior: Psychological costs and instrumental benefits. In M. S. Clark (Ed.), *Prosocial behavior.* Newbury Park, CA: Sage. (pp. 486–487)

Nadler, A., & Fisher, J. D. (1986). The role of threat to self-esteem and perceived control in recipient reaction to help: Theory development and empirical validation. In L. Berkowitz (Ed.), *Advances in Experimental Social Psychology,* vol. 19. Orlando, FL: Academic Press. (p. 484)

Nadler, A., Goldberg, M., & Jaffe, Y. (1982). Effect of self-differentiation and anonymity in group on deindividuation. *Journal of Personality and Social Psychology, 42,* 1127–1136. (p. 302)

Nagar, D., & Pandey, J. (1987). Affect and performance on cognitive task as a function of crowding and noise. *Journal of Applied Social Psychology, 17,* 147–157. (p. 290)

Nagourney, A. (2002, September 25). For remarks on Iraq, Gore gets praise and scorn. *New York Times* (www.nytimes.com). (p. 136)

Nail, P. R., MacDonald, G., & Levy, D. A. (2000). Proposal of a four-dimensional model of social response. *Psychological Bulletin, 126,* 454–470. (pp. 208–209, 238)

National Center for Health Statistics. (1991). Family structure and children's health: United States, 1988, *Vital and Health Statistics, Series 10, No. 178,* CHHS Publication No. PHS 91–1506 by Deborah A. Dawson. (p. 363)

National Council for Research on Women (1994). Women and philanthropy fact sheet. *Issues Quarterly, 1*(2), 9. (p. 183)

National Research Council (1993). *Understanding and preventing violence.* Washington, DC: National Academy Press. (p. 420)

National Research Council (2002). *Youth, pornography, and the Internet.* Washington, DC: National Academy Press. (p. 398)

National Safety Council (2001). Data from 1995 to 1999 summarized in personal correspondence from Kevin T. Fearn, NSC Research and Statistics Department. (p. 115)

National Television Violence Study (1997). Thousand Oaks, CA: Sage. (p. 403)

Naylor, T. H. (1990). Redefining corporate motivation, Swedish style. *Christian Century, 107,* 566–570. (p. 324)

NCTV (1988). TV and film alcohol research. *NCTV News, 9*(3–4), 4. (p. 408)

Needles, D. J., & Abramson, L. Y. (1990). Positive life events, attributional style, and hopefulness: Testing a model of recovery from depression. *Journal of Abnormal Psychology, 99,* 156–165. (p. 580)

Neimeyer, G. J., MacNair, R., Metzler, A. E., & Courchaine, K. (1991). Changing personal beliefs: Effects of forewarning, argument quality, prior bias, and personal exploration. *Journal of Social and Clinical Psychology, 10,* 1–20. (p. 595)

Nelson, L. J., & Miller, D. T. (1995). The distinctiveness effect in social categorization: You are what makes you unusual. *Psychological Science, 6,* 246. (p. 361)

Nelson, L., & LeBoeuf, R. (2002). Why do men overperceive women's sexual intent? False consensus vs. evolutionary explanations. Paper presented to the annual meeting of the Society for Personality and Social Psychology. (p. 85)

Nelson, T. E., Biernat, M. R., & Manis, M. (1990). Everyday base rates (sex stereotypes): Potent and resilient. *Journal of Personality and Social Psychology, 59,* 664–675. (p. 374)

Nemeth, C. (1977). Interactions between jurors as a function of majority vs. Unanimity decision rules. *Journal of Applied Social Psychology, 7,* 38–56. (p. 634)

Nemeth, C. (1979). The role of an active minority in intergroup relations. In W. G. Austin and S. Worchel (Eds.), *The social psychology of intergroup relations.* Monterey, CA: Brooks/Cole. (p. 322)

Nemeth, C. J. (1997). Managing innovation: When less is more. *California Management Review, 40,* 59–74. (p. 322)

Nemeth, C. J. (1999). Behind the scenes. In D. G. Myers, *Social psychology,* 6th edition. New York: McGraw-Hill. (p. 324)

Nemeth, C. J., Brown, K., & Rogers, J. (2001a). Devil's advocate versus authentic dissent: Stimulating quantity and quality. *European Journal of Social Psychology, 31*, 1–13. (p. 317)

Nemeth, C. J., Connell, J. B., Rogers, J. D., & Brown, K. S. (2001b). Improving decision making by means of dissent. *Journal of Applied Social Psychology, 31*, 48–58. (p. 317)

Nemeth, C., & Chiles, C. (1988). Modelling courage: The role of dissent in fostering independence. *European Journal of Social Psychology, 18*, 275–280. (pp. 229–230)

Nemeth, C., & Wachtler, J. (1974). Creating the perceptions of consistency and confidence: A necessary condition for minority influence. *Sociometry, 37*, 529–540. (pp. 322–323)

Neumann, R., & Strack, F. (2000). Approach and avoidance: The influence of proprioceptive and exteroceptive cues on encoding of affective information. *Journal of Personality and Social Psychology, 79*, 39–48. (pp. 159, 211)

New York Times (2002, May 26). Fighting to live as the towers died (www.nytimes.com). (p. 476)

Newcomb, T. M. (1961). *The acquaintance process.* New York: Holt, Rinehart and Winston. (pp. 426, 443)

Newell, B., & Lagnado, D. (2003). Think-tanks, or think *tanks. The Psychologist, 16*, 176. (p. 315)

Newman, A. (2001, February 4). Rotten teeth and dead babies. *New York Times Magazine* (www.nytimes.com). (pp. 257–258)

Newman, H. M., & Langer, E. J. (1981). Post-divorce adaptation and the attribution of responsibility. *Sex Roles, 7*, 223–231. (p. 75)

Newman, L. S. (1993). How individualists interpret behavior: Idiocentrism and spontaneous trait inference. *Social Cognition, 11*, 243–269. (p. 95)

Newman, L. S., Duff, K., Schnopp-Wyatt, N., Brock, B., & Hoffman, Y. (1997). Reactions to the O. J. Simpson verdict: "Mindless tribalism" or motivated inference processes? *Journal of Social Issues, 53*, 547–562. (p. 621)

Newport, F., Moore, D. W., Jones, J. M., & Saad, L. (2003, March 21). Special release: American opinion on the war. *Gallup Poll Tuesday Briefing* (www.gallup.com/poll/tb/goverpubli/s0030325.asp). (pp. 152, 246)

Newport, F., & Saad, L. (1997, February 7). Civil trial didn't alter public's view of Simpson case. Princeton, NJ: Gallup News Service, The Gallup Organization. (p. 99)

Nias, D. K. B. (1979). Marital choice: Matching or complementation? In M. Cook and G. Wilson (Eds.), *Love and attraction.* Oxford: Pergamon. (p. 446)

Nichols, J. (2003, February 9). Man overdoses online as chatters watch him die. *Grand Rapids Press*, p. A20. (p. 498)

Nicholson, N., Cole, S. G., & Rocklin, T. (1985). Conformity in the Asch situation: A comparison between contemporary British and U. S. university students. *British Journal of Social Psychology, 24*, 59–63. (p. 237)

Nickerson, C., Schwarz, N., Diener, E., & Kahneman, D. (2003). Zeroing in on the dark side of the American dream: A closer look at the negative consequences of the goal for financial success. *Psychological Science, 14*, 531–536. (p. 654)

Nie, N. H., & Erbring, L. (2000, February 17). Internet and society: A preliminary report. Stanford, CA: Stanford Institute for the Quantitative Study of Society. (p. 465)

Niedermeier, K. E., Kerr, N. L., & Messe, L. A. (1999). Jurors' use of naked statistical evidence: Exploring bases and implications of the Wells effect. *Journal of Personality and Social Psychology, 76*, 533–542. (p. 627)

Nielsen, M. E. (1998). Social psychology and religion on a trip to Ukraine. http://psychwww.com/psyrelig/ukraine/index.htm (pp. 31–32)

Niemi, R. G., Mueller, J., & Smith, T. W. (1989). *Trends in public opinion: A compendium of survey data.* New York: Greenwood Press. (pp. 197, 416)

Nigro, G. N., Hill, D. E., Gelbein, M. E., & Clark, C. L. (1988). Changes in the facial prominence of women and men over the last decade. *Psychology of Women Quarterly, 12*, 225–235. (p. 348)

Nisbett, R. (2003). *The geography of thought: How Asians and Westerners think differently . . . and why.* New York: Free Press. (pp. 46, 47)

Nisbett, R. E. (1990). Evolutionary psychology, biology, and cultural evolution. *Motivation and Emotion, 14*, 255–263. (p. 392)

Nisbett, R. E. (1993). Violence and U.S. regional culture. *American Psychologist, 48*, 441–449. (p. 392)

Nisbett, R. E., & Cohen, D. (1996). *Culture of honor: The psychology of violence in the South.* Boulder, CO: Westview Press. (p. 392)

Nisbett, R. E., Fong, G. T., Lehman, D. R., & Cheng, P. W. (1987). Teaching reasoning. *Science, 238*, 625–631. (p. 129)

Nisbett, R. E., & Ross, L. (1980). *Human inference: Strategies and shortcomings of social judgment.* Englewood Cliffs, NJ: Prentice-Hall. (pp. 127, 129)

Nisbett, R. E., & Schachter, S. (1966). Cognitive manipulation of pain. *Journal of Experimental Social Psychology, 2*, 227–236. (pp. 51–52)

Nix, G., Watson, C., Pyszczynski, T., & Greenberg, J. (1995). Reducing depressive affect through external focus of attention. *Journal of Social and Clinical Psychology, 14*, 36–52. (p. 581)

Noel, J. G., Forsyth, D. R., & Kelley, K. N. (1987). Improving the performance of failing students by overcoming their self-serving attributional biases. *Basic and Applied Social Psychology, 8*, 151–162. (p. 59)

Nolan, S. A., Flynn, C., & Garber, J. (2003). Prospective relations between rejection and depression in young adolescents. *Journal of Personality and Social Psychology, 85*, 745–755. (p. 424)

Noller, P. (1996). What is this thing called love? Defining the love that supports marriage and family. *Personal Relationships, 3*, 97–115. (p. 472)

Noller, P., & Fitzpatrick, M. A. (1990). Marital communication in the eighties. *Journal of Marriage and the Family, 52*, 832–843. (p. 470)

Noon, E., & Hollin, C. R. (1987). Lay knowledge of eyewitness behaviour: A

British survey. *Applied Cognitive Psychology*, **1**, 143–153. (p. 617)

NORC (1996). General social survey. National Opinion Research Center, University of Chicago (courtesy Tom W. Smith). (p. 197)

NORC (National Opinion Research Center) (2003). Marriage and happiness data from National Opinion Research Center General Social Surveys, 1972 to 2002 (www.csa.berkeley.edu:7502). (p. 600)

Norem, J. K. (2000). Defensive pessimism, optimism, and pessimism. In E. C. Chang (Ed.), *Optimism and pessimism*. Washington, DC: APA Books. (p. 71)

Norem, J. K., & Cantor, N. (1986). Defensive pessimism: Harnessing anxiety as motivation. *Journal of Personality and Social Psychology*, **51**, 1208–1217. (p. 72)

Notarius, C., & Markman, H. J. (1993). *We can work it out*. New York: Putnam. (p. 470)

Nunez, N., Poole, D. A., & Memon, A. (in press). Psychology's two cultures revisited: Implications for the integration of science and practice. *Scientific Review of Mental Health Practice*. (p. 568)

Nurmi, J-E., & Salmela-Aro, K. (1997). Social strategies and loneliness: A prospective study. *Personality and Individual Differences*, **23**, 205–215. (p. 582)

Nurmi, J-E., Toivonen, S., Salmela-Aro, K., & Eronen, S. (1996). Optimistic, approach-oriented, and avoidance strategies in social situations: Three studies on loneliness and peer relationships. *European Journal of Personality*, **10**, 201–219. (p. 582)

Nuttin, J. M., Jr. (1987). Affective consequences of mere ownership: The name letter effect in twelve European languages. *European Journal of Social Psychology*, **17**, 318–402. (p. 429)

O'Brien, L. T., & Crandall, C. S. (2003). Stereotype threat and arousal: Effects on women's math performance. *Personality and Social Psychology Bulletin*, **29**, 782–789. (p. 373)

Ochsner, K. N., & Lieberman, M. D. (2001). The emergence of social cognitive neuroscience. *American Psychologist*, **56**, 717–734. (p. 9)

Oddone-Paolucci, E., Genuis, M., & Violato, C. (2000). A meta-analysis of the published research on the effects of pornography. In C. Violata (Ed.), *The changing family and child development*. Aldershot, England: Ashgate Publishing. (p. 399)

O'Dea, T. F. (1968). Sects and cults. In D. L. Sills (Ed.), *International encyclopedia of the social sciences* (Vol. 14). New York: Macmillan. (p. 275)

Ohbuchi, K., & Kambara, T. (1985). Attacker's intent and awareness of outcome, impression management, and retaliation. *Journal of Experimental Social Psychology*, **21**, 321–330. (p. 395)

O'Leary, K. D., Christian, J. L., & Mendell, N. R. (1994). A closer look at the link between marital discord and depressive symptomatology. *Journal of Social and Clinical Psychology*, **13**, 33–41. (p. 469)

Olfson, M., & Pincus, H. A. (1994). Outpatient therapy in the United States: II. Patterns of utilization. *American Journal of Psychiatry*, **151**, 1289–1294. (p. 587)

Oliner, S. P., & Oliner, P. M. (1988). *The altruistic personality: Rescuers of Jews in Nazi Europe*. New York: The Free Press. (p. 514)

Oliver, M. B. (1994). Portrayals of crime, race, and aggression in "reality-based" police shows: A content analysis. *Journal of Broadcasting and Electronic Media*, **38**, 179–192. (p. 408)

Olson, J. M., & Cal, A. V. (1984). Source credibility, attitudes, and the recall of past behaviours. *European Journal of Social Psychology*, **14**, 203–210. (p. 252)

Olson, J. M., Roese, N. J., & Zanna, M. P. (1996). Expectancies. In E. T. Higgins & A. W. Kruglanski (Eds.), *Social psychology: Handbook of basic principles*. New York: Guilford Press, pp. 211–238. (p. 124)

Olson, J. M., & Zanna, M. P. (1993). Attitudes and attitude change. *Annual Review of Psychology*, **44**, 117–154. (p. 134)

Olweus, D. (1979). Stability of aggressive reaction patterns in males: A review. *Psychological Bulletin*, **86**, 852–875. (p. 383)

Olweus, D., Mattsson, A., Schalling, D., & Low, H. (1988). Circulating testosterone levels and aggression in adolescent males: A causal analysis. *Psychosomatic Medicine*, **50**, 261–272. (p. 385)

Omoto, A. M., & Snyder, M. (2002). Considerations of community: The context and process of volunteerism. *American Behavioral Scientist*, **45**, 846–867. (p. 510)

Omoto, A. M., Snyder, M., & Berghuis, J. P. (1993). The psychology of volunteerism: A conceptual analysis and a program of action research. In J. B. Pryor & G. D. Reeder (Eds.), *The social psychology of HIV infection*. Hillsdale, NJ: Erlbaum. (p. 508)

Opotow, S. (1990). Moral exclusion and injustice: An introduction. *Journal of Social Issues*, **46**, 1–20. (pp. 512–513)

Orbell, J. M., van de Kragt, A. J. C., & Dawes, R. M. (1988). Explaining discussion-induced cooperation. *Journal of Personality and Social Psychology*, **54**, 811–819. (p. 526)

Orenstein, P. (2003, July 6). Where have all the Lisas gone? *New York Times* (www.nytimes.com). (pp. 239–240)

Orive, R. (1984). Group similarity, public self-awareness, and opinion extremity: A social projection explanation of deindividuation effects. *Journal of Personality and Social Psychology*, **47**, 727–737. (p. 302)

Ornstein, R. (1991). *The evolution of consciousness: Of Darwin, Freud, and cranial fire: The origins of the way we think*. New York: Prentice-Hall. (pp. 144, 221, 274)

Osbeck, L. M., Moghaddam, F. M., & Perreault, S. (1996). Similarity and attraction among majority and minority groups in a multicultural context. *International Journal of Intercultural Relations*, **20**, 1–10. (p. 444)

Osberg, T. M., & Shrauger, J. S. (1986). Self-prediction: Exploring the parameters of accuracy. *Journal of Personality and Social Psychology*, **51**, 1044–1057. (p. 53)

Osborne, J. W. (1995). Academics, self-esteem, and race: A look at the underlying assumptions of the disidentification hypothesis. *Personality and Social Psychology Bulletin*, **21**, 449–455. (p. 372)

Osgood, C. E. (1962). *An alternative to war or surrender.* Urbana, IL: University of Illinois Press. (p. 558)

Osgood, C. E. (1966). *Perspective in foreign policy.* Palo Alto, CA: Pacific Books. (p. 559)

Osgood, C. E. (1980). GRIT: A strategy for survival in mankind's nuclear age? Paper presented at the Pugwash Conference on New Directions in Disarmament, Racine, Wis. (p. 558)

Oskamp, S. (1971). Effects of programmed strategies on cooperation in the prisoner's dilemma and other mixed-motive games. *Journal of Conflict Resolution,* **15,** 225–229. (p. 523)

Oskamp, S. (1991). Curbside recycling: Knowledge, attitudes, and behavior. Paper presented at the Society for Experimental Social Psychology meeting, Columbus, Ohio. (p. 138)

Oskamp, S. (2000). A sustainable future for humanity? How can psychology help? *American Psychologist,* **55,** 496–508. (p. 641)

Oskamp, S. (2003). Environmental sustainability is a crucial issue for psychologists. Address to the Western Psychological Association convention. (p. 642)

Osterhouse, R. A., & Brock, T. C. (1970). Distraction increases yielding to propaganda by inhibiting counterarguing. *Journal of Personality and Social Psychology,* **15,** 344–358. (p. 269)

Ostrom, T. M., & Sedikides, C. (1992). Out-group homogeneity effects in natural and minimal groups. *Psychological Bulletin,* **112,** 536–552. (p. 359)

Ouellette, J. A., & Wood, W. (1998). Habit and intention in everyday life: The multiple processes by which past behavior predicts future behavior. *Psychological Bulletin,* **124,** 54–74. (p. 139)

Oyserman, D., Coon, H. M., & Kemmelmeier, M. (2002a). Rethinking individualism and collectivism: Evaluation of theoretical assumptions and meta-analyses. *Psychological Bulletin,* **128,** 3–72. (p. 47)

Oyserman, D., Kemmelmeier, M., & Coon, H. M. (2002b). Cultural psychology, a new look: Reply to Bond (2002), Fiske (2002), Kitayama (2002), and Miller (2002). *Psychological Bulletin,* **128,** 110–117. (p. 47)

Ozer, E. M., & Bandura, A. (1990). Mechanisms governing empowerment effects: A self-efficacy analysis. *Journal of Personality and Social Psychology,* **58,** 472–486. (p. 44)

Padgett, V. R. (1989). Predicting organizational violence: An application of 11 powerful principles of obedience. Paper presented at the American Psychological Association Convention. (p. 219)

Pak, A. W., Dion, K. L., & Dion, K. K. (1991). Social-psychological correlates of experienced discrimination: Test of the double jeopardy hypothesis. *International Journal of Intercultural Relations,* **15,** 243–254. (p. 543)

Pallak, M. S., Mueller, M., Dollar, K., & Pallak, J. (1972). Effect of commitment on responsiveness to an extreme consonant communication. *Journal of Personality and Social Psychology,* **23,** 429–436. (p. 260)

Pallak, S. R., Murroni, E., & Koch, J. (1983). Communicator attractiveness and expertise, emotional versus rational appeals, and persuasion: A heuristic versus systematic processing interpretation. *Social Cognition,* **2,** 122–141. (p. 254)

Palmer, D. L. (1996). Determinants of Canadian attitudes toward immigration: More than just racism? *Canadian Journal of Behavioural Science,* **28,** 180–192. (p. 350)

Palmer, E. L., & Dorr, A. (Eds.) (1980). *Children and the faces of television: Teaching, violence, selling.* New York: Academic Press. (p. 281)

Paloutzian, R. (1979). Pro-ecology behavior: Three field experiments on litter pickup. Paper presented at the Western Psychological Association convention. (p. 263)

Pandey, J., Sinha, Y., Prakash, A., & Tripathi, R. C. (1982). Right-left political ideologies and attribution of the causes of poverty. *European Journal of Social Psychology,* **12,** 327–331. (p. 96)

Papastamou, S., & Mugny, G. (1990). Synchronic consistency and psychologization in minority influence. *European Journal of Social Psychology,* **20,** 85–98. (p. 322)

Pape, R. A. (2003, September 22). Dying to kill us. *New York Times* (www.nytimes.com). (p. 381)

Parachin, V. M. (1992, December). Four brave chaplains. *Retired Officer Magazine,* pp. 24–26. (p. 507)

Park, B., & Rothbart, M. (1982). Perception of out-group homogeneity and levels of social categorization: Memory for the subordinate attributes of in-group and out-group members. *Journal of Personality and Social Psychology,* **42,** 1051–1068. (p. 359)

Parke, R. D., Berkowitz, L., Leyens, J. P., West, S. G., & Sebastian, J. (1977). Some effects of violent and nonviolent movies on the behavior of juvenile delinquents. In L. Berkowitz (Ed.), *Advances in experimental social psychology* (Vol. 10). New York: Academic Press. (pp. 406–407)

Parker, K. D., Ortega, S. T., & VanLaningham, J. (1995). Life satisfaction, self-esteem, and personal happiness among Mexican and African Americans. *Sociological Spectrum,* **15,** 131–145. (p. 600)

Parks, C. D., & Rumble, A. C. (2001). Elements of reciprocity and social value orientation. *Personality and Social Psychology Bulletin,* **27,** 1301–1309. (p. 559)

Pascarella, E. T., & Terenzini, P. T. (1991). *How college affects students: Findings and insights from twenty years of research.* San Francisco: Jossey-Bass. (p. 306)

Patterson, D. (1996). *When learned men murder.* Bloomington, IN: Phi Delta Kappan Publishers. (p. 226)

Patterson, G. R., Chamberlain, P., & Reid, J. B. (1982). A comparative evaluation of parent training procedures. *Behavior Therapy,* **13,** 638–650. (p. 391)

Patterson, G. R., Littman, R. A., & Bricker, W. (1967). Assertive behavior in children: A step toward a theory of aggression. *Monographs of the Society of Research in Child Development* (Serial No. 113), **32,** 5. (p. 390)

Patterson, T. E. (1980). The role of the mass media in presidential campaigns: The lessons of the 1976 election. *Items,* **34,** 25–30. Social Science Research Council, 605 Third Avenue, New York, NY 10016. (p. 431)

Paulhus, D. (1982). Individual differences, self-presentation, and cognitive dissonance: Their concurrent operation in forced compliance. *Journal of Personality and Social Psychology, 43,* 838–852. (p. 151)

Paulhus, D. L., & Lim, D. T. K. (1994). Arousal and evaluative extremity in social judgments: A dynamic complexity model. *European Journal of Social Psychology, 24,* 89–99. (p. 120)

Paulhus, D. L., & Morgan, K. L. (1997). Perceptions of intelligence in leaderless groups: The dynamic effects of shyness and acquaintance. *Journal of Personality and Social Psychology, 72,* 581–591. (p. 584)

Pauling, L. (1962). Quoted by Etzioni, A. *the hard way to peace: A new strategy.* New York: Collier. (p. 530)

Paulus, P. B. (1998). Developing consensus about groupthink after all these years. *Organizational Behavior and Human Decision Processes, 73,* 362–375. (p. 317)

Paulus, P. B., Brown, V., & Ortega, A. H. (1997). Group creativity. In R. E. Purser and A. Montuori (Eds.), *Social creativity,* vol. 2. Cresskill, NJ: Hampton Press. (p. 319)

Paulus, P. B., Larey, T. S., & Dzindolet, M. T. (1998). Creativity in groups and teams. In M. Turner (Ed.), *Groups at work: Advances in theory and research.* Hillsdale, NJ: Erlbaum. (p. 319)

Paulus, P. B., Larey, T. S., & Dzindolet, M. T. (2000). Creativity in groups and teams. In M. Turner (Ed.), *Groups at work: Advances in theory and research.* Hillsdale, NJ: Hampton. (p. 319)

Paulus, P. B., Larey, T. S., & Ortega, A. H. (1995). Performance and perceptions of brainstormers in an organizational setting. *Basic and Applied Social Psychology, 17,* 249–265. (p. 319)

Payne, B. K. (2001). Prejudice and perception: The role of automatic and controlled processes in misperceiving a weapon. *Journal of Personality and Social Psychology, 81,* 181–192. (p. 339)

Pedersen, A., & Walker, I. (1997). Prejudice against Australian Aborigines: Old-fashioned and modern forms. *European Journal of Social Psychology, 27,* 561–587. (p. 336)

Pedersen, W. C., Gonzales, C., & Miller, N. (2000). The moderating effect of trivial triggering provocation on displaced aggression. *Journal of Personality and Social Psychology, 78,* 913–927. (p. 386)

Pegalis, L. J., Shaffer, D. R., Bazzini, D. G., & Greenier, K. (1994). On the ability to elicit self-disclosure: Are there gender-based and contextual limitations on the opener effect? *Personality and Social Psychology Bulletin, 20,* 412–420. (p. 463)

Pelham, B. W., Mirenberg, M. C., & Jones, J. T. (2002). Why Susie sells seashells by the seashore. Implicit egotism and major life decisions. *Journal of Personality and Social Psychology, 82,* 469–487. (p. 430)

Peng, Y., Zebrowitz, L. A., & Lee, H. K. (1993). The impact of cultural background and cross-cultural experience on impressions of American and Korean male speakers. *Journal of Cross-Cultural Psychology, 24,* 203–220. (p. 253)

Pennebaker, J. (1990). *Opening up: The healing power of confiding in others.* New York: William Morrow. (p. 598)

Pennebaker, J. W. (1982). *The psychology of physical symptoms.* New York: Springer-Verlag. (p. 585)

Pennebaker, J. W., & Lay, T. C. (2002). Language use and personality during crises: Analyses of Mayor Rudolph Giuliani's press conferences. *Journal of Research in Personality, 36,* 271–282. (p. 543)

Pennebaker, J. W., & O'Heeron, R. C. (1984). Confiding in others and illness rate among spouses of suicide and accidental death victims. *Journal of Abnormal Psychology, 93,* 473–476. (p. 598)

Pennebaker, J. W., Rimé, B., & Sproul, G. (1996). Stereotypes of emotional expressiveness of northerners and southerners: A cross-cultural test of Montesquieu's hypotheses. *Journal of Personality and Social Psychology, 70,* 372–380. (p. 333)

Penner, L. A. (2002). Dispositional and organizational influences on sustained volunteerism: An interactionist perspective. *Journal of Social Issues, 58,* 447–467. (pp. 506, 508)

Penner, L. A., Dertke, M. C., & Achenbach, C. J. (1973). The "flash" system: A field study of altruism. *Journal of Applied Social Psychology, 3,* 362–370. (p. 486)

Pennington, N., & Hastie, R. (1993). The story model for juror decision making. In R. Hastie (Ed.), *Inside the juror: The psychology of juror decision making.* New York: Cambridge University Press. (p. 625)

Penrod, S., & Cutler, B. L. (1987). Assessing the competence of juries. In I. B. Weiner & A. K. Hess (Eds.), *Handbook of forensic psychology.* New York: Wiley. (p. 629)

Penton-Voak, I. S., Jones, B. C., Little, A. C., Baker, S., Tiddeman, B., Burt, D. M., & Perrett, D. I. (2001). Symmetry, sexual dimorphism in facial proportions and male facial attractiveness. *Proceedings of the Royal Society of London, 268,* 1–7. (pp. 437–438)

People (2003, September 1). Nipped, tucked, talking. Pp. 102–111. (pp. 439–440)

Peplau, L. A., & Gordon, S. L. (1985). Women and men in love: Gender differences in close heterosexual relationships. In V. E. O'Leary, R. K. Unger, & B. S. Wallston (Eds.), *Women, gender, and social psychology.* Hillsdale, NJ: Erlbaum. (p. 455)

Pereira, J. (2003, January 10). Just how far does First Amendment protection go? *Wall Street Journal,* pp. B1, B3. (p. 411)

Perkins, H. W. (1991). Religious commitment, Yuppie values, and well-being in post-collegiate life. *Review of Religious Research, 32,* 244–251. (pp. 600, 654)

Perlman, D., & Rook, K. S. (1987). Social support, social deficits, and the family: Toward the enhancement of well-being. In S. Oskamp (Ed.), *Family processes and problems: Social psychological aspects.* Newbury Park, CA: Sage. (p. 600)

Perloff, L. S. (1987). Social comparison and illusions of invulnerability. In C. R. Snyder & C. R. Ford (Eds.), *Coping with negative life events: Clinical and social psychological perspectives.* New York: Plenum. (p. 71)

Perls, F. S. (1972). Gestalt therapy [interview]. In A. Bry (Ed.), *Inside psychotherapy.* New York: Basic Books. (p. 242)

Perls, F. S. (1973). *Ego, hunger and aggression: The beginning of Gestalt therapy.* Random House, 1969. Cited by Berkowitz in The case for bottling up rage. *Psychology Today*, July, pp. 24–30. (p. 416)

Perrin, S., & Spencer, C. (1981). Independence or conformity in the Asch experiment as a reflection of cultural or situational factors. *British Journal of Social Psychology*, **20**, 205–209. (p. 237)

Perry, L. C., Perry, D. G., & Weiss, R. J. (1986). Age differences in children's beliefs about whether altruism makes the actor feel good. *Social Cognition*, **4**, 263–269. (p. 481)

Pessin, J. (1933). The comparative effects of social and mechanical stimulation on memorizing. *American Journal of Psychology*, **45**, 263–270. (p. 287)

Pessin, J., & Husband, R. W. (1933). Effects of social stimulation on human maze learning. *Journal of Abnormal and Social Psychology*, **28**, 148–154. (p. 287)

Peterson, B. E., Doty, R. M., & Winter, D. G. (1993). Authoritarianism and attitudes toward contemporary social issues. *Personality and Social Psychology Bulletin*, **19**, 174–184. (p. 346)

Peterson, C., & Barrett, L. C. (1987). Explanatory style and academic performance among university freshmen. *Journal of Personality and Social Psychology*, **53**, 603–607. (p. 59)

Peterson, C., & Bossio, L. M. (2000). Optimism and physical well-being. In E. C. Chang (Ed.), *Optimism and pessimism.* Washington, DC: APA Books. (p. 591)

Peterson, C., Schwartz, S. M., & Seligman, M. E. P. (1981). Self-blame and depression symptoms. *Journal of Personality and Social Psychology*, **41**, 253–259. (p. 75)

Peterson, C., & Seligman, M. E. P. (1987). Explanatory style and illness. *Journal of Personality*, **55**, 237–265. (p. 590)

Peterson, C., Seligman, M. E. P., & Vaillant, G. E. (1988). Pessimistic explanatory style is a risk factor for physical illness: A thirty-five-year longitudinal study. *Journal of Personality and Social Psychology*, **55**, 23–27. (p. 590)

Peterson, C., & Steen, T. A. (2002). Optimistic explanatory style. In C. R. Snyder & S. J. Lopez (Ed.), *Handbook of positive psychology.* London: Oxford University Press. (p. 577)

Peterson, E. (1992). *Under the unpredictable plant.* Grand Rapids, MI: Eerdmans. (p. 34)

Peterson, J. L., & Zill, N. (1981). Television viewing in the United States and children's intellectual, social, and emotional development. *Television and Children*, **2**(2), 21–28. (p. 409)

Peterson, R. S., & Nemeth, C. J. (1996). Focus versus flexibility: Majority and minority influence can both improve performance. *Personality and Social Psychology Bulletin*, **22**, 14–23. (p. 322)

Pettigrew, T. F. (1958). Personality and socio-cultural factors in intergroup attitudes: A cross-national comparison. *Journal of Conflict Resolution*, **2**, 29–42. (p. 347)

Pettigrew, T. F. (1969). Racially separate or together? *Journal of Social Issues*, **2**, 43–69. (p. 539)

Pettigrew, T. F. (1978). Three issues in ethnicity: Boundaries, deprivations, and perceptions. In J. M. Yinger & S. J. Cutler (Eds.), *Major social issues: A multidisciplinary view.* New York: Free Press. (p. 350)

Pettigrew, T. F. (1979). The ultimate attribution error: Extending Allport's cognitive analysis of prejudice. *Personality and Social Psychology Bulletin*, **55**, 461–476. (p. 365)

Pettigrew, T. F. (1980). Prejudice. In S. Thernstrom et al. (Eds.), *Harvard encyclopedia of American ethnic groups.* Cambridge, MA: Harvard University Press. (p. 365)

Pettigrew, T. F. (1986). The intergroup contact hypothesis reconsidered. In M. Hewstone & R. Brown (Eds.), *Contact and conflict in intergroup encounters.* Oxford: Basil Blackwell. (p. 540)

Pettigrew, T. F. (1987, May 12). "Useful" modes of thought contribute to prejudice. *The New York Times*, pp. 17–20. (p. 337)

Pettigrew, T. F. (1988). Advancing racial justice: Past lessons for future use. Paper for the University of Alabama Conference: "Opening Doors: An Appraisal of Race Relations in America." (pp. 541–542)

Pettigrew, T. F. (1997). Generalized intergroup contact effects on prejudice. *Personality and Social Psychology Bulletin*, **23**, 173–185. (p. 541)

Pettigrew, T. F. (1998). Intergroup contact theory. *Annual Review of Psychology*, **49**, 65–85. (p. 541)

Pettigrew, T. F. (1998). Reactions toward the new minorities of western Europe. *Annual Review of Sociology*, **24**, 77–103. (p. 336)

Pettigrew, T. F. (2003). Peoples under threat: Americans, Arabs, and Israelis. *Peace and Conflict*, **9**, 69–90. (p. 388)

Pettigrew, T. F., Jackson, J. S., Brika, J. B., Lemaine, G., Meertens, R. W., Wagner, U., & Zick, A. (1998). Outgroup prejudice in western Europe. *European Review of Social Psychology*, **8**, 241–273. (p. 355)

Pettigrew, T. F., & Meertens, R. W. (1995). Subtle and blatant prejudice in western Europe. *European Journal of Social Psychology*, **25**, 57–76. (p. 350)

Pettigrew, T. F. & Tropp, L. R. (2000). Does intergroup contact reduce prejudice: Recent meta-analytic findings. In Oskamp, S., Ed., *Reducing prejudice and discrimination.* Mahwah, NJ: Lawrence Erlbaum Associates, Inc. 93–114. (pp. 540–541)

Petty, R. E., & Cacioppo, J. T. (1977). Forewarning cognitive responding, and resistance to persuasion. *Journal of Personality and Social Psychology*, **35**, 645–655. (p. 269)

Petty, R. E., & Cacioppo, J. T. (1979). Effects of forewarning of persuasive intent and involvement on cognitive response and persuasion. *Personality and Social Psychology Bulletin*, **5**, 173–176. *(a)* (pp. 260, 269)

Petty, R. E., & Cacioppo, J. T. (1986). *Communication and persuasion: Central and peripheral routes to attitude change.* New York: Springer-Verlag. (p. 248)

Petty, R. E., Cacioppo, J. T., & Goldman, R. (1981). Personal involvement as a determinant of argument-based persuasion. *Journal of*

Personality and Social Psychology, 41, 847–855. (pp. 256, 270)

Petty, R. E., Haugtvedt, C. P., & Smith, S. M. (1995). Elaboration as a determinant of attitude strength: Creating attitudes that are persistent, resistant, and predictive of behavior. In R. E. Petty & J. A. Krosnick (Eds.), *Attitude strength: Antecedents and consequences.* Hillsdale, NJ: Erlbaum. (p. 249)

Petty, R. E., & Krosnick, J. A. (Eds.). (1995). *Attitude strength: Antecedents and consequences.* Hillsdale, NJ: Erlbaum. (p. 247)

Petty, R. E., & Wegener, D. T. (1999). The elaboration likelihood model: Current status and controversies. In S. Chaiken & Y. Trope (Eds.). *Dual-process theories in social psychology* (pp. 41–72). New York: Guilford. (p. 248)

Petty, R. E., & Wegener, D. T. (1998). Attitude change: Multiple roles for persuasion variables. In D. Gilbert, S. Fiske, & G. Lindzey (eds), *Handbook of social psychology,* 4th edition. New York: McGraw-Hill. (p. 261)

Petty, R. E., Schumann, D. W., Richman, S. A., & Strathman, A. J. (1993). Positive mood and persuasion: Different roles for affect under high and low elaboration conditions. *Journal of Personality and Social Psychology, 64,* 5–20. (pp. 256–257)

Petty, R. E., Wegener, D. T., & Fabrigar, L. R. (1997). Attitudes and attitude change. *Annual Review of Psychology, 48,* 609–647. (p. 163)

Petty, R. E., Wheeler, S. C., & Bizer, G. Y. (2000). Attitude functions and persuasion: An elaboration likelihood approach to matched versus mismatched messages. In G. R. Maio & J. M. Olson (Eds.), *Why we evaluate: Functions of attitudes.* (pp. 133–162). Mahwah, NJ: Erlbaum. (p. 249)

Pew (2000, May 10). Tracking online life: How women use the Internet to cultivate relationships with family and friends. Washington, DC: Pew Internet and American Life Project. (p. 465)

Pew (2003). Views of a changing world 2003. The Pew Global Attitudes Project. Washington, DC: Pew Research Center for the People and the Press (http://people-press.org/ reports/pdf/185.pdf). (pp. 152, 196, 197, 245, 246, 544)

Phillips, D. L. (2003, September 20). Listening to the wrong Iraqi. *New York Times* (www.nytimes.com). (p. 536)

Phillips, D. P. (1982). The impact of fictional television stories on U.S. adult fatalities: New evidence on the effect of the mass media on violence. *American Journal of Sociology, 87,* 1340–1359. (p. 213)

Phillips, D. P. (1985). Natural experiments on the effects of mass media violence on fatal aggression: Strengths and weaknesses of a new approach. In L. Berkowitz (Ed.), *Advances in experimental social psychology,* Vol. 19. Orlando, FL: Academic Press. (p. 212)

Phillips, D. P., Carstensen, L. L., & Paight, D. J. (1989). Effects of mass media news stories on suicide, with new evidence on the role of story content. In D. R. Pfeffer (Ed.), *Suicide among youth: Perspectives on risk and prevention.* Washington, DC: American Psychiatric Press. (p. 212)

Phinney, J. S. (1990). Ethnic identity in adolescents and adults: Review of research. *Psychological Bulletin, 108,* 499–514. (p. 552)

Pierce, J. P., & Gilpin, E. A. (1995). A historical analysis of tobacco marketing and the uptake of smoking by youth in the United States: 1890–1977. *Health Psychology, 14,* 500–508. (p. 264)

Pierce, J. P., Lee, L., & Gilpin, E. A. (1994). Smoking initiation by adolescent girls, 1944 through 1988. *Journal of the American Medical Association, 27,* 608–611. (p. 264)

Piliavin, I. M., Rodin, J., & Piliavin, J. A. (1969). Good Samaritanism: An underground phenomenon. *Journal of Personality and Social Psychology, 13,* 289–299. (pp. 500, 502)

Piliavin, J. A. (2003). Doing well by doing good: Benefits for the benefactor. In C. L. M. Keyes & J. Haidt (Eds.), *Flourishing: Positive psychology and the life well-lived.* Washington, DC: American Psychological Association. (pp. 477, 478)

Piliavin, J. A., & Piliavin, I. M. (1973). The Good Samaritan: Why *does* he help? Unpublished manuscript, University of Wisconsin. (p. 479)

Piliavin, J. A., Evans, D. E., & Callero, P. (1982). Learning to "Give to unnamed strangers": The process of commitment to regular blood donation. In E. Staub, D. Bar-Tal, J. Karylowski, & J. Reykawski (Eds.), *The development and maintenance of prosocial behavior: International perspectives.* New York: Plenum. (pp. 515–516)

Pimentel, D., Bailey, O., Kim, P., Mullaney, E., Calabrese, J., Walman, J., Nelson, F., & Yao, X. (1999). Will limits of Earth's resources control human numbers? *Environment, Development and Sustainability, 1,* 19–39. (p. 644)

Pincus, J. H. (2001). *Base instincts: What makes killers kill?* New York: W. W. Norton & Co., Inc. (p. 383)

Pinel, E. C. (1999). Stigma consciousness: The psychological legacy of social stereotypes. *Journal of Personality and Social Psychology, 76,* 114–128. (p. 362)

Pinel, E. C. (2002). Stigma consciousness in intergroup contexts: The power of conviction. *Journal of Experimental Social Psychology, 38,* 178–185. (p. 125)

Pingitore, R., Dugoni, B. L., Tindale, R. S., & Spring, B. (1994). Bias against overweight job applicants in a simulated employment interview. *Journal of Applied Psychology, 79,* 909–917. (p. 332)

Pinker, S. (1997). *How the mind works.* New York: Norton. (p. 188)

Pinker, S. (2002). *The blank slate.* New York: Viking. (pp. 11, 171)

Pipher, M. (2002). *The middle of everywhere: The world's refugees come to our town.* Harcourt. (pp. 381–382)

Plaks, J. E., & Higgins, E. T. (2000). Pragmatic use of stereotyping in teamwork: Social loafing and compensation as a function of inferred partner-situation fit. *Journal of Personality and Social Psychology, 79,* 962–974. (p. 296)

Platz, S. J., & Hosch, H. M. (1988). Cross-racial/ethnic eyewitness identification: A field study. *Journal of Applied Social Psychology, 18,* 972–984. (p. 360)

Plaut, V. C., Markus, H. R., & Lackman, M. E. (2002). Place matters: Consensual features and regional variation in American well-being and self. *Journal of Personality and Social Psychology, 83,* 160–184. (p. 173)

Pliner, P., Hart, H., Kohl, J., & Saari, D. (1974). Compliance without pressure: Some further data on the foot-in-the-door technique. *Journal of Experimental Social Psychology, 10,* 17–22. (p. 144)

Plomin, R., & Daniels, D. (1987). Why are children in the same family so different from one another? *Behavioral and Brain Sciences, 10,* 1–60. (p. 199)

Plous, S. (1985). Perceptual illusions and military realities: A social-psychological analysis of the nuclear arms race. *Journal of Conflict Resolution, 29,* 363–389. (pp. 533–534)

Plous, S. (1993). The nuclear arms race: Prisoner's dilemma or perceptual dilemma? *Journal of Peace Research, 30,* 163–179. (pp. 533–534)

Pomazal, R. J., & Clore, G. L. (1973). Helping on the highway: The effects of dependency and sex. *Journal of Applied Social Psychology, 3,* 150–164. (p. 486)

Pomerleau, O. F., & Rodin, J. (1986). Behavioral medicine and health psychology. In S. L. Garfield & A. E. Bergin (Eds.), *Handbook of psychotherapy and behavior change,* 3rd ed. New York: Wiley. (p. 60)

Poniewozik, J. (2003, November 24). All the news that fits your reality. *Time,* p. 90. (pp. 99–100)

Poole, D. A., Lindsay, D. S., Memon, A., & Bull, R. (1995). Psychotherapy and the recovery of memories of childhood sexual abuse: U.S. and British practitioners' opinions, practices, and experiences. *Journal of Consulting and Clinical Psychology, 63,* 426–437. (p. 572)

Popenoe, D. (2002). The top ten myths of divorce. Unpublished manuscript, National Marriage Project, Rutgers University. (p. 468)

Porter, N., Geis, F. L., & Jennings (Walstedt), J. (1983). Are women invisible as leaders? *Sex Roles, 9,* 1035–1049. (p. 340)

Postmes, T., & Spears, R. (1998). Deindividuation and antinormative behavior: A meta-analysis. *Psychological Bulletin, 123,* 238–259. (p. 301)

Postmes, T., Spears, R., & Cihangir, S. (2001). Quality of decision making and group norms. *Journal of Personality and Social Psychology, 80,* 918–930. (p. 315)

Powell, J. (1989). *Happiness is an inside job.* Valencia, CA: Tabor. (p. 66)

Pozo, C., Carver, C. S., Wellens, A. R., & Scheier, M. F. (1991). Social anxiety and social perception: Construing others' reactions to the self. *Personality and Social Psychology Bulletin, 17,* 355–362. (p. 584)

Prager, I. G., & Cutler, B. L. (1990). Attributing traits to oneself and to others: The role of acquaintance level. *Personality and Social Psychology Bulletin, 16,* 309–319. (p. 94)

Pratkanis, A. R., Greenwald, A. G., Leippe, M. R., & Baumgardner, M. H. (1988). In search of reliable persuasion effects: III. The sleeper effect is dead. Long live the sleeper effect. *Journal of Personality and Social Psychology, 54,* 203–218. (pp. 251–252)

Pratkanis, A. R., & Turner, M. E. (1994a). The year cool Papa Bell lost the batting title: Mr. Branch Rickey and Mr. Jackie Robinson's plea for affirmative action. *Nine: A Journal of Baseball History and Social Policy Perspectives, 2,* 260–276. (p. 550–551)

Pratkanis, A. R., & Turner, M. E. (1994b). Nine principles of successful affirmative action: Mr. Branch Rickey, Mr. Jackie Robinson, and the integration of baseball. *Nine: A Journal of Baseball History and Social Policy Perspectives, 3,* 36–65. (pp. 550–551)

Pratkanis, A. R., & Turner, M. E. (1996). The procative removal of discriminatory barriers: Affirmative action as effective help. *Journal of Social Issues, 52,* 111–132. (p. 484)

Pratt, M. W., Pancer, M., Hunsberger, B., & Manchester, J. (1990). Reasoning about the self and relationships in maturity: An integrative complexity analysis of individual differences. *Journal of Personality and Social Psychology, 59,* 575–581. (p. 193)

Pratto, F. (1996). Sexual politics: The gender gap in the bedroom, the cupboard, and the cabinet. In D. M. Buss & N. M. Malamuth (Eds.), *Sex, power, conflict: Evolutionary and feminist perspectives.* New York: Oxford University Press. (p. 185)

Pratto, F., Sidanius, J., Stallworth, L. M., & Malle, B. F. (1994). Social dominance orientation: A personality variable predicting social and political attitudes. *Journal of Personality and Social Psychology, 67,* 741–763. (p. 345)

Pratto, F., Stallworth, L. M., & Sidanius, J. (1997). The gender gap: Differences in political attitudes and social dominance orientation. *British Journal of Social Psychology, 36,* 49–68. (p. 183)

Prentice, D. A., & Carranza, E. (2002). What women and men should be, shouldn't be, are allowed to be, and don't have to be: The contents of prescriptive gender stereotypes. *Psychology of Women Quarterly, 26,* 269–281. (p. 182)

Prentice-Dunn, S., & Rogers, R. W. (1980). Effects of deindividuating situational cues and aggressive models on subjective deindividuation and aggression. *Journal of Personality and Social Psychology, 39,* 104–113. (p. 302)

Prentice-Dunn, S., & Rogers, R. W. (1989). Deindividuation and the self-regulation of behavior. In P. B. Paulus (Ed.), *Psychology of group influence,* 2nd ed. Hillsdale, NJ: Erlbaum. (p. 302)

Pressley, C. A., & others (1997). *Alcohol and drugs on American college campuses: Issues of violence and harrassment.* Carbondale, IL: Core Institute, Southern Illinois University. (p. 384)

Presson, P. K., & Benassi, V. A. (1996). Illusion of control: A meta-analytic review. *Journal of Social Behavior and Personality, 11,* 493–510. (p. 117)

Price, G. H., Dabbs, J. M., Jr., Clower, B. J., & Resin, R. P. (1974). At first glance—Or, is physical attractiveness more than skin deep? Paper presented at the Eastern Psychological Association convention. Cited by K. L. Dion & K. K. Dion (1979). Personality and behavioral correlates of romantic love. In M. Cook & G. Wilson (Eds.), *Love and attraction.* Oxford: Pergamon. (p. 441)

Prislin, R., & Pool, G. J. (1996). Behavior, consequences, and the self: Is all well that ends well? *Personality* and Social Psychology Bulletin, **22**, 933–948. (p. 163)

Pritchard, I. L. (1998). The effects of rap music: On aggressive attitudes toward women. Master's thesis, Humboldt State University. (p. 407)

Prohaska, V. (1994). "I know I'll get an A": Confident overestimation of final course grades. *Teaching of Psychology, **21**, 141–143. (p. 72)

Pronin, E., Kruger, J., Savitsky, K., & Ross, L. (2001). You don't know me, but I know you: The illusion of asymmetric insight. *Journal of Personality and Social Psychology, **81**, 639–656. (p. 70)

Pronin, E., Lin, D. Y., & Ross, L. (2002). The bias blind spot: Perceptions of bias in self versus others. *Personality and Social Psychology Bulletin, **28**, 369–381. (p. 70)

Prothrow-Stith, D. (with M. Wiessman) (1991). *Deadly consequences.* New York: HarperCollins. (pp. 555–556)

Pruitt, D. G. (1986). Achieving integrative agreements in negotiation. In R. K. White (Ed.), *Psychology and the prevention of nuclear war.* New York: New York University Press. (p. 554)

Pruitt, D. G. (1998). Social conflict. In D. Gilbert, S. T. Fiske, & G. Lindzey (Eds.), *Handbook of social psychology,* 4th ed. New York: McGraw-Hill. (pp. 526, 554)

Pruitt, D. G., & Kimmel, M. J. (1977). Twenty years of experimental gaming: Critique, synthesis, and suggestions for the future. *Annual Review of Psychology, **28**, 363–392. (p. 527)

Pruitt, D. G., & Lewis, S. A. (1975). Development of integrative solutions in bilateral negotiation. *Journal of Personality and Social Psychology, **31**, 621–633. (p. 554)

Pruitt, D. G., & Lewis, S. A. (1977). The psychology of integrative bargaining. In D. Druckman (Ed.), *Negotiations: A social-psychological analysis.* New York: Halsted. (p. 554)

Pruitt, D. G., & Rubin, J. Z. (1986). *Social conflict.* San Francisco: Random House. (p. 527)

Pryke, S., Lindsay, R. C. L., Dysart, J. E., & Dupuis, P. (2004). Multiple independent identification decisions: A method of calibrating eyewitness identifications. *Journal of Applied Psychology, **89**, 73–84. (p. 617)

Pryor, J. B., DeSouza, E. R., Fitness, J., Hutz, C., Kumpf, M., Lubbert, K., Pesonen, O., & Erber, M. W. (1997). Gender differences in the interpretation of social-sexual behavior: A cross-cultural perspective on sexual harassment. *Journal of Cross-Cultural Psychology, **28**, 509–534. (p. 85)

Pryor, J. B. & Reeder, G. D. (1993). *The social psychology of HIV infection.* Hillsdale, NJ: Lawrence Erlbaum Associates, Inc. (p. 71)

Public Opinion (1984, August/September). Vanity fare, p. 22. (pp. 69, 70)

Purvis, J. A., Dabbs, J. M., Jr., & Hopper, C. H. (1984). The "opener": Skilled user of facial expression and speech pattern. *Personality and Social Psychology Bulletin, **10**, 61–66. (p. 463)

Putnam, R. (2000). *Bowling alone.* New York: Simon & Schuster. (pp.183, 409, 410, 465, 466, 509, 516, 543, 561–562, 648–649, 658)

Pyszczynski, T., & Greenberg, J. (1987). Self-regulatory perseveration and the depressive self-focusing style: A self-awareness theory of reactive depression. *Psychological Bulletin, **102**, 122–138. (p. 79)

Pyszczynski, T., Hamilton, J. C., Greenberg, J., & Becker, S. E. (1991). Self-awareness and psychological dysfunction. In C. R. Snyder & D. O. Forsyth (Eds.), *Handbook of social and clinical psychology: The health perspective.* New York: Pergamon. (pp. 579, 580)

Quartz, S. R., & Sejnowski, T. J. (2002). *Liars, lovers, and heroes: What the new brain science reveals about how we become who we are.* New York: Morrow. (p. 200)

Quattrone, G. A. (1982). Behavioral consequences of attributional bias. *Social Cognition, **1**, 358–378. (p. 96)

Quattrone, G. A., & Jones, E. E. (1980). The perception of variability within in-groups and out-groups: Implications for the law of small numbers. *Journal of Personality and Social Psychology, **38**, 141–152. (p. 364)

Raine, A. (1993). *The psychopathology of crime: Criminal behavior as a clinical disorder.* San Diego, CA: Academic Press. (p. 384)

Raine, A., Lencz, T., Bihrle, S., LaCasse, L., & Colletti, P. (2000). Reduced prefrontal gray matter volume and reduced autonomic activity in antisocial personality disorder. *Archives of General Psychiatry, **57**, 119–127. (p. 383)

Raine, A., Stoddard, J., Bihrle, S., & Buchsbaum, M. (1998). Prefrontal glucose deficits in murderers lacking psychosocial deprivation. *Neuropsychiatry, Neuropsychology, & Behavioral Neurology, **11**, 1–7. (p. 383)

Rajecki, D. W., Bledsoe, S. B., & Rasmussen, J. L. (1991). Successful personal ads: Gender differences and similarities in offers, stipulations, and outcomes. *Basic and Applied Social Psychology, **12**, 457–469. (p. 434)

Rank, S. G., & Jacobson, C. K. (1977). Hospital nurses' compliance with medication overdose orders: A failure to replicate. *Journal of Health and Social Behavior, **18**, 188–193. (p. 221)

Rapoport, A. (1960). *Fights, games, and debates.* Ann Arbor: University of Michigan Press. (p. 521)

Raven, P. H. (2002, August 9). Science, sustainability, and the human prospect. *Science, **297**, 954–958. (p. 644)

Rawls, J. (1971). *A theory of justice.* Cambridge, MA: Belknap Press of Harvard University Press. (p. 532)

Reed, D. (1989, November 25). Video collection documents Christian resistance to Hitler. Associated Press release in *Grand Rapids Press,* pp. B4, B5. (p. 347)

Reeder, G. D., McCormick, C. B., & Esselman, E. D. (1987). Self-referent processing and recall of prose. *Journal of Educational Psychology, **79**, 243–248. (p. 96)

Regan, D. T., & Cheng, J. B. (1973). Distraction and attitude change: A resolution. *Journal of Experimental Social Psychology, **9**, 138–147. (p. 269)

Regan, D. T., Williams, M., & Sparling, S. (1972). Voluntary expiation of guilt: A field experiment. *Journal of Personality and Social Psychology, **24**, 42–45. (p. 480)

Regan, P. C. (1998). What if you can't get what you want? Willingness to compromise ideal mate selection standards as a function of sex, mate value, and relationship context. *Personality and Social Psychology Bulletin*, **24**, 1294–1303. (p. 451)

Reicher, S., & Haslam, Z. (2002). Ethics and *The Experiment*. *Psychologist*, **15**, 282. (p. 142)

Reicher, S., Spears, R., & Postmes, T. (1995). A social identity model of deindividuation phenomena. In W. Storebe & M. Hewstone (Eds.), *European review of social psychology*, vol. 6. Chichester, England: Wiley. (p. 301)

Reid, P., & Finchilescu, G. (1995). The disempowering effects of media violence against women on college women. *Psychology of Women Quarterly*, **19**, 397–411. (p. 409)

Reifman, A. S., Larrick, R. P., & Fein, S. (1991). Temper and temperature on the diamond: The heat-aggression relationship in major league baseball. *Personality and Social Psychology Bulletin*, **17**, 580–585. (p. 394)

Reis, H. T., Nezlek, J., & Wheeler, L. (1980). Physical attractiveness in social interaction. *Journal of Personality and Social Psychology*, **38**, 604–617. (p. 432)

Reis, H. T., & Shaver, P. (1988). Intimacy as an interpersonal process. In S. Duck (Ed.), *Handbook of personal relationships: Theory, relationships and interventions*. Chichester, England: Wiley. (p. 462)

Reis, H. T., Wheeler, L., Spiegel, N., Kernis, M. H., Nezlek, J., & Perri, M. (1982). Physical attractiveness in social interaction: II. Why does appearance affect social experience? *Journal of Personality and Social Psychology*, **43**, 979–996. (p. 432)

Reis, T. J., Gerrard, M., & Gibbons, F. X. (1993). Social comparison and the pill: Reactions to upward and downward comparison of contraceptive behavior. *Personality and Social Psychology Bulletin*, **19**, 13–20. (p. 658)

Reisenzein, R. (1983). The Schachter theory of emotion: Two decades later. *Psychological Bulletin*, **94**, 239–264. (p. 396)

Reitzes, D. C. (1953). The role of organizational structures: Union versus neighborhood in a tension situation. *Journal of Social Issues*, **9**(1), 37–44. (p. 347)

Remley, A. (1988, October). From obedience to independence. *Psychology Today*, pp. 56–59. (p. 561)

Renaud, H., & Estess, F. (1961). Life history interviews with one hundred normal American males: "Pathogenecity" of childhood. *American Journal of Orthopsychiatry*, **31**, 786–802. (p. 572)

Renner, M. (1999). *Ending violent conflict*. Worldwatch Paper 146, Worldwatch Institute. (p. 380)

Ressler, R. K., Burgess, A. W., & Douglas, J. E. (1988). *Sexual homicide patterns*. Boston: Lexington Books. (p. 400)

Reychler, L. (1979). The effectiveness of a pacifist strategy in conflict resolution. *Journal of Conflict Resolution*, **23**, 228–260. (p. 523)

Rhine, R. J., & Severance, L. J. (1970). Ego-involvement, discrepancy, source credibility, and attitude change. *Journal of Personality and Social Psychology*, **16**, 175–190. (p. 260)

Rhodes, G., Sumich, A., & Byatt, G. (1999). Are average facial configurations attractive only because of their symmetry. *Psychological Science*, **10**, 52–58. (pp. 437–438)

Rhodes, N., & Wood, W. (1992). Self-esteem and intelligence affect influenceability: The mediating role of message reception. *Psychological Bulletin*, **111**, 156–171. (p. 267)

Rhodewalt, F. (1987). Is self-handicapping an effective self-protective attributional strategy? Paper presented at the American Psychological Association convention. (p. 78)

Rhodewalt, F., & Agustsdottir, S. (1986). Effects of self-presentation on the phenomenal self. *Journal of Personality and Social Psychology*, **50**, 47–55. (p. 592)

Rhodewalt, F., Saltzman, A. T., & Wittmer J. (1984). Self-handicapping among competitive athletes: The role of practice in self-esteem protection. *Basic and Applied Social Psychology*, **5**, 197–209. (p. 79)

Rholes, W. S., Newman, L. S., & Ruble, D. N. (1990). Understanding self and other: Developmental and motivational aspects of perceiving persons in terms of invariant dispositions. In E. T. Higgins & R. M. Sorrentino (Eds.), *Handbook of motivation and cognition: Foundations of social behavior*, Vol. 2. New York: Guilford. (p. 95)

Rice, B. (1985, September). Performance review: The job nobody likes. *Psychology Today*, pp. 30–36. (p. 68)

Rice, M. E., & Grusec, J. E. (1975). Saying and doing: Effects on observer performance. *Journal of Personality and Social Psychology*, **32**, 584–593. (p. 503)

Rich, F. (2001, May 20). Naked capitalists: There's no business like porn business. *New York Times* (www.nytimes.com). (p. 398)

Richard, F. D., Bond, C. F., Jr., & Stokes-Zoota, J. J. (2003). One hundred years of social psychology quantitatively described. *Review of General Psychology*, **7**, 331–363. (p. 20)

Richards, Z., & Hewstone, M. (2001). Subtyping and subgrouping: Processes for the prevention and promotion of stereotype change. *Personality and Social Psychology Review*, **5**, 52–73. (p. 370)

Richardson, J. T. E. (1990). Questionnaire studies of paramenstrual symptoms. *Psychology of Women Quarterly*, **14**, 15–42. (p. 586)

Richardson, J. T. E. (1993). The premenstrual syndrome: A brief history. Paper presented to the Annual Conference of the British Psychological Society. (p. 587)

Richardson, L. F. (1960). Generalized foreign policy. *British Journal of Psychology Monographs Supplements*, **23**. Cited by A. Rapoport in *Fights, games, and debates*. Ann Arbor: University of Michigan Press, 1960, p. 15. (p. 519)

Richeson, J. A., & Ambady, N. (2003). Effects of situational power on automatic racial prejudice. *Journal of Experimental Social Psychology*, **39**, 177–183. (p. 343)

Ridge, R. D., & Reber, J. S. (2002). "I think she's attracted to me": The effect of men's beliefs on women's behavior in a job interview scenario. *Basic and Applied Social Psychology*, **24**, 1–14. (p. 125)

Riess, M., Rosenfeld, P., Melburg, V., & Tedeschi, J. T. (1981). Self-serving attributions: Biased private perceptions and distorted public descriptions. *Journal of Personality and Social Psychology*, **41**, 224–231. (p. 79)

Riggs, J. M. (1992). Self-handicapping and achievement. In A. K. Boggiano & T. S. Pittman (Eds.), *Achievement and motivation: A social-developmental perspective*. New York: Cambridge University Press. (p. 79)

Riordan, C. A. (1980). Effects of admission of influence on attributions and attraction. Paper presented at the American Psychological Association convention. (pp. 451–452)

Riordan, C. A., & Ruggiero, J. (1980). Producing equal status interracial interaction: A replication. *Social Psychology Quarterly*, **43**, 131–136. (p. 542)

Rivkin, I. D., & Taylor, S. E. (1999). The effects of mental simulation on coping with controllable stressful events. *Personality and Social Psychology Bulletin*, **25**, 1451–1462. (p. 599)

Roach, M. (1998, December). Why men kill. *Discover*, pp. 100–108. (p. 383)

Robberson, M. R., & Rogers, R. W. (1988). Beyond fear appeals: Negative and positive persuasive appeals to health and self-esteem. *Journal of Applied Social Psychology*, **18**, 277–287. (p. 258)

Robertson, I. (1987). *Sociology*. New York: Worth Publishers. (p. 172)

Robins, L., & Regier, D. (Eds.). (1991). *Psychiatric disorders in America*. New York: Free Press. (p. 601)

Robins, R. W., & Beer, J. S. (2001). Positive illusions about the self: Short-term benefits and long-term costs. *Journal of Personality and Social Psychology*, **80**, 340–352. (p. 71)

Robins, R. W., Spranca, M. D., & Mendelsohn, G. A. (1996). The actor-observer effect revisited: Effects of individual differences and repeated social interactions on actor and observer attributions. *Journal of Personality and Social Psychology*, **71**, 375–389. (p. 96)

Robinson, J. (2002, October 8). What percentage of the population is gay? *Gallup Tuesday Briefing* (www.gallup.com). (p. 363)

Robinson, M. D., & Ryff, C. D. (1999). The role of self-deception in perceptions of past, present, and future happiness. *Personality and Social Psychology Bulletin*, **25**, 595–606. (p. 71)

Robinson, M. S., & Alloy, L. B. (2003). Negative cognitive styles and stress-reactive rumination interact to predict depression: A prospective study. *Cognitive Therapy and Research*, **27**, 275–291. (p. 580)

Robinson, R. J., Keltner, D., Ward, A., & Ross, L. (1995). Actual versus assumed differences in construal: "Naive realism" in intergroup perception and conflict. *Journal of Personality and Social Psychology*, **68**, 404–417. (p. 536)

Robinson, T. N., Wilde, M. L., Navracruz, L. C., Haydel, F., & Varady, A. (2001). Effects of reducing children's television and video game use on aggressive behavior. *Archives of Pediatric and Adolescent Medicine*, **155**, 17–23. (p. 419)

Rochat, F. (1993). How did they resist authority? Protecting refugees in Le Chambon during World War II. Paper presented at the American Psychological Association convention. (p. 224)

Rochat, F., & Modigliani, A. (1995). The ordinary quality of resistance: From Milgram's laboratory to the village of Le Chambon. *Journal of Social Issues*, **51**, 195–210. (pp. 224, 476)

Rodin, J. (1992). *Body traps*. New York: William Morrow. (p. 587)

Roehling, M. V. (2000). Weight-based discrimination in employment: psychological and legal aspects. *Personnel Psychology*, **52**, 969–1016. (p. 332)

Roese, N. J. (1994). The functional basis of counterfactual thinking. *Journal of Personality and Social Psychology*, **66**, 805–818. (p. 115)

Roese, N. J., & Hur, T. (1997). Affective determinants of counterfactual thinking. *Social Cognition*, **15**, 274–290. (pp. 115, 116)

Roese, N. L., & Olson, J. M. (1994). Attitude importance as a function of repeated attitude expression. *Journal of Experimental Social Psychology*, **66**, 805–818. (p. 163)

Roger, L. H., Cortes, D. E., & Malgady, R. B. (1991). Acculturation and mental health status among Hispanics: Convergence and new directions for research. *American Psychologist*, **46**, 585–597. (p. 552)

Rogers, C. R. (1958). Reinhold Niebuhr's *The self and the dramas of history*: A criticism. *Pastoral Psychology*, **9**, 15–17. (p. 66)

Rogers, C. R. (1980). *A way of being*. Boston: Houghton Mifflin. (p. 463)

Rogers, C. R. (1985, February). Quoted by Michael A. Wallach and Lise Wallach, "How Psychology Sanctions the Cult of the Self." *Washington Monthly*, pp. 46–56. (p. 242)

Rogers, R. W., & Mewborn, C. R. (1976). Fear appeals and attitude change: Effects of a threat's noxiousness, probability of occurrence, and the efficacy of coping responses. *Journal of Personality and Social Psychology*, **34**, 54–61. (p. 258)

Rogers, R. W., & Prentice-Dunn, S. (1981). Deindividuation and anger-mediated interracial aggression: Unmasking regressive racism. *Journal of Personality and Social Psychology*, **41**, 63–73. (p. 336)

Rohrer, J. H., Baron, S. H., Hoffman, E. L., & Swander, D. V. (1954). The stability of autokinetic judgments. *Journal of Abnormal and Social Psychology*, **49**, 595–597. (p. 210)

Rokeach, M. (1968). *Beliefs, attitudes, and values*. San Francisco: Jossey-Bass. (p. 444)

Rokeach, M., & Mezei, L. (1966). Race and shared beliefs as factors in social choice. *Science*, **151**, 167–172. (p. 359)

Romer, D., Gruder, D. L., & Lizzadro, T. (1986). A person-situation approach to altruistic behavior. *Journal of Personality and Social Psychology*, **51**, 1001–1012. (p. 506)

Roney, J. R. (2003). Effects of visual exposure to the opposite sex: Cognitive aspects mate attraction in human males. *Personality and Social Psychology Bulletin*, **29**, 393–404. (p. 191)

Rook, K. S. (1984). Promoting social bonding: Strategies for helping the lonely and socially isolated. *American Psychologist, 39*, 1389–1407. (p. 582)

Rook, K. S. (1987). Social support versus companionship: Effects on life stress, loneliness, and evaluations by others. *Journal of Personality and Social Psychology, 52*, 1132–1147. (p. 598)

Rosenbaum, M. E. (1986). The repulsion hypothesis: On the nondevelopment of relationships. *Journal of Personality and Social Psychology, 51*, 1156–1166. (p. 444)

Rosenbaum, M. E., & Holtz, R. (1985). The minimal intergroup discrimination effect: Out-group derogation, not in-group favorability. Paper presented at the American Psychological Association convention. (p. 354)

Rosenberg, L. A. (1961). Group size, prior experience and conformity. *Journal of Abnormal and Social Psychology, 63*, 436–437. (p. 228)

Rosenberg, R. (1984). Leta Hollingworth: Toward a sexless intelligence. In M. Lewin (Ed.), *In the shadow of the past: Psychology portrays the sexes*. New York: Columbia University Press. (p. 587)

Rosenblatt, A., & Greenberg, J. (1988). Depression and interpersonal attraction: The role of perceived similarity. *Journal of Personality and Social Psychology, 55*, 112–119. (p. 445)

Rosenblatt, R. (1994, April 24). The buck stops somewhere else. *Detroit Free Press Magazine*, pp. 6–13. (p. 134)

Rosenfeld, D., Folger, R., & Adelman, H. F. (1980). When rewards reflect competence: A qualification of the overjustification effect. *Journal of Personality and Social Psychology, 39*, 368–376. (p. 157)

Rosenhan, D. L. (1970). The natural socialization of altruistic autonomy. In J. Macaulay & L. Berkowitz (Eds.) *Altruism and helping behavior*. New York: Academic Press. (p. 514)

Rosenhan, D. L. (1973). On being sane in insane places. *Science, 179*, 250–258. (pp. 570–571)

Rosenthal, D. A., & Feldman, S. S. (1992). The nature and stability of ethnic identity in Chinese youth: Effects of length of residence in two cultural contexts. *Journal of Cross-Cultural Psychology, 23*, 214–227. (p. 552)

Rosenthal, R. (1985). From unconscious experimenter bias to teacher expectancy effects. In J. B. Dusek, V. C. Hall, & W. J. Meyer (Eds.), *Teacher expectancies*. Hillsdale, NJ: Erlbaum. (p. 121)

Rosenthal, R. (1991). Teacher expectancy effects: A brief update 25 years after the Pygmalion experiment. *Journal of Research in Education, 1*, 3–12. (p. 122)

Rosenthal, R. (2002). Covert communication in classrooms, clinics, courtrooms, and cubicles. *American Psychologist, 57*, 839–849. (p. 122)

Rosenthal, R. (2003). Covert communication in laboratories, classrooms, and the truly real world. *Current Directions in Psychological Science, 12*, 151–154. (p. 124)

Rosenthal, R., & Jacobson, L. (1968). *Pygmalion in the classroom: Teacher expectation and pupils' intellectual development*. New York: Holt, Rinehart & Winston. (p. 122)

Rosenzweig, M. R. (1972). Cognitive dissonance. *American Psychologist, 27*, 769. (p. 148)

Ross, C. (1979, February 12). Rejected. *New West*, pp. 39–43. (p. 111)

Ross, L. (1977). The intuitive psychologist and his shortcomings: Distortions in the attribution process. In L. Berkowitz (Ed.), *Advances in experimental social psychology* (Vol. 10). New York: Academic Press. (p. 88)

Ross, L. (1981). The "intuitive scientist" formulation and its developmental implications. In J. H. Havell & L. Ross (Eds.), *Social cognitive development: Frontiers and possible futures*. Cambridge, England: Cambridge University Press. (pp. 40, 95)

Ross, L. (1988). Situationist perspectives on the obedience experiments. Review of A. G. Miller's *The obedience experiments. Contemporary Psychology, 33*, 101–104. (p. 215)

Ross, L., Amabile, T. M., & Steinmetz, J. L. (1977). Social roles, social control, and biases in social-perception processes. *Journal of Personality and Social Psychology, 35*, 485–494. (pp. 89–90)

Ross, L., & Anderson, C. A. (1982). Shortcomings in the attribution process: On the origins and maintenance of erroneous social assessments. In D. Kahneman, P. Slovic, & A. Tversky (Eds.), *Judgment under uncertainty: Heuristics and biases*. New York: Cambridge University Press. (p. 101)

Ross, L., & Lepper, M. R. (1980). The perseverance of beliefs: Empirical and normative considerations. In R. A. Shweder (Ed.), *New directions for methodology of behavioral science: Fallible judgment in behavioral research*. San Francisco: Jossey-Bass. (p. 102)

Ross, L., & Ward, A. (1995). Psychological barriers to dispute resolution. In M. P. Zanna (Ed.), *Advances in experimental social psychology*, vol. 27. San Diego, CA: Academic Press. (pp. 556, 557)

Ross, L., & Ward, A. (1996). Naive realism in everyday life: Implications for social conflict and misunderstanding. In T. Brown, E. Reed, & E. Turiel (Eds.), *Values and knowledge*. Hillsdale, NJ: Erlbaum. (p. 528)

Ross, M., & Buehler, R. (1994). Creative remembering. In U. Neisser & R. Fivush (Eds.), *The remembering self*. New York: Cambridge University Press. (p. 103)

Ross, M., & Fletcher, G. J. O. (1985). Attribution and social perception. In G. Lindzey & E. Aronson (Eds.), *The Handbook of Social Psychology*, 3rd ed. New York: Random House. (p. 119)

Ross, M., McFarland, C., & Fletcher, G. J. O. (1981). The effect of attitude on the recall of personal histories. *Journal of Personality and Social Psychology, 40*, 627–634. (p. 104)

Ross, M., & Newby-Clark, I. R. (1998). Construing the past and future. *Social Cognition, 16*, 133–150. (p. 109)

Ross, M., & Sicoly, F. (1979). Egocentric biases in availability and attribution. *Journal of Personality and Social Psychology, 37*, 322–336. (pp. 67, 73)

Ross, M., Thibaut, J., & Evenbeck, S. (1971). Some determinants of the intensity of social protest. *Journal of Experimental Social Psychology, 7*, 401–418. (p. 531)

Rossi, A. S., & Rossi, P. H. (1990). *Of human bonding: Parent-child relations across the life course.* Hawthorne, NY: Aldine de Gruyter. (p. 183)

Roszell, P., Kennedy, D., & Grabb, E. (1990). Physical attractiveness and income attainment among Canadians. *Journal of Psychology*, **123**, 547–559. (p. 436)

Rotenberg, K. J. (1997). Loneliness and the perception of the exchange of disclosures. *Journal of Social and Clinical Psychology*, **16**, 259–276. (p. 582)

Rotenberg, K. J., Gruman, J. A., & Ariganello, M. (2002). Behavioral confirmation of the loneliness stereotype. *Basic and Applied Social Psychology*, **24**, 81–89. (pp. 124–125)

Rothbart, M., & Birrell, P. (1977). Attitude and perception of faces. *Journal of Research Personality*, **11**, 209–215. (pp. 100–101)

Rothbart, M., Fulero, S., Jensen, C., Howard, J., & Birrell, P. (1978). From individual to group impressions: Availability heuristics in stereotype formation. *Journal of Experimental Social Psychology*, **14**, 237–255. (pp. 363–364)

Rothbart, M., & Taylor, M. (1992). Social categories and social reality. In G. R. Semin & K. Fielder (Eds.), *Language, interaction and social cognition.* London: Sage. (p. 241)

Rothman, A. J., & Salovey, P. (1997). Shaping perceptions to motivate healthy behavior: The role of message framing. *Psychological Bulletin*, **121**, 3–19. (p. 588)

Rotter, J. (1973). Internal-external locus of control scale. In J. P. Robinson & R. P. Shaver (Eds.), *Measures of social psychological attitudes.* Ann Arbor, MI: Institute for Social Research. (p. 58)

Rotton, J., & Frey, J. (1985). Air pollution, weather, and violent crimes: Concomitant time-series analysis of archival data. *Journal of Personality and Social Psychology*, **49**, 1207–1220. (pp. 394, 395)

Rotundo, M., Nguyen, D-H., & Sackett, P. R. (2001). A meta-analytic review of gender differences in perceptions of sexual harrassment. *Journal of Applied Psychology*, **86**, 914–922. (p. 85)

Rouhana, N. N., & Bar-Tal, D. (1998). Psychological dynamics of intractable ethnonational conflicts: The Israeli-Palestinian case. *American Psychologist*, **53**, 761–770. (pp. 534–535)

Rowe, D. (1994). *The limits of family influence: Genes, experience, and behavior.* New York: Guilford Press. (p. 199)

Rowe, D. C., Almeida, D. M., & Jacobson, K. C. (1999). School context and genetic influences on aggression in adolescence. *Psychological Science*, **10**, 277–280. (p. 384)

Rowe, D. C., Vazsonyi, A. T., & Flannery, D. J. (1994). No more than skin deep: Ethnic and racial similarity in developmental process. *Psychological Review*, **101**, 396–413. (p. 33)

Ruback, R. B., Carr, T. S., & Hoper, C. H. (1986). Perceived control in prison: Its relation to reported crowding, stress, and symptoms. *Journal of Applied Social Psychology*, **16**, 375–386. (pp. 60–61)

Rubin, A. (2003, April 16). War fans young Arabs' anger. *Los Angeles Times.* (www.latimes.com) (p. 545)

Rubin, J. Z. (1986). Can we negotiate with terrorists: Some answers from psychology. Paper presented at the American Psychological Association convention. (p. 390)

Rubin, L. B. (1985). *Just friends: The role of friendship in our lives.* New York: Harper & Row. (p. 184)

Rubin, R. B. (1981). Ideal traits and terms of address for male and female college professors. *Journal of Personality and Social Psychology*, **41**, 966–974. (p. 560)

Rubin, Z. (1973). *Liking and loving: An invitation to social psychology.* New York: Holt, Rinehart and Winston. (p. 471)

Ruiter, R. A. C., Abraham, C., & Kok, G. (2001). Scary warnings and rational precautions: A review of the psychology of fear appeals. *Psychology and Health*, **16**, 613–630. (p. 258)

Ruiter, R. A. C., Kok, G., Verplanken, B., & Brug, J. (2001). Evoked fear and effects of appeals on attitudes to performing breast self-examination: An information-processing perspective. *Health Education Research*, **16**, 307–319. (p. 258)

Rule, B. G., Taylor, B. R., & Dobbs, A. R. (1987). Priming effects of heat on aggressive thoughts. *Social Cognition*, **5**, 131–143. (p. 394)

Rusbult, C. E. (1980). Commitment and satisfaction in romantic associations: A test of the investment model. *Journal of Experimental Social Psychology*, **16**, 172–186. (p. 450)

Rusbult, C. E., Johnson, D. J., & Morrow, G. D. (1986). Impact of couple patterns of problem solving on distress and nondistress in dating relationships. *Journal of Personality and Social Psychology*, **50**, 744–753. (pp. 469–470)

Rusbult, C. E., Martz, J. M., & Agnew, C. R. (1998). The investment model scale: Measuring commitment level, satisfaction level, quality of alternatives, and investment size. *Personal Relationships*, **5**, 357–391. (pp. 469–470)

Rusbult, C. E., Morrow, G. D., & Johnson, D. J. (1987). Self-esteem and problem-solving behaviour in close relationships. *British Journal of Social Psychology*, **26**, 293–303. (pp. 469–470)

Rusbult, C. E., Olsen, N., Davis, J. L., & Hannon, P. A. (2001). Commitment and relationship maintenance mechanisms. In J. Harvey & A. Wenzel (Eds.), *Close romantic relationships: Maintenance and enhancement.* Mahwah, NJ: Erlbaum. (p. 470)

Rushton, J. P. (1975). Generosity in children: Immediate and long-term effects of modeling, preaching, and moral judgment. *Journal of Personality and Social Psychology*, **31**, 459–466. (p. 503)

Rushton, J. P. (1976). Socialization and the altruistic behavior of children. *Psychological Bulletin*, **83**, 898–913. (p. 481)

Rushton, J. P. (1991). Is altruism innate? *Psychological Inquiry*, **2**, 141–143. (p. 488)

Rushton, J. P., Brainerd, C. J., & Pressley, M. (1983). Behavioral development and construct validity: The principle of aggregation. *Psychological Bulletin*, **94**, 18–38. (p. 236)

Rushton, J. P., & Campbell, A. C. (1977). Modeling, vicarious reinforcement and extraversion on blood donating in adults: Immediate and long-term effects. *European Journal of Social Psychology, 7,* 297–306. (p. 503)

Rushton, J. P., Chrisjohn, R. D., & Fekken, G. C. (1981). The altruistic personality and the self-report altruism scale. *Personality and Individual Differences, 2,* 293–302. (p. 506)

Rushton, J. P., Fulker, D. W., Neale, M. C., Nias, D. K. B., & Eysenck, H. J. (1986). Altruism and aggression: The heritability of individual differences. *Journal of Personality and Social Psychology, 50,* 1192–1198. (p. 384)

Russell, B. (1930/1980). *The conquest of happiness.* London: Unwin Paperbacks. (p. 432)

Russell, G. W. (1983). Psychological issues in sports aggression. In J. H. Goldstein (Ed.), *Sports violence.* New York: Springer-Verlag. (p. 416)

Rutkowski, G. K., Gruder, C. L., & Romer, D. (1983). Group cohesiveness, social norms, and bystander intervention. *Journal of Personality and Social Psychology, 44,* 545–552. (p. 502)

Ruvolo, A., & Markus, H. (1992). Possible selves and performance: The power of self-relevant imagery. *Social Cognition, 9,* 95–124. (p. 57)

Ruzzene, M., & Noller, P. (1986). Feedback motivation and reactions to personality interpretations that differ in favorability and accuracy. *Journal of Personality and Social Psychology, 51,* 1293–1299. (p. 80)

Ryan, R. (1999, February 2). Quoted by A. Kohn, In pursuit of affluence, at a high price. *New York Times* (via www.nytimes.com). (pp. 652, 654)

Ryckman, R. M., Robbins, M. A., Kaczor, L. M., & Gold, J. A. (1989). Male and female raters' stereotyping of male and female physiques. *Personality and Social Psychology Bulletin, 15,* 244–251. (p. 28)

Ryff, C. D., & Singer, B. (2000). Interpersonal flourishing: A positive health agenda for the new millennium. *Personality and Social Psychology Review, 4,* 30–44. (p. 597)

Saad, L. (2002, November 21). Most smokers wish they could quit. Gallup News Service (www.gallup.com/poll/releases/pr021121.asp). (p. 151)

Saad, L. (2003, April 22). Giving global warming the cold shoulder. The Gallup Organization (www.gallup.com). (p. 643)

Saad, L., & McAneny, L. (1994, April). Most Americans think religion losing clout in the 1990's. *Gallup Poll Monthly,* pp. 2–4. (p. 408)

Saal, F. E., Johnson, C. B., & Weber, N. (1989). Friendly or sexy? It may depend on whom you ask. *Psychology of Women Quarterly, 13,* 263–276. (p. 85)

Sabini, J., & Silver, M. (1982). *Moralities of everyday life.* New York: Oxford University Press. (pp. 225)

Sacco, W. P., & Dunn, V. K. (1990). Effect of actor depression on observer attributions: Existence and impact of negative attributions toward the depressed. *Journal of Personality and Social Psychology, 59,* 517–524. (p. 579)

Sack, K., & Elder, J. (2000, July 11). Poll finds optimistic outlook but enduring racial division. *New York Times* (www.nytimes.com). (p. 352)

Sacks, C. H., & Bugental, D. P. (1987). Attributions as moderators of affective and behavioral responses to social failure. *Journal of Personality and Social Psychology, 53,* 939–947. (p. 580)

Sagarin, B. J., Cialdini, R. B., Rice, W. E., & Serna, S. B. (2002). Dispelling the illusion of invulnerability: The motivations and mechanisms of resistance to persuasion. *Journal of Personality and Social Psychology, 83,* 526–541. (p. 277)

Sagarin, B. J., Rhoads, K. v. L., & Cialdini, R. B. (1998). Deceiver's distrust: Denigration as a consequence of undiscovered deception. *Personality and Social Psychology Bulletin, 24,* 1167–1176. (p. 72)

Saks, M. J. (1974). Ignorance of science is no excuse. *Trial, 10*(6), 18–20. (p. 634)

Saks, M. J. (1977). *Jury verdicts.* Lexington, MA: Heath. (p. 634)

Saks, M. J. (1996). The smaller the jury, the greater the unpredictability. *Judicature, 79,* 263–265. (p. 634)

Saks, M. J. (1998). What do jury experiments tell us about how juries (should) make decisions? *Southern California Interdisciplinary Law Journal, 6,* 1–53. (p. 634)

Saks, M. J., & Hastie, R. (1978). *Social psychology in court.* New York: Van Nostrand Reinhold. (pp. 606, 619, 629)

Saks, M. J., & Marti, M. W. (1997). A meta-analysis of the effects of jury size. *Law and Human Behavior, 21,* 451–467. (p. 634)

Sakurai, M. M. (1975). Small group cohesiveness and detrimental conformity. *Sociometry, 38,* 340–357. (p. 231)

Sales, S. M. (1972). Economic threat as a determinant of conversion rates in authoritarian and nonauthoritarian churches. *Journal of Personality and Social Psychology, 23,* 420–428. (p. 275)

Sales, S. M. (1973). Threat as a factor in authoritarianism: An analysis of archival data. *Journal of Personality & Social Psychology, 28,* 44–57. (p. 345)

Salmivalli, C., Kaukiainen, A., Kaistaniemi, L., & Lagerspetz, K. M. J. (1999). Self-evaluated self-esteem, peer-evaluated self-esteem, and defensive egotism as predictors of adolescents' participation in bullying situations. *Personality and Social Psychology Bulletin, 25,* 1268–1278. (p. 66)

Salovey, P., Mayer, J. D., & Rosenhan, D. L. (1991). Mood and healing: Mood as a motivator of helping and helping as a regulator of mood. In M. S. Clark (Ed.), *Prosocial behavior.* Newbury Park, CA: Sage. (p. 482)

Salovey, P., Schneider, T. R., & Apanovitch, A. M. (2002). Message framing in the prevention and early detection of illness. In J. P. Dillard & M. Pfau (Eds.), *The persuasion handbook: Theory and practice.* Thousand Oaks, CA: Sage. (p. 588)

Saltzstein, H. D., & Sandberg, L. (1979). Indirect social influence: Change in judgmental processor anticipatory conformity. *Journal of Experimental Social Psychology, 15,* 209–216. (p. 232)

Sampson, E. E. (1975). On justice as equality. *Journal of Social Issues, 31*(3), 45–64. (pp. 531–532)

Sanbonmatsu, D. M., Akimoto, S. A., & Gibson, B. D. (1994). Stereotype-based blocking in social explanation.

Personality and Social Psychology Bulletin, 20, 71–81. (pp. 368–369)

Sancton, T. 1997, October 13). The dossier on Diana's crash. *Time,* pp. 50–56. (p. 499)

Sande, G. N., Goethals, G. R., & Radloff, C. E. (1988). Perceiving one's own traits and others': The multifaceted self. *Journal of Personality and Social Psychology, 54,* 13–20. (p. 94)

Sanders, G. S. (1981). Driven by distraction: An integrative review of social facilitation and theory and research. *Journal of Experimental Social Psychology, 17,* 227–251. *(a)* (p. 291)

Sanders, G. S. (1981). Toward a comprehensive account of social facilitation: Distraction/conflict does not mean theoretical conflict. *Journal of Experimental Social Psychology, 17,* 262–265. *(b)* (p. 291)

Sanders, G. S., Baron, R. S., & Moore, D. L. (1978). Distraction and social comparison as mediators of social facilitation effects. *Journal of Experimental Social Psychology, 14,* 291–303. (p. 291)

Sanderson, C. A., & Cantor, N. (2001). The association of intimacy goals and marital satisfaction: A test of four mediational hypotheses. *Personality and Social Psychology Bulletin, 27,* 1567–1577. (p. 464)

Sanislow, C. A., III., Perkins, D. V., & Balogh, D. W. (1989). Mood induction, interpersonal perceptions, and rejection in the roommates of depressed, nondepressed-disturbed, and normal college students. *Journal of Social and Clinical Psychology, 8,* 345–358. (p. 579)

Sanitioso, R., Kunda, Z., & Fong, G. T. (1990). Motivated recruitment of autobiographical memories. *Journal of Personality and Social Psychology, 59,* 229–241. (p. 74)

Sanna, L. J., Parks, C. D., Meier, S., Chang, E. C., Kassin, B. R., Lechter, J. L., Turley-Ames, K. J., & Miyake, T. M. (2003). A game of inches: Spontaneous use of counterfactuals by broadcasters during major league baseball playoffs. *Journal of Applied Social Psychology, 33,* 455–475. (p. 116)

Sansone, C. (1986). A question of competence: The effects of competence and task feedback on intrinsic interest.

Journal of Personality and Social Psychology, 51, 918–931. (p. 160)

Sapadin, L. A. (1988). Friendship and gender: Perspectives of professional men and women. *Journal of Social and Personal Relationships, 5,* 387–403. (p. 184)

Sargent, J. D., Heatherton, T. F., Ahrens, M. B. (2002). Adolescent exposure to extremely violent movies. *Journal of Adolescent Health, 31,* 449–454. (p. 409)

Sartre, J-P. (1946/1948). *Anti-Semite and Jew.* New York: Schocken Books. (p. 4)

Sato, K. (1987). Distribution of the cost of maintaining common resources. *Journal of Experimental Social Psychology, 23,* 19–31. (p. 524)

Satterfield, A. T., & Muehlenhard, C. L. (1997). Shaken confidence: The effects of an authority figure's flirtatiousness on women's and men's self-rated creativity. *Psychology of Women Quarterly, 21,* 395–416. (p. 436)

Saucier, D. A., & Miller, C. T. (2003). The persuasiveness of racial arguments as a subtle measure of racism. *Personality and Social Psychology Bulletin, 29,* 1303–1315. (p. 100)

Savitsky, K., Epley, N., & Gilovich, T. (2001). Do others judge us as harshly as we think? Overestimating the impact of our failures, shortcomings, and mishaps. *Journal of Personality and Social Psychology, 81,* 44–56. (p. 40)

Savitsky, K., Medvec, V. H., & Gilovich, T. (1997). Remembering and regretting: The Zeigarnik effect and the cognitive availability of regrettable actions and inactions. *Personality and Social Psychology Bulletin, 23,* 248–257. (p. 116)

Sax, L. J., Lindholm, J. A., Astin, A. W., Korn, W. S., & Mahoney, K. M. (2002). *The American freshman: National norms for Fall, 2002.* Los Angeles: Cooperative Institutional Research Program, UCLA. (pp. 183, 188, 197, 247, 341)

Scarr, S. (1988). Race and gender as psychological variables: Social and ethical issues. *American Psychologist, 43,* 56–59. (p. 182)

Schachter, S. (1951). Deviation, rejection and communication. *Journal of Abnormal and Social Psychology, 46,* 190–207. (p. 234)

Schachter, S., & Singer, J. E. (1962). Cognitive, social and physiological determinants of emotional state. *Psychological Review, 69,* 379–399. (pp. 396, 454)

Schacter, D., Kaszniak, A., & Kihlstrom, J. (1991). Models of memory and the understanding of memory disorders. In T. Yanagihara & R. Petersen (Eds.), *Memory disorders: Research and clinical practice.* New York: Marcel Dekker. (p. 58)

Schafer, R. B., & Keith, P. M. (1980). Equity and depression among married couples. *Social Psychology Quarterly, 43,* 430–435. (p. 462)

Schaffner, P. E. (1985). Specious learning about reward and punishment. *Journal of Personality and Social Psychology, 48,* 1377–1386. (p. 118)

Schaffner, P. E., Wandersman, A., & Stang, D. (1981). Candidate name exposure and voting: Two field studies. *Basic and Applied Social Psychology, 2,* 195–203. (p. 431)

Schaller, M., & Cialdini, R. B. (1988). The economics of empathic helping: Support for a mood management motive. *Journal of Experimental Social Psychology, 24,* 163–181. (p. 491)

Scheier, M. F., & Carver, C. S. (1992). Effects of optimism on psychological and physical well-being: Theoretical overview and empirical update. *Cognitive Therapy and Research, 16,* 201–228. (p. 590)

Scheier, M. F., Carver, C. S., & Bridges, M. W. (2000). Optimism, pessimism, and psychological well-being. In E. C. Chang (Ed.), *Optimism and pessimism.* Washington, DC: APA Books. (p. 590)

Schein, E. H. (1956). The Chinese indoctrination program for prisoners of war: A study of attempted brainwashing. *Psychiatry, 19,* 149–172. (p. 150)

Schiffenbauer, A., & Schiavo, R. S. (1976). Physical distance and attraction: An intensification effect. *Journal of Experimental Social Psychology, 12,* 274–282. (p. 289)

Schiffmann, W. (1999, February 4). An heiress abducted: Patty Hearst, 25 years after her kidnapping. Associated Press (via www.abcnews.com). (p. 179)

Schimel, J., Arndt, J., Pyszczynski, T., & Greenberg, J. (2001). Being accepted for who we are: Evidence that social validation of the intrinsic self reduces general defensiveness. *Journal of Personality and Social Psychology*, **80**, 35–52. (p. 66)

Schimel, J., Pyszczynski, T., Greenberg, J., O'Mahen, H., Arndt, J. (2000). Running from the shadow: Psychological distancing from others to deny characteristics people fear in themselves. *Journal of Personality & Social Psychology*, **78**, 446–462. (p. 446)

Schimel, J., Simon, L., Greenberg, J., Pyszczynski, T., Solomon, S., & Waxmonsky, J. (1999). Stereotypes and terror management: Evidence that mortality salience enhances stereotypic thinking and preferences. *Journal of Personality and Social Psychology*, **77**, 905–926. (p. 355)

Schkade, D. A., & Kahneman, D. (1998). Does living in California make people happy? A focusing illusion in judgments of life satisfaction. *Psychological Science*, **9**, 340–346. (pp. 54–55)

Schkade, D. A., & Sunstein, C. R. (2003, June 11). Judging by where you sit. *New York Times* (www.nytimes.com). (p. 306)

Schlenker, B. R. (1976). Egocentric perceptions in cooperative groups: A conceptualization and research review. Final Report, Office of Naval Research Grant NR 170-797. (pp. 75–76)

Schlenker, B. R., & Leary, M. R. (1982). Social anxiety and self-presentation: A conceptualization and model. *Psychological Bulletin*, **92**, 641–669. *(b)* (p. 583)

Schlenker, B. R., & Leary, M. R. (1985). Social anxiety and communication about the self. *Journal of Language and Social Psychology*, **4**, 171–192. (p. 583)

Schlenker, B. R., & Miller, R. S. (1977). Egocentrism in groups: Self-serving biases or logical information processing? *Journal of Personality and Social Psychology*, **35**, 755–764. *(b)* (pp. 75–76)

Schlenker, B. R., & Miller, R. S. (1977). Group cohesiveness as a determinant of egocentric perceptions in cooperative groups. *Human Relations*, **30**, 1039–1055. *(a)* (pp. 75–76)

Schlenker, B. R., Phillips, S. T., Boniecki, K. A., & Schlenker, D. R. (1995). Championship pressures: Choking or triumphing in one's own territory? *Journal of Personality and Social Psychology*, **68**, 632–643. (p. 289)

Schlenker, B. R., & Weigold, M. F. (1992). Interpersonal processes involving impression regulation and management. *Annual Review of Psychology*, **43**, 133–168. (p. 79)

Schlenker, B. R., Weigold, M. F., & Hallam, J. R. (1990). Self-serving attributions in social context: Effects of self-esteem and social pressure. *Journal of Personality and Social Psychology*, **58**, 855–863. (p. 75)

Schlesinger, A., Jr. (1949). The statistical soldier. *Partisan Review*, **16**, 852–856. (p. 17)

Schlesinger, A., Jr. (1991, July 8). The cult of ethnicity, good and bad. *Time*, p. 21. (pp. 170, 561–562)

Schlosser, E. (2003, March 10). Empire of the obscene. *New Yorker*, pp. 61–71. (p. 398)

Schmader, T., & Johns, M. (2003). Converging evidence that stereotype threat reduces working memory capacity. *Journal of Personality and Social Psychology*, **85**, 440–451. (p. 372)

Schmidt, P. J., Nieman, L. K., Danaceau, M. A., Adams, L. F., & Rubinow, D. R. (1998). Differential behavioral effects of gonadal steroids in women with and in those without premenstrual syndrome. *New England Journal of Medicine*, **338**, 209–216. (p. 586)

Schmitt, D. P. (2003). Universal sex differences in the desire for sexual variety; tests from 52 nations, 6 continents, and 13 islands. *Journal of Personality and Social Psychology*, **85**, 85–104. (p. 188)

Schmuck, P., Kasser, T., & Ryan, R. M. (2000). Intrinsic and extrinsic goals: Their structure and relationship to well-being in German and U.S. college students. *Social Indicators Research*, **50**, 225–241. (p. 654)

Schnall, S., & Laird, J. D. (2003). Keep smiling: Enduring effects of facial expressions and postures on emotional experience and memory. *Cognition and Emotion*, **17**, 787–797. (p. 157)

Schneider, M. E., Major, B., Luhtanen, R., & Crocker, J. (1996). Social stigma and the potential costs of assumptive help. *Personality and Social Psychology Bulletin*, **22**, 201–209. (p. 484)

Schneider, P. (2000, February 13). Saving Konrad Latte. *New York Times Magazine* (www.nytimes.com). (p. 476)

Schneider, T. R., Salovey, P., Pallonen, U., Mundorf, N., Smith, N. F., & Steward, W. T. (2000). Visual and auditory message framing effects on tobacco smoking. *Journal of Applied Social Psychology*, in press. (p. 588)

Schoeneman, T. J. (1994). Individualism. In V. S. Ramachandran (Ed.), *Encyclopedia of Human Behavior*. San Diego, CA: Academic Press. (p. 46)

Schoenfeld, B. (1995, May 14). The loneliness of being white. *New York Times Magazine*, 34–37. (p. 336)

Schofield, J. (1982). *Black and white in school: Trust, tension, or tolerance?* New York: Praeger. (p. 540)

Schofield, J. W. (1986). Causes and consequences of the colorblind perspective. In J. F. Dovidio & S. L. Gaertner (Eds.), *Prejudice, discrimination, and racism*. Orlando, FL: Academic Press. (p. 540)

Schooler, J. W. (2002). Verbalization produces a transfer inappropriate processing shift. *Applied Cognitive Psychology*, **16**, 989–997. (p. 616)

Schor, J. B. (1998). *The overworked American*. New York: Basic Books. (pp. 649, 655, 656, 658)

Schroeder, D. A., Dovidio, J. F., Sibicky, M. E., Matthews, L. L., & Allen, J. L. (1988). Empathic concern and helping behavior: Egoism or altruism: *Journal of Experimental Social Psychology*, **24**, 333–353. (p. 492)

Schulz, J. W., & Pruitt, D. G. (1978). The effects of mutual concern on joint welfare. *Journal of Experimental Social Psychology*, **14**, 480–492. (pp. 556–557)

Schulz, R., & Decker, S. (1985). Long-term adjustment to physical disability: The role of social support, perceived control, and self-blame. *Journal of Personality and Social Psychology*, **48**, 1162–1172. (p. 657)

Schulz-Hardt, S., Frey, D., Luthgens, C., & Moscovici, S. (2000). Biased information search in group decision making. *Journal of Personality and Social Psychology, 78,* 655–669. (p. 315)

Schuman, H., & Kalton, G. (1985). Survey methods. In G. Lindzey & E. Aronson (Eds.), *Handbook of Social Psychology,* Vol. 1. Hillsdale, NJ: Erlbaum. (p. 26)

Schuman, H., & Ludwig, J. (1983). The norm of even-handedness in surveys as in life. *American Sociological Review, 48,* 112–120. (p. 26)

Schuman, H., & Scott, J. (1987). Problems in the use of survey questions to measure public opinion. *Science, 236,* 957–959. (p. 26)

Schuman, H., & Scott, J. (1989). Generations and collective memories. *American Sociological Review, 54,* 359–381. (p. 268)

Schutte, J. W., & Hosch, H. M. (1997). Gender differences in sexual assault verdicts. *Journal of Social Behavior and Personality, 12,* 759–772. (p. 85)

Schwartz, B. (2000). Self-determination: The tyranny of freedom. *American Psychologist, 55,* 79–88. (p. 61)

Schwartz, B. (2004). *The tyranny of choice.* New York: Ecco/HarperCollins. (p. 61)

Schwartz, S. H. (1975). The justice of need and the activation of humanitarian norms. *Journal of Social Issues, 31*(3), 111–136. (p. 485)

Schwartz, S. H., & Gottlieb, A. (1981). Participants' post-experimental reactions and the ethics of bystander research. *Journal of Experimental Social Psychology, 17,* 396–407. (p. 502)

Schwarz, N., & Clore, G. L. (1983). Mood, misattribution, and judgments of well-being: Informative and directive functions of affective states. *Journal of Personality and Social Psychology, 45,* 513–523. (p. 51)

Schwarz, N., & Kurz, E. (1989). What's in a picture? The impact of face-ism on trait attribution. *European Journal of Social Psychology, 19,* 311–316. (pp. 348–349)

Schwarz, N., Bless, H., & Bohner, G. (1991). Mood and persuasion: Affective states influence the processing of persuasive communications. In M. Zanna (Ed.), *Advances in experimental social*

psychology, vol. 24. New York: Academic Press. (p. 257)

Schwarz, N., Strack, F., Kommer, D., & Wagner, D. (1987). Soccer, rooms, and the quality of your life: Mood effects on judgments of satisfaction with life in general and with specific domains. *Journal of Applied Social Psychology, 17,* 69–79. (p. 119)

Schweinle, W. E., Ickes, W., Bernstein, I. H. (2002). Empathic inaccuracy in husband to wife aggression: The overattribution bias. *Personal Relationships, 9,* 141–159. (pp. 90–91)

Schweitzer, K., Zillmann, D., Weaver, J. B., & Luttrell, E. S. (1992, Spring). Perception of threatening events in the emotional aftermath of a televised college football game. *Journal of Broadcasting and Electronic Media,* pp. 75–82. (p. 119)

Scott, J. P., & Marston, M. V. (1953). Nonadaptive behavior resulting from a series of defeats in fighting mice. *Journal of Abnormal and Social Psychology, 48,* 417–428. (p. 389)

Scottish Life (2001, Winter). Isle of Muck without a crime for decades. P. 11. (p. 526)

Sears, D. O. (1979). Life stage effects upon attitude change, especially among the elderly. Manuscript prepared for Workshop on the Elderly of the Future, Committee on Aging, National Research Council, Annapolis, MD, May 3–5. (p. 267)

Sears, D. O. (1986). College sophomores in the laboratory: Influences of a narrow data base on social psychology's view of human nature. *Journal of Personality and Social Psychology, 51,* 515–530. (p. 267)

Sedikides, C. (1993). Assessment, enhancement, and verification determinants of the self-evaluation process. *Journal of Personality and Social Psychology, 65,* 317–338. (p. 74)

Sedikides, C., & Anderson, C. A. (1992). Causal explanations of defection: A knowledge structure approach. *Personality and Social Psychology Bulletin, 18,* 420–429. (p. 86)

Sedikides, C., Gaertner, L., & Toguchi, Y. (2003). Pancultural self-enhancement. *Journal of Personality and Social Psychology, 84,* 60–79. (p. 80)

Segal, H. A. (1954). Initial psychiatric findings of recently repatriated prisoners of war. *American Journal of Psychiatry, 61,* 358–363. (p. 150)

Segal, N. L. (1984). Cooperation, competition, and altruism within twin sets: A reappraisal. *Ethology and Sociobiology, 5,* 163–177. (p. 487)

Segal, N. L., & Hershberger, S. L. (1999). Cooperation and competition between twins: Findings from a Prisoner's Dilemma game. *Evolution and Human Behavior, 20,* 29–51. (p. 487)

Segall, M. H., Dasen, P. R., Berry, J. W., & Poortinga, Y. H. (1990). *Human behavior in global perspective: An introduction to cross-cultural psychology.* New York: Pergamon. (p. 188)

Segerstrom, S. C. (2001). Optimism and attentional bias for negative and positive stimuli. *Personality and Social Psychology Bulletin, 27,* 1334–1343. (p. 71)

Segerstrom, S. C., McCarthy, W. J., Caskey, N. H., Gross, T. M., & Jarvik, M. E. (1993). Optimistic bias among cigarette smokers. *Journal of Applied Social Psychology, 23,* 1606–1618. (p. 591)

Seibt, B., & Forster, J. (2004). Stereotype threat and performance: How self-stereotypes influence processing by inducing regulatory foci. *Journal of Personality and Social Psychology,* in press. (p. 372)

Selby, J. W., Calhoun, L. G., & Brock, T. A. (1977). Sex differences in the social perception of rape victims. *Personality and Social Psychology Bulletin, 3,* 412–415. (p. 620)

Seligman, C., Fazio, R. H., & Zanna, M. P. (1980). Effects of salience of extrinsic rewards on liking and loving. *Journal of Personality and Social Psychology, 38,* 453–460. (p. 448)

Seligman, M. (1994). *What You Can Change and What You Can't.* New York: Knopf. (p. 23)

Seligman, M. E. P. (1975). *Helplessness: On depression, development and death.* San Francisco: W. H. Freeman. (p. 60)

Seligman, M. E. P. (1989). Explanatory style: Predicting depression, achievement, and health. In M. D. Yapko (Ed.), *Brief therapy approaches to treating anxiety and depression.* New York: Brunner/Mazel. (p. 653)

Seligman, M. E. P. (1991). *Learned optimism.* New York: Knopf. (pp. 60, 580, 581)

Seligman, M. E. P. (1992). Power and powerlessness: Comments on "Cognates of personal control." *Applied & Preventive Psychology, 1,* 119–120. (p. 580)

Seligman, M. E. P. (1998). The prediction and prevention of depression. In D. K. Routh & R. J. DeRubeis (Eds.), *The science of clinical psychology: Accomplishments and future directions.* Washington, DC: American Psychological Association. (p. 581)

Seligman, M. E. P. (2002). *Authentic happiness: Using the new positive psychology to realize your potential for lasting fulfillment.* New York: Free Press. (p. 581)

Seligman, M. E. P., Nolen-Hoeksema, S., Thornton, N., & Thornton, K. M. (1990). Explanatory style as a mechanism of disappointing athletic performance. *Psychological Science, 1,* 143–146. (p. 59)

Seligman, M. E. P., & Schulman, P. (1986). Explanatory style as a predictor of productivity and quitting among life insurance sales agents. *Journal of Personality and Social Psychology, 50,* 832–838. (p. 59)

Semin, G. R., & De Poot, C. J. (1997). Bringing partiality to light: Question wording and choice as indicators of bias. *Social Cognition, 15,* 91–106. (p. 571)

Sengupta, S. (2001, October 10). Sept. 11 attack narrows the racial divide. *New York Times* (www.nytimes.com). (p. 543)

Sengupta, S. (2003, May 27). Congo war toll soars as U.N. pleads for aid. *New York Times* (www.nytimes.com). (p. 379)

Sentyrz, S. M., & Bushman, B. J. (1998). Mirror, mirror, on the wall, who's the thinnest one of all? Effects of self-awareness on consumption of fatty, reduced-fat, and fat-free products. *Journal of Applied Psychology, 83,* 944–949. (p. 302)

Seta, C. E., & Seta, J. J. (1992). Increments and decrements in mean arterial pressure levels as a function of audience composition: An averaging and summation analysis. *Personality and Social Psychology Bulletin, 18,* 173–181. (p. 291)

Seta, J. J. (1982). The impact of comparison processes on coactors' task performance. *Journal of Personality and Social Psychology, 42,* 281–291. (p. 290)

Shackelford, T. K., & Larsen, R. J. (1997). Facial asymmetry as an indicator of psychological, emotional, and physiological distress. *Journal of Personality and Social Psychology, 72,* 456–466. (p. 437)

Shaffer, D. R., Pegalis, L. J., & Bazzini, D. G. (1996). When boy meets girls (revisited): Gender, gender-role orientation, and prospect of future interaction as determinants of self-disclosure among same- and opposite-sex acquaintances. *Personality and Social Psychology Bulletin, 22,* 495–506. (pp. 462, 463)

Sharan, S., & Sharan, Y. (1976). *Small group teaching.* Englewood Cliffs, NJ: Educational Technology. (p. 549)

Sharan, Y., & Sharan, S. (1994). Group investigation in the cooperative classroom. In S. Sharan (Ed.), *Handbook of cooperative learning methods.* Westport, CT: Greenwood Press. (p. 549)

Sharma, N. (1981). Some aspect of attitude and behaviour of mothers. *Indian Psychological Review, 20,* 35–42. (p. 336)

Shaver, P. R., & Hazan, C. (1993). Adult romantic attachment: Theory and evidence. In D. Perlman & W. Jones (Eds.), *Advances in personal relationships,* vol. 4. Greenwich, CT: JAI. (p. 459)

Shaver, P. R., & Hazan, C. (1994). Attachment. In A. L. Weber & J. H. Harvey (Eds.), *Perspectives on close relationships.* Boston: Allyn & Bacon. (p. 459)

Shaver, P., Hazan, C., & Bradshaw, D. (1988). Love as attachment: The integration of three behavioral systems. In R. J. Sternberg & M. L. Barnes (Eds.), *The psychology of love.* New Haven, CT: Yale University Press. (p. 459)

Shavitt, S. (1990). The role of attitude objects in attitude functions. *Journal of Experimental Social Psychology, 26,* 124–148. (p. 249)

Shaw, J. S., III. (1996). Increases in eyewitness confidence resulting from postevent questioning. *Journal of Experimental Psychology: Applied, 2,* 126–146. (p. 614)

Shaw, M. E. (1981). *Group dynamics: The psychology of small group behavior.* New York: McGraw-Hill. (p. 286)

Sheldon, K. M., Elliot, A. J., Youngmee, K., & Kasser, T. (2001). What is satisfying about satisfying events? Testing 10 candidate psychological needs. *Journal of Personality and Social Psychology, 80,* 325–339. (p. 654)

Shell, R. M., & Eisenberg, N. (1992). A developmental model of recipients' reactions to aid. *Psychological Bulletin, 111,* 413–433. (p. 484)

Sheppard, B. H., & Vidmar, N. (1980). Adversary pretrial procedures and testimonial evidence: Effects of lawyer's role and machiavelianism. *Journal of Personality and Social Psychology, 39,* 320–322. (p. 613)

Shepperd, J. A. (2003). Interpreting comparative risk judgments: Are people personally optimistic or interpersonally pessimistic? Unpublished manuscript, University of Florida. (p. 71)

Shepperd, J. A., & Arkin, R. M. (1991). Behavioral other-enhancement: Strategically obscuring the link between performance and evaluation. *Journal of Personality and Social Psychology, 60,* 79–88. (p. 79)

Shepperd, J. A., Arkin, R. M., & Slaughter, J. (1995). Constraints on excuse making: The deterring effects of shyness and anticipated retest. *Personality and Social Psychology Bulletin, 21,* 1061–1072. (p. 584)

Shepperd, J. A., & Taylor, K. M. (1999). Ascribing advantages to social comparison targets. *Basic and Applied Social Psychology, 21,* 103–117. (pp. 44, 296)

Shepperd, J. A., & Wright, R. A. (1989). Individual contributions to a collective effort: An incentive analysis. *Personality and Social Psychology Bulletin, 15,* 141–149. (p. 296)

Sherif, M. (1935). A study of some social factors in perception. *Archives of Psychology*, No. 187. (pp. 210–211)

Sherif, M. (1937). An experimental approach to the study of attitudes. *Sociometry*, **1**, 90–98. (pp. 210–211)

Sherif, M. (1966). *In common predicament: Social psychology of intergroup conflict and cooperation*. Boston: Houghton Mifflin. (pp. 529–530, 547)

Sherif, M., & Sherif, C. W. (1969). *Social psychology*. New York: Harper & Row. (p. 211)

Sherman, D. K., Nelson, L. D., & Ross, L. D. (2003). Naive realism and affirmative action: Adversaries are more similar than they think. *Basic and Applied Social Psychology*, **25**, 275–289. (p. 535)

Sherman, J. W. (1996). Development and mental representation of stereotypes. *Journal of Personality and Social Psychology*, **70**, 1126–1141. (p. 363)

Sherman, J. W., Lee, A. Y., Bessenoff, G. R., & Frost, L. A. (1998). Stereotype efficiency reconsidered: Encoding flexibility under cognitive load. *Journal of Personality and Social Psychology*, **75**, 589–606. (p. 357)

Sherman, S. J. (1980). On the self-erasing nature of errors of prediction. *Journal of Personality and Social Psychology*, **39**, 211–221. (p. 126)

Sherman, S. J., Cialdini, R. B., Schwartzman, D. F., & Reynolds, K. D. (1985). Imagining can heighten or lower the perceived likelihood of contracting a disease: The mediating effect of ease of imagery. *Personality and Social Psychology Bulletin*, **11**, 118–127. (p. 114)

Sherman, S., Beike, D., & Ryalls, K. (1999). Dual-processing accounts of inconsistencies in response to general versus specific cases. In S. Chaiken & Y. Trope, *Dual process theories in social psychology*. New York: Guilford. (p. 259)

Shih, M., Pittinsky, T. L., & Ambady, N. (1999). Stereotype susceptibility: Identity salience and shifts in quantitative performance. *Psychological Science*, **10**, 80–83. (p. 373)

Shiller, R. (2000). *Irrational exuberance*. Princeton, NJ: Princeton University Press. (p. 122)

Short, J. F., Jr. (Ed.) (1969). *Gang delinquency and delinquent subcultures*. New York: Harper & Row. (p. 391)

Shostak, M. (1981). *Nisa: The life and words of a !Kung woman*. Cambridge, MA: Harvard University Press. (p. 456)

Shotland, R. L. (1989). A model of the causes of date rape in developing and close relationships. In C. Hendrick (Ed.), *Review of Personality and Social Psychology*, Vol. 10. Beverly Hills, CA: Sage. (p. 85)

Shotland, R. L., & Stebbins, C. A. (1983). Emergency and cost as determinants of helping behavior and the slow accumulation of social psychological knowledge. *Social Psychology Quarterly*, **46**, 36–46. (p. 485)

Shotland, R. L., & Straw, M. K. (1976). Bystander response to an assault: When a man attacks a woman. *Journal of Personality and Social Psychology*, **34**, 990–999. (p. 499)

Showers, C., & Ruben, C. (1987). Distinguishing pessimism from depression: Negative expectations and positive coping mechanisms. Paper presented at the American Psychological Association convention. (p. 72)

Shrauger, J. S. & Schoeneman, T. J. (1979, May). Symbolic interactionist view of self-concept: Through the looking glass darkly. *Psychological Bulletin*, **86**, 549–573. (p. 45)

Shrauger, J. S. (1975). Responses to evaluation as a function of initial self-perceptions. *Psychological Bulletin*, **82**, 581–596. (pp. 447–448)

Shrauger, J. S. (1983). The accuracy of self-prediction: How good are we and why? Paper presented at the Midwestern Psychological Association convention. (p. 52)

Shrauger, J. S., Ram, D., Greninger, S. A., & Mariano, E. (1996). Accuracy of self-predictions versus judgments by knowledgeable others. *Personality and Social Psychology Bulletin*, **22**, 1229–1243. (pp. 52–53)

Shure, G. H., Meeker, R. J., & Hansford, E. A. (1965). The effectiveness of pacifist strategies in bargaining games. *Journal of Conflict Resolution*, **9**(1), 106–117. (p. 523)

Sidanius, J., & Pratto, F. (1999). *Social Dominance: An Intergroup Theory of Social Hierarchy and Oppression*. New York: Cambridge University Press. (pp. 185–186, 345)

Sidanius, J., Pratto, F., & Bobo, L. (1994). Social dominance orientation and the political psychology of gender: A case of invariance? *Journal of Personality and Social Psychology*, **67**, 998–1011. (p. 186)

Sidanius, J., Pratto, F., & Bobo, L. (1996). Racism, conservatism, affirmative action, and intellectual sophistication: A matter of principled conservatism or group dominance? *Journal of Personality and Social Psychology*, **70**, 476–490. (p. 345)

Sieff, E. M., Dawes, R. M., & Loewenstein, G. F. (1999). Anticipated versus actual responses to HIV test results. *American Journal of Psychology*, **112**, 297–311. (p. 54)

Sigall, H. (1970). Effects of competence and consensual validation on a communicator's liking for the audience. *Journal of Personality and Social Psychology*, **16**, 252–258. (pp. 451–452)

Sigall, H., & Page, R. (1971). Current stereotypes: A little fading, a little faking. *Journal of Personality and Social Psychology*, **18**, 247–255. (p. 137)

Silke, A. (2003). Deindividuation, anonymity, and violence: Findings from Northern Ireland. *Journal of Social Psychology*, **143**, 493–499. (p. 301)

Silver, M., & Geller, D. (1978). On the irrelevance of evil: The organization and individual action. *Journal of Social Issues*, **34**, 125–136. (p. 225)

Silvia, P. J., & Duval, T. S. (2001). Objective self-awareness theory: Recent progress and enduring problems. *Personality and Social Psychology Review*, **5**, 230–241. (p. 93)

Simmons, W. W. (2000, December). When it comes to having children, Americans still prefer boys. *The Gallup Poll Monthly*, pp. 63–64. (p. 342)

Simon, H. A. (1957). *Models of man: Social and rational*. New York: Wiley. (p. 127)

Simon, P. (1996, April 17). American provincials. *Christian Century*, pp. 421–422. (p. 26)

Simonton, D. K. (1994). *Greatness: Who makes history and why.* New York: Guilford. (p. 325)

Simpson, J. A. (1987). The dissolution of romantic relationships: Factors involved in relationship stability and emotional distress. *Journal of Personality and Social Psychology, 53*, 683–692. (p. 469)

Simpson, J. A., Campbell, B., & Berscheid, E. (1986). The association between romantic love and marriage: Kephart (1967) twice revisited. *Personality and Social Psychology Bulletin, 12*, 363–372. (p. 457)

Simpson, J. A., Gangestad, S. W., & Lerma, M. (1990). Perception of physical attractiveness: Mechanisms involved in the maintenance of romantic relationships. *Journal of Personality and Social Psychology, 59*, 1192–1201. (p. 441)

Simpson, J. A., Rholes, W. S., Campbell, L., Tran, S., & Wilson, C. L. (2003). Adult attachment, the transition to parenthood, and depressive symptoms. *Journal of Personality and Social Psychology, 84*, 1172–1187. (p. 460)

Simpson, J. A., Rholes, W. S., & Nelligan, J. S. (1992). Support seeking and support giving within couples in an anxiety-provoking situation: The role of attachment styles. *Journal of Personality and Social Psychology, 62*, 434–446. (p. 459)

Simpson, J. A., Rholes, W. S., & Phillips, D. (1996). Conflict in close relationships: An attachment perspective. *Journal of Personality and Social Psychology, 71*, 899–914. (p. 460)

Singer, M. (1979). Cults and cult members. Address to the American Psychological Association convention. (a) (p. 275)

Singh, D. (1993). Adaptive significance of female physical attractiveness: Role of waist-to-hip ratio. *Journal of Personality and Social Psychology, 65*, 293–307. (pp. 438–439)

Singh, D. (1995b). Female judgment of male attractiveness and desirability for relationships: Role of waist-to-hip ratio and financial status. *Journal of*

Personality and Social Psychology, 69, 1089–1101. (pp. 438–439)

Singh, D., & Young, R. K. (1995). Body weight, waist-to-hip ratio, breasts, and hips: Role in judgments of female attractiveness and desirability for relationships. *Ethology and Sociobiology, 16*, 483–507. (p. 439)

Singh, R., & Ho, S. J. (2000). Attitudes and attraction: A new test of the attraction, repulsion and similarity-dissimilarity asymmetry hypotheses. *British Journal of Social Psychology, 39*, 197–211. (p. 444)

Singh, R., & Teoh, J. B. P. (1999). Attitudes and attraction: A test of two hypotheses for the similarity-dissimilarity asymmetry. *British Journal of Social Psychology, 38*, 427–443. (p. 444)

Sissons, M. (1981). Race, sex, and helping behavior. *British Journal of Social Psychology, 20*, 285–292. (p. 505)

Sittser, G. L. (1994, April). Long night's journey into light. *Second Opinion*, pp. 10–15. (p. 116)

Sivard, R. L. (1991). *World military and social expenditures.* Washington, DC: World Priorities. (p. 523)

Six, B., & Eckes, T. (1996). Metaanalysen in der Einstellungs-Verhaltens-Forschung. *Zeitschrift fur Sozialpsychologie*, pp. 7–17. (p. 138)

Skaalvik, E. M., & Hagtvet, K. A. (1990). Academic achievement and self-concept: An analysis of causal predominance in a developmental perpsective. *Journal of Personality and Social Psychology, 58*, 292–307. (pp. 23–24)

Skill, T., Robinson, J. D., Lyons, J. S., & Larson, D. (1994). The portrayal of religion and spirituality on fictional network television. *Review of Religious Research, 35*, 251–267. (p. 408)

Skinner, B. F. (1971). *Beyond freedom and dignity.* New York: Knopf. (p. 479)

Skitka, L. J. (1999). Ideological and attributional boundaries on public compassion: Reactions to individuals and communities affected by a natural disaster. *Personality and Social Psychology Bulletin, 25*, 793–808. (p. 96)

Skitka, L. J., & Tetlock, P. E. (1993). Providing public assistance: Cognitive and motivational processes underlying

liberal and conservative policy preferences. *Journal of Personality and Social Psychology, 65*, 1205–1223. (p. 485)

Slavin, R. E. (1980). Cooperative learning and desegregation. Paper presented at the American Psychological Association convention. (p. 549)

Slavin, R. E. (1985). Cooperative learning: Applying contact theory in desegregated schools. *Journal of Social Issues, 41*(3), 45–62. (pp. 548, 550)

Slavin, R. E. (1990, December/January). Research on cooperative learning: Consensus and controversy. *Educational Leadership*, pp. 52–54. (p. 550)

Slavin, R. E., & Cooper, R. (1999). Improving intergroup relations: Lessons learned from cooperative learning programs. *Journal of Social Issues, 55*, 647–663. (p. 549)

Slavin, R. E., Hurley, E. A., & Chamberlain, A. (2003). Cooperative learning and achievement: Theory and research. In W. M. Reynolds & G. E. Miller (Eds.), *Handbook of psychology: Educational psychology, Vol. 7.* New York: Wiley. (pp. 548, 550)

Slavin, R. E., & Madden, N. A. (1979). School practices that improve race relations. *Journal of Social Issues, 16*, 169–180. (p. 548)

Slotow, R., Van Dyke, G., Poole, J., Page, B., Klocke, A. (2000). Older bull elephants control young males. *Nature, 408*, 425–426. (p. 414)

Slovic, P. (1972). From Shakespeare to Simon: Speculations—and some evidence—about man's ability to process information. *Oregon Research Institute Research Bulletin, 12*(2). (p. 126)

Slovic, P., & Fischhoff, B. (1977). On the psychology of experimental surprises. *Journal of Experimental Psychology: Human Perception and Performance, 3*, 455–551. (p. 17)

Small, G. W., Propper, M. W., Randolph, E. T., & Eth, S. (1991). Mass hysteria among student performers: Social relationship as a symptom predictor. *American Journal of Psychiatry, 148*, 1200–1205. (p. 586)

Small, M. F. (1999, March 30). Are we losers? Putting a mating theory to the test. *New York Times* (www.nytimes.com). (p. 194)

Smedley, J. W., & Bayton, J. A. (1978). Evaluative race-class stereotypes by race and perceived class of subjects. *Journal of Personality and Social Psychology, 3,* 530–535. (p. 335)

Smelser, N. J., & Mitchell, F. (Eds.) (2002). *Terrorism: Perspectives from the behavioral and social sciences.* Washington, DC: National Research Council, National Academies Press. (p. 307)

Smith, A. (1976). *The wealth of nations.* Book 1. Chicago: University of Chicago Press. (Originally published, 1776.) (pp. 524–525)

Smith, A. E., Jussim, L., Eccles, J. (1999). Do self-fulfilling prophecies accumulate, dissipate, or remain stable over time? *Journal of Personality & Social Psychology, 77,* 548–565. (p. 121)

Smith, A. E., Jussim, L., Eccles, J., & others. (1998). Self-fulfilling prophecies, perceptual biases, and accuracy at the individual and group levels. *Journal of Experimental Social Psychology, 34,* 530–561. (p. 121)

Smith, D. E., Gier, J. A., & Willis, F. N. (1982). Interpersonal touch and compliance with a marketing request. *Basic and Applied Social Psychology, 3,* 35–38. (p. 220)

Smith, H. (1976) *The Russians.* New York: Balantine Books. Cited by B. Latané, K. Williams, and S. Harkins in, Many hands make light the work. *Journal of Personality and Social Psychology,* 1979, *37,* 822–832. (p. 296)

Smith, H. J., & Tyler, T. R. (1997). Choosing the right pond: The impact of group membership on self-esteem and group-oriented behavior. *Journal of Experimental Social Psychology, 33,* 146–170. (p. 351)

Smith, H. W. (1981). Territorial spacing on a beach revisited: A cross-national exploration. *Social Psychology Quarterly, 44,* 132–137. (p. 175)

Smith, M. B. (1978). Psychology and values. *Journal of Social Issues, 34,* 181–199. (p. 15)

Smith, P. B., & Tayeb, M. (1989). Organizational structure and

processes. In M. Bond (Ed.), *The cross-cultural challenge to social psychology.* Newbury Park, CA: Sage. (p. 325)

Smith, R. H., Turner, T. J., Garonzik, R., Leach, C. W., Urch-Druskat, V., & Weston, C. M. (1996). Envy and Schadenfreude. *Personality and Social Psychology Bulletin, 22,* 158–168. (p. 44)

Smith, S. M., & Shaffer, D. R. (1991). Celerity and cajolery: Rapid speech may promote or inhibit persuasion through its impact on message elaboration. *Personality and Social Psychology Bulletin, 17,* 663–669. (p. 253)

Smith, T. W. (1998, December). American sexual behavior: Trends, socio-demographic differences, and risk behavior. National Opinion Research Center GSS Topical Report No. 25. (p. 363)

Smith, T. W., & Ruiz, J. M. (2002). Psychosocial influences on the development and course of coronary heart disease: Current status and implications for research and practice. *Journal of Consulting and Clinical Psychology, 70,* 548–568. (p. 588)

Smith, V. L. (1991). Impact of pretrial instruction on jurors' information processing and decision making. *Journal of Applied Psychology, 76,* 220–228. (p. 626)

Smith, V. L. (1991). Prototypes in the courtroom: Lay representations of legal concepts. *Journal of Personality and Social Psychology, 61,* 857–872. (p. 623)

Smith, V. L., & Ellsworth, P. C. (1987). The social psychology of eyewitness accuracy: Misleading questions and communicator expertise. *Journal of Applied Psychology, 72,* 294–300. (p. 613)

Smolowe, J. (1994, August 1). Race and the O. J. case. *Time,* pp. 24–25. (p. 621)

Smoreda, Z., & Licoppe, C. (2000). Gender-specific use of the domestic telephone. *Social Psychology Quarterly, 63,* 238–252. (p. 182)

Snodgrass, M. A. (1987). The relationships of differential loneliness, intimacy, and characterological attributional style to duration of loneliness. *Journal of Social Behavior and Personality, 2,* 173–186. (p. 582)

Snyder, C. R. (1978). The "illusion" of uniqueness. *Journal of Humanistic Psychology, 18,* 33–41. (p. 70)

Snyder, C. R. (1980). The uniqueness mystique. *Psychology Today,* March, pp. 86–90. (p. 239)

Snyder, C. R., & Fromkin, H. L. (1980). *Uniqueness; The human pursuit of difference.* New York: Plenum. (p. 239)

Snyder, C. R., & Higgins, R. L. (1988). Excuses: Their effective role in the negotiation of reality. *Psychological Bulletin, 104,* 23–35. (p. 75)

Snyder, C. R., & Smith, T. W. (1986). On being "shy like a fox": A self-handicapping analysis. In W. H. Jones et al. (Eds.), *Shyness: Perspectives on research and treatment.* New York: Plenum. (p. 584)

Snyder, M. (1981). Seek, and ye shall find: Testing hypotheses about other people. In E. T. Higgins, C. P. Herman, & M. P. Zanna (Eds.), *Social cognition: The Ontario symposium on personality and social psychology.* Hillsdale, NJ: Erlbaum. *(a)* (p. 572)

Snyder, M. (1983). The influence of individuals on situations: Implications for understanding the links between personality and social behavior. *Journal of Personality, 51,* 497–516. (p. 203)

Snyder, M. (1984). When belief creates reality. In L. Berkowitz (Ed.), *Advances in Experimental Social Psychology,* Vol. 18. New York: Academic Press. (pp. 124, 571)

Snyder, M. (1987). *Public appearances/private realities: The psychology of self-monitoring.* New York: Freeman. (p. 79)

Snyder, M. (1988). Experiencing prejudice first hand: The "discrimination day" experiments. *Contemporary Psychology, 33,* 664–665. (p. 115)

Snyder, M., Campbell, B., & Preston, E. (1982). Testing hypotheses about human nature: Assessing the accuracy of social stereotypes. *Social Cognition, 1,* 256–272. (pp. 571–572)

Snyder, M., Grether, J., & Keller, K. (1974). Staring and compliance: A field experiment on hitch-hiking. *Journal of Applied Social Psychology, 4,* 165–170. (pp. 486, 510)

Snyder, M., & Haugen, J. A. (1994). Why does behavioral confirmation occur? A functional perspective on the role of the perceiver. *Journal of Experimental Social Psychology, 30,* 218–246. (p. 29)

Snyder, M., & Haugen, J. A. (1995). Why does behavioral confirmation occur? A functional perspective on the role of the target. *Personality and Social Psychology Bulletin, 21,* 963–974. (p. 29)

Snyder, M., & Ickes, W. (1985). Personality and social behavior. In G. Lindzey & E. Aronson (Eds.), *Handbook of social psychology* (3rd ed.). New York: Random House. (pp. 203, 345–346)

Snyder, M., & Swann, W. B., Jr. (1976). When actions reflect attitudes: The politics of impression management. *Journal of Personality and Social Psychology, 34,* 1034–1042. (p. 139)

Snyder, M., Tanke, E. D., & Berscheid, E. (1977). Social perception and interpersonal behavior: On the self-fulfilling nature of social stereotypes. *Journal of Personality and Social Psychology, 35,* 656–666. *(b)* (p. 124)

Snyder, M., & Thomsen, C. J. (1988). Interactions between therapists and clients: Hypothesis testing and behavioral confirmation. In D. C. Turk & P. Salovey (Eds.), *Reasoning, inference, and judgment in clinical psychology.* New York: Free Press. (p. 571)

Sober, E., & Wilson, D. S. (1998). *Unto others: The evolution and psychology of unselfish behavior.* Cambridge, MA: Harvard University Press. (p. 488)

Sokoll, G. R., & Mynatt, C. R. (1984). Arousal and free throw shooting. Paper presented at the Midwestern Psychological Association convention, Chicago. (p. 289)

Solano, C. H., Batten, P. G., & Parish, E. A. (1982). Loneliness and patterns of self-disclosure. *Journal of Personality and Social Psychology, 43,* 524–531. (p. 462)

Solberg, E. C., Diener, E., & Robinson, M. D. (2003). Why are materialists less satisfied? In T. Kasser & A. D. Kanner (Eds.), *Psychology and consumer culture: The struggle for a good life in a materialistic world.* Washington, DC: APA Books. (p. 654)

Solberg, E. C., Diener, E., Wirtz, D., Lucas, R. E., & Oishi, S. (2002). Wanting, having, and satisfaction: Examining the role of desire discrepancies in satisfaction with income. *Journal of Personality and Social Psychology, 83,* 725–734. (p. 389)

Solomon, H., & Solomon, L. Z. (1978). Effects of anonymity on helping in emergency situations. Paper presented at the Eastern Psychological Association convention. (p. 510)

Solomon, H., Solomon, L. Z., Arnone, M. M., Maur, B. J., Reda, R. M., & Rother, E. O. (1981). Anonymity and helping. *Journal Social Psychology, 113,* 37–43. (p. 510)

Solomon, L. Z., Solomon, H., & Stone, R. (1978). Helping as a function of number of bystanders and ambiguity of emergency. *Personality and Social Psychology Bulletin, 4,* 318–321. (p. 500)

Solomon, S., Greenberg, J., & Pyszczynski, T. (2000). Pride and prejudice: Fear of death and social behavior. *Current Directions in Psychological Science, 9,* 200–203. (p. 355)

Solomon, S., Ogilvie, D. M., Cohen, F., Greenberg, J., & Pyszczynski, T. (2004). The effects of reminders of death or the events of September 11, 2001 on evaluations of President Bush. Manuscript in preparation, Skidmore College. (p. 543)

Sommer, B. (1992). Cognitive performance and the menstrual cycle. In J. T. Richardson (Ed.), *Cognition and the menstrual cycle: Research, theory, and culture.* New York: Springer-Verlag. (p. 587)

Sommer, R. (1969). *Personal space.* Englewood Cliffs, NJ: Prentice-Hall. (p. 175)

Sommers, S. R., & Ellsworth, P. C. (2000). Race in the courtroom: Perceptions of guilt and dispositional attributions. *Personality and Social Psychology Bulletin, 26,* 1367–1379. (p. 621)

Sommers, S. R., & Ellsworth, P. C. (2001). White juror bias: An investigation of prejudice against Black defendants in the American courtroom. *Psychology, Public Policy, and Law, 7,* 201–229. (p. 621)

Sonne, J., & Janoff, D. (1979). The effect of treatment attributions on the maintenance of weight reduction: A replication and extension. *Cognitive Therapy and Research, 3,* 389–397. (p. 595)

Sparrell, J. A., & Shrauger, J. S. (1984). Self-confidence and optimism in self-prediction. Paper presented at the American Psychological Association convention. (p. 72)

Spector, P. E. (1986). Perceived control by employees: A meta-analysis of studies concerning autonomy and participation at work. *Human Relations, 39,* 1005–1016. (p. 324)

Speer, A. (1971). *Inside the Third Reich: Memoirs.* (P. Winston & C. Winston. trans.). New York: Avon Books. (p. 314)

Spencer, S. J., Fein, S., Wolfe, C. T., Fong, C., & Dunn, M. A. (1998). Automatic activation of stereotypes: The role of self-image threat. *Personality and Social Psychology Bulletin, 24,* 1139–1152. (p. 356)

Spencer, S. J., Steele, C. M., & Quinn, D. M. (1999). Stereotype threat and women's math performance. *Journal of Experimental Social Psychology, 3,* 4–28. (p. 371)

Spiegel, H. W. (1971). *The growth of economic thought.* Durham, NC: Duke University Press. (p. 71)

Spitz, H. H. (1999). Beleaguered *Pygmalion:* A history of the controversy over claims that teacher expectancy raises intelligence. *Intelligence, 27,* 199–234. (p. 122)

Spitzberg, B. H., & Hurt, H. T. (1987). The relationship of interpersonal competence and skills to reported loneliness across time. *Journal of Social Behavior and Personality, 2,* 157–172. (p. 572)

Spivak, J. (1979, June 6). *Wall Street Journal.* (p. 296)

Spivey, C. B., & Prentice-Dunn, S. (1990). Assessing the directionality of deindividuated behavior: Effects of deindividuation, modeling, and private self-consciousness on aggressive and prosocial responses.

Basic and Applied Social Psychology, 11, 387–403. (p. 301)

Sprecher, S. (1987). The effects of self-disclosure given and received on affection for an intimate partner and stability of the relationship. *Journal of Personality and Social Psychology, 4,* 115–127. (p. 464)

Sprecher, S., Aron, A., Hatfield, E., Cortese, A., Potapova, E., & Levitskaya, A. (1994). Love: American style, Russian style, and Japanese style. *Personal Relationships, 1,* 349–369. (p. 432)

Sprecher, S., & Sedikides, C. (1993). Gender differences in perceptions of emotionality: The case of close heterosexual relationships. *Sex Roles, 28,* 511–530. (p. 184)

Sprecher, S., Sullivan, Q., & Hatfield, E. (1994). Mate selection preferences: Gender differences examined in a national sample. *Journal of Personality and Social Psychology, 66,* 1074–1080. (p. 457)

Sprecher, S., & Toro-Morn, M. (2002). A study of men and women from different sides of earth to determine if men are from Mars and women are from Venus in their beliefs about love and romantic relationships. *Sex Roles, 46,* 131–147. (p. 457)

Srivastava, A., Locke, E. A., & Bartol, K. M. (2001). Money and subjective well-being: It's not the money, it's the motives. *Journal of Personality and Social Psychology, 80,* 959–971. (p. 654)

Stack, S. (1992). Marriage, family, religion, and suicide. In R. Maris, A. Berman, J. Maltsberg, and R. Yufits (Eds.), *Assessment and prediction of suicide.* New York: Guilford. (p. 600)

Stajkovic, A., & Luthans, F. (1998). Self-efficacy and work-related performance: A meta-analysis. *Psychological Bulletin, 124,* 240–261. (p. 57)

Stangor, C., Jonas, K., Stroebe, W., & Hewstone, M. (1996). Influence of student exchange on national stereotypes, attitudes and perceived group variability. *European Journal of Social Psychology, 26,* 663–675. (p. 540)

Stangor, C., Lynch, L., Duan, C., & Glass, B. (1992). Categorization of individuals on the basis of multiple social features. *Journal of Personality*

and Social Psychology, 62, 207–218. (p. 181)

Stangor, C., & McMillan, D. (1992). Memory for expectancy-congruent and expectancy-incongruent information: A review of the social and social developmental literatures. *Psychological Bulletin, 111,* 42–61. (pp. 368–369)

Staples, B. (1999a, May 2). When the 'paranoids' turn out to be right. *New York Times* (www.nytimes.com). (p. 336)

Staples, B. (1999b, May 24). Why 'racial profiling' will be tough to fight. *New York Times* (www.nytimes.com). (p. 336)

Staples, B. (2000, June 26). Playing 'catch and grope' in the schoolyard. *New York Times* (www.nytimes.com). (p. 385)

Stark, R., & Bainbridge, W. S. (1980). Networks of faith: Interpersonal bonds and recruitment of cults and sects *American Journal of Sociology, 85,* 1376–1395. (p. 275)

Stasser, G. (1991). Pooling of unshared information during group discussion. In S. Worchel, W. Wood, & J. Simpson (Eds.), *Group process and productivity.* Beverly Hills, CA: Sage. (p. 308)

Stasser, G., Kerr, N. L., & Bray, R. M. (1981). The social psychology of jury deliberations: Structure, process, and product. In N. L. Kerr & R. M. Bray (Eds.), *The psychology of the courtroom.* New York: Academic Press. (p. 633)

Statistics Canada. (2001). www.statcan.ca (p. 187)

Staub, E. (in press). The roots of goodness: The fulfillment of basic human needs and the development of caring, helping and nonaggression, inclusive caring, moral courage, active bystandership, and altruism born of suffering. In C. Edwards and G. Carlo (Eds.), *Moral motivation.* Nebraska Symposium on Motivation. Lincoln: University of Nebraska Press. (pp. 512–513)

Staub, E. (1978). *Positive social behavior and morality: Social and personal influences,* vol. 1. Hillsdale, NJ: Erlbaum. (p. 479)

Staub, E. (1989). *The roots of evil: The origins of genocide and other group*

violence. Cambridge: Cambridge University Press. (pp. 224, 514)

Staub, E. (1991). Altruistic and moral motivations for helping and their translation into action. *Psychological Inquiry, 2,* 150–153. (pp. 492, 514)

Staub, E. (1992). The origins of caring, helping and nonaggression: Parental socialization, the family system, schools, and cultural influence. In S. Oliner & P. Oliner (Eds.), *Embracing the other: Philosophical, psychological, and theological perspectives on altruism.* New York: New York University Press. (p. 514)

Staub, E. (1996). Altruism and aggression in children and youth: Origins and cures. In R. Feldman (Ed.), *The psychology of adversity.* Amherst: University of Massachusetts Press. (pp. 391, 414)

Staub, E. (1997). Blind versus constructive patriotism: Moving from embeddedness in the group to critical loyalty and action. In D. Bar-Tal and E. Staub (Eds.), *Patriotism in the lives of individuals and nations.* Chicago: Nelson-Hall. (p. 351)

Staub, E. (1997). Halting and preventing collective violence: The role of bystanders. Background paper for symposium organized by the Friends of Raoul Wallenberg, Stockholm, June 13–16. (p. 500)

Staub, E. (1999). Behind the scenes. In D. G. Myers, *Social psychology,* 6th edition. New York: McGraw-Hill. (p. 514)

Staub, E. (1999). The origins and prevention of genocide, mass killing, and other collective violence. *Peace and Conflict, 5,* 303–336. (p. 379)

Staub, E. (2003). *The psychology of good and evil: Why children, adults, and groups help and harm others.* New York: Cambridge University Press. (p. 224)

Staub, E., & Bar-Tal, D. (2003). Genocide, mass killing, and intractable conflict. In D. Sears, L. Huddy, & R. Jervis (Eds.), *Handbook of political psychology.* New York: Oxford University Press. (p. 533)

Staub, E., & Pearlman, L. A. (2004). Advancing healing and reconciliation. *Journal of Genocide Studies,* in press. (p. 557)

Steblay, N. M. (1987). Helping behavior in rural and urban environments: A meta-analysis. *Psychological Bulletin,* **102**, 346–356. (p. 488)

Steblay, N. M., Besirevic, J., Fulero, S. M., & Jimenez-Lorente, B. (1999). The effects of pretrial publicity on juror verdicts: A meta-analytic review. *Law and Human Behavior,* **23**, 219–235. (p. 623)

Steblay, N., Dysart, J. E., Fulero, S., & Lindsay, R. C. L. (2001). Eyewitness accuracy rates in sequential and simultaneous lineup presentations: A meta-analytic comparison. *Law and Human Behavior,* **25**, 459–473. (p. 617)

Steele, C. M. (1988). The psychology of self-affirmation: Sustaining the integrity of the self. In L. Berkowitz (Ed.), *Advances in experimental social psychology,* Vol. 21. Orlando, FL: Academic Press. (p. 162)

Steele, C. M. (1997). A threat in the air: How stereotypes shape intellectual identity and performance. *American Psychologist,* **52**, 613–629. (pp. 45, 371, 372)

Steele, C. M., & Aronson, J. (1995). Stereotype threat and the intellectual test performance of African Americans. *Journal of Personality and Social Psychology,* **69**, 797–811. (p. 372)

Steele, C. M., & Southwick, L. (1985). Alcohol and social behavior I: The psychology of drunken excess. *Journal of Personality and Social Psychology,* **48**, 18–34. (p. 385)

Steele, C. M., Southwick, L. L., & Critchlow, B. (1981). Dissonance and alcohol: Drinking your troubles away. *Journal of Personality and Social Psychology,* **41**, 831–846. (p. 162)

Steele, C. M., Spencer, S. J., & Lynch, M. (1993). Self-image resilience and dissonance: The role of affirmational resources. *Journal of Personality and Social Psychology,* **64**, 885–896. (p. 162)

Steele, C. M., Spencer, S. J., Aronson, J. (2002). Contending with group image: The psychology of stereotype and social identity threat. In Zanna, M. P. (Ed.), *Advances in experimental social psychology,* **34**, 379–440. San Diego, CA: Academic Press, Inc. (p. 372)

Stein, A. H., & Friedrich, L. K. (1972). Television content and young children's behavior. In J. P. Murray, E. A. Rubinstein, & G. A. Comstock (Eds.), *Television and social learning.* Washington, DC: Government Printing Office. (p. 514)

Stein, D. D., Hardyck, J. A., & Smith, M. B. (1965). Race and belief: An open and shut case. *Journal of Personality and Social Psychology,* **1**, 281–289. (p. 359)

Steinem, G. (1988). Six great ideas that television is missing. In S. Oskamp. (Ed.), *Television as a social issue: Applied Social Psychology Annual,* Vol. 8. Newbury Park, CA: Sage. (p. 403)

Stelzl, M., & Seligman, C. (2004). The social identity strategy of MOATING: Further evidence. Paper presented at the Society of Personality and Social Psychology convention. (p. 353)

Stephan, C. W., & Stephan, W. G. (1986). Habla Ingles? The effects of language translation on simulated juror decisions. *Journal of Applied Social Psychology,* **16**, 577–589. (p. 621)

Stephan, W. G. (1986). The effects of school desegregation: An evaluation 30 years after *Brown.* In R. Kidd, L. Saxe, & M. Saks (Eds.), *Advances in applied social psychology.* New York: Erlbaum. (p. 540)

Stephan, W. G. (1987). The contact hypothesis in intergroup relations. In C. Hendrick (Ed.), *Group processes and intergroup relations.* Newbury Park, CA: Sage. (pp. 541–542)

Stephan, W. G. (1988). School desegregation: Short-term and long-term effects. Paper presented at the national conference "Opening doors: An appraisal of race relations in America," University of Alabama. (p. 539)

Stephan, W. G., Berscheid, E., & Walster, E. (1971). Sexual arousal and heterosexual perception. *Journal of Personality and Social Psychology,* **20**, 93–101. (p. 454)

Stern, P. C. (2000). Psychology and the science of human-environment interactions. *American Psychologist,* **55**, 523–530. (p. 658)

Sternberg, R. J. (1988). Triangulating love. In R. J. Sternberg & M. L. Barnes (Eds.), *The psychology of love.* New Haven, CT: Yale University Press. (pp. 453, 471)

Sternberg, R. J. (1998). *Cupid's arrow: The course of love through time.* New York: Cambridge University Press. (p. 453)

Sternberg, R. J. (2003). A duplex theory of hate and its development and its application to terrorism, massacres, and genocide. *Review of General Psychology,* **7**, 299–328. (p. 380)

Sternberg, R. J., & Grajek, S. (1984). The nature of love. *Journal of Personality and Social Psychology,* **47**, 312–329. (p. 458)

Stiles, W. B., Shuster, P. L., & Harrigan, J. A. (1992). Disclosure and anxiety: A test of the fever model. *Journal of Personality and Social Psychology,* **63**, 980–988. (p. 462)

Stille, R. G., Malamuth, N., & Schallow, J. R. (1987). Prediction of rape proclivity by rape myth attitudes and hostility toward women. Paper presented at the American Psychological Association convention. (p. 401)

Stillinger, C., Epelbaum, M., Keltner, D., & Ross, L. (1991). The "reactive devaluation" barrier to conflict resolution. Unpublished manuscript, Stanford University. (p. 557)

Stinson, V., Devenport, J. L., Cutler, B. L., & Kravitz, D. A. (1996). How effective is the presence-of-counsel safeguard? Attorney perceptions of suggestiveness, fairness, and correctability of biased lineup procedures. *Journal of Applied Psychology,* **81**, 64–75. (p. 618)

Stinson, V., Devenport, J. L., Cutler, B. L., & Kravitz, D. A. (1997). How effective is the motion-to-suppress safeguard? Judges' perceptions of the suggestiveness and fairness of biased lineup procedures. *Journal of Personality and Social Psychology,* **82**, 211–220. (p. 618)

Stockdale, J. E. (1978). Crowding: Determinants and effects. In L. Berkowitz (Ed.), *Advances in experimental social psychology* (Vol. 11). New York: Academic Press. (p. 175)

Stocking, S. H. & Gross, P. H. (1989). *How do journalists think?: A proposal for the study of cognitive bias in newsmaking.* Bloomington, IN: Eric Clearinghouse on Reading and Communication Skills. (p. 128)

Stokes, J., & Levin, I. (1986). Gender differences in predicting loneliness from social network characteristics. *Journal of Personality and Social Psychology*, **51**, 1069–1074. (p. 582)

Stone, A. A., Hedges, S. M., Neale, J. M., & Satin, M. S. (1985). Prospective and cross-sectional mood reports offer no evidence of a "blue Monday" phenomenon. *Journal of Personality and Social Psychology*, **49**, 129–134. (p. 52)

Stone, A. L., & Glass, C. R. (1986). Cognitive distortion of social feedback in depression. *Journal of Social and Clinical Psychology*, **4**, 179–188. (p. 119)

Stone, J. (2000, November 6). Quoted by Sharon Begley, The stereotype trap. *Newsweek*. (p. 372)

Stone, J., Lynch, C. I., Sjomeling, M., & Darley, J. M. (1999). Stereotype threat effects on Black and White athletic performance. *Journal of Personality and Social Psychology*, **77**, 1213–1227. (pp. 163, 372)

Stone, L. (1977). *The family, sex and marriage in England, 1500–1800*. New York: Harper & Row. (p. 469)

Stoner, J. A. F. (1961). A comparison of individual and group decisions involving risk. Unpublished master's thesis, Massachusetts Institute of Technology, 1961. Cited by D. G. Marquis in, Individual responsibility and group decisions involving risk. *Industrial Management Review*, **3**, 8–23. (p. 303)

Stoppard, J. M., & Gruchy, C. D. G. (1993). Gender, context, and expression of positive emotion. *Personality and Social Psychology Bulletin*, **19**, 143–150. (p. 184)

Storms, M. D. (1973). Videotape and the attribution process: Reversing actors' and observers' points of view. *Journal of Personality and Social Psychology*, **27**, 165–175. (p. 92)

Storms, M. D., & Thomas, G. C. (1977). Reactions to physical closeness. *Journal of Personality and Social Psychology*, **35**, 412–418. (p. 289)

Stouffer, S. A., Suchman, E. A., DeVinney, L. C., Star, S. A., & Williams, R. M., Jr. (1949). *The American soldier: Adjustment during army life* (Vol. 1.). Princeton, NJ: Princeton University Press. (pp. 389, 539)

Strack, F., & Deutsch, R. (2004). Reflective and impulsive determinants of social behavior. *Personality and Social Psychology Review*, in press. (p. 107)

Strack, F., Martin, L. L., & Stepper, S. (1988). Inhibiting and facilitating conditions of the human smile: A nonobstrusive test of the facial feedback hypothesis. *Journal of Personality and Social Psychology*, **54**, 768–777. (p. 157)

Strack, S., & Coyne, J. C. (1983). Social confirmation of dysphoria: Shared and private reactions to depression. *Journal of Personality and Social Psychology*, **44**, 798–806. (p. 579)

Straus, M. A., & Gelles, R. J. (1980). *Behind closed doors: Violence in the American family*. New York: Anchor/Doubleday. (p. 391)

Strausberg, M. A. (2003, September 24). U.S. Muslim data. Personal correspondence from The Gallup Poll Data Librarian. (p. 363)

Streeter, S. A., & McBurney, D. H. (2003). Waist–hip ratio and attractiveness: New evidence and a critique of "a critical test." *Evolution and Human Behavior*, **24**, 88–98. (pp. 438–439)

Stroebe, W., & Diehl, M. (1994). Productivity loss in idea-generating groups. In W. Stroebe & M. Hewstone (Eds.), *European review of social psychology*, vol. 5. Chichester, England: Wiley. (p. 319)

Stroebe, W., Insko, C. A., Thompson, V. D., & Layton, B. D. (1971). Effects of physical attractiveness, attitude similarity, and sex on various aspects of interpersonal attraction. *Journal of Personality and Social Psychology*, **18**, 79–91. (p. 433)

Stroebe, W., Lenkert, A., & Jonas, K. (1988). Familiarity may breed contempt: The impact of student exchange on national stereotypes and attitudes. In W. Stroebe & A. W. Kruglanski (Eds.), *The social psychology of intergroup conflict*. New York: Springer-Verlag. (p. 540)

Stroebe, W., Stroebe, M., Abakoumkin, G., & Schut, H. (1996). The role of loneliness and social support in adjustment to loss: A test of attachment versus stress theory. *Journal of Personality and Social Psychology*, **70**, 1241–1249. (p. 582)

Stroessner, S. J., Hamilton, D. L., & Lepore, L. (1990). Intergroup categorization and intragroup differentiation: Ingroup-outgroup differences. Paper presented at the American Psychological Association convention. (p. 358)

Stroessner, S. J., & Mackie, D. M. (1993). Affect and perceived group variability: Implications for stereotyping and prejudice. In D. M. Mackie & D. L. Hamilton (Eds.), *Affect, cognition, and stereotyping: Interactive processes in group perception*. San Diego, CA: Academic Press. (p. 358)

Strong, S. R. (1978). Social psychological approach to psychotherapy research. In S. L. Garfield & A. E. Bergin (Eds.), *Handbook of psychotherapy and behavior change*, 2nd ed. New York: Wiley. (p. 277)

Strong, S. R. (1991). Social influence and change in therapeutic relationships. In C. R. Snyder & D. R. Forsyth (Eds.), *Handbook of social and clinical psychology*. New York: Pergamon Press. (p. 595)

Strong, S. R., Welsh, J. A., Corcoran, J. L., & Hoyt, W. T. (1992). Social psychology and counseling psychology: The history, products, and promise of an interface. *Journal of Personality and Social Psychology*, **39**, 139–157. (p. 591)

Stroufe, B., Chaikin, A., Cook, R., & Freeman, V. (1977). The effects of physical attractiveness on honesty: A socially desirable response. *Personality and Social Psychology*, **3**, 59–62. (p. 486)

Stuart, A. E., & Blanton, H. (2003). The effects of message framing on behavioral prevalence assumptions. *European Journal of Social Psychology*, **33**, 93–102. (p. 258)

Stukas, A. A., Snyder, M., & Clary, E. G. (1999). The effects of "mandatory volunteerism" on intentions to volunteer. *Psychological Science*, **10**, 59–64. (p. 154)

Sturm, M., Perovich, D. K., & Serreze, M. C. (2003, October). Meltdown in the North. *Scientific American*, pp. 60–67. (p. 642)

Sue, S., Smith, R. E., & Caldwell, C. (1973). Effects of inadmissible evidence on the decisions of simulated jurors: A moral dilemma. *Journal of Applied Social Psychology*, **3**, 345–353. (p. 622)

Suedfeld, P. (2000). Reverberations of the Holocaust fifty years later: Psychology's contributions to understanding persecution and genocide. *Canadian Psychology*, **41**, 1–9. (pp. 500–501)

Sullivan, A. (1999, September 26). What's so bad about hate? *New York Times Magazine* (www.nytimes.com). (p. 416)

Suls, J., & Tesch, F. (1978). Students' preferences for information about their test performance: A social comparison study, *Journal of Applied Social Psychology*, **8**, 189–197. (p. 44)

Suls, J., Wan, C. K., & Sanders, G. S. (1988). False consensus and false uniqueness in estimating the prevalence of health-protective behaviors. *Journal of Applied Social Psychology*, **18**, 66–79. (p. 73)

Summers, G., & Feldman, N. S. (1984). Blaming the victim versus blaming the perpetrator: An attributional analysis of spouse abuse. *Journal of Social and Clinical Psychology*, **2**, 339–347. (p. 367)

Sundstrom, E., De Meuse, K. P., & Futrell, D. (1990). Work teams: Applications and effectiveness. *American Psychologist*, **45**, 120–133. (p. 324)

Sunstein, C. R. (2001). *Republic.com*. Princeton, NJ: Princeton University Press. (p. 307)

Sussman, N. M. (2000). The dynamic nature of cultural identity throughout cultural transitions: Why home is not so sweet. *Personality and Social Psychology Review*, **4**, 355–373. (p. 178)

Svenson, O. (1981). Are we all less risky and more skillful than our fellow drivers? *Acta Psychologica*, **47**, 143–148. (p. 70)

Swann, W. B., Jr. (1984). Quest for accuracy in person perception: A matter of pragmatics. *Psychological Review*, **91**, 457–475. (p. 127)

Swann, W. B., Jr. (1987). Identity negotiation: Where two roads meet. *Journal of Personality and Social Psychology*, **53** 1038–1051. (pp. 125–126)

Swann, W. B., Jr. (1996). *Self-traps: The elusive quest for higher self-esteem*. New York: Freeman. (p. 74)

Swann, W. B., Jr. (1997). The trouble with change: Self-verification and allegiance to the self. *Psychological Science*, **8**, 177–180. (p. 74)

Swann, W. B., Jr., & Ely, R. J. (1984). A battle of wills: Self-verification versus behavioral confirmation. *Journal of Personality and Social Psychology*, **46**, 1287–1302. (p. 126)

Swann, W. B., Jr., & Gill, M. J. (1997). Confidence and accuracy in person perception: Do we know what we think we know about our relationship partners? *Journal of Personality and Social Psychology*, **73**, 747–757. (p. 110)

Swann, W. B., Jr., & Giuliano, T. (1987). Confirmatory search strategies in social interaction: How, when, why, and with what consequences. *Journal of Social and Clinical Psychology*, **5**, 511–524. (p. 571)

Swann, W. B., Jr., Milton, L. P., & Polzer, J. T. (2000). Should we create a niche or fall in line? Identity negotiation and small group effectiveness. *Journal of Personality and Social Psychology*, **79**, 238–250. (p. 112)

Swann, W. B., Jr., & Predmore, S. C. (1985). Intimates as agents of social support: Sources of consolation or despair? *Journal of Personality and Social Psychology*, **49**, 1609–1617. (p. 463)

Swann, W. B., Jr., & Read, S. J. (1981). Acquiring self-knowledge: The search for feedback that fits. *Journal of Personality and Social Psychology*, **41**, 1119–1128. (p. 112)

Swann, W. B., Jr., Rentfrow, P. J., & Gosling, S. D. (2003). The precarious couple effect: Verbally inhibited men + critical, disinhibited women = bad chemistry. *Journal of Personality and Social Psychology*, **85**, 1095–1106. (p. 470)

Swann, W. B., Jr., Stein-Seroussi, A., & Giesler, R. B. (1992a). Why people self-verify. *Journal of Personality and Social Psychology*, **62**, 392–401. (p. 112)

Swann, W. B., Jr., Stein-Seroussi, A., & McNulty, S. E. (1992b). Outcasts in a white lie society. The enigmatic worlds of people with negative self-conceptions. *Journal of Personality and Social Psychology*, **62**, 618–624. (p. 112)

Swann, W. B., Jr., Wenzlaff, R. M., Krull, D. S., & Pelham, B. W. (1991). Seeking truth, reaping despair: Depression, self-verification and selection of relationship partners. *Journal of Abnormal Psychology*, **101**, 293–306. (pp. 112, 449, 579)

Swap, W. C. (1977). Interpersonal attraction and repeated exposure to rewarders and punishers. *Personality and Social Psychology Bulletin*, **3**, 248–251. (p. 430)

Swedish Information Service (1980). *Social change in Sweden*, September, No. 19, p. 5. (Published by the Swedish Consulate General, 825 Third Avenue, New York, NY 10022.) (p. 419)

Sweeney, J. (1973). An experimental investigation of the free rider problem. *Social Science Research*, **2**, 277–292. (p. 294)

Sweeney, P. D., Anderson, K., & Bailey, S. (1986). Attributional style in depression: A meta-analytic review. *Journal of Personality and Social Psychology*, **50**, 947–991. (p. 577)

Swets, J. A., Dawes, R. M., & Monahan, J. (2000). Psychological science can improve diagnostic decisions. *Psychological Science in the Public Interest*, **1**, 1–26. (p. 572)

Swim, J., Borgida, E., Maruyama, G., & Myers, D. G. (1989). Joan McKay vs. John McKay: Do gender stereotypes bias evaluations? *Psychological Bulletin*, **105**, 409–429. (pp. 341–342)

Swim, J. K. (1994). Perceived versus meta-analytic effect sizes: An assessment of the accuracy of gender stereotypes. *Journal of Personality and Social Psychology*, **66**, 21–36. (pp. 182, 340–341)

Swim, J. K., Aikin, K. J., Hall, W. S., & Hunter, B. A. (1995). Sexism and racism: Old-fashioned and modern prejudices. *Journal of Personality and Social Psychology*, **68**, 199–214. (p. 337)

Swim, J. K., & Cohen, L. L. (1997). Overt, covert, and subtle sexism. *Psychology of Women Quarterly*, **21**, 103–118. (p. 337)

Swim, J. K., Cohen, L. L., & Hyers, L. L. (1998). Experiencing everyday prejudice and discrimination. In J. K. Swim & C. Stangor (Eds.), *Prejudice: The target's perspective.* San Diego, CA: Academic Press. (p. 361)

Swim, J. K., Ferguson, M. J., & Hyers, L. L. (1999). Avoiding stigma by association: Subtle prejudice against lesbians in the form of social distancing. *Basic and Applied Social Psychology*, **21**, 61–68. (p. 231)

Swim, J. K., & Hyers, L. L. (1999). Excuse me—What did you just say?!: Women's public and private reactions to sexist remarks. *Journal of Experimental Social Psychology*, **35**, 68–88. (p. 225)

Swim, J. K., & Stangor, C. (Eds.) (1998). *Prejudice: The target's perspective.* San Diego, CA: Academic Press. (p. 371)

Swindle, R., Jr., Heller, K., Bescosolido, B., & Kikuzawa, S. (2000). Responses to nervous breakdowns in America over a 40-year period: Mental health policy implications. *American Psychologist*, **55**, 740–749. (p. 581)

Symons, C. S., & Johnson, B. T. (1997). The self-reference effect in memory: A meta-analysis. *Psychological Bulletin*, **121**, 371–394. (p. 42)

Symons, D. (1979). *The evolution of human sexuality.* New York: Oxford University Press. (p. 188)

t'Hart, P. (1998). Preventing groupthink revisited: Evaluating and reforming groups in government. *Organizational Behavior and Human Decision Processes*, **73**, 306–326. (p. 315)

Tafarodi, R. W., & Vu, C. (1997). Two-dimensional self-esteem and reactions to success and failure. *Personality and Social Psychology Bulletin*, **23**, 626–635. (p. 44)

Tafarodi, R. W., Lo, C., Yamaguchi, S., Lee, W. W-S., & Katsura, H. (2004). The inner self in three countries. *Journal of Cross-Cultural Psychology*, **35**, 97–117. (p. 49)

Tajfel, H. (1970, November). Experiments in intergroup discrimination. *Scientific American*, pp. 96–102. (p. 352)

Tajfel, H. (1981). *Human groups and social categories: Studies in social psychology.* London: Cambridge University Press. (p. 352)

Tajfel, H. (1982). Social psychology of intergroup relations. *Annual Review of Psychology*, **33**, 1–39. (p. 352)

Tajfel, H., & Billig, M. (1974). Familiarity and categorization in intergroup behavior. *Journal of Experimental Social Psychology*, **10**, 159–170. (p. 352)

Takooshian, H., & Bodinger, H. (1982). Bystander indifference to street crime. In L. Savitz & N. Johnston (Eds.), *Contemporary criminology.* New York: Wiley. (p. 499)

Talbert, B. (1997, February 2). Bob Talbert's quote bag. *Detroit Free Press*, p. 5E, quoting *Allure* magazine. (p. 73)

Talbot, M. (2002, June 2). Hysteria hysteria. *The New York Times Magazine. www.nytimes.com*, 42. (p. 212)

Tamres, L. K., Janicki, D., & Helgeson, V. S. (2002). Sex differences in coping behavior: A meta-analytic review and an examination of relative coping. *Personality and Social Psychology Review*, **6**, 2–30. (p. 182)

Tang, S-H., & Hall, V. C. (1995). The overjustification effect: A meta-analysis. *Applied Cognitive Psychology*, **9**, 365–404. (p. 160)

Tangney, J. P., Baumeister, R. F., & Boone, A. L. (2004). High self-control predicts good adjustment, less pathology, better, grades, and interpersonal success. *Journal of Personality*, **72**, 271–324. (p. 59)

Tanke, E. D., & Tanke, T. J. (1979). Getting off a slippery slope: Social science in the judicial processes. *American Psychologist*, **34**, 1130–1138. (pp. 633, 634)

Tannen, D. (1990). *You just don't understand: Women and men in conversation.* New York: Morrow. (p. 182)

Tapp, J. L. (1980). Psychological and policy perspectives on the law: Reflections on a decade. *Journal of Social Issues*, **36**(2), 165–192. (p. 634)

Tarmann, A. (2002, May/June). Out of the closet and onto the Census long form. *Population Today*, **30**, 1, 6. (p. 363)

Taubes, G. (1992). Violence epidemiologists tests of hazards of gun ownership. *Science*, **258**, 213–215. (pp. 397, 420)

Tavris, C. (1988). Beyond cartoon killings: Comments on two overlooked effects of television. In S. Oskamp (Ed.), *Television as a social issue.* Newbury Park, CA: Sage. (p. 416)

Tavris, C. (1992). *The mismeasure of woman.* New York: Simon & Schuster. (p. 587)

Taylor, D. A., Gould, R. J., & Brounstein, P. J. (1981). Effects of personalistic self-disclosure. *Personality and Social Psychology Bulletin*, **7**, 487–492. (p. 462)

Taylor, D. G., Sheatsley, P. B., & Greeley, A. M. (1978). Attitudes toward racial integration. *Scientific American*, **238**(6), 42–49. (p. 148)

Taylor, D. M., & Doria, J. R. (1981). Self-serving and group-serving bias in attribution. *Journal of Social Psychology*, **113**, 201–211. (p. 76)

Taylor, K. M., & Shepperd, J. A. (1998). Bracing for the worst: Severity, testing, and feedback timing as moderators of the optimistic bias. *Personality and Social Psychology Bulletin*, **24**, 915–926. (p. 72)

Taylor, S. E. (1979). Remarks at symposium on social psychology and medicine, American Psychological Association convention. (p. 60)

Taylor, S. E. (1981). A categorization approach to stereotyping. In D. L. Hamilton (Ed.), *Cognitive processes in stereotyping and intergroup behavior.* Hillsdale, NJ: Erlbaum. (p. 359)

Taylor, S. E. (1989). *Positive illusions: Creative self-deception and the healthy mind.* New York: Basic Books. (pp. 71, 577, 658)

Taylor, S. E. (2002). The tending instinct: How nurturing is essential to who we are and how we live. New York: Times Books, Henry Holt. (p. 183)

Taylor, S. E., Crocker, J., Fiske, S. T., Sprinzen, M., & Winkler, J. D. (1979). The generalizability of salience effects. *Journal of Personality and Social Psychology*, **37**, 357–368. (p. 360)

Taylor, S. E., & Fiske, S. T. (1978). Salience, attention, and attribution: Top of the head phenomena. In L. Berkowitz (Ed.), *Advances in* *experimental social psychology* (Vol. 11). New York: Academic Press. (p. 360)

Taylor, S. E., Fiske, S. T., Etcoff, N. L., & Ruderman, A. J. (1978). Categorical and contextual bases of person memory and stereotyping. *Journal of Personality and Social Psychology,* **36,** 778–793. (p. 358)

Taylor, S. E., Lerner, J. S., Sherman, D. K., Sage, R. M., & McDowell, N. K. (2003). Are self-enhancing cognitions associated with healthy or unhealthy biological profiles? *Journal of Personality and Social Psychology* **85,** 605–615. (p. 75)

Taylor, S. E., Lerner, J. S., Sherman, D. K., Sage, R. M., & McDowell, N. K. (2003). Portrait of the self-enhancer: Well adjusted and well liked or maladjusted and friendless? *Journal of Personality and Social Psychology,* **84,** 165–176. (p. 75)

Taylor, S. E., Repetti, R. L., & Seeman, T. (1997). Health psychology: What is an unhealthy environment and how does it get under the skin? *Annual Review of Psychology,* **48,** 411–447. (p. 598)

Taylor, S. P., & Chermack, S. T. (1993). Alcohol, drugs and human physical aggression. *Journal of Studies on Alcohol,* Supplement No. **11,** 78–88. (p. 384)

Technical Working Group for Eyewitness Evidence (1999). Eyewitness Evidence: A Guide for Law Enforcement. A research report of the U.S. Department of Justice, Office of Justice Programs, National Institute of Justice. (p. 615)

Tedeschi, J. T., Nesler, M., & Taylor, E. (1987). Misattribution and the bogus pipeline: A test of dissonance and impression management theories. Paper presented at the American Psychological Association convention. (p. 151)

Teger, A. I. (1980). *Too much invested to quit.* New York: Pergamon Press. (p. 524)

Teigen, K. H. (1986). Old truths or fresh insights? A study of students' evaluations of proverbs. *British Journal of Social Psychology,* **25,** 43–50. (p. 18)

Teigen, K. H., Evensen, P. C., Samoilow, D. K., & Vatne, K. B. (1999). Good luck and bad luck: How to tell the difference. *European Journal of Social Psychology,* **29,** 981–1010. (p. 116)

Telch, M. J., Killen, J. D., McAlister, A. L., Perry, C. L., & Maccoby, N. (1981). Long-term follow-up of a pilot project on smoking prevention with adolescents. Paper presented at the American Psychological Association convention. (p. 280)

Tennen, H., & Affleck, G. (1987). The costs and benefits of optimistic explanations and dispositional optimism. *Journal of Personality,* **55,** 377–393. (p. 591)

Tennov, D. (1979). *Love and limerence: The experience of being in love.* New York: Stein and Day, p. 22. (p. 482)

Tesser, A. (1988). Toward a self-evaluation maintenance model of social behavior. In L. Berkowitz (Ed.), *Advances in experimental social psychology,* Vol. 21. San Diego, CA: Academic Press. (p. 63)

Tesser, A., Martin, L., & Mendolia, M. (1995). The impact of thought on attitude extremity and attitude-behavior consistency. In R. E. Petty and J. A Krosnick (Eds.), *Attitude strength: Antecedents and consequences.* Hillsdale, NJ: Erlbaum. (p. 309)

Tesser, A., Millar, M., & Moore, J. (1988). Some affective consequences of social comparison and reflection processes: The pain and pleasure of being close. *Journal of Personality and Social Psychology,* **54,** 49–61. (p. 353)

Tesser, A., Rosen, S., & Conlee, M. C. (1972). News valence and available recipient as determinants of news transmission. *Sociometry,* **35,** 619–628. (pp. 142–143)

Testa, M. (2002). The impact of men's alcohol consumption on perpetration of sexual aggression. *Clinical Psychology Review,* 22, 1239–1263. (p. 384)

Tetlock, P. E. (1983). Accountability and complexity of thought. *Journal of Personality and Social Psychology,* **45,** 74–83. (pp. 142–143)

Tetlock, P. E. (1985). Integrative complexity of American and Soviet foreign policy rhetoric: A time-series analysis. *Journal of Personality and Social Psychology,* **49,** 1565–1585. (p. 557)

Tetlock, P. E. (1988). Monitoring the integrative complexity of American and Soviet policy rhetoric: What can be learned? *Journal of Social Issues,* **44,** 101–131. (pp. 536–537)

Tetlock, P. E. (1998). Close-call counterfactuals and belief-system defenses: I was not almost wrong but I was almost right. *Journal of Personality and Social Psychology,* **75,** 639–652. (p. 111)

Tetlock, P. E. (1999). Theory-driven reasoning about plausible pasts and probable futures in world politics: Are we prisoners of our preconceptions? *American Journal of Political Science,* **43,** 335–366. (p. 111)

Tetlock, P. E., Peterson, R. S., McGuire, C., Chang, S., & Feld, P. (1992). Assessing political group dynamics: A test of the groupthink model. *Journal of Personality and Social Psychology,* **63,** 403–425. (p. 317)

TGM (2000). Canadian teens forsaking television for the Internet (an Angus Reid poll reported by the *Toronto Globe and Mail*). *Grand Rapids Press,* May 30, 2000. (p. 307)

Thibodeau, R. (1989). From racism to tokenism: The changing face of blacks in *New Yorker* cartoons. *Public Opinion Quarterly,* **53,** 482–494. (p. 349)

Thomas, G. C., & Batson, C. D. (1981). Effect of helping under normative pressure on self-perceived altruism. *Social Psychology Quarterly,* **44,** 127–131. (pp. 515–516)

Thomas, G. C., Batson, C. D., & Coke, J. S. (1981). Do Good Samaritans discourage helpfulness? Self-perceived altruism after exposure to highly helpful others. *Journal of Personality and Social Psychology,* **40,** 194–200. (pp. 515–516)

Thomas, G., & Fletcher, G. J. O. (2003). Mind-reading accuracy in intimate relationships: Assessing the roles of the relationship, the target, and the judge. *Journal of Personality and Social Psychology,* **85,** 1079–1094. (p. 185)

Thomas, K. W., & Pondy, L. R. (1977). Toward an "intent" model of conflict management among principal parties. *Human Relations,* **30,** 1089–1102. (p. 535)

Thomas, L. (1971). Notes of a biology watcher: A fear of pheromones. *New*

England Journal of Medicine, **285**, 292–293. (p. 191)

Thomas, L. (1978). Hubris in science? Science, **200**, 1459–1462. (p. 575)

Thomas, L. (1981). Quoted by J. L. Powell. Testimony before the Senate Subcommittee on Science, Technology and Space, April 22. (p. 379)

Thompson, D. (2001, September 14). Arab-Americans feel backlash. ABCNEWS.com (http://abcnews.go.com/sections/us/DailyNews/wtc_backlash-010914.html) (p. 332)

Thompson, L. (1990a). An examination of naive and experienced negotiators. Journal of Personality and Social Psychology, **59**, 82–90. (p. 554)

Thompson, L. (1990b). The influence of experience on negotiation performance. Journal of Experimental Social Psychology, **26**, 528–544. (p. 554)

Thompson, L. (1998b). The mind and heart of the negotiator. Upper Saddle River, NJ: Prentice-Hall. (p. 554)

Thompson, L. L., & Crocker, J. (1985). Prejudice following threat to the self-concept. Effects of performance expectations and attributions. Unpublished manuscript, Northwestern University. (p. 355)

Thompson, L., & Hrebec, D. (1996). Lose-lose agreements in interdependent decision making. Psychological Bulletin, **120**, 396–409. (p. 554)

Thompson, L., Valley, K. L., & Kramer, R. M. (1995). The bittersweet feeling of success: An examination of social perception in negotiation. Journal of Experimental Social Psychology, **31**, 467–492. (p. 554)

Thompson, S. C., Armstrong, W., & Thomas, C. (1998). Illusions of control, underestimations, and accuracy: A control heuristic explanation. Psychological Bulletin, **123**, 143–161. (p. 117)

Thompson, W. C., & Schumann, E. L. (1987). Interpretation of statistical evidence in criminal trials. Law and Human Behavior, **11**, 167–187. (p. 627)

Thompson, W. C., Cowan, C. L., & Rosenhan, D. L. (1980). Focus of attention mediates the impact of negative affect on altruism. Journal of

Personality and Social Psychology, **38**, 291–300. (p. 481)

Thompson, W. C., Fong, G. T., & Rosenhan, D. L. (1981). Inadmissible evidence and juror verdicts. Journal of Personality and Social Psychology, **40**, 453–463. (p. 635)

Thomson, R., & Murachver, T. (2001). Predicting gender from electronic discourse. British Journal of Social Psychology, **40**, 193–208 (and personal correspondence from T. Murachver, May 23, 2002). (p. 182)

Thornton, B., & Maurice, J. (1997). Physique contrast effect: Adverse impact of idealized body images for women. Sex Roles, **37**, 433–439. (p. 440)

Tice, D. M., & Baumeister, R. F. (1997). Longitudinal study of procrastination, performance, stress, and health: The costs and benefits of dawdling. Psychological Science, **8**, 454–458. (p. 590)

Tice, D. M., Butler, J. L., Muraven, M. B., & Stillwell, A. M. (1995). When modesty prevails: Differential favorability of self-presentation to friends and strangers. Journal of Personality and Social Psychology, **69**, 1120–1138. (p. 79)

Tideman, S. (2003, undated). Announcement (of Operationalizing Gross National Happiness conference, February 18–20, 2004). Distributed via the Internet. (p. 660)

Time (1992, March 30). The not so merry wife of Windsor. pp. 38–39. (p. 467)

Time (1994, November 7). Vox pop (poll by Yankelovich Partners Inc.). P. 21. (p. 26)

Time (1997, March 31). Local heroes. P. 26. (p. 475)

Timko, C., & Moos, R. H. (1989). Choice, control, and adaptation among elderly residents of sheltered care settings. Journal of Applied Social Psychology, **19**, 636–655. (p. 61)

Tindale, R. S., Davis, J. H., Vollrath, D. A., Nagao, D. H., & Hinsz, V. B. (1990). Asymmetrical social influence in freely interacting groups: A test of three models. Journal of Personality and Social Psychology, **58**, 438–449. (p. 633)

Tjaden, P., & Thoennes, N. (2000). Prevalence, incidence, and consequences of violence against women: Findings from

the National Violence Against Women Survey (National Institute of Justice Report No. NCJ-172837). Washington, DC: U.S. Department of Justice, National Institute of Justice. (p. 401)

Tobin, R. J., & Eagles, M. (1992). U.S. and Canadian attitudes toward international interactions: A cross-national test of the double-standard hypothesis. Basic and Applied Social Psychology, **13**, 447–459. (p. 533)

Tomorrow, T. (2003, April 30). Passive tense verbs deployed before large audience; stories remain unclear. (www240.pair.com/tomtom/pages/ja/ja_fr.html) (p. 246)

Tormala, Z. L., & Petty, R. E. (2002). What doesn't kill me makes me stronger: The effects of resisting persuasion on attitude change. Journal of Personality and Social Psychology, **83**, 1298–1313. (p. 278)

Totterdell, P., Kellett, S., Briner, R. B., & Teuchmann, K. (1998). Evidence of mood linkage in work groups. Journal of Personality and Social Psychology, **74**, 1504–1515. (p. 211)

Towson, S. M. J., & Zanna, M. P. (1983). Retaliation against sexual assault: Self-defense or public duty? Psychology of Women Quarterly, **8**, 89–99. (p. 620)

Travis, L. E. (1925). The effect of a small audience upon eye-hand coordination. Journal of Abnormal and Social Psychology, **20**, 142–146. (p. 287)

Trewin, D. (2001). Australian social trends 2001. Canberra: Australian Bureau of Statistics. (p. 403)

Triandis, H. C. (1981). Some dimensions of intercultural variation and their implications for interpersonal behavior. Paper presented at the American Psychological Association convention. (p. 174)

Triandis, H. C. (1982). Incongruence between intentions and behavior: A review. Paper presented at the American Psychological Association convention. (p. 136)

Triandis, H. C. (1994). Culture and social behavior. New York: McGraw-Hill. (pp. 46, 391, 468, 552)

Triandis, H. C. (2000). Culture and conflict. International Journal of Psychology, **55**, 145–152. (p. 49)

Triandis, H. C., Bontempo, R., Villareal, M. J., Asai, M., & Lucca, N. (1988). Individualism and collectivism: Cross-cultural perspectives on self-ingroup relationships. *Journal of Personality and Social Psychology*, **54**, 323–338. (p. 457)

Trimble, D. E. (1993). Meta-analysis of altruism and intrinsic and extrinsic religiousness. Paper presented at the Eastern Psychological Association convention. (p. 508)

Triplett, N. (1898). The dynamogenic factors in pacemaking and competition. *American Journal of Psychology*, **9**, 507–533. (p. 287)

Trolier, T. K., & Hamilton, D. L. (1986). Variables influencing judgments of correlational relations. *Journal of Personality and Social Psychology*, **50**, 879–888. (p. 117)

Tropp, L. R., & Pettigrew, T. F. (2004). Intergroup contact and the central role of affect in intergroup prejudice. In C. W. Leach & L. Tiedens (Eds.), *The social life of emotion*. Cambridge: Cambridge University Press. (pp. 539–540, 541)

Trost, M. R., Maass, A., & Kenrick, D. T. (1992). Minority influence: Personal relevance biases cognitive processes and reverses private acceptance. *Journal of Experimental Social Psychology*, **28**, 234–254. (p. 322)

Trouilloud, D. O., Sarrazin, P. G., Martinek, T. J., & Guillet, E. (2002). The influence of teacher expectations on student achievement in physical education classes: Pygmalion revisited. *European Journal of Social Psychology*, **32**, 591–607. (p. 121)

Tsang, J-A. (2002). Moral rationalization and the integration of situational factors and psychological processes in immoral behavior. *Review of General Psychology*, **6**, 25–50. (p. 227)

Tuan, Y-F. (1982). *Segmented worlds and self: Group life and individual consciousness*. Minneapolis: University of Minnesota Press. (p. 302)

Tumin, M. M. (1958). Readiness and resistance to desegregation: A social portrait of the hard core. *Social Forces*, **36**, 256–273. (p. 350)

Turner, C. W., Hesse, B. W., & Peterson-Lewis, S. (1986). Naturalistic studies of the long-term effects of television violence. *Journal of Social Issues*, **42**(3), 51–74. (p. 404)

Turner, J. C. (1981). The experimental social psychology of intergroup behaviour. In J. Turner & H. Giles (Eds.), *Intergroup behavior*. Oxford, England: Blackwell. (p. 350)

Turner, J. C. (1984). Social identification and psychological group formation. In H. Tajfel (Ed.), *The social dimensions: European developments in social psychology*, vol. 2. London: Cambridge University Press. (p. 351)

Turner, J. C. (1987). *Rediscovering the social group: A self-categorization theory*. New York: Basil Blackwell. (pp. 286, 350)

Turner, J. C. (1991). *Social influence*. Milton Keynes, England: Open University Press. (p. 350)

Turner, J. C., & Haslam, S. A. (2001). Social identity, organizations, and leadership. In M. E. Turner (Ed.), *Groups at work: Theory and research*. Mahwah, NJ: Erlbaum. (p. 350)

Turner, M. E., & Pratkanis, A. R. (1993). Effects of preferential and meritorious selection on performance: An examination of intuitive and self-handicapping perspectives. *Personality and Social Psychology Bulletin*, **19**, 47–58. (p. 79)

Turner, M. E., & Pratkanis, A. R. (1994). Social identity maintenance prescriptions for preventing groupthink: Reducing identity protection and enhancing intellectual conflict. *International Journal of Conflict Management*, **5**, 254–270. (pp. 312–313)

Turner, M. E., & Pratkanis, A. R. (1997). Mitigating groupthink by stimulating constructive conflict. In C. K. W. De Dreu & E. Van de Vliert (Eds.), *Using conflict in organizations*. London: Sage. (p. 315)

Turner, M. E., Pratkanis, A. R., Probasco, P., & Leve, C. (1992). Threat cohesion, and group effectiveness: Testing a social identity maintenance perspective on groupthink. *Journal of Personality and Social Psychology*, **63**, 781–796. (pp. 312–313)

TV Guide (1977, January 26), pp. 5–10. (p. 404)

Tversky, A. (1985, June). Quoted by Kevin McKean, Decisions, decisions. *Discover*, pp. 22–31. (p. 127)

Tversky, A., & Kahneman, D. (1973). Availability: A neuristic for judging frequency and probability. *Cognitive Psychology*, **5**, 207–302. (p. 114)

Tverksy, A., & Kahneman, D. (1974). Judgment under uncertainty: Heuristics and biases. *Science*, **185**, 1123–1131. (pp. 115, 117)

Tversky, A., & Kahneman, D. (1983). Extensional versus intuitive reasoning: The conjunction fallacy in probability judgment. *Psychological Review*, **90**, 293–315. (p. 113)

Twenge, J. M. (1997). Changes in masculine and feminine traits over time: A meta-analysis. *Sex Roles*, **36**, 305–325. (p. 202)

Twenge, J. M. (2001). Changes in women's assertiveness in response to status and roles: A cross-temporal meta-analysis, 1931–1993. *Journal of Personality and Social Psychology*, **81**, 133–145. (p. 187)

Twenge, J. M., Baumeister, R. F., Tice, D. M., & Stucke, T. S. (2001). If you can't join them, beat them: Effects of social exclusion on aggressive behavior. *Journal of Personality and Social Psychology*, **81**, 1058–1069. (p. 424)

Twenge, J. M., Catanese, K. R., & Baumeister, R. F. (2002). Social exclusion causes self-defeating behavior. *Journal of Personality and Social Psychology*, **83**, 606–615. (p. 424)

Twenge, J. M., Catanese, K. R., & Baumeister, R. F. (2003). Social exclusion and the deconstructed state: Time perception, meaninglessness, lethargy, lack of emotion, and self-awareness. *Journal of Personality and Social Psychology*, **85**, 409–423. (p. 424)

Tyler, T. R., & Lind, E. A. (1990). Intrinsic versus community-based justice models: When does group membership matter? *Journal of Social Issues*, **46**, 83–94. (pp. 512–513)

Tzeng, M. (1992). The effects of socioeconomic heterogamy and changes on marital dissolution for first marriages. *Journal of Marriage and the Family*, **54**, 609–619. (pp. 468–469)

U. S. Department of Justice. (1980). *Sourcebook of criminal justice statistics.* Washington, DC: Government Printing Office. (p. 606)

Uchino, B. N., Cacioppo, J. T., & Kiecolt-Glaser, J. K. (1996). The relationship between social support and physiological processes: A review with emphasis on underlying mechanisms and implications for health. *Psychological Bulletin,* **119,** 488–531. (p. 598)

Ugwuegbu, C. E. (1979). Racial and evidential factors in juror attribution of legal responsibility. *Journal of Experimental Social Psychology,* **15,** 133–146. (p. 620)

Uleman, J. S. (1989). A framework for thinking intentionally about unintended thoughts. In J. S. Uleman & J. A. Bargh (Eds.), *Unintended thought: The limits of awareness, intention, and control.* New York: Guilford. (p. 87)

Umberson, D., & Hughes, M. (1987). The impact of physical attractiveness on achievement and psychological well-being. *Social Psychology Quarterly,* **50,** 227–236. (p. 436)

Underwood, B., & Moore, B. (1982). Perspective-taking and altruism. *Psychological Bulletin,* **91,** 143–173. (p. 481)

Unger, R. K. (1979). Whom does helping help? Paper presented at the Eastern Psychological Association convention, April. (p. 478)

Unger, R. K. (1985). Epistomological consistency and its scientific implications. *American Psychologist,* **40,** 1413–1414. (p. 14)

United Nations (1991). *The world's women 1970–1990: Trends and statistics.* New York: United Nations. (pp. 195–196, 342)

United Nations Development Programme (1998). *Human development report 1998.* New York: Oxford. (pp. 646–647)

UPI. (1970/1967). September 23, 1967. Cited by P. G. Zimbardo, in The human choice: Individuation, reason, and order versus deindividuation, impulse, and chaos. In W. J. Arnold & D. Levine (Eds.), *Nebraska symposium on motivation,* 1969. Lincoln: University of Nebraska Press. (p. 298)

Usher, J. M. (1992). Research and theory related to female reproduction: Implications for clinical psychology. *British Journal of Clinical Psychology,* **31,** 129–151. (p. 587)

Vaillant, G. E. (1977). *Adaptation to life.* Boston: Little, Brown. (p. 103)

Valliant, G. E. (1997). Report on distress and longevity. Paper presented to the American Psychiatric Association convention. (pp. 588–589)

Vallone, R. P., Griffin, D. W., Lin, S., & Ross, L. (1990). Overconfident prediction of future actions and outcomes by self and others. *Journal of Personality and Social Psychology,* **58,** 582–592. (p. 110)

Vallone, R. P., Ross, L., & Lepper, M. R. (1985). The hostile media phenomenon: Biased perception and perceptions of media bias in coverage of the "Beirut Massacre." *Journal of Personality and Social Psychology,* **49,** 577–585. (p. 99)

van Baaren, R. B., Holland, R. W., Karremans, R. W., & van Knippenberg, A. (2003b). Mimicry and interpersonal closeness. Unpublished manuscript, University of Nijmegen. (p. 443)

van Baaren, R. B., Holland, R. W., Steenaert, B., & van Knippenberg, A. (2003a). Mimicry for money: Behavioral consequences of imitation. *Journal of Experimental Social Psychology,* **39,** 393–398. (p. 443)

Van Boven, L., & Gilovich, T. (2003). To do or to have? That is the question. *Journal of Personality and Social Psychology,* **85,** 1193–1202. (p. 656)

Van Boven, L., & Loewenstein, G. (2003). Social projection of transient drive states. *Personality and Social Psychology Bulletin,* **29,** 1159–1168. (p. 73)

van den Bos, K., Spruijt, N. (2002). Appropriateness of decisions as a moderator of the psychology of voice. *European Journal of Social Psychology,* **32,** 57–72. (p. 324)

Van Knippenberg, D., & Wilke, H. (1992). Prototypicality of arguments and conformity to ingroup norms. *European Journal of Social Psychology,* **22,** 141–155. (p. 254)

Van Lange, P. A. M. (1991). Being better but not smarter than others: The Muhammad Ali effect at work in interpersonal situations. *Personality and Social Psychology Bulletin,* **17,** 689–693. (p. 69)

Van Lange, P. A. M., & Visser, K. (1999). Locomotion in social dilemmas: How people adapt to cooperative, tit-for-tat, and noncooperative partners. *Journal of Personality and Social Psychology,* **77,** 762–773. (p. 559)

Van Lange, P. A. M., Taris, T. W., & Vonk, R. (1997). Dilemmas of academic practice: perceptions of superiority among social psychologists. *European Journal of Social Psychology,* **27,** 675–685. (p. 69)

Van Vugt, M., Van Lange, P. A. M., & Meertens, R. M. (1996). Commuting by car or public transportation? A social dilemma analysis of travel mode judgements. *European Journal of Social Psychology,* **26,** 373–395. (p. 528)

Van Yperen, N. W., & Buunk, B. P. (1990). A longitudinal study of equity and satisfaction in intimate relationships. *European Journal of Social Psychology,* **20,** 287–309. (p. 461)

Vandello, J. A., & Cohen, D. (1999). Patterns of individualism and collectivism across the United States. *Journal of Personality and Social Psychology,* **77,** 279–292. (p. 48)

Vandello, J. A., & Cohen, D. (2003). Male honor and female fidelity: Implicit cultural scripts that perpetuate domestic violence. *Journal of Personality and Social Psychology,* **84,** 997–1010. (p. 392)

Vanderslice, V. J., Rice, R. W., & Julian, J. W. (1987). The effects of participation in decision-making on worker satisfaction and productivity: An organizational simulation. *Journal of Applied Social Psychology,* **17,** 158–170. (p. 324)

Vanman, E. J., Paul, B. Y., Kaplan, D. L., & Miller, N. (1990). Facial electromyography differentiates racial bias in imagined cooperative settings. *Psychophysiology,* **27,** 563. (p. 356)

Vaughan, K. B., & Lanzetta, J. T. (1981). The effect of modification of expressive displays on vicarious emotional arousal. *Journal of*

Experimental Social Psychology, 17, 16–30. (p. 158)

Vaux, A. (1988). Social and personal factors in loneliness. *Journal of Social and Clinical Psychology, 6,* 462–471. (p. 582)

Verplanken, B. (1991). Persuasive communication of risk information: A test of cue versus message processing effects in a field experiment. *Personality and Social Psychology Bulletin, 17,* 188–193. (p. 249)

Veysey, B. M., & Messner, S. F. (1999). Further testing of social disorganization theory: An elaboration of Sampson and Groves's "Community structure and crime." *Journal of Research in Crime and Delinquency, 36,* 156–174. (p. 306)

Vidmar, N. (1979). The other issues in jury simulation research. *Law and Human Behavior, 3,* 95–106. (p. 634)

Vidmar, N., & Laird, N. M. (1983). Adversary social roles: Their effects on witnesses' communication of evidence and the assessments of adjudicators. *Journal of Personality and Social Psychology, 44,* 888–898. (p. 613)

Vignoles, V. L., Chryssochoou, X., & Breakwell, G. M. (2000). The distinctiveness principle: Identity, meaning, and the bounds of cultural relativity. *Personality and Social Psychology Review, 4,* 337–354. (pp. 240–241)

Visher, C. A. (1987). Juror decision making: The importance of evidence. *Law and Human Behavior, 11,* 1–17. (pp. 607, 619)

Visintainer, M. A., & Seligman, M. E. (1983, July/August). The hope factor. *American Health,* pp. 59–61. (p. 589)

Visintainer, M. A., & Seligman, M. E. P. (1985). Tumor rejection and early experience of uncontrollable shock in the rat. Unpublished manuscript, University of Pennsylvania. See also, M. A. Visintainer et al. (1982). Tumor rejection in rats after inescapable versus escapable shock. *Science, 216,* 437–439. (p. 589)

Visser, P. S., & Krosnick, J. A. (1998). Development of attitude strength over the life cycle: Surge and decline. *Journal of Personality and Social Psychology, 75,* 1389–1410. (p. 267)

Vitelli, R. (1988). The crisis issue assessed: An empirical analysis. *Basic and Applied Social Psychology, 9,* 301–309. (p. 31)

Vivian, J. E., & Berkowitz, N. H. (1993). Anticipated outgroup evaluations and intergroup bias. *European Journal of Social Psychology, 23,* 513–524. (p. 354)

Vollrath, D. A., Sheppard, B. H., Hinsz, V. B., & Davis, J. H. (1989). Memory performance by decision-making groups and individuals. *Organizational Behavior and Human Decision Processes, 43,* 289–300. (p. 633)

von Hippel, W., Silver, L. A., & Lynch, M. B. (2000). Stereotyping against your will: The role of inhibitory ability in stereotyping and prejudice among the elderly. *Personality and Social Psychology Bulletin, 26,* 523–532. (p. 356)

Vorauer, J. D., Main, K. J., & O'Connell, G. B. (1998). How do individuals expect to be viewed by members of lower status groups? Content and implications of meta-stereotypes. *Journal of Personality and Social Psychology, 75,* 917–937. (p. 362)

Vorauer, J. D., & Ratner, R. K. (1996). Who's going to make the first move? Pluralistic ignorance as an impediment to relationship formation. *Journal of Social and Personal Relationships, 13,* 483–506. (p. 309)

Wachtler, J., & Counselman, E. (1981). When increasing liking for a communicator decreases opinion change: An attribution analysis of attractiveness. *Journal of Experimental Social Psychology, 17,* 386–395. (p. 253)

Wackernagel, M. (2000). Carrying capacity, overshoot and the need to curb human consumption. In B. Heap & J. Kent (Eds.), *Towards sustainable consumption: A European perspective.* London: The Royal Society. (p. 644)

Wackernagel, M., Schulz, N. B., Deumling, D., Linares, A. C., Jenkins, M., Kapos, V., Monfreda, C., Loh, J., Myers, N., Norgaard, R., & Randers, J. (2002). Tracking the ecological overshoot of the human economy. *Proceedings of the National Academy of Sciences, 99,* 9266–9271. (p. 645)

Wagstaff, G. F. (1983). Attitudes to poverty, the Protestant ethic, and political affiliation: A preliminary investigation. *Social Behavior and Personality, 11,* 45–47. (p. 96)

Walfish, D. (2001). National count reveals major societal changes. *Science, 292,* 1823. (p. 342)

Walinsky, A. (1995, July). The crisis of public order. *The Atlantic Monthly,* pp. 39–54. (p. 419)

Walker, M., Harriman, S., & Costello, S. (1980). The influence of appearance on compliance with a request. *Journal of Social Psychology, 112,* 159–160. (p. 231)

Wall, B. (2002, August 24–25). Profit matures along with baby boomers. *International Herald Tribune,* p. 13. (p. 439)

Wallace, C. P. (2000, May 8). Germany's glass ceiling. *Time,* p. B8. (p. 196)

Wallace, D. S., Paulson, R. M., Lord, C. G., & Bond, C. F., Jr. (2004). Which behaviors do attitudes predict? Meta-analyzing the effects of social pressure and perceived difficulty. Unpublished manuscript, Fayetteville State University. (p. 138)

Wallace, M. *New York Times,* November 25, 1969. (p. 222)

Waller, J. (2002). *Becoming evil: How ordinary people commit genocide and mass killing.* New York: Oxford. (pp. 147, 234)

Walster (Hatfield), E. (1965). The effect of self-esteem on romantic liking. *Journal of Experimental Social Psychology, 1,* 184–197. (p. 448)

Walster (Hatfield), E., Aronson, V., Abrahams, D., & Rottman, L. (1966). Importance of physical attractiveness in dating behavior. *Journal of Personality and Social Psychology, 4,* 508–516. (p. 432)

Walster (Hatfield), E., & Festinger, L. (1962). The effectiveness of "overheard" persuasive communications. *Journal of Abnormal and Social Psychology, 65,* 395–402. (p. 252)

Walster (Hatfield), E., Walster, G. W., & Berscheid, E. (1978). *Equity: Theory and research.* Boston: Allyn and Bacon. (p. 530)

Ward, W. C., & Jenkins, H. M. (1965). The display of information and the judgment of contingency. *Canadian*

Journal of Psychology, **19**, 231–241. (p. 116)

Warnick, D. H., & Sanders, G. S. (1980). The effects of group discussion on eyewitness accuracy. *Journal of Applied Social Psychology*, **10**, 249–259. (p. 319)

Warr, P., & Payne, R. (1982). Experiences of strain and pleasure among British adults. *Social Science and Medicine*, **16**, 1691–1697. (p. 597)

Wason, P. C. (1960). On the failure to eliminate hypotheses in a conceptual task. *Quarterly Journal of Experimental Psychology*, **12**, 129–140. (p. 112)

Watkins, D., Akande, A., Fleming, J. (1998). Cultural dimensions, gender, and the nature of self-concept: A fourteen-country study? *International Journal of Psychology*, **33**, 17–31. (p. 182)

Watkins, D., Cheng, C., Mpofu, E., Olowu, S., Singh-Sengupta, S., & Regmi, M. (2003). Gender differences in self-construal: How generalizable are Western findings? *Journal of Social Psychology*, **143**, 501–519. (p. 182)

Watson, D. (1982, November). The actor and the observer: How are their perceptions of causality divergent? *Psychological Bulletin*, **92**, 682–700. (p. 94)

Watson, R. I., Jr. (1973). Investigation into deindividuation using a cross-cultural survey technique. *Journal of Personality and Social Psychology*, **25**, 342–345. (pp. 300–301)

Weary, G., & Edwards, J. A. (1994). Social cognition and clinical psychology: Anxiety, depression, and the processing of social information. In R. Wyer & T. Srull (Eds.), *Handbook of social cognition*, vol. 2. Hillsdale, NJ: Erlbaum. (p. 119)

Weary, G., Harvey, J. H., Schwieger, P., Olson, C. T., Perloff, R., & Pritchard, S. (1982). Self-presentation and the moderation of self-serving biases. *Social Cognition*, **1**, 140–159. (p. 79)

Webster, D. M. (1993). Motivated augmentation and reduction of the overattribution bias. *Journal of Personality and Social Psychology*, **65**, 261–271. (p. 96)

Wegner, D. M. (2002). *The illusion of conscious will.* Cambridge, MA: MIT Press. (p. 52)

Wegner, D. M., & Erber, R. (1992). The hyperaccessibility of suppressed thoughts. *Journal of Personality and Social Psychology*, **63**, 903–912. (p. 356)

Wehr, P. (1979). *Conflict regulation.* Boulder, CO: Westview Press. (p. 557)

Weiner, B. (1980). A cognitive (attribution)-emotion-action model of motivated behavior: An analysis of judgments of help-giving. *Journal of Personality and Social Psychology*, **39**, 186–200. (p. 485)

Weiner, B. (1981). The emotional consequences of causal ascriptions. Unpublished manuscript, UCLA. (p. 387)

Weiner, B. (1985). "Spontaneous" causal thinking. *Psychological Bulletin*, **97**, 74–84. (p. 84)

Weiner, B. (1995). Judgments of responsibility: A foundation for a theory of social conduct. New York: Guilford. (p. 85)

Weinstein, N. D. (1980). Unrealistic optimism about future life events. *Journal of Personality and Social Psychology*, **39**, 806–820. (p. 71)

Weinstein, N. D. (1982). Unrealistic optimism about susceptibility to health problems. *Journal of Behavioral Medicine*, **5**, 441–460. (p. 71)

Weiss, J., & Brown, P. (1976). Self-insight error in the explanation of mood. Unpublished manuscript, Harvard University. (p. 52)

Wells, G. L. (1984). The psychology of lineup identifications. *Journal of Applied Social Psychology*, **14**, 89–103. (p. 616)

Wells, G. L. (1986). Expert psychological testimony. *Law and Human Behavior*, **10**, 83–95. (p. 618)

Wells, G. L. (1992). Naked statistical evidence of liability: Is subjective probability enough? *Journal of Personality and Social Psychology*, **62**, 739–752. (p. 627)

Wells, G. L. (1993). What do we know about eyewitness identification? *American Psychologist*, **48**, 553–571. (p. 616)

Wells, G. L., & Bradfield, A. L. (1998). "Good, you identified the suspect": Feedback to eyewitnesses distorts their reports of the witnessing experience.

Journal of Applied Psychology, **83**, 360–376. (pp. 614–615)

Wells, G. L., & Bradfield, A. L. (1999). Distortions in eyewitnesses' recollections: Can the postidentification-feedback effect be moderated? *Psychological Science*, **10**, 138–144. (p. 614)

Wells, G. L., Ferguson, T. J., & Lindsay, R. C. L. (1981). The tractability of eyewitness confidence and its implications for triers of fact. *Journal of Applied Psychology*, **66**, 688–696. (pp. 613, 614)

Wells, G. L., & Leippe, M. R. (1981). How do triers of fact enter the accuracy of eyewitness identification? Memory for peripheral detail can be misleading. *Journal of Applied Psychology*, **66**, 682–687. (pp. 607–608)

Wells, G. L., Lindsay, R. C. L., & Ferguson, T. (1979). Accuracy, confidence, and juror perceptions in eyewitness identification. *Journal of Applied Psychology*, **64**, 440–448. (p. 607)

Wells, G. L., Lindsay, R. C. L., & Tousignant, J. P. (1980). Effects of expert psychological advice on human performance in judging the validity of eyewitness testimony. *Law and Human Behavior*, **4**, 275–285. (p. 607)

Wells, G. L., Malpass, R. S., Lindsay, R. C. L., Fisher, R. P., Turtle, J. W., & Fulero, S. M. (2000). Mistakes in eyewitness identification are caused by known factors. Collaboration between criminal justice experts and research psychologists may lower the number of errors. *American Psychologist*, **55**, 581–598. (p. 615)

Wells, G. L., & Murray, D. M. (1983). What can psychology say about the *Neil v. Biggers* criteria for judging eyewitness accuracy? *Journal of Applied Psychology*, **68**, 347–362. (p. 610)

Wells, G. L., Olson, E. A., & Charman, S. D. (2002). The confidence of eyewitnesses in their identifications from lineups. *Current Directions in Psychological Science*, **11**, 151–154. (pp. 608, 617)

Wells, G. L., & Olson, E. A. (2003). Eyewitness testimony. *Annual Review of Psychology*, **54**, 277–295. (pp. 608, 617)

Wells, G. L., & Petty, R. E. (1980). The effects of overt head movements on persuasion: Compatibility and incompatibility of responses. *Basic and Applied Social Psychology*, **1**, 219–230. (p. 158)

Wells, G. L., & Turtle, J. W. (1987). Eyewitness testimony research: Current knowledge and emergent controversies. *Canadian Journal of Behavioral Science*, **19**, 363–388. (p. 617)

Wener, R., Frazier, W., & Farbstein, J. (1987, June). Building better jails. *Psychology Today*, pp. 40–49. (pp. 60–61)

Wenzlaff, R. M., & Prohaska, M. L. (1989). When misery prefers company: Depression, attributions, and responses to others' moods. *Journal of Experimental Social Psychology*, **25**, 220–233. (p. 445)

Werner, C. M., Kagehiro, D. K., & Strube, M. J. (1982). Conviction proneness and the authoritarian juror: Inability to disregard information or attitudinal bias? *Journal of Applied Psychology*, **67**, 629–636. (p. 629)

Werner, C. M., Stoll, R., Birch, P., & White, P. H. (2002). Clinical validation and cognitive elaboration: Signs that encourage sustained recycling. *Basic and Applied Social Psychology*, **24**, 185–203. (p. 260)

West, S. G., & Brown, T. J. (1975). Physical attractiveness, the severity of the emergency and helping: A field experiment and interpersonal simulation. *Journal of Experimental Social Psychology*, **11**, 531–538. (p. 486)

West, S. G., Whitney, G., & Schnedler, R. (1975). Helping a motorist in distress: The effects of sex, race, and neighborhood. *Journal of Personality and Social Psychology*, **31**, 691–698. (p. 486)

Weyant, J. M. (1984). Applying social psychology to induce charitable donations. *Journal of Applied Social Psychology*, **14**, 441–447. (p. 512)

Weyant, J. M., & Smith, S. L. (1987). Getting more by asking for less: The effects of request size on donations of charity. *Journal of Applied Social Psychology*, **17**, 392–400. (p. 512)

Whatley, Mark A., Webster, J. M., Smith, R. H., & others. (1999). The effect of a favor on public and private compliance: How internalized is the norm of reciprocity? *Basic and Applied Social Psychology*, **21**, 251–261. (p. 484)

Wheeler, L., & Kim, Y. (1997). What is beautiful is culturally good: The physical attractiveness stereotype has different content in collectivistic cultures. *Personality and Social Psychology Bulletin*, **23**, 795–800. (p. 435)

Wheeler, L., Koestner, R., & Driver, R. E. (1982). Related attributes in the choice of comparison others: It's there, but it isn't all there is. *Journal of Experimental Social Psychology*, **18**, 489–500. (p. 44)

White, G. L. (1980). Physical attractiveness and courtship progress. *Journal of Personality and Social Psychology*, **39**, 660–668. (p. 433)

White, G. L., & Kight, T. D. (1984). Misattribution of arousal and attraction: Effects of salience of explanations for arousal. *Journal of Experimental Social Psychology*, **20**, 55–64. (pp. 454–455)

White, H. R., Brick, J., & Hansell, S. (1993). A longitudinal investigation of alcohol use and aggression in adolescence. *Journal of Studies on Alcohol*, Supplement No. **11**, 62–77. (p. 384)

White, J. A., & Plous, S. (1995). Self-enhancement and social responsibility: On caring more, but doing less, than others. *Journal of Applied Social Psychology*, **25**, 1297–1318. (p. 69)

White, J. W., & Kowalski, R. M. (1994). Deconstructing the myth of the nonaggressive woman. *Psychology of Women Quarterly*, **18**, 487–508. (p. 187)

White, M. (2000). *Historical atlas of the twentieth century*. http://users.erols.com/mwhite28/warstat8.htm. (p. 380)

White, M. J., & Gerstein, L. H. (1987). Helping: The influence of anticipated social sanctions and self-monitoring. *Journal of Personality*, **55**, 41–54. (p. 506)

White, P. A., & Younger, D. P. (1988). Differences in the ascription of transient internal states to self and other. *Journal of Experimental Social Psychology*, **24**, 292–309. (p. 90)

White, R. (1984). *Fearful warriors: A psychological profile of U.S.-Soviet relations*. New York: Free Press. (p. 533)

White, R. K. (1996). Why the Serbs fought: Motives and misperceptions. *Peace and Conflict: Journal of Peace Psychology*, **2**, 109–128. (p. 536)

White, R. K. (1998). American acts of force: Results and misperceptions. *Peace and Conflict*, **4**, 93–128. (p. 536)

Whitley, B. E., Jr. (1987). The effects of discredited eyewitness testimony: A meta-analysis. *Journal of Social Psychology*, **127**, 209–214. (p. 607)

Whitman, D. (1996, December 16). I'm OK, you're not. *U.S. News and World Report*, p. 24. (p. 76)

Whitman, D. (1998). *The optimism gap: The I'm OK—They're not syndrome and the myth of American decline*. New York: Walker & Co. (p. 334)

Whitman, R. M., Kramer, M., & Baldridge, B. (1963). Which dream does the patient tell? *Archives of General Psychology*, **8**, 277–282. (p. 572)

Whittaker, J. O., & Meade, R. D. (1967). Social pressure in the modification and distortion of judgment: A cross-cultural study. *International Journal of Psychology*, **2**, 109–113. (p. 237)

WHO (2002). *World health report 2002: Reducing risks, promoting healthy life*. Geneva: World Health Organization. (p. 133)

Whyte, G. (1993). Escalating commitment in individual and group decision making: A prospect theory approach. *Organizational Behavior and Human Decision Processes*, **54**, 430–455. (p. 305)

Wicker, A. W. (1969). Attitudes versus actions: The relationship of verbal and overt behavioral responses to attitude objects. *Journal of Social Issues*, **25**, 41–78. (p. 135)

Wicker, A. W. (1971). An examination of the "other variables" explanation of attitude-behavior inconsistency. *Journal of Personality and Social Psychology*, **19**, 18–30. (p. 136)

Widom, C. S. (1989). Does violence beget violence? A critical examination of the literature. *Psychological Bulletin*, **106**, 3–28. (p. 391)

Wiebe, D. J. (2003). Homicide and suicide risks associated with firearms in the home: A national case-control study. *Annals of Emergency Medicine,* **41**, 771–782. (p. 397)

Wiegman, O. (1985). Two politicians in a realistic experiment: Attraction, discrepancy, intensity of delivery, and attitude change. *Journal of Applied Social Psychology*, **15**, 673–686. (p. 251)

Wiesel, E. (1985, April 6). The brave Christians who saved Jews from the Nazis. *TV Guide*, pp. 4–6. (pp. 475–476)

Wieselquist, J., Rusbult, C. E., Foster, C. A., & Agnew, C. R. (1999). Commitment, pro-relationship behavior, and trust in close relationships. *Journal of Personality and Social Psychology*, **77**, 942–966. (p. 461)

Wilder, D. A. (1977). Perception of groups, size of opposition, and social influence. *Journal of Experimental Social Psychology*, **13**, 253–268. (pp. 228–229)

Wilder, D. A. (1978). Perceiving persons as a group: Effect on attributions of causality and beliefs. *Social Psychology*, **41**, 13–23. (p. 359)

Wilder, D. A. (1981). Perceiving persons as a group: Categorization and intergroup relations. In D. L. Hamilton (Ed.). *Cognitive processes in stereotyping and intergroup behavior.* Hillsdale, NJ: Erlbaum. (p. 352)

Wilder, D. A. (1990). Some determinants of the persuasive power of in-groups and out-groups: Organization of information and attribution of independence. *Journal of Personality and Social Psychology*, **59**, 1202–1213. (p. 254)

Wilder, D. A., & Shapiro, P. (1991). Facilitation of outgroup stereotypes by enhanced ingroup identity. *Journal of Experimental Social Psychology*, **27**, 431–452. (p. 354)

Wilder, D. A., & Shapiro, P. N. (1984). Role of out-group cues in determining social identity. *Journal of Personality and Social Psychology*, **47**, 342–348. (p. 543)

Wilder, D. A., & Shapiro, P. N. (1989). Role of competition-induced anxiety in limiting the beneficial impact of positive behavior by out-group members. *Journal of Personality and Social Psychology*, **56**, 60–69. (p. 369)

Wildschut, T., Pinter, B., Vevea, J. L., Insko, C. A., & Schopler, J. (2003). Beyond the group mind: A quantitative review of the interindividual-intergroup discontinuity effect. *Psychological Bulletin*, **129**, 698–722. (p. 529)

Wilkes, J. (1987, June). Murder in mind. *Psychology Today*, pp. 27–32. (p. 382)

Wilkinson, G. S. (1990, February). Food sharing in vampire bats. *Scientific American*, **262**, 76–82. (p. 488)

Willey, D. (1999). *Optimum world population.* Optimum Population Trust Brief 99/1. Manchester: Urmston. Cited by M. Wackernagel (2000). Carrying capacity, overshoot and the need to curb human consumption. In B. Heap & J. Kent (Eds.), *Towards sustainable consumption: A European perspective.* London: The Royal Society. (p. 644)

Williams, D. K., Bourgeois, M. J., & Croyle, R. T. (1993). The effects of stealing thunder in criminal and civil trials. *Law and Human Behavior,* **17**, 597–609. (p. 261)

Williams, J. E., & Best, D. L. (1990a). *Measuring sex stereotypes: A multination study.* Newbury Park, CA: Sage. (p. 185)

Williams, J. E., & Best, D. L. (1990b). *Sex and psyche: Gender and self viewed cross-culturally.* Newbury Park, CA: Sage. (p. 344)

Williams, J. E., Satterwhite, R. C., & Best, D. L. (1999). Pancultural gender stereotypes revisited: The Five Factor model. *Sex Roles*, **40**, 513–525. (p. 341)

Williams, J. E., Satterwhite, R. C., & Best, D. L. (2000). Five-factor gender stereotypes in 27 countries. Paper presented at the XV Congress of the International Association for Cross-Cultural Psychology, Pultusk, Poland. (p. 341)

Williams, K. D. (2002). *Ostracism: The power of silence.* New York: Guilford. (pp. 424, 429)

Williams, K. D., Cheung, C. K. T., & Choi, W. (2000). Cyberostracism: Effects of being ignored over the Internet. *Journal of Personality and Social Psychology*, **79**, 748–762. (pp. 425–426)

Williams, K. D., Harkins, S., & Latané, B. (1981). Identifiability as a deterrent to social loafing: Two cheering experiments. *Journal of Personality and Social Psychology*, **40**, 303–311. (p. 296)

Williams, K. D., Jackson, J. M., & Karau, S. J. (1992). Collective hedonism: A social loafing analysis of social dilemmas. In D. A. Schroeder (Ed.), *Social dilemmas: Social psychological perspectives.* New York: Praeger. (p. 294)

Williams, K. D., & Karau, S. J. (1991). Social loafing and social compensation: The effects of expectations of coworker performance. *Journal of Personality and Social Psychology,* **61**, 570–581. (p. 296)

Williams, K. D., Nida, S. A., Baca, L. D., & Latané, B. (1989). Social loafing and swimming: Effects of identifiability on individual and relay performance of intercollegiate swimmers. *Basic and Applied Social Psychology*, **10**, 73–81. (p. 295)

Williams, K. D. & Zadro, L. (2001). Ostracism: On being ignored, excluded and rejected. In M. Leary (Ed.), *Interpersonal rejection.* New York: Oxford. (p. 420)

Williams, R. (1993). *Anger kills.* New York: Times Books. (p. 588)

Williams, S., & Kohut, J. L. (1999). Psychologists in medical schools in 1997: Research brief. *American Psychologist*, **54**, 272–276. (p. 585)

Williams, T. M. (Ed.) (1986). *The impact of television: A natural experiment in three communities.* Orlando, FL: Academic Press. (p. 406)

Williamson, G. M., & Clark, M. S. (1989). Providing help and desired relationship type as determinants of changes in moods and self-evaluations. *Journal of Personality and Social Psychology,* **56**, 722–734. (p. 481)

Willis, F. N., & Hamm, H. K. (1980). The use of interpersonal touch in securing compliance. *Journal of Nonverbal Behavior,* **5**, 49–55. (p. 220)

Wills, T. A. (1981). Downward comparison principles in social psychology. *Psychological Bulletin*, **90**, 245–271. (p. 74)

Wilson, A. E., & Ross, M. (2001). From chump to champ: People's appraisals of their earlier and present selves.

Journal of Personality and Social Psychology, **80**, 572–584. (p. 68)

Wilson, D. K., Kaplan, R. M., & Schneiderman, L. J. (1987). Framing of decisions and selections of alternatives in health care. *Social Behaviour,* **2**, 51–59. (p. 588)

Wilson, D. W., & Donnerstein, E. (1979). Anonymity and interracial helping. Paper presented at the Southwestern Psychological Association convention. (p. 505)

Wilson, E. O. (1978). *On human nature.* Cambridge, MA: Harvard University Press. (p. 488)

Wilson, E. O. (2002, February). The bottleneck. *Scientific American,* **286**, 83–91. (p. 661)

Wilson, G. (1994, March 25). Equal, but different. *The Times Higher Education Supplement, Times of London.* (p. 191)

Wilson, J. P., & Petruska, R. (1984). Motivation, model attributes, and prosocial behavior. *Journal of Personality and Social Psychology,* **46**, 458–468. (p. 506)

Wilson, R. C., Gaft, J. G., Dienst, E. R., Wood, L., & Bavry, J. L. (1975). *College professors and their impact on students.* New York: Wiley. (p. 265)

Wilson, R. S., & Matheny, A. P., Jr. (1986). Behavior-genetics research in infant temperament: The Louisville twin study. In R. Plomin & J. Dunn (Eds.), *The study of temperament: Changes, continuities, and challenges.* Hillsdale, NJ: Erlbaum. (p. 384)

Wilson, T. D. (1985). Strangers to ourselves: The origins and accuracy of beliefs about one's own mental states. In J. H. Harvey & G. Weary (Eds.), *Attribution in contemporary psychology.* New York: Academic Press. (p. 55)

Wilson, T. D. (2002). *Strangers to ourselves: Discovering the adaptive unconscious.* Cambridge, MA: Harvard University Press. (p. 55)

Wilson, T. D., & Gilbert, D. T. (2003). Affective forecasting. *Advances in Experimental Social Psychology,* **35**, 346–413. (pp. 53, 55, 655)

Wilson, T. D., Dunn, D. S., Kraft, D., & Lisle, D. J. (1989). Introspection, attitude change, and attitude-behavior consistency: The disruptive effects of explaining why we feel the way we do. In L. Berkowitz (Eds.), *Advances in experimental social psychology,* Vol. 22. San Diego, CA: Academic Press. (p. 55)

Wilson, T. D., Laser, P. S., & Stone, J. I. (1982). Judging the predictors of one's mood: Accuracy and the use of shared theories. *Journal of Experimental Social Psychology,* **18**, 537–556. (p. 52)

Wilson, T. D., Lindsey, S., & Schooler, T. Y. (2000). A model of dual attitudes. *Psychological Review,* **107**, 101–126. (p. 56)

Wilson, T. D., Lisle, D. J., Schooler, J. W., Hodges, S. D., Klaaren, K. J., & LaFleur, S. J. (1993). Introspecting about reasons can reduce post-choice satisfaction. *Personality and Social Psychology Bulletin,* **19**, 331–339. (p. 55)

Wilson, W. R. (1979). Feeling more than we can know: Exposure effects without learning. *Journal of Personality and Social Psychology,* **37**, 811–821. (p. 429)

Winter, D. D. N. (2000). Some big ideas for some big problems. *American Psychologist,* **55**, 516–522. (p. 658)

Winter, F. W. (1973). A laboratory experiment of individual attitude response to advertising exposure. *Journal of Marketing Research,* **10**, 130–140. (p. 431)

Wiseman, R. (1998, Fall). Participatory science and the mass media. *Free Inquiry,* pp. 56–57. (p. 620)

Wisman, A., & Koole, S. L. (2003). Hiding in the crowd: Can mortality salience promote affiliation with others who oppose one's worldviews? *Journal of Personality and Social Psychology,* **84**, 511–526. (p. 424)

Wispe, L. G., & Freshley, H. B. (1971). Race, sex, and sympathetic helping behavior: The broken bag caper. *Journal of Personality and Social Psychology,* **17**, 59–65. (p. 505)

Wittenberg, M. T., & Reis, H. T. (1986). Loneliness, social skills, and social perception. *Personality and Social Psychology Bulletin,* **12**, 121–130. (p. 582)

Wittenbrink, B., Judd, C. M., & Park, B. (1997). Evidence for racial prejudice at the implicit level and its relationship with questionnaire measures. *Journal of Personality and Social Psychology,* **72**, 262–274. (p. 337)

Wixon, D. R., & Laird, J. D. (1976). Awareness and attitude change in the forced-compliance paradigm: The importance of when. *Journal of Personality and Social Psychology,* **34**, 376–384. (p. 103)

WMO (2003, July 2). According to the World Metereological Organization, extreme weather events might increase. World Metereological Association, press release WMO-No. 695. (p. 643)

Wohl, M. J. A., & Enzlc, M. E. (2002). The deployment of personal luck: Sympathetic magic and illusory control in games of pure chance. *Personality and Social Psychology Bulletin,* **28**, 1388–1397. (p. 117)

Wojciszke, B., Bazinska, R., & Jaworski, M. (1998). On the dominance of moral categories in impression formation. *Personality and Social Psychology Bulletin,* **24**, 1251–1263. (p. 451)

Wolf, S. (1987). Majority and minority influence: A social impact analysis. In M. P. Zanna, J. M. Olson, & C. P. Herman (Eds.), *Social influence: The Ontario symposium on personality and social psychology,* Vol. 5. Hillsdale, NJ: Erlbaum. (p. 323)

Wolf, S., & Latané, B. (1985). Conformity, innovation and the psycho-social law. In S. Moscovici, G. Mugny, & E. Van Avermaet (Eds.), *Perspectives on minority influence.* Cambridge: Cambridge University Press. (p. 323)

Wolf, S., & Montgomery, D. A. (1977). Effects of inadmissible evidence and level of judicial admonishment to disregard on the judgments of mock jurors. *Journal of Applied Social Psychology,* **7**, 205–219. (p. 622)

Wolsko, C., Park, B., Judd, C. M., & Wittenbrink, B. (2000). Framing interethnic ideology: Effects of multicultural and color blind perspectives on judgments of groups and individuals. *Journal of Personality and Social Psychology,* **78**, 635–654. (p. 354)

Women on Words and Images (1972). *Dick and Jane as victims: Sex stereotyping in children's readers.* Princeton: Women on Words and Images. Cited by C. Tavris & C. Offir (1977) in *The longest war: Sex differences in perspective.*

New York: Harcourt Brace Jovanovich, p. 177. (p. 348)

Wood, J. V. (1989). Theory and research concerning social comparisons of personal attributes. *Psychological Bulletin, 106,* 231–248. (p. 385)

Wood, J. V., Heimpel, S. A., & Michela, J. L. (2003). Savoring versus dampening: Self-esteem differences in regulating positive affect. *Journal of Personality and Social Psychology, 85,* 566–580. (p. 75)

Wood, J. V., Saltzberg, J. A., & Goldsamt, L. A. (1990a). Does affect induce self-focused attention? *Journal of Personality and Social Psychology, 58,* 899–908. (p. 580)

Wood, J. V., Saltzberg, J. A., Neale, J. M., Stone, A. A., & Rachmiel, T. B. (1990b). Self-focused attention, coping responses, and distressed mood in everyday life. *Journal of Personality and Social Psychology, 58,* 1027–1036. (p. 580)

Wood, W., & Eagly, A. H. (1981). Stages in the analysis of persuasive messages: The role of causal attributions and message comprehension. *Journal of Personality and Social Psychology, 40,* 246–259. (p. 253)

Wood, W., & Eagly, A. H. (2002). A cross-cultural analysis of the behavior of women and men: Implications for the origins of sex differences. *Psychological Bulletin, 128,* 699–727. (p. 202)

Wood, W., & Quinn, J. M. (2003). Forewarned and forewarmed? Two meta-analytic syntheses of forewarnings of influence appeals. *Psychological Bulletin, 129,* 119–138. (p. 269)

Wood, W., Rhodes, N., & Whelan, M. (1989). Sex differences in positive well-being: A consideration of emotional style and marital status. *Psychological Bulletin, 106,* 249–264. (p. 600)

Woodberry, R. D., & Smith, C. S. (1998). Fundamentalism et al: Conservative Protestants in America. *Annual Review of Sociology, 24,* 25–56. (p. 346)

Woodzicka, J. A., & LaFrance, M. (2001). Real versus imagined gender harassment. *Journal of Social Issues, 57*(1), 15–30. (p. 53)

Worchel, S., Andreoli, V. A., & Folger, R. (1977). Intergroup cooperation and intergroup attraction: The effect of previous interaction and outcome of combined effort. *Journal of Experimental Social Psychology, 13,* 131–140. (p. 547)

Worchel, S., Axsom, D., Ferris, F., Samah, G., & Schweitzer, S. (1978). Deterrents of the effect of intergroup cooperation on intergroup attraction. *Journal of Conflict Resolution, 22,* 429–439. (p. 547)

Worchel, S., & Brown, E. H. (1984). The role of plausibility in influencing environmental attributions. *Journal of Experimental Social Psychology, 20,* 86–96. (p. 289)

Worchel, S., & Norvell, N. (1980). Effect of perceived environmental conditions during cooperation on intergroup attraction. *Journal of Personality and Social Psychology, 38,* 764–772. (p. 547)

Worchel, S., Rothgerber, H., Day, E. A., Hart, D., & Butemeyer, J. (1998). Social identity and individual productivity within groups. *British Journal of Social Psychology, 37,* 389–413. (p. 296)

Word, C. O., Zanna, M. P., & Cooper, J. (1974). The nonverbal mediation of self-fulfilling prophecies in interracial interaction. *Journal of Experimental Social Psychology, 10,* 109–120. (p. 370)

Workman, E. A., & Williams, R. L. (1980). Effects of extrinsic rewards on intrinsic motivation in the classroom. *Journal of School Psychology, 18,* 141–147. (p. 160)

World Bank (2003, April 4). *Gender equality and the millennium development goals.* Washington, DC: Gender and Development Group, World Bank (www.worldbank.org/gender). (p. 186)

Worringham, C. J., & Messick, D. M. (1983). Social facilitation of running: An unobtrusive study. *Journal of Social Psychology, 121,* 23–29. (p. 290)

Wright, D. B., Boyd, C. E., & Tredoux, C. G. (2001). A field study of own-race bias in South Africa and England. *Psychology, Public Policy, & Law, 7,* 119–133. (p. 360)

Wright, D. B., & Stroud, J. N. (2002). Age differences in lineup identification accuracy: People are better with their

own age. *Law and Human Behavior, 26,* 641–654. (p. 360)

Wright, E. F., Lüüs, C. A., & Christie, S. D. (1990). Does group discussion facilitate the use of consensus information in making causal attributions? *Journal of Personality and Social Psychology, 59,* 261–269. (p. 319)

Wright, P., & Rip, P. D. (1981). Retrospective reports on the causes of decisions. *Journal of Personality and Social Psychology, 40,* 601–614. (p. 55)

Wright, R. (1995, March 13). The biology of violence. *New Yorker,* pp. 69–77. (pp. 385–386)

Wright, R. (1998, February 2). Politics made me do it. *Time,* p. 34. (p. 191)

Wright, R. (2003, June 29). Quoted by Thomas L. Friedman, "Is Google God?" *New York Times* (www.nytimes.com). (p. 307)

Wright, R. (2003, September 11). Two years later, a thousand years ago. *New York Times* (www.nytimes.com). (p. 535)

Wright, S. C., Aron, A., McLaughlin-Volpe, T., & Ropp, S. A. (1997). The extended contact effect: Knowledge of cross-group friendships and prejudice. *Journal of Personality and Social Psychology, 73,* 73–90. (pp. 540–541)

Wrightsman, L. (1978). The American trial jury on trial: Empirical evidence and procedural modifications. *Journal of Social Issues, 34,* 137–164. (p. 628)

Wuthnow, R. (1994). *God and mammon in America.* New York: Free Press. (pp. 508, 654)

Wylie, R. C. (1979). *The self-concept (Vol. 2): Theory and research on selected topics.* Lincoln: University of Nebraska Press. (p. 70)

Xu, X., & Whyte, M. (1990). Love matches and arranged marriages: A Chinese replication. *Journal of Marriage and the Family, 52,* 709–722. (p. 457)

Yarmey, A. D. (2003a). Eyewitness identification: Guidelines and recommendations for identification procedures in the United States and in Canada. *Canadian Psychology, 44,* 181–189. (pp. 615, 617)

Yarmey, A. D. (2003b). Eyewitnesses. In D. Carson and R. Bull, *Handbook of psychology in legal contexts*, 2nd ed. Chichester, England: Wiley. (p. 617)

Ybarra, O. (1999). Misanthropic person memory when the need to self-enhance is absent. *Personality and Social Psychology Bulletin*, 25, 261–269. (p. 66)

Yelsma, P., & Athappily, K. (1988). Marital satisfaction and communication practices: Comparisons among Indian and American couples. *Journal of Comparative Family Studies*, 19, 37–54. (p. 457)

Yik, M. S., Bond, M. H., & Paulhus, D. L. (1998). Do Chinese self-enhance or self-efface? It's a matter of domain. *Personality and Social Psychology Bulletin*, 24, 399–406. (p. 80)

Yinon, Y., Sharon, I., Gonen, Y., & Adam, R. (1982). Escape from responsibility and help in emergencies among persons alone or within groups. *European Journal of Social Psychology*, 12, 301–305. (p. 502)

Young, W. R. (1977, February). There's a girl on the tracks! *Reader's Digest*, pp. 91–95. (p. 475)

Yousif, Y., & Korte, C. (1995). Urbanization, culture, and helpfulness. *Journal of Cross-Cultural Psychology*, 26, 474–489. (p. 500)

Yovetich, N. A., & Rusbult, C. E. (1994). Accommodative behavior in close relationships: Exploring transformation of motivation. *Journal of Experimental Social Psychology*, 30, 138–164. (p. 470)

Yuchtman (Yaar), E. (1976). Effects of social-psychological factors on subjective economic welfare. In B. Strumpel (Ed.), *Economic means for human needs*. Ann Arbor: Institute for Social Research, University of Michigan. (p. 389)

Yuille, J. C., & Cutshall, J. L. (1986). A case study of eyewitness memory of a crime. *Journal of Applied Psychology*, 71, 291–301. (p. 608)

Yukl, G. (1974). Effects of the opponent's initial offer, concession magnitude, and concession frequency on bargaining behavior. *Journal of Personality and Social Psychology*, 30, 323–335. (p. 553)

Yzerbyt, V. Y., & Leyens, J-P. (1991). Requesting information to form an impression: The influence of valence and confirmatory status. *Journal of Experimental Social Psychology*, 27, 337–356. (p. 446)

Yzerbyt, V., Rocher, S., & Schadron, G. (1997). Stereotypes as explanations: A subjective essentialistic view of group perception. In R. Spears, P. J. Oakes, N. Ellemers, & S. A. Haslam (Eds.), *The social psychology of stereotyping and group life*. Oxford: Blackwell. (p. 343)

Zajonc, R. B. (1965). Social facilitation. *Science*, 149, 269–274. (pp. 287–288)

Zajonc, R. B. (1968). Attitudinal effects of mere exposure. *Journal of Personality and Social Psychology*, 9, Monograph Suppl. No. 2, part 2. (p. 428)

Zajonc, R. B. (1970, February). Brainwash: Familiarity breeds comfort. *Psychology Today*, pp. 32–35, 60–62. (p. 428)

Zajonc, R. B. (1980). Feeling and thinking: Preferences need no inferences. *American Psychologist*, 35, 151–175. (p. 429)

Zajonc, R. B. (1998). Emotions. In D. Gilbert, S. T. Fiske, & G. Lindzey (Eds.), *Handbook of social psychology*, 4th ed. New York: McGraw-Hill. (p. 429)

Zajonc, R. B. (2000). Massacres: Mass murders in the name of moral imperatives. Unpublished manuscript, Stanford University. (pp. 307, 414)

Zanna, M. P. (1993). Message receptivity: A new look at the old problem of open- vs. closed-mindedness. In A. Mitchell (Ed.), *Advertising: Exposure, memory and choice*. Hillsdale, NJ: Erlbaum. (p. 259)

Zanna, M. P., & Olson, J. M. (1982). Individual differences in attitudinal relations. In M. P. Zanna, E. T. Higgins, & C. P. Herman, *Consistency in social behavior: The Ontario symposium*, Vol. 2. Hillsdale, NJ: Erlbaum. (p. 79)

Zanna, M. P., & Pack, S. J. (1975). On the self-fulfilling nature of apparent sex differences in behavior. *Journal of Experimental Social Psychology*, 11, 583–591. (p. 196)

Zaragoza, M. S., & Mitchell, K. J. (1996). Repeated exposure to suggestion and the creation of false memories. *Psychological Science*, 7, 294–300. (p. 613)

Zebrowitz, L. A., Collins, M. A., & Dutta, R. (1998). The relationship between appearance and personality across the life span. *Personality and Social Psychology Bulletin*, 24, 736–749. (p. 441)

Zebrowitz, L. A., Olson, K., & Hoffman, K. (1993). Stability of babyfaceness and attractiveness across the life span. *Journal of Personality and Social Psychology*, 64, 453–466. (p. 441)

Zebrowitz-McArthur, L. (1988). Person perception in cross-cultural perspective. In M. H. Bond (Ed.), *The cross-cultural challenge to social psychology*. Newbury Park, CA: Sage. (p. 95)

Zeelenberg, M., van der Pligt, J., & Manstead, A. S. R. (1998). Undoing regret on Dutch television: Apologizing for interpersonal regrets involving actions or inactions. *Personality and Social Psychology Bulletin*, 24, 1113–1119. (pp. 115, 116)

Zeisel, H., & Diamond, S. S. (1976). The jury selection in the Mitchell-Stans conspiracy trial. *American Bar Foundation Research Journal*, 1, 151–174 (see p. 167). Cited by L. Wrightsman, The American trial jury on trial: Empirical evidence and procedural modifications. *Journal of Social Issues*, 1978, 34, 137–164. (pp. 628, 632)

Zill, N. (1988). Behavior, Achievement, and Health Problems Among Children in Stepfamilies: Findings From a National Survey of Child Health. In E. Mavis Hetherington and Josephine D. Arasteh (Eds.), *Impact of Divorce, Single Parenting, and Stepparenting on Children*. Hillsdale, NJ: Erlbaum. (p. 391)

Zillmann, D. (1988). Cognition-excitation interdependencies in aggressive behavior. *Aggressive Behavior*, 14, 51–64. (p. 396)

Zillmann, D. (1989). Aggression and sex: Independent and joint operations. In H. L. Wagner & A. S. R. Manstead (Eds.), *Handbook of psychophysiology: Emotion and social behavior*. Chichester, England: John Wiley. (pp. 407, 440)

Zillmann, D. (1989). Effects of prolonged consumption of pornography. In D. Zillmann & J. Bryant (Eds.), *Pornography: Research advances and policy considerations*. Hillsdale, NJ: Erlbaum. (p. 396)

Zillmann, D., & Paulus, P. B. (1993). Spectators: Reactions to sports events and effects on athletic performance. In R. N. Singer, N. Murphey, & L. K. Tennant (Eds.), *Handbook of research on sport psychology*. New York: Macmillan. (p. 289)

Zillmann, D., & Weaver, J. B., III. (1999). Effects of prolonged exposure to gratuitous media violence on provoked and unprovoked hostile behavior. *Journal of Applied Social Psychology*, **29**, 145–165. (p. 407)

Zillmer, E. A., Harrower, M., Ritzler, B. A., & Archer, R. P. (1995). *The quest for the Nazi personality: A psychological investigation of Nazi war criminals*. Hillsdale, NJ: Erlbaum. (p. 226)

Zimbardo, P. G. (1970). The human choice: Individuation, reason, and order versus deindividuation, impulse, and chaos. In W. J. Arnold & D. Levine (Eds.), *Nebraska symposium on motivation, 1969*. Lincoln: University of Nebraska Press. (p. 299)

Zimbardo, P. G. (1971). *The psychological power and pathology of imprisonment*. A statement prepared for the U.S. House of Representatives Committee on the Judiciary, Subcommittee No. 3: Hearings on Prison Reform, San Francisco, Calif., October 25. (p. 141)

Zimbardo, P. G. (1972). The Stanford prison experiment. A slide/tape presentation produced by Philip G. Zimbardo, Inc., P. O. Box 4395, Stanford, Calif. 94305. (p. 141)

Zimbardo, P. G. (1993). Personal communication of research findings on attributions and shyness. Department of Psychology, Stanford University. (p. 80)

Zimbardo, P. G. (2002, April). Nurturing psychological synergies. *APA Monitor*, pp. 5, 38. (p. 299)

Zimbardo, P. G. (2004). A situationist perspective on the psychology of evil: Understanding how good people are transformed into perpetrators. In A. G. Miller (Ed.), *The social psychology of good and evil*. New York: Guilford. (p. 535)

Zimbardo, P. G. (2004, May 3). Awful parallels: Abuse of Iraqi inmates and SPE. Comments to Social of Personality and Social Psychology listserv. (p. 142)

Zimbardo, P. G., Ebbesen, E. B., & Maslach, C. (1977). *Influencing attitudes and changing behavior*. Reading, MA: Addison-Wesley. (p. 302)

Zola-Morgan, S., Squire, L. R., Alvarez-Royo, P., & Clower, R. P. (1991). Independence of memory functions and emotional behavior. *Hippocampus*, **1**, 207–220. (p. 429)

Zucker, G. S., & Weiner, B. (1993). Conservatism and perceptions of poverty: An attributional analysis. *Journal of Applied Social Psychology*, **23**, 925–943. (p. 96)

Zuckerman, E. W., & Jost, J. T. (2001). What makes you think you're so popular? Self-evaluation maintenance and the subjective side of the "friendship paradox." *Social Psychology Quarterly*, **64**, 207–223. (p. 63)

Zuwerink, J. R., Monteith, M. J., Devine, P. G., & Cook, D. A. (1996). Prejudice toward blacks: With and without compunction? *Basic and Applied Social Psychology*, **18**, 131–150. (p. 357)

acknowledgments

TEXT/LINE ART CREDITS

Chapter 2

Figure 2–3 From S. Kitayama, S. Duffy, T. Hawamura & J. Larsen, 2003, "Perceiving an Object and its Context in Different Cultures: A Cultural Look at New Look," *Psychological Science*, 14, pp. 201–206. Reprinted by permission.

Figure 2-4 From H. Markus & S. Kitayama, 1991, "Culture and the Self: Implications for Cognition, Emotion and Motivation," *Psychological Review*, 98, pp. 224–253. Copyright © 1991 by the American Psychological Association. Reprinted by permission.

Figure 2–5 Reprinted by permission of Dr. Hazel Rose Markus.

Figure 2–7 From T. F. Heatherton & K. D. Vohs, 2000, "Interpersonal Evaluations Following Threats to Self: Role of Self-Esteem," *Journal of Personality and Social Psychology*, 78, pp. 725–736. Copyright © 2000 by the American Psychological Association. Reprinted by permission.

Chapter 3

Figure 3–7 From J. P. Forgas, G. H. Bower and S. E. Kranz, 1984, "The Influence of Mood on Perceptions of Social Interactions," *Journal of Experimental Social Psychology*, 20, pp. 497–513. Reprinted with permission of Academic Press.

Chapter 5

Figure 5–3 From D. M. Buss, "The Strategies of Human Mating," 1994, *American Scientist*, 82, pp. 239–249. Reprinted with permission of Sigma XI.

Figure 5–4 From D. M. Buss, "The Strategies of Human Mating," 1994, *American Scientist*, 82, pp. 239–249. Reprinted with permission of Sigma XI.

Figure 5–5 Reprinted with permission of the Pew Research Center for the People and the Press.

Figure 5–7 From A. H. Eagly & W. Wood, 1991, "Explaining Sex Differences in Social Behavior: A Meta-Analytic Perspective," *Personality and Social Psychology Bulletin*, 17, pp. 306–315. Reprinted by permission of Sage Publications, Inc.

Chapter 6

Figure 6–3 From the Milgram Obedience Experiment, from S. Milgram, 1965, "Some Conditions of Obedience and Disobedience to Authority," *Human Relations*, 18, pp. 57–76. Reprinted by permission.

Figure 6–4 From the Milgram Obedience Experiment, from S. Milgram, 1965, "Some Conditions of Obedience and Disobedience to Authority," *Human Relations*, 18, pp. 5–76. Reprinted by permission.

Table 6–1 From Stanley Milgram, 1974, *Obedience to Authority*, HarperCollins Publishers and Pinter & Martin, Ltd. Copyright © 1974 by Stanley Milgram. Reprinted by permission of the publishers.

Chapter 7

Figure 7–1 From W. J. McGuire, 1978, "An Information-Processing Model of Advertising Effectiveness," in *Behavioral and Management Sciences in Marketing*, H. L. Davis and A. J. Silk, eds. Copyright © 1978. Reprinted by permission of John Wiley & Sons, Inc.

Figure 7–9 From R. E. Pettry, T. J. Cacioppo & R. Goldman, 1981, "Personal Involvement as a Determinant of Argument-Based Persuasion," *Journal of Personality and Social Psychology*, 41, pp. 847–855. Copyright © 1981 by the American Psychological Association. Reprinted by permission.

Chapter 8

Figure 8–4 From Williams, Jackson & Karau, 1992, in *Social Dilemmas: Perspectives on Individuals and Groups*, D. A. Schroeder, ed. Copyright © 1992 by Praeger Publishers. Reproduced with permission of Greenwood Publishing Group, Inc., Westport, CT.

Chapter 9

Figure 9–6 From P. G. Devine & R. S. Malpass, 1985, "Orienting Strategies in Differential Face Recognition," *Personality and Social Psychology Bulletin*, 11, pp. 33–40. Reprinted by permission of Sage Publications, Inc.

Chapter 11

Figure 11–2 From R. B. Zajonc, 1968, "Attitudinal Effects of Mere Exposure," *Journal of Personality and Social Psychology*, 9, Monograph Supplement No. 2, part, 2. Copyright © 1968 by the American Psychological Association. Reprinted by permission.

Figure 11–3 From Opinion Dynamics Poll of Registered Voters, 1999, Fox News.

Figure 11–9 From A. L. Weber and J. H. Harvey, *Perspectives on Close Relationships*. Published by Allyn and Bacon, Boston, MA. Copyright © 1994 by Pearson Education. Reprinted by permission of the publisher.

Chapter 12

Figure 12–2 From M. A. Whatley, J. M. Webster, R. H. Smith & A. Rhodes, 1991, "The Effect of a Favor on Public and Private Compliance: How Internalized Is the Norm of Reciprocity?" *Basic and Applied Social Psychology*, 21, pp. 251–259. Reprinted by permission of Lawrence Erlbaum Associates.

Figure 12–3 From C. D. Batson, J. Fultz & P. A. Schoenrade, 1987, "Distress and Empathy: Two Qualitatively Distinct Vicarious Emotions with

Different Motivational Consequences," *Journal of Personality*, 55:1, Spring 1987. Reprinted by permission.

Figure 12–6 Reprinted by permission of Dr. Robert Levine.

Chapter 13

Figure 13–4 From P. E. Tetlock, 1988, "Monitoring the Integrative Complexity of American and Soviet Policy Rhetoric: What Can Be Learned?" *Journal of Social Issues*, Vol. 454, No. 2, pp. 101–131. Reprinted by permission.

Figure 13–6 Gallup 6/10/03. www.gallup.com.

Table 13–2 From S. Plous, 1993, "The Nuclear Arms Race: Prisoner's Dilemma or Perceptual Dilemma?" *Journal of Peace Research*, 30, pp. 163–179. Reprinted by permission of Sage Publications, Inc.

Chapter 14

Figure 14–1 From N. Nunez, D. Poole & A. Memon, (in press), "Psychology's Two Cultures Revisited: Implications for the Integration of Science and Practice," *Scientific Review of Mental Health Practice*. Reprinted by permission.

Figure 14–4 From J. Dill and C. Anderson, "Loneliness, Shyness and Depression: The Etiology and Interpersonal Relationships of Everyday Problems in Living," in *Recent Advances in Interpersonal Approaches to Depression*, T. Joiner & J. Coyne, eds., 1998. American Psychological Association. Copyright © 1998 by the American Psychological Association. Reprinted by permission.

Chapter 15

Figure 15–2 From G. H. Fisher, 1968, "Ambiguity of Form: Old and New," *Perception and Psychophysics*, 4, pp. 189–192. Reprinted with permission of Psychonomic Society, Inc.

Table 15–1 From S. Kassin, V. Tubb, H. Hosch & A. Memon, 2001, "On the 'General Acceptance' of Eyewitness Testimony Research: A New Survey of the Experts." *American Psychologist*, 56,

pp. 405–416. Copyright © 2001 by the American Psychological Association. Reprinted by permission.

Chapter 16

Figure 16–1 Reprinted by permission of the Population Reference Bureau.

Figure 16–2 From M. Wackernagel, N. Schulz, D. Deumling, A. Linares, M. Jenkins, V. Kapos, C. Manfreda, J. Loh, N. Myers, R. Norgaard & J. Randers, 2003, "Tracking the Ecological Overshoot of the Human Economy," *Proceedings of the National Academy of Sciences*, 99, pp. 9266–9271. Copyright © 2003 by National Academy of Sciences, USA.

Figure 16-4 From Ronald Inglehart, *Modernization and Postmodernization*. Copyright © 1997 Princeton University Press. Reprinted by permission of Princeton University Press.

PHOTO CREDITS

Chapter 1

p. 2: ©Kelvin Murray/Getty Images; p. 15: ©David Young-Wolff/Photo Edit; p. 23: ©Corrance/Still Digital; p. 25: Michael Newman/PhotoEdit; p. 27: Photo by Shannon Smith, Institute for Social Research, University of Michigan; p. 29: ©Mary Kate Denny/PhotoEdit.

Chapter 2

p. 37: ©Richard Lord/Image Works; p. 38: ©Bob Mahoney/Image Works; p. 47: Image courtesy of Takahiko Masuda, Ph.D. (see Masuda & Nisbett, 2001); p. 50 (left): Courtesy Hazel Rose Markus; p. 50 (right): Photo courtesy Mel Manis; p. 51: ©Haruyoshi Yamaguchi/Corbis Images; p. 54: ©Robert Holmes/Corbis Images; p. 61: ©Marc Deville/Gamma Press; p. 63: ©AP/Wide World Photos; p. 64: ©Michael Newman/PhotoEdit; p. 72: ©Larry Dale Gordon/Image Bank; p. 80: ©Dennis Budd Gray/Stock Boston/PictureQuest.

Chapter 3

p. 82: ©Ian Waldie/Reuters; p. 85: ©AP/Wide World Photos; p. 86:

©Ellen Senisi/Image Works; p. 89: ©AP/Wide World Photos; p. 91: ©Everett Collection; p. 92: ©Susan Van Etten/PhotoEdit; p. 93: ©AP/Wide World Photos; p. 94: ©Bill Bachmann/eStock Photography/PictureQuest; p. 95: ©Evan Kafka/Getty Images; p. 96: ©James Schnepf/Getty Images; p. 97: ©Esbin-Anderson/Image Works; p. 100 (left): ©AP/Wide World Photos; p. 100 (right): ©David M. Grossman/Image Works; p. 101, 111: ©Bettmann/Corbis Images; p. 116 (both): ©AP/Wide World Photos; p. 118: ©PhotoDisc/Vol.#67; p. 125: ©AP/Wide World Photos.

Chapter 4

p. 132: ©AP/Wide World Photos; p. 134: ©John Griffin/Image Works; p. 138: ©Prettyman/PhotoEdit; p. 141: ©Philip Zimbardo; p. 142: CBS News/60 Minutes II Website; p. 146: ©Paul Henry Versele/Gamma Press; p. 148: ©Donna Day/Getty Images; p. 149: ©AP/Wide World Photos; p. 153: Courtesy Leon Festinger; p. 154: ©Tom Stewart/Corbis Images; p. 155: ©Yellow Dog Productions/Getty Images; p. 156 (all): ©Colin Young-Wolff/PhotoEdit; p. 157 (both): Courtesy Fritz Strack; p. 158 (all): Bernieri, F., Davis, J., Rosenthal, R. & Knee, C. (1994). "Interactional synchrony and rapport: Measuring synchrony in displays devoid of sound and facial affect." *Personality and Social Psychology Bulletin*, 20, 303–311.

Chapter 5

p. 167: ©Pictor International/PictureQuest; p. 168: ©Steve Vidler/eStock Photography/PictureQuest; p. 173: ©Dorothy Littell/Stock Boston/PictureQuest; p. 176: ©Fujifotos/Image Works; p. 178 (left): ©Bettmann/Corbis Images; p. 178 (right): ©Peter Kramer/Getty Images; p. 183 (left): ©Audrey Gottlieb; p. 183 (right): ©Bob Daemmrich/Image Works; p. 184: ©Brian Potts; p. 192: ©Frederick M. Brown/Getty Images; p. 196 (left): ©Spencer Grant/PhotoEdit; p. 196 (right): ©Capital Features/Image

Works; p. 199: ©Bill Bachmann; p. 201: ©Evelyn Scolney; p. 202: Courtesy Alice Eagly.

Chapter 6

p. 206 (top left): ©European PressPhoto Agency, EPA/Wide World Photos; p. 206 (top right): ©PhotoDisc Website; p. 206 (center) : ©Barbara Stitzer/ PhotoEdit; p. 206 (bottom): ©Richard Hamilton Smith/Corbis Images; p. 214 (both): ©William Vandivert; p. 218: Stanley Milgram, 1965, from the film *Obedience,* distributed by the Pennsylvania State University, PCR; p. 220: ©AP/Wide World Photos; p. 222: Courtesy Alexandra Milgram; p. 223 (all): ©Benny Gool/Capetown Independent Newspaper; p. 224: ©European PressPhoto Agency/Wide World Photos; p. 229: ©James A. Sugar/Corbis Images; p. 230: ©PhotoFest; p. 231: ©IT Stock Int'l/Index Stock Imagery; p. 232: ©AP/Wide World Photos; p. 234: Congressional Photo Office; p. 237: ©Michael Grecco/Stock Boston; p. 239: ©Mark Peterson/SABA; p. 240: ©Michael Newman/PhotoEdit.

Chapter 7

p. 244 Topham/Image Works; p. 247: ©Bob Daemmrich/Image Works; p. 255: ©AP/Wide World Photos; p. 257 (all): ©Health Canada; p. 264: ©Time Life Pictures/Getty Images ; p. 270: ©Bettmann/Corbis; p. 272: ©AP/Wide World Photos; p. 276: ©Kate Brooks/Corbis Images; p. 279: ©Rachel Epstein/Image Works; p. 280: Courtesy William McGuire, Yale University; p. 282: ©Michelle D. Bridwell/PhotoEdit.

Chapter 8

p. 284: ©Stephanie Maze/Corbis Images; p. 287: ©Bob Winsett/Corbis Images; p. 290: ©Mike Okoniewski; p. 292: Courtesy Herman Miller, Inc.; p. 293: Courtesy Alan G. Ingham; p. 295 (top): ©Corbis/R-F Website; p. 295 (bottom): ©David Young-Wolff/ PhotoEdit; p. 296: ©Joel W. Rogers/ Corbis Images; p. 298: ©AP/Wide World Photos; p. 299: ©Philip

Zimbardo; p. 301: ©AP/Wide World Photos; p. 307: ©Tom Brakefield/Stock Connection/PictureQuest; p. 312: Courtesy Irving Janis; p. 314: ©Kobal Collection; p. 316: NASA; p. 318: ©Meyer Bruce/Corbis Images; p. 320: Courtesy Daniel Kahneman; p. 323: ©Time Life Pictures/Getty Images; p. 325: ©Mark Richards/PhotoEdit.

Chapter 9

p. 329: ©Richard Laird/Getty Images; p. 330: ©Kim Kulish/Corbis Images; p. 334: Andrew Redington/Getty Image—News; p. 336: ©Frank White; p. 338 (both): Correll, J., Park, B., Judd, C. M., & Wittenbrink, B. (2002). The police officer's dilemma: Using ethnicity to disambiguate potentially threatening individuals. *Journal of Personality and Social Psychology, 83,* 1316. Fig. 1. Images courtesy Josh Correll; pp. 338–339 (all): Figure created using stimuli from Hugenberg, K. and Bodenhausen, G. V. (2000). Facing Prejudice: Implicit Prejudice and the Perception of Facial Threat. *Psychological Science,* 6, 640–643. Used with permission of authors. Photos courtesy, Kurt Hugenberg (2000). Facing Prejudice: Implicit Prejudice and the Perception of Facial Threat. *Psychological Science,* 6, 640–643. Used with permission of authors; p. 340: Courtesy Dr. Natalie Porter; p. 344: ©AP/Wide World Photos; p. 349 (left): ©AP/Wide World Photos; p. 349 (right): ©Bonnie Kamin/Photo Edit; p. 351 (top): ©Brand X Photos/PhotoDisc Website; p. 351 (bottom): ©Digital Vision/ PhotoDisc Website; p. 353: ©AP/Wide World Photos; p. 354: ©1999 Allan Tannenbaum; p. 358: James Blascovich; p. 361: ©AP/Wide World Photos; p. 369: ©Bob Daemmrich/Stock Boston; p. 375: Photo by Ron P. Jaffe/NBC via Getty Images.

Chapter 10

p. 378: ©William Whitehurst/Corbis Images; p. 381: ©Granger Collection; p. 384: ©Jeff Share/Black Star; p. 385: ©Jose Mercado/Corbis Images; p. 387: ©O. Burriel/Photo Researchers; p. 390

(both): ©Albert Bandura; p. 394: ©AP/Wide World Photos; p. 395: ©John Barr/Getty Images; p. 400: ©Bettmann/Corbis Images; p. 413: Courtesy, Craig A. Anderson; p. 414: ©Gus van Dyk, Pilanesberg.

Chapter 11

p. 422: ©Myrleen Ferguson Cate/PhotoEdit; p. 425 (top): ©Getty Images; p. 425 (bottom): Eisenberger, N. I., Lieberman, M. D., & Williams, K. D. (2003). Does rejection hurt? An fMRI study of social exclusion. *Science,* 302, 290–292. ©2003 American Association for the Advancement of Science; p. 426: ©Pictor International/ Picture International, Ltd./ PictureQuest; p. 427: ©PhotoDisc Website; p. 431 (both): ©Christopher Morris/Corbis Images; p. 433: ©Tom Prettyman/PhotoEdit; p. 435: ©AP/ Wide World Photos; p. 437: Courtesy Ellen Berscheid, University of Minnesota; p. 438 (both): Victor Johnston © Reprinted with permission of *Discover Magazine*; p. 439 (left): ©Robert Giroux/Getty Images; p. 439 (right): ©AP/Wide World Photos; p. 441 (left): ©Rick Smolan/Stock Boston; p. 441 (center left): ©Paul Lau; p. 441 (center right): ©Catherine Karnow/Woodfin Camp; p. 441 (right): ©Marc Romanelli/Getty Images; p. 442: ©Granger Collection; p. 443: ©Reuters/Stefano Rellandini/ Corbis Images; p. 445: Courtesy James M. Jones; p. 451 (all): Dr. Pawel Lewicki, University of Tulsa, Oklahoma; p. 454: ©Joe Polillio; p. 456: ©Rob Nelson/Black Star; p. 459: ©AP/ Wide World Photos; p. 461: ©Mike Kagan.

Chapter 12

p. 474: ©Myrleen Ferguson Cate/ PhotoEdit; p. 476: Courtesy, Yad Vashem, The Holocaust Martyrs' and Heroes' Remembrance Authority; p. 477: ©National Gallery Collection; By kind permission of the Trustees of the National Gallery, London/Corbis Images; p. 481: ©Ellis Herwig/Stock Boston; p. 485: ©AP/Wide World

Photos; p. 486: ©Twentieth Century Fox/Shooting Star; p. 492: ©Hermine Dreyfus; p. 495: ©Robert Brenner/ PhotoEdit; p. 496: Courtesy John M. Darley, Princeton University; p. 498: ©Mark Zemnick; p. 499: ©Corbis Sygma; p. 504: Courtesy, Lisa DeBruine; p. 508: ©Lynn Burkholder/ First Impressions; p. 515: ©Page Collection/Gamma Press.

Chapter 13

p. 518: ©Pablo Torres Guerrero/El Pais/ Reuters/Corbis; p. 520: ©Bettmann/ Corbis Images; p. 526: ©Catherine Karnow/Corbis Images; p. 527: ©Joseph Sohm, ChromoSohm/Corbis Images; p. 530: Muzafer Sherif; p. 534: ©Chris Morris/Black Star; p. 535: ©Robert King/Getty Images; p. 537: ©European PressPhoto Agency, EPA/Wide World Photos; p. 541: Courtesy, John Dixon, Lancaster University; p. 542: ©AP/Wide World Photos; p. 544 (left): ©Ladd Co./ Paramount/Kobal Collection; p. 544 (right): Courtesy the author; p. 547: ©Ian Shaw/Getty Images; p. 548: ©AP/Wide World Photos; p. 549: ©Bettmann/Corbis Images; p. 550: ©AP/Wide World Photos; p. 553: ©Corbis Images; p. 556: ©Mark Antman/Image Works.

Chapter 14

p. 565: ©AP/Wide World Photos; p. 566: ©Bob Daemmrich/Image Works; p. 570: ©AP/Wide World Photos; p. 574: ©Bettmann/Corbis Images; p. 575: ©Robin Nelson/ PhotoEdit; p. 578: Courtesy Shelley Taylor; p. 580: ©Grant LeDuc; p. 583: ©Flip Chalfont/Image Bank; p. 584: ©David Young-Wolff/PhotoEdit; p. 590: ©Jacques Chenet/Getty Images; p. 593: ©Ellis Herwig/Stock Boston.

Chapter 15

p. 604: ©AP/Wide World Photos; p. 608 (both): Courtesy, Chicago Tribune; p. 609: ©AP/Wide World Photos; p. 612 (both): Courtesy Elizabeth Loftus; p. 623: ©Christopher Gardner/New Times/Corbis Images; p. 626: ©John Giordano/Corbis Images; p. 628: ©AP/Pool/Star Ledger/Wide World Photos; p. 635: ©Alexander Jason/Getty Images.

Chapter 16

p. 638 (both): ©2004 Peter Menzel/menzelphoto.com.; p. 642 (left): ©Ira Kirschenbaum/Stock Boston; p. 642 (right): ©Michele Burgess/Stock Boston; p. 643: ©Wolfgang Kaehler/Corbis Images; p. 645: ©Corbis Digital Stock.

name index

subject index